THE
Ultimate
FOOTBALL GUIDE
1997

Published by: SKY BLUE PUBLICATIONS LTD

Licensed by: BRITISH SKY BROADCASTING LIMITED

Publisher :- Bryan A Richardson
Editor :- Michael Williams
Editorial Assistant :- Sue Adams
Sky Introduction Text :- Chris Haynes
Colour Section Design :- Keenan Design Associates

ISBN 0-9526904-1-1

Sky Blue Publications Ltd
Highfield Road Stadium
King Richard Street
Coventry
CV2 4FW
Telephone: 01203 234017
Fax: 01203 234015

Foreword

Welcome to the 2nd edition of "Sky Sports The Ultimate Football Guide". Providing an in-depth focus on all of the 92 professional League clubs, this edition has managed to maintain the high standards of quality, content and presentation that has made it without doubt the best reference book in the market.

The Guide has been compiled by a dedicated team of expert statisticians, with the deliberate tactic of publishing after the season has started, enabling us to make this the most up to the minute footballing publication. It includes the pre-season transfers, up to date team photos in the latest strips, and all the big new signings.

With the invaluable support of Sky Sports, widely regarded as the absolute authority in football broadcasting, the Ultimate Football Guide has moved onto a higher level of sports publication. Not only has it become the essential supporters' guide, it has also become the definitive reference book for every serious sporting journalist and can be seen being vigorously thumbed through on Saturday afternoons in every press box, at every football ground, throughout the entire season. Truly "The Bible of Football".

The Ultimate Football Guide is a must for every true football fan, and will continue to remain so with the help and support of Sky Sports.

Bryan Richardson

Publisher

watch all your
heroes
all the time

Sky tv
the home
of football

The Sky Sports Channels

SKY TELEVISION has three channels devoted to sport with a combined output of around 270 hours of every week.

Sky Sports 1 was the first channel to be launched, in April 1991. The channel changed the way that the British public saw sport, offering greater access to major sports with more live coverage and a greater depth of highlights and analysis than ever seen before. Among its achievements, Sky Sports brought; the first live ball-by-ball coverage of England's cricket tours; regular live coverage of Rugby League and club Rugby Union; and live coverage of football's new FA Premier League, with many events previously unavailable to the British public.

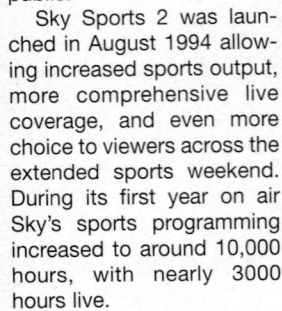

ACTION IMAGES

Sky Sports 2 was launched in August 1994 allowing increased sports output, more comprehensive live coverage, and even more choice to viewers across the extended sports weekend. During its first year on air Sky's sports programming increased to around 10,000 hours, with nearly 3000 hours live.

Sky Sports 3 was announced in July 1996, to begin on August 16. The service is scheduled twelve hours a day, seven days a week, with regular live programming including; the Nationwide Football League, Coca-Cola Cup, US PGA Tour golf, American Major League Baseball and NHL Ice Hockey. Its introduction will increase Sky's sports output further, to around 14,000 hours each year.

The sports channels cover all of the major sports; golf coverage amounts to 1000 hours each year, with live coverage from the European Tour, US PGA Tour, the US Open, and PGA Championship as well as the next two Ryder Cup tournaments; cricket programming includes live coverage of England's One-Day internationals and three of the domestic tournaments; rugby union for the new season is focused on the Courage Clubs Championship and Pilkington Cup; the new rugby Super League is exclusively live; and Big Time Boxing shows the biggest names in British boxing as well as the stars of the international stage. Sky Sports continues to offer classic sports programming - including Bobby Charlton's Football Scrapbook - on four nights of the week.

Across the sports channels, Sky has set new standards in the range and quality of its sports coverage, adopting new technology to take viewers to the heart of the action. Sky has pioneered new technology to improve graphics, camera angles, audio and replay systems introducing steadi-cams, super-slo-mo, Replay 2000, the constant clock and scoreline, and Dolby Surround Sound to change the look of British sports coverage. Support progamming for all of the major sports entertains and informs Skys sports fans and helps to promote interest and participation in a range of sports.

Sky Sports achievements have been recognised with award of the satellite channel of the year by the Television & Radio Industries Club and the Royal Television Society's prestigious Sports Coverage of the Year Award.

Live match coverage

Sky Television is set to screen more live football than ever before with more than 170 live matches planned for the new season.

Five seasons ago, in the year before Sky was awarded the live FA Premier League rights, Sky Sports broadcast 75 live matches. Then, with the advent of the FA Premier League, Sky's live coverage pushed past the 100 mark. And in 1994-95 Sky set a new benchmark as exclusive live coverage of the Copa America stretched Sky's live soccer through the summer months and took the end of season tally to 143 live games.

This season Sky Sports has added live coverage of the Nationwide Football League and the Coca-Cola Cup to the schedules, and viewers across the nation will be offered at least 70 more live domestic matches than ever before, making this the most televised season in the history of British football.

Whilst Sky is renowned for its award-winning exclusive live coverage of the FA Carling Premiership, the range of live coverage now stretches way beyond England's leading league. Sky Sports has shown live coverage of the FA Cup - the world's oldest cup competition - since the channel's launch in 1991, offering coverage of at least one live match and one replay from the First Round through to the Semi-Final. And every England international is exclusively live from Wembley Stadium as England embark on the qualifying campaign for the 1998 World Cup Finals.

A new five-year contract with the Football League will add; up to 60 live matches each season from across all three divisions of the Nationwide Football League; all three Wembley

play-offs live for the first time; and live coverage of the Coca-Cola Cup from the First Round through to the Final.

Every major domestic tournament in England can be seen live on Sky, and in Scotland, the third season of a four-year contract with the Scottish Football Association and Scottish Football League will again bring seventeen live games from the three major domestic tournaments; the Bell's Scottish League, Tennents Scottish Cup and the Scottish Coca-Cola Cup.

Each season a number of other live games have also been shown taking viewers to the Final of the FA Umbro Trophy, schoolboy international tournaments, Youth, Under-18, and Under-21 internationals.

Now, with live coverage of the FA Premier League, FA Cup, Football League and England internationals secured for the next five years, awarded through new TV contracts, Sky Sports viewers are guaranteed a season ticket to the game into the next millennium.

The FA Carling Premiership

Sky Television has broadcast 60 live games from the FA Carling Premiership every year since the league began in 1992.

Each season every club in the league has been seen at least three times, with a fairer distribution of live matches than ever before, and several clubs making their first live league appearance on national television.

In June 1996 the FA Premier League awarded Sky Television the exclusive live rights to the FA Premier League into the next century. The new deal extended Sky's live coverage up to the close of the 2000-01 season, under the biggest ever TV rights agreement in the UK.

For the 1996-97 season Sky, in agreement with the Premier League and the clubs, scheduled 34 televised games to launch the new season and take the coverage into the new year; more pre-scheduled games than ever before.

For the past two years the Premier League season has closed with two live games shown simultaneously on Sky Sports and Sky Sports 2. Viewers were able to choose which of the deciding games to watch, with regular updates of goals and crucial action from the other important game as well as the matches that settled the crucial relegation and European issues. Sky's ground-breaking coverage of the climax to the 1994-95 FA Carling Premiership was praised by the Royal Television Society as a marathon piece of live sport storytelling and recognised with the Sports Coverage of the Year Award.

Nationwide football league

The 1995-96 season introduces two new competitions to Sky Sports viewers; under a five-year deal secured in November 1995, Sky viewers will be offered live coverage of the Nationwide Football League and the Coca-Cola Cup - the two major competitions of the Football League. The five-year deal will bring up to 60 live matches each season from across all three Divisions of the Football League and - for the very first time - all three end-of season play-off finals broadcast live across the UK from Wembley Stadium.

Live league matches will be shown on Friday nights - Friday Night Football - and ahead of the day's Premier League coverage in Football League Live on Sunday afternoons. The presenter will be Russ Williams, with commentary by Rob Hawthorne, and the regular touchline reporter is George Gavin.

Coverage will begin on Friday 16 August with Manchester City at home to Ipswich Town, and the first Sunday match Birmingham City vs Crystal Palace on Sunday 18 August. All three clubs recently relegated from the FA Premier League are scheduled within the first fortnight, and every club in the First Division will be seen at least once within the first three months. The three clubs promoted from the Second Division will all be seen in September. The first live game from the Second Division will be the Lancashire derby between Preston North End and Blackpool on Friday 13 December. Further matches from the Second and Third Divisions of the Nationwide Football League will be scheduled as the season progresses.

The Football League Review, a new magazine show, will review the week and preview the weekend's games on Thursday evenings, and the League's competitions will also be seen within Sky's wide range of support programmes.

ACTION IMAGES

The Coca-Cola Cup

The Coca-Cola Cup is live from the first round for the first time, with Sky's live coverage kicking-off at the County Ground with Swindon vs Wolves on Tuesday 20 August. Reaching a climax with live coverage of the Coca-Cola Cup Final on Saturday 6 April, the tournament will bring up to ten games, exclusively live, to Sky Sports over the coming season. Sky's main sports presenter, Richard Keys, will present the live coverage, with new commentator, Alan Parry, the regular match commentator.

ENGLAND INTERNATIONALS

Since 1991 Sky has shown exclusive live coverage of every England international from Wembley Stadium, outside Euro 96. Now, with the contract extended until the close of the 2000-01 season Sky viewers will see England's matches into the next millennium.

Last season brought nine England internationals live to Sky Sports, from the international against Colombia to the tour of the Far East, as Terry Venables prepared his team for the European Championships. This season, following England's fine performances at Euro 96, Sky will show live coverage of England's qualifying campaign for the 1998 World Cup Finals, with the first home match against Poland on October 9 having the added significance of Glenn Hoddle's managerial

live all the
passion
all the time

Sky tv
the home
of football

debut at Wembley- the home of English football. Other opponents in World Cup Qualifying Group 2, over the next two seasons, will be Georgia, Moldova and Italy. And in future seasons Sky will have live coverage of the home qualifying ties for the European Championships for 2000.

FA Cup, sponsored by Littlewoods

This season Sky will show coverage from the first round stage through to the semi-final with at least one live tie and one replay from each round.

Since the channel's launch in 1991, Sky has shown live coverage of the FA Cup each season. To date, over 60 cup ties have been covered exclusively live, taking Sky viewers to clubs in the Premier League, across all three divisions of the Football League, the Vauxhall Conference and beyond. A new contract with the Football Association has extended Sky's live rights to the FA Cup until the close of the 2000-01 season.

This season's coverage will again begin at the First Round stage, in November. Following live ties and replays from the first two rounds, holders Manchester United and the other major clubs enter the competition in January, with Sky's live coverage continuing to offer at least one live tie and one replay (where required) up to and including the Semi-Final of the world's oldest cup competition.

Coverage will be presented by Richard Keys with Martin Tyler and Andy Gray the regular FA Cup commentators.

Ford Super Sunday

Ford Super Sunday follows Sky's coverage of the Nationwide Football League providing over six hours of live football on Sunday afternoons. Live Sunday football first came to British television in 1979, but it was Sky's regular live coverage, with major matches on most weekends right from the start of the season, that established Sunday as a footballing day throughout the year.

On Sundays with Sky it is possible to watch constant football programming from 7am - with Soccer Extra, through to 7pm - the end of Super Sunday - with more football programmes later in the evening. But the focus of the day are the live games, with Sky' double-header - the Football League Live (kick-off at 1pm) followed by Ford Super Sunday (kick-off at 4pm).

Super Sunday starts at 3pm with Richard Keys and his guests, live at the ground in a portable studio, setting the scene for the afternoon's entertainment. The viewer will see action, analysis, interviews and a reminder of the current league tables, before they are given a Story of the Season for each of the clubs, looking at the highlights and lowlights and analysing form.

Outside the ground, the cameras capture the players arriving, and ask fans of the teams - home and away - for their vox-pop views on the game and the likely result. The pace of the programme builds as the match approaches, and shortly before kick-off the commentators - Martin Tyler and Andy Gray - come into vision, high in the gantry, to look at the lineups and their likely formation.

At half time, and after the game, Richard Keys and his special studio guests discuss the game and any major incidents, with replays of relevant action. And at the end of the game, Andy Gray leaves his commentary position to return to the studio where he adds his opinion and analyses all the weekend's action. This season Super Sunday viewers will have the opportunity to vote for their Man of the Match who will be announced at the end of the programme.

The Super Sunday Outside Broadcast is the largest regular roadshow anywhere in Europe, now taking up to nine production trucks and tenders and up to ninety personnel the length of the country. Each game is produced at the ground, then sent by landline to an uplink centre which sends the pictures up to the Astra Satellite. And although highlights packages and most of the graphics are produced at Sky's HQ in advance of the game, the production is self-sufficient and can operate, if necessary, independently of the facilities back at west London.

Ford Monday Night Football

Sky's major transfer of the summer close-season has brought ITV's Alan Parry to Ford Monday Night Football. One of the country's most experienced commentators, Alan has moved to Sky after 12 years with ITV. He will be joined in the gantry by Trevor Francis who, will combine his task at Birmingham City with his role as co-commentator on Monday Night Football.

Last season saw a new-look Ford Monday Night Football with a sophisticated studio set, deeper tactical insights, and a revolutionary graphics and replay tool - Replay 2000 - for post-match analysis. The same successful formula, presented by Richard Keys, will be adopted this season as Ford Monday Night Football continues to evolve.

Each week Andy Gray previews the match in the 'technical area' at the front of the studio. Here a simple football pitch layout, situated beneath an overhead camera, allows Andy to talk through the likely game-plan that will be adopted by the teams. The final whistle is followed by further tactical talk where Andy uses the revolutionary Replay 20000 graphics and action-replay system. First seen last season, Replay 2000 complements Andy's intuitive tactical analysis.

Replay 2000 allows more advanced analysis than ever before, illustrating how the game was won and lost with graphics devices that; track the movements of players and the flight of the ball, highlight individual players as they run, measure distances, record velocity - as used with Tony Yeboah's spectacular goal against Liverpool last season recorded at over 90 mph - and draw cross-lines to help with off-side decisions.

Monday Night Football first changed the face of the game in August 1992. Since then Monday night matches have become an established and popular part of the extended football weekend and the coverage has continued to develop. Monday Night Football was launched with pre-match and half-time entertainment, live bands, and fireworks for the first season, and was soon established in football folklore with a four-page story - featuring Richard Keys and Andy Gray - in the classic comic-strip Roy of the Rovers. And research at the end of the first season showed that attendances at Monday Night matches were higher on average than similar Saturday fixtures.

Four seasons on, viewers can now watch nearly five hours of continuous prime-time football programming on Monday nights, starting with Sky Sports Centre at 18.00. Coverage continues with thirty minutes of Tartan Extra, before the live Monday match build-up begins at 19.00. Then, after the live match - which will normally kick-off at 20.00 - comes the analysis followed by the live late edition of Sky Sports Centre, which ends at 22.45.

Friday Night Football & Football League live

The 1996-97 season adds live coverage of The Nationwide Football League to Sky Sports, and provides a new platform and greater exposure for the game at this level.

Russ Williams presents live coverage of both Friday Night Football and Sunday's Football League Live. Based in Sky's west London studio, Russ will be joined on-set by regular guests and pundits such as Ray Clemence, Glenn Roeder, Clive Allen, Nigel Spackman and Steve Bruce.

The build-up begins at 7pm on Friday evenings, and at 12 noon on Sunday afternoons. Russ and his guests set the scene for the games ahead with player profiles, features on the clubs, and guides to the teams playing that day. The programmes also take a broader look at the whole

ACTION IMAGES

League and will appeal to fans of the other 70 clubs not involved in the day's live fixture. Friday Night Football will include team news for Saturday's games, transfer and ticket news, and match information from across the divisions. Football League Live on Sunday will review all of Saturday's Division One goals and take a look at the day's newspapers to see which stories are creating the headlines.

The programme then moves to live coverage of the match with Rob Hawthorne coming into view high up in the gantry as he runs through the team lists and possible formations. Rob will commentate on all Nationwide Football League games this season and will be supported by a team of co-commentators including former Ipswich Tower player Alan Brazil who will be a regular this season.

The standards that have become a hallmark of Sky's Premier League coverage will be adapted to coverage of the Nationwide Football League and viewers will enjoy greater access to the players and managers before, during and after the games. Touchline reporter George Gavin, will ask for the thoughts of the managers during the coverage and the opinions of fans at half-time and at the end of the game.

The weekend's Nationwide Football League action kicks-off on Thursday evenings with Football League Review presented by Paul Dempsey. The hour-and-a-half programme takes a look at the week's games and looks forward to the weekend's fixtures.

Live coverage of the Nationwide Football League begins on Friday 16 August with Manchester City's home game against Ipswich Town.

Support programmes

ACTION IMAGES

The new season sees; the start of Nationwide Football League coverage and support show The Football League Review, a fifth season of debate in The Footballers' Football Show, off-beat fun with Soccer AM and Soccer Extra and a global perspective with The Asian Football Show and Futbol Mundial. The weekends are the time for serious soccer and from Friday night's extended Sky Sports Centre through to Sunday's two live matches, Sky Sports has a total of almost 30 hours of football programming.

Sky Sports Centre

Sky Sports - Monday 6pm, 10.15pm, Tues-Thurs 6pm, 10pm
Sky Sports 3 - Monday-Friday 7pm, 11.30pm

Sky Sports Centre was first broadcast at the beginning of the 1995-96 season adding a daily sports news service to Sky Sports programming. Sky Sports Centre, sponsored by Strongbow, aims to break the big stories first with three live evening bulletins and two updates the following morning. The latest football news has always been central to the show with a team of reporters on hand to cover all the latest stories at home and abroad. Sky Sports Centre boasted a number of exclusives during the 1995-96 season; Terry Venables' views on the foreign players rule after the Ilie Dumitrescu case; Paul Merson discussing his personal problems one year after he hit the headlines, Birmingham City's signing of Steve Bruce; and the first pictures of Grimsby Town's injured Ivano Bonetti lying in hospital after a dressing room incident, were all seen first on Sky Sports Centre. Editor Nick Atkins, a former news editor at ITN and a dedicated team will again use their wealth of experience to structure the show in the traditionally fast, exciting format of a news bulletin. This season, regular presenters Dominik Holyer, Jeff

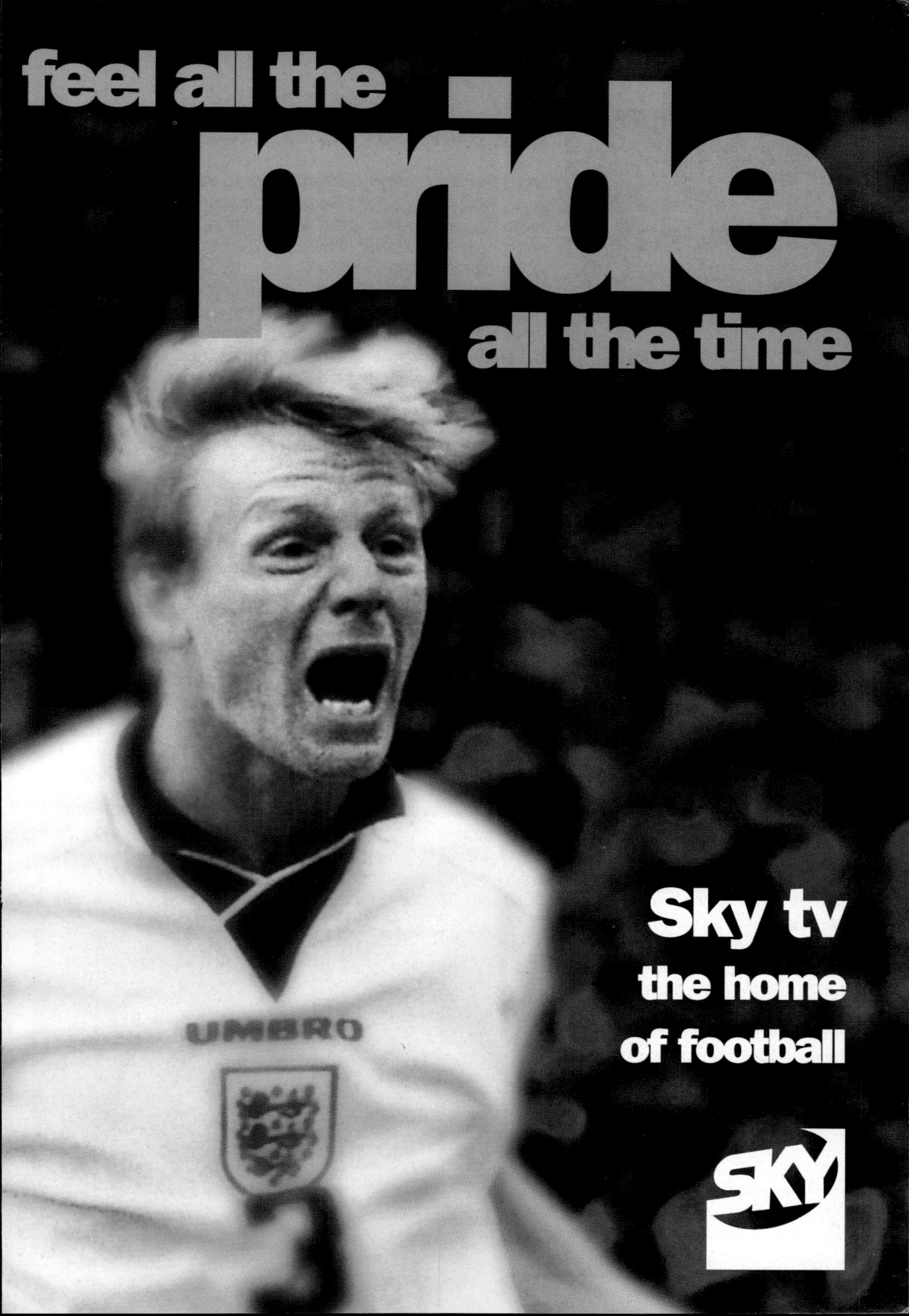

feel all the **pride** all the time

Sky tv
the home
of football

Stelling, David Bobin, Mark Durden Smith and Julian Waters will be joined by Sky's new signing Gabby Yorath.

Sky Sports - Fridays 6.30pm, 10pm / repeat at 10pm

Friday's Sky Sports Centre is dedicated to the weekend's football programme and the day's other sports headlines. This season, Sky Sports will show over 170 live matches across the whole spectrum of domestic and international football, and Friday's Sky Sports Centre will provide the perfect preview to the extended football weekend. As well as updates on the week's football news, Sky Sports Centre can also break the big stories before the weekend's games, bring the latest team news as it happens and interview the potential headline makers. Plus, there's action from the previous week and a host of features on the big matches over the following three days, including previews of Sky's live Nationwide Football League, FA Carling Premiership and Scottish matches. Friday's presenters will include Dominik Holyer, Gabby Yorath and Mark Durden-Smith.

Football League Preview & Tartan Extra

Sky Sports 3 - Thursdays 7.30-9.00pm

This season, Sky Sports will be showing up to sixty games from the Nationwide Football League and the new magazine support programme - The Football League Review - will be the perfect guide to Divisions One, Two and Three. Presented by Paul Dempsey, the show will look back on the week's games and look forward to the weekend's programme while a team of roving reporters will follow all the stories developing in the three divisions of the Football League. The show will also go behind the scenes with fly-on-the-wall video diaries featuring one club from each division. The programme aims to bring alive the teams, individual players and fans to viewers across the country as Sky Sports embarks on a new era of football coverage following all three divisions of The Nationwide Football League.

Sky Sports - Mondays 6.30-7.00pm

As Rangers face the final hurdle in their bid to equal Celtic's record nine successive Scottish League Championships, Tartan Extra will follow what promises to be a memorable campaign. Now in its third season, the Scottish football magazine show, sponsored by Littlewoods, will launch four hours of football in its familiar position on Monday evenings, preceding the Ford Monday Night live game. Tartan Extra is the ultimate guide to the Scottish scene, offering a complete round up of the week's action and reporting on teams from across the divisions of the Bell's Scottish League. In addition to a full round-up of goals from all divisions, Tartan Extra will also continue to run features on up-and-coming games following teams from every corner of Scotland and showcasing the Scottish game across the UK. Sky Sports will again show up to seventeen live games from Scotland's major competitions this season - The Bell's Premier Division, Coca-Cola Cup, and Tennent's Scottish Cup, in addition to the new extended coverage of the domestic competitions in England.

ACTION IMAGES

Sports Saturday & Goals On Sunday

Sky Sports - Saturdays. Football Preview 12.00-2.00pm. Results 4.15-5.30pm

This season Gillette Sports Saturday, Sky Sports' weekly Saturday afternoon sports show, has more football than ever before. Starting at 12.00pm the first half of the show will consist of a two-hour football preview, looking forward to all the day's key fixtures in the FA Carling Premiership, Nationwide Football League, and Bell's Scottish League with the opinions of special guests George Best and Mark Lawrenson. At 2.00pm there is a two hour break for live rugby union from the Courage Clubs Championship or Pilkington Cup, before Sports Saturday returns with the fastest results service on television. From 4.15pm, the scores are updated constantly, with a full classified check at 4.45pm. Reporters are ready with details at every Premiership game and selected games from the Football League. Sky Sports covers every corner of the sporting spectrum and features on events aside from football will remain a key part of the programme. But as producer Andy Hornett explains; "Football is such an integral part of a sports fans' Saturday afternoon that we will be trying harder than ever to capture that excitement in the build up, main body and finale of the show."

Sky Sports - Sundays. 11.00am-12.00pm

Anna Walker's Goals on Sunday is placed at the centre of the three-day football weekend. The Sunday morning show is in the perfect position to review Saturday's Premiership action and look ahead to the live games of Ford Super Sunday and Monday Night Football. This season, Goals on Sunday, sponsored by Ford, is a sixty-minute programme beginning at an earlier time of 11.00am. Once again, it will feature all the goals from the previous day's games in the FA Carling Premiership and is the perfect point to take stock of Sky Sports' football weekend. Presenter Anna Walker is also joined in the studio by the stars of the game and heroes of the previous afternoon to review the matches, analyse the goals, and discuss any of the big stories from the morning's newspapers. There is also a chance to review the latest league tables in the build-up to the afternoon's game and a look forward to the week's football on Sky Sports.

Soccer AM & Soccer Extra

Sky Sports 2 - Saturday 7-11am

Presented by Vince Henderson, Helen Chamberlain and Tim Lovejoy, Soccer AM goes out early on Saturday morning, ahead of the week's main games, and its carefree attitude is the perfect way to wake-up to the weekend. Britain's only all-football breakfast show contains lively chat and competitions galore, attracting the attention of the younger audience but also appealing to older football fans. This season, Soccer AM will mix a deluge of goals and off-beat features with studio-based fun, showing every Premiership goal from that week plus action from the Nationwide and Bell's Scottish football league. The usual mix of competitions and phone-ins will remain alongside more star interviews and special guests. For those off to the match in the afternoon there will be up-to-date ticket information, and travelling fans will be kept abreast of the situation on the roads and trains with a full travel report. For the ideal kick-start to your football weekend Soccer AM is just the ticket.

Sky Sports 2 - Sunday 7-11am

Soccer Extra gives Sunday's early-riser a detailed review of Saturday's action amid lively studio debate. There are highlights of the best games from the FA Carling Premiership and all three divisions of the Football League and a look ahead to Ford Super Sunday and Monday Night Football.

Studio guests will continue to provide lively discussion on Soccer Extra, with Sky Sports presenters acting as the referees, and the fans getting their say through regular phone-ins. This season, regular presenter Helen Chamberlain is joined by Andy Kerr, a former professional footballer with Wycombe Wanderers. There are also studio appearances from guests drawn from different corners of the game discussing the game's big issues, plus competitions and interactive TV games in a fast-moving four-hour show. For Sunday morning footballers or serious soccer addicts wanting an early start, Soccer Extra is vital viewing.

ACTION IMAGES

The Footballers' Football Show & Hold The Back Page

Sky Sports - Tuesdays 10.45-11.45pm. Repeat Wednesday am

Sun journalist Brian Woolnough returns to the table to host Sky Sports' longest running support programme. Now in its fifth season The Footballers' Football Show has become recognised by fans, players and managers alike as the platform for discussion and has featured some of the most well known and respected figures in the game talking about the issues that matter. Over 500 guests have passed through the studios through the years including the late Bobby Moore, George Graham and new England manager Glenn Hoddle. Other key figures in football, from coaches to writers, and agents to referees, have also added their contributions to the programme. Last season, the show tackled many of the game's biggest issues including the recent Bosman ruling and the difficulties surrounding the England manager's job, in addition to many topics stemming from the previous night's live football coverage. The show allows panelists to react to the major soccer stories and is fascinating viewing for all fans of football. In a game of opinions, The Footballer's Football Show is the perfect forum.

Sky Sports - Fridays 11.00-12.00pm

Brian Woolnough is the host of Friday night's sports discussion programme Hold the Back Page. This season, Hold the Back Page moves to Friday nights where Brian Woolnough will once again conduct an hour-long conversation with a panel of sports journalists looking at the stories behind the headlines with the people in the know.

Like The Footballer's Football Show, Hold the Back Page offers the ideal platform for informed debate but casts its net wider over the whole spectrum of sport. Many of the country's most renowned sports journalists have appeared on the show including; The Sun's Colin Hart, The Daily Express' Steve Curry, Neil Harman of the Daily Mail, David Lacey of The Guardian and The Sunday Telegraph's Patrick Barclay. With a mixture of journalists ready to express their opinions and share their stories, the debate is often lively, always informed and is compulsive viewing for those who want to look beyond the back pages. For those who are serious about their sport, Hold the Back Page gives a rare insight into the views of people who create the headlines in Britain's favourite papers.

Futbol Mundial & Asian Football Show

Sky Sports - Weekly

Futbol Mundial, as its name suggests, takes in all four corners of the globe, reviewing both the international scene and the world's leading domestic leagues. A review of the league news from across the world of soccer will form an essential part of the football fans weekly itinerary, giving a round-up of results and standings across Europe, Africa, Asia and South America. And Futbol Mundial will follow the big stories and transfers across

ACTION IMAGES

watch all your
heroes
all the time

live football on Sky
- FA Carling Premiership - Sundays and Mondays exclusively live on Sky Sports 1
- Nationwide Football League - Fridays and Sundays live on Sky Sports 3
- England's Wembley World Cup Campaign - exclusively live on Sky Sports 1
- FA Cup - live on Sky Sports 1 • Coca-Cola Cup - live on Sky Sports 3
- The best of Scottish Football - live on Sky Sports 1

programming line-up
- Sky Sports Centre - Weekdays, 6 & 10pm on Sky Sports 1, 7 & 11.30pm on Sky Sports 3
- The Footballers' Football Show - Tuesdays, 10.30pm on Sky Sports 1
- Goals on Sunday - Sundays, 11am on Sky Sports 1
- Sports Saturday - Saturdays, 12 noon on Sky Sports 1
- Soccer AM - Saturdays, 7-11am on Sky Sports 2
- Soccer Extra - Sundays, 7-11am on Sky Sports 2
- Netbusters - Thursdays, 6.30pm on Sky Sports 1
- Football League Review - Thursdays, 7.30pm on Sky Sports 3
- Tartan Extra - Mondays, 6.30pm on Sky Sports 1

get Sky for the best
football season ever

Europe and beyond, showing action of the greatest players in the global game. In the build-up to the World Cup finals in 1998, the 30-minute show will provide a vital insight into the European nations set to launch a challenge in the increasingly competitive international scene. And from further afield the show will keep track of major tournaments and international games across the five footballing continents in an imaginative mix of highlights, news and features.

Sky Sports - Tuesday evenings

Sky Sports' hour-long Asian Football Show focuses on one of the fastest growing footballing continents in the world. Three Asian nations are already ranked higher than Wales, Northern Ireland and the Republic of Ireland in FIFA's top 50 of international teams with Japan (30th), Saudi Arabia (35th) and China (50th). Japan were just three places behind England before Euro 96. Each programme consists of two main feature games, a goal of the week, trivia teasers and a news round-up, plus a fortnightly player profile and an A to Z of Asian football.

The show focuses on some of football's undiscovered areas, from Kazakhstan, with its 6,000 clubs and 260,000 players, to Japan's booming J-League where many of Brazil's 1994 World Cup winning side still play including Leonardo, Zinho, Jorginho, and Dunga. The show also features the leagues in: Hong Kong, Thailand, Malaysia, Korea, Pakistan, China, the Lebanon, Middle East, Afghanistan and Vietnam. Football is the global game - the most popular sport in the world. The Asian Football Show captures the spirit and skill of these emerging footballing nations.

Sky News & other media

Sky News

Sky News carries more sports news than any other broadcaster with reports every hour presented by a team of reporters including Steve Bottomley, Mark Saggers, Louise Moran, Jon Desborough, Chris Skudder, Pete Barraclough and Ian Woods. At the weekends, this commitment is extended with a half-hour preview programme, Saturday Sports Action at 8.30am followed by two half-hour round-ups - Sportsline at 7.30pm and Sportsline Extra at 11.30pm, offering even more comprehensive coverage of the day's football during the season. During the week, Sky News offers features on the previous night's action in all competitions and looks forward to the big games in the evening. There are bulletins every hour on Sky News plus an extra three during the morning's Sunrise show between 6.00am and 9.30am and additional bulletins between 12.00pm and 1.00pm and at 4.50pm and 10.00pm.

New media

Sky not only provides the best in television, but also new interactive media through Sky Internet, Sky Intertext and Sky Text.

Sky Internet is located at http://www.sky.co.uk. Launched in February 1996, the Sky Internet site is packed with information from all the Sky channels. Foremost are the Sky Sports pages which are home to the official Manchester United Web Site (http://www.sky.co.uk/sports/manu). The first site to be endorsed by the current Premiership champions, it gives fans a huge range of news and information including interviews, fixtures, statistics, match reports, player biographies, games and competitions. The Sky Internet site has quickly expanded to include world news updated by Sky News, a Sky One page, including the official X-Files site, an interactive TV Guide, the best in movies and a Sky shop, offering a range of merchandise.

Developed initially as a response to the Fantasy Football boom, Sky's Intertext service provides Sky subscribers with a range of services including Interactive Team Football. First launched as a record-breaking promotion in The Times newspaper, ITF enables the user to play Fantasy Football via a touch tone telephone and offers a range of opportunities for future development.

Sky Text offers viewers a full, fast sports information service featuring a unique page for every Premiership, First Division and Scottish Premier League club. All information is updated direct from Sky Television, while match information is on screen within moments of the ball hitting the net.

THE SKY SPORTS
ULTIMATE FOOTBALL
GUIDE 1997

Published by: SKY BLUE PUBLICATIONS LTD

Sponsored by: SKY SPORTS

CLUB PAGES
INTRODUCTION

There are no major changes to the layout of this year's edition of the Ultimate Football Guide. The only change you will have hopefully noticed is that you are reading this alot earlier than in previous years, thus giving you the guide for almost the whole football season.

The early publication date has, however, meant that we have had to use last year's squad photographs in most cases, with clubs having their photocalls after our deadline.

We have tried to maintain our policy of having the players at their clubs as at the beginning of the season, though some transfers may well have been missed, again due to the earlier deadline.

A new section can be found at the back of the book, with all of England's International matches and teams 1946-1996', which we hope you will find both interesting and informative.

To help you understand the notations used within this book and to give you a brief idea of the information that can be found within the club section, the following notes should be read.

FIRST PAGE: Includes a review of the 1995-96 season; Senior club personnel; Playing squad photograph plus caption.

SECOND & THIRD PAGES   Complete match by match details of the 1995-96 season. This year an 'X' has ben used to denote a player's appearance in a match throughout the four divisions. In the case of a substitution being made the following applies:
X1 (off) - S1 (on); X2 - S2; X3-S3; S - non-playing sub.

RECORDS PAGE(S)   Premier and First Division clubs' records and statistics cover two complete pages. Second and Third Division clubs' records and statistics are covered on one page with details of their Manager also included.

PLAYERS PAGE   This page is always left to the last minute so to include the summer signings, thus giving a list of players that are contracted to the club for the beginning of the **1996-97** season.
Details include - Height, Weight, Birth Date and Contract Date as well as League, FA Cup, League Cup and 'other'* appearances and goals. *All European competitions and any other domestic competition, such as The Associate Members Shield or Play-offs and alike, come under the heading of 'Other' Appearances and goals.

SEVENTH PAGE (Prem. & Div.1)   Overspill from the players page is then followed by details on the team manager.

GROUNDS PAGE   Contains 1996-97 matchday ticket prices along with details on the ground and easy to read directions.
Also included on this page are details plus the front cover (1995-96 cover) of the clubs' 1996-97 matchday programme.

F.A. CARLING PREMIERSHIP...

F.A. CARLING PREMIERSHIP 1995-96

FINAL LEAGUE TABLE

		P	W	D	L	F	A	W	D	L	F	A	Pts
			HOME					**AWAY**					
1	MANCHESTER UNITED (+1)	38	15	4	0	36	9	10	3	6	37	26	82
2	NEWCASTLE UNITED (+4)	38	17	1	1	38	9	7	5	7	28	28	78
3	LIVERPOOL (+1)	38	14	4	1	46	13	6	7	6	24	21	71
4	ASTON VILLA (+14)	38	11	5	3	32	15	7	4	8	20	20	63
5	ARSENAL (+7)	38	10	7	2	30	16	7	5	7	19	16	63
INTO EUROPE													
6	EVERTON (+9)	38	10	5	4	35	19	7	5	7	29	25	61
7	BLACKBURN ROVERS (-6)	38	14	2	3	44	19	4	5	10	17	28	61
8	TOTTENHAM HOTSPUR (-1)	38	9	5	5	26	19	7	8	4	24	19	61
9	NOTTINGHAM FOREST (-6)	38	11	6	2	29	17	4	7	8	21	37	58
10	WEST HAM UNITED (+4)	38	9	5	5	25	21	5	4	10	18	31	51
11	CHELSEA (-)	38	7	7	5	30	22	5	7	7	16	22	50
12	Middlesbrough	38	8	3	8	27	27	3	7	9	8	23	43
13	LEEDS UNITED (-8)	38	8	3	8	21	21	4	4	11	19	36	43
14	WIMBLEDON (-5)	38	5	6	8	27	33	5	5	9	28	37	41
15	SHEFFIELD WEDNESDAY (-2)	38	7	5	7	30	31	3	5	11	18	30	40
16	COVENTRY CITY (-)	38	6	7	6	21	23	2	7	10	21	37	38
17	SOUTHAMPTON (-7)	38	7	7	5	21	18	2	4	13	13	34	38
RELEGATED													
18	MANCHESTER CITY (-1)	38	7	7	5	21	19	2	4	13	12	39	38
19	QUEENS PARK RANGERS (-11)	38	6	5	8	25	26	3	1	15	13	31	38
20	BOLTON WANDERERS	38	5	4	10	16	31	3	1	15	23	40	29

The figure in brackets denotes the number of places lost or gained on the clubs 1994-95 final position.

European Qualification: Champions League - Manchester United.
UEFA Cup - Newcastle United, Aston Villa & Arsenal.   ECWC - Liverpool.

FA CARLING PREMERSHIP 1996-97

ARSENAL
(The Gunners)
F.A. CARLING PREMIERSHIP
SPONSORED BY: JVC (UK) LTD.

Back Row (L-R): Chris Kiwomya, Scott Marshall, Paul Merson, Lee Harper, Steve Bould, Andy Linighan, David Seaman, Steve Morrow, Nigel Winterburn, Vince Bartram, Ray Parlour, John Hartson, Ian Selley, George Armstrong (res. Coach). **Front Row:** Gary Lewin (Physio), Paul Dickov, Eddie McGoldrick, Lee Dixon, John Jensen, Ian Wright, Tony Adams, Bruce Rioch (Manager), Dennis Bergkamp, Glenn Helder, David Platt, Mark Flatts, David Hillier, Martin Keown, Stewart Houston (First Team Coach).

ARSENAL
FORMED IN 1886
TURNED PROFESSIONAL IN 1891
PLC IN 1990

CHAIRMAN: P D Hill-Wood
DIRECTORS:
D Dein (Vice-Chairman)
Sir Robert Bellinger CBE, DSO
R G Gibbs, C E B L Carr,
R C L Carr, K J Friar, D Fiszman.

SECRETARY/Managing Director:
Ken J Friar (0171 226 0304)
Assistant Secretary
David Miles
COMMERCIAL MANAGER
John Hazell (0171 359 0808)

MANAGER: Bruce Rioch
ASSISTANT: Stewart Houston/Pat Rice

RESERVE TEAM MANAGER
George Armstrong
YOUTH TEAM MANAGER
Tom Walley
PHYSIOTHERAPIST
Gary Lewin

CLUB STATISTICIAN FOR THE DIRECTORY
Chris Thompson

The summer months brought some much-needed stability to Highbury after the traumas caused by off-field scandals in the latter half of the 1994/5 season.

Bruce Rioch arrived as manager, and over £12 million was spent on two players, Dennis Bergkamp and David Platt. The high profile of these players meant that expectations were unrealistically high in some quarters, with some even thinking that the championship was a possibility. Good cup runs and a UEFA Cup place via a good league position were always going to be more realistic goals.

The Gunners made a solid, if unspectacular, start to the season, remaining unbeaten for seven games. The Highbury faithful had to wait until 23 September to see Dennis Bergkamp open his account with a brace against Southampton. David Platt, although appearing in two-thirds of the games, was injured in a pre-season game against Wolves and was not fully fit until the end of the season. Arsenal will surely see the best of him during 1996/7.

Arsenal's home form was, in stark contrast to the previous season, very good with both Manchester United and Newcastle being defeated. Indeed, Newcastle were to be beaten twice at Highbury when they succumbed to the Gunners in the quarter final of the Coca-Cola Cup. Arsenal really should have made the final of this competition, but squandered a two-goal advantage created by Dennis Bergkamp to go out on the away-goals rule at Villa Park. The FA Cup was a different story, with the team eliminated at Bramall Lane in a third-round replay.

The close season again sees Highbury in something of a turmoil. Goal-scoring icon Ian Wright is apparently unhappy with his role in the team, as well as the management, and requested a transfer before the end of the season. There is still much pruning to be done with the players on the periphery of the team and there is still a need for quality new faces, particularly in mid-field.

Highbury is drawing capacity crowds for every game and the fans deserve to have these problems resolved without further ado. Arsenal are a side who should always be in the forefront of the league.

CHRIS THOMPSON

ARSENAL

League: 5th   FA Cup: 3rd Rnd   Coca-Cola Cup: Semi-Finals

M	DATE	COMP	VEN	OPPONENTS	RESULT	HT	LP	GOAL SCORERS/GOAL TIMES	ATT.
1	A 20	PL	H	Middlesbrough	D 1-1	1-1	8	Wright 36	37308
2	23	PL	A	Everton	W 2-0	0-0	5	Platt 69, Wright 86	(35775)
3	26	PL	A	Coventry City	D 0-0	0-0			(20081)
4	29	PL	H	Nottingham Forest	D 1-1	1-0	5	Platt 41	38248
5	S 10	PL	A	Manchester City	W 1-0	0-0	6	Wright 90	(23994)
6	16	PL	H	West Ham United	W 1-0	0-0	5	Wright 75(pen)	38065
7	19	CC 2/1	A	**Hartlepool United**	W 3-0	2-0		**Adams 10, 85, Wright 40**	(4945)
8	23	PL	H	Southampton	W 4-2	2-0	4	Bergkamp 17, 68, Adams 23, Wright 73	38136
9	30	PL	A	Chelsea	L 0-1	0-0	8		(31048)
10	O 3	CC 2/2	H	**Hartlepool United**	W 5-0	2-0		**Bergkamp 29, 49, Wright 33, 58, 87 (3)**	27194
11	14	PL	A	Leeds United	W 3-0	1-0	3	Merson 43, Bergkamp 56, Wright 86	(38332)
12	21	PL	H	Aston Villa	W 2-0	0-0	4	Merson 47, Wright 78	38271
13	24	CC 3	A	**Barnsley**	W 3-0	2-0		**Bould 38, Bergkamp 42, Keown 76**	(18429)
14	30	PL	A	Bolton Wanderers	L 0-1	0-1	4		(18682)
15	N 4	PL	H	Manchester United	W 1-0	1-0	3	Bergkamp 14	38317
16	18	PL	A	Tottenham Hotspur	L 1-2	1-1	3	Bergkamp 14	(32894)
17	21	PL	H	Sheffield Wednesday	W 4-2	1-0	3	Bergkamp 3, Winterburn 53, Dickov 64, Hartson 86	34556
18	26	PL	H	Blackburn Rovers	D 0-0	0-0	3		37695
19	29	CC 4	H	**Sheffield Wednesday**	W 2-1	1-1		**Wright 39(pen), Hartson 64**	35361
20	D 2	PL	A	Aston Villa	D 1-1	0-0	3	Platt 60	(37770)
21	9	PL	A	Southampton	D 0-0	0-0	3		(15238)
22	16	PL	H	Chelsea	D 1-1	0-1	5	Dixon 88	38295
23	23	PL	A	Liverpool	L 1-3	1-1	7	Wright 8(pen)	(39806)
24	26	PL	H	Queens Park Rangers	W 3-0	1-0	5	Wright 44, Merson 61, 83	38259
25	30	PL	H	Wimbledon	L 1-3	1-1	5	Wright 27	37540
26	J 2	PL	A	Newcastle United	L 0-2	0-1	6		(36530)
27	6	FAC 3	H	**Sheffield United**	D 1-1	0-0		**Wright 70**	33453
28	10	CC QF	H	**Newcastle United**	W 2-0	1-0		**Wright 44, 89**	37857
29	13	PL	A	Middlesbrough	W 3-2	1-1	7	Merson 6, Platt 59, Helder 62	(29359)
30	17	FAC 3R	A	**Sheffield United**	L 0-1	0-0			(22255)
31	20	PL	H	Everton	L 1-2	1-0	8	Wright 38	38275
32	F 3	PL	H	Coventry City	D 1-1	1-1	8	Bergkamp 24	35623
33	10	PL	A	Nottingham Forest	W 1-0	0-0	7	Bergkamp 59	(27222)
34	14	CC SF1	H	**Aston Villa**	D 2-2	2-1		**Bergkamp 26, 32**	37562
35	21	CC SF2	A	**Aston Villa**	D 0-0	0-0			(39334)
36	24	PL	A	West Ham United	W 1-0	1-0	6	Hartson 2	(24217)
37	M 2	PL	A	Queens Park Rangers	D 1-1	0-1	7	Bergkamp 50	(17970)
38	5	PL	H	Manchester City	W 3-1	2-0	5	Hartson 29, 55, Dixon 41	34519
39	16	PL	A	Wimbledon	W 3-0	0-0	5	Winterburn 61, Platt 65, Bergkamp 83	(18335)
40	20	PL	A	Manchester United	L 0-1	0-0	5		(50028)
41	23	PL	H	Newcastle United	W 2-0	2-0	5	Marshall 3, Wright 17	38271
42	A 6	PL	A	Leeds United	W 2-1	1-0	5	Wright 44, 90	37619
43	8	PL	A	Sheffield Wednesday	L 0-1	0-0	5		(24349)
44	15	PL	H	Tottenham Hotspur	D 0-0	0-0	5		38273
45	27	PL	A	Blackburn Rovers	D 1-1	0-1	6	Wright 75(pen)	(29834)
46	M 1	PL	H	Liverpool	D 0-0	0-0	5		38323
47	5	PL	H	Bolton Wanderers	W 2-1	0-0	5	Platt 82, Bergkamp 84	38104

Best Home League Attendance: 38323 v Liverpool   Smallest: 34519 v Manchester City   Average: 37568

Goal Scorers:
PL(49):   Wright(15),Bergkamp(11),Platt(6),Merson(5),Hartson(4),Dixon(2),Winterburn(2),Dickov(1),Helder(1),Adams(1),Marshall(1)
CC(17):   Wright(7),Bergkamp(5),Adams(2),Hartson(1),Keown(1),Bould(1)
FAC(1):   Wright(1)

(D) Adams	(G) Bartram	(F) Bergkamp	(D) Bould	(F) Clarke	(F) Dickov	(D) Dixon	(F) Hartson	(F) Helder	(M) Hillier	(M) Hughes	(M) Jensen	(D) Keown	(D) Linighan	(D) Marshall	(M) McGoldrick	(M) McGowan	(F) Merson	(M) Morrow	(M) Parlour	(M) Platt	(M) Rose	(G) Seaman	(M) Selley	(D) Winterburn	(F) Wright	Referee	#
X	S	X	X			X	S	S1				X					X		X1	X		X		X	X	G.Ashby	1
X	S	X	X			X		S				S1	X1				X		X1	X		X		X	X	K.Burge	2
X	S	X	X			X2		S1				S2	X				X		X1	X		X		X	X	S.Dunn	3
X	S	X	X			X		S1				S	X				X		X1	X		X		X	X	L.R.Dilkes	4
X	S	X	X			X						X	X		S1		X		X1			X		X	X	D.Gallagher	5
X	S	X	X			X	S	X				X					X	S	X			X		X	X	A.Wilkie	6
X	S	X	X			X	S	X				X					X	S	X			X		X	X	E.Wolstenholme	7
X	S	X	X			X	S	X				X					X		X			X		X	X	R.Hart	8
X		X	X2			X		S1				X1	X	S2			X1		X			X		X	X	M.Bowdenham	9
X	S	X1	X			X	S1	S1				X	X				X1		X			X		X	X	S.W.Dunn	10
X	S	X	X			X	S	X				X	X				X		X			X		X	X	P.Crabtree	11
X	S	X	X			X	S	X				S	X				X		X			X		X	X	R.Hart	12
X		X	X			X	S1	X		S1		X1	X				X		X			X		X	X1	J.T.Winter	13
X	S	X	X			X	S	X					X1				X		X	S1		X		X	X	K.Cooper	14
X	S	X	X			X	S1	X				S	X				X		X			X		X	X1	P.Durkin	15
X	S	X	X			X	X	X1	S1			S	X				X		X			X		X		A.B.Wilkie	16
X		X	X	S1		X	X	X1	S			S	X				X		X			X		X		L.R.Dilkes	17
X		X	X	S2		X	X2	S1	X			S	X1				X		X			X		X		G.Poll	18
X		X1	X	S		X	S1	S1	S			X					X		X			X		X	X	K.Burge	19
X		X	S2	S1		X	X2	X1				X					X	S1	X			X		X	X	J.T.Winter	20
X		X	S1	S		X	X1					X	X	S			X		X			X		X	X	P.Danson	21
X		X	S		X	X	S1					X1	X	S			X		X			X		X	X	G.Ashby	22
X			S		X	X	S2	X2				X	X	X	S1		X		X1	X		X		X	X	K.Cooper	23
X			X	X	X	X	S	S				X	X	X	S		X		X			X		X	X	M.Reed	24
X		X	X2	S1		X						X1	X	X		S	X	S2	X			X		X	X	S.Lodge	25
X		X	X2	S1	S2	X						X	X		X1	X		X		X		X		X	X	D.Gallagher	26
X	S		X	S	X	X	X					X	X	S			X		X			X		X	X	P.Durkin	27
X		X	X1	X	S	S	X					X	X				X		X			X		X	X	G.Ashby	28
X		X	S	S	X		X					S1	X				X		X			X		X	X	G.Poll	29
X		X	S2	S	X1	X						X2	X	S1			X		X			X		X	X	P.Durkin	30
		X	X1	X		X						X	X	X		X	X	S			S	X		X	X	M.Bodenham	31
		X	X			X	S	X		S1	X1	X	X				X	S				X		X	X	S.W.Dunn	32
		X				X	X1	X1	X	S	X	X	X				X	S				X		X	X	R.A.Hart	33
		X				X	S	X1	X		X	X	X				X	S	S1			X		X	X	P.Durkin	34
		X				X	X		S	X		X	X				X	X	X	S1		X		X1	X	K.Burge	35
		X				X	X	X1		S		X	X				X	X	X	S1		X		X		D.Elleray	36
		X				X	X	S		S		X	X				X	X1	X	X	S1	X		X		P.Alcock	37
		X				X	X		S	S		X	X	S			X		X	X	X	X		X		P.Jones	38
		X				X	X	S	S			X	X	X			X		X	S	X	X		X	X	D.Gallagher	39
		X1				X	X	S2	S1			X	X	X			X2		X		X	X		X	X	G.Willard	40
		X				X	X	S2	S			X	X	X			X		X	S1	X	X		X2	X1	P.Durkin	41
		X				X	X	S				X	X	X			X		X	X	S1	X	S	X	X	G.Winter	42
		X				X	X1	X1				X	X	X			X		X	X	S1	X	S1	X	X	S.W.Dunn	43
		X				X	S	S1				X	X	X			X1		X	X	X	S1	X	S2	X	M.Reed	44
		X				X	S3					X	X2				X	X1	X	X	S1	X	S2	X	X3	K.Cooper	45
		X				X	X					X	X	X			X	X	X	S	S	X	S	X		G.Ashby	46
	S	X				X	S1					X	X	X2			X		X	X		X	S2	X	X1	G.Willard	47
21	0	33	19	4	1	38	15	15	3	0	13	34	17	10	0	1	38	3	20	27	1	38	0	36	31	PL Appearances	
0	0	0	0	2	6	0	4	9	2	1	2	0	1	1	1	0	0	1	2	2	3	0	3	0	0	PL Sub Appearances	
5	0	7	5	0	0	7	1+2	4+2	2	0+1	5+1	5	2	0	0	0	7	1	3+1	2+1	0	7	0	7	7	CC Appearances	
2	0	1	0	1+1	0	2	1	2	0	0	2	2	0+1	0	0	1	2	0	0	1	0	2	0	1	2	FAC Appearances	

ARSENAL

CLUB RECORDS

BIGGEST VICTORIES
League: 12-0 v Loughborough Town, Division 2, 12.3.1900.
F.A. Cup: 11-1 v Darwen, 3rd Round, 9.1.1932.
League Cup: 7-0 v Leeds United, 2nd Round, 4.9.1979.
Europe: (ECWC) 7-0 v Standard Liege, 2n Round 3.11.93.
(UEFA) 7-1 v Staevnet, 1st Round, 25.9.1963.
(Fairs Cup) 7-1 v Dinamo Bacau, Q/Final, 18.3.1970.

BIGGEST DEFEATS
League: 0-8 v Loughborough Town, Division 2, 12.12.1896.
F.A. Cup: 0-6 v Sunderland, 1st Round, 21.1.1893.
0-6 v Derby County, 1st Round, 28.1.1899.
0-6 v West Ham, 3rd Round, 5.1.1946.
League Cup: 2-6 v Manchester United, 4th Round,28.11.90.
0-3 v Liverpool, 4th Round, 8.12.1981.
Europe: (UEFA) 2-5 v Spartak Moscow, 1st Round, 29.9.82.

MOST POINTS
3 points a win: 83, 1990-91.
2 points a win: 66, 1930-31.

MOST GOALS SCORED
127, Division 1, 1930-31.
Lambert 38, Jack 31, Bastin 28, Hulme 14, James 5, Brain 4, John 2, Williams 2, Johnson 1, Roberts 1, Jones 1.

MOST GOALS CONCEDED
86, Division 1, 1926-27; Division 1, 1927-28.

MOST FIRST CLASS MATCHES IN A SEASON
70 - 1979-80 (League 42, FA Cup 11, League Cup 7, Charity Shield 1, ECWC 9).

MOST LEAGUE WINS
29, Division 1, 1970-71.

MOST LEAGUE DRAWS
18, Division 1, 1969-70.

MOST LEAGUE DEFEATS
23, Division 1, 1912-13; Division 1, 1924-25.

INDIVIDUAL CLUB RECORDS

MOST GOALS IN A SEASON
Ted Drake - 42, 1934-35.

MOST GOALS IN A MATCH
7. Ted Drake v Aston Villa, Division 1, 14.12.1935 (7-1).

OLDEST PLAYER
Jock Rutherford, 41 years 236 days v Manchester City, 20.3.1926.

YOUNGEST PLAYER
Gerry Ward, 16 years 321 days v Huddersfield, 22.8.1953.

MOST CAPPED PLAYER
Kenny Sansom (England) 77 1981-86.

BEST PERFORMANCES

League: 1930-31: Played 42, Won 29, Drawn 10, Lost 4, Goals for 127, Goals against 59, Points 66. First in Division 1.
Highest Position: Division 1 Champions.
F.A. Cup: Winners in 1929-30 v Huddersfield 2-0.
Winners in 1935-36 v Sheffield United 1-0.
Winners in 1949-50 v Liverpool 2-0.
Winners in 1970-71 v Liverpool 2-1.
Winners in 1978-79 v Manchester Utd 3-2.
Most Recent Success: 3rd Rnd, Yeovil Town (a) 3-1; 4th Rnd, Leeds United (h) 2-2, (a) 3-2 aet; 5th Rnd, Nottinghamshire Forest (h) 2-0; 6th Rnd Ipswich Town (a) 4-2; Semi-final Tottenham Hotspur 1-0; Final Sheffield Wednesday 1-1 aet, 2-1.
League Cup: Winners in 1986-87 v Liverpool 2-1.
Most Recent Success: 1992-93: 2nd Rnd Millwall (h) 1-1, (a) 1-1 (won 3-1 on pens.); 3rd Rnd, Derby County (a) 1-1, (h) 2-1; 4th Rnd, Scarborough (a) 1-0; 5th Rnd Nottingham Forest (h) 2-0; Semi-final, Crystal Palace (a) 3-1 (h) 2-0; Final Sheffield Wednesday 2-1.
Europe: (UEFA) 1969-70: 1st Rnd, Glentoran 5-0,0-1; 2nd Rnd Sp.ch.de Port 0-0,3-0; 3rd Rnd, Rouen 0-0,1-0; 4th Round Dinemo Bacau 2-0,7-1; Semi-final, Ajax 3-0,0-1; Final , Anderlect 1-3,3-0.
(ECWC) 1993-94: 1st Round Odense 2-1,1-1; 2nd Round Standard Leige 3-0,7-0; 2nd Round Torino 0-0,1-0; Semi-Final Paris St. Girman 1-1,1-0; Final Parma 1-0.

DIVISIONAL RECORD

	Played	Won	Drawn	Lost	For	Against	Points
Division 1/P	3,260	1,384	849	1027	5,214	4,324	**3,894**
Division 2	428	216	73	139	825	550	**505**
Total	**3,688**	**1,600**	**922**	**1,166**	**6,029**	**4,874**	**4,399**

ADDITIONAL INFORMATION
PREVIOUS NAME
None.

PREVIOUS LEAGUES
None.

Club Colours: Red with white sleeve shirts, white shorts, red and white stockings.
Change Colours: Blue with teal marked shirts, blue shorts, blue & teal stockings.

Reserve League: Football Combination.
Youth League: South Eastern Counties.

RECORDS AND STATISTICS

COMPETITIONS

Div 1/P	Div.2	Euro C	ECWC	UEFA
1904-13	1893-04	1971-72	1979-80	1963-64
1919-	1913-19	1991-92	1993-94	1969-70
			1994-95	1970-71
				1978-79
				1981-82
				1982-83

HONOURS

Div 1/P	FAC	Lge Cup	UEFA	ECWC	C/Sh'ld
1930-31	1929-30	1986-87	1969-70	1993-94	1930
1932-33	1935-36	1992-93			1931
1933-34	1949-50				1933
1934-35	1970-71				1934
1937-38	1978-79				1938
1947-48	1992-93				1948
1952-53					1953
1970-71					1992
1988-89					shared
1990-91					

MOST APPEARANCES

David O'Leary 682+40 (1975-93)
(Including 3 Charity Shield & 2 Others)

Year	League	FA Cup	Lge Cup	Europe
1975-76	27	1	2	
1976-77	33	3	4	
1977-78	41	6	6	
1978-79	37	11	1	5
1979-80	34	9	6	9
1980-81	24	1	2	
1981-82	40	1	5	4
1982-83	36	5	7	2
1983-84	36	1	4	
1984-85	36	3	3	
1985-86	35	5	7	
1986-87	39	4	9	
1987-88	23	4	6	
1988-89	26	2		
1989-90	28+6	3	4	
1990-91	11+10	5+1	0+1	
1991-92	11+14	1	0+1	1
1992-93	5+5	1+3	2	
	522+35	66+4	68+2	21

MOST GOALS IN A CAREER

Cliff Bastin - 178 (1929-37) includes 2 in Charity Shield

Year	League	FA Cup
1929-30	7	4
1930-31	28	1
1931-32	15	6
1932-33	33	
1933-34	13	2
1934-35	20	1
1935-36	11	6
1936-37	5	3
1937-38	15	2
1938-39	3	1
Total	150	26

Current top goalscorer: Ian Wright -144 (1991-1996)

RECORD TRANSFER FEE RECEIVED

Amount	Club	Player	Date
£2,000,000	Leeds United	David Rocastle	07/92
£1,500,000	Liverpool	Michael Thomas	12/91
£1,250,000	Crystal Palace	Clive Allen	08/80
£450,000	Liverpool	Ray Kennedy	07/74

RECORD TRANSFER FEE PAID

Amount	Club	Player	Date
£8,500,000	Inter Milan	Dennis Bergkamp	06/95
£4,750,000	Sampdoria	David Platt	07/95
£2,500,000	Luton Town	Jon Hartson	01/95
£2,500,000	Crystal Palace	Ian Wright	09/91

MANAGERS

Name	Seasons	Best	Worst
T E Mitchell	1897-98	5(2)	5(2)
George Excoat	1898-99	7(2)	7(2)
Harry Bradshaw	1899-04	2(2)	8(2)
Phil Kelso	1904-08	7(1)	15(1)
George Morrell	1908-15	6(1)	15(1)
Leslie Knighton	1919-25	9(1)	20(1)
Herbert Chapman	1925-34	1(1)	14(1)
George Allison	1934-47	1(1)	6(1)
Tom Whittaker	1947-56	1(1)	6(1)
Jack Crayston	1956-58	5(1)	12(1)
George Swindin	1958-62	3(1)	15(1)
Billy Wright	1962-66	8(1)	17(1)
Bertie Mee	1966-76	1(1)	17(1)
Terry Neill	1976-83	3(1)	17(1)
Don Howe	1983-86	6(1)	7(1)
George Graham	1986-95	1(1)	6(1)
Bruce Rioch	1995-	5(P)	5(P)

LONGEST LEAGUE RUNS

undefeated matches:	26 (28.4.1990 - 19.1.1991)	of league matches w/out a win:	23 (28.9.1912 - 1.3.1913)
undefeated home matches:	33 (1.10.1902-22.10.1904)	of undefeated away matches:	13 (5.51990 - 12.1.1991)
thout home win:	16 (23.4.1912 - 1.3.1913)	without an away win:	15 (7.1.1928 - 6.10.1928)
league wins:	10 (12.9.1987 - 14.11.1987)	of home wins:	15 (5.9.1903 - 4.4.1904)
league defeats:	7 (12.21977 - 12.3.1977)	of away wins:	6 (22.10.1977 - 27.12.1977)

ARSENAL

PLAYERS NAME / Honours	Ht	Wt	Birthdate	Birthplace / Transfers	Contract Date	Clubs	League	L/Cup	FA Cup	Other	Lge	L/C	FAC	Oth
G O A L K E E P E R S														
Bartram Vince	6.2	13.4	07/08/68	Birmingham	17/08/85	Wolves	5	2	3					
				Loan	27/10/89	Blackpool	9			2				
				£65000	24/07/91	Bournemouth	132	10	14	6				
				£400000	10/08/94	Arsenal	11	0+1						
Harper Lee	6.1	13.0	30/10/71	Chelsea		Sittingbourne								
				£150000	16/06/94	Arsenal								
Lukic John	6.4	13.7	11/12/60	Chesterfield	16.12.78	Leeds United (A)	146	7	9	3				
E: B.1, u21.7, Y.10. Div.1'89'92. LC'87. CT'89.				£50000	25.07.83	Arsenal	223	32	21	4				
				£1000000	14.06.90	Leeds United	181	16	14	11				
				Free		Arsenal								
Seaman David	6.2	13.0	10/09/63	Rotherham	22/09/81	Leeds United								
E:29,B.6,u21.10. Div.1'91.				£4000	13/08/82	Peterborough Utd	91	10	5					
LC'93. FAC'93. ECWC'94. FlgXl1				£100000	05/10/84	Birmingham City	75	4	5					
				£225000	07/08/86	Q.P.R.	141	13	17	4				
				£1300000	18/05/90	Arsenal	227	34	24	26				
D E F E N D E R S														
Adams Tony	6.1	12.1	10/10/66	Romford	30/01/84	Arsenal	364+3	53+1	31+1	28	24	5	5	3
E: 45,B.4,u21.5,Y.5,S. CT'89. Div.1'89'91.LC'87.'93.FAC'93														
Bould Steve	6.2	11.13	16/11/62	Stoke	15/11/80	Stoke City	179+4	13	10	5	6	1		
E:2,B.1. CT'89 Div.1'89.91.				Loan	19/10/82	Torquay United	9		2					
ECWC'94.				£390000	13/06/88	Arsenal	203+8	27	17	13+3	5	1		2
Dixon Lee	5.9	10.12	17/03/64	Manchester	21/07/82	Burnley	4	1						
E:21,B.4. CT'89 Div.1'89.91.				Free	16/02/84	Chester City	56+1	2	1	3	1			
FAC'93. ECWC'94. FLgXl.1.				Free	15/07/85	Bury	45	4	8	1	6		1	
				£40000	18/07/86	Stoke City	71	6	7	4	5			
				£400000	29/01/88	Arsenal	289+3	39	28	28	18		1	
Keown Martin	6.1	12.4	24/07/66	Oxford	02/02/84	Arsenal	22	5						
E:11,B.1,u21.8,Y.4.				Loan	15/02/85	Brighton & H.A.	21+2	2		2	1	1		1
				£200000	09/06/86	Aston Villa	109+3	12+1	6	2	3			
				£750000	07/08/89	Everton	92+4	11	12+1	6				
				£2000000	04/02/93	Arsenal	96+18	11+2	5+2	9+5	1	1		
Linighan Andy	6.3	12.6	18/06/62	Hartlepool	19/09/80	Hartlepool United	110	7+1	8	1	4	1		1
E: B.4. LC'93. FAC'93. ECWC'94				£200000	15/05/84	Leeds United	66	6	2	2	3	1		
				£65000	17/01/86	Oldham Athletic	87	8	3	4	6	2		
				£350000	04/03/88	Norwich City	86	6	10	4	8			
				£1250000	04/07/90	Arsenal	91+16	13+1	12+2	7+1	4	1	1	1
Marshall Scott	6.1	12.5	01/05/73	Islington	18/03/91	Arsenal	12+1				1			
S: u21.3,Y,S.				Loan	03/12/93	Rotherham United	10		1		1			
				Loan	25/08/94	Sheffield United	17							
Winterburn Nigel	5.10	10.7	11/12/63	Nuneaton	14/08/81	Birmingham City								
E:2,B.3,u21.1,Y.1. Div.1'89'91.				Free	22/09/83	Wimbledon	164+1	13	12	2	8			
CT'89. LC'93. FAC'93. ECWC'94				£407000	26/05/87	Arsenal	307+1	42	31	30	7	3		
M I D F I E L D														
Hillier David	5.10	11.6	18/12/69	Blackheath	11/02/88	Arsenal	82+20	13+2	13+2	5+4	2			
E: u21.1. FAYC'88. Div.1'91.														
Hughes Steve	6.0	12.12	18/09/76	Reading	01/08/94	Arsenal	1+1	0+1						
E: Y. FAYC'94.														
McGoldrick Eddie	5.10	11.7	30/04/65	Islington		Kettering Town		2						
Ei:15,B.1. Div.4'87. FMC'91.						Nuneaton Borough								
ECWC'94.				£10000	23/08/86	Northampton Town	97+10	9	6+1	7	9		1	1
				£200000	10/01/89	Crystal Palace	139+8	21+1	5	13+2	11	2		3
				£1000000	18/06/93	Arsenal	32+6	7+2	1+1	4+4				1
McGowan Gavin	5.11	12.03	16/01/76	Blackheath	01/07/94	Arsenal	2+2		1					
E: Y,S. FAYC'94.														
Morrow Steve	6.0	11.3	02/07/70	Belfast	05/05/88	Arsenal	34+14	7+2	3+2	1+4	1	2		
NI:19,u21.3,Y,S. FAYC'88.				Loan	16/01/91	Reading	10							
LC'93. ECWC'94.				Loan	14/08/91	Watford	7+1		1					
				Loan	30/10/91	Reading	3							
				Loan	04/03/92	Barnet	1							
Parlour Raymond	5.10	11.12	07/03/73	Romford	06/03/91	Arsenal	84+22	13+2	9	7+2	4		1	
E: u21.12, S. FLC'93. FAC'93.ECWC'94.														
Platt David	5.10	11.12	10/06/66	Oldham		Chadderton								
E:62,B.3,u21.4.					24/07/84	Manchester United								
				Free	23/02/85	Crewe Alexandra	134	8	3	7	56	4		1
				£200000	02/02/88	Aston Villa	121	14	4	6	50	10	2	6
				£5500000	01/07/91	Bari	29				11			
				£6500000	01/06/92	Juventus	16				3			
					01/08/93	Sampdoria	55				17			
				£4750000	14/07/95	Arsenal	27+2	2+1	1		6			
Rose Matthew			24/09/75	Dartford	01/08/94	Arsenal	1+3							
Selley Ian	5.9	10.1	14/06/74	Chertsey	06/05/92	Arsenal	35+5	5+1	3	8+2				2
E: u21.3,S. LC'93. FAC'93.ECWC'94.														

FORWARDS

Name / Notes	Ht	Wt	DOB	Birthplace	Date	Club	Lge App	FAC App	LC App	Eur App	Lge Gls	FAC Gls	LC Gls	Eur Gls
Bergkamp Dennis	6.0	12.05	18/05/69	Amsterdam		Ajax	185				103			
Dutch Int.						Inter Milan	52				11			
				£7500000	01/07/95	Arsenal	33	7	1		11	5		
Clarke Adrian	5.10	11.0	28/09/74	Cambridge	06/07/93	Arsenal	4+3		1+1					
E: Y.1,S.														
Dickov Paul	5.6	11.5	01/11/72	Livingston	28/12/90	Arsenal	6+14	2+2			3	3		
S: u21.5,Y,S. ECWC'94.				Loan	08/10/93	Luton Town	8+7				1			
				Loan	23/03/94	Brighton & H.A.	8				5			
Hartson John	6.1	14.6	05/04/75	Swansea	19/12/92	Luton Town	21+13	0+1	2+3	2	6		1	
				£2500000	13/01/95	Arsenal	29+5	1+2	1	6+1	11	1		1
Helder Glen	5.11	11.7	28/10/68	Leiden (Hol)	01/08/89	Sparta	93				9			
Dutch Int.					01/08/93	Vitesse Arnhem	52				12			
				£2300000	14/02/95	Arsenal	27+10	4+2	2		1			
Kiwomya Chris	5.9	10.7	02/12/69	Huddersfield	31/03/87	Ipswich Town	184+26	14	13	5+1	48	8	2	3
Div.2'92.				£1550000	13/01/95	Arsenal	5+9			1+2	3			
Merson Paul	5.10	11.9	20/03/68	Harlesdon	01/02/85	Arsenal	257+38	35+2	25+3		72	9	4	5
E:14,B.3,u21.4,Y. CT'89.				Loan	22/01/87	Brentford	6+1			1+1				
Div.1'89'91. LC'93. FAC'93.														
Shaw Paul	5.11	12.4	04/09/73	Burnham	18/09/91	Arsenal	0+4							
E: Y.1.				Loan	23/03/95	Burnley	8+1				4			
				Loan	20/10/95	Peterborough Utd	12		2		5			
Wright Ian	5.10	11.0	03/11/63	Woolwich		Greenwich Boro								
E:20,B.3. FMC'91. LC'93.			Free	02/08/85	Crystal Palace	206+19	19	9+2	19+3	90	9	3	16
FAC'93.				£2500000	24/09/91	Arsenal	160+2	25	14	18	95	23	12	14

ADDITIONAL CONTRACT PLAYERS

Name / Notes	Date	Club
Black Michael		Arsenal (T)
Crowe Jason	13/05/96	Arsenal (T)
E: Y.		
Gislason Valgur		Arsenal (T)
MacDonald James		Arsenal (T)
Rankin Isaiah	12/09/95	Arsenal (T)
Read Paul		Arsenal (T)
Taylor Ross	07/07/95	Arsenal (T)
Wicks Matthew	23/01/96	Arsenal (T)
Woolsey Jeff		Arsenal (T)

MANAGER
BRUCE RIOCH

Date of Birth . . . . 6th September 1947
Place of Birth . . . . Aldershot
Date of Appointment . . . . June 1995

PREVIOUS CLUBS
As Manager . . . . Millwall, Middlesbrough, Bolton Wanderers
As Player/Manager. . . . . Torquay United
As a Player. . . . . Luton, Aston Villa, Derby, Everton, Derby, Torquay,
. . . . Birmingham (loan), Sheffield United.

HONOURS
As a Manager
Middlesbrough: Promotion to Div.2 1987, Promotion to Div.1 1988.
Bolton: Promotion to Div.1 1993. Promotion to Premiership 1995.

As a Player
Derby: Division 1 Championship 1974-75.
International: 24 full caps for Scotland.

Arsenal Stadium

Highbury, London N5 1BU
Tel: 0171 226 0304

Capacity ....39,000.
First game...v Leicester Fosse, Division 2, 6.9.1913.
First floodlit game...v Glasgow Rangers, 1951.

ATTENDANCES
Highest ....73,295 v Sunderland, Div.1, 9.3.1935.
Lowest...600v Loughborough Town, Div.2, 12.3.1900.

OTHER GROUNDS ....Plumstead Common 1886-1887. Sportsman's Ground 1887-1888.
.................Manor Road 1888-1890/1893-1913. Invicta Ground 1890-1893. Highbury 1913 to date.

MATCHDAY TICKET PRICES

Centre Blocks - East & West Upper Tier £28
Next to Centre Blocks - East & West U.T. £21
Wing blocks - East & West Upper Tier £18.50
Lower Tiers - East & West £14.50
Lower Tiers - East & West Wing Blocks £13.50
North Bank - Upper Tier. £22
North Bank - Upper Tier Wing £17
North Bank - Lower Tier. £17
North Bank - Lower Tier Wing £13.50
North Bank - Lower Tier Outer Wing. £12
Clock End Stand £13
Family Enclosure: Adult - Lower Tier £14.50
Adult - Lower Tier Wing Block £13.50
Senior Citizen & Cannon Club £8Junior Gunners £7
Ticket Office Telephone No.. . . . . . . 0171 704 4242
(Recorded Message)

CLUBCALL
0898 20 20 20
Calls cost 39p per minute cheap rate and 49p per minute at all other times.
Call costings correct at time of going to press.

HOW TO GET TO THE GROUND

From the North
Leave Motorway M1 at junction 2 and follow signs to the City. In 6.2 miles pass Holloway Road Station and then take 3rd turning on left into Drayton Park Road. In 0.7 miles turn right into Avenell Road for Arsenal FC.

From the South
From London Bridge follow signs, to Bank of England, then follow signs to Angel (Islington). At traffic signals turn right (S.P. The North) and in 1 mile at Highbury roundabout forward into Holloway Road. Then take 3rd turning on right into Drayton Park Road. In 0.7 miles turn right into Avenell Road for Arsenal FC.

From the West
Leave motorway M4 at junction 1, Chiswick, and followed A315 (S.P. Chiswick). In 0.9 miles turn left A40 then follow signs to City to join motorway M41, then A40(M) at end forward into Ring Road A501. At Angel (Islington) turn left to Highbury roundabout, keep forward into Holloway Road. Then take 3rd turning on right into Drayton Park Road. In 0.7 miles turn right into Avenell Road for Arsenal FC.

Car Parking
Parking is permitted in adjacent streets with restrictions.
Nearest Railway Station
Finsbury Park and Highbury & Islington.

MATCHDAY PROGRAMME

Programme Editor . . . . Kevin Connolly.

Number of pages 48

Price £1.80

Subscriptions . . . . Subscription price on application to club shop.

Local Newspapers . . . . Islington Gazette.

Local Radio Stations . . . . Capital Radio, BBC Radio London.

ASTON VILLA
(The Villa)
F.A. CARLING PREMIERSHIP
SPONSORED BY: A.S.T. COMPUTER

Back Row (L-R): Neil Davis, Scott Murray, Phil King, Paul Browne (now Raith Rovers), Carl Tiler, Riccardo Scimeca, Gareth Farrelly, Darren Byfield, Lee Hendrie. **Middle Row:** Paul Barron, Paul McGrath, Gareth Southgate, Ian Taylor, Michael Oakes, Mark Bosnich, Ugo Ehiogu, Gary Charles, Tommy Johnson, Jim Walker. **Front Row:** Julian Joachim, Steve Staunton, Franz Carr, Mark Draper, Allan Evans (Asst. Manager), Brian Little (Manager), John Gregory (Coach), Savo Milosevic, Dwight Yorke, Andy Townsend, Alan Wright.

ASTON VILLA
FORMED IN 1874
TURNED PROFESSIONAL IN 1885
LTD COMPANY IN 1896

PRESIDENT: Harold Musgrove
CHAIRMAN: Doug Ellis
DIRECTORS:
J A Alderson, Dr D H Targett,
P D Ellis, S Stride
SECRETARY: Steven Stride
(0121 327 2299)
COMMERCIAL MANAGER
Abdul Rashid (0121 327 5399)

MANAGER: Brian Little
ASSISTANT: Allan Evans

RESERVE TEAM MANAGER
John Gregory
YOUTH TEAM MANAGER
Tony McAndrew
PHYSIOTHERAPIST
Jim Walker

**CLUB STATISTICIAN/STATISTICIAN FOR
THE DIRECTORY**
David Bridgewater/Dave Hodges

An emphatic 3-1 victory over 'The Champions' certainly set a high standard but this didn't worry Brian Little's side, they got even better.

The side settled down and grew in confidence as the season saw them develop from a solid unspectacular functional side into an attractive and exciting squad that could hold their own with any club in the Premier Division.

Bosnich, one of the competitions best goalkeepers, revelled in playing behind the sheer quality of McGrath, Ehiogu and Southgate. Little Alan Wright refused to give up his left-back position to Staunton and was one of the most consistent players in the side, while the creative midfield brought the best out of the truly exciting skills of Tommy Johnson, the quite inspirational Dwight Yorke and the very 'different' Savo Milosevic.

Johnston's sheer enthusiasm and Dwights talent were sometimes even over shadowed by Savo's quite amazing mistakes or breathtaking brilliance.

Brian Little has proved to be an excellent manager at every level, from The Conference to the Premier, and his man management and tactical skills have helped mould a squad that will surely be challenging for all honours next season.

They hold the Coca-Cola Cup of course, having completely outplayed Leeds United at Wembley. They also reached the Semi-Final of the F.A. Cup where they had to take on Liverpool only a week after their Wembley experience.

They have European football to look forward to and have a pedigree of course, as ex-European Cup holders, so it could be a memorable season which will be good for the Midlands, where other clubs could respond to their 'big brother' in the same way as we have sean the North-East come alive after Newcastle's resurgence.

TONY WILLIAMS.

ASTON VILLA

League: 4th   FA Cup: Semi-Final   Coca-Cola Cup: Winners

M	DATE	COMP	VEN	OPPONENTS	RESULT	HT	LP	GOAL SCORERS/GOAL TIMES	ATT.
1	A 19	PL	H	Manchester United	W 3-1	3-0	3	Taylor 14, Draper 27, Yorke 36(pen)	34655
2	23	PL	A	Tottenham Hotspur	W 1-0	0-0	5	Ehiogu 69	(26726)
3	26	PL	A	Leeds United	L 0-2	0-1	8		(35086)
4	30	PL	H	Bolton Wanderers	W 1-0	0-0	6	Yorke 75	31770
5	S 9	PL	A	Blackburn Rovers	D 1-1	1-0	6	Milosevic 33	(27084)
6	16	PL	H	Wimbledon	W 2-0	1-0	3	Draper 7, Taylor 47	26928
7	20	CC 2/1	H	Peterborough United	W 6-0	3-0		Draper 12, Yorke 15(pen), 42(pen), Johnson 69, Heald 81(og), Southgate 89	19602
8	23	PL	H	Nottingham Forest	D 1-1	0-0	6	Townsend 67	33972
9	30	PL	A	Coventry City	W 3-0	1-0	2	Yorke 1, Milosevic 84, 87	(21004)
10	O 3	CC 2/2	A	Peterborough United	D 1-1	0-0		Staunton 87	(5745)
11	14	PL	H	Chelsea	L 0-1	0-1	6		34992
12	21	PL	A	Arsenal	L 0-2	0-0	7		(38271)
13	25	CC 3	H	Stockport County	W 2-0	0-0		Ehiogu 57, Yorke 65	17679
14	28	PL	H	Everton	W 1-0	0-0	7	Yorke 76	32792
15	N 4	PL	A	West Ham United	W 4-1	1-0	5	Milosevic 33, 89, Johnson 49, Yorke 54	(23637)
16	18	PL	H	Newcastle United	D 1-1	1-0	3	Johnson 22	39167
17	20	PL	A	Southampton	W 1-0	1-0	3	Johnson 30	(13582)
18	25	PL	A	Manchester City	L 0-1	0-0	3		(28027)
19	29	CC 4	H	Queens Park Rangers	W 1-0	0-0		Townsend 60	24951
20	D 2	PL	H	Arsenal	D 1-1	0-0	4	Yorke 65	37770
21	10	PL	A	Nottingham Forest	D 1-1	0-0	6	Yorke 47	(25790)
22	16	PL	H	Coventry City	W 4-1	1-0	4	Johnson 12, Milosevic 48, 64, 80	28476
23	23	PL	A	Queens Park Rangers	L 0-1	0-0	6		(14778)
24	J 1	PL	A	Middlesbrough	W 2-0	2-0	5	Wright 21, Johnson 40	(28535)
25	6	FAC 3	A	Gravesend	W 3-0	1-0		Draper 2, Milosevic 47, Johnson 72	(26021)
26	10	CC QF	H	Wolverhampton Wand	W 1-0	0-0		Johnson 67	39277
27	13	PL	A	Manchester United	D 0-0	0-0	6		(42667)
28	21	PL	H	Tottenham Hotspur	W 2-1	1-1	5	McGrath 23, Yorke 79	35666
29	28	FAC 4	A	Sheffield United	W 1-0	0-0		Yorke 63(pen)	(18749)
30	31	PL	H	Liverpool	L 0-2	0-0	6		39332
31	F 3	PL	H	Leeds United	W 3-0	2-0	4	Yorke 11, 23, Wright 61	35982
32	10	PL	A	Bolton Wanderers	W 2-0	1-0	4	Yorke 40, 53	(18099)
33	14	CC SF1	A	Arsenal	D 2-2	1-2		Yorke 39, 72	(37562)
34	17	FAC 5	A	Ipswich Town	W 3-1	2-0		Draper 10, Yorke 19, Taylor 55	(20748)
35	21	CC SF2	H	Arsenal	D 0-0	0-0			39334
36	24	PL	A	Wimbledon	D 3-3	1-1	4	Reeves 33(og), Yorke 49 (pen), Cunningham 58(og)	(12193)
37	28	PL	H	Blackburn Rovers	W 2-0	0-0	4	Joachim 55, Southgate 71	28008
38	M 3	PL	A	Liverpool	L 0-3	0-3	4		(39508)
39	6	PL	H	Sheffield Wednesday	W 3-2	0-1	4	Milosevic 61, 62, Townsend 75	27893
40	9	PL	H	Queens Park Rangers	W 4-2	1-0	4	Milosevic 18, Yorke 65, 80, Yates 82(og)	28221
41	13	FAC QF	A	Nottingham Forest	W 1-0	1-0		Carr 26	(21067)
42	16	PL	A	Sheffield Wednesday	L 0-2	0-0	4		(22964)
43	19	PL	H	Middlesbrough	D 0-0	0-0	4		23933
44	24	CC F	N	Leeds United	W 3-0	1-0		Milosevic 20, Taylor 54, Yorke 89	77065
45	31	FAC SF	H	Liverpool	L 0-3	0-1			39072
46	A 6	PL	A	Chelsea	W 2-1	1-1	4	Milosevic 40, Yorke 59	(23530)
47	8	PL	H	Southampton	W 3-0	0-0	4	Taylor 64, Charles 78, Yorke 82	34059
48	14	PL	A	Newcastle United	L 0-1	0-0	4		(36510)
49	17	PL	H	West Ham United	D 1-1	1-0	4	McGrath 27	26768
50	27	PL	H	Manchester City	L 0-1	0-0	4		39336
51	M 5	PL	A	Everton	L 0-1	0-0	4		(40127)

Best Home League Attendance: 39336 v Manchester City   Smallest: 23933 v Middlesbrough   Average: 32616

Goal Scorers:
PL(52):   Yorke(17),Milosevic(12),Johnson(5),Taylor(3),Opponent(s)(3),Wright(2),Townsend(2),Draper(2),McGrath(2),Ehiogu(1),Joachim(1),Charles(1),Southgate(1)
CC(16):   Yorke(6),Johnson(2),Opponent(s)(1),Townsend(1),Staunton(1),Taylor(1),Milosevic(1),Southgate(1),Ehiogu(1),Draper(1)
FAC(8):   Draper(2),Yorke(2),Carr(1),Taylor(1),Milosevic(1),Johnson(1)

(G) Bosnich	(D) Browne	(F) Carr	(D) Charles	(F) Davis	(M) Draper	(D) Ehiogu	(M) Farrelly	(F) Fenton	(F) Hendrie	(F) Joachim	(F) Johnson	(M) McGrath	(F) Milosevic	(F) Murray	(G) Oakes	(D) Scimeca	(D) Southgate	(G) Spink	(D) Staunton	(M) Taylor	(D) Tiler	(M) Townsend	(D) Wright	(F) Yorke	Referee	No.
X			X		X	X					S1	X	X1			S2	X			X		X	X	X2	R.A.Hart	1
X			X		X	X						X	X			S	X	S		X		X	X	X	S.Dunn	2
X			X		X	X		S1			X1	X	X			S	X			X		X	X	X	D.Gallagher	3
X			X		X	X		S			S	X	X				X	S		X		X	X	X	P.James	4
X			X		X	X		S			S	X	X				X	S		X		X	X	X	R.Dilkes	5
X			X		X	X		S			S	X	X				X	S		X		X	X	X	D.Elleray	6
X			X		X	X	S2	S1			X	X					X	S	X1	X2		X	X		T.Heilbron	7
X			X		X	X		S	S	S1	X		X1				X	S		X		X	X	X	P.Danson	8
X	S		X		X	X		S				X					X		X	X		X	X	X	A.Wilkie	9
X			X		X1	X		S1				X	X				X	S	S2	X		X	X	X2	G.Ashby	10
X			X		X	X		S1		S1	X	X					X	S	X1	X		X	X		S.Dunn	11
X			X		X1	X		S3		S1	X3	S1					X		X1			X	X	X	R.Hart	12
X			X		X	X		S		S	X			S	X	X		X			X	X	X	D.Gallagher	13
X			X		X	X				S1	X				S1	X	S	X	X	X	X	X	X	K.Burge	14
X			X		X	X				S1	X	X			S	X		X	X1		X	X	X	P.Jones	15
X			X		X	X					X	X			S	X	S	S	X		X	X	X	S.Lodge	16
X			X		X	X					X	X			S	X	S	S	X		X	X	X	D.Elleray	17
X			X		X	X					X	X	X2		S2	X	S	S1	X1		X	X	X	G.Ashby	18
X			X		X2	X				X1	X				S2	X	S	S1			X	X	X	R.Bart	19
X			X		X	X				X	X				S	X	S		X		X	X	X	J.T.Winter	20
X			X		X	X	S			X	X				X	X	S		X		X	X	X	P.Durkin	21
X2			X		X	X				X	X	X3			S3	X	S2		X		X	X	X1	P.Alcock	22
X			X		X2	X	S2			X	X	X3			S3	X	S1	X1			X	X		A.B.Wilkie	23
X		S	X		X	X	S			X					X	X					X	X	X	M.Bodenham	24
X		S	X		X	X	S			X					X	X					X	X	X	K.Cooper	25
X			X		X	X				X1	X	X			S	X	S	S1			X	X	X	M.Bodenham	26
X			X		X	X				X1	X	X			S	X	S	S1			X	X	X	G.Willard	27
X			X		X	X					X	X			S	X	S	S			X	X	X	G.Poll	28
X			X		X	X					X	X			X	S	S	S			X	X	X	A.Wilkie	29
X			X		X	X					X	X1	X			S	X	S1	S	X1		X	X	X	R.Dilkes	30
X	S		X		X		S1				X	X				S	X		X	X		X1	X	X	R.Hart	31
X			X		X	X					X	S		S		S	X		X			X	X	X	G.Ashby	32
X			X		X	X					X1	S2		S		S	X		X1	S1		X	X	X	P.Durkin	33
X			X2		X						X1	S2		S		S	X		X2	X1		X	X	X	S.Lodge	34
X			X		X	X					S1	X		S		S2	X		X2	X1		X	X	X	K.Burge	35
X			X		X	X				S2	X2			S		X1	X		X			X	X	X	J.Winter	36
X			X		X1	X				S2	X2			S1		S1	X		X			X	X	X	S.Lodge	37
X			X		X	X				S				S1		X	X		X1			X	X	X	K.Cooper	38
X			X		X	X			S	S			S	X	X	X				X2		X	X	X	D.Elleray	39
X			X		X	X				S2	S1			X	X	X		X1				X	X	X	A.B.Wilkie	40
X		X1	X	S1	X	X				S				X	X	X				X		X	X	X	M.Bodenham	41
X		X	X		X	X				S	S1			X	X	X		X1				X	X	X	P.Jones	42
X	X		S1	X			S2		X	X1			X	X2	S				X		X	X	X		P.Alcock	43
X			X		X	X				S				X	X	X	S	X	S	X		X	X	X	R.Hart	44
X			X		X	X				S2	X			X2	X	X	S		X1	S1		X	X	X	P.Durkin	45
X			X		X	X			S	S1	X			X	X	S		X1		X		X	X	X	G.Poll	46
X			X		X	X				S	X1			X	X	X		X		X		X	X	X1	P.Danson	47
X			X		X	X				S1	X2			X	X	X	S	S2		X		X	X	X2	M.Bodenham	48
X			X1		X	X				S2	X			X	X	X	S	S1		X		X	X	X2	S.Dunn	49
X					S1	X				S	X1			X	X	X	S		X			X	X		D.Ellery	50
X	X				X	X		S			X	S1		X	X	X		X			X		X1	R.Heart	51
38	**2**	**1**	**34**	**0**	**36**	**36**	**1**	**0**	**2**	**4**	**17**	**29**	**36**	**3**	**0**	**7**	**31**	**0**	**11**	**24**	**1**	**32**	**38**	**35**	PL Appearances	
0	0	0	0	2	0	0	4	3	1	7	6	1	1	0	0	10	0	2	2	1	0	1	0	0	PL Sub Appearances	
8	0	0	8	0	8	8	0+1	0+2	0	0	4	5+1	7	0	0	1+2	8	0	2+2	5+1	0	8	8	8	CC Appearances	
5	0	1	5	0+1	5	5	0	0	0	0	3+1	3+1	5	0	0	2	4	0	1+1	2+1	0	4	5	5	FAC Appearances	

ASTON VILLA

CLUB RECORDS

BIGGEST VICTORIES
League: 12-2 v Accrington, Division 1, 12.3.1892.
11-1 v Charlton Athletic, Division 2, 24.11.1959.
10-0 v Sheffield Wednesday, Division 1, 5.10.1912.
10-0 v Burnley, Division 1, 29.8.1925.
7-1 v Wimbledon, Premier Division, 11.2.1995.
F.A. Cup: 13-0 v Wednesday Old Athletic, 3.10.1886
League Cup: 8-1 v Exeter City, Round 2 2nd leg, 7.10.1985.
Europe: 5-0 v Valur, Round 1, 16.9.1981.

BIGGEST DEFEATS
League: 0-7 v Blackburn Rovers, Division 1, 19.10.1989.
0-7 v Everton, Division 1, 4.1.1890.
0-7 v West Bromwich Albion, Division 1, 19.10.1935.
0-7 v Manchester United, Division 1, 8.3.1950.
0-7 v Manchester United, Division 1, 24.10.1964.
F.A. Cup: 1-8 v Blackburn Rovers, Round 3, 16.2.1889.
League Cup: 1-6 v West Bromwich Albion, Round 2, 14.9.1966.
Europe: (UEFA) 1-4 v Antwerp, Round 2, 17.9.1975.
0-3 v Inter Milan, Round 2, 17.11.1990.

MOST POINTS
3 points a win: 78, Division 2, 1987-88.
2 points a win: 70, Division 3, 1971-72. (Division 3 record)

MOST GOALS
128, 1930/31 (Division 1 record).
Waring 49, Houghton 30, Walker 15, Beresford 14, Mandley 8, Brown 5, Chester 3, Gibson 2, Talbot 1, Tate 1.

MOST LEAGUE GOALS CONCEDED
110, Division 1, 1935-36.

MOST FIRST CLASS MATCHES IN A SEASON
61 (42 League, 3FA Cup, 6 League Cup, 1 Charity Shield, 9 European Cup) 1981-82.

MOST LEAGUE WINS
32, Division 3, 1971-72.

MOST LEAGUE DRAWS
17, Division 1, 1975-76.

MOST LEAGUE DEFEATS
24, Division 1, 1966-67.

INDIVIDUAL CLUB RECORDS

MOST GOALS IN A SEASON
Tom 'Pongo' Waring, 50 (49 League, 1 FA Cup) 1930-31.

MOST GOALS IN A MATCH
5, Harry Hampton v Sheffield Wednesday 10-0, 5.10.1912.
5, Harold Halse v Derby County 5-1, 19.10.1912.
5, Len Capwell v Burnley 10-0, 29.8.1925.
5, George Brown v Leicester 8-3, 2.1.1932.
5, Gerry Hitchens v Charlton Athletic 11-1, 18.11.1959.

OLDEST PLAYER
Ernie Callaghan, 39 years 257 days v Grimsby Town, Division 1, 12.4.1947.

YOUNGEST PLAYER
Jimmy Brown, 15 years 349 days v Bolton (a), 17.9.1969.

MOST CAPPED PLAYER
Paul McGrath (Republic of Ireland) 82. (51 while at Villa)
David Platt (England) 22.

BEST PERFORMANCES

League: Division 3 Champions 1971-72: Matches played 46, Won 32, Drawn 6, Lost 8, Goals for 88, Goals against 32, Points 70.
Highest: Division 1 Champions.

F.A. Cup: Winners in 1886-87 v West Bromwich Albion 2-0.
1894-95 v West Bromwich Albion 1-0.
1896-97 v Everton 3-2.
1904-05 v Newcastle United 2-0.
1912-13 v Sunderland 1-0.
1919-20 v Huddersfield Town 1-0.
Most recent success: 1956-57: 3rd Rnd. Luton Town 2-2, 2-0; 4th Rnd. Middlesbrough 3-2; 5th Rnd. Bristol City 2-1; 6th Rnd. Burnley 1-1, 2-0; Semi-Final West Bromwich Albion 2-2, 1-0; Final Manchester United 2-1.

League Cup: Winners in 1960-61 v Rotherham 0-2, 3-0.
1974-75 v Norwich City 1-0.
1976-77 v Everton 0-0, 1-1, 3-2.
1993-94 v Manchester United 3-1.
Most recent success: 1995-96: 2nd Rnd Peterborough Utd 6-0,1-1 3rd Rnd Stockport Co. 2-0. 4th Rnd QPR 1-0. 5th Rnd Wolves 1-0. Semi-Final Arsenal 2-2, 0-0. Final Leeds United 3-0.

Europe: (EC) 1981-82: 1st Rnd. Valur 5-0, 2-0; 2nd Rnd. Dynamo Berlin 2-1, 0-1; 3rd Rnd. Dynamo Kiev 0-0, 2-0; Semi-Final Anderlecht 1-0, 0-0; Final Bayern Munich 1-0.

DIVISIONAL RECORD

	Played	Won	Drawn	Lost	For	Against	Points
Division 1/P	3,310	1,392	740	1,178	5,697	5,121	3,731
Division 2	422	179	111	132	617	487	491
Division 3	92	51	21	20	139	78	123
Total	3,824	1,622	872	1,330	6,453	5,686	4,345

ADDITIONAL INFORMATION
PREVIOUS NAME
None.

PREVIOUS LEAGUES
None

Club Colours: Claret shirts with light blue sleeves, light blue & yellow trim, white shorts claret & blue trim, claret socks light blue trim.
Change Colours: White shirt with claret & blue trim, claret shorts, white socks with claret & blue hoop.

Reserve League: Pontins Central League Division 2.
Youth League: Melville Youth League.

RECORDS AND STATISTICS

COMPETITIONS

Div 1/P	Div.2	Div.3	Euro C.	UEFA	W.C.C.
1888-36	1936-38	1970-72	1981-82	1975-76	1982-83
1938-59	1959-60		1982-83	1977-78	
1960-67	1967-70			1983-84	
1975-87	1972-75	E S Cup		1990-91	
1988-	1987-88		1982-83	1994-95	

HONOURS

Div 1/P	Div.2	Div.3	FAC	Lge Cup	Euro C.
1893-94	1937-38	1971-72	1887	1961	1981-82
1895-96	1959-60		1895	1975	
1896-97			1897	1977	E.S.C.
1898-99			1905	1994	1982-83
1899-00			1913	1996	
1909-10			1920	C/Sh'ld	
1980-81			1957	1981	

MOST APPEARANCES

Charlie Aitken 656+3 (1960-76)

Year	League	FA Cup	Lge Cup	Europe
1960-61	1			
1961-62	35	4	3	
1962-63	42	3	8	
1963-64	34	2	1	
1964-65	42	5	6	
1965-66	42	1	5	
1966-67	39	2	1	
1967-68	30+2	2	1	
1968-69	42	4	1	
1969-70	31	1	2	
1970-71	44	1	10	
1971-72	43	1	6	
1972-73	33	1	4	
1973-74	38	4	1	
1974-75	42	3	10	
1975-76	21	0+1	2	2
	559+2	34+1	61	2

MOST GOALS IN A CAREER

Billy Walker - 244 (1919-1934)

Year	League	FA Cup
1919-20	8	5
1920-21	27	4
1921-22	21	6
1922-23	23	0
1923-24	14	3
1924-25	19	6
1925-26	21	1
1926-27	15	0
1927-28	10	1
1928-29	19	0
1929-30	8	3
1930-31	15	1
1931-32	9	0
1932-33	5	0
1933-34	0	0
Total	214	30

Current top goalscorer: Dwight Yorke - 59 (1990-96)

RECORD TRANSFER FEE RECEIVED

Amount	Club	Player	Date
£5,500,000	Bari	David Platt	7/91
£1,750,000	Wolves	Andy Gray	9/79
£1,600,000	Everton	Earl Barrett	1/95
£1,500,000	Blackburn R.	Graham Fenton	11/95

RECORD TRANSFER FEE PAID

Amount	Club	Player	Date
£3,500,000	Partizen Belgrade	Savo Milosevic	7/95
£3,250,000	Leicester	Mark Draper	8/95
£2,500,000	Crystal Palace	Gareth Southgate	7/95
£2,100,000	Chelsea	Andy Townsend	7/93
£2,100,000	Liverpool	Dean Saunders	9/92

MANAGERS

Name	Seasons	Best	Worst
Jim McMullen	1934-36	13(1)	21(1)
Jim Hogan	1936-39	12(1)	9(2)
Alex Massie	1945-50	6(1)	12(1)
George Martin	1950-53	6(1)	15(1)
Eric Houghton	1953-58	6(1)	20(1)
Joe Mercer	1958-64	7(1)	1(2)
Dick Taylor	1964-67	16(1)	21(1)
Tony Cummings	1967-68	16(2)	16(2)
Arthur Cox (CT)	1968		
Tommy Docherty	1968-70	18(2)	21(2)
Vic Crowe	1970-74	3(2)	4(3)
Ron Saunders	1974-82	1(1)	2(2)
Tony Barton	1982-84	6(1)	11(1)
Graham Turner	1984-86	10(1)	16(1)
Billy McNeil	1986-87		
Graham Taylor	1987-90	2(1)	2(2)
Jozef Venglos	1990-91	17(1)	17(1)
Ron Atkinson	1991-94	2(P)	10(P)
Brain Little	1994-	4(P)	18(P)

LONGEST LEAGUE RUNS

of undefeated matches:	15 (16.1.1897 - 18.9.1897)	**of league matches w/out a win:**	12 (10.11.73 - 2.2.74)
	(18.12.1890 - 26.3.1910. 12.3.1949 - 27.8.1949)		(27.12. 1986 - 25.3.1987)
of undefeated home matches:	37 (24.4.1909 - 22.4.1911)	**of undefeated away matches:**	13 (5.9.1987 - 23.1.1988)
without home win:	8 (11.12.1920 - 28.3.1921)	**without an away win:**	27 (21.9. 1963 - 26.12.1964)
of league wins:	9 (22.3. - 18.9.1897. 15.10. - 10.12.1910)	**of home wins:**	14 (10.1.1903 - 25.11.1903)
of league defeats:	11 (22.3. 1963 - 4.4. 1963)	**of away wins:**	6 (6.2.1897 - 11.9. 1897)

ASTON VILLA

PLAYERS NAME Honours	Ht	Wt	Birthdate	Birthplace Transfers	Contract Date	Clubs	APPEARANCES				GOALS			
							League	L/Cup	FA Cup	Other	Lge	L/C	FAC	Oth
G O A L K E E P E R S														
Bosnich Mark	6.2	13.7	13/01/72	Sydney (Aus)		Sydney Croatia								
Australian Int. LC'94'96.				Free	05/06/89	Manchester United	3							
					01/01/90	Sydney Croatia								
				Free	28/02/92	Aston Villa	114	18+1	10	2				
Oakes Michael	6.1	12.6	30/10/73	Northwich	16/07/91	Aston Villa		1						
E: u21.7. LC'96.				Loan	26/11/93	Scarborough	1			1				
D E F E N D E R S														
Charles Gary	5.9	11.2	13/04/70	Newham	07/11/87	Nottingham Forest	54+2	9	8+2	4+2	1		1	
E: 2,u21.6. FMC'92. LC'96.				Loan	16/03/89	Leicester City	5+3							
				£750000	29/07/93	Derby County	61	5+1	1	9	3			
				£1450000	06/01/95	Aston Villa	48+4	8	5		1			
Ehiogu Ugochuku	6.1	12.0	03/11/72	Hackney	13/07/89	W.B.A.	0+2							
E:1,B.1,u21.15. LC'96.				£40000	12/07/91	Aston Villa	93+11	12+1	7+2	5	4			1
King Phillip	5.8	11.9	28/12/67	Bristol	07/01/85	Exeter City	24+3	1		1+2				
				£3000	14/07/86	Torquay United	24	2	1	2	3			
				£155000	06/02/87	Swindon Town	112+4	11	5	13	4			
				£400000	30/11/89	Sheffield Wed.	124+5	17	9	4	2			
				Loan	22/10/93	Notts County	6			2				
				£250000	01/08/94	Aston Villa	13+3	3		4				
				Loan	30/10/95	W.B.A.	4			1				
McGrath Paul	6.0	14.0	04/12/59	Ealing		St. Patricks								
Ei:82. FAC'85. LC'94'96.				£30000	30/04/82	Manchester United	159+4	13	15+2	9	12	2	2	
FLgeXI.				£400000	03/08/89	Aston Villa	248+5	29+1	23+1	15	9	1		
Scimeca Riccardo	6.1	12.09	13/06/75	Leamington	07/07/93	Aston Villa	7+10	1+2	2					
E: u21.1.														
Southgate Gareth	5.10	12.03	03/09/70	Watford	17/01/89	Crystal Palace	148+4	23+1	9	6	15	7		
E: 9. Div.1'94. LC'96.				£2500000	23/06/95	Aston Villa	31	8	4		1	1		
Staunton Steve	5.11	11.2	19/01/69	Dundalk		Dundalk								
Ei:62,u21.4. Div.1'90. FAC'89.				£20000	02/09/86	Liverpool	55+10	6+2	14+2	1		4		1
CS'89. LC'94'96.				Loan	13/11/87	Bradford City	7+1	2		1				
				£1100000	07/08/91	Aston Villa	148+3	16+2	15+1	6	13	1		
Tiler Carl	6.4	13.00	11/01/70	Sheffield	02/08/88	Barnsley	67+4	4	4+1	3+1	3			
E: u21.13.				£1400000	30/05/91	Nottingham Forest	67+2	10+1	6	1	1			
				Loan	18/11/94	Swindon Town	2							
				£750000	28/10/95	Aston Villa	1							
Wright Alan	5.4	9.4	28/09/71	Ashton-u-Lyne	13/04/89	Blackpool	91+7	10+2	8	11+2				
E: u21.2,Y,S. LC'96.				£400000	25/10/91	Blackburn Rovers	67+7	8+1	5	3	1			
				£1000000	10/04/95	Aston Villa	46	8	5		2			
M I D F I E L D														
Draper Mark	5.10	11.0	11/11/70	Long Eaton	12/12/88	Notts County	206+16	14+1	10	21+2	40	2	2	5
E: u21.3. LC'96.				£1250000	22/07/94	Leicester City	39	2	2		5			
				£3250000	05/07/95	Aston Villa	36	8	5		2	1	2	
Farrelly Gareth	6.0	12.07	28/08/75	Dublin		Home Farm								
Ei:3,u21					21/09/92	Aston Villa	1+4	0+1						
				Loan	21/03/95	Rotherham United	9+1				2			
Nelson Farnando						Sporting Lisburn								
				£1700000	02/08/96	Aston Villa								
Taylor Ian K	6.1	12.4	04/06/68	Birmingham		Moor Green								
AGT'93. LC'96.				£15000	13/07/92	Port Vale	83	4	6	13	28	2	1	4
				£1000000	12/07/94	Sheffield Wed.								
				£1000000	21/12/94	Aston Villa	46+1	5+1	4+1		4	1	1	
Townsend Andy	5.11	12.7	23/07/63	Maidstone		Welling								
Ei:60,B.1. Lc'94'96.				£13500		Weymouth		1						
				£35000	15/01/85	Southampton	77+6	7+1	2+3	3+2	5			
				£300000	31/08/88	Norwich City	66+5	3+1	10	3	8		2	
				£1200000	05/07/90	Chelsea	110	17	7	4	12	7		
				£2100000	26/07/93	Aston Villa	96+1	18	9	8	6	2		1

F O R W A R D S														
Byfield Darren	5.10	11.0	29/09/76	Birmingham	01/08/93	Aston Villa (T)								
Carr Franz	5.7	11.12	24/09/66	Preston	30/07/84	Blackburn Rovers								
E: u21.9,u19.1,Y.4. LC'90.				£100000	02/08/84	Nottingham Forest	122+9	16+2	4	5+2	17	5		1
SC'89. Div.1'93.				Loan	22/12/89	Sheffield Wed.	9+3		2					
				Loan	11/03/91	West Ham United	1+2							
				£250000	13/06/91	Newcastle United	20+5	2+2		3+1	3			
				£120000	12/01/93	Sheffield United	18		4	1	5			
				£100000	08/10/94	Leicester City	12+1				1			
				£250000	10/02/95	Aston Villa	1+2		1				1	
Davis Neil	5.8	11.0	15/08/73	Redditch	01/08/91	Aston Villa	0+2		0+1					
Hendrie Lee	5.9	10.3	18/05/77	Birmingham	01/08/93	Aston Villa	2+1							
E: u21,Y.														
Joachim Julian	5.6	11.11	20/09/74	Peterborough	15/09/92	Leicester City	77+22	7+2	4+1	4+2	25	3	1	2
E: u21.7,Y.8. UEFA Yth'93.				£1500000	24/02/96	Aston Villa	4+7				1			
Johnson Tommy	5.10	12.4	15/01/71	Newcastle-u-T.	19/01/89	Notts County	100+18	7+2	3+2	14+3	47	5	1	4
E: u21.7. LC'96.				£1300000	12/03/92	Derby County	91+7	9+1	5	16	30	2	1	8
				£1450000	06/01/95	Aston Villa	28+9	4	3+2		9	2	1	
Milosevic Savo	6.1	13.5	02/09/73			Patizan Belgrade								
Yugoslavian Int. LC'96.				£3500000	17/07/95	Aston Villa	36+1	7	5		12	1	1	
Murray Scott	5.10	11.00	26/05/74	Aberdeen	01/08/93	Aston Villa	3							
Yorke Dwight	5.10	11.12	03/11/71	Canaan (Tobago)		Signal Hill								
T&T Int.:20. LC'96.				£120000	19/12/89	Aston Villa	127+36	17+2	18+2	1	44	7	9	1
ADDITIONAL CONTRACT PLAYERS														
Barron Paul						Aston Villa (T)								
Walker Jim						Aston Villa (T)								

THE MANAGER
BRIAN LITTLE

Date of Birth . . . . 25th November 1953
Place of Birth . . . . Newcastle upon Tyne
Date of Appointment . . . . November 1994

PREVIOUS CLUBS
As Manager . . . . Darlington, Wolverhampton Wanderers, Leicester City
As Coach . . . . Wolverhampton Wanderers
As a Player . . . . Aston Villa

HONOURS
As a Manager
Darlington: GM Vauxhall Conference Championship 1989-90.
Division Four Championship 1990-91.
Leicester: Promotion to Premier League 1993-94.
Aston Villa: League Cup Winners 1995-96.
As a Player
Promotion to Div. 1 1975, League Cup Winners 1975 & 1977, FA Youth Cup Winners 1972.
International: 1 Full Cap and Youth for England.

Villa Park

Trinity Road, Birmingham B6 6HE
Tel: 0121 327 2299

Capacity 39,339
First game ....v Blackburn, Div.1, 17.4.1897 (3-0).
First floodlit game..v Portsmouth, Div.1, 25.8.1958 (3-2).
Internationals played at Villa Park..England v Scotland 8.4.1899, 3.5.1902, 8.4.1922.
 v Wales 10.11.1948, 26.11.1958. v Ireland 14.11.1951. Argentina v Spain 13.7.1966. v W.Germany 16.7.1966.
 ....Spain v W.Germany 20.7.1966. Brazil v Sweden 4.6.95. **Euro'96:** Holland v Scotland 10.6.96.
Switzerland v Holland 13.6.96. Scotland v Switzerland 18.6.96. Czech Republic v Portugal 23.6.96 (QF).

ATTENDANCES
Highest ....76,588 v Derby Co. FAC 6th Rnd, 2.3.1946.
Lowest ....2,900 v Bradford City, Div.1. 13.2.1915 (0-0).

OTHER GROUNDS...Aston Park 1874-76. Perry Barr 1876-1897.Villa Park 1897-

HOW TO GET TO THE GROUND

From North, East, South and West
Use Motorway, M6, junction 6.
Leave motorway and follow signs to Birmingham (NE).
Shortly at roundabout take fourth exit, A38 (Sign posted Aston).
In half a mile turn right into Aston Hall Road for Aston Villa FC.

Car Parking
Asda Park in Aston Hall Road, a Park & Ride. Street Parking also available.

Nearest Railway Station: Witton or Aston

CLUBCALL
0891 12 11 48
Calls cost 39p per minute cheap rate and 49p per minute at all other times.
Call costings correct at time of going to press.

MATCHDAY TICKET PRICES

North Stand £15
Juv/OAP £7.50

Holte End Upper £15
Juv/OAP £7.50
Lower. £13
Juv/OAP £6

Trinity Road Upper £17
Juv/OAP £9
Trinity Road Lower Tier. £14
Juv/OAP £8

Doug Ellis Stand Upper £17
Juv/OAP £9
Doug Ellis Stand Lower £14
Juv/OAP £8

Ticket Office Telephone No. 0121 327 5353

Credit Card Ticket Sales 0121 607 8000

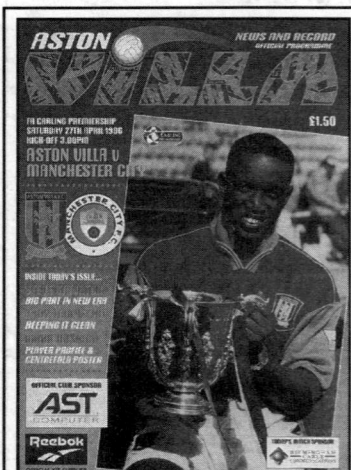

MATCHDAY PROGRAMME

Programme Editor . . . . Bernard Gallagher.

Number of pages. 32

Price £1.50

Subscriptions . . . . £53 within the UK.

Local Newspapers. . . . . Birmingham Post & Mail, Sports Argus,
. . . . Express & Star, Daily News, Sunday Mercury.

Local Radio Stations . . . . Xtra. AM, BRMB, BBC Radio W.M.

BLACKBURN ROVERS
(The Rovers)
F.A. CARLING PREMIERSHIP
SPONSORED BY: CIS CO-OPERATIVE INSURANCE

Back Row (L-R): Paul Warhurst, Nick Marker, Paul Harford, Ian Pearce, Colin Hendry, Chris Sutton, Mike Newell, Robbie Slater (new West Ham). **Middle Row:** Steve Foster (Physio), Lee Makel, Stuart Ripley, Jason Wilcox, Bobbie Mimms, Tim Flowers, Shay Given, Richard Witschge, Jeff Kenna, Graeme Le Saux, Tony Parkes (Chief Coach). **Front Row:** Henning Berg, Kevin Gallacher, Alan Shearer, Ray Harford (Manager), Kenny Dalglish (Director of Football), Tim Sherwood, David Batty, Mark Atkins.

**BLACKBURN ROVERS
FORMED IN** 1875
TURNED PROFESSIONAL IN 1880
LTD COMPANY IN 1897

PRESIDENT: W H Bancroft
SENIOR VICE PRESIDENT: J Walker
CHAIRMAN: R D Coar, BSC

DIRECTORS
R L Matthewson (Vice-Chairman),
K C Lee, I R Stanners, G A Root FCMA

SECRETARY
John Howarth FAA

COMMERCIAL MANAGER
Ken Beamish

DIRECTOR OF FOOTBALL
Kenny Dalglish
MANAGER: Ray Harford

YOUTH TEAM MANAGER
Jim Furnell

STATISTICIAN FOR THE DIRECTORY
Jim Norris/Harry Berry

Blackburn Rovers enjoyed mixed fortunes as defending champions.

Despite many exhilarating displays at Ewood Park, it was away results which baffled not only the management and players alike, but the supporters, who saw the team which had been consistent in performance and results the previous season, struggle to cash in on the outstanding home form.

The club's first excursion into the European Cup proved a very frustrating experience to say the least.

It was generally thought the group in which the team had been drawn would provide a passage through to the lucrative knock-out stages. Alas, this was not to be, but a couple of results which went against Rovers could have made all the difference in the final reckoning. The experience gained from this involvement will not be lost and if or when European competition is again a reality the Club would be in a better position to progress.

October brought the official opening of the stadium. A ceremony performed by the man responsible for the dramatic strides made by the Club since he became involved in 1991. None other than Mr Jack Walker. The team responded in the grand manner by thrashing Forest 7-0. Alan Shearer's hat-trick proved to be one of the five he would achieve before the end of the season.

Injuries to key players was a reasonable argument to the inconsistency and considering that the likes of Le-Saux, Sutton, Pearce, Wilcox and Gallacher were all out of action for long spells, only added weight to this theory. A final position of 7th would certainly have been surpassed with a full squad available.

The remarkable feats of Alan Shearer continued to hit the headlines - again. He was the first to register 100 Premiership goals; he was the first man for over 50 years to record over 30 goals in three consecutive seasons.

JIM NORRIS.

BLACKBURN ROVERS

League: 7th   FA Cup: 3rd Rnd   Coca-Cola Cup: 4th Rnd   European Cup: Group Stage

M	DATE	COMP	VEN	OPPONENTS	RESULT	HT	LP	GOAL SCORERS/GOAL TIMES	ATT.
1	A 13	CS	N	Everton	L 0-1	0-0			40149
2	19	PL	H	Queens Park Rangers	W 1-0	1-0	7	Shearer 6(pen)	25932
3	23	PL	A	Sheffield Wednesday	L 1-2	0-1	7	Shearer 60	(25544)
4	26	PL	A	Bolton Wanderers	L 1-2	0-1	12	Holmes 61	(20253)
5	29	PL	H	Manchester United	L 1-2	0-0	12	Shearer 59	29843
6	S 9	PL	H	Aston Villa	D 1-1	0-1	14	Shearer 52	27084
7	13	EC GB	H	Spartak Moscow	L 0-1	0-1			20940
8	16	PL	A	Liverpool	L 0-3	0-1	17		(39502)
9	20	CC 2/1	A	Swindon Town	W 3-2	2-2		Sutton 28, Shearer 42, 84	(14740)
10	23	PL	H	Coventry City	W 5-1	2-1	13	Shearer 8, 60, 67 (3), Hendry 23, Pearce 75	24382
11	27	EC GB	A	Rosenborg	L 1-2	0-1		Newell 62	(12210)
12	30	PL	A	Middlesbrough	L 0-2	0-1	15		(29462)
13	O 4	CC 2/2	H	Swindon Town	W 2-0	1-0		Shearer 37, 83	16924
14	14	PL	H	Southampton	W 2-1	1-0	11	Bohinen 19, Shearer 70	26780
15	18	EC GB	A	Legia Warsaw	L 0-1	0-1			(15000)
16	21	PL	A	West Ham United	D 1-1	0-1	11	Shearer 89	(21776)
17	24	CC 3	A	Watford	W 2-1	0-1		Shearer 58, Newell 79	(17035)
18	28	PL	H	Chelsea	W 3-0	1-0	11	Sherwood 39, Shearer 49, Newell 57	27733
19	N 1	EC GB	H	Legia Warsaw	D 0-0	0-0			20897
20	5	PL	A	Everton	L 0-1	0-1	11		(30097)
21	8	PL	A	Newcastle United	L 0-1	0-1	1		(36463)
22	18	PL	H	Nottingham Forest	W 7-0	2-0	10	Shearer 20, 58, 68,(3), Bohinen 28, 76, Newell 82, Le Saux 90	27660
23	22	EC GB	A	Spartak Moscow	L 0-3	0-1			(35000)
24	26	PL	A	Arsenal	D 0-0	0-0	13		(37695)
25	29	CC 4	A	Leeds United	L 1 -2	0-2		Kelly 51(og)	(26006)
26	D 2	PL	H	West Ham United	W 4-2	3-0	10	Shearer 3, 17, 65(pen) (3), Newell 32	26638
27	6	EC GB	H	Rosenborg	W 4-1	4-1		Shearer 16(pen), Newell 31, 38, 41 (3)	20677
28	9	PL	A	Coventry City	L 0-5	0-1	11		(13409)
29	16	PL	H	Middlesbrough	W 1-0	1-0	11	Shearer 42	27996
30	23	PL	A	Wimbledon	D 1-1	1-0	10	Sherwood 27	(7105)
31	26	PL	H	Manchester City	W 2-0	1-0	9	Shearer 11, Batty 50	28915
32	30	PL	H	Tottenham Hotspur	W 2-1	2-0	9	Marker 31, Shearer 41	30004
33	J 1	PL	A	Leeds United	D 0-0	0-0	10		(31285)
34	6	FAC 3	A	Ipswich Town	D 0-0	0-0			(21236)
35	13	PL	A	Queens Park Rangers	W 1-0	0-0	8	Shearer 77	(13957)
36	16	FAC 3R	H	Ipswich Town	L 0-1	0-0			19606
37	20	PL	H	Sheffield Wednesday	W 3-0	2-0	5	Shearer 28, Bohinen 31, Gallacher 84	24732
38	F 3	PL	H	Bolton Wanderers	W 3-1	1-1	6	Shearer 12, 83, 90 (3)	30419
39	10	PL	A	Manchester United	L 0-1	0-1	6		(42681)
40	24	PL	H	Liverpool	L 2-3	1-2	9	Wilcox 26, Sherwood 84	30895
41	28	PL	A	Aston Villa	L 0-2	0-0	9		(28008)
42	M 2	PL	A	Manchester City	D 1-1	0-0	10	Shearer 57	(29078)
43	13	PL	H	Leeds United	W 1-0	0-0	8	Fenton 47	23358
44	16	PL	A	Tottenham Hotspur	W 3-2	2-0	7	Shearer 7(pen), 34, 90 (3)	(31803)
45	30	PL	H	Everton	L 0-3	0-0	8		29468
46	A 6	PL	A	Southampton	L 0-1	0-0	9		(14793)
47	8	PL	H	Newcastle United	W 2-1	0-0	9	Fenton 86, 90	30717
48	13	PL	A	Nottingham Forest	W 5-1	3-1	8	Shearer 27, McKinlay 30, Wilcox 45, 69, Fenton 83	(25273)
49	17	PL	H	Wimbledon	W 3-2	1-1	6	Shearer 13, 46, Fenton 58	24174
50	27	PL	H	Arsenal	D 1-1	1-0	7	Gallacher 12	29834
51	M 5	PL	A	Chelsea	W 3-2	1-1	7	Sherwood 37, McKinlay 48, Fenton 59	(28436)

Best Home League Attendance: 30895 v Liverpool   **Smallest: 23358 v Leeds United**   **Average: 27713**

Goal Scorers:
PL(61): Shearer(31),Fenton(6),Sherwood(4),Bohinen(4),Newell(3),Wilcox(3),McKinlay(2),Gallacher(2),Pearce(1),Holmes(1),Hendry(1),Marker(1),Le Saux(1),Batty(1)
CC(8):   Shearer(5),Sutton(1),Opponent(s)(1),Newell(1)
FAC(0):
EC(5):   Newell(4),Shearer(1)

1995-96

(D) Atkins	(M) Batty	(D) Berg	(M) Bohinen	(D) Coleman	(F) Fenton	(M) Filtcroft	(G) Flowers	(F) Gallacher	(M) Gudmundsson	(D) Hendry	(D) Hitchin	(F) Holmes	(D) Kenna	(D) Le Saux	(D) Makel	(D) Marker	(M) McKinlay	(G) Mimms	(F) Newell	(M) Pearce	(M) Ripley	(F) Shearer	(M) Sherwood	(F) Sutton	(G) Talia	(F) Warhurst	(M) Whealing	(D) Wilcox		
S1	X						X	X3					X1	X		S2	S3		S	X	X	X2	X	X					D.Gallagher	1
S2	X	X					X	X1				X		X					S1	S	X	X2	X	X	X2				A.Wilkie	2
S1	X	X					X			X		X		X					S1	X	X1	X	X	X1					P.S.Danson	3
S2	X	X					X			X		X		X					S1	X	X2	X	X	X1					K.Burge	4
S1	X	X					X			X		X	X1	X				S	S2	X	X2	X	X	X					D.Elleray	5
X2	X	X								X		X	X1	X		S1		S	X	X	X	X	X	S					R.Dilkes	6
	X	X					X			X		X	S		X2	X	S2		X	X	X1	X	X	S2					M.Piraux	7
	X	X					X			X		X		X	X	S	S		X	X	X	X	X	X					G.Willard	8
	X	X					X			X		X		X	X1	S1			S	X	X	X	X	X					G.Singh	9
	X	X					X			X		S		X	X1	S		S	X	X	S1	X	X2	X		S2			K.Cooper	10
	X	X					X			X		X1	X		S				X	X	X	X	X	X		S1			G.Benko	11
X1	X						X			X		S	X						X	X	X	X	X	X	S	S1			P.Alcock	12
S	X	X	X				X			X		X	X				S		S	X	X	X	X	X	X	S1			R.Hart	13
	X	X					X			X		X	S	X			S		S	S1	X	X	X	X		X1			M.Reed	14
	X	X	X				X			X		X	S	X		S		S1	S2	X	X	X	X1	X2					A.Frisk	15
	X	X					X			X		S	X						X	X	X	X	X	S	X				S.Lodge	16
	X	X	X				X			X		X		X				S	X	X	X	X	S	S					P.Jones	17
	X	X					X			X		S	X	S1	S			S	X2	X	X	X	S2	X1					U.Meier	18
	X	X	X				X			X		X	X				X2	S	X	X	X	X	X1	S1					P.Durkin	19
	X	X					X			X		S	X				X		X	X	X	X	X2	X		S2			A.Wilkie	20
	X	X	X				X			X		X	S1	X1			X		X	X2	X	X	S2	X		S1			J.Winter	21
	X	X					X			X		X	X	X		S	S		X	X	X	X	X	S					P.Pairetto	22
	X	X	X				X			X		X1	X	X		X2	S	X1	X	X	X	X	S1	S2					G.Poll	23
S	X	X					X		X1			X1	X		X	X	S2	S	X1	X	X	X	X	X	X	X		S	P.Didler	24
	X	X	X2				X			X		X	X1	X	X	X2	S2	S	X1	X	X	X	X	X	S1				S.Dunn	25
	X	X	X	S1	S2		X			X			X	X2	X	S	X	X1	X	X									P.Danson	26
	X	X	X	X1			X	S1		X			X		X	S	X	S	X		X	X		S					M.Bodenham	27
	X	X	X	S			X			X			X		X	S	S	X	X		X	X	S	S					K.Cooper	28
X1	X	X	X	S2			X			X		X	X		X		S2	S	X1	X	X					S1			P.Jones	29
	X	X					X			X	X		X	X		X	X		X2		X	X							R.Dilkes	30
	X	X		X		S				X	S	X	S	X		S	X		X	X	X	X							D.Elleray	31
X1	X	X	X	X2			X			X			X	X		X2	X		X		X	X	X	S					G.R.Ashby	32
X2	X	X		X			X			X			X		X		S1	S1	X		X	X	S	S2					D.Elleray	33
	X	X	X				X	X	S2				X		X		S1	S	X	X1	X	X2	X	X			S		G.Willard	34
	X	X		X3	S1		X	X	X1	X			X				S1	S	X	X1	X	X				X2			K.Burge	35
	X		X	X			X	X	S2				X			S	X2		X1	X	X	X		S1			X		A.Wilkie	36
	X		X	S			X	X	X2				X				X	S	X		X	X		S			X1		S.Lodge	37
	X		X	S	S1		X	X	S	X			X				X	X	S		X	X		S			X		P.Danson	38
	X		X	X1			X	X	S	X			X				X	X		X	X	X					X		S.Dunn	39
	X		X	S2		X	X	X1					X			X2	S1				X	X	S1				X		P.A.Durkin	40
	X		X	S2	X	X	X	X1					X			X2	S1		X		X	X					X		J.Winter	41
	X		X	S1	X	X				X			X			X1		S	X		X	X					X		D.Elleray	42
	X		X	S1	X	S2				X			X			X1				X2	X	X					X		G.Willard	43
	X		X	S			X			X			X			S				X1	X	X			S1		X		T.Jones	44
	X		X	S2		X	X	X1					X			X2	S1		X		X	X					X		R.Hart	45
	X	S1		X2			X	X		X			X				X				X1		X			S2		X	K.Cooper	46
	X	S2		X2	S	X	X1			X			X				X				X		X			S1			M.Bodenham	47

Also Played: (D) Broomes S(27). (D) Croft S(46,47,50). (M) Gill S(15,27). (G) Given S(6). (F) Tallon S(1).

0	23	38	17	19	4	3	37	14	1	33	0	8	32	13	0	8	13	1	26	12	28	35	33	9	0	1	0	9	PL Appearances	
4	0	0	2	1	10	0	0	2	3	0	0	1	0	1	3	1	6	1	4	0	0	0	0	4	0	9	0	0	PL Sub Appearances	
0	4	4	0	0	0	0	3	0	0	4	0	0	4	2	0	0	1	1	4	3	3	4	2+1	1+2	0	0	0	0	CC Appearances	
0	1	2	1	2	0	0	2	2	0	2	0	0	2	0	0	0	2	1+1	0	2	0	2	2	1+1	0	0	0	0	FAC Appearances	
1	5	6	0	0	0	0	6	0+1	0	5	0	2+1	5	2+1	1+1	1	0	0	5+1	4	4+1	6	6	3+3	0	4+1	0	0	EC Appearances	
0+1	1	0	0	0	0	1	1	0	0	0	0	1	1	0+1	0+1	0	0	1	1	1	1	1	1	1	0	0	0	0	CS Appearances	

BLACKBURN ROVERS

CLUB RECORDS

BIGGEST VICTORIES
League: 9-0 v Middlesbrough, Division 2, 6.11.1954.
F.A. Cup: 11-0 v Rossendale, Round 1, 13.10.1884.
League Cup: 6-1 v Watford, Round 4, 9.12.1992.

BIGGEST DEFEATS
League: 0-8 v Arsenal, Division 1, 25.2.1933.
0-8 v Lincoln City, Division 2, 29.8.1953.
F.A. Cup: 0-6 v Nottingham Forest, Round 3, 1879-80.
1-6 v Manchester United, 1908-09.
1-6 v Luton Town, Round 3, 1952-53.
League Cup: 0-5 v Wimbledon, 24.9.1985.
1-6 v Nottingham Forest, 15.9.1979.
Europe: (UEFA) 0-1 v Trelleborgs, 27.9.1994.

MOST POINTS
3 points a win: 89, Premiership, 1994-95.
2 points a win: 60, Division 3, 1974-75.

MOST GOALS SCORED
114, 1954-55, Division 2.
Briggs 33, Quigley 28, Crossan 18, Mooney 16, Langton 13, Clayton 2, Bell 1, og 3.

MOST GOALS CONCEDED
102, Division 1, 1932-33.

MOST FIRST CLASS MATCHES IN A SEASON
60 - 1979-80 (League 46, FA Cup 7, League Cup 4, Anglo-Scottish Cup 3).
60 - 1988-89 (League 46, FA Cup 3, League Cup 4, Simod Cup 3, League Play-offs 4).

MOST LEAGUE WINS
27, Premiership, 1994-95.

MOST LEAGUE DRAWS
18, Division 2, 1980-81.

MOST LEAGUE DEFEATS
30, Division 1, 1980-81.

INDIVIDUAL CLUB RECORDS

MOST GOALS IN A SEASON
Ted Harper - 45, 1925-26 (League 43, FAC 2).

MOST GOALS IN A MATCH
7, Tommy Briggs v Bristol Rovers, Division 2, 5.2.1953.

OLDEST PLAYER
Bob Crompton, 40 years 151 days, 23.2.1920.

YOUNGEST PLAYER
Harry Dennison, 16 years 155 days, 8.4.1911.

MOST CAPPED PLAYER
Bob Crompton (England) 41.

BEST PERFORMANCES

League: 1994-95: Played 42, Won 27, Drawn 8, Lost 7, Goals for 80, Goals against 39, Points 89. Premiership Champions.
Highest Position: 1994-95 Premiership Champions.
F.A. Cup: Winners in 1884 v Queens Park, 2-1.
Winners in 1885 v Queens Park, 2-0.
Winners in 1886 v West Bromwich 0-0,2-0.
Winners in 1890 v Sheffield Wednesday 6-1.
Winners in 1891 v Notts County 3-1.
Most Recent Success: (1928) 3rd Rnd. Newcastle United 4-1; 4th Rnd. Exeter City 2-2,3-1; 5th Rnd. Port Vale 2-1; 6th Rnd. Manchester United 2-0; Semi-Final Arsenal 1-0; Final Huddersfield Town 3-1.
League Cup: Semi-Finalists in 1961-62 v Rochdale, 1-3.
Most Recent Success: (1992-93) 2nd Rnd. Huddersfield Town (a) 1-1, (h) 4-3 aet; 3rd Rnd. Norwich City 2-0; 4th Rnd. Watford (h) 6-1; 5th Rnd. Cambridge United (h) 3-2; Semi-Final Sheffield Wednesday (h) 2-4, (a) 1-2.
Europe: (UEFA) 1st Rnd. Trelleborg (h) 0-1, (a) 2-2.

ADDITIONAL INFORMATION
PREVIOUS NAME
None.
PREVIOUS LEAGUES
None.

Club Colours: Blue & white halved shirts, white shorts, white socks with blue trim.
Change Colours:

Reserve League: Pontins Central League Division 1.

DIVISIONAL RECORD

	Played	Won	Drawn	Lost	For	Against	Points
Division 1/P	2146	818	494	834	3571	3570	2193
Division 2	1446	583	364	499	2134	1981	1723
Division 3	230	104	59	67	299	249	267
Total	3822	1505	917	1400	6004	5800	4183

RECORDS AND STATISTICS

COMPETITIONS

Div 1/P	Div.2	Div.3	A/Scot
1888-1936	1936-39	1971-75	1975-76
1939-47	1947-57	1979-80	1976-77
1957-66	1966-71		1977-78
1992-	1975-79		1978-79
	1980-92	E.C.	1979-80
		1995-96	1980-81

HONOURS

Div 1/P	Div.2	Div.3	FAC	FMC	C/Sh'ld
1911-12	1938-39	1974-75	1884	1986-87	1912
1913-14			1885		
1994-95			1886		
			1890		
			1891		
			1928		

MOST APPEARANCES

D Fazackerley 689+3 (1970-87)

Year	League	FA Cup	Lge Cup	A/Scottish
1970-71	14			
1971-72	39	2	2	
1972-73	46	3	1	
1973-74	46	5	3	
1974-75	22+1	1	2	
1975-76	42	1	2	
1976-77	37+1	4	3	
1977-78	28	2	2	
1978-79	37	2	1	
1979-80	46	7	4	
1980-81	38	1	5	
1981-82	39	1	3	
1982-83	38	1	2	
1983-84	39	3	2	
1984-85	39	4	2	
1985-86	36+1	3	2	
1986-87	7		2	
	593+3	40	38	18

MOST GOALS IN A CAREER

Simon Garner - 192 (1978-92)

Year	League	FA Cup	Lge Cup	Others
1978-79	8			
1979-80	6			
1980-81	7		1	
1981-82	14	2	2	
1982-83	22	1		
1983-84	19	1	3	
1984-85	12		2	
1985-86	12			
1986-87	10		1	4
1987-88	14	1		
1988-89	20	1	2	
1989-90	18			2
1990-91	1	1		
1991-92	5			
Total	168	7	11	6

Current leading goalscorer: Jason Wilcox 24 (1994/96)

RECORD TRANSFER FEE RECEIVED

Amount	Club	Player	Date
£15,000,000	Newcastle United	Alan Shearer	7/96
£3,750,000	Newcastle United	David Batty	5/94
£1,250,000	Manchester Utd	David May	5/94
£700,000	Manchester City	Colin Hendry	11/89

RECORD TRANSFER FEE PAID

Amount	Club	Player	Date
£5,000,000	Norwich City	Chris Sutton	7/94
£3,300,000	Southampton	Alan Shearer	7/92
£2,750,000	Leeds United	David Batty	10/93
£2,700,000	Sheffield Wed.	Paul Warhurst	8/93

MANAGERS

Name	Seasons	Best	Worst
Eddie Hapgood	1946-48	17(1)	21(1)
Will Scott	1948-50	14(2)	16(2)
Jack Bruton	1950-52	6(2)	14(2)
Jackie Bestall	1952-53	9(2)	9(2)
John Carey	1953-58	2(2)	9(2)
Dally Duncan	1958-61	8(1)	17(1)
Jack Marshall	1961-69	7(1)	19(2)
Eddie Quigley	1969-71	8(2)	21(2)
John Carey	1971-72	10(3)	10(3)
Ken Furphy	1972-74	3(3)	13(3)
Gordon Lee	1974-75	1(3)	1(3)
Jim Smith	1975-78	5(2)	11(2)
Jim Iley	1978-79	22(2)	22(2)
Howard Kendall	1979-81	4(2)	2(3)
Bobby Saxton	1981-86	6(2)	19(2)
Don Mackay	1986-91		
Kenny Dalglish	1991-95	1(P)	6(2/1)
Ray Harford	1995-	7(P)	7(P)

LONGEST LEAGUE RUNS

of undefeated matches:	23 (30.9.1987-27.2.1988)	of league matches w/out a win:	16 (25.11.1978-28.3.1979)
of undefeated home matches:	30 (14.4.1911-21.12.1912)	of undefeated away matches:	11 (15.2.1912-1.11.1913)
			(30.9.1987-27.2.1988)
without home win:	11 (16.9.1978 - 24.3.1979)	without an away win:	24 (12.2.1910 - 27.2.1911)
of league wins:	8 (1.3.1980 - 7.4.1980)	of home wins:	13 (12.2.1954 - 20.11.1954)
of league defeats:	7 (12.3.1966 - 16.4.1966)	of away wins:	7 (12.1.1980 - 12.4.1980)

BLACKBURN ROVERS

PLAYERS NAME / Honours	Ht	Wt	Birthdate	Birthplace / Transfers	Contract Date	Clubs	APPEARANCES				GOALS			
							League	L/Cup	FA Cup	Other	Lge	L/C	FAC	Oth
G O A L K E E P E R S														
Flowers Tim	6.2	14.0	03/02/67	Kenilworth	28/08/84	Wolves	63	5	2	2				
E: 8,u21.3,Y.1. Prem'95.				£70000	13/06/86	Southampton	192	26	16	8				
				Loan	23/03/87	Swindon Town	2							
				Loan	13/11/87	Swindon Town	5							
				£2400000	04/11/93	Blackburn Rovers	105	7	8	10				
Given Shay	6.2	13.4	20/04/76	Lifford		Celtic								
Ei: 7, u21.					01/08/94	Blackburn Rovers								
				Loan	01/08/94	Swindon Town								
				Loan	04/08/95	Swindon Town	4							
				Loan	19/01/96	Sunderland	17							
D E F E N D E R S														
Berg Henning	6.0	11.9	01/09/69	Edsvill		Lillestrom (Swe)								
Norwegian Int. Prem'95.				£400000	26/01/93	Blackburn Rovers	118+5	13	8	9	2			
Broomes Marlon	6.0	12.7	28/11/77	Birmingham	01/08/94	Blackburn Rovers								
E: Y.														
Coleman Chris	6.2	14.06	10/06/70	Swansea		Manchester City								
W: 8, u21.10, Y, S. WC'89'91.				Free	01/09/87	Swansea City	159+1	8	13	15	2		1	
Div.1'94.				£275000	19/07/91	Crystal Palace	143+11	24+2	8	2	13	2	1	
				£2800000	16/12/95	Blackburn Rovers	19+1		2					
Croft Gary	5.9	10.8	17/02/74	Burton-on-Trent	07/07/92	Grimsby Town	139+10	7	8+2	3	3	1		
E: u21.3.				£1000000	29/03/96	Blackburn Rovers								
Hendry Colin	6.1	12.2	07/12/65	Keith		Dundee	17+24		2+3		2		1	
S: 21,B.1. FMC'87. Prem'95.				£30000	11/03/87	Blackburn Rovers	99+3	4	3	13	22			1
				£700000	16/11/89	Manchester City	57+6	4+1	5	4	5	1	2	2
				£700000	08/11/91	Blackburn Rovers	160+5	20	11+1	11	10			
Hitchin Steve						Blackburn Rov. (T)								
Kenna Jeff	5.11	11.7	27/08/70	Dublin	25/04/89	Southampton	82+4	2	5+1	3	4			
Ei: 12, B.1, u21.8.				£1500000	15/03/95	Blackburn Rovers	41	4	2	6	1			
Le Saux Graeme	5.10	11.2	17/10/68	Harrow		St. Pauls (Jersey)								
E:12,B.2,u21.4. Prem'95.				Free	09/12/87	Chelsea	77+13	7+6	7+1	8+1	8	1		
				25/03/93	Blackburn Rovers		101+2	10	6	6+1	6			
Marker Nick	6.0	12.11	03/05/65	Budleigh Salt.	04/05/83	Exeter City	196+6	11	8	8	3	1		3
				£95000	31/10/87	Plymouth Argyle	201+1	15	9	7	13	3	1	1
				£500000	23/09/92	Blackburn Rovers	36+11	3	4	1+1	1			
Reed Adam M	6.0	12.0	18/02/75	B.Auckland	16/07/93	Darlington	45+7	1+1	1	3	1			
				£200000	09/08/95	Blackburn Rovers								
Worrell David	5.9	11.0	12.01.78	Dublin	01/08/94	Blackburn Rov (T)								
M I D F I E L D														
Bohinen Lars	5.11	12.02	08/09/66	Vados		Young Boys of Berne								
Norwegian Int.				£450000	05/11/93	Nottingham Forest	59+5	7+1	2	1	7	2	1	
				£700000	14/10/95	Blackburn Rovers	17+2		1		4			
Chisholm Craig	5.10	10.4	21/09/77	Glasgow	01/08/94	Blackburn Rov. (T)								
Flitcroft Gary	5.10	11.0	06/11/72	Bolton	02/07/91	Manchester City	109+6	11+1	14		13		2	
E: u21.10,Y1,S.				Loan	05/03/92	Bury	12							
				£3200000	26/03/96	Blackburn Rovers	3							
Gill Wayne	5.10	11.3	28/11/75	Chorley	01/08/94	Blackburn Rovers								
Gudmundsson Niklas						Halmstads								
				£750000	01/03/96	Blackburn Rovers	1+3							
McKinlay Billy	5.9	9.13	22/04/69	Glasgow		Dundee United								
S: 18.				£1750000	14/10/95	Blackburn Rovers	13+6	1	1+1		2			
Morgan Thomas			30/03/77	Dublin	01/08/93	Blackburn Rovers								
Pearce Ian	6.1	12.4	07/05/74	Bury St.Ed.	01/08/91	Chelsea	0+4			0+1				
E: u21.1, Y.10. Prem'95.				£300000	04/10/93	Blackburn Rovers	35+10	3+3	1+2	6+1	1	1	1	
Ripley Stuart	5.11	12.6	20/11/67	Middlesbrough	23/12/85	Middlesbrough	210+39	21+2	17+1	20+1	26	3	1	1
E:1,u21.8,Y.4. Prem'95.				Loan	18/02/86	Bolton Wanderers	5			0+1	1			
				£1300000	20/07/92	Blackburn Rovers	142+3	18	11	8+1	11		2	
Sherwood Tim	6.0	11.6	06/02/69	St.Albans	07/02/87	Watford	23+9	4+1	9	4+1	2			
E: B.1,u21.4,u19.2. Prem'95.				£175000	18/07/89	Norwich City	66+5	7	4	5+1	10	1		2
				£500000	12/02/92	Blackburn Rovers	154+5	18	9+2	10	15		1	

F O R W A R D S

Name			DOB	From / Fee	Date	Club								
Beattie James	6.1	12.0	27/02/78		01/08/94	Blackburn Rov. (T)								
Cassin Graham	5.8	10.7	24/03/78	Dublin	01/08/94	Blackburn Rov. (T)								
Fenton Graham	5.10	11.03	22/05/74	Wallsend	13/02/92	Aston Villa	16+16	2+5			3			
				Loan	10/01/94	W.B.A.	7				3			
				£1500000	08/11/95	Blackburn Rovers	4+10				6			
Gallacher Kevin	5.8	10.10	23/11/66	Clydebank		Dundee United								
S:23,B.2,u21.7,Y.				£900000	29/01/90	Coventry City	99+1	11	4	2	28	7		
				£1500000	23/03/93	Blackburn Rovers	51+5	4	6	1+1	15		1	
Harford Paul	6.3	14.0	21/10/74	Chelmsford		Arsenal								
				Free	24/08/93	Blackburn Rovers								
				Loan	02/09/94	Wigan Athletic	3							
				Loan	15/12/94	Shrewsbury Town	3+3							
Holmes Matthew	5.7	10.7	01/08/69	Luton	22/08/88	Bournemouth	105+9	7	8+2	5	8			
				Loan	23/03/89	Cardiff City	0+1							
				£40000	19/08/92	West Ham United	63+13	4	6	3	5			1
				£1200000	15/08/95	Blackburn Rovers	8+1			2+1	1			
Sutton Chris	6.3	12.1	10/03/73	Nottingham	02/07/91	Norwich City	89+13	8+1	10	6	35	3	5	
E: B.1,u21.13. Prem'95.				£5000000	13/07/94	Blackburn Rovers	49+4	6+1	2	6+3	15	4	2	1
Warhurst Paul	6.1	12.10	26/09/69	Stockport	01/07/88	Manchester City								
E: u21.8. Prem'95.				£10000	27/10/88	Oldham Athletic	60+7	8	5+4	2	2			
				£750000	17/01/91	Sheffield Wed.	60+6	9	7+1	5	6	4	5	3
				£2700000	17/08/93	Blackburn Rovers	25+21	6+2	2	4+2	2			
Wilcox Jason	5.10	11.6	15/07/71	Farnworth	13/06/89	Blackburn Rovers	147+12	13+1	11	5	22	1	1	
E:1, B.1. Prem'95.														

ADDITIONAL CONTRACT PLAYERS

Coughlan Graham	Blackburn Rovers
Donis Georgios	Blackburn Rovers
Duff Damien	Blackburn Rovers
Hope Richard	Blackburn Rovers
Johnson Damien	Blackburn Rovers
Staton Luke	Blackburn Rovers
Whealing Tony	Blackburn Rov. (T)

THE MANAGER
RAY HARFORD

Date of Birth. . . . . 1st June 1945.
Place of Birth. . . . . Halifax.
Date of Appointment . . . . July 1995.

PREVIOUS CLUBS
As Manager . . . . Fulham, Luton Town, Wimbledon.
As Coach/Assistant . . . . . . Fulham, Luton Town, Wimbledon, Blackburn Rovers.
As a Player . . . . Charlton Athletic, Exeter City, LIncoln City, Mansfield Town,
. . . . Port Vale, Colchester United.

HONOURS
As a Manager
Luton Town: League Cup winners 1988, runners-up 1989. Simod Cup runners-up 1988.

As a Player
None.

Ewood Park

Blackburn, Lancashire BB2 4JF
Tel: 01254 698888

Capacity . . . . .31,141.
First game . . . . .v Accrington, (Friendly), 13.9.1890.
First floodlit game . . . . .v Werder (Friendly), 1958-59.
Second set . . . . .v Aberdeen (Friendly), 7.12.1976.

Internationals played at Ewood . . . . .England v Scotland, 6.4.1891. England v Wales, 3.3.1924.

ATTENDANCES
Highest . . . . .61,783 v Bolton Wanderers, FA Cup, 2.3.1929.
Lowest . . . . .1,200 v West Bromwich Albion, Div.1, 22.12.1894.

OTHER GROUNDS . . . . .Brookhouse Ground 1875-76. Alexandra Meadow 1876-81.
. . . . .Leamington Road 1881-1890. Ewood Park 1890 to date.

MATCHDAY TICKET PRICES

Jack Walker Stand
Upper Tier Central £19
Upper Tier Outer (Adult/Juv&OAP). . . . . . . £18/£9
Lower Tier Central. £18/£9
Lower Tier Outer . . . . £15/£8

Walker Steel Stand . . . . £15/£8

Darwen Stand Upper & Lower Tier . . . . . . £15/£8

Blackburn End Upper Family Stand & lower £15/£8

Ticket Office Telephone No.. . . . . . . 01254 696 767

CLUBCALL
0898 12 11 79
Calls cost 39p per minute cheap rate and 49p per
minute at all other times.
Call costings correct at time of going to press.

HOW TO GET TO THE GROUND

From the North and West
M6 to junction 31 or A666 into Blackburn. A666 into Bolton Road, left into Kidder Street for Ewood Park.

From the South
M6 to junction 31 as from North or A666 via Bolton. After Darwen turn right into Kidder Street for Ewood Park.

From the East
A679 or A677 to Blackburn then A666 toward Bolton into Bolton Road. Left into Kidder Street for Ewood Park.

Car Parking
Ewood car park within walking distance.

Nearest Railway Station
Blackburn Central (01254 662 537/8).

MATCHDAY PROGRAMME

Programme Editor . . . . Peter White.

Number of pages 32

Price £1.50

Subscriptions. . . . . £75 home & away, £40 home.

Local Newspapers . . . . Lancashire Evening Telegraph.

Local Radio Stations . . . . . . Red Rose Radio, BBC Radio Lancashire.

CHELSEA
(The Blues)
F.A. CARLING PREMIERSHIP
SPONSORED BY: COORS EXTRA GOLD

Back Row (L-R): Dave Collyer (Yth Dev. Officer), Terry Byrne (Asst. Physio), Robert Fleck, Gareth Hall, Michael Duberry, Nigel Spackman, Paul Furlong, Jakob Kjeldbjerg, Erland Johnsen, Paul Hughes, Mussie Izzet, Mark Nicholls, Junior Mendes, Christian McCann, Bernie Dixson (Yth Dev. Officer), Ian Oliver (Reflexologist). **Middle Row:** George Price (Res. Team Physio), Mike Banks (Physio), Scott Minto, Anthony Barness, Zeke Rowe, Andy Myers, Russell Kelly, Dmitri Kharine, Kevin Hitchcock, Steve Clarke, Craig Burley, David Lee, Terry Skiverton, Darren Barnard, Gwyn Williams (Scout/Admin Manager), Bob Orsborn (Kit Manager). **Front Row:** Eddie Niedzwiecki (res. Manager), Eddie Newton, Mark Stein, Andy Dow, Ruud Gullit, Dennis Wise, Glenn Hoddle (Manager), Peter Shreeves (Asst. Manager), Gavin Peacock, Mark Hughes, David Rocastle, Frank Sinclair, John Spencer, Graham Rix (Yth Manager).

CHELSEA
FORMED IN 1905
TURNED PROFESSIONAL IN 1905
LTD COMPANY IN 1905

CHAIRMAN: K W Bates

DIRECTORS
C Hutchinson (Managing), Y Todd, M Harding.
SECRETARY
Keith Lacy
COMMERCIAL MANAGER
Carole Phair

MANAGER: Ruud Gullit
ASSISTANT MANAGER: Gwyn Williams
FIRST TEAM COACH: Graham Rix
RESERVE TEAM MANAGER
Mick McGiven
YOUTH TEAM MANAGER
Ted Dale
PHYSIOTHERAPIST
Mike Banks

STATISTICIAN FOR THE DIRECTORY
Ron Hockings

With the sensational signings of Ruud Gullit (from Sampdoria) and Mark Hughes (from Manchester United), added to a squad, that under the influence of Glen Hoddle were starting to play good football whilst keeping it tight at the back, you might well have expected Chelsea to be in the running for some long awaited 'silver-ware'.,

Chelsea got off to a rather slow start, with three draws (two of them scoreless) and a defeat before they finally got it right away to London rivals West Ham (3-0). The following match, against Southampton, saw another good win (3-0) and Gullit's first goal for the club. However, this pick up in form was dented by a 0-0 draw against Stoke City in the Coca-Cola Cup followed by a 0-2 defeat at the hands of Newcastle United.

It was this inconsistency that would keep Chelsea out of the title race, but a 5-0 demolition of Middlesbrough, live on Sky TV, left the Chelsea supporters and the footballing world wondering why 'The Blues' were not further up the table than they were, a 0-1 defeat at the Highfield Road six days latter answered their questions.

A place in the semi-finals of the F.A. Cup was the closest Chelsea got to any domestic honours. Having beaten Newcastle at St. James Park in a 3rd Round replay (the first club to have beaten the Magpies at their home ground that season - albeit on penalties), the 'Blues' then beat Q.P.R. (2-1), Grimsby Town (4-0) after a 0-0 draw and finally Wimbledon, again in a replay, (3-1) before meeting Manchester United at Villa Park.

With Ruud Gullit's known ambitions of playing at Wembley and winning the F.A. Cup, you would have been excused for thinking they were on their way when the Dutch maestro netted after 35 minutes, to give Chelsea a 1-0 lead at half-time.

But this was Manchester United they were playing, a team that were hungry for not only the F.A Cup itself but the possible chance of the 'Double Double'. However, United's cause was made easier with two incidents that changed the dreams of both Chelsea supporters and Gullit alike. A struggling Terry Phelan, who had pulled up with a muscle injury, was aloud to play on after touch-line treatment. A fully fit David Beckham, taking advantage of normally one of the quickest full-backs obvious discomfort, ran down the wing before crossing the ball to Cantona who in turn found Cole, (1-1). Four minutes later and Craig Burley inexplicably tried to pass the ball back to Hitchcock from almost the half-way line, it found Beckham and United went through to the F.A. Cup final.

In the Coca-Cola Cup their 0-0 draw at Stoke City was followed by a humiliating 0-1 defeat, thus ending any hope of success in that competition.

The 1996/97 season promises to be an exciting time at Stamford Bridge. With Gullit at the reins and with the likes of Vialli, Di Matteo and Leboeff being brought into a team of quality players such as Hughes, Duberry and Wise surely this season will see Chelsea lift one of the major trophies. Indeed if the pre-season Umbro Cup final victory over Ajax (2-0) is anything to go by you would be foolish to bet against them.

CHELSEA

| League: 11th | | | FA Cup: Semi-Final | | | | Coca-Cola Cup: 2nd Rnd | |

M	DATE	COMP	VEN	OPPONENTS	RESULT	HT	LP	GOAL SCORERS/GOAL TIMES	ATT.
1	A 19	PL	H	Everton	D 0-0	0-0	10		30189
2	23	PL	A	Nottingham Forest	D 0-0	0-0	12		(27007)
3	26	PL	A	Middlesbrough	L 0-2	0-1	9		(28286)
4	30	PL	H	Coventry City	D 2-2	2-1	14	Wise 6(pen), Hughes 10	24398
5	S 11	PL	A	West Ham United	W 3-1	2-0	11	Wise 31, Spencer 33, 80	(19228)
6	16	PL	H	Southampton	W 3-0	0-0	9	Sinclair 74, Gullit 89, Hughes 90	26237
7	20	CC 2/1	A	Stoke City	D 0-0	0-0			(15574)
8	24	PL	A	Newcastle United	L 0-2	0-1	10		(36225)
9	30	PL	H	Arsenal	W 1-0	0-0	10	Hughes 51	31048
10	O 4	CC 2/2	H	Stoke City	L 0-1	0-0			16272
11	14	PL	A	Aston Villa	W 1-0	1-0	9	Wise 72	(34992)
12	21	PL	H	Manchester United	L 1-4	0-2	9	Hughes 76	31019
13	28	PL	A	Blackburn Rovers	L 0-3	0-1	10		(27733)
14	N 4	PL	H	Sheffield Wednesday	D 0-0	0-0	10		23216
15	18	PL	A	Leeds United	L 0-1	0-0	12		(36209)
16	22	PL	H	Bolton Wanderers	W 3-2	1-1	10	Lee 17, Hall 59, Newton 85	17495
17	25	PL	H	Tottenham Hotspur	D 0-0	0-0	11		31059
18	D 2	PL	A	Manchester United	D 1-1	0-0	11	Wise 53	(42019)
19	9	PL	H	Newcastle United	W 1-0	1-0	10	Petrescu 43	31098
20	16	PL	A	Arsenal	D 1-1	1-0	10	Spencer 25	(38295)
21	23	PL	A	Manchester City	W 1-0	0-0	9	Peacock 76	(28668)
22	26	PL	H	Wimbledon	L 1-2	1-2	11	Petrescu 12	21906
23	30	PL	H	Liverpool	D 2-2	2-1	12	Spencer 9, 44	31137
24	J 2	PL	A	Queens Park Rangers	W 2-1	0-0	12	Brazier 77(og), Furlong 90	(14904)
25	7	FAC 3	H	Newcastle United	D 1-1	1-0		Hughes 35	25151
26	13	PL	A	Everton	D 1-1	1-1	12	Spencer 20	(34968)
27	17	FAC 3R	A	Newcastle United	D 2-2	0-1		Wise 61(pen), Gullit 88 (Won on penalties))	(36534)
28	20	PL	H	Nottingham Forest	W 1-0	0-0	10	Spencer 55	24482
29	29	FAC 4	A	Queens Park Rangers	W 2-1	2-0		Peacock 19, Furlong 45	(18542)
30	F 4	PL	H	Middlesbrough	W 5-0	3-0	8	Peacock 29, 38, 55 (3), Spencer 31, Furlong 52	21060
31	10	PL	A	Coventry City	L 0-1	0-1	10		(20629)
32	17	PL	H	West Ham United	L 1-2	1-0	10	Peacock 13	25252
33	21	FAC 5	A	Grimsby Town	D 0-0	0-0			(9648)
34	24	PL	A	Southampton	W 3-2	2-2	8	Wise 20, 26(pen), Gullit 53	(15226)
35	28	FAC 5R	H	Grimsby Town	W 4-1	1-0		Duberry 21, Hughes 54, Spencer 56, Peacock 58	28545
36	M 2	PL	A	Wimbledon	D 1-1	1-1	8	Furlong 35	(17048)
37	9	FAC QF	H	Wimbledon	D 2-2	0-0		Hughes 70, Gullit 80	30805
38	12	PL	H	Manchester City	D 1-1	1-1	8	Gullit 25	17078
39	16	PL	A	Liverpool	L 0-2	0-0	9		(40820)
40	20	FAC QFR	A	Wimbledon	W 3-1	1-1		Petrescu 20, Duberry 79, Hughes 84	(21380)
41	23	PL	A	Queens Park Rangers	D 1-1	1-1	10	Spencer 9	25590
42	31	FAC SF	N	Manchester United	L 1-2	1-0		Gullit 35	38421
43	A 6	PL	H	Aston Villa	L 1-2	1-1	10	Spencer 8	23530
44	8	PL	A	Bolton Wanderers	L 1-2	1-2	10	Spencer 13	(18021)
45	13	PL	H	Leeds United	W 4-1	3-0	10	Hughes 18, 35 48(pen), Spencer 19	22131
46	17	PL	A	Sheffield Wednesday	D 0-0	0-0	10		(25094)
47	27	PL	A	Tottenham Hotspur	D 1-1	1-0	10	Hughes 35	(32918)
48	M 5	PL	H	Blackburn Rovers	L 2-3	1-1	11	Wise 35, Spencer 88	28436

Best Home League Attendance: 31137 v Liverpool　　　　　**Smallest: 17078 v Manchester City**　　　　　**Average: 25597**

Goal Scorers:
PL(46):　　　Spencer(13),Hughes(8),Wise(7),Peacock(5),Gullit(3),Furlong(3),Petrescu(2),Lee(1),Sinclair(1),Hall(1),Newton(1),Opponent(s)(1)
CC(0):
FAC(15):　　　Hughes(4),Gullit(3),Peacock(2),Duberry(2),Furlong(1),Spencer(1),Petrescu(1),Wise(1)

(D) Barness	(M) Burley	(D) Clarke	(D) Dow	(D) Duberry	(F) Fleck	(F) Furlong	(M) Gullit	(D) Hall	(G) Hitchcock	(F) Hughes	(F) Johnsen	(G) Kharine	(D) Kjeldbjerg	(D) Lee	(D) Minto	(M) Morris	(D) Myers	(M) Newton	(M) Peacock	(D) Petrescu	(D) Phelan	(M) Rocastle	(D) Sinclair	(M) Spackman	(F) Spencer	(F) Stein	(F) Wise		
	S2	X					X		S	X	X	X					X		X2				X	X	S1	X1	X	M.Reed	1
	S2	X					X			X	X	X					X	S2	X1				X	X	S1	X2	X	J.Winter	2
	S1	X					X		S	X	X	X		X			X	S2	X1				X		S1	X2	X	S.Lodge	3
		X					X			X	X	X		S1	X			X	X1				X		X	S	X1	G.Willard	4
	X1	X				S1	X		S	X	X	X			X			X					X	S	X		X	R.Hart	5
X1	X					S1	X		S	X	X	X			X			X					X	S	X		X	P.Alcock	6
	X					S2	X		S	X	X	X		X1				S1	X				X	X		X2	X	T.West	7
	X					X	X		S	X	X	X					X	S1	X1				X	X		S	X	P.Jones	8
X	X					X	X		S	X	X	X		S1					X1				X	X1	S1		X	M.Bowdenham	9
	X					X	X		S	X	X	X		X			X	X	X				X			S	X	K.Cooper	10
S1	X					X	X		S	X	X	X					X	X	X2					S2		X1	W.Wilkie	11
	X					X1	X			X	X	X		S2			X	X				X	X2			S1	X	P.Durkin	12
S	X					S1	X1	X	S	X	X	X		X			X						X		X	X	X	P.Danson	13
	X		X			S1	X		X	S	X	X1	X	X			X		X			S		X	X	X	M.Reed	14
	X1	X				S1	X		X	S	X	X	X	X			X		X				S1	X1		X	G.Poll	15
S1	X		X			X	X		X	S	X	X	X	X			X		X			X1	S		X	S.Lodge	16
	X		X			X	X		X	S	X	X	X				X		X			X1			X	M.Bodenham	17
S		X				X	X		S	S	X	X		X	X		X	X		X	X		X	X2	X	R.Dilkes	18
X	S1	X				S2			X	X	X		X	X		X	X1		X2	X	R.Dilkes	19

CHELSEA

CLUB RECORDS

BIGGEST VICTORIES
League: 7-0 v Lincoln City, Division 2, 29.10.1910.
7-0 v Port Vale, Division 2, 3.3.1906.
9-2 v Glossop N.E., Division 2, 1.9.1906.
7-0 v Portsmouth, Division 2, 21.5.1963.
7-0 v Walsall (a), Division 2, 4.2.1989.
F.A. Cup: 9-1 v Worksop, 1st Round, 31.1.1908.
League Cup: 7-0 v Doncaster Rovers, 3rd Round, 16.11.1960.
Europe: 13-0 v Jeunesse Hautcharge, ECWC, 29.9.1971.

BIGGEST DEFEATS
League: 1-8 v Wolverhampton W., Division 1, 26.9.1923.
0-7 v Leeds United, Division 1, 7.10.1967.
0-7 v Nottingham Forest, Division 1, 20.4.1991
F.A. Cup: 0-6 v Sheffield Wednesday, 2nd Round replay, 5.2.1913.
1-7 v Crystal Palace, 3rd Round, 16.11.1960.
League Cup: 2-6 v Stoke City, 3rd Round, 22.10.1974.
Europe: 0-5 v Barcelona, Semi-Final EUFA, 25.5.1966.

MOST POINTS
3 points a win: 99, Division 2, 1988-89 (Division 2 record, 46 games).
2 points a win: 57, Division 2, 1906-07.

MOST GOALS SCORED
98, Division 1, 1960-61.
Greaves 41, Tindall 16, Tambling 9, Brabrook 8, Livesey 8, Blunstone 5, Silett 2, Anderton 1, Bradbury 1, Bridges 1, Brooks 1, Gibbs 1, Mortimore 1, Harrison 1, opponents 2.

MOST GOALS CONCEDED
100, Division 1, 1960-61.

MOST FIRST CLASS MATCHES IN A SEASON
60 - 1965-66 (League 42, FA Cup 6, Fairs Cup 12).
60 - 1970-71 (League 42, FA Cup 3, League Cup 3, Charity Shield 1, ECWC 10).

MOST LEAGUE WINS
29, Division 2, 1988-89.

MOST LEAGUE DRAWS
18, Division 1, 1922-23.

MOST LEAGUE DEFEATS
27, Division 1, 1978-79.

INDIVIDUAL CLUB RECORDS

MOST GOALS IN A SEASON
Jimmy Greaves: 43 goals in 1960-61 (League 41, League Cup 2).

MOST GOALS IN A MATCH
6. George Hilsdon v Worksop, FA Cup (9-1), 11.1.1908.

OLDEST PLAYER
Dick Spence, 39 years 1 month, 1947-48.
Graham Rix made his Chelsea debut on 15.09.1994 (ECWC) aged 37 years 11 months, he made his League debut on 14.05.1995.
YOUNGEST PLAYER
Ian Hamilton, 16 years 4 months, 1966-67.

MOST CAPPED PLAYER
Glen Hoddle (England) 53.

BEST PERFORMANCES

League: 1988-89: Matches Played 46, Won 29, Drawn 12, Lost 3, Goals for 96, Goals against 50. Points 99. First in Division 2.
Highest Position: 1954-55, 1st in Division 1.
F.A. Cup: 1969-70: 3rd Round Birmingham City 3-0; 4th Round Burnley 2-2,3-1; 5th Round Crystal Palace 4-1; 6th Round Queens Park Rangers 4-2; Semi-Final Watford 5-1; Final Leeds United 2-2,2-1.
League Cup: 1964-65: 2nd Round Birmingham City 3-0; 3rd Round Notts County 4-0; 4th Round Swansea 3-2; 5th Round Workington 2-2,2-0; Semi-Final Aston Villa 3-2,1-1; Final Leicester City 0-0,3-2.
Europe: ECWC - 1970-71: 1st Round Aris Salonica 1-1,5-1; 2nd Round CSKA Sofia 1-0,1-0; 3rd Round Bruges 0-2,4-0; Semi-Final Manchester City 1-0,1-0; Final Real Madrid 1-1,2-1.
EUFA - 1965-66: 1st Round A.S.Roma 0-0,4-1; 2nd Round Wiener S.H. 0-1,2-0; 3rd Round A.C.Milan 2-1,1-2,1-1 (Chelsea won on toss of a coin); Semi-Final Barcelona 2-0,0-2, 0-5.

ADDITIONAL INFORMATION

PREVIOUS NAMES
None.
PREVIOUS LEAGUES
None.

Club colours: Royal blue shirts with white trim, blue shorts & socks.
Change colours: Grey shirts with orange trim, orange shorts, grey socks.

Reserve League: Avon Insurance Combination.

DIVISIONAL RECORD

	Played	Won	Drawn	Lost	For	Against	Points
Division 1/P	2,524	880	674	970	4,135	3,960	2,588
Division 2	786	383	202	201	1,323	887	1,018
Total	3,310	1,263	876	1,171	5,458	4,847	3,606

RECORDS AND STATISTICS

COMPETITIONS

Div 1/P	Div.2	ECWC	EUFA	A/Scot
1907-10	1905-07	1970-71	1965-66	1975-76
1912-24	1910-12	1971-72	1968-69	1976-77
1930-62	1924-30	1994-95		1977-78
1963-75	1962-63			
1977-79	1975-77			
1984-87	1979-84			
1989-	1988-89			

HONOURS

Div 1	Div.2	FA Cup	Lge Cup	ECWC	C/Shld
1954-55	1983-84	1970	1965	1971	1955
	1988-89				FMC
					1986
					1990

MOST APPEARANCES

RON HARRIS 791+12 (1961-80)

Year	League	FA Cup	Lge Cup	ECWC	EUFA	A/Scott
1961-62	3					
1962-63	7					
1963-64	41	3	1			
1964-65	42	5	6			
1965-66	36	6		10		
1966-67	42	7	3			
1967-68	40	5	1			
1968-69	40	5	3		4	
1969-70	30	8	3			
1970-71	38	3	4	9		
1971-72	41	3	9	4		
1972-73	42	3	7			
1973-74	36	2	1			
1974-75	42	2	4			
1975-76	38+2	4	1			3
1976-77	15+4	2	0+1			2
1977-78	37	4	1			2+1
1978-79	38+2	1	1			
1979-80	38+1	1	1+1			
	646+9	64	46+2	13	14	7+1

MOST GOALS IN A CAREER

BOBBY TAMBLING - 202 (1958-69)

Year	League	FA Cup	Lge Cup	EUFA
1958-59	1	-	-	-
1959-60	1	-	-	-
1960-61	9	-	3	-
1961-62	20	2	-	-
1962-63	35	2	-	-
1963-64	17	2	-	-
1964-65	15	4	6	-
1965-66	16	5	-	2
1966-67	21	6	1	-
1967-68	12	3	-	-
1968-69	17	1	-	2
Total	164	25	10	3

Current leading goalscorer: Dennis Wise - 52 (1990-96)

RECORD TRANSFER FEE RECEIVED

Amount	Club	Player	Date
£2,200,000	Tottenham H.	Gordon Durie	8/91
£1,700,000	Leeds United	Tony Dorigo	6/91
£925,000	Everton	Pat Nevin	7/88
£825,000	Manchester Utd	Ray Wilkins	8/79

RECORD TRANSFER FEE PAID

Amount	Club	Player	Date
£4,900,000	Lazio	Roberto Di Matteo	07/96
£2,500,000	Strasbourg	Franck Leboeff	07/96
£2,300,000	Watford	Paul Furlong	5/94
£2,100,000	Norwich City	Robert Fleck	8/92

MANAGERS

Name	Seasons	Best	Worst
J T Robertson	1905-06	3(2)	3(2)
David Calderhead	1907-33	8(1)	9(2)
Leslie Knighton	1933-39	8(1)	20(1)
Billy Birrell	1939-52	13(1)	19(1)
Ted Drake	1952-62	1(1)	22(1)
Tommy Docherty	1962-67	3(1)	2(2)
Dave Sexton	1967-74	3(1)	17(1)
Ron Stuart	1974-75	21(1)	21(1)
Eddie McCreadie	1975-77	2(2)	11(2)
Ken Shellitto	1977-78	16(1)	16(1)
Danny Blanchflower	1978-79	22(1)	22(1)
Geoff Hurst	1979-81	4(2)	12(2)
John Neal	1981-85	1(2)	18(2)
John Hollins	1985-88	6(1)	18(1)
Bobby Campbell	1988-91	5(1)	1(2)
Ian Porterfield	1991-93		
David Webb (Trail)	1993	11(P)	11(P)
Glenn Hoddle	1993-96	10(P)	11(P)
Ruud Gullit	1996-		

LONGEST LEAGUE RUNS

of undefeated matches:	27 (29.10.1988 - 15.4.1989)	of league matches w/out a win:	21 (3.11.1987 - 2.4.1988)
of undefeated home matches:	34 (28.4.1910 - 24.2.1912)	of undefeated away matches:	13 (5.11.1988 - 8.4.1989)
without home win:	11 (30.3.1974 - 28.9.1974)	without an away win:	22 (1.3.1952 - 14.3.1953)
of league wins:	8 (5.2.27 - 21.3.27 & 15.3.89 - 8.4.89)	of home wins:	13 (12.11.1910 - 2.9.1911)
of league defeats:	7 (1.11.1952 - 20.12.1952)	of away wins:	7 (4.2.1989 - 8.4.1989)

CHELSEA

PLAYERS NAME Honours	Ht	Wt	Birthdate	Birthplace Transfers	Contract Date	Clubs	League	L/Cup	FA Cup	Other	Lge	L/C	FAC	Oth
G O A L K E E P E R S														
Colgan Nick	6.1	12.0	19/09/73	Drogheda		Drogheda								
					01/10/92	Chelsea								
				Loan	01/08/93	Crewe Alexandra								
				Loan	01/08/94	Grimsby Town								
				Loan	29/09/95	Millwall								
Hitchcock Kevin	6.1	12.2	05/10/62	Canning Town		Barking								
AMC'87.				£15000	04/08/83	Nottingham Forest								
					01/02/84	Mansfield Town	182	12	10	20				
				£250000	25/03/88	Chelsea	80+1	8	12	13				
Kharine Dmitri	6.2	12.4	16/08/68	Moscow		CSKA Moscow								
CIS. USSR. Russian Int.				£200000	22/12/92	Chelsea	102	8	12	4				
Olympic G.Medal'88.														
D E F E N D E R S														
Clarke Steve	5.9	11.10	29/08/63	Saltcoats		St.Mirren	151	21	19	6	6		1	
S:6,B.3,u21.8,Y. SLgeXI.1.				£422000	19/01/87	Chelsea	268+5	17	26+2	21	6	1	1	1
Div.2'89.														
Duberry Michael	6.1	12.13	14/10/75	Enfield	01/08/93	Chelsea	22		8				2	
				Loan	29/09/95	Bournemouth	7		1					
Johnsen Erland	6.1	13.5	05/04/67	Frederikstad		Bayern Munich								
Norweigan Int.				£306000	06/12/89	Chelsea	121+6	6	15+1	12	1			
Kjeldbjerg Jakob	6.2	13.08	21/10/69			Silkeborg								
Norweigan Int.				£400000	13/08/93	Chelsea	52	6	6+1	1	2			
Leboeff Franck						Strasbourg								
French Int.				£2500000	01/06/96	Chelsea								
Lee David	6.3	13.12	26/11/69	Kingswood	01/07/88	Chelsea	117+32	12+5	10+4	6+2	10	1		1
E: u21.10,Y.1. Div.2'89.				Loan	30/01/92	Reading	5				5			
				Loan	12/08/94	Portsmouth	4+1							
McCann Christian	5.8	***	28/11/76		01/07/95	Chelsea								
Minto Scott	5.9	10.7	06/08/71	Heswall	02/02/89	Charlton Athletic	171+9	8	8+2	7	6	2		1
E: u21.6,Y.8.				£775000	28/05/94	Chelsea	29	1	3	5+1				
Myers Andrew	5.8	9.10	03/11/73	Hounslow	25/07/91	Chelsea	47+6	1+1	9	3	1			
E: u21.3,Y.12,S.3.														
Petrescu Dan	5.8	11.0	22/12/67	Bucharest		Steaua Bucharest								
Romanian Int. Rom.Div.1'85'86'						Foggia								
87'88. Rom.FAC'85'87'88.						Genoa								
				£1250000	06/08/94	Sheffield Wed.	28+9	2	0+2		3			
				£2300000	18/11/95	Chelsea	22+2		7		2		1	
Phelan Terry	5.8	10.0	16/03/67	Manchester	03/08/84	Leeds United	12+2	3		2				
Ei: 35, B.2, u23.1, u21.1,Y.				Free	30/07/86	Swansea City	45	4	5	3				
FAC'88.				£100000	29/07/87	Wimbledon	155+4	13+2	16	8	1		2	
				£2500000	25/08/92	Manchester City	102+1	11	8	1			1	
				£900000	15/11/95	Chelsea	12		8					
Sinclair Frank	5.8	11.2	03/12/71	Lambeth	17/05/90	Chelsea	126+1	13	12	7	5	1	1	2
				Loan	12/12/91	W.B.A.	6				1			
M I D F I E L D														
Burley Craig	6.1	11.7	24/09/71	Irvine	01/09/89	Chelsea	59+23	2	11+2	3	5		3	
S: 12.														
Clement Neil	5.10		03/10/78		06/10/95	Chelsea								
Gullit Ruud	6.0	13.0	01/09/62	Surinam		DWS Amsterdam								
Dutch Int. Euro'88.					01/08/79	Haalem	91				32			
					01/08/82	Feyenoord	85				30			
					01/08/85	PSV Eindhoven	68				46			
					01/08/87	AC Milan	117				35			
					01/08/93	Sampdoria	31				15			
					01/08/94	AC Milan	8				3			
					01/12/94	Sampdoria	22				9			
				Free	01/07/95	Chelsea	31	2	7		3		3	
Hughes John Paul	5.10		19/04/76	Hammersmith	01/07/94	Chelsea								
Di Matteo Roberto			22/01/68	Switzerland		Aarau (Switz)								
Italy: 15.						Lazio								
				£4900000	01/07/96	Chelsea								
Morris Jody					08/01/96	Chelsea	0+1							

Player / Honours	Ht	Wt	DOB	From/Fee	Date	Club									
Newton Edward	5.11	11.2	13/12/71	Hammersmith	17/05/90	Chelsea	108+17	12+1	10+2	5		8	1		
E: u21.2,Y.				Loan	23/01/92	Cardiff City	18					4			
Peacock Gavin	5.8	11.5	18/11/67	Eltham	19/11/84	Q.P.R.	7+10		0+1			1			
E: u19.3,S. Div.1'93.				£40000	05/10/87	Gillingham	69+1	4	2	5		11			1
				£250000	16/08/89	Bournemouth	56	6	2	2		8			
				£150000	30/11/90	Newcastle United	102+3	6	6	3		35	5	2	4
				£1250000	12/08/93	Chelsea	92+11	6	14+4	7		17	1	9	
Rocastle David	5.9	11.1	02/05/67	Lewisham	31/12/84	Arsenal	204+14	32+1	18+2	9		24	6	4	
E:14,B.2,u21.14. LC'87.				£2000000	04/08/92	Leeds United	17+8	0+3	0+3	2+1		2			
Div.1'89'91. CT'89.				£2000000	22/12/93	Manchester City	21		2			2			
				£1250000	12/08/94	Chelsea	27+2	3		7+1			1		1

F O R W A R D S

Player / Honours	Ht	Wt	DOB	From/Fee	Date	Club									
Hughes Mark	5.9	11.2	01/11/63	Wrexham	05/11/80	Manchester United	85+4	5+1	10	14+2		37	4	4	2
W: 60,u21.5,Y. FAC'85'90'94.ECWC'91. ESC'91.				£2500000	01/07/86	Barcelona	28					4			
LC'92. Prem'93'94. CS'93.						Bayern Munich	18					6			
				£1500000	20/07/88	Manchester United	251+5	32	34+1	27+1		82	12	13	8
				£1500000	01/06/95	Chelsea	31	2	6			8		4	
Nicholls Mark	5.10		30/05/77		01/07/95	Chelsea									
				Loan	15/12/95	Chertsey									
Spencer John	5.7	9.10	11/09/70	Glasgow		Glasgow Rangers	7+6	2		1+1		2			1
S: 12, u21.3.				Loan	04/03/89	Grennock Morton	4					1			
				£450000	01/08/92	Chelsea	75+24	2+4	16+4	4+1		36		4	1
Stein Mark E S	5.6	10.0	28/01/66	South Africa	31/01/84	Luton Town	41+13	4+1	9	3		19		3	1
E: u19.3. LC'88. AMC'92.				Loan	29/01/86	Aldershot	2					1			
Div.2'93.				£300000	26/08/88	Q.P.R.	20+13	4	2+1	4		4	2	1	
					15/09/89	Oxford United	72+10	4	2+1	3		18			
				£100000	15/09/91	Stoke City	94	8	4	17		50	8		10
				£1500000	28/10/93	Chelsea	44+4	0+1	9	2+1		16		2	2
Vialli Gianluca	5.9	12.7	09/07/64	Cremona		Cremonese	113					57			
Italy: 59, u21.11. Serie 'A91'95. IFAC'85'88'89'95.						Sampdoria	333					140			
SC'91'95. EC'96. UEFA'93. ECWC'90.						Juventus	137					25			
				Free	01/06/96	Chelsea									
Wise Dennis F	5.6	9.5	15/12/66	Kensington		Southampton									
E: 12, B.3, u21.1. FAC'88.				Free	28/03/85	Wimbledon	127+8	14	11	5		26		3	
				£1600000	03/07/90	Chelsea	184+3	16	18	10		34	6	3	3

THE MANAGER
RUUD GULLIT

Date of Birth . . . . 1st September 1962.
Place of Birth. . . . . Surinam.
Date of Appointment . . . . May 1996.

PREVIOUS CLUBS
As Manager . . . . None.
As Coach. . . . . None.
As a Player . . . . DWS Amsterdam, Haalem, Feyenoord, PSV Eindhoven,
. . . . AC Milan, Sampdoria, AC Milan, Sampdoria.

HONOURS
As a Manager
None.
As a Player
AC Milan: Serie A winners medals.
Holland: Full caps.

STAMFORD BRIDGE
Fulham Road, London SW6 1HS
Tel: 0171 385 5545

Capacity...31,544

First game...v Liverpool (friendly) 4-0, 4.9.1905.
First floodlit game..v Sparta, 19.3.1951.
Internationals ....England v Scotland, 1913. v Wales, 1929. v Austria, 1932.

ATTENDANCES
Highest..82,905 v Arsenal, Division 1, 12.10.1935.
Lowest...4,767 v Plymouth, Simod Cup, 9.11.1988.

OTHER GROUNDS...None.

MATCHDAY TICKET PRICES

Categories	A	B
North Stand		
Upper Tier (Members only)	£20	£15
Lower Tier	£20	£15
(Members only until one week prior to match)		
East Stand		
Upper Tier	£25	£17
Middle Tier	£40	£25
Lower Tier	£20	£18
Family Section		
1+1	£20	£16
Add. Juv/Unaccompanied Juv	£7	£5
Add. Qualifying Adult	£20	£16
West Stand	£20	£15
Western Enclosure	£13	£10
Concessions	£6	£5
Ticket Sales.	0898 12 10 11	

CLUBCALL 0898 12 11 59
Calls cost 39p per minute cheap rate and 49p per minute at all other times.
Call costings correct at time of going to press.

HOW TO GET TO THE GROUND

From the North
From motorway (M1) and A1. Follow signs to Central London to Hyde Park Corner, then follow signs to Guildford (A3) into Knightsbridge (A4). In 1 mile turn left (A308) into Fulham Road for Chelsea FC.

From the East
Via Hyde Park Corner as above or via Embankment and Cheyne Walk (A3212). Follow signs to Chelsea (A3220) then at crossroads turn left (A308) into Fulham Road for Chelsea FC.

From the South
Use A13 or A24 then A219 to cross Putney Bridge. Follow signs to the West End (A304), then join A308 into Fulham Road for Chelsea FC.

From the West
From motorway (M4). Follow signs to Central London, then Westminster (A3220). In 0.8 miles, at crossroads, turn right (A308) into Fulham Road for Chelsea FC.

Car Parking: Parking is available at Stamford Bridge Stadium. Matchday tariff £10 per day - underground car park with closed circuit television. Phone Janet Rainbow Chelsea Car Parks Ltd on 0171 610 2235 for further details. Very Limited street parking.
Nearest Tube Station: Fulham Broadway (District Line).

MATCHDAY PROGRAMME

Programme Editor . . . . Neil Barnett.

Number of pages . . . . 56.

Price . . . . £2.

Subscriptions . . . . £42 (UK postage).
. . . . All League and any FA Cup and Coca-Cola Cup.

Local Newspapers . . . . Evening Stanard, Fulham Chronicle,
. . . . Fulham Times, Kensington & Chelsea Times.

Local Radio Stations. . Capital Gold (1546AM), LNR (1152AM/97.3FM),
. . . . Capital Radio (95.8FM), GLR (BBC) 1458AM/94.9FM.

COVENTRY CITY
(The Sky Blues)
F.A. CARLING PREMIERSHIP
SPONSORED BY: PEUGEOT

1996-97 - Back Row (L-R): Isaias, Michael O'Neill, John Filan, Liam Daish, Steve Ogrizovic, Marcus Hall, Willie Boland.
Middle Row: George Dalton (Physio), Iyseden Christie, Paul Telfer, Noel Whelan, Gary McAllister, Paul Williams, Richard Shaw, David Busst, Gary Pendry (Reserve Team Manager).
Front Row: Brian Borrows, Kevin Richardson, Peter Ndlovu, Gordon Strachan, Dion Dublin, Ron Atkinson, Eoin Jess, David Burrows, John Salako.

COVENTRY CITY
FORMED IN 1883
TURNED PROFESSIONAL IN 1893
LTD COMPANY IN 1907

PRESIDENT: Eric Grove
CHAIRMAN: Bryan A Richardson
DEPUTY CHAIRMAN: Mike McGinnity
DIRECTORS
J F W Reason, A M Jepson,
G Robinson M.P. D A Higgs
SECRETARY
Graham Hover (01203 234 000)
DIRECTOR OF SALES & MARKETING
Mark Jones (01203 234 010)

MANAGER: Ron Atkinson
ASSISTANT MANAGER: Gordon Strachan
RESERVE TEAM COACH: Gary Pendry
DIRECTOR OF YOUTH FOOTBALL
Trevor Gould
YOUTH DEVELOPMENT MANAGER
Brian Roberts
PHYSIOTHERAPIST
George Dalton

STATISTICIAN FOR THE DIRECTORY
Jim Brown

Relegation was avoided by goal difference on the last day of the season after only one defeat in the final six games. The week before Easter it looked all over for the Sky Blues after twenty-nine years in the top-flight. They were in 19th place with only one win in twelve, and confidence was at its lowest ebb. Amazingly, Liverpool were beaten QPR were defeated in the vital six-pointer, and Wimbledon were beaten on their own ground by an inspired Peter Ndlovu. A goalless draw against Leeds was enough to survive by the narrowest margin on a nail-biting final day.

Nine months earlier everything had looked so rosy. Big Ron and his assistant Gordon Strachan had been given money in the close season and the signings looked to have given a blend of flair and fight: Salako and Isaias represented the former, Telfer and Williams the latter. Of the four, only Williams can now be described as a success. After a promising start it turned into a depressing autumn, and despite a memorable 3-2 Coca-Cola Cup win over Spurs after being 0-2 down, there was no league win from August to December.

The cheque book was out again with Richard Shaw and Noel Whelan - a record signing at £2 million - joining. Whelan was an immediate success, but the jury is still out on Shaw. The impetus given by Whelan's signing lasted well into the New Year and there appeared to be little danger until successive home draws with Middlesbrough and West Ham were followed by a dreadful home defeat by Bolton. By this time Ron had taken the spending to £13 million with the addition of Eoin Jess and Liam Daish - the latter to try and shore up the persistently-leaking defence. Fortunately, the last two signings proved to be sufficient to enable Coventry to escape the drop.

It would have been ironic if the club had been relegated. Under the chairmanship of Bryan Richardson there has been more ambition shown by the club than for many years. The vast sums put at the disposal of the management for players - funded in part by the novel 'buy a player' scheme - together with investments in ground improvements, have begun to convince the Coventry public that the club mean business. Gates are up almost 40% in two years and, whilst competition is hotter than ever, the club's ambition deserves some success. **JIM BROWN.**

COVENTRY CITY

League: 16th   FA Cup: 4th Rnd   Coca-Cola Cup: 4th Rnd

M	DATE	COMP	VEN	OPPONENTS	RESULT	HT	LP	GOAL SCORERS/GOAL TIMES	ATT.
1	A 19	PL	A	Newcastle United	L 0-3	0-1	20		(36485)
2	23	PL	H	Manchester City	W 2-1	1-0	11	Telfer 12, Dublin 86	16568
3	26	PL	H	Arsenal	D 0-0	0-0			20081
4	30	PL	A	Chelsea	D 2-2	1-2	11	Isaias 44, Ndlovu 54	(24398)
5	S 9	PL	H	Nottingham Forest	D 1-1	1-1	12	Dublin 12	17238
6	16	PL	A	Middlesbrough	L 1-2	0-0	15	Isaias 47	(27882)
7	20	CC 2/1	H	Hull City	W 2-0	2-0		Richardson 25, Lamptey 36	8915
8	23	PL	A	Blackburn Rovers	L 1-5	1-2	17	Ndlovu 34	(24382)
9	30	PL	A	Aston Villa	L 0-3	0-1	18		21004
10	O 4	CC 2/2	A	Hull City	W 1-0	1-0		Lamptey 10	(6929)
11	14	PL	A	Liverpool	D 0-0	0-0	18		(39079)
12	21	PL	H	Sheffield Wednesday	L 0-1	0-1	18		14002
13	25	CC 3	H	Tottenham Hotspur	W 3-2	0-2		Ndlovu 55(pen), Busst 61, Salako 76	18267
14	28	PL	A	Leeds United	L 1-3	1-2	18	Dublin 12	(30161)
15	N 4	PL	H	Tottenham Hotspur	L 2-3	1-2	18	Dublin 9, Williams 48	17545
16	19	PL	A	Queens Park Rangers	D 1-1	0-1	19	Dublin 75	(11189)
17	22	PL	H	Manchester United	L 0-4	0-1	20		23344
18	25	PL	H	Wimbledon	D 3-3	1-2	20	Heald 14(og), Dublin 67, Rennie 83	12496
19	29	CC 4	A	Wolverhampton Wand	L 1-2	0-2		Williams 67	(24628)
20	D 4	PL	A	Sheffield Wednesday	L 3-4	2-2	20	Dublin 18, 37, 55 (3)	(16229)
21	9	PL	H	Blackburn Rovers	W 5-0	1-0	19	Busst 40, Dublin 60, Rennie 64, Ndlovu 74, Salako 88	13409
22	16	PL	A	Aston Villa	L 1-4	0-1	19	Dublin 59	(28476)
23	23	PL	H	Everton	W 2-1	0-0	19	Busst 48, Whelan 84	16638
24	30	PL	A	Bolton Wanderers	W 2-1	1-1	18	Whelan 44, Salako 90(pen)	(16678)
25	J 1	PL	H	Southampton	D 1-1	0-0	18	Whelan 83	16822
26	6	FAC 3	A	Plymouth Argyle	W 3-1	0-1		Pickering 53, Salako 55, Telfer 58	(17721)
27	14	PL	H	Newcastle United	L 0-1	0-1	18		20532
28	20	PL	H	Manchester City	D 1-1	0-0	18	Dublin 66	(25710)
29	31	PL	A	West Ham United	L 2-3	0-0	18	Dublin 62, Whelan 82	(18884)
30	F 3	PL	A	Arsenal	D 1-1	1-1	18	Whelan 23	(35623)
31	7	FAC 4	H	Manchester City	D 2-2	1-1		Whelan 2, Dublin 90	18775
32	10	PL	H	Chelsea	W 1-0	1-0	18	Whelan 43	20629
33	14	FAC 4R	A	Manchester City	L 1-2	0-1		Dublin 85	(22419)
34	24	PL	H	Middlesbrough	D 0-0	0-0	18		17979
35	M 2	PL	H	West Ham United	D 2-2	2-2	13	Salako 7, Whelan 15	18884
36	9	PL	A	Everton	D 2-2	1-2	15	Daish 38, Williams 85	(34517)
37	16	PL	H	Bolton Wanderers	L 0-2	0-0	16		17168
38	25	PL	A	Southampton	L 0-1	0-1	17		(14461)
39	30	PL	A	Tottenham Hotspur	L 1-3	1-0	17	Dublin 20	(26808)
40	A 6	PL	H	Liverpool	W 1-0	1-0	18	Whelan 18	23137
41	8	PL	A	Manchester United	L 0-1	0-0	19		(50332)
42	13	PL	H	Queens Park Rangers	W 1-0	0-0	18	Jess 70	22906
43	17	PL	A	Nottingham Forest	D 0-0	0-0	18		(24629)
44	27	PL	A	Wimbledon	W 2-0	0-0	16	Ndlovu 52, 89	(15790)
45	M 5	PL	H	Leeds United	D 0-0	0-0	16		22757

Best Home League Attendance: 23344 v Manchester United   Smallest: 12496 v Wimbledon   Average: 18586

Goal Scorers:
PL(42):   Dublin(14),Whelan(8),Ndlovu(5),Salako(3),Isaias(2),Busst(2),Williams(2),Rennie(2),Opponent(s)(1),Telfer(1),Daish(1),Jess(1)
CC(7):   Lamptey(2),Salako(1),Williams(1),Richardson(1),Ndlovu(1),Busst(1)
FAC(6):   Dublin(2),Telfer(1),Whelan(1),Pickering(1),Salako(1)

(F) Barnwell-Edinboro	(M) Boland	(D) Borrows	(D) Burrows	(D) Busst	(M) Christie	(M) Cook	(D) Daish	(F) Dublin	(G) Filan	(D) Gillespie	(G) Gould	(D) Hall	(M) Isaias	(F) Jess	(F) Lampley	(F) Ndlovu	(G) Ogrizovic	(D) Pickering	(D) Rennie	(M) Richardson	(F) Salako	(D) Shaw	(F) Strachan	(M) Telfer	(F) Whelan	(D) Whyte (L)	(F) Williams	(M) Williams		
		X	X		S		X	X				X1					X		S1	X	X	X		X				X	R.Dilkes	1
		X		S			X	X				X	X				X			X	X	X		X				X	P.Alcock	2
		X	X	S			X	X			S	S	X				X			X	X	X		X				X	S.Dunn	3
		X	X	S			X	X			S	S	X				X			X	X	X		X				X	G.Willard	4
		X	X				X	X			S	S	X				X			X	X	X		X			S	X	P.Jones	5
S1		X					X1				S		X	X			X			X	X	X		X				X	G.Poll	6
		X			S					S	X	X	X		X	X	X			X	X	X		X				X	R.Poulain	7
		X		S1	X1			X				X	X		X	X	X	X1		X	X			X				X	K.Cooper	8
		X	X	S				X				X	X	X		X	X	X1		X	X		S1	X				X	A.Wilkie	9
	X	X	X					X					X	X		X	X1	S		X	X	X		X				X	S.J.Lodge	10
	S	X	X					X					X	X		X	X			X	X	S		X				X	P.Danson	11
		X1	X				S2	X			S	S1	X1	X			X	X		X	X	X		X				X	J.Winter	12
		X					X	X			S	X	X			S1	X1		X	X	X	X		X				X	S.Dunn	13
		X1	X				X	X			S	X	X			X1		S1	X	X	X		X				X	G.Ashby	14
						X	S	X				X			X1	X	X	X	S	S	X	X	S1	X1				X	J.Winter	15
		X	S1		X		X	S				X	X1			X	X	S	X	X	X	X	X	X	S1			X	M.Bodenham	16
		X	X2				X	S				X	S2			X	X	S1	X	X	X1	X		X				X	K.Burge	17
		X					X	X			S1	X	X1	S2	X	X2	X		X	X	X		X				X	R.Hart	18
		X	S				X	X				X	S		X	X	X	X1	X	X	X	S1	X				X	S.Lodge	19
		X					X	X			S	X	S	S	X	X	X	X	X	X			X	X			X	M.Reid	20
		X					X	X			S	X	X	S	S	X	X	X	X	X			X		X		X	S.Dunn	21
		X					X	X				X	S1	S2	X	X2		X	X	X		X	X	X			X	P.Alcock	22
		X					X	S			S	X	X1	S1	X	X	S		X	X	S	X	X	X			X	S.Lodge	23
	X	X					X	X				X	X	S			X	X	X	S	X	X	X		X	X	A.Wilkie	24
	S	X					X	S			S1	X	X			X	X	X	X	X1	X	X	X		X	X	K.Cooper	25
		S	X				X	S				X	X			X	X	X	X	X	X1	X		X		X	G.Willard	26
		S	X				X	S				X	S1	X	X	X	X	X	X	X1	S		X		X	P.Jones	27
	S	X					X	X				X	X	X	X	X	X	X	X	X	S	X	X		X	R.Hart	28
		X					X	X				X	S1	X	X	X1	X	X	S2	X	X	X	X	X	X2	G.Poll	29
		X					X	X				X	S1	X	S	X	X	X	X	X	X1	X	X	X	S.W.Dunn	30
		X					X	X				X	S1	X	X	X	X	X	X	X1	X	X	X	X	G.Ashby	31
	S	X					X	S				X1	X	X	X	X	X	X	X	X	X	X	X	S1	L.Dilkes	32
	S		X	X			X	S			S1	X	X	X	X	X	X	X	X1	X	X	X	X	K.Cooper	33
		X	S1				X	X	S		X	S2	X	X2	X	X	X	X	X1	X	X	P.Durkin	34
		X	X1				X	X	S		X	X	X	X	X	X	X	S	X	S1	M.Bodenham	35
		X	X				X	X	S		X	S1	X	X	X	S2	X2	X1	X	P.Danson	36
		X	X				X	X	S		X	X1	X	X	X	S1	S	X	X	K.Burge	37
		X	X				X	X	S		X	S1	X	X	X	X	S	X	S.Lodge	38
		X	X2				X	X	S		X1	X	X	X	S2	X	S1	X	R.Hart	39
		X1					X	X	S		S2	X2	X	X	X	S1	X	P.Jones	40
S1			X1				X	X		S2	X	X	X	X	X	X2	X	X	D.J.Gallagher	41
			X	X	S		X	S1	X	X	X	X1	X	S	X	X	K.Cooper	42
			X	X	S		X	X	X	X	X	X	S1	S	X1	X	M.D.Reed	43
	S		X				X	X	S	X	X	X	X	X	S	X	X	S.Dunn	44
		X					X	X	S	X	X	X	X	X	S	X	X	S	D.Ellery	45
0	2	21	11	16	0	2	11	34	13	0	0	24	9	9	3	27	25	26	9	33	34	21	5	31	21	0	30		PL Appearances	
1	1	0	0	1	1	1	0	0	0	0	0	1	2	3	3	5	0	4	2	0	3	0	7	0	0	0	2		PL Sub Appearances	
0	0	3	0	2	0+1	0	0	1+1	2	0	1+1	4	2	0	3+1	0+1	4	1	2+1	4	1	3	0	4	0	0	4		CC Appearances	
0	0	1	1	3	0	0	0	3	0	0	0	2	0	0	2	0	0	3	2	0	3	3	2	3	3	0	1		FAC Appearances	

Also Played: (D) Darby S(2,8,11,14). (g) Hunwick S(7). (G) Shilton S(1,2).

COVENTRY CITY

CLUB RECORDS

BIGGEST VICTORIES
League: 9-0 v Bristol City, Division 3(S), 28.4.1934.
F.A. Cup: 7-0 v Scunthorpe United, 1st Round, 24.11.1934.
League Cup: 7-2 v Chester City, 2nd Round, 9.10.1985.
5-0 v Watford, 5th Round replay, 9.12.1980.
5-0 v Sunderland 5th Round replay, 24.1.1990.
Europe: 4-1 v Trakia Plovdiv, 1st Round (UEFA) 16.9.1970.

BIGGEST DEFEATS
League: 2-10 v Norwich, Division 3(S), 15.3.1930.
1-9 v Millwall, Division 3(S), 19.11.1927.
F.A. Cup: 2-11 v Berwick Rangers, 2.11.1901. (Qualifying Round)
League Cup: 1-8 v Leicester City (h), 1.12.1964.
Europe: (UEFA) 1-6 v Bayern Munich, 20.10.1970.

MOST POINTS
3 points a win: 63, Division 1, 1986-87.
2 points a win: 60, Division 4, 1958-59, Division 3, 1963-64.

MOST GOALS SCORED
108, Division 3(S), 1931-32.
Bourton 49, Lauderdale 19, Lake 14, Shepperd 7, White 6, Holmes 5, Cull 3, Baker, Bowden, Heinmann, Johnson, Opponents.

MOST GOALS CONCEDED
97, Division 3(S) 1935-36; Division 4, 1958-59.

MOST FIRST CLASS MATCHES IN A SEASON
57, 1962-63 (League 46, FA Cup 9, League Cup 2).

MOST LEAGUE WINS
24, Division 3(S), 1935-36; Division 4, 1958-59.

MOST LEAGUE DRAWS
17, Division 3, 1962-63.

MOST LEAGUE DEFEATS
22, Division 2, 1919-20; Division 2, 1924-25; Division 3(S), 1927-28; Division 2, 1951-52; Division 1, 1984-85.

INDIVIDUAL CLUB RECORDS

MOST GOALS IN A SEASON
Clarrie Bourton: 50 goals in 1931-32 (League 49, FAC 1).
Previous holder: F.Herbert 27 (1926-27).

MOST GOALS IN A MATCH
5. C Bourton v Bournemouth, 6-1 (h), Division 3(S), 17.10.1931.
5. A Bacon v Gillingham, 7-3 (a), Division 3(S), 30.12.1933.
5. C Regis v Chester City, 7-2 (h), League Cup, 9.10.1985.

OLDEST PLAYER
Alf Wood, 44 years 207 days v Plymouth, FAC 2nd Rnd, 7.12.1958.

YOUNGEST PLAYER
Brian Hill, 16 years 281 days v Gillingham, Div.3 (S), 30.4.58.

MOST CAPPED PLAYER
Peter Ndlovu (Zimbabwe) 25.

BEST PERFORMANCES

League: 1966-67: Matches Played 42, Won 23, Drawn 13, Lost 6, Goals for 74, Goals against 43, Points 59. First in Division 2.
Highest Position: 1969-70: 6th Division 1.

F.A. Cup: 1986-87: 3rd Round Bolton Wanderers 3-0 (h); 4th Round Manchester United 1-0 (a); 5th Stoke City 1-0 (a); 6th Round Sheffield Wednesday 3-1 (a); Semi-Final Leeds United 3-2; Final Tottenham Hotspur 3-2.

League Cup: Semi-finalists in 1980-81.
Most recent success: 1989-90: 2nd Round Grimsby Town 1-3,3-0; 3rd round QPR 1-0; 4th Round Manchester City 1-0; 5th Round Sunderland 0-0,5-0; Semi-Final Nottingham Forest 1-2,0-0.

Europe: (UEFA) 1970-71: 1st Round Trakia Plovdiv 4-1,2-0; 2nd Round Bayern Munich 1-6,2-1.

DIVISIONAL RECORD

	Played	Won	Drawn	Lost	For	Against	Points
Division 1/P	1,200	378	339	483	1,398	1,689	1,287
Division 2	756	279	186	291	1,050	1,099	744
Division 3	230	93	66	71	403	347	252
Division 3(S)	696	282	158	256	1,278	1,102	722
Division 3(N)	42	16	6	20	73	82	38
Division 4	46	24	12	10	84	47	60
Total	**2,970**	**1,072**	**767**	**1,131**	**4,286**	**4,366**	**3,103**

ADDITIONAL INFORMATION
PREVIOUS NAMES
Singers FC, 1883-98.

PREVIOUS LEAGUES
Southern League, Birmingham & District League.

Club Colours: Sky blue & navy blue striped shirt, navy shorts, navy blue socks.
Change colours: Red & navy blue check shirts, navy blue shorts, red socks.

Reserves League: Pontins Central League Division 1.

RECORDS AND STATISTICS

COMPETITIONS

Div.1/P	Div.2	Div.3	Div.3(S)	Div.4	Texaco
1967-	1919-25	1959-64	1926-36	1958-59	1971-72
	1936-52		1952-58		1972-73
	1964-67				1973-74
			Div.3(N)		UEFA
			1925-26		1970-71

HONOURS

Div.2	Div.3	Div.3(S)	FA Cup
1966-67	1963-64	1935-36	1987

MOST APPEARANCES

George Curtis - 534+4 (1955-70)

Year	League	FA Cup	League Cup
1955-56	3		
1956-57	19		
1957-58	15	1	
1958-59	43	2	
1959-60	45	2	
1960-61	46	3	2
1961-62	46	2	1
1962-63	45	9	2
1963-64	46	2	2
1964-65	41	1	4
1965-66	42	4	4
1966-67	42	1	3
1967-68	3+1		
1968-69	28+2	2	3
1969-70	19+1		1
	483+4	29	22

MOST GOALS IN A CAREER

C Bourton - 181 (1931-37)

Year	League	FA Cup
1931-32	49	1
1932-33	40	3
1933-34	25	
1934-35	26	3
1935-36	23	2
1936-37	9	
Total	172	9

Current leading goalscorer - Peter Ndlovu 40 (1991-96)

RECORD TRANSFER FEE RECEIVED

Amount	Club	Player	Date
3,750,000	Liverpool	Phil Babb	8/94
1,500,000	Blackburn Rovers	Kevin Gallacher	3/93
£365,000	Portland Timbers	Gary Collier	3/80
£200,000	Arsenal	Jeoff Blockley	10/72

RECORD TRANSFER FEE PAID

Amount	Club	Player	Date
3,000,000	Leeds United	Gary McAllister	7/96
2,000,000	Leeds United	Noel Whelan	12/95
1,950,000	Manchester Utd	Dion Dublin	9/94
£900,000	Dundee United	Keith Gallacher	2/90

MANAGERS

Name	Seasons	Best	Worst
H Pollitt	1920-21	20(2)	20(2)
A Evans	1921-25	18(2)	22(2)
J Kerr	1926-28	15(3S)	20(3S)
J McIntyre	1928-31	6(3S)	14(3S)
H Storer	1931-45	4(2)	12(3S)
R Bayliss	1946-47	8(2)	8(2)
W Frith	1947-49	10(2)	16(2)
H Storer	1949-54	7(2)	14(3S)
J Fairbrother	1954-55	9(3S)	14(3S)
C Elliott		9(3S)	9(3S)
J Carver	1955-56	9(3S)	9(3S)
G Rayner			
H Warren	1957-58	8(3S)	19(3S)
W Frith	1958-62	4(3)	2(4)
J Hill	1962-68	20(1)	14(3)
N Cantwell	1968-72	6(1)	20(1)
R Dennison	1972		
J Mercer	1972-74	16(1)	19(1)
G Milne	1974-81	7(1)	19(1)
D Sexton	1981-83	14(1)	19(1)
R Gould	1983-84	18(1)	19(1)
D Mackay	1984-86	17(1)	18(1)
G Curtis/J Sillett	1986-87	10(1)	18(1)
J Sillett	1987-90	7(1)	12(1)
T Butcher	1990-92	16(1)	16(1)
D Howe	1992	19(1)	19(1)
R Gould	1992-93	16(1/P)	16(1/P)
P Neal	1993-95	11(P)	11(P)
R Atkinson	1995-	16(P)	16(P)

LONGEST LEAGUE RUNS

undefeated matches:	25 (26.11.1966 - 13.5.1967)	of league matches w/out a win:	19 (30.8.1919 - 20.12.1919)
undefeated home matches:	19 (11.4.1925 - 13.3.1926)	of undefeated away matches:	12 (19.11.1966 - 19.8.1967)
without home win:	10 (30.8.1919 - 20.12.1919 & 1.1.92 - 18.4.92)	without an away win:	28 (5.1.1924 - 4.4.1925)
league wins:	6 (20.4.1954 - 28.8.1954 & 24.4.1964 - 1.9.1964)	of home wins:	11 (18.10.1952 - 28.2.1953)
league defeats:	9 (30.8.1919 - 4.10.1919)	of away wins:	4 (24.5.1963 - 14.9.1963 & 19.8.1992 - 5.9.1992)

COVENTRY CITY

PLAYERS NAME Honours	Ht	Wt	Birthdate	Birthplace Transfers	Contract Date	Clubs	APPEARANCES				GOALS			
							League	L/Cup	FA Cup	Other	Lge	L/C	FAC	Oth
G O A L K E E P E R S														
Filan John	6.2	12.10	08/02/70	Sydney (Aus)		Sydney B'pest								
				£40000	12/03/93	Cambridge United	52	4	3	1				
				Loan	23/12/94	Nottingham Forest								
				Loan	02/03/95	Coventry City								
				£350000	17/03/95	Coventry City	15	2						
Hunwick Colin						Coventry City (T)								
Ogrizovic Steve	6.3	14.7	12/09/57	Mansfield	28/07/77	Chesterfield	16	2						
FAC'87. FLgeXI.1.				£70000	18/11/77	Liverpool	4		1					
				£70000	11/08/82	Shrewsbury Town	84	7	5					
				£82000	22/06/84	Coventry City	440	41	28	11	1			
D E F E N D E R S														
Blake Timothy	6.2	13.0	25/09/75	Merth										
Borrows Brian	5.10	10.12	20/12/60	Liverpool	23/04/80	Everton	27	2						
E: B.1.				£10000	24/03/83	Bolton Wanderers	95	7	4	4				
				£82000	06/06/85	Coventry City	380+6	38	23	10+1	11	1	1	
Burrows David	5.8	11.0	25/10/68	Dudley	08/11/86	W.B.A.	37+9	3+1	2	1	1			
E: B.3,u21.7. CS'89'90.				£550000	20/10/88	Liverpool	135	16	16+1	14	3			
Div.1'90. FAC'92. FlgeXI.					17/09/93	West Ham United	25	3	3		1	1		
					06/09/94	Everton	19	2	2					
				£1100000	02/03/95	Coventry City	22		1					
Busst David	6.1	12.7	30/06/67	Birmingham		Moor Green								
				Free	14/01/92	Coventry City	48+2	5+1	3+1		4	1		
Costello Lorcan	5.9	11.2	11/11/76	Dublin	01/08/93	Coventry City (T)								
Daish Liam	6.2	13.5	23/09/68	Portsmouth	29/09/86	Portsmouth	1			1+1				
Ei:1,u21.5. Div.3'91. Div.2'95				Free	11/07/88	Cambridge United	138+1	11	17	15	5			3
AMC'95.				£50000	10/01/94	Birmingham City	72+1	10	7	8	3	3		
				£1500000	24/02/96	Coventry City	11				1			
Genaux Reggis			31/08/73	Charleroi (Bel)		Standard Leige								
Belgium Int.				£750000	10/08/96	Coventry City								
Gillespie Gary	6.2	12.1	05/07/60	Stirling		Falkirk								
S:12,u21.8,S.3. Div.1'86'88'90 CS'88.				£75000	10/03/78	Coventry City	171+1	16	13					
				£325000	08/07/83	Liverpool	152+4	21	21+2	8+2	14	2		
				£900000	15/08/91	Celtic	67+2	3	4	6	2			
				Free	23/11/94	Coventry City	2+1	1						
Hall Marcus	6.1	12.02	24/04/76	Coventry	01/07/94	Coventry City	26+4	4	2					
Prenderville Barry	6.0	12.8	16/10/76	Dublin		Coventry City (T)								
Shaw Richard	5.9	11.5	11/09/68	Brentford	04/09/86	Crystal Palace	193+14	28+2	18	12+1	3			
FMC'91. Div.1'94.				Loan	14/12/89	Hull City	4							
				£650000	17/11/95	Coventry City	21		3					
M I D F I E L D														
Boland Willie	5.9	10.9	06/08/75	Ennis (Eire)	04/11/92	Coventry City	44+8	4						
Ei: u21.5,Y.														
Carlita	5.9	11.2	20/12/72			Farense (Portugal)								
				£250000	07/06/95	Coventry City								
Healy Brett	5.8	10.8	06/10/77	Coventry		Coventry City (T)								
Isaias	5.10	12.10	21/10/63			Benfica								
				£500000	17/07/95	Coventry City	9+2	2			2			
McAllister Gary	6.1	11.5	25/12/64	Motherwell		Motherwell	52+7	3+1	7		6		2	
S: 28, B.2, u21.1; SDiv1'85; Div1'92				£125000	15/08/85	Leicester City	199+2	14+1	5	4	46	3	2	
				£1000000	02/07/90	Leeds United	230+1	26	24	14	31	4	6	4
				£3000000	23.07.96	Coventry City								
O'Toole Scott	5.9	11.1	19/09/75	Dublin		Coventry City (T)								
Richardson Kevin	5.9	10.12	04/12/62	Newcastle	08/12/80	Everton	95+14	10+3	13	7+2	16	3	1	
E:1. Div.1'85'89. FAC'84.				£225000	04/09/86	Watford	39	3	7	1	2			
CS'84'86. ECWC'85. LC'94.				£200000	26/08/87	Arsenal	88+8	13+3	9	3	5	2	1	
				£750000	01/07/90	Real Sociedad								
				£450000	06/08/91	Aston Villa	142+1	15	12	10	13	3		
				£300000	16/02/95	Coventry City	47	4	3		1			
Shilton Sam	5.10	10.0	21/07/78	Nottingham		Plymouth Argyle (T)	1+1		0+1					
						Coventry City								
Telfer Paul	5.9	10.2	21/10/71	Edinburgh	07/11/88	Luton Town	91	3	10	2	10		2	1
S: B.1, u21.3.				£1150000	26/06/95	Coventry City	31	4	3		1		1	

Name	ht	wt	DOB	From	Date	Club									
Williams Paul D	5.11	12.0	26/03/71	Burton	13/07/89	Derby County	153+7	10+2	8	14+1	25	2	3	2
E: u21.6.				Loan	09/11/89	Lincoln City	3		2	1				
				£1000000	06/08/95	Coventry City	30+2	4	1		2	1		

F O R W A R D S

Name	ht	wt	DOB	From	Date	Club								
Christie Iyseden	6.0	12.2	14/11/76	Coventry		Coventry City (T)	0+1	0+1						
Dublin Dion	6.0	12.4	22/04/69	Leicester	24/03/88	Norwich City								
Div.3'91.				Free	02/08/88	Cambridge United	133+23	8+2	21	14+1	53	5	11	5
				£1000000	07/08/92	Manchester United	4+8	1+1	1+1	0+1	2	1		
				£1950000	09/09/94	Coventry City	65	4+1	7		27	2	3	
Ducros Andrew	5.4	9.8	16/09/77	Evesham		Coventry City (T)								
Jess Eoin	5.7	10.10	13/12/70	Aberdeen		Glasgow Rangers								
S:8,u21						Aberdeen	176				47			
				£1750000	24/02/96	Coventry City	9+3				1			
Ndlovu Peter	5.8	10.2	25/02/73	Zimbabwe		H'landers								
Zim: 25.				£20000	16/08/91	Coventry City	131+26	10	5+1	0+1	36	2	2	
O'Neill Michael	5.11	10.10	05/07/69	Portadown	01/08/87	Newcastle United	48				15			
NI: 25.					01/08/89	Dundee United	64				11			
					01/08/93	Hibernian	69				13			
				£300000	19/07/96	Coventry City								
Salako John	5.10	11.0	11/02/69	Nigeria	03/11/86	Crystal Palace	172+43	19+5	20	11+3	23	5	4	2
E:5. FMC'91. Div.1'94.				Loan	14/08/89	Swansea City	13			2	3			1
				£1500000	01/08/95	Coventry City	34+3	3	3		3	1	1	
Strachan Gordon	5.6	10.8	09/02/57	Edinburgh	01/06/71	Dundee	56+13	10+1	7		13	1	1	
S:50,u21.1,Y. SPD'80'84. SC'82'83'84.				£50000	01/11/77	Aberdeen	165+6	43+3	25	30+4	53	20	7	7
ECWC'83. ESC'83. FAC' 85. Div.2'90. Div.1'92.				£500000	13/08/84	Manchester United	155+5	12+1	22	10+2	33	1	2	3
				£300000	23/03/89	Leeds United	188+9	19	14	14+1	37	3	2	3
				Free	22/03/95	Coventry City	10+7	3	2					
Whelan Noel	6.2	11.3	30/12/74	Leeds	05/03/93	Leeds United	28+20	3+2	2	3	7	1		
				£2000000	16/12/95	Coventry City	21		3		8		1	

ADDITIONAL CONTRACT PLAYERS

Faulconbridge Craig						
Goodwin Scott						Coventry City (T)
Hawkins Colin						Coventry City (T)
Mitten Paul						Coventry City (T)
Nolan Carl						Coventry City (T)
Williams Jamie						Coventry City (T)

THE MANAGER
RON ATKINSON

Date of Birth . . . . 18th March 1939.
Place of Birth . . . . Liverpool.
Date of Appointment . . . . February 1995.

PREVIOUS CLUBS
As Manager . . . . Kettering Town, Cambridge Utd, West Bromwich Albion,
. . . . . . Manchester United, Athletico Madrid, Sheffield Wednesday, Aston Villa.
As a Player . . . . Aston Villa (A), Oxford United.

HONOURS
As a Manager
Cambridge United: Promotion to Division 3, 1977. Promotion to Division 2, 1978.
Manchester United: FA Cup Winners 1983.
Sheffield Wednesday: Promotion to Division 1 and League Cup winners, 1991.
Aston Villa: Premier League runners-up., 1992-93. League Cup winners 1993-94.

As a Player
Oxford United: Promotion to Division 3, 1965. Division 3 Champions 1968.

HIGHFIELD ROAD

King Richard Street, Coventry CV2 4FW
Tel: 01203 234 000

Capacity...23,662.

First game ....v Shrewsbury Town 9.9.1899
First floodlit game ....v Queen of the South, Friendly, 21.10.1953.
ATTENDANCES
Highest ....51,455 v Wolves, Div 2, 29.4.1967.
Lowest..1,086 v Millwall, FMC, 15.10.1985.

OTHER GROUNDS.................Binley Road 1883-87, Stoke Road 1887-99, Highfield Road since 1899.

MATCHDAY TICKET PRICES

Main Stand . . . . Adults - £20.
. . . . Juv & OAP - £10*.
M&B Stand . . . . Adults - £18.
. . . . Juv & OAP - £9.
East Stand . . . . Adults - 18.
. . . . Juv & OAP - £9.
McDonalds Family Stand . . . . Adults - £15.
. . . . Juv & OAP - £7.50.
Co-Op Bank West Terrace . . . . Adults - £15.
. . . . Juv & OAP - £7.50.
J.S.B. . . . . £4.
Visitors . . . . Adults - £18.
. . . . Juv & OAP - £10.
*J.S.B. & Senior Citizen members only.
Student discount - £3 (West Terrace only)
Ticket Office Telephone No.. . . . . . . 01203 234020.

CLUBCALL
0891 12 11 66
Calls cost 39p per minute cheap rate and 49p per
minute at all other times.
Call costings correct at time of going to press.

HOW TO GET TO THE GROUND

From the North and South
Exit the M6 at junction 2, take the A4600 and follow the signs for the City Centre.
Cross the roundabout keeping along Ansty Road (A4600). It bears left, and you
come to another roundabout. Take right exit and continue for a quarter-of-a-mile.
Turn right into Swan Lane. Coventry F.C. is directly ahead of you.

From the East
Exit the M69 at its junction with the M6 and then follow the directions given
above.

From the West
Exit the M40 at junction 15 and proceed along the A46 (dual carriageway) for
approximately 10 miles until you reach the island, cross the island and continue
until you reach the next island. At this point turn first left onto the B4110 signposted "Stoke", follow this road across all sets of traffic lights to a T-junction, then
turn left into Walsgrave Road and immediately right into Swan Lane.

MATCHDAY PROGRAMME

Programme Co-ordinator . . . . Mike Williams.

Number of pages . . . . 48.

Price . . . . £1.80.

Subscriptions. . . . . Please apply to the club.

Local Newspapers. . . . . Coventry Evening Telegraph.

Local Radio Stations . . . . . Mercia FM, BBC Coventry & Warwickshire.

DERBY COUNTY
(The Rams)
F.A. CARLING PREMIERSHIP
SPONSORED BY: PUMA

Back Row (L-R): Peter Melville (Physio), Lee Carsley, Jason Kavanagh, Darren Wassall, Gary Rowett, Dean Yates, Darryl Powell, Shane Nicholson, Andrew Tretton, Mark Stallard. **3rd Row:** Steve McLaren (Asst. Manager), Billy McEwan (Coach), Paul Trollope, Matt Warren, Ian Ashbee, Russell Hoult, Andy Quy, Martin Taylor, Steve Sutton, Craig Smith, John Harkes, Sean Flynn, Eric Steele (Goalkeeping coach), Gordon Guthrie (Asst. Physio). **2nd Row:** Steve Round, Wayne Sutton, Dean Sturridge, Paul Simpson, Marco Gabbiadini, Jim Smith (Manager), Robin van der Laan, Ron Willems, Chris Boden, Will Davies. **Front Row:** Nick Wright, Darren Wrack, Carl Cunningham, Matt Green, Steve Powell, Kevin Cooper.

DERBY COUNTY
FORMED IN 1884
TURNED PROFESSIONAL IN 1884
LTD COMPANY IN 1896

CHAIRMAN: L V Pickering
VICE-CHAIRMAN: P Gadsby

DIRECTORS
J N Kirkland BSc, CEng, MICE,
S Webb
CHIEF EXECUTIVE
Keith Loring (01332 340105)
SECRETARY
Keith Pearson (01332 340105)
COMMERCIAL MANAGER
Colin Tunnicliffe (01332 40105)

MANAGER: Jim Smith
FIRST TEAM COACH: Steve McLaren

YOUTH TEAM MANAGER
Richie Williams
PHYSIOTHERAPIST
Peter Melville

STATISTICIAN FOR THE DIRECTORY
Steve McGhee

After five years out of the top flight, Derby returned under the astute management of their experienced manager Jim Smith. Though their eventual promotion was rarely in doubt from the turn of the year, it required a victory over nearest challengers Crystal Palace to finally confirm what the club thoroughly deserved, despite a rather mediocre start to the campaign.

By the time the inspirational Igor Stimac agreed to sign from Croatia in November, the Rams had slipped to 17th place and were anxiously looking at a battle against relegation - indeed, his first game for the club ended in a 1-5 reverse at Tranmere. This, however, was the turning point for the club who embarked on a 20-match club record unbeaten run which was built around the solid defending of Stimac and a fit-at-last Dean Yates along with the potent strike force of Dean Sturridge and Marco Gabbiadini. By the time defeat eventually came in March at Sunderland, the question was really whether or not they could go up as Champions or runners-up. Sunderland's equally impressive late run gave the Roker club the title, but, just as Derby eased off, up came Dave Bassett's Crystal Palace with a late run of their own. The final home game of the season - against Palace - was live on TV with skipper Robin van der Laan's header ensuring promotion.

The cup games were of limited significance in view of the season's main objective, but Leeds United ended hopes in both competitions.

Next season will be a huge test for the club who have already made some very interesting signings in Christian Dailly, the Croatian midfielder Asanovic, and Danish full back Laursen.

This is, sadly, the final season at the famous old Baseball Ground before a move to the outskirts of the city. Whether the club can hold on to Premiership status in time to christen the new ground may well come down to the man-management skills of Jim Smith and his undoubted ability to get the best out of players.

STEVE MCGHEE

DERBY COUNTY

League: 2nd   FA Cup: 3rd Rnd   Coca-Cola Cup: 3rd Rnd

M	DATE	COMP	VEN	OPPONENTS	RESULT	HT	LP	GOAL SCORERS/GOAL TIMES	ATT.
1	A 13	EL	H	Port Vale	D 0-0	0-0	17		10869
2	19	EL	A	Reading	L 2-3	0-1	21	Sturridge 62, Preece 84	(9280)
3	26	EL	H	Grimsby Town	D 1-1	0-0	21	Sturridge 46	10564
4	30	EL	A	Wolverhampton Wand	L 0-3	0-3			(26053)
5	S 2	EL	A	Luton Town	W 2-1	1-0	17	Sturridge 15, Sturridge 63	(6427)
6	10	EL	H	Leicester City	L 0-1	0-1	20		11767
7	13	EL	H	Southend United	W 1-0	1-0	19	Sturridge 23	9242
8	16	EL	A	Portsmouth	D 2-2	1-1	18	Van der laan 32, Flynn 58	(14434)
9	19	CC 2/1	A	Shrewsbury Town	W 3-1	2-0		Simpson 29, Stallard 33, Gabbiadini 68	(3170)
10	23	EL	A	Barnsley	L 0-2	0-2	20		(8929)
11	O 1	EL	H	Millwall	D 2-2	1-2	20	Willems 9, Van der laan 66	9590
12	4	CC 2/2	H	Shrewsbury Town	D 1-1	1-0		Willems 30	8825
13	7	EL	A	Sheffield United	W 2-0	1-0	16	Gabbiadini 29, Willems 46	(12721)
14	14	EL	H	Ipswich Town	D 1-1	1-1	17	Gabbiadini 27	13034
15	22	EL	A	Stoke City	D 1-1	0-0	17	Van der laan 89	(9435)
16	25	CC 3	H	Leeds United	L 0-1	0-0			16030
17	28	EL	H	Oldham Athletic	W 2-1	1-0	14	Van der laan 33, Simpson 48	11545
18	N 4	EL	A	Tranmere Rovers	L 1-5	0-3	17	Stimac 52	(8565)
19	11	EL	H	West Bromwich Albion	W 3-0	2-0	14	Gabbiadini 16, 61, Sturridge 27(pen)	13765
20	18	EL	H	Charlton Athletic	W 2-0	1-0	11	Willems 43, Gabbiadini 62	12693
21	21	EL	A	Birmingham City	W 4-1	2-1	8	Sturridge 5, Willems 40, Gabbiadini 47, Powell 73	(19417)
22	25	EL	A	Crystal Palace	D 0-0	0-0	11		(13506)
23	D 2	EL	H	Sheffield United	W 4-2	1-1	8	Sturridge 29, Willems 65(pen), 67, Gabbiadini 74	13841
24	9	EL	H	Barnsley	W 4-1	1-0	4	Carsley 2, Gabbiadini 52, Sturridge 62, Willems 77(pen)	14415
25	16	EL	A	Millwall	W 1-0	1-0	3	Sturridge 43	(7694)
26	23	EL	H	Sunderland	W 3-1	1-1	1	Gabbiadini 35, Willems 64(pen), Sturridge 84	16882
27	26	EL	A	Huddersfield Town	W 1-0	0-0	1	Willems 77	(18495)
28	J 1	EL	H	Norwich City	W 2-1	1-0	1	Willems 37, Gabbiadini 90	16714
29	7	FAC 3	H	Leeds United	L 2-4	0-0		Gabbiadini 49, Simpson 50	16155
30	13	EL	H	Reading	W 3-0	0-0	1	Sturridge 47, 66, Flynn 81	15123
31	20	EL	A	Port Vale	D 1-1	1-0	1	Sturridge 44	(11947)
32	F 3	EL	A	Grimsby Town	D 1-1	0-1	1	Powell 49	(7818)
33	10	EL	H	Wolverhampton Wand	D 0-0	0-0	1		17460
34	17	EL	A	Southend United	W 2-1	0-1	1	Simpson 54, Willems 86	(8331)
35	21	EL	H	Luton Town	D 1-1	0-0	1	Powell 51	14825
36	24	EL	H	Portsmouth	W 3-2	0-0	1	Yates 71, Sturridge 76, Gabbiadini 83	16120
37	28	EL	A	Leicester City	D 0-0	0-0	1		(20911)
38	M 2	EL	H	Huddersfield Town	W 3-2	2-1	1	Simpson 12, 75, Van der laan 21	17097
39	5	EL	A	Watford	D 0-0	0-0	1		(8306)
40	9	EL	A	Sunderland	L 0-3	0-2	1		(21644)
41	16	EL	A	Watford	D 1-1	0-1	1	Simpson 84(pen)	15939
42	23	EL	A	Norwich City	L 0-1	0-0	2		(15348)
43	30	EL	H	Stoke City	W 3-1	0-1	2	Sturridge 53, 79, Powell 58	17245
44	A 2	EL	A	Ipswich Town	L 0-1	0-1	2		(16210)
45	6	EL	A	Oldham Athletic	W 1-0	0-0	2	Simpson 58(pen)	(8119)
46	8	EL	H	Tranmere Rovers	W 6-2	1-0	2	Powell 39, Yates 51, Simpson 55, 58, 69 (3), Sturridge 68	16723
47	14	EL	A	Charlton Athletic	D 0-0	0-0	2		(11334)
48	20	EL	H	Birmingham City	D 1-1	0-0	2	Simpson 56	16757
49	28	EL	H	Crystal Palace	W 2-1	1-1	2	Sturridge 3, Van der laan 65	17041
50	M 5	EL	A	West Bromwich Albion	L 2-3	1-2	2	Sturridge 16, Ward 87	(23858)

Best Home League Attendance: 17460 v Wolverhampton Wand   **Smallest: 9242 v Southend United**   **Average: 14315**

Goal Scorers:
EL(71):   Sturridge(20),Gabbiadini(11),Willems(11),Simpson(10),Van der laan(6),Powell(4),Yates(2),Flynn(2),Preece(1),Carsley(1),Powell(1),Ward(1),Stimac(1)
CC(4):   Willems(1),Stallard(1),Simpson(1),Gabbiadini(1)
FAC(2):   Simpson(1),Gabbiadini(1)

(D) Boden	(D) Carbon	(D) Carsley	(F) Davies	(M) Flynn	(F) Gabbiadini	(M) Harkes	(M) Hodges	(G) Hoult	(D) Kavanagh	(D) Nicholson	(D) Powell	(F) Powell	(M) Preece	(M) Rowett	(M) Simpson	(F) Stallard	(D) Stimac	(F) Sturridge	(G) Sutton	(D) Sutton	(M) Trollope	(M) Van der Laan	(F) Ward	(D) Wassall	(D) Webster	(M) Willems	(F) Wrack	(D) Yates	Referee	No.
				X	X	X		S			X		S1	X1	X		X2	S2	X			X	X	X					K.Breen	1
				X		X			S3		X		S1	X	X1	X1		S1		X	X3	X		X		X			M.Pierce	2
		X					S2		X	S1	X	X	X		X2			X	X	X	X1	X		X	X				J.Willard	3
		X1		X	X			X	S	X	X		X	X	S			X		X		S1	X				X		T.Heilbron	4
				X		X2		X	X	X	X1		X		X		S2	X		X		X		S1					J.Brandwood	5
		X2			S2	X	X1	X	X	X		X	S2		S1			X		X		X		X					T.West	6
				X		X1	X1		X	X	X		X		S			X	S		X2	X		X			S1	X	D.Allison	7
				X		X1	X1		X	X	X		X		S1			X	S1		X2	X		X			S3	X	R.Gifford	8
		X2		X					X	X	X		X1		X	X		X	X	S		S1	X		X		S2	X	J.A.Kirby	9
		S1		X	X				X	X	X		X		X	X1		X	S		S	X		X				X	G.Willard	10
				X					S	X		X	X	X	X1			X			S2	X		X2		X	S1	X	K.Lynch	11
	X			X	X1				S		X		X		X	X		X			X		S	X		X	S1	X	A.P.D'Urso	12
	X			X1	X3			S1		X		X	X	X	S3				X1		X			X	X1	X	E.Lomas	13
	X			S				X		X		X2	X	X	S2		S1		X			X		X	X1	X	N.S.Barry	14
	X			S2	X			X		X		X2	X	S1		S		X	X		X	X	X1	X	G.Furnandiz	15
	X			X1	X			X		X		S1	X	X1		S	X	X		X	X1	X	R.Dilkes	16
	X			X	X			X		X	X			X	X		S	S	X		X	S	X	C.R.Wilkes	17
	S			X1				X		X	X		X	X	X	S1	S	X		X		X	T.West	18
X	X			S1	X1			X		X			X	S	X	X	X	S	X		X	R.Poulain	19
X	X			S1	X1			X		X1			X	S	X	X	X	S	X2		X	U.D.Rennie	20
X	X			S1	X1			X		X1			X	S2	X	X	S	X2	X		X	J.J.Breen	21
X	X			S	X			X		X		X1	S1	X	X	X	X	X		X	M.Fletcher	22
	X			S2	X2			X		X1	X	X	S	X	X	S1	X	X2	S2	X	D.B.Allison	23
	X			X	X2			X		X	X1		X	S2	X	X	S1	X2	S2	X	G.Frankland	24
	X			X	X1			X		X	X	X	S1	X	X	X	X	X	S	X	D.Orr	25
	X			X	X			X		X	X	X	X	X	S	X1	S	X	P.Richards	26
	X			S3	X2			X		X1	X	X	S2	X	X	S1	X3	X	P.Rejer	27
	X2			X	X3			X		X	X	X	S1	X	S2	X1	X	S3	X	J.Rushton	28
				X	X2			X		X	X	X	X	X1		S	S1	X	X	S2	X	P.Jones	29
	X			X	S			X		X	X	X	X	S	X	S	X	X	X	K.Lynch	30
				X	X1			X		X	X	X	S1	X	S	X	X	X	X	R.Gifford	31
				X	X1			X	S	X	X	S1	X	X	S	X	X	X	X	K.Lynch	32
	X	X	S	X			X		X	X	X	S	X	X	X	S	X	X	T.Heilbron	33
	X1			S1	S1			X		X1	X	X	X	X	X	X	X	X	J.Kirby	34
	X1			S2	S1	S2		X		X	X	X	X2	X	X	X2	X	X	M.Riley	35
	S			X	S1	S2		X		X1	X	X	X	X	X	X2	X	X	X	W.Burns	36
	S2			X	S1	S		X		X	X1	X	X	X	X	X	X2	X	G.Singh	37
	S2			X	S1	S3		X		X	X3	X	X	X	X	X2	X1	X	E.Lomas	38
	S2			X	X	S1		X		X	X	X	X	X	X2	X1	X	R.Harris	39
	S3			X	S1	X		S1		X	X	X1	X	X	X1	X	X3	R.Richards	40
	S2	X		X	X	S1	X	S		X	X1	X2	X	X	X	X	C.Wilkes	41
				X	X1	X	X2	X		X3		S3	S2	X	S1	X	X	X	X	I.Hemley	42
				X	X	X	X		X	X	S2	X1	S1	S	X2	X	X	X	S.Mathieson	43
				X		S2	X	X2	X2	S2	X	X	X1	X	S1	X	G.Pooley	44
	S			X	S1	X	X	X2	X	X	X	X1	S2	X	X	N.Barry	45
	S1			X	S3	X	X	X2	X	X1	X	X	S2	X3	X	T.West	46
				X2	S1	X3	X	X	X1	X	X	X	X	S2	X	S3	X	M.Pierce	47
	S2	X2		S1	X	S3	X	X	X	X	X	X	X3	X	X1	S1	X	T.Heilbron	48
X	S			X	X1	X	X	X	X2	X	X	X	X	X	S2	D.Allison	49
	X	X2		X	X1	X	X	X	X	X	X	S2	G.Cain	50
4	**2**	**30**	**1**	**29**	**32**	**6**	**1**	**40**	**8**	**19**	**34**	**22**	**10**	**34**	**22**	**3**	**27**	**33**	**5**	**2**	**7**	**38**	**5**	**17**	**1**	**31**	**2**	**38**	EL Appearances	
0	4	4	0	13	6	1	8	1	1	1	0	0	3	1	17	0	0	6	0	0	10	0	2	1	0	2	7	0	EL Sub Appearances	
0	0	2	0	3	3	0	0	2	1	3	0	1+1	2	2	2	1	0	0	1	0	1+1	0	3	0	1	0	0+3	3	CC Appearances	
0	0	0	0	1	1	0	0	1	0	1	0	0	0	1	1	0	1	0	0	0	0	0	1	0	0	0	0+1	1	FAC Appearances	

Also Played: (M) Cooper S1(50). (G) Quy S(25). (F) Wright S(50).

DERBY COUNTY

CLUB RECORDS

BIGGEST VICTORIES
League: 9-0 v Wolverhampton Wanderers, 10.1.1891.
9-0 v Sheffield Wednesday, Division 1, 2.1.1899.
F.A. Cup: 8-1 v Barnsley, 1st Round, 30.1.1897.
League Cup: 7-0 v Southend, 2nd Round 2nd leg, 7.10.1992.
Europe: (UEFA) 12-0 v Finns Harps, 3rd Round, 15.9.1976.

BIGGEST DEFEATS
League: 0-8 v Blackburn Rovers, Division 1, 3.1.1891.
0-8 v Sunderland, Division 1, 1.9.1894.
F.A. Cup: 2-11 v Everton, 1st Round, 18.1.1890.
League Cup: 0-5 v Southampton, 8.10.1974.
0-5 v West Ham United, 3rd Round, 1.11.1988.
Europe: (UEFA) 1-5 v Real Madrid, 2nd Round, 5.11.1975.

MOST POINTS
3 points a win: 84, Division 3, 1985-86. Division 2, 1986-87.
2 points a win: 63, Division 3(N) 1955-56 & 1956-57, Division 2 1968-69.

MOST GOALS SCORED
111, Division 3(N), 1956-57.
Straw 37, Woodhead 14, Ryan 12, Brown 9, Parry 7, Crowshaw 6, Buchanan 5, Barrowcliffe 4, Ackerman 4, Mays 4, Powell 1, Pye 1, Davies 1, Wyer 1, Opponents 5.

MOST GOALS CONCEDED
90, Division 1, 1936-37.

MOST FIRST CLASS MATCHES IN A SEASON
64 - 1992-93 (League 46, FA Cup 5, League Cup 4, Anglo-Italian 9).

MOST LEAGUE WINS
28, Division 3(N), 1955-56.

MOST LEAGUE DRAWS
19, Division 1, 1976-77. Division 2, 1982-83.

MOST LEAGUE DEFEATS
26, Division 2, 1954-55.

INDIVIDUAL CLUB RECORDS

MOST GOALS IN A SEASON
Jack Bowers: 39 goals in 1930-31 (League 37, FAC 2).

MOST GOALS IN A MATCH
6. Steve Bloomer v Sheffield Wednesday, Division 1, 2.1.1899.

OLDEST PLAYER
Peter Shilton, 42 years 164 days v Watford, Division 2, 29.2.1992.

YOUNGEST PLAYER
Steve Powell, 16 years 33 days v Arsenal, Division 1, 23.10.1971.

MOST CAPPED PLAYER
Peter Shilton (England) 34.

BEST PERFORMANCES

League: 1956-57: Matches played 46, Won 26, Drawn 11, Lost 9, Goals for 111, Goals against 53, Points 63. First in Division 3(N).
Highest Position: Division 1 Champions 1971-72, 1974-75.
F.A. Cup: 1945-46: 3rd Round Luton Town 6-0,3-0; 4th Round West Bromwich Albion 1-0,3-1; 5th Round Brighton & H.A. 4-1,6-0; 6th Round Aston Villa 4-3,1-1; Semi-Final Birmingham City 1-1,4-0; Final Charlton 4-1.
League Cup: 1967-68: 2nd Round Hartlepool United 4-0; 3rd Round Birmingham City 3-1; 4th Round Lincoln City 1-1,3-1; 5th Round Darlington 5-4; Semi-Final Leeds United 0-1,2-3.
Europe: (European Cup) 1972-73: 1st Round Zelj Znicars 2-0,2-1; 2nd Round Benefica 3-0,0-0; 3rd Round Spartak Trnava 0-1,2-0; Semi-Final Juventus 1-3,0-0.

ADDITIONAL INFORMATION
PREVIOUS NAMES
None.

PREVIOUS LEAGUES
None.

Club colours: White shirts with black sleeves, gold piping, black shorts, white socks.
Change colours: Blue shirts & shorts, gold piping, black socks.

Reserves League: Pontins Central League Division 1.

DIVISIONAL RECORD

	Played	Won	Drawn	Lost	For	Against	Points
Division 1	2,202	838	515	849	3,493	3,490	2,236
Division 2/1	1,466	597	362	506	2,230	2,084	1,714
Division 3	92	42	28	22	145	95	154
Division 3(N)	92	54	18	20	221	108	126
Total	3,852	1,531	923	1,398	6,160	5,759	4,230

RECORDS AND STATISTICS

COMPETITIONS

Div.1/P	Div.2/1	Div.3	Div.3(N)	Euro C	Texaco
1889-07	1907-12	1984-86	1955-57	1972-73	1971-72
1912-14	1914-15			1975-76	
1919-21	1921-26				Wat C
1926-53	1953-54			UEFA	1970
1969-80	1957-69			1974-75	
1987-91	1980-84			1976-77	
1996-	1986-87				
	1991-96				

HONOURS

Div.1	Div.2	Div 3(N)	FAC	Texaco
1971-72	1911-12	1956-57	1945-46	1971-72
1974-75	1914-15			
	1968-69		Wat C	C/S'ld
	1986-87		1970	1975

MOST APPEARANCES
Kevin Hector 581+8 (1966-82)

Year	League	FA Cup	Lge Cup	Other
1966-67	30	1		
1967-68	41	1	7	
1968-69	41	1	8	
1969-70	41	4	6	
1970-71	42	3	3	
1971-72	42	5	2	6
1972-73	41	5	3	8
1973-74	42	4	3	
1974-75	38	2	2	6
1975-76	29+3	2	2	4
1976-77	28+1	4	2	3
1977-78	11		2	
1980-81	25	2		
1981-82	27+4		2	
	478+8	34	42	27

MOST GOALS IN A CAREER
Steve Bloomer - 331 (1892-1914)

Year	League	FA Cup
1892-93	11	
1893-94	19	
1894-95	10	
1895-96	22	5
1896-97	24	7
1897-98	15	5
1898-99	24	6
1899-1900	19	
1900-01	24	
1901-02	15	3
1902-03	12	1
1903-04	20	5
1904-05	13	
1905-06	12	
1910-11	20	4
1911-12	18	1
1912-13	13	1
1913-14	2	
Total	293	38

Current leading goalscorer: Marco Gabbiadini - 54 (1992-96)

RECORD TRANSFER FEE RECEIVED

Amount	Club	Player	Date
£2,900,000	Liverpool	Dean Saunders	7/91
£2,200,000	Liverpool	Mark Wright	6/91
£800,000	Millwall	Paul Goddard	12/89
£525,000	Aston Villa	Nigel Callaghan	2/89

RECORD TRANSFER FEE PAID

Amount	Club	Player	Date
£2,500,000	Notts County	Craig Short	9/92
£1,300,000	Notts County	Tommy Johnson	3/92
£1,200,000	Crystal Palace	Marco Gabbiadini	1/92
£1,000,000	Oxford United	Dean Saunders	10/88

MANAGERS

Name	Seasons	Best	Worst
Harry Newbould	1896-06	3(1)	15(1)
Jimmy Methvan	1906-22	7(1)	14(2)
Cecil Potter	1922-25	3(2)	14(2)
George Jobey	1925-41	2(1)	3(2)
Ted Magner	1941-46		
Stuart McMillan	1946-53	3(1)	22(1)
Jack Barker	1953-55	18(2)	22(2)
Harry Storer	1955-62	7(2)	2(3S)
Tim Ward	1962-67	8(2)	18(2)
Brian Clough	1967-73	1(1)	18(2)
Dave Mackay	1973-76	1(1)	4(1)
Colin Murphy	1976-77	15(1)	15(1)
Tommy Docherty	1977-79	12(1)	19(1)
Colin Addison	1979-81	19(1)	6(2)
John Newman	1981-83	13(2)	16(2)
Peter Taylor	1982-84	20(2)	20(2)
Arthur Cox	1984-93	5(1)	7(2)
Roy McFarland	1993-95	6(2/1)	6(2/1)
Jim Smith	1995-	2(1)	2(1)

LONGEST LEAGUE RUNS

of undefeated matches:	22 (8.3.1969 - 25.10.1969)	of league matches w/out a win:	20 (1.12.1990 - 4.5.1991)
of undefeated home matches:	23 (5.10.1929 - 11.10.1930)	of undefeated away matches:	13 (18.1.1969 - 27.9.1969)
without home win:	9 (24.11.1990 - 4.5.1991)	without an away win:	33 (1.9.1919 - 2.4.1921)
of league wins:	9 (15.3.1969 - 9.8.1969)	of home wins:	12 (23.10.1971 - 1.4.1972)
of league defeats:	8 (3.4.1965 - 15.9.1965 & 12.12.87 - 10.2.88)	of away wins:	7 (3.10.1992 - 20.12.1992)

DERBY COUNTY

PLAYERS NAME Honours	Ht	Wt	Birthdate	Birthplace Transfers	Contract Date	Clubs	League	L/Cup	FA Cup	Other	Lge	L/C	FAC	Oth
G O A L K E E P E R S														
Hoult Russell	6.4	13.2	22/11/72	Leicester	28/03/91	Leicester City	10	3		1				
				Loan	27/08/91	Lincoln City	2	1						
				Loan	22/07/93	Kettering Town								
				Loan	03/11/93	Bolton Wanderers	3+1							
				£200000	22/07/95	Derby County	55+1	2	1					
Quy Andrew	6.0	13.01	04/07/76	Harlow	12/07/94	Derby County								
				Loan	22/09/95	Stalybridge Celtic								
Sutton Stephen J	6.1	14.0	16/04/61	Hartington	16/04/79	Nottingham Forest	199	33	14	11				
LC'89'90; SC'89.														
				Loan	10/03/81	Mansfield Town	8							
				Loan	25/01/85	Derby County	14							
				Loan	01/02/91	Coventry City	1							
				Loan	28/11/91	Luton Town	14							
				£300000	06/03/92	Derby County	59+1	7	3	11				
				Loan	19/01/96	Reading	2							
Taylor Martin J	5.11	12.4	09/12/66	Tamworth		Mile Oak Rovers								
					02/07/86	Derby County	94	7	4	11				
				Loan	23/09/87	Carlisle United	10	1	1	2				
				Loan	17/12/87	Scunthorpe United	8							
D E F E N D E R S														
Ashbee Ian	6.1	12.10	06/09/76	Birmingham	09/11/94	Derby County	1							
Boden Christopher D	5.9	11.0	13/10/73	Wolverhampton	03/12/91	Aston Villa	0+1							
				Loan	15/10/93	Barnsley	4							
				£150000	23/03/95	Derby County	4+2							
				Loan	19/01/96	Shrewsbury Town	5							
Carbon Matthew P	6.2	12.4	08/06/75	Nottingham	13/04/93	Lincoln City	66+3	4	3	4+3	10	1		
				£400000	08/03/96	Derby County	2+4							
Carsley Lee K	5.11	11.11	28/04/74	Birmingham	31/05/94	Derby County	52+5	5+1	1	3	3			
Kavanagh Jason C	5.9	11.0	23/11/71	Meriden	09/12/88	Derby County	74+25	3+2	6	8+8	1			
E: Y14, S														
Laursen Jacob					01/07/96	Derby County								
Danish Int.														
Parker Paul A	5.7	10.8	04/04/64	West Ham	15/04/82	Fulham (A)	140+13	16	11	2	2	1		
E: 19, B.3, U21.8, Y.3. LC'92. Prem'93'94.														
FAC'94. CS'93.														
				£300000	18/06/87	Q.P.R.	121+4	14	16	5	1			
				£2000000	08/08/91	Manchester United	239+4	35	32+1	27+2	8		2	1
				Free	08/08/96	Derby County								
Powell Chris	5.10	11.07	08/09/69	Lambeth	24/12/87	Crystal Palace	2+1	0+1		0+1				
				Loan	11/01/90	Aldershot	11							
				Free	30/08/90	Southend United	219+2	11	7	17	3			
				£750000	01/06/95	Derby County	34				1			
Stimac Igor					£1500000	01/11/95	Derby County	27		1		1			
Sutton Wayne F	6.0	13.02	01/10/75	Derby	31/05/94	Derby County	2							
Tretton Andrew T	6.1	12.07	09/10/76	Derby	31/05/94	Derby County								
Wassall Darren P	5.11	12.3	27/06/68	Birmingham	01/06/86	Nottingham Forest	17+10	6+2	3+1	4+2				1
FMC'92														
				Loan	23/10/87	Hereford United	5		1	1				
				Loan	02/03/89	Bury	7				1			
				£600000	15/06/92	Derby County	91+8	9	4	11				
Yates Dean	6.1	11.0	26/10/67	Leicester	14/06/85	Notts County	291+2	20	20	32	33			4
E: u21.5														
				£350000	26/01/95	Derby County	49	3	1		3			
M I D F I E L D														
Aljosa Asanovic						01/07/96	Derby County								
Croation Int.														
Cooper Kevin L	5.6	10.7	08/02/75	Derby	31/05/94	Derby County	0+2		0+1					
Dailly Christian	5.10	10.11	23/10/73	Dundee	01/08/90	Dundee United	111				17			
				£500000	19/07/96	Derby County								
Flynn Sean M	5.7	11.2	13/03/68	Birmingham		Halesowen Town			5+2					
				£20000	03/12/91	Coventry City	90+7	5	3		9	1		
				£225000	01/06/95	Derby County	29+13	3	1		2			
Preece David	5.6	11.05	28/05/63	Bridgnorth	22/07/80	Walsall	107+4	18	6	1	5	5	1	
				£150000	06/12/84	Luton Town	328+8	23	27	8+1	21	3	2	1
				Free	11/08/95	Derby County	10+3	2			1			
				Loan	24/11/95	Birmingham City	6		1					
				Loan	21/03/96	Swindon Town	7				1			

Player	Ht	Wt	DOB	From / Fee	Date	Club								
Rowett Gary	6.0	12.0	06/03/74	Bromsgrove	10/09/91	Cambridge United	51+12	7	5+2	5	9	1		2
				£200000	21/05/94	Everton	0+2							
				£300000	20/07/95	Derby County	34+1	2	1					
Simpson Paul D	5.6	11.3	26/07/66	Carlisle	04/08/83	Manchester City	99+22	10+1	10+2	8+3	18	2	4	
E: u21.5, Y2														
				£200000	31/10/88	Oxford United	138+6	10	9	5	43	3	2	2
				£500000	02/02/92	Derby County	134+32	10+1	4+1	14+2	46	5	1	2
Trollope Paul J	6.0	12.2	03/06/72	Swindon	23/12/89	Swindon Town								
				Free	26/03/92	Torquay United	85+3	5+1	3	6+1	12	1		
				Loan	16/12/94	Derby County	4+1				1			
				£100000	19/01/95	Derby County	26+10	1+1	0+1		3			
Van der Laan Robin	5.10	12.0	05/09/68	Schiedam		Wageningen								
AGT'93														
				£80000	21/02/91	Port Vale	111+21	8	7+1	11+1	19	1	1	1
				£475000	02/08/95	Derby County	38	3	1		6			
Willems Ron						Grasshoppers-Zurich								
				£300000	01/08/95	Derby County	31+2	2	1		11	1		

F O R W A R D S

Player	Ht	Wt	DOB	From / Fee	Date	Club								
Davies William	6.2	13.4	27/09/75	Derby	12/07/94	Derby County	2+1			1+1				
				Loan	01/12/95	Buxton								
Gabbiadini Marco	5.10	12.4	20/01/68	Nottingham	05/09/85	York City	42+18	4+3		4	14	1		3
E: B1, u21.2, Y; FLgXI.2;														
Div3'88.														
				£80000	23/09/87	Sunderland	155+2	14	5	9	75	9		4
				£1800000	01/10/91	Crystal Palace	15	6	1	3	5	1		1
				£1000000	31/01/92	Derby County	157+16	12	8	16+1	50	7	3	8
Powell Darryl	6.0	12.3	15/01/71	Lambeth	22/12/88	Portsmouth	49+49	6+3	8	9+5	11			4
				£750000	27/07/95	Derby County	22	1+1			4			
Stallard Mark	6.0	12.6	24/10/74											
Sturridge Dean C	5.7	10.10	26/07/73	Birmingham	01/07/91	Derby County	49+13	0+1		2+1	21			
Ward Ashley A	6.1	12.4	24/11/70	Manchester	05/08/89	Manchester City	0+1		0+2		2			
				Loan	10/01/91	Wrexham	4				2			
				£80000	30/07/91	Leicester City	2+8	2+1	0+1	0+1				
				Loan	21/11/92	Blackpool	2				1			
				£80000	01/12/92	Crewe Alexandra	58+3	4	2	7	25	2	4	5
				£500000	08/12/94	Norwich City	28	6	1		18	3		
				£1000000	19/03/96	Derby County	5+2				1			
Wrack Darren	5.9	11.10	05/05/76	Cleethorpes	12/07/94	Derby County	2+7	0+3	0+1					
Wright Nicholas J	5.11	11.02	15/10/75	Derby	12/07/94	Derby County								
ADDITIONAL CONTRACT PLAYERS														
Radzki Lee M						Derby County								
Smith Craig						Derby County								

THE MANAGER
JIM SMITH

Date of Birth . . . . 17th November 1940.
Place of Birth . . . . Sheffield.
Date of Appointment . . . . August 1995.

PREVIOUS CLUBS
As Manager . . . . Boston Utd, Colchester Utd, Blackburn Rovers,
. . . . Birmingham City, Oxford Utd, Q.P.R., Newcaslte Utd, Portsmouth.
As Coach . . . . Middlesbrough.
As a Player . . . . Sheffield Utd, Aldershot, Halifax Town, Lincoln City,
. . . . Boston Utd, Colchester Utd.

HONOURS
As a Manager
Colchester Utd: Promotion to Division 3, 1974.
Birmingham City: Promotion to Division 1, 1980.
Oxford United: Division 3 Championship, 1984. Division 2 Championship, 1983.
Derby County: Promotion to the Premiership 1995-96.

As a Player
None.

BASEBALL GROUND

Shaftesbury Crescent, Derby DE3 8NB
Tel: 01332 40105

Capacity ....18,000.

First game ....v Sunderland, 2-0, 14.9.1885.
First floodlit game...
Internationals ....England v Ireland, 9.3.1895.

ATTENDANCES
Highest ....41,826 v Tottenham, Div. 1, 20.9.1969.
Lowest ....1,990 v W.B.A., 27.10.1894.

OTHER GROUNDS..Race Course Ground 1884-95. Baseball Ground since 1895.

MATCHDAY TICKET PRICES

Adults . . . . £12 & £11
Concessions £6

Normanton Lower Tier £7
Concessions £4

Ticket Office Telephone no. 01332 340105

HOW TO GET TO THE GROUND

From the North
Follow signs to Derby (A38) into Town Centre, then follow signs to Melbourne (A514). Then on nearside of Railway Bridge turn right into Shaftesbury Street for Derby County FC.

From East, South and West
Use Derby Ring Road, from East and South (sign posted Burton) and from West (sign posted Nottingham), as far as junction with A514, then follow signs to Town Centre into Osmaston Road. In 1.3 miles turn left into Shaftesbury Street for Derby County FC.

Car Parking
Eight parks within half-a-mile of the ground run by club in co-operation with local corporation. Street parking within same distance.

Nearest Railway Station
Derby Midland (-1332 32051)
Ramsline Halt (Specials only)

CLUBCALL
0891 12 11 87
Calls cost 39p per minute cheap rate and 49p per minute at all other times.
Call costings correct at time of going to press.

MATCHDAY PROGRAMME

Programme Editor . . . . J Fearn.

Number of pages . . . . 48.

Price . . . . £1.50.

Subscriptions . . . . £55 per season.

Local Newspapers . . . . Derby Evening Telegraph.

Local Radio Stations . . . . . . BBC Radio Derby, Ram FM (Commercial).

EVERTON
(The Toffeemen)
F.A. CARLING PREMIERSHIP
SPONSORED BY: DANKA

Back Row (L-R): Graham Stuart, John Ebbrell, Paul Holmes, Jason Kearton, Craig Short, Neville Southall, Joe Parkinson, Paul Rideout, Andy Hinchcliffe. **Middle Row:** Jim Martin(Kit Manager), Jim Gabriel (Res. Team Coach), Matthew Jackson, Vinny Samways, Neil Moore, Tony Grant, Earl Barrett, Andrei Kanchelskis, Willie Donachie (1st Team Coach), Les Helm (Physio). **Front Row:** David Unsworth, Stuart Barlow, Gary Ablett, Barry Horne, Joe Royle (Manager), Dave Watson (Capt), Duncan Ferguson, Daniel Amokachi, Anders Limpar.

EVERTON
FORMED IN 1878
TURNED PROFESSIONAL IN 1885
LTD COMPANY IN 1892

CHAIRMAN: Peter R Johnson
DIRECTORS
Sir Desmond Pitcher (Vice-Chairman),
B C Finch, R J Hughes, K M Tamlin,
A Abercromby, Dr D Marsh, Lord
Grantchester,
Sir Phillip Carter, CBE, W Kenwright
SECRETARY
Michael Dunford
COMMERCIAL MANAGER
Andrew Watson

MANAGER: Joe Royle
ASSISTANT MANAGER: Willie Donachie

RESERVE TEAM MANAGER
Jimmy Gabriel

PHYSIOTHERAPIST
Les Helm

STATISTICIAN FOR THE DIRECTORY
Richard Swift

Everton's season started well enough when they defeated the defending champions, Blackburn Rovers, by a single Vinnie Samways goal in the Charity Shield. However, basing the success of the season on that result was soon forgotten when the opening Premier League match against Chelsea was drawn 0-0 and the following game lost 0-2 at Highbury.

Their indifferent League form up to November coincided with their participation in the ECWC. Whether this competition was a distraction only the players will known, but on going out of the competition in the Second Round on November 2nd to Feyenoord, the 'Toffeemens'' League form dramatically picked up, stringing together a run of six matches without defeat and only then ending their run with 0-1 defeat at St James Park.

Both Cup competitions were ended by opposition from lower Divisions. A 2-4 defeat, after a 0-0 draw at Millwall's New Den, saw them exit the Coca-Cola Cup, while it took them two attempts to knock Stockport County out of the 3rd Round of the F.A. Cup before Everton lost 1-2 versus Port Vale, again after a replay.

From their exit of the F.A. Cup, Everton's league form (5 wins, 3 draws and 3 defeats) was enough to earn them the right to a possible place in European Football. If they could win their last match of the season and if other results went their way the 'Toffeemen' would been enjoying a second successive season on the continent.

With eight minutes remaining Everton were on their way to Europe, 1-0 to the good against Aston Villa, and Arsenal, their main rivals for the final European spot, were losing 0-1. However, two goals in the space of two minutes at Highbury meant that it would be the 'Gunners', not Everton, that would take their place in Europe.

If Joe Royal's side can start the 1996/97 season as they finished last season, with the inspirational Andrei Kanchelskis back to best, Everton in their own subtle way will be again fighting for a place in Europe, only this time they might well win the battle.

EVERTON

| League: 6th | | | | FA Cup: 4th Rnd | | | | Coca-Cola Cup: 2nd Rnd | | ECWC: 2nd Rnd | |

M	DATE	COMP	VEN	OPPONENTS	RESULT	HT	LP	GOAL SCORERS/GOAL TIMES	ATT.
1	A 13	CS	N	**Blackburn Rovers**	W 1-0	0-0		**Samways 57**	**(40149)**
2	19	PL	A	Chelsea	D 0-0	0-0	11		(30189)
3	23	PL	H	Arsenal	L 0-2	0-0	2		35775
4	26	PL	H	Southampton	W 2-0	2-0	10	Limpar 34, Amokachi 42	33668
5	30	PL	A	Manchester City	W 2-0	0-0	9	Parkinson 58, Amokachi 75	(28432)
6	S 9	PL	H	Manchester United	L 2-3	1-1	10	Limpar 27, Rideout 55	39496
7	14	ECWC 1/1	A	**Reykjavik**	**W 3-2**	**1-1**		**Ebbrell 22, Unsworth 57(pen), Amokachi 88**	**(6000)**
8	17	PL	A	Nottingham Forest	L 2-3	0-2	12	Rideout 62, 81	(24786)
9	20	CC 2/1	A	**Millwall**	**D 0-0**	**0-0**			**(12053)**
10	23	PL	A	West Ham United	L 1-2	1-2	14	Samways 40	(21085)
11	28	ECWC 1/2	H	**Reykjavik**	**W 3-1**	**0-1**		**Stuart 56, Grant 65, Rideout 87**	**18422**
12	O 1	PL	A	Newcastle United	L 1-3	0-1	15	Limpar 81	33080
13	4	CC 2/2	H	**Millwall**	**L 2-4**	**0-0**		**Hinchcliffe 47(pen), Stuart 55**	**14891**
14	14	PL	A	Bolton Wanderers	D 1-1	0-1	14	Rideout 85	(20427)
15	19	ECWC 2/1	H	**Feyenoord**	**D 0-0**	**0-0**			**27256**
16	22	PL	H	Tottenham Hotspur	D 1-1	1-1	15	Stuart 12	33629
17	28	PL	A	Aston Villa	L 0-1	0-1	16		(32792)
18	N 2	ECWC 2/2	A	**Feyenoord**	**L 0-1**	**0-1**			**(40000)**
19	5	PL	H	Blackburn Rovers	W 1-0	1-0	13	Stuart 23	30097
20	18	PL	A	Liverpool	W 2-1	0-0	13	Kanchelskis 53, 68	(40818)
21	22	PL	H	Queens Park Rangers	W 2-0	2-0	11	Stuart 18, Rideout 36	30009
22	25	PL	H	Sheffield Wednesday	D 2-2	1-2	12	Kanchelskis 45, Amokachi 53	35898
23	D 2	PL	A	Tottenham Hotspur	D 0-0	0-0	12		(32894)
24	11	PL	H	West Ham United	W 3-0	2-0	11	Stuart 33, Unsworth 43(pen), Ebbrell 68	31778
25	16	PL	A	Newcastle United	L 0-1	0-1	12		(36557)
26	23	PL	A	Coventry City	L 1-2	0-0	12	Rideout 67	(16638)
27	26	PL	H	Middlesbrough	W 4-0	2-0	12	Short 10, Stuart 45, 59, Kanchelskis 67	40019
28	30	PL	H	Leeds United	W 2-0	1-0	11	Wetherall 5(og), Kanchelskis 51	40009
29	J 1	PL	A	Wimbledon	W 3-2	3-0	9	Ebbrell 1, Ferguson 23, 25	(11121)
30	7	FAC 3	H	**Stockport County**	**D 2-2**	**2-1**		**Stuart 7, Ablett 44**	**28921**
31	13	PL	H	Chelsea	D 1-1	1-1	10	Unsworth 35(pen)	34968
32	17	FAC 3R	A	**Stockport County**	**W 3-2**	**0-1**		**Ferguson 71, Stuart 73, Ebbrell 89**	**(11283)**
33	20	PL	A	Arsenal	W 2-1	0-1	8	Stuart 50, Kanchelskis 84	(38275)
34	27	FAC 4	H	**Port Vale**	**D 2-2**	**1-0**		**Amokachi 39, Ferguson 88**	**33168**
35	F 3	PL	A	Southampton	D 2-2	0-0	8	Stuart 53, Horne 76	(15136)
36	10	PL	H	Manchester City	W 2-0	1-0	7	Parkinson 32, Hinchcliffe 47(pen)	37354
37	14	FAC 4R	A	**Port Vale**	**L 1-2**	**1-1**		**Stuart 32**	**(19197)**
38	21	PL	A	Manchester United	L 0-2	0-1	7		(42459)
39	24	PL	H	Nottingham Forest	W 3-0	0-0	6	Kanchelskis 52, Watson 56, Ferguson 60	33163
40	M 2	PL	A	Middlesbrough	W 2-0	2-0	6	Grant 28, Hinchcliffe 44(pen)	(29807)
41	9	PL	H	Coventry City	D 2-2	2-1	6	Ferguson 17, 25	34517
42	17	PL	A	Leeds United	D 2-2	1-2	6	Stuart 28, Kanchelskis 50	(29422)
43	23	PL	H	Wimbledon	L 2-4	1-1	7	Short 21, Kanchelskis 61	31382
44	30	PL	A	Blackburn Rovers	W 3-0	1-0	6	Amokachi 71, Kanchelskis 77, 90	(29468)
45	A 6	PL	H	Bolton Wanderers	W 3-0	1-0	6	Hottiger 21, Amokachi 86, Amokachi 90	37974
46	8	PL	A	Queens Park Rangers	L 1-3	0-2	7	Ebbrell 80	(18349)
47	16	PL	H	Liverpool	D 1-1	1-1	7	Kanchelskis 19	40120
48	27	PL	A	Sheffield Wednesday	W 5-2	3-1	5	Amokachi 4, Ebbrell 10, Kanchelskis 21, 54, 65 (3)	(32724)
49	M 5	PL	H	Aston Villa	W 1-0	0-0	6	Parkinson 78	40127

Best Home League Attendance: 40127 v Aston Villa　　　　Smallest: 30009 v Queens Park Rangers　　　Average: 35424

Goal Scorers:
PL(64):　Kanchelskis(16),Stuart(9),Rideout(6),Amokachi(6),Ferguson(5),Ebbrell(4),Limpar(3),Parkinson(3),Hinchcliffe(2),Short(2),Unsworth(2),Watson(1),Horne(1),Grant(1),
CC(2):　Stuart(1),Hinchcliffe(1)Opponent(s)(1),Samways(1),Hottiger(1)
FAC(8):　Stuart(3),Ferguson(2),Ebbrell(1),Amokachi(1),Ablett(1)
ECWC(6):　Unsworth(1),Stuart(1),Rideout(1),Grant(1),Ebbrell(1),Amokachi(1)
CS(1):　Samways(1)

(D) Ablett	(D) Allen	(F) Amokachi	(F) Barlow	(D) Barrett	(M) Branch	(M) Ebbrell	(F) Ferguson	(M) Grant	(D) Hinchcliffe	(D) Holmes	(M) Horne	(D) Hottiger	(D) Jackson	(F) Kanchelskis	(G) Kearton	(F) Limpar	(M) O'Connor	(M) Parkinson	(F) Rideout	(M) Samways	(D) Short	(G) Southall	(G) Speare	(F) Stuart	(D) Unsworth	(D) Watson	Official	
X		S		X		X		X1	X		X		S		S	X		X	X	X		X			X	S1	D.Gallagher	1
X			X				X	S	X	X		X				X1		X	X	S1		X			X	X	M.Reed	2
X		S2	S1	X			X	S	X1		X					X2		X	X			X			X	X	K.Burge	3
X		X	S	X	S						X		X	X	S	X		X	X			X			X	X	J.Winter	4
X		X	S	X			S1				X		X	X		X1		X	X			X			X	X	S.Lodge	5
X		X	S				S1		X	X			X	X1	S	X		X	X			X			X	X	G.Poll	6
X		X		X			S1	X	S1				X1			X1		X	X			X			X	X	R.Phillips	7
X1		X	S2	X			S1		X							X2		X	X		X	X				X	M.J.Bodenham	8
		X		X			X	X		X					S	S		X	X	X	X	X			S	X	D.Gallagher	9
		X		X		X2	X		X							S2		X	X1	X	X	X		S1		X	P.Durkin	10
S		X1		X		X	X		X				S			X		X	X		X	X		S1	X		N.Known	11
		X		X		X	X		X		X				S	S1	X1	X		S	X			X	X	X	K.Cooper	12
X		S1		X			X	X		X		X2			S	X		X			X	X		X1	S2		M.Reed	13
X1		S2		X			X			X		X	X2			S1		X			X	X		X			P.Alcock	14
X		S1		X	S			S1	X	X1			X1			X1		X	X	X	X	S	X	X			H.Weber	15
X				X	S			X1	X		X	X			S1		X	X		X	X	S	X	S	X		R.Dilkes	16
X	X1			X			X2				X	X	S	S2			X	X		X	X		X	S1	X		K.Burge	17
X2	X	S2		X1			S1	X	S	X		X						S	X		X	X	S	X		X	M.Nicchi	18
X	S1			X			S				X	X		X		X		X	X		X	X		X1	S	X	A.Wilkie	19
X1		S		X			S				X	X		X		X		X	X		X	X		X	S1	X	G.Ashby	20
		S		X				S		S		X	X		X		X	X		X	X		X	X	X		P.Danson	21
		S1		X			X		S		X	X	S	X		X	X1		X	X		X	X		X		M.Bodenham	22
		X		X			S1				X	X	S	X		X		X1			X	X		X	X	X	S.W.Dunn	23
		X		X	S1			S				X	X	S	X1		X			X	X		X	X	X		M.Reed	24
		X		X	S2			S1		X2	X	S	X		X1		X			X	X		X	X	X		P.Durkin	25
		X		X				S		X	X	S	X1		X	X	S1		X	X		X	X	X			S.Lodge	26
		S		X				S		X	X		X		X		X	X		X	X		X	X	X		P.Jones	27
		X	X1	S1			X	X	S	X	S		X		X	X		X	X		X	X	X				J.Winter	28
		X	X		S1			X	X1	S			X		X	X		X	X		X	X	X				A.Wilkie	29
X		X2		S1	S2			X		X	X	S	X1		X			X	X	X							G.Poll	30
X	S1			X			S	X1			X		X		X	X		X	X		X	X	X				R.Hart	31
X	S1			X	X				X		X	X	S	X1		X			X	X		X	X	S	X		G.Poll	32
X	X1			X	X				X		X	X	S	S		X			X	X		X	X	S1	X		M.Bodenham	33
X1	X1			X	X		S1		X		X	X	S	X1		X			X	X		X	X	X			M.Reed	34
S					X			X		X	X		X	X	S	X1		X	S1		X	X		X	X		D.Elleray	35
S	S				X			X		X	X		X	X	S	X		X	X		X	X		X	X		P.Alcock	36
		X			X			X		X	X		X2	X	S	S2		X			X	X		X	X1	X	M.Reed	37
		X		S1	X		X1	X		X	X			X	S	X		X	S1		X	X		X	X	X	M.Bodenham	38
		S1			X	X1	X	X					X	S	X	X		S	X	X		X	X		X	X	K.Cooper	39
		S			X	X	X	X				X	S	X	X		X	X		X	X		X	X	X		D.Gallagher	40
		S1			X	X	X	X		X		X		X	S	S2	X1		X2	X	X		X	X			P.Danson	41
		S			X	X	X	X		X	X	X	S	X		S		X	X		X	X	X				G.Ashby	42
		S2			X1	X	X	X		X	X	X		X1		S1		X	X		X2	S	X				R.Dilkes	43
		S2			X	X	X	X		X	X		X1		S1		X	X	S		X	X					J.Winter	44
		X		S1	X	X1	X		X	X		X		X	S	X		X			X	X		X3	X		M.Bodenham	45
				S1	X	X	S3	X		X2	X		X		X	X1		X		S2	X		X3	X			P.Durkin	46
		X1			X	X	X		X	X		X		S			S	X	S1	X		X	S1	X	X		D.Elleray	47
		X		X1	X		X				X		X		S		S1	X	X	S	X	X		X	X		M.Reed	48
		X2			X1			X	X	X	X		X		S1		X	S2		S	X		X	X	X		R.Heart	49
13	0	17	0	8	1	24	16	11	23	1	25	9	14	32	0	22	3	28	19	3	22	38	0	27	28	34	PL Appearances	
0	0	8	3	0	2	1	2	2	5	0	1	0	0	0	0	6	1	0	6	1	1	0	0	2	3	0	PL Sub Appearances	
1	0	1	0+1	2	0	0	0	2	2	0	2	0	1	0	0	1	0	2	2	1	2	2	0	1	0+1	1	CC Appearances	
3	0	2+1	0	0	4	2	0+1	1+2	0	4	0	2	4	0	2+2	0	2	1+1	0	3	4	0	4	2	4		FAC Appearances	
3	0	3	0+2	2	0	3	0	1+2	3	0+2	3	0	3	0	3	0	2	4	1	3	4	0	2+1	3	2		ECWC Appearances	
1	0	0	0	1	0	0	0	1	1	0	1	0	0	0	0	1	0	1	1	1	0	1	0	0	1	0+1	CS Appearances	

EVERTON

CLUB RECORDS

BIGGEST VICTORIES
League: 8-0 v Stoke City, Division 1, 2.11.1889.
9-1 v Manchester City, Division 1, 3.9.1906.
9-1 v Plymouth Argyle, Division 2, 27.12.1930.
8-0 v Southampton, Division 1, 20.11.1971.
F.A. Cup: 11-2 v Derby County, 1st Round, 18.1.1890.
League Cup: 8-0 v Wimbledon, 2nd Round, 24.8.1978.
Europe: (UEFA) 5-0 v Finn Harps, 1st Round 1st leg, 12.9.1978.
5-0 v Finn Harps, 1st Round 2nd leg, 26.9.1978.

BIGGEST DEFEATS
League: 0-7 v Sunderland, Division 1, 26.12.1934.
0-7 v Wolverhampton Wndrs., Division 1, 22.2.1939.
0-7 v Portsmouth, Division 1, 10.9.1949.
F.A. Cup: 0-6 v Crystal Palace (h), 1st Round, 7.1.1922.
League Cup: No more than 3 goal difference.
Europe: (UEFA) 0-3 v Ujpest Dozsa, 2nd Round 1st leg, 3.11.1965.

MOST POINTS
3 points a win: 90, Division 1, 1984-85 (Division 1 record)
2 points a win: 66, Division 1, 1969-70.

MOST GOALS SCORED
121, Division 1, 1930-31.
Dean 39, Down 14, Critchley 13, Johnson 13, Stein 11, White 10, Martin 7, Rigby 4, Griffith 3, Gee 2, Wilkinson 2, McPherson 1, McLure 1, Opponents 1.

MOST GOALS CONCEDED
92, Division 1, 1929-30.

MOST FIRST CLASS MATCHES IN A SEASON
63 - 1984-85 (League 42, FA Cup 7, League Cup 4, Charity Shield 1, ECWC 9).
63 - 1985-86 (League 42, FA Cup 7, League Cup 5, Charity Shield 1, Screen Super Cup 8).

MOST LEAGUE WINS
29, Division 1, 1969-70.

MOST LEAGUE DRAWS
18, Division 1, 1925-26, 1971-72, 1974-75.

MOST LEAGUE DEFEATS
22, Division 1, 1950-51, 1993-94.

INDIVIDUAL CLUB RECORDS

MOST GOALS IN A SEASON
William 'Dixie' Dean: 63 goals in 1927-28 (League 60, FAC 3). Previous holder: B Freeman 38 (1908-09).

MOST GOALS IN A MATCH
6. Jack Southwork v West Bromwich Albion, 7-1, Division 1, 30.12.1893.

OLDEST PLAYER
Ted Sager, 42 years, 1953.

YOUNGEST PLAYER
Joe Royle, 16 years, 1966.

MOST CAPPED PLAYER
Neville Southall (Wales) 85.

BEST PERFORMANCES

League: 1969-70: Matches played 42, Won 29, Drawn 8, Lost 5, Goals for 72, Goals against 34, Points 72. 1st Division 1.
Highest Position: Division 1 Champions nine times.
F.A. Cup: Winners in 1905-06, 1932-33, 1965-66, 1983-84. Most Recent success: 1994-95: 3rd Round Derby County 1-0; 4th Round Bristol City 1-0; 5th Round Norwich City 5-0; 6th Round Newcastle United 1-0; Semi-Final Tottenham Hotspur 4-1; Final Manchester United 1-0.
League Cup: 1976-77: 2nd Round Cambridge United 3-0; 3rd Round Stockport County 1-0; 4th Round Coventry City 3-0; 5th Round Manchester United 3-0; Semi-Final Bolton Wanderers 1-1,1-0; Final Aston Villa 1-1,2-3.
Europe: (ECWC) 1984-85: 1st Round University of Dublin 0-0,1-0; 2nd Round Inter Bratislav 1-0,3-0; 3rd Round Fortuna S 3-0,2-0; Semi-Final Bayern Munich 0-0,3-1; Final Rapid Vienna 3-1.

ADDITIONAL INFORMATION
Previous Names
None.
Previous Leagues
None.

Club colours: Blue & white trim shirts, white shorts, blue socks.
Change colours: Amber/black striped shirts, black shorts, amber socks.

Reserves League: Pontins Central League Premier Division.

DIVISIONAL RECORD							
	Played	Won	Drawn	Lost	For	Against	Points
Division 1/P	3,644	1,515	882	1,247	5,873	5,157	4,174
Division 2	168	77	45	46	348	257	199
Total	**3,812**	**1,592**	**927**	**1,293**	**6,221**	**5,414**	**4,373**

COMPETITIONS

Div 1/P	Div.2	Euro C	ECWC	UEFA	Texaco
888-30	1930-31	1963-64	1966-67	1962-63	1973-74
931-51	1951-54	1970-71	1984-85	1964-65	
1954-			1995-96	1965-66	
				1975-76	
				1978-79	
				1979-80	

HONOURS

Div 1/P	Div.2	FA Cup	ECWC	C/Sh'ld
1890-91	1930-31	1906	1984-85	1928
1914-15		1933		1932
1927-28		1966		1963
1931-32		1984		1970
1938-39		1995		1984
1962-63				1985
1969-70				1986
1984-85				1987
1986-87				

MOST APPEARANCES

NEVILLE SOUTHALL 649 (1981-95)

Year	League	FA Cup	Lge Cup	Europe	FMC	CT	CS
981-82	26	1					
982-83	17		2				
983-84	35	8	11				
984-85	42	7	4	9			1
985-86	32	5	5		6		1
986-87	31	3	3		2		
987-88	32	8	7		1		
988-89	38	8	5		3	1	
989-90	38	7	4				
990-91	38	6	3		6		
991-92	42	2	4		2		
992-93	40	1	6				
993-94	42	2	3				
994-95	41	6	2				
	494	64	59	9	20	1	2

MOST GOALS IN A CAREER

WILLIAM DEAN - 377 (1924-38)

Year	League	FA Cup
1924-25	2	
1925-26	32	1
1926-27	21	3
1927-28	60	3
1928-29	26	
1929-30	23	2
1930-31	39	9
1931-32	45	1
1932-33	24	5
1933-34	9	
1934-35	26	1
1935-36	17	
1936-37	24	3
1937-38	1	
Total	**349**	**28**

Current leading goalscorer: Paul Rideout - 39 (1992-96)

RECORD TRANSFER FEE RECEIVED

Amount	Club	Player	Date
2,800,000	Barcelona	Gary Lineker	6/86
2,500,000	Arsenal	Martin Keown	1/93
1,500,000	Glasgow Rangers	Trevor Steven	6/89
1,250,000	Glasgow Rangers	Stuart McCall	8/91

MANAGERS

Name	Seasons	Best	Worst
Theo Kelly	1939-48	1(1)	14(1)
Cliff Britton	1948-56	11(1)	16(2)
Ian Buchan	1956-58	15(1)	16(1)
John Carey	1958-61	5(1)	16(1)
Harry Catterick	1961-73	1(1)	17(1)
Billy Bingham	1973-77	4(1)	11(1)
Steve Burtenshaw	1977		
Gordon Lee	1977-81	3(1)	19(1)
Howard Kendall	1981-87	1(1)	8(1)
Colin Harvey	1987-90	4(1)	8(1)
Howard Kendall	1990-94	9(1)	13(1/P)
Mike Walker	1994	22(P)	22(P)
Joe Royle	1994-	6(P)	15(P)

RECORD TRANSFER FEE PAID

Amount	Club	Player	Date
5,000,000	Manchester Utd	Andrei Kanchelskis	8/95
4,000,000	Glasgow Rangers	Duncan Ferguson	12/94
3,500,000	Leeds Utd	Gary Speed	7/96
3,000,000	FC Club Brugge	Daniel Amokachi	8/94

LONGEST LEAGUE RUNS

undefeated matches:	20 (29.4.1978 - 16.12.1978)	of league matches w/out a win:	14 (6.3.1937 - 4.9.1937)
undefeated home matches:	39 (6.9.1961 - 7.9.1963)	of undefeated away matches:	11 (21.4.1908 - 27.9.1909)
thout home win:	12 (14.9.1957 - 22.3.1958)	without an away win:	35 (19.9.1970 - 8.4.1972)
league wins:	12 (27.3.1894 - 6.10.1894)	of home wins:	15 (4.10.1930 - 4.4.1931)
league defeats:	6 (5.3.30-12.4.30, 29.3.58-19.4.58, 4.11.72-9.12.72)	of away wins:	6 (2.9.1908 - 14.11.1908)

EVERTON

PLAYERS NAME Honours	Ht	Wt	Birthdate	Birthplace Transfers	Contract Date	Clubs	League	L/Cup	FA Cup	Other	Lge	L/C	FAC	Oth
G O A L K E E P E R S														
Gerrard Paul W	6.2	13.1	22/01/73	Heywood	02/11/91	Oldham Athletic	118+1	7	7	1				
						Everton								
Kearton Jason B	6.1	11.10	09/07/69	Ipswich (Aus)		Brisbane Lions								
				Free	31/10/88	Everton	3+3	1	1					
				Loan	13/08/91	Stoke City	16			1				
				Loan	09/01/92	Blackpool	14							
				Loan	20/01/95	Notts County	10			2				
				Loan	21/03/96	Preston North End								
Southall Neville	6.1	12.2	16/09/58	Llandudno		Bangor City								
W: 79. Div.1'85'87. FAC'84'95. CS'84'85'96						Winsford United								
ECWC'85.				£6000	14/06/80	Bury	39		5					
				£150000	13/07/81	Everton	532	62	68	37				
				Loan	27/01/83	Port Vale	9							
Speare James					01/07/95	Everton								
D E F E N D E R S														
Allen Graham	6.1	12.0	08/04/77	Bolton	01/08/94	Everton								
Barrett Earl D	5.10	11.2	28/04/67	Rochdale	26/04/85	Manchester City	2+1	1						
E:3,B.4,u21.4. Div.2'91.				Loan	01/03/86	Chester City	12							
FLgeXI.1. LC'94. CS'95.				£35000	24/11/87	Oldham Athletic	181+2	20	14	4	7	1	1	
				£1700000	25/02/92	Aston Villa	118+1	15	9	7	1	1		
				£1700000	30/01/95	Everton	25	2		3				
Hinchcliffe Andrew G	5.10	12.10	05/02/69	Manchester	17/06/86	Manchester City	107+5	11	12	4	8	1	1	1
E: u21.1, Y.7. FAC'95. CS'95.				£800000	17/07/90	Everton	137+10	16+2	12+2	8	6	1	1	
Hottiger Marc	5.10	12.09	07/11/67	Lausanne		Sion F.C.								
Swiss Int.				£600000	04/08/94	Newcastle United	38+1	6+1	4	4	1		1	
				£700000	09/03/96	Everton	9				1			
Jackson Matthew A	6.0	12.12	19/10/71	Leeds	04/07/90	Luton Town	7+2	2		0+1				
E: u21.10, u19.5, S. FAC'95.				Loan	27/03/91	Preston North End	3+1			1				
CS'95.				£600000	18/10/93	Everton	132+6	9	14	4	6			
				Loan	26/03/96	Charlton Athletic	8			2				
Moore Neil	6.0	12.3	21/09/72	Liverpool	04/06/91	Everton	4+1	0+1						
				Loan	09/09/94	Blackpool	7			1				
				Loan	16/02/95	Oldham Athletic	5							
				Loan	25/08/95	Carlisle United	12			2				
				Loan	20/03/96	Rotherham United	10+1							
Short Craig J	6.0	11.4	25/06/68	Bridlington		Pickering								
E: S.				Free	15/10/87	Scarborough	61+2	6	2	7	7			1
				£100000	27/07/89	Notts County	128	6	8	16	6	1	1	2
				£2500000	18/09/92	Derby County	118	11	7	7	9		4	
				£2400000	18/07/95	Everton	22+1	2	3	3	2			
Unsworth David G	6.0	13.0	16/10/73	Chorley	25/06/92	Everton	76+5	5+2	4	9	6			1
E:1, u21.5, y.14. FAC'95.														
Watson David	5.11	11.12	20/11/61	Liverpool	25/05/79	Liverpool								
E:12,u21.7. UEFAu21'84. LC'85.				£100000	29/11/80	Norwich City	212	21	18		11	3	1	
Div2'86.Div1'87.CS'87'95FAC'95				£900000	22/08/86	Everton	338+2	35	42	16+1	21	6	5	3
M I D F I E L D														
Branch Michael				18/10/78	Liverpool	24/10/95	Everton	1+2							
Ebbrell John K	5.7	9.12	01/10/69	Bromborough	07/11/86	Everton	200+10	16	20	9+2	13	1	3	2
E: B.1, u21.14, Y.4, S. GMAFS. FAC'95. CS'95.														
Grant Anthony J	5.10	10.2	14/11/74	Liverpool	08/07/93	Everton	12+6	2	0+1	2+2	1			1
CS'95.				Loan	18/01/96	Swindon Town	3				1			
Grugel Mark A	5.8	10.0	09/03/76	Liverpool	05/11/93	Everton								
Holcroft Peter I	5.8	10.0	03/11/76	Liverpool	01/07/94	Everton								
O'Connor Jonathan	5.10	11.03	29/10/76	Darlington	28/10/93	Everton	3+1							
E:Y.14, S.														
Parkinson Joseph S	5.8	12.2	11/06/71	Eccles	01/04/89	Wigan Athletic	115+4	11	9	8	6	1		
FAC'95. CS'95.				£35000	01/07/93	Bournemouth	30	4	4	1	1	1		
				£250000	24/03/94	Everton	60+2	3	8	3	4			
Price Christopher	5.9	11.09	24/10/75	Liverpool	01/07/94	Everton								
Samways Vincent	5.8	9.0	27/10/68	Bethnal Green	09/11/85	Tottenham Hotspur	165+28	27+4	15+1	7+1	11	4	2	
E: u21.5, u19.3, Y.3. FAC'91.CS'91'95.				£2200000	02/08/94	Everton	17+6	3		2	2	1		1
				Loan	21/12/95	Wolves	3							
				Loan	09/02/96	Birmingham City	12							

						Fee	Date	Club								
peed Gary A	5.11	10.12	08/09/69	Mancot			13/06/88	Leeds United (T)	231+17	25+1	21	14+3	39	11	5	2
/: 29, u21.3, Y. Div.2'90. Div.1'92.							01/06/96	Everton								
O R W A R D S																
erguson Duncan	6.4	14.6	27/12/71	Stirling			01/02/90	Dundee United	75+2	2+1	8		28	2	6	
:4, B, u21.7. SL'94. SLC'94.						£4000000	20/07/93	Glasgow Rangers	35	1+1	0+3	1	5			
AC'92.						£4400000	04/10/94	Everton	38+3	1	5+1		12		3	
anchelskis Andrei	5.10	12.4	23/01/69	Kirowograd (USSR)				Shakhtor Donetsk								
SSR,Russian Int. ESC'91.						£650000	26/03/91	Manchester United	96+27	15+1	11+1	10	28	3	4	1
C'92.Prem'93'94.FAC'94.CS'93.						£4500000	25/08/95	Everton	32		4		16			
ideout Paul D	5.11	12.2	14/08/64	Bournemouth			15/08/81	Swindon Town	90+5	3	7		38	2	1	
: u21.5, Y.9, S. FAC'95.						£200000	01/06/83	Aston Villa	50+4	4+2	1+1	1	19	3		
S'95.						£400000	01/07/85	Bari	80				24			
						£430000	05/07/91	Swindon Town	9				1			
						£250000	16/09/91	Notts County	9+2	2	1	2	3			
						£500000	10/01/92	Glasgow Rangers	7+5	0+1	1+1		1			
						£500000	14/08/92	Everton	82+20	10+1	8+1	5	29		8	2
tuart Graham C	5.8	11.6	24/10/70	Tooting			15/06/89	Chelsea	70+17	11	5+2	3+2	14	2	1	1
u21.5, Y.5, S. FAC'95.						£850000	19/08/93	Everton	53+6	3	5+1	2+1	12	1	3	1
ODITIONAL CONTRACT PLAYERS																
ills John								Everton (T)								
cCann Gavin								Everton (T)								
oore Richard								Everton (T)								
uayle Mark								Everton (T)								

THE MANAGER
JOE ROYLE

Date of Birth . . . . 8th April 1949.
Place of Birth . . . . Liverpool.
Date of Appointment . . . . November 1994.

PREVIOUS CLUBS
As Manager . . . . Oldham Athletic.
As Coach . . . . None.
As a Player . . . . Everton, Manchester City, Bristol City, Norwich City.

HONOURS
As a Manager
Oldham Athletic: League Cup finalists 1990. Division 2 champions 1990-91.
Everton: FA Cup winners 1994-95.

As a Player
Everton: League Championship 1970.
Manchester City: League Cup winners 1976.
International: 6 full caps and 10 U23 for England. Football League XI.

GOODISON PARK

Liverpool L4 4EL
Tel: 0151 330 2200

Capacity ....40,200.
First game ....v Bolton Wanderers, Division 1, 2.9.1892.
First floodlit game ....v Liverpool, 9.10.1957.
ATTENDANCES
Highest ....78,299 v Liverpool, Division 1, 18.9.1948.
Lowest...2,079 v WBA, 23.2.1899.
Internationals ....England v Scotland 1895, 1911.v Ireland 1907, 1924, 1928, 1935, 1947, 1953, 1973.
....v Eire 1949, v Portugal 1951, Poland 1966.
..Brazil v Bulgaria 1966, v Hungary 1966, Portugal 1966. Portugal v North Korea 1966. W.Germany v Russia 1966.
....Ireland v Wales 1973.

OTHER GROUNDS ....Stanley Park 1878-82, Priory Road 1882-84,
....Anfield Road 1884-92, Goodison Park 1892-

MATCHDAY TICKET PRICES

	Adults	Juv.	Sen.Cit
Main Stand	£18	-	-
Upper Bullens	£17	-	-
Park End Stand	£16	-	-
Top Balcony	£15	£7	-
Family Enclosure	£15	£7	£9
Paddock	£15	-	-
Lower Bullens	£15	£7	£9
Gwladys Stand	£15	-	£9
Gwladys Terrace Seating	£13	£7	-
Visitors			
Upper Bullens	£17	-	-
Lower Bullens	£15	£10	£10

Ticket Office Telephone no. 0151 330 2300

Dial a Seat (24 hour service) 0151 471 8000

HOW TO GET TO THE GROUND

From the North
Use motorway M6 until junction 28 then follow signs Liverpool on A58 then A580 and forward into Walton Hall Avenue for Everton FC.

From the East, and South
Use motorway M6 then M62 until end of motorway then turn right A5058 into Queens Drive. In 3.7 miles turn left A580 into Walton Hall Avenue for Everton FC.

From the West
Use Mersey Tunnel into Liverpool City Centre, then follow signs to Preston (A580) into Walton Hall Avenue for Everton FC.

Car Parking
Extensive parking is available on site at the corner of Prior and Utting Avenue.

Nearest Railway Station
Liverpool (Lime Street) 0151 709 9696.

CLUBCALL 0898 12 11 99
Calls cost 39p per minute cheap rate and 49p per minute at all other times.
Call costings correct at time of going to press.

MATCHDAY PROGRAMME

Programme Editor . . . . Mike Beddow.

Number of pages . . . . 32.

Price . . . . £1.70.

Subscriptions . . . . £58 UK. (For overseas apply to club).

Local Newspapers. . . . . Liverpool Daily Post, Liverpool Echo.

Local Radio Stations . . . . Radio Merseyside, Radio City.

LEEDS UNITED
(The Whites)
F.A. Carling Premiership
Sponsored by: Packard Bell

Back Row (L-R): David White, Brian Deane, Carlton Palmer, John Lukic, David Wetherall, Mark Beeney, Philemon Masinga, Lucas Radebe, Paul Beesley. **Middle Row:** Mike Hennigan (Asst. Manager), Matthew Smithard, Mark Ford, Noel Whelan, Robert Bowman, Mark Tinkler, Andy Couzens, Kevin Sharp, Tony Dorigo, Nigel Worthington, David O'Leary, David Williams (Coach), Geoff Ladley (Physio). **Front Row:** Rod Wallace, Anthony Yeboah, Gary McAllister, Howard Wilkinson (Manager), John Pemberton, Gary Speed, Gary Kelly.

LEEDS UNITED
FORMED IN 1919 (As United)
TURNED PROFESSIONAL IN 1919
LTD COMPANY IN 1920
PRESIDENT: Rt Hon Earl of Harewood
ACTING CHAIRMAN: W J Fotherby
VICE-CHAIRMAN: P J Gilman
DIRECTORS
R Barker MCIT, MBIM,
J W G Marjason (Dep. Chairman)
M J Bedford, E Carlile, A Hudson, R Feldman,
P Ridsdale, K Woolmer
SECRETARY
Nigel Pleasants (01132 716 037)
COMMERCIAL MANAGER
Bob Baldwin (01132 716 037)
MANAGER: Howard Wilkinson
ASSISTANT MANAGER: Michael Hennigan
COACHES
Peter Gunby, Robin Wray & David Williams
DIRECTOR OF YOUTH COACHING
Paul Hart
PHYSIOTHERAPISTS
Geoff Ladley & Alan Sutton

STATISTICIAN FOR THE DIRECTORY
Mark Evans

Following the outstanding run-in to the previous season, the club and its supporters entered the 1995/6 season optimistic about gaining some silverware.

The main pre-season addition was the £3.4 million signing of Tony Yeboah from Eintracht Frankfurt. Paul Beesley was also signed from neighbours Sheffield United.

Indeed, the side carried over its final form of 1994/5 into the new season, starting with three straight victories. Yeboah in particular began the season in blistering fashion: his right-foot volley from some thirty five yards to defeat Liverpool was an early contender for goal of the season, and he scored hat-tricks at Wimbledon and at AS Monaco in the UEFA Cup, in what to some was the result of the season.

Unfortunately, the early season momentum could not be maintained and although the club suffered more than its fair share of injuries, the number of defeats suffered at Elland Road - particularly against lowly opposition - led to a rather dismal league position of 13th. This after being fifth in November.

The side's much-awaited venture into Europe began in style with the victory over AS Monaco, but ended in the same manner at the hands of PSV Eindhoven , where the importance of not conceding goals at home was harshly learned.

The domestic cups brought about a much-needed and publicised change of fortune. After previous defeats against lowly opposition, the twin towers of Wembley were reached for the club's first domestic final in 23 years. Unfortunately, amid much anticipation and fervour, the side struggled to maintain any sort of performance and were resoundingly beaten by Aston Villa in the Coca-Cola Cup Final. Thus, the club's last hope of European qualification disappeared and the whole season went downhill from this point - particularly after the FA Cup Quarter-Final elimination at Liverpool.

Another major disappointment during the season concerned the two signings made: firstly the cruel injury sustained by Richard Jobson who had settled in easily and was beginning to look a class act, and secondly the Tomas Brolin situation. Signed in a record-breaking £4.5 million deal amid much anticipation, Brolin's career never really took off and his future hung in the balance at Elland Road by the end of the season.

In a season that began so promisingly and ended so disappointingly, one huge consolation can be drawn - that of the promise shown by the youngsters at the club, including Andy Cozens, Mark Ford and, particularly, Andy Gray, a young man of undoubted talent and ability.

Chairman Leslie Silver resigned before the season's end on ill-health grounds, so there will inevitably be a change at the top at Elland Road. Hopefully, Howard Wilkinson will receive the go-ahead to carry on the re-building programme at Leeds, which is viewed as a necessity by many of those who follow the club.

Mark Evans

LEEDS UNITED

League: 13th   FA Cup: Quarter Finals   Coca-Cola Cup: Runners Up   UEFA Cup: 2nd Rnd

M	DATE	COMP	VEN	OPPONENTS	RESULT	HT	LP	GOAL SCORERS/GOAL TIMES	ATT.
1	A 19	PL	A	West Ham United	W 2-1	0-1	5	Yeboah 48, 57	(22901)
2	21	PL	H	Liverpool	W 1-0	0-0	2	Yeboah 51	35852
3	26	PL	H	Aston Villa	W 2-0	1-0	1	Speed 4, White 87	35086
4	30	PL	A	Southampton	D 1-1	0-0	2	Dorigo 70	(15212)
5	S 9	PL	A	Tottenham Hotspur	L 1-2	0-1	5	Yeboah 53	(30034)
6	12	UEFA 1/1	A	Monaco	W 3-0	1-0		Yeboah 2, 65, 81 (3)	(14000)
7	16	PL	H	Queens Park Rangers	L 1-3	0-2	8	Wetherall 89	31504
8	19	CC 2/1	H	Notts County	D 0-0	0-0			12384
9	23	PL	A	Wimbledon	W 4-2	3-1	7	Palmer 32, Yeboah 42, 44, 74 (3)	(13307)
10	26	UEFA 1/2	H	Monaco	L 0-1	0-1			24501
11	30	PL	H	Sheffield Wednesday	W 2-0	1-0	4	Yeboah 33, Speed 59	34076
12	O 3	CC 2/2	A	Notts County	W 3-2	1-1		McAllister 19, Couzens 73, Speed 90	(12477)
13	14	PL	H	Arsenal	L 0-3	0-1	7		38332
14	17	UEFA 2/1	H	PSV Eindhoven	L 3-5	1-3		Speed 6, Palmer 48, McAllister 72	24846
15	21	PL	A	Manchester City	D 0-0	0-0	8		(26390)
16	25	CC 3	A	Derby County	W 1-0	0-0		Speed 72	(16030)
17	28	PL	H	Coventry City	W 3-1	2-1	8	McAllister 40, 44, 89(pen) (3)	30161
18	31	UEFA 2/2	A	PSV Eindhoven	L 0-3	0-2			(25750)
19	N 4	PL	A	Middlesbrough	D 1-1	1-1	8	Deane 44	(29467)
20	18	PL	H	Chelsea	W 1-0	0-0	4	Yeboah 80	36209
21	25	PL	A	Newcastle United	L 1-2	1-0	8	Deane 30	(36572)
22	29	CC 4	H	Blackburn Rovers	W 2-1	2-0		Deane 21, Yeboah 29	26006
23	D 2	PL	H	Manchester City	L 0-1	0-0	9		33249
24	9	PL	H	Wimbledon	D 1-1	0-1	9	Jobson 75	27984
25	16	PL	A	Sheffield Wednesday	L 2-6	1-3	9	Brolin 28, Wallace 84	(24573)
26	24	PL	H	Manchester United	W 3-1	2-1	9	McAllister 6(pen), Yeboah 35, Deane 72	39801
27	27	PL	A	Bolton Wanderers	W 2-0	1-0	8	Brolin 39, Wetherall 63	(18414)
28	30	PL	A	Everton	L 0-2	0-1	10		(40009)
29	J 1	PL	H	Blackburn Rovers	D 0-0	0-0	11		31285
30	7	FAC 3	A	Derby County	W 4-2	0-0		Speed 57, Deane 58, McAllister 90, Yeboah 90	(16155)
31	10	CC QF	H	Reading	W 2-1	2-1		Masinga 35, Speed 44	21023
32	13	PL	H	West Ham United	W 2-0	1-0	9	Brolin 25, 62	30658
33	20	PL	A	Liverpool	L 0-5	0-1	11		(40254)
34	31	PL	A	Nottingham Forest	L 1-2	0-1	11	Palmer 55	(24465)
35	F 3	PL	A	Aston Villa	L 0-3	0-2	11		(35982)
36	11	CC SF1	A	Birmingham City	W 2-1	0-1		Yeboah 54, Whyte 72(og)	(24781)
37	14	FAC 4	A	Bolton Wanderers	W 1-0	1-0		Wallace 1	(16694)
38	21	FAC 5	H	Port Vale	D 0-0	0-0			18607
39	25	CC SF2	H	Birmingham City	W 3-0	0-0		Masinga 54, Yeboah 56, Deane 86	35435
40	27	FAC 5R	A	Port Vale	W 2-1	0-1		McAllister 64, 89	(14023)
41	M 2	PL	H	Bolton Wanderers	L 0-1	0-1	11		30106
42	6	PL	A	Queens Park Rangers	W 2-1	2-1	11	Yeboah 10, 25	(13991)
43	10	FAC QF	H	Liverpool	D 0-0	0-0			34632
44	13	PL	A	Blackburn Rovers	L 0-1	0-0	12		(23358)
45	17	PL	H	Everton	D 2-2	2-1	12	Deane 6, 45	29422
46	20	FAC QFR	A	Liverpool	L 0-3	0-1			(30812)
47	24	CC F	N	Aston Villa	L 0-3	0-1			(77065)
48	30	PL	H	Middlesbrough	L 0-1	0-1	12		31778
49	A 3	PL	H	Southampton	W 1-0	0-0	12	Deane 73	26077
50	6	PL	A	Arsenal	L 1-2	0-1	12	Deane 53	(37619)
51	8	PL	H	Nottingham Forest	L 1-3	1-2	13	Wetherall 9	29220
52	13	PL	A	Chelsea	L 1-4	0-3	13	McAllister 65	(22131)
53	17	PL	A	Manchester United	L 0-1	0-0	13		(48382)
54	29	PL	H	Newcastle United	L 0-1	0-1	13		38862
55	M 2	PL	H	Tottenham Hotspur	L 1-3	1-2	13	Wetherall 13	30061
56	5	PL	A	Coventry City	D 0-0	0-0	13		(22757)

Best Home League Attendance: 39801 v Manchester United   Smallest: 26077 v Southampton   Average: 32617

Goal Scorers:
PL(40): Yeboah(12),Deane(7),McAllister(5),Brolin(4),Wetherall(4),Palmer(2),Speed(2),Dorigo(1),Wallace(1),White(1),Jobson(1)
CC(13): Speed(3),Yeboah(3),Masinga(3),Deane(2),Opponent(s)(1),Couzens(1),McAllister(1)
FAC(7): McAllister(3),Speed(1),Deane(1),Yeboah(1),Wallace(1)
UEFA(6): Yeboah(3),Speed(1),Palmer(1),McAllister(1)

1995-96

	(G) Beeney	(D) Beesley	(M) Blunt	(D) Bowman	(M) Brolin	(F) Chapman	(D) Couzens	(F) Deane	(D) Dorigo	(M) Ford	(M) Gray	(M) Harte	(D) Jobson	(D) Kelly	(F) Kewell	(G) Lukic	(F) Masinga	(M) McAllister	(M) Palmer	(D) Pemberton	(D) Radebe	(M) Speed	(M) Tinkler	(F) Wallace	(D) Wetherall	(F) Whelan	(F) White	(M) Worthington	(F) Yeboah	
		S2						X	X3					X		X		X	X2	X		X		X1	X	S1		S3	X	K.Burge 1
	S	S						X	X					X		X		X	X	X		X		X1	X	S1			X	D.Ellery 2
	S	S						X	X					X		X		X	X	X		X		X1	X		S1		X	D.Gallagher 3
								X	X					X		X		X	X	X		X		X1	X		S2	X2	X	K.Cooper 4
		S						X	X					X		X		X	X	X		X			X	X1	S1		X	P.Derkin 5
	S	S1				S		X	X1					X		X		X	X	X		X	S		X	X	S		X	J.Encinar 6
		S2						X						X		X		X	X	X		X			X	X1	S1	X2	X	S.Lodge 7
		S2						X			S1			X		X		X	X	X		X			X	X1	X2	X2	X	R.Hart 8
		X						X						X		X	X1	X	X	X		X			X	X	S		X	R.Dilkes 9
	S	S		S			S2	X			S			X		X		X	X2	X		X	S1		X	S1		X1	X	S.Muhmenthaler 10
	S	X	S					X	S1					X		X	X1	X	X			X		X	X			X	D.Allison 11
		X						X	X					X		S	X1	X			X	X2	S1		X		S2	X	A.Wilkie 12
		S						X	X	X				X		X		X	X			X	X	X	S1	X	S		X1	P.Crabtree 13
	S	S2						S1	X	X2				X		X		X	X	X		X		X1	S	S3	X	X3	X	A.J.Lopez Nieto 14
	S							X	X					X		X		X	X	X		X		S	X1	X	S1	X	X	M.Bodenham 15
		X						X	X					X		X		X	X	X		X			X	X1	X1		X	R.Dilkes 16
								S1	X1				X	X		X		X	X			X			X	X2		S	X	G.Ashby 17
	S	X3		X					S			S3		X		X		X	X			X	X1		X	X2	S2		X	M.Batta 18
								S	S					X	X	X		X	X	X		X			X	X		X	X	K.Burge 19
								S1	X1	X	X			X		X		X	X			X	S	S1	X	S			X	M.Reed 20
			S2	S1				X	X2	X1			X	X		X		X	X			X			X	X			X	S.Dunn 21
			S1	X1				X	X	X			X	X		X		X	X			X	X1		X	X			X	K.Cooper 22
				X1				X	X	X2			X	X		X		X	X		S2	X			X	S1		S	X	P.Alcock 23
	S			X				S	X1	X			X	X		X		X	X			X			X	S1			X	G.Poll 24
				X				X	X	S2	X		X	X1		X		X	X			X			X	S1			X2	R.A.Hart 25
X				X				X	X	X	X		X	X		X		X	X		S	X			X	S1	X	S	X1	D.Gallagher 26
X				X1			S	X	X	S	X		X	X		X		X	X		S1	X	S		X	S			X	D.Elleray 27
X				X				X	X	X1	X		X	X		X		X	X	X2	S	X	S		X	S1		S1	X	J.Winter 28
X				X1			S	X	X	X	X		X	X		S		X	X			X			X	S1	X1		X	R.Dilkes 29
X				X				X	X	X	X		X	X		X		S	X		X1	X			X	S1	X1			P.Jones 30
X			X					X	X	S2	X	S1		X		X		X	X1	X		X			X	X2				A.Wilkie 31
X			X1	X	S3		X3	X	X	S1	X	S1		X		X		X	X			X			X	X1	X			P.Danson 32
X	S		X2	X1	S1	S2	X							X		X		X	X			X			X	X		X		P.Durkin 33
X	S3		X1	X1	X	X3		X	S1					X		X		X	X			X		S1	X					A.B.Wilkie 34
X		X		X	X	X		S						X		X		X	X	X1		X		S2	X			S1		R.Hart 35
S	X						S1	X	X2					X		X		X	X			X	S2	X1	X	X1			X	K.Cooper 36
S	X						S1	X	X					X		X		X	X			X	S2	X1	X	X1			X2	J.Winter 37
S	X						S1	X	X					X		X		X	X			S	S1	X	X				X	P.Durkin 38
S	X					S2		X	X1					X		X		X	X			X	S1	X	X				X	R.Dilkes 39
	X					S		S1					X		X		X1	X	X		X	X2	X	X		X		X	P.Durkin 40
	X				S	X1			X	X	X		X		X		X	X			X		X	X			X1	X	G.Willard 41
	X				S	X1				X	X				X		X	S1			X		X	X			X	X	G.Powler 42
	X				X2				S2	X1	S	X		X		X		X	X		S1	X		X			X	X	D.Gallagher 43
	X1				S1			X					X		X		X	S	X		X		X	X			X		S.Dunn 44
	S			X2	X1			X	X	X			X		X		X	S2			X	X	X	X	X	S1			G.Ashby 45
	S			S2				S1	X	X1	X		X		X		X	X			X		X	X			X	X	D.Gallagher 46
				S2				S1	X1	X			X		X		X	X	X	X	X2		X				S	X	R.Hart 47
		S1						X		X			X	X2	X1	X	X	X	X2			X	S1	X	S2				D.Elleray 48
		X		X2				S1		X			X	X1	X	X		X	X	X		X	S	S2	X				M.Bodenham 49
				X					X		X	X	X		X		X	X	X		S	X1	S	S					G.Winter 50
	X1			X				X		X		S1	X		X		X	X	X		S	X1	S1	S					R.Hart 51
				X				X		X	X	X	X		X		X	X	X1		S1	X	S			S		X	D.Gallagher 52
X	X							X2		X1	X2		X				X		S2		X		S1	X	S2			X	K.Cooper 53
X	X							X		X2	X4		X				X		S2	X			X	X1	S	S1		X	K.Burge 54
	X		S					S1		X1	X	X	X		X		X	X		S	X		X	X			X	X	M.Bodenham 55
	S							S1		X1			X	S	X		X	X		X	X		X	X	X			X	D.Ellery 56
10	8	2	1	17	2	8	30	17	12	12	2	12	34	2	28	5	36	35	16	10	29	5	12	34	3	1	12	22	PL Appearances
0	2	1	2	2	0	6	4	0	0	3	2	0	0	0	4	0	0	1	3	0	4	0	5	3	4	0			PL Sub Appearances
1	4+1	0	0	2+2	0	1+1	5+2	4	4	1+1	0+1	1	0	8	0	7	2	8	8	3	1+2	7	1	3+1	8	0	1	2+1	7	CC Appearances
1	4	0	0	1+1	0	0	3+3	3	5	0+2	0	1	5	0	5	1	6	6	1+1	3+1	4	0	3+1	5	0	0	3	6	FAC Appearances
0	2+2	0	1	0	0	0+2	2	3	2	0+1	0	4	0	4	4	4	4	0	4	0+1	0+1	4	3	1+1	0	4			UEFA Appearances

Also Played: (M) Harrigan S(9). (M) Jackson S2(48). (D) Maybury X2(35). (G) Pettinger S(7,8). (D) Sharpe S(10),S2(17),S1(18).

LEEDS UNITED

CLUB RECORDS

BIGGEST VICTORIES:
League: 8-0 v Leicester City, Division 1, 7.4.1934.
F.A. Cup: 8-1 v Crystal Palace, 3rd Round, 11.1.1930.
7-0 v Leeds Steelworks, Preliminary Round, 25.9.1920.
League Cup: 5-1 v Mansfield Town, 2nd Round, 26.9.1963.
4-0 v Chesterfield, 2nd Round, 23.11.1960.
4-0 v Burnley, 2nd Round, 6.9.1972.
4-0 v Colchester, 3rd Round, 26.11.1977.
4-0 v York City, 2nd Round, 6.10.1987.
Europe: 10-0 v Lyn Oslo, European Cup 1st Round 1st leg, 17.9.1969.

BIGGEST DEFEATS
League: 1-8 v Stoke City, Division 1, 27.8.1934.
F.A. Cup: 2-7 v Middlesbrough, 3rd Round 2nd leg, 4.9.1979.
League Cup: 0-7 v Arsenal, 2nd Round 2nd leg, 4.9.1979.
0-7 v West Ham United, 4th Round, 7.11.1966.
Europe: 0-4 v Lierse, 1st Round, 2nd leg UEFA, 29.9.1971.

MOST POINTS
3 points a win: 85, Division 2, 1989-90.
2 points a win: 67, Division 1, 1968-69.

MOST GOALS SCORED
98, Division 2, 1927-28.
Jennings 21, White 21, Keetley 18, Wainscoat 18, Mitchell 8, Turnbull 8, Armand 2, Hart 1, Townsley 1.

MOST GOALS CONCEDED
92, Division 1, 1959-60.

MOST FIRST CLASS MATCHES IN A SEASON
66- 1967-68 (League 42, FA Cup 5, League Cup 7, UEFA 12).

MOST LEAGUE WINS
27, Division 1, 1968-69, Division 1, 1970-71.

MOST LEAGUE DRAWS
21, Division 2, 1982-83.

MOST LEAGUE DEFEATS
30, Division 1, 1946-47.

INDIVIDUAL CLUB RECORDS

MOST GOALS IN A SEASON
John Charles: 43 goals in 1953-54 (League 42, FA Cup 1).

MOST GOALS IN A MATCH
5. Gordon Hodgson v Leicester City, 8-2, Division 1, 1.10.1938.

OLDEST PLAYER
Peter Lorimer, 38 years 317 days v Barnsley, 27.10.1985.

YOUNGEST PLAYER
Peter Lorimer, 15 years 289 days v Southampton, 29.9.1962.

MOST CAPPED PLAYER
Billy Bremner (Scotland) 54.

BEST PERFORMANCES

League: 1968-69: Matches played 42, Won 27, Drawn 13, Lost 2, Goals for 66, Goals against 27, Points 67, 1st in Division 1.
Highest Position: Division 1 Champions 1968-69, 1973-74, 1991-92.
F.A. Cup: 1971-72: 3rd Round Bristol Rovers 4-1; 4th Round Liverpool 0-0,2-0; 5th Round Cardiff City 2-0; 6th Round Tottenham Hotspur 2-1; Semi-Final Birmingham City 3-0; Final Arsenal 1-0.
League Cup: 1967-68: 2nd Round Luton 3-1; 3rd Round Bury 3-0; 4th Round Sunderland 2-0; 5th Round Stoke City 2-0; Semi-Final Derby County 1-0, 3-2; Final Arsenal 1-0.
Europe: UEFA Cup winners in 1967-68.
Most recent success: 1970-71: 1st Round Sarpsborg 1-0,5-0; 2nd Round Dynamo Dresden 1-0,1-2; 3rd Round Sparta Prague 6-0,3-2; 4th Round Vitoria Setubul 2-1,1-1; Semi-Final Liverpool 1-0,0-0; Final Juventus 2-2,1-1 (Leeds won on away goals).

ADDITIONAL INFORMATION
PREVIOUS NAMES
Leeds United were formed in October 1919 after Leeds City (formed 1904) had been suspended 'sine die' by the F.A. earlier that same month.

PREVIOUS LEAGUES
Leeds City: West Yorkshire League 1904-05 prior to becoming a Football League club.
Leeds United: Gained admission to the Midland League in November 1919 and the first team competed in this League prior to gaining Football League status in the summer of 1920.

DIVISIONAL RECORD

	Played	Won	Drawn	Lost	For	Against	Points
Division 1/P	1,756	719	449	588	2,659	2,407	2,000
Division 2	1,144	483	309	1,731	1,731	1,451	1,369
Total	**3,180**	**1,202**	**758**	**940**	**4,390**	**3,858**	**3,369**

Club colours: All white with blue & yellow trim.

Change colours: All yellow with blue & white trim.

Reserves League: Pontins Central League Division 1.

RECORDS AND STATISTICS

COMPETITIONS

Div 1/P	Div.2	Euro C	ECWC	UEFA
1924-27	1920-24	1969-70	1972-73	1965-66
1928-31	1927-28	1974-75		1966-67
1932-47	1931-32	1992-93		1967-68
1956-60	1947-56			1968-69
1964-82	1960-64			1970-71
1990-				1971-72
				1973-74
				1979-80
				1995-96

HONOURS

Div.1	Div.2	FA Cup	Lge Cup	UEFA	C/S'ld
1968-69	1923-24	1972	1967-68	1967-68	1969
1973-74	1963-64			1970-71	1974
1991-92	1989-90				1992

MOST GOALS IN A CAREER
Peter Lorimer - 238 (1962-79 & 1983-85)

Year	League	FA Cup	Lge Cup	Europe
1965-66	13	3		3
1966-67	9	2	2	1
1967-68	17	2	4	8
1968-69	8	1		3
1969-70	14	2		3
1970-71	12	2		5
1971-72	23	3	2	1
1972-73	15	3	3	2
1973-74	12	2		
1974-75	9		3	4
1975-76	10		1	
1976-77	3			
1977-78	6		3	
1983-84	4			
1984-85	9		1	
1985-86	4			
Total	168	20	19	30

(plus 1 in the Charity Shield 1985-86)

Current leading goalscorer - Rod Wallace - 43 (1991-96)

MOST APPEARANCES
Jack Charlton 772 (1952-73)

Year	League	FA Cup	Lge Cup	Europe
1952-53	1			
1953-54				
1954-55	1			
1955-56	34	1		
1956-57	21	1		
1957-58	40	1		
1958-59	39	1		
1959-60	41	1		
1960-61	41	1	4	
1961-62	34	2	3	
1962-63	38	3	1	
1963-64	25		2	
1964-65	39	8	2	
1965-66	40	2	1	11
1966-67	29	6	4	7
1967-68	34	4	5	11
1968-69	41	2	2	7
1969-70	32	9	2	7
1970-71	40	4	1	10
1971-72	41	5	4	
1972-73	18	1	4	2
	629	52	35	55

includes 1 Charity Shield appearance 1969-70.

RECORD TRANSFER FEE RECEIVED

Amount	Club	Player	Date
3,500,000	Everton	Gary Speed	6/96
2,700,000	Blackburn Rovers	David Batty	10/93
1,200,000	Manchester Utd	Eric Cantona	11/92
1,000,000	Norwich City	Jon Newsome	6/94

RECORD TRANSFER FEE PAID

Amount	Club	Player	Date
4,500,000	Parma	Tomas Brolin	12/95
£400000	Manchester United	Lee Sharpe	08/96
3,400,000	Eintrach Frankfurt	Tony Yeboah	1/95
2,700,000	Sheffield United	Brian Deane	7/93

MANAGERS

Name	Seasons	Best	Worst
Arthur Fairclough	1920-27	18(1)	14(2)
Dick Ray	1927-35	5(1)	2(2)
Billy Hampson	1935-47	9(1)	22(1)
Willis Edwards	1947-48	18(2)	18(2)
Frank Buckley	1948-53	5(2)	15(2)
Raich Carter	1953-58	8(1)	10(2)
Bill Lambton	1958-59	15(1)	15(1)
Jack Taylor	1959-61	21(1)	14(2)
Don Revie	1961-74	1(1)	19(2)
Brian Clough	1974		
Jimmy Armfield	1974-78	5(1)	10(1)
Jock Stein	1978		
Jimmy Adamson	1978-80	5(1)	11(1)
Allan Clarke	1980-82	9(1)	20(1)
Eddie Gray	1982-85	7(2)	10(2)
Billy Bremner	1985-88	4(2)	14(2)
Howard Wilkinson	1988-	1(1/P)	10(2)

LONGEST LEAGUE RUNS

undefeated matches:	34 (26.10.1968 - 26.8.1969)	of league matches w/out a win:	17 (1.2.1947 - 26.5.1947)
undefeated home matches:	39 (14.8.1968 - 28.2.1970)	of undefeated away matches:	17 (2.11.1968 - 26.8.1969)
without home win:	10 (6.2.1982 - 12.5.1982)	without an away win:	27 (29.4.1938 - 30.8.1947)
of league wins:	9 (26.9.1931 - 21.11.1931)	of home wins:	13 (23.11.1968 - 9.8.1969)
of league defeats:	6 (26.4.1947 - 26.5.1947)	of away wins:	8 (1.10.1963 - 21.12.1963)

LEEDS UNITED

PLAYERS NAME Honours	Ht	Wt	Birthdate	Birthplace Transfers	Contract Date	Clubs	League	L/Cup	FA Cup	Other	Lge	L/C	FAC	Oth
G O A L K E E P E R S														
Beeney Mark R	6.4	14.7	30/12/67	Tunbridge Wells	17/08/85	Gillingham	2	1						
E: S-P 1; GMVC'89				Free	31/01/87	Maidstone	50	3	11	6				
				Loan	22/03/90	Aldershot	7							
				£30000	28/03/91	Brighton & H.A.	68+1	6	7	6				
				£350000	20/04/93	Leeds United	33	3	4					
Martyn Anthony Nigel	6.2	13.10	11/08/66	St.Austell		St.Blazey								
E:3,B.6,u21.11. Div.3'90.				Free	06/08/87	Bristol Rovers	101	6	6	11				
FMC'91. Div.1'94.				£1000000	21/11/89	Crystal Palace	272	36	22	19				
						Leeds United								
D E F E N D E R S														
Beesley Paul	6.1	11.5	21/07/65	Liverpool		Marine								
				Free	22/09/84	Wigan Athletic	153+2	13	6	11	3			
				£175000	20/10/89	Leyton Orient	32		1	2	1			1
				£300000	10/07/90	Sheffield United	162+6	12+1	9+2	3	5		1	1
				£250000	02/08/95	Leeds United	8+2	4+1	4	2+2				
Bowman Robert A	6.1	11.12	06/08/75	Durham City	20/11/92	Leeds United	4+3	0+1		1				
Couzens Andrew J	5.10	11.11	04/06/75	Shipley	05/03/93	Leeds United	10+8	1+1		0+2		1		
FAYC'93														
Dorigo Anthony R	5.8	10.7	31/12/65	Australia	19/07/83	Aston Villa	106+5	14+1	7	2	1			
E: 15, B.7, u21.11; Div1'92;				£475000	03/07/87	Chelsea	146	14	4	16	11	1		
Div2'89; ZDC'90				£1300000	06/06/91	Leeds United	153	12+1	12	9	5			
Jobson Richard I	6.1	13.05	09/05/63	Holderness		Burton Albion								
E: B.2; Div2'91				£22000	05/11/82	Watford	26+2	2	0+1	5+1	4			
				£40000	07/02/85	Hull City	219+2	12	13	9	17		1	
				£460000	30/08/90	Oldham Athletic	187+1	15	13	3	10	1		
				£1000000	26/10/95	Leeds United	12		1		1			
Kelly Garry	5.9	10.0	09/07/74	Drogheda		Home Farm								
Ei: 7, u21.4, Y					24/09/91	Leeds United	118+2	12+1	12	12				
Maybury Alan					17/08/95	Leeds United	1							
Pemberton John M	5.11	11.9	18/11/64	Oldham		Chadderton								
				Free	26/09/84	Rochdale	1							
				Free	29/03/85	Crewe Alexandra	116+5	7	3	7	1	1		
				£80000	24/03/88	Crystal Palace	76+2	6+1	8	12	2			
				£300000	27/07/90	Sheffield United	67+1	4	4	1				
				£250000	12/11/93	Leeds United	44+9	3+1	5+1	4				
Radebe Lucas	6.0	11.8	12/04/69	Johannesberg		Kaizer Chiefs								
				£250000	05/09/94	Leeds United	19+6	1+3	4+2					
Wetherall David	6.2	13.8	14/03/71	Sheffield	01/07/89	Sheffield Wed.								
E: S; Su19.3				£125000	15/07/91	Leeds United	116+2	13	13+2	4	9		3	
M I D F I E L D														
Blunt Jason	5.8	10.10	16/08/77	Penzance	01/08/94	Leeds United	2+1							
Bowyer Lee	5.9	9.11	03/01/77	London	13/04/94	Charlton Athletic	46	6+1	3	2	8	5	1	
E: Y				£2600000	04/07/96	Leeds United								
Evans Paul A						Witts University								
				£50000	29/12/95	Leeds United								
				Loan	18/03/96	Crystal Palace	1							
Ford Mark	5.7	9.3	10/10/75	Pontefract	05/03/93	Leeds United	12+1	4	5	0+1				
E: Y.5; FAYC'93														
Foster Martin	5.5	9.10	29/10/77	Sheffield	01/08/94	Leeds United								
Palmer Carlton L	6.2	11.10	05/12/65	Rowley Regis	21/12/84	W.B.A.	114+7	7+1	4	6	4	1		
E: 18, B.5, u21.4				£750000	23/02/89	Sheffield Wed.	204+1	31	18	8+1	14	3		1
				£2600000	30/06/94	Leeds United	74	10	9	4	5		1	1
Tinkler Mark	6.0	11.4	24/10/74	Bishop Auckland	29/11/91	Leeds United	13+9	1		0+1				
E: S, Y.7; UEFA Yth'93;														
FAYC'93														
F O R W A R D S														
Deane Brian C	6.3	12.7	07/02/88	Leeds	14/12/85	Doncaster Rovers	59+7	3	2+1	2+2	12		1	
E: 3, B.3				£30000	19/07/88	Sheffield United	197	16	23+1	2	83	11	11	2
				£2900000	14/07/93	Leeds United	104+6	8+3	9+3	3	27	2	3	

Name	Ht	Wt	DOB	Birthplace	Fee	Date	Previous Club								
ray Andy						01/07/95	Leeds United	12+3	1+1	0+2					
ewell Harry						23/12/95	Leeds United	2							
ush Ian	6.0	12.6	20/10/61	St Asaph		25/09/79	Chester City	33+1		5		14		3	
W: 68 (24 Gls Record Scorer), u21.2, S;					£300000	01/05/80	Liverpool	182	38	22	31+1	109	21	20	17
iv1'82'83'84'86'90;					Loan	01/07/86	Liverpool	42	9	3	3	30	4		6
					£3200000	01/07/86	Juventus	29				7			
					£2800000	23/08/88	Liverpool	223+22	30	30+6	16+1	90	23	19	7
					Free	24/05/96	Leeds United								
harpe Lee S	5.11	11.4	27/05/71	Halesowen		31/05/88	Torquay United	9+5			2+3	3			
8, B1, u21.8; ECWC'91; LC'92					£185000	10/06/88	Manchester United	160+32	15+8	22+7	18+2	21	9	3	3
					£4000000	10/08/96	Leeds United								
allace Rodney S	5.7	10.1	02/10/69	Greenwich		19/04/88	Southampton	11+17	18+1	10	3+1	44	6	3	2
B.2, u21.11; Div1'92					£1600000	07/06/91	Leeds United	141+17	11+1	8+5	1+4	40	3	1	1
eboah Anthony	5.10	13.11	06/06/66	Ghana			Saarsruken								
							Eintracht Frankfurt								
					£3400000	05/01/95	Leeds United	38+2	7	6+2	4	25	3	2	3

ADDITIONAL CONTRACT PLAYERS

Name				Date	Club			
oyle Wesley				26/04/96	Leeds United			
yrne Nicky				13/10/95	Leeds United (T)			
arte Ian P				15/12/95	Leeds United (T)	2+2	0+1	
ackson Mark G				01/07/95	Leeds United (T)	0+1		
atthews Lee J				15/02/96	Leeds United (T)			
hepherd Paul				15/09/95	Leeds United (T)			
right Andrew				26/10/95	Leeds United (T)			

THE MANAGER
HOWARD WILKINSON

Date of Birth . . . . 13th November 1943.
Place of Birth . . . . Sheffield.
Date of Appointment . . . . October 1988.

PREVIOUS CLUBS
As Manager . . . . Boston United (Player/Manager), England Semi-Pro,
. . . . Notts County, Sheffield Wednesday.
As Assistant . . . . Notts County, England Under-21 Team.
As a Player . . . . Sheffield Wednesday, Brighton & H.A. Boston United.

HONOURS
As a Manager
Notts County: Promotion to Division 1, 1981. Sheffield Wednesday: Division 2 Runners-up, 1984.
Leeds United: Division 2 Champions 1989-90. Division 1 Champions 1991-92.
As a Player
International: England youth.

ELLAND ROAD

Leeds, West Yorkshire LS11 0ES
Tel: 01532 716 037

Capacity 38,950

First game..1920.
First floodlit game..v Hibernian, 9.11.1953.

ATTENDANCES
Highest..57,892 v Sunderland FA Cup 5th Round replay, 15.3.1967.
Lowest ....2,274 v Sheffield United, AMC, 16.10.1985.

OTHER GROUNDS..None.

MATCHDAY TICKET PRICES

Categories	A+	A	B	C
West Stand				
Upper Tier & Paddock....	£25	£22	£21	£20
Stand B	£19	£16	£15	£14
Revie Stand..........	£19	£16	£15	£14
East Stand				
Upper Tier	£23	£20	£19	£18
Family Stand	£21	£18	£17	£16
South Stand				
Upper & Lower Tiers.....	£19	£16	£15	£14
North East &				
North West Stands	£21	£18	£17	£16

Concessions available - contact club.
Ticket Office Telephone no........ 01532 710 710

CLUBCALL
0891 12 11 80

Calls cost 39p per minute cheap rate and 49p per
minute at all other times.
Call costings correct at time of going to press.

HOW TO GET TO THE GROUND

From the North
Use A58 or A61 into Leeds City Centre, then follow signs to motorway (M621) to
join motorway. In 1.6 miles leave motorway and at roundabout join A643 into
Elland Road for Leeds United FC.

From the East
Use A63 or A64 into Leeds city centre, then follow signs to motorway (M621) to
join motorway. Then as above.

From the South
Use motorway (M1) then M621 until junction with A643, leave motorway and at
roundabout join A643 into Elland Road for Leeds United FC.

From the West
Use motorway (M62) then M621 until junction with A643. Leave motorway and a
roundabout join A643 into Elland Road for Leeds United FC.

Car Parking
Wesley Street Corner has park for 1,000 cars (approx), one minute walk from
ground.

Nearest Railway Station
Leeds City (01532 448 133)

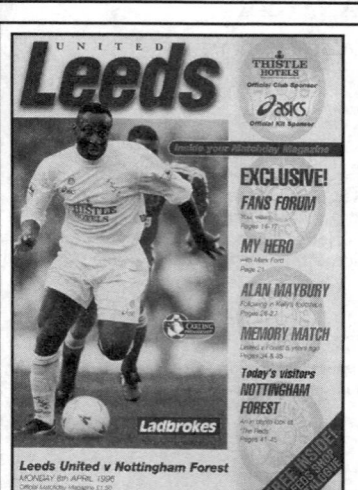

MATCHDAY PROGRAMME

Programme Editor .... Mike Beddow & John Curtis.

Number of pages .... 40.

Price .... £1.70.

Subscriptions .... £60 UK.

Local Newspapers......... Yorkshire Post, Yorkshire Evening Post,
.... Bradford Telegraph & Argus.

Local Radio Stations .... BBC Radio Leeds, Radio Aire (Leeds),
.... Pulse Radio (Bradford).

LEICESTER CITY
(The Foxes)
F.A. CARLING PREMIERSHIP
SPONSORED BY: WALKERS CRISPS

ck Row (L-R): Jamie Lawrence, Lee Philpott, Garry Parker, Simon Grayson, Colin Hill, Mark Blake, Phil Gee, Craig Hallam.
ddle Row: Mark McGhee (Manager), Colin Lee (Asst. Manager), Richard Smith, Jimmy Willis, Iwan Roberts, Kevin Poole, Steve Walsh, an Carey, Mike Whitlow, Mike Hickman (1st Team Coach), Alan Smith (Physio). **Front Row:** Taff Davies (Kit Manager), Julian Joachim, n McMahon, Neil Lewis, David Lowe, Scott Taylor, Mark Robins, Paul Bedder, Mick Yoeman (Physio).

LEICESTER CITY
FORMED IN 1884
TURNED PROFESSIONAL IN 1888
LTD COMPANY IN 1897

PRESIDENT: K R Brigstock
CHAIRMAN: Tom Smeaton
CHEIF EXECUTIVE: Barrie Pierpoint
DIRECTORS
M F George, J M Elsom FCA, R W Parker,
E Sharp, T W Shipman, W K Shooter FCA
FOOTBALL SECRETARY
Ian Silvester
HEAD OF PUBLICITY
Paul Mace

MANAGER: Martin O'Neill
COACHS: Paul Franklin & Steve Walford

YOUTH DEVELOPMENT & MANAGER
David Nish

PHYSIOTHERAPISTS
Alan Smith & Mick Yoeman

STATISTICIAN FOR THE DIRECTORY
Dave Smith

The one thing that has to be said about Leicester City supporters is that their lives are never dull. This roller-coaster of a season swung from triumph to disaster and back again, with as many twists as an Agatha Christie plot, and certainly as many heroes and villains as you could wish for.

Back in August, City started in stylish mode, racing to the head of the table with a pleasing passing style which was at times over-elaborate, but was producing results for Mark McGhee. A pinnacle of sorts came in early November with a stunning first-half display at the Hawthorns, but after the break previously unseen cracks began to appear. Giant goalkeeper Zeljko Kalac was thrust into the spotlight and suffered a nightmare second half and an even bigger midweek disaster in the League Cup. Trial by television consigned him back into the reserves and restored the consistent Kevin Poole to the starting line-up. Classy Swedish international Pontus Kamark made a huge impact but disappeared with knee ligament trouble after less than two games. Suddenly City's early season confidence had disappeared and, within weeks, so too had McGhee.

Lack of ambition at Filbert Street and the lure of the sleeping giant were quoted as McGhee's reasons for defection to Molineux, but the whole affair left an even more bitter taste with the Foxes fans than had Brian Little's switch to Villa Park exactly a year earlier.

Mike Walker looked set to be named as the new manager until Martin O'Neill's sudden resignation from Norwich. Days later, the former Wycombe boss was installed at Filbert Street, but his attempts to add a cutting edge to City's style were not immediately appreciated. The team sank almost to mid-table before O'Neill's new signings began to click and a late surge led to the play-offs once again.

Poole's Banksesque save in the opening moments of the semi-final against Stoke eventually proved decisive, as did the recall of Garry Parker - previously stripped of the captaincy following a public row with the new boss. Parker deservedly collected the Wembley Man of the Match trophy, though Neil Lennon ran him mighty close, as Leicester produced a wonderful display of relentless pressure to finally wear down Crystal Palace between the Twin Towers. The winning goal was gleefully miss-hit into the top corner in the dying seconds of extra time by Steve Claridge, who himself might not have finished the season if he had listened to his doctor's advice concerning a thyroid problem. And all this just after O'Neill had replaced Poole with the giant Kalac specifically to face a penalty shoot-out.

Come to think of it, if Agatha Christie had written this, everyone would have claimed it was too far-fetched for a real football story!

DAVE SMITH

LEICESTER CITY

League: 5th   **FA Cup: 3rd Rnd**   **Coca-Cola Cup: 3rd Rnd**

M	DATE	COMP	VEN	OPPONENTS	RESULT	HT	LP	GOAL SCORERS/GOAL TIMES	ATT
1	A 12	EL	A	Sunderland	W 2-1	1-1	9	Corica 9, Robins 69	(18593
2	19	EL	H	Stoke City	L 2-3	0-3	13	Walsh 71, Parker 74(pen)	17719
3	26	EL	A	Luton Town	D 1-1	0-1	12	Parker 64	(7612
4	30	EL	H	Portsmouth	W 4-2	4-1	4	Roberts 14, 37, 43, Parker 44	15170
5	S 2	EL	H	Wolverhampton Wand	W 1-0	1-0	3	Whitlow 26	18441
6	10	EL	A	Derby County	W 1-0	1-0	2	Joachim 32	(11767
7	12	EL	A	Port Vale	W 2-0	1-0	1	McMahon 44, Roberts 80	(8814
8	16	EL	H	Reading	D 1-1	0-1	1	Roberts 80	19103
9	20	CC 2/1	H	**Burnley**	**W 2-0**	**1-0**		**Robins 26, Joachim 55**	11142
10	23	EL	H	Southend United	L 1-3	1-2	2	Lowe 11	15278
11	30	EL	A	Norwich City	W 1-0	0-0	1	Heskey 87	(18435
12	O 3	CC 2/2	A	**Burnley**	**W 2-0**	**0-0**		**Robins 79, 85**	(4605
13	7	EL	A	Barnsley	D 2-2	1-1	2	Robins 11, Walsh 83	(13669
14	14	EL	H	Charlton Athletic	D 1-1	1-0	1	Lowe 26	16771
15	21	EL	A	Sheffield United	W 3-1	1-1	1	Roberts 5, Taylor 70, Lowe 79	(13100
16	24	CC 3	A	**Bolton Wanderers**	**D 0-0**	**0-0**			(9166
17	28	EL	H	Crystal Palace	L 2-3	0-2	2	Robins 76, Taylor 79	18376
18	N 5	EL	A	West Bromwich Albion	W 3-2	3-0	2	Taylor 14, Roberts 30, Taylor 44	16071
19	8	CC 3R	H	**Bolton Wanderers**	**L 2-3**	**0-1**		**Robins 50, 65**	14884
20	11	EL	H	Watford	W 1-0	1-0	2	Roberts 14	16230
21	19	EL	H	Tranmere Rovers	L 0-1	0-0	2		13128
22	21	EL	A	Huddersfield Town	L 1-3	1-1	2	Robins 45	(14300
23	26	EL	A	Birmingham City	D 2-2	2-1	4	Roberts 9, Grayson 15	(17350
24	D 2	EL	H	Barnsley	D 2-2	1-2	2	Roberts 14, Grayson 89	15128
25	9	EL	A	Southend United	L 1-2	1-1	2	Roberts 38	(5835
26	17	EL	H	Norwich City	W 3-2	1-2	4	Whitlow 36, Roberts 67, Heskey 79	14251
27	23	EL	A	Grimsby Town	D 2-2	0-1	4	Roberts 73, Walsh 90	(7713
28	J 1	EL	A	Millwall	D 1-1	1-0	3	Corica 45	(9953
29	6	FAC 3	H	**Manchester City**	**D 0-0**	**0-0**			20640
30	13	EL	A	Stoke City	L 0-1	0-1	5		(13669
31	17	FAC 3R	A	**Manchester City**	**L 0-5**	**0-2**			(19980
32	21	EL	H	Sunderland	D 0-0	0-0	5		16130
33	F 3	EL	H	Luton Town	D 1-1	0-0	7	Roberts 60	14821
34	10	EL	A	Portsmouth	L 1-2	1-1	10	Roberts 28	(9003
35	17	EL	H	Port Vale	D 1-1	1-0	8	Taylor 14	13758
36	21	EL	A	Wolverhampton Wand	W 3-2	1-2	6	Roberts 38, Heskey 60, 80	(27381
37	24	EL	A	Reading	D 1-1	0-0	6	Lewis 73	(9817
38	28	EL	H	Derby County	D 0-0	0-0	7		20911
39	M 3	EL	A	Ipswich Town	L 2-4	0-3	8	Roberts 55, Roberts 74	(9817
40	9	EL	H	Grimsby Town	W 2-1	1-0	7	Heskey 44, 86	13784
41	13	EL	H	Ipswich Town	L 0-2	0-2	8		17783
42	16	EL	A	Oldham Athletic	L 1-3	0-1	8	Whitlow 70	(5582
43	23	EL	H	Millwall	W 2-1	1-1	8	Carey 1, Taylor 57	12543
44	30	EL	H	Sheffield United	L 0-2	0-0	9		15230
45	A 2	EL	A	Charlton Athletic	W 1-0	1-0	7	Claridge 30	(11287
46	6	EL	A	Crystal Palace	W 1-0	1-0	7	Roberts 27	(17331
47	9	EL	H	West Bromwich Albion	L 1-2	0-1	8	Robins 56	17889
48	13	EL	A	Tranmere Rovers	D 1-1	1-0	8	Robins 16	(8882
49	17	EL	H	Oldham Athletic	W 2-0	0-0	7	Claridge 58, 78	12790
50	20	EL	H	Huddersfield Town	W 2-1	1-0	6	Walsh 40, Claridge 69	17619
51	27	EL	H	Birmingham City	W 3-0	2-0	6	Claridge 32, Heskey 39, Lennon 89	19702
52	M 5	EL	A	Watford	W 1-0	0-0	5	Izzet 59	(20089
53	12	PO SF1	H	**Stoke City**	**D 0-0**	**0-0**			20325
54	15	PO SF2	A	**Stoke City**	**W 1-0**	**0-0**		**Parker 46**	(21037
55	27	PO F	N	**Crystal Palace**	**W 2-1**	**0-1**		**Parker 76(pen), Claridge 120**	(73573

Best Home League Attendance: 20911 v Derby County   **Smallest: 12543 v Millwall**   **Average: 16197**

Goal Scorers:

EL(66):   Roberts(19),Heskey(7),Robins(6),Taylor(6),Claridge(5),Walsh(4),Whitlow(3),Parker(3),Lowe(3),Grayson(2),Corica(2),Joachim(1),Izzet(1),Carey(1),McMahon(1), Lennon(1),Lewis(1)

CC(6):   Robins(4),Roberts(1),Joachim(1)

FAC(0):

PO(3):   Parker(2),Claridge(1)

(D) Blake	(D) Carey	(F) Claridge	(F) Corica	(F) Gee	(M) Grayson	(F) Heskey	(D) Hill	(M) Izzet	(F) Joachim	(M) Kaamark	(G) Kalac	(F) Lawrence	(D) Lennon	(F) Lewis	(F) Lowe	(M) McMahon	(M) Parker	(M) Philpott	(G) Poole	(F) Roberts	(F) Robins	(M) Rolling	(D) Smith	(M) Taylor	(D) Walsh	(D) Watts	(M) Whitlow	(D) Willis		#
		X		X		S3	X					X1					X	S1	X	S2	X2			X	X		X	X3	W.C.Burns	1
		X		X2		S2	X					X1	S1				X		X	S2	X			X	X		X	X2	R.Gifford	2
S		X					X		X					S	S1		X		X	X	X1			X	X		X	X	M.Bailey	3
S1		X					X		X					S	S		X		X	X	S			X	X		X	X	G.Cain	4
S1		X		X					X2					S2			X		X	X	S			X	X		X	X1	J.Lloyd	5
		X	S2	S1		X1			X2								X2		X	X	S2			X	X		X	X	T.West	6
		X1		X					X								X	S1	X	X	S			X	X		X	X	G.Pooley	7
			X1	X		S			X2								X	S1	X	X	S2			X	X		X	X	U.Rennie	8
				X	S3	S1			X								X3	S1	X	X	X			X1	X1		X	X	P.Rejer	9
				X	S2	S3			X2								X3	S1	X	X	S1			X	X		X	X	E.Lomas	10
				X	S1	X			X								X	S	X	X	X1	X		X	X		X		N.Barry	11
X				X	X3	X			X2							S2	X		X	X	S3	X1			X		X	S1	M.Riley	12
X	S1			X	S1	X			X1			X1				S	X		X	X	X				X		X		D.B.Allison	13
X1	S3			X	S2	X						S1					X		X	X	X2			X3	X		X		I.Cruikshank	14
X	S			X		X											X		X	X	S	X		X	X		X		J.Rushton	15
X	X			X		X						S					X		X	X	S	X		X			X		A.Wilkie	16
X1	X1			X		X						S					X	S1	X	X	S1	X		X			X		K.Lynch	17
S1	X					X		X	X	X	S					X1	X		X	X	X			X			X		K.Gifford	18
	X2			S1		X		S2	X1	X						X	X		X	X	X			X			X		D.Elleray	19
	X		S	X1		X			S1							X	X	S2	X	X	X			X			X		E.Lomas	20
S	X			X1		X			S1			S2				X	X	X2	X	X	S						X		M.Bailey	21
	X			S1	S2	X			X1							X	X	X	X	X1	X	S		X2			X		B.Burns	22
	X			X	S1	X			X1							X	X	X	X2	X		S		X			X		D.Allison	23
	X	X		X	S1	X			S2							X1	X		X	X	X2			S	X		X		E.Wolstenholme	24
X1	X	X		X	S	X			S1							X2	X		X	X	S2			X			X		G.Pooley	25
	X			S1		X			S2								X		X	X	X2	X1	S	X	X		X		T.Heilbron	26
X1	X	X3			X1	X2			S1							S3	X		X	X	X			X	X		X		U.Rennie	27
		X2		X	X1	X			S1							S2	X		X	X	X			X	X		X		N.S.Barry	28
	X			X1	X		X		X			S					X	X	X	X	X	S	X	X			X		R.Gifford	29
	X			X	X		X		S2							S1	X	S3	X	X	X3		X1	X2	X		X		J.Kirkby	30
	X			X	X		X		X1			S					X	X2	X	X	S1	S2			X		X		R.Gifford	31
	X			X	S1	X			X1			S					X	X	X	X	X1	X			X		X		J.Rushton	32
X2				X	X	X			S							X1	X	S1	X	X	S2	X			X		X		G.Barber	33
S2				X		X			X2			X1					X	S1	X	X	X2	X			X		X		A.D'Urso	34
S				X	X				X			X2	S1				X		X	X	S2			X1			X		K.Lynch	35
S		X		X	X	X1			X			X	X	S			X		X	X	S			X			X	S1	T.West	36
X		X		X	X2				X			X1	X1	X			X		X	X	S			X			X		R.Poulain	37
X		X		X	X				S	X	X						X		X	X	X			X			X	S	G.Singh	38
X	X			X	S2							S1	X	X2			X		X	X				X1			X		S.Bennett	39
S	X			X	X				X	X	X						X		X	X	S2	X2		X			X	X	W.Burns	40
S		X		X	X				X	X1	S1						X		X	X				X			X	X	K.Leach	41
	X			X	X				X	X1	S3						X	S1	X		X1	X3		X			X	S1	T.Heilbron	42
X	X			X	X				S1	X							X		X	X1	S			X1	X		X		P.Richards	43
S	X	X1		X	X		S1		X			S1					X		X	X				X1	X	X	X		K.Breen	44
	S	X		X	X		X		X			S1	X				X		X	S				X1	X	X	X		D.Orr	45
	S	X		X	X		X1		X			S1	X				X		X	S				X1	X	X	X		K.Lynch	46
	S	X		X	X		X		X						S		X	X1	X	S1				X	X	X	X		I.Cruikshanks	47
	S	X		X	X	S	X		X						S		X		X	X				X	X	X	X		R.Harris	48
	S	X	X	X	X	X			X			S			S1		X		X	X1				X	X	X	X		J.Brandwood	49
	S	X	X	X	X	S	X		X						S1		X		X	X1				X	X	X	X		C.Wilkes	50
	S	X	X	X	X	X	S		X						S1		X		X	X1				X	X	X	X		J.Rushton	51
	S	X	X	X	X	S	X		X						S1		X		X	X1				X	X	X	X		J.Kirkby	52
	S	X	X	X	X	S	X		X						S1		X		X	X1				X	X	X	X		W.Burns	53
		X		X	X	S	X		X		S						X		X	S				X	X	X	X		J.Singh	54
		X		X	X	S2	X		S3			X					X	X3		S1				X1	X2	X	X		D.Allison	55
6	16	14	16	1	39	20	24	8	14	1	1	10	14	10	21	1	36	1	45	34	19	17	1	39	37	9	41	11	EL Appearances	
2	3	0	0	1	2	10	3	1	8	0	0	5	1	4	7	2	4	5	0	3	12	0	0	0	0	0	1	1	EL Sub Appearances	
2	2	0	0	0	3+1	1+1	3+1	0	2+1	1	1	0	0	0	0+1	0	4	0+1	4	0	3	2+1	3	0	3	2	0	4	1+1	CC Appearances	
0	0	0	2	0	2	0	2	0	1+1	0	0	1	0	0	0	1	0	2	2	2	1+1	0+1	1	1	2	0	0		FAC Appearances	
0	0	3	0	0	3	3	0+1	3	0	0	0+1	0	3	0	0	0	2+1	0	3	0	1+1	0	0	3	3	3	3	0	PO Appearances	

LEICESTER CITY

BIGGEST VICTORIES
League: 10-0 v Portsmouth (h) Division 1, 20.10.1928.
F.A. Cup: 13-0 v Notts Olympic (h), 1st Qual. Round, 13.10.1894.
7-0 v Crook Town (h) 3rd Round, 9.1.1932.
League Cup: 8-1 v Coventry City (a) 5th Round, 1.12.1964.
Europe: 4-1 v Glenavon (a) 1st Round, 13.9.1961.

BIGGEST DEFEATS
League: 0-12 v Nottingham Forest (a) Division 1, 21.4.1909.
F.A. Cup: No more than 4 clear goals (7 instances).
League Cup: 1-7 v Sheffield Wednesday (a) 3rd Round,
27.10.1992.
Europe: 0-2 v Atletico Madrid (a) 2nd Round, 15.11.1961.

MOST POINTS
3 points a win: 77, Division 2, 1991-92.
2 points a win: 61, Division 2, 1956-57.

MOST GOALS SCORED
109, Division 2, 1956-57.

MOST GOALS CONCEDED
112, Division 1, 1957-58.

MOST FIRST CLASS MATCHES IN A SEASON
61 - 1991-92 (League 46, FA Cup 2, League Cup 4, Zenith Data 6,
Play-offs 3).

MOST LEAGUE WINS
25, Division 2, 1956-57.

MOST LEAGUE DRAWS
19, Division 1, 1975-76.

MOST LEAGUE DEFEATS
25, Division 1/Premiership, 1977-78, 1994-95.

MOST GOALS IN A SEASON
Arthur Rowley: 44 goals in 1956-57 (League 44, 5 pens).

MOST GOALS IN A MATCH
6. John Duncan v Port Vale, 7-0, Division 2, 25.12.1924.
6. Arthur Chandler v Portsmouth, 10-0, Division 1, 20.10.1928.

OLDEST PLAYER
Joe Calvert, 40 years 313 days, 13.12.1947.

YOUNGEST PLAYER
Dave Buchanan, 16 years 192 days, 1.1.1979.

MOST CAPPED PLAYER
John O'Neill (Northern Ireland) 39.

League: 1956-57: Matches played 42, Won 25, Drawn 11, Lost 6,
Goals for 109, Goals against 67, Points 61. First in Division 2.
Highest Position: 1928-29: 2nd in Division 1.
F.A. Cup: Runners-up in 1948-49, 1960-61, 1962-63, 1968-69.
Most recent success: 1968-69: 3rd Round Barnsley 1-1,2-1; 4th
Round Millwall 1-0; 5th Round Liverpool 0-0,1-0; 6th Round
Mansfield Town 1-0; Semi-Final West Bromwich Albion 1-0; Final
Manchester City 0-1.
League Cup: 1963-64: 2nd Round Aldershot 2-0; 3rd Round
Tranmere Rovers 2-1; 4th Round Gillingham 3-1; 5th Round Norwich
City 1-1,2-1; Semi-Final West Ham United 4-3,2-0; Final Stoke City
1-1,3-2.
Europe: (ECWC) 1961-62: 1st Round Glenavon 4-1,3-1; Atletico
Madrid 1-1,0-2.

ADDITIONAL INFORMATION
PREVIOUS NAMES
Leicester Fosse 1884-1919.

PREVIOUS LEAGUES
Midland League.

Club colours: Royal blue shirts, white shorts, royal blue socks.
Change colours: Jade & navy halved shirts, jade & navy halved
shorts, navy socks with jade tops.

Reserves League: Pontins Central League Division 2.

	Played	Won	Drawn	Lost	For	Against	Points
Division 1/P	1,634	525	421	688	2,487	2,871	1,526
Division 2/1	2,074	854	514	706	3,312	2,933	2,401
Total	**3,708**	**1,379**	**934**	**1,394**	**5,799**	**5,804**	**3,927**

RECORDS AND STATISTICS

COMPETITIONS

Div 1/P	Div.2/1	ECWC	Texaco	A/Scot
1908-09	1894-08	1961-62	1972-73	1975-76
1925-35	1909-25		1973-74	
1937-39	1935-37			**A/Italian**
1954-55	1939-54			1971-72
1957-69	1955-57			1992-93
1971-78	1969-71			1993-94
1980-81	1978-80			
1983-87	1981-83			
1994-95	1987-94			
	1995-			

HONOURS

Div.2	League Cup	C/Shield
1924-25	1963-64	1971
1936-37		
1953-54		
1956-57		
1970-71		
1979-80		

MOST APPEARANCES

GRAHAM CROSS 596+3

Year	League	FA Cup	Lge Cup	Europe
1960-61	1			
1961-62	6			2
1962-63	29	6	2	
1963-64	39	1	6	
1964-65	35	5	9	
1965-66	38	4	1	
1966-67	41	1	3	
1967-68	29	6	1	
1968-69	37	8	2	
1969-70	42	5	6	
1970-71	42	6	5	
1971-72	39	3	1	
1972-73	38	2	1	
1973-74	40	7	1	
1974-75	38+2	5	2	
1975-76	1+1			
	495+3	**59**	**40**	**2**

MOST GOALS IN A CAREER

ARTHUR CHANDLER - 273 (1923-34)

Year	League	FA Cup
1923-24	24	
1924-25	32	6
1925-26	26	
1926-27	28	1
1927-28	34	
1928-29	34	
1929-30	32	
1930-31	18	
1931-32	12	2
1932-33	4	
1933-34	6	5
1934-35	9	
Total	**259**	**14**

Current leading goalscorer: Steve Walsh - 52 (1986-96)

RECORD TRANSFER FEE RECEIVED

Amount	Club	Player	Date
£3,250,000	Aston Villa	Mark Draper	07/95
£1,500,000	Wolves	Steve Corica	02/96
£1,500,000	Aston Villa	Julian Joachim	02/96
£1,400,000	Wolves	Iwan Roberts	07/96

RECORD TRANSFER FEE PAID

Amount	Club	Player	Date
£1.25m+£0.5m	Notts County	Mark Draper	07/94+07/95
£1,200,000	Birmingham City	Steve Claridge	03/96
£1,000,000	Norwich City	Mark Robins	01/95
£800,000	Chelsea	Mustafa Izzet	07/96

MANAGERS

Name	Seasons	Best	Worst
Peter Hodge	1919-26	17(1)	14(2)
Willie Orr	1926-32	2(1)	19(1)
Peter Hodge	1932-34	17(1)	19(1)
Arthur Lochhead	1934-36	21(1)	6(2)
Frank Womack	1936-39	16(1)	1(2)
Tom Bromilow	1939-45		
Tom Mather	1945-46		
John Duncan	1946-49	9(2)	19(2)
Norman Bullock	1949-55	21(1)	15(2)
David Halliday	1955-58	18(1)	5(2)
Matt Gillies	1959-68	4(1)	14(1)
Frank O'Farrell	1968-71	21(1)	3(2)
Jimmy Bloomfield	1971-77	7(1)	18(1)
Frank McLintock	1977-78	22(1)	22(1)
Jock Wallace	1978-82	21(1)	17(2)
Gordon Milne	1982-86	15(1)	3(2)
Bryan Hamlton	1986-87	20(1)	13(2)
David Pleat	1987-91	13(2)	22(2)
Gordon Lee	1991	22(2)	22(2)
Brian Little	1991-94	4(2/1)	6(2/1)
Mark McGhee	1994-95	21(P)	21(P)
Martin O'Neill	1995-		

LONGEST LEAGUE RUNS

of undefeated matches:	19 (6.2.1971 - 18.8.1971)	of league matches w/out a win:	18 (12.4.1975 - 1.11.1975)
of undefeated home matches:	40 (12.2.1898 - 17.4.1900)	of undefeated away matches:	10 (27.2.1971 - 14.8.1971)
without home win:	9 (3.12.1994 - 1.4.1995)	without an away win:	23 (19.11.1988 - 4.11.1989)
of league wins:	7 (15.2.08-28.3.08, 24.1.25-17.3.25)	of home wins:	13 (3.9.1906 - 29.12.1906)
	(26.12.62-9.3.1963, 28.2.93-27.3.93)		
of league defeats: 7 (28.11.1931 - 16.1.1932, 28.8.1990 - 29.9.1990)		of away wins:	4 (13.3.1971 - 12.4.1971)

LEICESTER CITY

PLAYERS NAME Honours	Ht	Wt	Birthdate	Birthplace Transfers	Contract Date	Clubs	APPEARANCES League	L/Cup	FA Cup	Other	GOALS Lge	L/C	FAC	Oth
G O A L K E E P E R S														
Kalac Zeljko						Sydney United								
				£760000	13/10/95	Leicester City	1	1		0+1				
Poole Kevin	5.10	11.11	21/07/63	Bromsgrove	26/06/81	Aston Villa	28	2	1	1				
				Loan	08/11/84	Northampton Town	3							
					27/08/87	Middlesbrough	34	4	2	2				
				Loan	27/03/91	Hartlepool United	12							
				£40000	30/07/91	Leicester City	156	9	8	12				
D E F E N D E R S														
Hill Colin F NI: 6	5.11	11.11	12/11/63	Uxbridge	07/08/81	Arsenal	46	4	1		1			
				Free	01/03/86	Maritime (Portugal)								
				Free	30/10/87	Colchester United	64+5	2	7	3+1	2			
				£85000	01/08/89	Sheffield United	77+5	5	10+2	3	3			
				Loan	26/03/92	Leicester City	10			3				
				£220000	31/07/92	Leicester City	124+4	9+1	8	6+1		1		
Lennon Neil NI: 1, B1, u23.1, u21.2	5.9	11.06	25/06/71	Lurgan, N.I.	26/08/89	Manchester City	1							
				Free	09/08/90	Crewe Alexandra	142+5	8+1	16	15+1	15	1	1	
				£750000	23/02/96	Leicester City	14+1		3	1	1			
Walsh Steven FRT'85	6.2	11.10	03/11/64	Preston	11/09/82	Wigan Athletic	123+3	7	6	10+2	4			
				£100000	24/06/86	Leicester City	285+2	23	9	22	44	3		4
Watts Julian	6.3	12.1	17/03/71	Sheffield	10/07/90	Rotherham United	17+3	1	4	2	1			
				£80000	13/03/92	Sheffield Wed.	12+4	1		1	1			
				Loan	18/12/92	Shrewsbury Town	9			1				
					29/03/96	Leicester City	9			3				
Willis James A	6.2	12.4	12/07/68	Liverpool		Blackburn Rovers								
				Free	21/08/86	Halifax Town								
				Free	30/12/87	Stockport County	10							
				£12000	24/03/88	Darlington	90	5	5	6	6			1
				£100000	20/12/91	Leicester City	58+2	4+1	4	5+1	3			
				Loan	26/03/92	Bradford City	9			1				
M I D F I E L D														
Grayson Simon N	5.11	10.7	16/12/69	Ripon	13/06/88	Leeds United	2			1+1				
				£50000	13/03/92	Leicester City	139+13	9+2	15+1	5	2			
Hallam Craig D						Leicester City (T)								
Izzet Mustafa	5.10	10.3	31/10/74	Mile End		Chelsea								
				£650000	05/07/96	Leicester City	8+1			3	1			
Kaamark Pontus S						Gothenburg								
				£840000	02/11/95	Leicester City	1	1						
McMahon Sam K	5.7	11.5	09/02/76	Newark	10/07/94	Leicester City	1+3	0+1			1			
Parker Garry S E: B, u21.6, u19.3, Y1; LC'89'90'94; SC'89	5.8	11.0	07/09/65	Oxford	05/05/83	Luton Town	31+11	1+3	6+2		3	1		
				£72000	21/02/86	Hull City	82+2	5	4	2	8			
				£260000	24/03/88	Nottingham Forest	93+4	22+1	16	9	17	4	5	3
				£650000	29/11/91	Aston Villa	79+2	8	10		11	1		
				£550000	10/02/95	Leicester City	50+4	4	3	2+1	5			2
Rolling Frank						Ayr								
				£100000	01/06/95	Leicester City	17	3	0+1					
Taylor Scott D	5.10	10.0	28/11/70	Portsmouth	22/06/88	Reading	164+43	7+5	11+2	12+4	24	1	3	1
				£500000	12/07/95	Leicester City	39	3	1	3	6			
Whitlow Michael W	6.1	11.6	13/01/68	Northwich		Witton Albion								
				£10000	11/11/88	Leeds United	62+15	4+1	1+4	9	4			
				£250000	27/03/92	Leicester City	127+3	8	6	16	6	1		

F O R W A R D S

	Fee	Date	Club								
Claridge Steve 5.11 11.08 10/04/66	Portsmouth		Portsmouth								
Div.3'91. Div.2'95. AWS'95		30/11/84	Bournemouth	3+4			1	1			
	£10000	01/10/85	Weymouth								
	£14000	13/10/88	Aldershot	58+4	2+1	6	5	19		1	2
	£75000	08/02/90	Cambridge United	56+23	2+4	1	6+3	28	2		1
	£160000	17/07/92	Luton Town	15+1	2		2	2	3		1
	£195000	20/11/92	Cambridge United	53	4	4	3	18	3		
	£350000	07/01/94	Birmingham City	85+2	14+1	7	9+1	28	2		5
	£1200000	01/03/96	Leicester City	14			3	5			1
Harrington Justin D 5.9 10.09 18/09/75	Truro	01/07/94	Norwich City (T)								
	Free	22/07/96	Leicester City								
Heskey Emile 6.1 13.0 11/01/78	Leicester		Leicester City	21+10	1+1		3	7			
Lawrence James H 5.10 12.3 08/03/70	Balham		Cowes								
		15/10/93	Sunderland	2+2	0+1						
	£20000	17/03/94	Doncaster Rovers	16+9	2	1	3	3			
	£175000	06/01/95	Leicester City	19+13				1			
Lewis Neil A 5.7 10.9 28/06/74	Wolverhampton	09/07/92	Leicester City	36+9	2+1	1	2	1			
Robins Mark G 5.7 10.1 22/12/69	Ashton-u-Lyme	23/12/86	Manchester United	19+29	0+7	4+4	4+3	11	2	3	1
E: u21.6; FAC'90; ECWC'91. ESC'91	£800000	14/06/92	Norwich City	57+10	6+3		1+1	20	1		
	£1000000	16/01/95	Leicester City	35+13	4+1	1+1	1+1	11	4		

THE MANAGER
MARTIN O'NEILL

Date of Birth. . . . . 1st March 1952.
Place of Birth . . . . Kilrea, Northern Ireland.
Date of Appointment . . . . December 1995.

PREVIOUS CLUBS
As Manager . . . . . . Grantham, Shepshed Charterhouse, Wycombe Wanderers,
. . . . Norwich City.
As Coach. . . . . None.
As a Player . . . . . . Distillery, Nottingham Forest, Norwich City, Manchester City,
. . . . Norwich City, Notts County.

HONOURS
As a Manager
Wycombe: FA Trophy 1991, 1993. Bob Lord Trophy 1992. GMVC champions & promoted to the Football League 1993. Promotion to Division Two via the play-offs 1994.
Leicester City: Promotion to the Premiership via the play-offs 1996.

As a Player
Irish Cup 1971. Division 1 championship 1978. League Cup 1978, 1979. European Cup 1980. Promotion to Division 1 1977, 1982.   **Northern Ireland:** 64 full caps.

FILBERT STREET
Leicester LE2 7EL
Tel: 01162 555 000

Capacity 22,517

First game ....v Nottingham Forest 'A' (F) 7.11.1891.
First floodlit game...v Borussia Dortmund (F) 23.10.1957.

ATTENDANCES
Highest..47,298 v Spurs, FAC 5th Rnd, 18.2.1928.
Lowest ....3,440 v Huddersfield, Simod 1st Rnd, 10.11.1987. (Post WW1)

OTHER GROUNDS ....Fosse Road/Racecourse 1884-85. Victoria Park 1885-87.
....Belgrave Road 1887-88. Victoria Park 1888-89. Mill Lane 1889-91.
.... Aylestone Road 1891. Filbert Street 1891-

MATCHDAY TICKET PRICES

Carling Executive Tier................ £20. £10
Carling Centre (D-F) . Adult £18/£20. Juvenile £9/10
Carling Wing (A-C, G-J) .... £16/£18. £8/9
Carling Members (WM 1-4) £13
Carling Family (WF1 -4)............. £13. £6.50
North Family (X) £12. £6
South Upper (M-S) £15. £8
South Lower.......................... £12
East (V) £12. £6
Visitors
East (U) £15. £8
East (T) £12. £6
Ticket Office Telephone no........ 0116 291 5232

CLUBCALL
0891 12 11 85
Calls cost 39p per minute cheap rate and 49p per minute at all other times.
Call costings correct at time of going to press.

HOW TO GET TO THE GROUND

From the North
Use motorway (M1) until junction 22 or A46/A607 into Leicester city centre. Follow signs to Rugby into Almond Road, then at end turn right into Aylestone Road. Shortly turn left into Walnut Street, then turn left into Filbert Street for Leicester City FC.
From the East
Use A47 into Leicester city centre. Follow signs to Rugby into Almond Road, then at end turn right into Aylestone Road. Shortly turn left into Walnut Street, then turn left into Filbert Street for Leicester City FC.
From the South
Use M1 or M69 until junction 21, then A46 (sign posted Leicester). Under railway bridge and in 0.2 miles turn right into Upperton Road, then turn right into Filbert Street for Leicester City FC.
From the West
Use motorway M69 or A50 into Leicester City centre and follow signs to Rugby into Almond Road, then at end turn into Aylestone Road. Shortly turn left into Walnut Street, then left into Filbert Street for Leicester City FC.

Car Parking: Parking adjacent to stadium for season ticket holders only. Street parking is available and there is also a public car park five minutes walk from the ground.

Nearest Railway Station: Leicester (0116 248 1000)

MATCHDAY PROGRAMME
(Voted top programme of 1995/96)

Programme Editor . . . . Paul Mace.

Number of pages . . . . 48 (full colour).

Price . . . . £2.

Local Newspapers . . . . . . Leicester Mercury, Leicester Herald & Post,
. . . . Melton Times, Coalville Times.

Local Radio Stations . . . . Leicester Sound, BBC Radio Leicester.

LIVERPOOL
(The Reds or Pool)
F.A. CARLING PREMIERSHIP
SPONSORED BY: CARLSBERG

Back Row (L-R): Doug Livermore, Lee Jones, Rob Jones, John Scales, David James, Michael Stensgaard, Tony Warner, Mark Wright, Mark Walters, Domini Matteo, Sammy Lee.
Middle Row: Joe Corrigan, Ronnie Moran, Michael Thomas, Stig Bjornebye, Stan Collymore, Phil Babb, John Barnes, Jan Molby, Mark Leather.
Front Row: Mark Kennedy, Robbie Fowler, Steve Harkness, Neil Ruddock, Roy Evans, Ian Rush, Jamie Redknapp, Steve McManaman, Nigel Clough.

LIVERPOOL
FORMED IN 1892
TURNED PROFESSIONAL IN 1892
LTD COMPANY IN 1892

HON VICE-PRESIDENT
H E Roberts, W D Corkish FCA,

CHAIRMAN: D R Moores
DIRECTORS
J T Cross, N White, FSCA, T D Smith,
P B Robinson, T W Saunders, K E B Clayton
CHIEF EXECUTIVE/SECRETARY
P B Robinson (0151 263 2361)
COMMERCIAL MANAGER
M L Turner

MANAGER: Roy Evans
ASSISTANT MANAGER: Doug Livermore
RESERVE TEAM MANAGER
Sammy Lee
YOUTH TEAM MANAGER
H McAuley
PHYSIOTHERAPIST
Mark Leather
STATISTICIAN FOR THE DIRECTORY
Brian Pead (0181 302 6446)

Liverpool's season was one in which they finally reassured their fans, and the footballing public at large, that they were once again a force to be reckoned with. With Newcastle and Manchester United claiming all the headlines, Liverpool went quietly about the business of laying firm foundations and building slowly on each small success.

Promises of UEFA Cup victory, which spawned after the defeat of Spartak Vladikavkaz, evaporated at Anfield against Brondby. It was a huge disappointment, which was followed by 'black November'. From third in the league, Liverpool slipped to eighth. They were dispatched from the Coca-Cola Cup by Newcastle at Anfield, and they failed to win a single game throughout that disastrous month, earning just one point in a goalless draw at West Ham.

Slowly things began to change - particularly after the 2-0 demolition of Manchester United in which Robbie Fowler scored both goals. Fowler was again a revelation, but the price to be paid for the young man's success was the impending departure of the Liverpool legend, Ian Rush, who could no longer be guaranteed a first-team place, particularly since new-signing Stan Collymore was linking up well with Fowler. But Rush had his moment of glory against Rochdale, when he scored to become this century's leading marksman in the FA Cup.

Progress was made in both the league and the FA Cup - so much so that there was premature talk of a possible double. But points were dropped unnecessarily in the league, leaving the top two to fight it out. Inadvertently, the Reds probably helped arch-rivals Manchester United to the title with a magnificent 4-3 victory over Newcastle. Defeat at Coventry meant that Liverpool could concentrate on the FA Cup, and progress was made with some remarkable wins against Leeds and Aston Villa. bur victory in the final was to prove beyond them in a drab encounter in which they failed to do themselves justice.

It has, however, been a season of solid improvement from Liverpool. The goalkeeper has matured into a safe last line of defence, whilst the defensive system introduced by Roy Evans appears to have settled down. The midfield is strong and inventive, even if, at times, it lacks a major ball-winner in the mould of Souness or McMahon. And the strike force is amongst the most potent in the league. Whilst there can never be room for complacency, the Anfield academy has had a good season. From the youth team to the Reserves and on to the first team, there is strength in depth and a positive attitude, allied to a will to win. The league title is a distinct possibility now that Evans, Moran and others have finally laid to rest the ghost of Souness, which shuddered through Anfield and almost brought the dynasty to its knees. But it was fitting that in a season when the legendary Bob Paisley finally succumbed to Alzheimer's Disease, the dynasty was once again able to build upon his legacy - and that of Shankly - as their protege raised the club back where it belongs: among the very best teams in England. There is still much work to be done to raise it to the heady heights of European Cup Winners, but at least the foundations are back in place. **BRIAN PEAD**

LIVERPOOL

League: 3rd		FA Cup: Runners Up			Coca-Cola Cup: 4th Rnd			UEFA Cup: 2nd Rnd	

M	DATE	COMP	VEN	OPPONENTS	RESULT	HT	LP	GOAL SCORERS/GOAL TIMES	ATT.
1	A 19	PL	H	Sheffield Wednesday	W 1-0	0-0	8	Collymore 60	40535
2	21	PL	A	Leeds United	L 0-1	0-0	8		(35852)
3	26	PL	A	Tottenham Hotspur	W 3-1	2-0	6	Barnes 7, 42, Fowler 55	(31254)
4	30	PL	H	Queens Park Rangers	W 1-0	1-0	4	Ruddock 30	37548
5	S 9	PL	A	Wimbledon	L 0-1	0-1	7		(19530)
6	12	UEFA 1/1	A	Spartak Vladikavkaz	W 2-1	1-1		McManaman 33, Redknapp 52	(43000)
7	16	PL	H	Blackburn Rovers	W 3-0	3-0	4	Redknapp 12, Fowler 22, Collymore 29	39502
8	20	CC 2/1	H	Sunderland	W 2-0	1-0		McManaman 9, Thomas 73	25579
9	23	PL	A	Bolton Wanderers	W 5 -2	2-0	3	Fowler 12, 30, 47, 65 (4), Harkness 84	40104
10	26	UEFA 1/2	H	Spartak Vladikavkaz	D 0-0	0-0			35042
11	O 1	PL	A	Manchester United	D 2-2	1-1	4	Fowler 32, 53	(34934)
12	4	CC 2/2	A	Sunderland	W 1-0	1-0		Fowler 39	(20560)
13	14	PL	H	Coventry City	D 0-0	0-0	3		39079
14	17	UEFA 2/1	A	Brondby	D 0-0	0-0			(37648)
15	22	PL	A	Southampton	W 3-1	1-1	4	McManaman 23, 55, Redknapp 73	(15245)
16	25	CC 3	H	Manchester City	W 4-0	1-0		Scales 9, Fowler 74, Rush 79, Harkness 82	29394
17	28	PL	H	Manchester City	W 6-0	2-0	3	Rush 3, 64, Redknapp 6, Fowler 47,60, Ruddock 53	39267
18	31	UEFA 2/2	H	Brondby	L 0-1	0-0			35878
19	N 4	PL	A	Newcastle United	L 1-2	1-1	3	Rush 11	(36547)
20	18	PL	H	Everton	L 1-2	1-0	6	Fowler 88	40818
21	22	PL	A	West Ham United	D 0-0	0-0	6		(24324)
22	25	PL	A	Middlesbrough	L 1-2	0-1	7	Ruddock 63	(29390)
23	29	CC 4	H	Newcastle United	L 0-1	0-0			40077
24	D 2	PL	A	Southampton	D 1-1	0-0	8	Collymore 67	38007
25	9	PL	A	Bolton Wanderers	W 1-0	0-0	6	Collymore 61	(21042)
26	17	PL	H	Manchester United	W 2-0	1-0	5	Fowler 44, 87	40546
27	23	PL	H	Arsenal	W 3-1	1-1	3	Fowler 40, 59, 78 (3)	39806
28	30	PL	A	Chelsea	D 2-2	1-2	3	McManaman 34, 76	(31137)
29	J 1	PL	H	Nottingham Forest	W 4-2	2-2	3	Fowler 31, 40, Collymore 61, Cooper 87(og)	39206
30	6	FAC 3	H	Rochdale	W 7-0	3-0		Fowler 21,C'more 43,44,70,Valentine 48(og), Rush 62, M'Ateer 86	28126
31	13	PL	A	Sheffield Wednesday	D 1-1	0-1	4	Rush 87	(32747)
32	20	PL	H	Leeds United	W 5-0	1-0	2	Ruddock 25, 90, Fowler 60 (pen), 67, Collymore 88	40254
33	31	PL	A	Aston Villa	W 2-0	0-0	2	Collymore 62, Fowler 65	(39332)
34	F 3	PL	H	Tottenham Hotspur	D 0-0	0-0	3		40628
35	11	PL	A	Queens Park Rangers	W 2-1	2-0	3	Wright 15, Fowler 30	(18405)
36	18	FAC 4	A	Shrewsbury Town	W 4-0	1-0		Collymore 8, Walton 69(og), Fowler 75, McAteer 84	(7752)
37	24	PL	A	Blackburn Rovers	W 3-2	2-1	9	Collymore 11, 21, Thomas 71	(30895)
38	28	FAC 5	H	Charlton Athletic	W 2-1	1-0		Fowler 12, Collymore 58	36818
39	M 3	PL	H	Aston Villa	W 3-0	3-0	3	McManaman 1, Fowler 5, 8	39508
40	10	FAC QF	A	Leeds United	D 0-0	0-0			(34632)
41	13	PL	H	Wimbledon	D 2-2	1-0	3	McManaman 35, Collymore 68	34063
42	16	PL	A	Chelsea	W 2-0	0-0	3	Wright 52, Fowler 62	40820
43	20	FAC QFR	H	Leeds United	W 3-0	0-0		McManaman 57, 73, Fowler 81	30812
44	23	PL	A	Nottingham Forest	L 0-1	0-1	3		(29058)
45	31	FAC SF	A	Aston Villa	W 3-0	1-0		Fowler 16, 85, McAteer 90	(39072)
46	A 3	PL	H	Newcastle United	W 4-3	1-2	3	Fowler 2, 57, Collymore 68, 90	40702
47	6	PL	A	Coventry City	L 0-1	0-1			(23137)
48	8	PL	H	West Ham United	W 2-0	2-0	3	Collymore 22, Barnes 38	40326
49	16	PL	A	Everton	D 1-1	0-1	3	Fowler 87	(40120)
50	27	PL	H	Middlesbrough	W 1-0	0-0	3	Collymore 70	40782
51	M 1	PL	A	Arsenal	D 0-0	0-0	3		(38323)
52	5	PL	A	Manchester City	D 2-2	2-0	3	Lomas 6(og), Rush 41	(31436)
53	11	FAC F	N	Manchester United	L 0-1	0-0			79007

Best Home League Attendance: 40820 v Chelsea	Smallest: 34063 v Wimbledon	Average: 39552

Goal Scorers:

PL(70): Fowler(28),Collymore(14),McManaman(6),Rush(5),Ruddock(5),Redknapp(3),Barnes(3),Opponent(s)(2),Wright(2),Thomas(1),Harkness(1)
CC(7): Fowler(2),Harkness(1),McManaman(1),Rush(1),Scales(1),Thomas(1)
FAC(19): Fowler(6),Collymore(5),McAteer(3),McManaman(2),Opponent(s)(2),Rush(1)
UEFA(2): Redknapp(1),McManaman(1)

1995-96

(D) Babb	(F) Barnes	(D) Bjorneby	(F) Clough	(F) Collymore	(F) Fowler	(D) Harkness	(G) James	(D) Jones	(F) Kennedy	(D) Matteo	(M) McAteer	(F) McManaman	(G) Pears	(M) Redknapp	(D) Ruddock	(F) Rush	(D) Scales	(M) Thomas	(G) Warner	(D) Wright	(M) Charnock		Referee	#
X	X			X2	S1	X	X	X		X		X		X		X1		S2	S	X			P.Durkin	1
X	X			X1	S1	X	X	X		X2		X		X		X		S2		X			D.Ellery	2
X	X				X	X	X	X			S	X1		X	X	X		S1	S	X			K.Cooper	3
X	X				X	X	X	X	S			X		X	X	X		S	S	X			S.Dunn	4
X	X				X	X1	X	X		S		X		X	X			S1	S	X			K.Burde	5
X	X		S	X1	S1	X	X	X	S	S		X		X	X			X		X			R.Havel	6
X	X1			X	X	X	X	X			S1	X		X1	X			S1	S	X			G.Willard	7
X				X1	X	X	X	X				X		X	X	S		S1	S	X			P.Jones	8
X	X			X	X	X	X	X			S	X		X	X	S			S	X			M.Bodenham	9
X	X		S		X1	X	X	X	S			X		X	X	S1	S	X		X			J.Ulrich	10
X				S	X	X	X	X		S		X		X	X	X	X	X	S				D.Elleray	11
X	X			S1	X1	X	X	X				S1		X	X	X1	X		S				R.Dilkes	12
X	X			X1	X	X	X	X2				S2		X	X	S1			S	X			P.Danson	13
X	X			S	X1	X	X	X	S	S		X		X	S	X	S1	S	X				G.Vilenberg	14
X	X			S	X1	X	X					X		X	S	X	X			X			D.Gallagher	15
X	X			S1	X1	X	X					X		X1	S1	X	X		S				S.Lodge	16
X	X1				X	X	X		S2			X		X	X	X			S	X			A.Wilkie	17
X	X			S2	X	X1	X	X2	S1			X		X	S	X	X	S		X			K.Ihring	18
X	X			S1	X	X	X	X			S	X		X	X	X1	X		S	X			M.Reed	19
X1	X				X	X2	X	X				X		X	X	S2	X	S1	S	X			G.Ashby	20
X	X			X	X	X	X	X	S			X		X				S	S	X			J.Winter	21
X	X			X	X	X	X	X1	S			X		X				S1	S	X			D.Gallagher	22
X	X		S	X	X	X	X	X	S1			X		X		X1			S	X			P.Durkin	23
X	X		S1	X	X	X	X	X1	X	S		X		X				X		S			R.Hart	24
	X	X	X	X	X	X	X	X				S		X				X	S	X	S		M.Bodenham	25
	X			X	X	X	X	X	S	S		X		X				X	X	S	X		G.Poll	26
	X		S	X	X	X	X	X	S			X		X				X	X	S	X		K.Cooper	27
	X		S	X	X	X	X	X	S		X	X	S					X	X		X		K.Burge	28
X	X		S	X	X	X	X	X	S		X	X	S					X	X				P.Alcock	29
	X			X	X	X	X1	S1		X	X	S			S2	X	X		X2				K.Leach	30
X	X			X	X		X	X1		S	X	X	S		X	S1	X	X					D.Elleray	31
X	X			X	X		X	X		S	X	X	S		X	S	X	X					P.Durkin	32
X	X			X	X		X	X			X	X			X	S	X	X	S	S			R.Dilkes	33
X	X			X	X		X	X1			X	X	S		S1	S	X	X	S	X			S.Lodge	34
X	X			X	X1	X	X	X			X	X		S1		S	X	X	S	X			D.Gallagher	35
X	X			X	X	X	X	X			X	X			S	S	X	X	S	X			M.Bodenham	36
X	X			X	X	X	X	X			X	X			S	X	X	X	S	X			A.Wilkie	37
X	X			X1	X	S	X	X			X	X			S1	X	X	X	S	X			J.Winter	38
X	X			X2	X		X	X			X	X		S1		S2	X	X	S	X1			K.Cooper	39
X	X1			X	X		X	X			X	X		S1		S	X	X	S	X			D.Gallagher	40
X	X			X	X		X	X1			X	X		S1		S	X	X	S	X			G.Willard	41
	X			X	X	X	X	X			X	X			S	S	X	X	S	X			S.Dunn	42
	X			X	X	X	X	X			X	X		S		S	X	X	S	X			D.Gallagher	43
	X			X1	X		X		X1	X	X	X			S1	X	S1	X	X				P.S.Danson	44
	X			X1	X	S	X	X			X	X			X	X	S1	X		S	X		P.Durkin	45
	X			X	X	S1	X	X2			X	X			X	X	S2	X		S	X1		M.Reed	46
	X			X	X	X1	X	X2		X	X	X			X	X	S2	X	S1	S	X		P.Jones	47
	X	X		X	X		X			S	X	X	X		X	X		S	X	X			P.Alcock	48
	X			X	X		X	X			X	X		X1	X1	S1	X	S1	X				D.Elleray	49
X	X			X	X1		X	X	S2			X		X	X	X	S1	X	X2	S			R.Dilkes	50
X	X			X1	X		X	X	S			X		X	X	X	S1	X	S				G.Ashby	51
X					X		X	X	S1	S	X	X		X1	X	X		X	S	X			S.Lodge	52
X	X			X1	X		X	X2			X	X		X			S1	S2	S	X			D.Gallagher	53
28	36	2	1	30	36	23	38	33	1	5	27	38	0	19	18	10	27	18	0	29	0		PL Appearances	
		1	1	2	1				3		2			4	2	10		9					PL Sub Appearances	
4	3	0	0	2+2	4	4	4	3	0+1	0	3+1	4	0	3	3+1	2	2	0+1	0	3	0		CC Appearances	
4	4	0	0	7	7	1	7	7	0+1	0	7	7	0	2+1	2	0+4	7	5+1	0	7	0		FAC Appearances	
4	4	0	0	1+1	3+1	4	4	4	0+1	0	0	4	0	4	2	2+1	2	2+1	0	4	0		UEFA Appearances	

LIVERPOOL

CLUB RECORDS

BIGGEST VICTORIES
League: 10-1 v Rotherham United, Division 2, 18.2.1896.
9-0 v Crystal Palace, Division 1, 12.9.1989.
6-1 v Crystal Palace, Premiership, 20.8.1994.
F.A. Cup: 8-0 v Swansea City, 3rd Round replay, 9.1.1990.
League Cup: 10-0 v Fulham, 2nd Round 1st leg, 23.9.1986.
Europe: 11-0 v Stromsgodset Gwc, ECWC, 17.9.1974.

BIGGEST DEFEATS
League: 1-9 v Birmingham City, Division 2, 11.12.1954.
0-8 v Huddersfield Town, Division 1, 10.11.1934.
F.A. Cup: 0-5 v Bolton Wanderers, 4th Round, 1945-46.
League Cup: 1-4 v West Ham, 4th Round, 30.11.1988.
Europe: (UEFA) 1-5 v Ajax, 2nd Round, 7.12.1966.

MOST POINTS
3 points a win: 90, Division 1, 1987-88 (equalled record).
2 points a win: 68, Division 1, 1978-79 (Division 1 record).

MOST GOALS SCORED
106, 1895-96.
Allan 25, Ross 23, Becton 17, Bradshaw 12, Geary 11, McVean 7, McQue 5, Hannah 3, Wilkie 1, Bull 1, McCartney 1.

MOST GOALS CONCEDED
97, Division 1, 1953-54.

MOST FIRST CLASS MATCHES IN A SEASON
67 - 1983-84 (League 42, FA Cup 2, League Cup 13, Charity Shield 1, European Cup 9).

MOST LEAGUE WINS
30, Division 1, 1978-79.

MOST LEAGUE DRAWS
19, Division 1, 1951-52.

MOST LEAGUE DEFEATS
23, Division 1, 1953-54.

INDIVIDUAL CLUB RECORDS

MOST GOALS IN A SEASON
Ian Rush: 47 goals in 1983-84 (League 32, FA Cup 2, League Cup 8, European Cup 5).

MOST GOALS IN A MATCH
5. Andy McGuigan v Stoke City (h) 7-0, Division 1, 4.1.1902.
5. John Evans v Bristol Rovers (h) 5-3, Division 2, 15.9.1954.
5. Ian Rush v Luton Town (h) 6-0, Division 1, 29.10.1983.
5. Robbie Fowler v Fulham (h) 5-0, League Cup 2nd Rnd, 5.10.93.

OLDEST PLAYER
Kenny Dalglish, 39 years 58 days v Derby County, 1.5.1990.

YOUNGEST PLAYER
Phil Charnock, ECWC, 16.09.92.

MOST CAPPED PLAYER
Ian Rush (Wales) 59.
Emlyn Hughes (England) 59.

BEST PERFORMANCES

League: 1978-79: Matches played 42, Won 30, Drawn 8, Lost 4, Goals for 85, Goals against 16, Points 68. First in Division 1.
Highest Position: Division 1 champions 18 times.
F.A. Cup: Winners in 1964-65, 1973-74, 1985-86, 1988-89.
Most recent success: 1991-92: 3rd Round Crewe Alexandra 4-0; 4th Round Bristol Rovers 1-1,2-1; 5th Round Ipswich Town 0-0,3-2; 6th Round Aston Villa 1-0; Semi-Final Portsmouth 1-1,0-0 (won 3-1 on penalties); Final Sunderland 2-0.
League Cup: Winners in 1980-81, 1981-82, 1982-83, 1983-84.
Most recent success: 1994-95: 2nd Round Burnley 2-0,4-1; 3rd Round Stoke City 2-1; 4th Round Blackburn Rovers 3-1; 5th Round Arsenal 1-0; Semi-Final Crystal Palace 1-0,1-0; Final Bolton Wanderers 2-1.
Europe: European Cup winners in 1976-77, 1977-78, 1980-81.
Most recent success: 1983-84: 1st Round Odense 1-0,5-0; 2nd Round Athletico Bilbao 0-0,1-0; 3rd round Benfica 1-0,4-1; Semi-Final Dynamo Bucharest 1-0,2-1; Final Roma 1-1 (Won on pens).
UEFA Cup winners in 1972-73.
Most recent success: 1975-76: 1st round Hibernian 0-1,3-1; 2nd Round Real Sociedad 3-1,6-0; 3rd Round Slask Wroclaw 2-1,3-0; 4th Round Dynamo Dresden 0-0,2-1; Semi-Final Barcelona 1-0,1-1; Final Bruges 3-2,1-1.

DIVISIONAL RECORD

	Played	Won	Drawn	Lost	For	Against	Points
Division 1/P	3,260	1,481	811	968	5,350	4,137	4,100
Division 2	428	243	82	103	977	571	568
Total	3,688	1,724	893	1,071	6,327	4,708	4,668

ADDITIONAL INFORMATION
PREVIOUS NAMES
None.
PREVIOUS LEAGUES
Lancashire League.

Club Colours: All red with white trim.
Change Colours: White and dark green quarters,dark green shorts with white trim, white socks with dark green trim.

Reserves League: Pontins Central League Division 1.

RECORDS AND STATISTICS

COMPETITIONS

Div 1/P	Div.2	Euro C	ECWC	UEFA	Sup.C	WCC
894-95	1893-94	1964-65	1965-66	1967-68	1977	1981
894-04	1895-96	1966-67	1971-72	1968-69	1978	1984
905-54	1904-05	1973-74	1974-75	1969-70		Sc Sp
1962-	1954-62	1976-77	1992-93	1970-71		Sup C
		1977-78		1972-73		1986
		1978-79		1975-76		
		1979-80		1991-92		
		1980-81		1995-96		
		1981-82				
		1982-83				
		1983-84				
		1984-85				

HONOURS

Div 1	Div.2	FAC	Lge C	Euro C	UEFA	C/Sh'd
1900-01	1893-94	1964-65	1980-81	1976-77	1972-73	1964
1905-06	1895-96	1973-74	1981-82	1977-78	1975-76	1965
1921-22	1904-05	1985-86	1982-83	1980-81		1966
1922-23	1961-62	1988-89	1983-84	1983-84		1974
1946-47		1991-92	1994-95		ESC	1976
1963-64					1977	1977
1965-66				Sc Sp		1979
1972-73				Sup C		1980
1975-76				1986		1982
1976-77						1986
1978-79						1988
1979-80						1989
1981-82						
1982-83						
1983-84						
1985-86						
1987-88						
1989-90						

MOST APPEARANCES

Ian Callaghan 839+7 (1959-78)

Year	League	FA Cup	Lge Cup	Europe
1959-60	4			
1960-61	3		2	
1961-62	24	5		
1962-63	37	6		
1963-64	42	5		
1964-65	37	8		9
1965-66	42	1		9
1966-67	40	4		5
1967-68	41	9	2	6
1968-69	42	4	3	2
1969-70	41	6	2	3+1
1970-71	21+1	4	1	5
1971-72	41	3	3	4
1972-73	42	4	8	12
1973-74	42	9	6	4
1974-75	41	2	3	4
1975-76	40	2	3	12
1976-77	32+1	4+1	2	7
1977-78	25+1	1	7	5
	637+3	77+1	42	87+1

MOST GOALS IN A CAREER

Ian Rush - 344 (1980-1996)

Year	League	FA Cup	Lge Cup	Europe	Other
1980-81					
1981-82	17	3	8	2	
1982-83	24	2	2	2	1
1983-84	32	2	8	5	
1984-85	14	7		5	
1985-86	22	6	3		2
1986-87	30		4		6
1988-89	7	3	1		
1989-90	18	6	2		
1990-91	16	5	5		
1991-92	3	1	3	1	
1992-93	14	1	1	5	1
1993-94	14	1	4		
1994-95	12	1	5		
1995-96	5	1	1		
Total	228	39	47	20	10

Current leading goalscorer: Robbie Fowler - 85 (1992-96)
Previous Holder: Roger Hunt - 285 (1959-70) Lge 245, FAC 18, Lge C 5, Europe 17

RECORD TRANSFER FEE RECEIVED

Amount	Club	Player	Date
£3,200,000	Juventus	Ian Rush	6/87
£650,000	Sampdoria	Graham Souness	6/84
£500,000	S V Hamburg	Kevin Keegan	6/77
£240,000	Coventry City	Larry Lloyd	8/74

RECORD TRANSFER FEE PAID

Amount	Club	Player	Date
£8,500,000	Nottingham Forest	Stan Collymore	07/95
£3,000,000	Coventry City	Phil Babb	09/94
£3,250,000	Borussia Dortmund	Patrik Berger	07/96
£2,900,000	Derby County	Dean Saunders	7/91

MANAGERS

Name	Seasons	Best	Worst
John McKenna	1892-96	16(1)	1(2)
Tom Watson	1896-15	1(1)	1(2)
Dave Ashworth	1920-23	1(1)	4(1)
Matt McQueen	1923-28	4(1)	16(1)
George Patterson	1928-36	7(1)	18(1)
George Kay	1936-51	1(1)	19(1)
Don Welsh	1951-56	9(1)	11(1)
Phil Taylor	1956-59	3(2)	4(2)
Bill Shankly	1959-74	1(1)	3(2)
Bob Paisley	1974-83	1(1)	5(1)
Joe Fagan	1983-85	1(1)	2(1)
Kenny Dalglish	1985-91	1(1)	2(1)
Graeme Souness	1991-94	6(P)	6(P)
Roy Evans	1994-	3(P)	4(P)

LONGEST LEAGUE RUNS

of undefeated matches: 31 (4.5.1987 - 16.3.1988)

of league matches w/out a win: 14 (5.12.1953 - 3.4.1954)

of undefeated home matches: 63 (25.2.1978 - 31.1.1981)

of undefeated away matches: 16 (2.9.1893-3.9.94, 9.5.87-16.3.88)

without home win: 10 (13.10.1951 - 22.3.1952)

without an away win: 24 (21.2.1953 - 7.4.1954)

of league wins: 12 (21.4.1990 - 6.10.1990)

of home wins: 21 (29.1.1972 - 30.12.1972)

of league defeats: 9 (29.4.1899 - 14.10.1899)

away wins: 6 (24.9.1904-19.11.1904, 31.12.04-11.3.05, 27.2.82-24.4.82)

LIVERPOOL

PLAYERS NAME / Honours	Ht	Wt	Birthdate	Birthplace / Transfers	Contract Date	Clubs	League	L/Cup	FA Cup	Other	Lge	L/C	FAC	Oth
G O A L K E E P E R S														
James David B	6.5	15.0	01/08/70	Welwyn Gard.	01/07/88	Watford	89	6	2	1				
E:u21.10;FAYC'89;LC'95				£1000000	06/07/92	Liverpool	122+1	13	14	5				
Pears Stephen	6.0	12.0	22/01/62	Brandon	25/01/79	Manchester United	4	1						
				Loan	01/11/83	Middlesbrough	12			2				
				£80000	09/07/85	Middlesbrough	322	30	33	27				
					01/08/95	Liverpool								
Stensgaard Michael	6.2	13.04	01/09/74	Denmark	21/05/92	HIV Donvere								
Danish u21				£400000	31/05/94	Liverpool								
Warner Anthony R	6.4	13.9	11/05/74	Liverpool	01/01/94	Liverpool								
D E F E N D E R S														
Babb Philip A	6.0	11.7	30/11/70	Lambeth	24/04/89	Millwall								
Ei: 20; LC'95;				Free	10/08/90	Bradford City	73+7	5+1	3	3+1	14			
				£500000	21/07/92	Coventry City	70+7	5	2		3	1		
				£3600000	01/09/94	Liverpool	61+1	11	10	4				
Bjorneby Stig I	5.10	11.9	11/12/69	Rosenborg		Rosenborg								
Norwegian Int. LC'95				£600000	18/12/92	Liverpool	50+3	7	7+2					
Brunskill Iain R	5.10	12.5	05/11/76	Ormskirk	21/05/94	Liverpool								
E:S														
Brydon Lee	6.0	11.4	15/11/74	Stockton	24/06/92	Liverpool								
E:S														
Harkness Steven	5.10	10.11	27/08/71	Carlisle	23/03/89	Carlisle United	12+1							
E:Y.13				£75000	17/07/89	Liverpool	57+7	8+2	3	8+2	3	1		
				Loan	24/09/93	Huddersfield Town	5		1					
				Loan	03/02/95	Southend United	6							
Harris Andrew D D	5.10	11.11	26/02/77	Springs	24/03/94	Liverpool								
Jones Robert M	5.11	11.0	05/11/71	Wrexham	20/12/88	Crewe Alexandra	59+16	9	0+3	3	2			
W: S; E:4, Y2, u21.2; FAC'92. LC'95				£300000	04/10/91	Liverpool	160	18+1	27	8				
Matteo Dominic	6.1	11.8	28/04/74	Dumfries	27/05/92	Liverpool	18+5	2	1					
E: u21.3, Y.1.														
Neal Ashley J	5.11	13.6	16/12/74	Northampton	27/04/93	Liverpool								
Ruddock Neil	6.2	12.0	09/05/68	Wandsworth	03/03/86	Millwall				3+1				1
E: 1, Y6, u21.4, u19.5. LC'95.				£50000	14/04/86	Tottenham Hotspur	7+2		1+1				1	
				£250000	13/02/89	Southampton	100+7	14+1	10	6	9	1	3	
				£750000	29/07/92	Tottenham Hotspur	38	4	5		3			
				£2500000	22/07/93	Liverpool	94+2	16+1	11	2	10	1		
Scales John R	6.2	12.7	04/07/66	Harrogate		Leeds United								
E: 3, B1: FAC'88; LC'95.				Free	11/07/85	Bristol Rovers	68+4	3	6	3+1	2			
				£70000	16/07/87	Wimbledon	235+5	18+1	20+1	7+1	11			
				£3500000	02/09/94	Liverpool	62	9	14	2	2	3		
Wright Mark	6.3	12.11	01/08/63	Dorchester	26/08/80	Oxford United	8+2		1					
E: 45, u21.4; FAC'92; FLgXI.1				£80000	25/03/82	Southampton	170	25	17	10	7	2	1	1
				£760000	27/08/87	Derby County	144	15	5	7	10			
				£2200000	15/07/91	Liverpool	118+2	11+2	16	12	5	1		
M I D F I E L D														
Berger Patrik				Borussia Dortmund										
Czech Int.				£3250000	01/08/96	Liverpool								
Cassidy Jamie	5.9	10.07	21/11/77	Liverpool	01/08/95	Liverpool								
E: Y.														
Charnock Philip A	5.10	11.3	14/02/75	Southport	27/05/92	Liverpool		1		0+1				
				Loan	09/02/96	Blackpool	0+4							
Clegg David L			23/10/76	Liverpool	01/08/95	Liverpool								
Jensen Michael S						Liverpool								
McAteer Jason	5.10	10.5	18/06/71	Birkenhead										
Ei: 18.					22/01/92	Bolton Wanderers	109+5	11	11	8+1	8	2	3	2
				£4500000	06/09/95	Liverpool	27+2	3+1	7				3	
Redknapp Jamie F	5.11	11.8	25/06/73	Barton	27/06/90	Bournemouth	6+7	3	3	2				
E: 5 , Y2, u21.16, S. LC'95				£350000	15/01/91	Liverpool	116+18	21	13+1	9+1	13	3	1	1
Thomas Michael L	5.10	12.4	24/08/67	Lambeth	31/12/84	Arsenal	149+14	22+2	14+3	5+2	24	5	1	1
E: 2, B5, u21.12, u19.6, Y14,S; LC'87'95;				Loan	30/12/86	Portsmouth	3							
Div1'89'91; FAC'92. CT'89. CS'91. FLgXI.1.				£1500000	16/12/91	Liverpool	57+25	2+3	14+2	4+1	5	1	2	

hompson David A	5.7	10.0	12/09/77	Birkenhead		01/08/94	Liverpool								
; Y.															
O R W A R D S															
arnes John C B	5.11	11.10	07/09/63	Jamaica			Sudbury Court								
79, u21.3; FAYC'82; Div1'88'90;					Free	14/07/81	Watford	232+1	21	31	7	66	7	11	
S'88'89'90; FAC'89. LC'95. FLgXI.1.£900000						19/06/87	Liverpool	276+3	23	49	9	80	3	16	2
ollymore Stan V	6.2	12.2	22/01/71	Stone		13/07/89	Wolves								
1					£100000	04/01/91	Crystal Palace	4+16	2+3			1	1		
					£100000	20/11/92	Southend United	30		3		15		3	
					£2000000	05/07/93	Nottingham Forest	64+1	9	2	2	41	7	2	
					£8500000	03/07/95	Liverpool	30+1	2+2	7	1+1	14		5	
alglish Paul							Celtic								
						25/07/96	Liverpool								
owler Robert B	5.8	10.3	09/04/75	Liverpool		23/04/92	Liverpool	105+3	12	15	3+1	65	12	8	
5, B.1, u21.8. Y. UEFAC'93. LC'95.															
nes Phillip L	5.9	10.5	29/05/73	Wrexham		05/07/91	Wrexham	24+15	2	1+2	4+1	9		1	2
: u21.10 (6 gls, record scorer for Wales u21)					£300000	12/03/92	Liverpool	0+1	0+1						
					Loan	03/09/93	Crewe Alexandra	4+4				1			
					Loan		Wrexham	20				8			
ennedy Mark	5.11	11.9	15/05/76	Dublin		06/05/92	Millwall	37+6	6+1	3+1		9	2	1	
: 10, u21. Y5.					£1500000	21/03/95	Liverpool	5+5	0+1	0+1	0+1				
cManaman Steve	5.11	10.2	11/02/72	Bootle		19/02/90	Liverpool	160+11	23+1	25+1	15	24	8	5	2
15 , Y2, u21.7; FAC'92. LC'95															
DDITIONAL CONTRACT PLAYERS															
aizer Phil						22/05/96	Liverpool (T)								
ars Sean						22/05/96	Liverpool (T)								
ior Lee						22/05/96	Liverpool (T)								
uinn Mark P						22/05/96	Liverpool (T)								
uinn Stuart						22/05/96	Liverpool (T)								
oberts Gareth						22/05/96	Liverpool (T)								
rkington Edmund						22/05/96	Liverpool (T)								

THE MANAGER
ROY EVANS

Date of Birth . . . . 5th June 1948.
Place of Birth . . . . Bootle.
Date of Appointment . . . . January 1994.

PREVIOUS CLUBS
As Manager . . . . None.
As Coach . . . . Liverpool.
As a Player . . . . Liverpool.

HONOURS
As a Manager
League Cup 1994/95.

As a Player
England Schools.

ANFIELD
Anfield Road, Liverpool L4 0TH
Tel: 0151 263 9199

Capacity 41,000

First game ....v Rotherham, 1.9.1892.
First floodlit game..v Everton, 30.10.1957.
Internationals...England v Ireland 1899, 1926. v Wales 1905, 1922, 1931.
.... Wales v Scotland 1977. **Euro'96:** Italy v Russia 10.6.96. Italy v Czech Republic 14.6.96.
....Czech Republic v Russia 19.6.96. France v Holland 22.6.96 (QF).

ATTENDANCES
Highest ....61,905 v Wolves, FA Cup 4th Round, 2.2.1952.
Lowest ....1,000 v Loughborough, Division 2, 7.12.1895.

OTHER GROUNDS..None.

MATCHDAY TICKET PRICES

Premium.. £16
Kop Grandstand.. £13
Family (1+1) - Andfield Rd Stand £24
Family (1+1) - Kop Grandstand £19.50

Standard.. £15
Kop Grandstand.. £12
Family (1+1) - Andfield Rd Stand........ £22.50
Family (1+1) - Kop Grandstand........... £18

Ticket Office Telephone no. .... 0151 260 8680.

CLUBCALL
0891 12 11 84
Calls cost 39p per minute cheap rate and 49p per
minute at all other times.
Call costings correct at time of going to press.

HOW TO GET TO THE GROUND

From the North
Use motorway (M6) until junction 28, then follow signs to Liverpool on A58 and
forward into Walton Hall Avenue past Stanley Park and turn left into Anfield Road
for Liverpool FC.

From the East and South
Use motorway M6 then M62 until end of motorway, then turn right (A5058 into
Queens Drive. In 3 miles turn left into Utting Avenue. In 1 mile turn right into
Anfield Road for Liverpool FC.

From the West
Use Mersey tunnel into Liverpool City Centre, then follow signs to Preston
(A580) into Walton Hall Avenue, then on nearside of Stanley Park turn right into
Anfield Road for Liverpool FC.

Car Parking
Limited street parking. Mainly privately-owned car park in Priory Road (5 minute
walk from ground).

Nearest Railway Station
Kirkdale or Lime Street (0151 709 9696)

MATCHDAY PROGRAMME

Programme Editor .... Vince Wilson.

Number of pages .... 40.

Price .... £1.50.

Subscriptions...................... £44 inc. postage UK/Ireland,
.... £50 inc. postage overseas.

Local Newspapers............ Liverpool Daily Post, Liverpool Echo.

Local Radio Stations .... Radio Merseyside, Radio City.

MANCHESTER UNITED
(The Red Devils)
F.A. CARLING PREMIERSHIP
SPONSORED BY: SHARP

ck Row (L-R): Norman Davies (Kit Manager), Ryan Giggs, Roy Keane, Nicky Butt, David May, John O'Kane, Phil Neville, Gary Neville, **dy** Cole, David Fevre (Physio). **Middle Row:** David Beckham, Patrick McGibbon, Eric Cantona, Gary Walsh, Peter Schmeichel, Kevin **kington**, Gary Pallister, Lee Sharpe, Chris Casper. **Front Row:** Paul Parker, Brian McClair, Steve Bruce, Alex Ferguson (Manager), Brian **Id** (Asst. Manager), Denis Irwin, Ben Thornley, Paul Scholes.

MANCHESTER UNITED
FORMED IN 1878
TURNED PROFESSIONAL IN 1885
LTD COMPANY IN 1907

CHAIRMAN: C M Edwards

DIRECTORS
J M Edelson, Sir Bobby Charlton CBE,
E M Watkins, A M Midani, R L Olive,
R P Launders
SECRETARY
Kenneth R Merrett (0161 872 1661/2)
COMMERCIAL MANAGER
Danny McGregor (0161 872 3488)

MANAGER: Alex Ferguson
ASSISTANT MANAGER: Brian Kidd

RESERVE TEAM MANAGER
Jimmy Ryan
YOUTH TEAM MANAGER
Eric Harrison
PHYSIOTHERAPIST
David Fevre

STATISTICIAN FOR THE DIRECTORY
Richard Facer

With the loss of three senior internationals and the introduction of so many youngsters it was the considered opinion of the football pundits that Alex Ferguson had blundered.

But nine months later United had won the double and produced some sparkling football inspired by Cantona, Giggs and Schmeichel and brilliantly served by the youngsters in the Neville brothers, David Beckham, Nicky Butt and Paul Scholes. Sadly Andy Cole and Lee Sharpe didn't consistently play to their full potential but there again Dennis Irwin was consistent enough to keep the England right-back out of his position and skipper Bruce and Pallister were as steady as ever when fit.

With the pressure off them and Newcastle United out in front, the exciting chase' created terrific end of season atmospheres and their flowing football plus some decisive goals from Eric Cantona saw United achieve thirteen victories in their last fifteen Premier games.

The club's second Championship and F.A. Cup double was achieved at Wembley when Liverpool were beaten in a very disappointing Final. The quality of play was forgotten however as a wonderful season full of sparkling football produced the ideal reward.

But in a season as glorious as this, United still managed to produce a memorable piece of history for York City by losing 0-3 at Old Trafford to them in the Coca-Cola Cup and then 3-4 on aggregate to go out in the Second Round, having also been eliminated by Volgograd (Roter) in the UEFA Cup First Round.

So 4th October would have been an excellent time to back Manchester United for the double! Two cup exits, a defeat by Villa and so many youngsters!

What a satisfying feeling it must have been for one of football's greatest managers. Can Alex Ferguson really do any better?

You wouldn't bet against it!

TONY WILLIAMS.

MANCHESTER UNITED

League: Champions   FA Cup: Winners   Coca-Cola Cup: 2nd Rnd   UEFA Cup: 1st Rnd

M	DATE	COMP	VEN	OPPONENTS	RESULT	HT	LP	GOAL SCORERS/GOAL TIMES	ATT.
1	A 19	PL	A	Aston Villa	L 1-3	0-3	18	Beckham 82	(34655)
2	23	PL	H	West Ham United	W 2-1	0-0	10	Scholes 50, Keane 68	31966
3	26	PL	H	Wimbledon	W 3-1	1-0	7	Keane 27, 79, Cole 59	32226
4	28	PL	A	Blackburn Rovers	W 2-1	0-0	3	Sharpe 46, Beckham 68	(29843)
5	S 9	PL	A	Everton	W 3-2	1-1	2	Sharpe 3, 49, Giggs 73	(39496)
6	12	UEFA 1/1	A	Volgograd (Rotor)	D 0-0	0-0			(40000)
7	16	PL	H	Bolton Wanderers	W 3-0	2-0	2	Scholes 17, 85, Giggs 33	32812
8	20	CC 2/1	H	York City	L 0-3	0-1			29049
9	23	PL	A	Sheffield Wednesday	D 0-0	0-0	1		(34101)
10	26	UEFA 1/2	H	Volgograd (Rotor)	D 2-2	1-1		Scholes 39, Schmeichel 89	29724
11	O 1	PL	H	Liverpool	D 2-2	1-1	3	Butt 1, Cantona 70(pen)	34934
12	3	CC 2/2	A	York City	W 3-1	2-1		Scholes 6, 80, Cooke 13	(9386)
13	14	PL	A	Manchester City	W 1-0	1-0	2	Scholes 4	35707
14	21	PL	A	Chelsea	W 4-1	2-0	2	Scholes 3, 10, Giggs 79, McClair 88	(31019)
15	28	PL	H	Middlesbrough	W 2-0	1-0	2	Pallister 43, Cole 87	36580
16	N 4	PL	A	Arsenal	L 0-1	0-1	2		(38317)
17	18	PL	H	Southampton	W 4-1	3-0	2	Giggs 1, 4, Scholes 8, Cole 69	39301
18	22	PL	A	Coventry City	W 4-0	1-0	2	Irwin 28, McClair 47, 76, Beckham 57	(23344)
19	27	PL	A	Nottingham Forest	D 1-1	0-1	2	Cantona 66(pen)	(29263)
20	D 2	PL	H	Chelsea	D 1-1	0-0	2	Beckham 60	42019
21	9	PL	H	Sheffield Wednesday	D 2-2	1-0	2	Cantona 17, 84	41849
22	17	PL	A	Liverpool	L 0-2	0-1	2		(40546)
23	24	PL	A	Leeds United	L 1-3	1-2	2	Cole 30	(39801)
24	27	PL	H	Newcastle United	W 2-0	1-0	2	Cole 5, Keane 53	42024
25	30	PL	H	Queens Park Rangers	W 2-1	1-0	2	Cole 44, Giggs 52	41890
26	J 1	PL	A	Tottenham Hotspur	L 1-4	1-2	2	Cole 36	(32852)
27	6	FAC 3	H	Sunderland	D 2-2	1-0		Butt 12, Cantona 79	41563
28	13	PL	H	Aston Villa	D 0-0	0-0	2		42667
29	16	FAC 3R	A	Sunderland	W 2-1	0-1		Scholes 70, Cole 89	(21378)
30	22	PL	A	West Ham United	W 1-0	1-0	2	Cantona 8	(24197)
31	27	FAC 4	A	Reading	W 3-0	1-0		Giggs 36, Parker 56, Cantona 89	(14780)
32	F 3	PL	A	Wimbledon	W 4-2	2-0	16	Cole 42, Perry 45(og), Cantona 70, 80(pen)	(25432)
33	10	PL	H	Blackburn Rovers	W 1-0	1-0	2	Sharpe 14	42681
34	18	FAC 5	H	Manchester City	W 2-1	1-1		Cantona 39(pen), Sharpe 77	42692
35	21	PL	H	Everton	W 2-0	1-0	2	Keane 30, Giggs 82	42459
36	25	PL	H	Bolton Wanderers	W 6-0	2-0	2	Beckham 5, Bruce 15, Cole 70, Scholes 76, 79, Butt 90	(21381)
37	M 4	PL	A	Newcastle United	W 1-0	0-0	2	Cantona 51	(36584)
38	11	FAC QF	H	Southampton	W 2-0	0-0		Cantona 49, Sharpe 90	45446
39	16	PL	A	Queens Park Rangers	D 1-1	0-0	1	Cantona 90	(18817)
40	20	PL	H	Arsenal	W 1-0	0-0	2	Cantona 66	50028
41	24	PL	H	Tottenham Hotspur	W 1-0	0-0	1	Cantona 50	50157
42	31	FAC SF	N	Chelsea	W 2-1	0-1		Cole 55, Beckham 59	(38421)
43	A 6	PL	A	Manchester City	W 3-2	2-1	1	Cantona 7(pen), Cole 41, Giggs 77	(29688)
44	8	PL	H	Coventry City	W 1-0	0-0	1	Cantona 47	50332
45	13	PL	A	Southampton	L 1-3	0-3	1	Giggs 89	(15262)
46	17	PL	H	Leeds United	W 1-0	0-0	1	Keane 72	48382
47	28	PL	H	Nottingham Forest	W 5-0	2-0	1	Scholes 41, Beckham 44, 54, Giggs 69, Cantona 89	53926
48	M 5	PL	A	Middlesbrough	W 3-0	1-0	1	May 15, Cole 54, Giggs 80	(29921)
49	11	FAC F	N	Liverpool	W 1-0	0-0		Cantona 86	(79007)

Best Home League Attendance: 53926 v Nottingham Forest   **Smallest: 31966 v West Ham United**   **Average: 41681**

Goal Scorers:

PL(73): Cantona(14),Giggs(11),Cole(11),Scholes(10),Beckham(7),Keane(6),Sharpe(4),McClair(3),Butt(2),May(1),Irwin(1),Bruce(1),Pallister(1),Opponent(s)(1)

CC(3): Scholes(2),Cooke(1)

FAC(14): Cantona(5),Sharpe(2),Cole(2),Giggs(1),Parker(1),Scholes(1),Butt(1),Beckham(1)

UEFA(2): Scholes(1),Schmeichel(1)

(M) Beckham	(D) Bruce	(F) Butt	(F) Cantona	(D) Casper	(F) Cole	(F) Cooke	(G) Coton	(M) Davies	(F) Giggs	(D) Irwin	(M) Keane	(D) May	(F) McClair	(M) Mustoe	(D) Neville. G	(D) Neville .P	(D) O'Kane	(D) Pallister	(D) Parker	(G) Pilkington	(M) Prunier	(G) Schmeichel	(M) Scholes	(M) Sharpe	(M) Thornley	(F) Tomlinson			Referee	No.
S1		X						S		X	X		X			X	X1	S2	X2	X			X	X	X				R.A.Hart	1
			X	X	X			S1		X	X		X2			X		X		S			X	X1	X	S2			D.Gallagher	2
X	X	X			X1			S2	S1	X	X					X		X					X	X2	X				P.Durkin	3
X1	X	X			X			S1	S1	X	X					X		X					X	X1	X				D.Elleray	4
X	X	X			X2			S2	S1	X	X					X		X					X	X1	X				G.Poll	5
X	X	X			X			S1	X	X	X1					X		S					X	X2	X				P.Mikkelsen	6
X	X	X			X			X1			X1				S	X		X	X				X	X	X				S.Dunn	7
X	S2				X		S		S1	X2	X	X			X	X		X1		X	X	X				S			J.Rushton	8
X	X	X		S				S1	X1	X	X				X			S		X	X		X	X					K.Burge	9
X2	X	X		S	S	X	S2			X		X			S			X	X1		S		X	S1	X					10
S1	X	X1	X		X				X		X				X	X2		X	S				X	S2	X				D.Elleray	11
X	X		X		X	X1			X		S1		S		X	S2		X					X	X	X2				J.Winter	12
X	X				X				X		X2		S2		X	X		X	S				X	X1	S1				R.Dilkes	13
S	X	X	X		X				X	X	X		S1		X			X					X	X1	S				W.Wilkie	14
S	X	X	X		X				X	X	X		S1		X			X					X	X1	S				S.Lodge	15
S1	X	X1	X		X				X	X3	X		S3		X			X					X	X1	S1				P.Durkin	16
X	X	X			X				X3	X1			S2		X	S1		X					X	X2	S3				P.Danson	17
X	X3	X2	X		X				X	X		S3	X		X1	S1		X					X		S2				K.Burge	18
X2	X	X	X		X				X	X			X1		X	S		X					X	S1					K.Cooper	19
X	X		X		X1	S1		S		X		X	X	S	X						X			X	X				M.Bodenham	20
X	X		X		X	S2		S1		X			X	X	X	X				S	X		X	X1	X2				P.Jones	21
X	X	X	X		X1				X	X		X	X	X	S	X					S		X	S1	X				G.Poll	22
X1	X3	X	X		X				X	X	S1	X	X	S3		X1							X	S1					D.Gallagher	23
X		X	X		X				X	X	X	X1	S1	S	X	X							X	S					P.Alcock	24
X3		X	X		X1				X	X	X		S1		X	X1		S1	X	X		X1			S3				R.Hart	25
X		X	X		X				X	X2			S2		X	X2		X	S1	X	X1				S2				G.Ashby	26
X1	X	X	X		X				X	X	X		S		X2	S2		X		X					S1				M.Reed	27
	X	X	X		X				X	X	X		S		X	X		S					X	S1	X1				G.Willard	28
	X	X2	X		X				X	X	X		S		X	X		X1					X	S2	S1				M.Reid	29
S1	X	X	X		X1				X	X	X				X	X		S					X	S	X				S.Lodge	30
X	X	X	X		X				X	X	X				X	X1		S1					X	S	X				J.Winter	31
S1	X1	X	X		X		S		X	X	X				X	X1							X	S	X				P.Durkin	32
X		X	X		X				X	X	X	X	S			X		X	S				X	S	X				K.Burge	33
	X	X	X		X		S		X	X	X	X	S			X		X					X	S	X				A.Wilkie	34
S1	X	X	X		X				X	X	X				S	X		X					X	S	X1				M.Bodenham	35
X	X	X	X2		X				X1	X	X		S1		S	X		X					X	S2					D.J.Gallagher	36
S	X	X	X		X				X	X	X	S			X	X							X	S	X				D.Elleray	37
S	X	X	X		X				X	X	X	S			X	X							X	S	X				S.Dunn	38
X2	X	S1	X		X				X	X	X	X2	X1		X								X		S1				R.A.Heart	39
X	X	X	X		X1				X		X	X	S	X	X								X	S1					G.Willard	40
S1	X	X	X		X2				X	X	X	S2		X	X1								X	S	X				G.Ashby	41
X	X	X	X		X				X	X	X	S		X	X			S					X	S	X				S.Lodge	42
X	X	X	X		X1				X	X	X	S1			X			X					X	S	X1				M.Reed	43
X	X	X1	X		X		S		X	X	X		X	X	X			S					X	S	X				D.J.Gallagher	44
X	S	X	X		X				X	X	X	S2			X								X	S1	X2				G.Poll	45
X	X1	X			X3				X	X	X	S1	X2			X							X	S2	S3				K.Cooper	46
X		X	X		S				X	X	X	X	S	S1	X1		X						X	X	X				J.Winter	47
X	S	X	X		S1				X	X	X	X			S	X		X					X	X1					P.Durkin	48
X2		X	X		X1				X	X	X	X			S2	X							X	S1	S				D.Gallagher	49
26	30	31	30	0	32	1	0	1	30	31	29	11	12	0	30	21	0	21	5	2	2	36	16	21	0	0			PL Appearances	
0	1	0	0	2	3	0	5	3	0	0	0	5	10	0	1	3	1	0	1	1	0	0	9	9	1	0			PL Sub Appearances	
2	1+1	0	1	0	1	1+1	0	1	2	1	0+1	1	1+1	0	1	1	1+1	0	2	1	1	0	1	1	1	2			CC Appearances	
3	5	7	7	0	7	0	0	0	7	6	7	2	0	0	5+1	6+1	0	3	1+1	1	0	6	0+2	4+2	0	0			FAC Appearances	
2	2	2	0	0	1	0+1	0	0+1	2	1	2	0	0	0	1	1	1	2	0+1	0	0	2	1+1	2	0	0			UEFA Appearances	

MANCHESTER UNITED

CLUB RECORDS

BIGGEST VICTORIES
League: 10-1 v Wolverhampton Wanderers, Division 2, 15.10.1892.
9-0 v Walsall, Division 2, 3.4.1895.
9-0 v Darwen, Division 2, 24.12.1898.
9-0 v Ipswich Town, Premiership, 4.3.95.
F.A. Cup: 8-0 v Yeovil Town, 5th Round, 12.2.1949.
League Cup: 7-2 v Newcastle United, 4th Round, 1976-77.
5-0 v Tranmere Rovers, 2nd Round, 1976-77.
5-0 v Rotherham United, 2nd Round, 12.10.1988.
5-0 v Hull City, 2nd Round, 23.9.1987.
Europe: 10-0 v Anderlecht, European Cup, 26.9.1956.

BIGGEST DEFEATS
League: 0-7 v Wolverhampton Wanderers, Division 2, 26.12.1931.
0-7 v Aston Villa, Division 1, 27.12.1930.
0-7 v Blackburn Rovers, Division 1, 10.4.1926.
F.A. Cup: 1-7 v Burnley, 1st Round, 1901
0-6 v Sheffield Wednesday, 2nd Round, 1904.
League Cup: 1-5 v Blackpool, 2nd Round, 1966-67.
0-4 v Manchester City, 4th Round, 12.11.1975.
Europe: (ECWC) 0-5 v Sporting Lisbon, Quarter-final, 18.3.1964.

MOST POINTS
3 points a win: 92, Premiership, 1993-94 (Divisional record).
2 points a win: 64, Division 1, 1956-57.

MOST GOALS SCORED
103, Division 1, 1956-57, 1958-59.
Whelen 26, Taylor 22, Viollet 16, Charlton 10, Berry 8, Pegg 6,
Edwards 5, Webster 3, Dawson 3, Scanlon 2, Colman 1, Opponents
1.
(58-59) Charlton 29, Violet 21, Scanlon 16, Bradley 12, Goodwin 6,
Webster 5, Dawson 4, Quixall 4, Cope 2, McGuinness 1, Pearson 1,
Opponents 2.

MOST GOALS CONCEDED
115, Division 1, 1930-31.

MOST FIRST CLASS MATCHES IN A SEASON
63 - 1993-94 (League 42, FA Cup 7, League Cup 9, European Cup
4, Charity Shield 1).

MOST LEAGUE WINS
28, Division 2, 1905-06, Division 1, 1956-57.

MOST LEAGUE DRAWS
18, Division 1, 1980-81.

MOST LEAGUE DEFEATS
27, Division 1, 1930-31.

INDIVIDUAL CLUB RECORDS

MOST GOALS IN A SEASON
Denis Law: 46 goals in 1963-64 (League 30, FA Cup 10, ECWC 6).

MOST GOALS IN A MATCH
6. Joe Cassidy v Walsall Town Swifts, 9-0, Division 2, 3.4.1895.
6. Harold Halse v Swindon Town, 8-4, Charity Shield, 1911.
6. George Best v Northampton Town (a), 8-2, FA Cup 5th Round,
7.2.1970.

OLDEST PLAYER
Billy Meredith, 46 years 285 days v Derby County, 7.5.1921.

YOUNGEST PLAYER
Duncan Edwards, 16 years 182 days v Cardiff City, 4.4.1953.

MOST CAPPED PLAYER
Bobby Charlton (England) 106.
(England's top goal scorer with 49).

BEST PERFORMANCES

League: 1956-57: Matches played 42, Won 28, Drawn 8, Lost 6,
Goals for 103, Goals against 54, Points 64. First in Division 1.
Highest Position: Division 1/Premiership champions on 10 occasions.
F.A. Cup: Winners in 1908-09,1947-48, 1962-63, 1976-77, 1982-83
1984-85, 1989-90, 1993-94.
1995-96: 3rd Round Sunderland 2-2, 2-1; 4th Round Readng 3-0;
5th Round Manchester City 2-1; 6th Round Southampton 2-0;
Semi-final Chelsea 2-1; Final Liverpool 1-0.
League Cup: 1991-92: 2nd Round Cambridge United 3-0,1-1, 3rd
round Portsmouth 3-1; 4th Round Oldham Athletic 2-0; 5th Round
Leeds United 3-1; Semi-Final Middlesbrough 0-0,2-1; Final
Nottingham Forest 1-0.
Europe: (European Cup) 1967-68: 1st Round Hibernians Valletta 4
0,0-0; 2nd Round Sarajevo 0-0,2-1; 3rd Round Gornik Zabrze 2-0,0
1; Semi-final Real Madrid 1-0,3-3; Final Benfica 4-1 aet.
(ECWC) 1990-91: 1st Round Pecsi Munkas 2-1,1-0; 2nd Round
Wrexham 3-0,2-0; 3rd Round Montpellier 1-1,2-0; Semi-final Legia
Warsaw 3-1,1-1; Final Barcelona 2-1.

DIVISIONAL RECORD

	Played	Won	Drawn	Lost	For	Against	Points
Division 1/P	2,904	1,264	744	896	4,820	4,007	3,579
Division 2	816	406	168	242	1,433	966	980
Total	**3,720**	**1,670**	**912**	**1,140**	**6,253**	**4,973**	**4,559**

ADDITIONAL INFORMATION
PREVIOUS NAMES
Newton Heath 1878-1902.

PREVIOUS LEAGUES
Football Alliance.

Club colours: Red shirts with black collar, white shorts, black
socks.
Change colours: White shirts, white shorts & black socks.

Reserves League: Pontins Central League Premier Division.

RECORDS AND STATISTICS

COMPETITIONS

Div.1/P	Div.2	Euro C	ECWC	UEFA	C/Shield	
1892-94	1894-06	1956-57	1963-64	1964-65	1908	1985
1906-22	1922-25	1957-58	1977-78	1976-77	1911	1990
1925-31	1931-36	1965-66	1983-84	1980-81	1952	1993
1936-37	1937-38	1967-68	1990-91	1982-83	1956	1994
1938-74	1974-75	1968-69	1991-92	1984-85	1957	
1975-		1993-94		1992-93	1965	Wat C
		1994-95		1995-96	1967	1970
					1977	1971
					1983	

HONOURS

Div.1/P	Div.2	FA Cup	Lge Cup	Euro C	C/Shield
1907-08	1935-36	1908-09	1991-92	1967-68	1908
1910-11	1974-75	1947-48			1911
1951-52		1962-63			1952
1955-56		1976-77		ECWC	1956
1956-57		1982-83		1991	1957
1964-65		1984-85			1965*
1966-67		1989-90			1977*
1992-93		**1993-94**		ESC	1983
1993-94		**1995-96**		1991	1990*
1995-96					1993
					1994
					*shared

MOST APPEARANCES

Bobby Charlton 756 (1956-73)

Year	League	FA Cup	Lge Cup	Europe
1956-57	14	2		1
1957-58	21	8		2
1958-59	38	1		
1959-60	37	3		
1960-61	39	3		
1961-62	37	7		
1962-63	28	6		
1963-64	40	7		6
1964-65	41	7		11
1965-66	38	7		8
1966-67	42	2		
1967-68	41	2		9
1968-69	32	6		8
1969-70	40	9	8	
1970-71	42	2	6	
1971-72	40	7	6	
1972-73	34+2	1	4	
	604+2	80	24	45

Includes 3 Charity Shield (1963-64, 1965-66 & 1967-68)

MOST GOALS IN A CAREER

Bobby Charlton - 248 (1956-73))

Year	League	FA Cup	Lge Cup	Europe
1956-57	10	1		1
1957-58	8	5		3
1958-59	29			
1959-60	17	3		
1960-61	21			
1961-62	8	2		
1962-63	7	2		
1963-64	9	2		4
1964-65	10			8
1965-66	16			2
1966-67	12			
1967-68	15	1		2
1968-69	5			2
1969-70	12	1	1	
1970-71	5		3	
1971-72	8	2	2	
1972-73	6		1	
Total	198	19	7	22

Includes 2 goals in the Charity Shield.

Current leading goalscorer: Brian McClair - 128 (1987-96)

RECORD TRANSFER FEE RECEIVED

Amount	Club	Player	Date
£7,000,000	Inter Milan	Paul Ince	07/95
£5,000,000	Everton	Andrei Kanchelskis	08/95
£2,500,000	Barcelona	Mark Hughes	6/86
£1,500,000	Chelsea	Mark Hughes	06/95
£1,500,000	AC Milan	Ray Wilkins	6/84

RECORD TRANSFER FEE PAID

Amount	Club	Player	Date
£7,000,000	Newcastle Utd	Andy Cole	1/95
£3,750,000	Nott'm Forest	Roy Keane	7/93
£3,500,000	Slavia Prague	Karel Poborsky	7/96
£2,300,000	Middlesbrough	Gary Pallister	8/89

MANAGERS

Name	Seasons	Best	Worst
E Magnall	1903-12	1(1)	3(2)
J R Robson	1914-21	12(1)	18(1)
J Chapman	1921-26	9(1)	14(2)
C Hilditch	1926-27	15(1)	15(1)
H Bamlett	1927-31	12(1)	22(1)
W Crickner	1931-32	12(1)	12(1)
A Scott Duncan	1932-37	21(1)	20(2)
M Busby	1945-69	1(1)	19(1)
J Murphy	1958		
W McGuinness	1969-70	8(1)	8(1)
M Busby	1970-71	8(1)	8(1)
F O'Farrell	1971-72	8(1)	8(1)
T Docherty	1972-77	3(1)	1(2)
D Sexton	1977-81	2(1)	10(1)
R Atkinson	1981-86	3(1)	8(1)
A. Ferguson	1986-	1(P)	13(1)

LONGEST LEAGUE RUNS

of undefeated matches:	26 (21.1.1956 - 20.10.1956)
of league matches w/out a win:	16 (19.3.1930 - 25.10.1930)
of undefeated home matches:	37 (27.4.1966 - 27.3.1968)
of undefeated away matches:	14 (21.1.1956 - 20.10.1956)
without home win:7 (30.3.1920 - 6.9.1920, 19.4.1930 - 1.10.1930)	
(9.12.1933 - 3.3.1934, 22.2.1958 - 21.4.1958, 5.2.1978 - 29.3.1978)	
without an away win:	26 (15.2.1930 - 3.4.1931)
of league wins:	14 (8.10.1904 - 1.2.1905)
of home wins:	18 (15.10.1904 - 30.4.1905)
of league defeats:	14 (26.4.1930 - 25.10.1930)
of away wins:	7 (5.4.1993 - 28.8.1993)

MANCHESTER UNITED

PLAYERS NAME / Honours	Ht	Wt	Birthdate	Birthplace / Transfers	Contract Date	Clubs	APPEARANCES League	L/Cup	FA Cup	Other	GOALS Lge	L/C	FAC	Oth
G O A L K E E P E R S														
Culkin Nicholas	6.2	12.13	06/07/78	York		York City								
				£250000	27/09/95	Manchester United								
Gibson Paul R	6.2	13.4	01/11/76	Sheffield	01/07/95	Manchester United								
Pilkington Kevin W	6.0	12.0	08/03/74	Hitchin	06/07/92	Manchester United	2+2	1	1					
ESFAu18.1; FAYC'92				Loan	02/02/96	Rochdale	6							
Schmeichel Peter B	6.4	13.6	18/11/68	Glostone (Den)		Brondby								
Den: ; DenFAC'89; Div1'87'88'89;				£550000	12/08/91	Manchester United	190	17	26	16				1
ESC'91; EuroC'92; E:														
D E F E N D E R S														
Casper Christopher M	6.0	10.7	28/04/75	Burnley	03/02/93	Manchester United		1						
E: Y.8; FAYC'92; UEFA Yth'93				Loan	11/02/96	Bournemouth	16		1					
Clegg Michael J	5.8	11.8	03/07/77	Thameside	01/08/95	Manchester United								
Curtis John C	5.9	11.3	03/09/78	Nuneaton	03/10/95	Manchester United								
E: Y.														
Hilton David	5.11	10.10	10/11/77	Barnsley	01/08/94	Manchester United								
E: Yth														
Irwin Joseph Dennis	5.8	10.10	31/10/65	Cork	03/11/83	Leeds United	72	5	3	2	1			
Ei: 40, B.1, u21.3, Y, S;				Free	22/05/86	Oldham Athletic	166+1	19	13	5	4	3		
ECWC'91; ESC'91; LC'92; CS'90				£625000	20/06/90	Manchester United	223+2	28+2	29	22	14		6	
Johnsen Ronnie						Besiktas								
Norway:				£1200000	05/07/96	Manchester United								
May David	6.0	11.4	24/06/70	Oldham	16/06/88	Blackburn Rovers	123	12+1	10	5	3	2	1	
FAC'96				£1400000	01/07/94	Manchester United	26+9	2	3	5	3	1		
McGibbon Patrick C G	6.2	12.12	06/09/73	Lurgan		Portadown								
NI: 2, B1, u21.1, S						Manchester United		1						
Murdock Colin J	6.1	12.0	02/07/75	Ballymena	21/07/92	Manchester United								
NI: 1, Y.4, S														
Neville Gary A	5.10	11.7	18/02/75	Bury	29/01/93	Manchester United	47+3	3+1	9+1	2+3				
E: 14. Y8; FAYC'92; UEFA Yth'93; FAC'96; Prem'96														
Neville Philip J	5.11	12.0	21/01/77	Bury	01/06/94	Manchester United	22+4	1+1	7+1	1				
E: 1. Y. FAYC'95; FAC'96; Prem'96														
O'Kane John A	5.10	11.5	15/11/74	Nottingham	29/01/93	Manchester United	0+1	1+1	1	1				
FAYC'92														
Pallister Gary	6.4	13.0	30/06/65	Ramsgate		Billingham Town								
E: 20, B9, FLgXI.1; FAC'90;				Free	07/11/84	Middlesbrough	156	10	10	13	5		1	
CS'90'93; ECWC'91; ESC'91;				Loan	18/10/85	Darlington	7							
				£2300000	29/08/89	Manchester United	254+3	36	34	29+1	9		1	1
Wallwork Ronald	5.9	12.9	10/09/77	Manchester	01/08/94	Manchester United								
E: Y.														
Westwood Ashley M	6.0	11.03	31/08/76											
M I D F I E L D														
Appleton Michael A	5.9	11.13	04/12/75	Salford	01/08/94	Manchester United								
				Loan	15/09/95	Lincoln City	4			1				
Beckham David R J	5.11	10.7	02/05/75	Leytonstone	29/01/93	Manchester United	28+9	5+1	4+1	3	7		1	1
E: Y.9; FAYC'92; Prem'96				Loan	28/02/95	Preston North End	4+1				2			
Brebner Grant I	5.9	11.3	06/12/77	Edinburgh	01/08/94	Manchester United								
Davies Simon I	5.11	11.8	23/04/74	Winsford	06/07/92	Manchester United	4+7	4		2+1				1
W: 1. FAYC'92				Loan	17/12/93	Exeter City	5+1		1		1			
Keane Roy M	5.10	11.3	10/08/71	Cork		Cobh Ramblers								
Ei: 30, u21.4, Y, FMC'92;				£10000	12/08/90	Nottingham Forest	114	37	18	5	22	6	3	2
Prem'94'96; FAC'94'96; CS'93				£3750000	22/07/93	Manchester United	86+5	7+2	19+1	10	13		1	3
Scholes Paul	5.6	10.8	16/11/74	Salford	29/01/93	Manchester United	22+20	4	1+4	1+3	15	4	1	1
E:Y4; UEFA Yth'93; FAC'96; Prem'96														
Smith Thomas E	5.9	10.10	25/11/77	Northampton	01/08/94	Manchester United								
Teather Paul	5.11	11.2	26/12/77	Rotherham	01/08/94	Manchester United								
E:Y														
Thornley Benjamin L	5.9	10.9	21/04/75	Bury	29/01/93	Manchester United	0+2							
E: Y, S; ESFAu15; FAYC'92				Loan	06/11/95	Stockport County		8+2					1	
				Loan	22/02/96	Huddersfield Town	12				2			
F O R W A R D S														
Brightwell Stuart	5.6	10.9	31/01/79	Easington	08/02/96	Manchester United								

Name	Ht	Wt	DOB	From	Date	Club								
Brown David A	5.9	12.6	02/10/78	Bolton	27/10/95	Manchester United								
Butt Nicholas E: Y.9; ESAu.15; FAYC'92 UEFA Yth'93; FAC'96; Prem'96	5.9	10.10	21/01/75	Manchester	29/01/93	Manchester United	42+14	3	10+2	7+1	3		1	
Cantona Eric Fra: 21, Fra.Div1'89-90; Fra. FAC'90. Div1'92; Prem'93'94'96	6.0	11.6	24/05/66	Paris		Auxerre (France)								
				£2200000		Marseilles (France)								
				Loan	01/01/02	Bordeaux (France)								
				Loan	01/01/03	Montpellier (France)								
				£1000000	01/01/04	Nimes (France)								
				£900000	06/02/92	Leeds United	18+10	1		6	9			4
				£1200000	27/11/92	Manchester United	106+1	6	14	8	53	1	10	3
Cole Andrew E: 1, B.1, u21.8, Y.20, S. Div1'93. FAC'96. Prem'96	5.10	11.2	15/10/71	Nottingham	18/10/89	Arsenal	0+1			0+1				
				Loan	05/09/91	Fulham	13		2		3			1
			Loan	12/03/92	Bristol City	12				8				
				£500000	21/07/92	Bristol City	29	3	1	4	12	4		1
				£1750000	12/02/93	Newcastle United	69+1	7	4	3	55	8	1	4
				£7000000	12/01/95	Manchester United	49+3	1	7	1	23		2	
Cooke Terence J E: Y.	5.7	9.09	05/08/76	Marston Green	01/08/94	Manchester United	1+3	1+1		0+1		1		
				Loan	29/01/96	Sunderland	6							
Giggs Ryan J W:16, u21.1, Y, ESAu.15; ESC'91; LC'92; FAYC'92; Prem'93'94'96. FAC'94'96	5.11	10.9	29/11/73	Cardiff	01/12/90	Manchester United	164+17	16+4	24+2	13+1	39	6	5	2
Cruyff Jordi Dutch Int.						Barcelona								
				£1300000	24/07/96	Manchester United								
McClair Brian J S:30, B1, u21.8; SPD'86; SC'85 Prem'93'94'96; FAC'90'94;	5.10	12.13	08/12/63	Belshill		Aston Villa								
				Free	01/08/81	Motherwell	33+7	9+1	2		15	4	1	
				£100000	01/07/83	Celtic	129+16	19+1	14+4	13+2	99	9	11	3
				£850000	30/07/87	Manchester United	290+33	41+1	35+4	23	88	19	14	7
Mulryne Philip P NI: 1.	5.8	10.4	01/01/78	Belfast	01/08/94	Manchester United								
Mustoe Neil J	5.8	12.0	01/07/95	Gloucester	05/07/93	Manchester United								
Poborsky Karel Czech. Int.						Slavia Prague								
				£3500000	19/07/96	Manchester United								
Solsjkar Ole Gunner Norway:						Molde								
				£1500000	05/07/96	Manchester United								
Tomlinson Graeme	5.9	11.7	10/12/75	Keighley		Bradford City	12+5		0+1		6			
				£100000	12/07/94	Manchester United		0+2						
				Loan	22/03/96	Luton Town	1+6							
Wilson Mark A	5.11	12.1	09/02/79	Scunthorpe	16/02/96	Manchester United								

MANAGER

ALEX FERGUSON

Date of Birth . . . . 31st December 1941.
Place of Birth . . . . Govan, Glasgow.
Date of Appointment . . . . 5th November 1986.

PREVIOUS CLUBS
As Manager. . . . . East Sterling, St Mirren, Aberdeen.
Alex was appointed caretaker manager of Scotland in 1985 on the death of Jock
Stein until Andy Roxburgh was made manager in July 1986.
As Coach. . . . . None.
As a Player. . . . . Rangers, Queens Park, Dunfermline.

HONOURS
As a Manager
Aberdeen: Scottish Champions 1980, 1984, 1985. Scottish Cup Winners 1982, 1983, 1984, 1986.
Scottish League Cup 1986. ECWC 1983.
Manchester United: FA Cup 1990,1994, 1996. ECWC 1991. Super Cup 1991. League Cup 1992.
Premier League Champions 1992-93, 1993-94, 1995-96. Charity Shield 1994, 1994.

As a Player
None.

OLD TRAFFORD
Manchester M16 0RA
Tel: 0161 872 1661

Capacity ....54,000.

First game ....v Liverpool, 19.2.1910.
First floodlit game..v Bolton Wanderers, 25.03.1957.

ATTENDANCES
Highest...76,962 Wolves v Grimsby, FA Cup Semi-final, 25.3.1939.
Lowest ....Not Known.

OTHER GROUNDS ....North Road, Monsall Road 1880-1893,Bank Street 1883-1910,
.... Old Trafford 1910-1941, Maine Road 1941-49, Old Trafford 1949-

---

MATCHDAY TICKET PRICES

Ticket Office Telephone no. . . . . . . 0161 872 0199.

CLUBCALL
0891 12 11 61
Calls cost 39p per minute cheap rate and 49p per
minute at all other times.
Call costings correct at time of going to press.

HOW TO GET TO THE GROUND
From the North
Use motorway M61 then M63 until junction 4. Leave motorway and follow signs
to Manchester A5081. In 2.5 miles turn right into Sir Matt Busby Way, then turn
right into United Road for Manchester United FC.
From the East
Use motorway M62 until junction 17 then A56 into Manchester. Follow signs
South then Chester into Chester Road. In 2 miles turn right into Sir Matt Busby
Way, then turn left into United Road for Manchester United FC.
From the South
Use motorway M6 until junction 19 then follow signs to Stockport A556 then
Altrincham A56. From Altrincham follow signs to Manchester. In 6 miles turn left
into Sir Matt Busby Way, then turn left into United Road for Manchester United
FC.
From the West
Use motorway M62 then M63 and route from north or as route from south.

Car Parking: Several large parks. Lancashire County Cricket Ground, Talbot
Road and Great Stone Road (1,200).
Nearest Railway Station: Manchester Piccadilly (0161 832 8353).
Nearest Metrolink Station: Old Trafford.

MATCHDAY PROGRAMME

Programme Editor . . . . Cliff Butler.

Number of pages . . . . 48.

Price . . . . £1.50.

Subscriptions . . . . UK £39, Eire £39, Europe £49, Overseas £85.

Local Newspapers . . . . Manchester Evening News, Sunday Pink.

Local Radio Stations . . . . . . BBC Radio Manchester, Piccadilly Radio.
. . . . Manchester Utd Radio (Match Days only) 1413 AM.

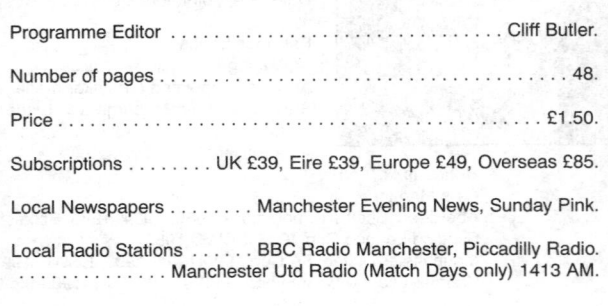

MIDDLESBROUGH
(The Boro)
F.A. CARLING PREMIERSHIP
SPONSORED BY: CELLNET

Back Row (L-R): John Hendrie, Jaime Moreno, Michael Barron, Craig Liddle, Phil Stamp, Craig Hignett, Jamie Pollock, Derek Whyte, Alan Moore, Keith O'Halloran. **Middle Row:** Gordon McQueen (Res. Coach), David Geddis (Yth Coach), Jan Fjortoft, Steve Vickers, Phil Whelan, Alan Miller, Ben Roberts, Paul Wilkinson, Robbie Mustoe, Curtis Fleming, Tommy Johnson (Physio), Mike Kelly (GK Coach). **Front Row:** Bob Ward (Chief physio), Chris Morris, Graham Kavanagh, Bryan Robson (Player-manager), Nigel Pearson (Capt), Viv Anderson (Player-Asst. Manager), Clayton Blackmore, Neil Cox, John Pickering (First team coach).

MIDDLESBROUGH
FORMED IN 1876
TURNED PROFESSIONAL IN 1899
LTD COMPANY IN 1899 (Amateur 1876-99)

CHAIRMAN: S Gibson

DIRECTOR
G Cooke
CHIEF EXECUTIVE
K Lamb, F.C.A.
HEAD OF MARKETING
J Knox

MANAGER: Bryan Robson
ASSISTANT MANAGER: Viv Anderson
FIRST TEAM COACH: John Pickering
RESERVE TEAM MANAGER
Gordon McQueen
YOUTH TEAM MANAGER
David Geddis
PHYSIOTHERAPIST
Bob Ward

STATISTICIAN FOR THE DIRECTORY
David Grey

If any Middlesbrough supporter had been asked at the beginning of 1995/6 what their realistic hopes were for the season, then a mid-table position would have been all that could have been hoped for. Yet as the season ended, this appeared to be a rather unsatisfactory position considering all that had gone before

The season started with high anticipation. Promotion had just been achieved. The Boro had just moved to a brand new stadium - one that reflected the current state of ambition within the club. The club's record transfer fee had been broken yet again, smashed by the signing of Nick Barmby from Tottenham.

The Riverside Stadium attracted nearly 30,000 people to its first match (and to every subsequent league match) which was incredible considering that crowds at Ayresome Park had hovered around the 10,000 mark only two seasons earlier. Early season results were superb, and the club soared to a high of fourth in the league during October, raising hopes for the possibility of a UEFA Cup place. The nation was watching the Boro's performances with interest. Then came the signing of the Brazilian, Juninho, surely one of the most imaginative buys the club had ever made. At this point the club was making the news headlines and consequently optimism grew even further for the remainder of the season. By this stage, the only way to see a Boro home match was with a season ticket - a move that alienated those fans not fortunate enough to possess one!

The team's performances dipped slightly, but they battled back to fourth position by December - although they were then surprisingly knocked out of the Coca-Cola Cup by Birmingham City.

Immediately after Christmas came the sudden, undignified decline: eight league defeats in a row and thirteen without a victory. The club slipped to 13th in the league, and were knocked out of the FA Cup by Wimbledon in a fourth round replay. Injuries were blamed, but really only showed up the squad's lack of strength in depth. By this time, relegation was at the back of some people's minds, rather than Europe. Another Brazilian, Branco, was signed under freedom of contract, which showed that the ambition was still present. Fortunately, results improved slightly, and the team finished the season in 12th place, without any real threat of relegation.

For the first time in recent years, Middlesbrough survived a season in the top division. The ambition is still present, but the squad needs to be strengthened - particularly in attack - if they are to seriously challenge for top honours.

DAVID GREY & NIGEL BALL

MIDDLESBROUGH

League: 12th   FA Cup: 4th Rnd   Coca-Cola Cup: 4th Rnd

M	DATE	COMP	VEN	OPPONENTS	RESULT	HT	LP	GOAL SCORERS/GOAL TIMES	ATT.
1	A 20	PL	A	Arsenal	D 1-1	1-1	9	Barmby 31	(37308)
2	26	PL	H	Chelsea	W 2-0	1-0	9	Hignett 39, Fjortoft 76	28286
3	30	PL	A	Newcastle United	L 0-1	0-0	10		(36483)
4	S 9	PL	A	Bolton Wanderers	D 1-1	0-1	11	Hignett 77	(18376)
5	12	PL	H	Southampton	D 0-0	0-0	11		29188
6	16	PL	H	Coventry City	W 2-1	0-0	10	Vickers 57, Fjortoft 78	27882
7	20	CC 2/1	H	**Rotherham United**	W 2-1	2-1		Mustoe 20, Fjortoft 41	13280
8	23	PL	A	Manchester City	W 1-0	1-0	8	Barmby 16	(25865)
9	30	PL	H	Blackburn Rovers	W 2-0	1-0	6	Barmby 44, Hignett 72	29462
10	O 3	CC 2/2	A	**Rotherham United**	W 1-0	0-0		Vickers 50	(6867)
11	15	PL	A	Sheffield Wednesday	W 1-0	0-0	3	Hignett 68(pen)	(21177)
12	21	PL	H	Queens Park Rangers	W 1-0	1-0	3	Hignett 15(pen)	29293
13	25	CC 3	A	**Crystal Palace**	D 2-2	2-2		Barmby 14, Hignett 20	(11873)
14	28	PL	A	Manchester United	L 0-2	0-1	5		(36560)
15	N 4	PL	H	Leeds United	D 1-1	1-1	6	Fjortoft 9	29467
16	8	CC 3R	H	**Crystal Palace**	W 2-0	1-0		Hignett 7, Fjortoft 76	16150
17	18	PL	A	Wimbledon	D 0-0	0-0	8		(13780)
18	21	PL	H	Tottenham Hotspur	L 0-1	0-0	9		29487
19	25	PL	H	Liverpool	W 2-1	1-0	6	Cox 2, Barmby 64	29390
20	29	CC 4	H	**Birmingham City**	D 0-0	0-0			28031
21	D 2	PL	A	Queens Park Rangers	D 1-1	1-1	6	Morris 8	(17546)
22	9	PL	H	Manchester City	W 4-1	1-1	3	Barmby 33, 54, Stamp 53, Juninho 74	29469
23	16	PL	A	Blackburn Rovers	L 0-1	0-1	6		(27996)
24	20	CC 4R	A	**Birmingham City**	L 0-2	0-2			(19878)
25	23	PL	H	West Ham United	W 4-2	3-0	5	Fjortoft 20, Cox 21, Morris 28, Hendrie 82	28640
26	26	PL	A	Everton	L 0-4	0-2	6		(40019)
27	30	PL	A	Nottingham Forest	L 0-1	0-1	7		(27027)
28	J 1	PL	H	Aston Villa	L 0-2	0-2	8		28535
29	6	FAC 3	A	**Notts County**	W 2-1	0-0		Pollock 46, Barmby 48	(12671)
30	13	PL	H	Arsenal	L 2-3	1-1	11	Juninho 38, Stamp 55	29359
31	20	PL	A	Southampton	L 1-2	1-0	12	Barmby 44	(15151)
32	F 4	PL	A	Chelsea	L 0-5	0-3	12		(21060)
33	7	FAC 4	H	**Wimbledon**	D 0-0	0-0			28915
34	10	PL	H	Newcastle United	L 1-2	1-0	12	Beresford 37(og)	30011
35	13	FAC 4R	A	**Wimbledon**	L 0-1	0-0			(5220)
36	17	PL	H	Bolton Wanderers	L 1-4	1-2	12	Pollock 36	29354
37	24	PL	A	Coventry City	D 0-0	0-0	12		(17979)
38	M 2	PL	H	Everton	L 0-2	0-2	12		29807
39	9	PL	A	West Ham United	L 0-2	0-1	13		(23850)
40	16	PL	H	Nottingham Forest	D 1-1	0-0	13	Mustoe 57	29392
41	19	PL	A	Aston Villa	D 0-0	0-0	13		(23933)
42	30	PL	A	Leeds United	W 1-0	1-0	13	Kavanagh 4 (pen)	(31778)
43	A 5	PL	H	Sheffield Wednesday	W 3-1	0-0	13	Fjortoft 53, 66, Freestone 71	29791
44	8	PL	A	Tottenham Hotspur	D 1-1	1-0	12	Whelan 85	(32036)
45	13	PL	H	Wimbledon	L 1-2	1-1	12	Fleming 23	29192
46	27	PL	A	Liverpool	L 0-1	0-0	12		(40782)
47	M 5	PL	H	Manchester United	L 0-3	0-1	12		29921

Best Home League Attendance: 30011 v Newcastle United   Smallest: 27882 v Coventry City   Average: 29259

Goal Scorers:

PL(35):   Barmby(7),Fjortoft(6),Hignett(5),Stamp(2),Juninho(2),Cox(2),Morris(2),Mustoe(1),Pollock(1),Kavanagh(1),Vickers(1),Freestone(1),Fleming(1),Whelan(1),
Hendrie(1),Opponent(s)(1)

CC(7):   Hignett(2),Fjortoft(2),Barmby(1),Vickers(1),Mustoe(1)

FAC(2):   Pollock(1),Barmby(1)

	(F) Barmby	(D) Barron	(D) Blackmore	(D) Branco	(F) Campbell	(D) Cox	(F) Fjortoft	(D) Fleming	(F) Freestone	(F) Hendrie	(M) Hignett	(F) Juninho	(M) Kavanagh	(M) Liddle	(G) Miller	(F) Moore	(F) Moreno	(D) Morris	(M) Mustoe	(D) O'Halloran	(D) Pearson	(M) Pollock	(M) Robson	(M) Stamp	(D) Vickers	(G) Walsh	(D) Whelan	(D) Whyte	(F) Wilkinson		
	X					X	X				X				X		S	X	X		X	X1			X	S	S1	X		G.Ashby	1
	X					X	X				X	S			X		S	X	X		X	X			X		S	X		S.Lodge	2
	X					X	X				X1	S			X		S1	X	X		X	X			X			X		R.Hart	3
	X					X	X				X						S	X	X		X	X			X	X	S	X		P.Danson	4
	X					X	X				X					S	S	X	X		X	X			X	X	S	X		P.Jones	5
	X					X	X				X					S	S	X	X		X	X			X	X	S	X		G.Poll	6
	X		S			X	X									S		X	X		X				X	X	X	X		W.Burns	7
	X					X	X				X						S	X	X		X	X			X	X	S	X		G.Willard	8
	X					X	X			S	X						S		X		X	X			X	X	S	X		P.Alcock	9
	X					X1	X			S	X			S1			S		X		X	X			X	X	X	X		P.Danson	10
	X					X	X1			S1	X			S			S	X	X		X	X			X	X	X	X		G.Ashby	11
	X					X	X		S2		X2						S		X		X	X			X	X	S1	X1		M.Reed	12
	X					X	X2		S2	X1								X	X		X	X			X	X	X			G.Poll	13
	X					X	X1			X							S1	X1	X		X	X			X	X	X			S.Lodge	14
	X		S1			X			S	X1		X		X		X	X	X	X	S	X	X	X		X	X				K.Burge	15
		S1				X		S	X1		X		X		X	X	X	X	S	X	X	X		X	X				P.Jones	16
	X					X	X					X		X	S		S	S2	X		X	X		X	X	X	X			K.Cooper	17
	X					X	X2					X		X			S	S2		X	X1	S1	X	X	X				M.Reed	18
	X					X	X		S			X		X			S	S	X		X	X		X	X	X	X			D.Gallagher	19
	X					X	X1			S1		X		X	S		S	X	X		X	X		X	X	X	X			B.Burns	20
	X					X	S		S	X1		X		X			S		X		X	X		X	X	X	X			P.Durkin	21
	X					X	X		S	S		X		X			S		X		X	X		X	X			X		S.Lodge	22
						X	X1	X	S1		X		X		S		S1				X	X		X	X			X		P.Danson	23
						X	X	X1		X		X		S	S	S1				X	X		X	X			X		M.E.Pierce	24
						X	X	X		X		X		S	S	S	X			X	X	X		X	X			X		S.Dunn	25
						X	X	X		X		X2		X		S2	S3	S1		X	X			X	X			X1	P.Jones	26
		S	X			X		X		X		X		X	S		X	S		X	X			X	X		S		G.Willard	27
		S2				X		X1		X2		X		X		X	S1			X3	X		X	X	X		X	S3	M.Bodenham	28
	X2					X1					X		X	S		S2				X	X	X	S1	X	X	X		X	G.Ashby	29
	X	X				X				X		X			S1	S			X	X1		X	X	X	X		X	G.Poll	30
	X	X				X	S			S2						X2		X		X	X	X	S1	X	X			X	K.Burge	31
	X	X				X	X1			X			X			S	X	X		X	X			X	X	X		S1	K.Cooper	32
	X					X		S1			S	X1	S		X			X		X	X	X		X	X	X			L.Dilkes	33
	X					X		S			S2	X2	S1		X			X		X	X	X1		X	X	X			S.Dunn	34
	X					X		X1			S1	X			X	S		X		X	X			X	X	X2	S1		S.Lodge	35
	X					X	X		S2	X						S2		X		X2	X1			X	X	X2	S1		P.Danson	36
	X					X	X	X		S		X						X		X	X			X	X	X	X	S	P.Durkin	37
	X	X	S	S1		X	X	X		S1	X1		X1		X		X			X				X			X		D.Gallagher	38
			S3			X	X1	X		S1	X1	S1	X				X3	X		X				X			X		M.Reid	39
	X		X			X	S			X	X		S				X	X		X				X			X		A.Wilkie	40
	X		X2			X		X		X	X1	X1	S2				X	X		X				X			X		P.Alcock	41
	X		S			X	S			X	X		X		S		X	X		X			X	X	S		X	K.Cooper	42
				S2		X	X	X	X	X2	S1	X1		X1				X		X				X	X	S	X		P.Jones	43
						X		X	X	X	X	X					X					X		X			X	X	G.Ashby	44
	X		S	S	S	X			X	S1	X	X1		X	X	X				X	X			X			X		R.Dilkes	45
	X		X2	X	S2	X					S	X				X		X			X1	X		X	X		S1	X	P.Durkin	46
	X		X2	X	X	X					X					S2		X		X	X1		S1	X	S	S	X	P.Durkin	47

PL Appearances	32	1	4	5	1	35	27	13	2	7	17	20	6	12	6	5	2	22	21	2	36	31	1	11	32	32	9	24	2		
PL Sub Appearances	0	0	1	2	1	0	1	0	1	6	5	1	1	1	0	7	5	1	0	1	0	0	1	1	0	0	4	1	1		
CC Appearances	4	0	0+1	0	0	5	6	1	0	1+1	3+1	2	0	2+1	0	1+2	2	4	3	0	5	6	1	2	6	6	3	3	0		
FAC Appearances	3	0	0	0	0	2	0	1	0+1	0	0+1	3	0	1	0	0	0	0+1	2	0	2	3	3	1	0+1	3	3	3	0		

Also Played: (M) Swalwell S1(44).

MIDDLESBROUGH

CLUB RECORDS

BIGGEST VICTORIES
League: 9-0 v Brighton & H.A., Division 2, 23.8.1958.
F.A. Cup: 11-0 v Scarborough, Qual. Round, 1890-91.
9-3 v Goole Town, 3rd Round, 1914-15.
League Cup: 5-0 v Brighton & H.A., 2nd Round, 21.9.93.

BIGGEST DEFEATS
League: 0-9 v Blackburn Rovers, Division 2, 6.11.1954.
F.A. Cup: 1-6 v Southampton, 3rd Round, 1905-06.
1-6 v Sheffield Wednesday, 2nd Round, 1894-95.
1-6 v Wolverhampton Wanderers, 3rd Round, 1936-37.
League Cup: 0-4 v Manchester City, Semi-final, 21.1.1976.

MOST POINTS
3 points a win: 94, division 3, 1986-87.
2 points a win: 65, Division 2, 1973-74.

MOST GOALS SCORED
122, Division 2, 1926-27.
Camsell 59, Pease 23, Birrell 16, Williams 9, Carr 6, McClelland 5, McKay 1, Ashman 1, J.Williams 1, Opponents 1.

MOST GOALS CONCEDED
91, Division 1, 1953-54.

MOST FIRST CLASS MATCHES IN A SEASON
60 - 1991-92 (League 46, FA Cup 4, League Cup 8, Zenith Data Cup 2).

MOST LEAGUE WINS
28, Division 3, 1986-87.

MOST LEAGUE DRAWS
19, Division 2, 1924-25.

MOST LEAGUE DEFEATS
27, Division 1, 1923-24.

INDIVIDUAL CLUB RECORDS

MOST GOALS IN A SEASON
George Camsell: 64 goals in 1926-27 (League 59, FA Cup 5).
(English record and League goals (59) is a Division 2 record)

MOST GOALS IN A MATCH
5. Andy Wilson v Nottingham Forest, 6.10.1923.
5. George Camsell v Manchester City 5-3 (a), 25.12.1926.
5. George Camsell v Aston Villa 7-2 (a), 9.9.1935.
5. Brian Clough v Brighton & H.A. 9-0, Division 2, 22.8.1958.

OLDEST PLAYER
Bryan Robson, 38 years, 360 days v Notts County, FAC, 6.1.96.

YOUNGEST PLAYER
Sam Lawrie, 16 years 323 days v Arsenal, Division 1, 3.11.51.
Stephen Bell, 16 years 323 days v Southampton, Division 1, 30.1.1982.

MOST CAPPED PLAYER
Wilf Mannion (England) 26, 1946-51.

BEST PERFORMANCES

League: 1986-87: Matches played 46, Won 28, Drawn 11, Lost 8, Goals for 67, Goals against 30, Points 94. Second in Division 3.
Highest Position: Third in Division 1, 1913-14.
F.A. Cup: 6th round in 1935-36, 1946-47, 1969-70, 1976-77.
Most recent success: 1980-81: 3rd Round Swansea City 5-0; 4th Round West Bromwich Albion 1-0; 5th Round Barnsley 2-1; 6th Round Wolverhampton Wanderers 1-1,1-3.
League Cup: Semi-final in 1975-76.
Most recent success: 1991-92: 2nd Round Bournemouth 1-1,2-1; 3rd Round Barnsley 1-0; 4th Round Manchester City 2-1; 5th Round Peterborough Utd 0-0,1-0; Semi-final Manchester United 0-0,1-2.

ADDITIONAL INFORMATION
PREVIOUS NAMES
None.

PREVIOUS LEAGUES
Northern League 1889-1899.

Club colours: Red shirts/white trim, white shorts/red trim, white socks.
Change colours: White shirts, black shorts, white socks.

Reserves League: Pontins Central League Premier Division.

DIVISIONAL RECORD

	Played	Won	Drawn	Lost	For	Against	Points
Division 1/P	1,944	675	466	803	2,867	3,097	1,855
Division 2/1	1,510	624	367	519	2,389	2,053	1,779
Division 3	92	51	19	22	154	94	149
Total	**3,546**	**1,450**	**852**	**1,344**	**5,410**	**6,244**	**3,783**

RECORDS AND STATISTICS

COMPETITIONS

DIVISION 1/P	DIVISION 2/1	DIVISION 3
1902-24	1899-02	1966-67
1927-28	1924-27	1986-87
1929-54	1928-29	
1974-82	1954-66	
1988-89	1967-74	
1992-93	1982-86	
1995-	1987-88	
	1989-92	
	1993-95	

HONOURS

DIVISION 2/1	ANGLO/SCOT	AMATEUR CUP
1926-27	1975-76	1895
1928-29		1898
1973-74		
1994-95		

MOST GOALS IN A CAREER
GEORGE CAMSELL - 345 (1925-39)

YEAR	LEAGUE	FA CUP
1925-26	3	
1926-27	59	4
1927-28	33	4
1928-29	30	3
1929-30	29	2
1930-31	32	
1931-32	20	
1932-33	17	1
1933-34	23	1
1934-35	14	
1935-36	28	4
1936-37	18	
1937-38	9	1
1938-39	10	
Total	325	20

Current leading goalscorer: John Hendrie - 56 (1990-96)

MOST APPEARANCES
TIM WILLIAMSON 602 (1902-23)

YEAR	LEAGUE	FA CUP
1901-02	2	
1902-03	16	
1903-04	34	4
1904-05	33	2
1905-06	34	5
1906-07	38	2
1907-08	37	1
1908-09	38	1
1909-10	38	2
1910-11	36	4
1911-12	36	4
1912-13	37	4
1913-14	29	1
1914-15	20	2
1919-20	37	2
1920-21	42	1
1921-22	26	1
1922-23	30	3
	563	39

MANAGERS

NAME	SEASONS	BEST	WORST
Peter McWilliam	1927-34	7(1)	1(2)
Wilf Gillow	1934-44	4(1)	20(1)
David Jack	1944-52	6(1)	19(1)
Walter Rowley	1952-54	13(1)	21(1)
Bob Dennison	1954-63	4(2)	14(2)
Raich Carter	1963-66	10(2)	21(2)
Stan Anderson	1966-73	4(2)	2(3)
Jack Charlton	1973-77	7(1)	1(2)
John Neal	1977-81	9(1)	14(1)
Bobby Murdoch	1981-82	22(1)	22(1)
Malcolm Allison	1982-84	16(2)	17(2)
Willie Maddren	1984-86	19(2)	21(2)
Bruce Rioch	1986-90	18(1)	2(3)
Colin Todd	1990-91	7(2)	21(2)
Lennie Lawrence	1991-94	21(1/P)	9(2/1)
Bryan Robson	1994-	12(P)	1(2/1)

RECORD TRANSFER FEE RECEIVED

AMOUNT	CLUB	PLAYER	DATE
2,300,000	Manchester Utd	Gary Pallister	8/89
1,600,000	Manchester City	Alan Kernaghan	9/93
1,500,000	Blackburn Rovers	Stuart Ripley	7/92
1,000,000	Celtic	Tony Mowbray	1/92

RECORD TRANSFER FEE PAID

AMOUNT	CLUB	PLAYER	DATE
7,000,000	Juventus	Fabrizio Ravanelli	07/96
5,250,000	Tottenham H.	Nick Barmby	8/95
4,750,000	Sao Paulo	Juninho	10/95
4,000,000	Porto	Emerson	05/96

LONGEST LEAGUE RUNS

f undefeated matches:	24 (8.9.1973 - 9.1.1974)	of league matches w/out a win:	19 (3.10.1981 - 6.3.1982)
f undefeated home matches:	27 (8.2.1935 - 10.4.1937)	of undefeated away matches:	14 (14.4.1973 - 12.1.1974)
without home win:	10 (10.11.1984 - 2.3.1985)	without an away win:	33 (7.3.1903 - 7.9.1907)
f league wins:	9 (16.2.1974 - 6.4.1974)	of home wins:	11 (22.11.1913 - 22.4.1914)
f league defeats: 8 (25.8.1954 - 2.10.1954 & 26.12.95 - 17.2.96)		of away wins:	5 (18.2.1974 - 30.3.1974, 21.3.1987 - 9.5.1987)

MIDDLESBROUGH

PLAYERS NAME / Honours	Ht	Wt	Birthdate	Birthplace / Transfers	Contract Date	Clubs	League	L/Cup	FA Cup	Other	Lge	L/C	FAC	Oth
GOALKEEPERS														
Miller Alan J	6.2	13.8	29/03/70	Epping	05/05/88	Arsenal	6+2							
E: u21.4,S. FAYC'88. ECWC'94.				Loan	24/11/88	Plymouth Argyle	13		2					
				Loan	15/08/91	W.B.A.	3							
				Loan	19/12/91	Birmingham City	15			1				
				£500000	12/08/94	Middlesbrough	47	1	2	2				
Roberts Ben J	6.0	12.6	22/06/75	Bishop Auck.	24/03/93	Middlesbrough				1				
				Loan	19/10/95	Hartlepool United	4			1				
				Loan	08/12/95	Wycombe Wand.	15							
Walsh Gary	6.3	14.0	21/03/68	Wigan	25/04/85	Manchester United	49+1	7		6				
E: u21.2. ECWC'91. ESC'91. FAC'94.				Loan	11/08/88	Airdrie	3	1						
				Loan	19/11/93	Oldham Athletic	6							
				£250000	11/08/95	Middlesbrough	32	6	3					
DEFENDERS														
Anderson Vivian A	6.0	11.1	29/08/56	Nottingham	01/08/74	Nottingham Forest	323+5	39	23+1	33	15	5	1	
E: 50,B,7,u12.1. ASC'77.				£250000	03/08/84	Arsenal	120	18	12		9	3	3	
Div.1'78.EC'79'80.ESC'79.LC'79				£250000	09/07/87	Manchester United	50+4	6+1	7	2	2	1	1	
				Free	10/01/91	Sheffield Wed.	60+10	9	8+2	5	8	1	2	2
				Free	01/07/93	Barnsley	20	2			3			
				Free	23/07/93	Middlesbrough	2							
Barron Michael J	5.10	11.3	22/12/74	Salford	02/02/93	Middlesbrough	2+1	1		3+3				
Blackmore Clayton G	5.9	11.3	23/09/64	Neath	28/09/82	Manchester United	150+36	23+2	15+6	19	19	3	1	4
W: 38,u21.3,Y,S. FAC'90. CS'90				Free	11/07/94	Middlesbrough	30+5	1+1		1	2			
ECWC'91. ESC'91. Prem'93.														
Branco			04/04/64	Bage		Internacional								
Brazil: 83. WC'94.				Free	06/02/96	Middlesbrough	5+2							
Cox Neil J	6.0	12.10	08/10/71	Scunthorpe	20/03/90	Scunthorpe United	17		4	4+1	1			
E: u21.6. LC'94.				£400000	12/02/91	Aston Villa	26+16	5+2	4+2	2	3		1	
				£1000000	19/07/94	Middlesbrough	74+1	7+1	2	2	3			
Fleming Curtis	5.8	11.4	08/10/68	Manchester		St.Patricks								
Ei: 7a, u21.5, u23.1. Ei: Div.1'90.				£50000	16/08/91	Middlesbrough	114+12	8+2	8	7+1	1			
Morris Christopher B	5.10	11.6	24/12/63	Newquay	£125000	10/08/87	Celtic	154+16	16+1		22	9	8		1
E:S. Ei: 35. SPD'88. SFAC'88'89					01/08/92	Middlesbrough	72+6	10	6	4	3			1
Div.1'95.					01/10/92	Sheffield Wed.	61+13	5+5	7+5		1	1		
O'Halloran Keith J	5.9	12.3	10/11/75	Dublin		Cherry Orchard								
					06/09/94	Middlesbrough	3+1		2	1				
				Loan	25/03/96	Scunthorpe United	6+1							
Pearson Nigel G	6.1	12.6	21/08/63	Nottingham		Heanor Town								
LC'91. Div.1'95.				£5000	12/11/81	Shrewsbury Town	153	19	6	3	5			
				£250000	16/10/87	Sheffield Wednesday	176+4	17+2	15	10	14	5		
				£750000	19/07/94	Middlesbrough	69	5	5		3			
Vickers Stephen	6.3	12.0	13/10/67	Bishop Auckland		Spennymoor Utd								
LDC'90. Div.1'95.					11/09/85	Tranmere Rovers	310+1	20+1	19	36	11	5	3	1
				£700000	03/12/93	Middlesbrough	101+1	9	7	2	7	1		
Whelan Phil	6.4	14.1	07/03/72	Stockport	02/07/90	Ipswich Town	64+5	6+1	2+1	1	2			
E: u21.4.				£300000	12/04/95	Middlesbrough	9+4	3	3		1			
White Alan	6.1	13.0	22/03/76	Darlington	08/07/94	Middlesbrough				1				
Whyte Derek	5.11	11.5	31/08/68	Glasgow		Celtic	211+5	18+1	26	15	7			1
S: 9,B3,u21.9,Y,S. SPD'88.SFAC'88'89. Div.1'95.					01/08/92	Middlesbrough	136+2	11	1+1	6	2			
MIDFIELD														
Emerson			12/04/72	Rio de Janeiro		Porto								
Portugusse Lge Champs'95'96.				£4000000	14/05/96	Middlesbrough								
Hignett Craig	5.10	11.0	12/01/70	Prescot		Liverpool								
Div.1'95.				Free	11/05/88	Crewe Alexandra	108+13	9+1	11+1	6+1	42	4	8	3
				£500000	27/11/92	Middlesbrough	79+19	9+2	2+1	5+1	22	8		
Kavanagh Graham A	5.9	11.5	02/12/73	Dublin		Home Farm								
Ei: u21.8, Y.				16/08/91	Middlesbrough		22+13	1	3+1	7	3		1	
				Loan	25/02/94	Darlington	5							
Liddle Craig	5.11	12.0	21/10/71	Chester-Le-Street		Blyth Spartans								
				Free	12/07/94	Middlesbrough	13+1	2+1	1	2				
Mustoe Robbie	5.11	11.6	28/08/68	Witney	02/07/86	Oxford United	78+13	2	2	3	10			
				£375000	05/07/90	Middlesbrough	171+9	24+1	10	12+1	13	7		1
Pollock Jamie	6.0	11.2	16/02/74	Stockton	18/12/91	Middlesbrough	144+11	17+2	13+1	4+1	18	1	1	
E: u21.2, Y.8. Div.1'95.														
Robson Bryan	5.10	12.12	11/01/57	Witton Gilbert	01/08/74	W.B.A.	193+4	17+1	10+2	12	39	2	2	3
E:90,B3,u21.7,Y.Flg.3.CS'83'93				£1500000	05/10/81	Manchester United	326+19	50+1	33+2	32+2	74	5	10	11
FAC'83'85'90.ECWC'91.Prem93'94				Free	01/05/94	Middlesbrough	22+2	1	1		1			
Stamp Philip L	5.9	11.9	12/12/75	Middlesbrough	04/02/93	Middlesbrough	20+5	4	1+1	5+1	2			
Summerbell Mark			30/10/76	Durham		Middlesbrough	0+1							
FORWARDS														
Barmby Nick	5.6	11.0	11/02/74	Hull	09/04/91	Tottenham Hotspur	81+6	7+1	12+1		20	2	5	
E: 9, B.1, u23.3. Y.8,S.				£5250000	08/08/95	Middlesbrough	32	4	3		7	1	1	
Beck Mikkel						Fortuna Koln								
Danish Int.					01/07/96	Middlesbrough								

Name	ft	st	DOB	From	Fee	Date	Club								
mpbell Andrew			18/04/79	Middlesbrough		09/07/96	Middlesbrough	1+1							
rtoft Jan A	6.0	12.8	10/01/67	Aalesund, Norway			Rapid Vienna								
					£500000	29/07/93	Swindon Town	62+10	9	3	1	27	9	2	
					£1300000	31/03/95	Middlesbrough	35+1	6			9	2		
eestone Christopher	5.11	11.7	04/09/71	Nottingham			Arnold								
					£10000	02/12/94	Middlesbrough	2+2		0+1		1			
ndrie John G	5.7	11.12	24/10/63	Lennoxtown		18/05/81	Coventry City	15+8	2			2			
Y. Div.3'85. Div.2'90.															
					Loan	10/01/84	Hereford United	6							
.1'95.															
					Free	02/07/84	Bradford City	173	17	11	11	46	3	6	4
					£500000	17/06/88	Newcastle United	34	2	4	3	4	1		
					£600000	20/06/89	Leeds United	22+5	1	1	2	5			
					£550000	05/07/90	Middlesbrough	181+11	21+1	10+2	6	44	6	2	4
ninho			22/02/73	Sao Paulo			Sao Paulo								
azil: 26. Brazilian P.O.Y'94															
					£4750000	07/10/95	Middlesbrough	20+1	2	3		2			
Garlge Stephen			24/10/75	Gateshead		01/08/93	Middlesbrough								
ore Alan	5.10	10.7	25/11/74	Dublin		05/12/91	Middlesbrough	82+11	7+2	1+1	3+1	14	1	2	
5, u21.3, Y. Div.1'95															
vanelli Fabrizio							Juventus								
ian Int. Serie'A'95. EC'96.					£7000000	22/07/96	Middlesbrough								
chardson Paul	5.8	11.1	22/07/77	Durham			Middlesbrough			1					

ADDITIONAL CONTRACT PLAYERS

Name	From	Date	Club
le Benjamin		09/07/96	Middlesbrough
nnor Paul		09/07/96	Middlesbrough
mmins Michael			Middlesbrough
al Claudio			Middlesbrough
e Patrick			Middlesbrough
rales Jaime			Middlesbrough
merod Anthony		09/07/96	Middlesbrough
alwell Andrew		09/07/96	Middlesbrough
ite Darren			Middlesbrough

THE MANAGER
BRYAN ROBSON

Date of Birth . . . . 11th January 1957.
Place of Birth . . . . Witton Gilbert.
Date of Appointment . . . . May 1994.

PREVIOUS CLUBS
As Manager. . . . . None.
As Coach. . . . . None.
As a Player. . . . . West Bromwich Albion, Manchester United.

HONOURS
As a Manager
Middlesbrough: Division 1 championship 1994-95.

As a Player
Manchester United: Premiership championship 1992-93, 1993-94. FA Cup 1983, 1985, 1990.
ECWC 1991.
Charity Shield 1983. Flg. XI.3.
International: 90 full caps, 7 U21, 3 'B' and Youth for England. (Currently England first team Coach).

Cellnet Riverside Stadium
Middlesbrough, Cleveland, TS3 6RS
Tel: 01642 227 227

Capacity..30,000.

First game...v Chelsea (2-0), Premier League, 26.08.1995.
First floodlit game ....v Southampton (0-0), Premier League, 12.09.1995.
ATTENDANCES
Highest ....30,011 v Newcastle United, 10.02.96.
Lowest..13,280 v Rotherham, League Cup, 20.09.95.

OTHER GROUNDS ....Old Archery Ground 1876-79. Breckon Hill Road 1879-80.
....Linthorpe Road 1880-1903. Ayresome Park 1903-1995.

HOW TO GET TO THE GROUND

From the North & South
Use A19 (sign posted Middlesbrough) until its junction with A66.
Continue along A66 through Middlesbrough. At the first roundabout
turn left. Cross the railway for Middlesbrough FC.

From the West
Use A66 through Middlesbrough. At the first roundabout turn left.
Cross the railway for MIddlesbrough FC.

MATCHDAY TICKET PRICES

Adults........................ £12.50 - £19

Juniors/OAP .... £7.50 - £12.50

BORO LIVEWIRE
0891 42 42 00
Calls cost 39p per minute cheap rate and 49p per
minute at all other times.
Call costings correct at time of going to press.

MATCHDAY PROGRAMME

Programme Editor . . . . Dave Allan.

Number of pages . . . . 48.

Price . . . . £1.50.

Subscriptions. . . . . . £31.99 home, £63.98 home & away (League only).

Local Newspapers . . . . Evening Gazette, Northern Echo,
. . . . Hartlepool Mail.

Local Radio Stations . . . . BBC Radio Cleveland, TFM,
. . . . Century Radio.

NEWCASTLE UNITED
(The Magpies)
F.A. CARLING PREMIERSHIP
SPONSORED BY: NEWCASTLE BREWERIES LTD

...ck row L-R: Chris Holland, Nicos Papavasiliou, Alan Neilson, Nathan Murray, Stephen Harper, Mike Jeffrey, Alex Mathie, Jason Drysdale, ...lcolm Allen. **Middle Row:** Paul Ferros (assistant physio), Derek Fazakerley (first team coach), Scott Sellers, Lee Clark, Steve Howey, ...ke Hooper, Steve Watson, Pavel Srnicek, Philippe Albert, Marc Hottiger, Steve Guppy, Bob elliott, Jeff Clark (reserve team coach), Derek ...ight (physio). **Front Row:** Barry Venison, John Beresford, Andy Cole, Peter Beardsley, Terry McDermott (asst.manager), Kevin Keegan ...anager), Arthur Cox (coach), Paul Bracewell, Ruel Fox, Robert Lee, Darren Peacock.

**NEWCASTLE UNITED
FORMED IN** 1892
TURNED PROFESSIONAL IN 1892
LTD COMPANY IN 1895

PRESIDENT: Trevor Bennett
CHAIRMAN: Sir John Hall

DIRECTORS
T B Bennett, Douglas Hall, R S Jones
Freddie Shepherd (Vice-chairman)
CHIEF EXECUTIVE
Freddie Fletcher
GENERAL MANAGER/SECRETARY
Russell Cushing
COMMERCIAL MANAGER
Trevor Garwood (0191 201 8400)

MANAGER: Kevin Keegan
ASSISTANT MANAGER: Terry McDermott

PHYSIOTHERAPIST
Derek Wright/Paul Ferris

STATISTICIAN FOR THE DIRECTORY
Dave Graham & David Stewart

So near and yet, in the end, so far!
Newcastle United started the 1995/96 season as though it was there last. Twelve victories in a 13 game sequence (their only defeat a surprise 0-1 defeat at Southampton) set the pace to which the rest of the Premiership would have to follow if the Magpie's were to be denied the title.

By the mid-way point in the season Newcastle had won 14, drawn 3, lost 2, and they were in the quarter finals of the Coca-Cola Cup. The Magpie's form owned mainly to the goal scoring of their record summer signing, Les Ferdinand. 21 goals in the first 23 games, 18 in the League made Ferdinand one of the most feared strikers in the country.

The second-half of the League season was kicked off with only their third defeat to date, their opponents though were Manchester United, this was followed by their F.A. Cup exit at St James' Park against Chelsea, and defeat against Arsenal in the Coca-Cola Cup. Rumours that the black and white army were starting to falter were soon dispelled when they reeled off three straight wins.

It was at this stage of the season that Keegan brought in the highly rated Faustino Asprilla from Parma. He made an immediate impact by coming on as a sub and setting Les Ferdinand up for his 21st League goal of the season.

However, the following six matches probably cost the Magpies the championship. Only four points were picked up (3-0 v. West Ham, 3-3 v. Manchester City), and the sixth game probably saw one of the best matches of modern times, the 3-4 defeat at the hands of Liverpool. Having lost in the last minute at St. James' Park and having been knocked out of the Coca-Cola Cup by Newcastle, Liverpool weren't out to do Keegan's men any favours, although the Magpies had the lead twice!

This was followed by victory against Queens Park Rangers but then another bad defeat this time at Ewood Park, and again having taken the lead, with only 14 minutes remaining.

Newcastle saw out the season with three wins and two draws, but with Manchester United at the top and not dropping points, the Championship dream had faded leaving all involved with Newcastle United Football Club thinking about what could have been.

There is no doubt that Newcastle's near championship season will be followed by another serious title charge this season, and with the World record signing of Alan Shearer during the summer the Magpies must surely be favourites.

NEWCASTLE UNITED

League: 2nd   FA Cup: 3rd Rnd   Coca-Cola Cup: Quarter Finals

M	DATE	COMP	VEN	OPPONENTS	RESULT	HT	LP	GOAL SCORERS/GOAL TIMES	ATT.
1	A 19	PL	H	Coventry City	W 3-0	1-0	2	Lee 7, Beardsley 82 (pen), Ferdinand 83	36485
2	22	PL	A	Bolton Wanderers	W 3-1	1-0	1	Ferdinand 17, 84, Lee 77	(20243)
3	27	PL	A	Sheffield Wednesday	W 2-0	0-0	1	Ginola 53, Beardsley 75	(24815)
4	30	PL	H	Middlesbrough	W 1-0	0-0	1	Ferdinand 67	36483
5	S 9	PL	A	Southampton	L 0-1	0-0	1		(15237)
6	16	PL	H	Manchester City	W 3-1	2-0	1	Beardsley 18(pen), Ferdinand 38, 59	36501
7	19	CC 2/1	A	**Bristol City**	**W 5-0**	**3-0**		**Peacock 8, Sellars 22, Ferdinand 30, Gillespie 46, Lee 85**	**(15952)**
8	24	PL	H	Chelsea	W 2-0	1-0	1	Ferdinand 41, 57	36225
9	O 1	PL	A	Everton	W 3-1	1-0	1	Ferdinand 20, Lee 59(pen), Kitson 65	(33080)
10	4	CC 2/2	H	**Bristol City**	**W 3-1**	**0-1**		**Barton 48, Albert 55, Ferdinand 65**	**36357**
11	14	PL	A	Queens Park Rangers	W 3-2	0-1	1	Gillespie 48, 72, Ferdinand 57	(18254)
12	21	PL	A	Wimbledon	W 6-1	3-0	1	Howey 31, Ferdinand 35, 41, 63 (3), Clark 59, Albert 84	36434
13	25	CC 3	A	**Stoke City**	**W 4-0**	**2-0**		**Beardsley 30, 39, Ferdinand 52, Peacock 73**	**(23000)**
14	29	PL	A	Tottenham Hotspur	D 1-1	0-1	1	Ginola 47	(32279)
15	N 4	PL	H	Liverpool	W 2-1	1-1	1	Ferdinand 3, Watson 89	36547
16	8	PL	H	Blackburn Rovers	W 1-0	1-0	1	Lee 13	36463
17	18	PL	A	Aston Villa	D 1-1	0-1	1	Ferdinand 58	(39167)
18	25	PL	H	Leeds United	W 2-1	0-1	1	Lee 70, Beardsley 72	36572
19	29	CC 4	A	**Liverpool**	**W 1-0**	**0-0**		**Watson 77**	**(40077)**
20	D 3	PL	A	Wimbledon	D 3-3	3-2	1	Ferdinand 8, 29, Gillespie 35	(18002)
21	9	PL	A	Chelsea	L 0-1	0-1	1		(31098)
22	16	PL	H	Everton	W 1-0	1-0	1	Ferdinand 17	36557
23	23	PL	H	Nottingham Forest	W 3-1	2-1	1	Lee 12, 74, Ginola 25	36531
24	27	PL	A	Manchester United	L 0-2	0-1	1		(42024)
25	J 2	PL	H	Arsenal	W 2-0	1-0	1	Ginola 1, Ferdinand 46	36530
26	7	FAC 3	A	**Chelsea**	**D 1-1**	**0-0**		**Ferdinand 90**	**(25151)**
27	10	CC QF	A	**Arsenal**	**L 0-2**	**0-1**			**(37857)**
28	14	PL	A	Coventry City	W 1-0	1-0	1	Watson 44	(20532)
29	17	FAC 3R	H	**Chelsea**	**D 2-2**	**1-0**		**Albert 43, Beardsley 64(pen)** *(Lost on penalties)*	**36534**
30	20	PL	A	Bolton Wanderers	W 2-1	2-1	1	Kitson 9, Beardsley 37	36543
31	F 3	PL	H	Sheffield Wednesday	W 2-0	0-0	1	Ferdinand 54, Clark 90	36567
32	10	PL	A	Middlesbrough	W 2-1	0-1	1	Watson 73, Ferdinand 78	(30011)
33	21	PL	A	West Ham United	L 0-2	0-1	1		(23834)
34	24	PL	A	Manchester City	D 3-3	1-1	1	Albert 44, 81, Asprilla 71	(31115)
35	M 4	PL	H	Manchester United	L 0-1	0-0	1		36584
36	18	PL	H	West Ham United	W 3-0	1-0	1	Albert 21, Asprilla 55, Ferdinand 65	36331
37	23	PL	A	Arsenal	L 0-2	0-2	1		(38271)
38	A 3	PL	A	Liverpool	L 3-4	2-1	2	Ferdinand 10, Ginola 14, Asprilla 57	(40702)
39	6	PL	H	Queens Park Rangers	W 2-1	0-0	2	Beardsley 77, 81	36583
40	8	PL	H	Blackburn Rovers	L 1-2	0-0	2	Batty 76	(30717)
41	14	PL	H	Aston Villa	W 1-0	0-0	2	Ferdinand 64	36510
42	17	PL	A	Southampton	W 1-0	1-0	2	Lee 10	36554
43	29	PL	A	Leeds United	W 1-0	1-0	2	Gillespie 17	(38862)
44	M 2	PL	A	Nottingham Forest	D 1-1	1-0	2	Beardsley 32	(28280)
45	5	PL	H	Tottenham Hotspur	D 1-1	0-0	2	Ferdinand 71	36589

Best Home League Attendance: 36589 v Tottenham Hotspur   Smallest: 36225 v Chelsea   Average: 36504

Goal Scorers:
PL(66):   Ferdinand(25),Lee(8),Beardsley(8),Ginola(5),Albert(4),Gillespie(4),Watson(3),Asprilla(3),Clark(2),Kitson(2),Howey(1),Batty(1)
CC(13):   Ferdinand(3),Peacock(2),Beardsley(2),Sellars(1),Lee(1),Watson(1),Gillespie(1),Barton(1),Albert(1)
FAC(3):   Ferdinand(1),Beardsley(1),Albert(1)

Albert (D)	Asprilla (F)	Barton (D)	Batty (M)	Beardsley (F)	Beresford (D)	Clark (M)	Crawford (M)	Drayson (F)	Elliott (D)	Ferdinand (F)	Fox (F)	Gillespie (F)	Ginola (F)	Hislop (G)	Holland (M)	Hottiger (D)	Howey (D)	Huckerby (F)	Keen (G)	Kitson (F)	Lee (F)	Peacock (D)	Sellars (M)	Srnicek (G)	Watson (D)	Referee	No.
		X		X	X	X			S	X	S1	X	X1	X			X				X	X				R.Dilkes	1
		X		X	X	X				X	S	X	X	X			X				X	X		S		S.Lodge	2
		X		X	X	X				X	S	X	X	X		S	X				S	X		S		P.E.Alcock	3
		X		X	X	X				X	S	X	X	X	S	X					X	X	S			R.Hart	4
		X		X		X			S	X	X1	X	X	X			X			S1	X	X				G.Ashby	5
	X3			X2	X1	X				X	S2	X	X	X			X				X	X	S1		S3	J.Winter	6
	X1						X	X	X	X	X1	X	X1	X	S1		X				X	X	X	S1	S1	K.Burge	7
	X1					X	X		X	X	X	X	X2	X			X				X	X	S2	S	S1	P.Jones	8
	X					X	X		X	X		X2	X1	X			X			S1	X	X	X		S2	K.Cooper	9
X	X				X		S2	X2	X	X		X		X	S1	X			S		X	X1		X		J.Kirkby	10
		X	X	X	X	X1			X	X	X	X		X	S1	X1				X1	X	S1		S		P.Durkin	11
S1		X	X	X			X	X	X	X	X	X		X1			X			X1	X	S1				G.Poll	12
S1		X		X					X	X	X	X	X1		X1					X	X	X	S	S		G.Ashby	13
S		X	X				S	X	X	X	X	X		X						X	X	S	S	X		M.Bodenham	14
S1		X	X					X	X1	X	X	X		X						X	X	S	S	X		M.Reed	15
S		X	X			S	X	X	X	X	X		X							X	X		S	X		D.Gallagher	16
S2		X	X	S1		X2			X	X	X		X							X	X		S	X1		S.Lodge	17
S		X	X	X		X	X	X	X	X		X							X	X	S		S			S.Dunn	18
		X	X	X	X1	X	X	X	X		X								X	X	S		S1			P.Durkin	19
S		X	X	X	X	X	X	X	X		X								X	X		S	S			G.Ashby	20
S		X	X	X	X	X	X	X1	X		X								X	X	S1	S				R.Dilkes	21
S1		X	X	X		X	X1	X	X		X								X	X	X	S				P.Durkin	22
X2		X	S2	X		X	X1	X		X							S	X	X	X	S1					D.Elleray	23
		X	X	X2	S	X	X1	X		X							S2	X	X	X	S1					P.Alcock	24
X		X	S2	X X	X	X		X		S	X1	X2	X	X	S1			D.Gallagher	25
X		X	X S S1	X	X		X	X	X1	X	X	X		S.Lodge	26
X		X	X X S	S	X	X		X	X	X	X	X	G.Ashby	27
X		X	X X X	S	X		X	S		X	X	X	X	P.Jones	28
X		X	X X X	X1		X	S	S1	X2	X	X	X	S.Lodge	29
X		X	X X X	S	X	S	S1	X1	X	X	X	K.Cooper	30
X	S1	X	X X X	S	S	X	X1	X	S1	X	X	X	P.Danson	31
X	X	X	X X X	X	X1	X		S1	X	X	S.Dunn	32
X	X	X	X X X	S	X	X	S	S	X	X	P.Alcock	33
X	X	X	X X X	S	X	X	S	X		X	X	M.Bodenham	34
X	X	X	X	X X S	X	S	X	X		X	S	D.Elleray	35
X	X1	X	X X X	X	S	X	X	X	S	X	S1	S.Lodge	36
X	X1	X	X X X	X	S	X	X	X	S	X	S1	P.Durkin	37
X	X	X	X X S	X	S	S	X1	X	S1	X	X	M.Reed	38
X	X	X	X X X	S	X	S1	X	X	X1	X		X	P.Sampson	39
X	X1	X	X X X	S	X	S1	X	X	X	X		X	G.Willard	40
X	X	S	X	X	X1	S	S1	X	X	X	X	X	M.Bodenham	41
X	X1	S	X	X	S	S1	X	X	X	X	X		X	D.Gallagher	42
X	X1	S2	X	X	S1	X	X	X	X	S	X	X	K.Burge	43
X	S2	S	X	X	S1	X	X	X2	X1	X	X	X	R.Dilkes	44
X	S1	S	X	X1	S1	X	X	X1	X	X	X	X	J.Gallagher	45

Albert	Asprilla	Barton	Batty	Beardsley	Beresford	Clark	Crawford	Drayson	Elliott	Ferdinand	Fox	Gillespie	Ginola	Hislop	Holland	Hottiger	Howey	Huckerby	Keen	Kitson	Lee	Peacock	Sellars	Srnicek	Watson		
9	11	30	11	35	32	23	0	0	5	37	2	26	34	24	0	0	28	0	0	2	36	33	2	14	15	PL Appearances	
4	3	1	0	0	1	6	0	0	1	0	2	2	0	0	0	1	0	1	0	5	0	1	4	1	8	PL Sub Appearances	
+1	0	5	0	3	2	3	0+1	1	2	5	1	4	4	4	0+1	1+1	4	0	0	4	5	2	1+1	2+3		CC Appearances	
2	0	2	0	2	1	1+1	0	0	1	2	0	0	2	0	0	0	0+1	0	2	1	2	0	2	1		FAC Appearances	

NEWCASTLE UNITED

CLUB RECORDS

BIGGEST VICTORIES
League: 13-0 v Newport County, Division 2, 5.10.1946 (joint record).
F.A. Cup: 9-0 v Southport, 4th Round, 1.2.1932.
League Cup: 7-1 v Notts County (A), 2nd Round, 5.10.1993.
Europe: 5-0 v Antwerp (h), (UEFA) 1st Round 1st leg, 13.9.1994. (2nd leg United won 5-2, 27.9.1994)
5-1 v Vittoria Setubal (UEFA) 12.3.1969.
4-0 v Bohemians (UEFA) 28.9.1977.
4-0 v Feyenoord (UEFA) 1st Round, 11.9.1968.

BIGGEST DEFEATS
League: 0-9 v Burton Wanderers, Division 2, 15.4.1895.
F.A. Cup: 1-7 v Aston Villa, 2nd Round, 16.2.1895.
League Cup: 2-7 v Manchester United, 4th Round, 27.10.1976.
Europe: No more than 2 goals difference.

MOST POINTS
3 points a win: 96, Division 1, 1992-93 (46 games).
2 points a win: 57, Division 2, 1964-65.

MOST GOALS SCORED
98, Division 1, 1951-52.
G.Robledo 33, Milburn 25, Mitchell 9, Foulkes 6, Davies 5, Hannah 5, Duncan 3, Keeble 3, Prior 2, Walker 2, Brennan 1, Crowe 1, Harvey 1, Taylor 1, Opponents 1.

MOST GOALS CONCEDED
109, Division 1, 1960-61.

MOST FIRST CLASS MATCHES IN A SEASON
95 - 1994-95 (League 67, FA Cup 9, League Cup 6, UEFA 13).

MOST LEAGUE WINS
29, Division 1, 1992-93.

MOST LEAGUE DRAWS
17, Division 2, 1990-91.

MOST LEAGUE DEFEATS
26, Division 1, 1977-78.

INDIVIDUAL CLUB RECORDS

MOST GOALS IN A SEASON
Andy Cole: 41 goals in 1993-94 (League 34, FA Cup 1, League Cup 6).

MOST GOALS IN A MATCH
6. L Shackleton v Newport, Division 2, 13-0, 5.10.1946.

OLDEST PLAYER
William Hampson, 44 years 225 days v Birmingham City, Division 1 9.4.1927.

YOUNGEST PLAYER
Stephen Watson, 16 years 223 days v Wolverhampton Wders., Division 2, 10.11.1990.

MOST CAPPED PLAYER
Alf McMichael (Northern Ireland) 40.

BEST PERFORMANCES

League: 1992-93: Matches played 46, Won 29, Drawn 9, LOst 8, Goals for 92, Goals against 38, Points 96. First in Division 2/1.
Highest Position: Division 1 champions four times.
F.A. Cup: Winners in 1909-10, 1923-24, 1931-32, 1950-51, 1951-52
Most recent success: 1954-55: 3rd Round Plymouth 1-0; 4th Round Brentford 3-2; 5th Round Nottingham Forest 1-1,2-2,2-1; 6th Round Huddersfield 1-1,2-0; Semi-final York City 1-1,2-0; Final Manchester City 3-1.
League Cup: 1975-76: 2nd Round Southport 6-0; 3rd Round Bristol Rovers 1-1,2-0; 4th Round Queens Park Rangers 3-1; 5th Round Notts County 1-0; Semi-final Tottenham 0-1,3-1; Final Manchester City 1-2.
Europe: (UEFA) 1968-69: 1st Round Feyenoord 4-0,0-2; 2nd Round Sporting Lisbon 1-1,1-0; 3rd Round Real Zaragossa 2-3,2-1; 4th Round Vittoria Setubal 5-1,1-3; Semi-final Rangers 0-0,2-0; Final Ujpest Dozsa 3-0,3-2.

DIVISIONAL RECORD

	Played	Won	Drawn	Lost	For	Against	Points
Division 1/P	2,666	1,058	631	976	4,168	3,899	2,877
Division 2/1	1,046	481	218	347	1,798	1,438	1,318
Total	**3,712**	**1,539**	**849**	**1,323**	**5,966**	**5,337**	**4,195**

ADDITIONAL INFORMATION
PREVIOUS NAMES
Newcastle East End 1882-92.

PREVIOUS LEAGUES
Northern League.

Club colours: Black/white striped shirts, black shorts, black socks/white tops.

Change colours: All gorge.

Reserves League: Pontins Central League Division 1.

RECORDS AND STATISTICS

COMPETITIONS

Div 1/P	Div.2/1	UEFA	A/Ital	A/Scot	Texaco
1898-1934	1893-98	1968-69	1972-73	1975-76	1971-72
1948-61	1934-48	1969-70		1976-77	1972-73
1965-78	1961-65	1970-71			1973-74
1984-89	1978-84	1977-78			1974-75
1993-	1989-93	1994-95			

HONOURS

Div.1	Div 2/1	FAC	UEFA	A/Ital	C/Shield
1904-05	1964-65	1909-10	1968-69	1972-73	1907
1906-07	1992-93	1923-24			1909
1908-09		1931-32		Texaco	
1926-27		1950-51		1973-74	
		1951-52		1974-75	
		1954-55			

MOST APPEARANCES

Jim Lawrence 496 (1904-22)

Year	League	FA Cup
1904-05	29	8
1905-06	33	8
1906-07	33	1
1907-08	38	6
1908-09	38	7
1909-10	34	8
1910-11	36	8
1911-12	27	
1912-13	34	8
1913-14	21	
1914-15	31	5
1919-20	20	1
1920-21	42	4
1921-22	16	
	432	**64**

MOST GOALS IN A CAREER

Jackie Milburn - 200 (1946-57)

Year	League	FA Cup
1945-46		2
1946-47	7	1
1947-48	20	
1948-49	19	
1949-50	18	3
1950-51	17	8
1951-52	25	3
1952-53	5	
1953-54	16	2
1954-55	19	2
1955-56	19	2
1956-57	12	
Total	**177**	**23**

Current leading goalscorer: Peter Beardsley - 111 (1983-87, 1993-96)

RECORD TRANSFER FEE RECEIVED

Amount	Club	Player	Date
£7,000,000*	Manchester Utd	Andy Cole	1/95
£2,300,000	Tottenham	Paul Gascoigne	7/88
£1,900,000	Liverpool	Peter Beardsley	7/87
£1,250,000	Chelsea	Gavin Peacock	7/93

*Included Keith Gillespie signing for Newcastle (valued at £1m)

RECORD TRANSFER FEE PAID

Amount	Club	Player	Date
£15,000,000	Blackburn Rovers	Alan Shearer	07/97
£7,500,000	Parma	Faustino Asprilla	02/96
£6,000,000	Q.P.R.	Les Ferdinand	06/95
£4,000,000	Blackburn	David Batty	03/96
£4,000,000	Wimbledon	Warren Barton	06/95
£2,700,000	Q.P.R.	Darren Peacock	03/94

MANAGERS

Name	Seasons	Best	Worst
A Cunningham	1930-35	5(1)	6(2)
T Mather	1935-39	4(2)	19(2)
S Seymour	1939-47	5(2)	5(2)
G Martin	1947-50	*3(1)	2(2)
S Seymour	1950-54	4(1)	16(1)
D Livingstone	1954-56	*5(1)	8(1)
C Mitten	1958-61	8(1)	21(1)
N Smith	1961-62	11(2)	11(2)
J Harvey	1962-75	7(1)	8(2)
G Lee	1975-77	*7(1)	15(1)
R Dinnis	1977	5(1)	*22(1)
W McGarry	1977-80	21(1)	*22(2)
A Cox	1980-84	*3(2)	11(2)
J Charlton	1984-85	14(1)	14(1)
W McFaul	1985-88	11(1)	*19(1)
J Smith	1988-91	20(1)	*11(2)
O Ardiles	1991-92	11(2)	*23(2)
K Keegan	1992-	2(P)	20(2)

*Indicates position when manager left club.

LONGEST LEAGUE RUNS

of undefeated matches:	14 (22.4.1950 - 30.9.1950)	of league matches w/out a win:	21 (14.1.1978 - 23.8.1978)
of undefeated home matches:	31 (9.12.1905 - 12.10.1907)	of undefeated away matches:	10 (16.11.1907 - 23.3.1908)
without home win:	12 (28.12.1977 - 26.8.1978)	without an away win:	18 (4.9.1984 - 20.4.1985)
of league wins:	13 (25.4.1992 - 18.10.1992)	of home wins:	20 (24.4.1906 - 1.4.1907)
of league defeats:	10 (23.8.1977 - 15.10.1977)	of away wins:	6 (2.5.1922 - 18.10.1992)

NEWCASTLE UNITED

PLAYERS NAME / Honours	Ht	Wt	Birthdate	Birthplace / Transfers	Contract Date	Clubs	APPEARANCES League	L/Cup	FA Cup	Other	GOALS Lge	L/C	FAC	Oth
G O A L K E E P E R S														
Harper Stephen	6.2	13.0	14/03/75	Easington		Seaham Red Star								
				Free	05/07/93	Newcastle United								
				Loan	18/09/95	Bradford City	1							
Hislop Shaka	6.6	12.0	22/02/69	London	09/09/92	Reading	104	10	3	9				
Div2'94				£1575000	10/08/95	Newcastle United	24	4						
Keen Peter	6.0		16/11/76	Middlesbrough	25/03/96	Newcastle United								
Srnicek Pavel	6.4	14.9	10/03/68	Ostrava (Czech)		Banik Ostrava								
Czech: .Div1'93				£350000	05/02/91	Newcastle United	125+1	9+1	11	10				
D E F E N D E R S														
Albert Phillippe	6.3	13.7	10/08/67	Bouillon (Belg)		Anderlecht								
Belgian International				£2650000	12/08/94	Newcastle United	36+4	6+1	2	4	6	2	1	
Arnison Paul S	5.9		18/09/77	Hartlepool	01/03/96	Newcastle United								
Barton Warren	6.0	11.0	19/03/69	Stoke Newington		Leyton Orient								
E: 2, B.2						Leytonstone Ilford								
				£10000	28/07/89	Maidstone	41+1	0+2	3	7			1	
				£300000	07/06/90	Wimbledon	178+2	16	11	2	10	1		
				£4000000	01/08/95	Newcastle United	30+1	5	2			1		
Beresford John	5.6	10.12	04/09/66	Sheffield	16/09/83	Manchester City								
E: B.1, Y.10, u19.3, S;				Free	04/08/86	Barnsley	79+9	5+2	5		5	2	1	
Div1'93				£300000	23/03/89	Portsmouth	102+5	12	11	2	8	2		
				£650000	02/07/92	Newcastle United	141+1	14	12	6	1		1	
Elliott Robert J	5.10	11.6	25/12/73	Newcastle	03/04/91	Newcastle United	42+8	3	6+1	1	2			
E: u21.2, Y1														
Elliott Stuart	5.10		27/08/77	Hendon	28/08/95	Newcastle United								
Howey Stephen N	6.2	10.9	26/10/71	Sunderland	11/12/89	Newcastle United	127+19	13+2	11+2	8	5	1		
E:4. Div1'93														
Peacock Darren	6.2	12.6	03/02/68	Bristol	11/02/86	Newport County	24+4	2	1	1+1				
WFAC'90				Free	23/03/89	Hereford United	56+3	6	6	6	4		1	
				£200000	22/12/90	Q.P.R.	123+3	12	3	2	6	1		
				£2700000	24/03/94	Newcastle United	77+1	9	7	4	1	2		
Watson Stephen C	6.0	12.7	01/04/74	North Shields	06/04/91	Newcastle United	92+24	8+4	8+2	4+3	10	1		
E: u21.6, u19.11, u18.4														
M I D F I E L D														
Batty David	5.8	12.00	02/12/68	Leeds	03/08/87	Leeds United	201+10	17	12	17	4			
E:15, B.5, u21.7, Y.2. Div1'92				£2750000	26/10/93	Blackburn Rovers	53+1	6	5	6	1			
Div2'90				£3750000	02/03/96	Newcastle United	11				1			
Clark Lee	5.8	11.7	27/10/72	Wallsend	09/12/89	Newcastle United	145+26	16	12+1	5+2	21		2	1
E: u21.11, Y6; Div1'93														
Crawford James	5.11	11.06	01/05/73	Dublin		Bohemians								
					01/08/94	Newcastle United		0+1						
Holland Christopher J	5.9	11.5	11/09/75	Whalley		Preston North End	0+1		1					
E: u21.6, Y.5, S				£100000	20/01/94	Newcastle United	2+1	0+1						
F O R W A R D S														
Allen Malcolm	5.8	11.2	21/03/67	Caernarfon	23/03/85	Watford	27+12	4+1	6+8		5	2	6	
W: 14, B.1, Y				Loan	03/09/87	Aston Villa	4							
				£175000	12/08/88	Norwich City	24+11	0+3	5	2+1	8		7	
				£400000	20/03/90	Millwall	64+17	7	0+1	1	24	2		
				£300000	13/08/93	Newcastle United	9+1	3			5	2		
Asprilla Faustino	5.9		10/11/69	Tulua		Parma								
				£6700000	10/02/96	Newcastle United	11+3				3			
Beardsley Peter A	5.8	11.7	18/01/61	Newcastle	09/08/79	Carlisle United	93+11	6+1	15		22		7	
E:59, B2; FLg.1; Div1'88'90;				£275000	01/04/82	Vancouver Wh'caps								
FAC'89; CS'88'89'90				£300000	09/09/82	Manchester United		1						
				Free	01/03/83	Vancouver Wh'caps								
				£150000	23/09/83	Newcastle United	146+1	10	6	1	61			
				£1900000	24/07/87	Liverpool	120+11	13+1	22+3	5	46	1	11	1
				£1000000	05/08/91	Everton	81	8	4	2	25	5	1	1
				£1400000	16/07/93	Newcastle United	104	9	8	4	42	3	3	2
Brayson Paul	5.4		16/09/77	Newcastle	01/08/95	Newcastle United								
E: Y.														

Name	Ht	Wt	DOB	Birthplace	Fee	Date	Club								
Eatock David	5.4		11/11/76	Blacklod			Chorley								
					£75000	30/08/95	Newcastle United								
Ferdinand Les	5.11	13.5	18/12/66	Acton			Hayes								
E: 10. Turkish FAC'89					£15000	12/03/87	Q.P.R.	152+11	11+2	6+1	1	60	7	3	
					Loan	24/03/88	Brentford	3							
					Loan	01/08/88	Besiktas								
					£6000000	01/08/95	Newcastle United	37	5	2		25	3	1	
Gillespie Keith R	5.10	10.11	18/02/75	Bangor		03/02/93	Manchester United	3+6	3			1			
NI: 4.					£1000000	10/01/95	Newcastle United	41+4	4	3		6	1	2	
Ginola David	6.0	13.0	25/01/67	Gossin			Toulon								
							Racing Paris								
							Brest								
							Paris St Germain								
					£2500000	06/07/95	Newcastle United	34	4	2		5			
Huckerby Darren	5.11	10.8	23/04/76	Nottingham		14/07/94	Lincoln City	20+8	2		1	5			2
					£500000	10/11/95	Newcastle United	0+1		0+1					
Kitson Paul	5.11	10.12	09/01/71	Peterlee		15/12/88	Leicester City	39+11	5	1+1	5	6	3	1	1
E: u21.7. FLg u18.1					£1300000	11/03/92	Derby County	105	7	5	13+1	36	3	1	9
					£2250000	24/09/94	Newcastle United	26+7	3	6+1		10	1	3	
Lee Robert M	5.10	11.6	01/02/66	West Ham			Hornchurch								
E: 28, B.1, u21.2; Div1'93					Free	12/07/83	Charlton Athletic	274+24	16+3	14	10+2	59	1	2	3
					£700000	22/09/92	Newcastle United	148	12	12	3	34	3	3	4
Shearer Alan	5.11	11.3	13/08/70	Newcastle		14/04/88	Southampton	105+13	16+2	11+3	8	23	11	4	5
E: 17,B.1,u21.12,Y.5. Prem'95.					£3600000	24/07/92	Blackburn Rovers	132+6	16	8	9	112	14	2	2
					£15,000,000	07/96	Newcastle United								
ADDITIONAL CONTRACT PLAYERS															
Barrett Paul						20/06/96	Newcastle United								
E: Y.															

MANAGER
KEVIN KEEGAN

Date of Birth . . . . 14th February 1951.
Place of Birth. . . . . Armthorpe.
Date of Appointment . . . . February 1992.

PREVIOUS CLUBS
As Manager. . . . . None.
As Coach. . . . . None.
As a Player. . . . . Scunthorpe, Liverpool, SV Hamburg, Southampton,
. . . . Newcastle United.

HONOURS
As a Manager
Division 1 championship 1992-93.

As a Player
Liverpool: Division 1 championship (3 times). FA Cup, European Cup (twice). UEFA (twice).
International: 63 full caps and 5 U23 for England.

St. James Park

Newcastle-upon-Tyne NE1 4ST
Tel: 0191 201 8400 (Fax: 0191 201 8600)

Capacity 36,610

First game ....v Celtic, 3.9.1892.
First floodlit game ....v Celtic, 25.2.1953.

ATTENDANCES
Highest...68,386 v Chelsea, Division 1, 3.9.1930.
Lowest..1,000 v Walsall T S, Div.2, 10.3.1894.

OTHER GROUNDS ....Chillingham Road, Heaton 1882-1892. St. James Park 1892-

HOW TO GET TO THE GROUND

From the North
Use A1 into Newcastle then follow sign Hexham into Percy Street, then turn right into Leazes Park Road (or turn left then right into St James' Street) for Newcastle United FC.

From the South
Use A1, A68 and then A6127, cross River Tyne and at roundabout take 1st exit into Mosley Street. One-way keep to left hand lane into Neville Street. At end turn right into Clayton Street for Newgate Street. Then turn left into Leazes Park Road (one-way) turn left then right into St James' Street for Newcastle United FC.

From the West
Use A69 (sign posted Newcastle) enter city centre then turn left into Clayton Street for Newgate Street. Then turn into Leazes Park Road (one-way) turn left then right into St James' Street for Newcastle United FC.

Car Parking
Parking on the north side of the ground. Also street parking is permitted.

Nearest Railway Station
Central Station (0191 232 6262).

MATCHDAY TICKET PRICES

Not known at the time of going to press.

Apply to club for prices.

Ticket Office Telephone no. 0191 261 1571

CLUBCALL
0891 12 11 90
Calls cost 39p per minute cheap rate and 49p per minute at all other times.
Call costings correct at time of going to press.

MATCHDAY PROGRAMME

Programme Editor . . . . Tony Hardisty.

Number of pages . . . . 40.

Price. . . . . T.BA.

Subscriptions . . . . Telephone: 0191 4871116.

Local Newspapers . . . . Newcastle Chronicle, Newcastle Journal, ... Sunday Sun, Northern Echo, South Shields Gazette.

Local Radio Stations. . . . . Metro Radio, Radio Newcastle, Radio Tees, ... Century Radio.

NOTTINGHAM FOREST
(The Reds)
F.A. CARLING PREMIERSHIP
SPONSORED BY: LABATTS

Back Row (R-L): Scot Gemmill, Paul McGregor, Lars Bohinen, Alf Haaland, Chris Bart-Williams, Kingsley Black, Neil Webb.
Middle Row: Richard Money (Res. Coach), Liam O'Kane (Coach), Andrea Silenzi, Jason Lee, Carl Tiler, Mark Crossley, Tommy Wright, Robert Rosario, Stephen Chettle, Kevin Campbell, John Haseldon (Physio), Peter Edwards (Fitness Consultant). **Front Row:** Des Lyttle, Stephen Stone, Bryan Roy, Frank Clark (Manager), Stuart Pearce (Capt), Alan Hill (Asst. Manager), Ian Woan, David Phillips, Colin Cooper.

NOTTINGHAM FOREST
FORMED IN 1865
TURNED PROFESSIONAL IN 1889
LTD COMPANY IN 1982

CHAIRMAN: F Reacher

DIRECTORS
G E McPherson JP, K R Gibson,
I I Korn (Vice-Chairman), R W Dove,
C Wootton, R A Fairhall
SECRETARY
R A Fairhall
Paul White (0115 952 6000)
COMMERCIAL MANAGER
Dave Pullan (0115 952 6006)

MANAGER: Frank Clark
ASSISTANT MANAGER: Alan Hill

PHYSIOTHERAPIST
John Haselden

STATISTICIAN FOR THE DIRECTORY
Ken Smales

A strange season for Forest started with a thrilling seven goal victory over Southampton followed by four draws, in which they could never score more than a single goal.

It was in fact the lack of a consistent goalscorer that took the edge off what could have been another memorable season for Forest.

Frank Clark's side were the last to lose their unbeaten Premier record. They did this in dramatic fashion on 18th November at Blackburn when Rovers recorded a 7-0 victory. In fact they let in another five to Blackburn in the home game - practically a quarter of Forest's goals conceded against one club!

Forest were also the last British club to be knocked out of European competition, although when defeat was suffered it was another trouncing at home (1-5) from Bayern Munich. Three excellent and well planned victories had been recorded against Malmo, Auxere and Lyon and did much for the English morale as our other representatives didn't cover themselves with glory.

With Collymore off to Liverpool and Bohinen choosing to go to Blackburn, Roy's form and consistency suffered.

Sadly three players bought to score goals Campbell, Lee and Selenci found life hard and it was the lightweight Roy and Ian Woan who were the only ones to reach double figures in the scoring charts.

As usual Forest were well served by the inspirational Stuart Pearce who also won back his England place, and a new national hero emerged from the City Ground when Steve Stone enjoying a purple patch mid-season was also capped by England.

The cups didn't bring the club much joy; losing to Bradford City in the Coca-Cola Cup, although they did reach the quarter finals of the FA Cup before losing to Aston Villa after beating Stoke City and Oxford United.

The club have bounced back impressively into Premier football and they looked as if they had never been away.

The quality of football was always there to be admired but the goals came in bursts, and so if consistency in front of goal is achieved, we should be seeing Nottingham Forest again challenging for honours.

TONY WILLIAMS.

NOTTINGHAM FOREST

League: 9th   **FA Cup: Quarter Finals**   **Coca-Cola Cup: 2nd Rnd**   **UEFA Cup: Quarter Finals**

M	DATE	COMP	VEN	OPPONENTS	RESULT	HT	LP	GOAL SCORERS/GOAL TIMES	ATT.
1	A 19	PL	A	Southampton	W 4-3	3-1	1	Cooper 8, Woan 36, Roy 41,79	(15164)
2	23	PL	H	Chelsea	D 0-0	0-0	1		27007
3	26	PL	H	West Ham United	D 1-1	1-1	2	Pearce 35(pen)	26641
4	29	PL	A	Arsenal	D 1-1	0-1	2	Campbell 61	(38248)
5	S 9	PL	A	Coventry City	D 1-1	1-1	3	Roy 23	(17238)
6	12	UEFA 1/1	A	Malmo	L 1-2	1-0		Woan 38	(12489)
7	17	PL	H	Everton	W 3-2	2-0	3	Watson 17(og), Lee 20, Woan 64	24786
8	19	CC 2/1	A	Bradford City	L 2-3	1-1		Bohinen 18, 90	(9288)
9	23	PL	A	Aston Villa	D 1-1	0-0	5	Lyttle 87	(33972)
10	26	UEFA 1/2	H	Malmo	W 1-0	0-0		Roy 69	23817
11	30	PL	H	Manchester City	W 3-0	1-0		Lee 10,46, Stone 82	25620
12	O 4	CC 2/2	H	Bradford City	D 2-2	1-0		Pearce 19, Silenzi 63	15321
13	14	PL	A	Tottenham Hotspur	W 1-0	0-0	10	Stone 65	(32876)
14	17	UEFA 2/1	A	Auxerre (France)	W 1-0	1-0		Stone 25	(20000)
15	21	PL	H	Bolton Wanderers	W 3-2	1-1	5	Roy 27, Lee 68, Cooper 90	25426
16	28	PL	A	Queens Park Rangers	D 1-1	0-0	4	Lee 47	(17549)
17	31	UEFA 2/2	H	Auxerre (France)	D 0-0	0-0			28064
18	N 6	PL	H	Wimbledon	W 4-1	2-1	3	Roy 8, Pearce 31, Lee 47, Gemmill 87	20810
19	18	PL	A	Blackburn Rovers	L 0-7	0-2	5		(27660)
20	21	UEFA 3/1	H	Lyon	W 1-0	0-0		McGregor 84	22141
21	27	PL	H	Manchester United	D 1-1	1-0	7	McGregor 19	29263
22	D 2	PL	A	Bolton Wanderers	D 1-1	1-0	7	Cooper 90	(17342)
23	5	UEFA 3/2	A	Lyon	D 0-0	0-0			(37000)
24	10	PL	H	Aston Villa	D 1-1	0-0	8	Stone 82	25790
25	18	PL	A	Manchester City	D 1-1	0-1	8	Campbell 69	(25660)
26	23	PL	A	Newcastle United	L 1-3	1-2	8	Woan 14	(36531)
27	26	PL	H	Sheffield Wednesday	W 1-0	1-0	8	Lee 7	27810
28	30	PL	H	Middlesbrough	W 1-0	1-0	5	Pearce 8(pen)	27027
29	J 1	PL	A	Liverpool	L 2-4	2-2	6	Stone 12, Woan 17	(39206)
30	6	FAC 3	A	Stoke City	D 1-1	0-1		Pearce 82	(18000)
31	13	PL	A	Southampton	W 1-0	1-0	5	Cooper 44	23321
32	17	FAC 3R	H	Stoke City	W 2-0	1-0		Campbell 16, Pearce 55(pen)	17372
33	20	PL	A	Chelsea	L 0-1	0-0	6		(24482)
34	31	PL	H	Leeds United	W 2-1	1-0	5	Campbell 39, Roy 57(pen)	24465
35	F 3	PL	A	West Ham United	L 0-1	0-1	9		(21257)
36	F 7	FAC 4	H	Oxford United	D 1-1	0-0		Campbell 54	15550
37	10	PL	A	Arsenal	L 0-1	0-0	9		27222
38	13	FAC 4R	A	Oxford United	W 3-0	1-0		Campbell 40, Woan 82(pen), Silenzi 85	(7948)
39	24	PL	A	Everton	L 0-3	0-0	10		(33163)
40	28	FAC 5	H	Tottenham Hotspur	D 2-2	1-2		Woan 4, 72	18600
41	M 2	PL	A	Sheffield Wednesday	W 3-1	1-0	9	Howe 10, McGregor 46, Roy 80	(21930)
42	5	UEFA QF1	A	Bayern Munich	L 1-2	1-2		Chettle 17	(38000)
43	9	FAC 5R	H	Tottenham Hotspur	D 1-1	1-1		Roy 9 (Won on penalties)	(31055)
44	13	FAC QF	H	Aston Villa	L 0-1	0-1			21067
45	16	PL	A	Middlesbrough	D 1-1	0-0	10	Allen 56	(29392)
46	19	UEFA QF2	H	Bayern Munich	L 1-5	0-2		Stone 82	28844
47	23	PL	H	Liverpool	W 1-0	1-0	9	Stone 43	29058
48	30	PL	A	Wimbledon	L 0-1	0-0	9		(9807)
49	A 6	PL	H	Tottenham Hotspur	W 2-1	0-0	8	Stone 40, Woan 61	27053
50	8	PL	A	Leeds United	W 3-1	2-1	8	Cooper 18, Lee 30, Woan 66	(29220)
51	13	PL	H	Blackburn Rovers	L 1-5	1-3	9	Woan 40	25273
52	17	PL	H	Coventry City	D 0-0	0-0	9		24629
53	28	PL	A	Manchester United	L 0-5	0-2	9		(53926)
54	M 2	PL	H	Newcastle United	D 1-1	0-1	9	Woan 75	28280
55	5	PL	H	Queens Park Rangers	W 3-0	1-0	9	Stone 44, Roy 63, Howe 77	22910

Best Home League Attendance: 29263 v Manchester United   Smallest: 20810 v Wimbledon   Average: 25915

Goal Scorers:

PL(50):	Woan(8),Roy(8),Lee(8),Stone(7),Cooper(5),Campbell(3),Pearce(3),Howe(2),McGregor(2),Allen(1),Lyttle(1),Opponent(s)(1),Gemmill(1)
CC(4):	Bohinen(2),Pearce(1),Silenzi(1)
FAC(10):	Campbell(3),Woan(3),Pearce(2),Roy(1),Silenzi(1)
UEFA(6):	Stone(2),Woan(1),Roy(1),McGregor(1),Chettle(1)

(F) Allen	(M) Armstrong	(M) Bart-Williams	(F) Black	(M) Bohinen	(F) Campbell	(D) Chettle	(G) Clark	(D) Cooper	(G) Crossley	(G) Fettis	(M) Gemmill	(F) Guinan	(M) Haaland	(M) Howe	(F) Irving	(F) Lee	(D) Lyttle	(F) McGregor	(D) Morgan	(D) Pearce	(M) Phillips	(G) Rigby	(F) Roy	(F) Silenzi	(M) Stone	(D) Tiler	(G) Tracey	(F) Woan		
				X	X2	X		X	X							S1	X			X	X		X1		X			X	G.S.Willard	1
		X	X1	X		X	X	X			S					S1	X			X	X		X2		X	S		X	J.Winter	2
				X1	X	X		X	X		S1					S2	X			X			X2		X	S		X	G.R.Ashby	3
				X	X		X	X			X					S1	X			X	X		X1	S	X			X	L.R.Dilkes	4
				X2	X1	X		X	X		S2						X			X	X		X	S1	X			X	P.Jones	5
	S1			S	X2	X		X	X		X		S			S2	X			X1	X		X		X			X	H.Krug	6
	X			X		X		X	X		S1		S	S		X	X			X			X1		X			X	M.J.Bodenham	7
	X			X	X	X		X	X		S		S			X	X			X			X		X			X	T.Lunt	8
	X			X		X		X	X		S		X	S		X	X			X			X		X	S		X	P.Danson	9
	X			X1		X	S	X	X		S1					X	X			X			X1	S1	X			X	M.Batta	10
	X			X1		X		X	X		S1					X	X			X			X2	S2	X	S		X	M.Reed	11
	X				X	S	X	X			X		S			X	X	S		X					X			X	P.E.Alcock	12
	X				X	X	X	X			X		S			X	X	S1	X	X			X1		X			X	R.Hart	13
	X				X	X	X	X			X		X			X1	X			X			S	S1	X	S		X	P.Collima	14
	X				X	X	X	X			X		S			X	X	S		X			X	S	X			X	D.Elleray	15
	X			S	X	X	X	X			X					X	X			X			X	S	X			X	S.Dunn	16
	X				X	X	X	X			X1		S1			X	X	S2		X	S		X2	S	X			X	S.Khussainov	17
	X				X	X	X	X			X		S			X1	X	S		X			X	S1	X			X	P.Alcock	18
	X				X	X		X1	X		X		X			X2	X	S		X	S1			S2	X			X	J.Winter	19
	X				X	X		X	X		X		S	S1			X	S1		X	S	S	X1	X1	X			X	S.Puhl	20
	X				X	X		X	X		X		S1	X2	S2		X	X1		X	S				X			X	K.Cooper	21
	X				X	X		X	X		X		X	S1			X1	X		X	S		X	X	X			X	R.Dilkes	22
	X				X	X		X	X		X1		S1	X		X2	X	S		X	S	S		S2	X			X	M.van der Ende	23
	X				X	X		X	X		X		X	X1	S	X	X			X	S			S1	X				P.Durkin	24
	X			X1	X	X		X	X		X		S	S	S	X				X				S1	X			X	K.Burge	25
	X				X	X		X	X		S		S			X	X	S1		X	X1				X			X	D.Elleray	26
	X			X1	X	X		X	X		X		S			X	X	S		X			S1		X			X	G.Ashby	27
	X				X	X		X	X		X		S			X1	X	S		X			S1		X			X	G.Willard	28
	X				X	X		X	X		X		S				X	X1		X		S	S1		X			X	P.Alcock	29
	X				X	X		X	X		X		S			S1	X			X			X1		X			X	D.Gallagher	30
	X			X1	X	X		X	X		X					S1	X	S		X	S		X		X			X	S.J.Lodge	31
	X			X1	X	S		X	X		X					S1	X			X	S2		X2		X			X	D.J.Gallagher	32
	X			X	X	X		X	X	X1		S				S1	X			X	S		X		X			X	J.Winter	33
	X			X	X	X		X	X		X		S2	S1		S	X2			X			X	X1	X			X	A.B.Wilkie	34
	X			X	X	X		X	X		X1		S1	S1		S	X			X			X	X	X			X	K.Burge	35
	X			X	X	X		X	X	S	X		S				X			X			X	X	X			X	D.R.Elleray	36
	X	X2		X	X	X		X	X		X1		S			S2	X	S1		X			X		X			X	R.A.Hart	37
	X			X	X	X	X	X	X	S	X		S				X			X			X	X	X			X	D.Elleray	38
S		X		X	X	X		X	X		X		S1	S			X			X			X		X			X1	K.Cooper	39
		X		X	X	X		X1	X	S	X		S1				X			X			X	S2	X2			X	G.S.Willard	40
S2	S	X	S1	X	X			X		X			X	X1		X	X2			X			X		X				G.Pole	41
		X		X	X		X	S	X		X		X	S		S	S	S		X			X		X			X	A.Lopez	42
		X		X3	X			X		X	X		X1			S3	X	S2		X	S1		X		X2			X	G.S.Willard	43
		X		X	X			X	X		X					S2	X	S1		X	X		X1		X		X2		M.Bodenham	44
X		X		X	X		X	X	S	X1				S1			X	X		X	X			S				X	A.Wilkie	45
		X1		X1	X		X	X		X			S3			S1	X3	S1		X	X		X		X			X	P.Ceccarini	46
S2		X			X		X	X		X1						X	X	S1		X	S1		X2		X			X	P.S.Danson	47
		X			X		X	X		X		X1	S			X	X	S1		X	S		X		X			X	K.Burge	48
		X			X		X	X		S2	S1		S			X	X	X2		X			X1		X			X	P.Alcock	49
		X		X1	X		X	X		X		X	S			X		S1		X					X			X	R.Hart	50
		X		X	X		X	X		X		X	S			X	X1	S1		X	S				X			X	T.Jones	51
		X		X1	X		X	X		X2		X	S			X	S			X	S2				X			X	M.D.Reed	52
		X			X		X	X		X		X	S			X	S	S		X			X		X			X	J.Winter	53
		X			X		X	X		X1		X	S2			X	S	S1		X			X2		X			X	R.Dilkes	54
		S			X		X	X			X1	X				S1	X2			X	S3		X	S2	X3			X	G.Ashby	55
1	0	32	1	7	21	37	0	37	38	0	26	1	12	4	0	21	32	7	1	31	12	0	25	0	3	34	0	33	PL Appearances	
2	0	0	1	0	0	0	0	0	0	0	4	1	5	5	1	7	1	7	0	0	4	0	3	0	7	0	0	0	PL Sub Appearances	
0	0	2	0	1	0	2	0	2	2	0	1	0	0	0	0	2	2	0	0	1	0	1	1	0	1	1	0	2	CC Appearances	
0	0	7	0	0	0	7	0	5	7	0	7	0	1+1	0	0	0+4	7	0+2	0	4	4+2	0	6	2+1	6	0	0	7	FAC Appearances	
0	0	7+1	0	1	3	8	0	7	8	0	6+1	0	2+3	1+1	0	4+2	7	0+3	0	8	3	0	6	0	1+3	8	0	8	UEFA Appearances	

Also Played: (D) Blatherwick S(35,45)

NOTTINGHAM FOREST

CLUB RECORDS

BIGGEST VICTORIES
League: 12-0 v Leicester City, Division 1, 12.4.1909 (Joint Division 1 record).
F.A. Cup: 14-0 v Clapton, 1st round, 17.1.1891 (a).
League Cup: 7-0 v Bury, 3rd Round 23.9.1980.
Europe: 5-1 v AEK Athens 2nd Round (Euro Cup), 15.11.1978.
4-0 v Eintracht Frankfurt, 1st Round (UEFA), 17.10.1967.

BIGGEST DEFEATS
League: 1-9 v Blackburn Rovers, Division 2, 10.4.1937.
0-8 v West Bromwich Albion, Division 1, 16.4.1900.
0-8 v Leeds City, Division 2, 29.11.1913.
0-8 v Birmingham City, Division 2, 10.3.1920.
0-8 v Burnley, Division 1, 21.11.1959.
F.A. Cup: 0-5 v Southampton, 6th Round, 1962-63.
League Cup: 0-4 v Manchester United, 5th Round, 19.1.1983.
Europe: 1-5 v Valencia, 1st Round, 14.10.1961.

MOST POINTS
3 points a win: 83, Division 1, 1993-94.
2 points a win: 70, Division 3(S), 1950-51 (Division 3(S) record).

MOST GOALS SCORED
110, Division 3(S), 1950-51.
Ardon 36, Capel 23, Collindridge 16, Johnson 15, Scott 9, Leverton 6, Gager 2, Love 1, Burkitt 1, Opponents 1.

MOST GOALS CONCEDED
90, Division 2, 1936-37.

MOST FIRST CLASS MATCHES IN A SEASON
65 - 1979-80 (League 42, FA Cup 2, League Cup 10, European Cup 9, European Super Cup 2).

MOST LEAGUE WINS
30, Division 3(S), 1950-51.

MOST LEAGUE DRAWS
18, Division 1, 1969-70 & 1978-79.

MOST LEAGUE DEFEATS
25, Division 1, 1971-72.

INDIVIDUAL CLUB RECORDS

MOST GOALS IN A SEASON
Wally Ardron: 36 goals in 1950-51 (All League).

MOST GOALS IN A MATCH
5. A Higgins v Clapton (a) 14-0, FA Cup 1st Round, 17.1.1891.

OLDEST PLAYER
Sam Hardy, 41 v Newcastle United, 4.10.1924.

YOUNGEST PLAYER
S J Burke, 16 years 22 days v Ayr United, Anglo-Scot Cup.

MOST CAPPED PLAYER
Stuart Pearce (England) 70.

BEST PERFORMANCES

League: 1950-51: Matches played 46, Won 30, Drawn 10, Lost 6, Goals for 110, Goals against 40, Points 70. First in Division 3(S).
Highest Position: Champions of Division 1, 1977-78.

F.A. Cup: Winners in 1897-98.
Most recent success: 1958-59: 3rd Round 2-2,3-0; 4th Round Grimsby Town 4-1; 5th Round Birmingham 1-1 (2); 6th Round Bolton Wanderers 2-1; Semi-final Aston Villa 1-0; Final Luton Town 2-1.

League Cup: Winners in 1977-78, 1978-79, 1988-89.
Most recent success: 1989-90: 2nd Round Huddersfield Town 1-1,3-3; 3rd Round Crystal Palace 0-0,5-0; 4th Round Everton 1-0; 5th Round Spurs 2-2,3-2; Semi-final Coventry City 2-1,0-0; Final Oldham Athletic 1-0.

Europe: (European Cup) Winners in 1978-79.
Most recent success: 1979-80: 1st Round Oester Vakjo 2-0,1-0; 2nd Round Agres Pitesti 2-1,2-0; 3rd Round Dynamo Berlin 0-1,3-1; Semi-final Real Madrid 2-0,0-1; Final S V Hamburg 1-0.

DIVISIONAL RECORD

	Played	Won	Drawn	Lost	For	Against	Points
Division 1/P	2,102	787	524	790	3,003	3,045	2,340
Division 2/1	1,538	571	384	592	2,332	2,311	1,549
Division 3(S)	88	50	19	19	177	79	119
Total	3,738	1,408	927	1,393	5,512	5,435	4,008

ADDITIONAL INFORMATION
PREVIOUS NAMES
None.

PREVIOUS LEAGUES
Football Alliance.

Club colours: Red shirts, white shorts, red socks.

Change colours: Yellow shirts with blue & red trim, blue shorts with red & yellow trim.

Reserves League: Pontins Central League Division 1.

RECORDS AND STATISTICS

COMPETITIONS

Div 1/P	Div.2/1	Div. 3(S)	Euro C	UEFA	Sup C
1892-06	1906-07	1949-51	1978-79	1961-62	1970-80
1907-11	1911-22		1979-80	1967-68	1980-81
1922-25	1925-49		1980-81	1983-84	
1957-72	1951-57			1984-85	Texaco
1977-93	1972-77		W.C.C.	1995-96	1970-71
1994-	1993-94		1982		
					A/Scot
					1976-77

HONOURS

Div.1	Div.2	Div.3(S)	FAC	Lge C	Euro C	A/Scot
1977-78	1906-07	1950-51	1898	1977-78	1978-79	1976-77
	1921-22		1959	1978-79	1979-80	
				1988-89		Sup C
			C/S'ld	1989-90	Sim. C.	1979-80
			1978		1988-89	
					1991-92	

MOST APPEARANCES

Bobby McKinlay 681+3 (1951-70)

Year	League	FA Cup	Lge Cup	Europe
1951-52	1	1		
1952-53	3			
1953-54	1			
1954-55	37	6		
1955-56	39	1		
1956-57	39	5		
1957-58	40	3		
1958-59	39	9		
1959-60	42	2		
1960-61	42	1	3	
1961-62	42	2	3	2
1962-63	42	7		
1963-64	42	2		
1964-65	42	3		
1965-66	41	1		
1966-67	42	7	2	
1967-68	42	2	2	4
1968-69	30+2	1	1	
1969-70	5+1			
	611+3	53	11	6

MOST GOALS IN A CAREER

Grenville Morris - 225 (1898-1913)

Year	League	FA Cup
1898-99	7	8
1899-1900	8	3
1900-01	14	1
1901-02	7	2
1902-03	24	2
1903-04	12	2
1904-05	12	1
1905-06	19	3
1906-07	21	1
1907-08	7	
1908-09	12	
1909-10	19	1
1910-11	11	1
1911-12	10	
1912-13	16	1
Total	**199**	**26**

Current leading goalscorer: Stuart Pearce - 77 (1985-95)

RECORD TRANSFER FEE RECEIVED

Amount	Club	Player	Date
8,500,000	Liverpool	Stan Collymore	07/95
2,100,000	Tottenham H	Teddy Sheringham	9/92
1,500,000	Sampdoria	Des Walker	5/92
1,500,000	Manchester Utd	Neil Webb	7/89

RECORD TRANSFER FEE PAID

Amount	Club	Player	Date
2,500,000	Arsenal	Kevin Campbell	7/95
2,500,000	Foggia	Bryan Roy	8/94
2,200,000	Southend United	Stan Collymore	7/93
2,000,000	Millwall	Teddy Sheringham	7/91

MANAGERS

Name	Seasons	Best	Worst
Harry Radford	1889-97	7(1)	13(1)
Harry Haslam	1897-09	4(1)	1(2)
F W Earp	1909-12	14(1)	15(2)
Bob Masters	1912-25	20(1)	20(2)
Jack Baynes	1925-29	5(2)	17(2)
Stan Hardy	1930-31	17(2)	17(2)
Noel Watson	1931-36	5(2)	19(2)
Harold Wightman	1936-39	18(2)	20(2)
Billy Walker	1939-60	10(1)	4(3S)
Andy Beattie	1960-63	9(1)	19(1)
John Carey	1963-68	2(1)	18(1)
Matt Gillies	1969-72	15(1)	21(1)
Dave Mackay	1972-73	14(2)	14(1)
Allan Brown	1973-75	7(2)	16(2)
Brian Clough	1975-93	1(1)	8(2)
Frank Clark	1993-	3(P)	2(1)

LONGEST LEAGUE RUNS

of undefeated matches:	42 (26.11.1977 - 25.11.1978)	of league matches w/out a win:	16 (8.2.1913 - 18.10.1913)
of undefeated home matches:	51 (27.4.1977 - 17.11.1979)	of undefeated away matches:	21 (3.12.1977 - 9.12.1978)
without home win:	10 (20.11.1909 - 9.4.1910)	without an away win:	37 (25.1.1913 - 23.1.1915)
of league wins: 7 (24.12.1892 - 25.2.1893, 29.8.1921 - 1.10.1921)		of home wins:	12 (23.2.1980 - 20.9.1980)
of league defeats:	14 (8.2.1913 - 18.11.1913)	of away wins:	5 (5.4.1983 - 29.8.1983, 31.12.1988 - 25.3.1989)
			(21.11.1993 - 16.01.1994)

NOTTINGHAM FOREST

PLAYERS NAME Honours	Ht	Wt	Birthdate	Birthplace Transfers	Contract Date	Clubs	League	L/Cup	FA Cup	Other	Lge	L/C	FAC	Oth
G O A L K E E P E R S														
Clark Richard	5.11	12.4	06/04/77	Nuneaton	12/04/94	Nottingham Forest								
Crossley Mark G	6.0	15.0	16/06/69	Barnsley	02/07/87	Nottingham Forest	237	31	29	18				
E: u21.3														
Fettis Alan	6.1	11.04	01/02/71	Belfast		Ards								
NI: 5, B.1					£50000	14/08/91	Hull City	131+3	7+1	5	7				
					£250000	13/01/96	Nottingham Forest								
Rigby Malcolm R	6.1	12.0	13/03/76	Nottingham		Notts County								
					£50000	01/08/94	Nottingham Forest								
Wright Thomas J	6.1	13.5	29/08/63	Belfast		Linfield								
NI: 22, u21.1; Div1'93					£30000	27/01/88	Newcastle United	72+1	6	4	1				
					Loan	14/02/91	Hull City	6							
					£450000	24/09/93	Nottingham Forest	10	2						
D E F E N D E R S														
Blatherwick Stephen	6.1	12.12	20/09/73	Nottingham	01/08/92	Nottingham Forest	3							
					Loan	01/08/93	Wycombe Wand.	2							
					Loan	11/09/95	Hereford United	10				1			
Chettle Stephen	6.1	13.3	27/09/68	Nottingham	28/08/86	Nottingham Forest	280+13	38+3	31+1	21+2	7	1	1	1
E: u21.12; LC'90; FMC'89'92														
Cooper Colin T	5.8	9.4	28/02/67	Sedgefield	17/07/84	Middlesbrough	188+5	18	13	19+1	6			2
E: u21.8					£300000	25/07/91	Millwall	77	6	2	2	6			
					£1700000	21/06/93	Nottingham Forest	108+1	10	8	7	13	1	1	
Lyttle Desmond	5.9	12.0	24/09/71	Wolverhampton	09/01/90	Leicester City								
						01/08/91	Worcester City								
					£12500	09/07/92	Swansea City								
					£375000	27/07/93	Nottingham Forest	107+1	12	11	8	2			
Morgan Ian	6.2	12.10	11/10/77	Birmingham	01/08/94	Nottingham Forest	1							
Pearce Stuart	5.10	13.0	24/04/62	Hammersmith		Wealdstone			2					
E: 70, u21.1; LC'90'; FMC'89'92					£25000	20/10/83	Coventry City	52		2		4			
					£200000	03/06/85	Nottingham Forest	368	58	35	24	58	10	9	6
Thom Stuart	6.2	11.8	27/12/76	Dewsbury	11/01/94	Nottingham Forest								
Todd Andrew J	5.9	12.3	21/09/74	Derby	06/03/92	Middlesbrough	7+1	1+1		5				
					Loan	27/02/95	Swindon Town	13							
						29/02/96	Nottingham Forest								
Warner Vance	6.0	11.12	03/09/74	Leeds	03/09/94	Nottingham Forest	2	1						
					Loan	02/02/96	Grimsby Town	3							
M I D F I E L D														
Archer Paul	5.7	9.04	25/04/78	Leicester	01/08/94	Nottingham Forest								
Armstrong S Craig	5.11	12.04	23/05/75	South Shields	02/06/92	Nottingham Forest								
					Loan	29/12/94	Burnley	4							
					Loan	05/01/96	Bristol Rovers	13+1							
Atkinson Craig	6.0	11.02	29/09/77	Rotherham	01/08/94	Nottingham Forest								
E: Y														
Barber Andrew J			13/02/96			Nottingham Forest								
Bart-Williams Chris	5.8	11.0	16/06/74	Sierra Leone	18/07/91	Leyton Orient	34+2	4		2	2			
E: B.1, u21.10, Y.12.					£275000	21/11/91	Sheffield Wed.	95+25	14+2	8+5	4	4	3	1	1
					£2500000	01/07/95	Nottingham Forest	32	2	7	7+1				
Burns John	5.8	10.08	04/12/77	Dublin	01/08/94	Nottingham Forest								
Cowling Lee	5.8	9.04	22/09/77	Doncaster	01/08/94	Nottingham Forest								
Finnigan John	5.8	10.05	29/03/76	Wakefield	01/08/92	Nottingham Forest								
Gemmill Scot	5.10	11.0	02/01/71	Paisley	05/01/90	Nottingham Forest	149+7	22+1	17	13+1	19	3	1	4
S: 6, B.1, u21.4; FMC'92														
Haaland Alf I R	5.10	12.0	23/11/72	Norway		Young Boys of Berne								
						25/01/94	Nottingham Forest	33+7	0+4	2+1	2+3	1			
Howe Stephen	5.7	10.04	06/11/73	Annisford	01/08/92	Nottingham Forest	4+5			1+1	2			
O'Neill Shane	5.10	12.00	20/06/78	Limavady	01/08/94	Nottingham Forest								
Phillips David O	5.10	11.2	29/07/63	Wegburg (Ger)	03/08/81	Plymouth Albion	65+8	2+1	12+1	4	15	1		
W: 55, u21.4, Y4; FAC'87					£65000	23/08/84	Manchester City	81	8	5	5	13			3
					£150000	05/06/86	Coventry City	93+7	8	9	5+1	8		1	2
					£525000	31/07/89	Norwich City	152	12	14	8	17		1	1
						20/08/93	Nottingham Forest	12+4	1	4+2	3				
Smith Paul A	5.11	11.03	25/01/76	Hastings	01/08/94	Nottingham Forest								
Stone Steve B	5.9	11.3	20/08/91	Gateshead	20/05/89	Nottingham Forest	131+2	10+1	10	10	18			2
E: 9.														
Stratford Lee	5.10	10.08	11/11/75	Barnsley	01/08/92	Nottingham Forest								
Walker Justin	5.10	11.08	06/09/75	Nottingham	01/08/92	Nottingham Forest								
E: Y														
F O R W A R D S														
Black Kingsley	5.8	10.11	22/06/68	Luton	07/07/86	Luton Town	123+4	16+2	5+1	3+2	25	1	2	1
NI: 31, u21.1, B, S; LC'88;					£1500000	02/09/91	Nottingham Forest	80+18	19+1	4	4+2	14	5		
FMC'92					Loan	02/03/95	Sheffield United	8+3				2			
					Loan	29/09/95	Millwall	2+2				1			
Campbell Kevin	6.0	13.1	04/02/70	Lambeth	11/02/88	Arsenal	105+38	9+10	12+5	12+2	42	5	2	5
E: B.1, u21.4. Div1'91.					Loan	16/01/89	Leyton Orient	16				9			
FAYC'88. LC'93. FAC'93. ECWC94					Loan	08/11/89	Leicester City	11		1		5			1
					£2500000	01/07/95	Nottingham Forest	21		7	3	3		3	

Player	Ht	Wt	DOB	From	Date	Club								
uinan Steve	6.1	12.12	24/12/75	Birmingham	01/08/92	Nottingham Forest	1+1							
				Loan	14/12/95	Darlington	3			1				
ring Richard	5.7	10.06	10/09/75	Halifax		Manchester United								
Y.4, S					19/07/95	Nottingham Forest	0+1							
rkan Nikola						Real Oviedo								
oatian Int.					08/07/96	Nottingham Forest								
e Jason	6.3	13.8	09/05/71	Forest Gate	02/06/89	Charlton Athletic	0+1		0+2					
				Loan	06/02/91	Stockport County	2							
				£35000	01/03/91	Lincoln City	86+7	6	2+1	4	21		1	
					06/08/93	Southend United	18+6	1	1	5+3	3			3
				£200000	04/03/94	Nottingham Forest	36+27	2+2	0+4	4+2	13			
cGregor Paul A	5.10	10.4	17/12/74	Liverpool	13/12/91	Nottingham Forest	7+18		0+2	0+3	3			1
r Stephen	5.7	10.0	19/01/78	Belper	01/08/94	Nottingham Forest								
oy Brian E S	5.10	10.08	12/02/70	Amsterdam		Foggia								
				£2500000	04/08/94	Nottingham Forest	62+3	5	8	6	21	1	1	1
aunders Dean	5.8	10.6	21/06/64	Swansea	24/06/82	Swansea City	42+7	2+1	1	1+1	12			
49. FAC'92. FLC'94.				Loan	29/03/85	Cardiff City	3+1							
				Free	07/08/85	Brighton & H.A.	66+6	4	7	3	21	5		
				£60000	12/03/87	Oxford United	57+2	9+1	2	2	22	8	2	1
				£1000000	28/10/88	Derby County	106	12	6	7	42	10		5
				£2900000	19/07/91	Liverpool	42	5	8	6	11	2	2	10
				£2300000	10/09/92	Aston Villa	111+1	15	9	8	37	7	4	1
					01/07/95	Galatasaray								
				£1500000	27/06/96	Nottingham Forest								
enzi Andrea	6.3	11.13	10/02/66	Sierra Leone		Reggiana								
ly: 5, u21.8						Napoli								
						Roma								
						Inter Milan								
						Torino								
				£1800000	01/08/95	Nottingham Forest	3+7	1	2+1	1+3			1	1
alley Mark	5.10	10.6	17/09/76	Barnsley	27/09/93	Nottingham Forest								
oan Ian S	5.10	12.4	14/12/67	Heswall		Runcorn								
				£80000	14/03/90	Nottingham Forest	147+8	12+2	17+1	13	29	1	4	2

DITIONAL CONTRACT PLAYERS

Player		Date	Club
ugh Gareth G		30/10/95	Nottingham Forest
wson Andrew		31/10/95	Nottingham Forest
chett Scott		23/02/96	Nottingham Forest
orge Daniel S		31/10/95	Nottingham Forest
im Robert J		03/10/95	Nottingham Forest
nry David		18/09/95	Nottingham Forest
lton Stephen		09/10/95	Nottingham Forest
rner Barry		23/01/96	Nottingham Forest
itney Scott			Nottingham Forest

THE MANAGER
FRANK CLARK

Date of Birth . . . . 9th October 1943.
Place of Birth . . . . Rowlands Gill.
Date of Appointment . . . . May 1993.

PREVIOUS CLUBS
As Manager . . . . Leyton Orient.
As Coach . . . . Sunderland, Nottingham Forest, Leyton Orient.
As a Player . . . . Crook Town, Newcastle United, Nottingham Forest.

HONOURS
As a Manager
Promotion to Division 3 1988-89. Promotion to the Premiership 1993-94.

As a Player
Crook Town: FA Amateur Cup 1961.
Newcastle: UEFA 1969. Division 2 1965.
Nottingham Forest: ECWC 1979. Division 1 1978. League Cup 1978, 1979.
International: England youth.

CITY GROUND

City Road, Nottingham NG2 5FJ
Tel: 01602 526 000

Capacity ....30,602.

First game ....v Blackburn Rovers, 0-1, 3.9.1898.
First floodlit game ....v Gillingham, 11.9.1961.
Internationals ....England v Wales, 1909.

ATTENDANCES
Highest ....44,946 v Manchester Utd, Div.1, 28.10.1967.
Lowest ....2,624 v WBA, 30.3.1904.

OTHER GROUNDS ....Forest Racecourse 1865-79. The Meadows 1879-80. Trent Bridge 1880-82.
.... Parkside Lenton 1882-85. Gregory Lenton 1885-90. Town Ground 1890-98. City Ground 1898-

MATCHDAY TICKET PRICES

Bridgford Stand
Upper Tier £19
Lower Tier (Visitors) £18

Main Stand £20

Trent End
Upper Tier £19
Lower Tier (Family) Adult £18
Lower Tier (Family) Junior £10

Executive Stand
Upper Tier £19
Lower Tier £18

Ticket Office Telephone no. 0115 952 6002

CLUBCALL 0898 12 11 74
Calls cost 39p per minute cheap rate and 49p per
minute at all other times.
Call costings correct at time of going to press.

HOW TO GET TO THE GROUND

From the North
Use motorway (M1) until junction 26, leave motorway and follow signs into
Nottingham A610. Follow signs to Melton Mowbray, Trent Bridge A606. Cross
river and turn left into Radcliffe Road, then turn left into Colwick Road for
Nottingham Forest FC.

From the East
Use A52 sign posted Nottingham, into West Bridgford, then turn left into Colwick
Road for Nottingham Forest FC.

From the South
Use motorway (M1) until junction 24, leave motorway and follow signs to
Nottingham (South) to Trent Bridge, turn right into Radcliffe Road, then turn left
into Colwick Road for Nottingham Forest FC.

From the West
USe A52 into Nottingham, then follow signs to Melton Mowbray, Trent Bridge
A606, cross river and turn left into Radcliffe Road, then turn left into Colwick
Road for Nottingham Forest FC.

Car Parking: Space for 300 cars in east Stand car park plus street parking off
Loughborough and Radcliffe Roads.
Nearest Railway Station: Nottingham Midland (0345 484 950).

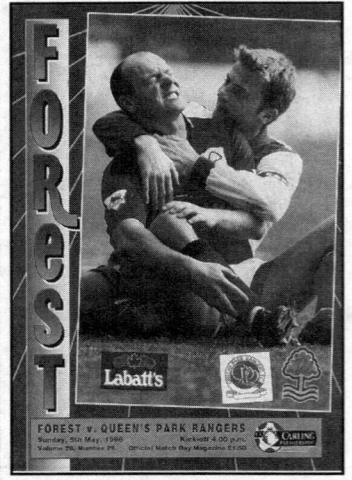

MATCHDAY PROGRAMME

Programme Editor . . . . John Lawson.

Number of pages . . . . 32.

Price . . . . £1.50.

Subscriptions . . . . Contact 'Temple Printers' 0115 928 6668.

Local Newspapers . . . . . . Nottingham Evening Post, Derby Telegraph.

Local Radio Stations . . . . Radio Nottingham, Radio Trent.

SHEFFIELD WEDNESDAY
(The Owls)
F.A. CARLING PREMIERSHIP
SPONSORED BY: SANDERSON ELECTRONICS PLC

ck Row (L-R): Andy Pearce, Mark Bright, Kevin Pressman, Julian Watts, Klas Ingesson, Chris Woods, Ryan Jones, Chris Waddle. **ddle Row:** Danny Bergara (First Team Coach), Mark Pembridge, Peter Atherton, John Sheridan, Michael Williams, Lee Briscoe, Ian **lan**, Guy Whittingham, Dave Galley (Physio). **Front Row:** David Pleat (Manager), Graham Hyde, Marc Degryse, Dan Petrescu, Des **lker**, Andy Sinton, David Hirst, Richie Barker (Football Devlopment/Manager's Assistant).

SHEFFIELD WEDNESDAY
FORMED IN 1867
TURNED PROFESSIONAL IN 1887
LTD COMPANY IN 1899

CHAIRMAN: D G Richards
DIRECTORS
K T Addy (Vice-Chairman), C Woodward,
E Barron, G K Hulley, R M Grierson FCA,
J Ashton MP, G Thorpe, H E Culley
SECRETARY
Graham Mackrell 0114 2343122)
COMMERCIAL MANAGER
Sean O'Toole

MANAGER: David Pleat
ASSISTANT MANAGER: Peter Shreeves

RESERVE TEAM MANAGER
Bobby Smith
YOUTH TEAM MANAGER
Albert Phelan
PHYSIOTHERAPIST
Dave Galley

STATISTICIAN FOR THE DIRECTORY
Michael Renshaw

Yet another very disappointing season for the Owls. A last day nail-biting draw, courtesy of a Jon Newsome last-minute goal at West Ham saw Sheffield Wednesday safe for another season. As it happened, other results had gone their way and so the point earned was that vital.

Despite the appointment of David Pleat to follow Trevor Francis, nothing much seems to have changed, with the team still short of pace, passion and pattern.

Lack of motivation of the players was an obvious weakness in Pleat's first season.

A poor start to the season was followed by a relatively more successful middle part, but then came an almost catastrophic ending.

Although player unrest doesn't seem to have been so noticeable as under the previous regime, the lack of spirit and camaraderie on the pitch was apparent to all fans. Until this is rectified and major amounts of money spent on the team and not the ground, then the Owls will continue to struggle along as also-rans in the chase for honours.

One of the bright spots of the season was the hundredth league goal scored by David Hirst, who had his most injury-free season for some time. He is the type of player the Owls will need to be in top form as the main goal threat.

MICK RENSHAW

SHEFFIELD WEDNESDAY

League: 15th   **FA Cup: 3rd Rnd**   **Coca-Cola Cup: 4th Rnd**

M	DATE	COMP	VEN	OPPONENTS	RESULT	HT	LP	GOAL SCORERS/GOAL TIMES	ATT.
1	A 19	PL	A	Liverpool	L 0-1	0-0	17		(40535)
2	23	PL	H	Blackburn Rovers	W 2-1	1-0	8	Waddle 18, Pembridge 83	25544
3	27	PL	H	Newcastle United	L 0-2	0-0	14		24815
4	30	PL	A	Wimbledon	D 2-2	1-1	12	Degryse 10, Hirst 46	(6352)
5	S 9	PL	A	Queens Park Rangers	W 3-0	0-0	9	Bright 56, 60, Donaldson 78	(12459)
6	16	PL	H	Tottenham Hotspur	L 1-3	1-1	13	Hirst 8	26565
7	19	CC 2/1	A	**Crewe Alexandra**	D 2-2	2-1		Degryse 2, 34	(5702)
8	23	PL	H	Manchester United	D 0-0	0-0	14		34101
9	30	PL	A	Leeds United	L 0-2	0-1	13		(34076)
10	O 4	CC 2/2	H	**Crewe Alexandra**	W 5-2	3-2		Degryse 7, Hirst 16, Bright 45, 63, 77 (3)	12039
11	15	PL	H	Middlesbrough	L 0-1	0-0	15		21177
12	21	PL	A	Coventry City	W 1-0	1-0	12	Whittingham 16	(14002)
13	25	CC 3	A	**Millwall**	W 2-0	1-0		Pembridge 15, Whittingham 64	(12822)
14	28	PL	H	West Ham United	L 0-1	0-1	13		23917
15	N 4	PL	A	Chelsea	D 0-0	0-0	13		(23216)
16	18	PL	H	Manchester City	D 1-1	1-0	14	Hirst 14(pen)	24422
17	21	PL	A	Arsenal	L 2-4	2-1	14	Hirst 9, Waddle 20	(34556)
18	25	PL	A	Everton	D 2-2	2-1	15	Bright 2, 35	(35898)
19	29	CC 4	A	**Arsenal**	L 1-2	1-1		Degryse 16	(35361)
20	D 4	PL	H	Coventry City	W 4-3	2-2	14	Whittingham 25, Hirst 39, Degryse 60, Bright 73	16229
21	9	PL	A	Manchester United	D 2-2	0-1	14	Bright 59, Whittingham 78	(41849)
22	16	PL	H	Leeds United	W 6-2	3-1	14	Degryse 5, 25, Whittingham 18, Bright 67, Hirst 72, 86	24573
23	23	PL	H	Southampton	D 2-2	1-1	14	Hirst 14(pen), 50(pen)	25115
24	26	PL	A	Nottingham Forest	L 0-1	0-1	14		(27810)
25	J 1	PL	H	Bolton Wanderers	W 4-2	2-0	13	Kovacevic 22, 45, Hirst 54(pen), 60	24872
26	6	FAC 3	A	**Charlton Athletic**	L 0-2	0-2			(13815)
27	13	PL	H	Liverpool	D 1-1	1-0	13	Kovacevic 7	32747
28	20	PL	A	Blackburn Rovers	L 0-3	0-2	13		(24732)
29	F 3	PL	A	Newcastle United	L 0-2	0-0	13		(36567)
30	10	PL	H	Wimbledon	W 2-1	0-0	13	Degryse 55, Watts 85	19085
31	17	PL	H	Queens Park Rangers	L 1-3	1-1	13	Hyde 22	22442
32	24	PL	A	Tottenham Hotspur	L 0-1	0-1	14		(32047)
33	M 2	PL	A	Nottingham Forest	L 1-3	0-1	14	Kovacevic 50	21930
34	6	PL	A	Aston Villa	L 2-3	1-0	14	Blinker 8, 63	(27893)
35	16	PL	H	Aston Villa	W 2-0	0-0	14	Whittingham 58, Hirst 87	22964
36	20	PL	A	Southampton	W 1-0	0-0	14	Degryse 1	(13216)
37	23	PL	A	Bolton Wanderers	L 1-2	1-1	14	Whittingham 37	(18368)
38	A 5	PL	A	Middlesbrough	L 1-3	0-0	13	Pembridge 54	(29791)
39	8	PL	H	Arsenal	W 1-0	0-0	14	Degryse 61	24349
40	13	PL	A	Manchester City	L 0-1	0-0	15		(30898)
41	17	PL	H	Chelsea	D 0-0	0-0	15		25094
42	27	PL	H	Everton	L 2-5	1-3	15	Hirst 9, Degryse 64	32724
43	M 5	PL	A	West Ham United	D 1-1	0-0	15	Newsome 89	(23790)

Best Home League Attendance: 34101 v Manchester United   **Smallest: 16229 v Coventry City**   **Average: 24877**

Goal Scorers:
PL(48): Hirst(13),Degryse(8),Bright(7),Whittingham(6),Kovacevic(4),Waddle(2),Pembridge(2),Blinker(2),Donaldson(1),Newsome(1),Watts(1),Hyde(1)
CC(10): Degryse(4),Bright(3),Pembridge(1),Whittingham(1),Hirst(1)
FAC(0):

1995-96

	(F) Blinker	(F) Bright	(F) Briscoe	(D) Burrows	(F) Degryse	(F) Donaldson	(F) Hirst	(D) Humphries	(M) Hyde	(M) Ingesson	(M) Kovacevic	(D) Newsome	(D) Nicol	(D) Nolan	(D) Pearce	(M) Pembridge	(D) Petrescou	(M) Platts	(G) Pressman	(M) Sheridan	(M) Sinton	(M) Stefanovic	(F) Waddle	(D) Walker	(D) Watts	(F) Whitingham	(M) Williams	(G) Woods	Referee	No.
	X						S1		X					X1		X	X		X	X	S2		X2	X	X			S	P.Durkin	1
	X			S			X		S					X		X	X		X	X	S1		X1	X	X				P.S.Danson	2
	X			X			X2		S1	S3				X		X	X3		X	X1	S2			X	X				P.E.Alcock	3
	X	S		X			X1			S1				X		X	X		X	X				X	X		S		A.Wilkie	4
	X	S		X		X1	X		X					X		X	X		X	X				X	X		S		M.Reed	5
	X			X			X							X		X	X		X	X2			S1	X	X1	S2	S		D.J.Gallagher	6
	X	S		X			S1							X	X	X	X		S		X		X	X		X1			P.Danson	7
	S2	S1	X	X			X2		X					X	X	X1	X		X	S			X	X					K.Burge	8
	S2	S3	X2	X			X		X					X1	X	X	X3		X	S1			X	X					D.Allison	9
	X	X	X1	X			X2		X					X		X			X				X	X		S1	S2	S	N.Barry	10
	X	X	X1						X2	S				X		X			X	S2	X		X	X		S1			G.Ashby	11
	X	X1							S2	X				X		X			X		X		X2	X		X	S1	S	J.Winter	12
	S1						X1		X					X	S	X			X		X		X	X	X	X			P.Durkin	13
	S2		S1		X		X		X					X		X			X		X		X	X		X2	X1		K.Cooper	14
	X	X			X		X		X					X	S	X1			X		X		X	X		S	S1		P.Danson	15
	X		X		X		X		S1					X	X1	X					X	X	X	X		S	S	X	G.Poll	16
	S2	X	S1		X		X		X					X	X1				X		X		X	X	X	X			L.R.Bilkes	17
	X	X1	S2				X		X			X		X					X		X		X	X		X	S1	S	M.Bodenham	18
	X1		X		S1		X		X					X					X		X		X	X	X1	X		S	K.Burge	19
	X	X	X		X		S1		X			X		X					X	S1	S		X1	X	S	X			M.Reid	20
	X	X	X		X		S		X			X		X					X		S		X1	X		X			P.Jones	21
	X	X	X		X		S1		X			X		X					X		S		X	X	S	X1			R.A.Hart	22
	X1	X	X1		X		S1		S1			X		X					X			S	X	X		X			J.T.Winter	23
	S2	X1	X		X2		S		X			X		X					X		S1		X	X		X			G.Ashby	24
	S1		X		X		S		X		X1			X					X	S	X		X	X		X			P.A.Durkin	25
	S		X		X		S		X			X		X					X		X		X	X		X			A.Wilkie	26
	S1	X	X2		X		S2		X		X1	X	X							S	X	S	X	X		X		X	D.Elleray	27
	S2		X		X		X		S1		X	X	X							X2	X1		X	X		X		X	G.Willard	28
	X				X		X1		S		S1	X	X				S	X					X	X	X	X			P.Danson	29
	S1		X1				X		X		X	X	X				S3	X		X1	X3		S1	X		X			M.Bodenham	30
	S1		X				X		X1		X	X	X				S	X		X	X		S	X		X			P.Durkin	31
		X2	X1		X		X		X		X3	X	X				S2						S1	X	S3	X		X	M.Reed	32
			X				S3	X1	X		X	X	X				S1					X3	S1	X	X	X		X1	G.Pole	33
X		X		S3		S2	X3		X2		S1	X1	X									X	X	X	X		X	D.Elleray	34
X		X		X			S1		S2	X	X		X1									X	S	X	X		X	P.Jones	35
X1		X		X		X2		S1		S2	X	X				X						X		X	X		X	M.Bodenham	36
		X		X		X1	X3	S2		S1	X		X								X2		X		X		X	J.Winter	37
X		S3		X		X1		S1		S1	X	X3				X	X1					X		X	X			K.Cooper	38
X1		X		X		X2				S2	X	S				X			X	X		X	S1	X	X			S.W.Dunn	39
X		X		X2	S2	X					X	X1				X3			X	S3		X	S1	X	X			R.Hart	40
X1		X		X	S	X				X	S					X			X	X		X	S1	X	X			G.Willard	41
X		X		X	S3	X3		S2			X					X2			X	X1		X	S1	X	X			M.Reed	42
X1		X		X2		X		S2	X		X	S				X						X	S1	X	X			R.Bilkes	43
6	**9**	**15**	**22**	**0**	**30**	**1**	**29**	**1**	**14**	**3**	**8**	**8**	**18**	**29**	**3**	**24**	**8**	**0**	**30**	**13**	**7**	**5**	**23**	**36**	**9**	**27**	**2**	**8**	**PL Appearances**	
0	**10**	**3**	**0**	**0**	**4**	**2**	**1**	**3**	**12**	**2**	**8**	**0**	**1**	**0**	**0**	**1**	**0**	**2**	**0**	**4**	**3**	**1**	**8**	**0**	**2**	**2**	**3**	**0**	**PL Sub Appearances**	
0	**3+1**	**1**	**0**	**0**	**3**	**0**	**1**	**0**	**2+1**	**0**	**2+1**	**1**	**0**	**0**	**0**	**4**	**1**	**3**	**0**	**0**	**4**	**0**	**3**	**4**	**4**	**1**	**3+1**	**1+1**	**0**	**CC Appearances**	
0	**0**	**0**	**0**	**0**	**1**	**0**	**1**	**0**	**0**	**0**	**0**	**1**	**0**	**0**	**1**	**0**	**0**	**0**	**0**	**0**	**1**	**0**	**1**	**1**	**1**	**0**	**1**	**0**	**FAC Appearances**	

SHEFFIELD WEDNESDAY

CLUB RECORDS

BIGGEST VICTORIES
League: 9-1 v Birmingham, Division 1, 13.12.1930
8-0 v Sunderland, Division 1, 26.12.1911
F.A. Cup: 12-0 v Halliwell, Round 1, 17.1.1891
League Cup: 8-0 v Aldershot (a), Round 2, 3.10.1989
Europe: 8-1 v Spora Luxembourg, UEFA Cup Rnd 1 1st leg, 16.9.1992

BIGGEST DEFEATS
League: 0-10 v Aston Villa, Division 1, 5.10.1912
F.A. Cup: 0-5 v Wolves, Round 3, 2.3.1889
1-6 v Blackburn Rovers, Final, 29.3.1890
0-5 v Everton (h), Round 3 replay, 27.1.1988
League Cup: 2-8 v Queens Park R., Round 2, 1973-74
Europe: No more than 2 goals

MOST POINTS
3 points a win: 88, Division 2, 1983-84
2 points a win: 62, Division 2, 1958-59

MOST GOALS
106, 1958-59 (Division 2).
Shiner 28, Froggatt 26, Fantham 12, Wilkinson 12, Finney 11, Curtis 5, JMcAnearney 3, Kay 3, Quixall 2, Ellis 1, T McAnearney 1, Young 1, og 1.

MOST LEAGUE GOALS CONCEDED
100, Division 1, 1954-55

MOST FIRST CLASS MATCHES IN A SEASON
61 (46 League, 4 FA Cup, 10 League Cup, 1 ZDS) 1990-91

MOST LEAGUE WINS
28, Division 2, 1958-59

MOST LEAGUE DRAWS
19, Division 3, 1978-79

MOST LEAGUE DEFEATS
26, Division 1, 1919-20; Division 2, 1974-75

INDIVIDUAL CLUB RECORDS

MOST GOALS IN A MATCH
6. Douglas Hunt v Norwich, Division 2, 19.11.1938 (7-0)

MOST GOALS IN A SEASON
Derek Dooley 47, (46 League, 1 FAC) 1951-52.
5 goals once=5; 4 goals twice=8; 3 goals 3 times=9; 2 goals 9 times=18; 1 goal 7 times=7
Previous holder: J Trotter, 37 League (1925-26 & 1926-27).

OLDEST PLAYER
Tom Brittleton 41 years v Oldham, 1.5.1920.

YOUNGEST PLAYER
Peter Fox 15 years 269 days, 31.3.1973

MOST CAPPED PLAYER
Nigel Worthington (N. Ireland) 50

BEST PERFORMANCES

League: 1958-59: Matches played 42, Won 28, Drawn 6, Lost 8, Goals for 106,Goals against 48, Points 62. 1st in Division 2

Highest: 1st in Division 1

F.A. Cup: 1895-96: 1st rnd. Southampton 3-2; 2nd rnd. Sunderland 2-1; 3rd rnd. Everton 4-0; Semi-Final Bolton 3-1; Final Wolves 2-1. 1906-07: 3rd rnd. Wolves 3-2; 4th rnd. Southampton 1-1, 3-1; 5th rnd. Sunderland 0-0, 1-0; 5th rnd. Liverpool 1-0; Semi-Final Arsenal 1-0; FinalEverton 2-1.
1934-35: 3rd rnd. Oldham 3-1; 4th rnd. Wolves 2-1; 5th rnd. Norwich City 1-0;6th rnd. Arsenal 2-1; Semi-Final Burnley 3-0; Final West Bromwich A. 4-2.

League Cup: 1990-91: 2nd rnd. Brentford 2-1, 2-1; 3rd rnd. Swindon 0-0, 1-0; 4th rnd. Derby Co. 1-1, 2-1; 5th rnd. Coventry City 1-0; Semi-Final Chelsea 2-0, 3-1; Final Manchester Utd 1-0

EUFA: 1963-64: 1st rnd. Olympique Lyonnais 2-4, 5-2; 2nd rnd. AS Roma 4-0, 0-1;Q/Final Barcelona 3-2, 0-2.

DIVISIONAL RECORD

	Played	Won	Drawn	Lost	For	Against	Points
Division 1/P	2,430	933	575	916	3,787	3,790	2,603
Division 2	1,088	460	281	347	1,693	1,401	1,285
Division 3	230	83	76	71	297	266	242
Total	3,750	1,476	932	1,340	5,785	5,457	4,130

ADDITIONAL INFORMATION
Previous Name
The Wednesday 1867-1929

Previous League
Football Alliance

Club colours: Blue & white striped shirts, blue shorts, blue socks.
Change colours: Green shirts, white shorts, white socks.

Reserves League: Pontins Central League Division 1.

RECORDS AND STATISTICS

COMPETITIONS

Div 1/P	Div.2	Div.3	EUFA
1892-99	1899-1900	1975-80	1961-62
1900-20	1920-26		1963-64
1926-37	1937-50		
1950-51	1951-52		
1952-55	1955-56		
1956-58	1958-59		
1959-70	1970-75		
1984-90	1980-84		
1991-	1990-91		

HONOURS

Div 1/P	Div.2	FA Cup	League Cup
1902-03	1899-1900	1896	1991
1903-04	1925-26	1907	
1928-29	1951-52	1935	C/Shield
1929-30	1955-56		1935
	1958-59		

MOST APPEARANCES

Andrew Wilson 546 (1900-20)

Year	League	FA Cup
1900-01	31	1
1901-02	25	1
1902-03	34	2
1903-04	29	3
1904-05	30	3
1905-06	35	5
1906-07	35	7
1907-08	34	1
1908-09	37	4
1909-10	30	2
1910-11	38	1
1911-12	37	2
1912-13	37	4
1913-14	31	5
1914-15	38	3
1919-20	1	
	502	44

MOST GOALS IN A CAREER

Andrew Wilson - 216 (1900-20)

Year	League	FA Cup
1900-01	13	
1901-02	9	
1902-03	12	
1903-04	10	2
1904-05	15	2
1905-06	16	2
1906-07	17	4
1907-08	19	
1908-09	18	3
1909-10	12	
1910-11	9	1
1911-12	12	
1912-13	9	2
1913-14	15	
1914-15	13	1
Total	199	17

Current leading goalscorer: David Hirst 122 (1986-96)

RECORD TRANSFER FEE RECEIVED

Amount	Club	Player	Date
£2,750,000	Blackburn Rov.	Paul Warhurst	8/93
£1,700,000	Real Sociedad	Dalian Atkinson	8/90
£800,000	Glasgow Rangers	Mel Sterland	3/89
£600,000	Arsenal	Brain Marwood	3/88

RECORD TRANSFER FEE PAID

Amount	Club	Player	Date
£2,750,000	Sampdoria	Des Walker	8/93
£2,750,000	Q.P.R.	Andy Sinton	8/93
£2,700,000	Huddersfield	Andy Booth	7/96
£1,200,000	Glasgow Rangers	Chris Woods	8/91

MANAGERS

Name	Seasons	Best	Worst
Rob Brown	1920-23	1(1)	14(2)
Bill Walker	1933-37	3(2)	22(2)
Jim McMullen	1937-42	3(2)	17(2)
Eric Taylor	1942-58	14(1)	20(2)
Harry Catterick	1958-61	2(1)	5(1)
Vic Buckingham	1961-64	6(1)	6(1)
Alan Brown	1964-67	8(1)	17(1)
Jack Marshall	1967-68	19(1)	19(1)
Tom McAnearney	1968-69	15(1)	15(1)
Danny Williams	1969-71	22(1)	15(1)
Derek Dooley	1971-74	10(2)	19(2)
Steve Burtenshaw	1974-75	22(2)	20(3)
Len Ashurst	1975-77	8(3)	14(3)
Jack Charlton	1977-83	4(2)	18(3)
Howard Wilkinson	1983-88	5(1)	2(1)
Peter Eustace	1989		
Ron Atkinson	1989-91	18(1)	3(2)
Trevor Francis	1991-95	3(1)	7(1/P)
David Pleat	1995-	15(P)	15(P)

LONGEST LEAGUE RUNS

of undefeated matches:	19 (3.12.1960 - 17.4.1961)	of league matches w/out a win:	20 (7.1.54-17.3.55, 11.1.75-6.9.75)
of undefeated home matches:	31 (13.12.1902 - 29.10.1904)	of undefeated away matches:	11 (6.11.1979 - 12.4.1980)
without home win:	13 (7.2.1974 - 6.9.1975)	without an away win:	35 (28.12.1974 - 16.10.1976)
of league wins:	9 (14.11.1903 - 16.1.1904)	of home wins:	19 (2.9.1899 - 6.10.1900)
of league defeats:	7 (7.1.1893 - 25.3.1893)	of away wins:	6 (28.4.1990 - 6.10.1990)

SHEFFIELD WEDNESDAY

PLAYERS NAME / Honours	Ht	Wt	Birthdate	Birthplace / Transfers	Contract Date	Clubs	League	L/Cup	FA Cup	Other	Lge	L/C	FAC	Oth
G O A L K E E P E R S														
Clarke Matt	6.3	11.7	03/11/73	Sheffield	28/07/92	Rotherham United	83+1		3	3				
				£300000	05/07/96	Sheffield Wed.								
Pressman Kevin	6.1	14.2	06/11/67	Fareham	07/11/85	Sheffield Wed.	158	25	8	4				
E: B.1, u21.1, u19.3, Y.6, S				Loan	10/03/92	Stoke City	4			2				
Scargill Jonathan M			09/04/77	Dewsbury	01/08/94	Sheffield Wed.								
				Loan	12/01/96	Matlock Town								
D E F E N D E R S														
Atherton Peter	5.11	12.3	06/04/70	Orrell	12/02/88	Wigan Athletic	145+4	8	7	12+1	1			
E: u21.1, S				£300000	23/08/91	Coventry City	113+1	4	2					
				£800000	01/06/94	Sheffield Wed.	67	8	4		1			
Humphreys Ritchie J					08/02/96	Sheffield Wed.	1+3							
Linighan Bryan	6.0	10.3	02/11/73	Hartlepool	16/07/92	Sheffield Wed.	1	1	1					
Newsome Jon	6.2	13.11	06/09/70	Sheffield	01/07/89	Sheffield Wed.	6+1	3						
Div1'92				£150000	11/06/91	Leeds United	62+14	3	3+1	5	3			
				£1000000	30/06/94	Norwich City	61+1	9	5		7		1	
				£1600000	16/03/96	Sheffield Wed.	8				1			
Nicol Stephen	5.10	11.2	11/12/61	Irvine		Aye United	68+2	16	3		7	1		
S:27, u21.14. Div1'84'86'88'90				£300000	26/10/81	Liverpool	328+15	42	50	32+2	36	4	3	3
FAC'86'89'92. EC'84. CS'89.				Free	20/01/95	Notts County	19		2					1
Nolan Ian	6.0	11.10	09/07/70	Liverpool	31/08/88	Preston North End								
				Free	01/08/89	Northwich Victoria				2				
					01/08/90	Marine								
				£100000	02/08/91	Tranmere Rovers	87+1	10	7	9	1	1		
				£1500000	01/08/94	Sheffield Wed.	71	8	4	3				
Walker Des	5.11	11.9	26/11/65	Hackney	02/12/83	Nottingham Forest	259+5	40	27	14	1			
E: 59, u21.7. LC'89'90.				£1500000	01/08/92	Sampdoria								
FMC'89'92				£2700000	22/07/93	Sheffield Wed.	116	14	8					
M I D F I E L D														
Blinker Regi						Feyenoord								
				£275000	05/03/96	Sheffield Wed.	9				2			
Hyde Graham	5.7	11.7	10/11/70	Doncaster	17/05/88	Sheffield Wed.	97+33	16+3	8+5	4	8	2	1	1
Jones Ryan	5.8	11.4	23/07/73	Sheffield	18/06/91	Sheffield Wed.	36+5	4+1	3		6	1		
W: 1, B.1, u21.1				Loan	12/01/96	Scunthorpe United	11				3			
Pembridge Mark	5.7	11.1	29/11/70	Merthyr Tydfil	01/07/89	Luton Town	60	2	4	4	6			
W: 8, B.1, u21.1				£1250000	02/06/92	Derby County	108+2	9	6	15	28	1	3	5
				£900000	19/07/95	Sheffield Wed.	24+1	3			2	1		
Poric Adam	5.9	11.13	22/04/72	Australia		St George (Aus)								
Australian Int.				£60000	01/10/93	Sheffield Wed.	3+7	0+2						
Sheridan John	5.9	10.8	01/10/64	Stretford		Manchester City								
Ei: 24, u23.1, u21.2, Y. LC'91				Free	02/03/82	Leeds United	225+5	14	11+1	11	47	3	1	
				£650000	03/08/89	Nottingham Forest		1						
				£500000	03/11/89	Sheffield Wed.	187+8	24	17+1	4	25	3	3	2
				Loan	09/02/96	Birmingham City								
Stefanovic Dejan						RS Belgrade								
				£2000000	22/12/95	Sheffield Wed.	5+1		1					
Williams Michael A	5.10	11.6	21/11/69	Bradford		Maltby MW								
				Free	13/02/91	Sheffield Wed.	16+6	2+2		1	1			
				Loan	18/12/92	Halifax Town	9				1			
F O R W A R D S														
Barker Richard	6.0	11.8	30/05/75	Sheffield	27/07/93	Sheffield Wed.								
				Loan	29/09/95	Doncaster Rovers	5+1			0+1				
Booth Andy	6.0	10.8	17/03/73	Huddersfield	01/07/92	Huddersfield Town	66+14	6+1	4	12+1	38		1	4
				£2700000	04/07/96	Sheffield Wed.								
Bright Mark	6.0	11.0	06/06/62	Stoke		Leek Town								
FMC'91				Free	15/10/81	Port Vale	18+11	1+1	0+1	2	10		1	
				£33000	19/07/84	Leicester City	26+16	3+1	1		6			
				£75000	13/11/86	Crystal Palace	224+3	22	13+1	23	90	11	2	9
				£1375000	11/09/92	Sheffield Wed.	112+20	20+1	13		48	11	7	
Briscoe Lee	5.10	10.9	30/09/75	Pontefract	22/05/94	Sheffield Wed.	28+4	1						
Donaldson O'Neill	6.0	11.4	24/11/69	Birmingham		Hinckley Town								
					13/11/91	Shrewsbury Town	15+13		1		4			
				Free	10/08/94	Doncaster Rovers	7+2	2		0+1	2			
				Loan	23/12/94	Mansfield Town	4+6		1+1					

						1	2	3	4	5	6	7	8
Donaldson continued...			£50000	09/01/95	Sheffield Wed.	1+3				1			
Hirst David	5.11 12.5 07/12/67	Cudworth		08/11/85	Barnsley	26+2	1			9			
E: 3, B.3, u21.7, u19.3, Y.8. LC'91			£200000	11/08/86	Sheffield Wed.	238+25	25+9	12+5	8	100	11	6	5
Oakes Scott J	5.10 9.12 05/08/72	Leicester		09/05/90	Leicester City	1+2							
E: u21.1				22/10/91	Luton Town	136+37	3+3	12+2	3+3	27	1	5	1
				01/08/96	Sheffield Wed.								
Smith Gavin D		24/09/77	Sheffield	01/08/94	Sheffield Wed.								
Waddle Chris	6.0 11.5 14/12/30	Felling			Tow Law Town								
E: 62, u21.1. FLg2. Fra: Div1'90'91'92. FFAC'92			£1000	28/07/80	Newcastle United	169+1	8	12		46	2	4	
			£590000	01/07/85	Tottenham Hotspur	137+1	21	14	4	33	4	5	
			£4250000	01/07/89	Marseilles (France)								
			£1000000	01/07/92	Sheffield Wed.	94+14	19	12+1	3+1	10		3	1
Whittingham Guy	5.10 11.12 10/11/64	Evesham			Oxford City								
LC'94					Waterlooville								
					Yeovil Town								
			Free	09/06/89	Portsmouth	149+11	7+2	7+3	9	88	3	10	3
			£1200000	01/08/93	Aston Villa	13+5	2		1	3			
			Loan	28/02/94	Wolves	13		1		8			
			£700000	21/12/94	Sheffield Wed.	43+7	3+1	3+1		15	1		
ADDITIONAL CONTRACT PLAYERS													
Batty Mark P					Sheffield Wed. (T)								
Daly Matthew				01/07/95	Sheffield Wed. (T)								
Pringle Alan				24/05/96	Sheffield Wed. (T)								
Stevens Andrew				24/05/96	Sheffield Wed. (T)								
Thorpe Steven				24/05/96	Sheffield Wed. (T)								
Weaver Simon				24/05/96	Sheffield Wed. (T)								

THE MANAGER
DAVID PLEAT

Date of Birth . . . . 15th January 1945.
Place of Birth . . . . Nottingham.
Date of Appointment . . . . June 1995.

PREVIOUS CLUBS
As Manager . . . . Nuneaton, Luton Town, Tottenham, Leicester City, Luton Town.
As Coach . . . . Luton Town.
As a Player . . . . Nott'm Forest, Luton Town, Shrewsbury, Exeter, Peterborough.

HONOURS
As a Manager
Div. 2 championship 1981-82.

As a Player
None.
International: England schoolboy 1961, Youth 1962, 1963, 1964.

HILLSBOROUGH

Sheffield S6 1SW
Tel: 01142 343 122

Capacity 39,859

First game .... v Chesterfield, Div 2, 5-1, 2.9.1899.
First floodlit game .... v International XI, 9.3.1955.
Internationals .... England v Scotland 1920, v France 1962.
.... W.Germany v Switzerland & v Uruguay 1966. Switzerland v Spain & v Argentina 1966.
...N.Ireland v Bulgaria 1974 **Euro'96:** Denmark v Portugal, Croatia v Denmark, Turkey v Denmark.
ATTENDANCES
Highest .... 72,841 v Man. City, FAC 5th Rnd, 17.2.1934.
Lowest .... 2,500 v Everton, 5.4.1902.
OTHER GROUNDS: .... Highfields 1867-69. Myrtle Rd 1869-77.
........Sheaf Close 1877-87. Olive Grove 1887-99. Owlerton (changed to Hillsborough 1912) 1899-

---

MATCHDAY TICKET PRICES

.... Premier Category/Standard
North & South Centre .... £18/£13
Concession .... £12/£9

Kop & West Lower .... £12/£9
Concession .... £7/£5.50

West Upper £13
Concession £9

Family Enclosure.................... £10.50
Concession........................ £6.50

Ticket Office Telephone no. 01142 337 233

CLUBCALL
0898 12 11 86
Calls cost 39p per minute cheap rate and 49p per
minute at all other times.
Call costings correct at time of going to press.

HOW TO GET TO THE GROUND

From the North
Use motorway (M1) until junction 34, leave motorway and follow signs to
Sheffield (A6109). in 1.5 miles at roundabout take 3rd exit (A6102). In 3.2 miles
turn left into Harries Road South for Sheffield Wednesday FC.

From East and South
Use A57 from motorway M1 (junction 31 or 33) then at roundabout junction with
Rign Road take 3rd exit A610 into Prince of Wales Road. In 5.8 miles turn left
into Herries Road South for Sheffield Wednesday FC.

From the West
Use A57 (sign posted Sheffield) then turn left A6101. In 3.8 miles at 'T' junction
turn left A61 into Penistone Road for Sheffield Wednesday FC.

Car Parking
Street parking is available.

Nearest Railway Station
Sheffield (01142 726 411).

MATCHDAY PROGRAMME

Programme Editor .... Roger Oldfield.

Number of pages .... 24.

Price .... £1.50.

Subscriptions .... 1st Class £62, 2nd Class £52, surface mail £62.

Local Newspapers .... Sheffield Newspapers Ltd. (The Star).

Local Radio Stations .... BBC Radio Sheffield, Radio Hallam.

SOUTHAMPTON
(The Saints)
F.A. CARLING PREMIERSHIP
SPONSORED BY: SANDERSON ELECTRONICS

Back Row (L-R): Frankie Bennett, Alan Neilson, Neil Shipperley, Dave Beasant, Ken Monkou, Richard Hall, Peter Whiston, Neil Heaney.
Middle Row: Paul McDonald, Craig Maskell, Gordon Watson, Simon Charlton, Jason Dodd, Tommy Widdrington, David Hughes, Paul Tisdale, Paul Allen.
Front Row: Lew Chatterley (Asst. Manager), Neil Maddison, Matthew Le Tissier, Lawrie McMenemy (Director of Football), Dave Merrington (Manager), Francis Benali, Jim Magilton, Jim Joyce (Physio).

SOUTHAMPTON
FORMED IN 1885
TURNED PROFESSIONAL IN 1894
LTD COMPANY IN 1897

PRESIDENT: John Corbett
VICE-PRESIDENT: E T Bates
CHAIRMAN: F G L Askham FCA
DIRECTORS
K St J Wiseman (Vice-Chairman),
I L Gordon, B D H Hunt, M R Richards FCA
Lawrie McMenemy
SECRETARY
Brian Truscott (01703 220 505)
COMMERCIAL MANAGER
John O'Sullivan

MANAGER: Graeme Souness
ASSISTANT MANAGER: Terry Cooper
FIRST TEAM COACH: Phil Boersma
RESERVE TEAM MANAGER
Ray Clarke
YOUTH TEAM MANAGER
Alan Murray
PHYSIOTHERAPIST
Jim Joyce & Don Taylor
STATISTICIAN FOR THE DIRECTORY
John Mason

The whole of the 1995-96 season was encapsulated within a final ten minutes of excruciating tension at The Dell in the last match of the campaign against Wimbledon. Never before has the club come so close to losing their record of eighteen unbroken years in the top division of English football.

Their task going into the final game was simply to match any result that Manchester City achieved at home to Liverpool, thus remaining above City by virtue of goal difference. The fans were quietly confident that this would be accomplished on the back of three straight home wins, and but for a three week period in March they had kept their heads above water and remained out of the dreaded bottom relegation positions since October.

The match though was turned into an occasion of surrealism when from early into the game concentration on the task in hand was broken and overshadowed by more important events happening elsewhere. Liverpool scored after six minutes to set off celibrative chants which with hindsight did not assist us in our predicament and was compounded just before half time when they scored again. Suddenly the match that was occurring in front of us was losing it's significance as long as the status quo remained. Worryingly though what we were watching took greater prominence when Manchester City scored after seventy-one minutes and monumental importance just seven minutes later when the news that it was two-two at Maine Road was conveyed to the team, causing anxious looks and conversations. After playing out the season in the mood of consolidation it became apparent that The Saints would not suddenly be able to raise their game enough to win it in the time remaining and that their fate would be sealed by whatever happened in Manchester.

The outcome is now history, but so unnerved were the directors by the experience, that they sacked Dave Merrington who had only taken up the manager's role in the previous July after thirteen years at the club. The general feeling was that it was harsh reward for his service and after three management changes in three summers suddenly the job of managing The Saints was no longer one of the most secure in football.

Graeme Souness was appointed on July 3rd as the first manager the south coast club has appointed with proven experience with top clubs. His task will be to build on the good victories last season against Newcastle, Blackburn, and the worldwide acclaim Southampton received for the famous grey day that Manchester United suffered at The Dell, and take The Saints into their new stadium on a more level playing field with the rest of the Premiership. JOHN MASON.

SOUTHAMPTON

League: 17th		FA Cup: Quarter Finals		Coca-Cola Cup: 4th Rnd					

M	DATE	COMP	VEN	OPPONENTS	RESULT	HT	LP	GOAL SCORERS/GOAL TIMES	ATT.
1	A 19	PL	H	Nottingham Forest	L 3-4	1-3	14	Le Tissier 10(pen), 68(pen), 81 (3)	15164
2	26	PL	A	Everton	L 0-2	0-2	20		(33668)
3	30	PL	H	Leeds United	D 1-1	0-0	19	Widdrington 81	15212
4	S 9	PL	H	Newcastle United	W 1-0	0-0	15	Magilton 65	15237
5	12	PL	A	Middlesbrough	D 0-0	0-0	11		(29188)
6	16	PL	A	Chelsea	L 0-3	0-0	16		(26237)
7	19	CC 2/1	A	Cardiff City	W 3-0	1-0		Le Tissier 27, 47, Shipperley 51	(9041)
8	23	PL	A	Arsenal	L 2-4	2-2	18	Watson 24, Monkou 45	(38136)
9	O 2	PL	H	West Ham United	D 0-0	0-0	17		13568
10	4	CC 2/2	H	Cardiff City	W 2-1	0-1		Watson 52, Hall 82	12709
11	14	PL	A	Blackburn Rovers	L 1-2	0-1	17	Maddison 90	(26780)
12	22	PL	H	Liverpool	L 1-3	1-1	17	Watson 3	15245
13	25	CC 3	H	West Ham United	W 2-1	1-1		Watson 4, Shipperley 79	11059
14	28	PL	A	Wimbledon	W 2-1	1-0	17	Shipperley 9, 75	(7982)
15	N 4	PL	H	Queens Park Rangers	W 2-0	1-0	14	Dodd 2, Le Tissier 76	15137
16	18	PL	A	Manchester United	L 1-4	0-3	15	Shipperley 85	(39301)
17	20	PL	H	Aston Villa	L 0-1	0-1	15		13582
18	25	PL	A	Bolton Wanderers	W 1-0	0-0	14	Hughes 74	14404
19	28	CC 4	A	Reading	L 1-2	1-1		Monkou 44	(13742)
20	D 2	PL	A	Liverpool	D 1-1	0-0	14	Shipperley 60	(38007)
21	9	PL	H	Arsenal	D 0-0	0-0	15		15238
22	16	PL	A	West Ham United	L 1-2	1-0	14	Bishop 22(og)	(18501)
23	23	PL	A	Sheffield Wednesday	D 2-2	1-1	15	Heaney 7, Magilton 80(pen)	(25115)
24	26	PL	H	Tottenham Hotspur	D 0-0	0-0	15		15238
25	J 1	PL	A	Coventry City	D 1-1	0-0	16	Heaney 64	(16822)
26	7	FAC 3	H	Portsmouth	W 3-0	1-0		Magilton 13, 46, Shipperley 80	15236
27	13	PL	A	Nottingham Forest	L 0-1	0-1	16		(23321)
28	20	PL	H	Middlesbrough	W 2-1	0-1	16	Shipperley 64, Hall 71	15151
29	31	PL	H	Manchester City	D 1-1	0-0	15	Shipperley 66	15172
30	F 3	PL	H	Everton	D 2-2	0-0	15	Watson 46, Magilton 77	15136
31	7	FAC 4	H	Crewe Alexandra	D 1-1	0-1		Le Tissier 63	13776
32	13	FAC 4R	A	Crewe Alexandra	W 3-2	3-0		Shipperley 9, Hall 20, Dodd 26	(5579)
33	17	FAC 5	A	Swindon Town	D 1-1	0-1		Watson 76	(15035)
34	24	PL	H	Chelsea	L 2-3	2-2	15	Widdrington 6, Shipperley 38	15226
35	28	FAC 5R	H	Swindon Town	W 2-0	0-0		Oakley 63, Shipperley 76	13962
36	M 2	PL	A	Tottenham Hotspur	L 0-1	0-0	17		(26320)
37	11	FAC QF	A	Manchester United	L 0-2	0-0			(45446)
38	16	PL	A	Manchester City	L 1-2	0-2	18	Tisdale 64	(29550)
39	20	PL	H	Sheffield Wednesday	L 0-1	0-1	18		13216
40	25	PL	H	Coventry City	W 1-0	1-0	18	Dodd 2	14461
41	30	PL	A	Queens Park Rangers	L 0-3	0-1	18		(17615)
42	A 3	PL	A	Leeds United	L 0-1	0-0	18		(26077)
43	6	PL	H	Blackburn Rovers	W 1-0	0-0	16	Le Tissier 80(pen)	14793
44	8	PL	A	Aston Villa	L 0-3	0-0	16		(34059)
45	13	PL	H	Manchester United	W 3-1	3-0	16	Monkou 11, Shipperley 23, Le Tissier 43	15262
46	17	PL	A	Newcastle United	L 0-1	0-1	17		(36554)
47	27	PL	A	Bolton Wanderers	W 1-0	1-0	17	Le Tissier 26	(18795)
48	M 5	PL	H	Wimbledon	D 0-0	0-0	17		15172

Best Home League Attendance: 15262 v Manchester United   **Smallest: 13216 v Sheffield Wednesday**   **Average: 14821**

Goal Scorers:
PL(34): Shipperley(8),Le Tissier(7),Watson(3),Magilton(3),Widdrington(2),Monkou(2),Dodd(2),Heaney(2),Tisdale(1),Hughes(1),Maddison(1),Hall(1),Opponent(s)(1)
CC(8): Watson(2),Shipperley(2),Le Tissier(2),Monkou(1),Hall(1)
FAC(10): Shipperley(3),Magilton(2),Oakley(1),Watson(1),Le Tissier(1),Hall(1),Dodd(1)

Beasant	Benali	Bennett	Charlton	Dodd	Grobbelaar	Hall	Heaney	Hughes	Le	Maddison	Magilton	Maskell	McDonald	Monkou	Nelson	Oakley	Robinson	Sheerin	Shipperley	Tisdale	Venison	Walters	Warren	Watson	Whiston	Widdrington	Referee	No.
X	X		S	X	S	X	X1	S1	X	X	X				X				X					X			G.S.Willard	1
X	X		X	X		X		S1	X	X	X				X1	S2								X2	X		J.Winter	2
X	X	S1	X1	X		S			S	X	X				X				X					X	X		K.Cooper	3
X	X	X1		X		S			S1	X	X				X				X			S			X		G.Ashby	4
X	X		X1	X		X			X	X	X				X				X					S1	X		P.Jones	5
X	X	X2		X		X			X	X	X			S1	X1				X					S2	X		P.Alcock	6
X	X			X		S	X		S	X	X				X				X					S	X		S.W.Dunn	7
X	X1			X		S	X	S1		X1	X	X			X				X				S1	X	X		R.Hart	8
X	X	S1	X1	X		S			X	X	X				X				X					S	X		G.Poll	9
X	X1	S2	S1	X		S			X	X	X				X				X					X		X2	M.Bodenham	10
X	X		S2		X			X	X	X					X				X	S1				X2	X1		M.Reed	11
X	X		X	X	S	X	S1	X			S1				X				X1	X				X	X1		D.Gallagher	12
X	X	S		X	S	X	X	X		X					X				X		X			X	S		P.Danson	13
X	X	S2		X	S	X	X2		X						X				X	S1	X			X	X1		J.Winter	14
X	X	S1		X	S	X	X		X				X		X				X		X			X1	S		L.R.Dilkes	15
X	X	S1		X	S	X	X1		S1	X					X				X					X1	X	X	P.Danson	16
X	X	S1		X	S	X	X	S	X		X1				X				X					X	X		D.Elleray	17
X	X	X2		X		X	S2	X		X					X		S		X		X		S1	X1			P.Jones	18
X	X1			X		X	S1	X	X3	X2					X				X		X		X	S1			M.Reed	19
X	X	X1	X		X			X	S	S					X		S1	S	X		X						R.Hart	20
X	X2		X		X	X1		X	S	X					X		S1		X		X			S2			P.Danson	21
X	X		X	X		X	S1	X	S1	X1					X		X	X		X		X					A.Wilkie	22
X			X	X	S	X	X		X1					X	S1	X	S	X		X					X		J.T.Winter	23
X			X	X	X	X	X1	S	X					X	S	X	X			S1						P.Durkin	24
X	S1		X1	X	S	X	X		X	X				X	X			X		X			X			K.Cooper	25
X		S	X	X			X1		X	S2	X	S1	X	X			X		X			X2			M.Bodenham	26
X	X1	X	X	S			X	X2	X	S1	X	X			X			X		S2					S.J.Lodge	27
X		X	X		X		X	X	S	X	S2	X1	X2		X	X		S1					K.Burge	28
X	X	X	X	S	X	X	S	X	X	S1	X	X1	X				S.Dunn	29
X	X	S	X	X	X	S1	X	X	S1	X	X1	X2	X			D.Elleray	30
X	X	S	X	X	S1	X	X	S2	X	X1	X2	X			P.Alcock	31
X	X	S2	X	X	X	S1	S	X	X1	X2	X		P.Alcock	32
X	X1	X	X	S	X	X	X	S1	X	X	S	X	X	X	R.Hart	33
X	X	X	S	X	X	X	S	X	X	S1	X1	X	X	G.Ashby	34
X	X	S	X	X	X	X	S1	X	S	X	X	X	R.Hart	35
X	X	X	S	X	X	X	S1	X	S2	X	X2	X	K.N.Burge	36
X	X	X	S	X	X	X	X	S1	X	X1	X	S.Dunn	37
X	X	S	X	X	X	X	X2	X1	S1	X	X	S2	J.Winter	38
X	X	X	X1	X	X	X	S1	X2	S	X	S2	X	X	M.Bodenham	39
X	X	X	X	X	X	X	X	S	X	S	X	S1	X1	S.Lodge	40
X	X1	X	X	X	X	X	X	X	S	X	S1	X	S	P.Jones	41
X	X	X2	X	S	X	X1	X	S1	X	X	X	S2	X	M.Bodenham	42
X	S	S1	X	X	X	X	S	X	X	X	X	X	D.Elleray	43
X	S	X	X	X	X	X	X	X	X	S1	X	P.Danson	44
S	X	X	X	X	X	X	X	X	X	S	S	G.Poll	45
X	X	X	X	X2	X	X1	S2	X	X	S1	D.Gallagher	46
X	X	X	S	X	X	X1	X	X	S1	X	X	G.Ashby	47
X	X	S	X	X	X	X	S	X	X	X	X	S	M.Reed	48
36	28	5	24	37	2	30	15	6	34	13	31	0	0	31	15	5	0	0	37	5	21	4	1	18	0	20	PL Appearances	
0	1	6	2	0	0	0	2	5	0	2	0	1	1	1	3	5	4	0	0	4	1	1	6	7	0	1	PL Sub Appearances	
4	4	0+1	0+1	4	0	4	2+1	2	4	2	4	3	0	0	4	0	0	0	4	0	2	0	1	2+1	0	2	CC Appearances	
6	1	0	6	5	0	5	1	0+1	5	0+2	6	0+1	0+1	6	1+1	2+1	0+2	0	6	0	3	4	0	5	0	4	FAC Appearances	

SOUTHAMPTON

CLUB RECORDS

BIGGEST VICTORIES
League: 8-0 v Northampton, Division 3S, 24.12.1921
F.A. Cup: 7-1 v Ipswich Town, Round 3, 7.1.1961
6-0 v Luton Town, Round 4, 8.2.1995
League Cup: 5-0 v Derby County, Round 3, 8.10.1974
5-0 v Wrexham, Round 2, 28.8.1979
5-0 v Rochdale, Round 2, 25.9.1990
Europe   (UEFA): 5-1 v Vittoria G, Round 2, 12.11.1969
(ECWC): 4-0 v Marseilles, Round 1, 15.9.1976

BIGGEST DEFEATS
League: 0-8 v Tottenham Hotspur, Division 2, 28.3.1936.
0-8 v Everton, Division 1, 20.11.1971.
F.A. Cup: 0-5 v Manchester City, Round 2, 5.2.1910.
League Cup: 1-7 v Watford, Round 2, 2.9.1980.
Europe: No more than 2 goal defeat.

MOST POINTS
3 points a win: 77, Division 1, 1983-84.
2 points a win: 61, Division 3S, 1921-22, Division 3 1959-60.

MOST GOALS
112, 1957-58 (Division 3S).
Reeves 31, Roper 18, Hoskins 18, Paine 12, Clifton 7, Mulgrew 8, Sydenham 4,Page 4, Walker 3, McGowan 2, Traynor 2, McLaughlin 1, og 2.

MOST FIRST CLASS MATCHES IN A SEASON
61 (42 League, 7 FA Cup, 6 League Cup, 6 ZDS) 1991-92

MOST LEAGUE GOALS CONCEDED
92, Division 1, 1966-67

MOST LEAGUE WINS
26, Division 3, 1959-60

MOST LEAGUE DRAWS
18, Division 2, 1924-25; Division 1/P, 1972-73, 1994-95.

MOST LEAGUE DEFEATS
23, Division 1, 1971-72,1993-94

INDIVIDUAL CLUB RECORDS

MOST GOALS IN A SEASON
Derek Reeves 45 (League 39, FAC 6) 1959-60.
4 goals twice=8; 3 goals twice=6; 2 goals 3 times=6; 1 goal 25 times=25.
Previous holder: C Wayman 32 (1948-49).

MOST GOALS IN A MATCH
5. Charlie Wayman v Leicester, Div 2, 23.10.1948 (6-0)
5. Derek Reeves v Leeds (LC4) 5.12.1960 (5-4)

OLDEST PLAYER
Peter Shilton, 37 years 233 days v Coventry (Div 1) 9.5.1987.

YOUNGEST PLAYER
Danny Wallace 16 years 313 days v Manchester Utd (Div 1) 29.11.1980.

MOST CAPPED PLAYER
Peter Shilton (England) 49

BEST PERFORMANCES

League: 1921-22: Matches played 42, Won 23, Drawn 15, Lost 4, Goals for 68,Goals against 21, Points 61. 1st in Division 3S.
Highest: 1983-84: 2nd in Division 1.

F.A. Cup: 1975-76 (Div 2): 3rd rnd. Aston Villa 1-1, 2-1; 4th rnd. Blackpool 3-1; 5th rnd. West Bromwich Albion 1-1, 4-0; 6th rnd. Bradford City 1-0; Semi-final Crystal Palace 2-0; Final Manchester United 1-0.

League Cup: 1978-79 (Div 1): 2nd rnd. Birmingham City 5-2; 3rd rnd. DerbyCounty 1-0; 4th rnd. Reading 0-0 2-0; 5th rnd. Manchester City 2-1; Semi-finalLeeds United 2-2, 1-0; Final Nottingham Forest 2-3.

Europe (ECWC): 1976-77 (Div 2): 1st rnd. Marseille 4-0, 1-2; 2nd rnd Carrick R.5-2, 4-1; 3rd rnd. Anderlecht 0-2, 2-1.
(UEFA): 1969-70: 1st rnd. Rosenburg 0-1, 2-0; 2nd rnd. Vittoria Guimariers 3-3,5-1; 3rd rnd. Newcastle 0-0, 1-1.

DIVISIONAL RECORD

	Played	Won	Drawn	Lost	For	Against	Points
Division 1/P	1,074	360	301	413	1,467	1,584	1,231
Division 2	1,428	559	353	516	2,221	2,140	1,471
Division 3	92	43	20	29	194	155	106
Division 3(S)	314	150	77	87	562	368	377
Total	2,908	1,112	740	1,027	4,444	4,247	3,185

ADDITIONAL INFORMATION
Previous Name
Southampton St. Mary's

Previous League
Southern League

Club colours: Red & white striped shirts, black shorts, red & white socks.
Change colours: Yellow & royal blue striped shirts, blue shorts, yellow & blue socks.

Reserves League: Avon Insurance Football Combination.

RECORDS AND STATISTICS

COMPETITIONS

Div 1/P	Div.2	Div.3	Div.3(S)	UEFA	ECWC
1966-74	1922-53	1920-21	1921-22	1969-70	1976-77
1978-	1960-66	1958-60	1953-58	1971-72	
	1974-78			1981-82	
				1982-83	TEXACO
				1984-85	1974-75

HONOURS

Division 3	Division 3(S)	FA Cup
1959-60	1921-22	1975-76

MOST GOALS IN A CAREER

Mike Channon - 227 (19966-77 & 1979-82)

Year	League	FA Cup	Lge Cup	Europe
1965-66	1			
1966-67				
1967-68	7	1		
1968-69	8	1	3	
1969-70	15	2	1	3
1970-71	18	1	1	
1971-72	14	1		1
1972-73	16		2	
1973-74	21	1	1	
1974-75	20	1	3	
1975-76	20	5		
1976-77	17	2	1	4
1979-80	10	1		
1980-81	10			
1981-82	8			1
Total	185	16	12	9

(Plus 5 in the Texaco Cup - 1974-75)

Current leading goalscorer: Matthew Le Tissier 168 (1986-96)

MOST APPEARANCES

Terry Paine 805+4 (1956-74)

Year	League	FA Cup	Lge Cup	Europe
1956-57	9			
1957-58	44	2		
1958-59	46	3		
1959-60	46	6		
1960-61	42	2	7	
1961-62	41	2	2	
1962-63	42	7	3	
1963-64	41	1	1	
1964-65	42	2	2	
1965-66	40	1	2	
1966-67	42	3	3	
1967-68	41	4	1	
1968-69	42	4	4	
1969-70	36	3	2	6
1970-71	41	4	1	
1971-72	37+3	2	2	2
1972-73	36+1	1	4	
1973-74	41	4	3	
	709+4	51	37	8

RECORD TRANSFER FEE RECEIVED

Amount	Club	Player	Date
£3,600,000	Blackburn Rov.	Alan Shearer	7/92
£1,600,000	Leeds United	Rodney Wallace	7/91
£1,200,000	Manchester Utd	Danny Wallace	9/89
£800,000	Q.P.R.	Colin Clarke	3/89

RECORD TRANSFER FEE PAID

Amount	Club	Player	Date
£1,200,000	Chelsea	Neil Shipperley	1/95
£1,000,000	Swindon Town	Alan McLoughlin	12/90
£750,000	Portsmouth	Barry Horne	3/89
£600,000	Middlesbrough	David Armstrong	8/81

MANAGERS

Name	Seasons	Best	Worst
George Swift	1911-12		
James McIntyre	1919-24	5(2)	2(3S)
Arthur Chadwick	1925-31	4(2)	17(2)
G Kay	1931-36	12(2)	19(2)
George Goss	1936-37	19(2)	19(2)
T Parker	1937-War	15(2)	18(2)
W Dodgin (Snr)	War-1949	3(2)	14(2)
Sid Cann	1949-51	13(2)	21(2)
George Roughton	1952-55	3(2)	6(3)
Ted Bates	1955-73	7(1)	14(3)
Lawrie McMenemy	1973-85	2(1)	13(2)
Chris Nicholl	1985-91	7(1)	14(1)
Ian Branfoot	1991-94	16(1)	18(1/P)
Alan Ball	1994-95	10(P)	18(P)
Dave Merrington	1995-96	17(P)	17(P)
Graeme Souness	1996-		

LONGEST LEAGUE RUNS

of undefeated matches:	19 (5.9.1921 - 14.1.1922)	of league matches w/out a win:	20 (30.8.1969 - 17.1.1970)
of undefeated home matches:	31 (22.1.1921 - 28.8.1922)	of undefeated away matches:	9 (19.11.77-29.3.78, 17.9.49-21.1.50)
without home win:	10 (6.9.1969 - 17.1.1970)	without an away win:	33 (22.4.1933 - 25.12.1934)
of league wins:	6 (5.9.1964 - 13.10.1964, 3.3.1992 - 8.4.1992)	of home wins:	11 (10.10.1959 - 19.3.1960)
of league defeats:	5 (7.5.1927 - 10.9.1927, 12.1.1957 - 25.2.1957)	of away wins:	3 (On 10 different occasions)
	(30.12.1967 - 10.2.1968, 31.12.1988 - 11.2.1989, Twice in 1993)		

SOUTHAMPTON

PLAYERS NAME Honours	Ht	Wt	Birthdate	Birthplace Transfers	Contract Date	Clubs	APPEARANCES League	L/Cup	FA Cup	Other	GOALS Lge	L/C	FAC	Oth
G O A L K E E P E R S														
Beasant Dave	6.3	13.0	20/03/59	Willesden		Edgware Town								
E: 2, B.7. Div4'83. Div2'89.				£1000	07/08/79	Wimbledon	340	21	27	3				
FAC'88. ZDC'90				£800000	13/06/88	Newcastle United	20	2	2	1				
				£735000	14/01/89	Chelsea	133	11	5	8				
				Loan	24/10/92	Grimsby Town	6							
				Loan	12/01/93	Wolves	4		1					
				£300000	04/11/93	Southampton	73+1	4	8					
Moss Neil	6.1	12.11	10/05/75	New Milton	29/01/93	Bournemouth	21+1	1	3+1	2				
				£250000	20/12/95	Southampton								
D E F E N D E R S														
Benali Francis	5.9	11.0	30/12/68	Southampton	05/01/87	Southampton	179+23	17+6	18	3+1				
Charlton Simon	5.7	11.1	25/10/71	Huddersfield	01/07/89	Huddersfield Town	121+3	9	10	14	1	1		
E: S				£250000	08/06/93	Southampton	78+6	3+2	8		2			
Dodd Jason	5.10	11.10	02/11/70	Bath		Bath City			0+1					
E: u21.8				£50000	15/03/89	Southampton	155+16	22+1	21	5	5		1	
Dryden Richard	6.0	12.0	14/06/69	Stroud	14/07/87	Bristol Rovers	12+1	2+1	0+2	2				
Div.4'90.				Loan	22/09/88	Exeter City	6							
					08/03/89	Exeter City	86	7	2	4	13	2		
				£250000	09/08/91	Notts County	30+1	1+1	2+1	2	1			
				Loan	18/11/92	Plymouth Argyle	5		1					
				£165000	19/03/93	Birmingham City	45	4	1					
				£200000	16/12/94	Bristol City	32+5	4	1+1	3	1			
				£150000	06/08/96	Southampton								
Monkou Kenneth	6.0	12.9	29/11/64	Surinam		Feyenoord								
Holland: u21. ZDC'90				£100000	02/03/89	Chelsea	92+2	12	3	10	2			
				£750000	21/08/92	Southampton	130+1	10	13		8	1	1	
Neilson Alan B	5.11	12.4	26/09/72	Wegburg (Ger)	11/02/91	Newcastle United	35+7	4		4	1			
W: 3, B.2, u21.7				£500000	01/08/95	Southampton	15+3		1+1					
Potter Graham	5.11	11.0	20/05/75	Solihull	01/07/92	Birmingham City	23+2		1	6	2			
E: Y.1				Loan	17/09/93	Wycombe Wand.	2+1	1		1				
				£75000	20/12/93	Stoke City	41+4	2+1	4	5	1			
					24/07/96	Southampton								
Venison Barry	5.10	11.09	16/08/64	Consett	20/01/82	Sunderland	169+4	21	7+1	3	2			1
				£200000	31/07/86	Liverpool	103+7	14+3	16+5	6+4	1			2
				£250000	31/07/92	Newcastle United	108+1	9	11	4	1			
					01/03/95	Galatasaray								
				£850000	25/10/95	Southampton	21+1	2	3					
M I D F I E L D														
Hughes David	5.9	11.0	30/12/72	St Albans	02/07/91	Southampton	8+17	2	0+5		3		1	
W: u21.1. E: u19.4, S														
Magilton Jim	5.10	12.7	06/05/69	Belfast	14/05/86	Liverpool								
NI: 22, u21.1, u23.1				£100000	03/10/90	Oxford United	150	9	8	6	34	1	4	3
				£600000	11/02/94	Southampton	88	6	11		9		3	
Oakley Matthew	5.10	11.0	17/08/77	Peterborough	01/08/94	Southampton	5+6		2+1				1	
Robinson Matt	5.10	10.8	23/12/74	Exeter	01/07/93	Southampton	0+5		0+2					
Tisdale Paul	5.9	10.9	14/01/73	Malta	05/06/91	Southampton	5+11	0+1	0+1		1			
E: u18.3, SFA				Loan	12/03/92	Northampton Town	5							
Warren Christer			10/10/74	Bournemouth		Cheltenham Town								
				£40000	01/08/95	Southampton	1+6	1						
Widdrington Tommy	5.8	11.1	01/10/71	Newcastle	10/05/90	Southampton	67+8	3+1	11		3			
				Loan	12/09/91	Wigan Athletic	5+1	2						
F O R W A R D S														
Bennett Frank	5.7	11.8	03/01/69	Birmingham		Halesowen Town								
				£7500	24/02/93	Southampton	5+14	1+2	0+1		1			
Heaney Neil	5.9	11.1	03/11/71	Middlesbrough	14/11/89	Arsenal	4+3	0+1						
E: u21.6, Y.3. FAYC'88				Loan	03/01/91	Hartlepool United	2+1							
				Loan	09/01/92	Cambridge United	9+4		1		2			

aney continued....				£300000	22/03/94	Southampton	38+15	4+2	6		4		2	
Tissier Matthew	6.0	11.10	14/10/68	Guernsey	17/10/86	Southampton	296+30	30+6	28+1	11+1	127	20	12	9
3, B.5, u19.2, Y.1. FLgXl.1														
eerin Paul	5.10	11.1	28/08/74	Edinburgh		Alloa	7+2	1						
				£60000	23/10/92	Southampton								
pperley Neil	5.11	13.2	30/10/74	Chatham	24/09/92	Chelsea	20+7	2+1	3		5	1	1	
u21.4				£1250000	08/01/95	Southampton	56	4	10		12	2	5	
tson Gordon	6.0	12.9	20/03/71	Sidcup	05/04/89	Charlton Athletic	20+11	2	0+1	1+1	7	1		
u21.2				£250000	20/02/91	Sheffield Wed.	29+27	6+5	5+2	2+2	15	3	2	1
				£1200000	17/03/95	Southampton	30+7	2+1	5		6	2	1	

DITIONAL CONTRACT PLAYERS

sham Steven	24/05/96	Southampton (T)	
mey Nathan		Southampton (T)	
havan Darryl	24/05/96	Southampton (T)	
er David	24/05/96	Southampton (T)	
dding Duncan	24/05/96	Southampton (T)	

THE MANAGER
GRAEME SOUNESS

Date of Birth . . . . 6th May 1953.
Place of Birth . . . . Edinburgh.
Date of Appointment . . . . 3rd July 1995.

PREVIOUS CLUBS
As Manager . . . . Glasgow Rangers, Liverpool, Galatasary.
As a Player . . . . Tottenham, Middlesbrough, Liverpool, Sampadoria,
. . . . Glasgow Rangers (player/manager).

HONOURS
As a Manager
Glasgow Rangers: League Champions 4 times, League Cup (4).
Liverpool: F.A. Cup winners 1992.
As a Player
Liverpool: Div.1 Champions (5), League Cup (4), European Cup (3).
Glasgow Rangers: League Champions (2), League Cup (4).
Sampadoria: Italian Cup (1).
Scotland: 53 full caps.

THE DELL

Milton Road, Southampton SO9 4XX
Tel: 01703 220 505

Capacity 15,200

First game...v Brighton, Sth League, 3.9.1898.
First floodlit game ....v Bournemouth, 31.10.1950.

ATTENDANCES
Highest ....31,044 v Manchester Utd, Div.1., 08.10.1969.
Lowest ....1,875 v Port Vale, Division 2, 30.3.1936.

OTHER GROUNDS ....Antelope Ground 1885-1897. County Cricket Ground 1897-98. The Dell 1898-

MATCHDAY TICKET PRICES

East/West Centre £18

Wings £17

Lower Tier £15
Juv £6

Milton Road £17

Archers Road. £17

Ticket Office Telephone no. 01703 337 171
(Visa/Access bookings only).

CLUBCALL
0891 12 11 78
Calls cost 39p per minute cheap rate and 49p per minute at all other times.
Call costings correct at time of going to press.

HOW TO GET TO THE GROUND

From the North
Use A33, sign posted Southampton, via The Avenue, then turn right into Northlands Road and at the end turn right into Archers Road for Southampton FC.

From the East
Use motorway M27 then A334 and follow signs to Southampton A3024. The follow signs to The West into Commercial Road then turn right into Hill Lane and take first turning right into Milton Road for Southampton FC.

From the West
Use M27 then A35 and follow signs to Southampton city centre A3024. Turn left over central station bridge, right into Fourpost Hill, then turn left into Hill Lane and take first turning right into Milton Road for Southampton FC.

Car Parking
Street parking and nearby municipal parks.

Nearest Railway Station
Southampton Central (01703 229 393).

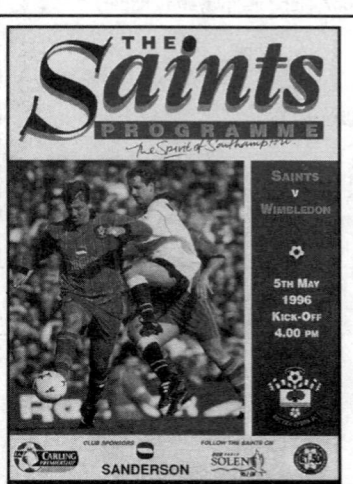

MATCHDAY PROGRAMME

Programme Editor . . . . Mr J Hughes.

Number of pages . . . . 48.

Price . . . . £1.50.

Subscriptions . . . . £58 for all home games.

Local Newspapers . . . . The Daily Echo, Portsmouth News, ... Hampshire Chronicle.

Local Radio Stations . . . . Radio Solent, Power FM.

SUNDERLAND
(The Rokerites)
F.A. CARLING PREMIERSHIP
SPONSORED BY: VAUX

Back Row (L-R): Martin Smith, Gary Bennett, Gordon Armstrong, Brett Angell, Richard Ord, Andy Melville, Lee Howey.
Middle Row: Mick Ferguson, Gordon Ellis, Paul Bracewell, Derek Furguson, Brain Atkinson, John Kay, Alec Chamberlain, David Preece,
Michael Gray, Steve Agnew, Phil Gray, Martin Gray, Martin Scott, Steven Grant, Bobby Saxton, Pop Robson, Steve Smelt.
Front Row: Ricky Sbragia, Scott Coates, Christopher Lawless, Paul Heckingbottom, Dariusz Kubicki, Kevin Ball, Peter Reid, Craig Russell,
David Mawson, Stephen Brodie, Sam Aiston, Joey McGiven, Stephen Pickering, John Cooke.

SUNDERLAND
FORMED IN 1879
TURNED PROFESSIONAL IN 1886
LTD COMPANY IN 1906

CHAIRMAN: Bob Murray
DIRECTORS
G S Wood (Vice-Chairman), J Wood,
J M Ficking
SECRETARY
Mark Blackbourne
MARKETING & COMMERCIAL
DEVELOPMENT MANAGER
Grahame McDonnell

MANAGER: Peter Reid
ASSISTANT MANAGER: Paul Bracewell
FIRST TEAM COACH: Bobby Saxton
RESERVE TEAM MANAGER
Bryan 'Pop' Robson
YOUTH TEAM MANAGER
Ricky Sbragia

STATISTICIAN FOR THE DIRECTORY
Eddie Brennan

To use a well-worn phrase, what a difference a year makes! Back in August, Sunderland's fans would happily have settled for a play-off place after years of relegation worries. As it was, the Rokerites secured an automatic promotion slot, setting a new club record of eighteen games unbeaten - a run which was ended on the final day of the season, by which time the First Division Championship trophy had already returned to Wearside.

Manager Peter Reid has stated that the team's achievements last season rank alongside any of his successes as a player. The structure of the side remained basically unchanged from the Division Two-bound outfit Reid had inherited the previous March. Indeed, his one major purchase - £1m.-striker David Kelly from Wolves in September - damaged ankle ligaments after nine games and missed the rest of the season. However, the return of midfielder Paul Bracewell as player-assistant manager, and the signings of striker Paul Stewart - on a free transfer from Liverpool - and £300,000 utility-man Gareth Hall from Chelsea, along with Shay Given on a three-month loan from Blackburn, proved to be masterstrokes by Reid, giving the squad vital stability in key areas.

The season began slowly but gathered momentum. Sunderland hovered around the play-off positions until three successive wins, culminating in the 6-0 demolition of then-leaders Millwall in December, put them in pole position. Although this stay at the summit ended at Derby a fortnight later, only four more defeats were suffered in the rest of the campaign. During this period, Sunderland strung together nine consecutive wins to reclaim the top spot in March, where they remained. Despite making an early exit in both the Coca-Cola and FA Cups, the Rokermen performed well against top-quality opposition in Liverpool and Manchester United respectively. Indeed, only a late Eric Cantona equaliser at Old Trafford denied them a famous victory over the Premiership champions.

Sunderland racked up the most number of victories in Division One (22), conceded the fewest amount of goals (32), and several personal performances were duly acknowledged. Full back Dariusz Kubicki and winger Michael Gray were named in the PFA 1st Division XI, whilst others such as Martin Scott and Richard Ord must have been in contention. Peter Reid himself was deservedly voted Manager of the Year by the FMA and, on a lighter note, saw his name appear in the pop charts via the song 'Cheer up Peter Reid'.

Inevitably, Sunderland have been tipped to struggle in the Premiership. However, whilst no one at Roker is under any illusions as to the magnitude of the step-up in class that the club has made, surely few will begrudge them the opportunity, for the close season at least, to bask in some well-earned and long-overdue glory. Hopefully, sufficient financial backing for new players, and the continued progress of home-grown talent such as strikers Sam Aiston and Michael Bridges, will see Peter Reid consolidate Sunderland's top-flight status in what will be the last season at Roker Park.

EDDIE BRENNAN

SUNDERLAND

M	DATE	COMP	VEN	OPPONENTS	RESULT	HT	LP	GOAL SCORERS/GOAL TIMES	ATT.
1	A 12	EL	H	Leicester City	L 1-2	1-1	17	Agnew 30	18593
2	15	CC 1/1	A	**Preston North End**	D 1-1	0-0		**Angell 50**	(6323)
3	19	EL	A	Norwich City	D 0-0	0-0	22		(16739)
4	23	CC 1/2	H	**Preston North End**	W 3-2	0-2		**Howey 47, 85, Kidd 48(og)**	7407
5	26	EL	H	Wolverhampton Wand	W 2-0	2-0	17	Melville 8, Gray 28	16816
6	30	EL	A	Port Vale	D 1-1	0-1	14	Gray 53	(7693)
7	S 2	EL	A	Ipswich Town	L 0-3	0-2	18		(12390)
8	9	EL	H	Southend United	W 1-0	0-0	16	Russell 40	13805
9	12	EL	H	Portsmouth	D 1-1	1-0	16	Melville 6	12282
10	16	EL	A	Luton Town	W 2-0	0-0	9	Mullin 51, Gray 80	(6995)
11	20	CC 2/1	A	**Liverpool**	**L 0-2**	**0-1**			(25579)
12	23	EL	A	Millwall	W 2-1	1-0	7	Scott 44(pen), Smith 78	(8691)
13	30	EL	H	Reading	D 2-2	0-0	6	Kelly 75, Melville 89	17503
14	O 4	CC 2/2	H	**Liverpool**	**L 0-1**	**0-1**			20560
15	7	EL	A	Crystal Palace	W 1-0	0-0	4	Kelly 75	(13754)
16	14	EL	H	Watford	D 1-1	0-0	5	Scott 72	17790
17	21	EL	A	Huddersfield Town	D 1-1	0-0	6	Gray 83	(16054)
18	28	EL	H	Barnsley	W 2-1	1-0	4	Russell 19, Howey 62	17024
19	N 5	EL	A	Charlton Athletic	D 1-1	1-1	5	Gray 18	(11626)
20	18	EL	H	Sheffield United	W 2-0	0-0	4	Gray 67, 72	16640
21	22	EL	A	Stoke City	L 0-1	0-1	8		(11754)
22	25	EL	A	West Bromwich Albion	W 1-0	1-0	4	Howey 10	(15931)
23	D 3	EL	H	Crystal Palace	W 1-0	1-0	2	Scott 39	12777
24	9	EL	H	Millwall	W 6-0	2-0	1	Scott 15(pen), Russell 32, 58, 72, 90, Gray 51	18951
25	16	EL	A	Reading	D 1-1	1-0	2	Smith 12	(9431)
26	23	EL	A	Derby County	L 1-3	1-0	3	Gray 34	(16882)
27	J 6	FAC 3	A	**Manchester United**	**D 2-2**	**0-1**		**Agnew 61, Russell 63**	(41563)
28	14	EL	H	Norwich City	L 0-1	0-1	8		14983
29	16	FAC 3R	H	**Manchester United**	**L 1-2**	**1-0**		**Gray 24**	21378
30	21	EL	A	Leicester City	D 0-0	0-0	7		(16130)
31	24	EL	H	Grimsby Town	W 1-0	0-0	4	Ord 65	14656
32	30	EL	H	Tranmere Rovers	D 0-0	0-0	3		17616
33	F 3	EL	A	Wolverhampton Wand	L 0-3	0-2	5		(26537)
34	10	EL	H	Port Vale	D 0-0	0-0	5		15954
35	17	EL	A	Portsmouth	D 2-2	1-1	5	Agnew 8, Howey 89	(12241)
36	20	EL	H	Ipswich Town	W 1-0	1-0	3	Russell 38	14052
37	24	EL	H	Luton Town	W 1-0	1-0	3	James 38(og)	16693
38	27	EL	A	Southend United	W 2-0	0-0	2	Scott 53(pen), Bridges 80	(5786)
39	M 3	EL	A	Grimsby Town	W 4-0	1-0	2	Ball 35, Russell 73, Gray 89, Bridges 90	(5318)
40	9	EL	H	Derby County	W 3-0	2-0	2	Russell 8,67, Agnew 32	21644
41	12	EL	A	Oldham Athletic	W 2-1	1-1	2	Gray 11, Ball 86	(7149)
42	17	EL	A	Birmingham City	W 2-0	1-0	1	Agnew 16, Melville 64	(23251)
43	23	EL	H	Oldham Athletic	W 1-0	0-0	1	Scott 82	20631
44	30	EL	H	Huddersfield Town	W 3-2	1-1	1	Ball 23, Bridges 83, 87	20131
45	A 2	EL	A	Watford	D 3-3	3-1	1	Agnew 16, Ball 18, Russell 41	(11195)
46	6	EL	A	Barnsley	W 1-0	1-0	1	Russell 24	(13189)
47	8	EL	H	Charlton Athletic	D 0-0	0-0	1		20914
48	13	EL	A	Sheffield United	D 0-0	0-0	1		(20050)
49	16	EL	H	Birmingham City	W 3-0	2-0	1	Gray 17, Stewart 20, Russell 62	19831
50	21	EL	H	Stoke City	D 0-0	0-0	1		21276
51	27	EL	H	West Bromwich Albion	D 0-0	0-0	1		22027
52	M 5	EL	A	Tranmere Rovers	L 0-2	0-1	1		(16193)

Best Home League Attendance: 22027 v West Bromwich Albion   Smallest: 12282 v Portsmouth   Average: 17503

Goal Scorers:
EL(59):   Russell(13),Gray(8),Scott(6),Agnew(5),Melville(4),Ball(4),Bridges(4),Gray(4),Howey(3),Smith(2),Kelly(2),Ord(1),Mullin(1),Stewart(1),Opponent(s)(1)
CC(4):   Howey(2),Opponent(s)(1),Angell(1)
FAC(3):   Gray(1),Agnew(1),Russell(1)

1995-96

	(M) Agnew	(M) Aiston	(F) Angell	(M) Armstrong	(M) Atkinson	(D) Ball	(M) Bracewell	(M) Bridges	(G) Chamberlain	(F) Cooke	(G) Given	(M) Gray Martin	(D) Gray Michael	(F) Gray Phil	(D) Hall	(D) Holloway	(F) Howey	(F) Kelly	(D) Kubicki	(D) Melville	(F) Mullin	(D) Ord	(F) Russell	(D) Scott	(F) Smith	(M) Stewart	
1	X1		X1	S1		X	X		X				X	X			S		X			X	S1	X	X		W.C.Burns
2	X1	X	S1			X	X		X				X	X			S		X			X	S1	X	X1		R.Fernandiz
3			X2		X	X	X		X			X	X	X			S2		X			X	S1		X1		I.Hemley
4					X	X	X		X			X	X2	X			X		X	X	S1		X1		S2		K.M.Lynch
5					X1	X	X		X			S	X2	X			X		X	X	S2		X	X	S2	S1	D.B.Allison
6		S2				X	X		X			X2					X		X	X	S3	S1	X3	X	X	X1	J.Kirkby
7		S3			S2	X	X		X			X1	X				X2		X	X		X	X	X	S1		G.Pooley
8		S1				X	X		X				X	X					X	X	X	X	X1	X	S		J.A.Kirkby
9		S2				X	X		X				X	X			S3		X	X	X2	X1	X1	X	S1		R.Poulain
10				X1	X2		X		X			S1	X	X3					X	X	X	S3	X	S2			P.Jones
11				X			X		X				X	X			S	X	X	X	X1	X	S	X	S1		J.Brandwood
12				X3	S2	X			X				X	X				X	X	X	X1	X2	S3	X	S1		S.W.Mathieson
13		S1			X1	X	X		X			X1	X				S	X	X	X			S1	X	X		R.Dilkes
14					S	X	X		X				X	X			S	X	X	X		X	S1	X	X1		P.Rejer
15		S1					X		X			X1	X				S		X	X	X2		S2	X	X1		K.J.Breen
16	S2	X1				X2	X		X				X	X			S3	X3	X	X		X	S1	X			G.Singh
17	S2	X2		S		X	X		X				X	X			S1		X	X		X	X1	X			W.C.Burns
18	S	S1				X	X		X				X	X			S	X	X	X		X	X1	X			K.Leach
19		S				X	X		X				X	X			S	X	X	X		X	X1	X	S1		R.D.Furnandiz
20		S3				X	X		X				X	X			S2	X3	X	X		X	X2	X	S1		R.Harris
21	X	X1		S1			X		X				X	X			X		X	X	S	X	S	X	S1		S.Baines
22	X			S1	X				X				X	S2		S	X2	X	X	X		X		X	X1		M.Riley
23	X		S				X		X			X	X	X			S		X	X	S	X	X	X	X		E.Lomas
24	X		S				X		X			X	X	X			S	S	X	X		X	X	X	X		R.Gifford
25	X1	S2					X		X			X3	X	X	S1			S3	X	X		X	X	X	X2		P.Richards
26	S1					X1	X		X				X	X3			S3	X2	X	X		X	X	X	S2		M.Reed
27	X					X			X				X	X	S		S2	X1	X2	X		X	X	X	S1		G.Cain
28	X2						X3		X			S2	X	X			S3		X	X	S1	X	X	X	X1		M.Reid
29	X						X2		X	X	S2	X	X	X			S1		X	X		X	X1	X			J.Rushton
30	X	X2							X	X	X	S1	X1	X	X		S		X	X	S2	X	X	X			D.B.Allison
31	X1							S	X	X	X	S1	X	X	X		X		X		S	X	X	X			E.K.Wolstenholme
32	S2						X2		X	X	X	X	X1	X	X		X		X		S1	X	X	X			U.Rennie
33	S				X	X	S1		X	X	S	X	X1				X		X	X			X	X			M.A.Riley
34	X				X	X	S2		X1	X		X2	S2	X			X		X	X	S1		X2				C.Wilkes
35		S			X	X	S		X	X		X	X	X			X		X	X			X	X	X		W.C.Burns
36	S				X	X	S1		X	X		X	X		S		X1		X	X			X	X	X		A.Butler
37	X				X	X	S1		X	S		X	X	X	S		X1		X	X			X	X2	X		G.Barber
38	X1				X	X	S2		X			X	X		S		S		X	X			X	X2	X		M.E.Pierce
39	X				X	X	S		X			X	X2	S1	S2				X	X			X	X	X	X1	R.Richards
40	X				X	X	S1		X			X	X	S	S		X		X	X			X	X1	X	X	K.J.Breen
41	X				X	X	S1		X			X	X	S2	S3				X	X			X	X1	X	X2	W.Burns
42	X				X	X	S1		X			X	X	S	S		S2		X	X			X	X2	X	X1	K.Lynch
43	X				X	X	S1		X			X	X	S	S		S		X	X			X	X1	X	X	N.Barry
44	X				X	X	S1		X			X	X	S2			S		X	X			X	X1	X	X	R.Gifford
45	X				X	X	S1		X			X	X	S			S2		X	X			X	X1	X	X	P.Richards
46	X1	S1			X	X	X2	X				X	X	S			S2		X	X			X	X1	X	X	E.Lomas
47	X				X	X	S1	X				X	X	S			S		X	X			X	X1	X	X	J.Brandwood
48	X				X	X	S	X				X	X	S			S		X	X			X	X	X	X	T.E.West
49	X2	S2			X	X	S1	X				X	X	S3			X		X	X			X	X1	X	X	G.Singh
50	X	S			X	X	S1	X				X	X		X1		X		X	X			X	X	X	S	R.D.Furnandiz
51	X	S1			X		X1	X				X2	X		X		S	X	X			X	X	X	S2		J.Lloyd
52																											
EL Appearances	*6	4	2	0	5	35	38	2	29	6	17	4	46	28	8	0	17	9	46	40	5	41	35	43	9	11	
EL Sub Appearances	3	11	0	1	2	1	0	13	0	0	3	0	0	0	0	6	0	10	1	0	0	5	1	6	0	11	
CC Appearances	1	0+1	1	0+1	3	4	4	0	4	0	4	1+1	4	4	0	1	1	4	2+1	1	3	1+3	3	2+2	0		
FAC Appearances	+1	0	0	0	0	1	2	0	2	0	0	0+1	2	2	0	0	0+2	1	2	2	0+1	2	2	2	1+1	0	

SUNDERLAND

CLUB RECORDS

BIGGEST VICTORIES
League: 9-1 v Newcastle, Division 1, 5.12.1908
8-0 v Derby County, Division 1, 1.9.1894
F.A. Cup: 11-1 v Fairfield, Round 1, 2.2.1895
League Cup: 7-1 v Oldham Athletic, Round 2, 24.9.1962

BIGGEST DEFEATS
League: 0-8 v Sheffield Wednesday, Division 1, 26.12.1911
0-8 v West Ham Utd, Division 1, 19.10.1968
0-8 v Watford, Division 1, 25.9.1982
F.A. Cup: 2-7 v Aston Villa, Round 4, 27.1.1934
0-5 v Arsenal, Round 2, 1905-06
0-5 v Liverpool, Round 1 replay, 1921-22
0-5 v Tottenham Hotspur, Round 6 replay, 1960-61
League Cup: 0-6 v Derby County, Round 3, 31.10.1990

MOST POINTS
3 points a win: 93, Division 3, 1987-88
2 points a win: 61, Division 2, 1963-64

MOST GOALS
109, Division 1, 1935-36
Carter 31, Gurney 31, Gallagher 19, Davis 10, Conner 6, Duns 5, Goddard 2,Hornby 2, Thompson 1, McNab 1, og 1.

MOST LEAGUE GOALS CONCEDED
97, Division 1, 1957-58

MOST FIRST CLASS MATCHES IN A SEASON
59 (46 League, 1 FA Cup, 8 League Cup, 1 Zenith, 3 Play-Offs) 1989-90

MOST LEAGUE WINS
27, Division 3, 1987-88

MOST LEAGUE DRAWS
18, Division 1, 1954-55, Division 2/1 1994-95

MOST LEAGUE DEFEATS
22, Division 1, 1956-57; Division 1, 1969-70; Division 1, 1984-85; Division2/1 1992-93

INDIVIDUAL CLUB RECORDS

MOST GOALS IN A MATCH
5. C Buchan v Liverpool, 7.12.1919 (7-0)
5. R Gurney v Bolton W., 7.12.1935 (7-2)
5. D Sharkey v Norwich, 20.2.1962 (7-1)

MOST GOALS IN A SEASON
Dave Halliday 43, 1928-29
4 goals once=4, 3 goals twice=6, 2 goals ten times=20, 1 goal 13 times=13

OLDEST PLAYER
Bryan `Pop' Robson, 38 years 128 days v Leicester, 12.5.1984

YOUNGEST PLAYER
Derek Forster, 15 years 184 days v Leicester, 22.8.1964

MOST CAPPED PLAYER
Martin Harvey (Northern Ireland) 34

BEST PERFORMANCES

League: 1963-64: Matches played 42, Won 25, Drawn 11, Lost 6, Goals for 87,Goals against 37, Points 61. 2nd in Division 2.

Highest: First in Division 1.

F.A. Cup: 1936-37: 3rd rnd. Southampton (A) 3-2; 4th rnd. Luton Town (A) 2-2,(H) 3-1; 5th rnd. Swansea (H) 3-0; 6th rnd. Wolverhampton W. 1-1 (A), 2-2 (H),4-0 (N); Semi-final Millwall 2-1; Final Preston North End 3-1.
1972-73: 3rd rnd. Notts County 1-1 (A), 2-0 (H); 4th rnd. Reading 1-1 (H), 3-1(A); 5th rnd. Manchester City 2-2 (A), 3-1 (H); 6th rnd. Luton 2-0 (H); Semi-final Arsenal 2-1; Final Leeds 1-0.

League Cup: 1984-85: 2nd rnd. Crystal Palace 2-1 (H), 0-0 (A); 3rd rnd.Nottingham Forest 1-1 (A), 1-0 (H); 4th rnd. Tottenham Hotspur 0-0 (H), 2-1(A); 5th rnd. Watford 1-0; Semi-final Chelsea 2-0 (H), 3-2 (A); Final Norwich 0-1.

Europe (ECWC): 1973-74: 1st rnd. VASAS Budapest 2-0 (A), 1-0 (H); 2nd rnd. Sporting Lisbon 2-1 (H), 0-2 (A).

DIVISIONAL RECORD

	Played	Won	Drawn	Lost	For	Against	Points
Division 1	2,732	1,107	621	1,004	4,531	4,217	2,889
Division 2/1	1,036	421	291	324	1,506	1,270	1,275
Division 3	46	27	12	7	92	48	93
Total	3,814	1,555	924	1,335	6,129	5,535	4,257

ADDITIONAL INFORMATION
Previous Names
Sunderland & District Teachers' Association F.C. 1879-80.

Previous League
Northumberland & District Football Association 1880-90.

Club colours: Red and white striped shirts, black shorts, red socks with white band.
Change colours: White shirts with red trim, white shorts with red trim, red and white socks with horizontal stripes.

Reserves League: Pontins Central League Division 2

RECORDS AND STATISTICS

COMPETITIONS

Div.1/P	Div.2/1	Div.3	ECWC
1890-58	1958-64	1987-88	1973-74
1964-70	1970-76		
1976-77	1977-80		
1980-85	1985-87		
1990-91	1988-90		
1996-	1991-96		

HONOURS

Div.1	Div.2/1	Div.3	FA Cup
1891-92	1975-76	1987-88	1937
1892-93	1995/96		1973
1894-95			
1901-02			
1912-13			
1935-36			

MOST APPEARANCES

Jim Montgomery 611+12 (1961-77)

Year	League	FA Cup	Lge Cup	Others
1961-62	12		1	
1962-63	42	4	7	
1963-64	42	6	1	
1964-65	9			
1965-66	29	1	2	
1966-67	42	5	2	
1967-68	39	2	3	
1968-69	42	1	1	
1969-70	41	1	1	4
1970-71	42	1	1	
1971-72	31	3	1	4
1972-73	41	9	1	
1973-74	41	2	4	
1974-75	40	1	1	
1975-76	38	5	1	
1976-77	6		4	
	537	41	33	8

Includes 4 appearances in the ECWC 1973-74.

MOST GOALS IN A CAREER

R Gurney - 228 (1925-39)

Year	League	FA Cup
1925-26	4	
1926-27	7	
1927-28	4	
1929-30	15	2
1930-31	31	2
1931-32	16	
1932-33	15	7
1933-34	21	1
1934-35	30	4
1935-36	31	
1936-37	20	6
1937-38	9	1
1938-39	2	
Total	**205**	**23**

Current leading goalscorer: Gordon Armstrong - 61 (1985-96)

RECORD TRANSFER FEE RECEIVED

Amount	Club	Player	Date
£1,800,000	Crystal Palace	Marco Gabbiadini	9/91
£275,000	Sheffield Wed.	Mark Proctor	9/87
£275,000	Manchester Utd	Chris Turner	7/85
£275,000	Everton	Paul Bracewell	4/84

RECORD TRANSFER FEE PAID

Amount	Club	Player	Date
£950,000	Wolves	David Kelly	8/95
£900,000	West Brom	Don Goodman	12/91
£450,000	Oxford United	Andy Melville	9/91
£400,000	Hull City	Tony Norman	12/88

MANAGERS

Name	Seasons	Best	Worst
Tom Watson	1890-96	1(1)	7(1)
Robert Campbell	1896-99	2(1)	15(1)
Alex Mackie	1899-05	1(1)	6(1)
Robert Kyle	1905-28	1(1)	16(1)
Johnny Cochrane	1928-39	1(1)	16(1)
William Murray	1939-57	3(1)	20(1)
Alan Brown	1957-64	21(1)	16(2)
George Hardwick	1964-65	15(1)	15(1)
Ian McColl	1965-68	15(1)	19(1)
Alan Brown	1968-72	17(1)	16(2)
Bob Stokoe	1972-76	1(2)	6(2)
Jimmy Adamson	1976-78	20(1)	6(2)
Billy Elliott	1978-79	4(2)	4(2)
Ken Knighton	1979-81	17(1)	2(2)
Alan Durban	1981-84	13(1)	19(1)
Len Ashurst	1984-85	21(1)	21(1)
Lawrie McMenemy	1985-87	18(2)	20(2)
Denis Smith	1987-91	19(1)	1(3)
Malcolm Crosby	1991-93	18(2)	18(2)
Terry Butcher	1993	21(2/1)	21(2/1)
Mick Buxton	1993-95	12(1)	12(1)
Peter Reid	1995-	1(1)	20(1)

LONGEST LEAGUE RUNS

of undefeated matches:	16 (11.11.1922 - 24.2.1923)	of league matches w/out a win:	14 (16.4.1985 - 14.9.1985)
of undefeated home matches:	44 (18.10.1890 - 6.12.1893)	of undefeated away matches:	14 25.11.1978 - 18.8.1979)
without home win:	12 (5.9.1981 - 27.2.1982)	without an away win:	28 (15.11.1952 - 2.1.1954)
of league wins:	13 (14.11.1891 - 22.4.1892)	of home wins:	19 (10.1.1891 - 16.4.1892)
of league defeats:	9 (23.11.1976 - 15.1.1977)	of away wins:	5 (1891-92, 1892, 1912-13, 1963)

SUNDERLAND

PLAYERS NAME Honours	Ht	Wt	Birthdate	Birthplace Transfers	Contract Date	Clubs	League	L/Cup	FA Cup	Other	Lge	L/C	FAC	Oth
G O A L K E E P E R S														
Coton Tony	6.2	13.07	19/05/61	Tamworth		Mile Oak Rovers								
E: B.1				Free	13/10/78	Birmingham City	94	10	10					
				£300000	27/09/84	Watford	233	18	32	8				
				£1000000	20/07/90	Manchester City	162+1	16	12	3				
				£500000	23/01/96	Manchester United								
				£350000	10/07/96	Sunderland								
Preece David	6.2	11.11	26/08/76	Sunderland	30/06/94	Sunderland								
D E F E N D E R S														
Ball Kevin	5.9	11.6	12/11/64	Hastings	06/10/82	Portsmouth	96+9	8+1	8	6	4			
				£350000	16/07/90	Sunderland	220+3	15	15	4	13	2		1
Gray Michael	5.7	10.8	03/08/74	Sunderland	01/07/92	Sunderland	95+16	6+3	3+1		7			
Hall Gareth D	5.8	10.07	20/03/69	Croydon	25/04/86	Chelsea	120+16	12+1	6	10+4	4			1
W: 9, u21.1. Div2'89. ZDC'90				£300000	19/01/96	Sunderland	8+6							
Holloway Darren						Sunderland (T)								
Kubicki Darisz	5.10	11.7	06/06/63	Warsaw		Legia Warsaw								
Polish Int.				£200000	28/08/91	Aston Villa	24+1	3	4+1	1				
				£100000	04/03/94	Sunderland	107	6	5					
Melville Andrew	6.1	12.6	29/11/68	Swansea	25/07/86	Swansea City	165+10	10	14+1	13	22		5	2
W: 20, B.1, u21.2. WFAC'89				£275000	23/07/90	Oxford United	135	12	6	6	13	1		1
					09/08/93	Sunderland	120	9+1	7	2	9			
Ord Richard	6.2	12.8	03/03/70	Murton	14/07/87	Sunderland	177+19	14+5	9+1	5+1	5		1	
E: u21.3				Loan	22/02/90	York City	3							
Scott Martin	5.9	11.0	07/01/68	Sheffield	10/01/86	Rotherham United	93+1	11	7+2	7	3	2		2
Div4'89				£200000	05/12/90	Bristol City	171	10	10	8	14	1		1
				£750000	23/12/94	Sunderland	67	3	5		6			
M I D F I E L D														
Agnew Steve	5.9	10.6	09/11/65	Shipley	10/11/83	Barnsley	185+9	13	20	6+1	29	3	4	
				£700000	25/06/91	Blackburn Rovers	2	2						
				Loan	21/11/92	Portsmouth	3+2							
				£250000	09/02/93	Leicester City	52+4	4+1	2	2	4			
				£250000	12/01/95	Sunderland	42+3	1	1+1		7		1	
Aiston Sam						Newcastle United								
				Free	14/07/95	Sunderland	4+11	0+1						
Armstrong Gordon	6.0	11.10	15/07/67	Newcastle	10/07/85	Sunderland	331+18	25+4	19	18+1	50	3	4	4
				Loan	24/08/95	Bristol City	6							
				Loan	05/01/96	Northampton Town	4		1		1			
Bracewell Paul	5.8	10.9	19/07/62	Heswell	06/02/80	Stoke City	123+6	6	6		5	1		
E: 3, u21.13. CS'84'85.				£250000	01/07/83	Sunderland	38	4	2		4			
Div1'85'93. ECWC'85. UEFA				£425000	25/05/84	Everton	95	11	19+2	17+2	7	2		1
				£250000	23/08/89	Sunderland	112+1	9	10	2	6			
				£250000	16/06/92	Newcastle United	67+9	3+1	6+2	2	3	1		
				£100000	01/08/95	Sunderland	38	4	2					
Pacheco Antonio						Sporting Lisbon								
				Free	07/96	Sunderland								
Rae Alex	5.8	11.8	30/09/69	Glasgow		Falkirk	71+12	5	2+1		20	1		
S: u21.9				£100000	20/08/90	Millwall	168+13	11+2	11	10	50		4	1
				£750000	14/05/96	Sunderland								
Stewart Paul	5.11	12.4	07/10/64	Manchester	13/10/81	Blackpool	188+13	11	7	6	56	3	2	1
E: 3, B5, u21.1, Y2; FAC'91;				£200000	19/03/87	Manchester City	51	6	4	2	6	2	1	1
CS'91; Div1'94				£1700000	21/06/88	Tottenham Hotspur	126+5	23	9	9	28	7	2	
				£2300000	29/07/92	Liverpool	28+4	6	1	3	1			2
				Loan	24/01/94	Crystal Palace	18				3			
				Loan	02/09/94	Wolves	5+3			2	2			
				Loan	08/12/95	Burnley	6							
				Free	05/03/96	Sunderland	11+1				1			
F O R W A R D S														
Angell Brett	6.2	12.8	20/06/68	Marlborough	01/08/86	Portsmouth								
					01/08/87	Cheltenham Town		1					1	
				£40000	19/02/88	Derby County								
				£33000	20/10/88	Stockport County	60+10	3	3	8	28		1	4
				£100000	02/08/90	Southend United	109+6	7+1	3	9+1	47	4	2	10
				£500000	17/01/94	Everton	16+4	0+1			1			
				£600000	23/03/95	Sunderland	10	1				1		

Name			DOB	From	Fee	Date	Club								
Angell continued....					Loan	30/01/96	Sheffield United	6				2			
					Loan	28/03/96	W.B.A.	0+3							
Bridges Michael						09/11/95	Sunderland	2+13				4			
Brodie Stephen	5.10	10.6	14/01/73	Sunderland		01/07/91	Sunderland	1+11							
					Loan	01/09/95	Doncaster Rovers	5				1			
Conlon Paul							Hartlepool United	11+4				4			
					Free	10/07/96	Sunderland								
Howey Lee	6.2	13.9	01/04/69	Sunderland			Ipswich Town								
							Seaham Red Star								
							Bishop Auckland								
					Free	25/03/95	Sunderland	30+27	1+4	2+4	0+1	8	2	1	
Kelly David	5.11	11.3	25/11/65	Birmingham			Alvechurch								
Ei: 17, B.2, u23.1, u21.3. Div1'93						21/12/83	Walsall	115+32	11+1	12+2	14+3	63	4	3	10
					£600000	01/08/88	West Ham United	29+12	11+3	6	2+1	7	5		2
					£300000	22/03/90	Leicester City	83+3	6	1	2	22	2		1
					£250000	04/12/91	Newcastle United	70	4	5	4	35	2	1	1
					£750000	23/06/93	Wolves	76+7	5	11	4	26	2	6	2
					£900000	19/09/95	Sunderland	9+1	1	1		2			
Mullin John	6.0	11.5	11/08/75	Bury		11/08/75	Burnley	7+11		2		2			
					£40000	12/08/95	Sunderland	5+5	1	0+1		1			
Russell Craig	5.10	12.0	04/02/74	South Shields		01/07/92	Sunderland	93+25	4+3	5+2	2	27	1	2	
Smith Martin	5.11	12.0	13/11/74	Sunderland		06/09/92	Sunderland	69+15	3+3	7+1		20		1	
E: S															
ADDITIONAL CONTRACT PLAYERS															
Grant Stephen							Athlone								
					Free	10/08/95	Sunderland								
Heckingbottom Paul							Manchester Utd (A)								
					Free	14/07/95	Sunderland								
Mawson David							Sunderland (T)								
Pickering Steven							Sunderland (T)								

THE MANAGER
PETER REID

Date of Birth. . . . . 20th June 1956.
Place of Birth . . . . Liverpool.
Date of Appointment . . . . March 1995.

PREVIOUS CLUBS
As Manager. . . . . Manchester City.
As Coach. . . . . None.
As a Player . . . . Bolton Wanderers, Everton, Q.P.R., Manchester City,
. . . . Southampton, Notts County, Bury.

HONOURS
As a Manager
Sunderland: Division 1 Champions 1995-96. Manager fo the Year 1995-96.

As a Player
Division 1 championship 1985, 1987. Division 2 championship 1978. FA Cup 1984. ECWC 1985.
P.F.A. Player of the Year 1985. CS 1984, 1985, 1987.
International: 13 full caps and 6 under-21 caps for England.

ROKER PARK

Sunderland, Tyne & Wear SR6 9SW
Tel: 0191 514 0332

Capacity...22,657
Covered Standing..9,000
Seating..7,765

First game..v Liverpool, 10.9.1898.
First floodlit game ....v Dundee, 11.12.52.

ATTENDANCES
Highest ....75,118 v Derby County, FA Cup 6th Round replay, 8.3.1933.
Lowest...68,004 v Newcastle United, Div 1, 29.4.1935.

OTHER GROUNDS ....Blue House Field, Groves Field, Horatio Street, ABBS Field.

MATCHDAY TICKET PRICES

Centre £15

Wings £13

Junior Family Enclosure £9
Clock Stand Wings

Standing is by payment at the turnstiles on the day
of the match.

Members £10
Non-Members £11
Juniors £6

Ticket Office Telephone no. 0191 514 0332

CLUBCALL
0898 12 11 40

Calls cost 39p per minute cheap rate and 49p per
minute at all other times.
Call costings correct at time of going to press.

HOW TO GET TO THE GROUND

From the North
Take A184 Newcastle - Sunderland road. After Boldon pass Greyhound Stadium
on left. Straight on at roundabout. After 150 yards bear left (signs for Fulwell,
Seaburn and Roker). At 'T' junction turn left to traffic lights at Blue Bell Public
House, then turn right. After about 0.5 miles ground is on the left up side street
(opposite Redby School) for Sunderland FC.

From the South
Use A1(M) North. Take A690 to Sunderland. Head for Town Centre. Follow signs
for Whitburn (A183) and South Shields (A1018). Pass over Wearmouth Bridge,
keep in right hand lane and take signs for Roker, Seafront and Whitburn. After
approximately 1 mile the ground is on the left up a side street.

From the West
Take A1231 towards Sunderland (north). Follow signs for Roker, Seafront and
Whitburn. After one mile ground is on left up side street.

Car Parking
Parking for 1,500 cars 200 yards from ground.

Nearest Railway Station
Seaburn.

MATCHDAY PROGRAMME

Programme Editor . . . . Clair Cogdon.

Number of pages . . . . 48.

Price . . . . £1.50.

Subscriptions . . . . Home, 1st class £16.50, 2nd class £15.50.
. . . . Home & away, 1st class £24.50. Overseas £27.00.

Local Newspapers . . Journal/Chronicle/Sunday Sun, Sunderland Echo,
. . . Northern Echo, Sunderland & Washington Times, Shields Gazette.

Local Radio Stations. . . . . Metro Radio, Radio Tees,
. . . . Radio Newcastle, Sun City 103.4.

TOTTENHAM HOTSPUR
(Spurs)
F.A. CARLING PREMIERSHIP
SPONSORED BY: HEWLETT PACKARD

Back Row (L-R): Andy Turner, Jason Cundy, Ronny Rosenthal, Darren Anderton, Erik Thorstvedt, Ian Walker, Kevin Scott, Colin Calderwood, Jason Dozzell, Stuart Nethercott. **Middle Row:** Tony Lenaghan (Physio), Danny Hill, Gerry McMahon, Clive Wilson, Ilie Dumitrescu, Chris Day, David Howells, Paul Mahorn, Kevin Watson, Steve Carr, Roy Reyland (Kit Manager). **Front Row:** Pat Jennings (Goalkeeping Coach), David Kerslake, Chris Armstrong, Justin Edinburgh, Gary Mabbutt, Gerry Francis (Manager), Roger Cross (Asst. Manager), Teddy Sheringham, Dean Austin, Sol Campbell, Darren Caskey, Chris Hughton (Reserve Team Manager).

TOTTENHAM HOTSPUR
FORMED IN 1882
TURNED PROFESSIONAL IN 1895
LTD COMPANY IN 1898

CLUB PRESIDENT: W E Nicholson OBE
CLUB VICE-PRESIDENT: N Soloman
DIRECTORS (EXECUTIVE)
CHAIRMAN: Alan M Sugar
CHIEF EXECUTIVE: C M Littner
FINANCE DIRECTOR: J Sedgwick
(NON-EXECUTIVE)
A G Berry (deputy-Chairman), D A Alexiou,
I Yawetz, C T Sandy,
COMPANY SECRETARY
J Ireland (0181365 5023)
CLUB SECRETARY
Peter Barnes (0181 365 5000)
COMMERCIAL MANAGER
Mike Rollo (0181 365 5010)

MANAGER: Gerry Francis
ASSISTANT MANAGER: Roger Cross
RESERVE TEAM MANAGER: Chris Hughton
YOUTH TEAM MANAGER: Des Bulpin
PHYSIOTHERAPIST: Tony Lenaghan
STATISTICIAN FOR THE DIRECTORY
Andy Shute

Tottenham began the season at Manchester City with record signing Chris Armstrong making his debut in a 1-1 draw. This was followed by successive home defeats against Aston Villa and Liverpool and the first league table of the season showed Tottenham one place off the bottom. Then five games unbeaten, including four straight league wins, lifted Spurs into the top half of the league. Although Armstrong had scored against Chester City in the cup the pressure was on him in the league and manager Gerry Francis' faith in him was rewarded with four goals in five games in late October. Up until then Teddy Sheringham had been scoring the goals, seven in four games, and had received an England call-up. Tottenham then embarked on an eleven-game unbeaten run lifting them into third place in the league, and during this run broke a club record by not conceding a goal for 602 minutes. The run was broken at Blackburn (1-2), Tottenham's first away defeat of the season after eleven away games. New Years' Day saw Manchester United visit White Hart Lane and a live TV audience saw Spurs produce an outstanding performance, winning 4-1. Tottenham's league form suffered as the FA Cup interrupted the early months of 1996 and just eight league games in three months brought four wins, three defeats and a draw. By now the partnership between Armstrong and Sheringham had blossomed - 46 goals in 47 league and cup games - but just one win in Tottenham's last six games denied them a European place next season.

In the Coca-Cola Cup a comfortable 7-1 aggregate score against Chester City was followed by an away tie at Coventry City. Spurs led 2-0 at half-time, but a Coventry revival ended Spurs' cup hopes, losing 3-2.

Tottenham played six games in the FA Cup but still only reached the fifth round. After drawing 1-1 at Hereford, a Sheringham hat-trick helped Tottenham to a 5-1 replay win, and a home tie against Wolverhampton Wanderers. Another 1-1 draw brought the TV cameras to Molineux for the replay, where Spurs won 2-0, both goals occurring in the opening 10 minutes. Spurs then travelled to Nottingham Forest, and after an abandoned game due to snow, drew 2-2 to force another replay. Forest, who had already won at Tottenham in the league, went through to the quarter finals, winning on penalties after a 1-1 draw at White Hart Lane.

Injuries to key players caused a major disruption to Tottenham's season; Darren Anderton was a long-term casualty, while Howells, Austin, Calderwood, Wilson, Dozzell and Edinburgh all missed part of the season at crucial times. Ruel Fox (from Newcastle) and Andy Sinton (from Sheffield Wednesday) were bought to strengthen the squad, while Sheringham and 'keeper Ian Walker - both ever-present - were rewarded with places in the England squad for the 1996 European Championships.

ANDY SHUTE

TOTTENHAM HOTSPUR

League: 8th   FA Cup: 5th Rnd   Coca-Cola Cup: 3rd Rnd

M	DATE	COMP	VEN	OPPONENTS	RESULT	HT	LP	GOAL SCORERS/GOAL TIMES	ATT.
1	A 19	PL	A	Manchester City	D 1-1	1-0	9	Sheringham 33	(30827)
2	23	PL	H	Aston Villa	L 0-1	0-0	14		26726
3	26	PL	H	Liverpool	L 1-3	0-2	18	Barnes 87(og)	31254
4	30	PL	A	West Ham United	D 1-1	1-1	18	Rosenthal 54	(23516)
5	S 9	PL	H	Leeds United	W 2-1	1-0	13	Howells 27, Sheringham 66	30034
6	16	PL	A	Sheffield Wednesday	W 3-1	1-1	11	Sheringham 32, 65(pen), Walker 60(og)	(26565)
7	20	CC 2/1	H	Chester City	W 4-0	3-0		Armstrong 20, 30, Sheringham 43, Rosenthal 90	17645
8	25	PL	A	Queens Park Rangers	W 3-2	0-1	9	Sheringham 48(pen), 75, Dozzell 73	(15659)
9	30	PL	H	Wimbledon	W 3-1	2-1	9	Sheringham 7, 32, Elkins 63(og)	25321
10	O 4	CC 2/2	A	Chester City	W 3-1	2-1		Sheringham 36, 68, Howells 45	(5372)
11	14	PL	H	Nottingham Forest	L 0-1	0-0	10		32876
12	22	PL	A	Everton	D 1-1	1-1	9	Armstrong 37	(33629)
13	25	CC 3	A	Coventry City	L 2-3	2-0		Armstrong 2, Busst 20(og)	(18267)
14	29	PL	H	Newcastle United	D 1-1	1-0	9	Armstrong 21	32279
15	N 4	PL	A	Coventry City	W 3-2	2-1	9	Fox 20, Sheringham 25, Howells 46	(17545)
16	18	PL	H	Arsenal	W 2-1	1-1	9	Sheringham 29, Armstrong 54	32894
17	21	PL	A	Middlesbrough	W 1-0	0-0	5	Armstrong 71	(29487)
18	25	PL	A	Chelsea	D 0-0	0-0	5		(31059)
19	D 2	PL	H	Everton	D 0-0	0-0	5		32894
20	9	PL	H	Queens Park Rangers	W 1-0	1-0	4	Sheringham 3	28851
21	16	PL	A	Wimbledon	W 1-0	0-0	3	Fox 85	(16193)
22	23	PL	H	Bolton Wanderers	D 2-2	0-0	4	Sheringham 53, Armstrong 71	30702
23	26	PL	A	Southampton	D 0-0	0-0	3		(15238)
24	30	PL	A	Blackburn Rovers	L 1-2	0-2	4	Sheringham 53	(30004)
25	J 1	PL	H	Manchester United	W 4-1	2-1	4	Sheringham 35, Campbell 45, Armstrong 48, 66	32852
26	6	FAC 3	A	Hereford United	D 1-1	1-0		Rosenthal 31	(8806)
27	13	PL	H	Manchester City	W 1-0	0-0	3	Armstrong 65	31438
28	17	FAC 3R	H	Hereford United	W 5-1	2-0		Sheringham 23, 54, 80 (3), Armstrong 29, 58,	31534
29	21	PL	A	Aston Villa	L 1-2	1-1	4	Fox 26	(35666)
30	27	FAC 4	H	Wolverhampton Wand	D 1-1	1-1		Wilson 12	32812
31	F 3	PL	A	Liverpool	D 0-0	0-0	5		(40628)
32	7	FAC 4R	A	Wolverhampton Wand	W 2-0	2-0		Rosenthal 7, Sheringham 9	(27846)
33	12	PL	H	West Ham United	L 0-1	0-1			29781
34	24	PL	H	Sheffield Wednesday	W 1-0	1-0	5	Armstrong 31	32047
35	28	FAC 5	A	Nottingham Forest	D 2-2	2-1		Armstrong 9, 28	(18600)
36	M 2	PL	H	Southampton	W 1-0	0-0	5	Dozzell 63	26320
37	9	FAC 5R	H	Nottingham Forest	D 1-1	1-1		Sheringham 32 (Lost 1-3 on penalties)	31055
38	16	PL	H	Blackburn Rovers	L 2-3	0-2	7	Sheringham 61, Armstrong 80	31803
39	20	PL	A	Bolton Wanderers	W 3-2	1-0	5	Howells 17, Fox 54, Armstrong 60	(17829)
40	24	PL	A	Manchester United	L 0-1	0-0	6		(50157)
41	30	PL	H	Coventry City	W 3-1	0-1	5	Sheringham 50, Fox 51, 64	26808
42	A 6	PL	A	Nottingham Forest	L 1-2	0-1	7	Armstrong 80	(27053)
43	8	PL	H	Middlesbrough	D 1-1	0-0	6	Armstrong 84	32036
44	15	PL	A	Arsenal	D 0-0	0-0	6		(38273)
45	27	PL	H	Chelsea	D 1-1	0-1	8	Armstrong 73	32918
46	M 2	PL	A	Leeds United	W 3-1	2-1	5	Armstrong 18, Anderton 24, 66	(30061)
47	5	PL	A	Newcastle United	D 1-1	0-0	8	Dozzell 57	(36589)

Best Home League Attendance: 32918 v Chelsea   Smallest: 25321 v Wimbledon   Average: 30517

Goal Scorers:

PL(50): Sheringham(16),Armstrong(15),Fox(6),Howells(3),Opponent(s)(3),Dozzell(3),Anderton(2),Campbell(1),Rosenthal(1)

CC(9): Armstrong(3),Sheringham(3),Howells(1),Opponent(s)(1),Rosenthal(1)

FAC(12): Sheringham(5),Armstrong(4),Rosenthal(2),Wilson(1)

(F) Anderton	(F) Armstrong	(D) Austin	(D) Calderwood	(D) Campbell	(M) Caskey	(D) Cundy	(G) Day	(M) Dozzell	(M) Dumitrescu	(D) Edinburgh	(M) Fox	(M) Howells	(M) Kerslake	(D) Mabbutt	(M) McMahon	(D) Nethercott	(F) Rosenthal	(D) Scott	(F) Sheringham	(M) Sinton	(F) Slade	(G) Thorstvedt	(G) Walker	(D) Wilson	Referee	No.
	X	X						X	X1		X	X	X	S	X	X	S1		X				X		G.Poll	1
	X	X	X					X	X		X	X1		X		S1			X	S	S		X		S.Dunn	2
	X		X					S1	X	X		X		X	X1	S	X		X	S			X	X	K.Cooper	3
S1	X	X	X					X			X			X	X1		X		X	S			X	X	M.Reed	4
X2	X	X	X					X			X1			X	S1		X		X		S		X	X	P.Derkin	5
X	X	X	X	X1						S1				X	X		X		X		S		X	X	D.J.Gallagher	6
X	X	X2						X		S1				X	X1		X	S2	X		S		X	X	P.E.Alcock	7
X1	X	X	X	S				X		S1		X		X			X		X				X	X	D.Elleray	8
	X	X	X	X				S1		S	X1			X	X		X		X		S		X	X	G.R.Ashby	9
	X	X	X1					S1		X				X	X2		X		X	S2	S	X	X		K.J.Breen	10
		X	X	X1				S1		X		X		X			X		X		S	X	X		R.Hart	11
	X	X	X	X1				S1			X	X		X	X2		S2	X			X	X		R.Dilkes	12
	X	X	X1	X				S1			X	X		X			X		X		S	X	X		S.Dunn	13
	X	X	S1	X1				X			X	X		X	S2		X2	X		S	X	X		M.Bodenham	14
	X	X	S1	X1				X			X	X		X	S		X	X		S	X	X		J.Winter	15
	X	X	X	X		S		X		S	X	X		X	S1		X1	X			X			A.B.Wilkie	16
	X	X	X	X		S		X		S	X	X		X	S		X	X			X			M.Reed	17
	X	X	X	X		S		X		S	X	X		X	S1		X1	X			X			S.Lodge	18
	X	X	X	X		S		X		S	X	X		X	S1		X1	X			X			S.W.Dunn	19
	X		X	X1		S				S1	X	X		X	S		X	X			X	X		K.Cooper	20
	X		X	X2				X1		S1	X	X		X			X	X		S2		X	X		D.Elleray	21
	X		X	X		S				X	X1	X		X		S1	X	X		S		X	X		P.Danson	22
	X	X	X	X	S			S		X				X	X1	S	X	X		S1		X	X		P.Durkin	23
	X	X	X	X	S			X	X			X		X		X	X	X		S		X			P.Jones	24
	X	X	X	X		S		X1	X			X			S1	X	X	X		S		X			G.Ashby	25
	X	X		X	X		S	S1	X			X	X1	X		X	X	X				X			M.A.Riley	26
	X	X		X	X		S	X				X		X		X	X	X		S		X	S		D.J.Gallagher	27
	X	X		X	X		S				X1	X		X		X	X2	X		S2		X	S1		S.Dunn	28
	X	X	X	X	X		S				X	X		X		S	S	X				X	X		G.Poll	29
	X	X	X	X1			S				X	X		X		S1	S2	X	X2			X	X		S.Lodge	31
	X	X	X	X	S			X			X			X		S	X	X				X	X		D.Allison	32
	X	X	X	X		S		X				X		X		S	X1	X	S1			X	X		J.Winter	33
	X		X	X		S	X			X1	X	X		X		S	S1	X	X			X	X		M.Reed	34
	X1		X	X		S		X			X	X		X	S1	S	X	X				X	X		G.S.Willard	35
			X	X		S		X			X	X		X		S	S1	X	X	X1		X	X		K.N.Burge	36
X1			X	X				X1	X		X	X		X		S1	X	X	S1	S		X	X		G.S.Willard	37
	X	X	X1			S1				X	X	X		X			X	X	X		S	X	X		P.A.Durkin	38
	X	X	X1	X				X		S1	X2	X		X			X		X	S2	S	X	X		S.Dunn	39
	X	X		X				X		S	X	X		X	X1	S1	X		X		S	X	X		G.Ashby	40
	X	X		X				X		S		X	X	X		X	S	X	X			X	X		R.Hart	41
	X	X		X		S		X		S2	X	X2			X	X	S1	X	X1			X	X		P.Alcock	42
	X	X		X		S		X		S	X	X1		X		X	X2		S2			X	X		P.Jones	43
S2	X		X1			S	X2	X		X	X	X		X		S1	X	X				X	X		M.Reed	44
X	X	S	X			S		X		X	X		X			S1		X	X1			X	X		A.B.Wilkin	45
X	X	S	X			S		X		X	X	X		X			S		X			X	X		M.Bodenham	46
X	X	S1	X1			S		X		X	X2	X		X			S2		X			X	X		J.Gallagher	47
6	36	28	26	31	3	0	0	24	5	15	26	29	2	32	7	9	26	0	38	8	1	0	38	28	PL Appearances	
2	0	0	3	0	0	1	0	4	0	7	0	0	0	0	0	7	4	7	2	0	1	4	0	0	PL Sub Appearances	
1	3	3	3	2	0	0	0	1+2	0	1+1	0	2	0	3	0	2	0+1	3	0	0+1	3	0	3	3	CC Appearances	
0	6	4	4	6	3	0	0	2+1	0	4	6	2	0	6	0+1	2+1	5	0	6	0	0+2	0	6	4+1	FAC Appearances	

TOTTENHAM HOTSPUR

CLUB RECORDS

BIGGEST VICTORIES
League: 9-0 v Bristol Rovers, Division 2, 22.10.1977
F.A. Cup: 13-2 v Crewe Alexandra, Round 4, 3.2.1960
League Cup: 5-0 v West Brom. Alb, Round 3, 28.10.1970
7-2 v Doncaster Rovers, Round 5, 3.12.1975
5-0 v Birmingham City, Round 3, 1986-87
5-0 v West Ham United, Round 5, 2.2.1987
5-0 v Hartlepool Utd, Round 1, 26.9.1990
Europe (UEFA): 9-0 v Keflavic, Round 1, 28.9.1971

BIGGEST DEFEATS
League: 0-7 v Liverpool, Division 1, 2.9.1979
F.A. Cup: 0-5 v Stoke City, Round 1, 1.2.1896
1-6 v Huddersfield, Round 6, 3.3.1928
League Cup: 0-4 v Middlesbrough (h), Round 2, 1974-75
Europe 0(UEFA): 1-4 v Bayern Munich, Round 2, 3.11.1982
1-4 v Manchester Utd, Cup Winners Cup Round 2, 10.12.1963

MOST POINTS
3 points a win: 77, Division 1, 1984-85
2 points a win: 70, Division 2, 1919-1920 (Div 2 record)

MOST GOALS
115, 1960-61 (Division 1)
Smith 28, Allen 22, Jones 15, White 13, Dyson 12, Blanchflower 6,
Medwin 5,Norman 4, Mackay 4, Saul 3, Baker 1, og 2

MOST FIRST CLASS MATCHES IN A SEASON
68 (42 League, 5 FA Cup, 7 League Cup, 12 UEFA Cup, 2 Anglos-
Ital. Cup WinnersCup) 1971-72

MOST LEAGUE GOALS CONCEDED
95, Division 1958-59

MOST LEAGUE WINS
32, Division 2, 1919-20
MOST LEAGUE DRAWS
17, Division 1, 1968-69
MOST LEAGUE DEFEATS
22, Division 1, 1934-35

INDIVIDUAL CLUB RECORDS

MOST GOALS IN A MATCH
5. Ted Harper v Reading, Division 2, 30.8.1930 (7-1)
5. Alf Stokes v Birmingham, Division 1, 18.9.1957 (7-1)
5. Les Allen v Crewe Alex., FAC Round 4, 3.2.1960 (13-2)
5. Bobby Smith v Aston Villa, Division 1, 29.3.1958 (6-2)
5. V Woodwood v West Ham Utd, 1904-05
Jack Rowley netted 7 in war-time games

MOST GOALS IN A SEASON
Clive Allen 49 (League 33, League Cup 12, FAC 4) 1986-87
3 goals 3 times=9; 2 goals 9 times=18; 1 goal 22 times=22
League Goals Only: Jimmy Greaves 37, Div 1, 1962-63

OLDEST PLAYER
Jimmy Cantrell, 40 years 349 days v Birmingham, 24.4.1923
YOUNGEST PLAYER
Ally Dick, 16 years 301 days v Manchester City, 20.2.1982
MOST CAPPED PLAYER
Pat Jennings (Northern Ireland) 74

BEST PERFORMANCES

League: 1919-20: Matches played 42, Won 32, Drawn 6, Lost 4,
Goals for 102,against 32, Points 70. Division 2 Champions.
Highest: 1950-51, 1960-61: Division 1 Champions.

F.A. Cup: 1900-01: 1st rnd. Preston North End 1-1, 4-2; 2nd rnd.
Bury 2-1; 3rd rnd. Reading 1-1, 3-0; Semi-final West Bromwich
Albion 4-0; Final SheffieldUnited 2-2, 3-1
1920-21: 1st rnd. Bristol Rov. 6-2; 2nd rnd. Bradford City 4-0; 3rd
rnd.Southend 4-1; Semi-final Preston N E 2-1; Final Wolverhampton
Wndrs 1-0
1960-61: 3rd rnd. Charlton Athletic 3-2; 4th rnd. Crewe Alexandra 5-
1; 5th rnd.Aston Villa 2-0; 6th rnd. Sunderland 1-1, 5-0; Semi-final
Burnley 3-0; Final Leicester 2-0
1961-62: 3rd rnd. Birmingham City 3-3, 4-2; 4th rnd. Plymouth 5-1;
5th rnd.West Brom. Alb 4-2; 6th rnd. Aston Villa 2-0; Semi-final
Manchester United 3-1;Final Burnley 3-1
1966-67: 3rd rnd. Millwall 0-0, 1-0; 4th rnd. Portsmouth 3-1; 5th rnd.
Bristol City 2-0; 6th rnd. Birmingham City 0-0, 6-0; Semi-final
Nottingham Forest 2-1;Final Chelsea 2-1
1980-81: 3rd rnd. Queens Park Rangers 0-0, 3-1; 4th rnd. Hull City
2-0; 5th rnd. Coventry City 3-1; 6th rnd. Exeter City 2-0; Semi-final
Wolverhampton W.2-2, 3-0; Final Manchester City 1-1, 3-2
1981-82: 3rd rnd. Arsenal 1-0; 4th rnd. Leeds United 1-0; 5th rnd.
Aston Villa1-0; 6th rnd. Chelsea 3-2; Semi-final Leicester City 2-0;
Final Queens Park Rangers 1-1, 1-0
1990-91: 3rd rnd. Blackpool 1-0; 4th rnd. Oxford Utd 4-2; 5th rnd.
Portsmouth2-1; 6-1 rnd. Notts County 2-1; Semi-Final Arsenal 3-1;
Final Nottingham Forest2-1

League Cup: 1970-71: 2nd rnd. Swansea City 3-0; 3rd rnd.
Sheffield United 2-1;4th rnd. West Bromwich Albion 5-0; 5th rnd.
Coventry 4-1; Semi-final BristolCity 1-1, 2-0; Final Aston Villa 2-0
1972-73: 2nd rnd. Huddersfield 2-1; 3rd rnd Middlesbrough 1-1, 0-0,
2-1; 4thrnd Millwall 2-0; 5th rnd. Liverpool 1-1, 3-1; Semi-final
Wolverhampton W. 2-1,2-2; Final Norwich 1-0

ECWC: 1962-63: 2nd rnd. Rangers 3-2, 5-2; 3rd rnd Slovan Bratisl.,
0-2, 6-0;Semi-final OFK Belgrade 2-1, 3-1; Final Athletico Madrid 5-
1
UEFA: 1971-72: 1st rnd. Keflavic 6-1, 9-0; 2nd rnd. Nantes 0-0, 1-0;
3rd rnd.Rapid Bucharest 3-0, 2-0; 4th rnd. UT Arad 2-0,
1-1; Semi-final AC Milan 2-1, 1-1; Final Wolverhampton W. 2-1, 1-1
1983-84: 1st rnd. Drogheda 6-0, 8-0; 2nd rnd. Feyenoord 4-2, 2-0;
3rd rnd.Bayern Munich 0-1, 2-0; 4th rnd. FK Austria 2-0, 2-2; Semi-
final Hadj. Split 1-2, 1-0; Final Anderlecht 1-1, 1-1, won on pens

DIVISIONAL RECORD							
	Played	Won	Drawn	Lost	For	Against	Points
Division 1/P	2,520	1,023	613	884	4,042	3,662	2,910
Division 2	668	311	172	185	1,253	851	794
Total	3,188	1,334	785	1,069	5,295	4,513	3,704

ADDITIONAL INFORMATION
Previous Name
Hotspur F.C. 1882-84

Previous League
None.

Club colours: White shirts, navy shorts, navy socks.
Change colours: All yellow.

Reserves League: Avon Insurance Football Combination.

RECORDS AND STATISTICS

COMPETITIONS

Div 1/P	Div.2	Euro C	ECWC	UEFA	Texaco
1909-15	1908-09	1961-62	1962-63	1971-72	1970-71
1920-28	1915-20		1963-64	1972-73	
1933-35	1928-33		1967-68	1973-74	
1950-77	1935-50		1981-82	1983-84	
1978-	1977-78		1982-83	1984-85	
			1991-92		

HONOURS

Div 1/P	Div.2	FAC	ECWC	Lge C	C/S'Ld
1950-51	1919-20	1900-01	1962-63	1970-71	1920
1960-61	1949-50	1920-21	1972-73		1951
		1960-61	**UEFA**		1961
		1961-62	1971-72		1962
		1966-67	1983-84		1967
		1980-81			1981
		1981-82			1992
		1990-91			shared

MOST APPEARANCES

STEVE PERRYMAN 860+4 (1969-86)

Year	League	FA Cup	Lge Cup	Europe
1969-70	21	4		
1970-71	42	5	6	
1971-72	40	5	6	12
1972-73	41	3	10	10
1973-74	40	1	1	12
1974-75	42	2	1	
1975-76	40	2	6	
1976-77	42	1	2	
1977-78	42	2	2	
1978-79	42	7	2	
1979-80	40	6	2	
1980-81	42	9	6	
1981-82	42	7	8	8
1982-83	32+1	3	2	2+1
1983-84	41	4	3	9
1984-85	42	3	5	8
1985-86	22+1	5	4	
	653+2	69	66	61+1

Including 1+1 Charity Shield, 10 Others.

MOST GOALS IN A CAREER

JIMMY GREAVES - 266 (161-70)

Year	League	FA Cup	Lge Cup	Europe
1961-62	21	9		
1962-63	37			5
1963-64	35			1
1964-65	29	4		
1965-66	15	3		
1966-67	25	6		
1967-68	23	3		3
1968-69	27	4	5	
1969-70	8	3		
Total	**220**	**32**	**5**	**9**

Current leading goalscorer: Teddy Sheringham - 89 (1992-96)

RECORD TRANSFER FEE RECEIVED

Amount	Club	Player	Date
£5,500,000	Lazio	Paul Gascoigne	7/91
£5,250,000	Middlesbrough	Nick Barmby	8/95
£4,500,000	Marseille	Chris Waddle	6/89
£2,800,000	Barcelona	Gica Popescu	5/95
£1,500,000	Rangers	Richard Gough	9/87
£1,500,000	Barcelona	Steve Archibald	7/84

RECORD TRANSFER FEE PAID

Amount	Club	Player	Date
£4,500,000	Crystal Palace	Chris Armstrong	6/95
£4,000,000	Newcastle Utd	Ruel Fox	10/95
£2,900,000	PSV Eindhoven	Gica Popescu	9/94
£2,600,000	Steaua Bucharest	Ilie Dumetrescu	8/94
£2,200,000	Chelsea	Gordon Durie	8/91
£2,000,000	Newcastle United	Paul Gascoigne	7/88

MANAGERS

Name	Seasons	Best	Worst
Frank Brettall	1895-88		
John Cameron	1898		
Fred Kirkham	1898-07		
Pete McWilliam	1907-08		
Billy Minter	1927-30	21(2)	12(2)
Percy Smith	1930-35	3(1)	8(2)
Jack Tresadern	1935-38	5(2)	10(2)
Pete McWilliam	1938-45	8(2)	8(2)
Arthur Turner	1942-46		
Joe Hulme	1945-49	5(2)	8(2)
Arthur Rowe	1949-55	1(1)	1(2)
Jim Anderson	1955-58	2(1)	18(1)
Bill Nicholson	1958-74	1(1)	11(1)
Terry Neill	1974-76	9(1)	19(1)
Keith Burkinshaw	1976-84	4(1)	3(2)
Peter Shreeves	1984-86	3(1)	10(1)
David Pleat	1986-87	3(1)	3(1)
Terry Venables	1987-91	3(1)	13(1)
Peter Shreeves	1991-92	15(1)	15(1)
Doug Livermore	1992-93	8(1/P)	8(1/P)
Ossie Ardiles	1993-94	15(P)	15(P)
Gerry Francis	1994-	7(P)	8(P)

LONGEST LEAGUE RUNS

of undefeated matches:	22 (31.8.1949 - 31.12.1949)	of league matches w/out a win:	16 (29.12.1934 - 13.4.1935)
of undefeated home matches:	33 (2.1.1932 - 23.9.1933)	of undefeated away matches:	16 (10.11.1984 - 21.8.1985)
without home win:	14 (23.10.1993 - 4.4.1994)	without an away win:	22 (25.2.1928 - 16.3.1929)
of league wins:	13 (23.4.1960 - 1.10.1960)	of home wins:	14)24.1.1987 - 3.10.1987)
of league defeats:	7 (1.1.94-27.2.94, 1.10.55-29.10.55)	of away wins:	10 (15.4.1960 - 29.10.1960)
	(18.2.75-22.3.75)		

TOTTENHAM HOTSPUR

PLAYERS NAME Honours	Ht	Wt	Birthdate	Birthplace Transfers	Contract Date	Clubs	League	L/Cup	FA Cup	Other	Lge	L/C	FAC	Oth
G O A L K E E P E R S														
Brown Simon J			01/07/95			Tottenham (T)								
Walker Ian	6.1	11.9	31/10/71	Watford	04/12/89	Tottenham Hotspur	125+1	9	14	2				
E: 2, u21.9, Y.17. FAYC'90. CS'91				Loan	31/08/90	Oxford United	2	1						
D E F E N D E R S														
Austin Dean	5.11	11.11	26/04/70	Hemel Hempstead		St.Albans								
				£12000	22/03/90	Southend United	96	4	2	7	2	1		
				£375000	04/06/92	Tottenham Hotspur	104+5	7+2	15+1					
Calderwood Colin	6.0	12.0	20/01/65	Stranraer	19/03/82	Mansfield Town	97+3	3+4	6	7	1		1	
S: 14. Div4'86				£30000	01/07/85	Swindon Town	328+2	35	17	32	20		1	
				£1250000	22/07/93	Tottenham Hotspur	87+4	9	13		2			
Campbell Sol	6.1	12.10	18/09/74	Newham	23/09/92	Tottenham Hotspur	87+9	10	10+2		2	1		
E: 2, u21.8, S, Y. UEFA Y'93														
Carr Stephen	5.9	12.02	29/08/76	Dublin	01/08/93	Tottenham Hotspur	1							
Ei: u21														
Cundy Jason	6.1	13.7	12/11/69	Wandsworth	01/08/88	Chelsea	40+1	6	6	4	2			
E: u21.3				£750000	26/03/92	Tottenham Hotspur	23+3	2						
				Loan	14/12/95	Crystal Palace	4							
Edinburgh Justin	5.9	11.6	18/12/69	Brentwood	05/08/88	Southend United	36+1	2+1	2	4+1				1
FAC'91. CS'91				£150000	30/07/90	Tottenham Hotspur	135+14	15+4	21	3	1			
Mabbutt Gary	5.10	10.6	23/08/61	Bristol	09/01/79	Bristol Rovers	122+9	10	5+1		10	1	1	
E:16, B.9, u21.7, Y.11.				£105000	11/08/82	Tottenham Hotspur	449+16	59+2	45+2	29+4	27	2	3	4
UEFA'84. FAC'91. CS'91														
Mahorn Paul	5.8	10.10	13/08/73	Whipps Cross	31/01/92	Tottenham Hotspur	1							
				Loan	23/09/93	Fulham	1+2			1				
				Loan	28/03/96	Burnley	3+5				1			
Nethercott Stuart	5.9	12.4	21/03/73	Ilford	17/08/91	Tottenham Hotspur	29+16		5+3				1	
				Loan	05/09/91	Maidstone	13+1			1				
				Loan	13/02/92	Barnet	3							
Scott Kevin	6.4	14.3	17/12/66	Easington	19/12/84	Newcastle United	227	18	15+1	12+1	8		1	2
FAYC'85. Div1'93				£850000	01/02/94	Tottenham Hotspur	16+2	0+1			1			
Wilson Clive	5.7	9.10	13/11/61	Manchester	08/12/79	Manchester City	107+2	10	2	5	9	2		
Div2'89				Loan	16/09/82	Chester City	21				2			
				£250000	19/03/87	Chelsea	68+13	3+3	4	10+2	5			
				£450000	04/07/90	Q.P.R.	170+2	16	8	2+1	12	1	1	
				Free	01/08/95	Tottenham Hotspur	28	3	4+1				1	
M I D F I E L D														
Dozzell Jason	6.2	12.0	09/12/67	Ipswich	20/12/84	Ipswich Town	312+20	29+1	22	22	52	3	12	4
E: u21.9, Y.5. Div2'92				£1900000	01/08/93	Tottenham Hotspur	58+9	7+2	4+1		12		1	
Fox Ruel Adrian	5.6	10.00	14/01/68	Ipswich	20/01/86	Norwich City	148+4	13+3	11+4	12+4	22	3		
E: B.1				£2250000	02/02/94	Newcastle United	56+2	3	5	1	12	1		1
				£4200000	06/10/95	Tottenham Hotspur	26		6		6			
Hill Danny	5.9	11.03	01/10/74	Enfield	09/09/92	Tottenham Hotspur	4+6	0+2						
E: S				Loan	24/11/95	Birmingham City	5	2						
				Loan	15/02/96	Watford	1							
Howells David	5.11	11.1	15/12/67	Guildford	28/01/85	Tottenham Hotspur	192+33	21+5	17+3	7	20	4	1	
E: u19.2, Y.8. FLgXI.1. FAC'91 CS'91														
Kerslake David	5.8	11.0	19/06/66	Stepney	01/06/83	Q.P.R.	38+20	6+2	2+2	2+2	6	4		
E: u21.1, u19.4, Y.27, S				£110000	24/11/89	Swindon Town	133+2	12	8	10	1			
				£500000	11/03/93	Leeds United	8							
				£450000	24/09/93	Tottenham Hotspur	34+3	5	1+1					
McMahon Gerry	5.11	11.6	29/12/73	Belfast		Glenavon								
NI: 4. B, u21.1				£100000	31/07/92	Tottenham Hotspur	9+7	3	0+1					
				Loan	20/09/94	Barnet	10		2	1	2		1	
Nielsen Allan						Brondby								
				£1650000	23/07/96	Tottenham Hotspur								
Sinton Andy	5.7	10.7	19/03/66	Newcastle	13/04/83	Cambridge United	90+3	6	3	2	13	1		1
E: 12, B.3, S. FLgXI.1				£25000	13/12/85	Brentford	149	8	11	14	28	3	1	2
				£350000	23/03/89	Q.P.R.	160	14	13	3	22		2	1
				£2750000	19/08/93	Sheffield Wed.	54+6	13	5		3			
				£1500000	23/01/96	Tottenham Hotspur	8+1							

ORWARDS (FORWARDS)

Name				Transfer	Date	Club								
nderton Darren	6.0	11.7	03/03/72	Southampton	05/02/90	Portsmouth	53+9	3+2	7+1	2	7	1	5	
16, Y.1, u21.12				£1750000	03/06/92	Tottenham Hotspur	110+6	10	13+1		19	2	2	
rmstrong Chris	6.0	11.0	19/06/71	Newcastle		Llay Welfare								
B.1. Div1.94				Free	03/03/89	Wrexham	40+20	2+1	0+1	5+1	13			3
				£50000	16/08/91	Millwall	11+17	3+1	0+1	0+1	5	2		
				£1000000	01/09/92	Crystal Palace	118	8	8	2	46	6	5	1
				£4500000	01/08/95	Tottenham Hotspur	36	3	6		15	3	4	
senthal Ronny	5.11	12.0	11/10/63	Haifa (Israel)		Maccabi Haifa								
ael. CS'90						FC Bruge								
						Standard Liege								
				Loan	22/03/90	Liverpool	5+3							
				£1000000	29/06/90	Liverpool	27+39	2+7	5+3	2+4	21	1		
				£250000	26/01/94	Tottenham Hotspur	51+17	3	7+2		7	1	2	
eringham Teddy	5.11	10.9	29/10/61	Walthamstow	19/01/84	Millwall	205+15	16+1	12	11+2	93	8	5	5
20, u21.1, Y.11. Div2'88.				Loan	01/02/85	Aldershot	4+1			1				
MC'92				£2000000	23/07/91	Nottingham Forest	42	10	4	6	14	5	2	2
				£2100000	28/08/92	Tottenham Hotspur	134+3	11	17		69	9	13	
rner Andy	5.9	10.4	28/03/75	Woolwich	08/04/92	Tottenham Hotspur	8+12	0+2	0+1		3	1		
u21.2				Loan	26/08/94	Wycombe Wand.	3+1							
				Loan	28/11/95	Huddersfield Town	2+3				1			
				Loan	28/03/96	Southend United	4+2							

ADDITIONAL CONTRACT PLAYERS

Name	Date	Club
en Rory	28/03/96	Tottenham (T)
ber Mark	27/03/96	Tottenham (T)
ady Gary		Tottenham (T)
apham James R		Tottenham (T)
emence Stephen N		Tottenham (T)
V.		
arcy Ross	01/07/95	Tottenham (T)
nn Neale M C	01/07/95	Tottenham (T)
in Peter	01/07/95	Tottenham (T)
her Kevin	01/07/95	Tottenham (T)
nnix Alan	01/07/95	Tottenham (T)
encer Simon	01/07/95	Tottenham (T)
wnley Leon		Tottenham (T)
bb Simon		Tottenham (T)
rmull Simon J	01/07/95	Tottenham (T)

THE MANAGER
GERRY FRANCIS

Date of Birth . . . . 6th December 1951.
Place of Birth . . . . Chiswick.
Date of Appointment . . . . November 1994.

PREVIOUS CLUBS
As Manager . . . . Bristol Rovers, Queens Park Rangers.
As Coach . . . . Wimbledon.
As a Player . . . . . QPR, C.Palace, QPR, Coventry City, Exeter City, Cardiff City,
. . . . Swansea City, Portsmouth, Bristol Rovers.

HONOURS
As a Manager
Bristol Rovers: Division 3 champions 1990.

As a Player
International: 12 full caps and six at U23 level for England.

WHITE HART LANE

748 High Road, Tottenham, London N17 0AP
Tel: 0181 365 5000

Capacity 33,083

First game...v Notts County (Friendly), 4-1, 4.9.1899.
Internationals ....England v France 1935, Germany 1935,
....Czechoslovakia 1937, v Italy 1949.

ATTENDANCES
Highest..75,038 v Sunderland, FAC 6th Rnd, 5.3.1938.
Lowest ....5,000 v Sunderland, Division 1, 19.12.1914.

OTHER GROUNDS.............Tottenham Marshes, 1882-1885. Northumberland Park 1885-1898. White Hart Lane 1898-

MATCHDAY TICKET PRICES

North Members Stand	Adults	Juv/OAP
Upper Tier - Standard/Premier . .	£17/£20	£8.50/£10
Lower Tier	£15/£18	£7.50/£9
West Stand		
Upper Tier	£28/£33	-
Lower Tier	£22/£27	-
East Stand		
Upper Tier Members	£20/£23	
£10/£11.50		
Upper Tier Non-Members	£24/£28	-
Lower Tier Members	£18/£21	£9/£10.50
Lower Tier Non-Members.	£20/£23	-
South Stand		
Upper Tier	£20/£23	-
Lower Tier	£17/£20	-

SPURSLINE
0891 33 55 55

Calls cost 39p per minute cheap rate and 49p per minute at all other times.
Call costings correct at time of going to press.

HOW TO GET TO THE GROUND

From all directions
Use A406 North Circular Road to Edmonton then at traffic signal follow signs to Tottenham A1010 into Fore Street for Tottenham Hotspur FC.

Car Parking
No street parking within a quarter-of-a-mile radius of the ground.

Nearest Railway Station
White Hart Lane (from Liverpool Street, Central London).
Northumberland Park (Liverpool Street).

Underground Stations
Manor House (Piccadilly Line) & Seven Sisters (Victoria Line)
Both stations change to bus routes 259, 279, 359 (Sundays only).
Also 149 from Seven Sisters.

MATCHDAY PROGRAMME

Programme Editor . . . . John Fennelly.

Number of pages . . . . 48.

Price . . . . £1.80.

Subscriptions . . . UK/BFPO £55.65, Overseas please contact the club.

Local Newspapers . . . . Waltham Forest Guardian,
. . . . North London News.

Local Radio Stations . . . . London News Radio, Greater London Radio,
. . . . Capital Radio.

WEST HAM UNITED
(The Hammers)
F.A. CARLING PREMIERSHIP
SPONSORED BY: DAGENHAM MOTORS

Back Row (L-R): Simon Webster, Ian Feuer, Marc Rieper, Ludek Miklosko, Jeroen Boere, Les Sealey, Alvin Martin.
Middle Row: Eddie Gillam (Kit Manager), Marco Boogers, Adrian Whitbread, Kenny Brown, Tim Breacker, Dale Gorden, John Moncur, Mark Watson, Matthew Rush, Danny Williamson, Martin Allen, John Green (Physio).
Front Row: Keith Rowland, Tony Cottee, Don Hutchison, Harry Redknapp (Manager), Steve Potts, Frank Lampard (Asst. Manager), Julian Dicks, Ian Bishop, Matt Holmes (Now with Blackburn).

WEST HAM UNITED
FORMED IN 1895
TURNED PROFESSIONAL IN 1900
LTD COMPANY IN 1900

CHAIRMAN: Terence W Brown
VICE-CHAIRMAN: Martin W Cearns
DIRECTORS
Charles Warner, P Storrie (Managing Director)
SECRETARY
Richard Skirrow (0181 548 2748)
COMMERCIAL MANAGER
Mrs Sue Page (0181 548 2777)

MANAGER: Harry Redknapp
ASSISTANT MANAGER: Frank Lampard

COACH
Farnk Burrows
YOUTH TEAM MANAGER
Tony Carr
PHYSIOTHERAPIST
John Green, BSC (Hons), MCSP, SRP

STATISTICIAN FOR THE DIRECTORY
John Northcutt & John Helliar

The opening day defeat by Leeds set the pattern for the early season's games. By mid-September, following disappointing defeats by Arsenal and Chelsea, the Hammers found themselves struggling in 19th place without a win.

To add height and aggression to the forward line, Iain Dowie was purchased and the dependable Alvin Martin was drafted into the side. Two goals from Julian Dicks against Everton gave West Ham their first league victory, and they then went on to beat Bristol Rovers both home and away in the Coca-Cola Cup. After three successive away wins the side were now in 11th place, although a 2-1 defeat at Southampton saw them go out of the Coca-Cola Cup.

Cottee and Dowie were forming a good partnership up front and young Danny Williamson was proving an inspiration in midfield. Narrow wins followed over QPR and Southampton, but the away form was causing concern, with three defeats and eleven goals conceded.

On New Years Day against Manchester City, 17 year-old goalkeeper Neil Finn became the Premiership's youngest ever player: West Ham's two regular keepers were both unavailable for the match and young Neil did well despite the 2-1 defeat.

In the FA Cup goals from Moncur and Hughes saw the Hammers safely through to the next round at the expense of Southend.

After a poor performance at Leeds, manager Harry Redknapp made some new signings and hit the headlines as an array of foreigners joined the Upton Park squad. The Rumanian forward Dumitrescu was soon joined by the Croatian centre-back Bilic and the Portuguese Dani. Five successive victories followed, including excellent wins at London rivals Spurs and Chelsea.

There was one setback, however, when West Ham slumped to a 3-0 FA Cup defeat at Grimsby.

Marc Rieper was in good form as he scored twice in games against Coventry - his partnership with the strong-tackling Bilic was excellent. A top ten place was the target, and two headed goals by Dowie against Manchester City helped the cause. Julian Dicks was in good form brought him a lot of media attention, and he was unlucky not to have been included in the England Squad. The team lacked a quality striker with pace which was evident in away defeats at Liverpool and Newcastle.

The final home game against Sheffield Wednesday saw Alvin Martin make his final league appearance for the club - the standing ovation he received was well deserved.

Julian Dicks is 'Hammer of the Year' and Iain Dowie runner up. The Youth Team won the South East Counties League Championship and finished runners up to Liverpool in the FA Youth Cup Final. A final league position of 10th was achieved, and if Harry Redknapp can sign a quality striker, then a European place is possible.

JOHN NORTHCUTT

WEST HAM UNITED

League: 10th   FA Cup: 4th Rnd   Coca-Cola Cup: 3rd Rnd

M	DATE	COMP	VEN	OPPONENTS	RESULT	HT	LP	GOAL SCORERS/GOAL TIMES	ATT.
1	A 19	PL	H	Leeds United	L	1-2	1-0	19	Williamson 5	22901
2	23	PL	A	Manchester United	L	1-2	0-0	19	Bruce 56(og)	(31966)
3	26	PL	A	Nottingham Forest	D	1-1	1-1	2	Allen 14	(26641)
4	30	PL	H	Tottenham Hotspur	D	1-1	1-1	17	Hutchison 24	23516
5	S 11	PL	H	Chelsea	L	1-3	0-2	19	Hutchison 73	19228
6	16	PL	A	Arsenal	L	0-1	0-0			(38065)
7	20	CC 2/1	A	Bristol Rovers	W	1-0	1-0		Moncur 34	(7103)
8	23	PL	H	Everton	W	2-1	2-1	16	Dicks 7(pen), 43(pen)	21085
9	O 2	PL	A	Southampton	D	0-0	0-0	16		(13568)
10	4	CC 2/2	H	Bristol Rovers	W	3-0	0-0		Dicks 47(pen), Bishop 49, Cottee 75	15375
11	16	PL	A	Wimbledon	W	1-0	1-0	13	Cottee 18	(9411)
12	21	PL	H	Blackburn Rovers	D	1-1	1-0	13	Dowie 25	21776
13	25	CC 3	A	Southampton	L	1-2	1-1		Cottee 33	(11059)
14	28	PL	A	Sheffield Wednesday	W	1-0	1-0	12	Dowie 40	(23917)
15	N 4	PL	H	Aston Villa	L	1-4	0-1	12	Dicks 85(pen)	23637
16	18	PL	A	Bolton Wanderers	W	3-0	0-0	11	Bishop 46, Cottee 68, Williamson 89	(19047)
17	22	PL	H	Liverpool	D	0-0	0-0	13		24324
18	25	PL	H	Queens Park Rangers	W	1-0	0-0	10	Cottee 84	21504
19	D 2	PL	A	Blackburn Rovers	L	2-4	0-3	13	Dicks 75(pen), Slater 86	(26638)
20	11	PL	A	Everton	L	0-3	0-2	13		(31778)
21	16	PL	H	Southampton	W	2-1	0-1	13	Cottee 80, Dowie 82	18501
22	23	PL	A	Middlesbrough	L	2-4	0-3	13	Cottee 80, Dicks 86	(28640)
23	J 1	PL	A	Manchester City	L	1-2	0-1	14	Dowie 74	(26024)
24	6	FAC 3	H	Southend United	W	2-0	0-0		Moncur 58, Hughes 87	23284
25	13	PL	A	Leeds United	L	0-2	0-1	14		(30658)
26	22	PL	H	Manchester United	L	0-1	0-1	16		24197
27	31	PL	H	Coventry City	W	3-2	0-0	14	Rieper 46, Cottee 59, Dowie 85	18884
28	F 3	PL	H	Nottingham Forest	W	1-0	1-0	10	Slater 19	21257
29	7	FAC 4	H	Grimsby Town	D	1-1	0-1		Dowie 35	22030
30	12	PL	A	Tottenham	W	1-0	1-0		Dani 4	(29781)
31	14	FAC 4R	A	Grimsby Town	L	0-3	0-1			(8382)
32	17	PL	A	Chelsea	W	2-1	0-1	14	Dicks 62, Williamson 72	(25252)
33	21	PL	H	Newcastle United	W	2-0	1-0	13	Williamson 7, Cottee 82	23834
34	24	PL	H	Arsenal	L	0-1	0-1	13		24217
35	M 2	PL	A	Coventry City	D	2-2	2-2	13	Cottee 2, Rieper 22	(18884)
36	9	PL	H	Middlesbrough	W	2-0	1-0	12	Dowie 1, Dicks 62(pen)	23850
37	18	PL	A	Newcastle United	L	0-3	0-1	12		(36331)
38	23	PL	H	Manchester City	W	4-2	0-1	11	Dowie 21, 53, Dicks 83, Dani 84	24017
39	A 6	PL	H	Wimbledon	D	1-1	1-1	11	Dicks 6	20402
40	8	PL	A	Liverpool	L	0-2	0-2	11		(40326)
41	13	PL	H	Bolton Wanderers	W	1-0	1-0	11	Cottee 28	23086
42	17	PL	A	Aston Villa	D	1-1	0-1	11	Cottee 84	(26768)
43	27	PL	A	Queens Park Rangers	L	0-3	0-0	11		(18828)
44	M 5	PL	H	Sheffield Wednesday	D	1-1	0-0	11	Dicks 72	23790

Best Home League Attendance: 24324 v Liverpool   Smallest: 18501 v Southampton   Average: 22316

Goal Scorers:
PL(43):   Cottee(10),Dicks(10),Dowie(8),Williamson(4),Slater(2),Rieper(2),Hutchison(2),Dani(2),Opponent(s)(1),Bishop(1),Allen(1)
CC(5):   Cottee(2),Dicks(1),Moncur(1),Bishop(1)
FAC(3):   Moncur(1),Hughes(1),Dowie(1)

	(M) Allen	(D) Bilic	(M) Bishop	(F) Boogers	(D) Breacker	(D) Brown	(F) Cottee	(F) Dani	(D) Dicks	(F) Dowie	(M) Dumitrescu	(G) Finn	(M) Gordon	(M) Harkes	(F) Hughes	(F) Hutchison	(M) Lampard	(M) Lazaridis	(D) Martin	(G) Miklosko	(M) Moncur	(D) Potts	(D) Rieper	(M) Rowland	(G) Sealey	(M) Slater	(F) Watson	(D) Whitbread	(M) Williamson	
K.Burge		X	S1		X		X		X							X			S2	X	X	X	X	X1					X2	1
D.Gallagher	X	X	S1		X		X		X							X			S	X	X	X	X			S			X1	2
G.R.Ashby	X	X	S		X		X1		X							X			S1	X	X	X	X				X			3
M.Reed	X	X			X		X		X						X1				S	X	X	X	X			S	X			4
R.Hart		X1			X		X2		X	X						X		S1	S	X	X	X1	X			S	X			5
A.Wilkie		X			X		X2		X	X						X3		S3	S2	X	X1	X	X			S1	X			6
K.Cooper		X			X		X		X	X2										X	X	X	X	S2		S	X1		S1	7
P.Durkin		X			X		X2		X	X										X	X	X	X1	S1		S	X		S2	8
G.Poll		X			X		S1		X							X		X1	X	X	X	X	X	S	X	S	X			9
R.Gifford		X	X		X		X		X	X					X	S			X	X	X	X	X	S	S	S	X			10
D.Gallagher		X			X		X		X	X					X	S1			X	X	X	X	X	S	S	X1				11
S.Lodge		X			X		X		X	X					X	S			X	X	X	X	X	S	S	X				12
P.Danson		X			X		X		X	X					X	S			X	X	X	X	X	S		X				13
K.Cooper		X	S		X		X		X	X				S1	X	S2			X	X	X2	X	X				X1			14
P.Jones		X	S1		X		X		X	X				S1	X	X1			X	X	X	X	X			S	X1			15
P.Durkin		X		S	X		X		X					X	X				X	X	X	X	X	S	S				X	16
J.Winter		X		S	X		X		X					X	X				X	X	X	X	X	X	S	S			X	17
P.Alcock		X		S1	X		X		X					X2	X		S3		X	X	X	X	X1	X	S2				X	18
K.Bulge		X3	S2	X	X2		X		X	X				X1	X				X	X	X	X			S1				X	19
M.Reed		X	S	X	X1		X		X	X				S	X				X	X	X	X	S1			X			X	20
A.Wilkie		X	S1		X		X		X	X				X	X		X1	X2	X	X	X	S	S2						X	21
S.Dunn		X	X		X		X		X	X				X1	X				X	X1	X	X	S1	S1		X			X	22
M.Reed		X			S		X	X	X	X	X		X	X1	X				X	X	X	X	S			X			X1	23
R.Dilkes		X			X		X	X	X	X		S		X	X	S			X	X	X	X	S							24
P.Danson		X			X		X	X	X	X				X	X				X	X	X	X	X1			S1				25
S.Lodge		X		X	X		X	X	X	X				X	X				X	X	X	X	S1			X1			SX	26
G.Poll		X		X	X2		X	X	X					X			S1		X	X1	X	X			S			S2	S2	27
K.Burge		X		X			X		X	X				X				S1	X		X	X			S	X2	S2	S2	X	28
G.Willard		X		X	X1	S1	X	X	X	X				X					X		X	X	S2		S	X1	X		X	29
J.Winter	X	X			S2	X2	X	X					S1	X1					X		X	X	X	S		X			X	30
R.A.Hart		X			X		X	X	X				S1	S1	X				X1		X	X	X	X1		S			X	31
G.Willard	X	X			S1	X1	X	X					S	X	X				X		X	X	X	X		S			X	32
P.Alcock	X1	X			X2		X	X	X				S2	S1	X				X		X	X	X	X		S			X	33
D.Elleray		X			X	S1	X	X	X					X1	X				X		X	X	X	X		S		S	X	34
M.Bodenham	X	X			X1	S	X	X	X					S1	X				X		X	X	X	X		S			X	35
M.Reid	X	X		X	X1		X	X	X	X					X				X		X	X	X	S					X	36
S.Lodge	X	X1		S1				S1	X	X	X1				X						X	X	X	X					X	37
K.Cooper	X	X		X				S1	X	X	X1				X				X			S	X	X	S				X	38
P.Durkin	X	X		X				X	X	X					X					S	X		X	X1	S	S1			X	39
P.Alcock	X	X		X				S1	X	X					X1					S	X		X	X		X			X	40
A.Wilkie	X	X		X		X		X	X						X1					X	S1		X	S2	S	X2			X	41
S.Dunn	X	X		X		X	X1	X	X											S	X	X1	X	X		S			X	42
G.S.Wilard	X	X		X	X1		X		X						X					S	X	X1	X	X	X1			S1	X	43
R.Bilkes		X			X	X1		X	X3						X			S1	S3	X		X	X	X1					X	44
PL Appearances	13	35	0	19	3	30	3	34	33	2	1	0	6	28	8	0	2	10	36	19	34	35	19	1	16	0	0	0	28	
PL Sub Appearances	0	0	4	0	3	0	3	6	0	0	1	0	5	0	4	2	4	2	0	1	0	1	4	1	6	1	2	1		
CC Appearances	0	3	0	2	0	3	0	3	3	0	0	0	0	2	0	0	1	2	3	3	2+1	0	3	0	0+1					
FAC Appearances	0	3	0	0	0	3	0	3	3	0	0	0+1	1+1	3	0	0+1	1	3	1	3	3	1+1	0	1	0	1	0	1	3	

Played: (F) Boere S1(4). (M) Ferdinand S1(43). (G) Shilton S(25,26). (M) Whyte S(25,26).

WEST HAM UNITED

CLUB RECORDS

BIGGEST VICTORIES
League: 8-0 v Rotherham United, Division 2, 8.3.1958
8-0 v Sunderland, Division 1, 19.10.1968
F.A. Cup: 6-0 v Bury, Round 2, 1919-20
6-0 v Arsenal, Round 3, 1945-46
League Cup: 10-0 v Bury, Round 2, 25.10.1984
Europe: No more than 4 goals

BIGGEST DEFEATS
League: 0-7 v Sheffield Wednesday, Division 1, 28.11.1959
0-7 v Everton, Division 1, 22.10.1927
0-7 v Barnsley, Division 2, 1.9.1919
F.A. Cup: 0-5 v Aston Villa, Round 2, 1912-13
0-5 v Tottenham Hotspur, Round 3, 1925-26
1-6 v Queens Park Rangers, Round 4 replay, 28.1.1978
League Cup: 0-6 v Oldham Athletic, Semi-Final, 14.2.1990
Europe 0(ECWC): No more than 3 goals

MOST POINTS
3 points a win: 88, Division 1, 1992-93
2 points a win: 66, Division 2, 1980-81

MOST GOALS
101, 1957-58, Division 2.
Dick 21, Keeble 19, Dare 14, Smith 11, Musgrove 9, Bond 8,
Cantwell 4, Malcolm3, Lewis 3, Newman 2, Grice 2, Landsowne 2,
Allison 2, og 2.

MOST LEAGUE GOALS CONCEDED
107 Division 1, 1931-32

MOST FIRST CLASS MATCHES IN A SEASON
62 (42 League, 4 FA Cup, 10 League Cup, 6 European Cup
Winners Cup) 1965-66

MOST LEAGUE WINS
28, Division 2, 1980-81

MOST LEAGUE DRAWS
18, Division 1, 1968-69

MOST LEAGUE DEFEATS
23, Division 1, 1931-32

INDIVIDUAL CLUB RECORDS

MOST GOALS IN A MATCH
6. Geoff Hurst v Sunderland, 8-0, Division 1, 19.10.1968
6. Vic Watson v Leeds United, 8-2, Division 1, 9.2.1929

MOST GOALS IN A SEASON
Vic Watson 50 (League 42, FAC 8) 1929-30.
4 goals once=4; 3 goals 3 times=9; 2 goals 8 times=16; 1 goal 21
times=21.
Previous holder: Vic Watson 34, 1926-27

OLDEST PLAYER
Billy Bonds 41 years 225 days v Southampton (Div 1), 30.4.1988

YOUNGEST PLAYER
Paul Allen, 17 years 32 days v Burnley, Div. 2, 29.9.1979

MOST CAPPED PLAYER
Bobby Moore (England) 108

BEST PERFORMANCES

League: 1980-81: Matches played 42, Won 28, Drawn 10, Lost 4,
Goals for 79.Goals against 29, Points 66. First in Division 2.

Highest: 1985-86: Third in Division 1.

F.A. Cup: 1963-64: 3rd rnd. Charlton Athletic 3-0; 4th rnd. Orient 1
1, 3-0;5th rnd. Swindon Town 3-1; 6th rnd. Burnley 3-2; Semi-final
Manchester United3-1; Final Preston North End 3-2.
1974-75: 3rd rnd. Southampton 2-1; 4th rnd. Swindon Town 1-1, 2-1
5th rnd.Queens Park Rangers 2-1; 6th rnd. Arsenal 2-0; Semi-final
Ipswich Town 0-0, 2-1; Final Fulham 2-0.
1979-80: 3rd rnd. West Bromwich Albion 1-1, 2-1; 4th rnd. Orient 3
2; 5th rnd.Swansea City 2-0; 6th rnd. Aston Villa 1-0; Semi-final
Everton 1-1, 2-1; Final Arsenal 1-0.

League Cup: 1965-66: 2nd rnd. Bristol Rovers 3-3, 3-2; 3rd rnd.
Mansfield Town4-0; 4th rnd. Rotherham United 2-1; 5th rnd. Grimsb
Town 2-2, 1-0; Semi-final Cardiff City 5-2, 5-1; Final West Bromwich
Albion 2-1, 1-4.

Europe (ECWC): 1964-65: 1st rnd. La Gantoise 1-0, 1-1; 2nd rnd.
Sparta Prague2-0, 1-2; 3rd rnd. Lausanne 2-1, 4-3; Semi-final Real
Zaragoza 2-1, 1-1; Final Munich 1860 2-0.

DIVISIONAL RECORD

	Played	Won	Drawn	Lost	For	Against	Points
Division 1/P	1,712	589	421	702	2,561	2,772	1,771
Division 2/1	1,230	537	300	393	1,958	1,622	1,444
Total	**2,942**	**1,126**	**721**	**1,095**	**4,519**	**4,394**	**3,215**

ADDITIONAL INFORMATION
Previous Name
Thames Ironworks 1895-1900

Previous League
Southern League

Club colours: Claret shirts with sky blue side panels & trim, white
shorts & socks with blue trim.
Change colours: White shirts, shorts & socks with claret & blue
piping.

Reserves League: Avon Insurance Football Combination.

RECORDS AND STATISTICS

COMPETITIONS

Div 1/P	Div.2/1	ECWC	Watney	A/Ital
1923-32	1919-23	1964-65	1973	1975
1958-78	1932-58	1965-66		1992-93
1981-89	1978-81	1975-76	Texaco	
1919-92	1989-91	1980-81	1974-75	
1993-	1992-93			

HONOURS

Div.2	FA Cup	C/Shield	ECWC
1957-58	1963-64	1964	1964-65
	1974-75		
	1979-80		

MOST APPEARANCES

Billy Bonds 781+12 (1967-88)

Year	League	FA Cup	Lge Cup	ECWC
1967-68	37	3	2	
1968-69	42	3	2	
1969-70	42	1	2	
1970-71	37	1	2	
1971-72	42	4	10	
1972-73	39	2	2	
1973-74	40	2	1	
1974-75	31	8	3	
1975-76	17+1		5	9
1976-77	41	2	3	
1977-78	29	3		
1978-79	39	1	1	
1979-80	34	5	9	
1980-81	41	3	8	6
1981-82	29	2	4	
1982-83	34	1	4	
1983-84	27	0+1	2	
1984-85	19+3		4	
1985-86				
1986-87	13+4	3+1	1+2	
1987-88	22	2		
	655+8	46+2	65+2	15

MOST GOALS IN A CAREER

Vic Watson - 326 (1920-35)

Year	League	FA Cup
1920-21	2	
1921-22	12	1
1922-23	22	5
1923-24	3	
1924-25	22	1
1925-26	20	
1926-27	34	3
1927-28	16	
1928-29	29	1
1929-30	42	8
1930-31	14	
1931-32	23	2
1932-33	23	4
1933-34	26	3
1934-35	10	
Total	298	28

Current leading goalscorer: Tony Cottee - 145 (1982-96 - 2 spells)

RECORD TRANSFER FEE RECEIVED

Amount	Club	Player	Date
£2,000,000	Everton	Tony Cottee	7/88
£850,000	Celtic	Frank McAvennie	10/87
£800,000	Manchester Utd	Paul Ince	9/89
£400,000	Newcastle Utd	Paul Goddard	10/86
£400,000	Tottenham H.	Paul Allen	6/85

RECORD TRANSFER FEE PAID

Amount	Club	Player	Date
£2,400,000	Espanol	Florin Raducioiu	7/96
£1,600,000	Tottenham H.	Ilie Dumitrescu	3/96
£1,500,000	Liverpool	Don Hutchison	8/94
£1,250,000	Celtic	Frank McAvennie	3/89

MANAGERS

Name	Seasons	Best	Worst
Syd King	1902-32	7(1)	7(2)
Charlie Paynter	1932-50	4(2)	20(2)
Ted Fenton	1950-61	6(1)	16(1)
Ron Greenwood	1961-77	6(1)	20(1)
John Lyall	1977-89	3(1)	7(2)
Lou Macari	1989-90		
Billy Bonds	1990-94	13(P)	7(2)
Harry Redknapp	1994-	14(P)	14(P)

LONGEST LEAGUE RUNS

of undefeated matches:	27 (27.12.1980 - 10.10.1981)	of league matches w/out a win:	17 (31.1.1976 - 21.8.1976)
of undefeated home matches:	27 (30.8.1980 - 21.11.1981)	of undefeated away matches:	13 (10.1.1981 - 3.10.1981)
without home win:	13 (29.10.1988 - 15.4.1989)	without an away win:	31 (12.12.1931 - 14.3.1933)
of league wins:	9 (19.10.1985 - 14.12.1985)	of home wins:	16 (30.8.1980 - 7.3.1981)
of league defeats:	9 (28.3.1932 - 29.8.1932)	of away wins:	5 (16.12.22-15.2.23, 26.12.35-15.3.36, 5.10.85-7.12.85)

WEST HAM UNITED

PLAYERS NAME / Honours	Ht	Wt	Birthdate	Birthplace / Transfers	Contract Date	Clubs	League	L/Cup	FA Cup	Other	Lge	L/C	FAC	Oth
G O A L K E E P E R S														
Miklosko Ludek	6.5	14.0	09/12/61	Ostrava		Banik Ostrava								
				£300000	19/02/90	West Ham United	266	20	23	8				
Sealey Les	6.0	11.6	29/09/57	Bethnal Green	01/03/76	Coventry City	158	11	9					
FAC'90. ECWC'91. CS'90				£100000	03/08/83	Luton Town	207	21	28	3				
				Loan	05/10/84	Plymouth Argyle	6							
				Loan	21/03/90	Manchester United	2		1					
				Free	06/06/90	Manchester United	31	8	3	9				
				Free	19/07/91	Aston Villa	18		4	2				
				Loan	25/03/92	Coventry City	2							
				Loan	02/10/92	Birmingham City	12			3				
				Free	06/01/93	Manchester United		1	0+1					
				Free	18/07/94	Blackpool	7	2						
				Free	28/11/94	West Ham United	1+1							
D E F E N D E R S														
Bilic Slaven				Karlsruhe										
					04/02/96	West Ham United	13							
Bowen Mark	5.8	11.6	07/12/63	Neath	01/12/81	Tottenham Hotspur	14+3		3	0+1	2			
W: 26, u21.3, Y, S				£97000	23/07/87	Norwich City	285+4	28	27	17	22	1	1	1
					04/07/96	West Ham United								
Breacker Tim	6.0	12.6	02/07/65	Bicester	15/05/83	Luton Town	204+6	22+2	21	7	3			
E: u21.2. LC'88				£600000	12/10/90	West Ham United	187+5	13	22	7	8			
Brown Kenny	5.8	11.6	11/07/67	Upminster	10/07/85	Norwich City	24+1			3				
				Free	10/08/88	Plymouth Argyle	126	9	6	3	4			
				£175000	02/08/91	West Ham United	55+8	1+1	7+2	2+2	5		1	
				Loan	07/09/95	Huddersfield Town	5							
				Loan	27/10/95	Reading	12	3			1			
				Loan	01/03/96	Southend United	6							
				Loan	28/03/96	Crystal Palace	5+1			3			1	
Dicks Julian	5.7	11.7	11/12/68	Bristol	12/04/86	Birmingham City	83+6	5+1	5	2	1			
E: u21.4, B.2				£300000	25/03/88	West Ham United	159	19	14	11	29	5	2	4
				£1500000	17/09/93	Liverpool	24	3	1		3			
				£1000000	20/10/94	West Ham United	63	5	5		15	1		
Hall Richard	6.1	12.8	14/03/72	Ipswich	20/03/90	Scunthorpe United	22	2	3	4	3			
E: u21.11				£200000	13/02/91	Southampton	89+7	7+1	10	3	11		2	
					01/07/96	West Ham United								
Potts Steve	5.8	10.5	07/05/67	Hartford (USA)	11/05/84	West Ham United	302+10	30+1	34	14+1	1			
E: Y.11														
Rieper Marc	6.4	14.2	05/06/68	Rodoure		Brondby								
				Loan	08/12/94	West Ham United	17+4				1			
				£500000	01/08/95	West Ham United	35+1	2+1	3		2			
Whitbread Adrian	6.2	11.8	22/10/71	Epping	13/11/89	Leyton Orient	125	10+1	11	8	2		1	
				£500000	29/07/93	Swindon Town	34+1		2		1			
				£650000	17/08/94	West Ham United	3+7	2+1	1					
				Loan	09/11/95	Portsmouth	13							
M I D F I E L D														
Bishop Ian	5.9	10.12	29/05/65	Liverpool	24/05/83	Everton	0+1							
E: B.1				Loan	22/03/84	Crewe Alexandra	4							
				£15000	11/10/84	Carlisle United	131+1	8	5	4	14	1	1	
				£35000	14/07/88	Bournemouth	44	4	5	1	2			
				£465000	02/08/89	Manchester City	18+1	4		1	2	1		
				£500000	28/12/89	West Ham United	211+11	16	20+1	4+1	11	1	3	1
Canham Scott W	5.7	11.07	05/11/74	London	02/07/93	West Ham United								
				Loan	03/11/95	Torquay United	3							
				Loan	19/01/96	Brentford	14							
Dumitrescu Ilie	5.9	10.07	06/01/69	Bucharest		Steaua Bucharest								
Romanian Int.				£2600000	03/08/94	Tottenham Hotspur	16+2	2			4	1		
				£1650000	09/03/96	West Ham United	2+1							
Lampard Frank	5.10	12.4	21/06/78	Romford	01/07/95	West Ham United	0+2							
Lazaridis Stan						West Adelaide								
				£300000	01/08/95	West Ham United	2+2	1	0+1					
Moncur John	5.7	9.10	22/09/66	Stepney	22/08/84	Tottenham Hotspur	10+11	1+2			1			
					25/09/86	Doncaster Rovers	4							
				Loan	27/03/87	Cambridge United	3+1							
				Loan	22/03/89	Portsmouth	7							
				Loan	19/10/89	Brentford	5			1	1			
				Loan	24/10/91	Ipswich Town	5+1							
				£80000	30/03/92	Swindon Town	53+5	4	1	4	5			1
				£900000	24/08/94	West Ham United	49+1	6	3		2	2	1	
Omoyimni Emmanuel	5.8	10.00	28/12/77	Nigeria	01/08/94	West Ham United								
Rowland Keith	5.10	10.0	01/09/71	Portadown	02/10/89	Bournemouth	65+7	5	8	3	2			
NI: Y. SLP'91. FLg u18.1				Loan	01/08/90	Farnborough			1					
				Loan	08/01/93	Coventry City	0+2							
				£110000	06/08/93	West Ham United	46+12	3	5+1					

Name	Ht	Wt	DOB	From	Fee	Date	Club								
Slater Robbie	5.11	13.0	22/11/64	Skelmersdale			Lens								
Australian International					£300000	04/08/94	Blackburn Rovers	12+6	1	1	2				
					£600000	15/08/95	West Ham United	16+6	3	1		2			
Williamson Daniel	5.11	12.3	05/12/73	Newham		03/07/92	West Ham United	34+2	0+1	3		5			
				Loan		04/02/93	Farnborough								
				Loan		08/10/93	Doncaster Rovers	10+3		2	1	1		2	

F O R W A R D S

Name	Ht	Wt	DOB	From	Fee	Date	Club								
Boogers Marco							Sparta								
					£800000	14/07/95	West Ham United	0+4							
Cottee Tony	5.8	11.5	11/07/65	West Ham		01/09/82	West Ham United	203+9	19	24	1	92	14	11	1
E: 7, u21.8, Y.3					£2300000	02/08/88	Everton	158+23	19+4	15+6	11+2	72	11	4	12
					£300000	07/09/94	West Ham United	61+3	6	5		22	3	1	
Dani							Sporting Lisbon								
				Loan		03/02/96	West Ham United	3+6				2			
Dowie Iain	6.1	12.12	09/01/65	Hatfield			Hendon								
NI: 25, u21.1					£30000	14/12/88	Luton Town	53+13	3+1	1+2	5	15			4
				Loan		13/09/89	Fulham	5				1			
					£480000	22/03/91	West Ham United	12				4			
					£500000	03/09/91	Southampton	115+7	8+3	6	4	30	1	1	
					£400000	13/01/95	Crystal Palace	19		6		6	4		
					£125000	07/09/95	West Ham United	33	3	3		8	1		
Futre Paulo							AC Millan								
Portuguese Int.					Free	07/96	West Ham United								
Hodges Lee L	5.4	9.06	02/03/78	Newham		01/08/94	West Ham United								
Hughes Michael E	5.6	10.8	02/08/71	Larne		17/08/88	Manchester City	25+1	5	1	1	1			
					£450000	01/04/92	Strasbourg								
				Loan		29/11/94	West Ham United	15+2		2		2			
					Free	04/07/96	West Ham United	28	2	3			1		
Jones Stephen G	6.0	12.12	17/03/70	Cambridge			Billericay Town								
					£22000	16/11/92	West Ham United	8+8		2+2	1+1	4		1	
				Loan		27/01/95	Bournemouth	27+3		1	1	8		1	
				Free		25/04/96	Bournemouth	44	4	2	2	18	3		
						17/05/96	West Ham United								
Raduciolu Florin							Espanol								
Romanian Int.					£2400000	04/07/96	West Ham United								

ADDITIONAL CONTRACT PLAYERS

Name	Date	Club	
Blaney Steven D	01/07/95	West Ham (T)	
Coyne Christopher	13/01/96	West Ham (T)	
Ferdinand Rio G	27/11/95	West Ham (T)	0+1
Mautone Steve	29/03/96	West Ham (T)	
Moore Jason M	28/02/96	West Ham (T)	
Omoyinmi Emmanuel	17/05/96	West Ham (T)	
Philson Graeme	15/01/96	West Ham (T)	
Phipp Daniel A	01/07/95	West Ham (T)	
	Loan	11/08/95	Dagenham & Red.

THE MANAGER
HARRY REDKNAPP

Date of Birth . . . . 2nd March 1947.
Place of Birth . . . . Poplar.
Date of Appointment . . . . 10th August 1994.

PREVIOUS CLUBS
As Manager . . . . Bournemouth.
As Coach. . . . . None.
As a Player. . . . . West Ham United, Bournemouth, Brentford.

HONOURS
As a Manager
Bournemouth: Division 3 champions 1987.

As a Player
None.

UPTON PARK

Green Street, London E13 9AZ
Tel: 0181 548 2700

Capacity ....25,985.

First game ....v Millwall, Sth Lge, 1.9.1904.
First floodlit game ....v Tottenham Hotspur, 16.4.1953.

ATTENDANCES
Highest ....42,322 v Tottenham, Div.1, 17.10.1970.
Lowest ....4,500 v Doncaster, Div.2, 24.2.1955.

OTHER GROUNDS ....Memorial Recreation Ground, Canning Town 1900-04. Upton Park 1904-

MATCHDAY TICKET PRICES

West Stand . . . . £18-£29
Juv/OAP £13
East Stand Upper Tier . . . . £18-£29
Lower Tier. £21-26
Juv/OAP £13
Bobby Moore Stand Upper . . . . £20-£25
Juv/OAP £13
Lower . . . . £16-£21
Juv/OAP £10
Centenary Stand Upper . . . . £10-£19
Lower . . . . Members £16.
Juv/OAP £8
Non Members & Away supporters . . . . . . £18-£22.
Juv/OAP £10
Ticket Office Telephone no. 0181 548 2700

CLUBCALL
0891 12 11 65

Calls cost 39p per minute cheap rate and 49p per
minute at all other times.
Call costings correct at time of going to press.

HOW TO GET TO THE GROUND

From the North and West
Take North Circular (A406) to A124 (East Ham), then on Barking Road for approx 1.5 miles until you approach traffic lights on crossroads. Turn right into Green Street, ground is on right hand side.

From the East
Use A13, sign posted London, then at crossroads turn right (A117). In 0.9 miles at crossroads turn left (A124). In 0.6 miles turn right into Green Street for West Ham United FC.

From the South
Use Blackwall Tunnel and A13 to Canning Town, then follow signs East Ham (A124). In 1.7 miles turn left into Green Street for West Ham United FC.

Car Parking
Ample side-street parking available.

Nearest Railway Station
Upton Park (District Line Tube).

MATCHDAY PROGRAMME

Programme Editor . . . . Peter Stewart.

Number of pages . . . . 48.

Price . . . . £2.

Subscriptions . . . . £63.50 for all 1st team home matches.

Local Newspapers. . . . . Stratford Express, Ilford Recorder.

Local Radio Stations . . . . Essex Radio.

WIMBLEDON
(The Crazy Gang)
F.A. CARLING PREMIERSHIP
SPONSORED BY: ELONEX

Back Row (L-R): Alan Reeves, Brian McAllister, Paul Heald, Neil Sullivan, Andy Thorn, Gary Elkins, Mick Harford.
Middle Row: Efan Ekoku, Neal Ardley, Grant Payne, Scott Fitzgerald, Aidan Newhouse, Vinny Jones, Marcus Gayle, Stewart Castledine, Jon Goodman, Robbie Earle. **Front Row:** Joe Kinnear, Steve Talboys, Alan Kimble, Chris Perry, Peter Fear, Mark Thomas.

WIMBLEDON
FORMED IN 1889
TURNED PROFESSIONAL IN 1964
LTD COMPANY IN 1964

CHAIRMAN: S G Reed
DEPUTY-CHAIRMAN: J H Lelliott
DIRECTORS
P E Cork, PR Lloyd Cooper,
S G N Hammam (Managing Director),
P. Miller
CHIEF EXECUTIVE
David Barnard
SECRETARY
Steve Rooke (0181 771 2233)
MARKETING MANAGER
Sharon Sillitoe
PR & MEDIA MANAGER: Reg Davis
MANAGER: Joe Kinnear
ASSISTANT MANAGER: Terry Burton
RESERVE TEAM MANAGER
Lawrie Sanchez
YOUTH TEAM MANAGER
Ernie Tippett
PHYSIOTHERAPIST
Steve Allen
STATISTICIAN FOR THE DIRECTORY
Simon Case

They've done it again!

Every season Wimbledon are expected to find life difficult in the Premier Division.

They regularly sell star players, they bring in youngsters and less experienced signings, they contrive to be 'unorthodox' in their preparations but there spirit is second to none, and they regularly achieve safety in the middle and sometimes near the top of the division.

Last season horrendous injuries stretched Joe Kinnear's squad to its limit and after a good start - three wins, a draw and ten goals in the first five games - the injuries really affected the teams confidence and a desperate run of sixteen games without a victory saw them plummet to eighteenth position.

Despite missing many games through injury, Robbie Earle (14 goals) gave Dean Holdsworth (16) great support from midfield. Once again 'The Crazy Gang' were magnificent at set pieces and although still very effective with the direct methods of play, they can certainly change their style to pass the ball around with the best when they feel the time is right.

Wimbledon were knocked out of the Coca-Cola Cup by Charlton Athletic during their dismal Autumn but there was F.A. Cup excitement to come. Watford, Middlesbrough and Huddersfield Town were all eliminated in home replays but then they were drawn at Selhurst Park but could only tie 2-2 with Chelsea. After two excellent cup ties their local rivals eventually won through to the Semi-Final. But this cup run lifted the club and although disappointed when missing the chance of another visit to Wembley, they once again showed their character by winning four of the next five Premier games.

When you realise the progress, development and achievement of Wimbledon Football Club, it is no wonder that they have won over so many neutrals who now actually admit to having a soft spot for them.

TONY WILLIAMS.

WIMBLEDON

League: 14th   FA Cup: Quarter Finals   Coca-Cola Cup: 2nd Rnd

M	DATE	COMP	VEN	OPPONENTS	RESULT	HT	LP	GOAL SCORERS/GOAL TIMES	ATT.
1	A 19	PL	H	Bolton Wanderers	W 3-2	2-2	4	Ekoku 5, Earle 23, Holdsworth 55	9317
2	23	PL	A	Queens Park Rangers	W 3-0	1-0	4	Leonhardsen 30, Holdsworth 56, Goodman 83	(11837)
3	26	PL	A	Manchester United	L 1-3	0-1	5	Earle 64	(32226)
4	30	PL	H	Sheffield Wednesday	D 2-2	1-1	8	Goodman 17, Holdsworth 84(pen)	6352
5	S 9	PL	H	Liverpool	W 1-0	1-0	4	Harford 28	19530
6	16	PL	A	Aston Villa	L 0-2	0-1	7		(26928)
7	19	CC 2/1	H	Charlton Athletic	L 4-5	1-2		Holdsworth 12, 71, Earle 72, Clarke 88	3717
8	23	PL	H	Leeds United	L 2-4	1-3	9	Holdsworth 43, Reeves 59	13307
9	30	PL	A	Tottenham Hotspur	L 1-3	1-2	11	Earle 39	(25321)
10	O 3	CC 2/2	A	Charlton Athletic	D 3-3	1-1		Holdsworth 31, 81(pen), Earle 46	(9823)
11	16	PL	H	West Ham United	L 0-1	0-1	12		9411
12	21	PL	A	Newcastle United	L 1-6	0-3	14	Gayle 60	(36434)
13	28	PL	H	Southampton	L 1-2	0-1	15	Euell 64	7982
14	N 6	PL	A	Nottingham Forest	L 1-4	1-2	15	Jones 11	(20810)
15	18	PL	H	Middlesbrough	D 0-0	0-0	16		13780
16	22	PL	A	Manchester City	L 0-1	0-0	17		(23617)
17	25	PL	A	Coventry City	D 3-3	2-1	16	Jones 28(pen), Goodman 43, Leonhardsen 58	(12496)
18	D 3	PL	H	Newcastle United	D 3-3	2-3	17	Holdsworth 19, 65, Ekoku 21	18002
19	9	PL	A	Leeds United	D 1-1	1-0	17	Leonhardsen 4	(27984)
20	16	PL	H	Tottenham Hotspur	L 0-1	0-0	18		16193
21	23	PL	H	Blackburn Rovers	D 1-1	0-1	18	Earle 82	7105
22	26	PL	A	Chelsea	W 2-1	2-1	16	Earle 35, Ekoku 39	(21906)
23	30	PL	A	Arsenal	W 3-1	1-1	15	Earle 38,67, Holdsworth 50	(37640)
24	J 1	PL	H	Everton	L 2-3	0-3	15	Holdsworth 55, Ekoku 74	11121
25	6	FAC 3	A	Watford	D 1-1	1-1		Leonhardsen 33	(11187)
26	13	PL	A	Bolton Wanderers	L 0-1	0-1	15		(16216)
27	17	FAC 3R	H	Watford	W 1-0	0-0		Clarke 78	5142
28	20	PL	H	Queens Park Rangers	W 2-1	1-0	14	Leonhardsen 40, Clarke 74	9123
29	F 3	PL	H	Manchester United	L 2-4	0-2	16	Gayle 68, Euell 78	25432
30	7	FAC 4	A	Middlesbrough	D 0-0	0-0			(28915)
31	10	PL	A	Sheffield Wednesday	L 1-2	0-0	16	Gayle 60	(19085)
32	13	FAC 4R	H	Middlesbrough	W 1-0	0-0		Holdsworth 73	5220
33	17	FAC 5	A	Huddersfield Town	D 2-2	0-1		Ekoku 66, 90	(17307)
34	24	PL	H	Aston Villa	D 3-3	1-1	16	Goodman 10, 48, Harford 90	12193
35	28	FAC 5R	H	Huddersfield Town	W 3-1	2-1		Ekoku 9, Goodman 42, 85	7015
36	M 2	PL	H	Chelsea	D 1-1	1-1	15	Clarke 38(og)	17048
37	9	FAC QF	A	Chelsea	D 2-2	0-0		Earle 54, Holdsworth 81	(30805)
38	13	PL	A	Liverpool	D 2-2	0-1	16	Ekoku 54, Holdsworth 60	(34063)
39	16	PL	H	Arsenal	L 0-3	0-0	17		18335
40	20	FAC QFR	H	Chelsea	L 1-3	1-1		Goodman 39	21380
41	23	PL	A	Everton	W 4-2	1-1	15	Gayle 12, Castledine 65, Clarke 85, Goodman 88	(31382)
42	30	PL	H	Nottingham Forest	W 1-0	0-0	15	Holdsworth 81	9807
43	A 6	PL	A	West Ham United	D 1-1	1-1	11	Jones 9	(20402)
44	8	PL	H	Manchester City	W 3-0	1-0	15	Earle 40, 47, Ekoku 52	11844
45	13	PL	A	Middlesbrough	W 2-1	1-1	14	Earle 12, Ekoku 64	(29192)
46	17	PL	A	Blackburn Rovers	L 2-3	1-1	14	Earle 22, Gayle 48	(24174)
47	27	PL	H	Coventry City	L 0-2	0-0	14		15790
48	M 5	PL	A	Southampton	D 0-0	0-0	14		(15172)

Best Home League Attendance: 25432 v Manchester United   Smallest: 6352 v Sheffield Wednesday   Average: 13245

Goal Scorers:

PL(55): Earle(11),Holdsworth(10),Ekoku(7),Goodman(6),Gayle(5),Leonhardsen(4),Jones(3),Harford(2),Euell(2),Clarke(2),Reeves(1),Castledine(1),Opponent(s)(1)

CC(7): Holdsworth(4),Earle(2),Clarke(1)

FAC(11): Ekoku(3),Goodman(3),Holdsworth(2),Leonhardsen(1),Earle(1),Clarke(1)

Appearance grid, season 1995-96.

(F) Ardley	(D) Blackwell	(F) Bissett	(M) Castledine	(F) Clarke	(D) Cunningham	(M) Earle	(F) Ekoku	(D) Elkins	(M) Euell	(M) Fear	(D) Fitzgerald	(F) Gayle	(F) Goodman	(F) Harford	(G) Heald	(F) Holdsworth	(M) Jones	(M) Kimble	(M) Leonhardsen	(D) McAllister	(D) Pearce	(D) Perry	(D) Reeves	(G) Segers	(G) Sullivan	(M) Talboys	(D) Thorn	(G) Tracey	Referee	No.
		S3				X	X2	S1	X				S2		X	X3	X	X1	X			X	X				X		K.Cooper	1
		S2				X	X3	S1		X1			S3		X	X	X	X	X2			X	X				X		G.Poll	2
		S2				X	X2	X1					S1		X	X	X	X	X2			X	X		S2		X		P.Durkin	3
		S2				X	X2	S2					S1	X	X	X	X	X	X2			X	X				X1		A.Wilkie	4
			S2	X	X	X2							X3	S3	X	X	X	X	X			S1	X				X1		K.Burde	5
				X	X3	X							S1	X1	S3	X2	X	S2	X			X	X						D.Elleray	6
				S1	X	X	X1			S			X	S1	X	X	X	X	X1			X	X						M.Reed	7
S				X	X	X	S1	X	X2			X1	S2	X	X	X	X					X	X						R.Dilkes	8
				S1	X	X		X		X1			X	S1	X	X	X	X1				X					X	G.R.Ashby	9
X		S2		X2	X2	X						X1		S1	X	X	X	S2			X				X	X		P.Durkin	10
		S2		X	X					S1	S2	X		X	X	X	X	X2	X		X					X1		D.Gallagher	11
				X	X					X	X	S2	X	X	X	X	S3	X1	X2	X				S1				G.Poll	12
				S1	X	X	X	X	X	X1	S	S	X	X	X		X	X	X2			X2						J.Winter	13
				S1	X	X	X	S		S1	X1	S1	X1	X	X	X				X	X				X	X	P.Alcock	14
					X	X	X1	X	X		S1	S	X	X	X	X		X	S				X				K.Cooper	15
				X1	X	X	X	X1	X		S1	S3	X	X3	X			X	S1				X	X				P.Durkin	16
			S3	S2	X	X				S1	X2	X1	X	X	X	X		X	X	X					X			R.Hart	17
				X	X	X1				S1	X	X	X	X	X	X1	X	S1	S								G.Ashby	18
				X	X	X2				S1	X	X1	X	S2	X	X	X	X	X				S				G.Poll	19
				X	X	X				S1	X	X2	X1	X	X	X	S2	X	X	S							D.Elleray	20
				X	X	X3				S3	X1	X	X2	X	S1	X	X	X	X	S2							M.Bodenham	21
				X	X	X3				S1	S2	X2	X1	X	X	X	X	S3	X	X	X						D.Gallagher	22
				X	X	X1				S1	S1	X1	X	X	X	X	S	X	X	X							S.Lodge	23
				X	X	X1				S1	X	X	X	X1	X	X	S	X	X	X							A.Wilkie	24
				X	X	X1	S1			X	X	X	X	X1	X	S	X	X	X								P.Danson	25
				X	X	X	S1			X	X	X	X	X1	X	S	X	X	X				X	S			M.Reed	26
S2			S1	X	X	X2	X			X1	X	X	X	X3	S3	X	X1			X				X			P.Danson	27
S2				X	X	S1	X			X1	X	X	X	X	X	X	X			X				X			S.Dunn	28
X2			X	X			S1			X	S2	X1	X	X	X	S	X	X1			X	X					P.Durkin	29
S2		X	X		S3					X	X	X2	X	X	S1	X	X1	X	X			X					L.Dilkes	30
	X2		S	X	X	X1	S2			X	X1	X3	X	X	X	X	X			X				S3			M.Bodenham	31
		S	X	X	X1	S1				X2	X	X	X	X	X	S	X	X	X				X				S.Lodge	32
		S1	X	X	X	S2				X2	X	X	X1	X	X	S	X	X	X				X		S		P.B.Alcock	33
X		X2	X	X		S2				X1	X	X		S1	X	X			X				X		S		J.Winter	34
X		S1	X	X	X2	S2				X	X			X	X1	X	X		X				X				P.Alcock	35
X		S1	X	X	S					X	X1			X	X	X			X				X		S		P.Jones	36
X			X	X	X					S2	X1	X2	S1	X	X	X			X				X				B.Poll	37
X			X	X	X					S1	S	X1	X2	X	X	X			X				X		S2		G.Willard	38
X			X	X	S					X	S1	X1	X2	X	X	X			X				X		S2		D.Gallagher	39
X		S1	X1	X	X					S1	X	X1	X	X	X			X				X		S				G.Poll	40
X		S1	X	X	X2					X	S2			X1	X	X			X				X		S		R.Dilkes	41
X		X	X	X	X1	X				X	S			S1	X	X			X				X		S		K.Burge	42
X		S2	X2	X	X					X1	S1			X	X	X			X				X		S		P.Durkin	43
X		S1	X	X	X2					X1	S2			X	X	X			X				X				G.Poll	44
X		S2	X	X	X					X2				X	X	X	X1	X	S1				X				G.Ashby	45
S1		X1	X	X	X					X	S1			X	X1	X	X	X	X				X		S		R.Hart	46
		X1	X	X	X					X1	S1	S1		X1	X	X	X1	X	X				X				S.Dunn	47
X			X	X	X					S1	S1		X1	X	X	X1	X	X	X				X				M.Reed	48
4	8	0	2	9	32	37	28	7	4	4	2	21	9	17	18	31	27	31	28	2	6	35	21	3	16	3	11	1	PL Appearances	
2	0	4	2	9	1	0	3	3	5	0	2	13	18	4	0	2	4	0	1	0	1	2	3	1	0	2	3	0	PL Sub Appearances	
1	0	0	0	0+2	2	2	1	0	0	0	2	0+1	0+1	2	2	2	1	1+1	0		0	2	1	0	0	1	1	0	CC Appearances	
0+2	3	0	1+1	1+3	8	7	7	0	1+5	0	0	6+2	3	7	0	4+1	3	8	7	0	1+2	7	6	0	8	1	0	0	FAC Appearances	

Also Played: (G) Murphy S(48). (D) Skinner X2(11).

WIMBLEDON

CLUB RECORDS

BIGGEST VICTORIES
League: 6-0 v Newport County, Division 3, 3.9.19830
F.A. Cup: 7-2 v Windsor & Eton, Rnd 1, 22.11.1980
League Cup: 5-0 v Blackburn, Round 1, 24.9.1985

BIGGEST DEFEATS
League: 1-7 v Aston Villa (A), Premier League, 11.2.95.
1-6 v Carlisle Utd., Division 2, 23.3.1985
1-6 v Gillingham, Division 2, 13.2.1982
1-6 v Newcastle Utd (A), Premier League, 21.10.95.
F.A. Cup: 0-6 v Fulham, Rnd 1 replay, 1930-31
League Cup: 0-8 v Everton, Round 2, 29.8.1978

MOST POINTS
3 points a win: 98, Division 4, 1982-83.
2 points a win: 61, Division 4, 1978-79.

MOST GOALS
97, 1983-84, Division 3
Cork 28, Hodges 16, Evans 12, Fishender 8, Ketteridge 7, Downes 4, Park 4,Morris 3, Peters 3, Smith 3, Thomas 3, Hatter 2, Galliers 1, Winterburn 1, og2.

MOST LEAGUE GOALS CONCEDED
81, Division 3, 1979-80

MOST FIRST CLASS MATCHES IN A SEASON
56 (46 League, 2 FA Cup, 2 League Cup, 6 Football League Group Cup) 1981-82

MOST LEAGUE WINS
29, Division 4, 1982-83

MOST LEAGUE DRAWS
16, Division 1, 1977-78, 1989-90

MOST LEAGUE DEFEATS
22, Division 3, 1979-80

INDIVIDUAL CLUB RECORDS

MOST GOALS IN A MATCH
4. Alan Cork v Torquay United, Division 4, 28.2.1979 (4-1).

MOST GOALS IN A SEASON
Alan Cork 33, (League 29, FAC 2, Lge C 2) 1983-84
3 goals once=3; 2 goals 6 times=12; 1 goal 17 times=17

OLDEST PLAYER
Dave Donaldson, 37 years 4 months. v Hartlepool (Div 4) 9.2.1979.

YOUNGEST PLAYER
Kevin Gage 17 years 15 days v Bury (Div 4), 2.5.1981.

MOST CAPPED PLAYER
Terry Phelan (Eire) 8

BEST PERFORMANCES

League: 1982-83: Matches played 46, Won 29, Drawn 11, Lost 6, Goals for 95,Goals against 45, Points 98. First in Division 4.

Highest: 1986-87,1993-94: 6th in Division 1.

F.A. Cup: 1987-88: 3rd rnd. West Bromwich Albion 4-1 (h); 4th rnd. MansfieldTown 2-1 (a); 5th rnd. Newcastle United 3-1 (a); 6th rnd. Watford 2-1 (a);Semi-final Luton Town 2-1; Final Liverpool 1-0.

League Cup: 1993-94: 5th Round

ADDITIONAL INFORMATION
Previous Name
Wimbledon Old Centrals 1887-1905

Previous Leagues
Isthmian League, Southern League

Club colours: Dark blue with yellow.

Change colours: White/black/black.

DIVISIONAL RECORD

	Played	Won	Drawn	Lost	For	Against	Points
Division 1/P	402	144	122	136	533	525	554
Division 2	84	37	23	24	129	113	134
Division 3	138	50	34	54	210	232	174
Division 4	184	91	47	46	304	204	258
Total	**808**	**322**	**226**	**260**	**1,176**	**1,074**	**1,120**

RECORDS AND STATISTICS

COMPETITIONS

Div.1/P	Div.2	Div.3	Div.4
1986-	1984-86	1979-80	1977-79
		1981-82	1980-81
		1983-84	1982-83

HONOURS

Division 4	FA Cup
1982-83	1988

MOST APPEARANCES

Alan Cork 414+96 (1977-92)

Year	League	FA Cup	Lge Cup	Others
1977-78	17			
1978-79	45	5	3	
1979-80	41+1	5	5	
1980-81	41	5	4	
1981-82	6		2	
1982-83	7			
1983-84	41+1	2	5	1
1984-85	26+2	5	1	
1985-86	36+2	1	3	
1986-87	22+8	0+3	1	
1987-88	28+6	5+1	2+1	0+1
1988-89	9+16	1+1	2+2	0+1
1989-90	12+19	0+1	0+1	1+1
1990-91	9+16	1+1	1+1	1+0
1991-92	12+7		0+2	0+1
	352+78	30+7	29+7	3+4

MOST GOALS IN A CAREER

Alan Cork - 167 (1977-92)

Year	League	FA Cup	Lge Cup
1977-78	4		
1978-79	22	2	1
1979-80	12		1
1980-81	23	2	1
1981-82			
1982-83	5		
1983-84	29	2	2
1984-85	11		
1985-86	11		4
1986-87	5		2
1987-88	9	1	2
1988-89	2		
1989-90	5		
1990-91	5	1	
1991-92	2		
Total	145	8	14

Current leading goalscorer: Dean Holdsworth - 67 (1992-96)

RECORD TRANSFER FEE RECEIVED

Amount	Club	Player	Date
£4,000,000	Newcastle Utd	Warren Barton	06/95
£3,500,000	Liverpool	John Scales	08/94
£2,500,000	Manchester City	Keith Curle	8/91
£2,500,000	Manchester City	Terry Phelan	9/92

MANAGERS

Name	Seasons	Best	Worst
Allen Batsford	1977-78	13(4)	13(3)
Dario Gradi	1978-81	22(3)	4(4)
Dave Bassett	1981-87	6(1)	1(4)
Bobby Gould	1987-90	7(1)	12(1)
Ray Harford	1990-91	7(1)	7(1)
Peter Withe	1991-92		
Joe Kinnear	1992-	6(P)	14(P)

RECORD TRANSFER FEE PAID

Amount	Club	Player	Date
£1,900,000	Millwall	Ben Thatcher	7/96
£920,000	Norwich City	Efan Ekoku	10/94
£775,000	Port Vale	Robbie Earle	7/91
£720,000*	Brentford	Dean Holdsworth	7/92

*Transfer included Kruszynski & Bennett in exchange.

LONGEST LEAGUE RUNS

of undefeated matches:	22 (15.1.1983 - 14.5.1983)	of league matches w/out a win:	14 (23.2.1980 - 15.4.1980 16.9.95 - 26.12.95)
of undefeated home matches:	21 (22.1.1983 - 3.12.1983)	of undefeated away matches:	12 (22.1.1983 - 27.8.1983)
without home win:	9 (23.9.95 - 20.1.96)	without an away win:	11 (5.4.1989-30.9.1989, 14.9.1991-25.2.1992)
of league wins:	7 (9.4.1983 - 7.5.1983)	of home wins:	8 (9.4.1983 - 17.9.1983, 8.4.1978 - 14.10.1978)
of league defeats:	7 (16.9.95 - 6.11.95)	of away wins:	3 (23.12.78-28.2.79, 31.3.84-14.4.84, 10.4.91-20.4.91)

WIMBLEDON

PLAYERS NAME Honours	Ht	Wt	Birthdate	Birthplace Transfers	Contract Date	Clubs	APPEARANCES League	L/Cup	FA Cup	Other	GOALS Lge	L/C	FAC	Oth
G O A L K E E P E R S														
Heald Paul A	6.2	12.5	20/09/68	Wath on Dearne	30/06/87	Sheffield United								
					02/12/88	Leyton Orient	176	13	9	21				
					10/03/92	Coventry City	2							
Loan (24/03/94) Swindon Town 1+1 Lge Apps.				£125000	25/07/95	Wimbledon	18	2						
Murphy Brendan	5.11	11.12	19/08/75	Wexford		Bradford City								
				Free	26/09/94	Wimbledon								
Sullivan Neil	6.0	12.1	24/02/70	Sutton	26/07/88	Wimbledon	31+1		8					
				Loan	01/05/92	Crystal Palace	1							
D E F E N D E R S														
Blackwell Dean	6.1	12.10	05/12/69	Camden	07/07/88	Wimbledon	75+17	3	10+1	1	1			
E: u21.6				Loan	15/03/90	Plymouth Argyle	5+2							
Cunningham Ken	5.11	11.2	28/06/71	Dublin		Tolka Rov								
Ei: u21.4, B.1					18/09/89	Millwall	132+4	10	1	5+1	1			
				£650000	09/11/94	Wimbledon	60+1	2	12					
Elkins Gary	5.9	11.13	04/05/66	Wallingford	03/12/83	Fulham	100+4	6	2+2	7+1	2			
E: Y.11				Loan	23/12/89	Exeter City	5							
				£20000	20/08/90	Wimbledon	100+10	8	7	1+1	3		1	
Fitzgerald Scott	6.0	12.2	13/08/69	Westminster	13/07/89	Wimbledon	95+11	13	5	1	1			
Ei: B.1, u21.2				Loan	23/11/95	Sheffield United	6							
Futcher Andrew	5.7	10.07	10/02/78	Enfield	01/08/94	Wimbledon								
Hodges Danny	6.0	12.7	14/09/76	Greenwich		Wimbledon								
Jupp Duncan A	6.0	13.4	25/01/75	Haslemere	12/07/93	Fulham	101+4	10+2	9+1	9+1	2		1	1
					27/06/96	Wimbledon								
Kimble Alan	5.10	12.4	06/08/66	Dagenham	08/08/84	Charlton Athletic	6							
Div3'91				Loan	23/08/85	Exeter City	1	1						
				Free	22/08/86	Cambridge United	295+4	23+1	29	22	24		1	
				£175000	27/07/93	Wimbledon	71	6	11					
Laidlaw Iain	6.2	12.9	10/12/76	Newcastle-u-Tyne		Wimbledon								
McAllister Brian	5.11	12.5	30/11/70	Glasgow	01/03/89	Wimbledon	51+4	5	3	1				
				Loan	05/12/90	Plymouth Argyle	7+1							
				Loan	08/03/96	Crewe Alexandra	13			2	1			
Pearce Andy	6.6	14.6	20/04/66	Bradford-on-Avon		Halesowen Town								
				£500000	24/06/93	Sheffield Wed.	66+3	11+1	6+1		3		1	
				£600000	22/11/95	Wimbledon	6+1		1+2					
Perry Chris	5.8	10.8	20/04/75	Surrey	02/07/91	Wimbledon	52+9	4	10					
Reeves Alan	6.0	12.0	19/11/67	Birkenhead		Heswell								
					20/09/88	Norwich City								
				Loan	09/02/89	Gillingham	18							
				£10000	18/08/89	Chester City	31+9	1+1	3	3	2			
				Free	02/07/91	Rochdale	114+2	10	6	5	9	1		
				£300000	06/09/94	Wimbledon	52+3	1	8		4			
Thatcher Ben	5.10	11.10	30/11/75	Swindon	08/06/92	Millwall	46+2	4	5	1	1			
				£1900000	01/07/96	Wimbledon								
Thorn Andrew	6.0	11.5	12/11/66	Carshalton	13/11/84	Wimbledon	106+1	7	9	1	2			
E: u21.5. FAC'88				£850000	01/08/88	Newcastle United	36	4		3	2	1		
				£650000	05/12/89	Crystal Palace	128	19	10	11	3	4		
				Free	05/10/94	Wimbledon	33+4	2	3		1			
M I D F I E L D														
Castledine Stewart	6.1	12.13	22/01/73	Wandsworth	02/07/91	Wimbledon	10+5		1+1		3			
				Loan	25/08/95	Wycombe Wand.								
Earle Robbie	5.9	10.10	27/01/65	N'castle-u-Lyme	05/07/82	Port Vale	284+10	21+2	20+1	18+1	77	4	4	5
				£775000	19/07/91	Wimbledon	170	14	21	1	41	5	3	1
Fear Peter	5.10	11.7	10/09/73	Sutton	02/07/92	Wimbledon	37+8	3+2	2		1			
E: u21.3														
Jones Vinnie	6.0	11.12	05/01/65	Watford		Wealdstone								
FAC'88. Div2'90				£10000	20/11/86	Wimbledon	77	6+2	11+2	3	9		1	
				£650000	20/06/89	Leeds United	44+2	2	1	4	5			
				£700000	13/09/90	Sheffield United	35	4	1	1	2			
				£575000	30/08/91	Chelsea	42	1	4	5	4		1	2
				£700000	10/09/92	Wimbledon	120+4	13	11		9	2		
Leonhardsen Oyvind	5.10	11.02	17/08/70	Norway		Rosenborg								
Norwegian International				Loan	01/10/94	Wimbledon	18+2		3		4		1	
				£660000	01/08/95	Wimbledon	28+1	1+1	7		4		1	
Piper Len	5.6	9.10	08/08/77	Camberwell		Wimbledon								
F O R W A R D S														
Ardley Neal	5.11	11.9	01/09/72	Epsom	29/07/91	Wimbledon	59+12	9+2	8+2		6	2		
E: u21.10														
Blissett Gary	6.0	12.7	29/06/64	Manchester		Altrincham								
Div3'92					23/08/83	Crewe Alexandra	112+10	9		6+1	39	3		4
				£60000	26/03/87	Brentford	220+13	16+3	14	23+2	79	9	7	10
				£350000	23/07/93	Wimbledon	10+21	1+2	1+2		3			
				Loan	07/12/95	Wycombe Wand.	4				2			
				Loan	11/03/96	Crewe Alexandra	10			1+1	1			

Name	Ht	Wt	DOB	Birthplace	Fee	Date	Club	App Lge	App FAC	App LC	App Oth	Gls Lge	Gls FAC	Gls LC	Gls Oth
arke Andrew	5.10	11.7	22/07/67	Islington			Barnet			5+1				1	
S-P.2. GMVC'91					£250000	21/02/91	Wimbledon	69+76	9+7	8+4		16	3	2	
oku Efangwu	6.1	12.0	08/06/67	Manchester			Sutton United	1							
					£100000	11/05/90	Bournemouth	43+19	0+2	5+2	3+1	21		2	2
					£500000	26/03/93	Norwich City	21+10	2	1+1	3	15	1		1
					£900000	14/10/94	Wimbledon	52+3	1	10		16		3	
ell Jason	6.2	12.7	06/02/77	London			Wimbledon	4+5		1+5		2			
yle Marcus	6.1	12.9	27/09/70	Hammersmith		06/07/89	Brentford	118+38	6+3	6+2	14+6	22		2	2
.1. Div3'92					£250000	24/03/94	Wimbledon	53+14	4	6+2		7	1		
odman Jon	6.0	12.3	02/08/71	Walthamstow			West Ham United								
				Free			Bromley								
					£50000	20/08/90	Millwall	97+20	5+4	5+1	3	27			
					£650000	09/11/94	Wimbledon	22+24	0+1	3+1		10		3	
rford Mick	6.2	12.9	12/02/59	Sunderland		06/07/77	Lincoln City	109+6	8	3		41	5		
2, B.1. LC'88					£180000	24/12/80	Newcastle United	18+1				4			
					£160000	24/08/81	Bristol City	30	5	5		11	1	2	
					£100000	26/03/82	Birmingham City	92	10	7		25	6	2	
					£250000	13/12/84	Luton Town	135+4	16	27	4	57	10	11	3
					£450000	18/01/90	Derby County	58	7	1	2	15	3		
					£325000	12/09/91	Luton Town	29	1		1	12			
					£300000	13/08/92	Chelsea	27+1	5	1		9	2		
					£250000	18/03/93	Sunderland	10+1				2			
					£200000	12/07/93	Coventry City	0+1				1			
					£70000	18/08/94	Wimbledon	34+14	2+2	9+2		8	1	1	
dsworth Dean	5.11	11.13	08/11/68	Walthamstow		12/11/86	Watford	2+14			0+4	3			
.1. Div3'92					Loan	11/02/88	Carlisle United	4				1			
					Loan	18/03/88	Port Vale	6				2			
					Loan	25/08/88	Swansea City	4+1				1			
					Loan	13/10/88	Brentford	2+5				1			
					£125000	29/09/89	Brentford	106+4	7+1	6	12+2	53	6	7	9
					£720000	20/07/92	Wimbledon	134+5	12+1	10+4		53	9	5	
whouse Aidan	6.1	13.5	23/05/72	Wallasey		01/07/89	Chester City	29+15	5+1	0+2	2+3	6			1
13					£100000	22/02/90	Wimbledon	7+16	1+1	2	0+1	2			
					Loan	21/01/94	Port Vale	0+2		0+1					
					Loan	02/12/94	Portsmouth	6				1			
					Loan	07/12/95	Torquay United	4				2			
ne Grant	5.9	10.6	25/12/75	Woking		02/07/92	Wimbledon								

TIONAL CONTRACT PLAYERS

Name						Date	Club								
t Carl						07/06/96	Wimbledon (T)								
onnor Richard						07/06/96	Wimbledon (T)								
rle Stuart						14/06/96	Wimbledon (T)								

THE MANAGER
JOE KINNEAR

Date of Birth . . . . 27th December 1946.
Place of Birth . . . . Dublin.
Date of Appointment . . . . January 1991.

PREVIOUS CLUBS
As Manager. . . . . None.
As Reserve Team Manager. . . . . Wimbledon.
As a Player . . . . Tottenham Hotspur, Brighton & Hove Albion.

HONOURS
As a Manager
5 Managers' Manager Awards - Managers' Manager of 1994-95.

As a Player
Tottenham: FA Cup winner 1967. League Cup winner 1970/71, 1971/72. UEFA Cup winner 1972/73.
International: 26 full caps for Eire.

SELHURST PARK

London SE25 6PY
Tel: 0181 771 2233

Capacity 26,309

First game..v Sheffield Wed., Division 2, 30.8.1924.
First floodlit game ....v Chelsea, 28.9.1953.
ATTENDANCES
Highest ....30,115 v Manchester Utd, Prem, 9.5.1993.
Lowest..2,151 v Hereford, Lge Cup, 5.9.1993.

OTHER GROUNDS ....Plough Lane

MATCHDAY TICKET PRICES

Stanley Stephenson Lounge . . . . £20.
Juv/OAP . . . . £10.
Players Lounge or Glaziers . . . . £20.
Juv/OAP . . . . £10.
Family Enclosures (Blocks A&J) . . . . £10.
u16 . . . . £5
Arthur Wait Stand (Visitors) . . . . £15.
Block R reserved for visiting families . . . . . £10/£5 .
(Advance only)
Whitehorse Lane Stand. . . . . £11.
Juv/OAP £6
Wheelchairs/blind & partially sighted
 . . . . Contact club re special enclosure.
Ticket Office Telephone no. . . . . . . 0181 771 8841.

CLUBCALL
0891 12 11 75

Calls cost 39p per minute cheap rate and 49p per
minute at all other times.
Call costings correct at time of going to press.

HOW TO GET TO THE GROUND

From the North
From motorway (M1) or A1, use A406 North Circular Road to Chiswick. Follow
signs South Circular Road (A205) to Wandsworth. Then use A3 to A214 and fo
low signs to Streatham. Join A23. In 1 mile turn left (B273). At the end turn left
into High Street then forward into Whitehorse Lane for Crystal Palace FC.

From the East
Use A232 (sign posted Croydon) to Shirley then join A215 (sign posted
Norwood). In 2.2 miles turn left (B266) into Whitehouse Lane.

From the South
Use A23 (sign posted London) then follow signs Crystal Palace (B266) via
Thornton Heath into Whitehorse Lane.

From the West
Use motorway (M4) to Chiswick then route from North or A232 (sign posted
Croydon) to Beddington, then follow signs London A23. After, follow signs
Crystal Palace (B266) via Thornton Heath into Whitehorse Lane.

Car Parking: Sainsbury's car park (468 spaces) on first come first served basis
Street parking is also available.

Nearest Railway Station: Thornton Heath/Norwood Junction/Selhurst.

MATCHDAY PROGRAMME

Programme Editor . . . . Reg Davis.

Number of pages . . . . 48.

Price . . . . £1.80.

Subscriptions . . . . Home matches £55 including postage.
. . . . Home & away £95 including postage.

Local Newspapers. . . . . . . Wimbledon Guardian, South London Press
. . . . Wimbledon News, Surrey Comet.

Local Radio Stations . . . . Capital Radio.

NATIONWIDE
LEAGUE DIVISION 1

FINAL LEAGUE TABLE

		P	W	D	L	F	A	PTS
1	Sunderland (+19)	46	22	17	7	59	33	83
2	Derby County (+7)	46	21	16	9	71	51	79
3	Crystal Palace	46	20	15	11	67	48	75
4	Stoke City (+7)	46	20	13	13	60	49	73
5	**Leicester City**	46	19	14	13	66	60	71
6	Charlton Athletic (+9)	46	17	20	9	57	45	71
7	Ipswich Town	46	19	12	15	79	69	69
8	Huddersfield Town	46	17	12	17	61	58	63
9	Sheffield United (-1)	46	16	14	16	57	54	62
10	Barnsley (-4)	46	14	18	14	60	66	60
11	West Bromwich A (+8)	46	16	12	18	60	68	60
12	Port Vale (+5)	46	15	15	16	59	66	60
13	Tranmere Rovers (-8)	46	14	17	15	64	60	59
14	Southend United (-1)	46	15	14	17	52	61	59
15	Birmingham City	46	15	13	18	61	64	58
16	Norwich City	46	14	15	17	59	55	57
17	Grimsby Town (-7)	46	14	14	18	55	69	56
18	Oldham Athletic (-4)	46	14	14	18	54	50	56
19	Reading (-17)	46	13	17	16	54	63	56
20	Wolverhampton W (-16)	46	13	16	17	56	62	55
21	Portsmouth (-3)	46	13	13	20	61	69	52
22	Millwall (-10)	46	13	13	20	43	63	52
23	Watford (-16)	46	10	18	18	62	70	48
24	Luton (-8)	46	11	12	23	40	64	45

The figure in brackets denotes the number of places lost or gained on the clubs 1994-95 final position.

NATIONWIDE LEAGUE DIVISION ONE - 1996-97

BARNSLEY
(The Tykes)
NATIONWIDE LEAGUE DIVISION 1
SPONSORED BY: ORA ELECTRONICS

ack Row (L-R): Scott Jones, Robert Hanby, Chris Jackson, Russell Harmer, Brendon O'Connell, Glynn Hurst, Steve Davies, Troy Bennett, harlie Bishop, Dean Fearon, Luke Bennett. **2nd Row:** Paul Smith (Physio), Eric Winstanley (Coach), Darren Clyde, David Brooke, Andy ammell, Adam Solite, Lee Butler, David Watson, Gerry Taggart (now Bolton), Andy Liddell, Mark Burton, Colin Walker (Yth Coach), alcolm Shotton (Res. Coach). **3rd Row:** Shane Hulson, Chris Morgan, Mark Feeney, Jonathan Perry, Andrew Gregory, Neil Redfearn, cky Eaden, Gary Fleming, Danny Wilson (Manager), Andy Payton, Owen Archdeacon, Martin Bullock, Darren Sheridan, Adrian Moses, mon Bochenski, Sean McClare, Richard Cannon. **Front Row:** Sean Hayes, Mark Hume, Craig Deacon, Dean Jones, Steven Clayton, ynn Clyde, Rudi Coleano, Ian Shaw, Duanne Beckett, Carl Rose, Paul Bashaw, Daniel Shenton, Chris Harris.

BARNSLEY
FORMED IN 1887
TURNED PROFESSIONAL IN 1888
LTD COMPANY IN 1899

PRESIDENT: Arthur Raynor
CHAIRMAN: John Dennis
VICE-CHAIRMAN: Barry Taylor
DIRECTORS:
Michael Hall, Christopher Harrison,
Michael Hayselden, John Kelly, Ian Potter.

GENERAL MANAGER/SECRETARY:
Michael Spinks
MARKETING MANAGER
Ian Davies

MANAGER: Danny Wilson
FIRST TEAM COACH: Eric Winstanley
RESERVE TEAM COACH: Malcolm Shotton

YOUTH TEAM COACH
Colin Walker

PHYSIOTHERAPIST
Michael Tarmey & Paul Smith

LUB STATISTICIAN FOR THE DIRECTORY
Ian Sawyer

Danny Wilson has built a very sound squad who could be setting their sights on a play-off place this season.

Finishing in tenth place last season, tucked in behind fellow Yorkshire challengers Huddersfield Town and Sheffield United, it was only two surprise home defeats in April that really put the 'The Tykes' out of the reckoning last season.

A settled defence was well served by under-21 International goalkeeper David Watson and another local lad Nick Eaden who were both ever present and the quality passing game adopted by the squad was reminiscent of the manager Danny Wilson's personal style of football.

Andy Liddell enjoyed his partnership with the experienced Neil Redfearn and also underlined the success of the club's excellent youth policy.

The highlight of the campaign was probably the visit of Arsenal, although the Gunners won 3-0 at Oakwell in the Coca-Cola Cup, after a thrilling 4-0 home victory over Huddersfield had given Barnsley a 4-2 aggregate victory in the First Round.

The attendance of 18,429 really gave the very smart stadium an exciting atmosphere and gave the loyal 6,000 regulars a treat.

Sadly there was no success in the F.A. Cup as Oldham Athletic left Oakwell with a goalless draw and won the replay 2-1.

However, the solid defence and neat, effective midfield will have the experienced Paul Wilkinson up front this season so watch out for a challenge from the Barnsley Reds.

TONY WILLIAMS.

BARNSLEY

League: 10th   FA Cup: 3rd Rnd   Coca-Cola Cup: 3rd Rnd

M	DATE	COMP	VEN	OPPONENTS	RESULT	HT	LP	GOAL SCORERS/GOAL TIMES	ATT.
1	A 12	EL	A	Crystal Palace	L 3-4	1-2	15	Davis 12, Viveash 63, Liddell 73	(12067)
2	19	EL	H	Oldham Athletic	W 2-1	1-0	11	Payton 37, Redfern 67(pen)	8793
3	26	EL	A	Watford	W 3-2	1-1	5	Rammell 25, 71, Davis 79	(8409)
4	29	EL	H	Tranmere Rovers	W 2-1	2-1	3	Payton 18, Davis 34	9710
5	S 2	EL	H	Birmingham City	L 0-5	0-0	7		11129
6	9	EL	A	Millwall	W 1-0	1-0	3	Redfern 2	(9272)
7	12	EL	A	Huddersfield Town	L 0-3	0-1	5		(14635)
8	17	EL	H	Sheffield United	D 2-2	2-0	7	Davis 9, Payton 35	7150
9	19	CC 2/1	A	**Huddersfield Town**	**L 0-2**	**0-1**			**(8264)**
10	23	EL	H	Derby County	W 2-0	2-0	4	Liddell 8, 44	8929
11	30	EL	A	Charlton Athletic	D 1-1	0-1	3	Redfern 90	(11219)
12	O 3	CC 2/2	H	**Huddersfield Town**	**W 4-0**	**2-0**		**Payton 27, 71, 77 (3), Rammell 88**	**8912**
13	7	EL	H	Leicester City	D 2-2	1-1	5	Payton 41, Bullock 69	13669
14	14	EL	A	Norwich City	L 1-3	1-0	8	Eaden 19	(14002)
15	21	EL	H	Port Vale	D 1-1	1-1	10	Archdeacon 2	7332
16	24	CC 3	H	**Arsenal**	**L 0-3**	**0-2**			**18429**
17	28	EL	A	Sunderland	L 1-2	0-1	12	Liddell 69	(17024)
18	N 4	EL	H	Wolverhampton Wand	W 1-0	0-0	8	Redfern 77	9668
19	11	EL	A	Grimsby Town	L 1-3	1-2	10	Davis 2	(6166)
20	18	EL	A	Reading	D 0-0	0-0	12		(6695)
21	21	EL	H	Portsmouth	D 0-0	0-0	13		6187
22	25	EL	H	Luton Town	W 1-0	0-0	12	Redfern 68	6437
23	D 2	EL	A	Leicester City	D 2-2	2-1	12	Payton 21, 40	(15125)
24	9	EL	A	Derby County	L 1-4	0-1	14	Rammell 76	(14415)
25	16	EL	H	Charlton Athletic	L 1-2	0-2	15	Payton 54	6140
26	22	EL	A	Ipswich Town	D 2-2	0-1	15	Zeeuw 54, Liddell 61	(11791)
27	26	EL	H	Stoke City	W 3-1	2-0	13	Redfern 30, Rammell 43, Liddell 62	9229
28	J 1	EL	A	Southend United	D 0-0	0-0	13		(6537)
29	6	FAC 3	H	**Oldham Athletic**	**D 0-0**	**0-0**			**9751**
30	13	EL	A	Oldham Athletic	W 1-0	0-0	10	Payton 72	(6029)
31	20	EL	H	Crystal Palace	D 1-1	0-1	12	Liddell 59	6620
32	23	FAC 3R	A	**Oldham Athletic**	**L 1-2**	**0-1**		**Redfern 57**	**(6670)**
33	F 3	EL	H	Watford	W 2-1	0-0	8	Archdeacon 49, Payton 77	6139
34	10	EL	A	Tranmere Rovers	W 3-1	0-0	6	Payton 49, 83, Redfern 80(pen)	(6376)
35	20	EL	A	Birmingham City	D 0-0	0-0	6		(14168)
36	24	EL	A	Sheffield United	L 0-1	0-1	7		(14584)
37	27	EL	H	Millwall	W 3-1	0-1	5	Payton 58, Payton 90, Liddell 90	6331
38	M 2	EL	A	Stoke City	L 0-2	0-1	6		(12663)
39	9	EL	H	Ipswich Town	D 3-3	2-0	8	Redfern 24(pen), 47, Liddell 32	7705
40	16	EL	A	West Bromwich Albion	L 1-2	0-2	10	Payton 57	(12701)
41	19	EL	H	Huddersfield Town	W 3-0	2-0	8	Eaden 2, Redfern 23, Archdeacon 50	10660
42	23	EL	H	Southend United	D 1-1	1-1	9	Payton 27	6754
43	30	EL	A	Port Vale	L 0-3	0-1	10		(7358)
44	A 2	EL	H	Norwich City	D 2-2	1-1	10	Redfern 8, Payton 62	6375
45	6	EL	H	Sunderland	L 0-1	0-1	11		13189
46	8	EL	A	Wolverhampton Wand	D 2-2	1-1	11	Moses 13, Payton 85	(23789)
47	13	EL	H	Reading	L 0-1	0-0	12		5488
48	20	EL	A	Portsmouth	D 0-0	0-0	14		(8744)
49	27	EL	A	Luton Town	W 3-1	2-0	13	Redfern 30, O'Connell 41, Redfern 72	(6194)
50	30	EL	H	West Bromwich Albion	D 1-1	1-1	10	Regis 20	6981
51	M 4	EL	H	Grimsby Town	D 1-1	1-1	10	Redfern 18	6108

Best Home League Attendance: 13669 v Leicester City   Smallest: 5488 v Reading   Average: 8118

Goal Scorers:
EL(60):   Payton(17),Redfern(14),Liddell(9),Davis(5),Rammell(4),Archdeacon(3),Eaden(2),Zeeuw(1),Viveash(1),Regis(1),Moses(1),O'Connell(1),Bullock(1)
CC(4):   Payton(3),Rammell(1)
FAC(1):   Redfern(1)

(F) Archdeacon	(D) Bishop	(F) Bochenski	(M) Bullock	(G) Butler	(D) Davis	(D) Eaden	(D) Fearon	(D) Fleming	(D) Hurst	(F) Jackson	(D) Jones	(M) Kane	(M) Laurens	(F) Liddell	(M) Molby	(D) Moses	(F) O'Connell	(F) Payton	(F) Rammell	(M) Redfern	(F) Regis	(M) Sheridan	(D) Shirtliff	(D) Shotton	(F) Van	(D) Viveash	(G) Watson	(D) Zeeuw	Referee	#
X	X		X1	S	X	X					X		X		S			X	S1	X						X	X		P.Rejer	1
X	X		S1	S	X	X		X		S		X		X1				X	X	X							X		T.West	2
	X		X1	S1	X	X						X		X1				X	X	X		X3	X4				X		M.Pierce	3
S	X		S1	S	X	X						X		X				X1	X	X		X	X				X		K.Leach	4
X	X		X	S1		X		S		S			X				X		X		X	X			X1		X		T.Heilbron	5
X	X		S1	S	X	X		S		X1			X				X		X		X	X					X		J.Rushton	6
X	X		X		X	X	S1		X1				X				X		X		X2	X					X		P.Richards	7
X		S	S1	X	X	X	X2		X				X		S2		X1		X		X		X	X					R.D.Furnandiz	8
X	X		X	S	X	X							X		S		X		X		X	X		X			X		I. Cruikshanks	9
X	X		X1	S	X	X							X		X		X		X		X		S				X		G.Willard	10
X	X		S2		X	X						X1	X	X			X		X		X		X2				X		R.Harris	11
X	X	S	S1	S	X	X					X				X1		X1		X2		X	X					X		J.W.Lloyd	12
X	X		S1	S	X	X					X				X	X1	X2		X		X		X				X		D.B.Allison	13
X	X		S1		X2		X				X1	X	X				S2		X		X						X		E.Lomas	14
X	X		X		X2		X1				X	X2		X	S1	S2		S2		X							X		S.W.Mathieson	15
X	X		X	S	X1		S				X			X	X	S1	X		X				X1				X		J.T.Winter	16
X			X		X		S				X			X	S1	X		X					X1		X		X		W.C.Burns	17
X			S1		X	X							X1		S		X	X		X	X				X		X	X	K.J.Breen	18
X			S1	S	X	X							X1		S		X	X		X	X				X		X	X	G.Cain	19
X			X	S	X	X		S					X				X	S		X	X				X		X	X	G.Barber	20
X			X	S	X	X			S1				X2				X1	S2		X	X				X		X	X	J.Rushton	21
X			X	S	X	X			S				X1				X	S1		X	X				X		X	X	A.R.Leake	22
X			X1		X	X							X2		S1		X	S2		X	X				X		X	X	E.Wolstenholme	23
X			X		X	X							X1		S2		S1	X		X2	X				X		X	X	G.Frankland	24
X			S2	S		X							X		X	S1	X2	X		X1	X				X		X	X	G.Singh	25
X	S		S			X							X1		X	X	S1	X		X	X				X		X	X	D.Orr	26
X	S		S		X	X							X		X	X	X	X		X	X				X		X	X	N.S.Berry	27
X			S2	S	X	X							X1		X	S1	X	X		X2	X				X		X	X	K.Breen	28
			S		X	X							X	S1	X	X	X	X		X1	X				X		X	X	G.Cain	29
X			S1	S	X	X							X	S	X	X		X	X1				X	X1			X	X	P.Rejer	30
X			S1	S	X	X							X	S		X	X		X				X	X1			X	X	T.Heilbron	31
X		S2	S1		X2	X							X		X	X1	X		X				X				X	X	G.Cain	32
X			X		X	X							X1		S	X	X	S1		X			S	X			X	X	M.Fletcher	33
X1			X		X		X						X		X	X	X			X			S1	X			X	X	R.Harris	34
	S		X		X	X		S					X		X	X	X			X			X	X			X	X	K.Lynch	35
	S1		X		X1	X							X		X	X			X	S2			X	X			X	X	E.Lomas	36
X	S		X			X							X		X1	X			X	S1			X	X			X	X	W.C.Burns	37
X			X	S		X		S1					X		S	X1	X			X			X	X			X	X	R.Gifford	38
X				S		X		S		X			X		S	X	X			X			X	X			X	X	I.Cruikshanks	39
X			S1	S		X				X1			X		S2	X	X			X			X	X2			X	X	B.Knight	40
X			S1	S		X							X		X	X1	X			X	S1		X	X			X	X	R.Gifford	41
X			S1	S		X							X1		X	X	X			X	S2		X	X2			X	X	K.Leach	42
			S2	S		X							X1		X	X	X			X	S1		X	X	X2		X	X	R.Pearson	43
			X	S		X			S1			S			X	X	X			X	X1		X		X		X	X	K.M.Lynch	44
			X			X					S			X	X2		X			X	S1		X	X		X1	X	X	P.Richards	45
			X			X					S			X	X	S	X			X	S1		X	X1		X	X	X	N.Barry	46
X			X			X			S1			S			X	X	S2	X2		X	S1			X1		X	X	X	K.Breen	47
X			X			X						S	X1	X		X	X			X	X					S	X	X	D.Orr	48
X			X			X			S1			S	S1	X		X	X			X1	X				S2		X	X	J.Brandwood	49
X			X			X						S	S1	X		X	X			X1	X			S2			X	X	G.Barber	50
S1			X1			X			S2			X	X2	X		X	X			X				X			X	X	T.Heilbron	51
36	12	0	26	1	27	45	1	2	0	6	4	4	1	43	4	21	19	36	11	45	4	37	32	2	6	2	45	31	EL Appearances	
1	1	0	15	2	0	0	0	1	5	2	0	0	2	0	0	3	4	3	9	0	8	2	0	0	1	0	0	0	EL Sub Appearances	
3	3	0	2+1	0	3	3	0	0	0	1	0	0	0	2	0	2	0	3	1+1	3	0	3	0	1	0	0	3	0	CC Appearances	
2	0	0+1	0+2	0	2	2	0	0	0	0	0	0	0	2	0	1	2	1+1	1	2	0	2	1	0	0	0	2	2	FAC Appearances	

BARNSLEY

BIGGEST VICTORIES
League: 9-0 v Loughborough Town, Division 2, 28.1.1899.
9-0 v Accrington Stanley, Division 3N, 3.2.1934 (a).
F.A. Cup: 8-0 v Leeds City, Qualifying Rnd, 3.11.1894.
League Cup: 6-0 v Peterborough, Round 1, 15.9.1981.

BIGGEST DEFEATS
League: 0-9 v Notts County, Division 2, 19.11.1927.
F.A. Cup: 1-8 v Derby County, Round 1, 30.1.1897.
League Cup: No defeat by more than 3 goals.

MOST POINTS
3 points a win: 74, Division 2, 1988-89.
2 points a win: 67, Division 3N, 1938-39.

MOST GOALS SCORED
118 Division 3(N), 1933-34.

MOST GOALS CONCEDED
108, Division 2, 1952-53.

MOST FIRST CLASS MATCHES IN A SEASON
58 - 1960-61 (46 League, 10 FA Cup, 2 League Cup).

MOST LEAGUE WINS
30, Division 3(N), 1938-39.
30, Division 3(N), 1954-55.

MOST LEAGUE DRAWS
18, Division 3, 1971-72.

MOST LEAGUE DEFEATS
29, Division 2, 1952-53.

INDIVIDUAL CLUB RECORDS

MOST GOALS IN A SEASON
Cecil McCormack: 34 - 1950-51 (League 33, FAC 1).

MOST GOALS IN A MATCH
5, F.Eaton v South Shields, 6-1, Division 3(N), 9.4.1927.
5, P.Cunningham v Darlington, 6-2, Division 3(N), 4.2.1933.
5, B.Asquith v Darlington, 7-1, Division 3(N), 12.11.1938.
5, C.McCormack v Luton, 6-1, Division 2, 9.9.1950.

OLDEST PLAYER
Beaumont Asquith, 37 years 3 months v Coventry City, 19.11.1927.

YOUNGEST PLAYER
Glyn Riley, 16 years 171 days v Torquay United, 11.1.1975.

MOST CAPPED PLAYER
Gerry Taggart (Northern Ireland) 24 caps.

BEST PERFORMANCES

League: 1938-39: Matches played 42, Won 30, Drawn 7, Lost 5, Goals for 94, Goals against 34, Points 67. First in Division 3(N).
Highest Position: 1914-15, 1921-22, Third Division 2.
F.A. Cup: 1911-12: 3rd Rnd. Birmingham City 0-0,3-1; 4th Rnd. Leicester City 1-0; Bolton Wanderers 2-1; 6th Rnd. Bradford City 0-0,0-0,0-0,3-0; Semi-Final Swindon Town 0-0, 1-0; Final West Bromwich Albion 0-0,1-0.
League Cup: 1981-82: 1st Rnd. Peterborough United 3-2,6-0; 2nd Rnd. Swansea City 2-0,2-3; 3rd Rnd. Brighton & Hove Albion 4-1; 4th Rnd. Manchester City 1-0; 5th Rnd. Liverpool 0-0,1-3.

ADDITIONAL INFORMATION
PREVIOUS NAMES
Barnsley St.Peters.
PREVIOUS LEAGUES
Midland.

Club Colours: Red shirts, white shorts, red & white hooped socks.
Change Colours:

Reserves League: Pontins League Division 2.
Youth League: Northern Intermediate League.

DIVISIONAL RECORD

	Played	Won	Drawn	Lost	For	Against	Points
Division 2/1	2,458	849	608	1,001	3,395	3,850	2,549
Division 3	552	183	159	210	736	838	525
Division 3N	218	130	38	50	467	278	298
Division 4	460	177	127	156	628	555	481
Total	3,688	1,339	932	1,403	5,226	5,521	3,853

RECORDS AND STATISTICS

COMPETITIONS

Div.2/1	Div.3	Div.3(N)	Div.4
1898-32	1959-65	1932-34	1965-68
1934-38	1968-72	1938-39	1972-79
1939-53	1979-81	1953-55	
1955-59			
1981-			

HONOURS

Div.3(N)	FA Cup
1933-34	1911-12
1938-39	
1954-55	

MOST APPEARANCES

BARRY MURPHY 564 (1962-78)

Year	League	FA Cup	Lge Cup
1962-63	21		2
1963-64	4		1
1964-65	22	1	1
1965-66	7+3		2
1966-67	14		
1967-68	46	1	1
1968-69	46	6	3
1969-70	46	4	1
1970-71	45	4	1
1971-72	46	3	3
1972-73	42	2	2
1973-74	10+1		2
1974-75	35	1	1
1975-76	36+1		2
1976-77	46	2	4
1977-78	43	2	3
	509+5	26	29

MOST GOALS IN A CAREER

ERNIE HINE - 130 (1921-26 & 1934-38)

Year	League	FA Cup
1921-22	12	1
1922-23	23	1
1923-24	19	
1924-25	15	
1925-26	12	
1934-35	9	
1935-36	14	5
1936-37	13	
1937-38	6	
Total	123	7

Current top goalscorer: Neil Redfern - 50 (1991-96)

RECORD TRANSFER FEE RECEIVED

Amount	Club	Player	Date
£1,400,000	Nott'm Forest	Carl Tiler	5/91
£750,000	Nott'm Forest	David Currie	1/90
£350,000	Huddersfield	Andy Payton	7/96
£300,000	Portsmouth	John Beresford	3/89

RECORD TRANSFER FEE PAID

Amount	Club	Player	Date
£250,000	Oldham Athletic	David Currie	9/91
£200,000	Aston Villa	Gareth Williams	8/91
£180,000	Burnley	Steve Davies	7/91
£175,000	Barnet	Phil Gridelet	9/90

MANAGERS

Name	Seasons	Best	Worst
John McCartney	1901-04	8(2)	11(2)
Arthur Fairclough	1904-12	6(2)	19(2)
John Hastie	1912-14	4(2)	5(2)
Harry Lewis	1914-19	3(2)	13(2)
Peter Sant	1919-26	3(2)	16(2)
John Commins	1926-29	11(2)	16(2)
Arthur Fairclough	1929-30	17(2)	17(2)
Brough Fletcher	1930-37	14(2)	8(3N)
Angus Seed	1937-53	9(2)	1(3N)
Tim Ward	1953-60	16(2)	17(3N)
John Steel	1960-71	7(3)	18(4)
John McSeventy	1971-72	22(3)	22(3)
John Steel	1972-73	14(4)	14(4)
Jim Iley	1973-78	6(4)	13(4)
Allan Clarke	1978-80	11(3)	4(4)
Norman Hunter	1980-84	6(2)	2(3)
Bobby Collins	1984-85	11(2)	11(2)
Alan Clarke	1985-89	7(2)	14(2)
Mel Machin	1989-93	8(2)	19(2)
Viv Anderson (P)	1993-94	18(1/2)	18(1/2)
Danny Wilson (P)	1994-	6(1)	10(1)

LONGEST LEAGUE RUNS

of undefeated matches:	21 (1.10.1933 - 5.5.1934)	of league matches w/out a win:	26 (13.12.52 - 29.8.53)
of undefeated home matches:	36 (6.2.1933 - 24.11.1934)	of undefeated away matches:	10 (27.12.1938 - 15.4.1939)
without home win:	11 (6.12.1952 - 24.9.1953)	without an away win:	29 (14.3.1908 - 19.11.1910)
of league wins:	10 (5.2.1955 - 23.4.1955)	of home wins:	12 (3.10.1914 - 8.3.1915)
of league defeats:	9 (14.3.1953 - 25.4.1953)	of away wins:	5 (27.12.1938 - 25.2.1939)

BARNSLEY

PLAYERS NAME Honours	Ht	Wt	Birthdate	Birthplace Transfers	Contract Date	Clubs	League	L/Cup	FA Cup	Other	Lge	L/C	FAC	Oth
G O A L K E E P E R S														
Watson David N	6.0	12.0	10/11/73	Barnsley	04/07/92	Barnsley	96	9	3	1				
E: u21.2,Y.8.														
D E F E N D E R S														
Appleby Matthew W	5.10	11.0	16/04/72	Middlesbrough	04/05/90	Newcastle United	18+2	2+1	2	2+2				
				Loan	25/11/93	Darlington	10		1		1			
				Free	15/06/94	Darlington	77+2	2	4	8	7			3
				£250000	16/07/96	Barnsley								
Clyde Darran	6.4	13.0	26/03/76	N.Ireland	28/03/95	Barnsley								
Davis Steven	6.0	12.7	26/07/65	Birmingham		Stoke City								
E: Y.1.				Free	17/08/83	Crewe Alexandra	140+5	10	3	7+1	1			
				£15000	03/10/87	Burnley	147	7	9	19	11			
				£180000	26/07/91	Barnsley	79+4	5	3		7			
De Zeeuw Arjan						Telstar								
				£250000	01/11/95	Barnsley	31		2		1			
Eaden Nicholas	5.10	11.3	12/12/72	Sheffield	04/06/91	Barnsley	126+3	6+1	7	2	5			
Fearon Dean	6.1	13.12	09/01/76	Barnsley	06/07/94	Barnsley	1							
Fleming Gary	5.9	11.1	17/02/67	Londonderry	19/11/84	Nottingham Forest	71+3	5+1	2+1	0+1				
NI: 28.				£150000	17/08/89	Manchester City	13+1	4		1				
				Loan	08/03/90	Notts County	3			1				
				£85000	23/03/90	Barnsley	236+3	14	12	6				
Hurst Glynn	5.10	11.06	17/01/76	Barnsley		Tottenham Hotspur								
				Free	13/07/94	Barnsley	0+7							
Jones Scott	5.10	11.06	01/05/75	Sheffield	01/02/94	Barnsley	4							
Moses Adrian	6.1	12.5	04/05/75	Doncaster	02/07/93	Barnsley	24+4	2	2		1			
Shirtliff Peter	6.0	13.3	06/04/61	Hoyland	31/10/78	Sheffield Wed.	188	17+1	17+1		4		1	
LC'91.				£125000	06/08/86	Charlton Athletic	102+1	10	5	7	7			
				£500000	26/07/89	Sheffield Wed.	104+4	18+1	9+2	4				
				£250000	18/08/93	Wolves	65+2	4	7	5				
				£200000	25/08/95	Barnsley	32		1					
Shotton Malcolm	6.3	13.12	16/02/57											
Viveash Adrian	6.1	11.2	30/09/69											
M I D F I E L D														
Bennett Tory	5.4	11.08	25/12/75	Barnsley		Barnsley	2							
E: Y.1.														
Bullock Martin	5.5	10.07	05/03/75	Derby		Eastwood Town								
				£15000	04/09/93	Barnsley	43+27	2+1	0+3	1	1			
Burton Marc	5.9	10.6	07/05/73	Barnsley	06/07/91	Barnsley	5		2					
Feeney Mark	5.7	11.0	26/07/74											
Kane Paul	5.8	9.9	20/06/65											
Redfern Neil	5.10	12.4	20/06/65	Dewsbury		Nottingham Forest								
Div.2'91.				Free	23/06/82	Bolton Wanderers	35	2	4		1			
				£8250	23/03/84	Lincoln City	96+4	4	3	7	13		1	
					22/08/86	Doncaster Rovers	46	2	3	2	14		1	
				£100000	31/07/87	Crystal Palace	57	6	1	1	10			
				£150000	21/11/88	Watford	22+2	1	6	5	3		3	1
				£150000	12/01/90	Oldham Athletic	56+6	3	7+1	1	16	1	3	
				£150000	05/09/91	Barnsley	209+3	14	12	5	44	3	3	
Sheridan Darren	5.6	10.12	08/12/67	Manchester		Winsford United			1					
				£10000	12/08/93	Barnsley	74+3	3	3	1+1	2			
Ten Heuvel Laurens						FC Den Bosch								
				£75000	12/03/96	Barnsley								
Wilson Danny	5.7	10.3	01/01/60	Wigan		Wigan Athletic			1					
NI:24. ASC'81. LC'88'91.				Free	21/09/77	Bury	87+3	4	11		8		2	
				£100000	22/07/80	Chesterfield	100	8	9		13	1	1	
				£50000	24/01/83	Nottingham Forest	9+1			0+1	1			
				Loan	07/10/83	Scunthorpe United	6				3			
				£100000	30/11/83	Brighton & H.A.	132+3	7	10	3	33	3	1	2
				£150000	16/07/87	Luton Town	110	20	8	4	24	3	2	
				£200000	08/08/90	Sheffield Wednesday	91+7	22	9+1	5+2	11	2		1
				£200000	01/07/93	Barnsley	77	6	5	1	2			
F O R W A R D S														
Bochenski Simon	5.8	11.13	06/12/75	Worksop	06/07/94	Barnsley			0+1					
Jackson Chris D	6.0	12.0	16/01/76	Barnsley	19/01/93	Barnsley	16+7	2+1		0+1	2			

E: Y.2, SFA u15.

Player	Ht	Wt	DOB	Birthplace	Fee	Date	Club								
Liddell Andrew	5.8	10.5	28/06/73	Leeds		06/07/91	Barnsley	101+25	5+1	4+1	2+1	25	1		
S: u21.1.															
Payton Andy	5.9	10.6	03/10/67	Whalley		29/07/85	Hull City	116+28	9+2	8	3	55	2		
					£750000	22/11/91	Middlesbrough	8+11		1+3		3			
						14/08/92	Celtic	20+18	3+2	1+1	3	15	5		
					£100000	25/11/93	Barnsley	99+8	7	6+1		41	3	1	
Regis David	6.3	13.0	03/03/64	Paddington			Dunstable								
Clubcall Cup. Div.3'92							Fisher Athletic								
					£8000		Barnet								
					£25000	28/09/90	Notts County	31+15	0+2		6	16			2
					£200000	07/11/91	Plymouth Argyle	28+3	2	1		4	3		
					Loan	13/08/92	Bournemouth	6+2							
					£100000	23/10/92	Stoke City	49+14	2	4+1	7+1	15	1	2	2
					£200000	01/08/94	Birmingham City	4+2	1			2			
					£100000	16/09/94	Southend United	9				1			
						21/02/96	Barnsley	29+12	1	1		9			
Van Der Velden Carel							FC Den Bosch								
					£75000	12/03/96	Barnsley	6+1							
Wilkinson Paul	6.0	11.9	30/10/69	Louth		08/11/82	Grimsby Town	69+2	10	4+2		27	5	1	
E: u21.4; CS'86; Div1'87					£250000	28/03/85	Everton	19+12	3+1	3	6+2	6	7	1	1
					£200000	26/03/87	Nottingham Forest	32+2	3	4+1	1	5	1	2	
					£300000	16/08/88	Watford	133+1	4	8+1	8	52	1		3
					£550000	16/08/91	Middlesbrough	159+4	16	11	5+1	53	8	5	4
					Loan	26/10/95	Oldham Athletic	4			1	1			1
					Loan	01/12/95	Watford	4							
					Loan	28/03/96	Luton Town	3							
					Free	19/07/96	Barnsley								
ADDITIONAL CONTRACT PLAYERS															
Beckett Luke J						11/05/96	Barnsley (T)								
Gregory Andrew							Barnsley (T)								
Rose Karl							Barnsley (T)								
Sollitt Adam						16/05/96	Barnsley (T)								
Thompson Neil						10/06/96	Barnsley (T)								

THE MANAGER
DANNY WILSON (PLAYER MANAGER)

Date of Birth . . . . 1st January 1960.
Place of Birth . . . . Wigan.
Date of Appointment . . . . July 1994.

PREVIOUS CLUBS
As Manager . . . . None.
As Coach . . . . Barnet.
As a Player . . . . Wigan Athletic, Bury, Chesterfield, Nottingham Forest,
. . . . Brighton & H.A., Luton Town and Sheffield Wednesday.

HONOURS
As a Manager
None.

As a Player

Luton Town: League Cup runner-up 1988.
Sheffield Wednesday: League Cup winner 1991
International: 25 full caps for Northern Ireland.

Oakwell Ground

Grove Street, Barnsley, Yorkshire S71 1ET
Tel: 01226 211211

Capacity . . . . .19006 (All seater).
First game . . . . .v Gawber (Friendly) 15.10.1887 (0-0).
First floodlit game . . . . .v Bolton W. (Friendly) 23.1.1962.

ATTENDANCES
Highest . . . . .40,255 v Stoke City, FA Cup 5th Rnd, 15.2.1936.
Lowest . . . . .1,627 v Grimsby Town, Anglo Italian Cup, 14.9.93.

MATCHDAY TICKET PRICES

East Stand Upper Tier £12.50
OAP/Juveniles. £6.50
East Stand Lower Tier £11
OAP/Juveniles £6
The Ora Stand £10.50
OAP/Juveniles £6

Visiting Supporters
West Stand Upper Tier £12.50
West Stand Lower Tier £11
Spion Kop £10.50

Ticket Office Telephone No. . . . . . 01226 295 353.

HOW TO GET TO THE GROUND

From The North
M1 to J37. Take A628 towards Barnsley and follow signs for Football Ground.

From The South
M1 to J37. Proceed as above.

From The East
A635 towards Barnsley and follow signs for Football Ground.

From The West
A628 towards Barnsley and shortly after crossing M1 Jnt 37 follow signs for Football Ground.

Car Parking: Official car parks for 1,200 vehicles adjacent to ground. Cost £1. Visitors use Queens Ground car park.

Railway Station: Barnsley 01742 26411.

CLUBCALL
0891 12 11 52
Calls cost 39p per minute cheap rate and 49p per minute at all other times.
Call costings correct at time of going to press.

MATCHDAY PROGRAMME

Programme Editor. . . . . Keith Lodge

Number of pages 32

Price . . . . £1.50.

Subscriptions. . . . . . . £34.50 for 23 home fixtures (inc post & packing)

Local Newspapers . Barnsley Chronicle (weekly), Barnsley Star (Daily)
. . . . Yorkshire Post, Yorkshire on Sunday.

Local Radio Stations . . . . Radio Sheffield, Hallam FM.

BIRMINGHAM CITY
(The Blues)
NATIONWIDE LEAGUE DIVISION 1
SPONSORED BY: AUTO-WINDSCREENS

Back Row (L-R): Lil Fuccillo (Chief Scout), Kenny Lowe, Ken Charlery, Peter Shearer, Dave Barnett, Simon Black, Ryan Price, Liam Daish (Team Capt), Andy Edwards, Chris Whyte, Steve Castle, John Frain (Club Capt), Neil McDairmid (Physio). **Middle Row:** David Howell (Res. Manager), Ian Muir, John Bass, Paul Challinor, Steve Claridge, Paul Harding, Ian Bennett, Gary Poole, Ben Sedgemore, Neil Doherty, Steve Finnan, Paul Tait, Edwin Stein (Asst. Manager). **Front Row:** Richard Forsyth, Ricky Otto, Jason Bowen, Steve Robinson, Jae Martin, Barry Fry (Manager), Jonathon Hunt, Louie Donowa, Mark Ward (Player coach), Scott Hiley, Gary Cooper.

**BIRMINGHAM CITY
FORMED IN** 1875
TURNED PROFESSIONAL IN 1885
LTD COMPANY IN 1888

CHAIRMAN: J F Wiseman
Managing Director: Karren Brady

DIRECTORS:
D Sullivan, A Jones, D Gold, B Gold, R Gold,
H Brandhan
SECRETARY: Alan G Jones, BA, MBA
COMMERCIAL MANAGER
Allan Robson

MANAGER: Trevor Francis
ASSISTANT: Mick Mills & Frank Barlow

DIRECTOR OF YOUTH COACHING
Brian Estick
YOTH DEVELOPMENT OFFICER
Bob Latchford
PHYSIOTHERAPIST
Neil McDiamond

CLUB STATISTICIAN FOR THE DIRECTORY
Dave Drage

What began as a season of promise, following the successful promotion campaign, faded badly after Christmas - so much so that the side eventually finished at a disappointing 15th place in the table.

There were a number of more obvious reasons for this sharp decline. Firstly, the club played a massive 66 competitive games, thus beating the previous record of 64 which was set only last season. Secondly, a total of 46 players appeared in first team matches (believed to be a new league record), which often meant a lack of cohesion, method or pattern in many games. Thirdly, there was an infuriating inability to score from the penalty spot. Fourth, was the constant media campaign waged against the club, particularly in regard to matches against Ancona and Millwall when the Blues were unfairly criticised for incidents that took place in both fixtures. Lastly came the loss of three mainstays of the promotion side: Liam Daish and Steve Claridge were transferred, and highly-rated goalkeeper Ian Bennett suffered a hand injury early in the New Year, which was to keep him out for the rest of the season.

Undoubtedly, the season's highlight was the team's progress to the Coca-Cola Cup semi-final - the first semi-final appearance in 21 years - before Leeds ended the dreams of an all-Brummie final against Villa. Twelve games were played during the cup run - another club record.

The ebullient Barry Fry, who seldom seemed to be off the back pages, paid the ultimate price for the club's fall-from-grace with the sack, and has been replaced by Blues legend Trevor Francis.

Trevor has already signed players of Premiership quality, and hopes of a successful season look very bright. It has been almost a dozen years since the Blues played in the top flight, which is far too long - the owners and the club's magnificent supporters deserve nothing less.

DAVE DRAGE

BIRMINGHAM CITY

League: 15th   FA Cup: 3rd Rnd   Coca-Cola Cup: Semi-Finals

M	DATE	COMP	VEN	OPPONENTS	RESULT	HT	LP	GOAL SCORERS/GOAL TIMES	ATT.
1	A 12	EL	H	Ipswich Town	W 3-1	0-0	3	Tait 63, Otto 73, Bowen 85	18910
2	15	CC 1/1	H	Plymouth Argyle	W 1-0	1-0		Cooper 44	7964
3	19	EL	A	Charlton Athletic	L 1-3	0-0	9	Bowen 54	(9692)
4	22	CC 1/2	A	Plymouth Argyle	W 2-1	0-1		Edwards 52, Hunt 54	(1871)
5	26	EL	H	Norwich City	W 3-1	1-0	4	Hunt 22, 48, 70(pen) (3)	19267
6	30	EL	A	Huddersfield Town	L 2-4	1-1	9	Ward 11, Ward 72	(12305)
7	S 2	EL	A	Barnsley	W 5-0	0-0	6	Hunt 55(pen), Claridge 60, Charlery 73, Forsyth 76, Doherty 86	(11129)
8	5	AIC	H	Genoa	L 2-3	0-0		Bowen 7, Bowen 9	20430
9	9	EL	H	Crystal Palace	D 0-0	0-0	5		19403
10	12	EL	H	Stoke City	D 1-1	1-0	7	Hunt 30	19005
11	17	EL	A	West Bromwich Albion	L 0-1	0-1	11		(18875)
12	20	CC 2/1	H	Grimsby Town	W 3-1	2-1		Claridge 23, Hunt 42, Daish 75	7446
13	23	EL	A	Watford	D 1-1	1-1	13	Finnan 11	(9422)
14	30	EL	H	Oldham Athletic	D 0-0	0-0	12		17269
15	O 3	CC 2/2	A	Grimsby Town	D 1-1	0-0		Bowen 82	(3280)
16	8	EL	H	Southend United	W 2-0	1-0	7	Claridge 45, 46	17341
17	11	AIC	A	Perugia	W 1-0	0-0		Castle 51	(1500)
18	14	EL	A	Portsmouth	W 1-0	1-0	6	Claridge 24	(10006)
19	21	EL	H	Grimsby Town	W 3-1	0-0	3	Claridge 52, Charlery 72, Claridge 89	16445
20	24	CC 3	H	Tranmere Rovers	D 1-1	1-0		McGreal 2(og)	13752
21	29	EL	A	Port Vale	W 2-1	1-0	2	Tait 7, Claridge 70	(8875)
22	N 4	EL	H	Millwall	D 2-2	1-0	2	Castle 24, Charlery 87	23016
23	8	CC 3R	A	Tranmere Rovers	W 3-1	0-0		Rushfeldt 47, Charlery 95, 115	(9151)
24	11	EL	A	Reading	W 1-0	0-0	3	Charlery 75	(10203)
25	15	AIC	A	Ancona	W 2-1	1-0		Edwards 43, og 72	(1500)
26	18	EL	A	Luton Town	D 0-0	0-0	3		(7920)
27	21	EL	H	Derby County	L 1-4	1-2	3	Ward 43	19417
28	26	EL	H	Leicester City	D 2-2	1-2	5	Hunt 30, Hunt 49(pen)	17350
29	29	CC 4	A	Middlesbrough	D 0-0	0-0			(28031)
30	D 2	EL	A	Southend United	L 1-3	1-2	6	Claridge 29	(7770)
31	9	EL	H	Watford	W 1-0	0-0	3	Francis 51	16970
32	13	AIC	H	Cesena	W 3-1	1-0		Donowa 32, Hunt 76, Claridge 87	7813
33	16	EL	A	Oldham Athletic	L 0-4	0-1	6		(6602)
34	20	CC 4R	H	Middlesbrough	W 2-0	2-0		Francis 11, 17	19878
35	23	EL	H	Tranmere Rovers	W 1-0	0-0	5	Hunt 75	18439
36	26	EL	A	Sheffield United	D 1-1	1-1	3	Francis 27	(17668)
37	J 6	FAC 3	H	Wolverhampton Wand	D 1-1	0-1		Poole 72	21349
38	10	CC QF	A	Norwich City	D 1-1	0-0		Francis 65	(13028)
39	14	EL	H	Charlton Athletic	L 3-4	1-3		Hunt 1(pen), Edwards 70, Forsyth 81	17688
40	17	FAC 3R	A	Wolverhampton Wand	L 1-2	0-1		Hunt 50	(28088)
41	20	EL	A	Ipswich Town	L 0-2	0-1	9		(12540)
42	24	CC QFR	H	Norwich City	W 2-1	0-0		Bowen 53, Daish 88	21097
43	30	AIC	H	West Bromwich Albion	D 2-2	0-1		Poole 57, Bull 88	9113
44	F 4	EL	A	Norwich City	D 1-1	0-0	11	Otto 76	(12612)
45	11	CC SF1	H	Leeds United	L 1-2	1-0		Francis 27	24781
46	17	EL	A	Stoke City	L 0-1	0-1	13		(15716)
47	20	EL	H	Barnsley	D 0-0	0-0	13		14168
48	25	CC SF2	A	Leeds United	L 0-3	0-0			(35435)
49	27	EL	A	Crystal Palace	L 2-3	1-1	13	Bowen 29, 77	(12965)
50	M 2	EL	H	Sheffield United	L 0-1	0-0	15		16799
51	5	EL	H	Wolverhampton Wand	W 2-0	2-0	13	Devlin 27(pen), 39	22051
52	9	EL	A	Tranmere Rovers	D 2-2	1-1	12	Legg 39, Hunt 62	(8696)
53	12	EL	H	Huddersfield Town	W 2-0	1-0	11	Devlin 12, Barnes 61	15296
54	17	EL	H	Sunderland	L -2	0-1	11		23251
55	20	EL	H	West Bromwich Albion	D 1-1	0-1	11	Hunt 80	19147
56	23	EL	A	Wolverhampton Wand	L 2-3	1-1	13	Devlin 6, 84	(26256)
57	30	EL	A	Grimsby Town	L 1-2	1-2	13	Barnes 4	(5475)
58	A 2	EL	H	Portsmouth	W 2-0	1-0	13	Barnes 18, Devlin 78(pen)	14886
59	6	EL	H	Port Vale	W 3-1	2-0	9	Barnes 16, Peschisolido 44, Tait 59	17469
60	10	EL	A	Millwall	L 0-2	0-1	10		(9271)
61	13	EL	H	Luton Town	W 4-0	1-0	9	Devlin 1, Francis 76, Barnes 77, 89	15426
62	16	EL	A	Sunderland	L 0-3	0-2	9		(19831)
63	20	EL	A	Derby County	D 1-1	0-0	9	Breen 74	(16757)
64	27	EL	A	Leicester City	L 0-3	0-2	12		(19702)
65	M 5	EL	H	Reading	L 1-2	1-2	15	Barnes 4	16233

Best Home League Attendance: 23251 v Sunderland   Smallest: 14168 v Barnsley   Average: 18054

Goal Scorers: **EL**(61): Hunt(11),Claridge(8),Devlin(7),Barnes(6),Charlery(4),Bowen(4),Tait(3),Ward(3),Francis(3),Otto(2),Forsyth(2),Edwards(1),Doherty(1),Finnan(1),Legg(1), Peschisolido(1),Castle(1),Breen(1),Barnes(1). **CC**(17): Francis(4),Hunt(2),Daish(2),Bowen(2),Charlery(2),Cooper(1),Edwards(1),Claridge(1),Opponent(s)(1),Rushfeldt(1)

FAC(2): Poole(1),Hunt(1) **AIC**(10): Bowen(2),Poole(1),Hunt(1),Edwards(1),Donowa(1),Claridge(1),Castle(1),Bull(1),Opponent(s)(1)

Appearance grid (EL = League; positions shown with each player surname). Columns left→right:

(F) Barnes	(G) Bennett	(M) Bowen	(D) Breen	(M) Castle	(F) Charlery	(F) Claridge	(D) Cooper	(M) Cornforth	(D) Daish	(F) Devlin	(F) Donowa	(M) Edwards	(M) Finnan	(M) Forsyth	(M) Frain	(F) Francis	(D) Grainger	(G) Griemink	(F) Hunt	(D) Johnson	(M) Legg	(F) Otto	(F) Peschisolido	(D) Poole	(M) Robinson	(M) Rushfeldt	(M) Tait	(M) Ward	Player / No.
X	S2			X					X		S1	X		X2	X				X2			S2		X			X	X	D.Allison 1
X	X			X3	X				X		S1	X		S1					S1			X		X			X1	X1	J.Lloyd 2
X	X			X1	X			X			S1	X		S1	X1				X			S1		X			X	X1	E.Lomas 3
X	X				X		X				S1	X		S2					X2					X			X	X1	C.Wilkes 4
X	X			S2	S	X	X				X2	X		S1					X					X			X	X1	R.Poulain 5
X	X			S2		X	X				X1	X		S2					X3	X				X				X	N.Barry 6
X	X1				X	X	X2				S2	X			X1				X3	X				X				X	T.Heilbron 7
	X																												8
X	X		S		X		X				X	X			S1				X	X				X				X1	M.Bailey 9
X	X			X2	X	X1	X				X								X	X1		X2		X			S2	X	I.Cruikshanks 10
X	X			S2	X	S1	X				X								X	X1	X2			X			X3	X	K.Breen 11
X	S1		X	X1	X		X				X		X1						X		S1			X				S	S.Mathieson 12
X	S2		X	X2	X	X	X				X		X	X1	S				X		S1			X				X	A.D'Urso 13
X	S1		X3	X1	X	X	X				X		X1	S3					X		S1			X				X	R.D.Furnandiz 14
X	X		X	X	S1	X	X				X		X1	X1					S1		X1			X				S1	K.M.Lynch 15
X	X3		X	X2	X	X	X				X		X1	S2					X	X	X			X					W.Burns 16
X			X	X		X	X				X		X						X1	X	X2	X		X	S1		S3		N. Known 17
X	X1		X	S3		X3	X3				X		X	X2					X	X	S1	X		X	S2		X		T.Helmley 18
X			X1	X		X	X				X		X	X1					X	X	X2	X		X	S2		X		M.Pierce 19
X			X1	X1		X	X				X		X	S1					X	X	X1	X		X	S1		X		T.Heilbron 20
X			X	X2		X	X	S2			X		X						X3	X				X		S1	X		R.Gifford 21
X			X	X		S2	X				X		X		S				X2	X	X1			X	X				J.A.Kirby 22
X			X2	X		S1	X				X		X						X2	X	S2	X		X		X1	X1	X	K.Lynch 23
X			X1	S1		X	X				X		X	S1					X1	X	S1			X		X1	X1	X	N.Barry 24
X			X2	X					S1		X		X	S3	X				X	X1				X	S2	X1	X3		N. Known 25
X			X2	X					X		X		X	X					X1	X3				X	S2	X1	X3	X	J.Rushton 26
X			S1	X							X		X1						S1	X				X1	X3	X	J.J.Breen 27
X			X1	S1			X						X	X	X1				X	X				X					D.Allison 28
X			X	S			X				S1		X	X	X				X1	X1					S2				B.Burns 29
X			X1	S2			X				X		X	X	X				X2						S2				R.Poulain 30
X			X1	S1			X				X		S2	X	S1				X	X					X				C.R.Wilkes 31
X1				S3			X				X		X2	X	X	X3	S1		X					X	X	X			N. Known 32
X				S1			X				X		X	X	X	X1			X		X1				X	X			S.J.Baines 33
X							X				X		X	X	X	X			X						X2	S			M.E.Pierce 34
X							X				X		S1	X	X	X			X						X				S.Mathieson 35
X			S2				X				X		S1	X	X	X2			X						X2	S2			I.Cruikshanks 36
X	S1				X			S			X		X	X	X	X			X1						X				R.Hart 37
	S1				X			S2			X		X	X	X	X			X1						X2				R.Poulain 38
S3				X2	S1						X		X	X	X1	X	X3		X3					X					P.Richards 39
	S1		X1		X						X		X	X	X3	X	X		S1	X				X		X1			R.Hart 40
	X3				X						X		X	S2	X	X	X		X	X							S1		I.Hemley 41
	S1		X2		X						X		X	X	X3		X		X	X1							S2		R.Gifford 42
	X1			S2							X		X		X3	X	X		X	X	X2			X			S3		J. Rushden 43
	X1										X		X	X	X	X			X	S1				X			X2		A.Butler 44
	S3								X	X1				S1	X1	X	X		X	X	S1								K.Cooper 45
	X1	S1	S1						X					S1	X1	X	X		X	X	S1								T.Heilbron 46
	X	X	X						X					S1	X1	X	X		X	X1									K.Lynch 47
	S2								X		S1		X	X1	X	X2	X		X	X	S2			X	X				R.Dilkes 48
			X						X		X		S3	S1	X	X2	X		X	X				X	X1				S.Baines 49
	X3	X	X3						X		X		X	S1	X		X		X1	X				X	X		S2		S.Mathieson 50
X1	S2	X	X		S		S				X		X	S1	X				X	X2				X			X		E.Lomas 51
X	S1	X	X								X1		X1		X		X		X	X			S				X		M.Riley 52
X		S	X	X							X1		X	S	X		X		X	X			S1				X		J.W.Lloyd 53
X3	S1	X									X1		X1	S1	X		X		X	X			S1				X		W.Burns 54
X	X2	X									X		X	X	X		X		X	X							X1		N.Barry 55
X	S	X	X								X	S	S	X	X		X		X	X									J.Kirkby 56
X1		X					X				X		X1	S1	X	X	X1	X	X1	X		S1					S1		D.B.Allison 57
X	S	X					X				X		X	X	X		X	X	X	X1							X		E.Wolstenholme 58
X		X	X				X				X		S	S	S	X	X	X	X	X							X		G.Cain 59
X		X	X			X			X				X	S1	X	X	X	X1	S1	X				S1			X		C.Wilkes 60
X		X	X						X3				X	S3	X	X	X2	S2	S1	X				X			X1		R.Gifford 61
		X	X						X				X1		X		X	X1	X1	X							X		T.E.West 62
X		X	X						X				X	S1	X		X	X	S	S2				X1			X		T.Heilbron 63
X		X	X						X1				X	X3	S1	X	X		X	X1				X			X		J.Rushton 64
X		X	X										X	X			X	X	X3	X				X	X		X		D.Orr 65
13	**24**	**16**	**17**	**12**	**8**	**27**	**16**	**8**	**16**	**15**	**5**	**1**	**36**	**6**	**12**	**21**	**11**	**8**	**20**	**43**	**31**	**9**	**6**	**7**	**27**	**3**	**3**	**22**	**EL Appearances**
0	0	7	0	1	3	9	0	2	0	1	0	8	1	5	13	1	7	0	0	2	3	12	2	1	4	3	4	0	EL Sub Apps.
0	8	3+5	0	7	3+1	11+1	6+1	0	7	0	3+5	0	11	2+2	7+2	6	6	0	3	8+3	5	0	3+3	0	10	3+1	1	3+1	CC Appearances
0	1	0+2	0	2	1+1	2	0	2	0	1	0	2	0	0	4	2+1	3	0	1	1+1	4	3	0	2	2	0	0	0	FAC Appearances
0	3	2	0	2	1+1	2+1	1	0	1	0	1	0	4	2+1	3	0	1	0	2	0	0	3	1+2	1	1+2	0			AIC Appearances

Also Played: (G) Barber X(52). (M) Barnes S2(34), S(35,59), S1(43,64), X(54,63), S3(65). (D) Bass X(45,46,51,52,53), X1(54). (F) Bull S1(37,46,47), X(39,43,49), S3(40,41,42), S(44), X2(50).
(D) Doherty S3(4), S(16), X(5), S(9), X1(42). (D) Hiley X(5,26,27), X2(6,41). (M) Hill (L) X3(28), X(29,30,34), X1(31,35,36). (M) Lowe S1(28,33). (F) Martin S3(16,26,27,50). S2(17,19), S(20), X1(21), S1(22).
(M) Muir X1(1), S3(2). (M) Preece (L) X(28,31,32,35,36,39), X2(30). (M) Richardson X(1), X3(17), S2(32), S3(64). (M) Samways X(46,47, 49,50,51,52,55,56,57,58), X1(53,54).
(M) Sansome (L) X(38,39), (M) Sheridan (L) X3(45), X4(6,48), S1(47), (D) Whyte X(2,4,5,6,7,28,45), S(2), X2(48).

BIRMINGHAM CITY

CLUB RECORDS

BIGGEST VICTORIES
League: 12-0 v Walsall Town Swifts, Division 2, 17.12.1892.
12-0 v Doncaster Rovers, Division 2, 1.4.1903.
F.A. Cup: 10-0 v Druids, 9.11.1889.
League Cup: 6-0 v Manchester City, 11.12.1962.
Europe: 5-0 v Boldklub Copenhag, 7.12.1960.

BIGGEST DEFEATS
League: 1-9 v Sheffield Wednesday, Division 1, 13.12.1930.
1-9 v Blackburn Rovers, Division 1, 5.1.1895.
0-8 v Derby County, Division 1, 30.11.1895.
0-8 v Newcastle United, Division 1, 23.11.1907.
0-8 v Preston North End, Division 1, 1.2.1958.
F.A. Cup: 0-6 v Wednesbury O.B., Qualifying Rnd., 17.10.1881.
0-6 v Tottenham Hotspur, 6th Rnd., 12.4.1967.
League Cup: 0-5 v Tottenham Hotspur, 3rd Rnd., 29.10.1986.
Europe: (Fairs) 1-4 v Barcelona, Final, 4.5.1960.

MOST POINTS
3 points a win: 89, Division 2, 1994-95.
2 points a win: 59, Division 2, 1947-48.

MOST GOALS SCORED
103, Division 2, 1893-94.
Mobley 24, Wheldon 22, Walton 16, Hands 14, Hallam 9, Jenkyns 6, Izon 4, Lee 3, Jolley 2, Pumfrey, Devey, Jackson 1 each.

MOST GOALS CONCEDED
96, Division 1, 1964-65.

MOST FIRST CLASS MATCHES IN A SEASON
63 - 1994-95 (46 League, 5 FA Cup, 4 League Cup, 8 AMC)

MOST LEAGUE WINS
27, Division 2, 1979-80.

MOST LEAGUE DRAWS
18, Division 1, 1937-38 & Division 2, 1971-72.

MOST LEAGUE DEFEATS
29, Division 1, 1985-86.

INDIVIDUAL CLUB RECORDS

MOST GOALS IN A SEASON
Walter Abbott 42 - 1898-99 (League 34, FAC 8).
5 goals once; 3 goals 5 times; 2 goals 7 times, 1 goal 8 times.

MOST GOALS IN A MATCH
5, Walter Abbott v Darwen (h), 8-0, Division 2, 26.11.1898.
5, John McMillan & R McRoberts v Blackpool (h), 10-1, Division 2, 2.3.1901.
5, Ben Green v Middlesbrough (h), 7-0, Division 1, 26.12.1905.
5, Jimmy Windridge v Glossop (h), 11-1, Division 2, 23.1.1915.

OLDEST PLAYER
Dennis Jennings, 40 years 190 days, 6.5.1950.

YOUNGEST PLAYER
Trevor Francis, 16 years 7 months v Cardiff City, 5.9.1970.

MOST CAPPED PLAYER
Malcolm Page (Wales) 28, 1971-79.
Harry Hibbs (For England), 25, 1951-54.

BEST PERFORMANCES

League: First in Division 2 - 1947-48: Matches played 42, Won 22, Drawn 15, Lost 5, Goals for 55, Goals against 24, Points 59.
Highest Position: 6th in Division 1, 1955-56.

F.A. Cup: Winners in 1930-31 v West Bromwich Albion, 1-2.
Most Recent Success: (1955-56) 3rd Rnd. Torquay United 7-1 (a); 4th Rnd. Leyton Orient 4-0 (a); 5th Rnd. West Bromwich Albion 1-0 (a); 6th Rnd. Arsenal 3-1 (a); Semi Final Sunderland 3-0 (n); Final Manchester City 1-3.
League Cup: (1962-63) 2nd Rnd. Doncaster Rovers 5-0; 3rd Rnd. Barrow 1-1 (a), 5-1 (h); 4th Rnd. Notts County 3-2 (h); 5th Rnd. Manchester City 6-0 (h); Semi-Final Bury 1-1 (a), 3-2(h); Final Astor Villa 0-0(a),3-1(h).
Europe: (Fairs Cup) Runners-up in 1958-60 v Barcelona, 0-0(h),1-4(a).
Most Recent Success: (1960-61) 1st Rnd. Ujpest Dozsa 3-2(h), 2-1(a); 2nd Rnd. Boldklub Copenhagen 4-4(a),5-0(h); Semi-Final Inter Milan 2-1(a),2-1(h); Final A.S.Roma 2-2(h),0-2(a).
Auto Windscreen Shield: Winners 1994-95.

DIVISIONAL RECORD

	Played	Won	Drawn	Lost	For	Against	Points
Division 1	2,040	651	501	888	2,776	3,296	1,845
Division 2/1	1,538	673	361	504	2,509	2,023	1,803
Division 3/2	184	82	55	47	258	197	310
Total	**3,762**	**1,406**	**917**	**1,439**	**5,543**	**5,516**	**3,958**

ADDITIONAL INFORMATION
Previous Names: Small Heath Alliance (1875-88); Small Heath (1888-1905).
Previous League: Football Alliance.

Club Colours: Royal blue/white & blue trim shirts, white with blue trim shorts, red stockings.
Change colours: Red and black stripes.

Reserves League: Pontins Central League Premier Division.

RECORDS AND STATISTICS

COMPETITIONS

Div 1/P	Div.2/1	Div.3/2
1894-96	1892-94	1989-92
1901-02	1896-1901	1994-95
1903-08	1902-03	
1921-39	1908-21	**Fairs Cup**
1948-50	1939-48	1955-58
1955-65	1950-55	1958-60
1972-79	1965-72	1960-61
1980-84	1979-80	1961-62
1985-86	1984-85	
	1992-94	
	1995-	

HONOURS

Div.2	Div.3/2	League Cup	A.M. Cup
1892-93	1994-95	1962-63	1990-91
1920-21			1994-95
1947-48			
1954-55			

MOST GOALS IN A CAREER

Joe Bradford - 267 (1920-35)

Year	League	FA Cup
1920-21	1	
1921-22	10	
1922-23	18	1
1923-24	24	
1924-25	11	
1925-26	26	1
1926-27	22	1
1927-28	29	3
1928-29	22	2
1929-30	23	
1930-31	14	8
1931-32	26	2
1932-33	14	
1933-34	5	
1934-35	4	
Total	249	18

Current Top goalscorer - John Frain - 24 (1986-96)

MOST APPEARANCES

Gil Merick 551 (1945-60)

AR	League	FA Cup	Europe
45-46		8	
46-47	41	4	
47-48	36		
48-49	41	2	
49-50	42	1	
50-51	42	6	
51-52	41	2	
52-53	35	7	
53-54	38	2	
54-55	27	4	
55-56	38	6	2
56-57	40	7	2
57-58	28	1	3
58-59	34	6	2
59-60	2		1
	485	56	10

MANAGERS

Name	Seasons	Best	Worst
Bob McRoberts	1910-15	3(2)	20(2)
Bill Beer	1923-27	8(1)	17(1)
Les Knighton	1928-33	9(1)	15(1)
George Liddell	1933-39	12(1)	20(1)
Willie Camkin	1939-45		
Ted Goodier	1945		
Harry Storer	1945-48	1(2)	3(2)
Bob Brocklebank	1949-54	17(1)	6(2)
Arthur Turner	1954-58	6(1)	1(2)
Albert Beasley	1958-60	9(2)	19(2)
Gil Merrick	1960-64	17(2)	20(2)
Joe Mallett	1964-65	22(2)	22(2)
Stan Cullis	1965-70	4(2)	18(2)
Fred Goodwin	1970-75	10(1)	9(2)
Willie Bell	1975-77	13(2)	19(2)
Sir Alf Ramsey	1977-78	11(1)	11(1)
Jim Smith	1978-82	13(1)	3(2)
Ron Saunders	1982-86	17(1)	2(2)
John Bond	1986-87	19(2)	19(2)
Gary Pendry	1987-89	19(2)	12(3)
Dave Mackay	1989-90	7(3)	7(3)
Lou Macari	1991		
Terry Cooper	1991-94	19(2/1)	2(3)
Barry Fry	1994-96	22(1)	22(1)
Trevor Francis	1996-		

RECORD TRANSFER FEE RECEIVED

Amount	Club	Player	Date
,180,000	Nottingham Forest	Trevor Francis	2/79
550,000	Coventry City	Liam Daish	2/96
500,000	Leicester City	Steve Claridge	3/96
350,000	Everton	B Latchford + PE	2/74

RECORD TRANSFER FEE PAID

Amount	Club	Player	Date
,500,000	Chelsea	Paul Furlong	7/96
800,000	Stockport County	Kevin Francis	1/95
800,000	Southend Utd	Ricky Otto	12/94
750,000	Blackburn Rovers	Mike Newell	7/96

LONGEST LEAGUE RUNS

undefeated matches:	20 (1994-95)	of league matches w/out a win:	17 (1985-86)
undefeated home matches:	36 (1970-72)	of undefeated away matches:	15 (1947-48)
hout home win:	11 (1962-63)	without an away win:	32 (1980-82)
eague wins:	13 (1892-93)	of home wins:	17 (1902-03)
eague defeats:	8 (1978-79, 1985)	of away wins:	9 (1897)

BIRMINGHAM CITY

PLAYERS NAME Honours	Ht	Wt	Birthdate	Birthplace Transfers	Contract Date	Clubs	League	L/Cup	FA Cup	Other	Lge	L/C	FAC	Oth
G O A L K E E P E R S														
Bennett Ian Div.2'95. AMC'95.	6.0	12.0	10/10/70	Worksop		Q.P.R.								
				Free	20/03/91	Newcastle United								
				Free	22/03/91	Peterborough Utd	72	10	3	4				
				£325000	17/12/93	Birmingham City	92	12	7	10				
Griemink Bart					09/11/95	Birmingham City	20	3	1	1+1				
D E F E N D E R S														
Ablett Gary E:B.1,u21.1. Div.1'88'90. CS'88'90'95. FAC'89'95.	6.0	11.4	19/11/65	Liverpool	19/11/83	Liverpool	103+6	10+1	16+2	9	1			
				Loan	25/01/85	Derby County	3+3			2				
				Loan	10/09/86	Hull City	5							
				£750000	14/01/92	Everton	128	12	12	4	5		1	
				Loan	01/03/96	Sheffield United	12							
					23/07/96	Birmingham City								
Barnett David K Div.2'95. AMC'95.	6.1	12.8	16/04/67	Birmingham		Windsor								
				25/08/88	Colchester United	19+1	2	3+2	3				
				01/06/89	Edmonton O. (Canada)								
				Free	13/10/89	W.B.A.								
				Free	17/07/90	Walsall	4+1	2						
				Free	01/10/90	Kidderminster H.			3					
				£10000	29/02/92	Barnet	58+1	5	3	5	2			
				£150000	20/12/93	Birmingham City	39+1	1	5	8				
Bass Jon	6.0	12.02	01/07/76	Weston-S-M.	27/06/94	Birmingham City	5	2						
Breen Gary Ei: u21.6.	6.1	12.00	12/12/73	London		Charlton Athletic								
				Free	06/03/91	Maidstone	19							
				Free	02/07/92	Gillingham	45+6	4	5	1				
				£70000	05/08/94	Peterborough Utd	68+1	6	6	6	1			1
					09/02/96	Birmingham City	17+1				1			
Bruce Steve E: B1, Y8; Prem'93'94'96; Div2'86; LC'85'92; FAC'90; ECW	6.0	12.6	31/12/60	Corbridge	27/10/78	Gillingham	203+2	15	14		29	6	1	
				£125000	24/08/84	Norwich City	141	20	9	10	14	5	1	
				£800000	18/12/87	Manchester United	279	31+1	36	30+2	35	6	3	7
				Free	15/06/96	Birmingham City								
Grainger Martin	5.10	11.7	23/08/72	Enfield	28/07/92	Colchester United	37+9	3	3+2	3	7			1
				£60000	21/10/93	Brentford	100+1	6	9	8	12	1		2
				£400000	25/03/96	Birmingham City	8							
Johnson Michael O	5.11	11.0	04/07/73	Nottingham	09/07/91	Notts County	102+5	9	4	15+1				
				£225000	01/09/95	Birmingham City	31+2	5	1	3				
Poole Gary GMVC'91. Div.2'95. AMC'95.	6.0	11.0	11/09/67	Stratford	15/07/85	Tottenham Hotspur								
				Free	14/08/87	Cambridge United	42+1	2	2	3				
				£3000	01/03/89	Barnet	39+1	2	7	6	2			1
				Free	05/06/92	Plymouth Argyle	39	6	2	0+1	5	2		
				£350000	09/07/93	Southend United	38		1	6	2			
				£50000	16/09/94	Birmingham City	61+1	10	7	10	1		1	2
Rea Simon	6.1	13.0	20/09/76	Coventry	01/08/94	Birmingham City	1+1			1+1				
				Loan	13/11/95	Kettering Town								
M I D F I E L D														
Barnes Steve						Welling								
				£75000	09/10/95	Birmingham City	2+2	0+1		0+1	1			
Bowen Jason W:1,u21.5,Y. AMC'94.	5.6	8.11	24/08/72	Merthyr Tydfil	01/07/90	Swansea City	93+31	6+1	9+2	15+3	26	2	1	8
				£275000	24/07/95	Birmingham City	16+7	3+5	0+2	2	4	2		2
Castle Steve	5.11	12.5	17/05/66	Barkingside	18/05/84	Leyton Orient	232+11	15+1	23+1	18+2	55	5	6	
				£195000	30/06/92	Plymouth Argyle	98+3	5	8	6	35	1		1
				£275000	21/07/95	Birmingham City	12+3	7	1	2	1			1
				Loan	15/02/96	Gillingham	5+1				1			
Cornforth John Div.3'88. AMC'94.	6.1	12.8	07/10/67	Whitley Bay	11/10/85	Sunderland	21+11	0+1		1+3	2			
				Loan	06/11/86	Doncaster Rovers	6+1		2		3			
				Loan	23/11/89	Shrewsbury Town	3		2					
				Loan	11/01/90	Lincoln City	9				1			
				£50000	02/08/91	Swansea City	147+2	14	14	19	16		1	1
				£350000	26/03/96	Birmingham City	8							
Edwards Andrew	6.2	12.7	17/09/71	Epping	14/12/89	Southend United	41+6	5	4	9	2			2
				£400000	06/07/95	Birmingham City	36+1	11	2	4	1	1		1
Finnan Steve				Kent		Woking								
				£100000	01/08/95	Birmingham City	6+5	2+2		2+1	1			
				Loan	05/03/96	Notts County	14+3			3	2			
Frain John AMC'91.	5.9	11.9	08/10/68	Birmingham	10/10/86	Birmingham City	263+9	28	12	22	23	1		2
Horne Barry W:49. WFAC'86. FAC'95. CS'95.	5.10	12.3	18/05/62	St.Asaph		Rhyl								
				Free	26/06/84	Wrexham	136	10	7	15	17	1	2	3
				£60000	17/07/87	Portsmouth	66+4	3	6		7			
				£700000	22/03/89	Southampton	111+1	15+2	15	7	6	3	3	1
				£675000	01/07/92	Everton	118+5	12+1	11+1	3	3			
					23/07/96	Birmingham City								
Legg Andy WFAC'89'91.	5.8	10.7	28/07/66	Neath		Britton Ferry								
				12/08/88	Swansea City	155+8	9+1	16	15+3	29		4	5
				£275000	23/07/93	Notts County	85+4	11	7+1	13+1	9		2	4
				£250000	01/03/96	Birmingham City	9+3				1			
Robinson Steven	5.4	10.11	17/01/75	Nottingham	09/06/93	Birmingham City	5+1			1				
				Loan	15/12/95	Kidderminster H.								
				Loan	15/03/96	Peterborough Utd	5							
Tait Paul Div.2'95. AMC'95.	6.1	10.0	31/07/71	Sutton C'dfield	02/08/88	Birmingham City	117+26	12+1	5+2	13+6	14			
F O R W A R D S														
Barnes Paul	5.10	12.09	16/11/67	Leicester	16/11/85	Notts County	36+17		0+1	4+6	14			5
				£30000	23/03/90	Stoke City	10+14	0+2		3+1	3			2
				Loan	08/11/90	Chesterfield	1		1				1	

Barnes continued....

Player / Fee	Date	Club								
£50000	15/07/92	York City	147+1	10	5	16	76	5		4
£350000	04/03/96	Birmingham City	13				6			
Devlin Paul J 5.8 10.10 14/04/72 — Birmingham	01/11/90	Stafford Rangers			0+1					
£40000	22/02/92	Notts County	132+9	11+1	8	17+2	25	1	1	6
£250000	01/03/96	Birmingham City	15				7			
Doherty Neil 5.9 10.09 21/02/69 — Barrow; NPL'89. FAT'90.	05/03/87	Watford								
	01/08/87	Barrow								
£40000	09/02/94	Birmingham City	16+7	2+1	0+1	0+2	2			
Loan	16/02/96	Northampton Town	3+6				1			
Donowa Louie 5.9 12.2 24/09/64 — Ipswich; E: u21.3. FAYC'83. MC'85.Div.2'95. AMC'95. 01/08/88 Willem II (Hol)	29/09/82	Norwich City	56+6	13+2	1+2		11	3	1	
Loan	23/12/85	Stoke City	4			0+1		1		
£40000	01/02/86	Real Deportivo								
Free	14/08/89	Ipswich Town	17+8	0+2	2	2+1	1			1
£55000	10/08/90	Bristol City	11+13	1	0+1		3			
£60000	30/08/91	Birmingham City	78+34	15+7	8	9+3	18		1	2
Loan	15/01/93	Burnley	4				2			
Loan	27/01/94	Shrewsbury Town	4							
Francis Kevin 6.7 15.08 06/12/67 — Birmingham; Div.2'95. AMC'95.		Mile Oak Rovers								
Free	02/02/89	Derby County	0+10	1+2	1+2	0+1			1	
£45000	21/02/91	Stockport County	131+4	8	9	25	76	4	6	18
£800000	20/01/95	Birmingham City	26+7	6	2	4	11	4		1
Furlong Paul A 6.0 11.8 01/10/68 — Wood Green; E: SP.5. FAT'88.		Enfield				4			1	
£130000	31/07/91	Coventry City	27+10	4	1+1	1	4	1		
£250000	24/07/92	Watford	79	7	2	2	3	37	4	
£2300000	26/05/94	Chelsea	44+20	3+1	5+4	7	13		1	3
£1500000	16/07/96	Birmingham City								
Hunt Jonathan 5.10 12.3 02/11/71 — Camden; Div.2'95. AMC'95.		Barnet	12+21	1	0+1	6+2				1
Free	20/07/93	Southend United	36+6	0+2	1	6+1	6			
£50000	16/09/94	Birmingham City	61+4	8+3	2+1	7	16	2	1	4
Martin Jae 5.11 11.0 05/02/76 — London	07/05/93	Southend United	1+3			0+1				
Free	01/07/95	Birmingham City	1+6			0+1				
Muir Ian 5.8 11.0 05/05/63 — Coventry; : Y.1. LCD'90.	03/09/80	Q.P.R.	2				2			
Loan	08/10/82	Burnley	1+1				1			
Free	27/08/83	Birmingham City	1			1				
Free	15/02/84	Brighton & H.A.	3+1							
Loan	28/01/85	Swindon Town	2			1				
Free	26/07/85	Tranmere Rovers	283+31	22+3	17+1	29+7	140	6	14	
£125000	01/08/95	Birmingham City	1	0+1						
Loan	08/09/95	Darlington								
Newell Mike 6.0 11.0 27/01/65 — Liverpool; : B.2,u21.4. AMC'85. Prem'95.		Liverpool								
Free	28/09/83	Crewe Alexandra	3							
Free	31/10/83	Wigan Athletic	64+8	6	8	5+1	25	1	6	3
£100000	09/01/86	Luton Town	62+1		5		18		1	
£350000	16/09/87	Leicester City	81	9	2	4	21	5		
£1100000	27/07/89	Everton	48+20	7+3	6+4	6	15	4		2
£1100000	15/11/91	Blackburn Rovers	113+17	14+2	9+2	9+1	28	8	6	6
£775000	23/07/96	Birmingham City								
Otto Ricky 5.10 10.10 09/11/67 — Hackney; Div.2'95. AMC'95.	07/11/90	Leyton Orient	41+15	3	2+1	5+1	13			2
£100000	09/07/93	Southend United	44+1	2	1	8	13			2
£800000	19/12/94	Birmingham City	24+18	3+3	2	8	6		1	1

ADDITIONAL CONTRACT PLAYERS

Hatton Paul (T) (18/05/96). **Webb Matthew** (T).

MANAGER
TREVOR FRANCIS

Date of Birth . . . . 19th April 1954.
Place of Birth . . . . Plymouth.
Date of Appointment . . . . May 1996.

PREVIOUS CLUBS
As Manager . . . . Queens Park Rangers, Sheffield Wednesday.
As Coach . . . . None.
As a Player. . . . . Birmingham City, Nottingham Forest, Manchester City, Sampdoria,
. . . . Atlanta (USA), Glasgow Rangers, QPR, Sheffield Wednesday.

HONOURS
As a Manager
None.

As a Player
Nottingham Forest: European Cup.
Glasgow Rangers: Premier League 1987.
England: 52 Full appearances.

St. Andrews

Birmingham B9 4NH
Tel: 0121 772 0101

Capacity ....25,899 (All seater).
First game..Not known.
First floodlit game ....Not known.

ATTENDANCES
Highest ....66,844 v Everton ,FA Cup 5th Round, 11.2.1939.
Lowest ....1,500 v Chesterfield, Division 2, 17.4.1909.

MATCHDAY TICKET PRICES

Seats. £11
Juveniles/OAP. £6.50

Ticket Office Telephone No. 0121 772 0101 Ext 5.

HOW TO GET TO THE GROUND

From North and East: M6 to J6, A38 (M). Branch left, first exit from round-abouts. A45 along Dartmouth Middleway. Left into St. Andrews Road for ground.

From South: M5 to J4, or A435 or A41 into Birmingham. A45 to Coventry Road then left into St. Andrews Road for ground.

From West: A456, A41 then A45 into Coventry Road, left into St. Andrews Road for ground.

Car Parking
Car parks in Coventry Road and Cattell Road. £2 per car on match days.

Nearest Railway Station
Buses from Birmingham New Street or Snow Hill, or walk from Bordesley Station from Birmingham Moor Street.

CLUBCALL
0891 12 11 88

Calls cost 39p per minute cheap rate and 49p per minute at all other times.
Call costings correct at time of going to press.

MATCHDAY PROGRAMME

Programme Editor. . . . . Peter Lewis

Number of pages. 48

Price £1.50

Subscriptions . . . . £40 for first 26 issues.

Local Newspapers . . . . Birmingham Post & Evening Mail, Sports Argus.

Local Radio Stations. . . . . BBC Radio W.M. & BRMB.

BOLTON WANDERERS
(The Trotters)
NATIONWIDE LEAGUE DIVISION 1
SPONSORED BY: REEBOK

...ck Row (L-R): Richard Sneekes, Jimmy Phillips, Scott Green, Chris Fairclough, Simon Coleman, Neil McDonald, Andy Todd, Nicky ...ooner. **Middle Row:** Ewan Simpson, Jason McAteer, Fabian de Freitas, Gudni Bergsson, Keith Branagan, Gerry Taggart, Aidan Davison, ...n Thompson, Mark Patterson, Steve Carroll, Ian McNeil. **Front Row:** David Lee, Owen Coyle, Alan Stubbs, Colin Todd, Roy McFarland, ...u Paatelainen, John McGinlay, Stewart Whittaker.

BOLTON WANDERERS
FORMED IN 1874
TURNED PROFESSIONAL IN 1880
LTD COMPANY IN 1895

PRESIDENT: Nat Lofthouse
CHAIRMAN: G Hargreaves
DIRECTORS
G Ball, G Seymour, G Warburton,
W B Warburton, P Gartside, B Scowcroft

SECRETARY/Chief Executive
D McBain (01204 389 200)
COMMERCIAL MANAGER
T Holland

MANAGER: Colin Todd
COACH: Phil Brown
RESERVE TEAM MANAGER
Steve Carroll
YOUTH TEAM MANAGER
Dean Crombie
PHYSIOTHERAPIST
Ewan Simpson

...UB STATISTICIAN FOR THE DIRECTORY
Simon Marland

The Wanderers went into their first Premiership season as favourites to return to the first division. By Christmas the pundits looked to have got their forecast spot on, but a spirited recovery at least gave the supporters something to shout about and took the issue to the last game.

A new management team of Colin Todd and Roy McFarland took over from Bruce Rioch, but the wanderers had a real baptism of fire having to face top three clubs and the previous term's champions in the opening weeks. Leading goalscorer John McGinlay missed the kick-off through injury whilst the press had a field day with the much-publicised transfer saga involving Jason McAteer and Alan Stubbs. McAteer went to Liverpool for a club record sale whilst Stubbs remained as team captain.

The Wanderers conceded a number of late goals that were to prove costly as time and again they matched sides blow for blow only to fail to convert chances that came their way.

Home victories over Blackburn and Arsenal were the highlights of the first half of the season, whilst the signing of Yugoslav international Sasa Curcic for a club record £1.5 million added another dimension to the midfield department.

Coca-Cola Cup interest ended when Norwich won a fourth-round replay 3-2 on penalties after both sides had failed to find a goal in 210 minutes. An FA Cup defeat by Leeds saw the club go out of both major competitions at home for the first season since 1973/4.

In the first week of the New Year Colin Todd took sole charge, with Roy McFarland leaving the club and Ian Porterfield coming in as coach. They had some early success with a cup win at Bradford and a league win over Wimbledon, but it wasn't until the middle of February that things really began to pick up. Four wins in six games began with a first away success of the season at Middlesbrough and, despite a six-goal reverse against Manchester United that equalised the club's worst home defeat, hopes of avoiding the drop became realistic.

The Wanderers came from behind to defeat Sheffield Wednesday at Burnden - a result that lifted them off the bottom for the first time in four months and put them just three points from safety. Unfortunately the final six games produced just one win and their fate was sealed in a home defeat by Southampton.

1996/7 will be the club's last at Burnden Park and a fitting finale would, of course, be a return to the Premiership in twelve month's time.

SIMON MARLAND

BOLTON WANDERERS

League: 20th   FA Cup: 4th Rnd   Coca-Cola Cup: 4th Rnd

M	DATE	COMP	VEN	OPPONENTS	RESULT	HT	LP	GOAL SCORERS/GOAL TIMES	ATT.
1	A 19	PL	A	Wimbledon	L 2-3	2-2	15	Thompson 26(pen), De Freitas 40	(9317)
2	22	PL	H	Newcastle United	L 1-3	0-1	19	Bergsson 51	20243
3	26	PL	H	Blackburn Rovers	W 2-1	1-0	13	De Freitas 21, Stubbs 80	20253
4	30	PL	A	Aston Villa	L 0-1	0-0	15		(31770)
5	S 9	PL	H	Middlesbrough	D 1-1	1-0	16	McGinlay 24	18376
6	16	PL	A	Manchester United	L 0-3	0-2	18		(32812)
7	20	CC 2/1	H	Brentford	W 1-0	0-0		Sneekes 79	5243
8	23	PL	A	Liverpool	L 2-5	0-2	19	Todd 78, Patterson 81(pen)	(40104)
9	30	PL	H	Queens Park Rangers	L 0-1	0-0	19		17362
10	O 3	CC 2/2	A	Brentford	W 3-2	0-1		Patterson 58, McGinlay 66, Thompson 81	(4861)
11	14	PL	H	Everton	D 1-1	1-0	19	Paatelainen 1	20427
12	21	PL	A	Nottingham Forest	L 2-3	1-1	19	Sneekes 24, De Freitas 78	(25426)
13	24	CC 3	H	Leicester City	D 0-0	0-0			9166
14	30	PL	H	Arsenal	W 1-0	1-0	18	McGinlay 35	18682
15	N 4	PL	A	Manchester City	L 0-1	0-1	18		(28397)
16	8	CC 3R	A	Leicester City	W 3-2	1-0		McGinlay 39, Sneekes 61, Curcic 76	(14884)
17	18	PL	H	West Ham United	L 0-3	0-0	18		19047
18	22	PL	A	Chelsea	L 2-3	1-1	19	Curcic 10, Green 67	(17495)
19	25	PL	A	Southampton	L 0-1	0-0	19		(14404)
20	29	CC 4	A	Norwich City	D 0-0	0-0			(13820)
21	D 2	PL	H	Nottingham Forest	D 1-1	0-0	19	De Freitas 67	17342
22	9	PL	H	Liverpool	L 0-1	0-0	20		21042
23	16	PL	A	Queens Park Rangers	L 1-2	1-1	20	Sellars 43	(11456)
24	20	CC 4R	H	Norwich City	D 0-0	0-0		(Lost on penalties)	8736
25	23	PL	A	Tottenham Hotspur	D 2-2	0-0	20	Green 76, Bergsson 78	(30702)
26	27	PL	H	Leeds United	L 0-2	0-1	20		18414
27	30	PL	H	Coventry City	L 1-2	1-1	20	McGinlay 16	16678
28	J 1	PL	A	Sheffield Wednesday	L 2-4	0-2	20	Curcic 51, Taggart 77	(24872)
29	6	FAC 3	A	Bradford City	W 3-0	1-0		McGinlay 40, Curcic 53, 66	(10265)
30	13	PL	H	Wimbledon	W 1-0	1-0	20	McGinlay 44(pen)	16216
31	20	PL	A	Newcastle United	L 1-2	1-2	20	Bergsson 19	(36543)
32	F 3	PL	A	Blackburn Rovers	L 1-3	1-1	20	Green 29	(30419)
33	10	PL	A	Aston Villa	L 0-2	0-1	20		18099
34	14	FAC 4	H	Leeds United	L 0-1	0-1			16694
35	17	PL	A	Middlesbrough	W 4-1	2-1	20	Blake 12, Coleman 45, De Freitas 62, Lee 73	(29354)
36	25	PL	H	Manchester United	L 0-6	0-2	20		21381
37	M 2	PL	A	Leeds United	W 1-0	1-0	20	Bergsson 16	(30106)
38	16	PL	A	Coventry City	W 2-0	0-0	20	Stubbs 68, 70	(17168)
39	20	PL	H	Tottenham Hotspur	L 2-3	0-1	20	Stubbs 74, Sellars 84	17829
40	23	PL	H	Sheffield Wednesday	W 2-1	1-1	19	Sellars 44, Curcic 52	18368
41	30	PL	H	Manchester City	D 1-1	0-1	20	McGinlay 74	21050
42	A 6	PL	A	Everton	L 0-3	0-1	20		(37974)
43	8	PL	H	Chelsea	W 2-1	2-1	20	McGinlay 40, Curcic 44	18021
44	13	PL	A	West Ham United	L 0-1	0-1	20		(23086)
45	27	PL	H	Southampton	L 0-1	0-1	20		18795
46	M 5	PL	A	Arsenal	L 1-2	0-0	20	Todd 76	(38104)

Best Home League Attendance: 21381 v Manchester United   **Smallest: 16216 v Wimbledon**   **Average: 18822**

Goal Scorers:
PL(39): McGinlay(6),De Freitas(5),Bergsson(4),Stubbs(4),Curcic(4),Sellars(3),Green(3),Todd(2),Taggart(1),Paatelainen(1),Patterson(1),Thompson(1),Sneekes(1),Coleman(1),Blake(1),Lee(1)
CC(7): Sneekes(2),McGinlay(2),Thompson(1),Patterson(1),Curcic(1)
FAC(3): Curcic(2),McGinlay(1)

(M) Burnett (L)	(M) Bergsson	(F) Blake	(G) Branagan	(D) Coleman	(F) Coyle	(F) Curcic	(G) Davison	(F) De	(D) Fairclough	(M) Green	(M) Lee	(D) McAnespie	(M) McAteer	(F) McGinlay	(F) Paatelainen	(D) Patterson	(D) Phillips	(M) Sellars	(D) Small	(M) Sneekes	(D) Strong	(D) Stubbs	(D) Taggart	(F) Taylor	(M) Thompson	(D) Todd	(G) Ward	(F) Whitaker	Referee	
	X1		X		S2		S	X	X	X	S1		X		X2	X	X						X	X					K.Cooper	1
	X		X		X		S	X	X2	X	S2		X			X	X			S1			X	X1					S.Lodge	2
	X		X		X1		S	X	X	X	X		X			X	X			S			X	X					K.Burge	3
	X		X					X	X	X2	S2		X	X1		X	X			S1			X	X					P.James	4
	X		X		S1		S	X	X	X	S			X1		X	X			X			X	X					P.Danson	5
	X		X					X	X	X	X			X2		S1	X			X			X	S2	X1	X			S.Dunn	6
	X		X		S1		S	X1	X	X	X	X		X		X2	X			X				X			S2		G.Cain	7
	X		X		S1		S	X	X	X	X			X1		X2	X			X				X	X2	S2			M.Bodenham	8
	X		X		S			X	S	S	X	X	X	X		X	X			X			X	X					J.Winter	9
	X		X			S		X	S1	X			X1	X2		X	X			X2			X	X1	S2				D.J.Gallagher	10
	X		X			S		X	S1	S2	X		X1	X2		X	X			X			X	X					P.Alcock	11
	X		X			S	S1	X			S2	X	X1	X2	X2	X	X			X			X	X					D.Elleray	12
	X		X			S	S2	X			S1	X	X	X2	X1	X	X			X			X	X					A.Wilkie	13
	X		X		X1		S	X	S2	X	X	X	X	X		S1	X			X				X2					K.Cooper	14
	X		X		X2		S2	X	S3	X	X	X	X	X1	X3	X	X			X				X					R.Hart	15
	X		X		X			X	S2	X	X	X	X	X		S1	X			X2			X1	X					D.Elleray	16
	X		X		X	S		X	S1	X1	X2		X			X	X			X				X	S2				P.Durkin	17
	X		X		X	S	S	X	X		S	X				X	X			S			X	X	X				G.Poll	18
	X		X		X	S	S	X	X		S	X				X	X						X	X	X				P.Jones	19
S			X		X	S	X	X	X		S	X				X	X						X	X	X				G.Singh	20
S			X		X	S	X	X	X		S	X				X	X						X	X	X				R.Dilkes	21
	X		X		X	S	X	X	X			X				S1	X	X					X		X1				M.Bodenham	22
	X		X		X	S	X	X	X		S1	X				S	X	X					X		X1				S.J.Lodge	23
	X		X		X	S	X	X	X		S	X				X	X1						X		X		X	S1	D.Allison	24
S1	X	X	X		X			S2	X	X		S		X2			X	X		S1			X		X1				P.Danson	25
S	X	X	X		X			S2	X	X		S		X		X2	X	X1					X						D.Elleray	26
S		X	X		X			X	X	X		S		X			X	X		X			X		X				A.Wilkie	27
		X	X		X	S	S2		X			X		X2			X	X		X	S1	X	X		X1				P.A.Durkin	28
		X	X		X			X	X			X		X			X	X		X		X	X	X				S	S.Dunn	29
	X	X1	X		X				X	S1	S			X	X		X	X		X		X	X		S				M.Reed	30
	X	X2	X		X1				X3	X	S3			X	S1		X	X		X		X	X		S2				K.Cooper	31
	X	S1	X		X			X2	X	S2				X1	X		X	X		X		X	X	S					P.Alcock	32
X1	X	X	X		X		X	X	X					S2	S		X	X2		X		X	X	S1					G.Ashby	33
	X2	X	X		X			X	X	X1				S1	S2		X	S		X	X	X	X					J.Winter	34
		X	X	X	X			X	X	X	X			S	S		X	X		S		X	X					P.Danson	35
		X	X	X	X			X	X	X	X1			S1	S		X	X				S	X					D.J.Gallagher	36
S	X	X1	X	X		X		S1	X	X	S					X	X			X		X							G.Willard	37
	X	X1		X		X		X	X	S3	X	X3				S1	X2			X		X		S2					K.Burge	38
	X		X		X		X	X	X	S						X	X		S	X	X	X		X					J.Winter	39
	X	S3	X		X			X1	X2	S1						X	S2			X	X	X		X3			X		R.Dilkes	40
	X	S2	X		X			S1	X	X1						X	X2			X		X		S			X		M.Bodenham	41
	X	X1	X		X					X	X					X	X			X		X		X			X		S.Lodge	42
	X	X1	X		X			S1	X	S						X	S			X		X		X			X		A.Wilkie	43
	X		X		X			X2	X1	S	S1					X	S2			X		X		X			X		G.Ashby	44
	X	S2	X	X2	X1					S				X	X		X	X		X	X			X	S1	X			G.Willard	45
																														46
0	**34**	**14**	**31**	**12**	**2**	**28**	**2**	**17**	**33**	**26**	**9**	**7**	**4**	**29**	**12**	**12**	**37**	**22**	**1**	**14**	**0**	**24**	**11**	**23**	**9**	**5**	**0**		PL Appearances	
1	0	4	0	0	3	0	0	10	0	5	9	2	0	3	3	4	0	0	0	3	1	1	0	3	3	0	0		PL Sub Appearances	
0	6	0	6	0	0+1	3	0	2+1	6	3+2	3+1	3	0	6	1	5+1	6	0	0	4	0	3	2	5	2+2	0	0+1		CC Appearances	
0	0	2	2	0	0	2	0	1	2	2	1	0	0	1+1	0+1	0	2	1	0	1	0	2	2	1	0	0	0		FAC Appearances	

On Loan (L): Burnett (Plymouth).

BOLTON WANDERERS

CLUB RECORDS

BIGGEST VICTORIES
League: 8-0 v Barnsley, Division 2, 6.10.1934.
F.A. Cup: 13-0 v Sheffield United, Round 2, 1.2.1890.
League Cup: 6-2 v Grimsby Town, Round 2, 26.10.1960.

BIGGEST DEFEATS
League: 0-7 v Burnley, Division 1, 1.3.1890.
0-7 v Sheffield Wednesday, Division 1, 1.3.1915.
0-7 v Manchester City, Division 1, 21.3.1936.
F.A. Cup: 1-9 v Preston North End, Round 2, 10.12.1887.
League Cup: 0-6 v Chelsea, Round 4 Replay, 8.11.1971.

MOST POINTS
3 points a win: 90, Division 3/2, 1992-93.
2 points a win: 61, Division 3, 1972-73.

MOST GOALS SCORED
96, 1934-35, Division 2.
Milsom 31, Westwood 30, Taylor 8, Cook 6, Eastham 6, Rimmer 4,
Gosling 2, Atkinson 2, Cameron, Chambers, Walton 1 each,
Opponents 4.

MOST GOALS CONCEDED
92, Division 1, 1932-33.

MOST FIRST CLASS MATCHES IN A SEASON
64 - (league 46, FA Cup 8, League Cup 4, Anglo Italian 6) 1993/94.

MOST LEAGUE WINS
27, Division 2, 1904-05, 1992-93.

MOST LEAGUE DRAWS
17, Division 3, 1991-92.

MOST LEAGUE DEFEATS
25, Division 2, 1970-71.
25, Premiership, 1995-96.

INDIVIDUAL CLUB RECORDS

MOST GOALS IN A SEASON
Joe Smith - 38, 1920-21 (League 38).

MOST GOALS IN A MATCH
5, J.Cassidy v Sheffield United, 13-0, FA Cup, 1.2.1890.
5, T.Caldwell v Walsall, 8-1, Division 3, 10.9.1983.

OLDEST PLAYER
Peter Shilton, 45 years 239 days v Wolves, 14.5.1995.

YOUNGEST PLAYER
Ray Parry, 15 years 267 days v Wolverhampton Wanderers,
13.10.1951.

MOST CAPPED PLAYER
Nat Lofthouse (England) 33.

BEST PERFORMANCES

League: Second in Division 2,1899-00: Matches played 34, Won 22,
Drawn 8, Lost 4, Goals for 79, Goals against 25, Points 52.
Highest Position: 3rd Division 1, 1891-92, 1920-21, 1924-25.

F.A. Cup: Winners in 1922-23 v West Ham United, 2-0.
Winners in 1925-26 v Manchester City, 1-0.
Winners in 1928-29 v Portsmouth, 2-0.
Most Recent Success: (1957-58) 3rd Rnd. Preston North End (a)
3-0; 4th Rnd. York City (a) 0-0, (h) 3-0; 5th Rnd. Stoke City (h) 3-1;
6th Rnd. Wolverhampton W. (h) 2-1; Semi-Final Blackburn Rovers 2-
1; Final Manchester United 2-0.

League Cup: (1994-95) 2nd Round Ipswich (A) 3-0, (H) 1-0,
3rd Round Sheffield Utd (A) 2-1, 4th Round West Ham (A) 3-1,
5th Round Norwich (H) 1-0, Semi-Final Swindon (A) 1-2, (H) 3-1,
Final Liverpool 1-2.

ADDITIONAL INFORMATION
PREVIOUS NAME
Christ Church FC 1874-1877.
PREVIOUS LEAGUES
None.

Club Colours: White shirts with red & blue trim, navy blue shorts,
red socks.
Change Colours: Two tone blue shirts, blue shorts, blue socks.

Reserves League: Pontins Central League Premier Division.
'A' Team: Lancashire League Division 1.

DIVISIONAL RECORD							
	Played	Won	Drawn	Lost	For	Against	Points
Division 1/P	2,346	876	518	952	3,620	3,793	2,278
Division 2/1	987	417	241	329	1,508	1,217	1,131
Division 3/2	513	201	137	175	672	598	692
Division 4	46	22	12	12	66	42	78
Total	3,892	1,516	908	1,468	5,866	5,650	4,179

RECORDS AND STATISTICS

COMPETITIONS

Div 1/P	Div.2/1	Div.3/2	Div.4
1888-99	1899-1900	1971-73	1987-88
1900-03	1903-05	1983-87	
1905-08	1908-09	1988-93	
1909-10	1910-11		
1911-33	1933-35		
1935-64	1964-71		
1978-80	1973-78		
1995-96	1980-83		
	1993-95		
	1996-		

HONOURS

Div.2	Div.3	FA Cup	AMC (SVT)
1908-09	1972-73	1922-23	1988-89
1977-78		1925-26	
		1928-29	
		1957-58	

MOST APPEARANCES

Edie Hopkinson 578 (1956-70)

Year	League	FA Cup	Lge Cup
956-57	42	1	
1957-58	33	7	
1958-59	39	6	
1959-60	26	3	
1960-61	42	3	5
1961-62	42	1	2
1962-63	39	1	1
1963-64	31	4	1
1964-65	40	3	1
1965-66	42	3	2
1966-67	41	3	1
1967-68	40	1	3
1968-69	42	2	1
1969-70	20		4
	519	38	21

MOST GOALS IN A CAREER

Nat Lofthouse - 290 (1945-61)

Year	League	FA Cup	Lge Cup	Others
1945-46		2		
1946-47	18	3		
1947-48	18			
1948-49	7	1		
1949-50	10	3		
1950-51	21	1		
1951-52	18			
1952-53	22	8		
1953-54	17	1		
1954-55	15			
1955-56	32	1		
1956-57	28			
1957-58	17	3		
1958-59	29	4		
1959-60				
1960-61	3		3	
Total	255	27	3	5

Current leading goalscorer: John McGinlay 86 (1992-96)

RECORD TRANSFER FEE RECEIVED

Amount	Club	Player	Date
£4,500,000	Liverpool	Jason McAteer	9/95
£3,500,000	Celtic	Alan Stubbs	6/96
£550,000	Celtic	Andy Walker	6/94
£340,000	Birmingham City	Neil Whatmore	8/81

RECORD TRANSFER FEE PAID

Amount	Club	Player	Date
£1,500,000	Partizan Belgrade	Sasa Cursic	10/95
£1,500,000	Barnsley	Gerry Taggart	8/95
£1,350,000	Sheffield Utd	Nathan Blake	12/95
£1,000,000	FC Copen Hagen	Michael Johansen	8/96

MANAGERS

Name	Seasons	Best	Worst
John Somerville	1908-10	19(1)	1(2)
Will Settle	1910-15	4(1)	2(2)
Tom Mather	1915-19		
Charles Foweraker	1919-44	3(1)	3(2)
Walter Rowley	1944-50	14(1)	18(1)
Bill Ridding	1951-68	4(1)	12(2)
Nat Lofthouse (x3)	1968-71	12(2)	22(2)
Jimmy McIlroy	1970		
Jimmy Meadows	1971		
Jimmy Armfield	1971-74	11(2)	7(3)
Ian Greaves	1974-80	17(1)	10(2)
Stan Anderson	1980-81	18(2)	18(2)
George Mulhall	1981-82	19(2)	19(2)
John McGovern	1982-85	22(2)	19(3)
Charles Wright	1985	17(3)	17(3)
Phil Neal	1985-92	4(3)	3(4)
Bruce Rioch	1992-95	3(2/1)	2(3/2)
Roy McFarland/Colin Todd	1995		
Colin Todd	1995-	20(P)	20(P)

LONGEST LEAGUE RUNS

of undefeated matches:	23 (13.10.1990 - 9.3.1991)	of league matches w/out a win:	26 (7.4.1902 - 10.1.1903)
of undefeated home matches:	27 (24.4.1920 - 24.9.1921)	of undefeated away matches:	11 (10.12.1904 - 21.4.1905)
without home win:	11 (19.4.1902 - 10.1.1903)	without an away win:	36 (25.9.1948 - 2.9.1950)
of league wins:	11 (5.11.1904 - 2.1.1905)	of home wins:	17 (11.10.1924 - 25.4.1925)
of league defeats:	11 (7.4.1902 - 18.10.1902)	of away wins:	5 (10.12.1904 - 18.3.1905)

BOLTON WANDERERS

PLAYERS NAME / Honours	Ht	Wt	Birthdate	Birthplace / Transfers	Contract Date	Clubs	League	L/Cup	FA Cup	Other	Lge	L/C	FAC	Oth
G O A L K E E P E R S														
Branagan Keith	6.0	11.0	10/07/66	Fulham	04/08/83	Cambridge United	110	12	6	6				
				£100000	25/03/88	Millwall	46	1	5	1				
				Loan	24/11/89	Brentford	2			1				
				Loan	01/10/91	Gillingham	1							
				Free	03/07/92	Bolton Wanderers	130	22	9	7				
Davison Aidan	6.1	13.2	11/05/68	Sedgefield		Spennymoor Utd								
						Billingham Synth.			1					
					25/03/88	Notts County	1							
				£6000	07/10/89	Bury								
				Free	14/08/91	Millwall	34	3	3	2				
				£25000	26/07/93	Bolton Wanderers	35+2		8	4				
Ward Gavin J Div.3'93. WFAC'93.	6.2	12.12	30/06/70	Sutton Coldfield		Aston Villa								
				Free	26/09/88	Shrewsbury Town								
				Free	18/09/89	W.B.A.								
				Free	05/10/89	Cardiff City	58+1		1	7				
				£175000	16/07/93	Leicester City	38	3	0+1	4				
				£175000	13/07/95	Bradford City	36	6	3	2				
				£300000	29/03/96	Bolton Wanderers	5							
D E F E N D E R S														
Coleman Simon	6.0	10.8	13/03/68	Worksop	29/07/85	Mansfield Town	96	9	7	7	7			1
				£400000	26/09/89	Middlesbrough	51+4		5	10	2			1
				£300000	15/08/91	Derby County	62+8	5+1	5	12	2			
				£250000	20/01/94	Sheffield Wed.	10+5	3	2		1			
				£350000	05/10/94	Bolton Wanderers	34	4	1		2			
Fairclough Chris	5.11	11.2	12/04/64	Nottingham	12/10/81	Nottingham Forest	102+5	9+1	6	9+2	1	1		
				£387000	03/07/87	Tottenham Hotspur	60	7	3		5			
				£500000	23/03/89	Leeds United	189+6	17+2	14+1	14	21	2		
				£500000	04/07/95	Bolton Wanderers	33	6	2					
McAnespie Stephen	5.9	10.7	01/02/72	Kilmarnock		Vasterhauringe								
					01/08/93	Raith	37							
				£900000	30/09/95	Bolton Wanderers	7+2	3						
Phillips James	6.0	12.0	08/02/66	Bolton	01/08/83	Bolton Wanderers	103+5	8	7	14	2			
				£95000	27/03/87	Glasgow Rangers	19+6	4		4				
				£110000	26/08/88	Oxford United	79	3	4	2	6			1
				£250000	15/03/90	Middlesbrough	139	16	10	5	6			2
				£250000	20/07/93	Bolton Wanderers	124+1	18	10	9	1			2
Small Bryan	5.9	11.09	15/11/71	Birmingham	09/07/90	Aston Villa	31+5	2	2+1	4				
				Loan	09/09/94	Birmingham City	3							
				Free	20/03/96	Bolton Wanderers	1							
Spooner Nicky	5.10	11.0	05/06/71	Manchester	12/07/89	Bolton Wanderers	22+1	2	3	0+1	2			
Strong Greg E: Y.S.	6.2	11.12	05/09/75	Bolton	01/10/92	Wigan Athletic	28+7	5	1	3+1	3			
					10/08/95	Bolton Wanderers	0+1							
Taggart Gerald NI:35,u21.1,Y.	6.1	13.4	18/10/70	Belfast	01/07/89	Manchester City	10+2		1		1			
				£75000	10/01/90	Barnsley	168+3	11	14	6	13		2	1
				£1500000	01/08/95	Bolton Wanderers	11	2	2		1			
Todd Andrew J J	5.9	10.6	21/09/74	Derby	06/03/92	Middlesbrough	7+1	1+1		5				
				Loan	27/02/95	Swindon Town	13							
				£250000	01/08/95	Bolton Wanderers	9+3	2+2			2			
M I D F I E L D														
Bergsson Gudni Icelandic Int. CS'91.	5.10	10.7	21/07/65	Reyjkavik		Valur (Iceland)								
				£100000	15/12/88	Tottenham Hotspur	51+20	4+2	2+2	5+1	3			
				£65000	21/05/95	Bolton Wanderers	42	6+1		3	4			
Burnett Wayne E: Y.1.	6.0	12.6	04/09/71	Lambeth	13/11/89	Leyton Orient (T)	34+6	3+1	3+1	4	1	1		
				£90000	19/08/92	Blackburn Rovers								
					09/08/93	Plymouth Argyle	61+9	3	8	3+1	3			
						Bolton Wanderers	0+1							
Green Scott	5.10	11.12	15/01/70	Walsall	20/07/88	Derby County								
				£50000	17/03/90	Bolton Wanderers	159+49	19+3	18+2	16+4	23	1	2	
Lee David	5.7	10.0	05/11/67	Blackburn	08/08/86	Bury	203+5	15	6	19+1	35	1		4
				£350000	27/08/91	Southampton	11+9		0+1	1+1				
				£300000	02/11/92	Bolton Wanderers	111+19	15+1	12+1	8+1	15	2		
Sellars Scott	5.8	10.0	27/11/65	Sheffield	25/07/83	Leeds United	72+4	4	4	2	12	1		1
				£20000	28/07/86	Blackburn Rovers	194+8	12	11	20	35	3	1	2

Player				Fee	Date	Club								
Sellars continued...				£800000	01/07/92	Leeds United	6+1	1+1		1				
				£700000	09/03/93	Newcastle United	56+5	6+1	3	4	5	2		1
				£750000	07/12/95	Bolton Wanderers	22		1		3			
Thompson Alan	6.0	12.5	22/12/73	Newcastle	11/03/91	Newcastle United	13+3		1	3				
E: u21.1,Y.11.				£250000	22/07/93	Bolton Wanderers	76+14	16+1	4+1	7+1	14	3	1	1

F O R W A R D S

Player				Fee	Date	Club								
Blake Nathan	6.0	12.8	27/01/72	Cardiff		Chelsea								
				Free	20/08/90	Cardiff City	113+18	6+2	10	13+2	35		4	1
				£300000	17/02/94	Sheffield United	55+14	3+1	1	1	34	1		
				£1200000	23/12/95	Bolton Wanderers	14+4		2		1			
Curcic Sasa						Patizan Belgrade								
				£1500000	28/10/95	Bolton Wanderers	28	3	2		4	1	2	
De Freitas Fabian	6.1	12.9	28/07/72	Paramaribo		Vollendam								
				£400000	19/08/94	Bolton Wanderers	24+16	2+4	1	0+2	7			2
McGinlay John	5.9	11.6	08/04/64	Inverness		Yeovil Town		5				2		
S:9,B.1. Isth Lge Prem'88.						Elgin		1				1		
					22/02/89	Shrewsbury Town	58+2	4	1	3	27		2	2
				£175000	11/07/90	Bury	16+9	1	1	1+1	9			
				£80000	21/01/91	Millwall	27+7	2+1	2	2	10			1
				£125000	30/09/92	Bolton Wanderers	133+9	16+1	15+1	11	63	7	9	7
Paatelainen Mixu	6.0	13.11	03/02/67	Helsinki		Valkeakosken Haka								
Finnish Int.					01/10/87	Dundee United	101+32	8+2	20+1	2+1	34	5	2	1
					31/03/92	Aberdeen	53+22	6	7+1	3	23	3	1	1
				£300000	29/07/94	Bolton Wanderers	55+4	8+1	1+1	3	13	2		1
Taylor Scott James	5.10	11.04	05/05/76	Chertsey		Staines								
				£15000	08/02/95	Millwall	13+15	0+2	1+1			2		
				£150000	29/03/96	Bolton Wanderers								
Whittaker Stuart	5.7	8.11	02/01/75	Liverpool		Liverpool								
				Free	14/05/93	Bolton Wanderers	2+1	0+1						
ADDITIONAL CONTRACT PLAYERS														
Feeney Gareth						Bolton Wand. (T)								
Whitehead Stuart						Bolton Wand. (T)								

THE MANAGER
COLIN TODD

Date of Birth . . . . 12th December 1948.
Place of Birth. . . . . Chester-le-Street.
Date of Appointment . . . . January 1995.

PREVIOUS CLUBS
As Manager. . . . . Whitley Bay, Middlesbrough.
As Assistant. . . . . Middlesbrough, Bolton Wanderers.
As a Player . . . . Sunderland, Derby County, Everton, Birmingham City,
. . . . Nottingham Forest, Oxford Utd, Vancouver Whitecaps, Luton.

HONOURS
As a Manager
None.

As a Player
Sunderland: FA Youth Cup 1967.
Derby County: Division 1 championship 1972, 1975.
England: 27 full, 14 u23 & Youth caps.   **FLgeXI:** 3 caps.

Burnden Park

Manchester Road, Bolton, Lancs BL3 2QR
Tel: 01204 389 200

Capacity . . . . .21,258.
First game . . . . .v P.N.E., Dai Jones Benefit, 11.9.1895.
First floodlit game . . . . .v Heart of Midlothian, 14.10.1957.

ATTENDANCES
Highest . . . . .69,912 v Manchester City, FA Cup 5th Round, 18.2.1933.
Lowest . . . . .1,507 v Rochdale, Autoglass Trophy, 10.12.1991.

OTHER GROUNDS . . . . .Pikes Lane.

MATCHDAY TICKET PRICES

Manchester Road Stand . . . . £15/£9

Burnden Stand . . . . £15/£9

Great Lever Stand . . . . £11/£8

Terrace . . . . £11/£8

Ticket Office Telephone No. 01204 521101

CLUBCALL
0898 12 11 64
Calls cost 39p per minute cheap rate and 49p per
minute at all other times.
Call costings correct at time of going to press.

HOW TO GET TO THE GROUND

From the North:
Leave M61 at junction 5 or enter Bolton via A666 or A676. Then follow signs for Farnworth B653 into Manchester Road. In 0.6 miles
ground is on the left.

From South, East and West:
Use M62 until junction 14 then join M61. In 2.1 miles leave Motorway
and at roundabout take first exit B6536. In 2.1 miles. Ground is on
the right.

Car Parking:
Private car parking only in forecourt. Large car park 200 yards from
ground. Limited street parking nearby. Multi-storey car parks are in
town centre.

Nearest Railway Station:
Bolton (01204 528216).

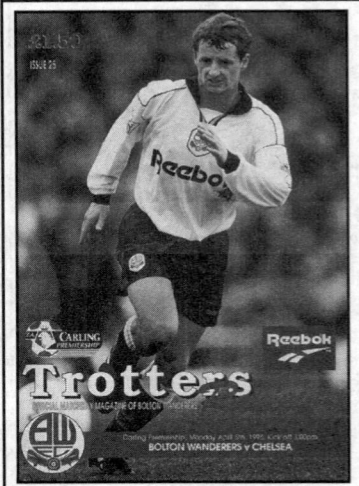

MATCHDAY PROGRAMME

Programme Editor. . . . . Simon Marland.

Number of pages . . . . 48.

Price . . . . £1.50.

Subscriptions. . . . . £40 (All home matches).

Local Newspapers. . . . . Bolton Evening News.

Local Radio Stations . . . . Piccadilly Radio, G.M.R.

BRADFORD CITY AFC
(The Bantams)
NATIONWIDE LEAGUE DIVISION 1
SPONSORED BY: DIAMOND SEAL LTD

Back Row (L-R): Wayne Benn, Richard Liburd, Scott Jackson, Carl Shutt, Richard Huxford, Andy Kiwomya, Paul Showler, Chris Stabb, Neil Grayston.
Middle Row: Steve Redmond (Physio), Graham Mitchell, John Ford, Nicky Mohan, Gavin Ward, Ian Ormondroyd, Neil Tolson, Des Hamilton, Steve Smith (Yth Coach).
Front Row: Chris Dolby, Wayne Jacobs, Craig Midgley, Lennie Lawrence (Manager), Eddie Youds (Capt), Chris Kamara (Asst Manager), Gary Robson, Shaun Murray, Tommy Wright.

BRADFORD CITY AFC
FORMED IN 1903
TURNED PROFESSIONAL IN 1903
LTD COMPANY IN 1983

CHAIRMAN: G Richmond

DIRECTORS
T Goddard, FCCA, Miss E Richmond,
D Richmond
ASSOCIATE DIRECTORS
A Biggin, M Scott, E Smith, M Smith,
H Williams

SECRETARY
Shaun Harvey (01274 773355)

COMMERCIAL MANAGER
Allan Guliver

MANAGER: Chris Kamara
FIRST TEAM COACH: Martin Hunter

RESERVE TEAM COACH:
P Jewek

YOUTH TEAM MANAGER
Steve Smith

PHYSIOTHERAPIST
Steve Redmond

STATISTICIAN FOR THE DIRECTORY
Terry Frost

Bradford City reclaimed their Division One status, after six years in Division Two, in dramatic fashion. Earning themselves a place in the play-offs by grabbing the last place on offer, Bradford City looked to have blown it in the first of their two legged semi-final matches against Blackpool.

There start to the season was impressive with only two points dropped in their first four games. Victory over Wrexham (2-1) took them to second, and they remained in the top four until two consecutive defeats in early October saw the clubs form decline. They were unable to recreate the early season form and slowly the 'Bantams' slipped down to 11th position.

The Third Round was reached in the two major Cup competitions. But it was in the Second Round Coca-Cola Cup that Bradford produced the shock result as they knocked out Premiership side Nottingham Forest 5-4 on aggregate. This was followed by their exit from the competition in a replay against Norwich City (3-5). Wins against non-League Burton Albion (4-3) in the First Round and Preston North End (2-1) in the Second set the club up for another possible 'giant killing' act against Bolton Wanderers, but it was not to be and the Premiership's relegation favourites won 0-3.

In the Auto Windscreen Shield two draws, one against Doncaster Rovers (1-1) and Carlisle United (1-1) was not enough to see them them through to the next round.

Back to the League and nine wins out of their last 13 matches was enough to get them a chance to prove themselves in the play-offs. However, after the first leg of the semi-finals Bradford looked destined to battle it out for yet another year in Division Two, as Blackpool came out 0-2 winners. With, what seemed, a mountain to climb Bradford pulled off the come-back of the season to win 3-0 at Blackpool to book a place in the final, where they had no trouble in beating Notts County (2-0) to earn themselves a place in Division One.

BRADFORD CITY

League: 6th   FA Cup: 3rd Rnd   Coca-Cola Cup: 3rd Rnd   Auto Windscreen Shield: 1st Rnd

M	DATE	COMP	VEN	OPPONENTS	RESULT	HT	LP	GOAL SCORERS/GOAL TIMES	ATT.
1	A 12	EL	H	Bournemouth	W 1-0	0-0	9	Tolsen 81	5107
2	15	CC 1/1	H	Blackpool	W 2-1	2-0		Showler 34, Wright 40	3670
3	19	EL	A	Brighton & H.A.	D 0-0	0-0	10		(5471)
4	22	CC 1/2	A	Blackpool	W 3-2	0-0		Wright 48, Hamilton 83, Youds 90	(4553)
5	26	EL	H	Shrewsbury Town	W 3-1	3-1	5	Youds 1, Youds 14, Shutt 26	5017
6	29	EL	A	Notts County	W 2-0	1-0	10	Youds 1, Showler 70	(6168)
7	S 2	EL	H	Wycombe Wanderers	L 0-4	0-1	4		9974
8	9	EL	A	Wrexham	W 2-1	0-0	2	Shutt 52, Youds 88	(3268)
9	13	EL	A	Swindon Town	L 1-4	1-2	4	Showler 31	(8203)
10	16	EL	H	Bristol City	W 3-0	1-0	3	Showler 37, Shutt 61, 65	5165
11	20	CC 2/1	H	Nottingham Forest	W 3-2	1-1		Showler 26, Youds 56, Ormondroyd 69	9288
12	23	EL	A	Peterborough United	L 1-3	1-1	5	Showler 25	(4509)
13	25	AWS 1/1	A	Doncaster Rovers	D 1-1	1-1		Murray 45	(1014)
14	30	EL	H	Blackpool	W 2-1	0-1	2	Ormondroyd 56, Tolsen 69	6820
15	O 4	CC 2/2	A	Nottingham Forest	D 2-2	0-1		Showler 62, Ormondroyd 88	(15321)
16	7	EL	A	Swansea City	L 0-2	0-1	4		(2207)
17	14	EL	A	Bristol Rovers	L 2-3	1-1	6	Wright 18(pen), Tolsen 65	5817
18	17	AWS 1/2	H	Carlisle United	D 1-1	0-0		Tolsen 46	1287
19	21	EL	A	Carlisle United	D 2-2	2-0	8	Shutt 74, Showler 88	(6274)
20	25	CC 3	A	Norwich City	D 0-0	0-0			(11649)
21	28	EL	H	Burnley	D 2-2	1-1	8	Mitchell 22, Hamilton 54	8356
22	31	EL	H	Walsall	W 1-0	0-0	7	Tolsen 87	4310
23	N 4	EL	A	Chesterfield	L 1-2	1-1	8	Tolsen 15	(5490)
24	7	CC 3R	H	Norwich City	L 3-5	1-2		Showler 23, Ormondroyd 49, Tolsen 56	8665
25	11	FAC 1	H	Burton Albion	W 4-3	3-3		Showler 17, 26, Robson 29, Ormondroyd 88	4920
26	18	EL	A	Hull City	D 1-1	0-1	9	Midgley 81	5830
27	25	EL	A	Brentford	L 1-2	0-2	11	Murray 85	(4237)
28	D 2	FAC 2	H	Preston North End	W 2-1	1-0		Jacobs 38, Jacobs 62	7602
29	9	EL	A	Peterborough United	W 2-1	1-0	11	Showler 20, Duxbury 51	4605
30	16	EL	A	Blackpool	L 1-4	0-1	10	Showler 77	(4857)
31	23	EL	H	Oxford United	W 1-0	1-0	10	Mohan 1	4637
32	26	EL	A	York City	W 3-0	1-0	19	Showler 21(pen), Duxbury 71, Jewell 90	(5213)
33	J 6	FAC 3	H	Bolton Wanderers	L 0-3	0-1			10265
34	10	EL	A	Stockport County	W 2-1	2-1	6	Jewell 4, Huxford 27	(6030)
35	13	EL	H	Brighton & H.A.	L 1-3	0-2	7	Ormondroyd 59	5139
36	20	EL	A	Bournemouth	L 1-3	1-1	8	Stallard 33	(3628)
37	23	EL	A	Rotherham United	L 0-2	0-0	8		(3052)
38	31	EL	H	Crewe Alexandra	W 2-1	0-0	5	Mohan 66, Shutt 77	4095
39	F 3	EL	A	Shrewsbury Town	D 1-1	0-0	6	Murray 79	(3405)
40	10	EL	H	Stockport County	L 0-1	0-0	6		5290
41	24	EL	A	Bristol City	L 1-2	0-1	11	Wright 64	(5400)
42	27	EL	H	Wrexham	W 2-0	2-0	10	Stallard 7, Jewell 44	3804
43	M 2	EL	H	York City	D 2-2	2-1	10	Mohan 29, Mohan 38	5208
44	9	EL	A	Oxford United	L 0-2	0-0	10		(5133)
45	16	EL	H	Rotherham United	W 2-0	0-0	10	Stallard 59, Ormondroyd 63	4047
46	19	EL	H	Notts County	W 1-0	1-0	10	Stallard 35	3622
47	23	EL	A	Crewe Alexandra	W 2-1	1-0	8	Stallard 15, Liburd 74	(3887)
48	26	EL	A	Wycombe Wanderers	L 2-5	1-2	9	Kiwomya 4, Shutt 71	(3021)
49	30	EL	H	Swansea City	W 5-1	0-0	8	Edwards 51(og), Stallard 61, 66, Tolsen 82, Hamilton 86	4183
50	A 2	EL	A	Bristol Rovers	L 0-1	0-0	9		(4008)
51	6	EL	A	Burnley	W 3-2	2-0	9	Tolsen 35, Winstanley 36(og), Kiwomya 89	(9714)
52	8	EL	H	Carlisle United	W 3-1	1-0	6	Tolsen 40, Ormondroyd 70, Stallard 76	6156
53	13	EL	A	Walsall	L 1-2	0-0	8	Wright 65(pen)	(3679)
54	20	EL	H	Chesterfield	W 2-1	0-1	7	Hamilton 59, Ormondroyd 78	6803
55	26	EL	H	Brentford	W 2-1	1-0	6	Ormondroyd 43, Duxbury 76	7730
56	30	EL	A	Swindon Town	D 1-1	0-0	6	Wright 51	9812
57	M 4	EL	A	Hull City	W 3-2	2-2	6	Stallard 11, Duxbury 26, Shutt 56	(8965)
58	12	PO SF1	H	Blackpool	L 0-2	0-0			14273
59	15	PO SF2	A	Blackpool	W 3-0	1-0		Shutt 39, Hamilton 68, Stallard 78	(9593)
60	26	PO F	H	Notts County	W 2-0	1-0		Hamilton 8, Stallard 75	39972

Best Home League Attendance: 9974 v Wycombe Wanderers   Smallest: 3622 v Notts County   Average: 5718

Goal Scorers:
EL(71):   Stallard(9),Showler(8),Tolsen(8),Shutt(8),Ormondroyd(6),Wright(4),Youds(4),Duxbury(4),Mohan(4),Hamilton(3),Jewell(3),Murray(2),Kiwomya(2),Opponent(s)(2),
            Huxford(1),Liburd(1),Midgley(1),Mitchell(1)
CC(13):   Showler(4),Ormondroyd(3),Wright(2),Youds(2),Hamilton(1),Tolsen(1)
FAC(6):   Jacobs(2),Showler(2),Ormondroyd(1),Robson(1)
AWS(2):   Tolsen(1),Murray(1)   PO(5):   Stallard(2),Hamilton(2),Shutt(1)

Brightwell (D)	Bullimore (M)	Dolby (F)	Duxbury (F)	Foley (M)	Ford (D)	Gould (G)	Grayston (D)	Hamilton (M)	Harper (G)	Huxford (D)	Jacobs (D)	Jewell (F)	Kernaghan (D)	Kiwomya (F)	Liburd (D)	Midgley (F)	Mitchell (D)	Mohan (D)	Murray (F)	Ormondroyd (F)	Robson (M)	Showler (F)	Shutt (F)	Stallard (F)	Tolsen (F)	Ward (G)	Wright (F)	Youds (D)	Player	#
										X					S2	X	X	X	X	X3	X1	S1	X2		S3	X	X	X	T.Heilbron	1
			S							X					S1	X	X	X	X	X2			X1		S2	X	X	X	N.Barry	2
			S							X					S	X	X	X	X				X		S	X	X	X	D.Orr	3
						X				X					S1	X	X	X	X			S	X	S	S	X	X	X	G.Cain	4
						X				X	X	X				S3	X	X	X	X2		S1	X3		S2	X	X1	X	T.West	5
			S							X	X	X				S	X	X	X				X		S	X		X	E.Wolstenholme	6
			S3							X	X3	X			S2		X	X	X2	X1			S1			X		X	K.Breen	7
					X					X	X		S				X	X	X1		X2	X1			S2	X	S1	X	E.Lomas	8
					X					X	X						X	X	X		X1		X2		S2	X	S1	X	J.Rushton	9
					X					X	X				S	S1	X1		X				X		S	X	X	X1	T.Heilbron	10
					X					X	X			S	S1		X1		X				X		S	X	X	X	T.Lunt	11
				X2						X					S1	X	S2		X				X	X1	S3	X	X3	X	S.G.Bennett	12
				X						X				X	S		X	X	X1				X		S	X	X	X	R.Pearson	13
				X						X	X						X	X	X				X	X1	S1	X	X	X	A.Wiley	14
				X						X	X			S			X	X			S	X			S	X	X	X	P.E.Alcock	15
				X2							X						X	X	S1	X1	S3	X	S4			X	X	X	G.P.Barber	16
				X3							X						X	X	S3			X2	X1		S1	X	X	X	A.R.Pearson	17
											X						X	X1	X	S3	S2	X2	X	S2	X	X	X3	X	G.Frankland	18
										X							X	X	X	S	S2	X1	X	X2	X2	X	X1	X	J.Lloyd	19
										X							X	X	X		S	S	S		X	X	X	X	D.Orr	20
										X							X	X	X		S	S	X		S	X	X	X	D.Allison	21
										X							X	X	X	S3	X2	S1	X		S2	X		X3	T.Lunt	22
										X			S				X	X	X	X	X		S		X1	X			B.Knight	23
										X					S1		X	X	S2	S3	X		X		X3	X	X2		N.Barry	24
		S								X			X				X		X2		X1		X		X	X			J.Winter	25
			X3		X		X	X1	X	X				S2			X		X	S3	X	X	X		X2				M.Fletcher	26
			X		X			X		X		X					X		X	S3	X	X	X		X2	X			R.Gifford	27
			X		X			X				X					X		S1	X2		X1	X3		S2	X	X	X	A.Wilkie	28
			X					X				S1		S			X	X		X			S1		X	X	X	X	P.Richards	29
	X3		X									X		X2		X1		X	X	S3	S2		X		S1	X	X	X	R.Furnandiz	30
X	S3		X							X1	X	X2		X			S	X	S		X	X3	S1		S2	X		X	I.Cruikshanks	31
X			X							X	X	X		X			S	X	S		X	X	S		X	X		X	K.Lynch	32
X			X							X	X2					X3	X	S3	S2		X	X1	X		S	X		X	S.Dunn	33
X			X							X			S				X	X	S		X	X	S		S	X		X	E.Wolstenholme	34
X3			X							X	X3	X					X1	X	S1	S3		X	X2	S2		X		X	P.Taylor	35
X			X									S1		S2		X	X	X	X	S3		X2	X	X1	X	X		X	M.Bailey	36
X1			X1				X					S2		S		X	X	X	X		X3	X2	X	S3	X	X	S1		D.B.Allison	37
X1			X2							X		S				X	X	X	X		X	X	X	S2	X	X			R.Pearson	38
			X					S		X		X	X	S2		X	X		X		X2	X1	S1	X1	X	X			M.J.Brandwood	39
			X							X			S3	X			X	X	X3		X	S1	X1	S2	X	X		X2	A.Butler	40
X			X									S2	X		X		X	X3	S1		X1	S3	X2		X	X			P.Rejer	41
X			X									S1	X		X		X	X	S		X	X	S	X1	X	X			A.Leake	42
X			X									X2	X	S3	X		X3	X	S1		X1	X2			X	X			R.Furnandiz	43
X			X		X							X1		S2	X	X	S3	X2	X	X3		S1			X	X			S.Baines	44
X			X		X1							S3		S1	X	X	X	X	X2					X3	S2	X	X		P.Richards	45
X			X				X					S		X	X	X	X	X	X		S		X	X	S	X	X		W.Burns	46
X			X		X							S3		X3		X	X	X	X				X1	S2	S1	X2	X	X1	R.Gifford	47
X3			X		S3									X	X		X	X			X1		S2	S1		X	X2		I.Hemley	48
X			X			X		S1				X		X2			X	X					S	X	X	S2	X1		E.Lomas	49
X			X			X		S2				X		X3			X	X2					S1	X1	S3	X	X		A.Wiley	50
X			X			X		S1				X		X			X	X1	S2				X3	X2	S3	X	X		M.Bailey	51
X			X			X		S2				X		X3			X	X2	S1				X	X1	S3	X	X		F.Stretton	52
X2			X	X		X		X		S3		X		X3							S1		S2	X	X1	X	X		C.Wilkes	53
			X	X		X		X		S2	X	S		X							S1		X	X	X1	X	X2		I.Cruikshanks	54
S2			X	X		X		X1		S1	X			X				X					X	X3	S3	X		X2	T.West	55
X			X2	X		X		X		S2	X			X				X	X	X1			S1	X3	S3	X	X		M.Fletcher	56
X			X	X		X		X		S2	X			X				X2	X				S1	X-	S		X1		U.Rennie	57
X1			X	X		X		X		S2	X			S1	X2			X					X	X3	S3				T.Heilbron	58
X			X			X		X		X	X	X	S		X			X	X			S		X	X		S2	X	W.Burns	59
S			X			X		X1		X	X				X			X				X	X	S				X	G.Singh	60
21	1	0	30	0	18	0	2	17	1	21	29	7	5	7	33	0	32	39	24	28	4	29	22	18	12	36	28	30	EL Appearances	
1	1	0	0	1	1	0	0	7	0	5	0	11	0	9	0	5	1	0	9	9	2	4	11	2	19	0	6	0	EL Sub Appearances	
0	0	0	0	0	4	0	0	4	0	5	4	0	0	0+2	3+2	0	6	6	2+2	6	0+1	5	3+1	1	3	1	1	5	CC Appearances	
1	0	0	2	0	0	0	0	2	0	1+1	3	1	0	0	1	0	2	2	1+2	2+1	1	3	1+1	0	2+1	0	1	2	FAC Appearances	
0	0	0	0	0	1	0	0	0+1	0	2	1	0	0	0	1	0	2	2	2	1+1	1	2	0+2	0	1	2	2	2	AWS Appearances	
2	0	0	3	0	0	3	0	3	0	2+1	3	0	0	2+1	1	0	2	3	0	1+1	0	0	3	3	0+1	0	0+1	2	PO Appearances	

BRADFORD CITY

CLUB RECORDS

BIGGEST VICTORIES
League: 11-1 v Rotherham United, Division 3(N), 25.8.1928.
FA Cup: 11-3 v Walker Celtic, FA Cup 1st Rnd. Replay, 1.12.1937.
League Cup: 4-0 v Rochdale, 2nd Rnd. 27.10.1982.

BIGGEST DEFEATS
League: 0-8 v Manchester City, Division 2, 7.5.1927.
1-9 v Colchester United, Division 4, 30.12.1961.
FA Cup: 1-6 v Newcastle United, 3rd Rnd, 7.3.1963.
0-5 v Burnley, 5th Rnd (R), 23.2.1960.
0-5 v Tottenham, 3rd Rnd, 7.1.1970.
League Cup: 1-7 v Aston Villa, 5th Rnd, 23.11.1964.

MOST POINTS
3 points a win: 94, Division 3, 1984-85.
2 points a win: 63, Division 3(N), 1928-29.

MOST GOALS SCORED
128, 1928-29 (Division 3(N))
Whitehurst 24, Moon 15, Edmunds 11, Scriven 10, Cairns 9, Cochrane 9, Bauld 8, Bedford 8, Randall 8, Moore 7, Barkas 5, White 4, Burkinshaw 4, Harvey 2, Mitchell 1, Russell 1, Opponents 2.

INDIVIDUAL CLUB RECORDS

MOST GOALS IN A SEASON
David Layne - 36 (League 34, FA Cup 2) Div 4, 1961-62.

MOST GOALS IN A MATCH
Albert Whitehurst - 7 v Tranmere Rovers, 8-0, Div 3(N), 6.3.1929.

MOST GOALS IN A CAREER
Robert Campbell - 143 (Lge 121, FAC 5, Lge Cup 11, Others 6).

MOST APPEARANCES
Cyril 'Cec' Podd 1970-84 (Lge 494+8, FAC 30, Lge C 33+1, Oth 8)
Total: 574

OLDEST PLAYER
Tommy Cairns, 41 years 7 days v Bradford P.A., 7.11.1931.

YOUNGEST PLAYER
Robert Cullingford, 16 years 141 days v Mansfield Town, 22.4.1970.

MOST CAPPED PLAYER
Harry Hampton (Northern Ireland) 9.
Evelyn Lintott (England) 4.

BEST PERFORMANCES

League: 1984-85: P 46 W 28 D 10 L 8 F 77 A 45 **Pts** 94. First in Division 3.

Highest: 5th in Division 1, 1910-11.

F.A. Cup: Winners in 1911.
1st Rnd. New Brompton 1-0. 2nd Rnd. Norwich City 2-1. 3rd Rnd. Grimsby Town 1-0. 4th Rnd. Burnley 1-0. Semi-Final Blackburn 3-0. Final Newcastle United 0-0, 1-0.

League Cup: 5th Round, 1964-65, 1987-88, 1988-89.

ADDITIONAL INFORMATION
Previous Names: None

Previous League: None (One of only two clubs to gain admission to Football League without playing a senior fixture - Chelsea being the other).

Club Colours: Amber/claret stripes, claret shorts, amber socks.
Change Colours: White shirts, white shorts, white socks.

Reserves League: Pontins Central League Division 2.

RECORDS AND STATISTICS

COMPETITIONS

Div.1/P	Div.2/1	Div.3/2	Div.3(N)	Div.4
1908-22	1903-08	1958-61	1927-29	1961-69
	1922-27	1969-72	1937-58	1972-77
	1929-37	1977-78		1978-82
	1985-90	1982-85		
	1996-	1990-96		

MOST APPEARANCES
Cecil Podd - 565+9 (1970-84)

Year	League	FA Cup	Lge Cup	Others
1970-71	19	3		
1971-72	9+1		2	
1972-73	40+1	4	1	
1973-74	36+1	2	1	
1974-75	44	1	2	
1975-76	45	6	2	
1976-77	43	2	1	
1977-78	34+3	1	1	
1978-79	39	2	3+1	
1979-80	37+2	2	4	
1980-81	35		4	
1981-82	46	1	6	4
1982-83	37	4	4	2
1983-84	30	2	2	2
	494+8	**30**	**33+1**	**8**

Previous holder: Ian Cooper - 493 (1965-77)

RECORD TRANSFER FEE RECEIVED

Amount	Club	Player	Date
£1,850,000	Wolves	Dean Richards	5/95
£875,000	Everton	Stuart McCall	6/88
£250,000	Newcastle United	Peter Jackson	10/86
£70,000	Derby County	Bobby Campbell	8/83

RECORD TRANSFER FEE PAID

Amount	Club	Player	Date
£300,000	Bristol Rovers	John Taylor	6/88
£290,000	Newcastle United	Peter Jackson	9/88
£250,000	Portsmouth	Mick Kennedy	7/87
£70,000	Aberdeen	Brian Mitchell	2/87

HONOURS

Division 2	Division 3	Division 3(N)	FA Cup	Division 3(N) C.
1907-08	1984-85	1928-29	1911	1938-39

MOST GOALS IN A CAREER
Bobby Campbell - 143 (1979-86)

Year	League	FA Cup	Lge Cup	Others
1979-80	8			
1980-81	19		3	
1981-82	24		3	2
1982-83	25	2	3	3
1983-84	9			1
1984-85	23	3		
1985-86	10		2	
1986-87	3			
	121	**5**	**11**	**6**

Current leading goalscorer:Paul Jewell - 67 (1988-96)

MANAGERS

Name	Seasons	Best	Worst
R.Campbell	1903-05		
P.O'Rourke	1905-21		
D.Menzies	1921-26		
C.Veitch	1926-28		
P O'Rourke	1928-30		
J Peart	1930-35		
R.Ray	1935-38		
F.Westgarth	1938-43		
R.Sharp (Hon.)	1943-46		
J.Barker	1946-47		
J.Milburn	1947-48		
D.Steele	1948-52		
A.Harris (Hon.)	1952		
I.Powell	1952-55		
P.Jackson Snr.	1955-61		
R.Brocklebank	1961-64		
W.Harris	1965-66		
W.Watson	1966-68		
G.Hair	1968		
J.Wheeler	1968-71		
B.Edwards	1971-75		
R.Kennedy	1975-78		
J.Napier	1978		
G.Mulhall	1978-81		
R.McFarland	1981-82		
T.Cherry	1982-87		
T.Dolan	1987-89		
T.Yorath	1989-90		
J.Docherty	1990-91		
F.Stapleton	1991-94		
Chris Kamara	1995-		

LONGEST LEAGUE RUNS

of undefeated matches:	21 (1968-69)	of league matches w/out a win:	16 (1948-49)
of undefeated home matches:	25 (1975-78)	of undefeated away matches:	10 (1968-69)
without home win:	10 (1962-64)	without an away win:	29 (1925-27)
of league wins:	10 (1983-84)	of home wins:	9 (1952-53, 1961-64)
of league defeats:	8 (1932-33)	of away wins:	5 (1928-29, 1981-82, 1984-85)

BRADFORD CITY

PLAYERS NAME Honours	Ht	Wt	Birthdate	Birthplace Transfers	Contract Date	Clubs	League	L/Cup	FA Cup	Other	Lge	L/C	FAC	Oth
G O A L K E E P E R S														
Gould Jonathan	6.1	12.6	18/07/68	Paddington		Clevedon Town								
				Free	18/07/90	Halifax Town	32	2	5	5				
				Free	30/01/92	W.B.A.								
				£17500	15/07/92	Coventry City	25	1+1						
				Loan	29/03/96	Bradford City	9			3				
				Free	01/07/96	Bradford City								
D E F E N D E R S														
Brightwell David	6.1	13.05	07/01/71	Lutterworth	11/04/88	Manchester City	35+8	2+1	5		1		1	
				Loan	22/03/91	Chester City	6							
				Loan	11/08/95	Lincoln City	5	2						
				Loan	11/09/95	Stoke City	0+1			1				
				£30000	29/12/95	Bradford City	21+1		1	2				
Ford Jonathan	6.1	13.1	12/04/68	Birmingham		Cradley Town								
AGT'94.				£5000	19/08/91	Swansea City	145+15	12+1	8+5	15+5	6		2	
				£210000	26/07/95	Bradford City	18+1	4	2	1				
Huxford Richard	5.10	11.6	25/07/69	Scunthorpe		Kettering Town								
					06/08/92	Barnet	33	2	2	2+1	1			
				Free	16/07/93	Millwall	25+7	1+1	1	3		1		
				Loan	21/02/94	Birmingham City	5							
				Loan	11/08/94	Bradford City								
				£50000	01/06/95	Bradford City	54+5	5	3+1	7+1	2			
Jacobs Wayne	5.9	10.2	03/02/69	Sheffield	03/01/87	Sheffield Wed.	5+1	3		1				
				£27000	25/03/88	Hull City	127+2	7	8	6	4			
				Free	05/08/93	Rotherham United	40+4	4	1	2	2			
				Free	05/08/94	Bradford City	67	8	4	5	1		2	
Liburd Richard	5.9	11.1	26/09/73	Nottingham		Eastwood Town								
				£20000	25/03/93	Middlesbrough	41	4	2	5	1			
				£200000	21/07/94	Bradford City	42	5+2	1	2	2			
Mitchell Graham	6.1	11.4	16/02/68	Shipley	16/06/86	Huddersfield Town	235+9	13+2	27	24	2	1	1	1
				Loan	24/12/93	Bournemouth	4							
					23/12/94	Bradford City	58+1	6	2	4	1			
Mohan Nicholas	6.0	11.10	06/10/70	Middlesbrough	18/11/87	Middlesbrough	93+6	11	9	11	4			
				Loan	26/09/92	Hull City	5				1			
				£330000	07/07/94	Leicester City	23	2	1					
				£225000	13/07/95	Bradford City	39	6	2	5	4			
Youds Edward	6.0	10.10	03/05/70	Liverpool	10/06/88	Everton	5+3	0+1		1				
				Loan	29/12/89	Cardiff City	0+1		0+1					
				Loan	08/02/90	Wrexham	20				2			
				£250000	15/11/91	Ipswich Town	38+12	1+2	5+1		1			
				Loan	20/01/95	Bradford City								
				£150000	17/03/95	Bradford City	47	5	2	4	7	2		
M I D F I E L D														
Bullimore Wayne A	5.1	11.07	12/09/70	Sutton-in-Ash.	16/09/88	Manchester United								
E: S.				Free	09/03/91	Barnsley	27+8	2+1	1+1		1			
				Free	11/10/93	Stockport County								
				Free	19/11/93	Scunthorpe United	62+5	2+1	7	5	11	1	1	1
				Free	15/12/95	Bradford City	1+1							
Cowans Gordon	5.7	10.6	27/10/58	Cornforth	01/09/76	Aston Villa (A)	276+10	23+4	19+1	23+1	42	5	3	2
E: 10, B.2, u21.5, Y. Div.1'81. EC'82. ESC'82.				£500000	01/07/85	Bari								
CS'81. LC'77'94.				£250000	13/07/88	Aston Villa	114+3	15	9	11+1	7			
				£200000	28/11/91	Blackburn Rovers	49+1	4	5	3	2		1	
				Free	05/07/93	Aston Villa	9+2	2		4				
				£80000	03/02/94	Derby County	19			3				1
				£25000	19/12/94	Wolves	31+6	2	5	2		1		
					29/12/96	Sheffield United	18+2		3					
				Free	18/07/96	Bradford City								
Hamilton Derick	5.7	10.12	06/07/65	Bradford	01/06/94	Bradford City	42+14	5	3	4+1	5	1		2
F O R W A R D S														
Duxbury Lee	5.8	11.0	07/10/69	Keighley	04/07/88	Bradford City	204+5	18+1	11	13	25	1		
				Loan	18/01/90	Rochdale	9+1		1					
				£250000	23/12/94	Huddersfield Town	29	1		3	2			
				£135000	15/11/95	Bradford City	30		2	3	4			
Jewell Paul	5.8	10.8	28/09/64	Liverpool	30/09/82	Liverpool								
AMC'85.				£15000	20/12/84	Wigan Athletic	117+20	5+2	9	14+4	35		5	7
				£80000	21/07/88	Bradford City	217+52	16+1	12+1	8+1	57	6	3	1
				Loan	16/08/95	Grimsby Town								
Kiwomya Andy	5.9	10.10	01/10/67	Huddersfield	16/07/85	Barnsley	1							
				£5000	07/10/86	Sheffield Wed.								
				Free	01/08/92	Dundee	11+10		0+1		1			
				Free	01/10/93	Rotherham United	4+3	0+1		0+2				
				Free	01/06/94	Halifax Town								
				Free	23/03/95	Scunthorpe United	9			3				

	Ht	Wt	DOB	Previous Club	Fee	Date	Club									
womya continued...					Free	04/07/95	Barnsley									
dgley Craig			24/05/76	Bradford		01/08/94	Bradford City	0+8		0+2	1	1				
					Loan	07/12/95	Scarborough	14+2				1				
urray Shaun	5.7	10.5	07/12/70	Newcastle		10/12/87	Tottenham Hotspur									
Y.7.					£100000	12/06/89	Portsmouth	21+13	2+1	1+3	2+2	1	1			
					Loan	16/08/93	Millwall									
						01/11/93	Scarborough	29		2	2	5				
					£200000	01/08/94	Bradford City	62+12	5+2	3+2	4	7	1		2	
mondroyd Ian	6.4	13.9	22/09/64	Bradford		06/09/85	Bradford City	72+15	12+2	7	7+2	20	4	2	1	
					Loan	27/03/87	Oldham Athletic	8+2				1				
					£600000	02/02/89	Aston Villa	41+15	4+2	5	6+1	6	2	2		
					£350000	19/09/91	Derby County	25	3	3		8		1		
						11/02/92	Leicester City	67+10	6	1+1	11	7	2		3	
					Loan	27/01/95	Hull City	10				6				
					£75000	13/07/95	Bradford City	28+9	6	2+1	2+2	6	3	1		
owler Paul	5.11	11.9	10/10/66	Doncaster			Sheffield Wed.									
SP.2. NPL'90. NPLD1'89.							Bentley Vics.									
							Goole Town									
						01/01/03	Colne Dynamoes									
						01/01/04	Altrincham			1						
					Free	15/08/91	Barnet	69+2	2	3+1	7	12		1		
					Free	04/08/93	Bradford City	72+16	8+1	6	4+1	15	5	2		
utt Carl	5.10	11.13	10/10/61	Sheffield		13/05/85	Sheffield Wed.	36+4	3	4+1		16	1	4		
v.1'92. Div.2'90.					£55000	30/10/87	Bristol City	39+7	5+2	7+1	10+1	10	4	4	4	
					£50000	23/03/89	Leeds United	46+33	6+2	10	4+5	17	2	1	4	
					£50000	23/08/93	Birmingham City	23+9	3			4				
					Loan	11/08/94	Bradford City									
					£75000	09/09/94	Bradford City	50+15	7+1	2+2	5+2	12	1		1	
allard Mark	6.0	12.04	24/10/74	Derby		06/11/91	Derby County	19+8	2+1	2+2	3	2	2		1	
					Loan	23/09/94	Fulham									
						18/01/96	Bradford City	18+2			3	9			2	
right Tommy E	5.7	9.9	10/01/66	Dunfermline		15/01/83	Leeds United	73+8	3+2	4		24	1	3		
u21.1.					£80000	24/10/86	Oldham Athletic	110+2	7+1	3	3	23	2	2		
					£350000	14/08/89	Leicester City	122+7	7+1	4	10	22			7	
					£650000	01/07/92	Middlesbrough	44+9	3+1	3	5+1	5		1		
					Free	04/07/95	Bradford City	28+6	6	1	2+1	4	2			

THE MANAGER
CHRIS KAMARA

Date of Birth . . . . 25th December 1957.
Place of Birth. . . . . Middlesbrough.
Date of Appointment . . . . November 1995.

PREVIOUS CLUBS
As Manager. . . . . None.
As Coach . . . . Bradford City.
As a Player . . . . Portsmouth, Swindon, Portsmouth, Brentford, Swindon,
. . . . Stoke, Leeds, Luton.

HONOURS
As a Manager
Bradford City: Gained promotion to Division 1, via the play-offs. 1995-96.

As a Player
None.

THE PULSE STADIUM

Valley Parade, Bradford, West Yorkshire BD8 7DY
Tel: 01274 773 355

Capacity 13,800
Covered Standing 7,234
Seating 6,270

First game .... v Gainsborough Trin., Div 2 5.9.1903
First floodlit game .... v Hull City, 20.12.1954

ATTENDANCES
Highest .... 39,146 v Burnley, FAC 4th Rnd, 11.3.1911
Lowest .... 1,179 v Hartlepool United, AMC, 22.2.1984

MATCHDAY TICKET PRICES

Sunwin Stand £13
. . . . OAP/Juv £7
HSG Stand £13
. . . . OAP £5
Diamond Seal Kop £9
. . . . OAP/Juv £5

Match and Ticket Information
N&P Stand tickets available four weeks in
advance of matches.

Ticket Office Telephone No. . 01274 773355

HOW TO GET TO THE GROUND

From the North
A650 to Bradford.
Join Ring Road, A6036.
Turn left into Valley Parade for ground.

From the South and West
M62 and A606 (M) to Bradford.
Fourth exit from roundabout to A6036 Ring Road.
Left at crossroads A650, left into Valley Parade.

From East
A647 to Bradford.
Right at crossroads, A6036.
Left at crossroads A650.
Left into Valley Parade.

MATCHDAY PROGRAMME

Programme Editor . . . . Kevin Mitchell.

Number of pages 48

Price £1.50

Subscriptions . . . . £40 per season

Local Newspapers . . . . Telegraph and Argus, Bradford Star

Local Radio Stations . . . . The Pulse 97.5 & 102.5 FM
. . . . BBC Radio Leeds (388 MW), Magic 828 (362 MW)

CHARLTON ATHLETIC
(The Addicks)
NATIONWIDE LEAGUE DIVISION 1
SPONSORED BY: VIGLEN

Back Row (L-R): Stuart Reynolds, Steve Brown, Richard Rufus, Mike Ammann, Mike Salmon, Andy Petterson, Carl Leaburn, Dean Chandler, Jamie Stuart. **Middle Row:** Jimmy Hendry (Physio), Gary Moss (Asst. Physio), Keith Dowson, Shaun Newton, Lee Bowyer, Paul Mortimer, Phil Chapple, Andy Larkin, Kim Grant, Peter Garland, Paul Linger, Steve Watts (Yth Dev. Officer). **Front Row:** John Humphrey, Paul Sturgess, David Whyte, Garry Nelson, Alan Curbishley (Manager), Keith Jones, Les Reed (First team coach), Stuart Balyer, Colin Walsh, John Robinson, Mark Robson.

CHARLTON ATHLETIC
FORMED IN 1905
TURNED PROFESSIONAL IN 1920
LTD COMPANY IN 1919

CHAIRMAN: M A Simons
VICE- CHAIRMAN & MANAGING DIRECTOR
R A Murray
DIRECTORS
R N Alwen, G P Bone, R D Collins, J Fuller,
D Hughes, C Norris, M C Stevens,
D Summer, D G Ufton
SECRETARY
Chris Parkes
COMMERCIAL MANAGER
Steve Dixon

MANAGER: Alan Curbishley
FIRST TEAM COACH: Les Reed
RESERVE TEAM MANAGER
Keith Peacock
YOUTH TEAM MANAGER
Terry Westley
PHYSIOTHERAPIST
Jimmy Hendry

STATISTICIAN FOR THE DIRECTORY
Paul Clayton

An eventful season saw the Addicks miss out on promotion in the play-offs after being in contention for an automatic promotion spot for most of the campaign. It was the home form that let them down, with only eight wins all season and eleven matches drawn. The away form was much better, with nine wins and nine draws, five of the victories coming in consecutive matches mid-season. Without a win in the last five home games, Charlton finished in sixth place. Goals were once again in short supply, with no player reaching double figures in the league, however, the defensive record was only bettered by champions Sunderland.

Charlton progressed to the third round of the Coca-Cola Cup, losing in extra time to Wolves at home in a replay, after beating Barnet and Premiership side Wimbledon in the previous rounds over two legs. Another Premiership scalp was taken in the FA Cup when Sheffield Wednesday were beaten at The Valley. Brentford were then put out before they were overcome by Liverpool at Anfield in the fifth round.

Former favourite John Humphrey - signed on a free transfer from Crystal Palace - and striker Marc Salmon from Harlow Town were the only close season signings, and another former player, Paul Williams, was signed early in the season. Experienced defender Chris Whyte was added to the squad in March, and Bradley Allen was signed for £400,000 from QPR just before the transfer deadline, with Kim Grant sold to Luton. Everton's Matt Jackson was also brought in on loan.

Success story of the season was Lee Bowyer who was outstanding in midfield and added 14 goals in the various competitions - he also made his England Under 21 debut, along with team-mates Richard Rufus and Jamie Stuart. Midfielder Shaun Newton must surely be on the verge of similar honours. Richard Rufus had another outstanding season alongside Stuart Balmer in the centre of defence and Supporters' Player of the Year John Robinson deservedly won a full Welsh Cap, as the culmination of a tremendous campaign. The goalkeeping duties were shared between the three 'keepers, with Andy Pettersen putting in some excellent performances during the promotion run-in. The play-off matches against Crystal Palace were disappointing as both games were lost, despite the Reds scoring in the first minute of the first leg and dominating both games.

Gates were up for the fifth successive season, with the average league gate topping the 11,000 mark.

Prospects for the new season would seem to depend on whether Charlton can hold on to their youngsters and whether David Whyte can regain his scoring touch or a new partner be found for Bradley Allen up front. **PAUL CLAYTON**

CHARLTON ATHLETIC

League: 6th   FA Cup: 5th Rnd   Coca-Cola Cup: 3rd Rnd

M	DATE	COMP	VEN	OPPONENTS	RESULT	HT	LP	GOAL SCORERS/GOAL TIMES	ATT.
1	A 12	EL	A	West Bromwich Albion	L 0-1	0-0	6		(14688)
2	15	CC 1/1	A	**Barnet**	**D 0-0**	**0-0**			**(1893)**
3	19	EL	H	Birmingham City	W 3-1	0-0	1	Nelson 68, Bowyer 69, Grant 88	9692
4	22	CC 1/2	H	**Barnet**	**W 2-0**	**1-0**		**Bowyer 27, 78**	**4418**
5	26	EL	A	Crystal Palace	D 1-1	1-0	1	Bowyer 20	(14124)
6	29	EL	H	Watford	W 2-1	0-1	1	Bowyer 49, Leaburn 70	8442
7	S 2	EL	H	Huddersfield Town	W 2-1	1-0	1	Newton 31, Stuart 71	9570
8	9	EL	A	Tranmere Rovers	D 0-0	0-0	1		(7402)
9	12	EL	A	Sheffield United	L 0-2	0-1	2		(9448)
10	16	EL	H	Oldham Athletic	D 1-1	0-1	3	Leaburn 65	8926
11	19	CC 2/1	A	**Wimbledon**	**W 5-4**	**2-1**		**Garland 25, Bowyer 42, 77, 79, Grant 85**	**(3717)**
12	23	EL	A	Ipswich Town	W 5-1	0-1	1	Chapple 55, Leaburn 69, 70, 90(pen) (3), Linger 90	(12815)
13	30	EL	H	Barnsley	D 1-1	1-0	2	Grant 40	11219
14	O 3	CC 2/2	H	**Wimbledon**	**D 3-3**	**1-1**		**Newton 21, Leaburn 80, Robinson 98**	**9823**
15	7	EL	H	Grimsby Town	L 0-1	0-1	3		8994
16	14	EL	A	Leicester City	D 1-1	0-1	4	Leaburn 83	(16771)
17	21	EL	H	Norwich City	D 1-1	0-0	5	Bowyer 69	13369
18	25	CC 3	A	**Wolverhampton Wand**	**D 0-0**	**0-0**			**(22481)**
19	29	EL	A	Luton Town	W 1-0	1-0	4	Nelson 16	(6270)
20	N 5	EL	H	Sunderland	D 1-1	1-1	4	Newton 10	11626
21	8	CC 3R	H	**Wolverhampton Wand**	**L 1-2**	**0-1**		**Robinson 57**	**10909**
22	12	EL	A	Wolverhampton Wand	D 0-0	0-0	4		(20450)
23	18	EL	A	Derby County	L 0-2	0-1	6		(12693)
24	21	EL	H	Reading	W 2-1	1-1	6	Chapple 20, Robinson 88	7840
25	25	EL	A	Port Vale	D 2-2	0-0	8	Mortimer 53(pen), Bowyer 73	10174
26	D 2	EL	A	Grimsby Town	W 2-1	1-0	4	Grant 44, Whyte 51(pen)	(6881)
27	5	EL	A	Millwall	W 2-0	1-0	1	Grant 7, 67	(11350)
28	9	EL	H	Ipswich Town	L 0-2	0-0	2		10316
29	16	EL	A	Barnsley	W 2-1	2-0	1	Robinson 23, Newton 39	(6140)
30	26	EL	H	Portsmouth	W 2-1	0-1	2	Newton 65, Nelson 89	11686
31	J 6	FAC 3	H	**Sheffield Wednesday**	**W 2-0**	**2-0**		**Grant 6, Mortimer 37(pen)**	**13815**
32	14	EL	A	Birmingham City	W 4-3	3-1		Edwards 18(og), Grant 37, Robinson 44, Leaburn 70	(17688)
33	20	EL	H	West Bromwich Albion	W 4-1	3-0	2	Robinson 3, 16, Stuart 44, Mortimer 64	11864
34	F 4	EL	H	Crystal Palace	D 0-0	0-0	2		13560
35	7	FAC 4	H	**Brentford**	**W 3-2**	**2-1**		**Robinson 20, Bowyer 44, Whyte 86**	**15000**
36	10	EL	A	Watford	W 2-1	0-1	2	Robinson 51, Bowyer 73	(8394)
37	17	EL	H	Sheffield United	D 1-1	0-0	2	Mortimer 90	11239
38	20	EL	A	Huddersfield Town	D 2-2	1-2	2	Bowyer 31, Robson 51(pen)	(10951)
39	24	EL	A	Oldham Athletic	D 1-1	0-0	2	Grant 70	(6570)
40	28	FAC 5	A	**Liverpool**	**L 1-2**	**1-0**		**Grant 86**	**36818**
41	M 2	EL	A	Portsmouth	L 1-2	1-1	3	Butters 24(og)	(9323)
42	5	EL	H	Southend United	L 0-3	0-1	3		11927
43	9	EL	H	Millwall	W 2-0	1-0	3	Bowyer 5, Leaburn 90	12204
44	16	EL	A	Southend United	D 1-1	1-1	4	Mortimer 32(pen)	(7382)
45	23	EL	H	Stoke City	W 2-1	0-1	4	Mortimer 85(pen), Whyte 90	12770
46	30	EL	A	Norwich City	W 1-0	0-0	4	Allen 54	(13434)
47	A 2	EL	H	Leicester City	L 0-1	0-1	4		11287
48	5	EL	H	Luton Town	D 1-1	0-1	4	Allen 69(pen)	14643
49	8	EL	A	Sunderland	D 0-0	0-0	4		(20914)
50	14	EL	H	Derby County	D 0-0	0-0	4		11334
51	17	EL	A	Stoke City	L 0-1	0-1	5		(12969)
52	20	EL	A	Reading	D 0-0	0-0	5		(9778)
53	27	EL	A	Port Vale	W 3-1	1-1	5	Balmer 42, Newton 47, Allen 70	(8428)
54	30	EL	H	Tranmere Rovers	D 0-0	0-0	5		10936
55	M 5	EL	H	Wolverhampton Wand	D 1-1	0-0	6	Leaburn 39	14023
56	12	PO SF1	H	**Crystal Palace**	**L 1-2**	**1-0**		**Newton 1**	**14618**
57	15	PO SF2	A	**Crystal Palace**	**L 0-1**	**0-1**			**(22880)**

Best Home League Attendance: 14643 v Luton Town   **Smallest: 7840 v Reading**   **Average: 11201**

Goal Scorers:
EL(57): Leaburn(9),Bowyer(8),Grant(7),Robinson(6),Newton(5),Mortimer(5),Nelson(3),Allen(3),Stuart(2),Whyte(2),Chapple(2),Opponent(s)(2),Robson(1),Linger(1),Balmer(1)
CC(11): Bowyer(5),Robinson(2),Garland(1),Grant(1),Newton(1),Leaburn(1)
FAC(6): Grant(2),Robinson(1),Whyte(1),Mortimer(1),Bowyer(1)
PO(1): Newton(1)

1995-96

Allen (F)	Ammann (G)	Balmer (D)	Bowyer (M)	Brown (D)	Chandler (D)	Chapple (D)	Garland (M)	Grant (F)	Humphrey (D)	Jackson (D)	Jones (M)	Leaburn (F)	Linger (F)	Mortimer (M)	Nelson (F)	Newton (M)	Nicholls (M)	Petterson (G)	Robinson (M)	Robson (F)	Rufus (D)	Salmon (G)	Stuart (D)	Sturgess (D)	Walsh (M)	Whyte (D)	Whyte (F)	Williams (F)	Opponent	#
	X	X	X2						X		X	X			S1				S2	X1	X	X	X				X		R.Poulain	1
	S	X	X	X				S	X		X				X				S1	X	X1	X	X				X		D.Orr	2
		X	X		S3			S1	X						X2					X	X	X	X	X1	S2		X3		E.Lomas	3
		X	X			S		S1	X		X				X					X	X1	X	X		S1		X1		A.D'Urso	4
		X	X					S2	X		X	S1			X1	X			X2	X	X	X				X		C.R.Wilkes	5
		X	X			S		S2	X		X	S1			X	X			X	X	X	X1				X2		B.Pooley	6
		X	X			S2		S1	X		X	X			X	X			X1	S	X2	X	X						M.Bailey	7
		X	X			S3		S1	X		X	X1			X3	X			X1	S1	X	X	X						J.Brandwood	8
		X	X					S1	X		X	X			X	X2			X	S2	X	X	X1						K.Breen	9
		X	X			S		S2	X		X	X			X	X			X	S1	X	X	X2						A.Butler	10
		X	X			S	X	S1	X			X			X2	X			X1	S2	X	X	X						M.Reed	11
	S	X	X3			X	X	X1				X	X1		X				X	S1	X	X							G.Barber	12
	S	X	X			X	X1	X				X	S1		X				X	S	X	X							R.Harris	13
	S	X	X			X	X1	X2	X			X	S2		X	X			X	S1	X	X							P.Durkin	14
	X1	X				X	X	X2	X			X			S2	X2			X	S2	S1	X	X					S1	I.Hemley	15
		X				X		X1	X3			X			S2	X			X	S1	X	X	X				X1	S1	I.Cruikshank	16
		X		S		X			X1			X			S1	X			X	S1	X	X	X				X1	X	P.Rejer	17
		X				X		S1	X			X			X	X			X1	S	X	X	X						R.Poulain	18
		X		S		X		S1	X			X			X1	X			X	S	X	X	X						J.Kirkby	19
	S1	X2				X		S2	X			S2			X	X			X		X2	X1	X				X		K.Leach	20
X		X				X		S1	X			S2			X	X1	S		X		X	X					X2		I.Hemley	21
X		X		S		X		X	X			X			S1	X1			X		X		X	X	S				C.Wilkes	22
X		X				X		X2	X			X	X		S2	X1	S		X		X		X				S1		U.D.Rennie	23
X		X				X		X1	X			X	X		S2	X2	S		X		X		X				S1		A.Butler	24
X		X				X		X	X			X	X		S1	X2	S		X		X		X1				S2		F.Streton	25
X		X				X		X	X			X			S1	X1			X		X		X				X2	S2	W.C.Burns	26
X	S1	X				X1		X3	X			X			S2	X			X		X		X				X2	S3	M.Pierce	27
X	X	X		S3				X3	X2			X			S1	X1			X		X		X				X	S2	A.D'Urso	28
X	X	X						X				X	X1	S2	S1	X			X		X		X				X2		G.Singh	29
	S	X						X	X			X		X	S1	X			X		X		X	X1	X2		S2		M.Bailey	30
	S	X	X					X1	X			X		X	S1	X			X		X	X	X				S		A.Wilkie	31
	S	X	X					X1	X			X		X	S1	X			X		X	X	X				S		P.Richards	32
	S	X	X	X				X1				X		X	S	X			X		X	X	X				S		R.Furnandiz	33
	S	X	X	X				X1				X		X	S	X			X		X	X	X				S1		R.Gifford	34
		X	X					X2	X1			X		X	S1	X			X		X	X	X				S2		S.Lodge	35
		X	S									X		X	X	S1			X2		X	X	X				X1	S2	J.Brandwood	36
		X	S						X2					X	S1				S2	X	X	X				X1		P.Rajer	37
	X	X	S2						X2			X	X	X	X1				S1	X	X	X						G.Cain	38
	S	X	X	X				S1				X			X2				X	X	X	X		X1			X1	S2	R.Pearson	39
	S	X	X	X1				S1				X			X2	S2			X	X	X	X					X	S2	J.Winter	40
		X		X3				X				X1	X		S2	S1			X	X2	X	X					S3		N.Barry	41
	X1	X		X				X				X	X		S2	X			X	S1	X	X	X2				S2	X2	J.Rushton	42
		X	X					X1				X		X	S1	X2			X	S2	X	X		X1			X	S	D.Alison	43
	S3	X						X3				X	X	S	S1	X			X	S1	X	X1		X1		X			G.R.Pooley	44
X	X		X	S				X1	X1			X		X	X	X			X	S1	X	X				X	S1		A.Butler	45
X	X		X	S						X		X		X	X				X	S1	X	X		X1		X	S		R.Poulina	46
X		X	S3							X3		X		X	X1				X	S1	X			X2		X	S2		D.Orr	47
X		X	X2	X							X	X	S1					X	X	X	X		X1			X	S2		B.Burns	48
X		X	X	X							X	X	S1		S	X			X	X1	X					X	S		E.Lomas	49
X1		X	X	X							X	X	X	S	S	X			X	X	X					X	S		M.Pierce	50
X		X	X1						X	X3	X		X		S1	X			X	S1	X		X1			X	S3		M.Riley	51
X2		X	X						X		X	X1	X	S2		S1			X	X	X	X				S2		J.Kirkby	52
X2		X	X1						X			X			X	X1			X	X	X	X				S1	S2		K.Lynch	53
X2		X	X	X1					X			X			S2	X	S		X	X	X	X	S1				S2		M.Bailey	54
X1			X						X2			X		X	S2	X			X	X	X	X		S			X	S1		I.Hemley	55
X1		X	X	S								X		X	S1	X			X	X2	X					X	S2		J.Kirkby	56
S3		X	X	X					X3			X			X2	X			X	X	X		S1			X1	S2		T.Heilbron	57
10	10	29	41	17	0	13	3	20	28	8	23	37	2	13	12	38	0	9	41	12	40	27	27	13	5	10	11	2	EL Appearances	
0	1	2	0	2	1	3	0	10	0	0	1	2	5	6	18	2	0	0	2	14	1	0	0	0	1	1	14	7	EL Sub Appearances	
0	1	4	6	1	0	3	2	1+4	6	0	2+1	4	0+1	0	6	4	0	0	5+1	2+2	5	5	1	2+1	0	2	0	0	CC Appearances	
0	0	3	3	2	0	0	0	2+1	2	0	1	3	0	2	1+2	2+1	0	0	3	1	2	3	3	0	0	0	0+1	0	FAC Appearances	
1+1	0	2	2	1	0	0	0	0	0	2	0	2	0	0	1+1	2	0	2	1	1	2	0	0+1	0	0	2	0+2	0	PO Appearances	

CHARLTON ATHLETIC

CLUB RECORDS

BIGGEST VICTORIES
League: 8-1 v Middlesbrough, Division 1, 12.9.1953.
F.A. Cup: 7-0 v Burton Albion, Round 3, 7.1.1956.
League Cup: 5-0 v Brentford, Round 1, 12.8.1980.

BIGGEST DEFEATS
League: 1-11 v Aston Villa, Division 2, 14.11.1959.
F.A. Cup: 0-6 v Wrexham, Round 3, 5.1.1980.
League Cup: 1-7 v Blackpool, Round 2, 25.9.1963.

MOST POINTS
3 points a win: 77, Division 2, 1985-86.
2 points a win: 61, Division 3(S), 1934-35.

MOST GOALS SCORED
107, Division 2, 1957-58.
Summers 28, Leary 17, Ayre 11, Ryan 10, Kierman 8, Hewie 6, Werge 6, Lucas 6, White 2, Firmani 2, Lawrie 2, Jago 1, Allen 1, Opponents 7.

MOST GOALS CONCEDED
120, Division 1, 1956-57.

MOST FIRST CLASS MATCHES IN A SEASON
60 - 1993-94 (League 46, FA Cup 6, League Cup 2, Anglo-Italian Cup 6).

MOST LEAGUE WINS
27, Division 3(S), 1934-35.

MOST LEAGUE DRAWS
17, Division 2, 1969-70, 1990-91.

MOST LEAGUE DEFEATS
29, Division 1, 1956-57.

INDIVIDUAL CLUB RECORDS

MOST GOALS IN A SEASON
Ralph Allen: 33 goals in 1934-35 (League 32, FA Cup 1).

MOST GOALS IN A MATCH
5. Wilson Lennox v Exeter (a), Division 3(S), 2.2.1929 (5-2).
5. Eddie Firmani v Aston Villa, Division 1, 5.2.1955 (6-1).
5. John Summers v Huddersfield, Division 2, 21.12.1957 (7-6).
5. John Summers v Portsmouth, Division 2, 1.10.1960 (7-4).

OLDEST PLAYER
Sam Bartram, 42 years 48 days v Arsenal, Division 1, 10.3.1956.

YOUNGEST PLAYER
Mark Penfold, 16 years 258 days v York City, Division 3, 25.8.1973.

MOST CAPPED PLAYER
John Hewie (Scotland) 19.

BEST PERFORMANCES

League: 1934-35: Matches Played 42, Won 27, Drawn 7, Lost 8, Goals for 103, Goals against 52, Points 61. First in Division 3(S).
Highest Position: 2nd in Division 1, 1936-37.
F.A. Cup: 1946-47: 3rd Round Rochdale 3-1; 4th round West Bromwich Albion 2-1; 5th round Blackburn Rovers 1-0; 6th Round Preston North End 2-1; Semi-Final Newcastle United 4-0; Final Burnley 1-0.
League Cup: 4th round in 1962-63, 1964-65, 1978-79. Most Recent Success: 1986-87: 2nd Round Lincoln City 3-1,1-0; 3rd Round Queens Park Rangers 1-0; 4th Round Arsenal 0-2.
Full Members Cup: 1986-87: 2nd Round Birmingham City 3-2; 3rd round Bradford City 2-0; 4th Round Everton 2-2 aet (won 6-5 on penalties); Semi-Final Norwich City 2-1 aet, Final Blackburn Rovers 0-1.

ADDITIONAL INFORMATION
PREVIOUS NAMES
None.
PREVIOUS LEAGUES
Southern League.

Club colours: Red shirts, white shorts, red socks.
Change colours: White shirts, black shorts, white socks.
Third strip: Green & purple striped shirts, purple shorts, green socks.

Reserves League: Avon Insurance Football Combination.

DIVISIONAL RECORD

	Played	Won	Drawn	Lost	For	Against	Points
Division 1	792	279	191	322	1,139	1,254	803
Division 2/1	1,490	517	384	589	2,206	2,423	1,577
Division 3	184	83	39	62	274	245	205
Division 3(S)	420	165	109	146	622	567	439
Total	2,886	1,044	723	1,119	4,241	4,489	3,024

RECORDS AND STATISTICS

COMPETITIONS

Div 1/P	Div.2/1	Div.3	Div 3(S)
1936-57	1929-33	1972-75	1921-29
1986-90	1935-36	1980-81	1933-35
	1957-72		
	1975-80		
	1981-86		
	1990-		

HONOURS

FA Cup	Div 3(S)
1947	1928-29
	1934-35

MOST APPEARANCES

SAM BARTRAM 623 (1934-56)		
YEAR	LEAGUE	FA CUP
1934-35	18	
1935-36	39	1
1936-37	42	1
1937-38	41	5
1938-39	42	1
1945-46	-	10
1946-47	41	6
1947-48	42	3
1948-49	41	1
1949-50	42	4
1950-51	37	2
1951-52	41	1
1952-53	38	1
1953-54	40	2
1954-55	42	3
1955-56	33	3
	579	44

MOST GOALS IN A CAREER

DEREK HALES - 168 (1973-76 & 1978-85)			
YEAR	LEAGUE	FA CUP	LGE CUP
1973-74	8	-	-
1974-75	20	-	1
1975-76	28	-	3
1976-77	16	-	2
1978-79	8	-	1
1979-80	8	-	1
1980-81	17	4	2
1981-82	11	-	2
1982-83	14	1	2
1983-84	10	-	1
1984-85	8	-	-
Total	148	5	15

Current leading goalscorer: Carl Leaburn - 53 (1987-96)

Stuart Leary scored most League goals (153) 1951-62.
(League 153, FA Cup 8, League Cup 2) Total 163.

RECORD TRANSFER FEE RECEIVED

AMOUNT	CLUB	PLAYER	DATE
£2,600,000	Leeds Utd	Lee Bowyer	7/96
£775,000	Chelsea	Scott Minto	5/94
£700,000	Newcastle Utd	Robert Lee	9/92
£650,000	Crystal Palace	Mike Flanagan	8/79

RECORD TRANSFER FEE PAID

AMOUNT	CLUB	PLAYER	DATE
£600,000	Chelsea	Joe McLaughlin	8/89
£430,000	Chelsea	Colin Pates	10/88
£350,000	Port Vale	Andy Jones	9/87
£324,000	Barcelona	Allan Simonsen	10/82

MANAGERS

NAME	SEASONS	BEST	WORST
Walter Rayner	1920-25	12(3S)	16(3S)
Alex McFarlane	1925-28	13(3S)	21(3S)
Albert Lindon	1928	11(3S)	11(3S)
Alex McFarlane	1928-32	10(2)	1(3S)
Albert Lindon	1932-33	22(2)	22(2)
Jimmy Seed	1933-56	2(1)	5(3S)
Jimmy Trotter	1956-61	22(1)	10(2)
Frank Hill	1961-65	4(2)	20(2)
Bob Stokoe	1965-67	16(2)	19(2)
Eddie Firmani	1967-70	3(2)	20(2)
Theo Foley	1970-74	20(2)	14(3)
Andy Nelson	1974-80	7(2)	3(3)
Mike Bailey	1980-81	3(3)	3(3)
Alan Mullery	1981-82	13(2)	13(2)
Ken Craggs	1982	17(2)	17(2)
Lennie Lawrence	1982-91	5(1)	17(2)
A Curbishley/ S Gritt	1991-95	7(2)	15 (2/1)
A Curbishley	1995-	6(1)	6(1)

LONGEST LEAGUE RUNS

of undefeated matches:	15 (4.10.80 - 20.12.80)	of league matches w/out a win:	16 (26.2.1955 - 22.8.1955)
of undefeated home matches:	28 (13.4.1935 - 3.10.1936)	of undefeated away matches:	7 (4.10.80-6.12.80 & 29.12.90- 1.4.91, 2.12.95 - 24.2.96)
without home win:	9 (5.3.1955 - 20.8.1955)	without an away win:	33 (29.3.1969 - 14.11.1970)
of league wins:	7 (7.10.1980 - 1.11.1980)	of home wins:	11 (4.12.1937 - 18.4.1938)
of league defeats:	10 (11.4.1990 - 15.9.1990)	of away wins:	5 (26.1.1935 - 23.3.1935, 2.12.95 - 10.2.96)

CHARLTON ATHLETIC

PLAYERS NAME Honours	Ht	Wt	Birthdate	Birthplace Transfers	Contract Date	Clubs	League	L/Cup	FA Cup	Other	Lge	L/C	FAC	Oth
G O A L K E E P E R S														
Petterson Andrew	6.2	14.2	26/09/69	Freemantle	30/12/88	Luton Town	16+3	2		2				
				Loan	26/03/93	Ipswich Town	1							
				£85000	15/07/94	Charlton Athletic	17+1	2		2				
				Loan	08/12/94	Bradford City	3							
Loan (26/09/95) Ipswich Town 1 Lge App.				Loan	23/01/96	Plymouth Argyle	6							
				Loan	08/03/96	Colchester United	5							
Salmon Michael	6.2	12.12	14/07/64	Leyland	16/10/81	Blackburn Rovers	1							
				Free	03/08/83	Stockport County	118	10	3	3				
				Free	31/07/86	Bolton Wanderers	26	2	4	4				
				£18000	07/03/87	Wrexham	100	4	4	9				
				£100000	06/07/89	Charlton Athletic	114	8	8	6				
				Loan	18/10/92	Chester City	16		2					
D E F E N D E R S														
Balmer Stuart	6.1	12.4	20/06/69	Falkirk	01/01/00	Celtic								
				£120000	24/08/90	Charlton Athletic	159+19	10	9	11	6		1	
Barness Anthony	5.10	10.12	25/03/73	Lewisham	06/03/91	Charlton Athletic	21+6	2	3	1+1	1		1	
				£350000	08/09/92	Chelsea	12+2	2		2+1				
				Loan	12/08/93	Middlesbrough				1				
				Loan	02/02/96	Southend United	5							
				£165000	07/08/96	Charlton Athletic								
Brown Steven B	6.1	12.0	13/05/72	Brighton	03/07/90	Charlton Athletic	77+4	3	9	3	3			
Chandler Dean A R	6.2	11.10	06/05/76	London	13/04/94	Charlton Athletic	1+1			1				
Chapple Philip Div3'91.	6.2	12.7	26/11/66	Norwich	10/07/85	Norwich City								
					29/03/88	Cambridge United	183+4	11	23	17	18	2	1	
				£100000	13/08/90	Charlton Athletic	74+7	7	4	5	9			
Rufus Richard R	6.1	11.2	12/01/75	Lewisham	01/07/93	Charlton Athletic	67+2	5	2	2				
Stuart Jamie C E: Y	5.10	10.7	15/10/76	Southwark	18/01/95	Charlton Athletic	39	5	3	0+1	2			
Sturgess Paul C	5.11	12.5	04/08/75	Dartford	01/07/93	Charlton Athletic	65+6	5		5				
M I D F I E L D														
Curbishley Alan E: u21.1, Y, S.	5.10	11.7	08/11/57	Forest Gate	14/08/75	West Ham United	78+7	3	5		5			
				£275000	11/07/79	Bristol City	128+2	12	10		11	3	1	
				£100000	25/03/83	Aston Villa	34+2	5		2	1			
				£40000	24/12/84	Charlton Athletic	62+1	1	3	2+1	6			
				£32000	21/08/87	Brighton & H.A.	111+5	4	6	6	13		2	
				Free	03/07/90	Charlton Athletic	22+6		1					
Garland Peter	5.10	12.0	20/01/71											
Jones Keith E: Y2, S	5.9	10.11	14/10/65	Dulwich	16/08/83	Chelsea	43+9	9+2	1	4+1	7	3		
				£40000	03/09/87	Brentford	167+12	15	13	16	13	2	4	1
				£175000	21/10/91	Southend United	81+2	2	5	9	11			1
				£150000	16/09/94	Charlton Athletic	54+1	2+1	1		1			
Mortimer Paul H E: u21.2	5.11	11.3	08/05/68	Kensington	01/01/00	Fulham								
				Free	01/01/01	Farnborough								
				Free	22/09/87	Charlton Athletic	108+5	4+1	8	3+1	17			
				£350000	24/07/91	Aston Villa	10+2	2			1			
				£500000	18/10/91	Crystal Palace	18+4	1	1	3	2			
				Loan	22/01/93	Brentford	6			2				
					05/07/94	Charlton Athletic	39+6		3		9		1	
Newton Shaun	5.8	10.4	20/08/75	Camberwell	01/07/93	Charlton Athletic	71+42	10	2+2	4+1	7	1		1
Robinson John R W: u21.2.	5.10	11.2	29/08/71	Bulawayo	21/04/89	Brighton & H.A.	57+5	5	2+1	1+1	6	1		2
				£75000	15/09/92	Charlton Athletic	99+7	6+2	7+1	3	12	2	1	
Walsh Colin	5.9	11.0	22/07/62											
F O R W A R D S														
Allen Bradley E: u21.8, Y.8.	5.7	10.0	13/09/71	Romford	30/09/88	Q.P.R.	56+25	5+2	3+2	1	27	5		
				£400000	28/03/96	Charlton Athletic	10			1+1	3			
Grant Kim	5.10	10.12	25/09/72											
Leaburn Carl E: Y1,u.19.	6.3	13.0	30/03/69	Lewisham	22/04/87	Charlton Athletic	222+41	15	16+2	9+5	42	4	3	4
				Loan	22/03/90	Northampton Town	9							
Linger Paul	5.6	9.5	20/12/74	Stepney	01/07/93	Charlton Athletic	5+17	0+1			1			
O'Connell Brendan	5.10	10.9	12/11/66	Lambeth	01/07/85	Portsmouth								
				Free	04/08/86	Exeter City	73+8	3+1	3	4	19	2		

					Fee	Date	Club								
O'Connell continued...					Free	01/07/88	Burnley	62+2	6	3	5	17	3	1	2
					Loan	30/11/89	Huddersfield Town	11				1			
					£50000	23/03/90	Barnsley	211+27	10+1	14	7+1	35	1	1	2
					£125000	23/07/96	Charlton Athletic								
Robson Mark A	5.7	10.2	22/05/69	Newham		17/12/86	Exeter City	26		2	2	7			
					£50000	17/07/87	Tottenham Hotspur	3+5	1						
					Loan	24/03/88	Reading	5+2							
					Loan	05/10/89	Watford	1							
					Loan	22/12/89	Plymouth Argyle	7							
					Loan	03/01/92	Exeter City	7+1			3	1			1
					Free	14/08/92	West Ham United	42+5	2	2	4+1	8		1	
					£125000	17/11/93	Charlton Athletic	72+17	4+2	8	2	6		1	
Whyte David	5.8	10.7	03/10/71	Greenwich		01/01/00	Greenwich Boro								
Div1'94					Free	15/02/89	Crystal Palace	17+10	5+2	0+1	0+3	4	2		1
					Loan	26/03/92	Charlton Athletic	7+1				2			
					£450000	05/07/94	Charlton Athletic	47+16	4	1+1	0+2	21	2	1	

ADDITIONAL CONTRACT PLAYERS

Kearley Dean			31/05/96	Charlton Athletic (T)
Lisbie Kevin			24/05/96	Charlton Athletic (T)
Nicholls Kevin J R				Charlton Athletic (T)
Wright Robert A			02/05/96	Charlton Athletic (T)

THE MANAGER
ALAN CURBISHLEY

Date of Birth . . . . 8th November 1957.
Place of Birth. . . . . Forest Gate.
Date of Appointment . . . . . 20th July 1991 as joint manager, June 1995 as sole.

PREVIOUS CLUBS
As Manager. . . . . None.
As Coach. . . . . None.
As a Player . . . West Ham, Aston Villa, Brighton, Birmingham, Charlton Athletic.

HONOURS
As a Manager
None.

As a Player
None.

THE VALLEY
Floyd Road, Charlton, London SE7 8BL
Tel: 0181 333 4000

Capacity 14,934

First game ....v Summerstown (Sth Suburban Lge) 13.9.19.
First Lge game..v Exeter City (Div 3(S)) 27.8.21.
First floodlit game ....Rotherham Utd (Div 2) 20.9.61.

ATTENDANCES
Highest..75,031 v Aston Villa, FA Cup, 12.2.1938.
Lowest..1,452 v Pisa, Anglo Italian Cup, 22.12.93)
OTHER GROUNDS.......Siemens Meadow 1906-07. Woolwich Common1907-08. Pound Park 1908-13.
.... Horn Lane 1913-19. The Valley 1919-23. The Mount 1923-24. The Valley 1924-85.
....Selhurst Park 1985-91. Upton Park 1991-92. The Valley 1992-

MATCHDAY TICKET PRICES

North Stand
Adult/Adult non-member . . . . £8/£13
Senior/Young member £6
Concession £6
Junior £4
West Stand
Adult/Adult non-member . . . . £13/£15
Senior/Young member £9
Concession £9
Junior £4
East Stand & Family Stand
Adult/Adult non-member . . . . £13/£15
Senior/Young member £9
Concession £9
Junior/Junior Red . . . . £4/£1
Ticket Office Telephone no. 0181 333 4010

CLUBCALL 0891 12 11 46
Calls cost 39p per minute cheap rate and 49p per
minute at all other times.
Call costings correct at time of going to press.

HOW TO GET TO THE GROUND

By Road
From M25 take junction 2 (A2 London bound) and follow until road becomes A102 (M). Take the turning marked 'Woolwich Ferry' and turn right along A206 Woolwich Road. This route takes you into Charlton.

Visitors Parking
Visiting coaches located in Anchor and Hope LAne, five minutes walk from ground. Also street parking.

By Rail
Charlton Station (British Rail main line) can be reached from Charing Cross, Waterloo (East) or London Bridge and is two minutes from the ground.

Nearest Railway Station
Charlton.

MATCHDAY PROGRAMME

Programme Editor. . . . . Peter Burrowes.

Number of pages 40

Price . . . . £1.50.

Subscriptions. . . . . £50 home, £50 away, £90 home & away.

Local Newspapers . . . . . . Kentish Times, South East London Mercury,
. . . . . South London Press, News Shopper, Greenwich Comet Leader,
. . . . Kent Messenger, Kent Today.

Local Radio Stations . . . . RTM, Capital Gold.

CRYSTAL PALACE
(The Eagles)
NATIONWIDE LEAGUE DIVISION 1
SPONSORED BY: TDK

Back Row (L-R): Danny Boxall, Bjorn Enqvist, Rory Ginty, Jason Harris, Robert Quinn, Paul Sparrow. **3rd Row:** Richard Shaw, George Ndah, Brian Launders, Andy Roberts, Jimmy Glass, Damian Matthew, Marc Edworthy, Jamie Vincent. **2nd Row:** Brian Sparrow, Peter McClean (Physio), Simon Rodger, Ian Cox, David Hopkin, Steve Taylor, Nigel Martyn, Rhys Wilmot, Bruce Dyer, Anthony Scully, Gareth Davies, Vic Bettonelli (Kit Manager), Steve Kember (Res. Manager). **Front Row:** Darren Patterson, Dean Gordon, Ray Houghton, Ray Lewington (First Team Coach), Steve Coppell (Technical Director), Peter Nicholas (First Team Coach), Iain Dowie, Darren Pitcher, Chris Coleman.

CRYSTAL PALACE
FORMED IN 1905
TURNED PROFESSIONAL IN 1905
LTD COMPANY IN 1905

CHAIRMAN: R G Noades
DIRECTORS
B Coleman OBE, A S C De'Souza,
M E Lee, S Hume-Kendall,
P H N Norman, R Anderson, S R Ebbs,
V E Murphy, D A Miller, P L Morley CBE JP
SECRETARY
Mike Hurst
LOTTERY MANAGER
Tony Shaw

DIRECTOR OF FOOTBALL: Steve Coppell
MANAGER: Dave Bassett
ASSISTANT MANAGERS
Ray Lewington/Peter Nicholas
RESERVE TEAM MANAGER
Steve Kember
YOUTH TEAM MANAGER
Peter Nicholas
PHYSIOTHERAPIST
Alistar Beattie
STATISTICIAN FOR THE DIRECTORY
Mike Purkiss

The 1995 close season dealt another bitter blow as the relegated side was totally dismembered, with Armstrong, Bowry, Newman, Preece, Salako and captain Southgate being sold, while Humphrey and Young were given free transfers. There were more sales later, with Coleman, Dowie, Patterson and Shaw leaving the club and only Gordon, Martyn, Matthew and Rodger remaining from the 1994 championship side. These sales produced a 1995 record of seven one-million-pound transfers - bettering the Premiership teams, with only Manchester United, at £12.5m, dealing with more cash than Palace.

We started in August with a 4-3 win at home, yet had to wait until mid-February before gaining our third home win - over struggling Watford - many games being drawn after taking the lead initially. The away record was far better, helping Palace to keep outside the relegation zone. After 11 November we were defeated only at champions Sunderland, and Huddersfield, and rose through the league to third place, thanks to a run of six consecutive wins at home. However, defeat against Leicester City and in the crunch match at Derby County lost us automatic second place. There was another chance via the play-offs, when we achieved a double over neighbours Charlton Athletic to reach Wembley - our fourth visit to the ground - for the final against Leicester. This started well as Player of the Year Andy Roberts gave us the lead in the 13th minute with his first goal of the season. But Leicester converted a penalty in the 76th minute to take the game into extra time and then scored in the last minute - courtesy of ex-Palace reserve Steve Claridge - to leave us in the first division for another season.

Several young players were signed and Freeman was top scorer with 20 league goals - his feat of three goals in 12 minutes against Grimsby beating Gordon's three in 25 minutes against West Bromwich Albion. Nigel Martyn was the only ever-present player, keeping 16 clean sheets in league games.

The cup games never reached the success of last season, with Palace going out in round three after replays in both competitions. The youth side, however, retained the Championship Cup for the third year running and was only beaten in the semi-final of the Youth Cup by winners Liverpool.

February saw the return of Dave Bassett as manager, who lasted longer than the four days in 1984 and was honoured as Manager of the Month for March. Palace came third in the league and were also placed third for league goals and for their defensive record - a successful season.

MIKE PURKISS

CRYSTAL PALACE

League: 3rd   FA Cup: 3rd Rnd   Coca-Cola Cup: 3rd Rnd

M	DATE	COMP	VEN	OPPONENTS	RESULT	HT	LP	GOAL SCORERS/GOAL TIMES	ATT.
1	A 12	EL	H	Barnsley	W 4-3	2-1	5	Houghton 16, Dowie 29, 58, Gordon 60(pen)	12067
2	19	EL	A	Ipswich Town	L 0-1	0-1	14		(12681)
3	26	EL	H	Charlton Athletic	D 1-1	0-1	13	Dyer 73	14124
4	29	EL	A	Sheffield United	W 3-2	0-0	5	Dyer 48, 89, Gordon 85	(10378)
5	S 9	EL	A	Birmingham City	D 0-0	0-0	15		(19403)
6	12	EL	A	Watford	D 0-0	0-0	14		(8780)
7	16	EL	H	Huddersfield Town	D 0-0	0-0	15		15645
8	19	CC 2/1	A	Southend United	D 2-2	0-1		Hopkin 68, 90	(4031)
9	23	EL	A	Oldham Athletic	L 1-3	1-0	17	Hopkin 36	(6586)
10	30	EL	H	Stoke City	D 1-1	1-1	17	Freedman 31	14613
11	O 3	CC 2/2	H	Southend United	W 2-0	1-0		Vincent 16, McKenzie 81	6588
12	7	EL	A	Sunderland	L 0-1	0-0	20		13754
13	15	EL	A	Port Vale	W 2-1	0-0	18	Freedman 54, Gordon 78	(6935)
14	22	EL	A	Millwall	L 1-2	1-2	19	Gordon 32	14338
15	25	CC 3	H	Middlesbrough	D 2-2	2-2		Hopkin 2, Hopkin 9	11873
16	28	EL	A	Leicester City	W 3-2	2-0	17	Dyer 4, Hopkin 26, Dyer 67	(18376)
17	N 4	EL	H	Reading	L 0-2	0-2	19		16058
18	8	CC 3R	A	Middlesbrough	L 0-2	0-1			(16150)
19	11	EL	A	Norwich City	L 0-1	0-1	20		(14156)
20	19	EL	H	Southend United	D 1-1	0-0	20	Lapper 68(og)	(5089)
21	22	EL	H	Wolverhampton Wand	W 3-2	2-0	16	Freedman 10, 29, 49 (3)	12571
22	25	EL	H	Derby County	D 0-0	0-0	17		13506
23	D 3	EL	A	Sunderland	L 0-1	0-1	18		(12777)
24	9	EL	H	Oldham Athletic	D 2-2	2-0	18	Davies 9, Freedman 33	12709
25	16	EL	A	Stoke City	W 2-1	1-0	16	Freedman 25, Taylor 70	(12090)
26	23	EL	A	West Bromwich Albion	W 3-2	3-0	16	Gordon 15(pen), 36(pen), 40 (3)	(13103)
27	J 1	EL	A	Portsmouth	W 3-2	2-0	15	Hopkin 14, 49, Freedman 45	(12926)
28	6	FAC 3	H	Port Vale	D 0-0	0-0			10456
29	13	EL	H	Ipswich Town	D 1-1	1-0	15	Davies 26	14097
30	16	FAC 3R	A	Port Vale	L 3-4	1-2		Taylor 30, Cox 76, Dyer 82	(6754)
31	20	EL	A	Barnsley	D 1-1	1-0	15	Gordon 13	6620
32	F 4	EL	A	Charlton Athletic	D 0-0	0-0	16		(13560)
33	10	EL	H	Sheffield United	D 0-0	0-0	15		15883
34	17	EL	H	Watford	W 4-0	2-0	14	Freedman 14, 38, Dyer 75, 77	13235
35	20	EL	A	Tranmere Rovers	W 3-2	0-2	8	Freedman 61, Boere 79, Houghton 85	(5253)
36	24	EL	A	Huddersfield Town	L 0-3	0-3	11		(13041)
37	27	EL	H	Birmingham City	W 3-2	1-1	8	Dyer 7, 55, 83 (3)	12965
38	M 2	EL	A	Luton Town	D 0-0	0-0	8		(8478)
39	5	EL	H	Grimsby Town	W 5-0	5-0	5	Freedman 15, 25, 26 (3), Hopkin 28, Houghton 38	11548
40	9	EL	H	West Bromwich Albion	W 1-0	1-0	5	Freedman 30	18336
41	12	EL	A	Tranmere Rovers	W 2-1	1-1	3	Ndah 38, Hopkin 86	13183
42	16	EL	H	Grimsby Town	W 2-0	1-0	3	Ndah 26, Tuttle 70	(5059)
43	19	EL	H	Luton Town	W 2-0	0-0	3	Dyer 82, 88	13609
44	23	EL	H	Portsmouth	D 0-0	0-0	3		17039
45	30	EL	A	Millwall	W 4-1	0-0	3	Hopkin 59, Brown 77, Ndah 86, 88	(13214)
46	A 2	EL	H	Port Vale	D 2-2	2-0	3	Freedman 25, 41	14180
47	6	EL	A	Leicester City	L 0-1	0-1	3		17331
48	8	EL	A	Reading	W 2-0	1-0	3	Freedman 45, Houghton 72	(12579)
49	13	EL	H	Southend United	W 2-0	1-0	3	Freedman 7, 57	15672
50	20	EL	A	Wolverhampton Wand	W 2-0	1-0	3	Hopkin 31, Dyer 55	(24350)
51	28	EL	A	Derby County	L 1-2	1-1	3	Brown 6	(17041)
52	M 5	EL	H	Norwich City	L 0-1	0-1	3		19354
53	12	PO SF1	A	Charlton Athletic	W 2-1	0-1		Brown 64, Veart 71	(14618)
54	15	PO SF2	H	Charlton Athletic	W 1-0	1-0		Houghton 4	22880
55	27	PO F	H	Leicester City	L 1-2	1-0		Roberts 13	73573

Best Home League Attendance: 19354 v Norwich City   Smallest: 11548 v Grimsby Town   Average: 14600

Goal Scorers:
EL(67):   Freedman(20),Dyer(13),Hopkin(8),Gordon(8),Ndah(4),Houghton(4),Davies(2),Dowie(2),Brown(2),Taylor(1),Tuttle(1),Boere(1),Opponent(s)(1)
CC(6):   Hopkin(4),Vincent(1),McKenzie(1)
FAC(3):   Taylor(1),Dyer(1),Cox(1)
PO(4):   Brown(1),Veart(1),Roberts(1),Houghton(1)

Appearance grid (X = full appearance, S/S1/S2/S3 = substitute, X1/X2/X3 = substituted). Player columns read left to right:

(F) Andersen	(F) Boere	(D) Brown (L)	(D) Coleman	(F) Cox	(M) Cundy (L)	(D) Davies	(F) Dowie	(M) Dyer	(D) Edworthy	(F) Freedman	(D) Gale	(M) Gordon	(M) Hopkin	(M) Houghton	(F) Launders	(G) Martyn	(M) Matthew	(F) McKenzie	(F) Ndah	(D) Pitcher	(D) Quinn	(M) Roberts	(D) Rodger	(D) Shaw	(D) Sparrow	(F) Taylor	(F) Veart	(D) Vincent	Opponent	#
		X		S1		X	X	X				X	X2	X		X	S1			X1	X			X					P.Rejer	1
		X		S2		X	X	X				X	X2	X		X	S1			X2	X1			X					G.Singh	2
		X				X	X	X				X	X	X		X	S1			X2	X1			X				S	C.R.Wilkes	3
		X			X	X	X					X	X	X		X	X1				X2			S1	X			S2	G.Cain	4
		X				X	X	X		X		X	X	X		X	X1			S2	X			S1	X			X	M.Bailey	5
		X				X	X	X		X		X	X	X		X				S1	X2			S2	X			X1	J.Brandwood	6
		X				X		X2	X	X		X	X	X		X	X3			S2				X1	X			S1	M.Pierce	7
		X				X		X	X			X1	X	X		X	X3			S2	S1		S3	X2	X			X	C.Wilkes	8
		X3						X1	X	X		X	X	X		X	X2				X		S3	S1	X			S2	K.A.Leach	9
		X						X	X	X		X	X	X	S2	X	S			X1		S1		X	X			X2	A.D'Urso	10
		X						X1	X			X	X	X	S1	X	S	X		X	S			X	X			X	A.N.Butler	11
		X						S2	X2	X		X	X	X		X	S	S1		X	X1			X	X			X1	P.Rejer	12
		X						X	S	X		X	X	X		X	S1			X	X1	X		X				S	W.Burns	13
		X						S2	X2	X		X	X	X		X	S1			X	X1	X		X				S	D.Orr	14
		X						X	X			X	X	X		X	S	X		X			X	S	X			S	G.Poll	15
		X						X1	X			X	X	X		X				X			X	X	X			S	K.Lynch	16
		X						X	X1	S1		X	X	X		X	S			X			X	X	X			S	G.Singh	17
		X						X	X			X1	X	X2		X	S2	X		X			X		X3			S1	P.Jones	18
		X						X1	X	X		X				X	S1			X			X	X				X	T.West	19
		X1						X2	X			X	X	X		X	S2			X			X		S1			S	R.B.Gifford	20
	S2					X		X	X1	X		X	X	X		X	S1			X			X		X2			X	G.Pooley	21
	S					X		X1	X			X	X	X		X	S1			X			X		X			X	M.Fletcher	22
	S2					X		X	X2			X	X	X		X	S1			X			X		X1			X1	M.Riley	23
	S2	X				X		S1	X	X		X	X1			X	X			X			X		X2			S	A.Butler	24
	S1				X			X	S2	X	X		X			X	X2			X			X		X1			X	K.Breen	25
	S2				X			S	X	X		X	S1	X		X	X1			X			X		X2			X1	G.Cain	26
		X	S1		X			S	X	X		X	X1	X		X	S1			X			X		X			X1	M.Brandwood	27
					X			X	X	X	S	X	X2	X		X	S1			X	S2		X		X1			X1	R.Poulain	28
					X	X1		S2	X	X2		X	X	X		X	S2			X			X	S1	X2				C.Wilkes	29
		S2						S1	X	X3	X1	X				X				X			X	S3	X				R.Poulain	30
		X						S1	X	X	S	X				X				X			X	X	X		X1		S	T.Heilbron	31
								X	S1	X	X2	S	X			X	X1			X			X	X		X1		S2	R.Gifford	32
X	S3							X	X2	X3		X	X2	X		X				S2	X		X	X1				S1	M.Pierce	33
S2	S1		S3					X	X	X3		X	X2	X		X				X2	X		X					X	G.Pooley	34
X	S1				S2			X	X	X1	X	X	X			X				X2	X		X	X1	S				P.Richards	35
X	S				X			X	X	X		X	X	X		X				X1			X	S1	S			X1	T.West	36
					X			X2	X	X		X	X	X		X				X			X	S	S2			X1	S.Baines	37
					X			X	X			X	X	X2	S1	X				X1	X		X	S2				X	J.Kirkby	38
X					X1			S2	X	X		X	X			X				X	X		X	S2					S.Bennett	39
X					X1			X2	X	X		X	X			X				X2	X3		X	S		S1			A.D'Urso	40
X					S2			X	X2			X	X	X		X				X1	X3		X	S3		X	S1		I.Hemley	41
X					S			X	X1			X	X			X				X	X		X	X		X	S1		M.Fletcher	42
X1					S1			X1	X1			X	X	X		X				X	X		X			X	S1		P.Taylor	43
X1			S1		X1	X1						X	X	X		X				X	X		X			X	S3		A.Wiley	44
	X				X	S	X					X	X			X				X	X		X	S		X	X		J.Rushton	45
	X				A.Butler	X		X	X1			X	X			X				X	X2		X	S2		X			A.Butler	46
X	S				X			X	X			X	X	X		X				X1	X		X			X2	S1		K.Lynch	47
S1	X				X	S2		X	X1			X	X	X		X				S	X		X	X		X	X2		G.Pooley	48
S1	X				X1	S2		X	X			X	X	X		X				S	X		X	X		X	X2		R.Poulain	49
X					S			X	X1			X	X			X			S	X		X			X	S1	X		J.Lloyd	50
X1	X				X2	X		X2				X	X			X			S1	X		X			X	S2	S2		D.Allison	51
	S1				X			X				X	X			X			X	X2		X1			X	X	X		G.Singh	52
X1	X				S	X	X					X	X			X			X	X	S1	X	S		X	X			J.Kirkby	53
	X				S1	X	X1					X				X			X	X	X	X	S		X	X			T.Heilbron	54
	X				S2	X	X2				X1	X				X			X	X	X	X	S3		X3	S1		D.Allison	55

	(F) Andersen	(F) Boere	(D) Brown	(D) Coleman	(F) Cox	(M) Cundy	(D) Davies	(F) Dowie	(M) Dyer	(D) Edworthy	(F) Freedman	(D) Gale	(M) Gordon	(M) Hopkin	(M) Houghton	(F) Launders	(G) Martyn	(M) Matthew	(F) McKenzie	(F) Ndah	(D) Pitcher	(D) Quinn	(M) Roberts	(D) Rodger	(D) Shaw	(D) Sparrow	(F) Taylor	(F) Veart	(D) Vincent
EL Appearances	2	0	5	17	1	4	17	4	21	44	37	2	34	41	41	0	46	4	4	17	36	1	36	14	15	18	9	5	19
EL Sub Appearances	4	8	1	0	3	0	3	0	14	0	2	0	0	1	0	2	0	4	8	6	0	0	2	9	0	2	1	7	6
CC Appearances	0	0	0	0	0	0	0	4	0	4	4	4	0+1	4	1+1	3	0+1	2+1	0	3+1	1	4	0	0	0	4	0	0	2+1
FAC Appearances	0	0	0	0	0+1	0	2	0	0+1	2	2	1	2	1	2	0	2	0	1+1	0	2	0	2	0+2	0	2	0	0	1
PO Appearances	1	0	3	0	0	0	0	0+2	3	3	0	0	1	3	0	3	0	0	3	3	2+1	3	0+1	0	3	2+1	0

Also Played: ((D) Boxall X(52), S(54). M) Connolly S(52). (M) Evans (L) X(45), S(46,52). (F) Ginty S2(52). (F) Scully S2(3), S3(7). (D) Tuttle S3(18), S(19,21,22,23), X(20). (G) Wilmot S(1,2,39).

CRYSTAL PALACE

CLUB RECORDS

BIGGEST VICTORIES
League: 9-0 v Barrow, Division 4, 10.10.1959.
F.A. Cup: 7-0 v Luton Town, 3rd Round, 16.1.1929.
League Cup: 8-0 v Southend, 2nd Round, 25.9.1990.

BIGGEST DEFEATS
League: 0-9 v Liverpool, Division 1, 12.9.1989.
F.A. Cup: 0-9 v Burnley, 2nd Round replay, 1908-09.
League Cup: 0-5 v Nottingham Forest, 3rd Round replay, 1.11.89.

MOST POINTS
3 points a win: 90, Division 1, 1993-94.
2 points a win: 64, Division 4, 1960-61.

MOST GOALS SCORED
110, Division 4, 1960-61.
Byrne 30, Summersby 25, Heckman 14, Woan 13, Gavin 8,
Petchley 7, Uphill 6, Barnett 2, Lunnis 1, McNicholl 1, Noakes 1,
Opponents 2.

MOST GOALS CONCEDED
86, Division 3(S), 1953-54.

MOST FIRST CLASS MATCHES IN A SEASON
59 - 1988-89 (League 46, FA Cup 1, League Cup 3, Simod Cup 5,
Play-offs 4).

MOST LEAGUE WINS
29, Division 4, 1960-61.

MOST LEAGUE DRAWS
19, Division 2, 1978-79.

MOST LEAGUE DEFEATS
29, Division 1, 1980-81.

INDIVIDUAL CLUB RECORDS

MOST GOALS IN A SEASON
Peter Simpson: 54 goals in 1930-31 (League 46, FA Cup 8).
Previous holder: P.A.Cherrett, 32 goals in 1926-27.

MOST GOALS IN A MATCH
6. Peter Simpson v Exeter, 7-2, Division 3(S), 4.10.1930.

OLDEST PLAYER
Wally Betteridge, 41 (Debut - Player/coach), 27.10.1928 (0-8).

YOUNGEST PLAYER
Phil Hoadley, 16 years 3 months, 27.4.1968.

MOST CAPPED PLAYER
Eric Young (Wales) 19.

BEST PERFORMANCES

League: 1960-61: Matches played 46, Won 29, Drawn 6, Lost 11,
Goals for 110, Goals against 69, Points 64. 2nd in Division 4.
Highest Position: 1990-91, 3rd in Division 1.
F.A. Cup: 1989-90: 3rd Round Portsmouth 2-1; 4th Round
Huddersfield Town 4-0; 5th Round Rochdale 1-0; 6th Round
Cambridge 1-0; Semi-Final Liverpool 4-3; Final Manchester United
3-3 aet, replay 0-1.
League Cup: 1992-93: 2nd Round Lincoln City (a) 3-1, (h) 1-1; 3rd
Round Southampton (a) 2-0; 4th Round Liverpool (a) 1-1, (h) 2-1
aet; 5th Round Chelsea (h) 3-1; Semi-Final Arsenal (h) 1-3, (a) 0-2.

ADDITIONAL INFORMATION
PREVIOUS NAMES
None.

PREVIOUS LEAGUES
Southern League.

Club colours: Red and blue shirts, white with red trim shorts and
socks.
Change colours: White with red & blue trim shirts, blue shorts and
socks.

Reserves League: Neville Ovenden Football Combination.

DIVISIONAL RECORD

	Played	Won	Drawn	Lost	For	Against	Points
Division 1/P	454	122	135	197	468	659	448
Division 2/1	938	358	255	325	1,193	1,141	1,150
Division 3	276	113	86	77	419	332	312
Division 3(S)	1,166	438	292	436	1,831	1,853	1,168
Division 4	138	68	30	40	284	204	166
Total	**2,972**	**1,099**	**798**	**1,075**	**4,195**	**4,189**	**3,244**

COMPETITIONS

Div .1/P	Div.2/1	Div.3	Div.3(S)	Div.4
1969-73	1921-25	1920-21	1925-58	1958-61
1979-81	1964-69			
1989-93	1973-74			Texaco
1994-95	1976-79			1972-73
	1981-89			
	1993-94			
	1995-			

HONOURS

Div. 2/1	Div. 3	FMC
1978-79	1920-21	1991
1993-94		

MOST APPEARANCES

JIM CANNON 665 + 4 (1972-86)

YEAR	LEAGUE	FA CUP	LGE CUP	OTHERS
1972-73	3			
1973-74	13+1		1	
1974-75	34+2	2	0+1	
1975-76	40	8	2	
1976-77	46	6	3	
1977-78	39	1	4	
1978-79	41	4	4	
1979-80	42	3	3	
1980-81	33	1	4	
1981-82	42	5	4	
1982-83	41	4	5	
1983-84	30	2	2	
1984-85	40	2	2	
1985-86	42	1	4	1
1986-87	42	2	4	1
1987-88	40	1	1	1
	568+3	42	43+1	3

MOST GOALS IN A CAREER

PETER SIMPSON - 166 (1929-34)

YEAR	LEAGUE	FA CUP
1929-30	36	1
1930-31	46	8
1931-32	24	1
1932-33	14	1
1933-34	20	1
1934-35	14	
Total	154	12

Current leading goalscorer: DougieFreedman - 20 (1995-96)

RECORD TRANSFER FEE RECEIVED

AMOUNT	CLUB	PLAYER	DATE
4,500,000	Tottenham H.	Chris Armstrong	06/95
2,500,000	Arsenal	Ian Wright	9/91
1,350,000	Arsenal	Kenny Sansom	8/80
£400,000	Derby County	Dave Swindlehurst	4/80

RECORD TRANSFER FEE PAID

AMOUNT	CLUB	PLAYER	DATE
2,300,000	Millwall	Andy Roberts	7/95
1,800,000	Sunderland	Marco Gabbiadini	9/91
1,350,000	Bristol Rovers	Nigel Martin	11/89
1,000,000	Arsenal	Clive Allen	8/80

MANAGERS

NAME	SEASONS	BEST	WORST
John Robson	1905-07	1(2)	19(1)
Eddie Goodman	1907-25	14(2)	1(3S)
Alec Maley	1925-27	6(3S)	13(3S)
Fred Maven	1927-30	2(3S)	9(3S)
Jack Tresadern	1930-35	2(3S)	12(3S)
Tom Bromilow	1935-36	6(3S)	6(3S)
R.S. Moyse	1936	14(3S)	14(3S)
Tom Bromilow	1937-39	2(3S)	7(3S)
George Irwin	1939-47	13(3S)	22(3S)
Jack Butler	1947-49	3(3S)	3(3S)
Ron Rooke	1949-50	3(3S)	3(3S)
F Dawes/C Slade	1950-51	24(3S)	24(3S)
Laurie Scott	1951-54	13(3S)	22(3S)
Cyril Spiers	1954-58	14(3S)	23(3S)
George Smith	1958-60	7(4)	8(4)
Arthur Rowe	1960-63	11(3)	2(4)
Dick Graham	1963-66	7(2)	2(3)
Arthur Rowe (Acting)	1966		
Bert Head	1966-72	18(1)	11(2)
Malcolm Allison	1972-76	21(1)	5(3)
Terry Venables	1976-80	13(1)	3(3)
Ernie Walley	1980	20(1)	22(1)
Malcolm Allison	1980-81	22(10	22(1)
Dario Gradi	1981	22(1)	15(2)
Steve Kember	1981-82	15(2)	15(2)
Alan Mullery	1982-84	15(2)	18(2)
Steve Coppell	1984-93	3(1)	15(2)
Alan Smith	1993-95	1(1)	1(1)
Dave Bassett	1996-	3(1)	3(1)

LONGEST LEAGUE RUNS

undefeated matches:	18 (1.3.1969 - 16.8.1969)	of league matches w/out a win:	20 (24.2.1962 - 13.10.1962)
undefeated home matches:	32 (28.2.1930 - 8.10.1932)	of undefeated away matches:	10 (22.12.1928 -1.4.1929,
			26.12.1968 - 10.8.1969, 16.8.1975 - 6.12.1975, 18.11.78 - 3.4.79).
without home win:	11 (14.4.1973 - 17.11.1973)	without an away win:	31 (15.3.1980 - 3.10.1981).
league wins:	8 (9.2.1991 - 26.3.1921)	of home wins:	12 (19.12.1925 - 28.8.1926).
league defeats:	8 (18.41925 - 19.9.1925)	of away wins:	4 (1931-32, 1932-33 & 1975-76)

CRYSTAL PALACE

PLAYERS NAME Honours	Ht	Wt	Birthdate	Birthplace Transfers	Contract Date	Clubs	APPEARANCES				GOALS			
							League	L/Cup	FA Cup	Other	Lge	L/C	FAC	Oth
G O A L K E E P E R S														
Day Chris	6.2	12.4	28/07/75	Waltham Cross	16/04/93	Tottenham Hotspur								
E: Y. UEFA Y'93				£450000	06/08/96	Crystal Palace								
Nash Carlo						Clitheroe								
				£35000		Crystal Palace								
D E F E N D E R S														
Boxall Danny J	5.8	10.05	24/08/77	Croydon	01/08/94	Crystal Palace	1							
Davies Gareth M	5.10	11.3	11/12/73	Hereford	10/04/92	Hereford United	91+4	5+2	4	5	2			
W: u21.7.				£120000	01/07/95	Crystal Palace	17+3		2		2			
Edworthy Marc	5.7	9.6	24/12/72	Barnstaple	30/03/91	Plymouth Argyle	52+17	5+2	5+2	2+2	1			
				£350000	01/06/95	Crystal Palace	44	4	2	3				
Muscat Kevin						South Melbourne								
				£75000		Crystal Palace								
Pitcher Darren E J	5.9	12.2	12/10/69	Stepney	12/01/88	Charlton Athletic	170+3	11	12	8	9		3	
E: S.				£40000	01/07/94	Crystal Palace	57+4	5+1	10	3		1	1	
Quinn Robert	5.11	11.02	08/11/76	Sidcup	01/08/94	Crystal Palace	1			2+1				
Rodger Simon L	5.9	10.13	03/10/71	Shoreham		Bognor Regis								
Div.1'94.				£1000	02/07/90	Crystal Palace	97+17	15	2+3	2+2	5			
Tuttle David	6.1	12.0	06/02/72	Reading	08/02/90	Tottenham Hotspur	10+3	3+1		1				1
				Loan	21/01/93	Peterborough United	7							
				£350000	01/08/93	Sheffield United	63	2	3		1			
				£300000	08/03/96	Crystal Palace	9+1			3	1			
Vincent Jamie R	5.10	11.6	18/06/75	London	13/07/93	Crystal Palace	19+6	2+1	1			1		
M I D F I E L D														
Dyer Bruce A	6.0	10.9	13/04/75	Ilford	19/04/93	Watford	29+2	4	1	2	6	2		1
E: u21.6. Div.1'94.				£1100000	10/03/94	Crystal Palace	30+24	5	1+1	0+2	14	1	1	
Enquist Bjorn	5.10	10.09	12/10/77	Lund		Malmo								
					01/08/94	Crystal Palace								
Gordon Dean D	6.0	11.5	10/02/73	Croydon	04/07/91	Crystal Palace	119+15	14+3	8+1	2+1	15	2	1	
E: u21.10. Div.1'94.														
Hopkin David	6.0	13.0	21/08/70	Greenock		Grennock Morton	33+15	2	2					
				£300000	25/09/92	Chelsea	14+11		3+2					
				£800000	29/07/95	Crystal Palace	41+1	4	1	1	8	4		
Houghton Raymond J	5.7	10.10	09/01/62	Glasgow	05/07/79	West Ham United	0+1							
Ei:64. LC'86'94. Div.1'88'90.				Free	07/07/82	Fulham	129	12	4		16	2	3	
CS'88'90. FAC'89'92.				£147000	13/09/85	Oxford United	83	13	3	6	10	3		1
				£825000	19/10/87	Liverpool	147+6	14	26+1	8	28	3	4	3
				£900000	28/07/92	Aston Villa	83+12	11+2	7	4+2	6	2	2	1
				£300000	23/03/95	Crystal Palace	51	4	4	3	6			1
Maddison Neil	5.9	11.8	02/10/69	Darlington	14/04/88	Southampton	130+15	7+3	7+5	1	17			
				£300000	24/07/96	Crystal Palace								
Roberts Andrew J	5.10	11.5	20/03/74	Dartford	29/10/91	Millwall	132+6	12	7	4	5	2		1
				£2520000	01/06/95	Crystal Palace	36+2	3+1	2	3				1
F O R W A R D S														
Andersen Leif					18/01/96	Crystal Palace	12+4			1				
Freedman Doug	5.9	11.0	21/01/74	Glasgow	15/05/92	Q.P.R.								
				Free	26/07/94	Barnet	47	6	2	2	27	5		
				£800000	08/09/95	Crystal Palace	37+2		2	3	20			
Ginty Rory V	5.9	10.02	23/01/77	Galway	01/08/94	Crystal Palace	0+1							
McKenzie Leon M						Crystal Palace	4+8	3	1+1		1			

Name			DOB	Birthplace	Signed	Club								
ah George E	6.1	10.0	23/12/74	Dulwich	10/08/92	Crystal Palace	21+16	2+4		4+1	4	1		
⁄3.				Loan	13/10/95	Bournemouth	12			1	2			
lly Anthony D T	5.7	11.12	12/06/76	Dublin	02/12/93	Crystal Palace	0+2							
rt Carl	5.11	12.8	21/05/70	Whyalla (Aus)		Adelaide C.								
				£250000	22/07/94	Sheffield United	47+19	2+1	2+1	2	16	1	1	
				£200000	08/03/96	Crystal Palace	5+7			2+1				1

ᴅITIONAL CONTRACT PLAYERS

ᴛTON-GODWIN Osagyef o			Crystal Palace (T)
us Andrew			Crystal Palace (T)
ins Thomas		14/06/96	Crystal Palace (T)
an Anthony			Crystal Palace (T)
ris Jason		14/06/96	Crystal Palace (T)
ry David			Crystal Palace (T)
ᴍson Steven			Crystal Palace (T)
es Danny			Crystal Palace (T)

MANAGER
DAVE BASSETT

Date of Birth . . . . 4th September 1944.
Place of Birth . . . . Wembley.
Date of Appointment . . . . 21st January 1996.

PREVIOUS CLUBS
As Manager . . . . Wimbledon, Watford, Sheffield United.
As Coach . . . . Wimbledon.
As a Player . . . . . . Walton & Hersham, Wimbledon, Hendon, Chelsea, Watford.

HONOURS
As a Manager
Wimbledon: Promotion to Div.3 1981. Div.4 Championship 1983. Promotion to Div.2 1984. Promotion to Div.1 1986.
Sheffield United: Promotion to Div.2 1989. Promotion to Div.1 1990.

As a Player
Amateur Cup Winners Medal 1973.

SELHURST PARK

London SE25 6PU
Tel: 0181 768 6000

Capacity 26,500

First game..v Sheffield Wed., Division 2, 30.8.1924.
First floodlit game ....v Chelsea, 28.9.1953.
ATTENDANCES
Highest...51,482 v Burnley, Division 2, 5.5.1979.
Lowest ....2,207 v Brighton, FMC, 16.10.1985.

OTHER GROUNDS............................Crystal Palace 1905-15. Herne Hill 1915-18. The Nest 1918-24.
.... Selhurst Park 1924-

MATCHDAY TICKET PRICES

Directors Box £25
Juv/OAP (*Junior Eagle) £15 (£13)
Main Stand £17
Juv/OAP £15 (£9)
Arthur Wait Stand £14
Juv/OAP £8 (£6)
Whitehorse Lane £11
Juv/OAP £6 (£4)
New Holmesdale Stand Upper - Gallery £15
Upper Tier £13
Lower. £11
Juv/OAP £6 (£4)
Ticket Office Telephone no. . . . . . . 0181 771 8841.
*Must be Junior Eagle members.

CLUBCALL
0891 400 333
Calls cost 39p per minute cheap rate and 49p per
minute at all other times.
Call costings correct at time of going to press.

HOW TO GET TO THE GROUND

From the North
From motorway (M1) or A1, use A406 North Circular Road to Chiswick. Follow
signs South Circular Road (A205) to Wandsworth. Then use A3 to A214 and fol
low signs to Streatham. Join A23. In 1 mile turn left (B273). At the end turn left
into High Street then forward into Whitehorse Lane for Crystal Palace FC.

From the East
Use A232 (sign posted Croydon) to Shirley then join A215 (sign posted
Norwood). In 2.2 miles turn left (B266) into Whitehouse Lane.

From the South
Use A23 (sign posted London) then follow signs Crystal Palace (B266) via
Thornton Heath into Whitehorse Lane.

From the West
Use motorway (M4) to Chiswick then route from North or A232 (sign posted
Croydon) to Beddington, then follow signs London A23. After, follow signs
Crystal Palace (B266) via Thornton Heath into Whitehorse Lane.

Car Parking: Club car park (468 spaces) on first come first served basis. Street
parking is also available.

Nearest Railway Station: Thornton Heath/Norwood Junction/Selhurst.

MATCHDAY PROGRAMME

Programme Editor. . . . . Pete King & James Coome.

Number of pages . . . . 56.

Price . . . . £1.80.

Subscriptions . . . . £54 (inland) Home only.

Local Newspapers . . . . Croydon Advertiser, South London Press.

Local Radio Stations . . . . G.L.R., Capital Gold.

GRIMSBY TOWN
(The Mariners)
NATIONWIDE LEAGUE DIVISION 1
SPONSORED BY: 'EUROPES FOOD TOWN'

...ck Row (L-R): Simon Buckley, Neil Woods, Jimmy Neil, Peter Handyside, Paul Crichton, Jason Pearcey, Graham Rodger, Stewart ...tchley, Mark Lever, Joby Gowshall, Mark Brookes.
...ddle Row: Mike Bielby (Kit Manager), Nicky Southall, Tommy Watson, Craig Shakespeare, Jack Lester, Steve Livingstone, Ashley ...kling, Jim Dobbin, Paul Groves, Gerry Delahunt (Physio).
...ont Row: Kevin Jobling, Clive Mendonca, Gary Childs, Kenny Swain (Asst. Manager), Brian Laws (Manager), John Cockerill (Yth ...anager), John McDermott, Gary Croft.

GRIMSBY TOWN
FORMED IN 1878
TURNED PROFESSIONAL IN 1890
LTD COMPANY IN 1890

LIFE PRESIDENT
T J Lindley, T Wilkinson
CHAIRMAN: W H Carr
VICE-CHAIRMAN: T Aspinall
DIRECTORS
J Teanby, G Lamming,
J Mager
CHIEF EXECUTIVE
Ian Fleming (01472 697 111)
COMMERCIAL MANAGER
Tony Richardson

MANAGER: Brian Laws
ASSISTANT MANAGER: Kenny Swain
RESERVE TEAM MANAGER
Kenny Swain
YOUTH TEAM MANAGER
John Cockerill
PHYSIOTHERAPIST
Gerry Delahunt

STATISTICIAN FOR THE DIRECTORY
Les Triggs

This has been a season of peaks and troughs for Grimsby Town. Unfortunately the troughs have predominated, and supporters can hardly credit that a side which at the end of November occupied second spot in the First Division table should experience a change of fortune which from that point on produced a run of fourteen league games without a win and from which only five were salvaged. Consequently what had been confident hopes of a play off place ended as a struggle for First Division survival.

One of the few peaks came in the F.A. Cup, where a 7-1 drubbing of Luton in the Third Round was followed by a magnificent 3-0 victory over West Ham in a Fourth Round replay at Blundell Park, the Hammers having being held to a 1-1 draw at Upton Park. In the next round a creditable 0-0 home draw against Chelsea which the Mariners may well have won, was followed by an ignominus 4-1 thrashing at Stamford Bridge. This marked the first of three successive matches in which the defence leaked 13 goals, the lowest point of the season.

One of the peaks was the surprise arrival at Blundell Park of ex Serie A star Ivano Bonetti, in a mysterious deal involving fans raising £50,000 to buy his services for the season from American based management company with whom the club were not allowed to deal. Bonetti is said to have contributed another £50,000. Quite what the attraction Grimsby held for the Italian is not clear. Bonnetti provided a level of ball control, and an ability to provide pin-point service to the centre of the box that few Mariners fans can have previously witnessed, and Bonetti became a cult figure at the club. The love affair came to an abrupt halt after the well publicised dressing room spat with manager Laws, and despite a superficial display of reconciliation, the rift was unbridgable and Bonetti left at the end of the season with threats of litigation in the air. So from a peak came another trough.

Speculation regarding the future of some of the clubs young players were partly justified when Gary Croft moved to Blackburn Rovers in a million pound plus add on deal. The future of skipper Paul Groves who has remarkable record of four seasons uninterrupted first team appearances is also certain despite offers of a lucrative new contract.

With money now available to strengthen the team, manager Laws promises a serious attempt on a promotion spot next season. With no details of the promised new ground yet emerging and with attendances regularly being the lowest in the First Division, the clubs potential for Premier League football must remain open to serious doubt.   LES TRIGGS.

GRIMSBY TOWN

League: 17th   FA Cup: 5th Rnd   Coca-Cola Cup: 2nd Rnd

M	DATE	COMP	VEN	OPPONENTS	RESULT	HT	LP	GOAL SCORERS/GOAL TIMES	ATT.
1	A 12	EL	A	Millwall	L 1-2	0-2	19	Livingstone 59	(8546)
2	19	EL	H	Portsmouth	W 2-1	0-0	15	Laws 72, Croft 78	4515
3	26	EL	A	Derby County	D 1-1	0-0	16	Shakespeare 75(pen)	(10564)
4	29	EL	H	Luton Town	D 0-0	0-0	10		4289
5	S 2	EL	H	Watford	D 0-0	0-0	14		3993
6	9	EL	A	Wolverhampton Wand	L 1-4	1-1	18	Groves 39	(23656)
7	12	EL	A	Reading	W 2-0	1-0	15	Woods 6, Livingstone 71	(7283)
8	16	EL	A	Port Vale	W 1-0	1-0	10	Livingstone 18	4066
9	20	CC 2/1	A	**Birmingham City**	L 1-3	1-2		**Woods 34**	(7446)
10	23	EL	H	Norwich City	D 2-2	2-1	12	Childs 31, Southall 32	5901
11	30	EL	A	Southend United	L 0-1	0-0	14		(4977)
12	O 3	CC 2/2	H	**Birmingham City**	D 1-1	0-0		**Southall 64**	3280
13	7	EL	A	Charlton Athletic	W 1-0	1-0	11	Jewell 39	(8994)
14	14	EL	A	Oldham Athletic	D 1-1	0-1	12	Dobbin 72	5509
15	21	EL	A	Birmingham City	L 1-3	0-0	12	Woods 77	(16445)
16	28	EL	H	Stoke City	W 1-0	0-0	10	Groves 45	5477
17	N 4	EL	A	Ipswich Town	D 2-2	0-2	11	Woods 62, Dobbin 69	(10500)
18	11	EL	H	Barnsley	W 3-1	2-1	9	Lever 11, Zeeuw 20(og), Livingstone 82	6166
19	18	EL	H	West Bromwich Albion	W 1-0	0-0	5	Bonetti 55	8155
20	21	EL	A	Sheffield United	W 2-1	0-0	5	Southall 51, Childs 72	(9884)
21	25	EL	A	Tranmere Rovers	W 1-0	1-0	2	Bonetti 26	(7500)
22	D 2	EL	H	Charlton Athletic	L 1-2	0-1	5	Groves 72	6881
23	9	EL	A	Norwich City	D 2-2	1-1	7	Livingstone 6, Groves 77	(13283)
24	16	EL	H	Southend United	D 1-1	0-0	5	Forrester 49	5269
25	23	EL	H	Leicester City	D 2-2	1-0	7	Walsh 4(og), Dobbin 67	7713
26	J 1	EL	H	Huddersfield Town	D 1-1	1-0	8	Livingstone 33	7524
27	6	FAC 3	H	**Luton Town**	W 7-1	4-1		**Forrester16,32, Livingstone23,72, Bonetti45, Southall81, Woods84**	5387
28	13	EL	A	Portsmouth	L 1-3	0-2	9	Groves 78	(6958)
29	20	EL	A	Millwall	L 1-2	1-0	13	Livingstone 28	4218
30	24	EL	A	Sunderland	L 0-1	0-0	13		(14656)
31	F 3	EL	A	Derby County	D 1-1	1-0	13	Bonetti 27	7818
32	7	FAC 4	A	**West Ham United**	D 1-1	1-1		**Laws 24**	(22030)
33	10	EL	A	Luton Town	L 2-3	1-1	14	Forrester 17, 58	(7158)
34	14	FAC 4R	H	**West Ham United**	W 3-0	1-0		**Childs 24, Woods 63, Forrester 89**	8382
35	17	EL	H	Reading	D 0-0	0-0	15		6546
36	21	FAC 5	H	**Chelsea**	D 0-0	0-0			9648
37	28	FAC 5R	A	**Chelsea**	L 1-4	0-1		**Groves 55**	(28545)
38	M 3	EL	H	Sunderland	L 0-4	0-1	17		5318
39	5	EL	A	Crystal Palace	L 0-5	0-5	17		(11548)
40	9	EL	A	Leicester City	L 1-2	0-1	19	Livingstone 84	(13784)
41	12	EL	H	Wolverhampton Wand	W 3-0	0-0	16	Shakespeare 51, Groves 66, Forrester 79	5013
42	16	EL	H	Crystal Palace	L 0-2	0-1	17		5059
43	24	EL	A	Huddersfield Town	W 3-1	1-1	17	Livingstone 7, Childs 70, Groves 73	(12090)
44	30	EL	H	Birmingham City	W 2-1	2-1	15	Groves 33, Livingstone 40	5475
45	A 2	EL	A	Oldham Athletic	L 0-1	0-0	17		(5037)
46	6	EL	A	Stoke City	W 2-1	0-1	15	Groves 47, Gallimore 55	(12524)
47	8	EL	H	Ipswich Town	W 3-1	0-0	13	Mendonca 66, 69, 86	5904
48	13	EL	A	West Bromwich Albion	L 1-3	1-2	14	Forrester 30	(16116)
49	16	EL	A	Port Vale	L 0-1	0-0	15		(5796)
50	20	EL	H	Sheffield United	L 0-2	0-2	17		7740
51	23	EL	A	Watford	L 3-6	1-4	17	Groves 34, Livingstone 49, Walker 82	(8909)
52	27	EL	H	Tranmere Rovers	D 1-1	0-1	17	Mendonca 38	5408
53	M 4	EL	A	Barnsley	D 1-1	1-1	17	McDermott 4	(6108)

Best Home League Attendance: 8155 v West Bromwich Albion   Smallest: 3993 v Watford   Average: 5821

Goal Scorers:

EL(55): Livingstone(11),Groves(10),Forrester(5),Mendonca(4),Woods(3),Bonetti(3),Childs(3),Dobbin(3),Shakespeare(2),Southall(2),Opponent(s)(2),Laws(1),Gallimore(1),
Jewell(1),Lever(1),Croft(1),Walker(1),McDermott(1)

CC(2): Woods(1),Southall(1)

FAC(12): Forrester(3),Woods(2),Livingstone(2),Laws(1),Southall(1),Groves(1),Childs(1),Bonetti(1)

(F) Bonetti	(M) Butler (L)	(F) Childs	(G) Crichton	(D) Croft	(M) Dobbin	(D) Fickling	(M) Flatts (L)	(F) Forrester	(M) Gallimore	(M) Groves	(D) Handyside	(M) Jewell	(M) Jobling	(D) Laws	(F) Lester	(D) Lever	(F) Livingstone	(D) McDermott	(F) Mendonca	(D) Neil	(G) Pearcey	(D) Rodger	(D) Smith (L)	(F) Southall	(M) Walker	(M) Warner	(M) Watson	(F) Woods		
		X	X	S						X	X		X1	S1			X				S	X	X		X			X	M.Bailey	1
		X	X	S						X	X				X	X	S					X	X		X			X	K.Breen	2
		X	X	S1						X	X	S2	X1		X		X				S	X	X	X2				X	J.Willard	3
		X	X	X1	S1					X	X	S			X	X	X				S		X		X			X	W.Burns	4
	X3		X	S1						X	X	S3	X2		X1	X	S2			X		X		X				X1	J.A.Kirkby	5
		X	X	S1						X	X	S1				X	X				X1	X	X		X			X1	R.Grifford	6
		X	X	S						X	X			S1		X	X1				X	X	X		X			X	G.Singh	7
	X2	X	X	S1						X	X	S			X		X				X1	X	X		X		S2	X	M.A.Riley	8
		X	X	X	X					X	X		X1	S1		X	X			S			X		X	X	X	S.Mathieson	9
	X1	X	X	X	S					X	X			S		X	X					X	X		S1	X	T.Heilbron	10
	X1	X	X	X						X	X	X2		S2		X					S1	X	X	S2		G.Barber	11
X		X1	X	X	X					X	X		X	X	X	S						X		S	K.M.Lynch	12
X		X	X	X	S					X	X	X	X	X	S				X	X	S	X	I.Hemley	13
X		X	X	X						X	X	X1	S1			X	X	X	R.Poulain	14
X		X	X	X	S1		S2			X	X	X			S	X1	X2	X	M.Pierce	15
X		X2	X	X			S1			X	X	X	X	S2		S		X1	X	T.West	16
		X	X	X			X1			X	X	X	X	S1		S	X	G.Pulley	17
X		X	X	X						X	X	X	X	X	S	S	S	X	G.Cain	18
X		X	X	X						X	X	X	X	X	S	S	S	A.N.Butler	19
		X	X	X		X				X	X	X	X	X	S	S	S1	X1	K.Leach	20
X		X	X	X				X1		X	S1		X	X	X	X	S	S	G.Frankland	21
X		X	X	X				X1		X	S		X	X	X	X	S	S1	W.C.Burns	22
X		X	X	X				X1		X	S1		X	X	X	S		S	R.Furnandiz	23
X		X	X	X				X1		X	X	X	X1	S	S		S1	R.Pearson	24
		X	X	X		X				X	X	X	X	S	S	X	X	U.Rennie	25
X		X	X	X		X1				X	X	X	X	S	S	S1	T.Heilbron	26
X		X1	X	X2		X3				X	X	X	X	S1	S3	S2	P.Richards	27
X		X	X	X1		X1				X	X	X	X	X1	S1	S1	I.Hemley	28
X		X	X	X1		X3				X	S1	X	X	X	X1	S1	S3	E.Wolstenholme	29
X2		S1	X	X		X1				X	X	X	X	X	X	S2	D.B.Allison	30
X	X	X	X	X			X1		X	S1	X2	X	S	X	X	K.Lynch	31
X2		X	X	X		X		X	X	X	S1	X	X	S2	X1	G.Willard	32
X	X	X1	X	X		X2		X	X	S2	X	S1	X	B.Knight	33
	X1	X	X	X		X	X	X	S1	X	S	X	X	R.A.Hart	34
	S	X	X	X		X	X1	X	X	S1	S	X	X	E.Lomas	35
		X	X	X	S	S	S	X	X	X	X	X	S.Dunn	36
	X2	X	X	S2	S2	S1	X	X2	X	X	X1	X	S.Dunn	37
	X	X1	X	X1	S1	X	X	X	X	S	X	X	S1	M.E.Pierce	38
		X	X	X		S	X	S	X	X	X	X	X	S.Bennett	39
	X1	X	X		S	X	S1	X	X	X	X	X1	X	W.Burns	40
		X	X	X		X	X	X	X1	X	X	S1	X	X	S	S	F.G.Stretton	41
	X2	X1	X	S1	X	X	X	X	X	X	X	S2	S	M.Fletcher	42
	X	X	X	S	X	X	X	X	X	X	X	X	S	J.Brandwood	43
		X	S	X	X	X	X	X	X	X	X	X	X	S	D.B.Allison	44
	S1	X	X	X2	X	X	S	X	X	X	X	X1	S2	G.Singh	45
	X	X	S1	X2	S3	X	X	X	X	X1	X3	X	X	S2	X	E.Wolstenholme	46
	X1	X	X	X	S2	X	X	S3	X	X3	X2	S1	X	M.C.Bailey	47
		X	S	X	S1	X1	X	X	S2	X	X	X	X	X	X2	K.Lynch	48
X		X	S	S	X	X	X	S	X	X	X	X	X	K.Breen	49
X		X	S2		X	X	X	X	X	X	X	X	S	N.Barry	50
		X	X	S1	X	X3	X	X1	X2	X	X	X	X	S3	S2	S.Baines	51
	X	X	S	X	X	X	X	X	X	X	X	X	S	S	A.N.Butler	52
		X	X	S2	X	X	X	X	X	X	X	X	X2	S1	T.Heilbron	53
3	19	33	44	36	21	5	4	23	10	46	30	2	3	21	0	23	33	27	8	2	14	24	18	28	1	3	0	24	EL Appearances	
0	0	2	0	0	4	6	1	5	0	0	0	3	0	6	5	1	5	1	0	0	2	4	0	5	1	0	2	9	EL Sub Appearances	
0	1	1	2	2	2	2	0	0	0	2	2	1	0	2	0+1	0	1	0	0	0	0	0	0	2	0	0	1	1	CC Appearances	
0	2	5	5	5	1+1	1+1	0	3+1	0	5	1	0	0	4	0	4	3+2	4	0	0	1	4+1	0	3+2	0	0	0	4+1	FAC Appearances	

Also Played: (M) Clare S1(12,50), S(53). (M) Gambaro S1(40). (D) Gowshall S(9). (M) Shakespeare X1(53).

GRIMSBY TOWN

CLUB RECORDS

BIGGEST VICTORIES
League: 9-2 v Darwen, Division 2, 15.4.1899.
7-0 v v Bristol Rovers (a), Division 2, 1957-58.
F.A. Cup: 10-0 v Boston, 2nd Round, 24.10.1981.
League Cup: 6-1 v Rotherham United, 2nd Round, 6.11.1984.

BIGGEST DEFEATS
League: 1-9 v Arsenal, Division 1, 28.1.1931.
F.A. Cup: 1-9 v Phoenix Bessemer, 2nd Round, 25.11.1982.
League Cup: 0-6 v Burnley, 2nd Round, 10.9.1968.

MOST POINTS
3 points a win: 83, Division 3, 1990-91.
2 points a win: 68, Division 3(N), 1955-56.

MOST GOALS SCORED
103, Division 2, 1933-34.
Glover 42, Craven 18, jennings 13, Bestall 11, Holmes 7, Kelly 3, Dyson 3, Ponting 2, Moralee 2, Dodds 1, Lewis 1.

MOST GOALS CONCEDED
111, Division 1, 1947-48.

MOST FIRST CLASS MATCHES IN A SEASON
59 - 1979-80 (League 46, FA Cup 4, League Cup 9).

MOST LEAGUE WINS
31, Division 3(N), 1955-56.

MOST LEAGUE DRAWS
20, Division 1, 1993-94.

MOST LEAGUE DEFEATS
28, Division 1, 1947-48.

INDIVIDUAL CLUB RECORDS

MOST GOALS IN A SEASON
Pat Glover: 43 goals in 1933-34 (League 42, FA Cup 1).

MOST GOALS IN A MATCH
6. Tommy McCairns v Leicester Fosse, Division 2, 11.4.1896.

OLDEST PLAYER
George Tweedy, 40 years 84 days v York City, 3.4.1953.

YOUNGEST PLAYER
Tony Ford, 16 years 143 days (Sub) v Walsall, 4.10.1975.

MOST CAPPED PLAYER
Pat Glover (Wales) 7.

BEST PERFORMANCES

League: 1925-26: Matches Played 42, Won 26, Drawn 9, Lost 7, Goals for 93, Goals against 40, Points 61. First in Division 3(N).
Highest Position: 5th Division 1, 1934-35.
F.A. Cup: Semi-finalists 1935-36.
Most recent success: 1938-39: 3rd Round Tranmere Rovers (h) 6-0; 4th round Millwall (a) 2-2, (h) 3-2; 5th Round Sheffield United (a) 0-0, (h) 1-0; 6th Round, Chelsea (a) 1-0; Semi-Final Wolverhampton Wndrs. 0-5.
League Cup: 5th Round 1979-80.
Most Recent success: 1984-85: 2nd Round Barnsley (h) 3-0, (a) 1-1; 3rd Round Rotherham United (a) 0-0, (h) 6-1; 4th Round Everton (a) 1-0; 5th Round Norwich City (h) 0-1.

ADDITIONAL INFORMATION
PREVIOUS NAMES
Grimsby Pelham.

PREVIOUS LEAGUES
Football Alliance; Midland League (1910).

Club colours: Black & white striped shirts, black shorts and white socks.
Change colours: Red & blue striped shirts, blue shorts and red socks.

Reserves League: Pontins Central League.
Youth: Midland Purity League.

DIVISIONAL RECORD

	Played	Won	Drawn	Lost	For	Against	Points
Division 1	488	167	97	224	756	940	431
Division 2/1	1,794	665	400	729	2,703	2,852	1,888
Division 3	690	272	170	248	976	913	750
Division 3(S)	42	15	9	18	49	59	39
Division 3(N)	432	200	85	147	672	534	485
Division 4	368	155	92	121	520	460	441
Total	**3,814**	**1,474**	**853**	**1,487**	**5,676**	**5,758**	**4,034**

RECORDS AND STATISTICS

COMPETITIONS

Div.1	Div.2/1	Div.3	Div.3(N)	Div.4
1901-03	1892-01	1920-21	1921-26	1968-72
1929-32	1903-10	1959-62	1951-56	1977-79
1934-48	1911-20	1964-68		1988-90
	1926-29	1972-77		
	1932-34	1979-80		
	1948-51	1987-88		
	1956-59	1990-91		
	1962-64			
	1980-87			
	1991-			

HONOURS

Div.2	Div.3(N)	Div.3	Div.4
1900-01	1925-26	1979-80	1971-72
1933-34	1955-56		

MOST APPEARANCES

KEITH JOBLING 493 (1953-66)

Year	League	FA Cup	Lge Cup
1953-54	9		
1954-55	6	1	
1956-57	6		
1957-58	13		
1958-59	42	3	
1959-60	42	2	
1960-61	36	1	1
1961-62	46	1	1
1962-63	41	1	1
1963-64	41	1	1
1964-65	46	4	2
1965-66	42	6	5
1966-67	21	2	4
1967-68	18	1	
1968-69	41	1	4
	450	24	19

MOST GOALS IN A CAREER

PAT GLOVER - 197 (1930-39)

Year	League	FA Cup
1930-31	2	
1931-32	12	4
1932-33	22	2
1933-34	42	1
1934-35	34	2
1935-36	31	4
1936-37	29	4
1937-38	4	
1938-39	4	
Total	180	17

RECORD TRANSFER FEE RECEIVED

Amount	Club	Player	Date
£1,000,000	Blackburn	Gary Croft	3/96
£650,000	Sunderland	Shaun Cunnington	7/92
£600,000	West Brom	Paul Groves	5/96
£500,000	Q.P.R.	Andy Tillson	12/90

RECORD TRANSFER FEE PAID

Amount	Club	Player	Date
£300,000	Southampton	Tommy Widdrington	7/96
£180,000	Carlisle Utd	Tony Gallimore	3/96
£140,000	Chelsea	Steve Livingstone	10/93
£135,000	Luton Town	Graham Rodger	1/92

MANAGERS

Name	Seasons	Best	Worst
Hayden Price	1920		
George Fraser	1921-24	3(3N)	14(3N)
Wilf Gillow	1924-32	13(1)	12(3N)
Frank Womack	1932-36	5(1)	13(2)
Charles Spencer	1937-51	16(1)	22(2)
Bill Shankly	1951-54	2(3N)	17(3N)
Bill Walsh	1954-55	17(3N)	23(3N)
Allenby Chilton	1955-59	13(2)	23(3N)
Tim Ward	1960-62	2(3)	6(3)
Tom Johnston	1962-64	19(2)	21(2)
Jimmy McGuigan	1964-67	10(3)	17(3)
Don McEvoy	1967-68	22(3)	22(3)
Bill Harvey	1968-69	22(3)	23(4)
Bobby Kennedy	1969-71	16(4)	23(4)
Lawrie McMenemy	1971-73	9(3)	19(4)
Ron Ashman	1973-75	6(3)	16(3)
Tommy Casey	1975-76	16(3)	18(3)
John Newman	1977-79	2(4)	6(4)
George Kerr	1979-82	7(2)	1(3)
Dave Booth	1982-85	5(2)	19(2)
Mick Lyons	1985-87	15(2)	21(2)
Bobby Roberts	1987-88	22(3)	22(3)
Alan Buckley	1988-94	9(2/1)	9(4)
Brain Laws	1994-	10(1)	10(1)

LONGEST LEAGUE RUNS

of undefeated matches:	19 (16.2.1980 - 30.8.1980)	of league matches w/out a win:	18 (10.10.1981 - 16.3.1982)
of undefeated home matches:	33 (8.10.1974 - 28.2.1976)	of undefeated away matches:	9 (23.2.80-30.8.80, 19.11.83-10.3.84)
without home win:	12 (27.9.1947 - 17.3.1948)	without an away win:	23 (2.10.1982 - 28.10.1983)
of league wins:	11 (19.1.1952 - 29.3.1952)	of home wins:	17 (9.3.1894 - 28.3.1895)
of league defeats:	9 (30.11.1907 - 18.1.1908)	of away wins:	5 (26.1.1952 - 22.3.1952)

GRIMSBY TOWN

PLAYERS NAME Honours	Ht	Wt	Birthdate	Birthplace Transfers	Contract Date	Clubs	League	L/Cup	FA Cup	Other	Lge	L/C	FAC	Oth
G O A L K E E P E R S														
Crichton Paul A	6.0	12.1	03/10/68	Pontefract	23/05/86	Nottingham Forest								
				Loan	19/09/86	Notts County	5							
				Loan	30/01/87	Darlington	5							
				Loan	27/03/87	Peterborough Utd	4							
				Loan	28/09/87	Darlington	3	1		1				
				Loan	24/12/87	Swindon Town	4							
				Loan	09/03/88	Rotherham United	6							
				Loan	25/08/88	Torquay United	13	2						
					03/11/88	Peterborough Utd	47		5	3				
				Free	25/08/90	Doncaster Rovers	77	5	3	5				
				Free	09/07/93	Grimsby Town	133	7	8	2				
Pearcey Jason	6.1	13.5	23/07/71	Leamington	18/07/89	Mansfield Town	74	5	2	6				
				Loan	03/11/94	Grimsby Town								
					16/12/94	Grimsby Town	5							
D E F E N D E R S														
Fickling Ashley E: u18.8.	5.10	11.0	15/11/72	Sheffield	26/07/91	Sheffield United		1						
				Loan	26/11/92	Darlington	14			1				
				Loan	12/08/93	Darlington	1	1						
				Free	23/03/95	Grimsby Town	6+6	2	1+1					
Gowshall Joby	6.1	13.0	07/08/75	Peterlee	13/07/94	Grimsby Town								
Handyside Peter D S: u21.5.	6.1	12.3	31/07/74	Dumfries	21/11/92	Grimsby Town	86+3	5	4	4				
Laws Brian	5.10	11.5	14/10/61	Wallsend	19/10/79	Burnley	125	14	15		12	2	1	
				£10000	26/08/83	Huddersfield Town	56	7	3		1			
				£30000	15/03/85	Middlesbrough	103+5	6+1	8+1	6+1	12	2		
				£120000	07/07/88	Nottingham Forest	136+11	28+4	16+2	11+1	4		4	
				Free	01/12/94	Grimsby Town	27+16	2	4		2		1	
Lever Mark	6.3	12.8	29/03/70	Beverley	09/08/88	Grimsby Town	236+7	15+1	14+1	9	8			
McDermott John	5.7	10.0	03/02/69	Middlesbrough	01/06/87	Grimsby Town	290+14	17+1	20+1	11	5			
Neil James D	5.8	10.05	28/02/76	Bury St.Ed	13/07/94	Grimsby Town	1							
Rodger Graham E: u21.4. FAC'87.	6.2	11.13	01/04/67	Glasgow		Wolves	1							
				Free	18/02/85	Coventry City	31+5	3+1	1+1	0+1	2			
				£150000	01/08/89	Luton Town	27+1	2		3	2			
				£135000	08/01/92	Grimsby Town	97+10	3	6	2	9			
M I D F I E L D														
Brookes Mark	5.9	10.06	19/09/75	Nottingham	23/02/95	Grimsby Town								
Clare Daryl						Grimsby Town	0+1	0+1						
Dobbin James S: Y.	5.9	10.7	17/09/63	Dunfermline		Celtic	1+1	4					1	
				Loan	01/02/84	Motherwell	1+1							
				£25000	19/03/84	Doncaster Rovers	56+8	5	2	3	13	1		
				£35000	19/09/86	Barnsley	116+13	3+1	11	4	12		1	
				£200000	15/07/91	Grimsby Town	154+9	13	7+1	5	21	3	1	1
Gallimore Anthony	5.11	11.3	21/02/72	Crewe	11/07/90	Stoke City	6+5							
				Loan	03/10/91	Carlisle United	8							
				Loan	26/02/92	Carlisle United	8							
				Loan	25/03/93	Carlisle United	8			1				
				£15000	13/07/93	Carlisle United	116	8	8	24	8	1		1
				£125000	28/03/96	Grimsby Town	10				1			
Jobling Kevin A	5.9	10.11	01/01/68	Sunderland	09/01/86	Leicester City	4+5		0+1	3				2
					19/02/88	Grimsby Town	210+17	12+1	4+3	5+4	9		1	
				Loan	10/01/94	Scunthorpe United				1				
Shakespeare Craig R	5.10	12.5	26/10/63	Birmingham	05/11/81	Walsall	276+8	31	22	18	45	6	6	2
				£300000	19/06/89	Sheffield Wed.	15+2	3		0+1	1			
				£275000	08/02/90	W.B.A.	104+8	6	5	5	12	1	2	1
				£115000	14/07/93	Grimsby Town	61+19	4+1	5+3	0+1	8			
Walker John						Clydebank								
					19/09/95	Grimsby Town	1+1				1			
Watson Thomas R	5.8	10.10	29/09/69	Liverpool	12/07/88	Grimsby Town	134+38	10+5	4	8+2	24	2		
				Loan	13/10/95	Hull City								

Name	Ht	Wt	DOB	Fee	Date	Club								
Childs Gary P C	5.7	10.8	19/04/64		13/02/82	Birmingham	2+1							
E: Y.4.				£15000	07/10/83	Walsall	120+11	14+2	9+1	7	17	2	2	2
				£50000	08/07/87	Birmingham City	39+16	0+2	3	2	2			
				Free	20/07/89	Grimsby Town	185+21	14	14	7+2	25	1	1	
Forrester Jamie	5.6	10.4	01/11/74			Bradford								
						Auxerre (France)								
				£60000	20/10/92	Leeds United	7+2		1+1			2		
				Loan	01/09/94	Southend United	3+2							
				Loan	10/03/95	Grimsby Town	7+2				1			
				Free	17/10/95	Grimsby Town	23+5		3+1		5	3		
Lester Jack W	5.10	11.2	08/10/75		08/07/94	Sheffield								
						Grimsby Town	1+11	0+2	0+1					
Livingstone Stephen	6.1	12.7	08/09/69		16/07/86	Middlesbrough								
						Coventry City	17+14	8+2		0+1	5	10		
				£450000	17/01/91	Blackburn Rovers	25+5	2	1		10		1	
				£350000	23/03/93	Chelsea	0+1							
				Loan	03/09/93	Port Vale	4+1							
				£140000	29/10/93	Grimsby Town	89+10	3	4+2		22		2	
Mendonca Clive P	5.10	10.7	09/09/68		10/09/86	Islington								
						Sheffield United	8+5	0+1		1	4			
				Loan	26/02/88	Doncaster Rovers	2							
				£35000	25/03/88	Rotherham United	71+13	5+2	4+1	4+2	27	1	2	1
				£110000	01/08/91	Sheffield United	4+6	0+2		0+1	1			
				Loan	09/01/92	Grimsby Town	10				3			
				£85000	13/08/92	Grimsby Town	106+5	8+1	7	2	39	4	2	1
Southall Nicholas	5.10	11.4	28/01/72			Stockton								
						Darlington								
				Free	21/02/91	Hartlepool United	118+20	6+1	4+4	6+2	24	3		
				£40000	12/07/95	Grimsby Town	28+5	2	3+2		2	1	1	
Woods Neil S	6.0	12.11	30/07/66		31/08/83	Bradford								
						Doncaster Rovers	55+10	4	5	5+2	16	1	2	3
				£120000	22/12/86	Glasgow Rangers	0+3							
				£120000	03/08/87	Ipswich Town	15+12			4	5		1	
					01/03/90	Bradford City	13+1				2			
				£82000	23/08/90	Grimsby Town	153+39	10+1	7+1	7	41	2	2	1

THE MANAGER
BRIAN LAWS

Date of Birth . . . . 14th October 1961.
Place of Birth . . . . Wallsend.
Date of Appointment . . . . November 1995.

PREVIOUS CLUBS
As Manager . . . . None.
As Coach . . . . None.
As a Player . . . Burnley, Huddersfield Town, Middlesbrough, Nottingham Forest.

HONOURS
As a Manager
None.

As a Player
Football League XI.
England 'B' cap.

BLUNDELL PARK

Cleethorpes, South Humberside DN35 7PY
Tel: 01472 697 111

Capacity 8,616
....(Away seating 1,874)

First game ....v Luton Town, 3-3, 2.9.1899.
First floodlit game ....v Gainsborough T, 9.3.1953.

ATTENDANCES
Highest ....31,657 v Wolves, FA Cup 5th Rnd, 20.2.1937.
Lowest ....970 v Scunthorpe Utd, AMC, 15.12.1987.

OTHER GROUNDS...None.

MATCHDAY TICKET PRICES

Upper John Smith's Stand & Main Stand

Adults £12

Children - all seats...................... £5

OAP's - all seats £6

Pontoon End & Lower John Smith's

Adults .... £10 (with Mariners Discount Card)

.... £12 without Card (Apply to club for Card)

Ticket Office Telephone no. 01472 697 111

HOW TO GET TO THE GROUND

From the North and West
Use motorway (M18) then A180, sign posted Grimsby, then follow signs to Cleethorpes A1098.

From the South
Use A1 then A16 and follow signs to Cleethorpes and at roundabout take first exit into Grimsby Road A1098 for Grimsby Town FC.

Car Parking
Street parking available.

Nearest Railway Station
Cleethorpes, Grimsby (01472 353 556).

HOTLINE
0891 55 58 55
Calls cost 39p per minute cheap rate and 49p per minute at all other times.
Call costings correct at time of going to press.

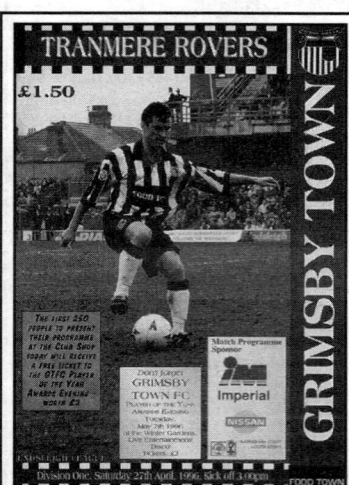

MATCHDAY PROGRAMME

Programme Editor .... Timothy Harvey.

Number of pages .... 32.

Price .... £1.50.

Subscriptions .... £40 per season.

Local Newspapers .... Grimsby Evening Telegraph,
.... Sports Telegraph, Grimsby Target.

Local Radio Stations............ Radio Humberside, Viking Radio.

HUDDERSFIELD TOWN
(The Terriers)
NATIONWIDE LEAGUE DIVISION 1
SPONSORED BY: PANASONIC

Back Row (L-R): Simon Baldry, Iain Dunn, Chris Billy, Jon Whitney, Ronnie Jepson, Andrew Booth, Simon Collins, Kevin Gray.
Middle Row: Dennis Booth (Coach), David Moss (Yth Coach), Craig Whittington, Simon Trevitt, Richard Logan, Tony Norman, Steve Francis, Jonathan Dyson, Patrick Scully, Dave Wilson (Physio).
Front Row: Rodney Rowe, Tom Cowan, Darren Bullock, Lee Sinnott, Brian Horton (Manager), Paul Reid, Lee Duxbury, Gary Crosby, Gary Clayton.

HUDDERSFIELD TOWN
FORMED IN 1908
TURNED PROFESSIONAL IN 1908
LTD COMPANY IN 1908

PRESIDENT: Lawrence Batley OBE
CHAIRMAN: D G Headey
DIRECTORS
J M Asquith, D A Taylor, E R Whiteley,
C Senior (Vice-President)
SECRETARY
A D Sykes (01484 420 335)
COMMERCIAL MANAGER
Alan Stevenson

MANAGER: Brian Horton
COACH: Dennis Booth
RESERVE TEAM MANAGER
David Moss
YOUTH DEVELOPMENT OFFICER
Gerry Murphy
YOUTH TEAM MANAGER
Mark Lillis
PHYSIOTHERAPIST
Dave Wilson

STATISTICIAN FOR THE DIRECTORY
Richard Stead

The disappointment at Towns failure to reach the 1st division play-offs following last seasons promotion shows just how much progress has been made in a short space of time. The season started with the need to replace manager Neil Warnock following his decision to resign and the man chosen to take over the role was Brian Horton. The promised to give the squad he inherited every chance to prove themselves before entering the transfer market and true to his word he used 29 players over the season as a whole.

The main question before the season started was how the players would react to life in the higher division, the answer was, surprisingly well, although an opening day away league defeat followed by defeat in the 1st leg of the Coca-Cola cup suggested that the pundits who had made Huddersfield favourites for an instant return to the 2nd division would be proved right. The first major test of the season came with the first home league game, which was won by the narrowest of margins to restore hope.

The early season games set the pattern for the rest of the season with Towns home form bettered only by Sunderland and Derby with their away form being the worst in the play-offs, although this was only confirmed in the second to last game of the season, inevitably an away defeat.

Horton led a 'quiet revolution' over the season to change the style of play and to recruit new players to fit the style. Notable recruits included Paul Dalton from Plymouth, in an exchange deal involving play-off scorer Chris Billy, record signing Lee Makel from Blackburn, Welsh international Steve Jenkins from Swansea and Rob Edwards from Crewe. The latter arriving with a bang by scoring 7 goals in 13 end of season games. On the scoring front Andy Booth continued to attract the attention of Premier league scouts with is 21 goals for the season, ably assisted by Ronnie Jepson.

In the cup competitions defeat in the Coca-Cola came in the second round but Town came within a whisker of reaching the F.A. Cup quarter finals. Only for a 'last kick of the game' equaliser by Wimbledon leading to a replay defeat, despite taking an early lead.

Once again the average attendance has increased and has now more than doubled from two seasons ago. Proof, if it were needed that the move to a new stadium has provided the catalyst for which the rewards are now being reaped.

The foundations for the future success have been laid but next season Towns away form will have to improve substantially if these hopes are to be realised. In some respects it may be harder as the element of ësurpriseí has now gone, however Horton will have the luxury of a full pre-season build-up with the squad and it is to be hoped that this, along with summer signings will provide the extra impetus for future success.

RICHARD STEAD.

HUDDERSFIELD TOWN

League: 8th   FA Cup: 5th Rnd   Coca-Cola Cup: 2nd Rnd

M	DATE	COMP	VEN	OPPONENTS	RESULT	HT	LP	GOAL SCORERS/GOAL TIMES	ATT.
1	A 12	EL	A	Oldham Athletic	L 0-3	0-1	23		(10259)
2	15	CC 1/1	H	Port Vale	L 1-2	1-1		Dalton 15	5363
3	19	EL	H	Watford	W 1-0	0-0	19	Jepson 67	10556
4	22	CC 1/2	A	Port Vale	W 3-1	2-0		Bullock 6, Booth 22, 70	(4380)
5	26	EL	A	Tranmere Rovers	L 1-3	0-0	20	Cowan 55	(9072)
6	30	EL	H	Birmingham City	W 4-2	1-1	11	Dalton 7, 51, Jepson 64, Bullock 70	12305
7	S 2	EL	A	Charlton Athletic	L 1-2	0-1	12	Booth 90	(9570)
8	9	EL	H	Ipswich Town	W 2-1	2-0	10	Collins 34, Sedgley 44(og)	12057
9	12	EL	H	Barnsley	W 3-0	1-0	4	Jepson 27, Collins 74, Booth 83	14635
10	16	EL	A	Crystal Palace	D 0-0	0-0	6		(15645)
11	19	CC 2/1	H	Barnsley	W 2-0	1-0		Collins 29, Booth 53	8264
12	24	EL	H	Sheffield United	L 1-2	0-2	10	Jepson 84	12840
13	30	EL	A	West Bromwich Albion	W 2-1	2-1	5	Cowan 38, Booth 40	(15945)
14	O 3	CC 2/2	A	Barnsley	L 0-4	0-1			(8912)
15	7	EL	H	Port Vale	L 0-2	0-1	8		11554
16	14	EL	A	Reading	L 1-3	1-1	14	Booth 25	(8534)
17	21	EL	H	Sunderland	D 1-1	0-0	11	Booth 69	16054
18	28	EL	A	Southend United	D 0-0	0-0	13		(5128)
19	N 4	EL	H	Norwich City	W 3-2	1-0	10	Jepson 15, Jenkins 49, Dalton 82	13747
20	11	EL	A	Portsmouth	D 1-1	1-1	12	Scully 35	(6876)
21	18	EL	A	Millwall	D 0-0	0-0	13		(9402)
22	21	EL	H	Leicester City	W 3-1	1-1	11	Bullock 22, 71, Dalton 85	14300
23	25	EL	H	Wolverhampton Wand	W 2-1	2-0	9	Booth 20, Dalton 38	16423
24	D 2	EL	A	Port Vale	L 0-1	0-1	11		(7701)
25	9	EL	A	Sheffield United	W 2-0	1-0	10	Booth 20, Bullock 52	(12126)
26	16	EL	H	West Bromwich Albion	W 4-1	0-0	4	Turner 52, Jepson 59, 83, Booth 63	12664
27	23	EL	A	Luton Town	D 2-2	0-1	6	Booth 56, Makel 64	(7076)
28	26	EL	H	Derby County	L 0-1	0-0	7		18495
29	30	EL	H	Stoke City	D 1-1	0-0	6	Prudhoe 73(og)	15071
30	J 1	EL	A	Grimsby Town	D 1-1	0-1	5	Jepson 76	(7524)
31	6	FAC 3	H	Blackpool	W 2-1	1-1		Jepson 44, 87	12424
32	13	EL	A	Watford	W 1-0	0-0	3	Bullock 46	(7568)
33	20	EL	H	Oldham Athletic	D 0-0	0-0	3		13013
34	F 3	EL	H	Tranmere Rovers	D 1-1	0-0	3	Collins 57	12041
35	5	FAC 4	H	Peterborough United	W 2-0	0-0		Bullock 52, Booth 74	11629
36	17	FAC 5	H	Wimbledon	D 2-2	1-0		Rowe 7, Cowan 48	17307
37	20	EL	H	Charlton Athletic	D 2-2	2-1	4	Booth 15, Rowe 20	10951
38	24	EL	A	Crystal Palace	W 3-0	3-0	4	Booth 11, Jepson 34(pen), Makel 44	13041
39	28	FAC 5R	A	Wimbledon	L 1-3	1-2		Booth 8	(7015)
40	M 2	EL	A	Derby County	L 2-3	1-2	5	Booth 2, Thornley 81	(17097)
41	9	EL	H	Luton Town	W 1-0	0-0	6	Edwards 75	11950
42	12	EL	A	Birmingham City	L 0-2	0-1	6		(15296)
43	16	EL	A	Stoke City	D 1-1	0-0	6	Edwards 87	(13157)
44	19	EL	A	Barnsley	L 0-3	0-2	7		(10660)
45	24	EL	H	Grimsby Town	L 1-3	1-1	7	Jepson 41	12090
46	30	EL	A	Sunderland	L 2-3	1-1	8	Edwards 21, Booth 58	(20131)
47	A 2	EL	H	Reading	W 3-1	0-1	6	Edwards 50, 68, Booth 84	11828
48	6	EL	H	Southend United	W 3-1	0-0	6	Jepson 51, Edwards 65, Booth 70	11558
49	8	EL	A	Norwich City	L 0-2	0-0	6		(13021)
50	13	EL	H	Millwall	W 3-0	1-0	6	Jepson 14, Edwards 74, Booth 79	11206
51	20	EL	A	Leicester City	L 1-2	0-1	8	Bullock 47	(17619)
52	27	EL	A	Wolverhampton Wand	D 0-0	0-0	8		(25290)
53	M 1	EL	A	Ipswich Town	L 1-2	1-1	8	Thornley 24	(17473)
54	5	EL	H	Portsmouth	L 0-1	0-1	8		14091

Best Home League Attendance: 18495 v Derby County   Smallest: 10556 v Watford   Average: 13150

Goal Scorers:
EL(61): Booth(16),Jepson(12),Edwards(7),Bullock(6),Dalton(5),Collins(3),Makel(2),Opponent(s)(2),Cowan(2),Thornley(2),Jenkins(1),Rowe(1),Scully(1),Turner(1)
CC(6): Booth(3),Collins(1),Dalton(1),Bullock(1)
FAC(7): Booth(2),Jepson(2),Rowe(1),Bullock(1),Cowan(1)

(F) Baldry	(F) Booth	(D) Brown	(M) Bullock	(M) Collins	(D) Cowan	(F) Crosby	(M) Dalton	(F) Dunn	(F) Duxbury	(D) Dyson	(F) Edwards	(G) Francis	(M) Gray	(D) Jenkins	(F) Jepson	(F) Lawson	(M) Logan	(M) Makel	(G) Norman	(M) Reid	(F) Rowe	(D) Scully	(D) Sinnott	(F) Thornley (L)	(D) Trevitt	(M) Turner (L)	(F) Ward	(D) Whitney		
	X		X	S1	X		X		X			X			X				S	X1		X	X	X				S	J.Rushton	1
	X		X	X	X		X	X	X1			X			X				S			X	X	X				S	D.Allison	2
	X		X	X	X		X	S1	X1			X			X		S		S			X	X	X				S1	J.Lloyd	3
	X		X	X	X	X	X1	S				X			X		S					X	X	X				S1	S.Matthieson	4
	X		X	X	X	S1	X					X	S		X							X	X			X1		X	E.Wolftenholme	5
S	X		X	X	X		X	S				X			X		X		S			X	X	X				X	N.Barry	6
S1	X		X	X	X		X	S2				X	X		X		X2						X1	X					M.Bailey	7
S1		X	X	X	X1		X	S				X			X						X	S	X	X					E.Wolstenholme	8
S		X	X	X	X		X	S				X			X				S	X		X	X	X					P.Richards	9
			X	X	X		X	S			X	X	X		X					X		X					X		M.Pierce	10
S	X		X	X	X		X1	X			X		S						X	X	X	S1	X	X					I.Cruikshanks	11
S1	X	X	X	X1	X		X	S2					S		X				X	X2		X	X						K.Lynch	12
S	X	X	X	X	X		X	S				X	X		X				X				X						G.Cain	13
S2	X		X	X			X1	S1			X	X	X		X				X				X					S	J.W.Lloyd	14
S1	X	X	X	X1	X2		X2	S2				X	X		X				X				X					S2	T.Hilbron	15
			X		X		X2	S2		X1		X	X		X				X		S1		X	X		X			A.D'Urso	16
X2			X	S	X		X	X1		X		X	X	X	X				X			S2	X						G.Singh	17
X1			X	S1	X		X			X		X	X	X	X				X			S	X						D.Orr	18
	X		X		X		X	X1		X	X	X	X	X				X	S	S1	S	S	X						E.Lomas	19
	X		X		X		X	X		X	X	X	X	X				X	S	S	S		X						R.Harris	20
	X		X	X	X		X1	X1		X	X	X	X	X				X	S	S1	S1	X							J.Brandwood	21
	X		X	S	X		X	S1		X	X	X	X	X				X	S	X1	X							B.Burns	22
	X		X	S	X		X	X1		X	X	X	X	X	S1			X	S		X	X	X					R.Pearson	23
	X		X	S	X		X	X		X	X	X	X	X	S1			X			X	X	X			S2		K.Lynch	24
	X		X	S	X		X2	X		X	X	X	X	X				X	S		X		X			S		I.Hemley	25
	X		X	S	S		X	X1		X	X	X	X	X	S1			X	S		X		X			S1		S.Mathieson	26
	X		X	S	S		X	S		X	X	X	X	X				X	S		X		X			X		D.Allison	27
	X		X2	S2	X		X1	S1		X	X	X	X	X				X	S		X		X			X		P.Rejer	28
	X		X		X		X2			X1	X	X	X	X				X		S2		X			S1			I.Cruikshanks	29
			X		X		X1	X		X1	X	X	X	X				X	S	S1	S1		X					T.Heilbron	30
	X		X	S1	X		X2	X2			X	X	X	X				X		S	X		X1					N.Barry	31
			X	X	X		X	S			X	X	X	X				X		S	S1	X1	X					K.Leach	32
	X		X	X1	X		X	S			X	X	X	X				X		S	S1		X					U.Rennie	33
	X		X	S1	X		X	S2			X	X	X	X1				X		S	X2		X					R.Furnandiz	34
	X		X	S	X		X	S			X	X	X	X				X		S	X	X	X					J.Rushton	35
	X		X	S1	X		X	S2			X	X	X	X1				X		S	X	X	X2					P.B.Alcock	36
	X		X	S2	X			S1			X	X	X	X			S	X		X1	X2		X					G.Cain	37
	X		X	X1	X			S1			X	X	X	X	X			X		S	S		X	X				T.West	38
	X		X	X	X			S			X	X	X	X	X			X		S	S1		X					P.Alcock	39
X2			X1		X			S2			X	X	X	X	X			X		S	S1		X	X				E.Lomas	40
	X		X		X			S		X	X	X	X	X	X			X		S			X	X				E.Wolstenholme	41
	X		X		X			S		X	X	X	X	X	X			X		S			X	X				J.W.Lloyd	42
S1	X		X	S	X		X	X1				X	X	X	X				X				X	X					K.Lynch	43
S2	X		X		X			S1			X	X	X	X	X1				X				X	X2					R.Gifford	44
S	X		X		S			S1			X	X	X	X	X2			X		X			X	X		X1		J.Brandwood	45
S	X		X		S			X			X	X	X	X				X		X		S	X	X			X		N.Barry	46
X	X		X		S		S					X	X	X	X							S	X				X		K.Leach	47
S	X		X		S		S					X	X	X	X			X					X		X		X		R.Pearson	48
S	X		S1									X	X	X	X				X				X	X1		X			A.Butler	49
S1	X	X3	S3									X	X	X	X	X2		X1				S2	X					X	P.Rejer	50
S1	X		S2									X	X	X	X	X2		X1				S2	X				X2		C.Wilkes	51
S1	X		X					S			X1	X	X	X	X				X				X	S			X		W.Burns	52
S1	X		X1	X								X	X	X	X				X				X	S	X2		S2		M.Pierce	53
X1	X		S2	X								X	X	X	X			X2					X	S	X				J.Rushden	54
3	43	5	42	18	43	0	29	3	3	15	13	43	38	31	40	0	2	33	3	8	6	25	32	12	4	2	7	3	EL Appearances	
1	0	0	0	11	0	1	0	11	0	2	0	0	0	0	3	0	0	0	0	5	8	0	0	0	0	3	1	1	EL Sub Appearances	
+1	4	0	4	3	4	1	4	1+1	0	1	2	0	3	1	0	3	0	0	0	1	2	0+1	3	4	0	2	0	0	CC Appearances	
0	4	0	4	1+2	4	0	4	1+1	0	0	0	4	4	4	2	0	0	4	0	2	3+1	0	4	0	0	0	0	0	FAC Appearances	

HUDDERSFIELD TOWN

CLUB RECORDS

BIGGEST VICTORIES
League: 10-1 v Blackpool, Division 1, 13.12.1930.
F.A. Cup: 7-0 v Lincoln City, 1st Round, 16.11.1991.
7-1 v Chesterfield (a), 3rd Round, 12.1.1929.

BIGGEST DEFEATS
League: 1-10 v Manchester City, Division 2, 7.11.1987.
F.A. Cup: 0-6 v Sunderland, 3rd Round, 1949-50.

MOST POINTS
3 points a win: 82, Division 3, 1982-83.
2 points a win: 66, Division 4, 1979-80.

MOST GOALS SCORED
101, Division 4, 1979-80.

MOST GOALS CONCEDED
100, Division 2, 1987-88.

MOST FIRST CLASS MATCHES IN A SEASON
61 - 1993-94 (League 46, Lge Cup 4, AMC 8, FA Cup 3)
61 - 1992-93 (League 46, Lge Cup 4, AMC 5, FA Cup 6)
61 - 1991-92 (League 46, Lge Cup 5, AMC 5, FA Cup 3, P/Off 2)

MOST LEAGUE WINS
28, Division 2, 1919-20.

MOST LEAGUE DRAWS
17, Division 1, 1926-27. Division 2, 1972-73.

MOST LEAGUE DEFEATS
28, Division 2, 1987-88.

INDIVIDUAL CLUB RECORDS

MOST GOALS IN A SEASON
Dave Mangnall: 42 goals in 1931-32 (League 33, FA Cup 9).

MOST GOALS IN A MATCH
5. D Mangnall v Derby County (h), 6-0, Division 1, 21.11.1931.
5. A P Lythgoe v Blackburn Rovers (h), 6-0, Division 1, 13.4.1935.

OLDEST PLAYER
W H Smith, 39 years, 1934.

YOUNGEST PLAYER
Dennis Law, 15 years 10 months, 1956.

MOST CAPPED PLAYER
Jimmy Nicholson (Northern Ireland) 31.
Ray Wilson (England) 30.

BEST PERFORMANCES

League: Champions of Division 1 (3).

F.A. Cup: Winners (1).
League Cup: Semi-Final 1967-68.

PREVIOUS NAMES
None.

PREVIOUS LEAGUES
Midland League.

Club colours: Blue & white striped shirts, white shorts, blue & white hoop on turnover socks.
Change colours: All yellow.

Reserves League: Pontins Central League.
Youth League: Northern Intermediate League.

DIVISIONAL RECORD

	Played	Won	Drawn	Lost	For	Against	Points
Division 1	1,306	497	329	480	1,935	1,912	1,340
Division 2/1	1,162	450	295	417	1,668	1,551	1,274
Division 3/2	552	217	148	187	753	674	750
Division 4	230	100	64	66	337	246	264
Total	3,250	1,264	836	1,150	4,693	4,383	3,628

RECORDS AND STATISTICS

COMPETITIONS

Div.1	Div.2/1	Div.3/2	Div.4
1919-51	1910-19	1972-74	1974-79
1952-55	1951-52	1979-82	
1969-71	1955-69	1987-88	
	1971-72	1987-95	
	1995-		

HONOURS

Div.1	Div.2	Div.4	FA Cup
1923-24	1969-70	1979-80	1922
1924-25			
1925-26			

Huddersfield were the first, of only three clubs, to win the Championship three years in succession.

MOST APPEARANCES

W H Smith 574 (1913-34)

Year	League	FA Cup
913-14	4	
914-15	24	1
915-16		
916-17		
917-18		
918-19		
919-20	39	5
920-21	33	2
921-22	40	9
922-23	35	5
923-24	39	3
924-25	41	1
925-26	28	2
926-27	39	1
927-28	38	8
928-29	32	6
929-30	33	5
930-31	30	
931-32	31	4
932-33	17	
933-34	18	1
934-35		
	521	53

MOST GOALS IN A CAREER

George Brown - 159 (1921-29)

Year	League	FA Cup
1921-22	4	
1922-23	6	
1923-24	8	
1924-25	20	
1925-26	35	
1926-27	27	1
1927-28	27	8
1928-29	15	8
Total	142	17

Current top goalscorer: Iain Dunn – 29 (1992-96)

MANAGERS

Name	Seasons	Best	Worst
F Walker	1908-10	5(ML)	16 (NEL)
D Pudan	1910-12	13(2)	17(2)
A Fairclough	1912-19	8(2)	13(2)
A Langley	1919-21	17(1)	2(2)
H Chapman	1921-25	1(1)	14(1)
C Potter	1925-26	1(1)	1(1)
J Chaplin	1926-29	2(1)	16(1)
C Stephenson	1929-42	2(1)	19(1)
T Magner	1942-43	5(FLNRS)	8(FLNRS)
D Steele	1943-47	15(1)	20(1)
G Stephenson	1947-52	15(1)	21(1)
A Beatie	1952-56	3(1)	12(2)
W Shankly	1956-60	6(2)	14(2)
E Boot	1960-64	6(2)	12(2)
T Johnston	1964-68	6(2)	14(2)
I Greaves	1968-74	15(1)	10(3)
R Collins	1974-75	24(3)	24(3)
T Johnston	1975-77	5(4)	9(4)
J Haselden	1977-78	11(4)	11(4)
M Buxton	1978-86	12(2)	9(4)
S Smith	1986-87	17(2)	17(2)
M MacDonald	1987-88	23(2)	23(2)
E Hand	1988-92	8(3)	14(3)
I Ross	1992-93	3(3)	15(3)
Neil Warnock	1993-95	1(2)	11(2)
Brian Horton	1995-	8(1)	8(1)

ML= Midland League.   NEL= North Eastern League.
FLNRS= Football League, North Regional Section.

RECORD TRANSFER FEE RECEIVED

Amount	Club	Player	Date
2,700,000	Sheffield Wed.	Andy Booth	07.96
£375,000	Southampton	Simon Charlton	6/93
£300,000	Leicester City	Iwan Roberts	10/93
£250,000	Reading	Craig Maskell	8/90
£250,000	Swindon	Duncan Shearer	6/88

RECORD TRANSFER FEE PAID

Amount	Club	Player	Date
1,200,000	Bristol Rovers	Marcus Stewart	7/96
£500,000	Blackpool	Andy Morrison	7/96
£312,500	Barnsley	Andy Payton	7/96
£325,000	Bradford City	Lee Duxbury	12/94

LONGEST LEAGUE RUNS

f undefeated matches:	27 (1924-25)	of league matches w/out a win:	22 (1971-72)
f undefeated home matches:	28 (1982-83)	of undefeated away matches:	18 (1924-25)
ithout home win:	11 (1971-72)	without an away win:	31 (1936-37)
f league wins:	11 (1919-21)	of home wins:	11 (1925-26)
f league defeats:	7 (1913-14, 1955-56)	of away wins:	5 (1924-25)

HUDDERSFIELD TOWN

PLAYERS NAME Honours	Ht	Wt	Birthdate	Birthplace Transfers	Contract Date	Clubs	League	L/Cup	FA Cup	Other	Lge	L/C	FAC	Oth
G O A L K E E P E R S														
Francis Stephen S	5.11	11.5	29/05/64	Billericay	24/08/82	Chelsea	71	6	10	1				
E: Y2; FMC'86'88				£20000	27/02/87	Reading	216	15	15	13				
				£150000	01/08/93	Huddersfield Town	132	11	8	12				
Norman Tony	6.2	12.8	24/02/58	Deeside	01/08/76	Burnley								
W: 5. B.1				£30000	14/02/80	Hull City	372	22	26	13				
				£200000	29/12/88	Sunderland	198	8	14	7				
				Free	07/07/95	Huddersfield Town	3	1						
O'Connor Derek P			09/03/78	Dublin		Crumplin Utd (Eire)								
					16/05/95	Huddersfield Town								
D E F E N D E R S														
Brown Kenny	5.8	11.6	11/07/67											
Collins Sam J	6.2	13.5	05/06/77	Pontefract	06/07/94	Huddersfield Town								
Cowan Thomas	5.8	10.8	28/08/69	Bellshill		Clydebank	16			2	2			
					01/02/89	Glasgow Rangers	8+4		0+1	2				
				£350000	01/08/91	Sheffield United	45	5	2	1				
				Loan	01/10/93	Stoke City	14	1		3				
				£150000	24/03/94	Huddersfield Town	90	8	6	6	4		1	
Dyson Jonathan P	6.1	12.0	23/03/72	Mirfield	29/12/90	Huddersfield Town	72+10	11	3	7+4	2			
Jenkins Steve R	5.10	10.9	16/07/72	Merthyr	01/07/90	Swansea City	155+10	12+1	10+1	26	1			
W: u21.2, Y.AGT'94				£275000	03/11/95	Huddersfield Town	31		4		1			
Ryan Robert P	5.11	11.05	16/05/77	Dublin		Belvedere								
				Free	26/07/94	Huddersfield Town								
Scully Patrick J	6.1	12.7	23/06/70	Dublin	16/09/87	Arsenal								
				Loan	07/09/89	Preston North End	13			1	1			
				Loan	23/08/90	Northampton Town	15			1				
				£100000	08/01/91	Southend United	114+1	3	4	5	6			
				Free	24/03/94	Huddersfield Town	74	7	2	6	2	1		
Sinnott Lee	6.1	11.9	12/07/65	Pelsall	16/11/82	Walsall	40	3	4		2			
E: u21.1, Y.4				£100000	15/09/83	Watford	71+7	6	11		2			
				£130000	23/07/87	Bradford City	173	19	9	12	6			1
				£300000	08/08/91	Crystal Palace	53+2	9+1	1	2				
					09/12/93	Bradford City	34	2	2	2	1			
				£105000	23/12/94	Huddersfield Town	57	4	4	3	1			
M I D F I E L D														
Bullock Darren J	5.8	12.4	12/02/69	Worcester		Nuneaton Borough								
				£55000	19/11/93	Huddersfield Town	101	7	6	9	15	1	2	1
Collins Simon	5.9	10.5	16/12/73	Pontefract	01/07/92	Huddersfield Town	21+14	3+1	1+2	1+3	3	1		
				Loan	14/01/94	Halifax Town								
Dalton Paul	5.11	12.0	25/04/67	Middlesbrough		Brandon United								
FLgXl.1				£35000	03/05/88	Manchester United								
				£20000	04/03/89	Hartlepool United	140+11	10	7	9	37	2	1	3
				£275000	11/06/92	Plymouth Argyle	93+5	5	7	6	25	2	5	
				£125000	11/08/95	Huddersfield Town	29	4	4		5	1		
Gray Kevin J	6.0	13.0	07/01/72	Sheffield	01/07/90	Mansfield Town	129+12	8	6+1	12+2	3	1		2
				£20000	18/07/94	Huddersfield Town	43	1	4	3				
Makel Lee	5.11	11.07	11/01/73	Sunderland	11/02/91	Newcastle United	6+6	1		0+1	1			
				£160000	20/07/92	Blackburn Rovers	1+5	0+3		1+3				
				£300000	13/10/95	Huddersfield Town	33		4		2			
Murphy Stephen			05/04/78	Dublin	16/05/95	Huddersfield Town								
Reid Paul R	5.9	10.8	19/01/68	Oldbury	09/01/86	Leicester City	140+22	13	5+1	6+2	21	4		
				Loan	19/03/92	Bradford City	7							
				£25000	27/07/92	Bradford City	80+2	3	3	5	15	2		1
				£70000	20/05/94	Huddersfield Town	50+5	5	4	1	6	1		

aldry Simon	5.10	11.0	12/02/76	Huddersfield	14/07/94	Huddersfield Town	21+14	2+1		1+2	2			1
rosby Gary	5.7	9.13	08/05/64	Sleaford		Lincoln United								
C'90. FMC'92				Free	23/08/86	Lincoln City	6+1	2						
					01/08/87	Grantham								
				£20000	21/12/87	Nottingham Forest	139+13	29+1	18+3	10+1	12	6	3	4
				Loan	23/08/93	Grimsby Town	2+1							
				Free	27/08/94	Huddersfield Town	16+4	2	1	5+2	4			1
unn Iain G W	5.10	11.7	01/04/70	Howden	07/07/88	York City	46+31	3+1	3+1	1+3	11			
u19.4				Free	14/08/91	Chesterfield	8+5			1				
					01/08/92	Scarborough								
				Free	29/09/92	Peterborough Utd				0+1				
				Free	01/10/92	Scarborough								
				Free	01/11/92	Goole Town								
				Free	04/12/92	Huddersfield Town	61+54	6+3	6+3	11+7	14	3	3	9
dwards Robert	5.8	11.7	23/02/70	Manchester	11/07/88	Crewe Alexandra	110+45	8	13+5	9+8	44	5	5	5
				£150000	08/03/96	Huddersfield Town	13				7			
awson Ian J	5.11	10.05	04/11/71	Huddersfield	27/01/95	Huddersfield Town								
owe Rodney C	5.8	12.8	30/07/75	Huddersfield	12/07/93	Huddersfield Town	13+14	0+1	6+1	3	2		2	1
				Loan	11/08/94	Scarborough	10+4	4		1	1			
				Loan	20/03/95	Bury	1+2							
DDITIONAL CONTRACT PLAYERS														
eary Thomas M						Huddersfield T. (T)								
ingworth Jeremy						Huddersfield T. (T)								
elly Mark A						Huddersfield T. (T)								

THE MANAGER
BRIAN HORTON

Date of Birth . . . . 4th February 1949.
Place of Birth . . . . Hednesford.
Date of Appointment . . . . June 1995.

PREVIOUS CLUBS
As Manager . . . . Hull City, Manchester City.
As Coach . . . . Oxford United.
As a Player. . . . . Walsall, Hednesford T., Port Vale, Brighton & H.A.,
. . . . Luton Town, Hull City.

HONOURS
As a Manager
Hull: Promotion to Division 2.

As a Player
Brighton: Promotion to 2nd & 1st Divisions.
Luton: Promotion to1st Division.

THE ALFRED MCALPINE STADIUM
Huddersfield, West Yorkshire
Tel: 01484 420 335

Capacity 19,600

First game .... v Wycombe W., Div 2. 8/94.
First floodlit game .... As above.

ATTENDANCES
Highest .... 18,775 v Birmingham City, Division 2, 06.05.95, (1-2).
Lowest .... 4,183 v York City, AMC, 18.10.94, (3-0).

OTHER GROUNDS .... Leeds Road

MATCHDAY TICKET PRICES

Kilner Bank & South £10
Juv/OAP £6

Riverside Upper £14
Juv/OAP £8

Riverside Lower £12.50
Juv/OAP £7

Match & Ticket Information
Advance reservations only for special matches,
otherwise admission to ground and stands on day of
matches.

Ticket Office Telephone no. 01484 420 335

CLUBCALL
0891 12 16 35
Calls cost 39p per minute cheap rate and 49p per
minute at all other times.
Call costings correct at time of going to press.

HOW TO GET TO THE GROUND

From the East and M1 (Junction 38)
Use A642, sign posted Huddersfield, into town centre, then follow signs Leeds
(A62) into Leeds Road, turn right down Bradley Mills Road for Huddersfield Town
FC.

From the South
Use A616 (sign posted Huddersfield) into town centre, then follow signs Leeds
(A62) into Leeds Road, turn right down Bradley Mills Road for Huddersfield Town
FC.

From the West
Use motorway M62 until junction 23 then A640 or A62 into Leeds Road, turn
right down Bradley Mills Road for Huddersfield Town FC.

Car Parking
Parking for 1,400 cars.

Nearest Railway Station
Huddersfield (01484 531 226).

MATCHDAY PROGRAMME

Programme Editor . . . . Alan Stevenson & Will Venters.

Number of pages . . . . 40.

Price . . . . £1.50.

Subscriptions . . . . Inland £40, Abroad £45.

Local Newspapers . . . . Huddersfield Examiner.

Local Radio Stations . . . . Radio Leeds, The Pulse.

IPSWICH TOWN
(The Blues or The Town)
NATIONWIDE LEAGUE DIVISION 1
SPONSORED BY: GREENE KING

ack Row (L-R): Leo Cotterell, Steve Palmer, Simon Portrey, Lee Chapman, Claus Thomsen, James Scowcroft, Kevin Ellis, Frank Yallop.
iddle Row: Bryan Klug (Coach), Geraint Williams, Simon Milton, David Linighan, Steve Sedgley, Richard Wright, Craig Forrest, Clive
aker, Richard Naylor, Chris Swailes, Tony Vaughan, Adam Tanner, Dale Roberts (Coach).
ont Row: Mauricio Taricco, Stuart Slater, Ian Marshall, Paul Mason, Alex Mathie, George Burley (Manager), John Wark, Neil Gregory,
ck Stockwell, Neil Thompson, Lee Norfolk, Lee Durrent.

IPSWICH TOWN
FORMED IN 1887
TURNED PROFESSIONAL IN 1936
LTD COMPANY IN 1936

CHAIRMAN: David R Sheepshanks
DIRECTORS
John Kerridge, R J Finbow,
Richard Moore, Philip Hope-Cobbold,
John Kerr MBE
SECRETARY
David Rose (01473 219 211)
COMMERCIAL MANAGER
Clive Turner (01473 219 211)

MANAGER: George Burley
ASSISTANT MANAGER: Dale Roberts

RESERVE TEAM COACH
Bryan Klug
YOUTH TEAM COACH
Phil Goddard
PHYSIOTHERAPIST
Dave Williams

STATISTICIAN FOR THE DIRECTORY
Paul Voller

The first season back in the Endsleigh League was not viewed with optimism by all supporters of the club - some felt that a play-off place was attainable while others were concerned that we might slip straight through the division.
The season started with a defeat at newly-promoted Birmingham, despite Marshall scoring the opening goal of the game - a situation that was to be repeated several times as the season unfolded. Uhlenbeek, the only summer signing, made his debut at St Andrews and was unfortunate to have a perfectly good goal ruled out.

There was a big improvement on the home form at the start of the season, with five consecutive wins recorded against Crystal Palace, Stoke, Sunderland, Reggiana and Watford. Mathie scored seven goals in these games, including a hat-trick against Sunderland. They came back down to earth, however, when they conceded five goals to Charlton after Forrest had been carried off and they did not have a substitute goalkeeper on the bench.

The team suffered an early departure from the Coca-Cola Cup at the hands of Stockport County, but progressed through to the English semi-finals of the Anglo-Italian Trophy after winning their group and remaining unbeaten in the process. It was this competition that enabled Taricco to have a second bite at holding down a first team place, and he did just that, with some classy left-back displays that questioned why he had been allowed to languish in the reserves for so long.

Ipswich lost their way in the league around Christmas and the New Year, but more than made up for this with a brilliant performance at Blackburn in the FA Cup in which young goalkeeper Richard Wright was outstanding. Thereafter their fortunes began to pick up - despite bowing out of the cup to Aston Villa - and there was a real chance of making the play-offs. The playing of Uhlenbeek at full back increased the attacking possibilities, and the arrival of Mowbray eventually improved the defence once he was given a regular partner. He never recovered from an injury sustained at Sunderland in February and took no further part in the season, his loss being a crucial factor in the team's failure to retain a place in the top six.

Marshall and Mathie both notched nineteen goals - despite missing large chunks of the season because of injuries - and were instrumental in Ipswich finishing the season as the leading goalscorer in the Premier and Endsleigh Leagues. How ironic, then, that in their last match of the season they were unable to score the one goal needed to earn a place in the play-offs.

PAUL VOLLLER

IPSWICH TOWN

League: 7th   FA Cup: 5th Rnd   Coca-Cola Cup: 2nd Rnd

M	DATE	COMP	VEN	OPPONENTS	RESULT	HT	LP	GOAL SCORERS/GOAL TIMES	ATT.
1	A 12	EL	A	Birmingham City	L 1-3	0-0	18	Marshall 47	(18910)
2	19	EL	H	Crystal Palace	W 1-0	1-0	14	Mathie 38	12681
3	26	EL	A	West Bromwich Albion	D 0-0	0-0	19		(14470)
4	30	EL	H	Stoke City	W 4-1	1-0	8	Slater 38, 62, Mathie 83, 88	10848
5	S 2	EL	H	Sunderland	W 3-0	2-0	4	Mathie 36, Mathie 41, 55	12390
6	5	AIC	H	Reggiana	W 2-1	0-1		Mathie 46, Tanner 84	9525
7	9	EL	A	Huddersfield Town	L 1-2	0-2	7	Sedgley 80(pen)	(12057)
8	12	EL	A	Oldham Athletic	D 1-1	0-0	8	Marshall 46	(5622)
9	16	EL	H	Watford	W 4-2	2-1	4	Gregory 5, 43, Thomsen 54, Uhlenbeek 85	11441
10	19	CC 2/1	A	Stockport County	D 1-1	1-1		Sedgley 7	(4865)
11	23	EL	H	Charlton Athletic	L 1-5	1-0	8	Thomsen 4	12815
12	30	EL	A	Sheffield United	D 2-2	0-2	7	Marshall 61, 68	(12557)
13	O 3	CC 2/2	H	Stockport County	L 1-2	1-0		Thomsen 25	8250
14	7	EL	H	Wolverhampton Wand	L 1-2	1-2	12	Sedgley 28(pen)	15335
15	11	AIC	A	Brescia	D 2-2	1-1		Sedgley 35, Mason 76	(1300)
16	14	EL	A	Derby County	D 1-1	1-1	13	Sedgley 2	(13034)
17	22	EL	H	Luton Town	L 0-1	0-1	14		9123
18	28	EL	A	Reading	W 4-1	1-0	11	Uhlenbeek 41, Mathie 67, Mason 83, Williams 90	(10281)
19	N 4	EL	H	Grimsby Town	D 2-2	2-0	12	Mason 17, 44	10500
20	8	AIC	A	Foggia	W 1-0	0-0		Mason 69	(2000)
21	11	EL	A	Millwall	L 1-2	1-1	15	Mason 37	(11360)
22	19	EL	A	Norwich City	L 1-2	0-1	15	Wark 82	(17862)
23	22	EL	H	Southend United	D 1-1	0-0	15	Uhlenbeek 48	9757
24	25	EL	H	Portsmouth	W 3-2	2-1	14	Milton 1, Marshall 26, Thompson 90	10286
25	D 3	EL	A	Wolverhampton Wand	D 2-2	1-0	15	Marshall 30, Mowbray 90	(20867)
26	9	EL	A	Charlton Athletic	W 2-0	0-0	13	Stockwell 49, Marshall 67	(10316)
27	13	AIC	H	Salernitana	W 2-0	0-0		Mowbray 52, Gregory 87	6429
28	16	EL	H	Sheffield United	D 1-1	0-0	14	Tuttle 60(og)	9630
29	22	EL	H	Barnsley	D 2-2	1-0	12	Marshall 9, Mathie 66	11791
30	J 1	EL	H	Port Vale	W 5-1	0-0	12	Milton 59, Sedgley 60, Marshall 73, Mathie 83, 90	9926
31	6	FAC 3	H	Blackburn Rovers	D 0-0	0-0			21236
32	13	EL	A	Crystal Palace	D 1-1	0-1	13	Mathie 58	(14097)
33	16	FAC 3R	A	Blackburn Rovers	W 1-0	0-0		Mason 116	(19606)
34	20	EL	H	Birmingham City	W 2-0	1-0	11	Milton 22, 55	12540
35	23	AIC	H	Port Vale	L 2-4	1-2		Mason 12, Gregory 75	5831
36	F 3	EL	H	West Bromwich Albion	W 2-1	1-0	6	Marshall 45, Mowbray 84	10798
37	10	EL	A	Stoke City	L 1-3	0-1	9	Scowcroft 54	(12239)
38	13	FAC 4	H	Walsall	W 1-0	1-0		Mason 6	18489
39	17	FAC 5	H	Aston Villa	L 1-3	0-2		Mason 84	20748
40	20	EL	A	Sunderland	L 0-1	0-1	12		(14052)
41	24	EL	A	Watford	W 3-2	0-2	10	Uhlenbeek 48, Mathie 66, 82	(11872)
42	M 3	EL	H	Leicester City	W 4-2	3-0	7	Wark 6, Milton 11, Marshall 12, 87	9817
43	9	EL	A	Barnsley	D 3-3	0-2	10	Marshall 85, 88, Milton 89	(7705)
44	13	EL	A	Leicester City	W 2-0	2-0	7	Marshall 12, Mathie 37	(17783)
45	16	EL	H	Tranmere Rovers	L 1-2	1-0	7	Marshall 13	11759
46	19	EL	H	Oldham Athletic	W 2-1	0-0	6	Mason 52, 85	9674
47	23	EL	A	Port Vale	L 1-2	1-1	6	Marshall 38	(7277)
48	30	EL	A	Luton Town	W 2-1	1-0	5	Milton 5, 51	(9151)
49	A 2	EL	H	Derby County	W 1-0	1-0	5	Vaughan 33	16210
50	6	EL	H	Reading	L 1-2	0-1	5	Mathie 70	17328
51	8	EL	A	Grimsby Town	L 1-3	0-0	5	Scowcroft 89	(5904)
52	14	EL	H	Norwich City	W 2-1	1-0	6	Marshall 22, Ullathorne 85(og)	20355
53	17	EL	A	Tranmere Rovers	L 2-5	1-1	6	Mason 5, Marshall 73	(6008)
54	20	EL	A	Southend United	L 1-2	1-1	7	Milton 6	(8363)
55	27	EL	A	Portsmouth	W 1-0	0-0	7	Mathie 80	(12954)
56	M 1	EL	H	Huddersfield Town	W 2-1	1-1	6	Mathie 45, 83	17473
57	5	EL	H	Millwall	D 0-0	0-0	7		17290

Best Home League Attendance: 20355 v Norwich City   **Smallest: 9123 v Luton Town**   **Average: 12598**

Goal Scorers:

EL(79): Marshall(19), Mathie(18), Milton(9), Mason(7), Uhlenbeek(4), Sedgley(4), Thomsen(2), Slater(2), Wark(2), Scowcroft(2), Mowbray(2), Opponent(s)(2), Gregory(2), Stockwell(1), Thompson(1), Vaughan(1), Williams(1)

CC(2): Sedgley(1), Thomsen(1)

FAC(3): Mason(3)

AIC(9): Mason(3), Gregory(2), Mathie(1), Mowbray(1), Sedgley(1), Tanner(1)

(M) Appleby	(G) Barber	(F) Chapman	(G) Forrest	(F) Gregory	(D) Linighan	(F) Marshall	(M) Mason	(F) Mathie	(M) Milton	(D) Mowbray	(M) Norfolk	(M) Palmer	(G) Petterson	(F) Scowcroft	(M) Sedgley	(F) Slater	(M) Stockwell	(D) Swailes	(M) Tanner	(D) Taricco	(D) Thompson	(M) Thomsen	(F) Uhlenbeek	(D) Vaughan	(M) Wark	(M) Williams	(G) Wright	(D) Yallop	Referee	No.
		S3	X			X		X	S2						X		X			X		X1	X	X	X2	X		S1	D.Allison	1
		S	X			X		X	X						X		X		S	S	X		X	X	X	X			G.Singh	2
		X	X	S1				X1	X		X				X	X2	X			S2			X	X		X			K.Lynch	3
		X	X	S				X	X1		X				X	X	X		S1	S2			X	X		X2			M.Bailey	4
		S	X			X		X	X1		X				X	X	X		S1	S2			X	X2		X			G.Pooley	5
		X1	X	S1				X	S2		X				X	X2	X			X	X		X			X	S			6
		S1	X			X		X1			X				X	X	X		X2	X	S2	X		X				E.Wolstenholme	7
		S2	X	X2		X					X				X	X1	X			X		X	X	S1		X			W.C.Burns	8
		S	X	X		X		S							X	X	X			X		X	X	S1	X1	X			R.Harris	9
		X	X	X				S1							X	X1	X		S	X		X	X	S	X	X			U.Rennie	10
		S2	X2	X				X	X						X	X		S1		X		X	X	X	X1	X			G.Barber	11
			S			X		X	X					S	X	S1		X1		X		X	X			X	X	X	P.Richards	12
			X1	X	X			X	S2					S1	X	X			S	X		X	X			X2	X	X	M.Bailey	13
			S					X	S	X			X	X	X	X			X1	X		X			X	X	X	M.Pierce	14
			S2	X		X		X	X1	X			S	X2	X	X		S1			X	S		X	X	15
			S3	X1		X	S2	X				X		X1	X		S1			X2		X3	X	N.S.Barry	16
		X	S2	X	X		X2		X			S	X1	X		S1	X		X	X		X	T.West	17
		X	S1		X	X2	X	X	X1	X			X		S2	X		X	X		X	J.Brandwood	18
		X	S2	X	X2	X	X1	X		X	S	X		S1	X		X	X		X	G.Pulley	19
	X	X	X		X		X1	X		S1	X		X2	X	S2		S	X	X	20
		X	S1	X	X	X1	X	X		S	X		X	X		X	X	G.Singh	21
		X	S1	X	X	X1	X	X		X	S2	S	X	X2	X	X	X	K.Lynch	22
		X	X2	X1	X		X	S2	X	S1	X	X	X	X	X	T.Lunt	23
		X		X	X	X	X	S	S1	X	X	X	X1	S	X	B.Knight	24
	X	S1	X	S1	X	X	X	X	X1	X1	X	X	S	X	G.Cain	25
	S	X	S	X	X	X	X	X1	X	X	X	S1	X	A.D'Urso	26
X3	X	X	X1	X	X	X	S1	X	X	X	X2	S2	27
S	X	S	X	X	X	X	X1	X	X	X	S1	X	J.Rushton	28
S1	X	S	X	X	X1	X1	X	X	X	X2	X	D.Orr	29
S1	X	S	X	X	X	X	X	X1	S	X	X	R.Furnandiz	30
	X	S	X	X	X	X	X	X	S1	X	X1	D.Elleray	31
	S	X	X	X	X	X	X1	X	S1	X	X	C.Wilkes	32
	S2	X2	S1	X1	X	X	X	X	X	X	X	D.Elleray	33
	S	X2	X1	X	X	S2	X	X	X	X	X2	X3	X	S1	I.Hemley	34
	S	X	X2	S3	S2	S	X1	X	X	X	X3	X	S1	T.Heilbron	35
	S	X	X1	X	X	S1	X	X1	S1	X	X	X	X	P.Taylor	36
	X	X	X2	X	X	X	S1	S2	X	X	X	X	G.Cain	37
	S	X	X	X	X	X	X1	X	S1	S	X	X	X	D.Gallagher	38
	S	X	X	X	X	X	X1	X	S1	S	X	X	X	S.Lodge	39
	S	X2	X	X	X1	X	S2	X	X	X	S1	X	X	W.C.Burns	40
	S2	X	X	X2	X	S1	X	X	X	X	X	P.Richards	41
	S	X	X1	X	X	S1	X	X	X	S	X	X	S.Bennett	42
	S	X	X1	X	X	S1	X	X	X	S1	X1	X	X	I.Cruickshanks	43
	S	X	S	X	X	S1	X	X1	X	X	X	X	K.Leach	44
	S	X	S2	X1	X	S1	X	X2	X	X	X	X	S.J.Baines	45
	S	X	X	X	X	X	S	X	X	S	X	X	G.Barber	46
	S3	X1	X	X	X	S1	X	S2	X	X	X2	X3	X	X	P.Rejer	47
	S	X	X	X1	X	X	S1	X	S	X	X	X	X	G.Singh	48
	S	S	X	X	X	X	S	X	X	X	X	X	G.Pooley	49
	S	S	X	X	S1	X	X	X1	X	X	X	X	C.Wilkes	50
	S1	X	X1	X	X	X	X	X	X	X	M.C.Bailey	51
S1	S	X	X	X	X	X	X1	X	S2	X2	X	X	J.Rushton	52
	S	X	X	X	X	S1	X	S	X	X1	X	X	J.A.Kirkby	53
	X	S1	X	X	X1	X	X	X	X	X	S	X	S	T.West	54
	S	X	X	X	S	X	X	S	X	X	X	M.Riley	55
	S1	X	X	X	X	X	X	X	X	X	M.Pierce	56
	S	X	X1	X	S1	X	X	X	X2	X	X	K.Lynch	57

	(M) Appleby	(G) Barber	(F) Chapman	(G) Forrest	(F) Gregory	(D) Linighan	(F) Marshall	(M) Mason	(F) Mathie	(M) Milton	(D) Mowbray	(M) Norfolk	(M) Palmer	(G) Petterson	(F) Scowcroft	(M) Sedgley	(F) Slater	(M) Stockwell	(D) Swailes	(M) Tanner	(D) Taricco	(D) Thompson	(M) Thomsen	(F) Uhlenbeek	(D) Vaughan	(M) Wark	(M) Williams	(G) Wright	(D) Yallop
EL Appearances	0	1	2	21	5	2	35	24	39	34	19	0	5	1	13	40	11	33	4	3	36	5	36	37	19	13	42	23	3
EL Sub Appearances	3	0	4	0	13	0	0	2	0	3	0	0	0	0	10	0	0	6	4	1	7	3	0	1	2	5	1	0	3
CC Appearances	0	0	0	1	0+1	0	4	2+1	2	4	4	0	0	0	0	2	2	1	0	0	3	0	0	3	0	3	1+3	1	1
FAC Appearances	1	0	2	3	3+2	1	0	3	4+1	3	1	1	0	1+2	3	2+2	2	0	3+1	3	0	2+1	4	2	2	2	2	1+2	AIC Appearances

Also Played: (G) Baker S(6,20,27,31). (M) Durrant S3(27). (F) Naylor S(15,56).

IPSWICH TOWN

CLUB RECORDS

BIGGEST VICTORIES
League: 7-0 v Portsmouth, Division 2, 7.11.1964.
7-0 v Southampton, Division 1, 2.2.1974.
7-0 v West Bromwich Albion, Division 1, 6.11.1976.
F.A. Cup: 11-0 v Cromer, 3rd Qualifying Round, 31.10.1936.
League Cup: 5-0 v Northampton, 2nd Round, 30.8.1977
6-1 v Swindon, 4th Round, 26.11.1985.
Europe: 10-0 v Floriana, 25.9.1962.

BIGGEST DEFEATS
League: 0-9 v Manchester Utd, 4.3.95.
1-10 v Fulham, Division 1, 16.12.1983.
F.A. Cup: 1-7 v Southampton, 3rd Round, 2.2.1974.
League Cup: 0-4 v Arsenal, 2nd Round, 9.9.1971.
2-6 v Aston Villa, 4th Round, 30.11.1988.
Europe: 0-4 v Bruges, 2nd Round, 5.11.1975.

MOST POINTS
3 points a win: 84, Division 2, 1991-92.
2 points a win: 64, Division 3(S), 1953-54, 1955-56.

MOST GOALS SCORED
106, Division 3(S), 1955-56.
Parker 30, Garneys 19, Grant 16, Reed 12, Blackman 8, McLuckie 6, Elsworthy 3, Leadbetter 4, Acres 2, Brown 2, Myles 1, Snell 1, Opponents 2.

MOST GOALS CONCEDED
121, Division 1, 1963-64.

MOST FIRST CLASS MATCHES IN A SEASON
66 - 1980-81 (League 42, FA Cup 7, League Cup 5, UEFA Cup 12).

MOST LEAGUE WINS
27, Division 3(S), 1953-54.

MOST LEAGUE DRAWS
18, Division 2, 1990-91.

MOST LEAGUE DEFEATS
29, Premiership 1994-95.

INDIVIDUAL CLUB RECORDS

MOST GOALS IN A SEASON
Ted Phillips: 46 goals in 1956-57 (League 41, FA Cup 5).

MOST GOALS IN A MATCH
5. Ray Crawford v Florina, 10-0, European Cup, 25.9.1962.
5. Alan Brazil v Southampton, 5-2, Division 1, 16.2.1982.

OLDEST PLAYER
Mick Burns, 43 years 219 days v Gateshead, FA Cup, 12.1.1952.

YOUNGEST PLAYER
Jason Dozzell, 16 years 56 days v Coventry, 4.2.1984.

MOST CAPPED PLAYER
Allan Hunter (Northern Ireland) 47.

BEST PERFORMANCES

League: 1955-56: Matches played 46, Won 25, Drawn 14, Lost 7, Goals for 106, Goals against 64, Points 64. Third in Division 3(S).
Highest Position: First in Division 1, 1961-62.
F.A. Cup: 1977-78: 3rd Round Cardiff City 2-0; 4th Round Hartlepool United 4-1; 5th Round Bristol Rovers 2-2,3-0; 6th Round Millwall 6-1; Semi-final W.B.A. 3-1; Final Arsenal 1-0.
League Cup: Semi-finalists in 1981-82.
Most recent success: 1984-85: 2nd Round Derby County 4-2,1-1; 3rd Round Newcastle United 1-1,2-1; 4th Round Oxford United 2-1; 5th Round Q.P.R. 0-0,2-1; Semi-final Norwich City 1-0,0-2.
Europe: (UEFA) 1980-81: 1st Round Aris Salonika 5-1,1-3; 2nd Round Bohemians 0-2,3-0; 3rd Round Widzew Lodz 5-0,0-1; 4th Round St. Ettiene 4-1,3-1; Semi-final Cologne 1-0,1-0; Final AZ67 Alkmaar 3-0,2-4.

DIVISIONAL RECORD

	Played	Won	Drawn	Lost	For	Against	Points
Division 1/P	1,008	373	250	385	1,344	1,392	1,104
Division 2	694	291	187	226	1,113	1,001	892
Division 3(S)	486	214	112	160	806	695	540
Total	2,188	878	539	769	3,263	3,088	2,536

ADDITIONAL INFORMATION
PREVIOUS NAMES
None.

PREVIOUS LEAGUES
Southern League.

Club colours: Royal blue shirts fading into white, royal blue shorts fading into white, white socks with blue tops.
Change colours: Jade shirts with maroon sleaves and mustard trim, maroon shorts with jade side panels, maroon socks with jade tops. **Additional change kit:** Black & cream stripes, black shorts & cream socks.

Reserves League
Avon Insurance Football Combination.

RECORDS AND STATISTICS

COMPETITIONS

DIV 1/P	DIV.2/1	DIV.3(S)	EURO C	UEFA	ECWC
1961-64	1954-55	1938-54	1962-63	1973-74	1978-79
1968-86	1957-61	1955-57		1974-75	
1992-95	1964-68			1975-76	TEXACO
	1986-92			1977-78	1972-73
	1995-			1979-80	
				1980-81	
				1981-82	
				1982-83	

HONOURS

DIV.1	DIV.2	DIV.3(S)	FA CUP	UEFA
1961-62	1960-61	1953-54	1977-78	1980-81
	1967-68	1956-57		TEXACO
	1991-92			1972-73

MOST GOALS IN A CAREER
RAY CRAWFORD - 227 (1958-69)

YEAR	LEAGUE	FA CUP	LGE CUP	EUROPE
1958-59	25	1		
1959-60	18			
1960-61	40			
1961-62	33	1	3	
1962-63	25			8
1963-64	2			
1965-66	8			
1966-67	21	3	1	
1967-68	16		5	
1968-69	16		1	
Total	204	5	10	8

Current top goalscorer - John Wark 179 (1974-1996 - 3 spells)

MOST APPEARANCES
MICK MILLS 737+4 (1966-82)

YEAR	LEAGUE	FA CUP	LGE CUP	EUROPE
1965-66	2			
1966-67	21+1	1	2	
1967-68	9+1	1	1+1	
1968-69	35+1	1		
1969-70	40	1	3	
1970-71	42	6	2	
1971-72	35	2	1	
1972-73	42	2	2	
1973-74	42	3	4	8
1974-75	42	9	5	
1975-76	42	3	1	4
1976-77	37	3	2	
1977-78	34	7	2	5
1978-79	42	5	1	6
1979-80	37	4	2	3
1980-81	33	6	5	10
1981-82	42	3	8	2
1982-83	11		2	2
	588+3	57	43+1	40

Plus 8 Texaco Cup 1972-73 & 1 Charity Shield 1978-79.

MANAGERS

NAME	SEASONS	BEST	WORST
Michael O'Brien	1936-37		
Adam Scott Duncan	1937-55	1(1)	3(3S)
Alf Ramsey	1955-63	1(1)	3(3S)
Jackie Milburn	1963-64	22(1)	22(1)
Bill McGarry	1964-68	1(2)	15(2)
Bobby Robson	1968-82	2(1)	19(1)
Bobby Ferguson	1982-87	9(1)	5(2)
John Duncan	1987-90	8(2)	9(2)
John Lyall	1990-95	1(2)	14(2)
George Burley	1995-	20(P)	20(P)

RECORD TRANSFER FEE RECEIVED

AMOUNT	CLUB	PLAYER	DATE
£1,750,000	Tottenham H	Jason Dozzell	8/93
£800,000	Sheffield Utd	Brian Gayle	9/91
£750,000	Glasgow Rangers	Terry Butcher	8/86
£500,000	Tottenham H	Alan Brazil	3/83

RECORD TRANSFER FEE PAID

AMOUNT	CLUB	PLAYER	DATE
£1,000,000	Tottenham Hotspur	Steve Sedgley	6/94
£750,000	Oldham Athletic	Ian Marshall	8/93
£650,000	Derby County	Geraint Williams	5/92
£400,000	Aberdeen	Paul Mason	6/93

LONGEST LEAGUE RUNS

of undefeated matches:	23 (8.12.1979 - 26.4.1980)	of league matches w/out a win:	21 (28.8.1963 - 20.12.1963)
of undefeated home matches:	33 (27.10.1979 - 28.3.1981)	of undefeated away matches:	11 (15.12.1979 - 18.4.1980)
without home win:	9 (24.8.1963 - 28.12.1963)	without an away win:	27 (10.5.1963 - 29.9.1964)
of league wins:	8 (19.8.1953 - 16.9.1953)	of home wins:	14 (19.9.1956 - 9.3.1957)
of league defeats:	10 (9.9.1954 - 16.10.1954)	of away wins:	5 (10.9.1976 - 27.12.1976)

IPSWICH TOWN

PLAYERS NAME Honours	Ht	Wt	Birthdate	Birthplace Transfers	Contract Date	Clubs	League	L/Cup	FA Cup	Other	Lge	L/C	FAC	Oth
							APPEARANCES				**GOALS**			
G O A L K E E P E R S														
Forrest Craig L	6.4	14.4	20/09/67	Vancouver	31/08/85	Ipswich Town	257	19	14	14				
Can; Div2'92				Loan	01/03/88	Colchester United	11							
Wright Richard I	6.2	13.0	05/11/77	Ipswich	02/01/95	Ipswich Town	26	1	3	2				
E: S														
D E F E N D E R S														
Ellis Kevin	5.10	11.5	12/05/77	Gt Yarmouth	01/08/94	Ipswich Town	1							
Gaughan Kevin			06/03/78	Glasgow		Ipswich Town								
Mowbray Tony	6.1	13.0	22/11/63	Saltburn		Guisborough								
E: B					27/11/81	Middlesbrough	345+3	33+2	26	24+1	25	2	1	1
					01/11/91	Celtic	78					6		
				£300000	06/10/95	Ipswich Town	19		4	3	2			1
Swailes Christopher W	6.1	12.11	11/10/70	Gateshead	23/05/89	Ipswich Town								
FA Vase'93				£10000	28/03/91	Peterborough Utd								
				£8000	01/09/91	Boston United								
					01/08/92	Kettering Town								
					01/08/93	Bridlington								
				Free	27/10/93	Doncaster Rovers	49	2	1	2		1		
				£150000	23/03/95	Ipswich Town	8+1							
Taricco Mauricio	5.9	11.7	10/03/73	Buenos Aires		Argentinos Jnrs.								
				£175000	09/09/94	Ipswich Town	36+3	3	3	3				
Vaughan Anthony J	6.1	11.02	11/10/75	Manchester	01/07/94	Ipswich Town	29+5		2	2	1			
E: S														
M I D F I E L D														
Mason Paul D	5.8	12.1	03/09/63	Liverpool		Everton								
SLC'90; SFAC'90				Free		F.C. Groningen								
				£200000	01/08/88	Aberdeen	138+20	13+2	11+1	7	27	8	1	1
				£400000	18/06/93	Ipswich Town	61+8	3	4+3	3	13	1	3	3
Milton Simon C	5.10	11.0	23/08/63	Fulham		Bury Town								
Div2'92				£5500	17/07/87	Ipswich Town	202+36	11+5	12	14+2	48	2	1	3
				Loan	01/11/87	Exeter City	2			1	3			
				Loan	01/03/88	Torquay United	4				1			
Norfolk Lee R	5.10	11.3	17/10/75	Dunedin, NZ	01/07/94	Ipswich Town	1+2			1				
Sedgley Stephen P	6.1	12.6	26/05/68	Enfield	02/06/86	Coventry City	81+3	9	2+2	5+1	3	2		
E: u21.11; FAC'91; CS'91			£750000		28/07/89	Tottenham Hotspur	147+17	24+3	12+1	5+3	8	1	1	
				£1000000	15/06/94	Ipswich Town	66	4	5	3	8	1		1
Stockwell Michael T	5.6	10.3	14/02/65	Chelmsford	17/12/82	Ipswich Town	332+20	24+3	21+3	18+2	21	2	1	1
Div2'92														
Tanner Adam D	6.0	12.1	25/10/73	Maldon	13/07/92	Ipswich Town	12+8		1	3+1	2			1
Thomsen Claus	6.3	11.6	31/05/70	Aarhus, Denmark		Aarhus								
Den:				£250000	15/06/94	Ipswich Town	67+3	4	4	2+1	7	1		
Wark John	5.10	12.10	04/08/57	Glasgow	01/08/74	Ipswich Town	295+1	24+1	36+1	25	94	12	10	18
S: 29, u21.9, UEFA'81; FAC'78			£450000	10/03/84	Liverpool	64+6	11+2	13+2	28	3	6	5	
SC'86; Div2'92				£100000	04/01/88	Ipswich Town	87+2	4	3	9	23			2
				£50000	23/08/90	Middlesbrough	31+1	5	2	1	3			
				Free	21/09/91	Ipswich Town	149+3	13+1	16	5	18		2	
Williams David Geraint	5.7	10.6	05/01/62	Treorchy	12/01/80	Bristol Rovers	138+3	14	9+2	5	8		2	
W: 12, u21.2, Y: Div2'92				£40000	29/03/85	Derby County	276+1	26+1	17	11	9	1		
				£650000	01/07/92	Ipswich Town	151	11+1	13	2	2			
F O R W A R D S														
Gregory Neil R	6.0	11.10	07/10/72	Ndola (Zambia)	21/02/92	Ipswich Town	6+15	2	0+1	3+2	2			2
				Loan	03/02/94	Chesterfield	2+1				1			
				Loan	03/03/95	Scunthorpe United	10				7			

Player						Club								
Marshall Ian P	6.1	12.12	20/03/66	Liverpool	23/03/84	Everton	9+6	1+1		7	1	1		
Div2'91; CS'86				£100000	24/03/86	Oldham Athletic	165+5	17	14	2+1	36		3	1
				£750000	09/08/93	Ipswich Town	77+5	3	9		32	2	3	
Mathie Alexander	5.10	10.7	20/12/68	Bathgate	15/05/87	Celtic	7+4		1	0+1				
				£100000	01/08/91	Grennock Morton	73+1	2	5	7	31	1	3	9
				Loan	30/03/93	Port Vale	0+3							
				£285000	30/07/93	Newcastle United	3+22	2+2			4			
				£500000	24/02/95	Ipswich Town	52	1	2	4	20			1
Scowcroft James B	6.1	12.2	25/10/73	Bury St. Edmunds	01/07/94	Ipswich Town	13+10	0+1	2	1+2	2			
Slater Stuart I	5.7	10.5	27/03/69	Sudbury	02/04/87	West Ham United	134+7	16+1	16	5	11	2	3	2
E: B2, u21.3				£1500000	14/08/92	Celtic	40+4	3+2	3	4	3			
				£750000	30/09/93	Ipswich Town	33+11	4	1	2+2	3			
Uhlenbeek Guss	5.9	12.5				SV Tops								
				£100000	11/08/95	Ipswich Town	37+2	2	1+3	4	4			
ADDITIONAL CONTRACT PLAYERS														
Bell Lyon					16/05/96	Ipswich Town (T)								
Brown Wayne					16/05/96	Ipswich Town (T)								
Hollman James					18/05/96	Ipswich Town (T)								
Naylor Richard (F)						Ipswich Town (T)								
Petta Bob					04/06/96	Ipswich Town (T)								
Sonner Daniel					01/06/96	Ipswich Town (T)								

THE MANAGER
GEORGE BURLEY

Date of Birth . . . . 3rd June 1956.
Place of Birth. . . . . Cumnock.
Date of Appointment . . . . December 1994.

PREVIOUS CLUBS
As Manager. . . . . Aye United, Colchester United.
As Coach . . . . Motherwell, twice.
As a Player . . . . Ipswich Town, Sunderland, Gillingham.

HONOURS
As a Manager
None.

As a Player
Ipswich Town: FA Cup 1978, UEFA 1981.
International: 11 full caps, 2 U23, 5 U21, Y, S for Scotland.

PORTMAN ROAD

Ipswich, Suffolk IP1 2DA
Tel: 01473 219 211

Capacity 22,600

First game ....v V Beccles Caxton,
....Suffolk Challenge Cup, 7-1, 2.3.1889.
First floodlit game...v Arsenal, Friendly, 16.2.1960.

ATTENDANCES
Highest ....38,010 v Leeds Utd, FAC 6th Rnd, 8.3.1975.
Lowest...3,116 v Leyton Orient, 25.3.1953.

OTHER GROUNDS..None.

MATCHDAY TICKET PRICES

Cobbold Stand
B Block (Adult/Juv/OAP) - . . . . £16/£6/£7.50
C & E Blocks - . . . . £18/£6*/-
D. . . . . £20/£6*/-
Cobbold Lower . . . . £10/£5/£7.50
Pioneer Stand - Y. £20/£6*/-
H, N, O Blocks . . . . £18/£6*/-
G, I M, P Blocks . . . . £16/£6/£7.50
Q, J, R Blocks . . . . £14/£6/£7.50
Pioneer Lower - FF GG II JJ . . . . £11/£6/£7.50
Pioneer Family F, K, L Blocks . . . . £14/£4/£7.50
Churchmans Stand. . . . . £11/£6/£7.50
North Stand . . . . £11 for all ages.
*Accompanied children only.
Ticket Office Telephone no. 01473 221 133

HOW TO GET TO THE GROUND

From the North and West
Use A45 sign posted to Ipswich West.
Proceed straight through Constable County Hotel traffic lights.
At the second set of traffic lights turn right into West End Road.
The ground is 400 metres along on the left.

From the South
Follow signs for Ipswich West, then proceed as above.

Car Parking
Large parks in Portman Road, Portman's Walk & West End Road.

Nearest Railway Station
Ipswich (01473 57373)

CLUBCALL

0839 66 44 88

Calls cost 49p per minute
Call costings correct at time of going to press.

MATCHDAY PROGRAMME

Programme Controller . . . . Mike Noye.

Number of pages . . . . 36.

Price . . . . £1.50.

Subscriptions . . . . Apply to club.

Local Newspapers . . . . East Anglian Daily Times, Evening Star.

Local Radio Stations. . . . . . SGR FM, Saxon Radio, BBC Radio Suffolk.

MANCHESTER CITY
(City or The Blues)
NATIONWIDE LEAGUE DIVISION 1
SPONSORED BY: BROTHER

Back Row (L-R): Rae Ingram, Ian Brightwell, Garry Flitcroft, Martyn Margetson, Michael Vonk, Alan Kernaghan, Steve Lomas.
Middle Row: Neil McNab (Yth Coach), Les Chapman (Res. Coach), Scott Thomas, Nick Summerbee, John Foster, Tony Coton, Andy Dibble, Paul Lake, Uwe Rosler, Keith Curle, Tony Book (First Team Coach), Asa Hartford (Asst. Manager). **Front Row:** Roy Bailey (Physio), Niall Quinn, Terry Phelan, Georgiou Kinkladze, Alan Ball (Manager), Peter Beagrie, Paul Walsh, Richard Edghill, Ronnie Evans (Coach).

MANCHESTER CITY
FORMED IN 1887
TURNED PROFESSIONAL IN 1887
LTD COMPANY IN 1894

CHAIRMAN: Francis Lee
MANAGING DIRECTOR: Colin Barlow
DIRECTORS
D Bernstein, J Dunkerley, G Grant,
D Holt, A Lewis, A Thomas
SECRETARY
Bernard Halford (0161 224 5000)
COMMERCIAL MANAGER
Geoff Durbin (0161 248 9999)

MANAGER: Alan Ball
ASSISTANT MANAGER: Asa Hartford
RESERVE TEAM MANAGER
Kevin Bond
YOUTH COACH
Neil McNab
PHYSIOTHERAPIST
Roy Bailey

STATISTICIAN FOR THE DIRECTORY
Dennis Chapman

In the close season of 1995, Brian Horton left the manager's position. Speculation was rife as to his successor. Then quite surprisingly Alan Ball was approached and within a short period of time was installed as manager.

In the weeks leading up to the start of the season he signed three players, Immel, Symons and Kinkladze. Although partly being unknown quantities they turned out to be exceptionally good acquisitions, where all three had an excellent season.

The season started with a creditable home draw against Tottenham Hotspur. What followed was something that any club would dread - eight League defeats on the run (a new club record!), followed by a home draw against Leeds United then a hammering 0-6 defeat at Liverpool. After eleven League games played City could only show three goals scored and well entrenched at the bottom of the table.

The spear head of Quinn and Rosler was just not producing goals that everyone expected. It was rumoured that the manager was expecting his ideas and methods to bring success overnight. Some senior players appeared to resent being highlighted for lack of commitment. This, on can form their own opinion, but the fact was that success was just not happening on the field.

However, the first home win against Bolton at the beginning of November heralded an excellent four weeks where City won four and drew one of the next five games and confidence rose tremendously. After this encouraging run, results were again disappointing through to the end of the season, winning five, drawing eight and nine defeats. It was a case of just "keeping up with the Jones" and not being able to break away from the bottom pack to give a little room to concentrate on putting their game together.

Towards the end of the season it became nail biting stuff. Hope gleamed at Villa Park with an excellent win but in the end City ran out of steam and lost out by the burden of goals scored against during the first half of the season. This culminated by being relegated on goal difference.

One must give credit however to new signings Hiley and Phillips who can look to a successful future. Summerbee, now more matured, had a very good consistent season. Brown and Lomas gave their all and should be stars of the future. Quinn and Rosler scored some exciting goals and one must applaud their commitment even though the goals dried up.

The one bright asset of the season was Kinkladze. Small in stature but with ball skills and confidence to run at defences he is a gem that can inspire the team to quickly return the the Premiership.

DENNIS CHAPMAN.

MANCHESTER CITY

League: 18th   FA Cup: 5th Rnd   Coca-Cola Cup: 3rd Rnd

M	DATE	COMP	VEN	OPPONENTS	RESULT	HT	LP	GOAL SCORERS/GOAL TIMES	ATT.
1	A 19	PL	H	Tottenham Hotspur	D 1-1	0-1	12	Rosler 52	30827
2	23	PL	A	Coventry City	L 1-2	0-1	16	Rosler 82	(16568)
3	26	PL	A	Queens Park Rangers	L 0-1	0-1	19		(14212)
4	30	PL	H	Everton	L 0-2	0-0	20		28432
5	S 10	PL	H	Arsenal	L 0-1	0-0	20		23994
6	16	PL	A	Newcastle United	L 1-3	0-2	20	Creaney 81	(36501)
7	19	CC 2/1	A	**Wycombe Wanderers**	D 0-0	0-0			(7443)
8	23	PL	H	Middlesbrough	L 0-1	0-1	20		25865
9	30	PL	A	Nottingham Forest	L 0-3	0-1			(25620)
10	O 4	CC 2/2	H	**Wycombe Wanderers**	W 4-0	2-0		**Rosler 31, 34, Quinn 60, Curle 63(pen)**	11474
11	14	PL	A	Manchester United	L 0-1	0-1	20		(35707)
12	21	PL	H	Leeds United	D 0-0	0-0	20		26390
13	25	CC 3	A	**Liverpool**	L 0-4	0-1			(29394)
14	28	PL	A	Liverpool	L 0-6	0-2	20		(39267)
15	N 4	PL	H	Bolton Wanderers	W 1-0	1-0	20	Summerbee 11	28397
16	18	PL	A	Sheffield Wednesday	D 1-1	0-1	20	Lomas 55	(24422)
17	22	PL	H	Wimbledon	W 1-0	0-0	18	Quinn 90	23617
18	25	PL	H	Aston Villa	W 1-0	0-0	17	Kinkladze 85	28027
19	D 2	PL	A	Leeds United	W 1-0	0-0	15	Creaney 60	(33249)
20	9	PL	A	Middlesbrough	L 1-4	1-1	16	Kinkladze 14	(29469)
21	18	PL	A	Nottingham Forest	D 1-1	1-0	16	Rosler 16	25660
22	23	PL	H	Chelsea	L 0-1	0-0	17		28668
23	26	PL	A	Blackburn Rovers	L 0-2	0-1	18		(28915)
24	J 1	PL	H	West Ham United	W 2-1	1-0	17	Quinn 21, 78	26024
25	6	FAC 3	A	**Leicester City**	D 0-0	0-0			(20640)
26	13	PL	A	Tottenham Hotspur	L 0-1	0-0	17		(31438)
27	17	FAC 3R	H	**Leicester City**	W 5-0	2-0		**Rosler 10, Kinkladze 18, Quinn 51, Lomas 54, Creaney 80**	19980
28	20	PL	H	Coventry City	D 1-1	0-0	17	Rosler 55	25710
29	31	PL	A	Southampton	D 1-1	0-0	17	Rosler 84	(15172)
30	F 3	PL	H	Queens Park Rangers	W 2-0	1-0	17	Clough 25, Symons 50	27509
31	7	FAC 4	A	**Coventry City**	D 2-2	1-1		**Busst 33(og), Flitcroft 81**	(18775)
32	10	PL	A	Everton	L 0-2	0-1	17		(37354)
33	14	FAC 4R	H	**Coventry City**	W 2-1	1-0		**Clough 29, Quinn 46**	22419
34	18	FAC 5	A	**Manchester United**	L 1-2	1-1		**Rosler 11**	(42692)
35	24	PL	H	Newcastle United	D 3-3	1-1	17	Quinn 16, 62, Rosler 77	31115
36	M 2	PL	H	Blackburn Rovers	D 1-1	0-0	16	Lomas 84	29078
37	5	PL	A	Arsenal	L 1-3	0-2	16	Creaney 54	(34519)
38	12	PL	A	Chelsea	D 1-1	1-1	16	Clough 43	(17078)
39	16	PL	H	Southampton	W 2-1	2-0	15	Kinkladze 32, 37	29550
40	23	PL	A	West Ham United	L 2-4	0-1	16	Quinn 76, 90	(24017)
41	30	PL	A	Bolton Wanderers	D 1-1	1-0	16	Quinn 2	(21050)
42	A 6	PL	H	Manchester United	L 2-3	1-2	17	Kavelashvili 39, Rosler 71	29688
43	8	PL	A	Wimbledon	L 0-3	0-1	17		(11844)
44	13	PL	H	Sheffield Wednesday	W 1-0	0-0	17	Rosler 65	30898
45	27	PL	A	Aston Villa	W 1-0	0-0	17	Lomas 70	(39336)
46	M 5	PL	H	Liverpool	D 2-2	0-2	17	Rosler 71(pen), Symons 78	31436

Best Home League Attendance: 31436 v Liverpool   Smallest: 23617 v Wimbledon   Average: 27941

Goal Scorers:
PL(33):   Rosler(9),Quinn(8),Kinkladze(4),Lomas(3),Creaney(3),Symons(2),Clough(2),Kavelashvili(1),Summerbee(1)
CC(4):   Rosler(2),Curle(1),Quinn(1)
FAC(10):   Quinn(2),Rosler(2),Opponent(s)(1),Lomas(1),Kinkladze(1),Flitcroft(1),Creaney(1),Clough(1)

(F) Beagrie	(M) Brightwell	(M) Brown	(F) Clough	(G) Coton	(F) Creaney	(D) Curle	(D) Edghill	(M) Ekelund	(M) Flitcroft	(D) Foster	(D) Frontzeck	(D) Hiley	(G) Immel	(D) Ingram	(F) Kavelashvili	(D) Kernaghan	(M) Kerr	(F) Kinkladze	(M) Lomas	(G) Margetson	(M) Mazzarelli	(D) Phelan	(F) Phillips	(F) Quinn	(F) Rossler	(D) Summerbee	(D) Symons	(F) Walsh	Referee	No.
	X						X		X				X			S		X	X	S			X	S1	X1	X	X	X	G.Poll	1
	X1						X		X				X			S1		X	X2	S			X	S2	X	X	X	X	P.Alcock	2
		S2							X	X			X			X		X	X2				X	S1	X	X	X	X1	P.Danson	3
	X1								X	X			X	X2		S2	S1	X					X	X	X	X	X	X	S.Lodge	4
X	X					X	X		X				X					X1	S	S			X	S1	X	X	X		D.Gallagher	5
X	X				X	X	X		X1				X					X2	S1				X		X	S2	X		J.Winter	6
X	X	S				X							X					X1	X	S			X	X	X	S1	X		M.Pierce	7
S1	X	X1				X	X						X					X2	X	S				X	X	S2	X		G.Willard	8
X	X	X				X1	X			X			X					X	X	S				S	X	S1	X		M.Reed	9
X	X	S1				X	X3		X1				X					X2	X	S3				X	X	S2	X		K.Burge	10
X1					S2	X	X		X				X			S		X	X			X		X2	X	S1	X		R.Dilkes	11
	S1				S2	X	X		X1				X					X	X	S		X2		X	X	X	X		M.Bodenham	12
	X	S1				X	X		X				X			S		X	X					X	X1	X	X		S.Lodge	13
	X2	S1			S2	X	X		X				X					X1	X					X	X	X	X		A.Wilkie	14
	S1				S2	X	X		X	X1	X2		X					X	X	S				X	X	X	X		R.Hart	15
	X		S		S1	X1	X		X				X			S		X						X	X	X	X		G.Poll	16
	X		S		S1	X	X1		X				X			S		X						X	X	X	X		P.Durkin	17
	X		S		S	X	X		X				X			S		X						X	X	X	X		G.Ashby	18
	X				S1	X1	X		X				X			S		X						X	X	X	X		P.Alcock	19
	X	X	S		X	X			X				X	X		X1		X	X					X	X	X	X		S.Lodge	20
	X	S1	S		S	X			X				X	X		X1		X	X					X	X	X	X		K.Burge	21
	X	X	S		X	X			X				X	X		S		X						X	X1	X	X		G.Willard	22
	X	X	S			X1	X		X				X			S		X						X	X	X	X		K.Cooper	23
	X	X	S			X	X			S1	X1		X					X					S2	X	X2	X	X		M.Reed	24
	X	X				S	X		X	X	X		X					X						X	X	X	X		R.Gifford	25
	S1						X		S1	X1	X		X	X		S		X	X	S				X	X	X	X		D.J.Gallagher	26
	X					S1	X		S2	X1	X		X	X		S		X	X				X2	X	X	X	X		R.Gifford	27
X	X					S	X		X				X					X	X1	S			S1	X	X	X	X		R.Hart	28
	S2	X				S	X		X	X2			X					X	X1	S			S1	X1	X	X	X		S.Dunn	29
	S1	X				S1	X		X	X			X					X	X1	S			X		X1	X	X	X		G.Poll	30
	X	X				S	X		X				X					X	X						X	X	X	X		G.Ashby	31
		X1	X			S1	X1			X			X					X	S				X1	S1	X	X	X	X		P.Alcock	32
	X	X				S1	X1		X				X					X	X	S				X	X	X	X		K.Cooper	33
	X	X				S1	X		X				X					X	X				X1	X	X	X	X		A.Wilkie	34
	X	X	S				X			X			X					X	X	S		S	X	X	X	X	X		M.Bodenham	35
	S	X					X			X			X1	S1	X			X	X	S			S1	X1	X	X	X	X	P.Danson	36
		X	X				X			X			X1	S1	X		X	X	X	S			S1		X	X1	X	X	P.Jones	37
	X		X				X			X			X		S	X		X	X	S				S1		X	X1	X	P.Durkin	38
X		X				X			X				X1	S1	X			X	X1					S	S1	X	X	X	J.Winter	39
X	X	X				X			X				X2	S2	X			X	X		S3			S1	X1	X3	X	X	K.Cooper	40
X	X	X				X			X				S1	X1	X		S	X	X					S	X	S2	X	X	R.Dilkes	41
X	X	X				X			X				X1	X	X2			X		S				S1	X	X	X	X	M.Reed	42
X	X	X				X			X				X	X	X	S		X	X					S1	X1	S1	X1	X	G.Poll	43
X	X	X				X			X				X1	X	X1			X	X	S				S1	S1	X	X	X	R.Hart	44
X	X	X				X			X				S		X	S		X	X					S	X	X	X	X	D.Ellery	45
X	X	X2				X			X				S		X	S2		X	X					S1	X1	X	X	X	S.Lodge	46
4	26	16	15	0	6	32	13	2	25	4	11	2	38	5	3	4	0	37	32	0	0	9	2	24	34	33	38	3	PL Appearances	
1	3	5	0	0	9	0	0	2	0	1	4	0	0	1	2	1	0	1	0	2	1	0	2	9	8	2	4	0	PL Sub Appearances	
2	3	0+2	0	0	0	3	3	0	1	1	0	0	3	0	0	0	0	3	3	0+1	0	1	0	3	3	1+2	3	0	CC Appearances	
0	2	5	3	0	0+3	5	0	1+1	4	0	1	0	5	1	0	0	0	4	5	0	0	4	5	5	5	5	5	0	FAC Appearances	

Also Played: (F) Beech S(33). (M) Crooks S(20). (M) Rowlands S(31).

MANCHESTER CITY

CLUB RECORDS

BIGGEST VICTORIES
League: 10-0 v Darwen, Division 2, 18.2.1899.
F.A. Cup: 10-1 v Swindon Town, 4th Round (Replay), 29.1.1930.
9-0 v Gateshead, 3rd Round (Replay), 18.1.1933.
League Cup: 6-0 v Scunthorpe United, 2nd Round, 10.9.1974.
6-0 v Torquay United, 2nd Round, 25.10.1983.
Europe: 5-0 v S K Lierse, 2nd Round, 26.11.1969.

BIGGEST DEFEATS
League: 0-8 v Burton Wanderers, Division 2, 26.12.1894.
1-9 v Everton, Division 1, 3.9.1906.
0-8 v Wolverhampton Wndrs, Division 1, 23.12.1933.
F.A. Cup: 0-6 v Preston North End, 30.1.1897.
2-8 v Bradford Park Avenue (h), 4th Round, 30.1.1946.
League Cup: 0-6 v Birmingham City, 5th Round, 11.12.1962.
Europe: No more than two goals. (4 games)

MOST POINTS
3 points a win: 82, Division 2, 1988-89.
2 points a win: 62, Division 2, 1946-47.

MOST GOALS SCORED
108, Division 2, 1926-27.
Johnson 25, Hicks 21, Roberts 14, W Cowan 11, Austin 10, Barrass 7, Broadhurst 7, Bell 4, McMullan 3, S Cowan 2, Gibson 2, Pringle 1, Opponents 1.

MOST GOALS CONCEDED
102, Division 1, 1962-63.

MOST FIRST CLASS MATCHES IN A SEASON
62 - 1969-70 (League 42, FA Cup 2, League Cup 7, Charity Shield 1, ECWC 10).

MOST LEAGUE WINS
26, Division 2, 1946-47, Division 1, 1967-68.

MOST LEAGUE DRAWS
18, Premiership, 1993-94.

MOST LEAGUE DEFEATS
22, Division 1, 1958-59, Division 1, 1959-60.

INDIVIDUAL CLUB RECORDS

MOST GOALS IN A SEASON
Tom Johnson: 38 goals in 1928-29 (Division 1).
Previous holder: F Roberts 31.

MOST GOALS IN A MATCH
5. Tom Johnson v Everton (a), 6-2, Division 1, 15.9.1928.
5. R.S. Marshall v Swindon Town, 10-1, FA Cup 4th Rnd (replay), 29.1.1930.
5. George Smith v Newport, 5-1, Division 2, 14.6.1947.

OLDEST PLAYER
Billy Meredith, 49 years 245 days v Newcastle United, FA Cup sem final, 29.3.1924.

YOUNGEST PLAYER
Glyn Pardoe, 15 years 314 days v Birmingham City, Division 1, 11.4.1961.

MOST CAPPED PLAYER
Colin Bell (England) 48.

BEST PERFORMANCES

League: 1902-03: Matches played 34, Won 25, Drawn 4, Lost 5, Goals for 95, Goals against 29, Points 54. First in Division 2.
Highest Position: Champions of Division 1, 1936-37, 1967-68.
F.A. Cup: 1968-69: 3rd Round Luton Town 1-0; 4th Round Newcastle United 0-0,2-0; 5th Round Blackburn Rovers 4-1; 6th Round Tottenham Hotspur 1-0; Semi-final Everton 1-0; Final Leicester City 1-0.
League Cup: Winners in 1969-70.
Most recent success: 1975-76: 2nd Round Norwich City 1-1,2-6 1; 3rd Round Nottingham Forest 2-1; 4th Round Manchester United 4-0; 5th Round Mansfield Town 4-2; Semi-final Middlesbrough 0-1,4 0; Final Newcastle United 2-1.
Europe: ECWC 1969-70: 1st Round Athletico Bilbao 3-3,3-0; 2nd Round Lierse 3-0,5-0; 3rd Round Academica Coimbra 0-0,1-0; Semi-final Schalke 04 0-1,5-1; Final Gornik Zabrze 2-1.

DIVISIONAL RECORD

	Played	Won	Drawn	Lost	For	Against	Points
Division 1/P	2,936	1,106	731	1,099	4,457	4,464	3,084
Division 2	786	402	173	211	1,652	1,072	1,060
Total	3,722	1,508	904	1,310	6,109	5,536	4,144

ADDITIONAL INFORMATION

PREVIOUS NAMES
Ardwick F.C. 1887-95 (an amalgamation of West Gorton and Gorton Athletic).

PREVIOUS LEAGUES
Football Alliance.

Club colours: Sky blue shirts, white shorts, sky blue socks.
Change colours: Maroon & white shirt, maroon shorts, white socks with maroon trim.

Reserves League: Pontins Central League Division 2.

COMPETITIONS

Div 1/P	Div.2/1	Euro C	ECWC	UEFA	Texaco
1899-02	1892-99	1968-69	1969-70	1972-73	1971-72
1903-09	1902-03		1970-71	1976-77	1974-75
1910-26	1909-10	FMC		1977-78	
1928-38	1926-28	1985-86		1978-79	A/Ital
1947-50	1938-47	1986-87			1970-71
1951-63	1950-51	1987-88			
1966-83	1963-66	1988-89			A/Scot
1985-87	1983-85	1989-90			1975-76
1989-96	1987-89	1990-91			
	1996-	1991-93			

HONOURS

Div.1	Div.2	FA Cup	Lge Cup	ECWC
1936-37	1898-99	1903-04	1969-70	1969-70
1967-68	1902-03	1933-34	1975-76	
	1909-10	1955-56		C/Sh'd
	1927-28	1968-69		1937
	1946-47			1968
	1965-66			1972

MOST GOALS IN A CAREER

Eric Brook - 177 (1927-39)

Year	League	FA Cup
1927-28	2	
1928-29	14	
1929-30	16	1
1930-31	16	
1931-32	10	3
1932-33	15	6
1933-34	8	3
1934-35	17	
1935-36	13	3
1936-37	20	2
1937-38	16	1
1938-39	11	
Total	158	19

Current leading goalscorer: Niall Quinn - 78 (1990-96)

MOST APPEARANCES

Alan Oakes 672+4 (1959-76)

Year	League	FA Cup	Lge Cup	Europe
959-60	18	1		
960-61	22			
961-62	25			
962-63	34	2	4	
963-64	41	1	6	
964-65	41	2	1	
965-66	41	8	2	
966-67	39	6	2	
967-68	41	4	4	
968-69	39	7	3	2
969-70	40	2	7	9
970-71	30	3	1	4
971-72	31+1	2		
972-73	13+1		0+1	2
973-74	28		5	
974-75	40	1	2	
975-76	38+1	2	9	
	561+3	41	46+1	17

Also: 2 A/Ital Cup 70-71; 3 Texaco 74-75; 3 A/Scot 75-76.

MANAGERS

Name	Seasons	Best	Worst
L Furniss	1892-93	5(2)	5(2)
J Parlby	1893-95	9(2)	13(2)
S Ormrod	1895-02	7(1)	6(2)
T Maley	1902-06	2(1)	1(2)
H W Newbould	1906-12	3(1)	1(2)
E Magnell	1912-24	2(1)	13(1)
D Ashworth	1924-25	10(1)	21(1)
P Hodge	1926-32	3(1)	3(2)
W Wild	1932-46	1(1)	5(2)
S Cowan	1946-47	1(2)	1(2)
J Thompson	1947-50	7(1)	21(1)
L McDowell	1950-63	4(1)	2(2)
G Poyser	1963-65	6(2)	11(2)
J Mercer OBE	1965-71	1(1)	1(2)
M Allison	1971-73	4(1)	11(1)
J Hart	1973		
R Saunders	1973-74	14(1)	14(1)
T Book	1974-79	2(1)	15(1)
M Allison	1979-80	17(1)	17(1)
J Bond	1980-83	10(1)	20(1)
J Benson	1983		
W McNeill MBE	1983-86	15(1)	4(2)
J Frizzell	1986-87	21(1)	21(1)
M Machin	1987-89	2(2)	9(2)
H Kendall	1989-90	14(1)	14(1)
P Reid	1990-93	5(1)	9(1/P)
B Horton	1993-95	16(P)	17(P)
A Ball	1995-	18(P)	18(P)

RECORD TRANSFER FEE RECEIVED

Amount	Club	Player	Date
£3,200,000	Garry Flitcroft	Blackburn Rovers	3/96
£2,000,000	Leeds United	David White*	01/94
£1,700,000	Tottenham	Paul Stewart	6/88
£900,000	Everton	Mark Ward	6/91

*- Deal included David Rocastle joining Manchester City.

RECORD TRANSFER FEE PAID

Amount	Club	Player	Date
£2,500,000	Wimbledon	Keith Curle	8/91
£1,150,000	Wolves	Steve Daley	9/79
£350,000	Luton Town	Paul Futcher	6/78
£275,000	Sunderland	Denis Tueart	3/74

LONGEST LEAGUE RUNS

of undefeated matches:	22 (16.11.46-9.4.47, 26.12.36-1.5.37)	of league matches w/out a win:	17 (26.12.1979 - 7.4.1980)
of undefeated home matches:	41 (25.12.1919 - 19.11.1921)	of undefeated away matches:	12 (23.11.1946 - 14.5.1947)
without home win:	9 (26.12.1979 - 7.4.1980)	without an away win:	34 (11.2.1986 - 17.10.1987)
of league wins:	9 (8.4.1912 - 28.9.1912)	of home wins:	16 (13.11.1920 - 27.8.1921)
of league defeats:	8 (23.08.95 - 14.10.95)	of away wins:	6 (7.3.1903 - 26.9.1903)

MANCHESTER CITY

PLAYERS NAME Honours	Ht	Wt	Birthdate	Birthplace Transfers	Contract Date	Clubs	League	L/Cup	FA Cup	Other	Lge	L/C	FAC	Oth
G O A L K E E P E R S														
Dibble Andy	6.2	13.7	08/05/65	Cwmbran	27/08/82	Cardiff City	62	4	4					
W: 3, u21.3, Y, S. LC'88				£125000	16/07/84	Luton Town	30	4	1	1				
				Loan	21/02/86	Sunderland	12							
				Loan	26/03/87	Huddersfield Town	5							
				£240000	01/07/88	Manchester City	101+2	12	8+1	2				
				Loan	12/10/90	Aberdeen	5							
				Loan	20/02/91	Middlesbrough	19			2				
				Loan	06/09/91	Bolton Wanderers	13			1				
				Loan	27/02/92	W.B.A.	9							
Immel Eike				VfB Stuttgart										
				£400000	17/08/95	Manchester City	38	3	5					
Margetson Martyn	6.0	13.10	08/09/71	Neath	05/07/90	Manchester City	6	0+2		1				
W: B.2, u21.7, Y, S				Loan	08/12/93	Bristol Rovers	2+1							
				Loan	23/03/95	Luton Town								
D E F E N D E R S														
Bentley James	6.1	12.7	11/06/76	Liverpool	13/07/93	Manchester City								
Edghill Richard	5.8	10.6	23/09/74	Oldham	15/07/92	Manchester City	49	10	1					
E: B.1, u21.2														
Foster John	5.11	11.2	19/09/73	Manchester	15/07/92	Manchester City	5	1	1					
Frontzeck Michael				BM'gladbach										
				£350000	31/01/96	Manchester City	11+1		1					
Hiley Scott	5.9	10.4	27/09/68	Plymouth	04/08/86	Exeter City	205+5	17	14	16+2	12			
Div4'90. Div2'95				£100000	12/03/93	Birmingham City	45	6	1	1				
				£250000	01/04/96	Manchester City	2+4							
Ingram Rae	5.11	11.7	06/12/74	Manchester	09/07/93	Manchester City	5		1					
Kernaghan Alan	6.1	12.13	25/04/67	Otley	08/03/85	Middlesbrough	172+40	22+7	7+4	14+2	16	1	3	2
Ei: 11				Loan	17/01/91	Charlton Athletic	13							
				£1600000	20/09/93	Manchester City	45+7	7	5		1		1	
				Loan	18/08/94	Bolton Wanderers	9+2							
				Loan	02/02/96	Bradford City	5							
Summerbee Nicholas	5.8	11.8	26/08/71	Altrincham	20/07/89	Swindon Town	89+23	9+1	2+4	7	6	3		1
E: B.1, u21.3				£1500000	24/06/94	Manchester City	72+6	7+2	9		2	2		
Symons Kit	6.1	10.10	08/03/71	Basingstoke	30/12/88	Portsmouth	180	19	10	13+1	10			1
W: 13, u21.2, Y				£1200000	17/08/95	Manchester City	38	3	5		2			
M I D F I E L D														
Brightwell Ian	5.10	11.7	09/04/68	Lutterworth	07/05/86	Manchester City	230+33	27+2	15+4	4+3	16		1	
E: u21.4, S, Y.3														
Brown Michael	5.7	10.06	25/01/77	Hartlepool	01/08/94	Manchester City	16+5	0+2	5					
Crooks Lee	6.1	11.1	14/01/78	Wakefield	01/08/94	Manchester City								
Kerr David W	5.11	11.2	06/09/74	Dumfries	10/09/91	Manchester City	2+2							
				Loan	22/09/95	Mansfield Town	4+1		1					
Lomas Stephen	6.0	11.10	18/01/74	Hanover (Ger)	22/01/91	Manchester City	67+9	14	7+1		5	1	1	
NI: 4, B.1, Y														
F O R W A R D S														
Beagrie Peter	5.8	9.10	28/11/65	Middlesbrough	10/09/83	Middlesbrough	24+8	1		1+1	2			
E: B.2, u21.2				£35000	16/08/86	Sheffield United	81+3	5	5	4	11			
				£210000	29/06/88	Stoke City	54	4	3		7		1	
				£750000	02/11/89	Everton	88+26	7+2	7+2	5+1	12	3		1
				Loan	26/09/91	Sunderland	5				1			
				£1000000	24/03/94	Manchester City	46+5	8	4		3	1	1	
Beech Chris	5.9	11.0	05/11/75	Congleton	12/11/92	Manchester City								
Clough Nigel	5.9	11.8	19/03/66	Sunderland		Heanor Town								
E: 14, B.3, u21.15; LC'89'90;				Free	15/09/84	Nottingham Forest	307+4	46	28	11+3	101	22	6	1
FMC'89'92; FLgXI.1				£2275000	07/06/93	Liverpool	29+10	3	2		7	2		
Nigel Clough continued....				£1500000	24/01/96	Manchester City	15		3		2		1	
Creaney Gerry	5.10	10.7	13/04/70	Coatbridge		Glasgow Rangers	85+28	9+1	9+1	7+3	36	7	8	3
S: u21.12				£500000	25/01/94	Portsmouth	60	7	2		32	3	1	
				£1500000	08/09/95	Manchester City	6+9		0+3		3		1	
				Loan	28/03/96	Oldham Athletic	8+1				2			

Name	Ht	Wt	DOB	Previous/Club	Fee	Date	Club								
avelashvila Mikhail				Spartak Vladikavkaz											
				Manchester City	£1400000	28/03/96		3+1				1			
nkladze Georgiou				Dinamo Tbilisi											
				Manchester City	£2000000	01/08/95		37	3	4		4		1	
hillips Martin J	5.11	12.8	13/03/76	Exeter		04/07/94	Exeter City	36+16	1+2	2+2	1+5	5			
				Manchester City	£500000	25/11/95		2+9							
uinn Niall	6.4	12.4	06/10/66	Dublin		30/11/83	Arsenal	59+8	14+2	8+2	0+1	14	4	2	
: 42, B.1, u23.1, u21.5,Y.LC'87				Manchester City	£800000	21/03/90		183+20	20+2	13+3	3	65	6	4	1
osler Ulve	6.0	12.4	15/11/68	Attenburg			Dynamo Dresden								
Germany: 5. Germany B.1.				Manchester City	£750000	02/03/94		75+4	6+1	9		29	4	7	
Ger. Div1. FAC'90															
homas Scott L	5.11	11.4	30/10/74	Bury		26/03/92	Manchester City								

ADDITIONAL CONTRACT PLAYERS

Name	Date	Club
allaghan Anthony S	04/12/95	Manchester City (T)
eeman Nathan	04/10/95	Manchester City (T)
reenacre Christopher	01/07/95	Manchester City (T)
arris Samuel R	16/04/96	Manchester City (T)
lly Raymond		Athlone
	£30000 01/08/94	Manchester City
cGlinchey Brian K		Manchester City (T)
orley David T	03/01/96	Manchester City (T)
mmer Stephen	29/05/96	Manchester City (T)
owlands Aled	01/07/95	Manchester City (T)
rpey Gerard E	01/07/95	Manchester City (T)
hitley James		Manchester City (T)
hitley Jeffrey	19/02/96	Manchester City (T)

THE MANAGER
ALAN BALL

Date of Birth . . . . 12th May 1945.
Place of Birth . . . . Farnworth.
Date of Appointment . . . . 14th July 1995.

PREVIOUS CLUBS
As Manager . . . . Blackpool, Vancouvr Whitecaps (as player/manager),
. . . . Portsmouth, Stoke City, Exeter City, Southampton.
As Coach . . . . Bristol Rovers, Portsmouth.
As a Player . . . . Blackpool, Everton, Arsenal, Southampton (twice),
. . . . Bristol Rovers.

HONOURS
As a Manager
Portsmouth: Promotion to Division 1, 1987.

As a Player
Everton: Division 1 Championship 1970.
International: 72 full caps and 8 u23. World Cup Winner 1966.

MAINE ROAD

Moss Side, Manchester M14 7WN
Tel: 0161 224 5000 Fax: 0161 248 8449

Capacity ....31,000.

First game ....v Sheffield Utd, 2-1, 25.8.1923.
First floodlit game ....v Hearts, 14.10.1953.

ATTENDANCES
Highest ....84,569 v Stoke City, FA Cup 6th Round, 3.3.1934 (record outside London).
Lowest..4,029 v Leeds United, FMC, 14.10.1985.

OTHER GROUNDS ....Clowes Street 1880-81; Kirkmanshulme C.C. 1881-82; Queens Road 1882-84;
...............................Pink Bank Lane 1884-85; Bulls Head Ground, Reddish Lane 1885-87; Hyde Road 1887-1923;
.... Maine Road 1923-

MATCHDAY TICKET PRICES

Main Stand
Blocks B, C £16
Other Blocks £15
Block G (OAP only) £5
North Stand £10
Juv/OAP £7
Blocks K,L (Juv/OAP). £5
Umbro Stand
Main Section £11
JD Sports Famiy Enclosure £8
Juv/OAP £5
Kippax Stand
Upper Tier £14
Lower Tier £11

Ticket Office telephone no. 0161 226 2224

CLUBCALL 0898 12 11 91

Calls cost 39p per minute cheap rate and 49p per
minute at all other times.
Call costings correct at time of going to press.

HOW TO GET TO THE GROUND

From the North
Use motorway M61 then M63 until junction 9. Leave motorway and follow signs
Manchester A5103. In 2.8 miles at crossroads turn right in Claremont Road. In
0.4 miles turn right into Maine Road for Manchester City FC.

From the East
Use motorway M61 until junction 17 then A56 into Manchester. Follow signs to
Manchester Airport then turn left to join motorway A57(M). Follow signs to
Birmingham to join A5103. Then in 1.3 miles turn left into Claremont Road. In 0
miles turn right into Maine Road for Manchester City.

From the South
Use motorway M6 until junction 19 then A556 and M56 until junction 3. Keep for
ward A5103 sign posted Manchester. In 2.8 miles at crossroads turn right into
Claremont Road. In 0.4 miles turn right into Maine Road for Manchester City FC

From the West
Use motorway M62 then M63 and route as from north. Or use M56 route as from
south.

Car Parking: Kippax Street car park holds 400 vehicles (approx). Some street
parking is permitted, parking at local schools.
Nearest Railway Station: Manchester Piccadilly (0161 832 8353).

MATCHDAY PROGRAMME

Programme Editor . . . . Mike Beddow.

Number of pages . . . . 32.

Price . . . . £1.70.

Subscriptions . . . . Apply to the club.

Local Newspapers . . . . Manchester Evening News, Football Pink.

Local Radio Stations . . . . GMR Talk, Piccadilly Radio.

NORWICH CITY
(The Canaries)
NATIONWIDE LEAGUE DIVISION 1
SPONSORED BY: NORWICH & PETERBOROUGH BUILDING S.

Back Row (L-R): Ade Akinbiyi, Daryl Sutch, Mike Sheron, Ashley Ward, Rob Newman, Lee Bray, Jon Newsome, Spencer Prior, Andy Johnson, Keith O'Neill, Danny Mills. **Middle Row:** Tim Sheppard (Physio), Stacey Kreft, Johnny Wright, Shaun Carey, Jeremy Goss, Andrew Brownrigg, Steve Walford (Res. Manager), Paul Franklin (Asst. Manager), John Faulkner (Coach), Carl Bradshaw, Mark Bowen, Robert Fleathorne, Ali Gibb, Justin Harrington, Keith Webb (Yth Manager). **Front Row:** Darren Eadie, Neil Adams, Karl Simpson, John Polston, Bryan Gunn, Martin O'Neill (Manager), Andy Marshall, Ian Crook, Mike Milligan, Jamie Cureton, Jamie Mitchell.

NORWICH CITY
FORMED IN 1902
TURNED PROFESSIONAL IN 1905
LTD COMPANY IN 1905

PRESIDENT: G C Watling
HON.SENIOR LIFE VICE-PRESIDENT
Sir Arthur South J.P.
DIRECTORS
B W Lockwood, G A Paterson, T J Nicholls,
R.J.Munby, M Armstrong
SECRETARY
Andrew Neville (01603 760 760)
COMMERCIAL MANAGER
Trevor Bond
MANAGER: Mike Walker
ASSISTANT MANAGER: John Faulkner

RESERVE TEAM MANAGER

YOUTH TEAM MANAGER
Keith Webb
PHYSIOTHERAPIST
Tim Sheppard MCSP, SRP

STATISTICIAN FOR THE DIRECTORY
John Brock

What a season of horror for Norwich City supporters! Following relegation from the Premier League in 1995, chairman Robert Chase stated that he would 'put everything on the back burner' to ensure immediate promotion back to the top. The board appointed Martin O'Neill as manager, and it looked as if the club would make a serious attempt at promotion.

The first crisis arrived in October, when the board turned down O'Neill's request to buy Dean Windass from Hull City. Relations between chairman and manager were clearly strained. Nevertheless, it still came as a shock when O'Neill resigned in December. The board quickly appointed former player Gary Megson as the new manager; he had been caretaker-manager at the time the club was relegated from the Premier League.

At the first home game following O'Neill's departure (Boxing Day, versus Southend United) the atmosphere in the ground was hostile. Protests in the past had been mainly confined to before the kick-off, half-time, and after the final whistle. The fans' feelings towards the chairman were clear throughout the entirety of this match, however. At the beginning of February a petition of over 10,000 signatures was presented to Chase calling on him to resign.

At the end of February there was a further shock for the long-suffering supporters: it was revealed that the club was millions of pounds in debt. This was despite the fact that Norwich City had sold most of its best players for large amounts of money over the years. Chase's business sense was now seriously brought into question. Chase responded to the revelation of the debt by selling two more of the club's best players at bargain prices a fortnight later: captain Jon Newsome and leading goal-scorer Ashley Ward.

Eventually, on 2nd May, came the news that most supporters had hoped for: Chase resigned from the board. Former chairman and current president Geoffrey Watling bought his shares, and he has the awesome task of trying to establish a new regime in the boardroom that can rebuild the club. Unfortunately the club has had to cut back very severely on its wage bill, and many back-room staff are being made redundant. Experienced players - presumably high earners - are sadly being released on free transfers: Ian Crook, Mark Bowen, and Jeremy Goss - all heroes from the club's UEFA Cup run just two and a half years ago.

As for the football - after a reasonable start in the first half of the season, the Canaries' fortunes plummeted, and at one stage a second successive relegation looked a distinct possibility. As it was, the club finished in its lowest league position for thirty-two years.

JOHN BROCK

NORWICH CITY

M	DATE	COMP	VEN	OPPONENTS	RESULT	HT	LP	GOAL SCORERS/GOAL TIMES	ATT.
1	A 13	EL	A	Luton Town	W 3-1	0-0	8	Newsome 14, 55, Adams 70	(27064)
2	19	EL	H	Sunderland	D 0-0	0-0	8		16739
3	26	EL	A	Birmingham City	L 1-3	0-1	15	Sheron 88	(19267)
4	30	EL	H	Oldham Athletic	W 2-1	0-0	7	Bowen 56, Johnson 80	14816
5	S 2	EL	H	Port Vale	W 2-1	2-1	5	Johnson 19, Fleck 24	13908
6	9	EL	A	Sheffield United	L 1-2	1-1	8	Ward 17	(11205)
7	13	EL	A	Wolverhampton Wand	W 2-0	0-0	4	Johnson 59, Ward 68	(27064)
8	16	EL	H	Millwall	D 0-0	0-0	5		15952
9	20	CC 2/1	H	**Torquay United**	**W 6-1**	**3-0**		**Akinbiyi 15, 46, Crook 19, Sheron 44, 58, Gore 81(og)**	**7542**
10	23	EL	A	Grimsby Town	D 2-2	1-2	5	Fleck 20, Akinbiyi 90	(5901)
11	30	EL	H	Leicester City	L 0-1	0-0	10		18435
12	O 4	CC 2/2	A	**Torquay United**	**W 3-2**	**0-0**		**Ullathorne 65, Eadie 86, Mills 88**	**(1790)**
13	7	EL	A	Stoke City	D 1-1	1-0	9	Akinbiyi 32	(12016)
14	14	EL	H	Barnsley	W 3-1	0-1	7	Newsome 53, Johnson 62, Fleck 72	14002
15	21	EL	A	Charlton Athletic	D 1-1	0-0	9	Bowen 73	(13369)
16	25	CC 3	H	**Bradford City**	**D 0-0**	**0-0**			**11649**
17	29	EL	H	Tranmere Rovers	D 1-1	1-0	8	Johnson 11	15513
18	N 4	EL	A	Huddersfield Town	L 2-3	0-1	9	Ward 65, 77	(13747)
19	7	CC 3R	A	**Bradford City**	**W 5-3**	**2-1**		**Ward 11, 34, 88, Fleck 91, Johnson 109**	**(8665)**
20	11	EL	H	Crystal Palace	W 1-0	1-0	8	Johnson 44	14156
21	19	EL	H	Ipswich Town	W 2-1	1-0	6	Newsome 8, Fleck 71	17862
22	21	EL	A	West Bromwich Albion	W 4-1	1-1	4	Fleck 45, Scott 48, Adams 57, Ward 66	(13680)
23	26	EL	A	Watford	W 2-0	1-0	2	Ward 31, Scott 46	(7798)
24	29	CC 4	H	**Bolton Wanderers**	**D 0-0**	**0-0**			**13820**
25	D 2	EL	H	Stoke City	L 0-1	0-0	3		15707
26	9	EL	A	Grimsby Town	D 2-2	1-1	4	Ward 33, Eadie 62	13283
27	17	EL	A	Leicester City	L 2-3	2-1	8	Eadie 1, Fleck 31	(14251)
28	20	CC 4R	A	**Bolton Wanderers**	**D 0-0**	**0-0**			**(8736)**
29	23	EL	A	Portsmouth	L 0-1	0-0	9		(9966)
30	26	EL	H	Southend United	L 0-1	0-0	11		17029
31	30	EL	H	Reading	D 3-3	1-1	10	Johnson 21, Ward 48, Fleck 52	13556
32	J 1	EL	A	Derby County	L 1-2	0-1	11	Fleck 64	(16714)
33	6	FAC 3	H	**Brentford**	**L 1-2**	**0-1**		**Newsome 65**	**10082**
34	10	CC QF	H	**Birmingham City**	**D 1-1**	**0-0**		**Fleck 69**	**13028**
35	14	EL	A	Sunderland	W 1-0	1-0	6	Ward 10	(14983)
36	20	EL	H	Luton Town	L 0-1	0-1	8		12474
37	24	CC QFR	A	**Birmingham City**	**L 1-2**	**0-0**		**Molby 78**	**(21097)**
38	F 4	EL	H	Birmingham City	D 1-1	0-0	10	Ward 74	12612
39	10	EL	A	Oldham Athletic	L 0-2	0-1	12		(5604)
40	17	EL	H	Wolverhampton Wand	L 2-3	2-2	12	Crook 24, Eadie 25	14691
41	24	EL	A	Millwall	L 1-2	0-0	14	Milligan 84	(8218)
42	28	EL	H	Sheffield United	D 0-0	0-0	13		10945
43	M 2	EL	A	Southend United	D 1-1	0-1	13	Bradshaw 64	(6208)
44	9	EL	H	Portsmouth	D 1-1	1-1	14	Milligan 14	13004
45	16	EL	A	Reading	W 3-0	1-0	13	Prior 16, Eadie 55, O'Neil 90	(8501)
46	20	EL	A	Port Vale	L 0-1	0-1	13		(6085)
47	23	EL	H	Derby County	W 1-0	0-0	12	Goss 66	15348
48	30	EL	H	Charlton Athletic	L 0-1	0-0	14		13434
49	A 2	EL	A	Barnsley	D 2-2	1-1	14	Fleck 3, Newman 88	(6375)
50	6	EL	A	Tranmere Rovers	D 1-1	1-0	16	Eadie 29	(6613)
51	8	EL	H	Huddersfield Town	W 2-0	1-0	16	Fleck 62, Akinbiyi 81	13021
52	14	EL	A	Ipswich Town	L 1-2	0-1	16	Cureton 62	(20355)
53	20	EL	H	West Bromwich Albion	D 2-2	0-1	16	Cureton 78, Eadie 84	14667
54	27	EL	H	Watford	L 1-2	0-1	17	Crook 55	14188
55	M 5	EL	A	Crystal Palace	W 1-0	1-0	16	Hopkin 5(og)	(19354)

Best Home League Attendance: 18435 v Leicester City   Smallest: 10945 v Sheffield United   Average: 14580

Goal Scorers:

EL(59): Ward(10),Fleck(10),Johnson(7),Eadie(6),Newsome(4),Akinbiyi(3),Adams(2),Milligan(2),Scott(2),Cureton(2),Crook(2),Bowen(2),Newman(1),Sheron(1), Bradshaw(1),O'Neil(1),Prior(1),Goss(1),Opponent(s)(1)

CC(16): Ward(3),Fleck(2),Akinbiyi(2),Sheron(2),Opponent(s)(1),Eadie(1),Ullathorne(1),Crook(1),Molby(1),Mills(1),Johnson(1)

FAC(1): Newsome(1)

(F) Adams	(F) Akinbiyi	(D) Bowen	(F) Bradshaw	((M) Carey	(M) Crook	(F) Cureton	(M) Eadie	(F) Fleck	(M) Goss	(G) Gunn	(M) Johnson	(G) Marshall	(M) Milligan	(D) Mills	(M) Molby	(D) Newman	(D) Newsome	(M) O'Neil	(D) Polston	(D) Prior	(D) Quinn	(F) Scott	(M) Sheron	(M) Simpson	(M) Sutch	(D) Ullathorne	(F) Ward	(F) Wright		
X	X	X					X			X	X1		X2	X			X			S3	X					S1	S2	X	T.West	1
X	X	X					X			X	X1		X	X			S2		X	S			X2						I.Hemley	2
X	X	X				S2	X			X	X2		X1	X			X			X			X		S1				R.Poulain	3
X	X	X		S			X	X1		X	X			X			X		X	X			S1		X	X			A.D'Urso	4
X	S	X					X	X		X	X2			X			X		X1	S1		S2			X	X	X	X	D.Orr	5
X	S3	X			X2		X	X1		X	X3		S2	X		S1	X			X								X	A.Butler	6
X	X	X			X1		X	X		X	X		S1	X			X			X						S	X		T.West	7
X	S1	X			X2		X	X		X	X		S2	X			X			X						S	X	X1	J.Kirkby	8
	X	X		S2	X2		X1			X3	X		S3				X	S1		X			X	X	X				R.D.Furnandiz	9
X2	X	X			X		X	X3		X	X					S3	X			X			S2		X1	S1			T.Heilbron	10
X1	X	X			X		X	X2		X	X					X	S1	S	X	X			S2			X			N.Barry	11
X	X1			X			S2	S1		X		S	X	X		X		X	X	X			X2			X			J.Rushton	12
X1	X				X		X2			X	X		S1			X	X3	S3	X	X			S2			X			G.Cain	13
	S	X			X		X			X	X	S	X			X	X	S	X	X				X1		X	X		E.Lomas	14
	S	X			X		X			X	X	S	X			X	X	S	X	X						X	X		P.Rejer	15
	S	X			X		X	S1		X	X		X1			X	X	S	X	X						X	X		D.Orr	16
	S2	X3			X1		X	X2		X	X		S1			X	X	S3	X	X						X	X		G.Singh	17
	X1				X		X	S1		X	X	S	S	X		X			X	X						X	X		E.Lomas	18
	S1		X		X		X	X1		X	X		X	S2		X1			X2	X						X	X		N.Barry	19
S1	S2	X	X		X1		X	X		X	X2	S					X			X						X	X		T.West	20
X	S2	X	X1				X			X			X2				X	X		X		S				S1	X	X	K.Lynch	21
X	S2	X1		S1			X2			X		S					X	X	X	X		X			X	X	X	X	J.Kirkby	22
X2		X	S1		S2		S3	X3		X							X	X	X	X		X			X1	X	X	X	S.Bennett	23
X		X		X1			X	X		X		S					X	X	X	X		S1			S	X	X	X	G.Singh	24
X	S1	X	S				X	X		X		S					X	X	X	X		X			X1	X	X	X	I.Hemley	25
X		X		X			X	X1		X							X	S	X	X		S1			S	X	X	X	R.Furnandiz	26
S1		X		X			X1	X2		X		S	X				X		X	X		S2				X	X	X	T.Heilbron	27
S1		X		X			X	X1		X		S	X		S		X		X	X					X	X	X		D.Allison	28
X		X		X			X2			X	X1	S					X		X	X		S2				X	X		G.Pooley	29
X		X					X2	S1	X	X		X1			S3	X	X3		X	X		S2				X	X		D.Orr	30
X		X					X	S1	X	X	X1			X2	S2	X	X		X	X		S				X	X		W.Burns	31
X		X		X2			S2	X	X	X		S3			S1		X3	X	X1	X						X	X		J.Rushton	32
X	X1	X3					S2	X2	X	X					X	X	S3		X	X						S1	X	X	J.Kirkby	33
X	X	X					X	X		X					X	X1	X3	S1	S2	X						S3	X2	X	R.Poulain	34
X	X	X					X	X2		X					X	S	X1	X	S2	X						S1	X	X	G.Cain	35
X	X2	X3					X1	X	S1	X					X	S2	X	X	X	X		S3						X	C.Wilkes	36
X		X					X1	X		X					X	S	X	X	X	X								X	R.Gifford	37
X	X2	X1	X		X			X	S3	X	X3					S1			X	X		S2						X	A.Butler	38
X	X1		X			X3	S1		X2	X2	S2		X	X		S3	X		X	X								X	T.E.West	39
X		X		S2	X2	S1	X	X1		X	X						X		X	X								X	A.D'Urso	40
X	S2	X	S		X1		X		S1	X			X				X		X	X		X1						X2	K.Leach	41
X2	X1		X		X		X	S1	S	X	X		X				X		S2	X		X							N.Barry	42
X			X	X1	X		X	S1	X1	X						X	X	X	S	S		S						X	W.C.Burns	43
X			X		X		X	S1	X1	X			X				X	X	X	X								X	P.Taylor	44
X		X			X2	S	X1	X	X	X						X	S2		X	S1		X							J.Brandwood	45
X		X			X2	S1	X	X1	X3	X	S2		X	X		X	S3		X	X									C.Wilkes	46
X		X			X1	X2	X3	X	X	X			X	S1		X			S3	X									I.Hemley	47
X	S2	X			X		X1	X2		X			X	S1		X			X	X							X		R.Poulina	48
X		X			X		X	S3	X2	X3	X1		X	S2		X			S1	X						X			K.M.Lynch	49
X2		X			X			X	X		X		X	S	S	X			X	X				X1			X		T.Heilbron	50
X	X2	X			X1	S2	X3	X		X			X	S3		X				X					S1	X			A.Butler	51
X	X2	X			X		X2	X		X		X	S3			X3			X	X		X1	S1			X			J.Rushton	52
X		X		S1			X	S2	X	X		X	S3			X3			X	X		X1	X2			X			U.Rennie	53
X			S1	S3	X3	X1		X	X2	X			X			X			S2	X	X						X		S.Mathieson	54
X	S				X			X	S				X	X	X				X	X	X	X					S1	X	X1	G.Singh	55
40	13	30	18	6	27	3	29	37	9	43	23	3	21	8	3	15	26	12	27	42	1	5	2	1	7	26	28	1	EL Appearances	
2	9	1	3	3	1	8	2	4	7	0	3	0	7	6	0	8	1	7	3	2	0	7	5	0	6	3	0	0	EL Sub Appearances	
4+1	2+1	6	3	2+1	4	0	6+1	5+2	0	7	3+1	1	4	1+2	2	2	5	4+1	5	6+1	0	0+2	2	1	2	5+1	6	0	CC Appearances	
1	0	1	1	0	0	0	0+1	1	1	1	0	0	0	0	0	0	1	1	0+1	1	0	0	0	0	0	0+1	1	1	0	FAC Appearances	

Also Played: (M) Rush S1(2).

265

NORWICH CITY

CLUB RECORDS

BIGGEST VICTORIES
League: 10-2 v Coventry City, Division 3(S), 15.3.1930.
8-0 v Walsall, Division 3(S), 29.12.1951.
F.A. Cup: 8-0 v Sutton United, 4th Round, 28.1.1989.
League Cup: 7-1 v Halifax Town, 4th Round, 27.11.1963.

BIGGEST DEFEATS
League: 0-7 v Walsall, Division 3(S), 13.9.1930.
0-7 v Sheffield Wednesday, Division 2, 19.11.1938.
F.A. Cup: 0-6 v Luton Town, 2nd Round, 10.12.1927.
0-6 v Manchester City, 4th Round, 24.1.1981.
League Cup: 1-6 v Manchester City, 2nd Round 2nd replay, 29.9.1975.

MOST POINTS
3 points a win: 84, Division 2, 1985-86.
2 points a win: 64, Division 3(S), 1950-51.

MOST GOALS SCORED
99, Division 3(S), 1952-53.
Ackerman 20, Gavin 20, Johnston 15, Summers 10, Ashman 9, Kinsey 7, McCrohan 7, Rattray 5, Adams 3, Coxon 2, Opponents 1.

MOST GOALS CONCEDED
100, Division 3(S), 1946-47.

MOST FIRST CLASS MATCHES IN A SEASON
60 - 1972-73 (League 42, FA Cup 3, League Cup 7, Texaco Cup 8).

MOST LEAGUE WINS
26, Division 3(S), 1951-52.

MOST LEAGUE DRAWS
23, Division 1, 1978-79.

MOST LEAGUE DEFEATS
24, Division 3(S), 1930-31 & 1946-47. Division 2, 1938-39.

INDIVIDUAL CLUB RECORDS

MOST GOALS IN A SEASON
Ralph Hunt: 31 goals in 1955-56, Division 3(S).

MOST GOALS IN A MATCH
5. Roy Hollis v Walsall, Division 3(S), 29.12.1951.
5. T Hunt v Coventry City, 10-2, Division 3(S), 15.3.1930.

OLDEST PLAYER
Albert Sturgess, 42 years 249 days v Millwall Athletic, Division 3(S), 14.2.1925.

YOUNGEST PLAYER
Ian Davies, 17 years 29 days (sub) v Birmingham City, Division 1, 27.4.1974.

MOST CAPPED PLAYER
Mark Bowen (Wales) 34.

BEST PERFORMANCES

League: 1950-51: Matches played 46, Won 25, Drawn 14, Lost 7, Goals for 82, Goals against 45, Points 64. Second in Division 3(S).
Highest Position: 3rd in Premier League, 1992-93.
F.A. Cup: Semi-finalists 1958-59, 1988-89.
Most recent success: 1991-92: 3rd Round Barnsley 1-0; 4th Round Millwall 2-1; 5th Round Notts County 3-0, 6th Round Southampton 0-0,2-1 (aet); Semi-final Sunderland 0-1.
League Cup: Winners in 1961-62.
Most recent success: 1984-85: 2nd Round Preston North End 3-3, 6-1; 3rd Round Aldershot 0-0, 4-0; 4th Round Notts County 3-0; 5th Round Grimsby Town 1-0; Semi-final Ipswich Town 0-1,2-0; Final Sunderland 1-0.
Europe: 1993-94: 1st Round Vitesse Arnhem 0-0,0-3; 2nd Round Bayern Munich 1-2,1-1; 3rd Round Inter Milan 0-1,0-1.

ADDITIONAL INFORMATION
PREVIOUS NAMES
None.

PREVIOUS LEAGUES
Southern League.

Club colours: Yellow shirts with green trim, green shorts with yellow trim, yellow socks with green tops.
Change colours:

Reserves League: Avon Insurance Football Combination.

DIVISIONAL RECORD

	Played	Won	Drawn	Lost	For	Against	Points
Division 1/P	826	257	251	318	970	1,177	930
Division 2	886	343	224	319	1,290	1,243	971
Division 3	92	46	24	22	171	116	116
Division 3(S)	1,124	423	291	410	1,779	1,725	1,137
Total	**2,928**	**1,069**	**790**	**1,069**	**4,210**	**4,261**	**3,154**

RECORDS AND STATISTICS

COMPETITIONS

Div 1/P	Div.2	Div.3	Div.3(S)	A/Scot	Texaco
1972-74	1934-39	1958-60	1920-34	1975-76	1972-73
1975-81	1960-72		1939-58	1976-77	1973-74
1982-85	1974-75		1977-78	1974-75
1986-95	1981-82		**UEFA**	1978-79	
	1985-86		1993-94		
	1995-				

HONOURS

Division 2	Division 3(S)	League Cup
1971-72	1933-34	1961-62
1985-86		1984-85

MOST APPEARANCES

Kevin Keelan 680 (1963-80)

Year	League	FA Cup	Lge Cup	Others
1963-64	16		1	
1964-65	23	1		
1965-66	42	4	1	
1966-67	39	3	1	
1967-68	30	3	3	
1968-69	32	1	3	
1969-70	33		1	
1970-71	38	1	4	
1971-72	42	1	5	
1972-73	42	3	7	7
1973-74	42	1	7	4
1974-75	38	1	9	3
1975-76	42	5	3	3
1976-77	38	1	2	3
1977-78	26	2	1	1
1978-79	22	1	3	
1979-80	26	3	6	
	571	31	57	21

MOST GOALS IN A CAREER

John Gavin - 132 (1949-58)

Year	League	FA Cup
1949-50	1	
1950-51	17	1
1951-52	19	1
1952-53	20	
1953-54	13	1
1954-55	6	
1955-56	13	2
1956-57	16	
1957-58	17	5
Total	**122**	**10**

Current leading goalscorer: Robert Fleck 90 (1987-92 & 1995-96)

MANAGERS

A Turner 1902-05, J Bowman 1905-07, J McEwen 1907-09,
A Turner 1909-10, J Stansfield 1910-15, F Buckley 1919-20,
C O'Hagan 1920.

Name	Seasons	Best	Worst
A Gosnell	1921-26	11(3S)	18(3S)
J Stansfield	1926	-	-
C Potter	1926-29	16(3S)	17(3S)
J Kerr	1929-33	3(3S)	22(3S)
T Parker	1933-37	11(2)	1(3S)
R Young	1937-39	14(2)	14(2)
A Jewell	1939	21(2)	21(2)
R Young	1939-45	-	-
D Lochhead	1945-46	-	-
C Spiers	1946-47	21(3S)	21(3S)
D Lochhead	1947-50	10(3S)	21(3S)
N Low	1950-55	2(3S)	11(3S)
T Parker	1955-57	7(3S)	24(3S)
A Macaulay	1957-61	4(2)	8(3S)
W Reid	1961-62	17(2)	17(2)
G Swindin	1962	-	-
R Ashman	1962-66	6(2)	17(2)
L Morgan	1966-69	9(2)	13(2)
R Saunders	1969-73	20(1)	11(2)
J Bond	1973-80	10(1)	3(2)
K Brown	1980-87	5(1)	3(2)
D Stringer	1987-92	4(1)	18(1)
Mike Walker	1992-94	3(P)	3(P)
John Deehan	1994-95	12(P)	20(P)
Martin O'Neill	1995	-	-
Gary Megson	1995-96	-	-
Mike Walker	1996-		

RECORD TRANSFER FEE RECEIVED

Amount	Club	Player	Date
£5,000,000	Blackburn Rovers	Chris Sutton	7/94
£2,250,000	Newcastle Utd	Ruel Fox	2/94
£2,100,000	Chelsea	Robert Fleck	8/92
£1,200,000	Glasgow Rangers	Dale Gordon	11/91
£1,200,000	Chelsea	Andy Townsend	7/90
£1,200,000	Arsenal	Andy Linighan	7/90

RECORD TRANSFER FEE PAID

Amount	Club	Player	Date
£1,000,000	Leeds United	Jon Newsome	6/94
£925,000	Port Vale	Darren Beckford	6/91
£700,000	Derby County	Paul Blades	7/90
£580,000	Glasgow Rangers	Robert Fleck	12/87

LONGEST LEAGUE RUNS

of undefeated matches:	20 (31.8.1950 - 11.1.1951)	of league matches w/out a win:	25 (22.9.1956 - 2.3.1957)
of undefeated home matches:	31 (21.8.1971 - 2.12.1972)	of undefeated away matches:	12 (14.9.1985 - 8.3.1986)
without home win:	12 (29.9.1956 - 2.3.1957)	without an away win:	41 (3.9.1977 - 18.8.1979)
of league wins:	10 (23.11.1985 - 1.2.1986)	of home wins:	12 (15.3.1952 - 4.10.1952)
of league defeats:	7 (4.9.1935 - 5.10.1935, 12.1.1957 - 2.3.1957)	of away wins:	5 (3.9.1988 - 19.11.1988)
	(1.4.1995 - 14.5.1995)		

NORWICH CITY

PLAYERS NAME / Honours	Ht	Wt	Birthdate	Birthplace / Transfers	Contract Date	Clubs	League	L/Cup	FA Cup	Other	Lge	L/C	FAC	Oth
G O A L K E E P E R S														
Gunn Bryan	6.2	12.5	22/12/63	Thurso		Aberdeen	15	4	1	1				
S: 6, u21.9, Y, S, B.3				£150000	23/10/86	Norwich City	347	32	25	22				
Marshall Andrew J	6.2	12.7	14/04/74	Bury St. Edmunds	06/07/93	Norwich City	23+1	2	2+1					
D E F E N D E R S														
Brownrigg Andrew D	6.0	11.13	02/08/76	Sheffield	03/01/95	Hereford United	8							
S: Y				£100000	09/03/95	Norwich City								
				Loan	01/12/96	Kettering Town								
Mills Daniel	5.11	11.09	18/05/77	Norwich		Norwich City	8+6	1+2				1		
Newman Robert N	6.2	12.0	13/12/63	B'ford on Avon	05/10/81	Bristol City	382+12	29+1	27	33	52	2	2	5
FRT'86				£600000	15/07/91	Norwich City	127+19	19+1	11	7	13	2	1	
Polston John D	5.11	11.3	10/06/68	Walthamstow	16/07/85	Tottenham Hotspur	17+7	3+1						
E: Y6				£250000	24/07/90	Norwich City	166+6	16+1	16+1	9	6	2		1
Prior Spencer	6.3	12.10	22/04/71	Southend	22/05/89	Southend United	135	9	5	7	3			1
				£200000	24/06/93	Norwich City	67+7	10+1	0+2	2	1	1		
Wright Jonathan	5.8	11.04	24/11/75	Belfast	01/07/94	Norwich City	2+1							
M I D F I E L D														
Carey Shaun P	5.9	10.06	13/05/76	Kettering	01/07/94	Norwich City	6+3	2+1						
Eadie Darren M	5.8	10.6	10/06/75	Chippenham	05/02/93	Norwich City	60+12	15+1	4+1	1+1	11	2	1	
E: u21.2, Y2														
Johnson Andrew J	6.0	11.6	02/05/74	Bristol	04/03/92	Norwich City	32+7	5+1	1		8	1		
E: Y1														
Milligan Michael J	5.8	11.0	20/02/67	Manchester	02/03/85	Oldham Athletic	161+1	19+1	12	4	17	1	1	
Ei:1, B1, u21.1				£1000000	24/08/90	Everton	16+1	0+1	1	4+1	1			1
				£600000	17/07/91	Oldham Athletic	117	11	9	1	6	1		1
				£800000	27/06/94	Norwich City	46+8	8	3		4			
O'Neil Keith P	6.1	11.0	16/02/76	Dublin	01/07/94	Norwich City	12+8	4+1	1		1			
Rush Matthew	5.11	12.10	06/08/71	Hackney	24/03/90	West Ham United	29+19	4		2+1	5			
				Loan	12/03/93	Cambridge United	4+6							
				Loan	10/01/94	Swansea City	13		4					
				£330000	18/08/95	Norwich City	0+1							
Shore James A	5.9	10.09	01/09/77	Bristol		Norwich City (T)								
Simpson Karl	5.7	10.12	18/09/75	Portsmouth		Norwich City (T)								
Sutch Daryl	5.11	10.12	11/09/71	Beccles	06/07/90	Norwich City	49+32	8+3	4+2	2+3	3			
E: u21.4, Y2														
F O R W A R D S														
Adams Neil J	5.8	10.8	23/11/65	Stoke	01/07/85	Stoke City	31+1	3	1	3	4			
E: u21.1; Div1'87; CS'86;				£150000	07/07/86	Everton	17+3	4+1		5+1		1		
Div2'91				Loan	11/01/89	Oldham Athletic	9							
				£100000	21/06/89	Oldham Athletic	93+36	13+2	10+2	1+1	23	1	2	
				£250000	17/02/94	Norwich City	74+15	10+1	4		5	1		
Akinbiyi Adeola P	6.1	12.0	10/10/74	Hackney	05/02/93	Norwich City	19+18	2+2	1+2	0+1	3	2		
				Loan	21/01/94	Hereford United	3+1				2			
				Loan	24/11/94	Brighton & H.A.	7				4			
Bradshaw Carl	6.0	11.0	02/10/68	Sheffield	23/08/86	Sheffield Wed.	16+16	2+2	6+1	1	4		3	
E: Y4				Loan	24/08/86	Barnsley	6							
				£50000	30/09/88	Manchester City	1+4		0+1	0+1				
				£50000	07/09/89	Sheffield United	122+25	10+1	12+1	4	8	2	3	
				£500000	28/07/94	Norwich City	43+4	5	2		2	1		
Cureton Jamie	5.8	10.0	28/08/76	Bristol	05/02/93	Norwich City	12+16	0+1	0+2		6			
E: Y4				Loan	08/09/95	Bournemouth	0+5			0+1				
Fleck Robert	5.10	10.3	11/08/65	Glasgow		Glasgow Rangers	61+24	3+5	1+1	3+4	29	2		3
S: 4, u21.7,Y. SPD'87.				£580000	17/12/87	Norwich City	130+13	13	16+2	7	40	11	11	4
SLC'87'88				£2100000	13/08/92	Chelsea	35+5	7	1		3	1		
				Loan	01/11/93	Partick Thistle	1+1				1			
				Loan	17/12/93	Bolton Wanderers	6+1		1		1			
				Loan	12/01/95	Bristol City	10				1			
				£650000	29/09/95	Norwich City	37+4	5+2	1		10	2		
Scott Keith	6.3	13.4	10/06/67	London		Hinckley United								
GMVC'93, FAT'91'93				Free		Leicester United								
				Free	22/03/90	Lincoln City	7+9	0+1		1+1	2			

Scott continued...											
	£30000	05/07/93	Wycombe Wand.	15	4	8	10	10	2	1	2
	£300000	18/11/93	Swindon Town	43+8	5		3	12	3		1
	£300000	30/12/94	Stoke City	16+2		2		3		1	
		11/11/95	Norwich City	5+7	0+2			2			
	Loan	16/02/96	Bournemouth	8				1			

TRAINEES

Barber Paul		Norwich City (T)
Bellamy Craig		Norwich City (T)
Broughton Drewe		Norwich City (T)
Coote Adrian		Norwich City (T)
Davis Kori		Norwich City (T)
Forbes Adrian		Norwich City (T)
Green Joseph		Norwich City (T)
Hilton Damian		Norwich City (T)
Kenton Darren		Norwich City (T)
Lewis Craig		Norwich City (T)
Llewellyn Christopher		Norwich City (T)
McCullough Stephen		Norwich City (T)
O'Connor Westley		Norwich City (T)
Roche Stewart		Norwich City (T)
Tipple Gaven		Norwich City (T)
Wigger Christopher		Norwich City (T)
Wilson Che		Norwich City (T)
Winston Samuel		Norwich City (T)

THE MANAGER
MIKE WALKER

Date of Birth . . . . 28th November 1945.
Place of Birth . . . . Colwyn Bay.
Date of Appointment . . . . June 1996.

PREVIOUS CLUBS
As Manager. . . . . Colchester United, Norwich City, Everton.
As Reserve Team Manager . . . . Norwich City (Nov.1987 - June 1992).
As a Player . . . . Reading, Shrewsbury, York, Watford, Charlton Ath (Loan),
. . . . Colchester United.

HONOURS
As a Manager
None.

As a Player
Promotion from Div.4 1973-74 & 1976-77.
Wales: under-23 caps.

CARROW ROAD

Norwich NR1 1JE
Tel: 01603 760 760

Capacity 21,994

First game ....v West Ham, Div.2, 31.8.1935.
First floodlit game ....v Sunderland, 17.10.1956.

ATTENDANCES
Highest ....43,984 v Leicester City, FAC 6th Rnd, 30.3.1963.
Lowest..1,801 v Northampton, FLT, 14.8.1982.

OTHER GROUNDS ....Newmarket Road 1902-08.The Nest, Rosary Road 1908-35.
....Carrow Road 1935-

MATCHDAY TICKET PRICES

Category A

Lounges.	£25
Reserved.	£15
Juv.	£10

Category B

Lounges.	£15
Reserved.	£10
Juv.	£5

Match and Ticket Information
Applications to Box Office 28 days before match with payment and SAE.

Ticket Office Telephone no. 01603 761 661

CLUBCALL
0891 12 11 44

Calls cost 39p per minute cheap rate and 49p per minute at all other times.
Call costings correct at time of going to press.

HOW TO GET TO THE GROUND

From the North
Use A140 to junction with Ring Road, then follow signs to Yarmouth (A47). In 3.5 miles at 'T' junction turn right. In half-a-mile turn left into Carrow Road for Norwich City FC.

From the East
Use A47, sign posted Norwich, on entering city keep left into Ring Road for Carrow Road for Norwich City FC.

From the South and West
Use A11, A140 into Norwich and follow signs to Yarmouth (A47) into Ring Road, Carrow Road for Norwich City FC.

Car Parking
Numerous private parks nearby. Multistory parks in Malt House Road and St Andrews Street. Street parking nearby in Rose Lane, Carrow Hill and side streets of King Street. Coaches must park at Lower Clarence Road Car Park.

Nearest Railway Station
Norwich (01603 -1603 632 055)

MATCHDAY PROGRAMME

Programme Editor. . . . . Kevan Platt.

Number of pages . . . . 32.

Price . . . . £1.50.

Subscriptions . . . . £40 for all games (£47 Europe).

Local Newspapers . . . . Eastern Counties Newspapers.

Local Radio Stations . . . . Radio Norfolk, Radio Broadland.

OLDHAM ATHLETIC
(The Latics)
NATIONWIDE LEAGUE DIVISION 1
SPONSORED BY: J D SPORTS

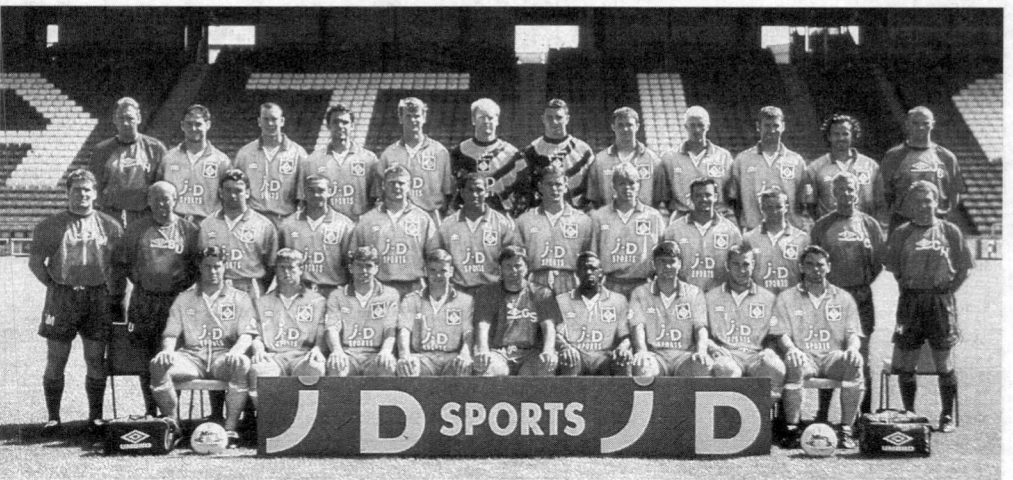

Back Row (L-R): Andy Holden (Res. Coach), Steve Redmond, Richard Graham, Craig Fleming, Richard Jobson, Jon Hallworth, Paul Gerrard, Simon Kay, Ian Olney, Ricky Evans, Lee Richardson, John Bowden (Kit Manager). **Middle Row:** Alexis Moreno (Physio), Billy Urmson (Yth Coach), Rick Holden, Carl Serrant, Darren Lonergan, Martin Pemberton, Paul Bernard, Gunnar Halle, Nicky Banger, David Beresford, Jim Cassell (Chief Scout), Colin Harvey (First Team Coach). **Front Row:** Sean McCarthy, Paul Rickers, Mark Brennan, Nick Henry, Graeme Sharp (Manager), Darren Beckford, Ian Snodin, Chris Makin, Neil Pointon.

OLDHAM ATHLETIC
FORMED IN 1895
TURNED PROFESSIONAL IN 1899
LTD COMPANY IN 1906

PRESIDENT: R Schofield
CHAIRMAN: I H Scott

DIRECTORS
D A Brierley (Vice-Chairman),
G T Butterworth, P Chadwick, J C Slevin,
D R Taylor, N Holden
SECRETARY
J T Cale (0161 624 4972)
COMMERCIAL MANAGER
A Hardy (0161 624 0966)

MANAGER: Graeme Sharp
ASSISTANT MANAGER: Colin Harvey
RESERVE TEAM MANAGER
Andy Holden
YOUTH TEAM MANAGER
Bill Urmson
PHYSIOTHERAPIST
Alexis Moreno

STATISTICIAN FOR THE DIRECTORY
Gordon A Lawton

Phew!...."that was a close shave", were the words on many supporters lips as Latics strung together five wins and two draws from their last nine games to escape the dreaded drop in to the Second Division.

The season started brightly enough with a 3-0 thrashing of newly promoted Huddersfield Town and then Latics celebrated their Centenary with a visit from Manchester United, but from then onwards it was disappointment after disappointment.

Some say Latics involvement in the Anglo Italian Cup was a big mistake and distracted them from the important bread and butter matches at home.

Latics crashed out of the Coca-Cola Cup at the hands of their "bogey" team Tranmere Rovers, the next time Latics beat TRanmere it will be the first for 23 years!!

Autumn saw events pick up slightly with draws against Portsmouth and Grimsby and wins over Reading and Wolves, before another "bogey" team arrived in Southend United to complete their customary win at Boundary Park.

Birmingham City arrived just before Christmas and were duly thrashed 4-0. But from then onwards it was all downhill.

Dreadful results followed against football giants such as Barnsley, Watford, and Reading, and when Second Division Swindon sent us packing in the FA Cup it left a cloud of doom and gloom over Boundary Park, as Latics found themselves next to bottom in the division after a home defeat against Sunderland in mid March.

A run of seven defeats from eight games spelled disaster for Latics fans - had twelve years good work by Joe Royle been thrown away or could another ex Evertonian pair in Graeme Sharp and Colin Harvy turn things around?

The answer thankfully, was yes.

Lee Richardson returned to the side, Gerry Creaney arrived on loan from Manchester City and Latics began to claw their way to safety.

Port Vale were beaten 3-1 at Vale Park, Millwall were beaten at the Den, Stoke City and Luton Town both never had a kick as they were well beaten at Boundary Park and Latics finished the season in eighteenth spot in the League, but it was all too close for many fans.

But as they say in football........there's always next year!

G A LAWTON.

OLDHAM ATHLETIC

League: 18th   FA Cup: 4th Rnd   Coca-Cola Cup: 2nd Rnd

M	DATE	COMP	VEN	OPPONENTS	RESULT	HT	LP	GOAL SCORERS/GOAL TIMES	ATT.
1	A 12	EL	H	Huddersfield Town	W 3-0	1-0	7	Brennan 35, 63, Richardson 69	10259
2	19	EL	A	Barnsley	L 1-2	0-1	12	McCarthy 83	(8793)
3	26	EL	H	Sheffield United	W 2-1	0-0	6	Banger 63, McCarthy 67	6851
4	30	EL	A	Norwich City	L 1-2	0-0	10	Halle 46	(14816)
5	S 2	EL	A	Stoke City	W 1-0	0-0	8	Overson 69(og)	(8663)
6	5	AIC	A	Ancona	L 0-1	0-0			(311)
7	9	EL	H	West Bromwich Albion	L 1-2	1-1	9	Bernard 44	8397
8	12	EL	H	Ipswich Town	D 1-1	0-0	9	McCarthy 78	5622
9	16	EL	A	Charlton Athletic	D 1-1	1-0	12	McCarthy 7	(8926)
10	19	CC 2/1	A	Tranmere Rovers	L 0-1	0-0			(5223)
11	23	EL	H	Crystal Palace	W 3-1	0-1	9	McCarthy 49, Brennan 67, Banger 84	6586
12	30	EL	A	Birmingham City	D 0-0	0-0	8		(17269)
13	O 4	CC 2/2	H	Tranmere Rovers	L 1-3	1-1		Halle 24	5335
14	7	EL	H	Portsmouth	D 1-1	0-0	7	McCarthy 79	5937
15	14	EL	A	Grimsby Town	D 1-1	1-0	9	Richardson 43	(5509)
16	21	EL	H	Reading	W 2-1	1-1	8	Richardson 24, Beresford 66	5709
17	28	EL	A	Derby County	L 1-2	0-1	7	McCarthy 63	(11545)
18	N 5	EL	H	Port Vale	D 2-2	1-1	9	Wilkinson 6, Richardson 86(pen)	5138
19	8	AIC	H	Perugia	W 2-0	0-0		McCarthy 52, Wilkinson 86	3760
20	11	EL	A	Luton Town	D 1-1	0-1	11	Halle 65	(6047)
21	18	EL	A	Wolverhampton Wand	W 3-1	0-1	7	Makin 62, McCarthy 64, Beresford 78	(23128)
22	21	EL	H	Millwall	D 2-2	1-0	10	McCarthy 44, Barlow 80	6161
23	25	EL	H	Southend United	L 0-1	0-0	13		6474
24	D 2	EL	A	Portsmouth	L 1-2	1-1	14	Beckford 20	(6002)
25	9	EL	A	Crystal Palace	D 2-2	0-2	15	Vonk 63, Redmond 72	(12709)
26	13	AIC	A	Genoa	D 0-0	0-0			(1200)
27	16	EL	H	Birmingham City	W 4-0	1-0	12	Poole 26(og), Francis 56(og), Barlow 58, Halle 68	6602
28	23	EL	H	Watford	D 0-0	0-0	12		5878
29	26	EL	A	Tranmere Rovers	L 0-2	0-0	14		9787
30	J 6	FAC 3	A	Barnsley	D 0-0	0-0			(9751)
31	13	EL	H	Barnsley	L 0-1	0-0	17		6029
32	20	EL	A	Huddersfield Town	D 0-0	0-0	17		(13013)
33	23	FAC 3R	H	Barnsley	W 2-1	1-0		Beckford 17, Beckford 68(pen)	6670
34	F 3	EL	A	Sheffield United	L 1-2	1-1	17	Hughes 35	(10956)
35	10	EL	H	Norwich City	W 2-0	1-0	16	Makin 12, Barlow 63	5604
36	12	FAC 4	A	Swindon Town	L 0-1	0-0			(9508)
37	24	EL	H	Charlton Athletic	D 1-1	0-0	18	Richardson 65	6570
38	27	EL	A	West Bromwich Albion	L 0-1	0-1	19		(10959)
39	M 3	EL	H	Tranmere Rovers	L 1-2	0-1	21	Graham 71	4225
40	9	EL	A	Watford	L 1-2	0-1	21	McCarthy 72	(10961)
41	12	EL	H	Sunderland	L 1-2	1-1	23	Richardson 43	7149
42	16	EL	H	Leicester City	W 3-1	1-0	19	Barlow 18, Serrant 76, Richardson 88(pen)	5582
43	19	EL	A	Ipswich Town	L 1-2	0-0	20	Richardson 72(pen)	(9674)
44	23	EL	A	Sunderland	L 0-1	0-0	22		(20631)
45	30	EL	A	Reading	L 0-2	0-1	22		(7025)
46	A 2	EL	H	Grimsby Town	W 1-0	0-0	22	Barlow 58	5037
47	6	EL	A	Derby County	L 0-1	0-0	22		8119
48	8	EL	A	Port Vale	W 3-1	1-0	22	Barlow 33, Beckford 46, Richardson 78(pen)	(7796)
49	13	EL	H	Wolverhampton Wand	D 0-0	0-0	22		75f92
50	17	EL	A	Leicester City	L 0-2	0-0	22		(12790)
51	20	EL	A	Millwall	W 1-0	0-0	22	Richardson 57	(9574)
52	27	EL	A	Southend United	D 1-1	1-0	20	Creaney 3	(5397)
53	30	EL	H	Stoke City	W 2-0	1-0	18	Richardson 26, Creaney 72	10271
54	M 5	EL	H	Luton Town	W 1-0	0-0	18	Barlow 84	6623

Best Home League Attendance: 10271 v Stoke City   Smallest: 4225 v Tranmere Rovers   Average: 6626

Goal Scorers:

EL(54): McCarthy(10),Barlow(7),Richardson(6),Richardson(5),Halle(3),Opponent(s)(3),Brennan(3),Beresford(2),Beckford(2),Banger(2),Makin(2),Creaney(2),Wilkinson(1), Vonk(1),Graham(1),Serrant(1),Hughes(1),Redmond(1),Bernard(1)

CC(1): Halle(1)

FAC(2): Beckford(2)

AIC(2): Wilkinson(1),McCarthy(1)

(F) Banger	(F) Barlow	(F) Beckford	(M) Beresford	(M) Bernard	(M) Brennan	(D) Fleming	(M) Gannon	(F) Creaney (L)	(G) Gerrard	(M) Graham	(D) Halle	(G) Hallworth	(M) Henry	(M) Hughes	(D) Jobson	(M) Makin	(F) McCarthy	(F) McNiven	(M) Orlygsson	(M) Pemberton	(D) Pointon	(D) Redmond	(M) Richardson	(M) Rickers	(D) Serrant	(M) Snodin	(D) Vonk (L)	(F) Wilkinson (L)	Player	No.
	S		X	X			X		X	X	S		X	X	X	X	X				S1		X			X1			J.Rushton	1
	S1		X	X1			X		X	X	S		X		X	X	X	S			X	S	X						T.West	2
S1			X	X1			X		X	X	S		X		X	X	X	S				X	X1						T.Heilbron	3
S1				X			X		X				X	X2	X	X	X	S2				X	X	X1					A.D'Urso	4
X1			X	X			X		X				X	X	X	X	X	S		S1	X	X	S						K.Lynch	5
S2				X	X3				S				X	X	X	X1	X	X			S	S3	X2	S1					N.Known	6
S1				X					X				S	X	X	X	X	S			X	X	X						N.S.Barry	7
			S1	X	X1		X		X	S			X		X	X	X				X	X	X						W.C.Burns	8
X1			S1	X	X1		X		X	S			X		X	X	X				X	X	X						A.Butler	9
S			S1	X	X1		X		X	X	X		X		X	X	X				X	X	X						D.B.Allison	10
X			S				X		X	X	X		X	X	X	X	X				X	X	X		S				K.A.Leach	11
X1			S1				X		X	X			X	X	X	X	X				X	X				S			R.D.Furnandiz	12
			X		X				X	X	X1		X	S	X	X	X				X	X				S			C.R.Wilks	13
		S2	X1						X	X			X	X	X	X	X				X	X					S1		J.W.Lloyd	14
		S2	S1		X				X	X	X1		X	S	X	X	X2	X			X						X		R.Poulain	15
		X1	S1		X2				X	X	X		X	S	X	X	X					S2	X				X		M.A.Bailey	16
			S1		X2				X	X	X				X	X	X					S2	X1				X	X	C.R.Wilkes	17
			S1		X		X		X	X	X	S			X	X1						X	X	S			X	X	P.R.Richards	18
			S1		X		X		S	S	S		X			S3	S2	X2	X			X	X3	X	X		X1		(—)	19
			S1				X		X	X			X	X		X	X1					X	X	X	S	X	X	X1	A.D'Urso	20
			X						X				X	X		X	X1					X	X	X	S	X	X	X	W.Burns	21
X			X			S1			X	S			X	X		X						X	X	X	X	X	S	X	K.M.Lynch	22
X	S1		X						X				X	S		X						S2	X2	X	X	X	S	X1	E.K.Wolstenholme	23
			X	X			X		X	X				X1	S	X				S1		X	X		X	X			G.Barber	24
	X1		S1				X		X1				S1			X						X	X		X	X3			A.Butler	25
	X3		X		X2				X	X			X1	S		S1		X	X			S3	X	S2		X			(—)	26
	X		S		X				X	X	X		S			X	X					X			X	X			S.J.Baines	27
	X		S2		X2				X	X	X		S			X	X					X			X	X1			G.Singh	28
	X	S2			S1				X	X	X		S			X	X		X2	X1		X			X				R.Poulain	29
	X		S						X	X	X		S			X	X		X	X		X			X				G.Cain	30
	X		S2						X	X	X		S			X	X	X	X1			X			X				P.Rejer	31
	X		S						X	X	X		S			X	X		X			X			S	X			U.Rennie	32
	X1								X	X	X		S			X	X		S1			X			S	X			G.Cain	33
	X1								X	X	X		S			X	X		S1			X			S	X			P.Richards	34
	X1								X	X	X		S			X	X		X1			X			S	X	S		T.E.West	35
S1	X				X				X	X	X		S				X		X1			X			X	X	S		P.Danson	36
S1	X1				S1				X	X	X		S				X					X	X	X1		X			R.Pearson	37
S1	S2	X	X2						X	X	X		S				X1					X	X			X			A.Butler	38
X	S1	X	X						X	X	X1		S		S1		X					X	X	X1		X			G.B.Frankland	39
X1	S1					X	X		X	X	X		S2		X	X						X	X	X2		X			F.Stretton	40
X2		S2				X	X1		X	S1	X		S		X	X						X	X		S	X			K.J.Breen	41
X			S1			X			X	X	X		S		X							X	X	X1	X	X			T.Heilbron	42
X			S1						X	X	X		X		X							X	X	X	X	X			G.Barber	43
X			S1			X1			X	X	X		S									X	X	X	X	X			K.Lynch	44
X2	X		S1					X	X	X												S2	X1	X	X	X			M.Pierce	45
X	X							X	X	X			S									X	X	X	X	X			G.Singh	46
X	S3	S2							X1	X	X									S1		X2	X	X	X	X	X3		N.Barry	47
X	X	S							X	X					X		S		X1			X	X	X	X	X			R.Poulain	48
X2	X	S3			S1		S2	X3	X						X		X	X				X	X	X	X	X			I.Cruikshanks	49
X	S1	S3				S		X1	X		X				X							X	X1	X	X	X			J.Brandwood	50
X1	S				X			X			X				S1		X		X1			X	X	X	X	X3			G.Pooley	51
S	X							X			X				X		S	S		X		X	X	X	X	X			G.Singh	52
S	X					X		X		X	S		X		X							X	X	X	X	X			K.Leach	53
S1	X1					X		X2		X	X		X						S2			X2	X	X	X	X	S2		M.A.Riley	54
8	22	12	8	7	22	8	21	5	36	31	37	10	14	10	11	39	30	14	15	0	3	37	28	23	20	24	5	4	EL Appearances	
5	4	8	20	0	2	1	1	0	0	1	0	0	0	0	4	0	0	5	1	1	2	1	3	0	0	0	2	0	EL Sub Appearances	
0	0	0	1+1	1	2	0	1	0	2	2	2	0	2	2	0	2	2	0	0	0	1	0	0	1	0	0	0	0	CC Appearances	
0+1	3	1	0	0	2	0	0	0	3	3	3	0	0	3	0	2	2	1	0	0	3	0	0	3	0	1+1	2	1	FAC Appearances	
0+1	1	0+1	2	1	2	0	3	0	1	1	3	2	1	0+2	1	1+1	3	3	0	0+1	0	1+1	3	1+2	2	0	0	1	AIC Appearances	

Also Played: (G) Darnborough S(21). (D) Lonergan S(26,45), S(48), X1(49). (F) Olney S1(13), X2(14).

OLDHAM ATHLETIC

CLUB RECORDS

BIGGEST VICTORIES
League: 11-0 v Southport, Division 4, 26.12.1962
F.A. Cup: 11-1 v Lytham, Round 1, 18.11.1925
League Cup: 7-0 v Scarborough, Round 3, 25.10.1989

BIGGEST DEFEATS
League: 4-13 v Tranmere Rovers, Division 3N, 26.12.1935
0-9 v Hull City, Division 3N, 5.4.1958
F.A. Cup: 0-6 v Huddersfield Town, Round 3, 13.1.1932
0-6 v Tottenham H, Round 3, 14.1.1933 (h)
League Cup: 1-7 v Sunderland, Round 2, 24.9.1962

MOST POINTS
3 points a win: 88, Division 2, 1990-91
2 points a win: 62, Division 3, 1973-74

MOST GOALS
95, 1962-63, Division 4.
Lister 30, Whittaker 17, Colquhoun 13, Ledger 8, Frizzell 5, Johnstone 5, Bowie5, Williams 5, McCall 4, og 3

MOST LEAGUE GOALS CONCEDED
95, Division 2, 1934-35

MOST FIRST CLASS MATCHES IN A SEASON
65 (46 League, 9 FA Cup, 9 League Cup, 1 Zenith Data) 1989-90

MOST LEAGUE WINS
25, Division 3, 1973-74
25, Division 2, 1990-91

MOST LEAGUE DRAWS
21, Division 2, 1988-89

MOST LEAGUE DEFEATS
26, Division 2, 1934-35; Division 4, 1958-59; Division 4, 1959-60

INDIVIDUAL CLUB RECORDS

MOST GOALS IN A SEASON
Tom Davis 35 (League 33, FAC 2) Div 3N, 1936-37
3 goals four times=12, 2 goals 3 times=6, 1 goal 17 times
Previous holder: W Walsh 32 (1935-36)

MOST GOALS IN A MATCH
7. Eric Gemmill v Chester, Division 3N, 19.1.1953 (11-2)
7. Bert Lister v Southport, Division 4, 20.12.1962
Frank Bunn scored 6 goals against Scarborough, Lge Cup, 25.10.1989, thus setting a record for the competition

OLDEST PLAYER
Bobby Collins, 42 years, 63 days v Rochdale 20.04.1973.

YOUNGEST PLAYER
Eddie Hopkinson, 16 years, 76 days v Crewe Alexandra 12.01.1952

MOST CAPPED PLAYER
Gunnar Halle 53 (Norway)

BEST PERFORMANCES

League: 1990-91: Matches played 46, Won 25, Drawn 13, Lost 8, Goals for 83,Goals against 53, Points 88. First in Division 2
Highest: 1914-15: Second in Division 1
F.A. Cup: 1912-13: 3rd rnd. Bolton Wanderers 2-0, 4th rnd. Nottingham Forest 5-1; 5th rnd. Manchester City 0-0, 2-1; 6th rnd. Everton 1-0; Semi-final Aston Villa 0-1.
1989-90: 3rd rnd. Birmingham City 1-1, 1-0; 4th rnd. Brighton & H.A. 2-1; 5th rnd. Everton 2-2, 1-1, 2-1; 6th rnd. Aston Villa 3-0; Semi-Final Manchester Utd3-3, 1-2
1993-94: 3rd rnd. Derby County 2-1; 4th rnd. Stoke City 0-0, 0-1; 5th rnd.Barnsley 1-0; 6th rnd. Bolton W. 0-1; Semi-Final Manchester Utd 1-1, 1-4
League Cup: 1989-90: 2nd rnd. Leeds Utd 2-1, 2-1; 3rd rnd. Scarborough 7-0; 4th rnd. Arsenal 3-1; 5th rnd. Southampton 2-2, 2-0; Semi-Final West Ham United 6-0, 0-3; Final Nott'm Forest 0-1

DIVISIONAL RECORD

	Played	Won	Drawn	Lost	For	Against	Points
Division 1/P	484	159	129	196	604	713	483
Division 2/1	1,480	551	383	546	2,109	2,129	1,684
Division 3	414	156	96	162	593	609	408
Division 3(N)	658	256	171	231	1,085	1,002	683
Division 4	320	121	70	129	499	513	312
Total	3,356	1,243	849	1,264	4,890	4,966	3,570

ADDITIONAL INFORMATION

PREVIOUS NAME
Pine Villa

PREVIOUS LEAGUE
Lancashire League

Club colours: Royal blue & red hooped shirts, white shorts with blue & red hooped socks.

Change colours:

Reserves League: Pontins Central League Division 1.

RECORDS AND STATISTICS

COMPETITIONS

DIV 1/P	DIV.2/1	DIV.3	DIV.3(N)	DIV.4	TEXACO	A/SCOT
1910-23	1907-10	1963-69	1935-53	1958-63	1974-75	1977-78
1991-94	1923-35	1971-74	1954-58	1969-71		1978-79
	1953-54					1979-80
	1974-91					1980-81
	1994-					

HONOURS

DIVISION 2	DIVISION 3	DIVISION 3(N)
1990-91	1973-74	1952-53

MOST APPEARANCES

IAN T WOOD 562+8 (1965-80)

YEAR	LEAGUE	FA CUP	LGE CUP
1965-66	1		
1966-67	14		
1967-68	25+3	1+1	1
1968-69	40	1	
1969-70	46	3	1
1970-71	45	1	2
1971-72	46	1	2
1972-73	46	2	1
1973-74	44	6	2
1974-75	40	1	1
1975-76	35+2	1	2
1976-77	30+1	3	2
1977-78	33	2	2
1978-79	36	3	
1979-80	36+1	1	2
	517+7	27+1	18

MOST GOALS IN A CAREER

ROGER PALMER - 157 (1980-92)

YEAR	LEAGUE	FA CUP	LGE CUP	OTHER
1980-81	6			
1981-82	7	3		
1982-83	15			
1983-84	13	1		
1984-85	9			
1985-86	15		1	
1986-87	16	1		
1987-88	17	3		
1988-89	15			
1989-90	16	1	3	
1990-91	9			1
1991-92	3	1	1	
Total	141	10	5	1

Current leading goalscorer: Greame Sharpe - 39 (1991-96)

RECORD TRANSFER FEE RECEIVED

AMOUNT	CLUB	PLAYER	DATE
£1,700,000	Aston Villa	Earl Barrett	2/92
£850,000	Everton	Mike Milligan	8/90
£700,000	Manchester Utd	Dennis Irwin	7/90
£350,000	Leicester City	Tommy Wright	7/89

RECORD TRANSFER FEE PAID

AMOUNT	CLUB	PLAYER	DATE
£700,000	Aston Villa	Ian Olney	5/92
£600,000	Everton	Mike Milligan	7/91
£500,000	Everton	Graeme Sharp	7/91
£480,000	Nott'm Forest	David Currie	7/90

MANAGERS

NAME	SEASONS	BEST	WORST
David Ashworth	1906-14	4(1)	6(2)
Herbert Bamlett	1914-21	2(1)	19(1)
Charles Roberts	1921-22	19(1)	19(1)
David Ashworth	1923-24	7(2)	7(2)
Robert Mellor	1924-27	7(2)	18(2)
Andrew Wilson	1927-32	3(2)	18(2)
Robert Mellor	1932-33	16(2)	16(2)
Jim McMullen	1933-34	9(2)	9(2)
Robert Mellor	1934-35	21(2)	7(3)
Frank Womack	1945-47	6(3N)	19(3N)
Bill Wooton	1947-50	6(3N)	11(3N)
George Hardwick	1950-56	22(2)	15(3N)
Ted Goodier	1956-58	15(3N)	19(3N)
Norman Dodgin	1958-60	21(4)	23(3N)
Danny McLennan	1960		
Jack Rowley	1960-63	2(4)	12(4)
Les McDowell	1963-65	9(3)	20(3)
Gordon Hurst	1965-66	20(3)	20(3)
Jimmy McIlroy	1966-68	10(3)	16(3)
Jack Rowley	1968-69	24(3)	24(3)
Jimmy Frizzell	1970-82	8(2)	3(4)
Joe Royle	1982-94	17(1)	16(2)
Graham Sharp	1994-	14(1)	14(1)

LONGEST LEAGUE RUNS

of undefeated matches:	20 (1.5.1990 - 10.11.1990)	of league matches w/out a win:	17 (4.9.1920 - 18.12.1920)
of undefeated home matches:	28 (3.2.23-18.4.24, 14.1.89-28.3.90)	of undefeated away matches:	11 (14.4.1973 - 10.11.1973)
without home win:	9 (4.9.1920 - 18.12.1920)	without an away win:	31 (24.4.1974 - 15.11.1975)
of league wins:	10 (12.1.1974 - 12.3.1974)	of home wins:	14 (11.1.1903 - 25.11.1903)
of league defeats:	8 (27.12.32-18.2.33, 15.12.34-2.2.35)	of away wins:	5 (12.1.1974 - 5.3.1974)

OLDHAM ATHLETIC

PLAYERS NAME Honours	Ht	Wt	Birthdate	Birthplace Transfers	Contract Date	Clubs	League	L/Cup	FA Cup	Other	Lge	L/C	FAC	Oth
G O A L K E E P E R S														
Darnborough Lee			15/09/77	Ashton	27/09/94	Oldham Athletic								
Hallworth Jonathan G	6.2	13.10	26/10/65	Stockport	25/05/83	Ipswich Town	45	4	1	6				
				Loan	01/01/85	Bristol Rovers	2			1				
				£75000	03/02/89	Oldham Athletic	167+2	18	20	3				
D E F E N D E R S														
Fleming Craig	6.0	11.7	06/10/71	Halifax	21/03/90	Halifax Town	56+1	4	3	3+2				
				£80000	15/08/91	Oldham Athletic	114+6	8+1	10	4	1			
Halle Gunner	5.11	11.2	11/08/65	Oslo		Lilestrom (Sweden)								
				£280000	15/02/91	Oldham Athletic	167+5	11	7	3	14	2	2	
Lonergan Darren			28/01/74	Cork		Waterford (Eire)								
					09/09/95	Oldham Athletic	1+1							
Redmond Stephen	5.10	11.2	02/11/67	Liverpool	03/12/84	Manchester City	231+4	24	17	11	7			
				£300000	10/07/92	Oldham Athletic	139+8	13	7+2	1+1	2			
Serrant Carl			12/09/75	Bradford	22/07/94	Oldham Athletic	20		2	2	1			
M I D F I E L D														
Beresford David	5.8	10.09	11/11/76	Middlesbrough	22/07/94	Oldham Athletic	8+23	1+1		2	2			
Gannon John	5.8	10.10	18/12/66	Wimbledon	19/12/84	Wimbledon	13+3	1+1		1	2			
				Free	23/02/89	Sheffield United	150+12	13+1	13	6	6			1
				Loan	05/11/93	Middlesbrough	6+1			2				
				Free	08/03/96	Oldham Athletic	5							
Graham Richard E	6.2	12.1	28/11/74	Dewsbury	16/07/93	Oldham Athletic	64+5	6	5	1	3			
Henry Nicholas I	5.6	10.8	21/02/69	Liverpool	06/07/87	Oldham Athletic	243+8	27+3	20	5	18	3		
Hughes Andrew														
Makin Christopher	5.10	10.6	08/05/73	Manchester	02/11/91	Oldham Athletic	93+1	7	11	1+1	4			
				Loan	28/08/92	Wigan Athletic	14+1				2			
Orlygsson Thorvaldur	5.11	10.13	02/08/66	Odense		KA Akureyri								
				£175000	09/12/89	Nottingham Forest	31+6	5+1	1	0+1	2	2		
				Free	05/08/93	Stoke City	80+3	7	6	6	16	1	1	1
				£180000	22/12/95	Oldham Athletic	15+1		3					
Pemberton Martin C			01/02/76	Bradford	22/07/94	Oldham Athletic	0+2			0+1				
Richardson Lee	5.11	11.0	12/03/69	Halifax	06/07/87	Halifax Town	43+13	4	4+2	6	2			
				£175000	09/02/89	Watford	40+1	1+1	1		1			
				£250000	15/08/90	Blackburn Rovers	50+12	1		2+2	3			
					16/09/92	Aberdeen	59+5	2+2	9	3	6	1	2	1
				£300000	12/08/94	Oldham Athletic	49+2	2	2	3	12	1		
Richardson Lloyd M			07/01/77	Dewsbury	11/10/94	Oldham Athletic								
Rickers Paul S	5.10	11.0	09/05/75	Leeds	16/07/93	Oldham Athletic	27		1+1	1+2	1			
Snodin Ian	5.7	9.0	15/08/63	Rotherham	18/08/80	Doncaster Rovers	181+7	9	11+1	3	25	1	1	
				£200000	22/05/85	Leeds United	51	3	1		6	2		
				£840000	16/01/87	Everton	142+6	19+4	26	3	3	2	2	
				Loan	13/10/94	Sunderland	6							
				Free	09/01/95	Oldham Athletic	41+2		1					
F O R W A R D S														
Banger Nicholas L	5.8	10.6	25/02/71	Southampton	25/04/89	Southampton	18+37	2+2	0+2	1	8	3		
				£250000	04/10/94	Oldham Athletic	28+13	2	1+1	0+1	5			
Barlow Stuart	5.10	11.0	16/07/68	Liverpool	06/06/90	Everton	24+47	3+5	4+3	0+2	10	1	2	
				Loan	10/01/92	Rotherham United				0+1				
				£350000	20/11/95	Oldham Athletic	22+4		3	1	7			
Beckford Darren R	6.1	11.1	12/05/67	Manchester	21/08/84	Manchester City	7+4	0+1						
				Loan	10/10/85	Bury	12				5			
				£150000	26/03/87	Port Vale	169+9	12	14	9+1	71	3	4	3
				£925000	14/06/91	Norwich City	32+6	3+2	4+1	1	8	3	1	1
				£300000	25/03/93	Oldham Athletic	31+21	2	6+3	0+1	11	1	5	
Holden Andy	6.1	13.2	14/09/62	Flint		Rhyl								
				£3000	18/08/83	Chester City	100	8	2	4	17	1	2	2
				£45000	30/10/86	Wigan Athletic	48+1	3	7	7	4			
				£130000	12/01/89	Oldham Athletic	23		2		4			

Name	Height	Weight	DOB	Birthplace	Fee	Date	Club									
McCarthy Sean C	6.1	11.7	12/09/67	Bridgend			Bridgend Town									
						22/10/85	Swansea City	76+15	4+1	5+2	9+1	25	3	4	6	
					£50000	18/08/88	Plymouth Argyle	67+3	7	3	0+1	19	5	1	1	
					£250000	04/07/90	Bradford City	127+4	10+2	8	8+1	60	10	2	7	
					£500000	03/12/93	Oldham Athletic	84+10	6	3	3	32			1	
McNiven Scott			08/07/72	Leeds		27/09/94	Oldham Athletic	14+1	2	1	3					
Sharpe Graeme M	6.1	11.8	16/10/60	Glasgow			Dumbarton	37+3	2	2		17		2		
					£125000	04/04/80	Everton	306+16	46+2	52+2	21+1	111	15	20		
					£500000	17/07/91	Oldham Athletic	103+6	12+1	11+1	1	31	4	2		

ADDITIONAL CONTRACT PLAYERS

Allot Mark							Oldham Athletic (T)									
Innes Mark							Oldham Athletic (T)									
McNiven Scott							Oldham Athletic (T)									

TRAINEES

Agg Nathan							Oldham Athletic (T)									
Carroll Stephen							Oldham Athletic (T)									
Clark Allan							Oldham Athletic (T)									
Clitheroe Lee							Oldham Athletic (T)									
Dixon Alan							Oldham Athletic (T)									
Earnshaw Mark							Oldham Athletic (T)									
Gorman Darren							Oldham Athletic (T)									
Hart Barrie							Oldham Athletic (T)									
Holt Andrew							Oldham Athletic (T)									
Hotte Mark							Oldham Athletic (T)									
Jablonski Mark							Oldham Athletic (T)									
Johnson Alan							Oldham Athletic (T)									
Levendis Andreas							Oldham Athletic (T)									
Mather Gregg							Oldham Athletic (T)									
Morrison Alastair							Oldham Athletic (T)									
Murphy Gerard							Oldham Athletic (T)									
Oldham Gavin							Oldham Athletic (T)									
Ramsden Gavin							Oldham Athletic (T)									
Randall Lee							Oldham Athletic (T)									
Morrow John							Glasgow Rangers									
						08/08/96	Oldham Athletic									

THE MANAGER
GRAEME SHARP

Date of Birth . . . . 16th October 1960.
Place of Birth . . . . Glasgow.
Date of Appointment . . . . November 1994.

PREVIOUS CLUBS
As Manager . . . . None.
As Coach . . . . None.
As a Player . . . . Dumbarton, Everton, Oldham Athletic.

HONOURS
As a Manager
None.

As a Player
Everton: FA Cup 1984. Charity Shield 1984, 1987. Division 1 championship 1985, 1987. ECWC 1985.
International: 12 full caps and 1 U21 cap for Scotland.

BOUNDARY PARK

Oldham, Lancashire OL1 2PA
Tel: 0161 624 4972

Capacity 13,599

First game .... v Colne (Lancs. Comb), 1.9.1906.
First floodlit game .... v Burnley, 1961-62.

ATTENDANCES
Highest .... 47,671 v Sheffield Wednesday, FA Cup 4th Round, 25.1.1930.
Lowest .... 1,841 v WBA, Simod Cup, 10.11.1987.

OTHER GROUNDS .... Sheepfoot Lane 1895-1905. Boundary Park 1905-
.... (In 1986 En Tout Cas Sporturf laid an artificial surface, new grass was laid in 1991)

MATCHDAY TICKET PRICES

George Hill Stand........	Matchday Members
Blue block	£13
Grey block	£12
Juv/OAP	£8
White block	£12
Green block	£11
Juv/OAP	£7.50

Existing S/T holders only.

Lookers Stand

Seats..............................	£12
Juv/OAP	£8
Paddock or uncovered..............	£7.50
Juv/OAP	£5

Seton Stand

Seats	£10.50
Juv/OAP	£6.50

Rochdale Road Stand.........	**Non-Members**
Visitors...........................	£12
Juv/OAP	£8
Home Supporters .... £12 (Members £10.50)	
Juv/OAP................. £8 (Members £6.50)	

Ticket Office Telephone no. 0161 624 4972

HOW TO GET TO THE GROUND

From North, East, South and West
Use motorway M62 until junction 20, then A627 to junction A664.
Leave motorway and at roundabout take 1st exit onto Broadway.
1st right off Broadway into Hilbre Avenue, which leads to car park.

Car Parking
Parking for 1,200 cars on site adjacent to ground.

Nearest Railway Station
Werneth.

CLUBCALL
0891 12 11 42
Calls cost 39p per minute cheap rate and 49p per
minute at all other times.
Call costings correct at time of going to press.

MATCHDAY PROGRAMME

Programme Editor .... Alan Hardy.

Number of pages .... 44.

Price .... £1.50.

Subscriptions................... £1.60 per programme (UK only).

Local Newspapers .... Oldham Chronicle,
..... Manchester Evening News (Saturday Pink), Oldham Advertiser.

Local Radio Stations.......... Radio Piccadilly, Radio Manchester,
.... Radio Cavell (Hospital), Key 103, Sunset Radio, Radio Latics.

OXFORD UNITED
(The U's)
NATIONWIDE LEAGUE DIVISION 1
SPONSORED BY: UNIPART

Back Row (L-R): Mickey Lewis, Matt Murphy, Paul Milsom, Elliot Jackson, Phil Whitehead, Danny Cullip, Mark Druce, Chris Allen.
Middle Row: John Clinkard (Physio), Maurice Evans (General Manager), Simon Marsh, Alex Dyer (departed), Steve Wood, Paul Moody, Matt Elliott, Phil Gilchrist, Malcolm Elias (Youth Dev.), Mark Harrison (Res/Youth Coach).
Front Row: Bobby Ford, Stuart Massey, Wayne Biggins, Les Robinson, Denis Smith (Director of COaching), Malcolm Crosby (1st Team Coach), Mike Ford, David Smith, David Rush.

OXFORD UNITED
FORMED IN 1893
TURNED PROFESSIONAL IN 1949
LTD COMPANY IN 1949

PRESIDENT: The Duke of Marlborough
CHAIRMAN: R Herd CBE
DIRECTORS
K Cox, G Coppock, N Harris, D Smith
SECRETARY
Mick Brown (01865 61503)
MARKETING
Trevor Baxter

MANAGER: Denis Smith
ASSISTANT MANAGER: Malcolm Crosby
RESERVE/YOUTH TEAM MANAGER
Mark Harrison
PHYSIOTHERAPIST
John Clinkard

STATISTICIAN FOR THE DIRECTORY
Roy Grant

Season 1995/6 saw promotion clinched on the final day of the season when Peterborough were eventually eased aside with a 4-0 win. The success was gained by virtue of a marvellous 17-game run at the end which saw just one defeat and was aided in no small way by Blackpool - who held a nine-point lead over United at Easter - collapsing.

Few United fans could have seen this happening even as late as February when we were lying in mid-table, held there by virtue of good home form which remained throughout as the best in the division. However, during that final spell, just nine points were dropped (from 54), the only defeat coming at Stockport in the one game that Player of the Year Matt Elliott missed.

A vital game in that period saw a cracking late goal from prodigal son Joey Beauchamp beat Blackpool. Joey had returned for a 'song' in October after unhappy times at West Ham and arch-rivals Swindon.

The whole squad played its part and looked likely to beat any side at the Manor Ground. Twenty-four goals came in the final nine home games during which time champions Swindon were crushed 3-0. The defence, too, was very tight - virtually unchanged since Christmas, it kept a club record 23 clean sheets.

It is easy to dwell on the final third of the season, but there were other highlights. A new record score of 9-1 against Dorchester in the FA Cup helped start a run which only ended in Round Four with a defeat against Nottingham Forest in a Manor Ground replay after a draw at the City Ground.

The Coca-Cola Cup saw defeat at QPR in Round Two when many thought Oxford were the better side. Home league form was good with just two home defeats - one of them a 4-1 disaster at the hands of Wycombe which was avenged later with a 3-0 win at Adams Park. It was the performances away from the Manor which were frustrating - the first success at Burnley in January coming at the thirteenth attempt.

On the playing front, Martin Aldridge came in on a free transfer from Northampton and soon scored nine goals at nearly a goal per game, and formed a striking partnership with David Rush. Top-scorer Paul Moody at this time was on the bench, coming on to score at regular intervals - including one of his three hat-tricks during the campaign.

Space does not permit the mention of everyone, but the central-defensive partnership of Elliott and Phil Gilchrist will not be out of place in Division One. If the end of season form is continued, United will do well in the new campaign: they have the players to make an impact and with Dennis Smith in the position of being able to strengthen the squad, the last season at the Manor should be interesting.

With derbies with Swindon and Reading, and the likes of Manchester City, Wolves, Birmingham, etc. to come, the Manor will be heaving again - United Fans have a great deal to look forward to. **ROY GRANT**

OXFORD UNITED

| League: 2nd | | FA Cup: 4th Rnd | | Coca-Cola Cup: 2nd Rnd | | Auto Windscreen Shield: 2nd Rnd | | |

M	DATE	COMP	VEN	OPPONENTS	RESULT	HT	LP	GOAL SCORERS/GOAL TIMES	ATT.
1	A 12	EL	H	Chesterfield	W 1-0	0-0	8	Allen 86	5563
2	15	CC 1/1	A	Hereford United	W 2-0	1-0		Biggins 35(pen), Murphy 88	(3021)
3	19	EL	A	Brentford	L 0-1	0-1	15		(5516)
4	22	CC 1/2	H	Hereford United	W 3-2	3-0		Allen 7, Smith 24, Moody 33	3571
5	26	EL	H	Rotherham United	D 1-1	0-1	14	Ford 90	4282
6	30	EL	A	Swindon Town	D 1-1	0-1	14	Moody 63	(13041)
7	S 3	EL	H	York City	W 2-0	2-0	10	Elliot 7, Biggins 19(pen)	4304
8	9	EL	A	Hull City	D 0-0	0-0	10		(4608)
9	12	EL	A	Walsall	D 2-2	0-1	10	Gilchrist 81, Rush 86	(3905)
10	16	EL	H	Carlisle United	W 4-0	2-0	6	Gilchrist 10, Ford 20, Rush 62, Murphy 77	5046
11	19	CC 2/1	H	Queens Park Rangers	D 1-1	0-1		Allen 69	7484
12	23	EL	A	Swansea City	D 1-1	1-0	8	Ford 14	(2505)
13	26	AWS 1/2	H	Bristol City	W 3-0	3-0		Rush 10, Murphy 12, Rush 16	2558
14	30	EL	H	Bristol Rovers	L 1-2	0-2	11	Allen 61	6091
15	O 3	CC 2/2	A	Queens Park Rangers	L 1-2	1-0		Robinson 12	(9207)
16	7	EL	H	Stockport County	W 2-1	0-1	8	Gilchrist 6, Moody 45	5646
17	14	EL	A	Wrexham	L 1-2	0-1	11	Elliot 48	(3189)
18	21	EL	H	Wycombe Wanderers	L 1-4	0-3	12	Smith 54	7731
19	28	EL	A	Blackpool	D 1-1	0-0	14	Rush 53	(5303)
20	31	EL	A	Shrewsbury Town	L 0-2	0-1	14		(2186)
21	N 4	EL	H	Bristol City	W 2-0	0-0	12	Angel 83, Murphy 90	5665
22	7	AWS 1/2	A	Barnet	W 3-2	0-0		Pardew 49(og), Murphy 72, Moody 79	(1072)
23	11	FAC 1	H	Dorchester	W 9-1	2-0		Ford 9,57, Wood 33,70 Rush 56, Moody 63,69,82, Beauchamp 78	3819
24	18	EL	A	Peterborough United	D 1-1	1-0	13	Ford 36	(4720)
25	25	EL	A	Crewe Alexandra	W 1-0	1-0	12	Rush 12	5287
26	28	AWS 2	H	Colchester United	L 1-2	1-1		Angel 40	1943
27	D 2	FAC 2	H	Northampton Town	W 2-0	1-0		Massey 6, Moody 84	6355
28	9	EL	H	Swansea City	W 5-1	0-0	10	Moody 59, 68, 81, Elliot 73, Elliot 90	4674
29	16	EL	A	Bristol Rovers	L 0-2	0-0	11		(4051)
30	23	EL	A	Bradford City	L 0-1	0-1	13		(4637)
31	26	EL	H	Bournemouth	W 2-0	2-0	12	Ford 11, Massey 15	6347
32	J 6	FAC 3	A	Millwall	D 3-3	1-0		Massey 11, Moody 58, Ford 88	(7564)
33	13	EL	H	Brentford	W 2-1	1-1	12	Aldridge 35, 64	5566
34	16	FAC 3R	H	Millwall	W 1-0	0-0		Massey 55	8122
35	20	EL	A	Chesterfield	L 0-1	0-1	14		(4589)
36	30	EL	A	Burnley	W 2-0	1-0	10	Massey 26, Allen 69	(6815)
37	F 3	EL	A	Rotherham United	L 0-1	0-0	13		(2842)
38	7	FAC 4	A	Nottingham Forest	D 1-1	0-0		Massey 88	(15550)
39	10	EL	H	Brighton & H.A.	D 1-1	1-0	13	Elliot 28	5967
40	13	FAC 4R	H	Nottingham Forest	L 0-3	0-2			7948
41	17	EL	H	Walsall	W 3-2	0-1	9	Moody 66(pen), Aldridge 79, 90	4369
42	20	EL	A	York City	L 0-1	0-0	10		(2112)
43	24	EL	A	Carlisle United	W 2-1	0-0	8	Elliot 78, Aldridge 90	(5525)
44	27	EL	H	Hull City	W 2-0	1-0	6	Rush 14, 69	4650
45	M 2	EL	A	Bournemouth	W 1-0	1-0	6	Beauchamp 7	(3996)
46	9	EL	H	Bradford City	W 2-0	0-0	6	Moody 62, Aldridge 69	5133
47	12	EL	A	Brighton & H.A.	W 2-1	1-0	5	Murphy 43, 63	(3953)
48	16	EL	A	Notts County	D 1-1	1-0	5	Rush 33	(5140)
49	19	EL	H	Swindon Town	W 3-0	1-0	4	Elliot 19, Aldridge 54, Beauchamp 89	8585
50	23	EL	H	Burnley	W 5-0	1-0	4	Aldridge 37, Moody 77, 80, 90, Beauchamp 86	6529
51	30	EL	A	Stockport County	L 2-4	1-2	5	Beauchamp 25, Aldridge 69	(6096)
52	A 2	EL	H	Wrexham	D 0-0	0-0	5		5554
53	6	EL	H	Blackpool	W 1-0	0-0	4	Beauchamp 83	7875
54	8	EL	A	Wycombe Wanderers	W 3-0	1-0	3	Rush 41, Massey 68, Moody 75	(6727)
55	16	EL	H	Notts County	D 1-1	1-0	3	Moody 5(pen)	6934
56	20	EL	A	Bristol City	W 2-0	0-0	3	Rush 57, Moody 73	(7674)
57	23	EL	H	Shrewsbury Town	W 6-0	2-0	3	Moody 16, 57, Massey 34, Rush 67, Beauchamp 81, Murphy 90	5800
58	27	EL	A	Crewe Alexandra	W 2-1	1-0	2	Moody 10, Beauchamp 62	(4605)
59	M 4	EL	H	Peterborough United	W 4-0	0-0	2	Grazioli 53(og), Moody 66, Elliot 68, Rush 72	7535

Best Home League Attendance: 8585 v Swindon Town   **Smallest: 4282 v Rotherham United**   **Average: 5875**

Goal Scorers:
EL(76): Moody(17),Rush(11),Aldridge(9),Elliot(8),Beauchamp(7),Murphy(5),Massey(4),Gilchrist(3),Ford(3),Allen(3),Ford(2),Biggins(1),Angel(1),Smith(1),Opponent(s)(1)
CC(7):   Allen(2),Biggins(1),Moody(1),Smith(1),Robinson(1),Murphy(1)
FAC(16): Moody(5),Massey(4),Wood(2),Ford(2),Rush(1),Ford(1),Beauchamp(1)
AWS(7): Murphy(2),Rush(2),Opponent(s)(1),Moody(1),Angel(1)

Opp	(F) Aldridge	(F) Allen	(F) Angel	(M) Beauchamp	(F) Biggins	(G) Carter	(F) Druce	(D) Elliot	(D) Ford	(M) Ford	(D) Gilchrist	(M) Gray	(M) Jackson	(M) Lewis	(F) Marsh	(M) Massey	(M) Milson	(F) Moody	(M) Murphy	(D) Powell	(G) Reeves	(D) Robinson	(F) Rush	(M) Smith	(G) Whitehead	(D) Wood	#
G.Barber		X	S1		X1	X		X	X	X			S					X	S2			X	X	X2		X	1
R.Gifford		X	S		X1	X		X	X	X	X		S					X	S1			X		X			2
A.D'Urso		X			X	X		X	X		X			X2		X1		X	S1			X	S2	X	S		3
A.Wiley		X	S2		X	X		X	X		X				S1			X2	X1			X	X	X	S		4
D.Orr		X2	S2		X			X	X	S1	X							X	X1			X	X	X	S		5
M.Brandwood		X1			X	X		X	X	X	X							X	S1			X	X	X	S	S	6
R.Poulain		X	S2		X	X		X	X	X	X							X1	S1			X	X2	X	S		7
M.Riley		X			X1	X		X	X	X	X					S2		X	S1			X	X2	X	S		8
E.Wolstenholme		X2	S2			X		X	X	X	X					X1		X	S1			X	X	X	S		9
E.Lomas		X	S			X		X	X	X	X					X		X1	X			X	X	X	S		10
G.Pooley		X	S		X1	X		X	X	X	X					X			S1			X	X	X	S		11
G.Cain		X	S1		X			X	X	X	X					X1		X				X	X	X	S		12
A.Butler		X	S1		X			X	X	X	X					X1		S2	X2			X	X2	X	S		13
P.Taylor		X	S1					X	X	X	X				S2			X1	X			X	X2	X	S		14
G.Pole		X				S1			X	X	X				S2			X1	X			X	X2	X	S		15
C.Wilkes		X	S2	X		X		X	X	X	X							X1	X			X	X	X	S		16
T.West		X1		X2	S2	X		X	X	X	X				S1			X	X			X	X	X	S		17
S.Bennett		X3	S2	X2	S1			X	X	X								X	S3			X	X1	X	X		18
F.Stretton		S2	X2		X1			X	X	X					S	X			S1			X	X	X	X	X	19
J.W.Lloyd			X	S2	X1			X	X	X	X					X		S1				X3	X	X2	X	S3	20
I.Hemley			X	S1		S		X	X	X	X					X		X	S2			X1	X2	X	X		21
D'Urso			X3	S2	S1			X	X	X	X2					X		X	X	S3			X1	X	X	X	22
M.Bodenham			X2	S2		S		X	X	X						X1		X	S1				X	X	X	X	23
S.Baines			X	S		S		X	X	X	X					X		X1	S1				X	X	X	X	24
U.Rennie			X1	S1		S		X	X	X	X					X		X	S2				X2	X	X	X	25
D.Orr			X	S1				X	X	X	X					X		X	S2	S3		X1	X3	X	X2	X	26
M.Reed		S	X	S1				X	X	X1	X					X		X	X				X	X	X	X	27
J.Brandwood			X	S1				X	X	X	X			S		X		X	S			X1	X	X	X	X	28
C.Wilkes			X	S2				X	X	X	X			S		X2		X	S1			X1	X	X	X	X	29
I.Cruikshanks			X	S1				X	X	X	X			S		X1		X	X2			S2	X		X	X	30
G.Cain	S2	S1	X1	S				X	X	X	X					X		X				X	X2		X	X	31
C.Wilkes	S2	S1	X					X	X	X	X			S		X		X2				X	X1		X	X	32
T.West	X2	S3	X	X3			S2		X	X1	X				S1	X						X	X1		X	X	33
C.Wilkes	X	S1	X1						X	X	X			S	X2	X						X	S2		X	X	34
T.Leake	S2			X			S3	X		X	X				S1	X1		X		X3		X	X2		X	X	35
A.Butler	S	S1		X2			S2	X		X	X			X		X		X				X	X		X	X	36
K.Breen		S2		X				S1	X	S3						X3		X	X1			X	X2		X	X	37
D.R.Elleray	S	X1		X			S	X	X	X						X		X	S1			X	X		X	X	38
G.Barber		X		X				S2	X	X						X3		X	S3			X	X1	X	X	X2	39
D.Elleray	S2		S3	X				X	X	X	X					X2		X2	X1			X	S1	X3	X		40
R.Furnandiz	X		X3	S2			X1	X	X	X2	X					S1						X	X		X		41
E.Lomas	X2		X	X					X	X	X1		X			X		X				X	S2	X	X		42
G.Frankland	X		X2	X3				X	X		X					S3		X		S2		S1	X	X1	X		43
R.Gifford	X		X	X2				X	X		S1					X		S3				X	X3	X1	X		44
F.Stretton	X2		X1	X				X	X		X					S3		S2				X	X2	X	X		45
S.Baines	X3		X1	X				X	X		X				X	S3		S2	S1			X	X2	X	X		46
B.Knight	X1			X2			S3	X	X		X				X	S2		S1	X			X	X3	X	X		47
R.Pearson	X			X1			S1		X		X					S2		X			S	X	X2		X		48
N.Barry	X1		X3					X	X		X					S2		S1	X		S3	X	X2		X		49
M.Fletcher	X		S3	X				X	X		X					S2	X3	S1	X2			X	X1	X	X		50
W.C.Burns	X	S2		X					X		X					S1	X1	S2	X2			X	X2		X	X	51
S.Bennett	X3		S2	X				X	X		X		X			S3		S1	X1			X	X2		X		52
J.Brandwood	S2	S3		X				X	X		X		X1			S1		X	X3			X	X2		X		53
E.Wolstenholme	X2	S3		X				X	X		X					X	S1	S2	X1			X	X3		X		54
S.Mathieson	X1	S3		X2				X	X		X		S2			X		X	S1			X	X		X		55
P.Rejer			S	X				X	X		X		X			S		X	S			X	X	X	X		56
P.Taylor			S2	X				X	X		X		X			S		X1	X			X	S1	X	X		57
K.Breen			S	X1				X	X		X		X			S2		X	S1			X	X2	X	X		58
G.Pooley			S	X				X	X		X		X1			S1		X	S			X	X	X	X		59
EL Appearances	15	13	16	25	8	11	1	44	43	26	42	6	0	5	2	33	0	30	13	1	0	40	41	43	34	10	
EL Sub Appearances	3	11	11	7	2	0	7	0	1	2	0	1	0	14	3	2	0	12	21	2	0	1	2	0	0	1	
CC Appearances	0	4	0+1	0	3+1	4	0	4	4	3	4	0	0	0	0+2	2	0	3	2+2	0	0	4	3	4	0	0	
FAC Appearances	1+2	1+2	4+1	2+2	0	0	0	6	5	5	5	0	0	0	1	6	0	6	2+2	0	0	4	2+2	6	6	3	
AWS Appearances	0	1	2+1	0+2	0+1	1	0	3	3	3	3	0	0	0	0	2	0+1	2	2+1	0+2	0	1	3	3	2	2	

Player numbers (right column):
1 G.Barber, 2 R.Gifford, 3 A.D'Urso, 4 A.Wiley, 5 D.Orr, 6 M.Brandwood, 7 R.Poulain, 8 M.Riley, 9 E.Wolstenholme, 10 E.Lomas, 11 G.Pooley, 12 G.Cain, 13 A.Butler, 14 P.Taylor, 15 G.Pole, 16 C.Wilkes, 17 T.West, 18 S.Bennett, 19 F.Stretton, 20 J.W.Lloyd, 21 I.Hemley, 22 D'Urso, 23 M.Bodenham, 24 S.Baines, 25 U.Rennie, 26 D.Orr, 27 M.Reed, 28 J.Brandwood, 29 C.Wilkes, 30 I.Cruikshanks, 31 G.Cain, 32 C.Wilkes, 33 T.West, 34 C.Wilkes, 35 T.Leake, 36 A.Butler, 37 K.Breen, 38 D.R.Elleray, 39 G.Barber, 40 D.Elleray, 41 R.Furnandiz, 42 E.Lomas, 43 G.Frankland, 44 R.Gifford, 45 F.Stretton, 46 S.Baines, 47 B.Knight, 48 R.Pearson, 49 N.Barry, 50 M.Fletcher, 51 W.C.Burns, 52 S.Bennett, 53 J.Brandwood, 54 E.Wolstenholme, 55 S.Mathieson, 56 P.Rejer, 57 P.Taylor, 58 K.Breen, 59 G.Pooley

OXFORD UNITED

CLUB RECORDS

BIGGEST VICTORIES
League: 7-0 v Barrow,Division 4, 19.12.1964.
F.A. Cup: 9-1 v Dorchester Town, 1st Rnd, 11.11.1995.
League Cup: 6-0 v Gillingham, Rnd 2, 24.9.1986.

BIGGEST DEFEAT
League: 0-6 v Liverpool, Div. 1, 22.3.1986.
F.A. Cup: by 4 goals on three occasions.
League Cup: 0-5 v Nottingham Forest, 4.10.78.

MOST LEAGUE POINTS
(3pts for win) 95, Div 3, 1983-84
(2pts for win) 61, Div 4,1964-65

MOST GOALS SCORED
91, Division 3, 1983-84.
Biggins 19, Hebberd 11, Vinter 11, Lawrence 9, Thomas 7, Aldridge 4, McDonald 4, Rhodes-Brown 4, Briggs 3, Brock 3, Whatmore 3, Opponents 3, Jones 2, Shotton 1.
MOST GOALS CONCEDED
80, Division 1, 1985-86; Division 1, 1987-88.

MOST FIRST CLASS MATCHES IN A SEASON
65, 1983-84 (46 League, 7 FA Cup, 11 League Cup, 1 AMC).

MOST LEAGUE WINS
28 (from 46), Division 3, 1983-84. 25 (from 42) Division 2, 1984-85.

MOST LEAGUE DRAWS
19, Division 2, 1990-91.

MOST LEAGUE DEFEATS
22, Division 2, 1989-90; Division 2, 1991-92.

INDIVIDUAL CLUB RECORDS

MOST GOALS IN A SEASON
John Aldridge 34 (League 30, FAC 1,League Cup 3) 1984-85.
3 goals twice = 6; 2 goals 8 times = 16; 1 goal 12 times = 12.

MOST GOALS IN A MATCH
4, Tony Jones v Newport County (5-1), Div.4, 22.9.1962.
4, Arthur Longbottom v Darlington (5-0), Div.4, 26.10.1963.
4, Bill Calder v Walsall (6-1), League Cup 1st Rnd. replay, 7.9.1964.
4, John Aldridge v Gillingham (6-0), League Cup 2nd Rnd., 24.9.1986.
4, Richard Hill v Walsall (a) (5-1), Div.2, 26.12.1988.

OLDEST PLAYER IN A LEAGUE MATCH
Colin Todd, 35 years 4 months.

YOUNGEST PLAYER IN A LEAGUE MATCH
Jason Seacole, 16 years 5 months

MOST CAPPED PLAYER
Jim Magilton (N. Ireland) 18

BEST PERFORMANCES

League:Div3 1983-84: **P** 46 **W** 28 **D** 11 **L** 7 **F** 91 **A** 50 **Pts** 95.
Div 2 1984-85: **P** 42 **W** 25 **D** 9 **L** 8 **F** 84 **A** 36 **Pts** 84.
(The only team to win succesive championships of Div.3 & 2.)
Highest: 18th Div 1 1983-84 & 1986-87.
FA Cup: 6th Rnd. 1963-64
League Cup: Winners in 1985-86, v Q.P.R. (3-0).

ADDITIONAL INFORMATION
Previous League: Southern League
Previous Names: Headington United (until 1960)

Club colours: Yellow shirts navy trim, navy shorts, navy socks with yellow trim.

Change colours: Red & black striped shirts, black shorts & socks with red trim
Reserves League: Avon Insurance Football Combination.

DIVISIONAL RECORD

	Played	Won	Drawn	Lost	For	Against	Points
Division 1/P	124	27	38	59	150	229	119
Division 2/1	654	213	182	259	765	841	716
Division 3/2	598	236	171	191	826	711	757
Division 4/3	138	50	43	45	216	178	143
Total	**1,514**	**526**	**434**	**554**	**1,977**	**1,959**	**1,735**

RECORDS AND STATISTICS

COMPETITIONS

Div.1/P	Div.2/1	Div.3/2	Div.4
1985-88	1968-76	1965-68	1962-65
	1984-85	1976-84	1965-70
	1988-94	1994-96	
	1996-		

HONOURS

Division 2	Division 3	Lge Cup
1984-85	1967-68	1985-86
	1983-84	

MOST APPEARANCES

John Shuker 529+5 (1962-77)

Year	League	FA Cup	Lge Cup	Ang/Ital
1962-63	18			
1963-64	12	4		
1964-65	11			
1965-66	33+1	2	1	
1966-67	24+2	3	1	
1967-68	36+1	3	2	
1968-69	34	2	1	
1969-70	34	2	5	
1970-71	42	5	2	
1971-72	41	1	3	
1972-73	36	2	3	3
1973-74	41	1	1	
1974-75	32	1	1	
1975-76	40	1	3	
1976-77	29+1	2	1	
	473+5	29	24	3

Previous holder: Ron Atkinson 425+1 (162-71)

MOST GOALS IN A CAREER

John Aldridge 90 (1983-87)

Year	League	FA Cup	Lge Cup	FMC
1983-84	4			
1984-85	30	1	3	
1985-86	23	1	5	2
1986-87	15		6	
	72	2	14	2

Current leading goalscorer: Paul Moody 53 (1994-96)

RECORD TRANSFER FEE RECEIVED

Amount	Club	Player	Date
£1,100,000	Derby Co.	Dean Saunders	10/88
£825,000	Liverpool	Ray Houghton	10/87
£750,000	Liverpool	John Aldridge	1/87
£600,000	Southampton	Jim Magilton	2/94

RECORD TRANSFER FEE PAID

Amount	Club	Player	Date
£285,000	Gillingham	Colin Grenall	2/88
£275,000	Swansea	Andrew Melville	7/90*
£250,000	Liverpool	John Durnin	2/89
£200,000	Man. City	Paul Simpson	10/88

*League Tribunal ordered further sums to Swansea City on sale in 8/93 of Andrew Melville to Sunderland. These figures have not been disclosed.

MANAGERS

Name	Seasons	Best	Worst
A Turner	1959-69	22(2)	18(4)
R Saunders	1969	20(2)	20(2)
G Summers	1969-75	8(2)	17(2)
M Brown	1975-79	20(2)	18(3)
W Asprey	1979-80	17(3)	17(3)
R Barry (caretaker)	1980	-	-
I Greaves	1980-82	5(3)	14(3)
J Smith	1982-85	1(2)	5(3)
M Evans	1985-88	18(1)	18(1)
M Lawrenson	1988	21(1)	8(2)
B Horton	1988-93	10(2)	21(2)
Denis Smith	1993-		

LONGEST LEAGUE RUNS

of undefeated matches:	20 (17.3.1984 - 29.9.1984)	of league matches w/out a win:	27 (14.11.1987 - 27.8.1988)
of undefeated home matches:	20 (3.10.1964 - 25.8.1965)	of undefeated away matches:	12 (28.2.1984 - 22.9.1984)
without home win:	13 (21.11.1987 - 2.5.1988)	without an away win:	24 (14.9.1974 - 27.9.1975)
of league wins:	6 (14.1.67-26.2.67, 16.3.68-6.4.68, 4.12.82-3.1.83)	of home wins:	10 (15.9.1984 - 29.12.1984)
of league defeats:	7 (4.5.1991 - 7.9.1991)	of away wins:	4 (4.12.1982 - 3.1.1983, 7.5.1984 - 22.9.1984)

OXFORD UNITED

PLAYERS NAME / Honours	Ht	Wt	Birthdate	Birthplace / Transfers	Contract Date	Clubs	APPEARANCES League	L/Cup	FA Cup	Other	GOALS Lge	L/C	FAC	Oth
G O A L K E E P E R S														
Reeves Stephen	5.11	13.0	24/09/74	Dagenham	01/08/93	Everton								
					01/08/95	Oxford United								
Whitehead Philip M	6.3	13.7	17/12/69	Halifax	01/07/88	Halifax Town	42	2	4	4				
				£60000	09/03/90	Barnsley	16							
				Loan	07/03/91	Halifax Town	9							
				Loan	29/11/91	Scunthorpe United	8			2				
				Loan	04/09/92	Scunthorpe United	8	2						
				Loan	19/11/92	Bradford City	6			4				
				£75000	01/11/93	Oxford United	111	4	11	3				
D E F E N D E R S														
Elliot Matthew S	6.3	13.6	01/11/68	Wandsworth		Epsom & Ewell								
				£5000	09/09/88	Charlton Athletic		1						
				£10000	23/03/89	Torquay United	123+1	9	9	16	15	2	2	1
				£50000	26/03/92	Scunthorpe United	61	6	2	8	8			
				£150000	05/11/93	Oxford United	121	8	11	6	18		2	
Ford Michael P	6.0	11.6	09/02/66	Bristol	11/02/84	Leicester City								
				Free	19/09/84	Cardiff City	144+1	6	9	7	13			
				£150000	10/06/88	Oxford United	209+16	17+1	10+1	8	12	1	2	
				Free	01/08/94	Devizes Town								
Gilchrist Philip A	6.0	11.12	25/08/73	Stockton-on-T	05/12/90	Nottingham Forest								
				Free	10/01/92	Middlesbrough								
				Free	27/11/92	Hartlepool United	77+5	4+1	4	5				
				£100000	17/02/95	Oxford United	60	4	5	3	4			
Powell Paul						Oxford United (T)	1+2			0+2				
Robinson Leslie	5.8	11.1	01/03/67	Shirebrook		Chesterfield								
				Free	06/10/84	Mansfield Town	11+4			1				
					27/11/86	Stockport County	67	2	4	4	3			
				£10000	24/03/88	Doncaster Rovers	82	4	5	5	12		1	1
				£150000	19/03/90	Oxford United	207+3	18	12+1	10	2	2		
M I D F I E L D														
Beauchamp Joey FLge.u18.1.	5.10	11.10	13/03/71	Oxford	16/05/89	Oxford United	117+7	6+1	8	5+1	20	2	3	
				Loan	30/10/91	Swansea City	5		1		2			
				£1000000	22/06/94	West Ham United								
				£850000	22/06/94	Swindon Town	39+6	7+2	2	4	3	1		
				£300000	12/10/95	Oxford United	25+7		2+2	0+2	7		1	
Ford Robert J	5.8	11.0	22/09/74	Bristol	06/10/92	Oxford United	58+7	3+1	8	7	5		2	1
Gray Martin D	5.9	10.11	17/08/71	Stockton	01/02/90	Sunderland	46+18	6+2	0+3	3+1	1			
				Loan	09/01/91	Aldershot	3+2			1				
				Loan	20/10/95	Fulham	6			1				
				£100000	28/03/96	Oxford United	6+1							
Jackson Elliot						Oxford United (T)								
Lewis Michael E: Y.7.	5.6	10.6	15/02/65	Birmingham	18/02/82	W.B.A	22+2	4+1	4					
				£25000	16/11/84	Derby County	37+6	2	0+1	4	1			
					25/08/88	Oxford United	276+24	15+2	12+1	11+1	7			
Massey Stuart A	5.11	11.8	17/11/64	Crawley		Sutton United								
				£20000	17/07/92	Crystal Palace	1+1			1				
				Free	05/07/94	Oxford United	53+4	6	7	3	4	1	4	
Murphy Matthew S	5.10	11.5	20/08/71	Northampton		Corby								
				£20000	12/02/93	Oxford United	32+26	2+2	2+2	3+3	12	1		3
Smith David C	5.8	11.2	26/12/70	Liverpool	04/07/89	Norwich City	13+5		2+1	1+1				
				£100000	05/07/94	Oxford United	84+1	8	7	7	1		1	
F O R W A R D S														
Aldridge Martin J	5.11	11.4	06/12/74	Northampton	27/08/92	Northampton Town	50+20	1+2	1+1	5+2	17		1	4
				Loan	09/12/95	Dagenham & Red.								
				Free	22/12/95	Oxford United	15+3		1+2		9			
Allen Chris A	5.11	12.2	18/11/72	Oxford	14/05/91	Oxford United	110+40	11+2	5+5	5+3	12	4	1	
				Loan	24/02/96	Nottingham Forest	1+2				1			
Angel Mark	5.8	11.01	23/08/75	Newcastle	31/12/92	Sunderland								
				Free	09/08/95	Oxford United	16+11	0+1	4+1	2+1	1			1
Druce Mark A	5.11	11.11	03/07/74	Oxford	03/12/91	Oxford United	18+34	1+3		2+1	4			

Player		Fee	Date	Club								
Jemson Nigel 5.10 11.10 10/08/69	Hutton		06/07/87	Preston North End	28+4		2	5+1	8		1	5
E: u21.1. LC'90. AMC'96.		£150000	24/03/88	Nottingham Forest	45+2	9	3+1	1	13	4	3	
		Loan	03/12/88	Bolton Wanderers	4+1							
		Loan	15/03/89	Preston North End	6+3			2	2			1
		£800000	17/09/91	Sheffield Wed.	26+25	3+4	3+3	2+2	9	1		1
		Loan	10/09/93	Grimsby Town	6			1	1			
		£300000	08/09/94	Notts County	5+6	1+1		1	1	1		
		Loan	13/01/95	Watford	3+1							
		Loan	25/04/95	Coventry City								
		Loan	15/02/96	Rotherham United	16			3	5			4
		£60000	10/07/96	Oxford United								
Marsh Simon T 5.11 11.2 29/01/77	Ealing		22/11/94	Oxford United	10+3	2+2	2	2				
Moody Paul 6.3 12.6 13/06/67	Portsmouth			Fareham								
		£4000		Waterlooville								
		£50000	15/07/91	Southampton	7+5	1	0+1					
		Loan	09/12/92	Reading	5			1	1			
		£60000	19/02/94	Oxford United	79+19	7	7	3	46	2	5	3
Rush David 5.11 10.3 15/05/71	Sunderland			Notts County								
		Free	21/07/89	Sunderland	40+19	1+1	9	1+1	12		1	
		Loan	15/08/91	Hartlepool United	8				2			
		Loan	27/10/93	Peterborough Utd	2+2	1			1	1		
		Loan	12/09/94	Cambridge United	2							
		£100000	23/09/94	Oxford United	63+14	3+1	2+3	6+1	20		1	2

THE MANAGER
DENIS SMITH

Date of Birth . . . . 19th November 1947.
Place of Birth . . . . Stoke.
Date of Appointment. . . . . September 1993.

PREVIOUS CLUBS
As Manager . . . . York City, Sunderland, Bristol City.
As Coach. . . . . None.
As a Player . . . . Stoke City, York City.

HONOURS
As a Manager
York: Division 4 champions 1984.
Sunderland: Promotion to Division 1, 1990.
Oxford: Promotion to Division 1, 1996.

As a Player
Stoke: League Cup 1972.

MANOR GROUND

London Road, Headington, Oxford OX3 7RS
Tel: 01865 61503

Capacity...9,572
Standing...6,769
Seating..2,803

First game...1.10.1898
First floodlit game......................................v Banbury, 18.12.1950(first club to stage a floodlit game)
ATTENDANCES
Highest...22,750 v Preston North End, FA Cup 6th Round, 29.2.1964.
Lowest ....1,055 v Portsmouth, ZDS Cup, 12.12.1990.

OTHER GROUNDS...None.

MATCHDAY TICKET PRICES

Seats . . . . £9 - £12
Juv/OAP. . . . . £4.50 - £8

Terraces. . . . . £7.50 - £9
Juv/OAP. . . . . £4.50 - £6
(all prices dependant on category of match)

Ticket Office Telephone no. 01865 61503

CLUBLINE
0891 44 00 55
Calls cost 39p per minute cheap rate and 49p per
minute at all other times.
Call costings correct at time of going to press.

HOW TO GET TO THE GROUND

From the North: From North (M40) leave at junction 9. Follow signs for A34 to Oxford. Take slip road A44 marked Witney, Woodstock. At roundabout take first exit (Pear Tree). Follow to next roundabout A44 junction with A40 Woodstock Road, take second exit marked A40 London. Down to next roundabout (Banbury Road), take second exit on to Northern by-pass. Cars should take next left turn at slip road marked New Marston half-a-mile and JR Hospital 1 mile. (Coaches should follow diversions to avoid weak bridge, next roundabout A40, Green Road, take fifth exit, follow signs for A40 junction with (B4105) Marston). Down to mini-roundabout turn left. Straight up Headley Way, coaches should take second junction right marked Franklin Road which leads into coach park.

From South: A34 by-pass to junction A44 Pear Tree. Follow directions as North.

From the East: Cars and coaches should follow coach diversion directions as from Green Road roundabout.

From the West: Take A34 following signs to M40. Take exit A44 marked Woodstock, take third exit Pear Tree, follow as North.

Car Parking: Street parking near ground. Take care for matchday parking restrictions.

Nearest Railway Station: Oxford (01865 722 333)

MATCHDAY PROGRAMME

Programme Editor . . . . Ian Davies.

Number of pages. . . . . 32 (sometimes 36).

Price . . . . £1.50.

Subscriptions . . . . £45 per season.

Local Newspapers . . . . Oxford Mail, Oxford Times.

Local Radio Stations . . . . Thames Valley FM, Fox FM.

PORT VALE
(The Valiants)
NATIONWIDE LEAGUE DIVISION 1
SPONSORED BY: TUNSTALL ASSURANCE LTD.

Back Row (L-R): Martin Foyle, Allen Tankard, Stewart Talbot, Jermaine Holwyn, Paul Musselwhite, Gareth Griffiths, Arjan van Heusden, Lee Mills, Neil Aspin (Capt), Dean Glover, Steve Guppy. **Middle Row:** Mark Grew (Yth Coach), Stan Nicholls (Kit manager), John Jeffers, Ray Walker, Wayne Corden, Kevin Kent, Richard Eyre, Bradley Sandeman, Jim Cooper Community Officer), Rick Carter (Physio). **Back Row:** John Rudge (Manager), Ian Bogie, Craig Lawton, John McCarthy, Tony Naylor, Andy Porter, Dean Stokes, Dean Cunningham, Bill Dearden (First Team Coach).

PORT VALE
FORMED IN 1876
TURNED PROFESSIONAL IN 1885
LTD COMPANY IN 1911

PRESIDENT: J Burgess
CHAIRMAN: W T Bell, L.A.E., MIMI

DIRECTORS
D Bundy (Vice-Chairman), I McPherson,
A Belfield
SECRETARY
R A Allan ((01782 814 134)
COMMERCIAL MANAGER
Margaret Moran-Smith (01782 835 524)

MANAGER: John Rudge
COACH: Bill Dearden

YOUTH TEAM MANAGER
Mark Grew
PHYSIOTHERAPIST
R Carter

STATISTICIAN FOR THE DIRECTORY
Philip Sherwin

A season of mixed fortunes, in which the team played a record number of games, finally ended with the team in a comfortable mid-table position being just two goals short of their best finish since 1934.

Confidence was high after an opening-day televised draw at favourites Derby County, but soon afterwards skipper Neil Aspin dislocated his shoulder and striker Martin Foyle missed three months with a foot injury. Without arguably the club's best defender and striker the team struggled and a run of only one win - against local rivals Stoke City - from eleven outings saw the team slump to the foot of the table.

Although the away form was reasonable, the side mustered only three points from their first nine home games in the league and didn't record their first victory on home soil until December - co-incidentally in the game that marked Foyle's Vale Park return and he scored the only goal of the game, in the seventh minute.

Four successive victories, including a remarkable 5-3 win in Perugia in the Anglo-Italian Cup, promised a brighter future, along with Tony Naylor scoring in five consecutive league games.

The New Year was dominated by cup-ties, with a run to Wembley in the much-maligned Anglo-Italian Cup and an appearance in the fifth round of the FA Cup. A replay victory over Crystal Palace in the third round earned a trip to the cup-holders Everton and after a 2-2 draw, the unthinkable happened in the replay with the Vale winning 2-1 to clinch the FA Giant-Killers Cup. In the next round Leeds United came close to being embarrassed before clinching victory in the last minute of the replay.

Wembley was a great occasion, despite bowing to Genoa's superior skills, and then it was back to a back-log of league games caused by the cup successes, which still left the club in the bottom two in the second week of March.

Six successive league victories - including the completion of the team's first double over Stoke for 70 years - immediately banished any thoughts of relegation, and the tightness of the league even suggested an outside bid for the play-offs, especially when they came back from 2-0 down to draw 2-2 at Crystal Palace. Three successive defeats at Easter soon ended that particular dream and the season then petered out into mid-table mediocrity.

Player of the Year was Jon McCarthy, who scored the winner against Everton and made it into the full international line-up for Northern Ireland, whilst the leading scorer was Tony Naylor. In all competitions five players reached double figures, equalling a club record last achieved in 1959-60.

PHIL SHERWIN

PORT VALE

League: 12th   FA Cup: 5th Rnd   Coca-Cola Cup: 1st Rnd   Anglo/Italian Cup: Finalists

M	DATE	COMP	VEN	OPPONENTS	RESULT	HT	LP	GOAL SCORERS/GOAL TIMES	ATT.
1	A 13	EL	A	Derby County	D 0-0	0-0	16		(10869)
2	15	CC 1/1	A	Huddersfield Town	W 2-1	1-1		Glover 2, Mills 55	(5363)
3	19	EL	H	Millwall	L 0-1	0-0	23		8202
4	22	CC 1/2	H	Huddersfield Town	L 1-3	0-2		Glover 72	4380
5	27	EL	W	Stoke City	W 1-0	0-0	20	Bogie 48	(14283)
6	30	EL	H	Sunderland	D 1-1	1-0	18	Porter 4	7693
7	S 2	EL	A	Norwich City	L 1-2	1-2	21	Mills 41	(13908)
8	5	AIC	A	Cesena	D 2-2	0-1		Glover 53, Mills 57	(820)
9	9	EL	H	Portsmouth	L 0-2	0-1	22		7374
10	12	EL	H	Leicester City	L 0-2	0-1	24		8814
11	16	EL	A	Grimsby Town	L 0-1	0-1	24		(4066)
12	23	EL	A	Reading	D 2-2	2-1	23	Mills 26, Glover 42	(7819)
13	30	EL	H	Wolverhampton Wand	D 2-2	1-2	24	Richards 38(og), Porter 61(pen)	11550
14	O 7	EL	A	Huddersfield Town	W 2-0	1-0	23	McCarthy 12, Guppy 60	(11554)
15	11	AIC	H	Ancona	W 2-0	0-0		Talbot 50, Guppy 70	3440
16	15	EL	H	Crystal Palace	L 1-2	0-0	23	Glover 60	6935
17	21	EL	A	Barnsley	D 1-1	1-1	22	Guppy 38	(7332)
18	29	EL	A	Birmingham City	L 1-2	0-1	24	Porter 80(pen)	8875
19	N 5	EL	A	Oldham Athletic	D 2-2	1-1	23	Mills 18, 90	(5138)
20	8	AIC	H	Genoa	D 0-0	0-0			3282
21	11	EL	H	Sheffield United	L 2-3	1-1	24	Naylor 34, Mills 83	7284
22	18	EL	H	Watford	D 1-1	0-1	24	Samuel 64	6265
23	22	EL	A	Tranmere Rovers	L 1-2	0-1	24	Naylor 84	(6681)
24	25	EL	A	Charlton Athletic	D 2-2	0-0	24	Porter 61, Griffiths 79	(10174)
25	D 2	EL	H	Huddersfield Town	W 1-0	1-0	24	Foyle 6	7701
26	9	EL	H	Reading	W 3-2	3-1	20	Foyle 2, Guppy 17, Porter 35(pen)	6376
27	13	AIC	A	Perugia	W 5-3	3-1		Porter 17(pen), McCarthy 20, Mills 42, 74, 90 (3)	(200)
28	16	EL	A	Wolverhampton Wand	W 1-0	1-0	20	Porter 6	(23329)
29	20	EL	A	Southend United	L 1-2	1-2	20	Naylor 33	(4506)
30	26	EL	H	West Bromwich Albion	W 3-1	0-0	18	Naylor 48, Foyle 52, Guppy 88	10807
31	J 1	EL	A	Ipswich Town	L 1-5	0-0	19	Naylor 86	(9926)
32	6	FAC 3	A	Crystal Palace	D 0-0	0-0			(10456)
33	13	EL	A	Millwall	W 2-1	1-1	18	Foyle 5, Naylor 62	(14220)
34	16	FAC 3R	H	Crystal Palace	W 4-3	2-1		Walker 18, 111, Porter 28(pen), Foyle 60	6754
35	20	EL	H	Derby County	D 1-1	0-1	19	Naylor 76	11947
36	23	AIC	A	Ipswich Town	W 4-2	2-1		Naylor 44, 45, 74 (3), Foyle 90	(5831)
37	27	FAC 4	A	Everton	D 2-2	0-1		Foyle 59, Bogie 89	(33168)
38	F 10	EL	A	Sunderland	D 0-0	0-0	21		(15954)
39	14	FAC 4R	H	Everton	W 2-1	1-1		Bogie 17, McCarthy 69	19197
40	17	EL	A	Leicester City	D 1-1	0-1	21	McCarthy 70	(13758)
41	21	FAC 5	A	Leeds United	D 0-0	0-0			(18607)
42	24	AIC	A	West Bromwich Albion	D 0-0	0-0			(10862)
43	27	FAC 5R	H	Leeds United	L 1-2	1-0		Naylor 37	14023
44	M 2	EL	A	West Bromwich Albion	D 1-1	0-1	23	McCarthy 46	(13707)
45	5	AIC	H	West Bromwich Albion	W 3-1	1-0		McCarthy 6, Glover 85, Foyle 87	7640
46	9	EL	H	Southend United	W 2-1	1-0	23	McCarthy 10, Glover 54	6222
47	12	EL	H	Stoke City	W 1-0	1-0	19	Bogie 1	16737
48	17	AIC F	N	Genoa	L 2-5	0-3		Foyle 68, 82	12663
49	20	EL	H	Norwich City	W 1-0	1-0	17	Foyle 16	6085
50	23	EL	A	Ipswich Town	W 2-1	1-1	17	Bogie 41(pen), McCarthy 86	7277
51	27	EL	A	Portsmouth	W 2-1	2-1	14	Naylor 5, Griffiths 43	(6335)
52	30	EL	H	Barnsley	W 3-0	1-0	12	Foyle 9, Porter 62, Naylor 78	7358
53	A 2	EL	A	Crystal Palace	D 2-2	0-2	11	McCarthy 51, Foyle 75	(14180)
54	6	EL	A	Birmingham City	L 1-3	0-2	12	Porter 68	(17469)
55	8	EL	H	Oldham Athletic	L 1-3	0-1	16	Mills 87	7796
56	13	EL	H	Watford	L 2-5	1-2	17	Porter 44(pen), McCarthy 66	(9066)
57	16	EL	H	Grimsby Town	W 1-0	0-0	10	Aspin 84	5796
58	20	EL	H	Tranmere Rovers	D 1-1	0-0	12	Naylor 84	7419
59	23	EL	H	Luton Town	W 1-0	1-0	9	Mills 34	6054
60	27	EL	H	Charlton Athletic	L 1-3	1-1	10	McCarthy 26	8428
61	30	EL	A	Luton Town	L 2-3	1-1	11	Porter 7, Mills 87	(5443)
62	M 4	EL	A	Sheffield United	D 1-1	0-0	11	Naylor 62	(18741)

Best Home League Attendance: 16737 v Stoke City   Smallest: 5796 v Grimsby Town   Average: 8217

Goal Scorers:

EL(59): Naylor(11), Porter(10), Mills(8), McCarthy(8), Foyle(7), Guppy(4), Bogie(3), Glover(3), Griffiths(2), Samuel(1), Opponent(s)(1), Aspin(1)

CC(3): Mills(1), Glover(1), Glover(1)

FAC(9): Foyle(2), Bogie(2), Walker(2), Porter(1), Naylor(1), McCarthy(1)

AIC(18): Foyle(4), Mills(4), Naylor(3), McCarthy(2), Glover(2), Guppy(1), Porter(1), Talbot(1)

(D) Aspin	(M) Bogie	(M) Corden	(F) Foyle	(D) Glover	(F) Glover	(D) Griffiths	(M) Guppy	(D) Hill	(F) Kent	(M) Lawton	(M) McCarthy	(F) Mills	(G) Musselwhite	(F) Naylor	(M) Porter	(D) Samuel	(M) Sandeman	(D) Stokes	(M) Talbot	(D) Tankard	(G) Van Heusden	(M) Walker	Player	No.
X	S		X	X	X1	X	X				X	S1	X		X					X	S	X	K.Breen	1
X	X		S	X	X	X	X				X	X	X		X					X	S	S	D.Allison	2
X2	S2		X	X	X3	X1	X				X	S3	X		X			S1		X		X	I.Cruikshank	3
X			X2	X	S2		X				X	X	X	X1	S1					X	S	X	S.Matthieson	4
X			X	X	X1	X	X	X			X	X	X	S1	X					X		S	G.Singh	5
X			X	X	X	X	X				X	X1	X	S1	X			S		X		S	J.Kirkby	6
X1			X	X	X	X	X				X2	X	X	S2	X			S		X		S1	D.Orr	7
X			X	X	X	X	X1				X	X	X	S	X			S1		X				8
X1			X	X	X	X		S			X	X1	X	S1	X	X		S1		X			R.Poulain	9
X1			X	X	X	X1	X				X1	S1	X	S1	X			S1		X		X	G.Pooley	10
X1			X	X	X	X2	X	S2			X		S		X			X		X	X	S1	M.A.Riley	11
	S		X	X	X	X2					X	X		S2	X			S1	X	X	X	X1	P.Rejer	12
	S		X	X1	X	X					X	X		S1	X			S	X	X	X	X	U.Rennie	13
	S		X	X	X	X					X	X		S	X			S	X	X	X	X	T.Hilbron	14
	X		X	X	X	X					X3	X		X	S3			S1	X2	X1	X	S2	G. Rosica	15
	S		X	X	X	X					X1	X2		S2	X			X	X		X	X	W.Burns	16
	S		X	X	X	X					X	S1		X	X1			S	X			X	S.W.Mathieson	17
	S1		X	X1	X	X					X1	S1		X	X			S1	X			X1	R.Gifford	18
	S1		X1	S		X					X	X		X	X			X	X				P.R.Richards	19
X		S3				S2	X1		X	X	X	X	X3		X	X2					S1		S. Racalbuto	20
X			X	S1	X	X					X1	X	X		X			S	X1			S1	T.Lunt	21
X1		S1	X	X		S	X				X1	X	X	X1	X			X	X			S1	E.Wolstenholme	22
	X	X		S1	X			S			X	X1	X	X	X			X	X			S1	M.Riley	23
	S	X		X							X	S	X	X	X	X		S	X			X	F.Streton	24
	S	X	X	S		X	X1				X	S	X	X	X	X		S	X			X	K.Lynch	25
	S	X	X			X	X1				X	S	X	X	X	X		S1	X			X	A.Leake	26
	X		S2	X	X2	X				S1	X	X	X	X2	X	X		X1			S		I. Cruikshanks	27
	X	X		X	X	X					X	S1	X	X1	X						S	X	J.Kirkby	28
		X		X	X	X					X	X	X	X	X	X1		S	S1		S	X	N.S.Barry	29
X		X	X	X	X	X					X	S	X	X	X			S	X	S			T.West	30
X1		X	X	X	X						X	S	X	X	X			S1	X	S			R.Furnandiz	31
X		X	X	X		X					X	S	X	X1	X			X	X			S1	R.Poulain	32
X		X	X	X	S						X	X	X	S	X			X	X				U.Rennie	33
X		X	X1	X1							X	S2	X	X2	X			X	X			S1	R.Poulain	34
X	S1		X		S2	X2	X				X	S	X	X	X			X1	X			X	R.Gifford	35
X	X		X			X	X1				X	S	S	X	X		S1		X	X	X		T. Heilbron	36
X	S1		X			X	X1	X			X	S	X	X	X				X	S	X		M.Reed	37
X	X1		X	S1		X	X				X		X	X1	X			S	X		S	S1	M.A.Riley	38
X	X		X		X1	X	X2	X			X	S	X	X	X			S	X	S	S1		M.Reed	39
X	X1		X			X	X	X			X	S2	X	X2	X			S	X			S1	K.Lynch	40
X	X		X			X	X	X			X	S	X	X	X			S	X			X	P.Durkin	41
	X2				S1	X	X3	X			X	X1	X	X	X			X	S2	S3	S	X	S.Mathieson	42
X	X		S			X	X	X2			X	S1	X	X1	X			S2	X			X	P.Durkin	43
X	X		X		X1	X	X				X	X	X		X			S1	S	X	S	X	P.Richards	44
X	X		S2			X	X	X			X	X	X		X			S1		X1	S	X	J. Kirkby	45
X	X		X			X	X	X1	X		X	S	X		X			X	S			S1	J.Lloyd	46
X	X1		X		X1	X	X				X		X	S1	X			X	S			X1	E.Lomas	47
X	X		X		X1	X	X2	X			X		X	S1	X			X3	S2			S3	I. Koho	48
X	X		X	S	S	X	X				X1		X	X				X	S1			X	C.Wilkes	49
X	X		X		S2	X	X	X			X		X	X2	S1			X	S			X1	P.Rejer	50
X	X1		X			X	X	X			S1	S2	X	X2	X			X	S			X	S.Bennett	51
X	X1		X			X	X	X			X	S1	X	X1	X			X		S		S1	R.Pearson	52
X	X		X		X1	X	X				X	S2	X	X	X2			X	S1			S	A.Butler	53
X	X3		X			X	X				X2	S2	X	X1	X	X		X	S1			S3	G.Cain	54
X	X3		X			X	X				X	S1	X	X	X1	X1		X	S1			S3	R.Poulain	55
X	X		X	S	S1	X	X				X	X	X	X1	X			X	S			X	A.D'Urso	56
X	X		X	S1		X	X				X	X	X	S						X1		S	K.Breen	57
X	X1		X		S	X1	X				X	X	X	X				X				S1	G.Barber	58
X		X1		S2	S	X	X			X2		X		X	X			X	S1	X			R.Furnandiz	59
X	S1	X1		S		X	S1	X		X1	X	X		X	X			X		X			K.Lynch	60
X	X1		X	S2		X	X				X	X2	X	X	X		S	X				S1	N.Barry	61
X	S			S	S	X	X				X	X	X	X	X			X				X	B.Burns	62
22	27	2	24	27	17	40	43	35	0	2	44	20	39	30	44	9	1	16	8	28	7	21	EL Appearances	
0	5	0	1	2	7	1	1	0	1	0	1	12	0	9	1	0	0	2	12	1	0	14	EL Sub Appearances	
1	2	0	1	2	1+1	1	2	0	0	0	2	2	2	0	2	0	1	0+1	0	2	0	1	CC Appearances	
4	5+1	0	4	2	0	4	6	6	0	0	6	0+2	6	6	6	0	0	0	2+1	6	0	3+3	FAC Appearances	
3	8	0	2+2	2	3+2	7	7+1	6	0	1+1	8	6	6	5+1	7+1	1	0	4+3	2+3	5+1	2	3+3	AIC Appearances	

289

PORT VALE

CLUB RECORDS

BIGGEST VICTORIES
League: 9-1 v Chesterfield, Division 2, 24.9.1932
8-0 v Gateshead, Division 4, 26.12.1958
F.A. Cup: 8-2 v Alfreton (a), 6th Qual. Rnd, 13.12.1924.
League Cup: 5-1 v Wrexham, Rnd 1, 13.9.1983

BIGGEST DEFEATS
League: 0-10 v Sheffield United, Division 2, 10.12.1892
0-10 v Notts County, Division 2, 26.2.1895
F.A. Cup: 0-7 v Small Heath, 5th Qual. Round, 10.12.1898
League Cup: 0-4 v Northampton Town, Rnd 1, 2.9.1987

MOST POINTS
3 points a win: 89, Division 2, 1992-93
2 points a win: 69, Division 3N, 1953-54

MOST GOALS
110, 1958-59 (Division 4)
Steele 23, Wilkinson 21, Barnett 20, Poole 17, Cunliffe 14, Jackson 8, Kinsey3, Hall 2, Sproson 1, og 1.

MOST LEAGUE GOALS CONCEDED
106, Division 2, 1935-36

MOST GOALS IN A SEASON
Wilf Kirkham (1926-27) 38 League, 3 FA Cup, Total 41

MOST FIRST CLASS MATCHES IN A SEASON
62, 1995-96 (46 League, 6 FA Cup, 2 League Cup, 8 Anglo/Italian).

MOST LEAGUE WINS
30, Division 3N, 1929-30

MOST LEAGUE DRAWS
20, Division 3, 1977-78

MOST LEAGUE DEFEATS
28, Division 2, 1956-57

INDIVIDUAL CLUB RECORDS

MOST GOALS IN A MATCH
6. Stewart Littlewood v Chesterfield, Division 2, 24.9.1932 (9-1)

OLDEST PLAYER
Tom Holford, 46 yrs 3 months, 5.4.1924

YOUNGEST PLAYER
Malcolm McKenzie, 15yrs 347 days, 12.4.1965

MOST CAPPED PLAYER
Sammy Morgan (Northern Ireland) 7

BEST PERFORMANCES

League: 1953-54: Matches played 46, Won 26, Drawn 17, Lost 3, Goals for 74,Goals against 21, Points 69. 1st in Division 3N.

Highest: 5th Division 2, 1930-31.

F.A. Cup: 1953-54: 1st rnd. Darlington 3-1; 2nd rnd. Southport 1-1 2-0; 3rd rnd. Queens Park Rangers 1-0; 4th rnd. Cardiff City 2-0; 5th rnd. Blackpool 2-0; 6th rnd. Leyton Orient 1-0; Semi-Final West Bromwich Albion 1-2.

League Cup: 1991-92: 1st rnd. Bye, 2nd rnd. Notts County 2-1, 2-3, 3rd rnd.Liverpool 2-2, 1-4.
2nd rnd. 1960-61; 1962-63; 1963-64; 1967-68; 1972-73; 1981-82; 1983-84; 1984-85; 1985-86; 1986-87; 1988-89; 1989-90; 1990-91; 1994-95.

ADDITIONAL INFORMATION
Previous Leagues: Midland League
Previous Name: Burslem Port Vale 1884-1909

Club colours: White shirts, black shorts.
Change colours: Yellow/black quarted shirts, yellow shorts.

Reserves League: Pontins Central League Division 2
Youth League: Midland Melville Youth League.

DIVISIONAL RECORD

	Played	Won	Drawn	Lost	For	Against	Points
Division 2/1	1,444	487	319	638	2,003	2,451	1,363
Division 3/2	920	336	255	329	1,240	1,237	1,047
Division 3(N)	218	105	66	47	367	230	276
Division 3(S)	348	122	89	137	458	460	333
Division 4	598	220	185	193	802	713	704
Total	**3,528**	**1,270**	**914**	**1,344**	**4,870**	**5,091**	**3,723**

(Excluding Leeds City results 1919-20)

Records and Statistics

COMPETITIONS

Div.2/1	Div.3(N)	Div.3(S)	Div.3/2	Div.4
1892-96	1929-30	1938-52	1959-65	1958-59
1898-07	1936-38	1957-58	1970-78	1965-70
1919-29	1952-54		1983-84	1978-83
1930-36			1986-89	1984-86
1954-57			1992-94	
1989-92				
1994-				

MOST APPEARANCES

Roy Sproson 831+5 (1950-72)

Year	League	FA Cup	Lge Cup
1950-51	10		
1951-52	28		
1952053	45	2	
1953-54	45	8	
1954-55	42	3	
1955-56	42	2	
1956-57	39	2	
1957-58	37	3	
1958-59	21	1	
1959-60	41	6	
1960-61	43	3	3
1961-62	46	7	1
1962-63	42	4	1
1963-64	46	5	1
1964-65	45	2	1
1965-66	28+2	4	
1966-67	30+1	2	1
1967-68	32	1	1
1968-69	41+1	5	
1969-70	46	5	1
1970-71	5+1		1
1971-72	1		
	755+5	65	11

RECORD TRANSFER FEE RECEIVED

Amount	Club	Player	Date
1,000,000	Sheffield Wed.	Ian Taylor	08/94
£925,000	Norwich City	Darren Beckford	6/91
£350,000	Charlton Athletic	Andy Jones	8/87
£135,000	Stoke City	Mark Chamberlain	8/82

RECORD TRANSFER FEE PAID

Amount	Club	Player	Date
£450,000	York City	Jon McCarthy	07/95
£375,000	Oxford United	Martin Foyle	6/91
£200,000	Middlesbrough	Dean Glover	2/89
£40,000	Leicester City	Gary Ford	12/87

HONOURS

Division 3(N)	Division 4	AGT
1929-30	1958-59	1992-93
1953-54		

MOST GOALS IN A CAREER

Wilf Kirkham - 164 (1923-29 & 1931-33)

Year	League	FA Cup
1923-24	7	
1924-25	26	7
1925-26	35	
1926-27	38	3
1927-28	13	1
1928-29	15	
1931-32	4	
1932-33	15	
Total	153	11

Current leading goalscorer: Martin Foyle - 80 (1991-96)

MANAGERS

Name	Seasons	Best	Worst
T Clare	1905-06	17(2)	17(2)
S Gleaves	1906-07	16(2)	16(2)
A Walker	1911-13		
H Myatt	1913-14		
T Holford	1914-17		
J Cameron	1918-19		
J Schofield	1919-29	8(2)	21(2)
T Morgan	1929-32	5(2)	1(3N)
T Holford	1932-36	8(2)	21(2)
W Cresswell	1936-37	11(3N)	11(3N)
T Morgan	1937-39	15(3N)	18(3S)
W Frith	1944-46		
G Hodgson	1946-51	8(3S)	13(3S)
I Powell	1951		
F Steele	1951-57	12(2)	13(3S)
N Low	1957-62	7(3)	15(3S)
F Steele	1962-65	3(3)	22(3)
J Mudie	1965-67	13(4)	19(4)
S Matthews	1967-68	18(4)	18(4)
G Lee	1968-74	6(3)	13(4)
R Sproson	1974-77	6(3)	19(3)
C Harper	1977		
R Smith	1977-78	21(3)	21(3)
D Butler	1978-79	16(4)	16(4)
A Bloor	1979		
J McGrath	1979-83	23(3)	20(4)
J Rudge	1983-	11(2)	12(4)

LONGEST LEAGUE RUNS

f undefeated matches:	19 (16.8.1969 - 18.11.1969)	of league matches w/out a win:	17 (7.12.1991 - 21.03.1992)
f undefeated home matches:	43 (20.12.1952 - 18.9.1954)	of undefeated away matches:	12 (16.9.1953 - 9.1.1954)
without home win:	13 (28.3.1978 - 21.10.1978)	without an away win:	24 (2.12.1893 - 23.3.1895)
f league wins:	8 (8.4.1893 - 30.9.1893)	of home wins: 12 (9.2.1952 - 8.9.1952, 31.8.1953 - 25.12.1953)	
f league defeats:	9 (9.3.1957 - 20.4.1957)	of away wins:	5 (20.3.1993 - 24.4.1993)

PORT VALE

PLAYERS NAME Honours	Ht	Wt	Birthdate	Birthplace Transfers	Contract Date	Clubs	League	L/Cup	FA Cup	Other	Lge	L/C	FAC	Oth
G O A L K E E P E R S														
Musselwhite Paul	6.2	12.9	22/12/68	Portsmouth	01/12/86	Portsmouth								
AGT'93				Free	21/03/88	Scunthorpe United	132	11	7	13				
				£20000	30/07/92	Port Vale	170	8	17	19				
Van Heusden Arjan	6.4	12.0	11/12/72	Alphen (Holland)		Noordwijk								
				£4500	15/08/94	Port Vale	9			2				
D E F E N D E R S														
Aspin Neil	6.0	12.8	12/04/65	Gateshead	06/10/82	Leeds United	203+4	9	17	11	5	1		
AGT'93				£200000	28/07/89	Port Vale	257+2	13	20	18	3			
Glover Dean	5.9	11.2	29/12/63	West Bromwich	30/12/81	Aston Villa	25+3	7	3	1		1		
AGT'93				Loan	17/10/86	Sheffield United	5							
					17/06/87	Middlesbrough	44+6	4	5	7	5			2
				£200000	03/02/89	Port Vale	193+3	20	18	22	13	1		3
Griffiths Gareth	6.4	14.0	10/04/70	Winsford		Rhyl								
				£1000	08/02/93	Port Vale	43+2	1	4	7	4			
Hill Andy	5.11	12.0	20/01/65	Maltby	26/01/83	Manchester United								
E: Y.2				Free	04/07/84	Bury	264+10	22+1	212	19+1				
				£200000	21/12/90	Manchester City	91+7	11	2+1	1	6			
				£150000	25/08/95	Port Vale	35		6	6				
Holwyn Jermaine	6.0	11.10	16/04/73	Amsterdam		Ajax								
				£5000	01/07/95	Port Vale								
Stokes Dean	5.7	10.7	23/05/70	Birmingham		Halesowen Town								
					15/01/93	Port Vale	40+2	0+1	3	5+3				
Tankard Allen	5.10	11.7	21/05/69	Fleet	27/05/87	Southampton	5			2				
				Free	04/07/88	Wigan Athletic	205+4	15	13	20	4	1		
				£87500	26/07/93	Port Vale	89+5	8	10	8+1	1		1	
M I D F I E L D														
Bogie Ian	5.7	10.2	06/12/67	Newcastle	18/12/85	Newcastle United	7+7	0+1	1+2	3				1
					09/02/89	Preston North End	67+12	3+1	3	4+1	12			
				£145000	16/08/91	Millwall	44+7	1	2	3	1			
				£50000	23/03/93	Port Vale	34+7	2	5+1	8	5	2		
				£100000	14/10/93	Leyton Orient	62+3	2	2	8+1	5			
Corden S Wayne	5.9	10.6	01/11/75	Leek	20/07/94	Port Vale	2+1							
Eyre Richard P	5.10	11.7	15/09/76	Poynton	01/07/95	Port Vale								
Guppy Stephen	5.11	10.10	29/03/69	Winchester		Wycombe Wand.	41	4	8	10	8		2	
E: S-P.1. GMVC'93. FAT'91'93				£15000	02/08/94	Newcastle United								
				£225000	25/11/94	Port Vale	68+3	2	7	7+1	6			1
McCarthy Jon	5.9	11.5	18/08/70	Middlesbrough	07/11/87	Hartlepool United	0+1							
NI: 1, B.1				Free	01/08/88	Shepshed Albion								
				Free	22/03/90	York City	198+1	8	11	15	31	1	3	3
				£450000	01/08/95	Port Vale	44+1	2	6	8	8		1	2
Porter Andy	5.9	11.2	17/09/68	Macclesfield	29/06/87	Port Vale	241+31	16	17+4	26+2	14		3	1
AGT'93														
Talbot Stewart	6.0	13.0	14/06/73	Birmingham	10/08/94	Port Vale	10+12		2+1	2+3				1
Walker Ray	5.10	12.0	28/09/63	North Shields	26/09/81	Aston Villa	15+8	2+1	2					
E: Y.6 FAYC'80				Loan	07/09/84	Port Vale	15				1			
				£12000	05/08/86	Port Vale	313+21	17+1	25+3	22+3	32	1	5	3
				Loan	23/09/94	Cambridge United	5			2				
F O R W A R D S														
Cunningham Dean	5.5	10.6	28/05/77	Burslem	01/07/95	Port Vale								
Foyle Martin	5.10	11.2	02/05/63	Salisbury	13/08/80	Southampton	6+6	0+2			1	2		
AGT'93				£10000	03/08/84	Aldershot	98	10	8	6	35	5	5	
				£140000	26/03/87	Oxford United	120+6	16	5	3+1	36	4	3	1
				£375000	25/06/91	Port Vale	153+10	13	13+1	13+3	56	6	9	9
Glover Edward Lee	5.10	12.1	24/04/70	Kettering	02/05/87	Nottingham Forest	61+15	6+5	8+2	4+1	9	2	1	1
S: u21.3, Y. FMC'92				Loan	14/09/89	Leicester City	3+2				1			
				Loan	18/01/90	Barnsley	8		4					
				Loan	02/09/91	Luton Town	1							
				£200000	02/08/94	Port Vale	38+14	5+1	0+2	3+2	7	4		2

							Club										
ills R Lee	6.1	12.11	10/07/70	Mexborough			Stocksbridge										
						09/12/92	Wolves	12+13	1	3+1	3	2		1	1		
				£400000	24/02/95	Derby County	16				7						
				£200000	01/08/95	Port Vale	20+12	2	0+2	6	8	1		4			
aylor Tony	5.5	9.0	29/03/67	Manchester			Droylsden										
				£20000	22/03/90	Crewe Alexandra	104+18	7+2	9	12	45	5	6	9			
				£150000	16/07/94	Port Vale	59+13	3	6	5+1	20	1	1	3			

ADDITIONAL CONTRACT PLAYERS

Reilly Justin M	Port Vale (T)

TRAINEES

oor Darren	Port Vale (T)
oyd Stephen	Port Vale (T)
own Mark	Port Vale (T)
urns Liam	Port Vale (T)
utler Robert	Port Vale (T)
ommander Andrew	Port Vale (T)
avis Neal	Port Vale (T)
ancock Darren	Port Vale (T)
ale Andrew	Port Vale (T)
cShane Antony	Port Vale (T)
ant Robert	Port Vale (T)
eynolds Craig	Port Vale (T)
ochester Daniel	Port Vale (T)
illiams Stephen	Port Vale (T)
orth Matthew	Port Vale (T)

THE MANAGER
JOHN RUDGE

Date of Birth . . . . 21st October 1944.
Place of Birth . . . . Wolverhampton.
Date of Appointment . . . . December 1983.

PREVIOUS CLUBS
As Manager . . . . None.
As Coach . . . . Torquay United.
As a Player . . . . Huddersfield Town, Carlisle United, Torquay United,
. . . . Bristol Rovers, Bournemouth.

HONOURS
As a Manager
Port Vale: Promotion to Division 3, 1986. Promotion to Division 2, 1989. AGT Winners 1993.
Promotion to Division 1, 1994.

As a Player
Bristol Rovers: Promotion to Division 2, 1974.

VALE PARK
Burslem, Stoke-on-Trent ST6 1AW
Tel: 01782 814 134

Capacity 22,356
Seating 17,616

First game .... v Newport Co., Div.3(S), 24.8.1950.
First floodlit game .... v WBA (Friendly), 24.9.1958.

ATTENDANCES
Highest .... 49,768 v Aston Villa, FAc 5th Rnd, 20.2.1960.
Lowest .... 994 v Hereford Utd, AMC, 22.12.1986.

OTHER GROUNDS .... Limekiln Lane 1876-81. Westport 1881-84. Moorland Road 1884-86.
.... Athletic Ground 1886-1913. Recreation Ground 1913-1950. Vale Park 1950-

MATCHDAY TICKET PRICES

Railway Stand	£12
Juv/OAP	£9
Railway Paddock	£11
Juv/OAP	£8
Sential Stand	£11
Juv/OAP	£8
Family Stand	£11
Juv/OAP	£8
Terraces . . . . Lome Street	£9.50
Juv/OAP	£6.50

Visiting Supporters. . . . . Caudwell End £12

Ticket Office Telephone no. 01782 814 134

CLUBCALL
0891 12 16 36
Calls cost 39p per minute cheap rate and 49p per minute at all other times.
Call costings correct at time of going to press.

HOW TO GET TO THE GROUND

From the North
Use motorway (M6) until junction 16 then join A500, sign posted Stoke. In 5.9 miles branch left and at roundabout take 1st exit A527. In 0.4 miles turn right B5051 into Newcastle Street and at end over crossroads into Moorland Road. Shortly turn left into Hamil Road for Port Vale FC.

From the East
Use A50 or A52 into Stoke-on-Trent then follow signs to Burslem A50 into Waterloo Road. At Burslem crossroads turn right into Moorland Road. Shortly turn left into Hamil Road for Port Vale FC.

From the South and West
Use motorway (M6) until junction 15 then A5006 and A500. In 6.3 miles branch left and at roundabout take 3rd exit A527. In 0.4 miles turn right B5051 into Newcastle Street and at end over crossroads into Moorland Road. Shortly turn left into Hamil Road for Port Vale FC.

Car Parking
(Ample) behind the Railway Stand, on Hamil Road car park and streets.

Nearest Railway Station
Longport, Stoke-on-Trent (01345 484950)

MATCHDAY PROGRAMME

Programme Editor . . . . Chris Harper.

Number of pages . . . . 40.

Price . . . . £1.50.

Subscriptions . . . . . £40 (home only), £75 (home & away) inc. postage.

Local Newspapers . . . . The Sentinel, The Green'Un.

Local Radio Stations . . . . Radio Stoke, Signal Radio.

PORTSMOUTH
(The Pompey)
NATIONWIDE LEAGUE DIVISION 1
SPONSORED BY: THE NEWS

ack Row (L-R): Danny Hounsell, Alan McLoughlin, Mark Stimson, Kevin Braybrook, Aaron Flahavan, Tony Dobson, Jimmy Carter, Jimmy azer, Deon Burton, Alex Totten. **Middle Row:** Gordon Neave (Kit), Neil Sillett (Physio), Jason Rees, Lloyd McGrath, Mart Poom, Kieth aldon (First Team Coach), Alan Knight, Guy Butters, Russell Perrett, Larry May (Youth Team Coach), Martin Hinshelwood (Res. Manager). ront Row: Sammy Igoe, Paul Hall, Andy Awford, Simon Barnard, David Waterman, Gerry Creaney, Terry Fenwick (Manager), Kit Symons, hn Durnin, Paul Wood, Lee Russell, Robbie Pethick, Anthony Tilley.

PORTSMOUTH
FORMED IN 1898
TURNED PROFESSIONAL IN 1898
LTD COMPANY IN 1898

MANAGING DIRECTOR: M H Gregory

DIRECTORS
Brady, B A V Henson FCA, J S Hutchinson,
R G Smith, V J Jenner JP. MBA. FIMgt,
F E Dinenage

SECRETARY
P A Weld (01705 731 204)
COMMERCIAL MANAGER
Julie Baker

MANAGER: Terry Fenwick

YOUTH TEAM MANAGER
L May
PHYSIOTHERAPIST
N Sillett

STATISTICIAN FOR THE DIRECTORY
Peter Macey

It is said that over time luck will even itself out. Pompey went into the final game of the season needing nothing short of a miracle; they were away at Huddersfield Town and Millwall, the only team they could catch, away at play-off chasing Ipswich Town. In the end the results came down in our favour and we stayed in the first division on goals scored. This was the moment luck evened itself out, as three years earlier we were piped for promotion to the Premiership on goals scored. What bitter sweet irony.

Last season was one of the worst the club has seen in some time and lessons must be learnt very quickly for next season to make sure the same thing does not happen again next year. During the season Terry Brady, father of Birmingham City's Karen, joined the board of directors. Hopefully next season Mr BRady will, along with the rest of the board sanction money to be made available for the strengthening of the squad. If they have the ambition to try and make the club great again then this is a must and if they don't then the club can only go one way.

All too much last season there was allot of talk on transfer deals and no action, talk which towards the end of the season most of the fans were dismissing as rubbish after watching none of the said transfer deals go through. Next season there must be less talk and more action, and certainly a more consistent performance on the pitch than we saw last year.

Last season saw Alan Knight pick up his third player of the year award from the fans; the season also saw Alan break the league record for league appearances by a goalkeeper for one club, a record previously held by Peter Bonetti, 600 with Chelsea.

PETER MACEY.

PORTSMOUTH

League: 21st   FA Cup: 3rd Rnd   Coca-Cola Cup: 1st Rnd

M	DATE	COMP	VEN	OPPONENTS	RESULT	HT	LP	GOAL SCORERS/GOAL TIMES	ATT.
1	A 12	EL	H	Southend United	W 4-2	2-1	4	Creaney 40,76, Tilson 42(og), Rees 73	10630
2	16	CC 1/1	H	Cardiff City	L 0-2	0-1			4203
3	19	EL	A	Grimsby Town	L 1-2	0-0	10	McLoughlin 81(pen)	(4515)
4	22	CC 1/2	A	Cardiff City	L 0-1	0-0			(4341)
5	26	EL	H	Reading	D 0-0	0-0	11		9917
6	30	EL	A	Leicester City	L 2-4	1-4	19	Creaney 35(pen), Hall 60	(15170)
7	S 2	EL	H	Millwall	L 0-1	0-1	22		8023
8	9	EL	A	Port Vale	W 2-0	1-0	17	Burton 14, Griffiths 83(pen)	(7374)
9	12	EL	A	Sunderland	D 1-1	0-1	18	McLoughlin 86(pen)	(12282)
10	16	EL	H	Derby County	D 2-2	1-1	16	Gittens 19, McLoughlin 89	14434
11	23	EL	H	Tranmere Rovers	L 0-2	0-0	18		11127
12	30	EL	A	Luton Town	L 1-3	1-2	21	Walsh 43	(7795)
13	O 7	EL	A	Oldham Athletic	D 1-1	0-0	21	Simpson 49	(5937)
14	14	EL	H	Birmingham City	L 0-1	0-1	22		10006
15	21	EL	A	West Bromwich Albion	L 1-2	0-0	23	McLoughlin 59(pen)	(16257)
16	28	EL	H	Watford	W 4-2	2-0	20	Stimson 12, 15, Allen 63, Carter 88	7025
17	N 4	EL	A	Sheffield United	L 1-4	1-2	21	Simpson 20	(11281)
18	11	EL	H	Huddersfield Town	D 1-1	1-1	21	Simpson 28(pen)	6876
19	18	EL	H	Stoke City	D 3-3	2-1	21	McLoughlin 16(pen), 56, Walsh 44	8030
20	21	EL	A	Barnsley	D 0-0	0-0	21		(6187)
21	25	EL	A	Ipswich Town	L 2-3	1-2	21	Walsh 25, Allen 75	(10286)
22	D 2	EL	H	Oldham Athletic	W 2-1	1-1	20	Allen 19, McLoughlin 77(pen)	6002
23	9	EL	A	Tranmere Rovers	W 2-1	2-0	19	Durnin 9, Hall 36	(6678)
24	16	EL	H	Luton Town	W 4-0	3-0	17	Hall 3, 43, Walsh 45, Carter 47	7012
25	23	EL	H	Norwich City	W 1-0	0-0	17	Durnin 56	9966
26	26	EL	A	Charlton Athletic	L 1-2	1-0	17	Hall 9	(11686)
27	30	EL	A	Wolverhampton Wand	D 2-2	0-2	16	Carter 58, Burton 65	(25294)
28	J 1	EL	H	Crystal Palace	L 2-3	0-2	17	Butters 57, Simpson 65	12926
29	7	FAC 3	A	Southampton	L 0-3	0-1			(15236)
30	13	EL	H	Grimsby Town	W 3-1	2-0	16	Walsh 10, Wood 12, Carter 77	6958
31	20	EL	A	Southend United	L 1-2	1-0	16	Hall 41	(5560)
32	27	EL	A	Millwall	D 1-1	0-1	16	Burton 75	(7710)
33	F 4	EL	A	Reading	W 1-0	0-0	14	McLoughlin 69	(7924)
34	10	EL	H	Leicester City	W 2-1	1-1	11	Burton 30, Hall 89	9003
35	17	EL	H	Sunderland	D 2-2	1-1	10	Hall 33, Griffiths 89	12241
36	24	EL	A	Derby County	L 2-3	0-0	12	Hall 61, McLoughlin 86(pen)	(16120)
37	M 2	EL	H	Charlton Athletic	W 2-1	1-1	11	Burton 44, 57	9323
38	9	EL	A	Norwich City	D 1-1	1-1	11	Hall 38	(13004)
39	16	EL	H	Wolverhampton Wand	L 0-2	0-2	15		11732
40	23	EL	A	Crystal Palace	D 0-0	0-0	16		(17039)
41	27	EL	H	Port Vale	L 1-2	1-2	17	Allen 18	6335
42	30	EL	H	West Bromwich Albion	L 0-2	0-1	18		8126
43	A 2	EL	A	Birmingham City	L 0-2	0-1	19		(14886)
44	6	EL	A	Watford	W 2-1	1-1	18	Awford 28, McLoughlin 61	(8226)
45	8	EL	H	Sheffield United	L 1-2	0-2	18	Durnin 56	8978
46	13	EL	A	Stoke City	L 1-2	0-1	21	Butters 61	(11471)
47	20	EL	H	Barnsley	D 0-0	0-0	21		8744
48	27	EL	H	Ipswich Town	L 0-1	0-0	22		12954
49	M 5	EL	A	Huddersfield Town	W 1-0	1-0	21	Burton 9	(14091)

Best Home League Attendance: 14434 v Derby County   Smallest: 6002 v Oldham Athletic   Average: 9407

Goal Scorers:
EL(61):   McLoughlin(10),Hall(10),Burton(7),Walsh(5),Simpson(5),Carter(4),Allen(4),Creaney(3),Durnin(3),Griffiths(2),Butters(2),Rees(1),Stimson(1),Gittens(1),Wood(1), Awford(1),Opponent(s)(1)

CC(0):
FAC(0):

1995-96

(M) Allen	(D) Awford	(M) Bradbury	(F) Burton	(D) Butters	(F) Carter	(F) Creaney	(D) Dobson	(F) Durnin	(G) Flahavan	(D) Gittens	(F) Griffiths	(F) Hall	(D) Hinshelwood	(M) Igoe	(G) Knight	(M) McLoughlin	(D) Perrett	(D) Pethick	(G) Poom	(M) Rees	(D) Russell	(F) Simpson	(D) Simson	(D) Symons	(D) Thomson	(F) Walsh	(D) Whitbread	(F) Wood	Player	#
	S1		S3	X	X1	X		X				X3		S1		X1		X	X	X	X				X				R.Gifford	1
	X		S2	X	X1	X2	S	X				X		S1	X	X		X	X	X	X				X				A.D.Urso	2
	X		S1	X	X1	S3						X		S1		X3		X	X	X	X	X1							K.Breen	3
X1			X	X	S2	X2		X				X		S1				X	X	X2	X	X							J.Brandwood	4
			X	X	X2		S	X		X	S1	X		S2				X	X	X1	X	X							G.Pooley	5
		S2			X1	X2	X	X		X		X		S1				X	X	X	X								G.Cain	6
		S2	X3		X2		X1			X		X	S3	X	X			X		X	X	X							C.Wilkes	7
		S1	X1	X	X							X	S2	X2		X	X			X	X	X							R.Poulain	8
X3			X	X	X1			S1				X	S3	X		S2		X			X2	X							T.Lunt	9
X			X1	X				S1				X	S3	X		X	S2	X3			X2	X				X			R.Gifford	10
		S1	X1	X				S2				X		X		X	X	X2			X		X3			X		S3	D.Orr	11
			X	X				S2				X	X	S3	X2	X1	X	X			X	X				X		S1	P.Rejer	12
			X1	X		X	X	X			S1			X	X	S3	X2				X	X					X3	X	J.W.Lloyd	13
			X2	X		X	X	X			X	S2	S3	X	X		S1			X1		X3				X		X	T.Helmley	14
X			S2	X		X	X	X			X	S	X1	X	X		S1					X				X2		X	U.Rennie	15
X			X		S2	X	X1				X	S		X	X		S1				X	X	X2			X			K.Leach	16
X			X				S1				X	X	X2	S	X	X	X	S2			X	X	X1			X			T.Heilbron	17
X			X				S3				X1	X3	S2	X	X			S1			X2	X	X			X	X		R.Harris	18
X			S1	X			X1					X		S	X	X		X			S	X				X	X		C.Wilkes	19
X			S1	X	X2		X3				X1	X		S3	X	X		X			S2	X						X	J.Rushton	20
X			X	X3			X				S1	X2	S2	X	X1			X			S3		X			X	X	X	B.Knight	21
X			X	S1			X					X		X	X			X					X	X1		X	X	X	G.Barber	22
X			X	X1	S		X					S2		X	X			X			S1		X	X		X2		X	M.Fletcher	23
			X	X			X					S		X	X			X			S	S	X	X		X	X	X	E.Lomas	24
X		S	X	X1			X					X		S1	X			X					S			X	X	X	G.Pooley	25
X			S2	X	X1		X					X2		X	X						S	X	S1			X	X		M.Bailey	26
X			X2	X	X		X1					X	S2	X	X			X			S	X	S1			X		X	A.Butler	27
X			S2	X	X2		S1					X	S3	X	X			X					X3	X1		X	X		M.Brandwood	28
			S2	X	S1		X			X		X2		X	X			X					X	X		X		X1	M.Bodenham	29
			S	X	X		X					X		S1	X	X		X					S	X		X	X	X1	I.Hemley	30
			S	X	X		X1	S1				X		X	X			X			S		X	X		X	X	X	G.Singh	31
			S1	X	X3		X2					X		X	X	X	X	X			S3		X		S2	X1		X	J.Kirkby	32
			X	X	X		S1				X1	X		S2	X	X	X	X					X			X		X2	D.Orr	33
	X		X	X	X		S1					X		S2	X	X	X2					S			X	X1		X	A.D'Urso	34
	X		X2	X	X1		S1					X		S	X	X		X					S1			X		X1	C.Wilkes	35
X2	X		X	X	X1		S1					X		X	X	X		X								X		X	W.Burns	36
X	X		X	X	X1		S1					S		X	X	X	S	X								X		X	N.Barry	37
X	X		X2	X	X		S1					X		X	X	X		X								X		X1	P.Taylor	38
X	X		X3	X1	X		S1					X		X	X	X		S1	X1							X		X	G.Barber	39
X	X	S2	X2		X							X	X		X	X	X1	X					X			X			A.Wiley	40
X	X	S2	X		X1							X	X2	S1	X		X				S3		X3			X			S.Bennett	41
X	X	S2			X							X2		X	X		X		S1			S	X1	X		X			R.Gifford	42
X	X1	S	X									X	X	S2	X	X	X					S1	X2			X			E.K.Wolstenholme	43
X	X		X	S								X	X	S	X	X	X	S					X		X				R.Poulain	44
X	X		X	X								X	X1	X	X	X		S1				S	X			X			C.Wilkes	45
X	X		X	X1			X	S				X		S1	X	X		X			S					X			M.Bailey	46
X	X	S1	X1	X				S				X		X	X	X		X2			S2		X						D.Orr	47
	X	S1	X	X2				S				X		X1	X	X		X			S2		X			X			M.Riley	48
X	X	S	X	X				S				X		S	X	X		X			X		X			X			J.Rushden	49
27	17	3	24	37	31	3	7	30	0	14	2	44	5	4	42	38	8	30	4	15	17	27	14	1	15	21	13	13	EL Appearances	
0	1	9	8	0	4	0	1	11	0	1	13	2	0	18	0	2	1	8	0	6	2	3	0	0	1	0	0	2	EL Sub Appearances	
0	2	0	1+1	2	1+1	2	0	2	0	0	0+1	2	0	0+2	1	1	0	2	1	2	2	1	0	0	0	0	0	0	CC Appearances	
0	0	0	0+1	0	0+1	0	0	1	0	1	0	1	0	0	1	0	1	1	0	1	0	0	0	1	1	0	1	1	FAC Appearances	

PORTSMOUTH

CLUB RECORDS

BIGGEST VICTORIES
League: 9-1 v Notts County, Division 2, 9.4.1927
F.A. Cup: 7-0 v Stockport (h), Rnd 3, 8.1.1949
League Cup: 5-0 v Rotherham United Rnd 2, 5.10.1993

BIGGEST DEFEATS
League: 0-10 v Leicester City, Division 1, 20.10.1928
F.A. Cup: 0-5 v Everton, Round 1, 1902-03
0-5 v Tottenham H, Round 3, 16.1.1937
0-5 v Blackburn Rov, Rnd 1 2nd Replay, 1899-90
League Cup: 0-5 v Queens Park Rangers, Round 2, 6.10.1981

MOST POINTS
3 points a win: 91, Division 3, 1982-83
2 points a win: 65, Division 3, 1961-62

MOST GOALS
91, 1979-80 (Division 4)
Garwood 17, Laidlaw 16, Hemmerman 13, Brisley 12, Rogers 9,
Gregory 5, Ashworth4, Aizelwood 2, Bryant 2, Perrin 2, Davey 1,
McLaughlin 1, Purdie 1, Todd 1,Showers 1, og 4

MOST LEAGUE GOALS CONCEDED
112, Division 1, 1958-59

MOST FIRST CLASS MATCHES IN A SEASON
61 (46 League, 2 FA Cup, 7 League Cup, 6 Anglo Italian) 1993-94

MOST LEAGUE WINS
27, Division 3, 1961-62; Division 3, 1982-83

MOST LEAGUE DRAWS
19, Division 3, 1981-82

MOST LEAGUE DEFEATS
27, Division 1, 1958-59

INDIVIDUAL CLUB RECORDS

MOST GOALS IN A MATCH
5. Alf Strange v Gillingham, Division 3, 27.1.1923 (6-1)
5. Peter Harris v Aston Villa, Division 1, 3.9.1958 (5-2)
(Peter Harris's 5th goal was his 200th league & cup goal for
Portsmouth)

MOST GOALS IN A SEASON
Guy Whittingham 47 (Lge 42, Lg Cup 2, Anglo-Ital 3) 1992-93
4 goals once=4, 3 goals three times=9, 2 goals 6 times=12, 1 goal
22 times=22
Previous holder: Billy Haines 43 (Lg 40, FAC 3) 1926-27

OLDEST PLAYER
Jimmy Dickinson MBE, 40 exactly v Northampton, 24.4.1965

YOUNGEST PLAYER
Clive Green, 16 years 259 days v Wrexham, 21.8.1976
(also youngest goalscorer when 16 yrs 280 days v Lincoln City,
11.9.1976)

MOST CAPPED PLAYER
Jimmy Dickenson (England) 48

BEST PERFORMANCES

League: 1961-62: Matches played 46, Won 27, Drawn 11, Lost 8,
Goals for 87,Goals against 47, Points 65. 1st in Division 3.
Highest: 1948-49, 1949-50: 1st in Division 1.

F.A. Cup: 1938-39: 3rd rnd. Lincoln 4-0; 4th rnd. West Bromwich
Albion 2-0; 5th rnd. West Ham United 2-0; 6th rnd. Preston North
End 1-0; Semi-final Huddersfield 2-1; Final Wolves 4-1.

League Cup: 1960-61: 2nd rnd. Coventry 2-0; 3rd rnd. Manchester
City 2-0; 4th rnd. Chelsea 1-0; 5th rnd. Rotherham 0-3. 1993-94: 5th
rnd.
1993-94: 2nd rnd. Rotherham 0-0, 5-0; 3rd rnd. Swindon 2-0; 4th
rnd.Peterborough 0-0, 1-0; 5th rnd. Manchester Utd 2-2, 0-1.

ADDITIONAL INFORMATION
Previous League: Southern League.

Club colours: Royal blue shirts, white shorts, red socks.
Change colours: Red & black striped shirts, black shorts, red
socks.

Reserves League: Avon Insurance Football Combination.

DIVISIONAL RECORD

	Played	Won	Drawn	Lost	For	Against	Points
Division 1	1,090	405	257	428	1,729	1,828	1,074
Division 2/1	1,334	480	355	512	1,886	1,940	1,498
Division 3	318	120	95	103	412	379	376
Division 3(S)	126	61	36	29	207	121	158
Division 4	92	44	24	24	153	97	112
Total	**2,960**	**1,110**	**767**	**1,096**	**4,387**	**4,365**	**3,218**

RECORDS AND STATISTICS

COMPETITIONS

Div.1	Div.2/1	Div.3	Div.3(S)	Div.4
1927-59	1924-27	1920-21	1921-24	1978-80
1987-88	1959-61	1961-62		
	1962-76	1976-78		
	1983-87	1980-83		
	1988-			

HONOURS

Div.1	Div.3	Div.3(S)	FA Cup	C/Shield
1948-49	1961-62	1923-24	1938-39	1949
1949-50	1982-83			

MOST APPEARANCES

Jimmy Dickinson 829 (1946-65)

Year	League	FA Cup	Lge Cup	C/Shield
1946-47	40	2		
1947-48	42	2		
1948-49	41	5		
1949-50	40	5		1
1950-51	41	1		
1951-52	40	4		
1952-53	40	2		
1953-54	40	7		
1954-55	25			
1955-56	39	2		
1956-57	42	2		
1957-58	42	2		
1958-59	39	4		
1959-60	42	1		
1960-61	40	1	4	
1961-62	46	1	4	
1962-63	42	5	3	
1963-64	42	1	2	
1964-65	41	2	2	
	764	49	15	1

MOST GOALS IN A CAREER

Peter Harris - 208 (1946-60)

Year	League	FA Cup
1946-47	1	
1947-48	13	1
1948-49	17	5
1949-50	16	1
1950-51	5	
1951-52	9	1
1952-53	23	
1953-54	20	4
1954-55	23	
1955-56	23	1
1956-57	12	2
1957-58	18	
1958-59	13	
1959-60	1	
Total	193	15

Current leading goalscorer: Alan McCloughlin - 40 (1992-96)

MANAGERS

Name	Seasons	Best	Worst
Since joining the League			
John McCartney	1920-27	2(2)	12(3S)
John Tinn	1927-47	4(1)	20(1)
J R Jackson	1947-52	1(1)	8(1)
Eddie Lever	1952-58	3(1)	20(1)
Freddie Cox	1958-61	22(1)	21(2)
Bill Thompson	1961		
George Smith	1961-70	5(2)	1(3)
Ron Tindall	1970-73	16(2)	17(2)
John Mortimore	1973-74	15(2)	15(2)
Ron Tindall	1974		
Ian St John	1974-77	17(2)	20(3)
Jimmy Dickinson	1977-79	24(3)	7(4)
Frank Burrows	1979-82	6(3)	4(4)
Bobby Campbell	1982-84	16(2)	1(3)
Alan Ball	1984-89	20(1)	4(2)
John Gregory	1989-90		
Frank Burrows	1990-91		
Jim Smith	1991-95	3(2/1)	17(2/1)
Terry Fenwick	1995-	21(1)	21(1)

RECORD TRANSFER FEE RECEIVED

Amount	Club	Player	Date
£1,700,000	Tottenham H.	Darren Anderton	6/92
£1,000,000	Inter Milan	Mark Hateley	6/84
£130,000	Brighton & H.A.	Steve Foster	6/79
£75,000	Carlisle United	David Kemp	3/78

RECORD TRANSFER FEE PAID

Amount	Club	Player	Date
£500,000	Celtic	Gerry Creaney	1/94
£450,000	Q.P.R.	Colin Clarke	5/90
£315,000	Aston Villa	Warren Aspinall	8/88
£300,000	Barnsley	John Beresford	3/89

LONGEST LEAGUE RUNS

of undefeated matches:	15 (18.4.1924 - 18.10.1924)	of league matches w/out a win:	25 (22.1.1958 - 17.10.1959)
of undefeated home matches:	32 (3.1.1948 - 27.8.1949)	of undefeated away matches:	14 (1.3.1924 - 18.10.1924)
without home win:	16 (6.2.1958 - 17.10.1959)	without an away win:	24 (26.1.1938 - 11.3.1939)
of league wins:	7 (19.4.1980-30.8.1980, 22.1.1983-1.4.1983)	of home wins:	14 (13.9.1986 - 28.2.1987)
of league defeats:	9 (22.11.1959-17.1.1960, 21.3.1959-29.8.1959)	of away wins:	6 (1.4.1980 - 30.8.1980)
	(3.11.1963 - 22.12.1963, 21.10.1975 - 6.12.1975)		

PORTSMOUTH

PLAYERS NAME Honours	Ht	Wt	Birthdate	Birthplace Transfers	Contract Date	Clubs	League	L/Cup	FA Cup	Other	Lge	L/C	FAC	Oth
G O A L K E E P E R S														
Flahavan Aaron	6.1	12.10	15/12/75	Southampton	15/02/94	Portsmouth				0+1				
Knight Alan	6.1	13.1	03/07/61	Balham	12/03/79	Portsmouth	620	49	35	21				
E: u21.2, Y.3, Div3'83														
D E F E N D E R S														
Awford Andrew	5.9	11.9	14/07/72	Worcester	24/07/89	Portsmouth	155+1	18	10	12	1			
E: u21.9, Y.13														
Butters Guy	6.3	13.0	30/10/69	Hillingdon	05/08/88	Tottenham Hotspur	34+1	2+1	1		1			
E: u21.3				Loan	13/01/90	Southend United	16			2	3			
				£375000	28/09/90	Portsmouth	141+6	13+1	7	7+2	6	1		
				Loan	04/11/94	Oxford United	3			1	1			
Dobson Tony	6.1	12.10	05/02/69	Coventry	07/07/86	Coventry City	51+3	5+3		0+1	1			
E: u21.4				£300000	17/01/91	Blackburn Rovers	36+5	5	2	1				
				£150000	22/09/93	Portsmouth	44+2	5	1+1	4	2			1
				Loan	15/12/94	Oxford United	5							
				Loan	29/01/96	Peterborough Utd	4							
Hinshelwood Danny	5.9	10.11	04/12/75	Bromley	01/08/92	Nottingham Forest								
E: Y					28/02/96	Portsmouth	5							
Perrett Russell						Lymington AFC								
					02/10/95	Portsmouth	8+1							
Pethick Robert	5.10	11.7	08/09/70	Tavistock		Plymouth Argyle								
						Weymouth								
				£30000	01/10/93	Portsmouth	83+17	7+2	3	3+1				
Russell Lee	5.10	11.4	03/09/69	Southampton	12/07/88	Portsmouth	77+18	4+1	3+2	5+2	1			
				Loan	09/09/94	Bournemouth	3							
Thomson Andrew	6.3	14.12	28/03/74	Swindon	01/05/93	Swindon Town	21+1	5		3		1		
				£75000	29/12/95	Portsmouth	15+1							
M I D F I E L D														
Allen Martin	5.10	11.0	14/08/65	Reading	27/05/83	Q.P.R.	128+8	15+3	9	2	16	1	1	1
E: u21.2, u19.3, Y				£675000	24/08/89	West Ham United	160+27	15+3	14	10	25	5	4	
				Loan	11/09/95	Portsmouth								
				£500000	22/02/96	Portsmouth	27				4			
Igoe Samuel	5.6	10.8	30/09/75	Spelthorne										
McGrath Lloyd	5.8	10.6	24/02/65	Birmingham		Coventry City	200+14	22	16	6	4	1		
				Free	01/06/94	Hong Kong								
					17/10/94	Portsmouth	15+3	1	2					
McLoughlin Alan	5.8	10.0	20/04/67	Manchester	25/04/85	Manchester United								
Ei: 16, B.2				Free	15/08/86	Swindon Town	101+5	11+3	4+2	10	18	5		1
				Loan	13/03/87	Torquay United	21+3				4			
				£1000000	13/12/90	Southampton	22+2	0+1	4	1	1			
				Loan	30/09/91	Aston Villa				1				
				£400000	17/02/92	Portsmouth	171+5	15	7+1	9	33	3	5	1
Rees Jason	5.5	9.8	22/12/69	Aberdare	01/07/88	Luton Town	58+23	3+2	2+1	5+1				2
W: 1, u21.3, B.1, Y				Loan	23/12/93	Mansfield Town	15		1	1	1			
				Free	18/07/94	Portsmouth	29+11	2+1	0+1		2			
Tilley Anthony J						Brighton & H.A.								
				Free	04/09/95	Portsmouth								
F O R W A R D S														
Bradbury Lee					03/10/95	Portsmouth	3+9							
				Loan	02/01/96	Exeter City	14				5			
Burton Deon	5.8	10.10	25/10/76	Reading	15/02/94	Portsmouth	30+11	1+2	0+1		9			
Carter Jimmy	5.10	10.4	09/11/65	Hammersmith	15/11/83	Crystal Palace								
Div2'88				Free	30/09/85	Q.P.R.								
				£15000	12/03/87	Millwall	99+11	6+1	6+1	5+1	11		2	
				£800000	10/01/91	Liverpool	2+3		2	0+1				
				£500000	08/10/91	Arsenal	18+7	1	2+1		2			
				Loan	23/03/94	Oxford United	8+1							
				Free	06/07/95	Portsmouth	31+4	1+1	0+1		4			
Durnin John	5.10	11.4	18/08/65	Bootle		Waterloo Dock								
				Free	29/03/86	Liverpool		1+1						
				Loan	20/10/88	W.B.A.	5				2			
				£225000	10/02/89	Oxford United	140+21	7	7	4+1	44	1	1	1
				£200000	15/07/93	Portsmouth	61+24	9+1	2+1	4+2	11	2		1

Name			DOB	From	Date	Club								
Hall Paul	5.9	10.2	03/07/72	Manchester	09/07/90	Torquay United	77+16	7	4+1	5+1	1		2	1
				£70000	25/03/93	Portsmouth	90+27	6+2	1+1	6+2	19	1		2
Simpson Fitzroy	5.6	10.4	26/02/70	Trowbridge	06/07/88	Swindon Town	78+27	15+2	2+1	3+2	9	1		
				£500000	06/03/92	Manchester City	58+13	5+1	4+1		5			
				£200000	17/08/95	Portsmouth	27+3	1	1		5			
Simpson Robert	5.10	10.7	03/03/76	Luton		Tottenham (T)								
				Free	15/07/96	Portsmouth								
Walsh Paul	5.8	10.4	01/10/62	Plumstead	02/10/79	Charlton Athletic	85+2	9	4		24	6	1	
E: 5, u21.7, Y.10. Div1'86.				£400000	26/07/82	Luton Town	80	5	4		24	1	3	
SC'86. FAC'91. CS'91				£700000	21/05/84	Liverpool	63+14	10+2	6+2	13+2	25	4	3	5
				£500000	16/02/88	Tottenham Hotspur	84+44	9+6	4+4	1+3	19	2		
				Loan	16/09/91	Q.P.R.	2							
				£400000	03/06/92	Portsmouth	67+6	7+1	3	6+1	13	4		3
				£750000	10/03/94	Manchester City	53	6	3		16	2	1	
				£500000	11/09/95	Portsmouth	21		1		5			
Wood Paul A	5.9	10.1	01/11/64	Saltburn	03/11/82	Portsmouth	25+22	5+3	2	2+2	7	1		3
				£40000	28/08/87	Brighton & H.A.	77+15	4	2+2	5	8			
				£90000	09/02/90	Sheffield United	19+9	1		1	3			
				Loan	31/01/91	Bournemouth	20+1							
				£40000	03/10/91	Bournemouth	73+5	1+1	13	5	18		2	2
					18/02/94	Portsmouth	25+7		2		3			

ADDITIONAL CONTRACT PLAYERS

Waterman David G		Portsmouth (T)

THE MANAGER
TERRY FENWICK

Date of Birth . . . . 17th November 1959.
Place of Birth . . . . Seaham.
Date of Appointment . . . . February 1995.

PREVIOUS CLUBS
As Manager. . . . . None.
As Coach. . . . . None.
As a Player Crystal Palace, Queens Park Rangers, Tottenham, Leicester (Loan)

HONOURS
As a Manager
None.

As a Player
Crystal Palace: Division 2 championship 1979. FAYC 1977, 1978.
Queens Park Rangers: Division 2 championship 1983.
Tottenham Hotspur: FA Cup 1991.
International: 20 full caps and 11 U21 caps for England. UEFA U21 1982.

FRATTON ROAD
Frogmore Road, Portsmouth PO4 8RA
Tel: 01705 731 204

Capacity 26,452
Covered standing 2,700
Seating 6,652

First game ....v Southampton (Friendly) 2-0, 6.9.1899.
First floodlit game ....v Newcastle, 2.3.1953.
Second Set ....v Burnley, 10.10.1962.

ATTENDANCES
Highest ....51,385 v Derby County, FAC 6th Rnd, 20.2.1949.
Lowest ....2,499 v Wimbledon, Z.Data 1st Rnd, 5.12.1989.

OTHER GROUNDS ....None.

MATCHDAY TICKET PRICES

South Stand
A Section (Adults/Concessions). . . . . £13/£9
B Section . . . . £15/£10
C Section . . . . £15/£10

North Stand
E Section . . . . £11/£7
F Section . . . . £13/£8
G Section. . . . . £11/£5*
Terrace . . . . £8/£5
Family Section . . . . £8/£3*
*Family Section passes must be produced to gain
access into these sections and Adults must be
accompanied by a Junior passholder.
Ticket office Telephone no. 01705 750 825

CLUBCALL
0898 12 11 82

Calls cost 39p per minute cheap rate and 49p per
minute at all other times.
Call costings correct at time of going to press.

HOW TO GET TO THE GROUND

From the North and West
Use motorway (M27) and (M275) and at end at roundabout take 2nd exit and in
0.2 miles, at 'T' junction turn right (A2047) into London Road.
In 1.3 miles over railway bridge and turn left into Goldsmith Avenue. In 0.6 miles
turn left into Frogmore Road for POrtsmouth FC.

From the East
Use A27 then follow signs to Southsea (A2030). In 3 miles at roundabout turn
left (A288). Then turn right into Priory Crescent then take next turning right into
Carisbrooke Road for Portsmouth FC.

Car Parking
Side-street parking only.

Nearest Railway Station
Fratton (by Fratton Park), Portsmouth 01705 825 711)

MATCHDAY PROGRAMME

Programme Editor . . . . Julie Baker.

Number of pages . . . . 40.

Price . . . . £1.50.

Subscriptions . . . . Available from Club.

Local Newspapers . . . . Portsmouth Evening News.

Local Radio Stations . . . . Ocean F.M., Radio Solent.

QUEENS PARK RANGERS
(The Rangers or The R's)
NATIONWIDE LEAGUE DIVISION 1
SPONSORED BY: ERICSSON

Back Row (L-R): John Cross, Danny Maddix, Karl Ready, Chris Plummer, Daniele Dichio, Tony Roberts, Richard Hurst, Alan McDonald, Alan McCarthy, Kevin Gallen, Simon Osborn, Steven Parmenter. **Middle Row:** Brian Morris (Physio), Terry Warren (Asst. Physio), Les Boyle (Kit Manager), Matthew Lockwood, David Bardsley, Michael Mahoney-Johnson, Trevor Sinclair, Sieb Dykstra, Steve Yates, Dennis Bailey, Graeme Power, Nigel Quashie, Phil Parkes (GK coach), Billy Bonds (Yth Manager), John Nolan (Asst. Kit Man.), John Hollins (Res. Manager). **Front Row:** Andrew McDermott, Mark Graham, Bradley Allen, Matthew Brazier, Steve Hodge, Andrew Impey, Ray Wilkins (Manager), Frank Sibley (Coach), Simon Barker, Gary Penrice, Trevor Challis, Rufus Brevett, Ian Holloway, Lee Charles.

QUEENS PARK RANGERS
FORMED IN 1885
TURNED PROFESSIONAL IN 1898
LTD COMPANY IN 1899

CHAIRMAN: C B Berlin
COMPANY DIRECTORS
A J Hedges (Managing), PA Hart (Finance)
CLUB DIRECTORS
A Ellis, P D Ellis, A Ingham, K Westcott.
SECRETARY
Miss S F Marson
COMMERCIAL MANAGER
Leon Gold (0181 743 0262)

MANAGER: Ray Wilkins MBE
ASSISTANT MANAGER: Frank Sibley

RESERVE TEAM MANAGER
John Hollins MBE
YOUTH TEAM MANAGER
Billy Bonds MBE
PHYSIOTHERAPIST
Brian Morris

STATISTICIAN FOR THE DIRECTORY
Andy Shute

For the third time in four seasons Rangers started their league campaign at the home of the current league champions, this year Blackburn Rovers. A controversial 1-0 defeat set the tone for the season ahead, as did four defeats in their opening five games. The only victory in these five games was a 1-0 home win versus Manchester City.

Rangers then won two away games (Leeds 3-1, Bolton 1-0) to climb to 12th in the league, their highest position all season. However, nine league games without a win plunged Rangers into the bottom three as injuries and suspensions took their toll. Two successive victories against Bolton and Aston Villa just before Christmas coincided with the arrival of £1.5m Mark Hateley. Rangers fans were given false optimism: seven successive defeats followed and Rangers seemed destined for the Endsleigh League even by mid-February. A rare win at Sheffield Wednesday and a superb performance against Manchester United at Loftus Road raised hopes again. The battle against relegation was on . . . an away draw at Chelsea, followed by home victories against Southampton and Everton, lifted Rangers to within sight of safety. However, a 0-1 defeat at fellow relegation-strugglers Coventry left Rangers in need of a miracle from their final two games - although they beat West Ham 3-0, other results went against them and condemned QPR to relegation. Rangers on the whole lacked a killer instinct up front - 15 of the 22 defeats were by the odd goal - and eventually the poor run of just three wins in 23 games in mid-season sealed Rangers' fate.

In the Coca-Cola League Cup QPR finally beat Second Division Oxford United in extra time of the second leg (1-1, 2-1). In the third round, York City were the visitors but QPR ran out 3-1 winners. The cup run came to an end 0-1 at Aston Villa in the fourth round.

In the FA Cup QPR were drawn away to Tranmere Rovers, and came away with a superb 2-0 win, but in the fourth round Rangers lost 1-2 at home to rivals Chelsea.

Due to the injuries and suspensions that QPR suffered throughout the season, Ray Wilkins was able to bring in young talent in the form of Nigel Quashie, Trevor Challis and Matthew Brazier, who had all come in from Rangers youth team and who look excellent prospects. Of the more established players Steve Yates, Alan McDonald, Trevor Sinclair and Simon Barker all had a good season and goalkeeper Jergen Sommer performed well in his first season. Sadly for QPR supporters, Bradley Allen was sold to Charlton Athletic for just £400,000 in March.

The QPR reserve side won the Championship of their respective league, and depending on whether QPR can keep hold of their young stars, Rangers have the experience and youth in their squad to gain promotion at the first attempt. Let's hope so . . . **ANDY SHUTE**

QUEENS PARK RANGERS

League: 19th   FA Cup: 4th Rnd   Coca-Cola Cup: 4th Rnd

M	DATE	COMP	VEN	OPPONENTS	RESULT	HT	LP	GOAL SCORERS/GOAL TIMES	ATT.
1	A 19	PL	A	Blackburn Rovers	L 0-1	0-1	16		(25932)
2	23	PL	H	Wimbledon	L 0-3	0-1	20		11837
3	26	PL	H	Manchester City	W 1-0	1-0	15	Barker 31	14212
4	30	PL	A	Liverpool	L 0-1	0-1	16		(37548)
5	S 9	PL	H	Sheffield Wednesday	L 0-3	0-0	18		12459
6	16	PL	A	Leeds United	W 3-1	2-0	14	Dichio 15, 64, Sinclair 39	(31504)
7	19	CC 2/1	A	Oxford United	D 1-1	1-0		Dichio 15	(7484)
8	25	PL	H	Tottenham Hotspur	L 2-3	1-0	15	Dichio 36, Impey 46	15659
9	30	PL	A	Bolton Wanderers	W 1-0	0-0	12	Dichio 89	(17362)
10	O 3	CC 2/2	H	Oxford United	W 2-1	0-1		Ready 70, Gallen 90	9207
11	14	PL	H	Newcastle United	L 2-3	1-0	14	Dichio 43, 68	18254
12	21	PL	A	Middlesbrough	L 0-1	0-1	15		(29293)
13	25	CC 3	H	York City	W 3-1	1-1		Sinclair 24, Impey 55, Dichio 65	12972
14	28	PL	H	Nottingham Forest	D 1-1	0-0	14	Sinclair 76	17549
15	N 4	PL	A	Southampton	L 0-2	0-1	15		(15137)
16	19	PL	H	Coventry City	D 1-1	1-0	16	Barker 37	11189
17	22	PL	A	Everton	L 0-2	0-2	16		(30009)
18	25	PL	A	West Ham United	L 0-1	0-0	18		(21504)
19	29	CC 4	A	Aston Villa	L 0-1	0-0			(24951)
20	D 2	PL	H	Middlesbrough	D 1-1	1-1	17	McDonald 15	17546
21	9	PL	A	Tottenham Hotspur	L 0-1	0-1	18		(28851)
22	16	PL	H	Bolton Wanderers	W 2-1	1-1	16	Osborn 40, Impey 76	11456
23	23	PL	H	Aston Villa	W 1-0	0-0	16	Gallen 54	14778
24	26	PL	A	Arsenal	L 0-3	0-1	17		(38259)
25	30	PL	A	Manchester United	L 1-2	0-1	17	Dichio 68	(41890)
26	J 2	PL	H	Chelsea	L 1-2	1-0	19	Allen 71	14904
27	6	FAC 3	A	Tranmere Rovers	W 2-0	0-0		Quashie 55, Sinclair 59	(10230)
28	13	PL	H	Blackburn Rovers	L 0-1	0-0	19		13957
29	20	PL	A	Wimbledon	L 1-2	0-1	19	Hateley 56	(9123)
30	29	FAC 4	H	Chelsea	L 1-2	0-2		Quashie 67	18542
31	F 3	PL	A	Manchester City	L 0-2	0-1	19		(27509)
32	11	PL	H	Liverpool	L 1-2	0-2	19	Dichio 66	18405
33	17	PL	A	Sheffield Wednesday	W 3-1	1-1	19	Barker 33, 67, Goodridge 87	(22442)
34	M 2	PL	H	Arsenal	D 1-1	1-0	19	Gallen 20	17970
35	6	PL	H	Leeds United	L 1-2	1-2	19	Gallen 30	13991
36	9	PL	A	Aston Villa	L 2-4	0-1	19	Dichio 50, Gallen 59	(28221)
37	16	PL	H	Manchester United	D 1-1	0-0	19	Dichio 65	18817
38	23	PL	A	Chelsea	D 1-1	1-1	20	Barker 20	(25590)
39	30	PL	H	Southampton	W 3-0	1-0	19	Brevett 25, Dichio 61, Gallen 76	17615
40	A 6	PL	A	Newcastle United	L 1-2	0-0	19	Holloway 53	(36583)
41	8	PL	H	Everton	W 3-1	2-0	18	Gallen 15, Hateley 42, Impey 61	18349
42	13	PL	A	Coventry City	L 0-1	0-0	19		(22906)
43	27	PL	H	West Ham United	W 3-0	0-0	19	Ready 60, Gallen 70, 79	18828
44	M 5	PL	A	Nottingham Forest	L 0-3	0-1	19		(22910)

Best Home League Attendance: 18828 v West Ham United   **Smallest: 11189 v Coventry City**   **Average: 15672**

Goal Scorers:
PL(38):   Dichio(11),Gallen(8),Barker(5),Impey(3),Sinclair(2),Hateley(2),Holloway(1),Goodridge(1),McDonald(1),Osborn(1),Brevett(1),Ready(1),Allen(1)
CC(6):   Dichio(2),Ready(1),Sinclair(1),Gallen(1),Impey(1)
FAC(3):   Quashie(2),Sinclair(1)

Player appearance grid (Queens Park Rangers, season 1995-96). Column headers are players; each row is a match with the referee named at right.

#	Referee	(F) Allen	(D) Bardsley	(M) Barker	(D) Brazier	(D) Brevett	(D) Challis	(F) Charles	(F) Dichio	(F) Gallen	(F) Goodridge	(F) Hateley	(M) Hodge	(M) Holloway	(G) Hurst	(M) Impey	(M) Maddix	(D) McDonald	(D) Murray	(M) Osborn	(F) Penrice	(D) Plummer	(M) Quashie	(D) Ready	(G) Roberts	(M) Sinclair	(G) Sommer	(M) Wilkins	(D) Yates	(M) Zelic
1	A.Wilkie		X1	X		X			X	X				X		X	X	X		S1						X	X	S		
2	G.Poll		X	X2		X			X	X				X		X	X	X1		S						X	X	S2		S1
3	P.Danson		X	X		X			X	X1				X		X	X	X		S	S1			S		X	X			
4	S.Dunn		X	X		X			X							X	X	X		X	S1			S		X	X	X1		
5	M.Reed		X	X		X1			X	X						X	X	X		S	S1			S		X	X			
6	S.Lodge		X	X		X			X	S			S	X		S	X	X		X				X		X	X		X	
7	G.Pooley		X			X	S		X	S				X		X	X	X		X				X	X	X		S		
8	D.Elleray	S1	X			X	S		X	S				X		X	X	X		X1				X		X	X	S		
9	J.Winter		X			X	S		X	S				X1		X	X	X		X				X		X	X	S1		
10	G.Pole			X2	S2	X			X	X	S1			X		X	X	X1		X2				X	X			S2		
11	P.Durkin		X			X			X	S	S1			X		X	X			X1				X		X	X	S	X	
12	M.Reed	X	X			X1	S		X	S1				X		X	X							X	X	X		X	X	
13	M.Bodenham	X	X			X	S		X	S	S			X			X							X	X	X		X	X	
14	S.Dunn	X	X1		S3	X			X	S1				X3			X			S1				X1		X	X	X	X	
15	L.R.Dilkes	X	X			X			X	S1					S		X			S				X1		X	X	X	X	X
16	M.Bodenham		X		X1	S1	X		X	X				X		X	S							X		X2	X	S2	X	X
17	P.Danson		X		X	X2			X	X				X		X	S2							X		X1	X	S	X	X
18	P.Alcock		X		X		S2		X	X				X		X2	S1	X		S				X		X	X	X1	X	
19	R.Bart	X	X						X1			S1				X		X		S				X	X	X	X	X	X	
20	P.Durkin	S	X		X				S1	X1		X		X		X		X		S				X		X	X	X	X	
21	K.Cooper		X2			X	S2		X1			X		X		X	X	S		S1				X		X	X	X	X	
22	S.J.Lodge		X			X1			S2			X		X		X		X		X2				S1		X	X	S	X	
23	A.B.Wilkie	S1	X	X	S1	X			X1			X3		X		X		X						S3		X	X	X1	X	
24	M.Reed		X	X		X			S2	X1		X		X		S1		X						S		X	X	X2	X	
25	R.Hart	X1	X2		X	X			S1			X		X		X	X	X					X	S2	S	X	X		X	
26	D.Elleray	X	S1		X	X	X		S2			X		X		X	X						X2	X1		X	X	S	X	
27	J.Winter	X3			X	X			S3	S2						X	S1	X					X	X2		X	X	X	X1	
28	G.R.Ashby	X	X		X1	X				S2	S1						X2	S3	X				X	X		X	X	X3	X	
29	S.Dunn	X1	X	X	X	X2			S1	S2		X						S	X				X	X		X	X		X	
30	P.Durkin	X	X1		S	X				S		X		X		X	X			S1			X	X		X	X		X	
31	G.Poll	X1	X		S3	X			S1	S1		X1		X		X		X					X3	X		X	X		X	
32	D.Gallagher	S	X		X	S			X	X		S		X		X		X					X	X		X	X		X	
33	P.Durkin	S2	X		X	X	S			X2	S1			X		X1	X	X					X	X		X	X		X	
34	P.Alcock		X		X	X			S1	X	S	X		X		X1		X					X	S		X	X		X	
35	G.Powler		X	X1	S1	X			X	X2	S2	X		X									X	S		X	X		X	
36	A.B.Wilkie		X	X	S	X			X	X	S1	X		X						X1			X	X		X	X		X	
37	R.A.Heart		X	X		X			X2	X2			S2	X		S1	X			X1			X	S2		X	X		X	
38	M.Reed		X	X	S3	X			X2	X2		X		X			X	X1						S1		X	X		X	X3
39	P.Sampson		X		S	X			X	X	S	S1		X		X	X	X					S			X	X	X	X	
40	P.Durkin		X		S	X				S		X		X		X	X	X					S			X	X	X	X	
41	P.Durkin		X	X		X				X		X1		X		X	X	X					S	S		X	X	X	S1	
42	K.Cooper		X		S	X		S1	X	X		X1		X									S	X	S	X	X	X	X	
43	G.S.Wilard			X		X	S1		X	X		X1								X1	X			S		S3	X	X	X1	X
44	G.Ashby	X3		X		X	S1		X	X								X1	X	S1			S3			X	X	X1	X	

Statistic	Allen	Bardsley	Barker	Brazier	Brevett	Challis	Charles	Dichio	Gallen	Goodridge	Hateley	Hodge	Holloway	Hurst	Impey	Maddix	McDonald	Murray	Osborn	Penrice	Plummer	Quashie	Ready	Roberts	Sinclair	Sommer	Wilkins	Yates	Zelic
PL Appearances	5	28	33	6	27	10	0	21	26	0	10	0	26	0	28	20	25	1	6	0	0	11	16	5	37	33	11	30	3
PL Sub Appearances	3	1	0	5	0	1	4	8	4	7	4	0	1	0	1	2	1	0	3	3	1	0	6	0	0	0	4	0	1
CC Appearances	0	2	4	1+1	3	0	0	3	2	0+1	0+1	0	2	0	4	3	3	0	2	0	0	0	4	4	3	0	2+1	2	0
FAC Appearances	2	1	0	1	0	2	0	0	0	0+1	1	0	1	0	2	0+2	2	0	0	0	0	2	1	0	2	2	1	2	0

QUEENS PARK RANGERS

CLUB RECORDS

BIGGEST VICTORIES
League: 8-0 v Merthyr, Division 3S, 9.3.1929
F.A. Cup: 8-1 v Bristol Rovers (a), Round 1, 27.11.1937
7-0 v Barry Town, Round 1, 1961-62
League Cup: 8-1 Crewe, Round 2, 3.10.1983
Europe (UEFA): 7-0 v Brann Bergen, Round 1, 29-9-1976

BIGGEST DEFEATS
League: 1-8 v Mansfield, Division 3, 15.3.1965
1-8 v Manchester United, Division 1, 19.3.1969
0-7 v Southend United, Division 3S, 7.4.1928
0-7 v Coventry City, Division 3S, 4.3.1933
0-7 v Torquay United, Division 3S, 22.4.1935
0-7 v Barnsley, Division 2, 4.11.1950
F.A. Cup: 0-5 v Huddersfield, Round 4, 23.1.1932
0-5 v Derby County, Round 6, 12.3.1948
0-5 v Huddersfield (h), Round 3, 1948-49
1-6 v Burnley, Round 3, 1961-62
1-6 v Hereford, Round 2, 1957-58
League Cup: 0-4 v Reading, Round 2, 23.9.1964
0-4 v Newcastle, Round 2, 8.10.1974
Europe (UEFA): 0-4 v Partizan Belgrade, 7.11.1984

MOST POINTS
3 points a win: 85, Division 2, 1982-83
2 points a win: 67, Division 3, 1966-67

MOST GOALS
111, Division 3, 1961-62.
Bedford 36, Evans 19, Lazarus 12, Towers 12, McClelland 11,
Angell 6, Collins 6, Barber 4, Keen 2, Francis 1, og 2.

MOST LEAGUE GOALS CONCEDED
95, Division 1, 1968-69

MOST FIRST CLASS MATCHES IN A SEASON
59 (42 League, 2 FA Cup, 7 League Cup, 8 UEFA Cup) 1976-77

MOST LEAGUE WINS
26, Div 3S, 1947-48; Div 3, 1966-67; Div 2, 1982-83

MOST LEAGUE DRAWS
18, Division 1, 1991-92

MOST LEAGUE DEFEATS
28, Division 1, 1968-69

INDIVIDUAL CLUB RECORDS

MOST GOALS IN A SEASON
Rodney Marsh, 44 (League 30, FAC 3, League Cup 11) 1966-67.
(League Only) George Goddard, 37, Div 3S, 1929-30

MOST GOALS IN A MATCH
5. Alan Wilks v Oxford, Round 3, League Cup, 10.10.1967.

OLDEST PLAYER
Jimmy Langley, 38 years 96 days.

YOUNGEST PLAYER
Frank Sibley, 15 years 274 days.

MOST CAPPED PLAYER
Alan McDonald (Northern Ireland) 51

BEST PERFORMANCES

League: 1966-67: Matches played 46, Won 26, Drawn 15, Lost 5, Goals for 103, Goals against 38, Points 67. First in Division 3

Highest: 1975-76: 2nd in Division 1.

F.A. Cup: 1981-82: 3rd rnd. Middlesbrough 1-1, 3-2; 4th rnd. Blackpool 0-0, 5-1; 5th rnd. Grimsby 3-1; 6th rnd. Crystal Palace 1-0; Semi-final West Bromwich Albion 1-0; Final Tottenham 1-1, 0-1.

League Cup: 1966-67: 1st rnd. Colchester 5-0; 2nd rnd. Aldershot 1-1, 2-0; 3rnd. Swansea 2-1; 4th rnd. Leicester 4-2; 5th rnd. Carlisle 2-1; Semi-final Birmingham 4-1, 3-1; Final West Bromwich Albion 3-2.

UEFA Cup: 1976-77: 1st rnd. Brann Bergen 4-0, 7-0; 2nd rnd. Slovan Bratislava 3-2, 5-2; 3rd rnd FC Cologne 3-0, 1-4; 4th rnd. AEK Athens 3-0, 0-3.

ADDITIONAL INFORMATION
Previous Name: St. Judes 1885-87

Previous League: Southern League

Club colours: Blue and white shirts, white shorts, white socks.

Change colours: All red.

Reserves League: Avon Insurance Football Combination.

DIVISIONAL RECORD

	Played	Won	Drawn	Lost	For	Against	Points
Division 1/P	822	277	223	322	1,028	1,111	969
Division 2	546	233	141	172	809	671	654
Division 3	414	188	98	128	782	601	474
Division 3(S)	1,158	466	276	416	1,781	1,692	1,208
Total	**2,940**	**1,164**	**738**	**1,038**	**4,400**	**4,075**	**3,205**

RECORDS AND STATISTICS

COMPETITIONS

Div 1/P	Div.2/1	Div.3	Div.3(S)	UEFA
1968-69	1948-52	1958-67	1920-48	1976-77
1973-79	1967-68		1952-58	1984-85
1983-96	1969-73			
	1979-83			
	1996-			

HONOURS

Div.2	Div.3	Div.3(S)	League Cup
1982-83	1966-67	1947-48	1966-67

MOST APPEARANCES

Tony Ingham 548 (1950-63)

Year	League	FA Cup	Lge Cup
1950-51	24		
1951-52	17		
1952-53	43	3	
1953-54	40	4	
1954-55	38	3	
1955-56	41	1	
1956-57	46	3	
1957-58	46	3	
1958-59	46	2	
1959-60	46	3	
1960-61	46	2	2
1961-62	40	4	2
1962-63	41	2	
	514	30	4

MOST GOALS IN A CAREER

George Goddard - 186 (1926-33)

Year	League	FA Cup
1926-27	22	
1927-28	26	
1928-29	36	1
1929-30	37	2
1930-31	24	4
1931-32	17	2
1932-33	12	3
Total	174	12

Current leading goalscorer: Simon Barker 34 (1988-96)

RECORD TRANSFER FEE RECEIVED

Amount	Club	Player	Date
£6,000,000	Newcastle Utd	Les Ferdinand	6/95
£2,700,000	Newcastle Utd	Darren Peacock	3/94
£2,700,000	Sheffield Wed.	Andy Sinton	8/93
£1,700,000	Manchester Utd	Paul Parker	7/91

RECORD TRANSFER FEE PAID

Amount	Club	Player	Date
£1,500,000	Glasgow Rangers	Mark Hateley	9/95
£1,250,000	Borussia Dortmund	Ned Zelic	7/95
£1,100,000*	Reading	Simon Osborn	7/95
£1,000,000	Luton Town	Roy Wegerle	12/89

*Included Michael Meaker going to Reading.

MANAGERS

Name	Seasons	Best	Worst
James Cowan	1907-13		
James Howie	1919-20		
Ned Liddell	1920-25	3(3S)	22(3S)
Bob Hewison	1925-31	3(3S)	22(3S)
John Browman	1931		
Archie Mitchell	1931-33	13(3S)	16(3S)
Mitchell O'Brien	1933-35	4(3S)	13(3S)
Billy Birrell	1935-39	3(3S)	9(3S)
Ted Vizard	1939-44		
Dave Mangall	1944-52	13(2)	3(3S)
Jack Taylor	1952-59	10(3)	21(3S)
Alex Stock	1959-68	2(2)	15(3)
Tommy Docherty	1968		
Les Allen	1969-71	22(1)	11(2)
Gordon Jago	1971-74	4(1)	8(2)
Dave Sexton	1974-77	2(1)	14(1)
Frank Sibley	1977-78	19(1)	19(1)
Steve Burtenshaw	1978-79	20(1)	20(1)
Tommy Docherty	1979-80	5(2)	5(2)
Terry Venables	1980-84	5(1)	8(2)
Alan Mullery	1984		
Frank Sibley	1984-85	19(1)	19(1)
Jim Smith	1985-88	5(1)	16(1)
P Shreeve (Caretaker)	1988-89		
Trevor Francis	1989-90	9(1)	9(1)
Don Howe	1990-91	12(1)	12(1)
Gerry Francis	1991-94	5(1/P)	11(1)
Ray Wilkins	1994-	8(P)	19(P)

LONGEST LEAGUE RUNS

of undefeated matches:	20 (19.11.1966 - 11.4.1967)	of league matches w/out a win:	20 (23.11.1968 - 12.4.1969)
of undefeated home matches:	25 (18.11.1972 - 5.2.1974)	of undefeated away matches:	17 (27.8.1966 - 11.4.1967)
without home win:	10 (23.11.1968 - 10.4.1969)	without an away win:	22 (27.12.1954-26.12.1955, 11.5.69-13.9.70)
of league wins:	8 (7.11.1931 - 28.12.1931)	of home wins:	11 (26.12.1972 - 28.4.1973)
of league defeats:	9 (15.2.1969 - 12.4.1969)	of away wins:	7 (2.4.1927 - 4.9.1927)

QUEENS PARK RANGERS

PLAYERS NAME Honours	Ht	Wt	Birthdate	Birthplace Transfers	Contract Date	Clubs	League	L/Cup	FA Cup	Other	Lge	L/C	FAC	Oth
G O A L K E E P E R S														
Dykstra Sieb	6.5	14.7	20/10/66	Kerkrade		Roda JC								
						Motherwell								
				£250000	22/07/94	Q.P.R.	11	1						
				Loan	22/09/95	Bristol City	8			2				
				Loan	07/03/96	Wycombe Wand.	13							
Hurst Richard	6.0	12.0	23/12/76	Hammersmith	01/08/94	Q.P.R.								
Roberts Anthony W: 1, B.2, u21.2, Y	6.1	12.4	04/08/69	Holyhead	24/07/87	Q.P.R.	99	11	6+1	2				
Sommer Juergen	6.4	15.12	27/02/64	New York	05/09/91	Luton Town	80	4	11					
				Loan	13/11/91	Brighton & H.A.	1							
				Loan	31/10/92	Torquay United	10			1				
				£600000	29/08/95	Q.P.R.	33		2					
D E F E N D E R S														
Bardsley David E: 2, Y.2	5.10	10.0	11/09/64	Manchester	05/11/82	Blackpool	45	2+1	2					
				£150000	23/11/83	Watford	97+3	6	13+1	1	7	1	1	
				£265000	18/09/87	Oxford United	74	12	5	3	7			
				£500000	15/09/89	Q.P.R.	240+1	20	19	3	4	1		1
Brazier Matthew	5.8	10.07	02/07/76	Leytonstone	01/07/94	Q.P.R.	6+5	1+1	1					
Brevett Rufus	5.8	11.0	24/09/69	Derby	08/07/88	Doncaster Rovers	106+3	5	4	10+1	3			
				£250000	15/02/91	Q.P.R.	77+8	5+1	2		1			
Challis Trevor E: Y.2, S	5.7	10.0	23/10/75	Paddington	01/07/94	Q.P.R.	10+1		2					
Maddix Daniel	5.10	11.7	11/10/67	Ashford	25/07/85	Tottenham Hotspur								
				Loan	01/11/86	Southend United	2							
				Free	23/07/87	Q.P.R.	163+25	18	18+2	2+3	7	2	2	
McDonald Alan E: Y1	6.2	12.7	12/10/63	Belfast	12/08/81	Q.P.R.	357+6	42	30	5	11	2	1	
				Loan	24/03/83	Charlton Athletic	9							
Plummer Chris E: S	6.3	11.06	12/10/76	Hounslow	01/07/94	Q.P.R.	0+1							
Ready Karl W: B.2, u21.5	6.1	12.2	14/08/72	Neath	13/08/90	Q.P.R.	49+12	4+2	1		3	1		
Yates Steve Div3'90	5.11	11.0	29/01/70	Bristol	01/07/88	Bristol Rovers	196+1	9	11	21				
				£650000	16/08/93	Q.P.R.	79+3	5	4		1			
M I D F I E L D														
Barker Simon E: u21.4, FMC'87	5.9	11.0	04/11/64	Farnworth	06/11/82	Blackburn Rovers	180+2	11	12	8	35	4		2
				£400000	20/07/88	Q.P.R.	233+21	25+2	20+1	7	22	5	3	
Hodge Stephen	5.8	10.3	25/10/62											
Impey Andrew FAV'90, E: u21.1	5.8	10.6	30/09/71	Hammersmith		Yeading								
				£35000	14/06/90	Q.P.R.	151+4	13+1	6+2	0+2	11	2	1	1
Murray Paul	5.8	10.5	31/08/76	Carlisle	14/06/94	Carlisle United	12+6			3+2				
					08/03/96	Q.P.R.	1							
Quashie Nigel					01/08/95	Q.P.R.	11		2				2	
Sinclair Trevor E: u21.8, Y.1, S	5.10	11.2	02/03/73	Dulwich	21/08/90	Blackpool	84+28	8	6+1	8+5	15			1
				£600000	12/08/93	Q.P.R.	99+3	9	4		10	3	1	
Wilkins Ray E: 84, u23.2, u21.1, Y, S. FAC'83. SPD'90	5.8	11.2	14/09/56	Hillingdon	01/10/73	Chelsea	176+3	6+1	10+1		30	2	2	
				£825000	01/08/79	Manchester United	158+2	14+1	10	9	7	1	1	1
				£1500000	01/07/84	AC Milan								
					01/08/86	Paris St Germain								
				£250000	01/11/87	Glasgow Rangers	69+1	10	8+1	7	2	1		
				Free	30/11/89	Q.P.R.	153+1	13	13	2	7		2	1
				Free	26/05/94	Crystal Palace	1							
				Free	17/11/94	Q.P.R.	12+5	2+1	1					
F O R W A R D S														
Charles Lee						Chertsey								
				£67500	04/08/95	Q.P.R.	0+4							
				Loan	22/09/95	Barnet	2+3			0+1				
Dichio Daniel E: Y,S	6.2	11.0	19/10/74	Hammersmith	17/05/93	Q.P.R.	25+13	4	1+1		14	2		
				Loan	18/02/94	Welling								
				Loan	24/03/94	Barnet	9				2			
Gallen Kevin E: Y.11, S. UEFA Y'93	6.0	12.0	21/09/75	Chiswick	22/09/92	Q.P.R.	57+10	3+1	4		18	2	1	

Name	ht	wt	DOB	Birthplace	Date	Club	League App	League Gls	FA Cup	FL Cup	Other App	Other Gls		Other
Goodridge Greg	5.6	10.0	10/02/75	Barbados		Lambada WI								
Barbados International				Free	24/03/94	Torquay United	32+6	4	2+1	3+1	4	1		1
				£100000	09/08/95	Q.P.R.	0+7	0+1	0+1		1			
Graham Mark	5.7	10.0	24/10/74	Newry	26/05/93	Q.P.R.								
NI: Y, S														
Mateley Mark	6.1	11.07	07/11/61	Liverpool	01/12/78	Coventry City	86+6				25			
					01/06/83	Portsmouth	38	4	2		21	2	1	
					01/08/84	AC Milan	66				17			
						Monaco								
					01/08/90	Glasgow Rangers	165				85			
					04/11/95	Q.P.R.	10+4	0+1	1		2			
Slade Steve	5.11	10.10	06/10/75	Romford	01/07/94	Tottenham Hotspur	1+4	0+1	0+2					
				£350000	08/07/96	Q.P.R.								
ADDITIONAL CONTACT PLAYERS														
Bruce Paul (F)						Q.P.R. (T)								
Cross John (M)	5.8	10.10		Barking		Q.P.R. (T)								
Graham Mark (M)	5.7	10.0	24/10/74	Newry		Q.P.R. (T)								
Lockwood Matthew (M)	5.9	10.7	17/10/76	Rochford		Q.P.R. (T)								
McDermott Andrew (D)				Australia		IOS Australia								
					04/08/95	Q.P.R.								
Mahoney-Johnson Michael(F)	5.10	11.0	06/11/76	Paddington	01/08/94	Q.P.R. (T)								
Parmenter Steve (F)	5.9	10.7	22.01.77	Chelmsford		Q.P.R. (T)								
Power Graham ((M)						Q.P.R. (T)								
Perry Mark J					26/10/95	Q.P.R. (T)								
Sharp Lee					14/09/95	Lincoln United								
					27/10/95	Q.P.R. (T)								

THE MANAGER
RAY WILKINS

Date of Birth . . . . 14th September 1956.
Place of Birth . . . . Hillingdon.
Date of Appointment . . . . November 1994.

PREVIOUS CLUBS
As Manager. . . . . None.
As Coach. . . . . None.
As a Player . . . . Chelsea, Manchester Utd, A.C. Milan, Paris St Germain,
. . . . Glasgow Rangers, Q.P.R., Crystal Palace.

HONOURS
As a Manager
None.

As a Player
Manchester United: FA Cup 1983.
Glasgow Rangers: Scottish Premier Division Championship.
International: 84 full caps, 2 U23, 1 U21, Yth & S for England.

RANGERS STADIUM
South Africa Road, London W12 7PA
Tel: 0181 743 0262

Capacity 19,000
First game..v West Ham Utd, FA Cup, 8.9.1917.
First floodlit game ....v Arsenal, 5.10.1953.
2nd Set...v Colchester, 23.8.1966.

ATTENDANCES
Highest ....35,353 v Leeds Utd, Div.1, 12.1.1974.
Lowest ....3,245 v Coventry City, Div 3, 22.5.1963.

OTHER GROUNDS.................... Welfords Field 1885-89. London Scottish Ground, Brondesbury Home Farm,
........Kensall Rise Green Gun Club, Wormwood Scrubs, Kilburn C.C. 1889-99, Kensal Rise 1899-1901, Latimer Rd,
....Knotting Hill 1901-04, Agriculture Soc, Park Royal 1904-07, Park Royal Ground 1907-17.
..... Loftus Road 1917-31, White City 1931-33, Loftus Road 1933-62. White City 1962-63. South Africa Road 1963-

MATCHDAY TICKET PRICES

South Africa Road	£15
Ellerslie Road.	£13
Juveniles	£7.50/£6.50
Loftus Road Upper Level (Members only)	£10
Juv/OAP	£5
Lower Level (Members)	£10
Juv/OAP	£5
Non-Members	£12
Juv/OAP	£6
East & West Paddocks (Members)	£8
Juv/OAP	£4
Non-Members	£10
Juv/OAP	£5
Ticket Office Telephone no.	**0181 749 7798.**

CLUBCALL 0891 12 11 62

Calls cost 39p per minute cheap rate and 49p per
minute at all other times.
Call costings correct at time of going to press.

HOW TO GET TO THE GROUND

From the North
Use motorway (M1) and A406 North Circular Road as for Neasden. In 0.7 miles
turn left then join A404, sign posted Harlesden, then follow signs Hammersmith
and turn right in to White City Road then turn left into South Africa Road for
Queens Park Rangers.

From the East
Use A12, A406 then A503 then join Ring Road and follow signs Oxford to join
A40 (M). In 2 miles branch left (sign posted The West) to join M41. At roundabout take 3rd exit (A40) then join A4020, sign posted Acton. In 0.3 miles turn
right into Loftus Road for Queens Park Rangers FC.

From the South
Use A206, A3 to cross Putney Bridge and follow signs Hammersmith. Follow
signs Oxford (A219) to Shepherds Bush then join A4020, sign posted Acton. In
0.3 miles turn right into Loftus Road for Queens Park Rangers FC.

From the West
Use motorway (M4) to Chiswick then A315 and A402 to Shepherds Bush, then
join A4020 sign posted Acton. In 0.3 miles turn right into Loftus Road for Queens
Park Rangers FC.

Car Parking
Limited side-street parking available.
Nearest Railway Station
Shepherds Bush (Tube), White City (Central Line)

MATCHDAY PROGRAMME

Programme Editor . . . . Sheila Marson.

Number of pages . . . . 36.

Price . . . . £1.50.

Subscriptions . . . . Please apply to club.

Local Newspapers . . . . Shepherds Bush Gazette, Acton Gazette.

Local Radio Stations . . . . Capital Radio.

READING

(The Royals)

NATIONWIDE LEAGUE DIVISION 1

SPONSORED BY: AUTOTRADER (SHIRTS)

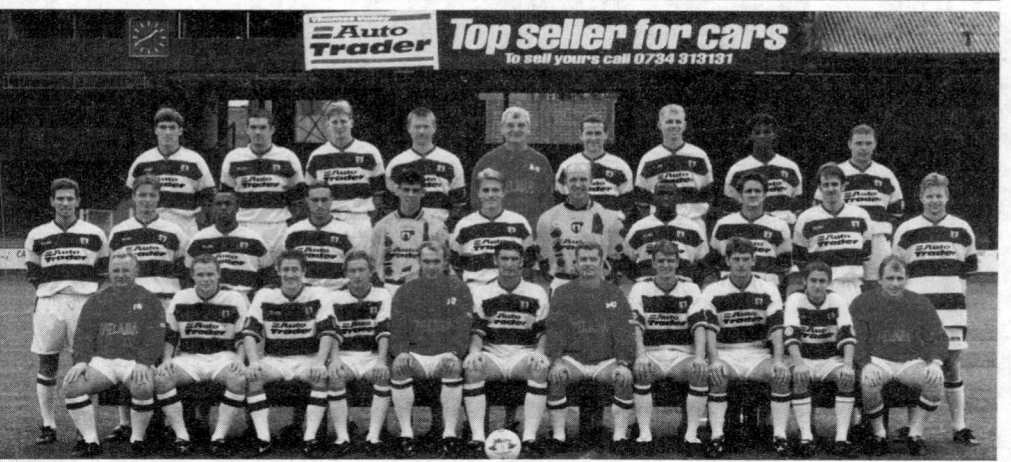

Back Row (L-R): Trevor Morley, Jeff Hopkins, Michael Thorp, Matthew Stowell, Ron Grant (Kitman), Stuart Lovell, David Bass, Martin Williams, Alan Carey. **Middle Row:** Lee Nogan, Michael Murphy, Michael Gilkes, Andy Bernal, Stuart Jones, Phil Parkinson, Simon Sheppard, Keith McPherson, Michael Meaker, Paul Holsgrove, Dylan Kerr. **Front Row:** Phil Holder (Coach), Derek Simpson, James Lambert, Steven Swales, Jimmy Quinn (joint player/Manager), Adrian Williams (capt), Mick Gooding (joint player/Manager), Dariusz Wdowczyk, Tom Jones, Gareth Randell, Paul Turner (Physio).

READING
FORMED IN 1871
TURNED PROFESSIONAL IN 1895
LTD COMPANY IN 1895

CHAIRMAN: J Madejski
CHEIF EXECUTIVE: Nigel Howe
DIRECTORS
I Wood-Smith
GENERAL MANAGER
Adrian Porter
SECRETARY
Andrea Barker
COMMERCIAL MANAGER
Kevin Girdler

PLAYER MANAGERS
Mick Gooding & Jimmy Quinn
COACH: Richard Hill
YOUTH TEAM COACH
Steve Kean
PHYSIOTHERAPIST
P Turner

STATISTICIAN FOR THE DIRECTORY
David Downs

Reading just managed to hold on to their Division One status, survival only being ensured in the last home game of the season, which brought an exciting 3-0 victory over Wolverhampton Wanderers. A final position of 19th was in stark contrast to the previous campaign, which had seen Royals within four minutes of the Premiership. That near-miss contributed to the change in fortunes, as the players had a very short close season, and the preparations for 1995-96 were hampered by injuries along with the departure of key players Hislop, Osborn and Taylor.

Players came and went so quickly that Royals set a new club record by using 32 players in the first team. Featured in that total were eight goalkeepers, including Bulgarian World Cup star Bobby Mikhailov and , unusually, player-manager and striker Jimmy Quinn who appeared as a second-half substitute between the posts in the home win over West Bromwich Albion, after Simon Sheppard had broken an arm. Quinn was leading goalscorer with 17 strikes, and his joint player-manager, Nick Gooding, was another to lead by example, being voted the supporters' 'Player of the Season'.

If the league programme gave little cause for celebration, there was more to admire in the team's exploits in the cup competitions. For the first time in its history, Reading reached the quarter-finals of the Football League Cup, beating Premier League Southampton 2-1 before succumbing by the same score - very unluckily - away to Leeds United. The FA Cup brought a brave 3-1 win over a physical Gillingham side, then the mouth-watering prospect of a home tie against Manchester United. Reading lost that fourth round game 0-3, but there was consolation in the receipts for the match - a record for any game played at Elm Park, £110,741.

More records were established in the transfer market. Goalkeeper Hislop was sold to Newcastle United for £1,575,000, then replaced by Mikhailov, who arrived from Botev Plovdiv for £300,000. That club record lasted for only five months, from September until February, when Darren Caskey arrived from Spurs for £700,000. However, another mainstay of the team, skipper and Welsh international Adrian Williams, transferred to Wolves during the close season for £1,000,000. Only time will tell how much his departure will affect the club.

The playing squad still includes a mixture of experienced internationals such as Bernal, Hopkins, Hunter, Mikhailov, Nogan, Quinn and Wdowczyk, plus promising youngsters like Bass, Lambert, Scales and Thorp. It could be a successful combination, providing the lessons learned from the last two traumatic seasons are put to good use. Up the Royals!

DAVID DOWNS

READING

League: 19th   FA Cup: 4th Rnd   Coca-Cola Cup: 4th Rnd

M	DATE	COMP	VEN	OPPONENTS	RESULT	HT	LP	GOAL SCORERS/GOAL TIMES	ATT.
1	A 12	EL	A	Stoke City	D 1-1	0-1	14	Williams 83	(11932)
2	19	EL	H	Derby County	W 3-2	1-0	6	Lovell 36, Morley 59, Nogan 90	9280
3	26	EL	A	Portsmouth	D 0-0	0-0	8		(9917)
4	29	EL	H	Millwall	L 1-2	1-0	9	Gooding 35	10143
5	S 2	EL	A	Southend United	D 0-0	0-0	13		(4962)
6	9	EL	H	Luton Town	W 3-1	1-1	11	Nogan 17, 69, Lovell 60(pen)	8550
7	12	EL	H	Grimsby Town	L 0-2	0-1	13		7283
8	16	EL	A	Leicester City	D 1-1	0-1	14	Bernal 24	(19103)
9	20	CC 2/1	H	West Bromwich Albion	D 1-1	0-0		Lovell 81	6948
10	23	EL	H	Port Vale	D 2-2	1-2	14	Lambert 30, 90	7819
11	30	EL	A	Sunderland	D 2-2	0-0	16	Lovell 55, Kerr 87	(17503)
12	O 3	CC 2/2	A	West Bromwich Albion	W 4-2	1-1		Lovell 11, Quinn 50(pen), 66, Lambert 89	(8165)
13	7	EL	A	West Bromwich Albion	L 0-2	0-0	18		(12956)
14	14	EL	H	Huddersfield Town	W 3-1	1-1	15	Lambert 15, Williams 70, Quinn 79	8534
15	21	EL	A	Oldham Athletic	L 1-2	1-1	15	Lovell 42	(5709)
16	28	EL	H	Ipswich Town	L 1-4	0-1	18	Lovell 64	10281
17	N 4	EL	A	Crystal Palace	W 2-0	2-0	16	Lovell 14, Nogan 25	(16058)
18	7	CC 3	H	Bury	W 2-1	0-0		Lucketti 52(og), Quinn 89	10329
19	11	EL	H	Birmingham City	L 0-1	0-0	18		10203
20	18	EL	H	Barnsley	D 0-0	0-0	16		6695
21	21	EL	A	Charlton Athletic	L 1-2	1-1	17	Brown 45	(7840)
22	25	EL	A	Sheffield United	D 0-0	0-0	18		(9737)
23	28	CC 4	H	Southampton	W 2-1	1-1		Nogan 29, Morley 64	13742
24	D 2	EL	A	West Bromwich Albion	W 3-1	2-1	17	Morley 6, Holsgrove 41, Nogan 71	7910
25	9	EL	A	Port Vale	L 2-3	1-3	17	Morley 31, Quinn 78(pen)	(6376)
26	16	EL	H	Sunderland	D 1-1	0-1	18	Quinn 86	9431
27	30	EL	A	Norwich City	D 3-3	1-1	19	Lambert 14, Nogan 72, Kerr 83	(13556)
28	J 1	EL	H	Tranmere Rovers	W 1-0	0-0	18	Morley 79	8421
29	6	FAC 3	H	Gillingham	W 3-1	0-1		Morley 58, Quinn 73, 77	10324
30	10	CC QF	A	Leeds United	L 1-2	1-2		Quinn 17	(21023)
31	13	EL	A	Derby County	L 0-3	0-0	19		(15123)
32	20	EL	H	Stoke City	W 1-0	0-0	18	Gooding 67	8082
33	27	FAC 4	H	Manchester United	L 0-3	0-1			14780
34	F 4	EL	H	Portsmouth	L 0-1	0-0	19		7924
35	10	EL	A	Millwall	D 1-1	1-0	19	Bowry 32(og)	(8875)
36	17	EL	A	Grimsby Town	D 0-0	0-0	20		(6546)
37	24	EL	H	Leicester City	D 1-1	0-0	18	Lovell 76(pen)	9817
38	27	EL	A	Luton Town	W 2-1	1-1	18	Booty 45, Lovell 78	(6683)
39	M 2	EL	H	Watford	D 0-0	0-0	18		8933
40	9	EL	A	Wolverhampton Wand	D 1-1	1-1	18	Gooding 17	(25954)
41	16	EL	H	Norwich City	L 0-3	0-1	22		8501
42	19	EL	H	Southend United	D 3-3	1-0	19	Nogan 45, 54, 66	5321
43	23	EL	A	Tranmere Rovers	L 1-2	1-1	21	Caskey 36	(6249)
44	30	EL	H	Oldham Athletic	W 2-0	1-0	21	Quinn 42, 52	7025
45	A 2	EL	A	Huddersfield Town	L 1-3	1-0	21	Williams 32	(11828)
46	6	EL	A	Ipswich Town	W 2-1	1-0	21	Bernal 22, Quinn 53	(17324)
47	8	EL	H	Crystal Palace	L 0-2	0-1	21		12579
48	13	EL	A	Barnsley	W 1-0	0-0	20	Quinn 78(pen)	(5488)
49	16	EL	A	Watford	L 2-4	0-2	20	Caskey 62, Quinn 90	(8113)
50	20	EL	H	Charlton Athletic	D 0-0	0-0	20		9778
51	27	EL	H	Sheffield United	L 0-3	0-1	21		9769
52	30	EL	H	Wolverhampton Wand	W 3-0	2-0	20	Williams 22, Quinn 40, 86	12828
53	M 5	EL	A	Birmingham City	W 2-1	2-1	19	Nogan 10, Quinn 23	(16233)

Best Home League Attendance: 12828 v Wolverhampton Wand   Smallest: 5321 v Southend United   Average: 8917

Goal Scorers:
EL(54):   Quinn(11),Nogan(10),Lovell(8),Morley(4),Lambert(4),Gooding(3),Williams(3),Caskey(2),Bernal(2),Kerr(2),Opponent(s)(1),Williams(1),Brown(1),Holsgrove(1),Booty(1)
CC(10):   Quinn(4),Lovell(2),Opponent(s)(1),Nogan(1),Morley(1),Lambert(1)
FAC(3):   Quinn(2),Morley(1)

(D) Bernal	(D) Booty	(F) Carey	(M) Caskey	(M) Freeman	(F) Gilkes	(F) Gordon	(G) Hammond	(F) Holsgrove	(D) Hopkins	(M) Jones	(D) Kerr	(M) Law	(M) Lovell	(D) McPherson	(M) Meaker	(G) Mihailov	(G) Nixon	(F) Nogan	(M) Parkinson	(F) Quinn	(G) Sutton	(D) Swales	(D) Thorp	(D) Wdowczyk	(D) Williams	(M) Williams	(G) Woods		
X2					X	X				X			X	X			S1	X1	X		X			S2	X	X		J.Kirkby	1
				X2	X					X			X1	X	S1			X	X	X		X	S2		X	X	S	M.Pierce	2
X				X1	X								X	X	S2		X2	X	X		X	S1		X	X	S		G.Pooley	3
X				S1	X								X2	X	X			X	X1		X	X		X	X	S2		P.Rejer	4
X				S1	X								X	X	X2		X3	X	S3	X	X1			X	X	S2		R.J.Harris	5
X				X	X2					S1			X	X			X	X	S2	X				X1	X	X		K.Leach	6
X				X	X					X		S1	X	X1			X	X	S1	X	S			X	X1			G.Singh	7
X				X	X		X			X			X	X			X		S	S		X		X	S			U.Rennie	8
X				X	X2					X	S2	X	X	X			X	X	S3	X		X1			S1			I.Hemley	9
X			X1	X						X	X	S3	X	X	S2	X		X	X1	X2								P.Rejer	10
X			S2	X	X					X2			S1	X1		X		X3	X	S3		X	X					S.W.Mathieson	11
X			S	X	X					X	S	S	X	X				X	X	X				X	X			D.Orr	12
X				X	X					X	S	S	X	X				X	X1	X				X	X			M.Bailey	13
X				X	S1					X1		S	X	X		X		S	X	X				X	X			A.D'Urso	14
X			S	X	S1					X			X	X2	X			S2	X	X	X			X1	X			M.A.Bailey	15
X		X		X3	X							X	S2	X		X2	S3	S1		X1					X		X	J.Brandwood	16
	X			X1	X					X		S1		S	X	X		X	X			S			X		X	G.Singh	17
X	X			X1	X					X		S		S1	X2	X		X	X	S2	X				X			J.Kirkby	18
X	X		S	X	X					X		S		X1	X			X	X			S1			X		X	N.Barry	19
X	X			X1	X					S1				S1	X		X	X1	X	S					X	X	X	G.Barber	20
X	X			X	X					S1		X1	X2	X				X	S2	S					X		X	A.Butler	21
X	X			S1	X1					X			X	X			X2		X	S2	X	S		X	X			A.Wiley	22
X1	X			S2	X					X2			X	X			X3	X	S3	X	S1		X					M.Reed	23
X1	X			S2	X					X			X	X			X	X	S3	S3	X3		X2					F.Stretton	24
	X			X						X3		X1		S3	X		X	X	X	S2		X2		X		S1		A.Leake	25
	X			X1		X	X			X1	S3	S1		X			X	X	X3	S1				X	X			R.Gifford	26
	X			X3		X	X			S3	S1	X1		X1	X1		X	X	S1					X	X			W.Burns	27
	X				X	X	X			S2	X1	X1	S3				X3	X2	X					X	X			C.Wilkes	28
				S	X					X		S1	S2			X	X	X	X2		X1	X			X			P.Alcock	29
	X			S1	X					X		S2					X	X	X2	X			X1		X			A.Wilkie	30
X				S2	X	X				X2			S1				X	X1	X	X					X			K.Lynch	31
X	X			S1	X					S		S2					X2	X	X	X				X1	X			G.Pooley	32
X				X	X	X				X		S1		S1	S1		X	X1	X1	X3					X			J.Winter	33
X	X			X	X	X				S1		X1	S1		S1	X1	X1	X1						X			D.Orr	34
	X			X	X					X			X		S		X	X	X	X		S		X	X	S		I.Hemley	35
	X			S	X	X	X			X			X	S1	X	X1	X1		S			X		X	X		E.Lomas	36
S	X			S1	X			X1	X				X		X		X	X	S			X		X	X			R.Poulain	37
X	X			S1						X	X	S		X			X	X	X2	X	S2			X1	X			P.Rejer	38
X	X		X		X	S1				S	S		X			X	X	X1	X					X			E.Wolstenholme	39
X	X		X2		X	X				S2	X			X1			X	X	S1	X	S			X			T.Heilbron	40
X2	X		X		X	X				S2	X			X			X	X			X1	S1	X		X			J.Brandwood	41
	X		X		X1	X				S	X			X2			X	X	S1	X				X	X			M.Bailey	42
	X		X		X	X				X				X1			X1	X	S1	S1				X	X			I.Cruikshanks	43
X	X		X		X	X				S	X			X			X	X	X1	S2	S1	X		X2	X			M.Pierce	44
X	X		X		X	X				X			S				X	X	X1	X	X	S1		X				K.Leach	45
X	X		X		X	X				S2					S1		S		X	X				X	X2	X1		C.Wilkes	46
X	X		X		X	X				X					S1		S2		S2	X2	X2	X		X		X1		G.Pooley	47
X	X		X		X	X									S	X		S1	X	X1	X			X		X		K.Breen	48
X	X		X		X1	X					X	S2					S1		X	X2	X			X		X2		B.Knight	49
X	X		X		X	X				X		S					S	X	S1	X	X			X		X1		J.Kirkby	50
X	X		X		X	X				X	S	S					X	X	S1	X1	X			X		X		P.Richards	51
X		X1			X	X				X	X	S		S				X	S1	X				X		X		G.Pooley	52
		X1			X	X				X			X		S			X	S1	X	X	X		X		X		D.Orr	53
34	17	12	15	3	36	37	5	27	14	12	4	9	28	16	15	16	14	32	37	20	18	4	2	29	31	11	5	EL Appearances	
0	0	0	0	1	8	3	0	3	0	8	4	5	7	0	6	0	3	7	6	15	0	5	0	1	0	3	0	EL Sub Appearances	
4	0	3	0	1	3+2	4	0	5	0	3	0+1	2+2	3	0	3	0	0	4	5	2	4	0+1	2	2	2	0+1	0	CC Appearances	
1	0	0	0	0	1	2	1	2	0	2	0	0+2	0+2	0	0+1	1	2	2	2	2	2	2	2	0	1	1	0	FAC Appearances	

lso Played: (M) Bass S(41,45). (D) Brown S(6). (M) Codner S2(49), S(53). (M) Gooding S1(13). (F) Lambert S(4). (F) Morley X(30). (G) Sheppard X(32,35).

READING

CLUB RECORDS

BIGGEST VICTORIES
League: 10-2 v Crystal Palace, Division 3S, 4.9.1946
F.A. Cup: 8-3 v Corinthians, Rnd.1, 1935-36
6-0 v Leyton, Round 2, 1925/26
League Cup: 4-0 v QPR, Round 2, 23.9.1964
5-1 v Southend United, Round 2, 1965/66
5-1 v Oxford United, Round 1, 1979/80

BIGGEST DEFEATS
League: 1-8 v Burnley, Division 2, 13.9.1930
F.A. Cup: 0-18 v Preston North End, Round 1, 27.1.1894
League Cup: 0-5 v Leicester City, Round 2, 1966/67
0-5 v Watford, Round 2, 1977/78

MOST POINTS
3 points a win: 94, Division 3, 1985-86
2 points a win: 65, Division 4, 1978-79

MOST GOALS
112, 1951-52 (Division 3S)
Blackman 39, Bainbridge 18, Lewis 15, Edelston 14, Henley 10, Simpson 8, Owens4, Brice 2, Brooks 1, 1og.

MOST FIRST CLASS MATCHES IN A SEASON
60 (46 league + 10 FA Cup + 4 Lge Cup) 1989-90

MOST LEAGUE GOALS CONCEDED
96, Division 2, 1930-31

MOST LEAGUE WINS
29, Division 3, 1985-86

MOST LEAGUE DRAWS
19, Division 4, 1973-74
Division 3, 1989-90

MOST LEAGUE DEFEATS
24, Division 2, 1930-31
Division 3, 1976-77

INDIVIDUAL CLUB RECORDS

MOST GOALS IN A MATCH
6. Arthur Bacon v Stoke City, Division 2, 3.4.1931 (7-3)

MOST GOALS IN A SEASON
Trevor Senior, 36 League, 1 FA Cup, 4 Lge Cup, Total 41 (1983-84)
3 goals 2 times = 6, 2 goals 10 times = 20, 1 goal 15 times = 15.
Previous holder: Ronnie Blackman, 40 (39 league, 1 FA Cup) 1951-52.

OLDEST PLAYER
Beaumont Ratcliffe, 39 years 336 days v Northampton Town, 1947-48

YOUNGEST PLAYER
S Hetkze, 16 years 184 days v Darlington, 4.12.71

MOST CAPPED PLAYER
Jimmy Quinn (Northern Ireland) 17

BEST PERFORMANCES

League: 1985-86: Matches played 46, Won 29, Drawn 7, Lost 10, Goals for 67,Goals against 51, Points 94. 1st in Division 3.

Highest: 2nd, Division 1, 1994-95.

F.A. Cup: 1926-27: 1st rnd. Weymouth 4-4, 5-0; 2nd rnd. Southend, 3-2; 3rd rnd.Manchester United, 1-1,2-2,2-1; 4th rnd. Portsmouth, 3-1; 5th rnd. Brentford,1-0; 6th rnd, Swansea, 3-1; Semi-Final, Cardiff City, 0-3.

League Cup: 1965-66: 1st rnd, Port Vale, 2-2, 1-0; 2nd rnd, Southend, 5-1; 3rd rnd, Derby County, 1-1, 2-0; 4th rnd, Cardiff City 1-5.
1978-79: 1st rnd, Gillingham, 3-1, 2-1; 2nd rnd, Wolves, 1-0; 3rd rnd,Rotherham, 2-2, 1-0, 4th rnd, Southampton, 0-0, 0-2.
1995-96: 2nd rnd, WBA H1-1,A4-2. 3rd rnd, Bury H2-1.
4th rnd, Southampton H2-1. 5th rnd, Leeds A1-2.

ADDITIONAL INFORMATION
Previous League: Southern League

Club colours: Royal Blue & white hooped shirts, white shorts and socks.

Change colours: Toro red & white shirts, toro red shorts and toro red & white socks.

Reserves League: Capital League.
Youth League: S E Counties, Allied Counties Youth League.

DIVISIONAL RECORD

	Played	Won	Drawn	Lost	For	Against	Points
Division 2/1	388	126	100	162	469	565	332
Division 3/2	1,196	471	296	429	1,779	1,722	1,238
Division 3(S)	1,124	480	260	384	1,892	1,585	1,220
Division 4	368	161	110	97	513	392	432
Total	3,076	1,238	766	1,072	4,707	4,327	3,278

RECORDS AND STATISTICS

COMPETITIONS

Div.2/1	Div.3.2	Div.3(S)	Div.4	Watney C.
1926-31	1958-71	1920-26	1971-76	1970
1986-88	1976-77	1931-58	1977-79	
1994-	1979-83		1983-84	
	1984-86			
	1986-94			

HONOURS

Div.3/2	Div.3(S)	Div.4	Div.3(S) Cup
1985-86	1925-26	1978-79	1937-38
1993-94			
			Simod Cup
			1987-88

MOST APPEARANCES

Martin Hicks 601+2 (178-91)

Year	League	FA Cup	Lge Cup	Others
1977-78	19			
1978-79	46	4	7	
1979-80	1		2	
1980-81	27	1	1	
1981-82	43+1	1	2	3
1982-83	32		1	5
1983-84	46	3	2	
1984-85	40	2	2	2
1985-86	34	6	2	1+1
1986-87	34	1	4	
1987-88	44	1	5	6
1988-89	45	7	4	3
1989-90	44	10	4	3
1990-91	44	1	2	2
	499+1	39	38	25+1

MOST GOALS IN A CAREER

Trevor Senior - 154 (1983-92)

Year	League	FA Cup	Lge Cup	Others
1983-84	36	1	4	
1984-85	22	4	1	
1985-86	27	4		
1986-87	17	1	6	
1988-89	16	4		4
1989-90	14	4	3	
1990-91	15			
1991-92	7			
Total	154	18	14	4

Current leading goalscorer: Jimmy Quinn - 85 (1992-96)

RECORD TRANSFER FEE RECEIVED

Amount	Club	Player	Date
£1,575,000	Newcastle Utd	Shaka Hislop	08/95
£1,005,000	Wolves	Adrian Williams	7/96
£500,000	Wimbledon	Keith Curle	10/88
£320,000	Watford	Trevor Senior	07/87

RECORD TRANSFER FEE PAID

Amount	Club	Player	Date
£700,000	Tottenham	Darren Caskey	02/96
£350,000	Wrexham	Barry Hunter	8/96
£300,000	FC Botev Flodrid	Borislav Mihailov	09/95

MANAGERS

Name	Seasons	Best	Worst
Harry Matthews	1902-22	13(3S)	20(3S)
Arthur Chadwick	1923-25	14(3S)	19(3S)
Angus Wylie	1926-31	14(2)	1(3S)
Joe Smith	1931-35	2(3S)	4(3S)
Billy Butler	1935-39	3(3S)	6(3S)
John Cochrane	1939		
Joe Edelston	1939-47	9(3S)	9(3S)
Ted Drake	1947-52	2(3S)	10(3S)
Jack Smith	1952-55	8(3S)	18(3S)
Harry Johnson	1955-63	4(3S)	20(3)
Roy Bentley	1963-69	4(3)	14(3)
Jack Mansell	1969-72	8(3)	16(4)
Charlie Hurley	1972-77	21(3)	6(4)
Maurice Evans	1977-84	7(3)	8(4)
Ian Branfoot	1984-89	13(2)	18(3)
Ian Porterfield	1989-91	10(3)	15(3)
Mark McGhee	1991-94	1(2/3)	15(3)
M Gooding & J Quinn	1994-	2(1)	19(1)

LONGEST LEAGUE RUNS

of undefeated matches:	19 (1973)	of league matches w/out a win:	14 (1927)
of undefeated home matches:	55 (1933-36)	of undefeated away matches:	11 (1985)
without home win:	8 (1954, 1991)	without an away win:	21 (1952-53)
of league wins:	13 (1985, record for start of a season)	of home wins:	19 (1931-32)
of league defeats:	6 (1971)	of away wins:	7 (1951-52, 1985)

READING

PLAYERS NAME Honours	Ht	Wt	Birthdate	Birthplace Transfers	Contract Date	Clubs	League	L/Cup	FA Cup	Other	Lge	L/C	FAC	Oth
G O A L K E E P E R S														
Hammond Nicky	6.0	11.13	07/09/67	Hornchurch	12/07/85	Arsenal								
				Loan	23/08/86	Bristol Rovers	3							
				Free	01/07/87	Swindon Town	65+2	11	10	6				
				£40000	14/08/95	Plymouth Argyle	4	2						
				Loan	13/12/95	Reading								
				£40000	09/01/96	Reading	5		1					
Mihailov Borislav			12/02/63			FC Bolev								
				£300000	19/09/95	Reading	16		1					
D E F E N D E R S														
Bernal Andrew Aus: 21	5.10	12.5	16/07/66	Canberra (Aus)		Sporting Gijon								
				Free	24/09/87	Ipswich Town	4+5			0+2				
					01/08/90	Sydney Olympic								
				£30000	26/07/94	Reading	67	7	2	3	2			
Bodin Paul W: 22, u21.1, Y	5.10	10.11	13/09/64	Cardiff		Chelsea								
				Free	28/01/82	Newport County								
				Free	01/08/82	Cardiff City	68+7	11	4		4			
				Free	01/02/85	Bath City			8				3	
				£15000	27/01/88	Newport County	6			1				
				£30000	07/03/88	Swindon Town	87+6	12	6	8	9			1
				£550000	20/03/91	Crystal Palace	8+1	1						
				Loan	05/12/91	Newcastle United	6							
				£225000	10/01/92	Swindon Town	135+6	14	10	8	28		1	1
				Free	09/07/96	Reading								
Booty Martyn J	5.8	11.2	30/05/71	Kirby Muxloe	30/05/89	Coventry City	4+1	2	2					
				Free	07/10/93	Crewe Alexandra	95+1	6	8	13	5		1	
					18/01/96	Reading	17				1			
Hopkins Jeff W: 16, u21.5, Y. Div2'94	6.0	12.11	14/04/64	Swansea	10/09/81	Fulham	213+6	26	12	3	4	2		
				£240000	17/08/88	Crystal Palace	70	7	4	12	2	1	1	
				Loan	24/10/91	Plymouth Argyle	8			1				
				Free	05/03/92	Bristol Rovers	4+2							
				Free	13/07/92	Reading	110+3	8+1	6+1	6+2	3	1		
Hunter Barry	6.4	12.0	18/11/68	Coleraine		Crusaders								
				£50000	20/08/93	Wrexham	88+3	6	7+1	15	4		1	1
				£400000	09/07/96	Reading								
Kerr Dylan Div2'94	5.9	11.4	14/01/67	Valetta (Malta)	01/09/84	Sheffield Wednesday								
				Free	01/08/85	Arcadia Shepherds								
				Free	08/02/89	Leeds United	6+7	2	1	0+4				
				Loan	22/08/91	Doncaster Rovers	7				1			
				Loan	31/12/91	Blackpool	12			1	1			
				£75000	15/07/93	Reading	84+5	8+1	2	3+1	5			
McPherson Keith FAYC'81. Div4'87. Div2'94	5.11	11.0	11/09/63	Greenwich	12/09/81	West Ham United	1							
				Loan	30/09/85	Cambridge United	11				1			
				£15000	23/01/86	Northampton Town	182	9	12	13	8	1		
					24/08/90	Reading	188+5	13+1	10+1	20+1	7			
Swales Steve	5.8	10.0	26/12/73	Whitby	03/08/92	Scarborough	51+3		5	3				
				£70000	13/07/95	Reading	4+5	0+1	1					
Thorp Michael			05/12/75	Wallingford		Reading	2	2	1					
Wdowczyk Dariusz Poland: 53	5.11	11.11	21/09/62	Warsaw		Legia Warsaw								
				£450000	17/11/89	Celtic	112+4	11	13	6+1	4		2	
				Free	01/08/94	Reading	66+2	4	1	3				
Williams Adrian	6.2	12.6	16/08/71	Reading										
M I D F I E L D														
Bass David	5.11	12.7	29/11/74	Frimley	14/07/93	Reading	7+2							
Caskey Darren E: S, Y.15. UEFA Y'93	5.8	10.7	21/08/74	Basildon	06/03/92	Tottenham Hotspur	20+12	3+1	6+1		4	1		
				Loan	27/10/95	Watford	6				1			
				£700000	01/02/96	Reading	15				2			
Gooding Mick Div3'81'89. Div2'94	5.9	10.7	12/04/59	Newcastle		Bishop Auckland								
					18/07/79	Rotherham United	90+12	9	3		10	3		
					24/12/82	Chesterfield	12							
					09/09/83	Rotherham United	149+7	18	13	7	32	3	4	
				£18000	13/08/87	Peterborough Utd	47	8	1	4	21	2	2	2
				£85000	20/09/88	Wolves	43+1	4		5+1	4			1
				£65000	26/12/89	Reading	263+8	17	16+1	16	26		2	2
Lovell Stuart Div2'94	5.10	11.0	09/01/72	Sydney (Aus)	13/07/90	Reading	152+34	12	5+7	7+3	53	5	2	2
Meaker Michael W: u21.2	5.11	11.5	18/08/71	Greenford	07/02/90	Q.P.R.	14+12	1	1	0+1	1	1		
				Loan	20/11/91	Plymouth Argyle	4			1				
				£550000	19/07/95	Reading	15+6		0+1					
Parkinson Phil Div2'94	6.0	11.6	01/12/67	Chorley	07/12/85	Southampton								
				£12000	08/03/88	Bury	133+12	6+1	4	13	5		1	1
				£37500	10/07/92	Reading	142+13	14	8	4+2	6	1	1	
Simpson Derek F	***	***	23/12/78	Lanark	01/07/94	Reading								
Williams Martin	5.9	11.12	12/07/73	Luton		Leicester City								
				Free	13/09/91	Luton Town	12+28	1	0+1	2+1	2			
				Free	13/07/95	Reading	11+3	0+1			1			

F O R W A R D S					

Carey Alan 5.7 10.2 21/08/75

Type	Date	Club	Lge	FAC	LC	Oth	Gls Lge	Gls FAC	Gls LC	Gls Oth
Greenwich	20/07/94	Reading	0+3							
Loan	06/03/95	Weymouth								

Gilkes Michael 5.8 10.10 20/07/65 FMC'88. FLgXI'88. Div2'94

Type	Date	Club	Lge	FAC	LC	Oth	Gls Lge	Gls FAC	Gls LC	Gls Oth
Hackney		Leicester City								
Free	10/07/84	Reading	321+40	25+6	29+2	26+2	42	6	1	2
Loan	28/01/92	Chelsea	0+1			0+1				
Loan	04/03/92	Southampton	4+2							

Holsgrove Paul 6.11 11.10 26/08/69

Type	Date	Club	Lge	FAC	LC	Oth	Gls Lge	Gls FAC	Gls LC	Gls Oth
Wellington	09/02/87	Aldershot	0+3		1					
Free	01/03/90	Wokingham Town								
Loan	01/08/90	Farnborough			1					
£25000	01/01/91	Luton Town	1+1							
Free	01/11/91	Heracles								
Free	13/08/92	Millwall	3+8	0+1	0+1	2				
Free	10/08/94	Reading	50+4	7+2	3		4	1		

Lambert James 5.7 10.4 14/09/73

Type	Date	Club	Lge	FAC	LC	Oth	Gls Lge	Gls FAC	Gls LC	Gls Oth
Henley	03/07/92	Reading	22+36	2+3	4+2	2+3	8	1		1

Morley Trevor 5.11 12.1 20/03/61 E: S-P.6. Sthrn Lge'82. Div4'87

Type	Date	Club	Lge	FAC	LC	Oth	Gls Lge	Gls FAC	Gls LC	Gls Oth
Nottingham		Derby County								
Free		Corby								
£10000		Nuneaton Borough			3					
£20000	21/06/85	Northampton Town	107	10	6	7	39	4	2	
£175000	22/01/88	Manchester City	69+3	7	1	2	18	3		
£500000	28/12/89	West Ham United	159+19	10+1	14+5	5+1	57	5	7	1
Free	01/08/95	Reading	14+3	2	2		4	1	1	

Nogan Lee 5.10 11.0 21/05/69 W: 1, B.1, u21.1

Type	Date	Club	Lge	FAC	LC	Oth	Gls Lge	Gls FAC	Gls LC	Gls Oth
Cardiff	25/03/87	Oxford United	57+7	4+1	2+1	4+1	10		1	1
Loan	25/03/87	Brentford	10+1				2			
Loan	17/09/87	Southend United	6	2		1	1			1
£350000	12/12/91	Watford	97+8	5+2	2	1+2	26	3	1	
Loan	17/03/94	Southend United	4+1							
£250000	13/01/95	Reading	50+9	4	2	3	20	1	2	

Quinn Jimmy 6.0 11.6 18/11/59 NI: 41. Div2'94

Type	Date	Club	Lge	FAC	LC	Oth	Gls Lge	Gls FAC	Gls LC	Gls Oth
Belfast		Oswestry								
£10000	31/12/81	Swindon Town	34+15	1+1	5+3	1	10		6	2
£32000	15/08/84	Blackburn Rovers	58+13	6+1	4	2	17	2	3	1
£50000	19/12/86	Swindon Town	61+3	6	5	10+1	30	8		5
£210000	20/06/88	Leicester City	13+18	2+1	0+1	0+1	6			
	17/03/89	Bradford City	35	2		1	13	1		
£320000	30/12/89	West Ham United	34+13	3	4+2	1	19	1	2	
£40000	05/08/91	Bournemouth	43	4	5	2	19	2	2	1
£55000	27/07/92	Reading	139+19	11+3	9	6+3	68	11	5	6

PLAYER-MANAGERS
MICK GOODING AND JIMMY QUINN

Date of Birth . . . . 12th April 1959 (MG). 18th November 1959 (JQ).
Place of Birth. . . . . Newcastle (MG). Belfast (JQ).
Date of Appointment . . . . January 1995.

PREVIOUS CLUBS
As Manager. . . . . None.
As Coach. . . . . None.
As a Player . . . . MG - Bishop Auckland, Rotherham (x2), Chesterfield, Peterborough, Wolves, Reading. JQ - Oswestry, Swindon, Blackburn, Leicester, ... Bradford, West Ham, Bournemouth, Reading.

HONOURS
As a Manager
None.
As a Player
MG - Rotherham: Division 3 championship 1983
Reading: Division 3 championship 1989, Division 2 1994.
JQ - Reading: Division 2 championship 1994.
International: 49 full caps and 1 B cap for Northern Ireland.

ELM PARK
Norfolk Road, Reading RG3 2EF
Tel: 0118 950 7878

Capacity 15,000
Seating 2,242

First game ....v London XI, 05.09.1896.
First floodlit game ....v Racing Club de Paris, 06.10.1954.

ATTENDANCES
Highest ....33,042 v Brentford, FAC, 19.2.1927.
Lowest ....1,403 v Orient, FRT, 6.3.1986.

OTHER GROUNDS...........Reading Recreation Ground 1871. Reading CC 1882. Coley Park 1882-89.
....Caversham CC 1889-96. Elm Park 1896-

MATCHDAY TICKET PRICES

B & D Stand. £11

C Stand £12

E Stand (Family Area) Adult £9
Juv. £5

Terrace £8.50

Ticket Office Telephone no. 01189 507 878

CLUBCALL
0891 12 10 00
Calls cost 39p per minute cheap rate and 49p per
minute at all other times.
Call costings correct at time of going to press.

HOW TO GET TO THE GROUND

From the North
From Oxford use A423, A4074 and A4155 and cross railway bridge into Reading, follow signs Newbury (A4) into Castle Hill, turn right into Tilehurst Road. In 0.7 miles turn right into Cranbury Road, turn left, then take 2nd left into Norfolk Road for Reading FC.
From the East
Use motorway (M4) until junction 10, leave motorway and use A329 and A4 into Reading. Follow signs to Newbury into Bath Road. Over railway bridge then take 3rd turning on right into Liebenrood Road. At end turn left then right into Waverley Road, turn right into Norfolk Road for Reading FC.
From the South
Use A33 into Reading then follow signs to Newbury (A4) into Bath Road. Over railway bridge then take third turning on right into Liebenrood Road. Then proceed as from the East.
From the West
Use motorway (M4) until junction 12, leave motorway and follow signs to Reading (A4). In 3.3 miles turn left into Liebenrood Road. Then proceed as from the East.

Car Parking: Park & ride - Plospect Park - £1.50 per car.
Nearest Railway Station: Reading (01734 595 911) and bus or Reading West (1o minutes walk).

MATCHDAY PROGRAMME

Programme Editor . . . . Maurice O'Brien.

Number of pages . . . . 48.

Price . . . . £1.50.

Subscriptions. . . . . Contact supporters club.

Local Newspapers . . . . Reading Evening Post, Reading Chronicle.

Local Radio Stations . . . . BBC Thames Valley FM, Radio 210.

SHEFFIELD UNITED
(The Blades)
NATIONWIDE LEAGUE DIVISION 1
SPONSORED BY: WARDS BREWERY LTD

Back Row (L-R): Denis Circuit (Physio), Rob Scott, Doug Hodgson, Brian Gayle, Mark Foran, Alan Kelly, Jostein Flo, Dave Tuttle, Paul Rogers, Andy Scott, Brian Eastick (Coach). **Middle Row:** Derek French (Physio), John Greaves (Kitman), Mark Blount, Phil Starbuck, Carl Veart, Billy Mercer, Glyn Hodges, Salvatore Bibbo, Charlie Hartfield, Roger Nilsen, Nathan Blake, Geoff Taylor (Asst.Manager). **Front Row:** John Reed, Paul Holland, Dane, Whitehouse, Dave Bassett (Manager), Mitch Ward, Kevin Gage, Ross Davidson.

SHEFFIELD UNITED
FORMED IN 1889
TURNED PROFESSIONAL IN 1889
LTD COMPANY IN 1889

CHAIRMAN: Mike McDonald

DIRECTORS
A H Laver, B Proctor, A M McDonald,
J Plant, JP, S L Hinchcliffe, K McCabe,
S White
SECRETARY
David Capper (0114 273 8956)
COMMERCIAL MANAGER
Andy Daykin

MANAGER: Howard Kendall
ASSISTANT MANAGER: Nigel Spackman

COACH: Viv Busby

YOUTH TEAM MANAGER
Russell Slade
PHYSIOTHERAPIST
Denis Circuit

STATISTICIAN FOR THE DIRECTORY
Andrew Treherne

In another season of contrasts at Bramall Lane, the season began with five successive league defeats and a place at the bottom of the table. It ended with an unbeaten run of nine matches, including seven victories and a near miss for a play off spot. In between, there was almost total change at the club with the final conclusion to the Reg Brearley era, bought out by Mike McDonald, and management moving from Dave Bassett to Howard Kendall.

The first victory of the season did not arrive until September, and was only achieved with difficulty against Norwich, despite them playing the whole of the second half with only ten men. A mini run of six unbeaten games was brought to an end by Bury in the Coca-Cola Cup second leg, who triumphed 5-3 on aggregate, in what Dave Bassett considered the worst performance by the team in twenty years.

By this time Mike McDonald had joined the Board, and the seeds of change were sown. By the middle of December only two more League games had been won, and a home defeat by Huddersfield led to Dave Bassett leaving by mutual consent. Within two days Howard Kendall was installed as manager and the revolution began. This began slowly, as period of team changing by Kendall led to a run of five draws, but improved team performances. The first win was achieved with a memorable FA Cup replay victory over Arsenal, the winning goal coming from Carl Veart one of twenty two players transfer listed or released by Kendall.

The speed of change gathered pace, as Don Hutchinson became United's first Million Pound player and transfer deals became almost daily events as the team was totally rebuilt. The players brought in were undoubtedly of Premier League quality, and, as they blended into a unit, the results and standard of football improved. Defeat to Aston Villa in the FA Cup fourth round was to a debatable penalty award, and only three league games were lost in the remainder of the season. At the end of February the team was still in the relegation zone, and the league was so close that as they climbed the table to finish in ninth place, relegation or a play off spot was still mathematically possible until the last two weeks of the season.

The season ended with two 'Manager of the Month' awards for Kendall and the team already installed as one of the promotion favourites for next season. A fine return to form for Simon Tracey could lead to the departure of Alan Kelly, which could, in turn, lead to further additions to the squad and a successful promotion campaign. **ANDREW TREHERNE.**

SHEFFIELD UNITED

League: 9th   **FA Cup: 4th Rnd**   **Coca-Cola Cup: 2nd Rnd**

M	DATE	COMP	VEN	OPPONENTS	RESULT	HT	LP	GOAL SCORERS/GOAL TIMES	ATT.
1	A 12	EL	A	Watford	L	1-2	1-2	12	Blake 30	(8667)
2	19	EL	H	Tranmere Rovers	L	0-2	0-1	20		11247
3	26	EL	A	Oldham Athletic	L	1-2	0-0	22	Blake 76	(6851)
4	29	EL	H	Crystal Palace	L	2-3	0-0	24	Flo 52, Whitehouse 71	10378
5	S 2	EL	A	West Bromwich Albion	L	1-3	0-2	24	Scott 87	(14377)
6	9	EL	H	Norwich City	W	2-1	1-1	23	Blake 45, Veart 72	11205
7	12	EL	A	Charlton Athletic	W	2-0	1-0	19	Blake 40, 80	9448
8	17	EL	A	Barnsley	D	2-2	0-2	19	Blake 60, 82	(7150)
9	20	CC 2/1	H	Bury	W	2-1	1-0		Whitehouse 6(pen), Veart 77	4075
10	24	EL	A	Huddersfield Town	W	2-1	2-0	14	Flo 13, Hodges 20	(12840)
11	30	EL	H	Ipswich Town	D	2-2	0-1	15	Blake 10, Whitehouse 33(pen)	12557
12	O 3	CC 2/2	A	Bury	L	2-4	0-2		Flo 72, Holland 90	(2888)
13	7	EL	H	Derby County	L	0-2	0-1	17		12721
14	14	EL	A	Southend United	L	1-2	1-1	19	Holland 19	(5292)
15	21	EL	H	Leicester City	L	1-3	1-1	20	Flo 16	13100
16	28	EL	A	Wolverhampton Wand	L	0-1	0-1	21		(23881)
17	N 4	EL	H	Portsmouth	W	4-1	2-1	20	Veart 32, 74, Flo 34, Battersby 79	11281
18	11	EL	A	Port Vale	W	3-2	1-1	17	Blake 43, 53, Hodges 69	(7284)
19	18	EL	A	Sunderland	L	0-2	0-0	18		(16640)
20	21	EL	H	Grimsby Town	L	1-2	0-0	18	Blake 80	9884
21	25	EL	H	Reading	D	0-0	0-0	19		9737
22	D 2	EL	A	Derby County	L	2-4	1-1	19	Blake 38, Veart 50	(13841)
23	9	EL	H	Huddersfield Town	L	0-2	0-1	21		12126
24	16	EL	A	Ipswich Town	D	1-1	0-0	23	Starbuck 65	(9630)
25	23	EL	A	Stoke City	D	2-2	1-1	23	Patterson 7, White 74	(12265)
26	26	EL	H	Birmingham City	D	1-1	1-1	22	Patterson 42	17668
27	J 6	FAC 3	A	Arsenal	D	1-1	0-0		Whitehouse 78	(33453)
28	13	EL	A	Tranmere Rovers	D	1-1	0-0	22	Hodges 72	(7321)
29	17	FAC 3R	H	Arsenal	W	1-0	0-0		Veart 68	22255
30	20	EL	H	Watford	D	1-1	0-0		Tuttle 55	12782
31	28	FAC 4	H	Aston Villa	L	0-1	0-0			18749
32	31	EL	A	Luton Town	L	0-1	0-0	23		(6995)
33	F 3	EL	H	Oldham Athletic	W	2-1	1-1	22	White 37, 81	10956
34	10	EL	A	Crystal Palace	D	0-0	0-0	23		(15883)
35	13	EL	H	Millwall	W	2-0	1-0	22	Veart 45, Hutchison 53	10007
36	17	EL	A	Charlton Athletic	D	1-1	0-0	22	White 65	(11239)
37	20	EL	H	West Bromwich Albion	L	1-2	1-2	23	Angell 34	10944
38	24	EL	H	Barnsley	W	1-0	1-0	20	Angell 21	14584
39	28	EL	A	Norwich City	D	0-0	0-0	21		(10945)
40	M 2	EL	A	Birmingham City	W	1-0	0-0	17	Walker 78	(16799)
41	9	EL	H	Stoke City	D	0-0	0-0	17		14468
42	16	EL	A	Millwall	L	0-1	0-0	20		(7795)
43	23	EL	H	Luton Town	W	1-0	0-0	19	Hutchison 78	14395
44	30	EL	A	Leicester City	W	2-0	0-0	20	Walker 63, Ward 83(pen)	(15230)
45	A 2	EL	A	Southend United	W	3-0	3-0	16	White 19, Walker 28, 38	11319
46	6	EL	H	Wolverhampton Wand	W	2-1	2-1	14	Taylor 21, White 31	16658
47	8	EL	A	Portsmouth	W	2-1	2-0	12	Whitehouse 33(pen), White 40	(8978)
48	13	EL	A	Sunderland	D	0-0	0-0	10		20050
49	20	EL	A	Grimsby Town	W	2-0	2-0	10	Walker 9, Taylor 23	(7685)
50	27	EL	A	Reading	W	3-0	1-0	9	Walker 28, 90, Whitehouse 86	(9769)
51	M 4	EL	H	Port Vale	D	1-1	0-0	9	Walker 73	18741

Best Home League Attendance: 20050 v Sunderland   **Smallest: 9448 v Charlton Athletic**   **Average: 12880**

Goal Scorers:

EL(57): Blake(12),Walker(8),White(7),Veart(5),Flo(4),Whitehouse(4),Hodges(3),Patterson(2),Taylor(2),Hutchison(2),Angell(2),Holland(1),Scott(1),Starbuck(1),Battersby(1), Tuttle(1),Ward(1)

CC(2): Whitehouse(1),Veart(1),Holland(1),Flo(1)

FAC(4): Whitehouse(1),Veart(1)

(D) Ablett (L)	(F) Battersby	(D) Beard	(F) Blake	(M) Blount	(M) Cowans	(F) Flo	(D) Foran	(M) Gannon	(F) Hodges	(M) Hodgson	(M) Holland	(F) Hutchison	(G) Kelly	(D) Nilsen	(M) Patterson	(M) Rogers	(F) Scott	(D) Short	(F) Starbuck	(F) Taylor	(G) Tracey	(D) Tuttle	(F) Veart	(D) Vonk	(F) Walker	(M) Ward	(F) White	(M) Whitehouse	Player	No.
		X			S2						X3		X	X		X	X1		S3			X	X			X		X	G.Singh	1
	S1	X									X		X	X		X2	X					X	S2			X		X	B.Burns	2
		X	S1				X1				X		X	X		X						X	X			X		X	T.Heilbron	3
		X	X	X2			X3		S1					X		X	S2						X1			X		X	G.Cain	4
		X	X	X							X		X	X		X1							X1			X		X	D.Allison	5
	S	X	X	X			X				X		X	X		X2						X1	S1			X		X	A.Butler	6
	S2	X3	X				X2				X1	X	S1	X		X			S3							X		X	K.Breen	7
X		X	X								X	X	S1	X		X1					S		S1			X1		X	R.D.Furnandiz	8
X2		X	X								S1	X1	X	X		S2							S2			X		X	J.Brandwood	9
			X1	X		X	X				X		X	X		X	S1					X	S					X	K.Lynch	10
		X1	X3	X			X2	X			X	S2	X	X		X	S1					X	S3					X	P.Richards	11
	S2	X2		X			X				S1		X	X		X	X1				S	X	X					X	G.Singh	12
	S3	X	X2	X			X				X		X	X								X	S2		S1			X	E.Lomas	13
	X2	S2					X	X	X		X		X	X		S1						X1	X3			X		X	C.Wilkes	14
		X					X				X		X	X					X		S	X	S			X		X	J.Rushton	15
		X					X	X1			S1		X	X				X	X2			X	X		S2			X	S.W.Mathieson	16
	S1	S2	X1				X				X3		X	X					S3			X	X			X		X	T.Heilbron	17
		X	X				X	X	X2	S1	S2			X1								X	X			X		X	T.Lunt	18
		X	X	S2			X	X	X		X	X2	X									S	X1			X	X	X	R.D.Furnandiz	19
	S3	X	X				X3	X1	S1				X		S1							X	X1			X	X	X	K.Leach	20
	S2	X1	X2				X		X		S		X		S1							X	X			X	X	X	A.Wiley	21
	S2	X	X				X2	X					X	X									X1		S1	X		X1	D.B.Allison	22
		X1						X2	X2	X	S2		X									X	X2				X2	X1	I.Hemley	23
		X1						X2	S2	X			X	X					S1			X	X2			X	X		J.Rushton	24
X								X1	S2				X	X	X	X			S			X		X2		X	X		E.Wolstenholme	25
							S2	X1	X				X	X	X	X			X2			S	X			X	X	X	I.Cruikshanks	26
			X						X2	X		S2	X	X				X	X1							X	X	X	P.Durkin	27
			X						X2	X1	S2	X	X	X				X	X1							X	X	X	W.Burns	28
			X							S1			X	X	X			X	S			X	X			X	X	X1	P.Durkin	29
			X							S1		X	X	X	X			X	S			S	S2	X		X1	X	X2	A. D'Urso	30
			X	X2									X1	X	X			X	S			S	S1			X	X	X	A.Wilkie	31
			X	X1									X	X	X			X	S			X1	S1			X	X1	X	D.Orr	32
			X	X									X	X	X			X	S			X1	S1			X	X	X	P.Richards	33
			X	X							S2		X	X	X			X					X			X	X	X2	M.Pierce	34
			X	X							S		X	X	X			X	S1			S	X1			X	X	X	J.Lloyd	35
			X	X									X	X1	X			X	X				X			X	X	S1	P.Rajer	36
			S	X							S		X	X	X			X	X			S	X			X	X	X	E.Wolstenholme	37
			X	X									X	X	X			S2	S			X	S1	X	X1	X	X	X	E.Lomas	38
			X	X									X	X	X			S1	S2			S	X2	X	X1	X	X	X	N.Barry	39
X	S								X				X	X	X			X	X	X					S1	X	X	X1	S.Mathieson	40
X									X				X	X1	X			X	S	X	S				S1	X	X	X	R.Furnandiz	41
X		S2							X2				X	S1	X			X			S	X1			X	X	X	X	R.Gifford	42
X									S3				X	X	X			X1	X1			X			X	X	X	X3	T.West	43
X									X				X	X	X		S		X1			X	X		X	X	S1		K.Breen	44
X	S1								X				X	X	X							X	X			X	X2	S1	G.Cain	45
X	S2			X1									X	X	X							X	X			X	X2	S1	J.Rushton	46
X	S2			S1									X	X	X							X	X		X1	X2	X	X	C.Wilkes	47
X				X							S1		X	X	X		S					X	X		X1	X	X	X	J.Brandwood	48
X				X							S		X	X	X							X	X		X1	X	S1	X	N.Barry	49
X	S1			X									X	X					X3			X2	X		X	X	X1	X	P.Richards	50
X				X1							X2		X	X			S3		X			X3	X			X		X	B.Burns	51
12	3	13	20	6	18	17	6	12	15	12	11	18	34	39	21	13	3	13	5	10	11	26	17	17	12	39	24	36	EL Appearances	
0	7	7	2	1	2	2	1	0	7	4	7	1	1	0	0	3	4	2	6	0	0	0	10	0	2	3	4	2	EL Sub Appearances	
0	1+1	2	1	2	0	1	0	0	0+2	1+1	0	1	3	2	2	0	1+1	1	0	0	1	1+1	0	0	1	0	0	2	CC Appearances	
0	0	0	0	0	3	0	0	1	1+2	1+1	0	1	3	3	2	0	3	1	0	0	2	1+1	2	0	3	3	3		FAC Appearances	

Also Played: (F) Angell X(32,3337,39), X1(34), X2(38). (M) Anthony X2(9), S(36). (D) Davidson X3(13). (D) Fitzgerald X(13,21,23,24,25,26). (D) Gage S(15) X(16), X2(17). (D) Gayle S1(1), S(2), X(3,4,5), S2(51). (M) Hawes S1(5), X1(13). (F) Heath S1(25,26,27,32,34), S (29,33). (G) Mercer S(3), X(4). (G) Muggleton S(44,45,46,48,49) S3(50). (M) Reed S2(50), S1(51). (M) Scott.R X2(1), X1(2), S2(6), S3(4), S1(5).

SHEFFIELD UNITED

CLUB RECORDS

BIGGEST VICTORIES
League: 10-0 v Port Vale (a), Div 2, 10.12.1892 (The only time a club has scored 10 Lge goals away from home)
10-0 v Burnley, Division 1, 19.1.1929
(Most goals) 11-2 v Cardiff City, 1.1.1926
F.A. Cup: 5-0 v Corinthians, Round 1, 10.1.1925
5-0 v Newcastle, Round 1, 10.1.1914
5-0 v Barrow, Round 3, 7.1.1956
League Cup: 4-0 v Fulham, Round 1, 25.9.1961
5-1 v Grimsby, Round 2, 26.10.1982
5-1 v Rotherham United, Round 1, 3.9.1985

BIGGEST DEFEATS
League: 1-8 v Arsenal, Division 1, 12.4.1930
2-9 v Arsenal, Division 1, 24.12.1932
3-10 v Middlesbrough, Division 1, 18.11.1933
0-7 v Tottenham Hotspur, Division 2, 12.11.1949
F.A. Cup: 0-13 v Bolton Wanderers, Round 2, 1.2.1890
League Cup: 0-5 v West Ham United, Round 5, 17.11.1971

MOST POINTS
3 points a win: 96, Division 4, 1981-82
2 points a win: 60, Division 2, 1952-53

MOST GOALS
102, Division 1, 1925-26.
Johnson 23, Tunstall 20, Boyle 13, Gillespie 12, Menlove 12, Mercer 8,Partridge 6, Hoyland 3, Roxborough 1, Waugh 1, Longworth 1, Grew 1, og 1.

MOST FIRST CLASS MATCHES IN A SEASON
61 (46 League, 7 FA Cup, 5 League Cup, 3 Sherpa Van Trophy) 1988-89

MOST LEAGUE GOALS CONCEDED
101, Division 1, 1933-34

MOST LEAGUE WINS
27, Division 4, 1981-82

MOST LEAGUE DRAWS
18, Division 1, 1920-21, Premier Division 1993-94

MOST LEAGUE DEFEATS
26, Division 1, 1975-76

INDIVIDUAL CLUB RECORDS

MOST GOALS IN A SEASON
Jimmy Dunne 46 (League 41, FAC 5) 1930-31
4 goals once=4; 3 goals 5 times=15; 2 goals 4 times=8; 1 goal 19 times=19.
Previous holder: Jimmy Dunne 36, 1928-29.

MOST GOALS IN A MATCH
5. Harry Hammond v Bootle, 8-3, Division 2, 26.11.1892
5. Harry Johnson v West Ham Utd, 6-2, Division 1, 26.12.1927

OLDEST PLAYER
Jimmy Hagan, 39 years 236 days v Derby County, 14.9.1957

YOUNGEST PLAYER
Steve Hawes, 17 years 47 days v WBA 2.9.96.

MOST CAPPED PLAYER
Billy Gillespie (Northern Ireland) 25

BEST PERFORMANCES

League: 1981-82: Matches played 46, Won 27, Drawn 15, Lost 4, Goals for 94,Goals against 41, Points 96. First in Division 4.
Highest: Division 1 Champions.
F.A. Cup: 1898-99: 1st rnd. Burnley 2-2, 2-0; 2nd rnd. Preston North End 2-2,2-1; 3rd rnd. Notts County 1-0; Semi-final Liverpool 2 2, 4-4, 1-0; Final Derby 4-1.
1901-02: 1st rnd. Northampton 2-0; 2nd rnd. Bolton Wanderers 2-1; 3rd rnd. Newcastle Utd. 1-1, 2-1; Semi-final Derby County 1-1, 1-1, 1-0; Final Southampton 1-1, 2-1.
1914-15: 3rd rnd. Blackpool 2-1; 4th rnd. Liverpool 1-0; 5th rnd. Bradford 1-0; 6th rnd. Oldham 0-0, 3-0; Semi-final Bolton Wanderers 2-1; Final Chelsea 3-0.
1924-25: 3rd rnd. Corinthians 5-0; 4th rnd. Sheffield Wednesday 3-2; 5th rnd.Everton 1-0; 6th rnd. West Bromwich Albion 2-0; Semi-final Southampton 2-0;Final Cardiff 1-0.
League Cup: 1961-62: 1st rnd. Fulham 1-1, 4-0; 2nd rnd. Newcastle 2-2, 2-0; 3rd rnd. Portsmouth 1-0; 4th rnd. Bye; 5th rnd Blackpool 0-0, 0-2.
1966-67: 1st rnd. Bye; 2nd rnd. Sunderland 1-1, 1-0; 3rd rnd. Burnley 2-0; 4th rnd. Walsall 2-1; 5th rnd. Birmingham 2-3.
1971-72: 1st rnd. Bye; 2nd rnd. Fulham 3-0; 3rd rnd. York City 3-2; 4th rnd.Arsenal 0-0, 2-0; 5th rnd. West Ham United 0-5.

DIVISIONAL RECORD							
	Played	Won	Drawn	Lost	For	Against	Points
Division 1/P	2,318	861	552	905	3,499	3,707	2,325
Division 2/1	1,170	510	292	368	1,945	1,559	1,362
Division 3	230	100	49	81	366	300	317
Division 4	46	27	15	4	94	41	96
Total	3,764	1,498	908	1,358	5,904	5,607	4,162

ADDITIONAL INFORMATION
Club colours: Red/white striped shirts, black shorts, red/black socks.
Change colours: Yellow and purple halved shirts, yellow shorts, yellow/purple socks.

Reserves League
Pontins League Division 1.

RECORDS AND STATISTICS

COMPETITIONS

Div 1/P	Div.2/1	Div.3	Div.4	Texaco	Watney
893-1934	1892-93	1979-81	1981-82	1972-73	1970
1945-49	1934-39	1982-84		1973-74	1972
1953-56	1949-53	1988-89		1974-75	
1961-68	1956-61				A/Scot
1971-76	1968-71				1975-76
1990-94	1976-79			A/Ital	1977-78
	1984-88			1994-95	1978-79
	1989-90				1979-80
	1994-				1980-81

HONOURS

Div.1	Div.2	Div.4	FA Cup
1897-98	1952-53	1981-82	1899
			1902
			1915
			1925

MOST APPEARANCES

Joe Shaw 689 (1948-66)

Year	League	FA Cup	Lge Cup
1948-49	19		
1949-50	37	3	
1950-51	36		
1951-52	39	5	
1952-53	42	3	
1953-54	35	2	
1954-55	41	1	
1955-56	19		
1956-57	30	1	
1957-58	41	4	
1958-59	41	6	
1959-60	39	3	
1960-61	42	7	1
1961-62	37	5	5
1962-63	40	3	1
1963-64	41	3	
1964-65	25	3	
1965-66	27	2	
	631	51	7

MOST GOALS IN A CAREER

J Johnson - 223 (1919-31)

Year	League	FA Cup
1919-20	12	1
1920-21	12	
1921-22	17	
1922-23	17	1
1923-24	15	
1924-25	16	5
1925-26	23	1
1926-27	23	1
1927-28	33	9
1928-29	33	
1929-30	3	
1930-31	1	
Total	205	18

Current leading goalscorer: Dane Whitehouse - 38 (1989-96)

MANAGERS

Name	Seasons	Best	Worst
J Wolstinholm	1898-99	16(1)	16(1)
J Nicholson	1899-32	2(1)	20(1)
J Davison	1932-52	6(1)	11(2)
R Freeman	1952-54	13(1)	1(2)
J Mercer	1954-59	22(1)	7(2)
J Harris	1959-68	5(1)	4(2)
A Rowley	1968-69	9(2)	9(2)
J Harris	1969-73	10(1)	6(2)
K Furphy	1973-76	6(1)	13(1)
J Sirrell	1976-78	22(1)	11(2)
C Coldwell	1978	12(2)	12(2)
H Haslam	1978-81	20(2)	12(3)
M Peters	1981	21(3)	21(3)
I Porterfield	1981-86	7(2)	1(4)
B McEwan	1986-88	9(2)	9(2)
D Bassett	1988-95	9(1)	2(3)
H Kendall	1995-	9(1)	9(1)

RECORD TRANSFER FEE RECEIVED

Amount	Club	Player	Date
£2,700,000	Leeds United	Brian Deane	7/93
£1,750,000*	Bolton Wanderers	Nathan Blake	12/95
£750,000	Notts County	Tony Agana	11/91
£575,000	Chelsea	Vinny Jones	9/91

Included Mark Patterson coming to United.

RECORD TRANSFER FEE PAID

Amount	Club	Player	Date
£1,000,000*	West Ham	Don Hutchinson	12/95
£700,000	Ipswich Town	Brain Gayle	9/91
£650,000	Leeds United	Vinny Jones	9/90
£375,000	Leyton Orient	Paul Beesley	7/90

Could increase to £1.2m after so many appearances.

LONGEST LEAGUE RUNS

of undefeated matches:	22 (2.9.1899 - 20.1.1900)	of league matches w/out a win:	19 (27.9.1975 - 14.2.1976)
of undefeated home matches:	27 (31.8.1936 - 6.11.1937)	of undefeated away matches:	11 (3.12.1892 - 30.10.1893)
without home win:	10 (26.3.1949 - 22.10.1949)	without an away win:	20 (19.4.1975 - 14.4.1976)
of league wins:	8 (6.2.1893-12.4.1893, 5.9.1903-31.10.1903)	of home wins:	11 (30.4.1960 - 3.12.1960)
	(1.2.1958 - 5.4.1958, 14.9.1960 - 22.10.1960)		
of league defeats:	7 (19.8.1975 - 23.9.1975)	of away wins:	6 (10.12.1891 - 12.4.1892)

SHEFFIELD UNITED

PLAYERS NAME / Honours	Ht	Wt	Birthdate	Birthplace / Transfers	Contract Date	Clubs	League	L/Cup	FA Cup	Other	Lge	L/C	FAC	Oth
G O A L K E E P E R S														
Kelly Alan	6.2	12.5	11/08/68	Preston	25/09/85	Preston North End	142	1	8	13				
Ei: 3, u23.1, u21.1, Y				£150000	24/07/92	Sheffield United	133+3	8	12					
Tracey Simon	6.0	12.0	09/12/67	Woolwich	03/02/86	Wimbledon	1			1				
				£7500	19/10/88	Sheffield United	152+2	7	10	7				
				Loan	28/10/94	Manchester City	3							
				Loan	03/01/95	Norwich City	1		2					
				Loan	04/08/95	Nottingham Forest								
				Loan	02/11/95	Wimbledon	1							
D E F E N D E R S														
Beard Mark	5.10	10.12	08/10/74	Roehampton	18/03/93	Millwall	32+13	3+1	4		2		1	
				£117000	18/08/95	Sheffield United	13+7	2						
Hartfield Charles	6.0	12.0	04/09/71	Lambeth	20/09/89	Arsenal								
E: Y.4				Free	06/08/91	Sheffield United	44+10	2	4	1	1			
Nilsen Roger	5.9	11.8	08/08/69	Norway		Viking Stavanger								
Norwegian International				£550000	02/11/93	Sheffield United	93+1	3	4+1					
Sandford Lee	6.1	12.2	22/04/68	Basingstoke	04/12/85	Portsmouth	66+6	11	4	2+1	1			
E: Y, S. AGT'92. Div2'93				£140000	22/12/89	Stoke City	255+3	19	16	31	8		2	4
				£500000	05/07/96	Sheffield United								
Short Chris	5.1	12.02	09/05/70	Munster		Pickering								
				Free	11/07/88	Scarborough	42+1	5	1	3+1	1			
				£100000	05/09/90	Notts County	77+17	7	5+1	8+1	2		1	
				Loan	23/12/94	Huddersfield Town	6			1				
					29/12/95	Sheffield United	13+2		3					
Vonk Michel	6.2	12.2	28/10/68	Alkmaar		SW Dordrecht								
				£500000	11/03/92	Manchester City	87+4	3+2	6+1		4	1	1	
				Loan	17/11/95	Oldham Athletic	5				1			
				£350000	21/12/95	Sheffield United	17		2					
M I D F I E L D														
Anthony Graham	5.7	9.7	09/08/75	South Shields	07/07/93	Sheffield United	0+1	1		2				
				Loan	01/03/96	Scarborough	2							
Hodgson Doug	6.2	13.10	27/02/69	Frankston (Aus)		Heidelberg Alex								
				£30000	22/07/94	Sheffield United	12+5	2	1+1	1				
Patterson Mark	5.6	10.10	24/05/65	Darwen	01/05/83	Blackburn Rovers	89+12	4	3+1	2+4	20	1		1
FMC'87				£20000	15/06/88	Preston North End	54+1	4+1	4	7	19			
				£80000	01/02/90	Bury	42	2	1	4	10			
				£65000	10/01/91	Bolton Wanderers	158+11	16+4	17	9	11	2	1	
				£300000	22/12/95	Sheffield United	21		2		2			
Quinn Wayne	5.10	11.7	19/11/76	Cornwall	06/12/94	Sheffield United								
Reed John	5.6	8.11	27/08/72	Rotherham	03/07/90	Sheffield United	11+4	1		1	2			1
				Loan	10/01/91	Scarborough	14				5			
				Loan	26/09/91	Scarborough	5+1	1			2			
				Loan	19/03/93	Darlington	8+2				2			
				Loan	23/09/93	Mansfield Town	12+1		1	3	2			2
Spackman Nigel	6.1	12.4	02/12/60	Romsey		Andover								
Div.2'84. FMC'86. Div.1'88. SPD'90'91'92.				Free	08/05/80	Bournemouth	118+1	5	7		10			
SCL'91. SFAC'92.				£40000	20/06/83	Chelsea	139+2	22+1	8	7	12		1	1
				£400000	24/02/87	Liverpool	39+12	6+1	5					
				£500000	02/02/89	Q.P.R.	27+2	2		2	1	1		
				£500000	30/11/89	Glasgow Rangers	100	10	9	5	1	1	1	
				£487000	08/09/92	Chelsea	47+4	4	6	7				
				Free		Sheffield United								
Ward Mitchum	5.8	10.7	19/06/71	Sheffield	01/07/89	Sheffield United	98+16	4+3	7+2	2+1	6	1	2	1
				Loan	01/11/90	Crewe Alexandra	4		1	2	1		1	
Whitehouse Dane	5.9	10.12	14/10/70	Sheffield	01/07/89	Sheffield United	157+27	11+1	14+3	3	29	5	2	2
FLg u18.1														
F O R W A R D S														
Hutchison Don	6.2	11.08	09/05/71	Gateshead	20/03/90	Hartlepool United	19+5	1+1	2	1	3			
S: B.1				£175000	27/11/90	Liverpool	33+12	7+1	1+2	3+1	7	2		1
				£1500000	30/08/94	West Ham United	30+5	3	0+1		11	2		
				£1200000	11/01/96	Sheffield United	18+1		1		2			
Katchouro Peter						Dinamo Minsk								
Belarus Int				£650000	11/07/96	Sheffield United								

	Ht	Wt	DOB	From	Date	Club								
cott Andrew	6.1	12.0	02/08/72	Epsom		Sutton United			2					
				£50000	01/12/92	Sheffield United	34+27	3	1+1	3+1	4	1		3
arbuck Phil	5.11	12.4	24/11/68	Nottingham	19/08/86	Nottingham Forest	9+27	1+3	2+5	0+4	2			
				Loan	07/03/88	Birmingham City	3							
				Loan	19/02/90	Hereford United	6		1					
				Loan	06/09/90	Blackburn Rovers	5+1				1			
				Free	17/08/91	Huddersfield Town	116+12	10+2	5+1	14+3	35	4		6
				Loan	28/10/94	Sheffield United								
				£150000	06/01/95	Sheffield United	25+9		1+1		2			
				Loan	15/09/95	Bristol City	5			1	1			
aylor Gareth K	6.2	12.05	25/02/73	Weston-s-Mare		Southampton								
				Free	29/07/91	Bristol Rovers	24+16	0+1	1+1	5	12			
				£1250000	27/09/95	Crystal Palace	18+2		2		1		1	
					08/03/96	Sheffield United	10				2			
alker Andy	5.8	10.07	06/04/65	Glasgow		Motherwell	65+12	2+4	9+2		17	1	2	
1, u21.1. S.Div1'85. SPD'88.				£350000		Celtic	86+22	9+6	8+3	5+2	40	8	6	3
FAC'88.				Loan	01/09/91	Newcastle United	2	1						
				£160000	09/01/92	Bolton Wanderers	61+6	3	9+3	5	44	1	8	2
					01/08/94	Celtic	26				6			
				£500000	23/02/96	Sheffield United	12+2				8			
hite David	6.1	12.9	30/10/67	Manchester	07/11/85	Manchester City	273+12	24+2	22	9	81	11	4	2
1, Y1, u21.6, B2				£2000000	22/12/93	Leeds United	28+14	1	6	1+1	9		2	
				£500000	29/12/95	Sheffield United	24+4		3		7			

ADDITIONAL CONTRACT PLAYERS

yer Liam D						Sheffield Utd (T)								
ettney Christopher J					15/05/96	Sheffield Utd (T)								
awes Steven R						Sheffield Utd (T)	1+1							
eritage Paul					04/06/96	Sheffield Utd (T)								
ocking Matthew J					16/05/96	Sheffield Utd (T)								
ood Paul J					02/05/96	Sheffield Utd (T)								

MANAGER

HOWARD KENDALL

Date of Birth. . . . . 22nd May 1946.
Place of Birth. . . . . Co. Durham.
Date of Appointment . . . . December 1995.

PREVIOUS CLUBS
As Manager. . . . . Blackburn Rovers, Everton, Bilbao, Manchester City,
. . . . Everton, Notts County.
As a Player . . . . Preston North End, Everton, Birmingham City, Stoke City.

HONOURS
As a Manager
Everton: FA Cup 1984. Div.1 champions 1984-85, 1986-87. ECWC 1984-85.

As a Player
Div.1 championship 1969-79.

BRAMALL LANE GROUND
Sheffield S2 4SU
Tel: 0114 273 8955

Capacity ....Up to 30,000 by October 1996.

First game...Sheffield Club v Hallam (Charity Match), 0-0, 28.12.1862.
As Sheffield Utd... v Birmingham St Georges (friendly) 0-4, 28.9.1889.
First floodlit game...v Rotherham, 16.3.1954.

ATTENDANCES
Highest...68,287 v Leeds United, FAC 5th Rnd, 15.1.1936.
Lowest...1,500 v Bootle, Division 1, 10.9.1892.

OTHER GROUNDS..None.

MATCHDAY TICKET PRICES

South Stand.........................£14
Juv/OAP £7
Kop £9
Juv/OAP £6
Stone Best Bitter Stand £9
Juv/OAP £6
Family Enclosure £10
Juv/OAP £5
Visiting..............................£14
Juv/OAP £7
(in the Stones Best Bitter Upper Stand)

Ticket Office telephone no. 0114 276 6771

HOW TO GET TO THE GROUND

From the North
Use motorway M1 until junction 34. Leave motorway and follow signs, Sheffield (A6109). In 3.4 miles turn left and shortly at roundabout take 4th exit into Sheaf Street. Then at 2nd roundabout take 5th exit into St Mary's Road (sign posted Bakewell). In half-a-mile left into Bramall Lane for Sheffield United FC.

From the East and South
Use (A57) from motorway M1 (junction 31 or 33) then at roundabout take 3rd exit into Sheaf Street. Then at 2nd roundabout take 5th exit in St Mary's Road and proceed as above.

From the West
Use A57, sign posted Sheffield, and at roundabout take 4th exit A6134 into Upper Hanover Street. Then at 2nd roundabout take 3rd exit into Bramall Lane.

Car Parking
The ground is five minutes away from car parks in the City Centre. Side-street parking is ample.

Nearest Railway Station
Sheffield Midland (0114 272 6411)

CLUBCALL
0891 888 650

Calls cost 39p per minute cheap rate and 49p per minute at all other times.
Call costings correct at time of going to press.

MATCHDAY PROGRAMME

Programme Editor............................... Andy Pack

Number of pages .... 48.

Price .... £1.50.

Subscriptions.................. £27.30 + £9.45 postage (homes).
.... Double price for aways also.

Local Newspapers..................... Sheffield Newspaper Ltd
.... (The Star, Sheffield Telegraph)

Local Radio Stations .... BBC Radio Sheffield, Radio Hallam.

SOUTHEND UNITED
(The Shrimpers)
NATIONWIDE LEAGUE DIVISION 1
SPONSORED BY: TELEWEST COMMUNICATIONS

ack Row (L-R): Domonic Iorfa, Luke Morrish, Andy Sussex, Paul Sansome, Dave Regis, Simon Royce, Mark Hone, Danny Foot, Leo **oget. Middle Row:** Danny Greaves, Ijah Anderson, Declan Perkins, Gary Jones, Roger Willis, Phil Gridlet, Steve Tilson, Keith Dublin, John **owans. Front Row:** Andy Ansah, Andy Thompson, Theo Foley, Mick Bodley, Ronnie Whelan, Julian Hails, Chris Powell.

SOUTHEND UNITED
FORMED IN 1906
TURNED PROFESSIONAL IN 1906
LTD COMPANY IN 1919

PRESIDENT: N J Woodcock
CHAIRMAN: V T Jobson
VICE-CHAIRMAN/CHIEF EXECUTIVE
J W Adams
DIRECTORS
J Bridge, B R Gunner, W R Kelleway,
D M Markscheffel, C Wooldridge
MARKETING DIRECTOR
C Wooldridge

PLAYER/MANAGER: Ronnie Whelan
ASSISTANT MANAGER: Theo Foley
COACH: Peter Trevivian
YOUTH TEAM MANAGER
Peter Johnson

SPORTS THERAPISTS
John Gowens and Spencer Barham

STATISTICIAN FOR THE DIRECTORY
Dave Goody

The 1995/6 season turned out to be one of those 'what might have been' seasons in more than one way for Southend United, with the excitement of a possible play-off place with only eight games to go being tempered by the realisation that relegation was eventually only avoided by a three-win margin.

The season started with a trip to Portsmouth and a 2-4 defeat was made all the worse by an injury to player-manager Ronnie Whelan which proved to be bad enough to rule him out for the rest of the season, and may yet prove to have finished his long and illustrious career. By mid-October, a comfortable mid-table position had been reached, with an exceptional 3-1 victory against Leicester City at Filbert Street being the highlight as Julian Hails notched a hat-trick. By this time, record £500,000-signing Mike Marsh had taken the role vacated by Ronnie Whelan and his skills and artistry was something that had never before been seen in the blue shirt of Southend United. He was joined by ex-Celtic stars Paul Byrne and Mark McNally, both of whom are surely destined for greater things.

By December, the need for a new striker was apparent and many were tried, including Pettar Belsvik (Norway), Ken Charlery (Birmingham City) and Paul Reed (Arsenal), but none of them fitted Ronnie Whelan's bill until the signing of Andy Rammell (Barnsley) and Jeroen Boere (Crystal Palace) at the start of March. By this time, the Blues were in a play-off position, with no little thanks to goalkeeper Simon Royce, whose elevation from reserve to automatic first-choice had been dramatic. He continued to receive fine reviews all through the season, including a televised pat-on-the-back from England manager Terry Venables, and a move to a Premiership club looks to be in the offing during the close season.

Unfortunately, a bad run of injuries robbed the Blues of key players during the second half of the season, including broken-leg victim Mike Lapper, whose arrival from the USA meant that no one missed the departing Andy Edwards. Both Rammell (cartilage) and Boere (badly-broken finger) were sidelined for six games apiece, as was last year's top scorer Andy Thomson. With Keith Dublin being asked to fill in as temporary centre-forward, three wins in the last eighteen games was nowhere near good enough, and a play-off spot was well out of reach by the end of the season. When looking at the final table, the importance of a good mid-season run could be seen, with only a few points separating the top from the bottom.

Ronnie Whelan's excellent transfer activity this season has shown that the Blues could mount a challenge in the coming season, but I am sure that most of the long-standing fans will be more than happy with a season of consolidation.

DAVE GOODY

SOUTHEND UNITED

League: 14th   FA Cup: 3rd Rnd   Coca-Cola Cup: 2nd Rnd

M	DATE	COMP	VEN	OPPONENTS	RESULT	HT	LP	GOAL SCORERS/GOAL TIMES	ATT.
1	A 12	EL	A	Portsmouth	L 2-4	1-2	16	Thomson 4, 78	(10630)
2	19	EL	H	Luton Town	L 0-1	0-0	24		4630
3	26	EL	A	Millwall	D 0-0	0-0	23		(10536)
4	29	EL	H	West Bromwich Albion	W 2-1	1-0	17	Thomson 22, Regis 66	4628
5	S 2	EL	H	Reading	D 0-0	0-0	19		4962
6	5	AIC	H	Brescia	D 0-0	0-0			2849
7	9	EL	A	Sunderland	L 0-1	0-1	21		(13805)
8	13	EL	A	Derby County	L 0-1	0-1	23		(9242)
9	16	EL	H	Wolverhampton Wand	W 2-1	1-1	20	Gridelet 44, Jones 73	6322
10	19	CC 2/1	H	Crystal Palace	D 2-2	1-0		Byrne 35, Jones 81	4031
11	23	EL	A	Leicester City	W 3-1	2-1	15	Hails 3, 29, 90	(15276)
12	30	EL	H	Grimsby Town	W 1-0	0-0	11	Regis 84	4977
13	O 3	CC 2/2	A	Crystal Palace	L 0-2	0-1			(6588)
14	8	EL	A	Birmingham City	L 0-2	0-1	14		(17341)
15	14	EL	H	Sheffield United	W 2-1	1-1	11	Regis 11, Tilson 62	5292
16	21	EL	A	Tranmere Rovers	L 0-3	0-1	13		(6584)
17	28	EL	H	Huddersfield Town	D 0-0	0-0	15		5128
18	N 4	EL	A	Watford	D 2-2	1-1	14	Regis 5, Read 46	(7091)
19	11	EL	H	Stoke City	L 2-4	1-1	16	Belsvik 25, Hails 54	5967
20	19	EL	A	Crystal Palace	D 1-1	0-0	16	Regis 47	5089
21	22	EL	A	Ipswich Town	D 1-1	0-0	17	Regis 60	(9757)
22	25	EL	A	Oldham Athletic	W 1-0	0-0	16	Snodin 51(og)	(6474)
23	D 2	EL	H	Birmingham City	W 3-1	2-1	13	Bodley 44, Regis 45, Byrne 71	7770
24	9	EL	H	Leicester City	W 2-1	1-1	12	Dublin 9, Gridelet 48	5835
25	16	EL	A	Grimsby Town	D 1-1	0-0	11	Byrne 88	(5269)
26	20	EL	H	Port Vale	W 2-1	2-1	10	Marsh 19, 40(pen)	4506
27	26	EL	A	Norwich City	W 1-0	0-0	6	Jones 56	(17029)
28	J 1	EL	H	Barnsley	D 0-0	0-0	7		6537
29	6	FAC 3	A	West Ham United	L 0-2	0-0			(23284)
30	13	EL	A	Luton Town	L 1-3	0-1	8	Byrne 80	(6566)
31	20	EL	H	Portsmouth	W 2-1	0-1	4	McNally 71, Tilson 84	5560
32	F 3	EL	H	Millwall	W 2-0	1-0	4	McNally 34, Regis 77	7302
33	10	EL	A	West Bromwich Albion	L 1-3	0-1	4	Marsh 87	(12906)
34	17	EL	H	Derby County	L 1-2	1-0	6	Thomson 30	8331
35	24	EL	A	Wolverhampton Wand	L 0-2	0-1	8		(24677)
36	27	EL	H	Sunderland	L 0-2	0-0	9		5786
37	M 2	EL	H	Norwich City	D 1-1	1-0	9	Byrne 43	6208
38	5	EL	A	Charlton Athletic	W 3-0	1-0	7	Dublin 35, Tilson 51, Thomson 53	(11927)
39	9	EL	A	Port Vale	L 1-2	1-1	9	Boere 33	(6222)
40	16	EL	H	Charlton Athletic	D 1-1	1-1	9	Thomson 36	7382
41	19	EL	A	Reading	D 3-3	0-1	9	Willis 59, 78, Rammell 87	(5321)
42	23	EL	A	Barnsley	D 1-1	1-1	10	Rammell 37	(6754)
43	30	EL	H	Tranmere Rovers	W 2-0	0-0	7	Byrne 78, Boere 89	4738
44	A 2	EL	A	Sheffield United	L 0-3	0-3	9		(11319)
45	6	EL	A	Huddersfield Town	L 1-3	0-0	10	Willis 52	(11558)
46	8	EL	H	Watford	D 1-1	0-1	9	Roget 90	5348
47	13	EL	A	Crystal Palace	L 0-2	0-1	11		(15672)
48	20	EL	H	Ipswich Town	W 2-1	1-1	11	Dublin 30, Marsh 90	8363
49	27	EL	H	Oldham Athletic	D 1-1	0-1	11	Marsh 63(pen)	5397
50	M 5	EL	A	Stoke City	L 0-1	0-1	14		(18897)

Best Home League Attendance: 8363 v Ipswich Town   Smallest: 4506 v Port Vale   Average: 5915

Goal Scorers:

EL(52): Regis(8), Thomson(6), Byrne(5), Marsh(5), Hails(4), Tilson(3), Dublin(3), Willis(3), Rammell(2), Jones(2), Gridelet(2), McNally(2), Boere(2), Read(1), Bodley(1), Belsvik(1), Roget(1), Opponent(s)(1)

CC(2): Jones(1), Byrne(1)

FAC(0:

AIC(0):

(F) Ansah	(D) Barness	(M) Belsvik	(D) Bodley	(F) Boere	(D) Brown	(M) Byrne	(M) Charlery	(D) Dublin	(M) Gridelet	(M) Hails	(D) Hone	(F) Jones	(D) Lapper	(F) Marsh	(D) McNally	(D) Powell	(F) Rammell	(F) Read	(F) Regis	(M) Roget	(G) Royce	(G) Sansome	(D) Stimson	(F) Sussex	(F) Thomson	(F) Tilson	(F) Turner	(F) Willis	Player	No.
			X			X				X	S	X	X	X		X			X		X		S		X	X			R.Gifford	1
S1			X						X2	X	S2	X3	X1	X		X			X		X		S		X	X			G.R.Pooley	2
S			X		X			X	X	X	X			S	X				X		X				X	X			K.Leach	3
S1			X		X	X	X1	X	X	X		S	S1	X					X		X				X1				M.Pierce	4
S1			X		X	X	X	X	X	X		X	X1	X					X		X					X			R.J.Harris	5
X			X			X		X	X	X	S		X	X	X				X		X					S			M.Cardona	6
			X			X3		X	X	X	S1	S3	S2	X	X				X		X				X2	X1			J.A.Kirkby	7
			X			X	X	X	X2	X	S1	X	X						X1		X				X				D.Allison	8
			X			X	X	S	X	X	X	X	X						S		X		X		X	S			M.C.Bailey	9
		X				X	X	X	S1	S2	X	X2	X						S		X		X1		X				C.Wilkes	10
		X				X	X	X	X	X	X	X							S1		X				X1				E.Lomas	11
		X				X	X	X2	X	S	X	X							S1		X				X1	S2			G.Barber	12
S1		X				X1		X	S3	X1	X		X						S1		X				S1	X3			A.N.Butler	13
		X				X2		X	S2	S3	X	X			X	X3	S1		X					S1	X			W.Burns	14
S		X				X		X	X	S2	X	X	X2				X1		X					S1	X			C.Wilkes	15
S2			X			X		X2	X	S1	X	X						X		X				X1	X			J.Kirkby	16
S			X			X	X	X	S	X	X		X			X		X					S1				D.Orr	17
		S	X			X1	X	X	X	S		X	X	X			X	X					S1				P.Rejer	18
		X2	X			X	X	X	X1		X	X			X	S2	X					S1	S			M.D.Pierce	19
		X1	X			X	X	X	S	X	X	X			X		X					S1	S			R.B.Gifford	20
		X1	X			X	X	X	S1	X	X			X		X					S	S			T.Lunt	21
			X			X	X	X	X	X	X	X			X	S	X					S	S			E.K.Wolstenholme	22
			X			X	X	X	X	X	X	X	X			S	X					S	S			R.Poulain	23
			X			X	X	X	X	X	X	X	X	S	X						S	S			G.Pooley	24
			X			X	X	X	X	X1	X	X			X		X				S1	S			R.Pearson	25
			X			X	X	X	X	X	X	X1	X	X	X		X				S	S			N.S.Barry	26
			X			X	X	X	X	S1	X	X1	X	X	X		X				S	S			D.Orr	27
		X				X	X	X	X	S	X1		X	X	X		X				S1	S			K.Breen	28
		X				X	X	X	X	S	X1		X	X	X		X				S1				R.Dilkes	29
		X				X	S2	X1	X2	X	S1		X	X	X		X				X2	S2			A.Wiley	30
		X					X1	X	X	S		X	X	X		X				S1	X		S	G.Singh	31
	X					X	X	X	X	X	X		X	X		X		X	S			S	X	R.J.Harris	32
	X					X	X	X	X	X		X	X1	X		X	S	X	S		S1	X	U.Rennie	33
X		X				X	X	X	X	X	S1	X		X	S		X			X1	X1	J.Kirby	34
X		X				S1	X	X	X	X	S		X		X			X		X	X1	M.Riley	35
X		X				S1	X	X	X	X	S1		X		X		S2	X		X1	S	G.Barber	36
		X	X	X		X	X	X	X	S		X	X	X1		X			S1	X	W.C.Burns	37
		X	X	X	X	X	S	X	S		X	X		X			X	X	J.Rushton	38
	S2	X2	X	X1		X	S1	X		X	X		X		X	X	J.Lloyd	39
	X	X2	X	X		S	S1	X1		X	X		X	X		S2	G.R.Pooley	40
		X	X	X2	S1	S3	S2		X	X		X		X	X1	X3	X	M.Bailey	41
		X	X	S1	X	X			X	X		X		X	X1	S	X	K.Leach	42
		X	X	X1	X	S		X		S1	X		X	X1	S1	X	X	D.Orr	43
	X	X	X	X			X		X1	X	X	X	X1	S	S1	X1	G.Cain	44
	X	X		X	X		X		S	X	S	S	X	X1	S1	X	R.Pearson	45
		X	X		X	X		X		S2	X	S		X	S1	X2	X	M.Pierce	46
		X	X1	X	X	X	S1		X		X1	X	S		X	S2	X2	X	R.Poulain	47
		X	X	X	S	X		X		X	S	S	X	X	X	T.West	48
		X	X	X	X		S	X	X	S1	S	X	X	X1	G.Singh	49
		X1	X	X	X		S1	X	X	X2	S2	X	X	S	M.Barry	50
0	5	3	37	6	6	38	2	42	37	39	11	14	24	40	20	27	6	3	25	4	46	0	10	1	22	23	4	9	EL.Appearances	
4	0	0	1	0	0	3	1	1	3	3	5	9	1	0	0	0	1	1	4	0	0	0	1	1	1	5	2	1	EL Sub Appearances	
0+1	0	0	2	0	0	2	0	2	1+1	0+2	2	2	2	0	2	0	0	0	1	0	2	0	0	1	1+1	1	0	0	CC Appearances	
0	0	0	1	0	0	1	0	1	1	1	0	1	0	1	0	1	0	0	1	0	1	0	0	0	0	0+1	0	0	FAC Appearances	
1	0	0	1	0	0	1	0	1	1	1	0	1	0	1	0	1	0	0	0	0	1	0	0	0	0	0	0	0	AIC Appearances	

Also Played: (F) Hayes S95), X1(6). (F) Iorfa X(1), S3(2), S1(6). (M) Morrish S(16). ((F) Tolson S(11). M) Whelan X(1).

SOUTHEND UNITED

CLUB RECORDS

BIGGEST VICTORIES
League: 9-2 v Newport Co., Div 3S, 5.9.1936
7-0 v QPR, Div 3S, 7.4.1928
8-1 v Cardiff City, Div 3S, 20.2.1937
7-0 v Workington, Div 4, 29.3.1968
F.A. Cup: 10-1 v Golders Green, Round 1, 24.11.1934
9-0 v Kings Lynn, Round 1, 16.11.1968
10-1 v Brentwood, Round 2, 7.12.1968
League Cup: 6-1 v Bournemouth, 13.8.1968

BIGGEST DEFEATS
League: 0-8 v Northampton Town, Div 3S, 22.3.1924
1-9 v Brighton, Div 3, 27.11.1965
F.A. Cup: 0-6 v Burnley, Round 2, 30.1.1915
League Cup: 0-8 v Crystal Palace, Rnd 2, 25.9.1990

MOST POINTS
3 points a win: 85, Division 3, 1990-91
2 points a win: 67, Division 4, 1980-81

MOST GOALS
92, Division 3S, 1950-51
Stubbs 19, Wakefield 15, Davies 12, Tippett 12, Grant 12, French 5, Sibley 5, Lawler 4, McAlinden 2, Anderson 1, Butler 1, Woods 1, og 3

MOST LEAGUE GOALS CONCEDED
85, Division 4, 1969-70

MOST FIRST CLASS MATCHES IN A SEASON
57 (46 League, 1 FA Cup, 2 League Cup, 8 Anglo Italian Cup)
1993-94

MOST LEAGUE WINS
30, Division 4, 1980-81

MOST LEAGUE DRAWS
19, Division 4, 1976-77

MOST LEAGUE DEFEATS
26, Division 3, 1965-66

INDIVIDUAL CLUB RECORDS

MOST GOALS IN A MATCH
5. Jim Shankly v Merthyr Tydfil, 6-0, Div 3S, 1.3.1930
5. H. Johnson v Golders Green, 10-1, FAC Rnd 1, 24.11.1934
5. Billy Best v Brentwood, 10-1, FAC Rnd 2, 7.12.1968

MOST GOALS IN A SEASON
Jim Shankly 35 (League 34, FAC 1) 1928-29
3 goals 2 times=6; 2 goals 6 times=12; 1 goal 17 times=17. Total 35

OLDEST PLAYER
Not known.

YOUNGEST PLAYER
Phil O'Connor, 16 years 76 days, 26.12.1969.

MOST CAPPED PLAYER
George McKenzie (Eire) 9

BEST PERFORMANCES

League: 1980-81: Matches Played 46, Won 30, Drawn 7, Lost 9, Goals for 79, Goals against 31, Points 67. First in Division 4

Highest: 12th Division 2, 1991-92

F.A. Cup: 1920-21: Last sixteen
1925-26: 1st rnd. Dulwich (h) 5-1; 2nd rnd. Gillingham (h) 1-0; 3rd rnd. Southport (h) 5-2; 4th rnd. Derby County (h) 4-1; 5th rnd. Nottingham Forest (h) 0-1
1951-52: 1st rnd. Bournemouth (h) 6-1; 2nd rnd. Oldham Athletic (h) 5-0; 3rd rnd. Southampton (h) 3-0; 4th rnd. Bristol Rovers (h) 2-1; 5th rnd. Sheffield Utd (h) 1-2
1975-76: 1st rnd. Swansea City (h) 2-0; 2nd rnd. Dover (h) 4-1; 3rd rnd. Brighton (h) 2-1; 4th rnd. Cardiff City (h) 2-1; 5th rnd Derby County (a) 0-1
1992-93: 3rd rnd. Millwall (h) 1-0; 4th rnd. Huddersfield (h) 2-1; 5th rnd. Sheffield Wednesday (a) 0-2

League Cup: Never past Round 3

DIVISIONAL RECORD

	Played	Won	Drawn	Lost	For	Against	Points
Division 2/1	230	80	54	96	286	328	294
Division 3	920	319	238	363	1,266	1,358	972
Division 3(S)	1,334	503	312	519	2,074	2,065	1,318
Division 4	598	262	144	192	871	742	746
Total	**3,082**	**1,164**	**748**	**1,170**	**4,497**	**4,493**	**3,330**

ADDITIONAL INFORMATION
Previous Names
None.

Previous League
Southern League

Club colours: Blue shirts with red collar & cuff, blue shorts, blue socks.
Change colours: All red

Reserves League: Capital League.

RECORDS AND STATISTICS

COMPETITIONS

Div.2/1	Div.3(S)	Div.3	Div.4
1991-	1921-58	1920-21	1966-72
		1958-66	1976-78
		1972-76	1980-81
		1978-80	1984-87
		1981-84	1989-90
		1987-89	
		1990-91	

HONOURS

Division 4
1980-81

MOST APPEARANCES

A W (Sandy) Anderson 452 (1950-63)

Year	League
1950-51	30
1951-52	46
1952-53	23
1953-54	45
1954-55	45
1955-56	9
1956-57	27
1957-58	40
1958-59	41
1959-60	38
1960-61	43
1961-62	45
1962-63	20
	452

MOST GOALS IN A CAREER

Roy Hollis - 120 (1953-60)

Year	League
1953-54	10
1954-55	27
1955-56	23
1956-57	18
1957-58	18
1958-59	17
1959-60	7
Total	120

Current leading goalscorer: Andrew Sussex - 14 (1991-96)

MANAGERS

Name	Seasons	Best	Worst
Tom Mather	1920-21	3(3S)	22(3S)
F L Birnie	1921-24	3(3S)	22(3S)
D B Jack	1924-39	10(3S)	21(3S)
Harry Warren	1946-56	3(3S)	18(3S)
Eddie Perry	1956-60	7(3S)	12(3)
Frank Broome	1960	20(3)	20(3)
Ted Fenton	1961-65	8(3)	16(2)
Alvin Williams	1965-67	21(3)	6(4)
Ernie Shepherd	1967-69	6(4)	7(4)
Geoff Hudson	1969-70	17(4)	17(4)
Arthur Rowley	1970-76	12(3)	18(4)
Dave Smith	1976-82	7(3)	10(4)
Peter Morris	1982-84	22(3)	22(3)
Bobby Moore	1984-86	9(3)	20(4)
David Webb	1986-87	7(3)	20(4)
Dick Bate	1987		
Paul Clark	1987-88	19(3)	19(3)
Dave Webb	1988-92	12(3)	3(4)
Colin Murphy	1992-93		
Barry Fry	1993-94	18(2/1)	18(2/1)
Peter Taylor	1993-95	15(2/1)	15(2/1)
Steve Thompson	1995		
Ronnie Whelan	1995-	14(1)	14(1)

RECORD TRANSFER FEE RECEIVED

Amount	Club	Player	Date
£2,200,000	Nott'm Forest	Stan Collymore	7/93
£375,000	Tottenham H.	Dean Austin	7/92
£150,000	Wolves	Shane Westley	6/89
£120,000	Crystal Palace	Peter Taylor	10/73

RECORD TRANSFER FEE PAID

Amount	Club	Player	Date
£400,000	Galataray	Mike Marsh	8/95
£350,000	Plymouth Argyle	Gary Poole	7/93
£175,000	Brentford	Keith Jones	10/91
£111,111	Blackpool	Derek Spence	12/79

LONGEST LEAGUE RUNS

of undefeated matches:	16 (20.2.1932 - 29.8.1932)	of league matches w/out a win:	7 (31.12.1983 - 14.4.1984)
of undefeated home matches:	32 (16.2.1980 - 1.5.1981)	of undefeated away matches:	9 (4.3.1972 - 29.4.1972)
without home win:	8 (2.10.1948 - 22.1.1949)	without an away win:	27 (13.11.1920 - 4.2.1922)
of league wins:	7 (4.10.1924 - 6.11.1924, 24.4.1990 - 18.9.1990)	of home wins:	18 (4.4.1980 - 9.1.1981)
of league defeats:	6 (29.8.1987 - 19.9.1987)	of away wins:	5 (31.8.1931 - 3.10.1931, 9.4.1991 - 3.9.1991)

SOUTHEND UNITED

PLAYERS NAME / Honours	Ht	Wt	Birthdate	Birthplace / Transfers	Contract Date	Clubs	League	L/Cup	FA Cup	Other	Lge	L/C	FAC	Oth
G O A L K E E P E R S														
Royce Simon	6.1	12.0	09/09/71	Forest Gate		Heybridge Swifts								
				£10000	15/10/91	Southend United	67+2	4	2	2				
Sansome Paul	6.0	13.8	06/10/61	New Addington		Crystal Palace								
FLT'83				Free	18/04/80	Millwall	156	12	13	9				
				£40000	24/03/88	Southend United	305	18	8	22				
				Loan	09/01/96	Birmingham City								
D E F E N D E R S														
Bodley Michael	5.11	12.0	14/09/67	Hayes	17/09/85	Chelsea	6	1		1	1			
GMVC'91				£50000	12/01/89	Northampton Town	20			2				
				£15000	01/10/89	Barnet	69	2	10	9	3			
				Free	15/07/93	Southend United	65+1	3	2	4	2			
				Loan	23/11/94	Gillingham	6+1			1				
				Loan	23/01/95	Birmingham City	3							
Dublin Keith	5.7	10.0	29/01/66	H. Wycombe	28/01/84	Chelsea	50+1	6	5	5+1				
E: u19.4. Y				£3500	14/08/87	Brighton & H.A.	132	5	7	7	5		1	
				£275000	17/07/90	Watford	165+3	12	4	6	2			
					21/07/94	Southend United	82+1	4	2	1	5			
Lapper Michael S						USSF								
				£150000	11/08/95	Southend United	24+1	2		1				
McNally Mark	5.9	10.7	10/03/71	Belshill		Celtic								
				£50000	08/12/95	Southend United	20		1		2			
Stimson Mark	5.11	11.0	27/12/67	Plaistow	15/07/85	Tottenham Hotspur	1+1							
				Loan	15/03/88	Leyton Orient	10							
				Loan	19/01/89	Gillingham	18							
				£200000	16/06/89	Newcastle United	82+4	5	7	6	2		1	
				Loan	10/12/92	Portsmouth	3+1							
				£100000	23/07/93	Portsmouth	57+1	9	3	3	2	1		
				£25000	15/03/96	Southend United	10							
M I D F I E L D														
Byrne Paul	5.11	13.0	30/06/72	Dublin	04/07/89	Oxford United	4+2							
				Free	01/09/91	Bangor City								
					26/05/93	Celtic	24+5	1	1		3			
				Loan	10/03/95	Brighton & H.A.	8			1				
				£80000	25/08/95	Southend United	38+3	2	1	1	5	1		
Gridelet Phil	5.11	12.0	30/04/67	Hendon		Hendon								
E: S-P4				£25000	01/09/90	Barnet			0+1					
				£175000	21/09/90	Barnsley	3+3		1	1				
				Loan	05/03/93	Rotherham United	9							
				Free	01/08/95	Southend United	84+14	1	2	5	6			1
Hails Julian	5.9	11.0	20/11/67	Lincoln		Hemel Hempstead								
					29/08/90	Fulham	99+13	5+1	2	9	12			
				Free	02/12/94	Southend United	59+9	1+1	1		6			
Neilsen John						Ikast								
				Free	31/07/96	Southend United								
Roche David	5.11	12.1	13/12/70	Newcastle	30/08/88	Newcastle United	23+13	2	1	1+2				
				Loan	08/01/93	Peterborough Utd	4							
					01/10/93	Doncaster Rovers	49+1		3	3	8			1
				£55000	23/03/95	Southend United	0+4							
Roget Leo Thomas Erl					05/07/95	Southend United	4+4				1			
				Loan	01/12/95	Dover Athletic								
Whelan Ronnie	5.9	10.13	25/09/61	Dublin		Home Farm								
Ei: 45, u21.1. Div1'82'83'84''86'88'90.				Free	01/10/79	Liverpool	351+11	46+4	40+1	38+2	46	14	7	6
FAC'86'89. EC'84. LC'82'83'84.				Free	14/10/94	Southend United	34+1		1					

F O R W A R D S															
Boere Jeroen	6.3	13.5	18/11/67	Arnheim			Go Ahead Eagles								
Netherlands: u21.					£250000	22/09/93	West Ham United	15+9	1+1	2		7	1		
					Loan	24/03/94	Portsmouth	4+1							
					Loan	08/09/94	W.B.A.	5							
					£375000	07/09/95	Crystal Palace	0+8				1			
					£150000	01/03/96	Southend United	6				2			
Marsh Mike	5.8	11.0	21/07/69	Liverpool			Kirby Town								
FAC'92					Free	21/08/87	Liverpool	42+27	10+1	6+2	12+1	2	3		1
						17/09/93	West Ham United	46+3	6	6		1		1	
					£450000	30/12/94	Coventry City	15+2		4					
						01/05/95	Galatasaray								
					£500000	04/09/95	Southend United	40	2	1	1	5			
Rammell Andrew	5.10	11.7	10/02/67	Nuneaton			Atherstone			0+1					
					£40000	26/09/89	Manchester United								
					£100000	14/09/90	Barnsley	149+36	11+3	12+1	8	44	1	4	1
						22/02/96	Southend United	6+1				2			
Sussex Andrew	6.0	11.6	23/11/64	Enfield		25/11/82	Leyton Orient	126+18	7+1	8	5+3	17	2	1	
					£16000	23/06/88	Crewe Alexandra	86+16	10	7+1	5	24	6	4	2
					£100000	04/07/91	Southend United	49+12	6	2+1	3+1	13			1
					Loan	12/12/95	Brentford	3							
Thomson Andy	5.10	10.07	01/04/71	Motherwell			Queen of the South								
					£250000	04/07/94	Southend United	57+15	2+1	1+1		17			
Tilson Stephen	5.11	12.6	27/07/66	Wickford			Witham Town								
						07/02/89	Southend United	169+31	7+1	3	10+1	3			
					Loan	16/09/93	Brentford	2							

THE MANAGER (PLAYER)
RONNIE WHELAN

Date of Birth . . . . 25th September 1961.
Place of Birth . . . . Dublin.
Date of Appointment . . . . July 1995.

PREVIOUS CLUBS
As Manager . . . . None.
As Coach . . . . None.
As a Player . . . . Home Farm, Liverpool, Southend United.

HONOURS
As a Manager
None.

As a Player
Liverpool: Division 1 championship 1982, 1983, 1984, 1986, 1988, 1990. FA Cup 1986, 1989.
League Cup 1982, 1983, 1984. European Cup 1984.
International: 45 full caps and 1 u21 cap for Eire.

ROOTS HALL

Victoria Avenue, Southend-on-Sea SS2 6NQ
Tel: 01702 304050

Capacity..12,435

First game ....v Norwich City, Div. 3(S) (3-1, 20.08.55. Att: 17,700.
First floodlit game..Not Known.
ATTENDANCES
Highest ....31,033 v Liverpool, FAC 3rd Rnd, 10.1.1979.
Lowest...653 v Northampton, AMC, 13.3.1986.
OTHER GROUNDS..Roots Hall 1909-1919. The Kursaal 1919-1934.
....Southend Stadium 1934-1955. Played at New Writtle Street,Chelmsford in 1940, during the war.

MATCHDAY TICKET PRICES

East Stand . . . . Blue Block £14
. . . . Yellow Block £14
. . . . Red Block £15
. . . . Black Block £14/£7
. . . . Green Block £15
South Stand (Home) . . . . Lower Tier £8/£4
. . . . Upper Tier £12
UB40 Members £5

Family Stand . . . . £10/£8/£12
Juv/OAP . . . . ££5/£4/£6/£8/£12

North Stand (away supporters) . . . . . . £12/£8, £4

Ticket Office Telephone no. 01702 304090

CLUBCALL
0839 66 44 44

Calls cost 39p per minute cheap rate and 49p per
minute at all other times.
Call costings correct at time of going to press.

HOW TO GET TO THE GROUND

From the North and East
Use A127, sign posted Southend, and then at roundabout take 3rd
exit into Victoria Avenue for Southend United FC.

From the South
Use A13, sign posted Southend, and then turn left into West Road
and at end turn left into Victoria Avenue for Southend United FC.

Car Parking
Reserved car park on match days. Ample street parking is available.

Nearest Railway Station
Southend Central (01702 611 811) Prittlewell.

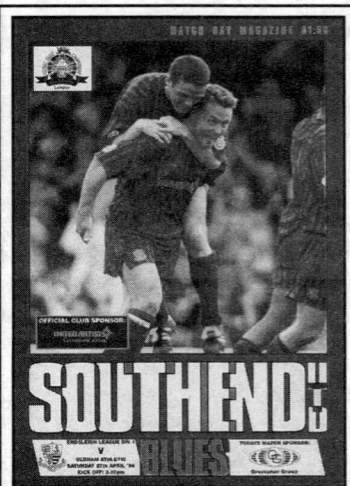

MATCHDAY PROGRAMME

Programme Editor . . . . Kevin O'Donnell.

Number of pages . . . . 40.

Price . . . . £1.50.

Subscriptions . . . . Apply to club.

Local Newspapers . . . . Evening Echo, Standard Recorder,
. . . . Yellow Advertiser.

Local Radio Stations . . . . Essex Radio, BBC Essex.

STOKE CITY
(The Potters)
NATIONWIDE LEAGUE DIVISION 1
SPONSORED BY: ASICS UK

Back Row (L-R): Ian Clarkson, Keith Scott, Lee Sandford, Ian Cranson, Graham Potter, Vince Overson (Captain), John Dreyer, John Gayle Carl Beeston. **Middle Row:** Ashley Grimes, Lou Macari, Mohammed Gargo, Toddy Orlygsson, Ronnie Sinclair, Carl Muggleton, Mark Prudhoe, Nigel Gleghorn, Larus Sigurdsson, Ian Liversage (Physio), Chic Bates. **Front Row:** Kevin Keen, Simon Sturridge, Paul Peschisolido, Ray Wallace, Martin Carruthers.

STOKE CITY
FORMED IN 1868
TURNED PROFESSIONAL IN 1885
LTD COMPANY IN 1908

PRESIDENT: Sir Stanley Matthews
CHAIRMAN: P Coates

DIRECTORS
K A Humphreys (Vice-Chairman)
D J Edwards, M E Moors
SECRETARY
M J Potts (01782 413 511)
CHIEF EXECUTIVE
Jez Moxey

MANAGER: Lou Macari
ASSISTANT MANAGER: Chic Bates

RESERVE TEAM MANAGER
Ashley Grimes
YOUTH TEAM MANAGER
Ashley Grimes
PHYSIOTHERAPIST
Ian Liversedge

STATISTICIAN FOR THE DIRECTORY
Wade Martin

With Lou Macari in full charge from the start of the season the Stoke fans' were subdued as again there was an absence of new faces in the squad. There had also been much talk in the press at the club's policy of paying players' signing on fees linked to the number of games played rather than the traditional form of lump sum one off payment at the outset. The club's board received a lot of support from other clubs' but the players had no time for it and there was the traditional delay in players' signing the contracts on offer.

Toddy Orlygsson was the principal rebel and although he was in the team as the season kicked off his heart was clearly not in it and after a particularly lack lustre 'derby game' at home to Port Vale he was dropped. The other significant event at the start of the season was Lou Macari wished to take up a role that seemed close Director of Football, leaving playing matters in the hands of his coaching staff headed by Chic Bates. With a draw at home to Reading on the opening day, followed by a truly sensational 3-2 win at eventually promoted Leicester, the scene was brighter than might have been expected. The rot set in and four bad defeats saw the team in the bottom two.

Whether Macari was told by the board to replace his lounge suit with a track suit or whether he worked it out himself is incidental. He did and turned the club around with no money and an absence of quality players. There was growing tension in the dressing room and Keith Scott and Carl Beeston were allegedly suspended and sent home. Macari then pulled off a deal that will be long remembered by Stoke fans. He swapped Keith Scott for Mike Sheron of Norwich City a cash adjustment of £150,000 for Stoke to pay on completion of a set number of appearances. Orlygsson finally left for Oldham Athletic for £180,000 set by tribunal.

The team responded memorably and games against Chelsea (with Ruud Gullit) and Newcastle United (when David Ginola captivated the home crowd) in the League Cup will stick in the mind. The 1-0 win at Stamford Bridge was the performance of the year.

With the club's board concerned with a move or stay stadium dilemma money was desperate and on transfer deadline day Paul Peschisolido was sold back to Birmingham City for £400,000. The Canadian international had cost Stoke £460,000 plus Dave Regis at £120,000 and had been their record signing.

The striking partnership of Sheron and Simon Sturridge netted 28 League goals between them with Sheron breaking a League record for the club scoring in seven successive matches.

A play off place was secured and after drawing 0-0 at Leicester the scene was set for the return leg at Stoke. However, it turned out to be one game to many and the team, which had played so tremendously well, slipped out 0-1 and were clearly second best on the night. End of season injuries to Kevin Keen, Ian Cranson and Vince Overson were just too much to cover, although the likes of Mark Devlin and Justin Whittle took their chance with great promise for the future.

WADE MARTIN.

STOKE CITY

League: 4th   FA Cup: 3rd Rnd   Coca-Cola Cup: 3rd Rnd

M	DATE	COMP	VEN	OPPONENTS	RESULT	HT	LP	GOAL SCORERS/GOAL TIMES	ATT.
1	A 12	EL	H	Reading	D 1-1	1-0	13	Wallace 12	11932
2	19	EL	A	Leicester City	W 3-2	3-0	5	Peschisolido 10, 24, Gleghorn 32	(17719)
3	27	EL	H	Port Vale	L 0-1	0-0	14		14283
4	30	EL	A	Ipswich Town	L 1-4	0-1	21	Peschisolido 85	(10848)
5	S 2	EL	H	Oldham Athletic	L 0-1	0-0	23		8663
6	5	AIC	A	Foggia	D 1-1	0-0		Peschisolido 65	(1000)
7	9	EL	A	Watford	L 0-3	0-2	24		(7130)
8	12	EL	A	Birmingham City	D 1-1	0-1	20	Carruthers 51	(19005)
9	16	EL	H	Tranmere Rovers	D 0-0	0-0	22		8618
10	20	CC 2/1	H	Chelsea	D 0-0	0-0			15574
11	24	EL	H	West Bromwich Albion	W 2-1	0-0	21	Peschisolido 14, Keen 51	9612
12	30	EL	A	Crystal Palace	D 1-1	1-1	20	Carruthers 36	(14613)
13	O 4	CC 2/2	A	Chelsea	W 1-0	0-0		Peschisolido 75	(16272)
14	7	EL	H	Norwich City	D 1-1	0-1	19	Wallace 68	12016
15	11	AIC	H	Salernitana	D 2-2	1-1		Peschisolido 3, Wallace 47	5071
16	14	EL	A	Wolverhampton Wand	W 4-1	2-1	16	Gleghorn 39, Potter 41, Wallace 85, Carruthers 89	(26483)
17	22	EL	H	Derby County	D 1-1	0-0	16	Keen 66	9435
18	25	CC 3	H	Newcastle United	L 0-4	0-2			23000
19	28	EL	A	Grimsby Town	L 0-1	0-0	19		(5477)
20	N 4	EL	H	Luton Town	W 5-0	1-0	15	Peschisolido 14, Sturridge 73, 87, Gayle 75, Gleghorn 90	9382
21	8	AIC	H	Brescia	D 1-1	0-0		Dreyer 90	4193
22	11	EL	A	Southend United	W 4-2	1-1	13	Sturridge 33, 64, 76, Gleghorn 67	(5967)
23	18	EL	A	Portsmouth	D 3-3	1-2	14	Gayle 33, 61, Sturridge 63	(8030)
24	22	EL	H	Sunderland	W 1-0	1-0	12	Wallace 21	11754
25	25	EL	H	Millwall	W 1-0	0-0	10	Gleghorn 62	12590
26	D 2	EL	A	Norwich City	W 1-0	0-0	7	Gleghorn 53	(15707)
27	9	EL	A	West Bromwich Albion	W 1-0	1-0	6	Peschisolido 34	(14819)
28	16	EL	H	Crystal Palace	L 1-2	0-1	7	Sheron 85	12090
29	23	EL	H	Sheffield United	D 2-2	1-1	8	Gleghorn 28, Sheron 47	12265
30	26	EL	A	Barnsley	L 1-3	0-2	9	Gleghorn 69	(9229)
31	30	EL	A	Huddersfield Town	D 1-1	0-0	8	Sheron 48	(15071)
32	J 6	FAC 3	H	Nottingham Forest	D 1-1	1-0		Sturridge 45	18000
33	13	EL	H	Leicester City	W 1-0	1-0	4	Sturridge 27	13669
34	17	FAC 3R	A	Nottingham Forest	L 0-2	0-1			(17372)
35	20	EL	A	Reading	L 0-1	0-0	5		8082
36	F 10	EL	H	Ipswich Town	W 3-1	1-0	7	Sheron 37, 75, Gleghorn 65	12239
37	17	EL	H	Birmingham City	W 1-0	1-0	3	Sturridge 25	15716
38	24	EL	A	Tranmere Rovers	D 0-0	0-0	5		(8312)
39	28	EL	H	Watford	W 2-0	1-0	4	Cranson 48, Wallace 62	10114
40	M 2	EL	H	Barnsley	W 2-0	1-0	4	Keen 38, Sheron 70	12663
41	9	EL	A	Sheffield United	D 0-0	0-0	4		(14468)
42	12	EL	A	Port Vale	L 0-1	0-1	5		(16737)
43	16	EL	H	Huddersfield Town	D 1-1	0-0	5	Sturridge 67	13157
44	23	EL	A	Charlton Athletic	L 1-2	1-0	5	Sheron 41	(12770)
45	30	EL	A	Derby County	L 1-3	1-0	6	Sheron 22	(17245)
46	A 3	EL	H	Wolverhampton Wand	W 2-0	1-0	6	Sheron 3, Sturridge 59	16361
47	6	EL	H	Grimsby Town	L 1-2	1-0	8	Sheron 34	12524
48	9	EL	A	Luton Town	W 2-1	0-1	5	Sturridge 86, Sheron 90	(7689)
49	13	EL	H	Portsmouth	W 2-1	1-0	5	Wallace 8, Sheron 90	11471
50	17	EL	H	Charlton Athletic	W 1-0	1-0	4	Sheron 29	12969
51	21	EL	A	Sunderland	D 0-0	0-0	4		(21276)
52	27	EL	A	Millwall	W 3-2	2-0	4	Sheron 29, Sturridge 33, 71(pen)	(10105)
53	30	EL	A	Oldham Athletic	L 0-2	0-1	4		(10271)
54	M 5	EL	H	Southend United	W 1-0	1-0	4	Sheron 12	18897
55	12	PO SF1	A	Leicester City	D 0-0	0-0			(20325)
56	15	PO SF2	H	Leicester City	L 0-1	0-0			21037

Best Home League Attendance: 18897 v Southend United   Smallest: 8618 v Tranmere Rovers   Average: 12279

Goal Scorers:
EL(60):   Sheron(15), Sturridge(13), Gleghorn(9), Wallace(6), Peschisolido(6), Keen(3), Gayle(3), Carruthers(3), Potter(1), Cranson(1)
CC(1):   Peschisolido(1)
FAC(1):   Sturridge(1)
AIC(4):   Peschisolido(2), Wallace(1), Dreyer(1)

(D) Beeston	(D) Brightwell	(F) Carruthers	(D) Clarkson	(D) Cranson	(M) Devlin	(D) Dreyer	(F) Gayle	(M) Gleghorn	(M) Keen	(M) Macari	(G) Muggleton	(M) Orlygsson	(D) Overson	(F) Peschisolido	(D) Potter	(G) Prudhoe	(D) Sandford	(F) Scott	(M) Sheron	(M) Sigurdsson	(G) Sinclair	(F) Sturridge	(D) Wallace	(D) Whittle	Referee	No.
	S	X						X	X		X	X	X	X	X1	S	X	X		X		S1	X		J.Kirkby	1
		X				S2		X	X		X	X	X	X	X1	S	X	X2		X		S1	X		R.Gifford	2
		X				S		X	X		X	X1	X	X	S2		X	X2		X		S1	X		G.Singh	3
		X						X	X1		X	X	X	X	S		X	X		X		S1	X		M.Bailey	4
	S	X						X	X1		X	X	X	X	S		X	X		X		S1	X		K.Lynch	5
	X	X					S1	X	X1		S	X	X	X	X				S	X	X		X		G.Pooley	6
	X	X			S1	S1		X	X1			X1	X	X			X3	S3		X	X		X		P.Rejer	7
S2	S1	X						X2	X3		X		X		X	X1				X		S3	X		I.Cruikshanks	8
S	X	X						X	X1		S1		X		X	X	X			X		S	X		S.Mathieson	9
	X	X				S	S	X	X				X		X	X	X			X		S	X		T.West	10
	S	X1	X			S		X	X				X		X	X	X			X		S1	X		T.Lunt	11
	S	X	X					X	X				X		X1	X	X			X		S1	X		A.D'Urso	12
		X	X			S		X					X		X	X	X			X		X	X		K.Cooper	13
	S	X	X			S	S	X					X		X	X	X			X		X	X		G.Cain	14
X1	X	X				S1	X	S					X		X	X	X				S	X	X		F.Treossi	15
	X1	X					S	X	X				X		X	X	X			X		S1	X		D.Allison	16
	X	X				S1		S	X				X		X	X1	X			X		S	X		G.Furnandiz	17
	X	X	S1					S	X				X		X	X1	X			X			X		G.Ashby	18
	X	X				S1		X	X1				X		X	X	X			X			X		T.West	19
	X1	X3	S3				S2	X	X				X		X2	X	X			X		S1	X		J.Lloyd	20
		X	S2	S1				X	X2				X		X1	X	X			X	S	X	X		E. Pellegrino	21
	S2		X	S1			X2	X3	X				X			X	X			X		X	X1	S3	M.D.Pierce	22
	S		X2	S1				X	X				X		X1	X	X		S2	X		X	X		C.Wilkes	23
	S3		X			S1		X	X					X2	X1	X	X		S2	X		X3	X		R.Harris	24
	S2		X			S1	X2	X1							X	X	X		S3	X		X3	X		P.Taylor	25
S2	S		X	X		X		X						X1	X2	X	X		S1			X	X		I.Hemley	26
	S3		X	X		X		X	S2					X1	X	X	X		S1			X3	X2		T.Heilbron	27
	S		X	X		S		X	X1					S1	X	X	X		X	X		X	X		K.Breen	28
			X	X		S	S1	X	S						X	X	X		X1	X		X	X		E.Wolstenholme	29
			X1	X		S1		X							X	X	X		X			S	X		N.S.Berry	30
	S2		X	X				X	X						X1	X	X		X2	X		S1	X		I.Cruikshanks	31
S			X	X				X	S							X	X		X			X	X	S	D.Gallagher	32
S1	X2		X	X		S3	S2	X	X1						X3	X	X		X			X	X		J.Kirkby	33
S			X	X		S	S1	X	X						X1	X	X		X			X	X		D.J.Gallagher	34
			X	X		S	S	X1	X						X	X	X		X			X	X		G.Pooley	35
X	X		X			S2	S	X							S1	X2	X		X			X1	X		G.Cain	36
X1			X	X		S2	S	X								X2	X		X			X	X		T.Heilbron	37
X	S		X	X				X	S						S1	X	X		X1			X	X		D.Allison	38
X			X	X		S		X	S2						S1	X	X		X1			X	X2		T.West	39
X			X	X		S1	S	X							S	X1	X		X			X	X		R.Gifford	40
X			X	X		S2		X	S						S1	X2	X		X1			X	X		R.Furnandiz	41
X1			X	X			S	X	X2						S1	X	X		X			X	X		E.Lomas	42
X			X	X		S1	X	S								X	X		X			X	X		K.Lynch	43
X			X	X		S1		X	S2						X2	X	X		X1			X	X	S	A.Butler	44
X	S1		X			S		X	X						X1	X	X		X			X	X	S	S.Mathieson	45
X1			X	X		S3		X	S1						X3	X	X		X2			X	X		M.Pierce	46
S2	S1		X	X		S		X2	X1						X	X	X		X			X	X		E.Wolstenholme	47
X2	S2		X			X1		X	S3						S1	X	X		X3			X	X	X	U.Rennie	48
X1	S		X	S1				X	S							X	X		X			X	X	X	M.Bailey	49
X1	S		X			X	S1	X								X1	X		X			X	X	X	M.Riley	50
	S2		X	S1				X								X1	X	S	X2			X	X	X	G.Singh	51
	S2		X	X		S1		X								X1	X	S	X2			X	X	X	R.Harris	52
	S1		X1	X		S		X								X	X	S	X			X	X	X	K.Leach	53
	S		X	X		S1		X								X1	X	S	X			X	X	X	M.Barry	54
	S		X	X		S		X								X	X	S	X			X	X	X	W.Burns	55
	S1		X	X		S		X								X1	X	S	X			X	X	X	J.Singh	56
13	0	10	43	23	5	4	5	46	27	0	6	6	18	20	38	39	46	6	23	46	1	30	44	7	EL Appearances	
3	1	13	0	1	5	16	5	0	6	0	0	1	0	6	3	0	0	1	5	0	0	11	0	1	EL Sub Appearances	
0	0	3	3	0+1	0	0	0	3	2	0	0	0	3	3	2	3	3	0	0	3	0	1	3	0	CC Appearances	
0	0	1	2	1	0	0	0+1	2	2	0	0	0	1	2	2	2	2	0	2	2	0	2	2	0	FAC Appearances	
0	1	2	2	1	0	1+1	1+1	3	2	0	0	1	2	2	2	2	2	0	0	2	1	2	3	0	AIC Appearances	
0	0	0+1	2	0	2	0	2	0	0	0	0	0	0	0	0	2	2	0	2	2	0	2	2	2	PO Appearances	

STOKE CITY

CLUB RECORDS

BIGGEST VICTORIES
League: 9-0 v Plymouth Argyle,Division 2, 17.12.1960
F.A. Cup: 7-1 v Burnley, Round 2, 20.2.1896
League Cup: 6-2 v Chelsea, Round 2, 22.10.1974
Europe: 3-1 v Kaiserslautern, UEFA Cup, 1972-73

BIGGEST DEFEATS
League: 0-10 v Preston North End, Division 1, 4.2.1937
F.A. Cup: 0-7 v Leicester City, 14.11.1910
League Cup: No more than 3 goals
Europe: 0-4 v Kaiserslautern, UEFA Cup 1972-73

MOST POINTS
3 points a win: 93, Division 3/2, 1992-93
2 points a win: 63, Division 3N, 1926-27

MOST GOALS
92, Division 3N, 1926-27
Wilson 25, Davies 14, Eyres 12, Bussey 8, Williams 6, Archibald 6,
Johnson 5,Armitage 5, Williams 5, Watkin 3, Cull 1, Beswick 1,
Opponents 1

MOST LEAGUE GOALS CONCEDED
91, Division 1, 1984-85

MOST FIRST CLASS MATCHES IN A SEASON
67 (42 League, 9 FA Cup, 12 League Cup, 4 Texaco Cup) 1971-72

MOST LEAGUE WINS
27, Division 3(N), 1926-27
27, Division 3/2, 1992-93

MOST LEAGUE DRAWS
19, Division 2, 1989-90

MOST LEAGUE DEFEATS
31, Division 1, 1984-85

INDIVIDUAL CLUB RECORDS

MOST GOALS IN A MATCH
7. Neville Coleman v Lincoln, Div 2, 23.2.1957

MOST GOALS IN A SEASON
Charles Wilson, 38, (32 League, 6 FA Cup) 1927-28
3 goals twice=6, 2 goals seven times=14, 1 goal 18 times=18

OLDEST PLAYER
Sir Stanley Matthews, 50 years 5 days v Fulham, 6.2.1965

YOUNGEST PLAYER
Peter Bullock, 16 years 163 days v Swansea, 19.4.1958

MOST CAPPED PLAYER
Gordon Banks (England) 36

BEST PERFORMANCES

League: 1926-27: Matches played 42, Won 27, Drawn 9, Lost 6,
Goals for 92,Goals against 40, Points 63. 1st in Division 3N

Highest: Fourth in Division 1, 1935-36 & 1946-47

F.A. Cup: 1898-99: 3rd rnd. Sheffield Wednesday (a) 2-2, (h) 2-0;
4th rnd.Birmingham City (h) 2-2, (a) 2-1; 5th rnd. Tottenham H (h) 4
1; Semi-final Derby County 1-3
1970-71: 3rd rnd. Millwall 2-1; 4th rnd. Huddersfield 3-3, 0-0, 1-0;
5th rnd.Ipswich Town 0-0 1-0; 6th rnd. Hull City 3-2; Semi-final
Arsenal 2-2, 0-2
1971-72: 3rd rnd. Chesterfield 2-1; 4th rnd. Tranmere Rov 2-2, 2-0;
5th rnd.Hull City 4-1; 6th rnd. Manchester Utd 1-1, 2-1; Semi-final
Arsenal 1-1, 1-2

League Cup: 1971-72: 2nd rnd. Southport 2-1; 3rd rnd. Oxford
United 1-1, 1-0;4th rnd. Manchester Utd 1-1, 0-0, 2-1; 5th rnd.
Bristol Rov 4-2; Semi-final West Ham Utd, 1-2, 1-0, 0-0, 3-2; Final
Chelsea 2-1.

DIVISIONAL RECORD

	Played	Won	Drawn	Lost	For	Against	Points
Division 1	1,992	662	474	856	2,447	3,137	1,842
Division 2/1	1,404	551	361	492	2,009	1,843	1,585
Division 3/2	138	64	38	36	197	142	230
Division 3(N)	42	27	9	6	92	40	63
Total	3,576	1,304	882	1,380	4,745	5,162	3,720

ADDITIONAL INFORMATION
Previous Name: Stoke Ramblers, Stoke-upon-Trent, Stoke.

Previous League: Southern League; Birmingham League; Football
Alliance

Club colours: Red and white striped shirts, white shorts, red &
white socks.

Change colours: Green & black striped shirts, black shorts, green
& black socks.

Reserves League: Pontins Central League Division 1

RECORDS AND STATISTICS

COMPETITIONS

Div.1	Div.2/1	Div.3/2	Div.3(N)
1888-90	1890-91	1890-93	1926-27
1891-1907	1907-08		
1922-23	1919-22		
1933-53	1923-26		
1963-77	1927-33		
1979-86	1953-63		
	1977-79		
	1986-90		
	1993-		

HONOURS

Div.2	Div.3/2	Div.3(N)	Lge Cup	Watney
1932-33	1992-93	1926-27	1971-72	1973
1962-63				AMC
				1991-92

MOST APPEARANCES

Eric Skeels 591 (1959-76)

Year	League	FA Cup	Lge Cup	Europe
1959-60	2			
1960-61	37	6	1	
1961-62	42	3	1	
1962-63	38	1	2	
1964-64	39	5	10	
1964-65	42	3	5	
1965-66	41	1	5	
1966-67	40	1	1	
1967-68	34	3	4	
1968-69	35+1	4		
1969-70	34+1	0+1	1+1	
1970-71	27+2	9+1	1	
1971-72	13+6	4	1+1	
1972-73	30+1	1	2	1
1973-74	15	1	1	
1974-75	22+1		1	
1975-76	4			
	495+12	42+2	36+2	1

Including 1 appearance in the Texaco Cup.

RECORD TRANSFER FEE RECEIVED

Amount	Club	Player	Date
£1,500,000	Chelsea	Mark Stein	11/93
£750,000	Everton	Peter Beagrie	10/89
£700,000	Everton	Adrian Heath	1/82
£600,000	Tottenham H.	Garth Crooks	7/80

RECORD TRANSFER FEE PAID

Amount	Club	Player	Date
£450,000	Sheffield Wed	Ian Cranston	7/89
£350,000	Manchester Utd	Sammy McIlroy	2/82
£325,000	Leicester City	Peter Shilton	11/74
£240,000	Chelsea	Alan Hudson	1/74

MOST GOALS IN A CAREER

John Ritchie - 171 (1962-66 & 1969-75)

Year	League	FA Cup	Lge Cup	Others
1963-64	18	2	10	
1964-65	25	2	2	
1965-66	13			
1966-67	8		1	
1969-70	14	2		
1970-71	13	6		
1971-72	12	2	4	2
1972-73	14		1	1
1973-74	14	1		
1974-75	4			
Total	135	15	18	3

Current leading goalscorer: Nigel Gleghorn - 31 (1992-96)

MANAGERS

Name	Seasons	Best	Worst
Tom Slaney	1874-83		
Walt Cox	1883-84		
Harry Lockett	1884-90	12(1)	12(1)
Joe Bradshaw	1890-92	13(1)	13(1)
Arthur Reeves	1892-95	7(1)	14(1)
William Rowley	1895-97	6(1)	13(1)
H Austerberry	1897-08	6(1)	10(2)
A J Barker	1908-14		
Peter Hodge	1914-15		
Joe Schofield	1915-19		
Arthur Shallcross	1919-23	21(1)	20(2)
John Rutherford	1923		
Tom Mather	1923-25	6(2)	20(2)
Bob McGory	1935-52	4(1)	1(3N)
Frank Taylor	1952-60	21(1)	17(2)
Tony Waddington	1960-77	5(1)	18(2)
George Eastham	1977-78	7(2)	7(2)
Alan A'Court	1978		
Alan Durban	1978-81	11(1)	3(2)
Ritchie Barker	1981-83	13(1)	18(1)
Bill Asprey	1984-85	18(1)	22(1)
Mick Mills	1985-89	8(2)	13(2)
Alan Ball	1989-91	22(2)	14(3)
Lou Macari	1991-93	1(3/2)	4(3)
Joe Jordan	1993-94	10(2/1)	19(2/1)
Lou Macari	1994-	4(1)	4(1)

LONGEST LEAGUE RUNS

of undefeated matches:	25 (5.9.1992 - 20.2.1993)	of league matches w/out a win:	7 (15.9.1984 - 22.12.1984)
of undefeated home matches:	23 (15.12.1973 - 21.12.1974)	of undefeated away matches:	12 (12.9.1992 - 30.1.1993)
without home win:	9 (15.4.1963 - 30.11.1963)	without an away win:	30 (16.1.1897 - 18.12.1899)
of league wins:	7 (2.9.1905 - 23.9.1905, 4.4.1947 - 26.5.1947)	of home wins:	11 (30.3.1895 - 21.12.1895)
of league defeats:	11 (6.4.1985 - 17.8.1985)	of away wins:	5 (14.1.1922 - 11.3.1922, 4.4.1947 - 26.5.1947)

STOKE CITY

PLAYERS NAME Honours	Ht	Wt	Birthdate	Birthplace Transfers	Contract Date	Clubs	League	L/Cup	FA Cup	Other	Lge	L/C	FAC	Oth
G O A L K E E P E R S														
Morgan Phil	6.1	13.0	18/12/74	Stoke-on-Trent	01/07/93	Ipswich Town								
E: S				Free	06/07/95	Stoke City								
				Loan	06/10/95	Macclesfield Town								
Muggleton Carl	6.0	11.13	13/09/68	Leicester	17/09/86	Leicester City	46		3	5				
E:u21.1				Loan	10/09/87	Chesterfield	17			2				
				Loan	01/02/88	Blackpool	2							
				Loan	28/10/88	Hartlepool United	8			2				
				Loan	01/03/90	Stockport County	4							
				Loan	13/08/93	Stoke City	6	1		2				
				£150000	11/01/94	Celtic	12		1					
				£200000	21/07/94	Stoke City	30	3		4				
				Loan	01/11/95	Rotherham United	6			1				
				Loan	28/03/96	Sheffield United	0+1							
Prudhoe Mark	6.0	13.0	11/11/63	Washington	11/09/81	Sunderland	7							
GMVC'90. Div4'91. FLgXI				Loan	04/11/83	Hartlepool United	3							
				£22000	24/09/84	Birmingham City	1	4						
				£22000	27/02/86	Walsall	26	4	1					
				Loan	11/12/86	Doncaster Rovers	5							
				Loan	26/03/87	Grimsby Town	8							
				Loan	29/08/87	Hartlepool United	13							
				Loan	06/11/87	Bristol City	3			2				
				£10000	11/12/87	Carlisle United	34	2						
				£10000	16/03/89	Darlington	146	8	9	6				
				£120000	24/06/93	Stoke City	69	6	4	7				
				Loan	30/09/94	Peterborough UTD	6							
				Loan	29/11/94	Liverpool								
D E F E N D E R S														
Beeston Carl	5.9	10.3	30/06/67	Stoke	01/07/85	Stoke City	207+11	12	7+1	15	13	1	1	2
E: u21.1. Div2'93														
Clarkson Ian	5.11	11.8	04/12/70	Solihull	15/12/88	Birmingham City	125+11	12	5+1	17+1				
AMC'91				£40000	13/09/93	Stoke City	72+3	6	5	8+2				
Cranson Ian	5.11	12.4	02/07/64	Easington	05/07/82	Ipswich Town	130+1	15	11+1	7	5			
E: u21.5. AGT'92. Div2'93				£450000	24/03/88	Sheffield Wed.	29+1	2	2	1				
				£450000	25/07/89	Stoke City	214+3	16+1	14	27	9	1	1	1
Dreyer John	6.0	11.6	11/06/63	Alnwick		Wallingford								
					08/01/85	Oxford United	57+3	10+1	2	3	2			
				Loan	13/12/85	Torquay United	5							
				Loan	27/03/88	Fulham	12			2				
				£140000	27/06/88	Luton Town	212+2	13	14	8	14	1		
				Free	15/07/94	Stoke City	20+18	2	1	4+1	2			1
				Loan	23/03/95	Bolton Wanderers	1+1			1+1				
Overson Vince	6.0	13.0	15/05/62	Kettering	16/11/79	Burnley	207+4	9	19	10	6	1		
Div3'82. Div2'93. AMC'91'92				Free	11/06/86	Birmingham City	179+3	11+1	8	11	3		1	
				£55000	29/08/91	Stoke City	167+3	13	10	23	6	1		
Wallace Ray	5.6	10.2	02/10/69	Greenwich	21/04/88	Southampton	33+2	8	2	2				
E: u21.4				£100000	08/07/91	Leeds United	5+2							
				Loan	20/03/92	Swansea City	2							
				Loan	11/03/94	Reading	3							
				Free	12/08/94	Stoke City	60+4	4	3	11	7			1
				Loan	16/12/94	Hull City	7							
Whittle Justin	6.1	12.12	18/03/71	Derby		Celtic								
				Free	20/10/94	Stoke City	7+1			2				
Worthington Nigel	5.10	12.6	04/11/61	Ballymena		Bellymena								
NI: 50, Y.1. UC'81. IFAC'81. LC'91.				£100000	01/07/81	Notts County	67+11	4		4				
				£125000	06/02/84	Sheffield Wed.	334+4	41	29	9	12	1		1
				£325000	04/07/94	Leeds United	33+10	4+1	6+1		1			
				Free	19/07/96	Stoke City								
M I D F I E L D														
Devlin Mark	5.9	11.3	18/01/73	Irvine	06/04/91	Stoke City	26+8	1+1		2+2	2			
Forsyth Richard			03/10/70	Dudley		Kidderminster H.								
GMVC. FAXI.				£50000	13/07/95	Birmingham City	12+13	7+2	2	3	2			
				£200000	22/07/96	Stoke City								
Gleghorn Nigel	6.0	12.13	12/08/62	Seaham		Seaham Red Star								
AMC'91. Div2'93				Free	30/08/85	Ipswich Town	54+12	3+2	3+1	7+2	11		2	

Player	Ht	Wt	DOB	From	Fee/Type	Date	Club								
eghorn continued...					£47500	04/08/88	Manchester City	27+7	2	0+1	1	7	2	1	1
					£175000	09/09/89	Birmingham City	142	13	7	14	33	5	3	2
					£100000	24/10/92	Stoke City	162+4	10	10	22	26	2	2	1
en Kevin	5.6	10.3	25/02/67	Amersham		08/03/84	West Ham United	187+32	21+1	15+7	14+2	21	5	1	3
Y.10,S					£600000	07/07/93	Wolves	37+5	2+1	5	4	7		1	1
					£300000	19/10/94	Stoke City	42+12	2	2	2	5			
acari Michael			04/02/73	Kilwinning		31/07/91	Stoke City								
eron Michael N	5.9	11.3	11/01/72	Liverpool		05/07/90	Manchester City	82+18	9+1	5+3	1	24	1	3	
u21.16					Loan	28/03/91	Bury	1+4			2	1			
					£1000000	26/08/94	Norwich City	19+9	6	4		2	3	2	
						13/11/95	Stoke City	23+5			2	15			
gurdsson Larus	6.0	11.5	04/06/73	Iceland			Iceland								
elandic Int. u21, Y.					£150000	21/10/94	Stoke City	68+2	3	2+1	4	1			
okoe Graham	6.0	11.11	17/12/75	Newcastle			Stoke City								
					Loan	23/02/96	Hartlepool United	8							
orthington Nigel	5.10	12.6	04/11/61	Ballymena			Ballymena	67							
50. Y1; UC'81; IC'81;					£100000	01/07/81	Notts County	62+5	11	4		4			
'91					£125000	06/02/84	Sheffield Wednesday	334+4	41	29	9	12	1		1
					£250000	04/07/94	Leeds United	21+6	2	3+1		1			

F O R W A R D S

Player	Ht	Wt	DOB	From	Fee/Type	Date	Club								
arruthers Martin	5.11	11.9	07/08/72	Nottingham		04/07/90	Aston Villa	2+2		0+1	0+1				
					Loan	31/10/92	Hull City	13			3	6			
					£300000	05/07/93	Stoke City	60+29	7+2	3+1	10+4	13	1	3	3
ayle John	6.4	13.1	30/07/64	Bromsgrove			Burton Albion								
MVC'91					£30000	01/03/89	Wimbledon	17+3	3			2			
					£175000	21/11/90	Birmingham City	39+5		2	8+1	10			4
					Loan	20/08/93	Walsall	4				1			
					£100000	13/09/93	Coventry City	3	1+2						
					£70000	17/08/94	Burnley	7+7	1+1	1+1		3	1	1	
					£70000	23/01/95	Stoke City	6+8		0+1	3+1	3			
					Loan	14/03/96	Gillingham	9				3			
urridge Simon	5.5	10.7	09/12/69	Birmingham		08/07/88	Birmingham City	129+21	10+4	8	14	30	1	2	5
MC'91						24/09/93	Stoke City	37+25	2	3+3	7+3	14		1	

ADDITIONAL CONTRACT PLAYERS

rch Mark	Stoke City (T)
llan Aidan J	Stoke City (T)
oods Stephen J	Stoke City (T)

THE MANAGER
LOU MACARI

Date of Birth . . . . 7th June 1949.
Place of Birth . . . . Edinburgh.
Date of Appointment . . . . September 1994.

PREVIOUS CLUBS
As Manager . . . . Swindon, West Ham, Birmingham, Celtic.
As Coach . . . . None.
As a Player . . . . Celtic, Manchester United.

HONOURS
As a Manager
Swindon: Promotion to Div.3, 1985-86. Promotion to Div.2, 1986-87.
Birmingham: Leyland Daf Cup 1991.
Stoke: Promotion to Div.1, 1992-93.
As a Player
Celtic: League Championship 3 times. Scottish Cup twice.
Manchester United: FA Cup 1977.
International: 24 full caps for Scotland.

VICTORIA GROUND

Stoke-on-Trent, Staffordshire ST4 4EG
Tel: 01782 413 511

Capacity 24,054
Seating 8,979

First game ....v Talke Rangers (Friendly) 25.3.1878.
First floodlit game...v Port Vale, 10.10.1956.
Internationals..England v Wales 1889, 1893, v Ireland 1936.

ATTENDANCES
Highest ....51,380 v Arsenal, Division 1, 29.3.1937.
Lowest ....3,516 v Coventry City, FMC, 18.9.1985.

OTHER GROUNDS..Sweeting Fields 1875-78.   Victoria Ground 1878-

---

MATCHDAY TICKET PRICES

Boothen Stand Blocks B, C & D.
Adults £13
Juv/OAP £7
Butler Street Stand Block C.
Adults £13
Juv/OAP £7
Stoke End Stand . . . . £13 (£7 Juv)
Family Ticket . . . . Adult £11
Junior £3 (u13), £6 (u17/OAP)
Boothen End
Adult £9
Juv/OAP £6

Ticket Office Telephone no. 01782 413 961

CLUBCALL
0891 12 10 40
Calls cost 39p per minute cheap rate and 49p per
minute at all other times.
Call costings correct at time of going to press.

HOW TO GET TO THE GROUND

From the North, West and South
Use motorway M6 until junction 15, leave motorway and follow signs to Stoke(A5006) then join A500. In 0.8 miles branch left and shortly at roundabout take 2nd exit into Campbell Road for Stoke City FC.

From the East
Use A50 into Stoke town centre and at crossroads turn left into Lonsdale Street for Campbell Road for Stoke City FC.

Car Parking
Whieldon Road Car Park - £1.
Also street parking.

Nearest Railway Station
Stoke (01782 411 411).

MATCHDAY PROGRAMME

Programme Editor . . . . Tony Tams.

Number of pages . . . . 48.

Price . . . . £1.50.

Subscriptions . . . . £42 UK, £50 Overseas.

Local Newspapers. . . . . . . The Sentinel, North Staffordshire Advertiser.

Local Radio Stations . . . . BBC Radio Stoke, Signal Radio.

SWINDON TOWN
(The Robins)
NATIONWIDE LEAGUE DIVISION 1
SPONSORED BY: CASTROL (UK) LTD.

Back Row (L-R): Wayne Allison, Paul Bodin, Shaun Taylor, Fraser Digby, Mark Seagreaves, Andy Thomson, Peter Thorne.
Middle Row: Ian Culverhouse, Kevin Horlock, Jason Drysdale, Stephen Finney, Dean Hooper, Mark Robinson, Luc Nijholt, Ty Gooden, Edwin Murray.
Front Row: Martin Ling, Wayne O'Sullivan, Andy Rowland (1st Team Coach), Steve McMahon (Player/Manager), Ross MacLaren (Reserves Manager), Jonathan Trigg (Physio), Jamie Pitman, Ben Worrall.

SWINDON TOWN
FORMED IN 1879
TURNED PROFESSIONAL IN 1894
LTD COMPANY IN 1894

PRESIDENT: C Green
CHAIRMAN: J M Spearman
VICE-CHAIRMAN
P T Archer
DIRECTORS
P R Godwin CBE, Sir D Seton Wills, Bt,
C J Puffett, J R Hunt (Associate Director)
CHEIF EXECUTIVE/SECRETARY
Steve Jones
MARKETING MANAGER
Martin Stevens

MANAGER: Steve McMahon
FIRST TEAM COACH: Andy Rowland
RESERVE TEAM MANAGER
Ross MacLaren
YOUTH TEAM MANAGER
Thomas Wheeldon
PHYSIOTHERAPIST
Jonathan Trigg

STATISTICIAN FOR THE DIRECTORY
Vacant

Steve McMahon's first full season as Swindon Town manager brought back a habit that he was use to in his playing days at Liverpool, winning silverware! Swindon were only off the top twice during the season, briefly in December and for a spell of five games in March.

The Robins lost their first game in the League on September 30th in a thrilling 3-4 tussle with Wrexham, this was preceded by eight wins and two draws. This, not surprisingly, installed the confidence in the side that made them almost invincible.

In the Coca-Cola Cup a set-back away to Cambridge (1-2) was overcome in the second leg with a 2-0 win, this in turn would bring the Premiership Champions, Blackburn Rovers, to the County Ground. But the shock result looked on the cards at Ewood Park, with Swindon taking an early 2-0 lead, however Mr Shearer had other ideas and helped Blackburn turn the tie around eventually coming out 2-3 victors. The match at the County Ground was lost 0-2.

The 5th Round of the F.A. Cup was reached with victories over Cambridge United again (2-0), Cardiff City (2-0), non-League Woking (2-0), Oldham Athletic (1-0) before losing to Southampton in a replay at the Dell (0-2).

There winning ways in the League however had not faltered and they were looking good for the title. A sticky patch in March however saw their championship hopes threatened. McMahon and his players soon overcame this minor hic-cup and remained unbeaten from March 23rd to the end of the season, this was enough to win the Second Division title, that had been well deserved.

If Swindon Town can start the 1996/97 season as they did the 1995/96 then there is no reason why they wouldn't be fighting for a play-off place if not an automatic place.

SWINDON TOWN

| League: Champions | | FA Cup: 5th Rnd | | | Coca-Cola Cup: 2nd Rnd | | | Auto Windscreen Shield: 2nd Rnd | |

M	DATE	COMP	VEN	OPPONENTS	RESULT	HT	LP	GOAL SCORERS/GOAL TIMES	ATT.
1	A 12	EL	A	Hull City	W 1-0	0-0	1	Finney 68	(6525)
2	15	CC 1/1	A	**Cambridge United**	L 1-2	1-1		**Gooden 2**	(2530)
3	19	EL	H	York City	W 3-0	2-0	1	Finney 2, 66, Bodin 42(pen)	7746
4	23	CC 1/2	H	**Cambridge United**	W 2-0	0-0		**Beauchamp 78, Horlock 90**	6724
5	26	EL	A	Carlisle United	W 1-0	0-0	1	Murray 65	(6325)
6	30	EL	H	Oxford United	D 1-1	1-0	1	Allison 40	13041
7	S 2	EL	A	Brentford	W 2-0	1-0	1	O'Sullivan 38, Finney 76	(7878)
8	9	EL	H	Chesterfield	D 1-1	0-1	1	Allison 46	8687
9	13	EL	H	Bradford City	W 4-1	2-1	1	Robinson 10, Allison 18, Finney 58, Horlock 85	8203
10	16	EL	A	Bristol Rovers	W 4-1	1-1	1	Horlock 5, 62, 82, Taylor 58	(7025)
11	20	CC 2/1	H	**Blackburn Rovers**	L 2-3	2-2		**Allison 25, Finney 26**	14740
12	23	EL	A	Rotherham United	W 1-0	0-0	1	Gooden 64	8470
13	30	EL	A	Wrexham	L 3-4	2-1	1	Allison 11, 23, Thorne 56	(4396)
14	O 4	CC 2/2	A	**Blackburn Rovers**	L 0-2	0-1			(16924)
15	7	EL	H	Bristol City	W 2-0	1-0	1	O'Sullivan 12, Allison 89	11797
16	14	EL	A	Brighton & H.A.	W 3-1	3-0	1	Finney 17, Finney 37, Horlock 44	(7808)
17	17	AWS 1/2	A	**Torquay United**	D 1-1	1-1		**Ling 45**	(1135)
18	21	EL	H	Crewe Alexandra	W 2-1	0-0	1	Allison 58, Finney 89(pen)	12633
19	28	EL	A	Notts County	W 3-1	2-1	1	Taylor 7, 78, Bodin 45	(8725)
20	31	EL	A	Bournemouth	D 0-0	0-0	1		(6352)
21	N 4	EL	H	Blackpool	D 1-1	0-0	1	Finney 50	12470
22	8	AWS 1/2	H	**Colchester United**	W 2-0	0-0		**Finney 46, Thorne 47**	6222
23	11	FAC 1	H	**Cambridge United**	W 4-1	2-0		**Horlock 41, 44, Finney 48, Allen 85**	7383
24	18	EL	A	Stockport County	D 1-1	1-0	1	Allison 45	(7196)
25	25	EL	H	Shrewsbury Town	L 0-1	0-0	1		9306
26	29	AWS 2	H	**Hereford United**	L 0-1	0-1			6650
27	D 2	FAC 2	H	**Cardiff City**	W 2-0	0-0		**Allison 58, Finney 83**	8274
28	9	EL	A	Rotherham United	W 2-0	0-0	1	Finney 70, Finney 89	(3042)
29	16	EL	H	Wrexham	D 1-1	0-0	1	O'Sullivan 76	8418
30	23	EL	A	Walsall	D 0-0	0-0	2		(5624)
31	26	EL	H	Wycombe Wanderers	D 0-0	0-0	2		12976
32	J 6	FAC 3	H	**Woking**	W 2-0	0-0		**Allison 17, Bodin 83**	10322
33	10	EL	H	Swansea City	W 3-0	1-0	1	Allison 20, Thorne 61, 76	6555
34	13	EL	A	York City	L 0-2	0-0	1		(3613)
35	20	EL	H	Hull City	W 3-0	0-0	1	Thorne 49, Grant 68, Horlock 82	8118
36	F 3	EL	H	Carlisle United	W 2-1	0-0	1	Thorne 52, Allison 71	8242
37	10	EL	A	Swansea City	W 1-0	1-0	1	Taylor 28	(4452)
38	12	FAC 4	H	**Oldham Athletic**	W 1-0	0-0		**Ling 89**	9508
39	17	FAC 5	H	**Southampton**	D 1-1	1-0		**Horlock 32**	15035
40	21	EL	H	Brentford	D 2-2	2-2	1	Allison 27, Gooden 31(pen)	8814
41	24	EL	H	Bristol Rovers	W 2-1	0-1	1	Allison 78, Taylor 81	11724
42	28	FAC 5R	A	**Southampton**	L 0-2	0-0			(13962)
43	M 2	EL	A	Wycombe Wanderers	W 2-1	2-0	1	Gooden 4, Thorne 19	(6457)
44	5	EL	A	Peterborough United	W 2-0	1-0	1	Allison 24, Finney 70	(4196)
45	9	EL	H	Walsall	D 1-1	0-0	1	Taylor 84	9564
46	16	EL	A	Burnley	D 0-0	0-0	2		(9360)
47	19	EL	A	Oxford United	L 0-3	0-1	2		(8585)
48	23	EL	H	Peterborough United	W 2-0	2-0	2	Allison 11, Thorne 16	9066
49	30	EL	A	Bristol City	D 0-0	0-0	2		(11370)
50	A 3	EL	H	Brighton & H.A.	W 3-2	1-0	2	Thorne 44, 85, Allison 46	8610
51	6	EL	H	Notts County	W 1-0	0-0	1	Horlock 89	10928
52	8	EL	A	Crewe Alexandra	W 2-0	1-0	1	Horlock 27, Preece 47	(5162)
53	13	EL	H	Bournemouth	D 2-2	1-1	1	Horlock 16, 72(pen)	10508
54	17	EL	H	Burnley	D 0-0	0-0	1		10480
55	20	EL	A	Blackpool	D 1-1	1-0	1	Horlock 14	(9175)
56	23	EL	A	Chesterfield	W 3-1	2-1	1	Cowe 26, Thorne 31, Allison 79	(5523)
57	27	EL	H	Shrewsbury Town	W 2-1	1-1	1	Horlock 30, Taylor 56	(4233)
58	30	EL	A	Bradford City	D 1-1	0-0	1	Allison 68	(9812)
59	M 4	EL	H	Stockport County	D 0-0	0-0	1		14697

Best Home League Attendance: 14697 v Stockport County **Smallest: 6555 v Swansea City** **Average: 10045**

Goal Scorers:

EL(71): Allison(17),Horlock(12),Finney(12),Thorne(10),Taylor(7),Gooden(3),O'Sullivan(3),Bodin(2),Murray(1),Preece(1),Cowe(1),Grant(1),Robinson(1)

CC(5): Beauchamp(1),Allison(1),Gooden(1),Finney(1),Horlock(1)

FAC(10): Horlock(3),Allison(2),Finney(2),Bodin(1),Allen(1),Ling(1)

AWS(3): Thorne(1),Ling(1),Finney(1)

(M) Allen	(F) Allison	(F) Beauchamp	(M) Bodin	(M) Collins	(M) Cowe	(D) Culverhouse	(G) Digby	(D) Drysdale	(F) Finney	(G) Given	(M) Gooden	(M) Grant	(M) Hooper	(D) Horlock	(F) Leitch	(F) Ling	(M) McMahon	(G) Mildenhall	(D) Murray	(M) O'Sullivan	(M) Preece	(M) Robinson	(D) Seagraves	(D) Smith	(G) Talia	(D) Taylor	(F) Thorne	Opponent	No.
	X	S1		X		X		X1	X		X						X	S		X		X	X			X		E.Lomas	1
	X		X			X			X	X	X			S2			X1	S	S	X		X2	X			X		S.T.Bennett	2
	X		X			X			X	X	X			S1			X1	S	S	X		X	X			X		M.Bailey	3
		S2	X			X			X		X			X	S1		X	X	X	X			X1			X	X2	K.Leach	4
	X		X			X	S		X	X	X			X			X	X	X	X		X	X			X		K.Breen	5
	X	S2	X			X	S		X	X	X			X			X2	S1	S	X		X1	X			X		M.Brandwood	6
	X	S	X			X	S		X	X	X			X			X1	S1	S	X		X	X			X		P.Rejer	7
	X		X1			X	S		X		S1			X			X		S	X		X	X		X	X		M.Pierce	8
X1	X	S2	X			X	S		X		S1			X			X2			X		X	X		X	X		J.Rushton	9
		S	X			X	S		X		S1			X			X	X1		X		X	X		X	X		E.Wolstenholme	10
	X		X			X	X		X		S1			X			X1			X		X	X		X	X	S	G.Singh	11
	X		X1			X	S		X2		S1			X						X		X	X		X	X	S2	M.Fletcher	12
	X		S			X	S		S1		X			X						X		X	X	X	X	X1	T.Leake	13
	X		X			X	X		X		S	S	X	X			S			X		X	X			X		R.Hart	14
	X		X			X	X		X		S	S	X	X			S			X		X	X			X		R.Gifford	15
S1	X		X			X	X		X		S			X1			X			X		X	X			X		G.Pooley	16
X	X		X				X		X		X2			S3	X3		X	S1		X	X1		X			X		C.Wilkes	17
X	X		X				X		X		S			X	S	X			S	X		X				X		G.Barber	18
X	X		X				X		X		X			X	S	S	X		X			X				X		A.Wiley	19
X	X		X				X		X		S1			X	S	S	X		X1			X				X		A.D'urfo	20
	X		X1				X	S1	X	X	X			S2		S	X2			X		X				X		G.Bennett	21
	X					X	X	X	X2		X1	X3	X	S1					X		X				X	S3			22
X	X3		X1			X	X	S1	X		S2			X			X2			X		X				X	S3	P.Alcock	23
	X		X			X	X	X1	S		X			X	X		X			X		S			S	X1	G.Frankland	24
	X					X	X	X	X		S1			X	X2		X1			X		S			S	X2	I.Hemley	25
				X		X	X	X	S2		X2	X	X3	S1						S3	X				X	X1		26
X	X					X	X	X	X		X			S			X			X		X	X	S	X	S	P.Jones	27
X	X					X	X	X	X		S1			X			X			X	X1	S	X	S	X	S	G.Singh	28
X	X1					X	X	X	X2		X			X			S2			X	S	X	S	X	S1	B.Knight	29
X	X		X			X	X	X			S1			X			X1			X2		X	S	X	X	X	S.J.Baines	30
X	X	X				X	X	S1			X			X	S			X1		S	X		S	X	X	C.Wilkes	31
X	X		X			X	X	S2			X			X	S1				S	X		X	X1	X2	J.Rushton	32
X	X		X			X	X	S2	S1		X			X2			X		X	X1	S		X	Thorne X	M.Pierce	33
X	X		X			X	X	S1	S2		X3	X	X1			X3		S2	X			X	I.Cruikshanks	34
X3	X	X2	X			X	X	S1	X	X	X	X1			S3	X	S2		X	G.Cain	35
	X1	X	X			X	X	S	S1	X	X	X			S	X		X	X	T.Leake	36
	X	X	S			X	X	S	X	X	X			X	S	X	X	P.Rejer	37
X	X2	X				X	X	S2	X		S1	X1			X	S	X	X	P.Danson	38
X	X2	X1				X	X	X	X3		X	S3	X	X	R.Hart	39
X	X		S			X	X	X	S1	X	X1			X	S	X	X	N.Barry	40
X1	X					X	X	X	S2	X2	X	S1	S	X	X	J.Lloyd	41
	X	X1				X	X	S1	X	X	S	S	X	X	R.Hart	42
	X	X				X	X	X	X	X	S	X	X	S	X	X1	K.Breen	43
X	X		S			X	S	X	X	X	X	S	X	X	X	A.Butler	44
X	X		S1			X	S	X	X	X1	S	X	X	X	G.Barber	45
X	X	S	X			X	X1	X	X	X	X	S	X	X	M.Riley	46
X	X		X			X	S1	X2	X3	S3	X	X1	S2	X	X	X	N.Barry	47
X	X		X	S2		X	X	S1	X1	X	X	S	X	X	X2	T.Heilbron	48
X	X		X	S		X	X	S	X	X	X	S	X	X	X	I.Hemley	49
X	X		X2	S3		X	X	X3	S2	X	X1	S	X	X	X1	A.Leake	50
X	X		X	S1		X	X	X2	S2	X	X	S	X	X	G.Pooley	51
X	X2		X	S2		X	X	X1	X	S	S1	X	X	E.Lomas	52
X	X		X1	S2		X	X	X	X	S1	X	X	X2	K.Leach	53
X	X		X	S1		X	X	X	X1	X	S	X	X	K.Leach	54
X2	X		X	S3		X	X	X1	S1	X	X	S2	X	X3	J.Rushton	55
	X		X	S		X1	X	X	S1	X	X	X	S	X	X	D.Allison	56
S1	X		X	S3	X	X	X	S2	X2	X	X3	X	X	X	X1	J.A.Kirkby	57
	X	S	X	S1	S1	X	X	S2	X	X	X1	X	X	X2	X	M.Fletcher	58
S1	X		X1	X		X	X	S3	X	X3	X	X1	S1	X	K.Breen	59

25	42	1	32	2	4	46	25	10	22	4	14	3	0	44	7	12	20	0	3	26	7	46	25	2	16	43	22	EL Appearances	
2	1	2	1	3	7	0	0	3	8	0	12	0	0	1	0	4	1	0	2	7	0	0	3	6	0	0	4	EL Sub Appearances	
0	3	0	4	0	0	2	0	4	0	1+1	0	0+1	3+1	0	0	4	2	1	4	0	3	4	0	0	4	0	1	CC Appearances	
5	6	0	4	1	0	6	6	2+2	2+4	0	3+1	0	0	6	0	2+1	3+1	0	0	1	0	6	3+1	0	0	6	4+1	FAC Appearances	
1	3	0	1	0	1	0	1	3	2	2+1	0	3	0	2	1+2	0	3	0+1	0	1	0+2	0	2+1	2	0	0	3	1+1	AWS Appearances	

Also Played: (M) Nijholt S(1), S1(2). (M) Pitman S(4,5). (D) Thorne S2(17, X(22).

SWINDON TOWN

CLUB RECORDS

BIGGEST VICTORIES
League: 9-1 v Luton Town, Division 3S, 28.4.1921
8-0 v Newport County, Div 3S, 26.12.1938
8-0 v Bury, Division 3, 8.12.1979
F.A. Cup: 10-1 v Farnham United Breweries FC (a), Round 1, 28.11.1925
League Cup: 6-0 v Torquay United (a), Rnd 2 1st leg 23.9.1992

BIGGEST DEFEATS
League: 0-9 v Torquay United, Division 3S, 8.3.1952
F.A. Cup: 1-10 v Manchester City, Round 2, 29.1.1930
League Cup: 0-5 v Notts County, Round 3, 1962-63
0-5 v Liverpool, Round 3, 1980-81

MOST POINTS
3 points a win: 102, Division 4, 1985-86 (League record)
2 points a win: 64, Division 3, 1968-69

MOST GOALS
100, 1926-27, Division 3S.
Morris 47, Eddelston 11, Thom 8, Wall 7, Petrie 6, Denyer 5, Dickinson 3, Flood 3, Jeffries 3, Archer 1, Weston 1, Brown 1, Bailey 1, Johnson 1, Daniel 1, og1.

MOST LEAGUE GOALS CONCEDED
105, Division 3S, 1932-33

MOST FIRST CLASS MATCHES IN A SEASON
64 (46 League, 4 FA Cup, 4 League Cup, 5 Freight Rover Trophy, 5 Play-offs)1986-87

MOST LEAGUE WINS: 32, Division 4, 1985-86

MOST LEAGUE DRAWS: 17, Division 3, 1967-68

MOST LEAGUE DEFEATS: 25, Division 3S, 1956-57

INDIVIDUAL CLUB RECORDS

MOST GOALS IN A MATCH
5. Harry Morris v Queens Park Rangers, 18.12.1927, Div 3S (6-2).
5. v Norwich City, 26.4.1930, Div 3S (5-1).
5. Keith East v Mansfield, 20.11.1965, Div 3. (6-2).

MOST GOALS IN A SEASON
Harry Morris 48, (47 League, 1 FA Cup) 1926-27.
5 goals once=5; 4 goals once=4; 3 goals 3 times=9; 2 goals 5 times=10; 1 goal 20 times=20.

OLDEST PLAYER
Alex Ferguson 43 years 103 days, v Bristol City (Div. 3S), 15.11.1947.

YOUNGEST PLAYER
Paul Rideout, 16 years 107 days v Hull (Div 3), 29.11.1980).

MOST CAPPED PLAYER
Rod Thomas (Wales) 30

BEST PERFORMANCES

League: 1985-86: Matches played 46, Won 32, Drawn 6, Lost 8, Goals for 82,Goals against 43, Points 102. First in Division 4.
Highest: 1989-90: 4th Division 2.
F.A. Cup: 1910: 1st rnd. Crystal Palace 3-1; 2nd rnd. Burnley 2-0; 3rd rnd.Tottenham Hotspur 3-2; 4th rnd. Manchester City 2-0; Semi-Final Newcastle Utd. 0-2.
1912: 1st rnd. Sutton 5-0; 2nd rnd. Notts County 2-0; 3rd rnd. West Ham United1-1, 4-0; 4th rnd. Everton 2-1; Semi-Final Barnsley 0-0, 0-1.
League Cup: 1968-69: 1st rnd. Torquay 2-1; 2nd rnd. Bradford City 1-1;4-3; 3rd rnd. Coventry City 2-2, 3-0; 4th rnd. Derby County 0-0, 1-0; Semi-Final Burnley 2-1; Final Arsenal 3-1.

ADDITIONAL INFORMATION
Previous Name: None.

Previous League: Southern League.

Club colours: Red shirts, shorts & socks with white & green trim.

Change colours: Blue & black shirts, blue shorts, blue socks.

Reserves League: Avon Insurance Combination Division 1.

DIVISIONAL RECORD

	Played	Won	Drawn	Lost	For	Against	Points
Premier	42	5	15	22	47	100	30
Division 2/1	614	211	177	226	849	859	718
Division 3/2	874	358	237	279	1,315	1,101	1,016
Division 3(S)	1,334	491	333	510	2,058	2,130	1,315
Division 4	184	87	39	58	263	211	300
Total	**3,048**	**1,152**	**801**	**1,095**	**4,480**	**4,401**	**3,379**

RECORDS AND STATISTICS

COMPETITIONS

Div.1/P	Div.2/1	Div.3/2	Div.3(S)	Div.4
1993-94	1963-65	1920-21	1921-58	1982-86
	1969-74	1958-63		
	1987-93	1965-69		
	1994-95	1974-82		
	1996-	1986-87		
		1995-96		

HONOURS

Division 2	Division 4	League Cup	Anglo/Ital
1995-96	1985-86	1968-69	1970

MOST APPEARANCES

John Trollope 886+3 (1960-81)

Year	League	FA Cup	Lge Cup	Other
1960-61	44	3	3	
1961-62	46	2	3	
1962-63	46	4	2	
1963-64	42	3	4	
1964-65	42	1	1	
1965-66	46	3	1	
1966-67	46	8	5	
1967-68	46	4	2	
1968-69	19+1	1	2	
1969-70	42	4	2	7
1970-71	39	2	3	4
1971-72	42	1	1	
1972-73	34	2	1	
1973-74	36	2	3	
1974-75	46	5	1	
1975-76	46	5	4	
1976-77	35	7		
1977-78	40	4	6	
1978-79	16+2		2	
1979-80				
1980-81	14			
	767+3	61	47	11

MOST GOALS IN A CAREER

Harry Morris 230 (1926-33)

Year	League	FA Cup
1926-27	47	1
1927-28	38	6
1928-29	27	5
1929-30	28	1
1930-31	35	
1931-32	29	
1932-33	12	1
Total	216	14

Current leading goalscorer: Shaun Taylor - 33 (1991-96)

MANAGERS

As secretary, Sam Allen took control of team matters between 1902-1948. However, a team manager was appointed in 1933.

Name	Seasons	Best	Worst
Ted Vizard	1933-39	8(3S)	19(3S)
Neil Harris	1939		
Louis Page	1945-53	4(3S)	18(3S)
Maurice Lindley	1953-58	4(3S)	24(3S)
Bert Head	1958-65	14(2)	16(3)
Danny Williams	1965-69	2(3)	10(3)
Fred Ford	1969-71	5(2)	12(2)
Dave Mackay	1971-72	11(2)	11(2)
Les Allen	1977-74	11(2)	22(2)
Danny Williams	1974-78	4(3)	19(3)
Bob Smith	1978-80	5(3)	10(3)
John Trollope	1980-83	17(3)	8(4)
Ken Beamish	1983-84	17(4)	17(4)
Lou Macari	1984-89	12(2)	8(4)
Osvaldo Ardiles	1989-91	4(2)	
Glenn Hoddle	1991-93	5(2/1)	8(2)
John Gorman	1993-94	22(P)	
Steve McMahon	1994-	1(2)	1(2)

RECORD TRANSFER FEE RECEIVED

Amount	Club	Player	Date
£1,300,000	Middlesbrough	Jan Aage Fjortoft	3/95
£1,250,000	Tottenham	Colin Calderwood	8/93
£1,150,000	Manchester City	Nicky Summerbee	6/94
£1,000,000	Southampton	Alan McLoughlin	11/90

RECORD TRANSFER FEE PAID

Amount	Club	Player	Date
£850,000	West Ham	Joey Beauchamp	6/94
£600,000	Newcastle	Mark Robinson	7/94
£500,000	Leyton Orient	Adrian Whitbread	7/93
£500,000	Rapid Veienna	Jan Aage Fjortoft	7/93

LONGEST LEAGUE RUNS

of undefeated matches:	22 (12.1.1986 - 23.8.1986)	of league matches w/out a win:	9 (17.4.1993 - 20.11.1993)
of undefeated home matches:	26 (24.2.1968 - 29.3.1969)	of undefeated away matches:	13 (18.1.1986 - 6.9.1986)
without home win:	10 (28.2.56-15.9.56, 17.4.93-20.11.93)	without an away win:	30 (25.11.1972 - 15.4.1974)
of league wins:	8 (2.1.26-27.3.26, 12.1.86-15.3.86)	of home wins:	14 (26.8.1985 - 15.3.1986)
of league defeats:	6 (1967, 3.5.8.1980 - 6.9.1980)	of away wins:	6 (18.1.1986 - 8.3.1986.

SWINDON TOWN

PLAYERS NAME Honours	Ht	Wt	Birthdate	Birthplace Transfers	Contract Date	Clubs	League	L/Cup	FA Cup	Other	Lge	L/C	FAC	Oth
							APPEARANCES				**GOALS**			
G O A L K E E P E R S														
Digby Fraser	6.1	12.12	23/04/67	Sheffield	25/04/85	Manchester United								
E: u21.5, u19.1, Y.7, S.Div.2'96.				£32000	25/09/86	Swindon Town	348	32	19	33+1				
Mildenhall Stephen						Swindon Town (T)		2						
Talia Frank	6.1	13.6	20/07/72	Melbourne		Sunshine George								
Div.2'96.				Free	28/08/92	Blackburn Rovers								
				Loan	29/12/92	Hartlepool United	14		1					
				Loan	08/09/95	Swindon Town								
				£150000	10/11/95	Swindon Town	16							
D E F E N D E R S														
Culverhouse Ian	5.10	11.2	22/09/64	Bishop's Stort	24/09/82	Tottenham Hotspur	1+1							
E: Y.6. Div.2/1'86. Div.2'96.				£50000	08/10/85	Norwich City	295+1	23	28	22	1			
				£250000	30/12/94	Swindon Town	55	5	8	1				
Drysdale Jason	5.10	12.0	17/11/70	Bristol	08/09/88	Watford	135+10	8+1	2	4	11	2		
E: Y.5. FAYC'89. Div.2'96.			£425000		02/08/94	Newcastle United								
				£340000	23/03/95	Swindon Town	11+3		2+2					
Horlock Kevin	6.0	12.0	01/11/72	Bexley	01/07/91	West Ham United								
NI: 2, B.1. Div.2'96.				Free	27/08/92	Swindon Town	123+12	10+2	11	5+2	14	1	3	
MacLaren Ross	5.10	12.12	14/04/62	Edinburgh		Glasgow Rangers								
Div.2'87. WFAC'85.				Free	15/08/80	Shrewsbury Town	158+3	11	7+1		18	3	1	
				£67000	11/07/85	Derby County	113+9	13	9	5	4	1		
				£165000	04/08/88	Swindon Town	195+2	21	11	16	9	2		1
Murray Edwin	5.11	12.0	31/08/73	Ilford	09/07/91	Swindon Town	7+5	3	1+1	1	1			
Seagraves Mark	6.0	12.10	22/10/66	Bootle	04/11/83	Liverpool		1	1					
E: Y.4,S. Div.2'96.				Loan	21/11/86	Norwich City	3							
				£100000	25/09/87	Manchester City	36+6	3	3	2				
				£100000	24/09/90	Bolton Wanderers	152+5	8	17	13	8		1	1
				Free	01/06/95	Swindon Town	25+3	4	3+1	2				
Smith Alex P	5.7	9.00	15/02/76	Liverpool	01/08/94	Everton								
				Free	12/01/96	Swindon Town	2+6							
Taylor Shaun	6.1	12.8	26/02/63	Plymouth		Bideford								
Div.4'90. Div.2'96.				Free	10/12/86	Exeter City	200	12	9	12	17			
				£200000	26/07/91	Swindon Town	210	21	14	10	30	2		1
M I D F I E L D														
Allen Paul K	5.7	11.03	28/08/62	Aveley	29/08/79	West Ham United	149+3	20+4	15+3	2+1	6	2	3	
E: u21.3, Y.27. FAC'80'81.				£400000	19/06/85	Tottenham Hotspur	276+16	42+2	26+1	12+2	23	4	1	
UEFAY'80. CS'91. Div.2'96.				£550000	16/09/93	Southampton	40+3	4	2		1			
				Loan	23/12/94	Luton Town	4							
					20/01/95	Stoke City	17		2		1			
				Free	11/10/95	Swindon Town	25+2		5	1			1	
Collins Lee						Albion Rovers								
				£15000	15/11/95	Swindon Town	2+3		1	1				
Cowe Steve	5.7	10.2	29/09/74	Gloucester	01/08/93	Aston Villa								
				£100000	28/03/96	Swindon Town	4+7				1			
Darras Frederic						Bastia (Corsica)								
					08/08/96	Swindon Town								
Gooden Ty	5.8	12.6	23/10/72	Canvey Island		Arsenal								
Div.2'96.				Free		Wycombe Wanderers								
				Free	31/01/94	Swindon Town	29+17	2+1	3+1	3+1	5	1		
Hooper Dean	5.10	11.6	13/04/71	Harefield		Hayes								
					03/03/95	Swindon Town	0+4	0+2		2				
				Loan	15/12/95	Peterborough Utd	4							
McMahon Steve	5.9	12.1	20/08/61	Liverpool	29/08/79	Everton	99+1	11	9		11	3		
E:17,u21.6,B.2. Div.1'86'88'90. FAC'86'89.				£175000	20/05/83	Aston Villa	74+1	9	3	4	7			
CS'86'88'89.SC'86. FLgXI.1. Div.2'96.				£375000	12/09/85	Liverpool	202+2	27	30	16	29	13	7	1

	Fee	Date	Club								
McMahon continued....	£900000	24/12/91	Manchester City	77+3	7	3		1			
	Free	01/12/94	Swindon Town	36+2	4	3+1	0+1				
O'Sullivan Wayne 5.11 11.2 25/02/74		Cyprus	01/05/93	Swindon Town	48+15	9	1+2	2+2	3		1
Div.2'96.											
Robinson Mark 5.9 10.6 21/11/68		Rochdale	10/01/87	W.B.A.	2	0+1					
Div.2'96.	Free	23/06/87	Barnsley	117+20	7+2	7+1	3+2	6			1
	£450000	09/03/93	Newcastle United	14+11		1					
	£600000	22/07/94	Swindon Town	86	10	8	6+1	1			

F O R W A R D S

	Fee	Date	Club								
Allison Wayne 6.1 13.5 16/10/68		Huddersfield	06/07/87	Halifax Town	74+10	3	4+1	8+1	21	2	2	3
Div.2'96.	£250000	26/07/89	Watford	6+1							
	£300000	09/08/90	Bristol City	112+46	4+5	9+1	6+2	35	2	5	3
	£475000	22/07/95	Swindon Town	42+1	3	6	3	17	1	2	
Finney Stephen K 5.10 12.0 31/10/73		Hexham	02/05/92	Preston North End	1+5		0+1	1+1	1		
Div.2'96.	Free	12/02/93	Manchester City	1		1					
		01/08/95	Swindon Town	22+8	4	2+4	2+1	12	1	2	1
Lietch Scott			Hearts								
		28/07/96	Swindon Town								
Thorne Peter 6.0 12.3 21/06/73		Manchester	20/06/91	Blackburn Rovers							
Div.2'96.	Loan	11/03/94	Wigan Athletic	10+1							
	£200000	18/01/95	Swindon Town	42+5	3	4+2	1+1	19	2		1
Walters Mark 5.9 11.5 02/06/64		Birmingham	18/05/82	Aston Villa (A)	168+13	20+1	11+1	7+3	39	6	1	2
E: 1, B.1, u21.9, Y.10, S. FAYC'80. ESC'82.	£500000	31/12/87	Glasgow Rangers	101+5	13	14	10	32	11	6	2
SPD'89'90'91. SLC'89'91. FAC'92. LC'95.	£1250000	13/08/91	Liverpool	58+36	10+2	6+3	8+1	14	4		1
	Loan	24/03/94	Stoke City	9				2			
	Loan	09/09/94	Wolves	11				3			
	Free	18/01/96	Southampton	4+1		4					
	Free	28/07/96	Swindon Town								

THE MANAGER
STEVE MCMAHON

Date of Birth . . . . 29th August 1979.
Place of Birth . . . . Liverpool.
Date of Appointment . . . . November 1994.

PREVIOUS CLUBS
As Manager . . . . None.
As Asst.Man/Coach . . . . None.
As a player . . . . Everton, Aston Villa, Liverpool, Manchester City, Swindon.

HONOURS
As a Manager
Swindon: Division 2 Championship 1995/96.

As a Player
Liverpool: Division 1 championship 1986, 1988, 1990. FA Cup 1986, 1989.
Charity Shield 1986,1988,1989. Super Cup 1986.

COUNTY GROUND
Swindon SN1 2ED
Tel: 01793 430 430

Capacity 15,728

First game .... v Old St Stephens, 13.5.1893.
First floodlit game .... v Bristol City, 02.04.1951.

ATTENDANCES
Highest .... 32,000 v Arsenal, FA Cup, 15.1.1972. 29,106 v Watford, Division 3, 29.3.1969.
Lowest .... 1,681 v Darlington, Division 4, 17.4.1984.

OTHER GROUNDS .... Bradford's Field, Globe Field, The Croft (1884-1895)

MATCHDAY TICKET PRICES

Seats . . . . £10 - £13.50

Juv/OAP . . . . £5 - £7.50

Family package (2+2) £20
Additional child . . . . £1. (Rover Family Stand)

Ticket Office Telephone no. 01793 529 000

HOW TO GET TO THE GROUND

From all directions
Two miles towards Town Centre from M4, junction 15.

Car Parking
Town centre car parks. No off street parking.

Nearest Railway Station
Swindon (01793 536 804) 10-15 minutes walk.

CLUBCALL
0891 12 16 40
Calls cost 39p per minute cheap rate and 49p per
minute at all other times.
Call costings correct at time of going to press.

MATCHDAY PROGRAMME

Programme Editor . . . . Jason Harris.

Number of pages . . . . 48.

Price . . . . £1.50.

Subscriptions . . . . £50.

Local Newspapers . . . . . . Wiltshire Newspapers (Evening Advertiser),
. . . . Western Daily Press.

Local Radio Stations . . . . GWR, BBC Wiltshire Sound.

TRANMERE ROVERS
(The Rovers)
NATIONWIDE LEAGUE DIVISION 1
SPONSORED BY: WIRRAL BOROUGH COUNCIL

Back Row (L-R): Alan Morgan, John McGreal, Dave Challinor, Graham Branch, Jamie Jardine, Shaun Garnett, Gary Jones, Gary Bennett, Kenny Irons, John Morrissey. **Middle Row:** Norman Wilson (Club Secretary), Warwick Rimmer (Youth Dev. Officer), Kenny Jones (trainer), Alan Rogers, Dave Higgins, Jamie Hughes. Martin Jones, Eric Nixon, Danny Coyne, Nick Edwards, Ian Moore, Phil Davies, Ronnie Moore (First Team Coach), Les Parry (Physio),Ray Marthias (Reserve Team Manager), **Front Row:** Alan Mahon, Ged Brannan, Tony Thomas, Gary Stevens, Steve Mungall, John King (Manager), John Aldridge, Pat Nevin, Jon Kenworthy, Liam O'Brien, Billy Woods. (Liverpool Senior Cup)

TRANMERE ROVERS
FORMED IN 1885
TURNED PROFESSIONAL IN 1912
LTD COMPANY IN 1912

PRESIDENT: H B Thomas
CHAIRMAN: Frank Corfe
DIRECTORS
F Williams, A J Adams,
J Holsgrove, H Jones, C N Wilson
SECRETARY
Norman Wilson (0151 608 4194)
COMMERCIAL MANAGER
Janet Ratcliffe (0151 608 0371)

DIRECTOR OF FOOTBALL: John King
PLAYER/MANAGER: John Aldridge
COACH: Steve Mungall

RESERVE TEAM MANAGER
Ray Mathias
YOUTH DEVELOPMENT OFFICER
Warwick Rimmer
PHYSIOTHERAPIST
Les Parry

STATISTICIAN FOR THE DIRECTORY
Peter Bishop

For once the chairman, manager and supporters were in unison, and Tranmere had their strongest squad of players ever - yet in the end Rovers only just escaped relegation! Pre-season had seen Shaun Teale arrive for a club record £450,000, along with the nation's top goalscorer Gary Bennett of Wrexham at £300,000 and Irish hopeful Billy Woods for £40,000, while Chris Malkin and Ian Muir left for pastures new.

The fourth challenge, as it was dubbed, was beginning to look a distinct possibility in November, but then for some reason, Rovers began free-falling towards the relegation zone and only recovered to finish 13th when John King was relieved of his duties and replaced with John Aldridge on 12 April.

Injuries certainly played a part with the likes of Teale, McGreal and O'Brien out for long spells, however, it was a collective loss of form and confidence which did the real damage and cost John King the role he had enjoyed for almost 9 years.

Despite the gloom, there were positive points in the season. John Aldridge, now installed as player-manager, was once again the Division's leading marksman with 29 goals; Ian Moore emerged as a striker of genuine class - a fact recognised by England who gave him his first U21 cap; goalkeeper Danny Coyne - having displaced Eric Nixon as the club's regular number one - gained his first full Welsh Cap; and youngsters like Alan Rogers and Alan Mahon emerged from the Youth Scheme to show great promise. In a bid to boost flagging attendances, the club introduced several innovative ideas including 'Ladies' and 'Schools' days and family fun nights which are now being copied by other clubs.

Rovers FA Cup run ended after just 90 minutes when QPR - later to be relegated - proved there is still a gap between the Premiership and the First Division, while Birmingham City ended their interest in the Coca-Cola Cup in the 3rd round.

There is, however, renewed optimism following Aldridge's elevation to the hot seat, and a belief that he may be able to get the best out of the resources available - though with the club deeply in debt, he will have to follow Peter Reid's example and do it on a shoestring budget.

John King, meanwhile, has moved upstairs into a 'Director of Football' role a la Kenny Dalglish.

PETER BISHOP

TRANMERE ROVERS

League: 13th   FA Cup: 3rd Rnd   Coca-Cola Cup: 3rd Rnd

M	DATE	COMP	VEN	OPPONENTS	RESULT	HT	LP	GOAL SCORERS/GOAL TIMES	ATT.
1	A 12	EL	H	Wolverhampton Wand	D 2-2	0-1	11	O'Brien 51, Aldridge 81	11880
2	19	EL	A	Sheffield United	W 2-0	1-0	4	Aldridge 42, 87	(11247)
3	26	EL	H	Huddersfield Town	W 3-1	0-0	2	O'Brien 73, Aldridge 78, Moore 86	9072
4	29	EL	A	Barnsley	L 1-2	1-2	4	Aldridge 58	(9710)
5	S 9	EL	H	Charlton Athletic	D 0-0	0-0	14		7402
6	12	EL	H	West Bromwich Albion	D 2-2	1-0	11	Bennett 18, Aldridge 68	7196
7	16	EL	A	Stoke City	D 0-0	0-0	13		(8618)
8	19	CC 2/1	H	Oldham Athletic	W 1-0	0-0		Aldridge 50	5223
9	23	EL	A	Portsmouth	W 2-0	0-0	10	Nevin 57, Bennett 62	(11127)
10	30	EL	H	Watford	L 2-3	1-1		Bennett 28, Aldridge 74	7041
11	O 4	CC 2/2	A	Oldham Athletic	W 3-1	1-1		Jones 13, 78, Brannan 53	(5335)
12	7	EL	H	Luton Town	W 1-0	1-0	10	Aldridge 4	6680
13	14	EL	A	Millwall	D 2-2	0-0	10	Moore 57, Bennett 89(pen)	(9293)
14	21	EL	H	Southend United	W 3-0	1-0	7	Moore 42, 90, Bennett 79	6584
15	24	CC 3	H	Birmingham City	D 1-1	0-1		Moore 75	(13752)
16	29	EL	A	Norwich City	D 1-1	0-1	7	Moore 46	(15513)
17	N 4	EL	H	Derby County	W 5-1	3-0	4	Nevin 13, Moore 24, Aldridge 31, 87, Bennett 80	8565
18	8	CC 3R	H	Birmingham City	L 1-3	0-0		Aldridge 90	9151
19	19	EL	A	Leicester City	W 1-0	0-0	5	Moore 66	(13125)
20	22	EL	H	Port Vale	W 2-1	1-0	5	Aldridge 31, 79	6681
21	25	EL	A	Grimsby Town	L 0-1	0-1	7		7500
22	D 2	EL	A	Luton Town	L 2-3	1-1	10	Bennett 2, Jones 52	(6025)
23	9	EL	H	Portsmouth	L 1-2	0-2	11	Moore 80	6678
24	16	EL	A	Watford	L 0-3	0-0	13		(7257)
25	23	EL	A	Birmingham City	L 0-1	0-0	14		(18439)
26	26	EL	H	Oldham Athletic	W 2-0	0-0	12	Aldridge 67, 71	9787
27	J 1	EL	A	Reading	L 0-1	0-0	14		(8421)
28	6	FAC 3	H	Queens Park Rangers	L 0-2	0-0			10230
29	13	EL	H	Sheffield United	D 1-1	0-0	14	Moore 85	7321
30	20	EL	A	Wolverhampton Wand	L 1-2	0-1	14	Aldridge 55	(24173)
31	30	EL	A	Sunderland	D 0-0	0-0	14		(17616)
32	F 3	EL	A	Huddersfield Town	L 0-1	0-0	14		(12041)
33	10	EL	H	Barnsley	L 1-3	0-0	17	Aldridge 76	6376
34	17	EL	A	West Bromwich Albion	D 1-1	0-1	16	Branch 57	(15014)
35	20	EL	H	Crystal Palace	L 2-3	2-0	16	Bennett 13, Aldridge 25	5253
36	24	EL	A	Stoke City	D 0-0	0-0	17		8312
37	M 3	EL	A	Oldham Athletic	W 2-1	1-0	15	Nevin 19, Aldridge 52	(4225)
38	9	EL	H	Birmingham City	D 2-2	1-1	16	Aldridge 40, Rogers 70	8696
39	12	EL	A	Crystal Palace	L 1-2	1-1	17	Branch 40	(13183)
40	16	EL	A	Ipswich Town	W 2-1	0-1	16	Aldridge 83, Bennett 84	(11759)
41	23	EL	H	Reading	W 2-1	1-1	14	Aldridge 23, Hopkins 61(og)	6249
42	30	EL	A	Southend United	L 0-2	0-0	16		(4738)
43	A 2	EL	H	Millwall	D 2-2	0-1	15	Rogers 47, Aldridge 59(pen)	5850
44	6	EL	H	Norwich City	D 1-1	0-1	17	Aldridge 60	6613
45	8	EL	A	Derby County	L 2-6	1-1	17	Cook 6, Aldridge 82(pen)	(16723)
46	13	EL	H	Leicester City	D 1-1	0-1	19	Lennon 61(og)	8882
47	17	EL	H	Ipswich Town	W 5-2	1-1	16	O'Brien 29, Irons 61, 63, Aldridge 81, Morgan 88	6008
48	20	EL	A	Port Vale	D 1-1	0-0	15	O'Brien 70	(7419)
49	27	EL	A	Grimsby Town	D 1-1	0-1	15	Aldridge 47	(5408)
50	30	EL	A	Charlton Athletic	D 0-0	0-0	15		(10936)
51	M 5	EL	H	Sunderland	W 2-0	1-0	13	Irons 38, Aldridge 58(pen)	16193

Best Home League Attendance: 16193 v Sunderland   Smallest: 5253 v Crystal Palace   Average: 7861

Goal Scorers:
EL(64):   Aldridge(27),Moore(9),Bennett(9),O'Brien(4),Nevin(3),Irons(3),Rogers(2),Opponent(s)(2),Branch(2),Cook(1),Morgan(1),Jones(1)
CC(6):   Jones(2),Aldridge(2),Moore(1),Brannan(1)
FAC(0):

(F) Aldridge	(F) Bennett	(F) Branch	(D) Brannan	(M) Cook	(G) Coyne	(D) Garnett	(D) Higgins	(M) Irons	(F) Jones	(G) Jones	(F) Kenworthy	(M) Mahon	(D) McGreal	(F) Moore	(M) Morgan	(F) Morrissey	(D) Mungall	(F) Nevin	(G) Nixon	(M) O'Brien	(D) Rogers	(M) Scott	(D) Stevens	(D) Teale	(D) Thomas	(M) Woods		
X	X		X		X	X2		X					X	S2			S1	X	S	X		X1	X				I.Cruikshanks	1
X	X		X		X	X		X	S				X	S				X	S	X			X	X			B.Burns	2
X	X		X		X	X		X1	S				X	S1				X	S	X			X	X			E.Wolfenholme	3
X	X		X		X	X		X					X	S				X		X			X	X			K.Leach	4
X	X		X		X			X					X	S	X1			X	S	X		S1	X	X			J.Brandwood	5
X	X		X		X			S					X	S	X			X	S	X		X	X	X			E.Lomas	6
X	X		X		X			X	S1				X	S2				X		X2		X1	X	X			S.Mathieson	7
X	X		X		X			X	S				X	S1	X1			X	S			X	X	X			D.B.Allison	8
X2	X		X		X	X1		X	X			S2	X	S1				X	S			X	X	X			D.Orr	9
X	X		X		X			X		X		S2	X	S1				X2	S			X1	X	X			A. Butler	10
	X	S	X		X	X		X		X	X	S	X	X				S				X	X	X			C.R.Wilks	11
X	X1		X		X			X	X				X	S1		S		X	S			X	X	X			P.Richards	12
X1	X	S1	X		X				X				X	X				X	S			X	X	X			R.Harris	13
X	X	S	X		X	S							X	X				X	S			X	X	X			J.Kirkby	14
X	X1	S1	X		X	S			X				X	X				X				X	X	X			T.Heilbron	15
X	X	S	X		X	S			X				X	X				X	S			X	X	X			G.Singh	16
X	X	S	X		X				X				X	X				X	S		S	X	X	X			T.West	17
X	X1	S1	X		X	S			X				X	X				X	S			X	X	X			K.Lynch	18
X	X	S1	X		X				X				X	X1				X				X	X	X			M.Bailey	19
X	X	S	X		X	X		S1	X				X	X				X	S			X1	X	X			M.Riley	20
X	X	S2	X		X	X		X1	X				X					X2	S		S1		X	X			G.Frankland	21
X	X2	S2	X		X	X1			X				X					X		S1	X		X	X			K.Leach	22
	X	X2	X		X		X		X1				X		S2			X	S	S1	X		X	X			M.Fletcher	23
X	X		X		X		X	S2	X				X1					X2	S1		S1			X	X			A.Wiley	24
X	X		X		X	X			X				X			S	X	S	S	S				X			S.Mathieson	25
X	X1		X		X	X			X				X		S1		X	S	S	S				X			R.Poulain	26
X	X		X		X	X			X				X		S1		X1	S	S					X			C.Wilkes	27
X	S		X		X				X		X		X	X		X	S	X	S	S				X			J.Winter	28
X		X2	X		X			X1	S1				X	X			S2	S	X	X				X			W.Burns	29
X		S1	X		X	X	X1	S					X	X				X	S	X	X			X			M.Pierce	30
X		S2	X		X	X							X	X			S1	X2	S	X1		X	X				E.K.Wolstenholme	31
X		S2	X		X	X	X					S1	X	X	S		X1	X	X2			X	X				R.Furnandiz	32
X		S3	X		X	X	X2					S2	X	X		S1	X	X3				X	X	X1			R.Harris	33
X	X		X		X	S1	X	X				S	X1				S				X	X	X					A.Leake	34
X	X	X1	X		X		X		S				S			S1	S			X	X	X					P.Richards	35
X	X3		X		X	X2		X	S1							S3	S2			X1	X	X	X				D.Allison	36
X	S2	X2	X	X1	X	X	S3	S1					X					X			X3	X		X			G.B.Frankland	37
X	S	X2	X	X	X	X	S1						X				S2			X	X1						M.Riley	38
X	S1	X1	X	X	X			S	S				X					X			X	X	X	X			I.Hemley	39
X	S1	X1	X	X	X			S2	S				X					X2			X	X	X	X			S.J.Baines	40
X	S		X	X	X			S2					X	X		S1		X2			X	X	X	X1			I.Cruikshanks	41
X		S1	X	X	X			S	X1	S			X	X				X			X	X	X				D.Orr	42
X		X2	X	X1	X			S1	S2				X	X				X			X	X	X		S		S.Mathieson	43
X		S1	X	X	X			X1	S				X	X	S			X			X	X	X				T.Heilbron	44
X		X1	X	X	X			S			S1		X	X				X			X	X	X				T.West	45
X2		X	X	X	X			X	X2	S2		S1	X				X1	X			S2	X	X				R.Harris	46
X		X	X	X	X			X	S				X		S2	X1		S1			X	X2	X				J.A.Kirkby	47
X2		X	X	X	X			X	X1	S2			X				S1	X			X		X	S			G.Barber	48
X2		X	X	X	X			X	X				X	S2	S1	X		X1			X	X1	X	S			A.N.Butler	49
X2		X	X	X	X			X	X				X	S2	S1	X		X			X1	X	X				M.Bailey	50
X		X	X	X	X			X	X1				X	S1	S	X		S			X	X	X				J.Lloyd	51
45	26	11	44	15	46	17	16	25	15	1	0	0	32	27	0	8	2	39	0	18	25	33	29	31	0		EL Appearances	
0	3	10	0	0	0	1	1	7	6	0	4	2	0	9	4	8	4	1	0	4	1	1	0	0	0		EL Sub Appearances	
3	4	0+2	4	0	4	1	0	2	2	1	0	0	4	3+1	0	1	0	3	0	0	0	4	4	4	0		CC Appearances	
1	0	0	1	0	1	1	0	0	1	0	0	0	0	1	1	0	1	0	1	0	0+1	0	0	1	0		FAC Appearances	

TRANMERE ROVERS

CLUB RECORDS

BIGGEST VICTORIES
League: 11-1 v Durham City, Div 3N, 7.1.1928
13-4 v Oldham, Div 3N, 26.12.1935
F.A. Cup: 13-0 v Oswestry, 10.10.1914
League Cup: 5-1 v Oxford Utd, Rnd 2, 21.9.1993

BIGGEST DEFEATS
League: 2-9 v Q.P.R., Div 3, 3.12.1960
0-8 v Grimsby Town, Div 3N, 14.9.1925
0-8 v Bradford City, Div 3N, 6.3.1929
0-8 v Lincoln City, Div 3N, 21.4.1930
0-8 v Bury, Div 3, 10.1.1970
F.A. Cup: 1-9 v Tottenham, Rnd 3 replay, 14.1.1953
League Cup: 0-6 v Q.P.R., Rnd 3, 23.9.1969
0-6 v West Ham Utd, Rnd 2, 11.9.1974

MOST POINTS
3 points a win: 80, Division 4, 1988-89, Div 3, 1989-90
2 points a win: 60, Division 4, 1964-65

MOST GOALS
111, Division 3N, 1930-31
J Kennedy 34, Dixon 32, Watts 27, Meston 8, Urmson 7, Barton 1,
Lewis 1, og 1

MOST LEAGUE GOALS CONCEDED
115, Division 3, 1960-61

MOST FIRST CLASS MATCHES IN A SEASON
65 (46 League, 1 FA Cup, 7 League Cup, 8 Leyland Daf, 3 Play-
Offs) 1989-90

MOST LEAGUE WINS
27, Division 4, 1964-65

MOST LEAGUE DRAWS
22, Division 3, 1970-71

MOST LEAGUE DEFEATS
31, Division 2, 1938-39

INDIVIDUAL CLUB RECORDS

MOST GOALS IN A MATCH
9. Robert `Bunny' Bell v Oldham Athletic, 26.12.1935

MOST GOALS IN A SEASON
Robert `Bunny' Bell 40 (League 35, FA Cup 5,) 1933-34
4 goals twice=8; 3 goals 4 times=12; 1 goal 12 times=12. Total 40
John Aldridge 40 (League 22, Lge Cup 8, FA Cup 3, AMC 7) 1991-92
3 goals 4 times=12; 2 goals 5 times=10, 1 goal 18 times=18. Total 40

OLDEST PLAYER
George Payne, 39 years 202 days, Div 3, 11.3.1961

YOUNGEST PLAYER
William `Dixie' Dean, 16 years 355 days, Div 3N, 12.1.1924

MOST CAPPED PLAYER
John Aldridge (Eire) 28

BEST PERFORMANCES

League: 1992-93: Matches Played 46, Won 23, Drawn 10, Lost 13,
Goals for 72,Goals against 56, Points 79.
Fourth in Division 1

Highest: 4th Division 1, 1992-93

F.A. Cup: 1967-68: 1st rnd. Rochdale (h) 5-1; 2nd rnd. Bradford P.A.
(a) 3-2;3rd rnd. Huddersfield (h) 2-1; 4th rnd. Coventry City 1-1, 2-0;
5th rnd.Everton (a) 0-2

League Cup: 1993-94: 2nd Rnd. Oxford United 5-1,1-1; 3rd Rnd.
Grimsby 4-1; 4th Rnd. Oldham Ath. 3-0; 5th Rnd. Nottingham F. 1-
1,2-0; Semi-Final Aston Villa 3-1,1-3 (lost 5-4 on pens).

DIVISIONAL RECORD

	Played	Won	Drawn	Lost	For	Against	Points
Division 2/1	272	100	70	102	367	382	364
Division 3	736	242	213	281	980	1,028	743
Division 3(N)	1,240	506	255	479	2,073	1,987	1,267
Division 4	780	318	185	277	1,179	1,057	955
Total	3,028	1,166	723	1,139	4,599	4,454	3,329

ADDITIONAL INFORMATION
Previous Name
Belmont 1884-85

Previous League
Central League 1919-21

Club colours: All white with green & blue trim.
Change colours: Old gold & black stripes, black shorts and socks.

Reserves League: Pontins Central League Division 1.
Youth League: Lancashire League Divisions 1 & 2.

RECORDS AND STATISTICS

COMPETITIONS

DIV.2/1	DIV.3(N)	DIV.3	DIV.4
1938-39	1921-38	1958-61	1961-67
1991-	1939-58	1967-75	1975-76
		1976-79	1979-89
		1989-91	

HONOURS

DIVISION 3(N)	LEYLAND DAF	WELSH CUP
1937-38	1990	1934-35

MOST APPEARANCES

RAY MATHIAS 626+11 (1967-84)

YEAR	LEAGUE	FA CUP	LGE CUP
1967-68	13		
1968-69	26	1	5
1969-70	20+4		
1970-71	46	3	3
1971-72	46	7	3
1972-73	45	2	1
1973-74	38+1	2	3
1974-75	40	1	3
1975-76	46	1	2
1976-77	46	1	3
1977-78	46	2	2
1978-79	45	3	2
1979-80	38+4	3	4
1980-81	37	3	4
1981-82	1		1
1982-83	16		3
1983-84	6+1	1	
1984-85	2		
	557+10	29+1	40

MOST GOALS IN A CAREER

IAN MUIR -180 (1985-95)

YEAR	LEAGUE	FA CUP	LGE CUP	OTHERS
1985-86	14	1		
1986-87	20	3		2
1987-88	27	2		
1988-89	21	5	2	1
1989-90	23		4	8
1990-91	13			8
1991-92	5			
1992-93	2			
1993-94	9			
1994-95	7	3		
Total	141	14	6	19

Current leading goalscorer: John Aldridge - 149 (1991-96)

RECORD TRANSFER FEE RECEIVED

AMOUNT	CLUB	PLAYER	DATE
£1,500,000	Sheffield Wed.	Ian Nolan	08/94
£750,000	Middlesbrough	Steve Vickers	11/93
£120,000	Cardiff City	Ronnie Moore	2/79
£60,000	Manchester Utd	Steve Coppell	3/75

RECORD TRANSFER FEE PAID

AMOUNT	CLUB	PLAYER	DATE
£500,000	Aston Villa	Shaun Teale	8/95
£350,000	Glasgow Rangers	Gary Stevens	10/94
£350,000	Glasgow Celtic	Tommy Coyne	3/93
£300,000	Everton	Pat Nevin	8/92

MANAGERS

NAME	SEASONS	BEST	WORST
Bert Cooke	1912-35	4(3N)	21(3N)
Jack Carr	1935-36	3(3N)	3(3N)
Jim Knowles	1936-39	22(2)	19(3N)
Bill Ridding	1939-45		
Ernie Blackburn	1946-55	4(3N)	19(3N)
Noel Kelly	1955-57	16(3N)	23(3N)
Peter Farrall	1957-60	7(3)	20(3)
Walter Galbraith	1961	21(3)	21(3)
Dave Russell	1961-69	7(3)	15(4)
Jackie Wright	1969-72	16(3)	20(3)
Ron Yeats	1972-75	10(3)	22(3)
John King	1975-80	12(3)	15(4)
Bryan Hamilton	1980-85	6(4)	21(4)
Frank Worthington	1985-87	19(4)	20(4)
Ronnie Moore	1987		
John King	1987-96	4(2/1)	20(4)
John Aldridge	1996-	13(2/1)	

LONGEST LEAGUE RUNS

of undefeated matches:	18 (16.3.1970 - 4.9.1970)	of league matches w/out a win:	15 (19.2.1979 - 18.4.1979)
of undefeated home matches:	26 (24.10.1988 - 10.11.1989)	of undefeated away matches:	10 (27.12.1983 - 21.4.1984)
without home win:	11 (19.2.1979 - 9.5.1979)	without an away win:	35 (19.11.1977 - 14.4.1979)
of league wins:	9 (9.2.1990 - 19.3.1990)	of home wins:	18 (22.8.1964 - 28.3.1965)
of league defeats:	8 (29.10.1938 - 17.12.1938)	of away wins:	4 (17.2.1990 - 17.3.1990)

TRANMERE ROVERS

PLAYERS NAME / Honours	Ht	Wt	Birthdate	Birthplace / Transfers	Contract Date	Clubs	League	L/Cup	FA Cup	Other	Lge	L/C	FAC	Oth
						APPEARANCES					GOALS			
GOALKEEPERS														
Coyne Daniel	6.0	12.7	27/08/73	Prestatyn	08/05/92	Tranmere Rovers	56+1	4	1	2				
W: full, u21.2, S, Y														
Jones Martin	6.1	12.0	27/03/75	Liverpool	14/07/93	Tranmere Rovers	1	1		0+1	2			
				Loan	04/09/95	Altrincham								
Nixon Eric	6.4	14.3	04/10/62	Manchester		Cuzon Ashton								
LDC'90				£1000	10/12/83	Manchester City	58	8	10	8				
				Loan	29/08/86	Wolves	16							
				Loan	28/11/86	Bradford City	3							
				Loan	23/12/86	Southampton	4							
				Loan	23/01/87	Carlisle United	18							
				£60000	24/03/88	Tranmere Rovers	316	34	18	45+1				
				Loan	09/01/96	Reading		1						
				Loan	05/02/96	Blackpool	20			2				
DEFENDERS														
Brannan Gerald	6.0	13.3	15/01/72	Prescot	03/07/90	Tranmere Rovers	196+8	23	9+1	26+1	14	4		1
Challinor David	6.1	12.0	02/10/75	Chester	18/07/94	Tranmere Rovers								
Higgins Dave	6.0	11.0	19/08/61	Liverpool		Eagle								
				Free	22/08/83	Tranmere Rovers	27+1		2	5				
				Free	01/03/85	South Liverpool			1					
				Free	01/08/86	Carnarfon								
				Free	20/07/87	Tranmere Rovers	294+3	25	17	34	10			
McGreal John	5.11	10.11	02/08/72	Liverpool	30/07/90	Tranmere Rovers	91+2	9	3	5+1	1			
Mungall Steve	5.8	11.5	22/05/58	Bellshill		Motherwell	14+6	11+2						
LDC'90				Free	03/07/79	Tranmere Rovers	478+34	32+3	30+1	43+2	14	2	1	
Rogers Alan	5.10	11.8	03/01/77	Liverpool	01/07/95	Tranmere Rovers	25+1		1		2			
Stevens Michael Gary	5.11	10.12	27/03/63	Barrow-in-Furness		Everton	207+1	30	39	10	9	1	3	
E: 46, B.1, u21.1. Div1'85'87.				£1000000	19/07/88	Glasgow Rangers	186+1	22	22	14	8		1	
FAC'84, CS'84'85. ECWC'85				£350000	14/10/94	Tranmere Rovers	70+1	7	3	4	1			
Teale Shaun	6.0	13.7	10/03/64	Southport		Weymouth								
E: SP.1. LC'94				£50000	22/01/89	Bournemouth	99+1	8	5	3	4		1	
				£300000	25/07/91	Aston Villa	118+11	13	11	6	2	3		
				£500000	14/08/95	Tranmere Rovers	29	4						
Thomas Tony	5.11	12.5	12/07/71	Liverpool	01/02/89	Tranmere Rovers	226+1	22+1	6	26	12	1		1
LDC'90														
MIDFIELD														
Cook Paul	5.11	10.10	22/02/67	Liverpool		Marine								
					20/07/84	Wigan Athletic	77+6	4	6+1	5+1	14			1
				£73000	23/05/88	Norwich City	3+3			1+1				
				£250000	01/11/89	Wolves	191+2	7	5+2	6+1	19	1		1
				£500000	18/08/94	Coventry City	35+2	3	3		3			
				£250000	29/03/96	Tranmere Rovers	15				1			
Irons Kenneth	5.9	11.0	04/11/70	Liverpool	09/11/89	Tranmere Rovers	200+24	15+3	11+1	28+3	30	4	3	3
Mahon Alan	5.10	11.5		Dublin	19/04/95	Tranmere Rovers	0+2							
Ei: S														
Morgan Alan	5.10	11.0	02/11/73	Aberystwyth	08/05/92	Tranmere Rovers	0+4				1			
O'Brien Liam	6.1	11.10	05/09/64	Dublin		Shamrock Rovers								
Ei: 11, Y. Ei Lge'84'85'86.				£60000	14/10/86	Manchester United	16+15	1+2	0+2		2			
Ei Cup'85'86. Div1'93				£250000	15/11/88	Newcastle United	131+20	9	12+2	9+2	19	1	1	1
				£300000	21/01/94	Tranmere Rovers	73+4	7	3+1	5+1	6		1	
Woods Billy	6.0	12.0	24/10/73	Cork		Cork City								
Ei: u21				£50000	10/07/95	Tranmere Rovers								

Player				Birthplace	Fee	Date	Club	App				Gls			
ldridge John	5.11	12.1	18/09/58	Liverpool			South Liverpool								
.63. Div1'88. Div2'85. LC'86					£3500	02/05/79	Newport County	159+11	11	12+1	4	69	5	7	2
FAC'80. CS'88, FAC'89			£78000			21/03/84	Oxford United	111+3	17	5	5	72	14		2
					£750000	27/01/87	Liverpool	69+14	7+1	12	1	50	3	8	2
					£1100000	01/09/89	Real Sociedad								
					£250000	11/07/91	Tranmere Rovers	182+3	21	7+1	18	115	20	4	10
ranch Graham	6.2	13.0	12/02/72	Liverpool			Heswell								
					Free	02/07/91	Tranmere Rovers	17+25	0+4	0+1	2+1	2			
					Loan	20/11/92	Bury	3+1			1	1			
ones Gary S	6.3	14.0	11/05/75	Chester		05/07/93	Tranmere Rovers	17+10	2	1		3			
enworthy Jonathan R	5.7	10.6	18/08/74	St Asaph		14/07/93	Tranmere Rovers	14+12	3		1+2	2			
u21.3, Y					Loan	08/12/95	Chester City	5+2				1			
oore Ian	5.11	12.0	26/08/76	Liverpool		06/07/94	Tranmere Rovers	27+9	3+1	1		9	1		
u21, Y															
orrissey John	5.8	11.9	08/03/65	Liverpool		10/03/83	Everton	1			0+1				
Y.2					Free	02/08/85	Wolves	5+5	1			1			
					£8000	02/10/85	Tranmere Rovers	343+35	30+2	26+1	39+3	47		5	6
evin Pat	5.6	11.9	06/09/63	Glasgow			Clydebank	60+13	5+3	10		17		3	
22. B.3, u21.5, Y. SDiv2'82					£95000	14/07/83	Chelsea	190+3	25+1	8+1	13	36	5	1	4
v2'84. FMC'86.					£925000	13/07/88	Everton	81+28	10+1	12+6	9+3	16	2	2	1
					Loan	04/03/92	Tranmere Rovers	8							
					£300000	18/08/92	Tranmere Rovers	171+1	16	7	14	28	5	2	2
DDITIONAL CONTRACT PLAYERS															
awford Keith							Tranmere Rov. (T)								
rdine Jamie							Tranmere Rov. (T)								
					Loan	21/08/95	Chorley								
nes Paul N							Tranmere Rov. (T)								
ott Gary C							Tranmere Rov. (T)								

THE MANAGER
JOHN ALDRIDGE

Date of Birth . . . . 18th September 1958.
Place of Birth . . . . Liverpool.
Date of Appointment . . . . March 1996.

PREVIOUS CLUBS
As Manager . . . . None.
As Coach . . . . None.
As a Player . . . . Newport Co., Oxford Utd, Liverpool, Real Sociedad.

HONOURS
As a Manager
None.

As a Player
Newport County: Welsh FA Cup 1980.
Oxford United: League Div.2 1985. League Cup 1986.
Liverpool: League Div.1 1988. CS 1988. FA Cup 1989.
Eire: 28 full caps.

Prenton Park
Prenton Road West, Birkenhead,
Merseyside L42 9PN
Tel: 0151 608 4194

Capacity 16,789

First game ....v Lancaster, 8-0, 9.3.1912.
First floodlit game ....v Rochdale, 2-1, 29.9.1958.

ATTENDANCES
Highest ....24,424 v Stoke City, FAC 4th Rnd, 5.2.1972.
Lowest ....937 v Halifax, AMC, 20.2.1984.

OTHER GROUNDS ..Steeles Field 1884-87. Ravenshaws Field (later renamed Prenton Park) 1887-1912.

MATCHDAY TICKET PRICES

Main Stand . . . . £11.50\£10.00.
Juniors/OAP . . . . £6.50/£8

Cow Shed, Borough Rd, Kop Stand £10
Juniors/OAP . . . . £5/£7

Family Area Seating . . . . Members Only

Ticket Office Telephone no. 0151 609 0137

HOW TO GET TO THE GROUND

From the North
Use Mersey Tunnel and motorway M53 until junction 3. Leave motorway and at roundabout take 1st exit (A552). In 1.3 miles at Half-way House crossroads turn right (B5151) then turn left into Prenton Road West for Tranmere Rovers FC.

From the South
Use motorway M53 until junction 4, leave motorway and at roundabout take 4th exit B5151. In 2.5 miles turn right into Prenton Road West for Tranmere Rovers FC.
Away supporters should use the Kop end of the ground. Entrance from main car park.

Car Parking
No car parking available at ground on match days, except for visiting coaches. Car park tickets cost £50 for season.

Nearest Railway Station
Hamilton Square, Rock Ferry (1 mile).
Liverpool Lime Street (Main Line).

CLUBCALL
0891 12 16 46
Calls cost 39p per minute cheap rate and 49p per minute at all other times.
Call costings correct at time of going to press.

MATCHDAY PROGRAMME

Programme Editor. . . . . Peter Bishop.

Number of pages . . . . 40.

Price . . . . £1.50.

Subscriptions. . . . . Details available from Club.

Local Newspapers. . . . . Liverpool Daily Post & Echo, Wirral News, ... Wirral Globe.

Local Radio Stations. BBC Radio Merseyside, ... City Gold and City FM (Radio City), MFM (Marcher Sound).

WEST BROMWICH ALBION
(The Throstles, 'Baggies' or 'Albion')
NATIONWIDE LEAGUE DIVISION 1
SPONSORED BY: GUEST MOTORS

Back Row (L-R): Tony Brien, Daryl Burgess, Andy Hunt, Paul Raven, Bob Taylor, Mike Phelan, Paul Agnew. **Middle Row:** Richard O'Kelly (th Coach), Paul Michell (Physio), Ian Hamilton, Stuart Naylor, Gary Germaine, Chris Hargreaves, Ronnie Allen (Coach), John Trewick Res. Coach). **Front Row:** Tony Rees, Stacy Coldicott, Lee Ashcroft, Arthur Mann (Asst. Manager), Paul Mardon, Alan Buckley (Manager), aul Edwards, Kevin Donovan, David Smith.

WEST BROMWICH ALBION
FORMED IN 1878-79
TURNED PROFESSIONAL IN 1885
LTD COMPANY IN 1891

PRESIDENT: Sir F A Millichip
VICE-PRESIDENT: J Silk
CHAIRMAN: A B Hale
DIRECTORS
J W Brandrick, T Guy, B Hurst,
C M Stapleton, P Thompson
SECRETARY
Dr. John Evans (0121 525 8888)
COMMERCIAL EXECUTIVE
Tom Cardall

MANAGER: Alan Buckley
ASSISTANT MANAGER: Arthur Mann

RESERVE TEAM MANAGER
Richard O'Kelly
YOUTH TEAM MANAGER
John Trewick
PHYSIOTHERAPIST
Paul Mitchell
HAWTHORNS CURATOR &
STATISTICIAN FOR THE DIRECTORY
Tony Matthews

What an extraordinary season this was for Albion. Not many clubs can say they have been second and 23rd in the same division in the same campaign! That's precisely what happened to Albion - at one stage in early January they looked doomed to relegation after a run of 11 straight defeats (a club record).

Albion started off the season very well, with new signing Dave Gilbert (from Grimsby Town), striker Bob Taylor and defenders Paul Mardon and Paul Raven all in fine form. By the end of October, with 13 league games played, they found themselves in second place with the opportunity of going top if they won at Millwall. Sadly, they were beaten 2-1 at the New Den and this reverse set the Baggies on an astonishing run of successive league defeats, only one win being achieved in fifteen games. However, manager Alan Buckley didn't panic and with the supporters still behind the team despite an early FA Cup exit at Crewe, Albion slowly but surely picked themselves up, beginning to produce the type of sweet-flowing, attacking football they had displayed earlier in the season. And with more new recruits - Nigel Spink (signed at the age of 37 from Aston Villa), full-backs Paul Holmes and Shane Nicholson, on-loan midfielder Paul Butler and the flying Dutchman Richard Sneekes who cost £400,000 from Bolton Wanderers - Albion started to climb the table. They almost reached Wembley, but were ousted in the English Final of the Anglo-Italian Cup by Port Vale. Amazingly, from their last 13 league games - when the new Hawthorns cult hero Sneekes was in the line-up - Albion suffered only one defeat, a 2-0 home reverse against relegated Luton. They amassed 24 out of a possible 39 points and finished 11th in the table.

It was a season split into three - each period being totally different in terms of performances. T Taylor, who was skipper during the second half of the campaign, top-scored with 23 goals, netting his 100th for Albion in the last-day win over promoted Derby-County. Sneekes scored 10 in 13 outings, while Messrs Mardon and Raven, along with Daryl Burgess, were outstanding in defence. Albion's average gate was over 15,000 and with a new share issue being introduced to supporters, along with a £2.5 million investment into the club by newly-appointed director Paul Thompson, the future certainly looks much brighter for a revitalised Albion side who could be one of the stronger sides in the division in 1996/7.

TONY MATTHEWS

WEST BROMWICH ALBION

League: 11th   FA Cup: 3rd Rnd   Coca-Cola Cup: 2nd Rnd

M	DATE	COMP	VEN	OPPONENTS	RESULT	HT	LP	GOAL SCORERS/GOAL TIMES	ATT.
1	A 12	EL	H	Charlton Athletic	W 1-0	0-0	10	Gilbert 65	14688
2	15	CC 1/1	H	Northampton Town	D 1-1	1-0		Taylor 41	6489
3	20	EL	A	Wolverhampton Wand	D 1-1	0-0	9	Taylor 46	(26329)
4	22	CC 1/2	A	Northampton Town	W 4-2	1-0		Taylor 45, 72, Donovan 55, Hunt 70	(7083)
5	26	EL	H	Ipswich Town	D 0-0	0-0	9		14470
6	29	EL	A	Southend United	L 1-2	1-1	11	Raven 42	(4628)
7	S 2	EL	H	Sheffield United	W 3-1	2-0	9	Burgess 12, Hamilton 23, Hunt 88	14377
8	5	AIC	A	Salernitana	D 0-0	0-0			(3000)
9	9	EL	A	Oldham Athletic	W 2-1	1-1	4	Taylor 11, Gilbert 54	(8397)
10	12	EL	A	Tranmere Rovers	D 2-2	0-1	6	Hunt 46, Ashcroft 87(pen)	(7196)
11	17	EL	H	Birmingham City	W 1-0	1-0	4	Hunt 29	18875
12	20	CC 2/1	A	Reading	D 1-1	0-0		Burgess 70	(6948)
13	24	EL	A	Stoke City	L 1-2	0-1	6	Hunt 62(pen)	(9612)
14	30	EL	H	Huddersfield Town	L 1-2	1-2	9	Taylor 46	15945
15	O 3	CC 2/2	H	Reading	L 2-4	1-1		Burgess 44, Donovan 72	8165
16	7	EL	H	Reading	W 2-0	0-0	6	Gilbert 59, Taylor 65	12956
17	11	AIC	H	Foggia	L 1-2	1-1		Herbert 42	8155
18	14	EL	A	Luton Town	W 2-1	0-1	3	Ashcroft 74, Hunt 83	(8042)
19	21	EL	H	Portsmouth	W 2-1	0-0	2	Ashcroft 64, Hunt 90	16257
20	28	EL	A	Millwall	L 1-2	1-1	3	Hunt 21	(9717)
21	N 5	EL	H	Leicester City	L 2-3	0-3	7	Hamilton 57, Raven 87	16071
22	8	AIC	H	Reggiana	W 2-1	0-1		Hunt 72, Taylor 75	6009
23	11	EL	A	Derby County	L 0-3	0-2	7		(13765)
24	18	EL	A	Grimsby Town	L 0-1	0-0	9		(8155)
25	21	EL	H	Norwich City	L 1-4	1-1	12	Hunt 5	13680
26	25	EL	H	Sunderland	L 0-1	0-1	15		15931
27	D 2	EL	A	Reading	L 1-3	1-2	16	Ashcroft 8	(7910)
28	9	EL	H	Stoke City	L 0-1	0-1	16		14819
29	13	AIC	A	Brescia	W 1-0	0-0		Taylor 87	(196)
30	16	EL	A	Huddersfield Town	L 1-4	0-0	19	Hamilton 75	(12664)
31	23	EL	H	Crystal Palace	L 2-3	0-3	18	Hunt 62, Darby 85	13103
32	26	EL	A	Port Vale	L 1-3	0-0	19	Gilbert 63	10807
33	J 6	FAC 3	A	Crewe Alexandra	L 3-4	1-3		Hunt 27, Raven 63, Coldicott 86	(5750)
34	13	EL	H	Wolverhampton Wand	D 0-0	0-0	21		21642
35	20	EL	A	Charlton Athletic	L 1-4	0-3	21	Hunt 49(pen)	(11864)
36	30	AIC	A	Birmingham City	D 2-2	1-0		Rees 17, Raven 79	(9113)
37	F 3	EL	A	Ipswich Town	L 1-2	0-1	23	Taylor 66	(10798)
38	10	EL	H	Southend United	W 3-1	1-0	22	Hunt 34, Taylor 46, 86	12906
39	17	EL	H	Tranmere Rovers	D 1-1	1-0	23	Hunt 12(pen)	15014
40	20	EL	A	Sheffield United	W 2-1	2-1	21	Burgess 6, Hunt 10	(10944)
41	24	AIC	H	Port Vale	D 0-0	0-0			10862
42	27	EL	H	Oldham Athletic	W 1-0	1-0	21	Taylor 37	10959
43	M 2	EL	H	Port Vale	D 1-1	1-0	21	Taylor 18	13707
44	5	AIC	A	Port Vale	L 1-3	0-1		Taylor 70	(7640)
45	9	EL	A	Crystal Palace	L 0-1	0-1	22		(18336)
46	12	EL	H	Watford	D 4-4	3-2	21	Taylor 13, 27,79 (3), Sneekes 15	11836
47	16	EL	H	Barnsley	W 2-1	2-0	18	Raven 2, Sneekes 28	12701
48	20	EL	A	Birmingham City	D 1-1	1-0	19	Sneekes 19	(19147)
49	23	EL	A	Watford	D 1-1	0-0	18	Taylor 78	(10334)
50	30	EL	A	Portsmouth	W 2-0	1-0	19	Sneekes 20, 79	(8126)
51	A 2	EL	H	Luton Town	L 0-2	0-1	20		15131
52	6	EL	H	Millwall	W 1-0	0-0	19	Sneekes 88	13793
53	9	EL	A	Leicester City	W 2-1	1-0	17	Sneekes 17, Raven 90	(17889)
54	13	EL	H	Grimsby Town	W 3-1	2-1	13	Taylor 25, 29, Sneekes 64	16116
55	20	EL	A	Norwich City	D 2-2	1-0	13	Taylor 30, Sneekes 61	(14667)
56	27	EL	A	Sunderland	D 0-0	0-0	14		22027
57	30	EL	A	Barnsley	D 1-1	1-1	14	Gilbert 23	(6981)
58	M 5	EL	H	Derby County	W 3-2	2-1	11	Hunt 13, Sneekes 37, Taylor 89	23858

Best Home League Attendance: 23858 v Derby County   **Smallest: 10959 v Oldham Athletic**   **Average: 15166**

Goal Scorers:
EL(60):   Taylor(17),Hunt(14),Sneekes(10),Gilbert(5),Raven(4),Ashcroft(4),Hamilton(3),Burgess(2),Darby(1)
CC(8):   Taylor(3),Donovan(2),Burgess(2),Hunt(1)
FAC(3):   Raven(1),Hunt(1),Coldicott(1)
AIC(7):   Taylor(3),Rees(1),Raven(1),Hunt(1),Herbert(1)

(D) Agnew	(F) Angell	(F) Ashcroft	(D) Brien	(D) Burgess	(M) Butler	(M) Coldicott	(D) Comyn	(M) Cunnington	(D) Darby	(M) Donovan	(D) Edwards	(G) Fettis	(M) Gilbert	(M) Hamilton	(F) Hargreaves	(D) Holmes	(F) Hunt	(D) King	(D) Mardon	(G) Naylor	(D) Nicholson	(M) Raven	(G) Reece	(F) Rees	(M) Smith	(M) Sneekes	(G) Spink	(F) Taylor	Opponent	No.
		S		X		X		X1		X	X		X				X		X	X		X			S1			X	R.Poulain	1
		X1		X		X				X	X		X				X1		X	X		X		S	S1	S1		X	J.Kirkby	2
				X		X				X	X		X	X			X		X	X		X			S	S		X	C.Wilkes	3
				X		X				X	X		X	X			X1		X	X		X			S1	S		X	T.West	4
		S1		X		X				X	X		X1	X			X		X	X		X		S	S			X	K.Lynch	5
		S1		X		X				X1	X		X	X			X1		X	X		X		S	S1			X	M.Pierce	6
		S1		X		X				X	X		X	X			X		X	X		X1		S	S			X	D.Allison	7
		S1	X	X		X				X	X		X	X			X1		X	X		X		S			X	X	R. Poulain	8
		S	X	X		X				X	X		X	X			X		X	X		X		S				X	N.S.Barry	9
		S1	X1	X		X				X			X				X		X	X		X			S2	X2		X	E.Lomas	10
		S		X		X				X	X		X	X			X		X	X		X		S	S			X	K.Breen	11
		S		X		X				X	X		X	X			X		X	X		X			S	S		X	I.Hemley	12
		S1		X		X				X	X1		X	X			X		X	X		X			S	S1		X1	T.Lunt	13
X1		S1		X		S1		X1		X			X				X		X	X		X		S				X	G.Cain	14
X		S1		X		X		X		X			X1				X1		X	X		X		S	S			X	D.Orr	15
X		X		X		X		X		X			X				S		X	X		X		S	S			X	M.Bailey	16
		X2		X		X		X		X			X				S1			X		X		S	S2	X		X	D. Tombolini	17
X2		X		X		X		X		X			X1				S1		X	X		X			S2			X	G.Barber	18
		X		X		X			X2	X1	X		S1	S2			X		X	X		X		S				X	U.Rennie	19
		X		X		X				X	X2		X1	X			X		X	X		X		S	S1			X	G.Pooley	20
		X		X		X		S1		S			X	X			X	X1	X	X		X		S				X	K.Gifford	21
		X		X		X				X1			X	X			X	X	X	X		X					S1		A. Bonfrisco	22
		S1		X		X1		S2		X2			X	S			X	X	X	X		X						X	R.Poulain	23
		S2		X				X		X2	S3		X	X			X		X3	X		X	X	X1			S1		A.N.Butler	24
		S2		X		X				X	S1	X	X	X			X		X1	X		X				S3		X2	J.Kirkby	25
				X		X				X		X	X2	X	S2		X		X			X		S	X				S.Baines	26
				X		X				X	X1	X	X	X			X		X			X		S		S1			F.Stretton	27
		X2		X		S2				X	S1	X	S	X1			X		X			X						X	T.Heilbron	28
				X		S1				X	X1	X	X	X	S2				X			X		S	X2	X		X	C. Wilkes	29
		S2		X						X	X1		X	X			X		X	X		X			S1			X2	S.Mathieson	30
		X1		X						X	S1	S3	X3	X			X		X	X		X			S1			S1	G.Cain	31
				X						X	X	S	X1	X			X		X	X		X		S	S1			X	T.West	32
		S1		X		X				X3	X	X2	X1	S3			X		X	X		X				S2		X	G.Cruikshanks	33
				X		X				X	X		S	S		X	X		X	X		X			S			X	R.Poulain	34
		S3		X		X2				X	X		S1	S2		X	X		X1	X		X			X3			X3	R.Furnandiz	35
		S1		X		S2			X1	X			X2			X	X		X1			X		X3				S3	J. Rushden	36
		S3		X		S1			X1	X			X3			X	X					X		X2			X	S2	P.Taylor	37
		S		X		S				X	X		X	X		X	X				X	X		S			X	X	U.Rennie	38
		S2		X1		S3			X3	X			X2	X		X	X		S1		X	X					X	X	A.Leake	39
		S		X		S1				X	X		X	X		X	X1				X	X					X	X	E.Wolstenholme	40
		X1		X		S				X	X1		X	X		X	X3	S			S	X		S1			X	X	S.Mathieson	41
				X		S1				X	X1		X2	X		X	X		S2		X	X		S			X	X	A.Butler	42
				X		S2				X1			X	S		X	X1	X			S	X		S1	X		X	X2	P.Richards	43
				X		X				X1			X	X		X	X	X			S	X		S	S1		X	X	J. Kirkby	44
				X3		S2				X1	X		X2	X		X	X				S1	X		S3				X	A.D'Urso	45
				X						S1	X1		X2	X		X	X		S2		S	X					X	X	D.Allison	46
				X						X1				X		X	X	X	X		S	X		S	S		X	X	B.Knight	47
		S2		X		S1				X1				X		X	X		X2		X	X					X	X	N.Barry	48
		S2		X		X1				S1				S		X	X		X2		X	X					X	X	E.Lomas	49
	S			X	X					S1				S2		X	X1	X	X2		X	X					X	X	R.Gifford	50
	S3			X	X					X3	S2			S1		X2	X		X		X	X	X1				X	X	J.Lloyd	51
	S				X	X1	X			S	S1			X		X	X		X			X				X	X	X	M.Pierce	52
	S			X	X	X1								S1		X	X		X			X				X	X	X	I.Cruikshanks	53
	S			X	X					S	S			X		X	X		X			X				X	X	X	K.Lynch	54
	S2			X	X					S	S1			X		X	X	X	X2			X				X1	X	X	U.Rennie	55
	S1			X	X		X			X				S		X	X		X			X			X1		X	X	R.D.Furnandiz	56
	S			X	X		S	X1		S1				X		X	X		X			X					X	X	G.Barber	57
	S			X	X			S		S				X		X	X		X			X					X	X	G.Cain	58
3	0	11	2	45	9	21	3	8	19	28	13	3	35	38	0	18	44	4	35	27	18	40	1	3	9	13	15	39	EL Appearances	
0	3	15	0	0	0	12	0	1	3	6	3	0	5	2	1	0	1	0	4	0	0	0	0	6	7	0	0	3	EL Sub Appearances	
1	0	0+1	1	4	0	4	0	1	0	4	3	0	4	2	0	0	4	0	4	4	0	4	0	0+2	0+2	0	0	4	CC Appearances	
0	0	0+1	0	1	0	1	0	0	1	1	0	0+1	1	1	0	0	1	0	1	0	1	1	0	0	0+1	0	0	1	FAC Appearances	
0	0	4+2	1	6	0	3+2	0	2	4	6	2	0	7	5	0+1	3	5+1	1	2	5	2	6	0	2+2	4+1	0	2	5+2	AIC Appearances	

Also Played: (G) Germaine S(22). (D) Herbert X1(17). (M) Phelan X1(31).

WEST BROMWICH ALBION

CLUB RECORDS

BIGGEST VICTORIES
League: 12-0 v Darwen, Division 1, 4.4.1892 (League Record)
F.A. Cup: 10-1 v Chatham, Round 3, 2.3.1889.
League Cup: 6-1 v Coventry City, Round 4, 10.11.1965; v Aston Villa, Round 2,14.9.1966
Europe (UEFA): 4-0 v Dynamo Bucharest, Round 2, 27.11.1968

BIGGEST DEFEATS
League: 3-10 v Stoke City, Division 1, 4.2.1937.
F.A. Cup: 0-5 v Leeds United, Round 4, 18.2.1967
League Cup: 0-5 v Tottenham Hotspur, Round 4, 28.10.1970
1-6 v Nottingham Forest, Round 2, 6.10.1982
Europe: No more than 3 goals.

MOST POINTS
3 points a win: 85, Division 2, 1992-93
2 points a win: 60, Division 1, 1919-20

MOST GOALS
105, Division 2 1929-30
Cookson 33, Glidden 20, Carter 19, Wood 7, Cresswell 6, Evans 5, Shaw 4, Boston 3, Edwards 3, W.G. Richardson 2, Fitton 1, og 2.

MOST LEAGUE GOALS CONCEDED
98, Division 1, 1936-37

MOST FIRST CLASS MATCHES IN A SEASON
59 (42 League, 6 FA Cup, 3 League Cup, 8 UEFA Cup) 1978-79

MOST LEAGUE WINS: 28, Division 1, 1919-20

MOST LEAGUE DRAWS: 19, Division 1, 1979-80

MOST LEAGUE DEFEATS: 26, Division 1, 1985-86

INDIVIDUAL CLUB RECORDS

MOST GOALS IN A MATCH
6, Jimmy Cookson v Blackpool, Div 2, 17.9.1927

MOST GOALS IN A SEASON
'W.G.' Richardson 40 (League 39, FA Cup 1) 1935-36
4 goals twice=8, 3 goals twice=6, 2 goals 5 times=10, 1 goal 17 times=17

OLDEST PLAYER
George Baddeley, 39 years, 345 days v Sheffield Wed. 18.04.1914

YOUNGEST PLAYER
Charlie Wilson, 16 years, 73 days v Oldham (Div 1), 1.10.1921
(Frank Hodgetts was 16 yrs 26 days when he played for Albion v Notts County in a wartime game on 26.10.1940)

BEST PERFORMANCES

League: 1919-20: Matches played 42, Won 28, Drawn 4, Lost 10, Goals for 104,Goals against 47, Points 60. (Champions)

F.A. Cup: 1887-88: 1st rnd. Wednesbury O.A. (a) 7-1; 2nd rnd. Mitchell St,George (a) 1-0; 3rd rnd. Wolves (h) 2-0; 4th rnd. bye; 5th rnd. Stoke City (h)4-1. 6th rnd. Old Carthusians (h) 4-2; Semi-Final, Derby Junction 3-0; Final Preston North End, 2-1
1891-92: 3rd rnd. Old Westminsters (a) 3-2; 4th rnd. Blackburn Rovers (h) 3-1;5th rnd. Sheffield Weds. (h) 2-1; Semi-Final Nottingham Forest 1-1, 1-1, 6-2;Final Aston Villa 3-0
1930-31: 3rd rnd. Charlton Athletic (h) 2-2, (a) 1-1, (n) 3-1; 4th rnd.Tottenham Hotspur (h) 1-0; 5th rnd. Portsmouth (a) 1-0; 6th rnd. Wolves (h) 1-1, (a) 2-1; Semi-Final Everton, 1-0; Final Birmingham 2-1
1953-54: 3rd rnd. Chelsea (h) 1-0; 4th rnd. Rotherham United (h) 4-0; 5th rnd.Newcastle United (h) 3-2; 6th rnd. Tottenham Hotspur (h) 3-0; Semi-Final Port Vale, 2-1; Final Preston North End, 3-2
1967-68: 3rd rnd. Colchester (a) 1-1, (h) 4-0; 4th rnd. Southampton (h) 1-1,(a) 3-2; 5th rnd. Portsmouth (a) 2-1; 6th rnd. Liverpool (h) 0-0, (a) 1-1, (n)2-1; Semi-Final Birmingham City, 2-0; Final Everton, 1-0

League Cup: 1965-66: 2nd rnd. Walsall (h) 3-1; 3rd rnd. Leeds United (a) 4-2;4th rnd. Coventry City (a) 1-1, (h) 6-1; 5th rnd. Aston Villa (h) 3-1; Semi-Final Peterborough United (h) 2-1, (a) 4-2; Final West Ham United (a) 1-2, (h)4-1

Europe (UEFA): 1978-79: 1st rnd. Galatasary, 3-1, 3-1; 2nd rnd. Sporting Braga,2-0, 1-0. 3rd rnd. Valencia, 1-1, 2-0; 4th rnd. Red Star, 0-1, 1-1.

ADDITIONAL INFORMATION
In 1956-57 Albion played 42 First Division games. They won 14, drew 14,and lost 14 for a total of 42 points and finished halfway in the table (11th)

Previous Name
West Bromwich Strollers 1878-80
Previous League:
None

Club colours: Navy blue/white striped shirts, white shorts, white socks.
Change colours: Yellow shirts light blue sleeves, blue shorts, yellow/blue socks.

Reserves League
Pontins Central League Division 2.

DIVISIONAL RECORD

	Played	Won	Drawn	Lost	For	Against	Points
Division 1	2,652	988	637	1,027	4,134	4,224	2,673
Division 2/1	1,120	478	273	369	1,806	1,441	1,339
Division 3/2	92	44	24	24	152	103	156
Total	3,864	1,510	934	1,420	6,092	5,768	4,168

RECORDS AND STATISTICS

COMPETITIONS

Div.1	Div.2/1	Div.3.2	ECWC	FMC	Texaco	A/Scot
1888-01	1901-02	1991-93	1968-69	1986	1970-71	1975-76
1902-04	1904-11			1987	1972-73	1976-77
1911-27	1927-31		EUFA	1988	1974-75	A/Ital.
1931-38	1938-49		1966-67	SC	Watney C	1969-70
1949-73	1973-76		1978-79	1988-89	1971-72	1970-71
1976-86	1986-91		1979-80	ZC		1994-95
	1993-		1981-82	1989-91	AGT	1995-96
					1991-92	T/Cal
						1977-78
						1978-79

HONOURS

Div.1	Div.2	FAC	Lge Cup	C/Shield
1919-20	1901-02	1887-88	1965-66	1920
	1910-11	1891-92		1954
		1930-31		
		1953-54		
		1967-68		

MOST GOALS IN A CAREER

Tony Brown - 261 (1963-80)

Year	League	FA Cup	Lge Cup	Europe
1963-64	5			
1964-65	9			
1965-66	17		10	
1966-67	14	1	1	3
1967-68	11	4		
1968-69	17	2	1	3
1969-70	10	1	2	
1970-71	28	2		
1971-72	17	1		
1972-73	12	1	1	
1973-74	19	4		
1974-75	12	1		
1975-76	8	4		
1976-77	8			
1977-78	19	3	1	
1978-79	10	2	1	2
1979-80	2	1	1	
Total	**218**	**27**	**18**	**8**

Current leading goalscorer: Bob Taylor - 100 (1992-96)

MOST APPEARANCES

Tony Brown 704+16 (1963-80)

Year	League	FA Cup	Lge Cup	Europe	Other
1963-64	13				
1964-65	17				
1965-66	35	1	9		
1966-67	31	2	4	3	
1967-68	35	10	1		
1968-69	42	4	2	6	1
1969-70	40	1	8+1		4
1970-71	42	4	2		6
1971-72	40	1	1		3
1972-73	38+1	5	3		4
1973-74	41	4	2		
1974-75	32+2	3	2		3
1975-76	37+3	4	1		1
1976-77	36+1	2	3		3
1977-78	41	6	2		1
1978-79	29+2	6	1	5+1	2
1979-80	12+4	0+1	5	2	
	561+13	53+1	46+1	16+1	28

MANAGERS

Name	Seasons	Best	Worst
Thomas Foster	1885-87	5(1)	6(1)
Louis Ford	1887-90	5(1)	6(1)
W. Pierre Dix	1890-92	12(1)	12(1)
Henry Jackson	1892-94	8(1)	8(1)
E Stephenson	1894-95	13(1)	13(1)
Clement Keys	1895		
Frank Heaven	1896-02	7(1)	1(1)
Fred Everiss	1902-48	1(1)	11(2)
Jack Smith	1948-52	14(1)	3(2)
Jesse Carver	1952-53	4(1)	4(1)
Vic Buckingham	1953-59	2(1)	17(1)
Gordon Clark	1959-61	4(1)	10(1)
Archie Macauley	1961-63	9(1)	14(1)
Jimmy Hagan	1963-67	6(1)	14(1)
Alan Ashman	1967-71	8(1)	18(1)
Don Howe	1971-75	16(1)	16(2)
Johnny Giles	1975-77	7(1)	3(2)
Ronnie Allen	1977		
Ron Atkinson	1978-81	3(1)	10(1)
Ronnie Allen	1981-82	17(1)	17(1)
Ron Wylie	1982-84	11(1)	17(1)
Johnny Giles	1984-85	12(1)	12(1)
Nobby Stiles	1985		
Ron Saunders	1986-87	22(1)	22(1)
Ron Atkinson	1987-88	20(2)	20(2)
Brain Talbot	1988-91	9(2)	9(2)
Bobby Gould	1991-92	7(3)	7(3)
Ossie Ardiles	1992-93	4(3/2)	4(3/2)
Keith Burkinshaw	1993-94	21(1/2)	21(1/2)
Alan Buckley	1994-	19(1)	19(1)

RECORD TRANSFER FEE RECEIVED

Amount	Club	Player	Date
£1,500,000	Manchester Utd	Bryan Robson	10/81
£995,000	Real Madrid	Laurie Cunningham	6/79
£225,000	Manchester City	Asa Hartford	6/79
£75,000	Norwich City	Colin Suggett	2/73

RECORD TRANSFER FEE PAID

Amount	Club	Player	Date
£748,000	Manchester City	Peter Barnes	7/79
£516,000	Middlesbrough	David Mills	1/79
£138,000	Rangers	Willlie Johnson	12/72
£100,000	Sunderland	Colin Suggett	8/69

LONGEST LEAGUE RUNS

of undefeated matches:	17 (23.11.1901 - 29.3.1902)	of league matches w/out a win:	14 (28.10.95 - 3.2.96)
of undefeated home matches:	19 (2.9.01-11.10.02, 7.9.08-6.9.09)	of undefeated away matches:	11 (23.4.57-14.12.57, 26.1.80-13.9.80)
without home win:	9 (2.5.21-26.11.21, 21.8.71-11.12.71)	without an away win:	27 (27.12.1969 - 12.4.1971)
of league wins:	11 (5.4.1930 - 8.9.1930)	of home wins:	11 (20.10.1906 - 1.4.1907)
of league defeats:	11 (28.10.95 - 26.11.95)	of away wins:	7 (22.4.1953 - 31.10.1953)

WEST BROMWICH ALBION

PLAYERS NAME / Honours	Ht	Wt	Birthdate	Birthplace / Transfers	Contract Date	Clubs	League	L/Cup	FA Cup	Other	Lge	L/C	FAC	Oth
GOALKEEPERS														
Cutler Neil — E: S	6.1	12.0	03/09/76	Birmingham	06/09/93	W.B.A.								
				Loan	09/12/94	Cheltenham Town								
				Loan	03/02/95	Cheltenham Town								
				Loan	28/10/95	Coventry City								
				Loan	09/12/95	Tamworth								
				Loan	27/03/96	Chester City	1							
Germaine Gary	6.2	14.0	02/08/76	Birmingham	05/07/94	W.B.A.								
				Loan	09/12/95	Telford								
				Loan	08/03/96	Scunthorpe United	11							
Reece Paul J	5.10	12.7	16/07/68	Nottingham	18/07/86	Stoke City	2							
				Free	01/03/87	Kettering Town								
				£10000	18/07/88	Grimsby Town	54	3	5	4				
				Free	25/09/92	Doncaster Rovers	1							
				Free	02/10/93	Oxford United	39	3	2	1				
				Free	02/08/94	Notts County	11	1		2+1				
				Free	11/08/95	W.B.A.	1							
				Loan	01/03/96	Ilkeston Town								
Spink Nigel — E: 1, B.2. EC'82. ESC'82. LC'94. FLgXI	6.2	14.6	08/08/58	Chelmsford		Chelmsford								
				£4000	01/01/77	Aston Villa	357+4	45	28	25+1				
				Free	31/01/96	W.B.A.	15		2					
DEFENDERS														
Agnew Paul — NI: u23.1, Y, S	5.9	10.7	15/08/65	Lisburn		Cliftonville								
				£4000	15/02/84	Grimsby Town	219+23	17+1	23+1	12+2	3			
				£65000	23/02/95	W.B.A.	17	1			1			
Brien Tony	5.11	11.9	10/02/69	Dublin	13/02/87	Leicester City	12+4	1	1	3				
				£90000	16/12/88	Chesterfield	201+3	14	7	14	8			
					08/10/93	Rotherham United	41+2	2	4	6	4			
				Free	13/07/95	W.B.A.	2	1		1				
				Loan	16/02/96	Mansfield Town	4							
				Loan	22/03/96	Chester City	8							
Burgess Daryl	5.11	12.3	24/01/71	Birmingham	01/07/89	W.B.A.	218+5	12+2	7	14	7	3		
Darby Julian — E: S. SVT'89	6.0	11.4	03/10/67	Bolton	22/07/86	Bolton Wanderers	258+12	25	19	31+1	36	8	3	5
				£150000	28/10/93	Coventry City	25+1		1		5			
				£250000	23/11/95	W.B.A.	19+3		1	4	1			
Hamner Gareth	5.10	11.0	12/10/73	Shrewsbury		Shrewsbury Town								
						Newtown								
				£20000	17/05/96	W.B.A.								
Herbert Craig	6.0	12.0	09/11/75	Coventry		Torquay United								
				Free	18/03/94	W.B.A.	8	2		1				1
Holmes Paul	5.10	11.0	18/02/68	Stocksbridge	24/02/86	Doncaster Rovers	42+5		3+1	1	1		1	
				£6000	12/08/88	Torquay United	127+11	9	9+2	13+3	4			
				£40000	05/06/92	Birmingham City	12		1					
				£100000	19/03/93	Everton	20	4	1					
				Loan	12/01/96	W.B.A.								
				£80000	15/02/96	W.B.A.	18			3				
Mardon Paul	6.0	12.0	14/09/69	Bristol	29/01/88	Bristol City	29+13	3+3		1		1		
				Loan	13/09/90	Doncaster Rovers	3							
				£115000	16/08/91	Birmingham City	54+10	11+1	1	3				
				£220000	18/11/93	W.B.A.	84+4	4	3	2	2			
Nicholson Shane — APL (GMVC)'88	5.10	11.0	03/03/70	Newark	19/07/88	Lincoln City	122+11	8+3	6	7+1	7		1	
				£100000	24/02/92	Derby County	63+1	4	4	5	1		1	
				£150000	01/03/96	W.B.A.	18		2					
MIDFIELD														
Buckley Simon J	5.10	11.0	29/02/76	Stafford	12/07/94	Grimsby Town								
					01/05/96	W.B.A.								
Coldicott Stacy	5.10	11.8	20/04/74	Redditch	04/03/92	W.B.A.	44+19	7+1	2+1	7+3			1	
Cunnington Shaun — WFAC'86	5.9	11.0	04/01/66	Bourne	11/01/84	Wrexham	196+3	13	9	21	12	1		2
				£55000	19/02/88	Grimsby Town	182	11	11	9	13	3		
				£650000	17/07/92	Sunderland	52+6	3	2	2	8	1		
				£220000	11/08/95	W.B.A.	8+1	1		2				
Donovan Kevin	5.9	11.0	17/12/71	Halifax	11/10/89	Huddersfield Town	11+9	1+1	1	4	1			2
				Loan	13/02/92	Halifax Town	6							
				£25000	01/10/92	W.B.A.	122+14	9	7+1	15+1	19	5	3	4
Gilbert Dave — Div4'87	5.4	10.4	22/06/63	Lincoln	29/06/81	Lincoln City	15+15	5	3		1			
				Free	18/08/82	Scunthorpe United	1	1						
				Free	01/01/83	Boston United			4				2	
					30/06/86	Northampton Town	120	10	6	9	21	2	3	1
				£55000	23/03/89	Grimsby Town	259	18	11	9	41	4	2	
					08/08/95	W.B.A.	35+5	4	1	7	5			
Groves Paul	5.11	11.5	28/02/66	Derby	01/10/86	Burton Albion				2+1				
				£12000	18/04/88	Leicester City	7+9	1	0+1	0+1	1	1		
				Loan	20/08/89	Lincoln City	8	2			1			
				£60000	25/01/90	Blackpool	106+1	6	9	13	21	1	4	3
				£125000	12/08/92	Grimsby Town	183+1	10+1	12	4	38	2	2	1
				£600000	16/06/96	W.B.A.								

Player	Ht	Wt	DOB	From / Fee	Date	Club	Lge App	FAC App	FLC App	Oth App	Lge Gls	FAC Gls	FLC Gls	Oth Gls
Hamilton Ian	5.9	11.3	14/12/67	Stevenage	24/12/85	Southampton								
					29/03/88	Cambridge United	23+1	1	2	2	1			
					23/12/88	Scunthorpe United	139+6	6	6+1	14+1	18			3
				£170000	19/06/92	W.B.A.	160+3	8	7+1	14+2	17		1	3
Raven Paul ESFA U18.4	6.0	12.3	28/07/70	Salisbury	06/06/88	Doncaster Rovers	52	2	5	2	4			
				£100000	23/03/89	W.B.A.	175+4	11	7	15	13		3	1
				Loan	27/11/91	Doncaster Rovers	7							
Rodosthenous Michael					30/05/96	W.B.A.								
Smith David E: u21.10	5.8	10.2	29/03/68	Stonehouse	07/07/86	Coventry City	144+10	17	6	4+1	19			
				Loan	06/01/93	Bournemouth	1							
					12/03/93	Birmingham City	35+3	4	0+1	1	3			
				£90000	31/01/94	W.B.A.	43+13	1+2	0+3	4+1				
Sneekes Richard	5.11	12.2	30/10/68	Amsterdam		Ajax								
						Fortuna Sittard								
				£200000	12/08/94	Bolton Wanderers	51+4	11+1	2		7	3	1	
				£400000	11/03/96	W.B.A.	13				10			

F O R W A R D S

Player	Ht	Wt	DOB	From / Fee	Date	Club	Lge App	FAC App	FLC App	Oth App	Lge Gls	FAC Gls	FLC Gls	Oth Gls
Ashcroft Lee E: u21.1	5.10	11.0	07/09/72	Preston	16/07/91	Preston North End	78+13	3	5	6+2	13			1
				£225000	01/08/93	W.B.A.	64+21	2+2	3+1	9+3	17		1	
				Loan	28/03/96	Notts County	4+2							
Butler Peter J	5.9	11.1	27/08/66	Halifax	21/08/84	Huddersfield Town	0+5							
				Loan	24/01/86	Cambridge United	14			1	1			
				Free	08/07/86	Bury	9+2	2	1			1		
				Free	10/12/86	Cambridge United	55	4	2	2	9			
				£75000	12/02/88	Southend United	135+7	12	2	11	9	1		2
Loan (24/03/92) Huddersfield T. 7 Lge Apps.				£125000	12/08/92	West Ham United	70	4	3	1	3			
				£350000	04/10/94	Notts County	20	2	2	3				
				Loan	30/01/96	Grimsby Town	3							
Loan (28/03/96) W.B.A. 9 Lge Apps.				£175000	01/08/96	W.B.A.								
Hargreaves Chris	5.11	11.0	12/05/72	Cleethorpes	06/12/89	Grimsby Town	15+36	2+2	1+2	2+4	5	1	1	
				Loan	04/03/93	Scarborough	2+1							
					26/07/93	Hull City	34+15	1	2+1	3+1			1	
				Free	13/07/95	W.B.A.	0+1			0+1				
				Loan	19/02/96	Hereford United								
Hunt Andrew	6.0	12.0	09/06/70	Grays		Kings Lynn								
				Free		Kettering Town								
				£150000	29/01/91	Newcastle United	34+9	3	2	3	11	1	2	
				£100000	25/03/93	W.B.A.	121+8	7	4	8+1	48	2	2	3
Peschisolido Paolo Canadian Int.	5.4	10.5	25/05/71	Canada	01/01/00	Toronto Bl (Canada)								
				£25000	11/11/92	Birmingham City	37+6	2	0+1	1+1	16	1		
				£400000	01/08/94	Stoke City	39+1	3	2	3+1	13	2		
				£400000	29/03/96	Birmingham City	7+2				1			
				£600000	22/07/96	W.B.A.								
Taylor Bob	5.10	11.9	03/02/67	Horden		Horden								
				Free	27/03/86	Leeds United	33+9	5+1	1	4+1	9	3		1
				£175000	23/03/89	Bristol City	96+10	6+1	9+1	3	50	2	5	1
				£300000	31/01/92	W.B.A.	184+7	11	6+1	16+3	84	5	3	8

ADDITIONAL CONTRACT PLAYERS:
Wills James (21/06/96). Knight Lee (10/06/96).

THE MANAGER
ALAN BUCKLEY

Date of Birth . . . . 20th April 1951.
Place of Birth . . . . Eastwood.
Date of Appointment . . . . October 1995.

PREVIOUS CLUBS
As Manager . . . . Walsall, Kettering Town, Grimsby Town.
As Coach . . . .
As a Player . . . . Nottingham Forest, Walsall, Birmingham City, Walsall.

HONOURS
As a Manager
Guided Grimsby Town to promotion from Division 4 in 1990 and from Division 3 in 1991.

As a Player
None.

THE HAWTHORNS
West Bromwich B71 4LF
Tel: 0121 525 8888

Capacity ....25,296 (all seater)

First game ....v Derby County, 1-1, 3.9.1900.
First floodlit game ....v Chelsea, Div.1, 1-1, 18.9.1957)
Internationals ....England v N.Ireland 1922, v Belgium 1924, v Wales 1945.

ATTENDANCES
Highest ....64,815 v Arsenal, FAC 6th Rnd, 6.3.1937.
Lowest ....405 v Derby County, Div 1, 29.11.1890.
OTHER GROUNDS ....Coopers Hill 1878. Dartmouth Park 1879-81.Bunns Field 1881-82.
.... Four Acres (Dartmouth CC) 1882-85.Stoney Lane 1885-1900. The Hawthorns 1900-

MATCHDAY TICKET PRICES

Halford Lane Centre £16
Concessions £10
Halford Lane Wings £15
Concessions £9

WBBS Centre £15
Concessions £9
WBBS Wings £14
Concessions £8

BRE/SME/Paddock £11
Concessions £6

Ticket Office Telephone no. . . . . . . 0121 553 5472.

CLUBCALL
0898 12 11 93
Calls cost 39p per minute cheap rate and 49p per
minute at all other times.
Call costings correct at time of going to press.

HOW TO GET TO THE GROUND

From all directions
Use motorway (M5) until junction 1.
Leave motorway and follow local signs on matchdays to ground.
Signs for Hawthorne Station Park & Ride are useful!.

Car Parking
Car parks of Halfords Lane and Middlemore Road, street parking in
some areas within 10 minutes walk of ground.

Nearest Railway Station
Rolfe St. Smethwick (One and a quarter miles).
Hawthorns Halt (400 yards).

MATCHDAY PROGRAMME

Programme Editor . . . . Tom Cardall.

Number of pages . . . . 40.

Price . . . . £1.50.

Subscriptions . . . . (Home only): UK £50, Eire & Europe £52.50.
. . . Outside Europe: Air £78.50. For home & away the cost is doubled.

Local Newspapers . . . . Sandwell Evening Mail,
. . . Birmingham Post & Evening Mail, Express & Star Wolverhampton,
. . . . Sports Argus, Sporting Pink.l, Sunday Mercury.

Local Radio Stations . . . . BRMB Radio, Radio WM, Beacon Radio,
. . . . Mercia Sound, W.A.B. Radio.

WOLVERHAMPTON WANDERERS
(Wolves)
NATIONWIDE LEAGUE DIVISION 1
SPONSORED BY: GOODYEAR

Back Row (L-R): Jamie Smith, Gordon Cowans, Darren Ferguson, Geoff Thomas, Mike Stowell, Paul Jones, Neil Emblen, Neil Masters, Jermaine Wright, Robbie Dennison. **Middle Row:** Barry Holmes (Physio), Andy Thompson, Don Goodman, Brian Law, Dean Richards, Andy Debont, David Kelly, Jimmy Kelly, Mark Rankine, Paul Birch, Dave Hancock (Asst. Physio). **Front Row:** Chris Evans (Yth Dev. Officer), Ian Miller (Res. Coach), Steve Froggatt, Tony Daley, Peter Shirtliff (Capt), Graham Taylor (Manager), Bobby Downes (Asst. Manager), John De Wolf, Mark Venus, Steve Bull, Rob Kelly (Yth Manager), Steve Harrison (First team coach).

WOLVERHAMPTON WANDERERS
FORMED IN 1877
TURNED PROFESSIONAL IN 1888
LTD COMPANY IN 1892

PRESIDENT: Sir Jack Hayward
CHAIRMAN: Jonathan Hayward
DIRECTORS
Jack Harris, John Harris, John Richards,
Nic Stones, Michael Blackburn
SECRETARY
Tom Finn
COMMERCIAL DIRECTOR
David Clayton

MANAGER: Mark McGhee
ASSISTANT MANAGER: Colin Lee
COACH: Mike Hickmen
YOUTH COACH
Chris Turner
PHYSIOTHERAPISTS
Barry Holmes & Dave Hanock

STATISTICIAN FOR THE DIRECTORY
Les Smith

Once again Wolves did not live up to their 'big club' reputation. Not only were they out of the battle for a Premiership place, but they came very close to the relegation zone with a final position of 20th.

Expectations were high of Graham Taylor , money had been spent and now it was time to bring out the performances on the pitch. This alas did not happen. Victory over Derby (3-0) gave the supporters a glimpse of what could be achieved but performances such as that became scarce and finally Graham Taylor had no choice but to leave the club.

However, Taylor did see some sort of glory in the form of the Coca-Cola Cup. Victories over Fulham (2-0, 5-1) and Charlton Athletic (0-0, 2-1) brought a tie against Premiership side Coventry City. Taylor and his men once again showed what could be done by beating their Midland rivals 2-1 and set up a quarter final tie against the Villa. This they lost 0-1.

The man they chose to take over from Graham Taylor was Mark McGhee, who had done so well with Reading before moving to Leicester City, from which he left to come to Molineux. He made an immediate impact as a run of seven games without defeat proved. This form put some of the confidence back into the team, this saw the club move from 21st place to 11th with thoughts very much on a play-off place. But four points from their last eight games saw Wolves dramatically slip down the table to finish the season only two places above the relegation zone.

The fourth round of the F.A. Cup was reached by beating Birmingham City 2-1 in a replay before Tottenham knocked them out 0-2, also in a replay.

If Mark McGhee can have a fully fit squad at his disposal for the 1996/97 season then maybe we'll finally see Wolves challenging for a place in the Division where they belong, The Premiership, but then we've heard that before!

WOLVERHAMPTON WANDERERS

League: 20th   FA Cup: 4th Rnd   Coca-Cola Cup: Quarter Finals

M	DATE	COMP	VEN	OPPONENTS	RESULT	HT	LP	GOAL SCORERS/GOAL TIMES	ATT.
1	A 12	EL	A	Tranmere Rovers	D 2-2	1-0	1	Bull 40, Goodman 54	(11880)
2	20	EL	H	West Bromwich Albion	D 1-1	0-0	3	Mardon 66(og)	26329
3	26	EL	A	Sunderland	L 0-2	0-2	7		(16816)
4	30	EL	H	Derby County	W 3-0	3-0		Daley 13, Goodman 16, De Wolf 32	26053
5	S 2	EL	A	Leicester City	L 0-1	0-1	15		(18441)
6	9	EL	H	Grimsby Town	W 4-1	1-1	12	Bull 42, 69, Goodman 51, 76	23656
7	13	EL	H	Norwich City	L 0-2	0-0	17		27064
8	16	EL	A	Southend United	L 1-2	1-1	19	Goodman 29	(6322)
9	20	CC 2/1	H	Fulham	W 2-0	1-0		Goodman 4, Wright 50	20381
10	23	EL	H	Luton Town	D 0-0	0-0	19		23659
11	30	EL	A	Port Vale	D 2-2	2-1	18	Goodman 16, Daley 31	(11550)
12	O 3	CC 2/2	A	Fulham	W 5-1	1-0		Daley 27, Williams 69, Atkins 78, Goodman 85, 87	(6625)
13	7	EL	A	Ipswich Town	W 2-1	2-1	15	Goodman 35, Williams 42	(15335)
14	14	EL	H	Stoke City	L 1-4	1-2	18	Thompson 71(pen)	26483
15	21	EL	A	Watford	D 1-1	1-0	16	Daley 45	(11319)
16	25	CC 3	H	Charlton Athletic	D 0-0	0-0			22481
17	28	EL	H	Sheffield United	W 1-0	1-0	16	Bull 37	23881
18	N 4	EL	A	Barnsley	L 0-1	0-0	18		(9668)
19	8	CC 3R	A	Charlton Athletic	W 2-1	1-0		Emblen 23, Atkins 97	(10909)
20	12	EL	H	Charlton Athletic	D 0-0	0-0	19		20450
21	18	EL	H	Oldham Athletic	L 1-3	1-0	19	Emblen 27	23128
22	22	EL	A	Crystal Palace	L 2-3	0-2	20	Thompson 64(pen), Young 83	(12571)
23	25	EL	A	Huddersfield Town	L 1-2	0-2	20	Bull 79	(16423)
24	29	CC 4	H	Coventry City	W 2-1	2-0		Venus 33, Ferguson 34	24628
25	D 3	EL	H	Ipswich Town	D 2-2	0-1	21	Goodman 60, 70	20867
26	10	EL	A	Luton Town	W 3-2	3-1	20	Richards 7, Goodman 18, Bull 41	(6997)
27	16	EL	H	Port Vale	L 0-1	0-1	21		23329
28	26	EL	H	Millwall	D 1-1	1-0	21	Bull 10	25593
29	30	EL	H	Portsmouth	D 2-2	2-0	20	Bull 5, Goodman 35	25294
30	J 6	FAC 3	A	Birmingham City	D 1-1	1-0		Bull 25	(21349)
31	10	CC QF	A	Aston Villa	L 0-1	0-0			(39277)
32	13	EL	A	West Bromwich Albion	D 0-0	0-0	20		(21642)
33	17	FAC 3R	H	Birmingham City	W 2-1	1-0		Ferguson 17, Bull 62	28088
34	20	EL	H	Tranmere Rovers	W 2-1	1-0	20	Bull 35, Goodman 67	24173
35	27	FAC 4	A	Tottenham Hotspur	D 1-1	1-1		Goodman 28	(32812)
36	F 3	EL	H	Sunderland	W 3-0	2-0	18	Thompson 15(pen), Goodman 18, Atkins 61	26537
37	7	FAC 4R	H	Tottenham Hotspur	L 0-2	0-2			27846
38	10	EL	A	Derby County	D 0-0	0-0	18		(17460)
39	17	EL	A	Norwich City	W 3-2	2-2	17	Bull 12, 37, Goodman 75	(14691)
40	21	EL	H	Leicester City	L 2-3	2-1	18	Bull 26, Law 42	27381
41	24	EL	H	Southend United	W 2-0	1-0	16	Young 29, Thompson 50	24677
42	M 2	EL	A	Millwall	W 1-0	0-0	14	Bull 69	(9131)
43	5	EL	A	Birmingham City	L 0-2	0-2	15		(22051)
44	9	EL	H	Reading	D 1-1	1-1	15	Atkins 42	25954
45	12	EL	A	Grimsby Town	L 0-3	0-0	15		(5013)
46	16	EL	A	Portsmouth	W 2-0	2-0	14	Emblen 39, Goodman 41	(11732)
47	23	EL	H	Birmingham City	W 3-2	1-1	11	Goodman 37, Thompson 88(pen), Bull 89	26256
48	30	EL	H	Watford	W 3-0	2-0	11	Froggatt 32, Osborn 42, 54	25885
49	A 3	EL	A	Stoke City	L 0-2	0-1	12		(16361)
50	6	EL	A	Sheffield United	L 1-2	1-2	13	Thompson 45	(16658)
51	8	EL	H	Barnsley	D 2-2	1-1	15	Bull 16, Ferguson 51(pen)	23789
52	13	EL	A	Oldham Athletic	D 0-0	0-0	15		(7592)
53	20	EL	H	Crystal Palace	L 0-2	0-1	18		24350
54	27	EL	H	Huddersfield Town	D 0-0	0-0	18		25290
55	30	EL	A	Reading	L 0-3	0-2	18		(12828)
56	M 5	EL	A	Charlton Athletic	D 1-1	0-1	20	Crowe 53	(14023)

Best Home League Attendance: 27381 v Leicester City   Smallest: 20450 v Charlton Athletic   Average: 24786

Goal Scorers:

EL(56): Goodman(16), Bull(15), Thompson(6), Daley(3), Osborn(2), Atkins(2), Emblen(2), Young(2), DeWolf (1), Crowe(1), Ferguson(1), Law(1), Opponent(s)(1), Froggatt(1), Williams(1), Richards(1)

CC(11): Goodman(3), Atkins(2), Williams(1), Venus(1), Ferguson(1), Emblen(1), Daley(1), Wright(1)

FAC(4): Bull(2), Ferguson(1), Goodman(1)

1995-96

(D) Atkins	(M) Birch	(F) Bull	(M) Corica	(M) Cowans	(F) Daley	(D) De Wolf	(D) Emblen	(M) Ferguson	(M) Foley	(M) Froggatt	(F) Goodman	(G) Jones	(F) Kelly	(D) Law	(D) Masters	(M) Osborn	(D) Pearce	(F) Rankine	(D) Richards	(M) Samways	(F) Smith	(G) Stowell	(D) Thompson	(D) Venus	(F) Williams	(F) Wright	(D) Young			
		X		X	X		X				X	X	X		X				X				X						I.Cruikshanks	1
		X		X	X		X			S1	X		X1		X			S	X			X	X						C.Wilkes	2
		X		X	S1	X				X	X1		X		X1			X	X			X	X						D.B.Allison	3
		X			X	X	X	X		X	X		S	S			S1	X1	X			X	X						T. Heilbron	4
		X			X1	X	X2	X			X		S1				X	X	X			X	X						J.Lloyd	5
		X		S1	X	X		X		X	X		S				X1	X	X			X	X			S			R.Grifford	6
		X		S1	X	X	S1	X1		X	X1		S1				X1	X	X			X	X						T.West	7
		X		S	X		S	X		X	X		S					X	X		X	X	X				X		M.C.Bailey	8
		X		S	X2		S1	X			X							X	X		X1	X	X		S2	X	X		R.Lomas	9
X1		X		S1	X			X			X							X	X			X	X	S	S2	X2	X		N.Barry	10
X				X	X			X			X							X	X			X	X	S1	X1	S	X		U.Rennie	11
X					X			X			X							X	X			X	X	X	X		X		R.Harris	12
X				S2	X2		S	X			X							X	X			X	X	X	X1	S1	X		M.Pierce	13
X		S1		S1			X	X1			X								X		S3	X3	X	X1	X	X	X		D.Allison	14
X	X	X		X	X		S				X	X						X	X				X			S	X		T.Lunt	15
X	X1	X		X	X		S				X	X						X	X				X			S1	X		R.Poulain	16
X	X	X		X			S1				X	X						X	X1				X		S	X	X		S.W.Mathieson	17
X	X1	X		X	X1	X	S1				X	X						X					X			S1	X		K.J.Breen	18
X	S2	S1		X	X	X2	X				X	X						X					X		X1		X		I.Hemley	19
X		S2		X	X	X	X				X	X						X2					X		X1	S1	X		C.Wilkes	20
S2	X2	X		X	X1	X	X		S2		X	X						X					X		S1		X		W.Burns	21
S	X1	X		X		X	X		S1		X	X						X	S1				X			X1	X		G.Pooley	22
X		X				X	X	S1	X1		X	X		S				X	X				X	X	S				R.Pearson	23
X	X	X						X			X	S		X				X	X		S	X	X	X	S				S.Lodge	24
X	S1	X					X1	X			X	S		X				X	X			X	X	X	S				G.Cain	25
X	S	X				S	X	X			X			X				X	X			X	X	X					K.Lynch	26
X1	S1	X			S1	X1	X	X			X	S						X	X			X	X	X					J.Kirkby	27
X1		X		S3	X2		X	S1			X					X		S2	X	X3		X	X	X					R.Gifford	28
X		X			X2		X	S2			X					X		S1	X	X1		X	X	X			S		A.Butler	29
X		X					X1		S2		X					X	X2	S1	X			X	X		X		X		R.Hart	30
X		X						X	S2		X			S3			X1	X	X			X	X3	X2			X		M.Bodenham	31
S1		X						X1	S2		X					X		X	X	X2		X	X	X			X		R.Poulain	32
X		X			S			X	S		X			X		X	S	X				X	X	X			X		R.Hart	33
X		X						X	S		X			S		X	S	X	X			X	X	X			X		M.Pierce	34
X		X					X	X			X	S				X		X	X			X	X	S			X		D.Allison	35
X		X			S	S	X	X	S		X					X		X				X	X	X			X		U.Rennie	36
X		X			S1	S	X	X			X	S				X		X1				X	X	X			X		D.Allison	37
X		X				X	X	X	S		X					X		S				X	X	X			X		T.Heilbron	38
X		X	X			X1	X	X			X			S1		X		S				X	X		S		X		A.D'Urso	39
X		X	X1				X	S		S1	X			X2		X						X	X	X	S2		X		T.West	40
X		X	X				X	X		S	X			X		X						X	X	S	S		X		M.Riley	41
X		X	X				X	X		S	X			S		X			X1			X	X	S1			X		G.Cain	42
X1		X	X				X	X		S1	X			X2		X						X	X		S2		X		E.Lomas	43
X		X	X				X	X1		S1	X					X			X			X	X	S	S		X		T.Heilbron	44
X1		X					X2	X		S1	X					X			X		S2	X	X	X2	S2		X		F.G.Stretton	45
S		X	X				X			X	X					X	S		X		X	X	X		S		X		G.Barber	46
S1		X	X				X			X	X					X	S		X		X	X	X		S		X1		J.Kirkby	47
		X	X2				X1	S2		X	X					X		S	X		X	X	X	S1			X		T.Leake	48
S1		X	X					S2		X	X					X3		S3	X		X1	X	X	X2			X		M.Pierce	49
X		X	X			X		X3		X1	X							S3	X2		S1	X	X		S2		X		J.Rushton	50
X1		X	X					X		X	X							X	X		X	X		S1	S		X		N.Barry	51
		X	X2				X	X		X	X1							S2	X		X	X	X	S	S1		X		I.Cruikshanks	52
		X	X			S2	X		S3	X2	S1					X		X3	X			X	X	X	X1				J.Lloyd	53
		X	X				X	S1			X1					X		X	X		X	X	X	X			S		W.Burns	54
S2		X	X				X	X1								X		X2	X		X	X	X	X			S		G.Pooley	55
S2		X	X2					S2								X	S1	X2	X1		X	X	X	X			X		I.Hemley	56
26	5	42	17	10	16	14	30	26	1	13	43	8	3	5	3	21	3	27	36	3	10	38	45	19	5	4	30		EL Appearances	
6	2	2	0	6	2	1	3	7	4	5	1	0	2	1	0	0	2	5	1	0	3	0	0	4	7	3	0		EL Sub Appearances	
5	2+1	4+1	0	2	4	1	1+1	4	0+1	0	6	2	0	1+1	0	0	1	6	5	0	1	4	6	3	2+1	1+1	5		CC Appearances	
4	0	4	0	0	0+1	0	3	3	0+1	0	4	0	0	1	0	4	1	3+1	2	0	0	4	4	2	1	0	4		FAC Appearances	

o Played: (F) Crowe S(54), S1(55), X(56). (G) De Bont S(1,15,16,17,18,20). (F) Dennison S1(31), S(51). (D) Shirtliff X(1,2). (M) Thomas S(1), S1(3), S2(5).

WOLVERHAMPTON WANDERERS

CLUB RECORDS

BIGGEST VICTORIES
League: 10-1 v Leicester City, Division 1, 15.4.1938
9-0 v Fulham, Division 1, 16.9.1959
F.A. Cup: 14-0 v Crosswells Brewery, Rnd 2, 13.11.1886
League Cup: 6-1 v Shrewsbury, Rnd 2, 24.9.1991
Europe: 5-0 v F K Austria, 30.11.1960

BIGGEST DEFEATS
League: 1-10 v Newton Heath, Division 1, 15.10.1892
0-9 v Derby County, Division 1, 10.1.1891
F.A. Cup: 0-6 v Rotherham Utd, Rnd 1, 16.11.1985
League Cup: 0-5 v Fulham, Rnd 3, 5.10.1966
0-5 v Sunderland, Rnd 2 replay, 27.10.1982
Europe: 0-4 v Barcelona, European Cup Q-Final, 2.10.1960

MOST POINTS
3 points a win: 92, Division 3, 1988-89
2 points a win: 64, Division 1, 1957-58

MOST GOALS
115, Division 2, 1931-32.
Hartill 30, Bottrill 21, Phillips 18, Deacon 13, Lowton 9, Baraclough 7, Buttery 6, Hollingworth 4, Crook 2, Martin 1, Redfern 1, Richards 1, Smalley 1,og 1.

MOST FIRST CLASS MATCHES IN A SEASON
61 (46 League, 3 FA Cup, 4 League Cup, 8 Sherpa Van Trophy) 1987-88

MOST LEAGUE GOALS CONCEDED
99, Division 1, 1905-06

MOST LEAGUE WINS
28, Division 1, 1957-58; Division 1, 1958-59

MOST LEAGUE DRAWS
19, Division 2, 1990-91

MOST LEAGUE DEFEATS
25, Division 1, 1964-65; Division 1, 1983-84; Division 2, 1984-85; Division3, 1985-86

INDIVIDUAL CLUB RECORDS

MOST GOALS IN A MATCH
5. J Brodie v Stoke, 8-0, FA Cup 3, 22.2.1890
5. J Butcher v Accrington, 5-3, Div 1, 19.11.1892
5. T Phillipson v Bradford City, 7-2, Div 2, 25.12.1926
5. W Hartill v Notts County, 5-1, Div 2, 12.10.1929
5. W Hartill v Aston Villa, 5-2, Div 1, 3.9.1934

MOST GOALS IN A SEASON
Steve Bull, 52, 1987-88.
League 34, FA Cup 3, League Cup 3, SVT 12.
League only: D Westcott 38, 1946-47

OLDEST PLAYER
Lawrie Madden 37 yrs 222 days v Derby County, 8.5.1993

YOUNGEST PLAYER
Jimmy Mullen, 16 years 43 days v Leeds United, 18.2.1939
Wartime: Cameron Buchanan, 14 yrs 57 days v W.B.A., 26.9.1942

MOST CAPPED PLAYER
Billy Wright, 105 for England

BEST PERFORMANCES

Wolverhampton are the only League Club to have been Champions of all Four Divisions: Div 1, 1954, 1958, 1959; Div 2, 1932, 1977; Div 3N 1924; Div 3,1989; Div 4, 1988

League: 1957-58: Played 42, Won 28, Drawn 8, Lost 6, Goals For 103, Goals Against 47, Points 64. First in Division One

Highest: Division One Champions 3 times

F.A. Cup: 1892-93: 1st rnd. Bolton Wanderers 1-1, 2-1; 2nd rnd. Middlesbrough 2-1; 3rd rnd. Darwen 5-0; Semi-Final Blackburn Rovers 2-1; Final Everton 1-0
1907-08: 1st rnd. Bradford City 1-1, 1-0; 2nd rnd. Bury 2-0; 3rd rnd. Swindon Town 2-0; 4th rnd. Stoke City 1-0; Semi-Final Southampton 2-0; Final Newcastle United 3-1
1948-49: 3rd rnd. Chesterfield 6-0, 4th rnd. Sheffield Utd 3-0; Liverpool 3-1;6th rnd. West Bromwich Albion 1-0; Semi-Final Manchester United 1-1, 1-0; Final Leicester City 3-1
1959-60: 3rd rnd. Newcastle United 2-2, 4-2; 4th rnd Charlton Athletic 2-1; 5th Luton Town 4-1; 6th rnd. Leicester City 2-1; Semi-Final Aston Villa 1-0; Final Blackburn Rovers 3-0

League Cup: 1973-74: 2nd rnd. Halifax Town 3-0; 3rd rnd. Tranmere Rovers 1-1,2-1; 4th rnd. Exeter City 5-1; 5th rnd. Liverpool 1-0; Semi-Final Norwich City 1-1, 1-0; Final Manchester City 2-1
1979-80: 2nd rnd. Burnley 1-1, 2-0; 3rd rnd. Crystal Palace 2-1; 4th rnd. Queens Park Rangers 1-1, 1-0; 5th rnd. Grimsby Town 0-0, 1-1, 2-0; Semi-Final Swindon Town 1-2, 3-1; Final Nottingham Forest 1-0

UEFA Cup: 1971-72: 1st rnd. Academica 3-0, 4-1; 2nd rnd. Den Haag 3-1, 4-0; 3rd rnd. Carl Zeiss 1-0, 3-0; Quarter-Final Juventus 1-1, 2-1; Semi-Final Ferencvaros 2-2, 2-1; Final Tottenham Hotspur 1-2, 1-1

ADDITIONAL INFORMATION
Previous Name: None.
Previous League: None.

Club colours: Gold shirts, black shorts, gold socks.

Change colours: All white.

Reserves League: Pontins Central League Division 1.

DIVISIONAL RECORD

	Played	Won	Drawn	Lost	For	Against	Points
Division 1	2,270	911	506	853	3,874	3,671	2,344
Division 2/1	1,378	548	322	508	2,161	1,957	1,562
Division 3	92	37	24	31	153	147	135
Division 3(N)	42	24	15	3	76	27	63
Division 4	92	51	16	25	151	93	169
Total	3,874	1,571	883	1,420	6,415	5,895	4,273

RECORDS AND STATISTICS

COMPETITIONS

Div.1	Div.2/1	Div.3N	Euro C	Texaco	Watney	C/Sld
1888-06	1906-23	1923-24	1958-59	1970-71	1972-73	1949-50
1932-65	1924-32		1959-60	1972-73		1954-55
1967-76	1965-67	Div.3	ECWC		F/SVT	1958-59
1977-82	1976-77	1985-86	1960-61	A/Ital	1985-86	1959-60
1983-84	1982-83	1988-89	UEFA	1969-70	1986-87	1960-61
	1984-85		1971-72		1987-88	
	1989-	Div.4	1973-74		1988-89	
		1986-88	1974-75			
			1980-81			

HONOURS

Div.1	Div.2	Div.3	Div.4	FAC	Lge C	C/S/sld
1953-54	1931-32	1923-24	1987-88	1892-93	1973-74	1949-50*
1957-58	1976-77	1988-89		1907-08	1979-80	1954-55*
1958-59				1948-49		1959-60
				1959-60		1960-61*

*Shared

Also won the Texaco Cup - 1970-71 & SVT 1987-88

MOST APPEARANCES

Derek Parkin 607+2 (167-82)

Year	League	FA Cup	Lge Cup	Europe
1967-68	15			
1968-69	42	2	3	
1969-70	42	1	3	
1970-71	39	2	1	
1971-72	32	2	1	7
1972-73	18	3		
1973-74	39	3	6	4
1974-75	41	1	1	2
1975-76	30	6	3	
1976-77	42	5	1	
1977-78	38	3	1	
1978-79	42	7	1	
1979-80	40	3	11	
1980-81	19+1	6+1	1	2
1981-82	21	1	2	
	500+1	45+1	35	15

Includes 7 Texaco Cup 70-71, 4 Anglo-Itl 69-70, 1 Watney C. 72-73.

MOST GOALS IN A CAREER

Steve Bull - 268 (1986-96)

Year	League	FA Cup	Lge Cup	Others
1986-87	15			4
1987-88	34	3	3	12
1988-89	37		2	11
1989-90	24	1	2	
1990-91	26			1
1991-92	20		3	
1992-93	16	1	1	1
1993-94	14			1
1994-95	16		2	1
1995-96	15	2		
Total	217	7	13	31

RECORD TRANSFER FEE RECEIVED

Amount	Club	Player	Date
£1,125,000	Manchester City	Steve Daley	9/79
£240,000	Arsenal	Alan Sunderland	11/77
£100,000	Liverpool	Alun Evans	6/68

RECORD TRANSFER FEE PAID

Amount	Club	Player	Date
£1,300,000	Bradford City	Dean Richards	5/95
£1,250,000	Aston Villa	Tony Daley	5/94
£1,150,000	Aston Villa	Andy Gray	9/80
£185,000	Hull City	Peter Daniel	3/78

MANAGERS

Name	Seasons	Best	Worst
Jack Addenbrooke	1885-1922	3(1)	19(2)
George Jobey	1922-24	22(2)	1(3)
Albert Hoskins	1924-26	4(2)	6(2)
Fred Scotchbrook	1926-27	15(2)	15(2)
Major Frank Buckley	1927-44	2(1)	17(2)
Ted Vizard	1944-48	3(1)	5(1)
Stan Cullis	1948-64	1(1)	18(1)
Andy Beattie	1964-65	21(1)	21(1)
Ronnie Allen	1965-68	17(1)	6(2)
Bill McGarry	1968-76	4(1)	20(1)
Sammy Chung	1976-78	15(1)	1(2)
John Barnwell	1978-81	6(1)	18(1)
Ian Greaves	1982		
Graham Hawkins	1982-84	22(1)	2(2)
Tommy Docherty	1984-85	22(2)	22(2)
Sammy Chapman	1985		
Bill McGarry	1985		
Sammy Chapman	1985-86	23(3)	23(3)
Brian Little	1986		
Graham Turner	1986-94	10(2)	4(4)
Graham Taylor	1994-95	4(1)	4(1)
Mark McGhee	1995-	20(1)	20(1)

LONGEST LEAGUE RUNS

of undefeated matches:	20 (24.11.1923 - 5.4.1924)	of league matches w/out a win:	19 (1.12.1984 - 6.4.1985)
of undefeated home matches:	27 (24.3.1923 - 6.9.1924)	of undefeated away matches:	11 (5.9.1953 - 2.1.1954)
without home win:	13 (17.11.1984 - 27.4.1985)	without an away win:	32 (4.3.1922 - 6.10.1923)
of league wins:	8 (13.3.1915-17.4.1915, 4.2.1967-28.3.1967)	of home wins:	14 (7.3.1953 - 28.11.1953)
	(14.3.1987 - 20.4.1987, 15.10.1988 - 26.11.1988)		
of league defeats:	8 (5.12.1981 - 13.2.1982)	of away wins:	5 (1.1.38-26.2.38, 20.8.62-22.9.62, 9.2.80-7.4.80)

WOLVERHAMPTON WANDERERS

PLAYERS NAME Honours	Ht	Wt	Birthdate	Birthplace Transfers	Contract Date	Clubs	League	L/Cup	FA Cup	Other	Lge	L/C	FAC	Oth
G O A L K E E P E R S														
Stowell Michael	6.2	11.10	19/04/65	Preston		Leyland Motors								
				Free	14/02/85	Preston North End								
				Free	12/12/85	Everton			1					
				Loan	03/09/87	Chester City	14			2				
				Loan	24/12/87	York City	6							
				Loan	02/02/88	Manchester City	14		1					
				Loan	21/10/88	Port Vale	7			1				
				Loan	17/03/89	Wolves	7							
				Loan	08/02/90	Preston North End	2							
				£250000	28/06/90	Wolves	232	16	13	9				
D E F E N D E R S														
Atkins Mark E: S	6.0	12.5	14/08/68	Doncaster	09/07/86	Scunthorpe United	45+5	3+1	5	6+1	2			
				£45000	16/06/88	Blackburn Rovers	224+33	20+4	11+3	17+2	34	4		1
				£1000000	21/09/95	Wolves	26+6	5	4		2	2		
Curle Keith E: 3, B.4. FRT'86. SC'88. FLgXI.1	6.0	12.0	14/11/63	Bristol	20/11/81	Bristol Rovers	21+11	3	1		4			
				£5000	04/11/83	Torquay United	16		1	1	5		1	
				£10000	03/03/84	Bristol City	113+8	7+1	5	14+1	1			
				£150000	23/10/87	Reading	40	8		5				
				£500000	21/10/88	Wimbledon	91+2	7	5	6	3			1
				£2500000	14/08/91	Manchester City	171	18	14	1	11	2		
				£650000	31/07/96	Wolves								
Emblen Neil	6.1	12.07	19/06/71	Bromley		Tonbridge								
						Sittingbourne								
				£175000	08/11/93	Millwall	12			1				
				£600000	14/07/94	Wolves	53+7	2+2	6+2	2+1	9	1		
Law Brian W: 1, u21.1, Y. S	6.2	11.12	01/01/70	Merthyr Tydfil	15/08/87	Q.P.R.	19+1	2+1	3	1				
				£134000	23/12/94	Wolves	22+1	1+1	7		1			
Masters Neil	6.1	13.3	25/05/72	Ballymena	31/08/90	Bournemouth	37+1	4	5+2	2	2	1	1	
				£600000	22/12/93	Wolves	10+2							
Pearce Dennis	5.9	11.0	10/09/74	Wolverhampton	07/06/93	Aston Villa								
					03/07/95	Wolves	3+2	1	1					
Richards Dean	6.0	12.0	09/06/74	Bradford	10/07/92	Bradford City	52+4	4	3	2+2	3			
				£1850000	30/06/95	Wolves	36+1	5	2		1			
Thompson Andy Div4'88. Div3'89. SVT'88	5.4	10.6	09/11/67	Cannock	16/11/85	W.B.A.	18+6	0+1	2	1+1	1			
				£35000	21/11/86	Wolves	330+14	20	20	32	41	1	1	1
Venus Mark Div3'89	6.0	11.8	06/04/67	Hartlepool	06/09/85	Leicester City	58+3	3	2	2+1	1			
				£40000	23/03/88	Wolves	235+13	15+1	14+1	17	7	1		2
					22/03/91	Hartlepool United	4			0+1				
Young Eric W: 20; FAC'88; IsthPL'81; FMC'91; Div1'94	6.3	12.6	25/03/60	Singapore		Staines								
					Slough			2						
				£10000	01/11/82	Brighton & H.A.	126	8	11	2	10		1	
				£70000	29/07/87	Wimbledon	96+3	12	6+1	7	9		1	
				£850000	15/08/90	Crystal Palace	161	25	10	6	15	1		1
					16/09/95	Wolves	30	5	4		2			
M I D F I E L D														
Corica Steve						Marconi								
				£100000	11/08/95	Leicester City	16		2		2			
				£1100000	16/02/96	Wolves	17							
De Jong Davy						Willem II (Hol)								
				Free		Wolves								
Ferguson Darren S: u21.8, Y. Prem'93	5.10	10.9	09/02/72	Glasgow	11/07/90	Manchester United	20+7	2+1						
				£250000	13/01/94	Wolves	60+11	7	7	4	1	1	1	
Foley Dominic						Wolves	1+4	0+1	0+1					
Froggatt Stephen E: u21.2	5.10	11.0	09/03/73	Lincoln	26/01/91	Aston Villa	30+5	1+1	5+2		2		1	
				£1000000	11/07/94	Wolves	33+5	3			3	1		
Osborn Simon	5.10	11.4	19/01/72	Croydon	03/01/90	Crystal Palace	47+8	11	2	1+3	4	1		
				£90000	17/08/94	Reading	31+1	4		3	5			
				£1100000	07/07/95	Q.P.R.	6+3	2			1			
				£1000000	22/12/95	Wolves	21		4		2			
Robinson Carl P						Wolves								
				Loan	28/03/96	Shrewsbury Town	2+2		1					
Thomas Geoff E: 9, B.3. FMC'91	6.1	12.0	05/08/64	Manchester	13/08/82	Rochdale	10+1		0+1	1				
				Free	22/03/84	Crewe Alexandra	120+5	8	2	2+1	21			

Thomas continued...					£50000	08/06/87	Crystal Palace	192+3	24	13+1		15+1	26	3	2	4
					£800000	18/06/93	Wolves	21+3	1			4	5			
Westwood Christopher							Wolves									
O R W A R D S																
Bull Steve	5.11	11.4	28/03/65	Tipton			Tipton Town									
E: 13, B.5, u21.5. Div4'88.					Free	24/08/85	W.B.A.	2+2	2			1+2	2	1		
Div3'89. SVT'88					£35000	21/11/86	Wolves	383+2	23+1	16		31+1	216	13	7	32
Daley Tony	5.8	10.8	18/10/67	Birmingham	31/05/85		Aston Villa	189+44	22+2	15+1		15+2	31	4	2	1
E: 7, B.1, Y.8. LC'94					£1250000	06/06/94	Wolves	16+3	4	0+1			3	1		
Dennison Robert	5.7	11.0	30/04/63	Banbridge			Glenavon									
NI: 17, B.1. Div4'88. Div3'89.					£40000	13/09/85	W.B.A.	9+7	1	2		1	1			
SVT'88					£20000	13/03/87	Wolves	255+24	12+4	15+2		24+2	40	3	2	4
Goodman Don	5.10	11.7	09/05/66	Leeds			Collingham									
Div3'85					Free	10/07/84	Bradford City	65+5	5+1	2+3		4+1	14	2	4	2
					£50000	27/03/87	W.B.A.	140+18	11	7		5	60	1	1	1
					£900000	06/12/91	Sunderland	95+3	7	3		4	37	1	1	2
					£1100000	06/12/94	Wolves	67+1	6	9+1		2	19	3	1	
Rankine S Mark	5.10	11.8	30/09/69	Doncaster	04/07/88		Doncaster Rovers	160+4	8+1	8		14	20	1	2	2
					£70000	31/01/92	Wolves	112+20	9+1	14+2		7+2	1			
Roberts Iwan	6.3	12.6	26/06/68	Bangor	04/07/86		Watford	40+23	6+2	1+6		5	9	3		
W: 4, Y					£275000	02/08/90	Huddersfield Town	141+1	13+1	12		14	51	6	4	8
					£100000	25/11/93	Leicester City	92+8	18	5			28	1	2	
					£1000000	04/07/96	Wolves									
Smith James	5.6	10.8	17/09/74	Birmingham	07/06/93		Wolves	34+4	4	1		2				
Wright Jermaine	5.9	10.13	21/10/75	Greenwich	27/11/92		Millwall									
					£60000	29/12/94	Wolves	4+9	1+1			0+1		1		
					Loan	01/03/96	Doncaster Rovers	13								

THE MANAGER
MARK McGHEE

Date of Birth . . . . 25th May 1957.
Place of Birth . . . . Glasgow.
Date of Appointment . . . . December 1995.

PREVIOUS CLUBS
As Manager . . . . Reading, Leicester City.
As Coach. . . . . None.
As a Player. . . Bristol City (A), Morton, Newcastle Utd, Aberdeen, SV Hamburg,
. . . . Celtic, Newcastle Utd, Reading (player-manager).

HONOURS
As a Manager
Reading: Division 2 champions 1993-94.

As a Player
Scottish League Chapions 1980, 1984, 1986, 1988. Scottish Cup 1982, 1983, 1984, 1988, 1989.
ECWC 1983.
Scotland: 4 full caps and 1 u21 cap.

MOLINEUX GROUND

Waterloo Road, Wolverhampton WV1 4QR
Tel: 01902 655 000

Capacity 28,500

First game ....v Aston Villa, 2.9.1889.
First floodlit game ....v South Africa XI, 30.9.1953.

ATTENDANCES
Highest...61,315 v Liverpool, FA. Cup 5th Rnd, 11.2.1939.
Lowest ....900 v Notts County, Div.1, 17.10.1891.

OTHER GROUNDS ....Three previous to Molineux.

MATCHDAY TICKET PRICES

Jack Harris/Stand Cullis £11
Juv/OAP £7.50

John Ireland Stand Upper £13
Juv/OAP £8.50
John Ireland Stand Lower. £11
Juv/OAP £7.50

Billy Wright Upper Wing £14
Juv/OAP £9
Billy Wright Upper Centre. £15
Juv/OAP £9.50

Young Wolves Family Enclosure £8

Ticket Office Telephone no. 01902 25899

CLUBCALL 0891 12 11 03

Calls cost 39p per minute cheap rate and 49p per
minute at all other times.
Call costings correct at time of going to press.

HOW TO GET TO THE GROUND

From the North
Use motorway M6 until junction 12, leave motorway and follow signs to
Wolverhampton (A5) then A449 and at roundabout take 2nd exit into Waterloo
Road, then turn left in Molineux Street for Wolverhampton Wanderers FC.
From the East
Use motorway M6 until junction 10, leave motorway and follow signs to
Wolverhampton 9A454). Then at crossroads turn right into Stafford Street. In 0.2
miles turn left into Ring Road. Then at next crossroads turn right into Waterloo Road
and shortly turn right into Molineux Street for Wolverhampton Wanderers FC.
From the South
Use motorway M5 until junction 12, leave motorway and follow signs to
Wolverhampton (A4123) turn right then shortly turn left into Ring Road. In 1 mile
turn left into Waterloo Road and shortly turn left into Molineux Street for
Wolverhampton Wanderers FC.
From the West
Use A454, sign posted Wolverhampton, and at roundabout turn left into Ring Road,
then left into Molineux Street for Wolverhampton FC.

Car Parking: Available around 'The West Park', in side streets and at the rear of the
North Bank.

Nearest Railway Station
Wolverhampton (01902 595 451)

MATCHDAY PROGRAMME

Programme Editor . . . . Lorraine Hennessy.

Number of pages . . . . 48.

Price . . . . £1.50.

Subscriptions . . . . Please contact club.

Local Newspapers . . . . Express & Star, Evening Mail,
. . . . Wolverhampton's Saturday night Pink.

Local Radio Stations . . . . Beacon Radio, BRMB, Radio WM.

NATIONWIDE
LEAGUE DIVISION 2

...1996-97

FINAL LEAGUE TABLE

		P	W	D	L	F	A	Pts
1	Swindon Town	46	25	17	4	71	34	92
2	Oxford United (+5)	46	24	11	11	76	39	83
3	Blackpool (+9)	46	23	13	10	67	40	82
4	Notts County	46	21	15	10	63	39	78
5	Crewe Alexandra (-2)	46	22	7	17	77	60	73
6	Bradford City (+8)	46	22	7	17	71	69	73
7	Chesterfield	46	20	12	14	56	51	72
8	Wrexham (+5)	46	18	16	12	76	55	70
9	Stockport County (+2)	46	19	13	14	61	47	70
10	Bristol Rovers (-6)	46	20	10	16	57	60	70
11	Walsall	46	19	12	15	60	45	69
12	Wycome Wanderers (-6)	46	15	15	16	63	59	60
13	Bristol City	46	15	15	16	55	60	60
14	Bournemouth (+5)	46	16	10	20	51	70	58
15	Brentford (-13)	46	15	13	18	43	49	58
16	Rotherham United (+1)	46	14	14	18	54	62	56
17	Burnley	46	14	13	19	56	68	55
18	Shrewsbury Town (-)	46	13	14	19	58	70	53
19	Peterborough United (-4)	46	13	13	20	59	66	52
20	York City (-11)	46	13	13	20	58	73	52
21	Carlisle United	46	12	13	21	57	72	49
22	Swansea City (-12)	46	11	14	21	43	79	47
23	Brighton & Hove A. (-7)	46	10	10	26	46	69	40
24	Hull City (-16)	46	5	16	25	36	78	31

The figure in brackets denotes the number of places lost or gained on the clubs 1994-95 final position.

NATIONWIDE LEAGUE DIVISION TWO 1996-97

BLACKPOOL
(The Seasiders)
NATIONWIDE LEAGUE DIVISION 2
SPONSORED BY: REBECCA'S JEWELLERS

Back Row (L-R): Paul Symons, Darren Bradshaw, Jamie Murphy, Jason Lydiate, Craig Allardyce, Andy Preece, Phil Horner, Tony Ellis, Jon Sunderland, Scott Darton.
Middle Row: David Carroll, Stephen Torre, John Hooks, Graeme Craggs, Lee Martin, Tim Carter, Melvin Capleton, James Quinn, David Burke, Robert Ward, Jamie Sheppard.
Front Row: Stuart Parkinson, Micky Mellon, Chris Beech, Andy Morrison, Billy Bingham (Director of Football), Sam Allardyce (Manager), Phil Brown (Player Coach), Brian Croft, Andy Gouck, Mark Bonner, Andy Barlow.

BLACKPOOL
FORMED IN 1887
TURNED PROFESSIONAL IN 1887
LTD COMPANY IN 1896

PRESIDENT: C A Sagar B.E.M.
HON VICE PRESIDENTS: R P Gibrail,
J Armfield, K Chadwick,
Sir Stanley Matthews, W Beaumont
CHAIRMAN: O J Oyston
DIRECTORS:
Mrs V Oyston (Deputy Chairman)
Mrs R Bincham, W L Bingham MBE,
Mrs G Bridge (Managing), K Chadwick,
M Joyce, C Muir OBE (Associate Director)
G Warburton, J Wilde MBE.
SECRETARY: Carol Banks
(01253 404 331)
COMMERCIAL MANAGER
Geoff Warburton (01253 752 222)

MANAGER: Sam Allardyce
PLAYER/COACH: Phil Brown
YOUTH TEAM MANAGER
Alan Crawford
PHYSIOTHERAPIST
Mark Taylor

CLUB STATISTICIAN FOR THE DIRECTORY
Roger Harrison

Blackpool appeared to be one of the favourites, along with Swindon Town, for automatic promotion, until a disasterous run in April in which two points were gained from seven games. This left them in third place, while Oxford United only needed to win the final game to gain promotion - which they did 4-0. Blackpool entered the promotion play-offs, but after winning 2-0 at Bradford City in the first leg they lost 3-0 at home three days later, leaving the club and supporters in dismay after what had been - until April - a tremendous season. The gates had been up by 22% at home and the away support had been great.

The promotion run had been built around a spell of one defeat in 22 league games between 25 November and 30 March during which Sam Allardyce won the Divisional Manager of the Month award twice. Unfortunately the season will be remembered by many for its last few weeks.

We went out in the first round of the Coca-Cola Cup, losing in both legs against Bradford City who we eventually met six times during the season. In the FA Cup we beat Chester City and Colwyn Bay, and were then drawn at Huddersfield Town in the third round - only to lose 2-1 to a late goal.

In the Auto Windscreens Shield we reached the third round, but lost to Chesterfield who were a tricky side during the season, keeping three clean sheets against us.

Tony Ellis, with 17 goals overall, was leading scorer, followed by Andy Preece (15) and James Quinn (14) who also made his international debut for Northern Ireland. The summer will be spent sorting out contracts. Let's hope that the success of this season will stand Blackpool in good stead for the next year.

ROGER HARRISON

BLACKPOOL

League: 3rd   FA Cup: 3rd Rnd   Coca-Cola Cup: 1st Rnd   Auto Windscreen Shield: Quarter Finals

M	DATE		COMP	VEN	OPPONENTS	RESULT		HT	LP	GOAL SCORERS/GOAL TIMES	ATT.
1	A	12	EL	A	Bristol City	D	1-1	1-1	16	Quinn 1	(7734)
2		15	CC 1/1	A	**Bradford City**	L	1-2	0-2		Ellis 78	**(3670)**
3		19	EL	H	Wrexham	W	2-0	2-0	7	Ellis 2, 40	4799
4		22	CC 1/2	H	**Bradford City**	L	2-3	0-0		**Mellon 67, Ellis 68**	**4553**
5		26	EL	A	Hull City	L	1-2	1-1	10	Lydiate 24	(4755)
6		29	EL	H	Peterborough United	W	2-1	1-1	6	Preece 22, Quinn 47	3902
7	S	2	EL	A	Shrewsbury Town	W	2-0	2-0	2	Preece 17, 44	(3182)
8		9	EL	H	Stockport County	L	0-1	0-1	6		6602
9		12	EL	H	Bournemouth	W	2-1	1-1	3	Preece 36, Morrison 70	3884
10		16	EL	A	Brighton & H.A.	W	2-1	2-0	4	Ellis 6, Mellon 18	(6158)
11		23	EL	A	Crewe Alexandra	W	2-1	1-0	2	Preece 56, Ellis 65	7301
12		26	AWS 1/1	H	**Crewe Alexandra**	W	1-0	1-0		Quinn 4	**2560**
13		30	EL	A	Bradford City	L	1-2	1-0	3	Preece 36	(6820)
14	O	7	EL	A	Brentford	W	2-1	0-1	2	Preece 56(pen), Ellis 80	(5313)
15		14	EL	H	Chesterfield	D	0-0	0-0	3		6855
16		21	EL	A	Rotherham United	L	1-2	0-0	4	Preece 57(pen)	(3663)
17		28	EL	H	Oxford United	D	1-1	0-0	5	Quinn 72	5303
18		31	EL	H	Bristol Rovers	W	3-0	1-0	3	Gouck 7, Quinn 11, Ellis 18	3877
19	N	4	EL	A	Swindon Town	D	1-1	0-0	5	Quinn 71(pen)	(12470)
20		7	AWS 1/2	A	**Hartlepool United**	L	2-3	2-2		Beech 15, Quinn 33	**(895)**
21		11	FAC 1	H	**Chester City**	W	2-1	0-0		**Quinn 84, Lydiate 86**	**5004**
22		18	EL	H	York City	L	1-3	1-1	5	Holden 27	4514
23		25	EL	A	Walsall	D	1-1	0-0	4	Mellon 58	(4459)
24		28	AWS 2	H	**Hull City**	W	2-1	0-0		**Beech 71, Mellon 77**	**(1422)**
25	D	2	FAC 2	H	**Colwyn Bay**	W	2-0	0-0		**Preece 52, Quinn 64**	**4581**
26		9	EL	A	Crewe Alexandra	W	2-1	1-0	4	Watson 56, Ellis 68	(4551)
27		16	EL	H	Bradford City	W	4-1	1-0	4	Watson 15, 70, Ellis 56, Bonner 78	4857
28		23	EL	A	Notts County	D	1-1	0-0	4	Arkins 68(og)	(5522)
29	J	1	EL	A	Carlisle United	W	2-1	1-0	3	Bryan 43, Linighan 89	(7532)
30		6	FAC 3	A	**Huddersfield Town**	L	1-2	1-1		**Quinn 24**	**(12424)**
31		9	AWS QF	H	**Chesterfield**	L	0-1	0-0			**2469**
32		13	EL	A	Wrexham	D	1-1	0-0	3	Preece 88	(5479)
33		20	EL	A	Bristol City	W	3-0	1-0	3	Morrison 34, Ellis 56, Preece 73(pen)	4838
34		23	EL	H	Wycombe Wanderers	D	1-1	1-0	3	Preece 27	3887
35	F	3	EL	H	Hull City	D	1-1	1-0	4	Holden 17	4713
36		10	EL	A	Wycombe Wanderers	W	1-0	1-0	3	Watson 34	(5285)
37		13	EL	H	Swansea City	W	4-0	2-0	2	Watson 15, Mellon 38, Bonner 65, Preece 71	4092
38		17	EL	A	Bournemouth	L	0-1	0-0	3		(4157)
39		20	EL	H	Shrewsbury Town	W	2-1	0-0	2	Quinn 36, Seabury 84(og)	4210
40		24	EL	H	Brighton & H.A.	W	2-1	0-1	2	Mellon 68, 89	4937
41		27	EL	A	Stockport County	D	1-1	0-0	2	Ellis 90	(7711)
42	M	2	EL	A	Burnley	W	1-0	0-0	2	Preece 62	(10082)
43		9	EL	A	Notts County	W	1-0	1-0	2	Ellis 11	7187
44		12	EL	H	Burnley	W	3-1	1-1	2	Mellon 25, Bonner 59, Ellis 78	8941
45		16	EL	A	Swansea City	W	2-0	0-0	1	Ellis 89, Watson 90	(4478)
46		23	EL	H	Carlisle United	W	3-1	1-1	1	Linighan 39, 86, Quinn 71(pen)	8144
47		26	EL	A	Peterborough United	D	0-0	0-0	1		(4425)
48		30	EL	H	Brentford	W	1-0	1-0	1	Quinn 42(pen)	5899
49	A	2	EL	A	Chesterfield	L	0-1	0-0	1		(7002)
50		6	EL	A	Oxford United	L	0-1	0-0	4		(7875)
51		8	EL	H	Rotherham United	L	1-2	1-1	2	Preece 10	6850
52		13	EL	A	Bristol Rovers	D	1-1	0-1	2	Linighan 50	(5626)
53		20	EL	H	Swindon Town	D	1-1	0-1	2	Barlow 61	9175
54		27	EL	H	Walsall	L	1-2	1-1	3	Quinn 41(pen)	9148
55	M	4	EL	A	York City	W	2-0	1-0	3	Morrison 6, Ellis 85	(7147)
56		12	PO SF1	A	**Bradford City**	W	2-0	0-0		**Ellis 71, Bonner 78**	**(14273)**
57		15	PO SF2	H	**Bradford City**	L	0-3	0-1			9593

Best Home League Attendance: 9175 v Swindon Town   Smallest: 3877 v Bristol Rovers   Average: 5822

Goal Scorers:
EL(67):   Preece(14),Ellis(14),Quinn(9),Watson(6),Mellon(6),Linighan(4),Morrison(3),Bonner(3),Holden(2),Opponent(s)(2),Lydiate(1),Bryan(1),Barlow(1),Gouck(1)
CC(3):   Ellis(2),Mellon(1)
FAC(5):   Quinn(3),Preece(1),Lydiate(1)
AWS(5):   Quinn(2),Beech(2),Mellon(1)
PO(2):   Bonner(1),Ellis(1)

(D) Allardyce	(G) Banks	(M) Barber	(M) Barlow	(M) Beech	(M) Bonner	(M) Bradshaw	(D) Brown	(D) Brown	(F) Bryan	(G) Capleton	(M) Charnock	(D) Darton	(F) Ellis	(M) Gouck	(M) Holden	(D) Linighan	(D) Lydiate	(M) Mellon	(M) Mitchell	(D) Morrison	(G) Nixon	(M) Parkinson	(F) Pascoe	(M) Philpott	(F) Preece	(F) Quinn	(M) Watson	(D) Yallop	Player	No
		X	S	X	X	X	S	X	S1	X				X	X			X		X					X	X1			G.Pooley	1
	X		S2	X1	X		X2	S1	X				S	X	X			X		X					X	X			N.Barry	2
		X	X	X	S		X	S	X					X	X			X		X					X	X1			T.Heilbron	3
	X		X2	X	S2	X	S	X	S1					X	X1			X		X					X	X			G.Cain	4
	X		X1	X	S2	X		X	S1					X	X2			X		X			S		X	X			I.G.Cruikshanks	5
	X		S1	X	X	S		X	X				X	X				X		X	S				X	X1			J.Lloyd	6
	X		S1	X	X	S		X	X				X	X				X		X1	S				X	X			R.D.Furnandiz	7
	X			X	X			X	X				X	X		S1	X	X1		X					X	X1			K.M.Lynch	8
	X	X	S	X	X	S		X	X					X		S1		X		X					X	X1			M.Fletcher	9
	X	X	X2	X3	S2			X	X				X	S3		X	X	X		X					X1	S1			F.Stretton	10
	X	X	S1		X			X	X				X	X			X	X		X					X	X1			R.Pearson	11
	X	X	S1		X			X	X				X2	S2		X	X	X		X					X	X1			G.Frankland	12
	X		S2	X	S			X	X				X	X			X2	X		X					X	X1	S1		A.Wiley	13
	X		S1	X				X	X				S	X1			X	X		X					X	X	S		K.A.Leach	14
S	X	X		X				X	X				X2	S2		X	X	X		X					X	X1	S1		J.Rushton	15
	X		S1		X	S		X	X				X		X	X	X		X					X	X1	X1		W.Burns	16
	X		S2	X				X	X				X2	S	X	X	X		X					X1	X	S1		F.Stretton	17
	X		X2					X	X				X	X	X	X	X		X1					S2	X	S		M.Riley	18
	X		X	X			S1	X	X				X	X	X1	X	X							S	X	S	X	G.Bennett	19
S	X		X	X1	X			X	X				S	X	S1	X	X							X	X	X	X	T.West	20
	X		X		X	X		X	X				S	X1	X2	X	X		X					S1	X	S2		J.Kirkby	21
	X		S2	X1	S			X	X				X	X2	S	X	X	X		X					X	S1	X1	R.Pulain	22
	X		X2					X	X			S1	X	X2	X3	X	X		X					S2	X	X1		C.Wilkes	23
	X	X	S2		X			X	S3	X	X2	X3	X	X	X		X		X					X1	S1			T.Leake	24
	X		X	X	X	S2		X	X				X1			X	X		X					X	X2	X1		S.Mathieson	25
S	X		X	S1				X	S	X			X	X	X		X		X					X	X1			D.Allison	26
S2		X	X	S3	X3			X	S1	X1	X2	X	X	X	X		X		X					X	X			R.Furnandiz	27
	X	S	X	S				X	S	X			X	X	X		X		X					X	X			M.Bailey	28
	X	S	X	X1				X	S1	X			X	X	X		X		X				S2	X2	X			E.Wolstenholme	29
	X	X2	X	X3	S3			X	X	S2			X	X	X		X		X					S1	X1	X		N.Barry	30
	X	X1	S		X1			X	S	X			X	X	X		X		X					X	X	X2		K.Leach	31
	X	X1	S		X	S1	X	X				X	X	X		X		X				S2	X2	X			J.Rushton	32
	X		X2	S	X			X	X	S2			X	X	X		X		X					X	X1	X		T.West	33
	X		X	X	X	S3		X	X	S1	X2	X	X	X1		X		X					X	X	S3		I.Cruikshank	34
S		X1	X	X				X	S1	X2	X	X	X		X		X							X	X1	S2		E.Lomas	35
S		X	X			S1		X			X	X				X		X		X			X	X1	X			G.Singh	36
		X1	X			X2	S1	X	S		X	X		X	X		S2	X		X			X	X	X1	X		U.Rennie	37
	X3	X	X			X	S3	X	S2	X2	X	S1	X	X	X		X		X			X	X	X1	X		M.Pierce	38
		X	S1			X	S	X	X1		X	X	X	S		X	X	X			X	X		X				J.Lloyd	39
		X	X			X	S	X	X		X	X	X	X1		X	X	X			X	X		X				S.Baines	40
	X2	X				X	S2	X	X		X	S	X	X		X	X	X			X	X1		X1	X			A.Riley	41
	X	S				X	S	X	X		X	X		X	X		X			X	X		X1	X1	S1		K.Lynch	42
	X	S1				X	X2	X	X		X	X		X	X		X			X	X		X	X1	S2		G.Cain	43
	X	S1	X1		S		X	X		X	X		X	X		X	X			X	X		X2	X	S2		T.Heilbron	44
S	X1	X				X	S1	X		X	X		X	X		X	X			X		X	X				A.Butler	45
	X	X			X	S	X		X	X		X	X		X	X			X	S1	X	X	X1			W.Burns	46
	X	S1	X2	S2		X	X		X	S		X	X		X	X			X	X	X	X1			F.Stretton	47
	X	S1	X			S	X		X	X	X	X	S		X	X			X	X1	X	S			M.Fletcher	48
S	X	X1			X		X		X	X		X	X		X	X			X	S1	X2	X	S3			G.Frankland	49
S	X	X1			X		X1		X	X		X	X		X	X			X	S1	X	X2	S3			J.Brandwood	50
	X	X			S2		X		X	X	X3	X1	X	X	X		X	S1	X	X2	S3			K.Breen	51
	X	X	S				X	X2	S2	X	X		X	X		X1	X	X	S1			S.Mathieson	52
	X	X	S2			X	S1	X	X	S	X1	X	S3	X1	S1		X2	J.Rushton	53
	X	X	X2			X	X		X	X	S2	S3	X3	X1	S1		R.Poulain	54
	X1	X	X	X	X	X	X3	X	S3	X2	S2	X		G.Barber	55
	X	X	S	X	X	X	X	S	X1	S1	S1	X	T.Heilbron	56
	X	X	S3	X	X3	X	X	S1	X2	S2	X1	W.Burns	57

0	24	1	34	3	41	25	5	2	44	1	0	5	41	8	19	29	30	45	0	29	20	0	0	4	37	42	14	3	EL Appearances	
1	0	0	0	15	1	0	8	1	2	0	4	4	2	8	3	0	2	0	0	0	0	0	1	6	4	2	13	0	EL Sub Appearances	
0	1	0	2	1+1	1+1	2	0	2	0+2	1	0	0	2	2	0	0	2	2	0	0	0	0	0	2	2	0	0	0	CC Appearances	
0	3	0	2	0	3	2	1+2	0	3	0	0	0	3	1+1	2	0	3	3	0	2	0	0	0	0	1+2	3	1+2	0	FAC Appearances	
0	4	0	3	1+3	3	2	0	4	0	0	0	3	2+1	2+1	2	0	3	3	0	2	0	0	0	0	4	3	2+1	1	AWS Appearances	
0	0	0	0	0	2	2	0+1	0	2	0	0	0	2	2	0	2	0	2	0	1	2	0	0	0+1	2	0+2	2	0	PO Appearances	

Also Played: (G) Martin S(8,25). (F) Thorpe S(36).

CLUB RECORDS

BIGGEST VICTORIES
League: 8-4 v Charlton Athletic, Division 1, 27.9.1952.
7-0 v Reading, Division 2, 10.11.1928.
7-0 v Preston North End, Division 1, 1.5.1948.
7-0 v Sunderland, Division 1, 13.10.1957.
Most Goals Scored in a Cup Tie: 10-0 v Lanerossi, Anglo-Italian Cup, 10.6.1972.

BIGGEST DEFEATS
League: 1-10 v Small Heath, Division 2, 2.3.1901.
1-10 v Huddersfield Town, Division 1, 13.12.1930.
In a Cup Competition: 0-6 v Barnsley, FA Cup Round 1 Replay, 1909-10.

MOST POINTS
3 points a win: 86, Division 4, 1984-85.
2 points a win: 58, Division 2, 1929-30, 1967-68.

BEST PERFORMANCES
League: 2nd Division 1, 1955-56.
F.A. Cup: Winners in 1953.
League Cup: Semi-Final 1962.

HONOURS
Division 2 Champions 1929-30.
FA Cup Winners 1953.
Anglo-Italian Cup Winners 1971.

LEAGUE CAREER
Elected to Div 2 1896, Failed to gain re-election 1899, Re-elected to Div 2 1900, Promoted to Div 1 1929-30, Relegated to Div 2 1932-33, Promoted to Div 1 1936-37, Relegated to Div 2 1966-67, Promoted to Div 1 1969-70, Relegated to Div 2 1970-71, Relegated to Div 3 1977-78, Relegated to Div 4 1980-81, Promoted to Div 3 1984-85, Relegated to Div 4 1989-90, Promoted to Div 3 1991-92 (Now Div 2).

INDIVIDUAL CLUB RECORDS

MOST GOALS IN A SEASON
Jimmy Hampson - 46, Division 2,1929-30 (League 45, FA Cup 1).

MOST GOALS IN A MATCH
5, Jimmy Hampson v Reading, Division 2, 10.11.1928.
5, Jimmy McIntosh v Preston North End, Division 1, 01.05.1948.

OLDEST PLAYER
Sir Stanley Matthews, 46.

YOUNGEST PLAYER (In a League match)
Trevor Sinclair, 16 years 170 days v Wigan Athletic, 19.8.1989.

MOST CAPPED PLAYER
Jimmy Armfield (England) 43.

PREVIOUS MANAGERS

Since 1946: Joe Smith, Ron Stuart, Stan Mortensen, Les Shannon, Jimmy Meadows, Bob Stokoe, Harry Potts, Allan Brown, Jimmy Meadows, Bob Stokoe, Stan Ternent, Alan Ball (jnr), Allan Brown, Sam Ellis, Jimmy Mullen, Graham Carr, Billy Ayre.

ADDITIONAL INFORMATION
PREVIOUS NAME
In 1899 South Shore amalgamated with Blackpool who had been formed when Blackpool St John disbanded in 1887.

PREVIOUS LEAGUE
Lancashire League.

Club colours: Tangerine shirts with white collar, white shorts with tangerine trim, tangerine socks with navy trim.

Change colours: White shirts, tangerine shorts.

Reserves League: Pontins Central League Div 2.
Youth League: Lancashire League.

LONGEST LEAGUE RUNS

of undefeated matches:	17 (1968)	of league matches w/out a win:	19 (1970-71)
of undefeated home matches:	24 (1990-91)	of undefeated away matches:	10 (1973-74)
without home win:	16 (1966-67)	without an away win:	41 (1907-09)
of league wins:	9 (1936-37)	of home wins:	15 (1990-91)
of league defeats:	8 (1898-99)	of away wins:	6 (1936-37)

THE MANAGER

Sam Allardyce . . . . appointed in July 1994.

PREVIOUS CLUBS
As a Manager . . . . Limerick.
As an Assistant/Coach . . . . Preston North End (caretaker/Youth team coach).
As a Player . . . . Bolton Wanderers, Sunderland, Millwall, Tampa Bay, Coventry City, Huddersfield Town, ... Bolton wanderers, Preston North End, West Bromwich Albion.

HONOURS
As a Manager . . . . None.
As a Player . . . . Division 2 Championship 1978, FLT 1983.

BLACKPOOL

PLAYERS NAME / Honours	Ht	Wt	Birthdate	Birthplace / Transfers	Contract Date	Clubs	League	L/Cup	FA Cup	Other	Lge	L/C	FAC	Oth
G O A L K E E P E R S														
Banks Steve	5.11	12.4	09/02/72	Hillingdon	24/03/90	West Ham United				1				
Loan (25/03/93) Gillingham				Free	24/06/93	Gillingham	67		7	2				
				£60000	18/08/95	Blackpool	24	1	3	4				
Martin Lee B	5.11	11.8	09/09/68	Huddersfield	01/07/87	Huddersfield Town	54		4	5				
				Free	31/07/92	Blackpool	98	8	4	7				
				Loan	25/01/96	Bradford City								
D E F E N D E R S														
Allardyce Craig	6.3	13.07	09/06/75	Bolton		Preston North End	1							
					19/09/94	Blackpool	0+1							
Butler Phillip Tony	6.2	10.10	28/09/72	Stockport	13/05/91	Gillingham	142+6	12	12+1	5+1	5			1
					29/07/96	Blackpool								
Darton Scott	5.11	11.02	27/03/75	Ipswich	28/10/92	W.B.A.	15	1		5				1
Loan (20/01/95) Blackpool					22/03/95	Blackpool	23+4			0+1				
Linighan David	6.2	12.6	09/01/65	Hartlepool	03/03/82	Hartlepool United	84+7	3+1	4	3	2			4
£25000 (11/08/86) Derby County				£30000	04/12/86	Shrewsbury Town	65	5	3	1	1			
				£300000	23/06/88	Ipswich Town	275+3	21	18	11	12		1	
Loan (17/11/95) Blackpool				£90000	26/01/96	Blackpool	29		4	4				
Lydiate Jason	5.11	12.3	29/10/71	Manchester	01/07/90	Manchester United								
				Free	19/03/92	Bolton Wanderers	29+1	4	2	1				
				£75000	02/03/95	Blackpool	41+2	2	3	3	1	1		
Morrison Andy	5.11	12.0	30/07/70	Inverness	06/07/88	Plymouth Argyle	105+8	10+1	6	2+1	6	1		
				£500000	05/08/93	Blackburn Rovers	1+4		1					
				Free	09/12/94	Blackpool	47		2	3	3			
M I D F I E L D														
Barlow Andrew	5.9	11.1	24/11/65	Oldham	31/07/84	Oldham Athletic	243+16	22	19	6	5			
Div.2'91.				Free	01/11/93	Bradford City	2							
				Free	13/07/95	Blackpool	34	2	2	3	1			
Beech Chris	5.10	11.0	16/09/74	Blackpool	09/07/93	Blackpool	53+29	4+4	1	3+3	4			2
E: Y.S.														
Bonner Mark	5.10	10.10	07/06/74	Ormskirk	18/06/92	Blackpool	99+18	7+3	7	8+3	10			1
Brabin Gary	5.11	14.8	09/12/70	Liverpool	14/12/89	Stockport County	1+1			1+1				
E: SP. via Gateshead, Runcorn				£45000	26/07/94	Doncaster Rovers	58+1	2	2	4	11			
				£125000	29/03/96	Bury	5							
					29/07/96	Blackpool								
Bradshaw Darren	5.10	11.3	19/03/67	Sheffield		Matlock Town								
E: Y.2.				Loan	12/08/87	Chesterfield	18	2						
				Free	14/11/87	York City	58+1	2	2	3	3			
				£10000	16/08/89	Newcastle United	32+6	3	2+1	3				
				Free	13/08/92	Peterborough Utd	70+3	7	4	2	1	1		
					20/10/94	Blackpool	51	2	3	5	1			
Dixon Ben	6.1	11.0	16/09/74	Lincoln	04/11/92	Lincoln City	33+10	2	0+1	2+2				
E: U18.			Loan (28/10/93) Witton Albion		11/07/96	Blackpool								
Gouck Andrew	5.9	11.12	08/06/72	Blackpool	04/07/90	Blackpool	121+27	9+3	4+1	11+1	12			3
Hooks John						Q.P.R.								
				Free	05/07/95	Blackpool								
Mellon Michael	5.8	11.3	18/03/72	Paisley	06/12/89	Bristol City	26+9	3	1+1	5+3	1			
				£75000	11/02/93	W.B.A.	38+7	3+2	0+1	6	6			1
				£50000	23/11/94	Blackpool	71	2	3	5	10	1		1
Mitchell Neil N	5.6	10.0	07/11/74	Lytham	28/11/92	Blackpool	39+28	0+3	2+1	5+1	8		1	1
E: S.				Loan	08/12/95	Rochdale	3+1							
				Loan	28/03/96	Southport								
Philpott Lee	5.9	11.8	21/02/70	Hackney	17/07/86	Peterborough Utd	1+3		0+1	0+2				
					31/05/89	Cambridge United	118+16	10	19	15	17	1	3	2
				£350000	24/11/92	Leicester City	57+18	2+1	6+1	4+1	3			
				£350000	22/03/96	Blackpool	4+6		0+1					
Watson Andrew	5.9	11.2	01/04/67	Leeds	23/08/88	Halifax Town	75+8	5+1	6	7	15	2	1	1
WFAC'91.				£40000	31/07/90	Swansea City	9+5	0+1		1+1	1			
				£30000	19/09/91	Carlisle United	55+1	4	3	1	22	1	1	1
				£55000	05/02/93	Blackpool	88+27	6	3+2	7+1	23	5		1
F O R W A R D S														
Bryan Marvin	6.0	12.2	02/08/75	Paddington	17/08/92	Q.P.R.								
Loan (08/12/94) Doncaster R. 5 Lge Apps 1gl.				Free	10/08/95	Blackpool	44+2	0+2	3	6	1			
Ellis Tony	5.11	11.0	20/10/64	Salford		Northwich								
				Free	22/08/86	Oldham Athletic	5+3	1		1				
				£23000	06/10/87	Preston North End	80+6	3	5	11+1	26			5
				£250000	20/12/89	Stoke City	66+11	5+1	1+4	3+2	19	1		
				£50000	14/08/92	Preston North End	70+2	4	6	6	48	2	3	3
				£165000	25/07/94	Blackpool	81+2	4	4	6	32	3		1
Pascoe Colin	5.10	10.0	09/04/65	Port Talbot	12/04/83	Swansea City	167+7	11	9	7	39	3	2	1
W:10,u21.4,Y. WFAC'83. AMC'94.				£70000	25/03/88	Sunderland	116+10	12	4+2	5	22	3		
Loan (24/07/92) Swansea 15 Lge, 4gls. 2 LC.			£70000	01/08/93	Swansea City	72+9	7	3	13+1	11	2	2	1
					27/04/96	Blackpool	0+1							
Preece Andrew P	6.1	12.0	27/03/67	Evesham		Evesham								
				Free	31/08/88	Northampton Town	0+1	0+1		0+1				
Free (01/08/89) Worcester City		Free		22/03/90	Wrexham	44+7	5+1	1	5	7	1	2	1
				£10000	18/12/91	Stockport County	89+8	2+1	7	12+1	42	3		9
				£350000	23/06/94	Crystal Palace	17+3	4+2	2+3		4	1		
				£200000	05/07/95	Blackpool	37+4	2	1+2	6	14		1	
Quinn Jimmy	6.2	11.11	15/12/74	Coventry		Birmingham City	1+3							
				£25000	05/07/93	Blackpool	117+23	5+5	3+3	7+2	27	3	3	2
				Loan	04/03/94	Stockport County	0+1							
Symons Paul	5.11	12.0	20/04/76	North Shields		Blackpool	0+1							
				Loan	12/09/94	Southport								
Thorpe Lee	6.0	11.06	14/12/75	Wolverhampton	18/07/94	Blackpool	0+4							
				Loan	11/02/95	Horwich RMI								

Bloomfield Road

Blackpool, Lancashire FY1 6JJ
Tel: 01253 404 331   Fax: 01253 405 011

Capacity . . . . .9,701.
Covered Standing . . . . .2,800.
Seating . . . . .2,987.
First game . . . .(League) v Gainsborough Town, 1-1, 8.9.1900.
First floodlit game . . . . .v Hearts, 2-1, 13.10.1958.

ATTENDANCES
Highest . . . . .38,098 v Wolves, Division 1, 17.9.1955.
Lowest . . . . .1,228 v Rochdale, Sherpa Van Trophy, 6.12.1988.

MATCHDAY TICKET PRICES

Seats . . . . £11/£10
Concessions . . . . £7.50/£6.50

Terraces £8.50
Concessions £5

Ticket Office Telephone No. 01253 404 331

HOW TO GET TO THE GROUND

From the North, East and South
Leave M6 Motorway at junction 32 and follow signs to Blackpool M55. At end of motorway the ground is immediately on the right hand side of the Municipal Car Park.

Car Parking
Parking for 1,000 cars. Street Parking also available.

Nearest Railway Station
Blackpool North (01772 594 39).

TANGERINE CALL
0891 12 16 48

Calls cost 39p per minute cheap rate and 49p per minute at all other times.
Call costings correct at time of going to press.

MATCHDAY PROGRAMME

Programme Editor . . . . Geoff Warburton & Roger Harrison

Number of pages 40

Price £1.50

Subscriptions . . . . £55 for all home programmes.

Local Newspapers. . . . . Blackpool Evening Gazette.

Local Radio Stations . . Red Rose Radio, Radio Lancashire, Radio Wave.

AFC BOURNEMOUTH
(The Cherries)
NATIONWIDE LEAGUE DIVISION 2
SPONSORED BY: FRIZZELL

Back Row (L-R): Neil Young, Eddie Howe, Steve Strong, Michael Dean, John O'Neill, Dale Gordon (Player/Coach), Leo Cotterill, Owen Coll.
Middle Row: Larry Clay (Youth & Community Development Officer), Mike McElhatton, Robert Murray, Mark Watson, Jimmy Glass, David Wells, Mark Morris, Steve Fletcher, Ian Cox, John Williams (Asst. Manager).
Front Row: Sean O'Driscoll (Youth Manager), David Town, Marcus Oldbury, John Bailey, Jason Brissett, Mel Machin (Manager), Matt Holland, Steve Robinson, Russell Beardsmore, Mark Rawlinson, Steve Hardwick (Physio).

AFC BOURNEMOUTH
FORMED IN 1899
TURNED PROFESSIONAL IN 1912
LTD COMPANY IN 1914

PRESIDENT: P W Hayward
CHAIRMAN: K Gardiner
VICE-CHAIRMAN
B E Willis
DIRECTORS
E G Keep, G M C Hayward, G W Legg,
N Hayward, A J C Griffiths
SECRETARY
Keith MacAlister
COMMERCIAL MANAGER
Terry Lovell

MANAGER: Mel Machin
ASSISTANT MANAGER: John Williams
RESERVE TEAM MANAGER
John Williams
YOUTH TEAM MANAGER
Sean O'Driscoll
PHYSIOTHERAPIST
Steve Hardwick

STATISTICIAN FOR THE DIRECTORY
Andy Shute

After the 'great escape' of the 1994/5 season, and the form shown in the latter part of that season, expectations were actually quite high of Bournemouth this year. Although the club had stated that this would be a consolidation year, a final position of 14th was seen as a bit of a disappointment by AFCB supporters, especially given the start to the season that AFCB had.

Having lost at Bradford on the opening day, three wins from their following four games saw AFCB climb to 3rd in the league, but in line with Bournemouth's inconsistency they then lost their next three, including a very controversial 0-4 home defeat by Crewe in which AFCB had two players dismissed. By the end of October AFCB were mid-table, and 'keeper Neil Moss came into the side and kept seven consecutive clean sheets (five league and 2 cup), equalling a club record, as AFCB embarked on an eight-game unbeaten run. However, again the inconsistency crept into their play and after an amazing 5-4 away win at Peterborough, followed by home wins against Bradford and promotion-chasing Blackpool, AFCB then went seven games without a win and dropped into the fringes of the relegation zone. AFCB won just four of their final 17 league games, but a fine 2-2 draw away at champions Swindon Town ensured Bournemouth's safety.

All three cup competitions came to an end in the second round: a Coca-Cola Cup victory over Luton Town was followed by defeat from Watford, albeit on penalties. In the FA Cup after beating Bristol City in a replay, Brentford came to Dean Court and won 1-0. Brentford also beat AFCB in the Auto Windscreen's Shield, but after beating Exeter away it was Bristol Rovers who finally ended AFCB's hopes of a cup run.

The inconsistency of AFCB's season was caused mainly by having an unsettled side, injuries and suspensions taking their toll as AFCB managed just three consecutive games (twice) with an unchanged side, and used over 30 players all season. Russell Beardsmore, Jason Brissett and top-scorer Steve Jones missed just two league games each. Matthew Holland, in his first full season at Bournemouth, walked away with all the 'Player of the Year' awards after some superb midfield performances. During the season AFCB had six loan players, the pick of which were Chelsea's Michael Duberry and Manchester United's young defender Chris Casper.

Having had the 'consolidation season' AFCB must hope to be pushing for a top-six place next season as their young team gels together, and as a result will hope to start the 98/99 season in Division One and their new stadium.

AFC Bournemouth reserves won the Avon League Division Two championship.

ANDY SHUTE

BOURNEMOUTH

League: 14th   FA Cup: 2nd Rnd   Coca-Cola Cup: 2nd Rnd   Auto Windscreen Shield: 2nd Rnd

M	DATE	COMP	VEN	OPPONENTS	RESULT	HT	LP	GOAL SCORERS/GOAL TIMES	ATT.
1	A 12	EL	A	Bradford City	L 0-1	0-0	24		(5107)
2	15	CC 1/1	A	Luton Town	D 1-1	1-0		Jones 16	(2728)
3	19	EL	H	Peterborough United	W 3-0	1-0	13	Jones 3, 72, 81 (3)	4175
4	22	CC 1/2	H	Luton Town	W 2-1	1-1		Jones 12, Morris 98	4884
5	26	EL	A	Wycombe Wanderers	W 2-1	2-0	7	Jones 20, Murray 43	(4749)
6	29	EL	H	Wrexham	D 1-1	0-1	7	Jones 61	4825
7	S 2	EL	H	Rotherham United	W 2-1	2-1	3	Brissett 6, Holland 43	4906
8	9	EL	A	Notts County	L 0-2	0-0	7		(4875)
9	12	EL	A	Blackpool	L 1-2	1-1	9	Jones 24	(3884)
10	16	EL	H	Crewe Alexandra	L 0-4	0-2	13		4488
11	19	CC 2/1	H	Watford	D 1-1	1-0		Jones 10	(5037)
12	24	EL	H	Brighton & H.A.	W 3-1	2-0	11	Robinson 25, Robinson 28, Jones 73	4560
13	27	AWS 1/1	H	Brentford	L 0-1	0-1			1092
14	30	EL	A	Stockport County	L 1-3	0-1	12	Bailey 78	(5655)
15	O 3	CC 2/2	H	Watford	D 1-1	0-0		Oldbury 120 (lost on penalties)	4365
16	7	EL	A	Bristol Rovers	W 2-0	1-0	10	Brissett 18, Bailey 50	(5171)
17	14	EL	A	Burnley	L 0-2	0-1	12		4954
18	21	EL	A	Swansea City	D 1-1	1-0	14	Jones 17	(1988)
19	28	EL	H	Carlisle United	W 2-0	1-0	9	Brissett 20, Fletcher 89	4250
20	31	EL	H	Swindon Town	D 0-0	0-0	10		6352
21	N 4	EL	A	Walsall	D 0-0	0-0	11		(3626)
22	7	AWS 1/2	A	Exeter City	W 2-0	0-0		Brissett 46, Brissett 47	(1898)
23	11	FAC 1	H	Bristol City	D 0-0	0-0			5304
24	18	EL	H	Brentford	W 1-0	0-0	10	Victory 46	3894
25	21	FAC 1R	A	Bristol City	W 1-0	1-0		Robinson 5	(5069)
26	25	EL	A	Chesterfield	L 0-3	0-2	13		(4034)
27	28	AWS 2	A	Bristol Rovers	L 1-2	0-0		Robinson 46	(1979)
28	D 2	FAC 2	H	Brentford	L 0-1	0-1			4451
29	9	EL	A	Brighton & H.A.	L 0-2	0-1	13		(5414)
30	16	EL	H	Stockport County	W 3-2	1-1	12	Ndah 22, Jones 70, Holland 75	3638
31	23	EL	H	Hull City	W 2-0	1-0	11	Jones 22, Holland 75	3491
32	26	EL	A	Oxford United	L 0-2	0-2	12		(6347)
33	J 2	EL	H	Shrewsbury Town	L 0-2	0-1	13		3245
34	6	EL	H	Bristol City	D 1-1	0-1	12	Morris 52	3667
35	13	EL	A	Peterborough United	W 5-4	1-1	12	Ndah 8, Casper 67, Mean 70, Jones 84, 85	(4596)
36	20	EL	H	Bradford City	W 3-1	1-1	7	Jones 13, Holland 56, Robinson 58	3628
37	F 3	EL	H	Wycombe Wanderers	L 2-3	2-1	10	Bailey 12, Holland 41	4447
38	10	EL	A	Bristol City	L 0-3	0-2	12		(6217)
39	17	EL	H	Blackpool	W 1-0	0-0	10	Robinson 70	4157
40	20	EL	A	Rotherham United	L 0-1	0-1	11		(2092)
41	24	EL	A	Crewe Alexandra	L 0-2	0-0	12		(3535)
42	27	EL	H	Notts County	L 0-2	0-1	13		3191
43	M 2	EL	H	Oxford United	L 0-1	0-1	13		3996
44	9	EL	A	Hull City	D 1-1	1-1	16	Scott 2	(2853)
45	12	EL	A	Wrexham	L 0-5	0-3	17		(2004)
46	16	EL	H	York City	D 2-2	1-0	16	Robinson 28, 63	3505
47	23	EL	A	Shrewsbury Town	W 2-1	0-1	15	Holland 52, 63	(2534)
48	26	EL	A	York City	L 1-3	0-1	15	Holland 75	(2055)
49	30	EL	H	Bristol Rovers	W 2-1	1-0	14	Robinson 36, Jones 79	4607
50	A 2	EL	A	Burnley	D 0-0	0-0	13		(7912)
51	6	EL	A	Carlisle United	L 0-4	0-0	15		(5401)
52	9	EL	H	Swansea City	W 3-1	1-1	14	Jones 5, Bailey 59, Holland 72	4049
53	13	EL	A	Swindon Town	D 2-2	1-1	15	Jones 31, 68	(10508)
54	20	EL	H	Walsall	D 0-0	0-0	14		4380
55	27	EL	H	Chesterfield	W 2-0	1-0	14	Robinson 32, Jones 63	4483
56	M 4	EL	A	Brentford	L 0-2	0-0	14		(6091)

Best Home League Attendance: 6352 v Swindon Town   **Smallest: 3191 v Notts County**   **Average: 4212**

Goal Scorers:
EL(51): Jones(18),Holland(9),Robinson(8),Bailey(4),Brissett(3),Ndah(2),Morris(1),Murray(1),Scott(1),Fletcher(1),Casper(1),Mean(1),Victory(1)
CC(5): Jones(3),Morris(1),Oldbury(1)
FAC(1): Robinson(1)
AWS(3): Brissett(2),Robinson(1)

(G) Andrews	(F) Bailey	(M) Beardsmore	(F) Brissett	(M) Casper	(D) Coll	(F) Cox	(D) Dubbery	(F) Fletcher	(G) Glass	(M) Holland	(F) Jones	(F) McElhatton	(M) Mean	(D) Mitchell	(D) Morris	(G) Moss	(F) Murray	(M) Ndah	(F) O'Neill	(M) Oldbury	(D) Pennock	(M) Rawlinson	(D) Robinson	(F) Scott	(D) Strong	(F) Town	(D) Victory	(D) Young		
X	S3	X	X				X			X2	X		X		X1		X				S2		X3				S1	X	T.Heilbron	1
X	S1	X	X					X1		X	X	S2	X		X		X				S		X2					X	G.Singh	2
X	X	X	X							X	X		X		X		X				S		X			S	S	X	K.Leach	3
X	X	X	X2							X	X		X		X		X				X1	S3				S2	S1	X	D.Orr	4
X	X	X2	X							X	X3		X		X		X				X1	S				S3	S1	X	G.Barber	5
X	X	X2	X							X	X		X		X		X				X1	S				S2	S1	X	C.Wilkes	6
X	X	X	X							X	X		X		X		X				X	S				S	S	X	S.Bennett	7
X	X2	X3	X								X	S3	X		X		X				X	S2				X1	X		G.Pooley	8
X	X3	X	X								X	X2	X		X		X				X	S2				S1	X1		M.Fletcher	9
X	X	X	X1							X	X	S1	X2		X		X				X	S2					X		B.Knight	10
X	S	X	X							X	X		X		X		X			S	X		X			S		X	R.Gifford	11
X	S1	X	X							X	X		X1		X		X				X	X3				S2	X2	X	I.Hemley	12
X	S1	X	X3							X	X				X1		X				X	X2				S2	X			13
X	X	X	X1			X				X	X				X1		X			S1		S1	X				X1	X	T.Lunt	14
X	X	X	X1							X	X2				X		X			S1	X	S	X			S2	X		G.Barber	15
X	X	X	X3							X	X				X		X			S	X	S	X				S		G.Singh	16
X		X	X			X	S			X	X				X		X	X		S	X	S	X					S	M.Pierce	17
X		X	X			X	S			X	X				X		X	S1	X	S	X	S	X1					X	M.Fletcher	18
	S2	X	X2			X	S3			X	X3				X	X	S1	X	S1	X	X		X1					X	P.Taylor	19
	X	X	X1			X	S1			X	X				X	X	S	X	S	X	X	S					X	A.D'urfo	20
X2	X	X	X			X	S2			X	X3				X	X	S1	X	S1	X	X	S3					X1		U.Rennie	21
	X	X	X			X	X			X	X	S				X	S	X	S	X	X	X						D.Orr	22
	X1	X	X				X			X	X	S			X	X	X	X		X	X	S1						G.Barber	23
	S3	X	X				X			X1	X				X	X	X2		X	S2	S2	X					S1	X	G.Singh	24
	X	X	X1				X			X	X		S	S1	X	X	X			X	X	X					S	X	G.Barber	25
	X	X	X				X2				X1	X	X3	X		X		X	S3	S2	X					S1	X	S.Mathieson	26
	X	X	X3								X2		X1	X		X		X	X	X	X					S1	X		27
	X	X	X						X	X1		X2		X		X		S1	X	S3	X	S2	S		S	X	G.Singh	28
	S1	X	X2							X		X3	X	X	X	X1	X2	S3	X			X	R.J.Harris	29
	S1	X	X							X		S2	X	X	X	X1	X2	X			S	X	P.Rejer	30
X	X	X								X		X	X	X	S	S1	X		X	X	A.Wiley	31
X	X	X								X		X	X	S2	S	X		X1	X	G.Cain	32
X	X	X								X		X	X	S2	S	X		X1	X	A.D'Urso	33
X	X	X								X	X2	S1	X	X1	X	S	X		X	I.Hemley	34
X	X	X	X3	X						X	X	X	X2	X1	X	S2	S1	S3	X	S.J.Baines	35
X	X	X	X	X						X	X	X	X1	X	S1	X	S2	X	M.Bailey	36
X	X	X	X	X						X	X	X	X	S	X	S	X	R.Poulaine	37
X	X	X	X	X						X	X	X2	X	X1	S3	X	S1	X	K.Leach	38
X	X3	X	X1							X	X	S3	S2	X	X	S	S1	X	M.Pierce	39
X	X3	X	X1							X	X	X	S2	X	X	S1	S1	X	A.Leake	40
X	X	X	X1	X						X	X	X	S1	S	X	X	S2	X	C.Wilkes	41
X	X	X	X3	X						X	X	X1	S2	S3	X	X	S1	X2	S.Bennett	42
X	X	X	X2	X1						X	X	S2	X	X	S3	X	F.Stretton	43
	X	X	X1					X	X	X		X	S	S1	X	X	X	P.R.Richards	44
X1	X	X2	X					X	X	X	X	S1	S2	X3	X	X	K.Lynch	45
X	X	X	X					X	X	X	X	S	X	S	X	A.D'Orso	46
X	X	X	X					X	X	X	X2	X	X	S	X	R.D.Furnandiz	47
X2	X	X1	X					X	X	X	X	S1	X	S2	X	S3	X3	G.Frankland	48
S1	X	X	X	X	X			X	X	X	X1	S	S	X	G.Pooley	49
S1	X	X2	X	X	X			X	X	X	X1	S2	S	X	K.Breen	50
X	X	X1	X2	X	X			X	X	X	S3	S1	S2	X	X3	T.West	51
S	X	X		X	X			X	X	X	S	S	X	B.Harris	52
X	X	X2		X	X			X	X	S2	X	S1	S	X1	X	E.Lomas	53
X	X	X1		X	X			X	X2	S	X	S1	S2	X	P.Taylor	54
X	X	S		X	X			X	X	S	X	X	S	X	J.Lloyd	55
X		X1		X	X			X	X	X	S	X	S1	X	P.Rejer	56
26	36	44	43	16	8	8	7	3	13	43	44	2	13	2	28	7	30	12	2	2	16	3	36	8	0	1	5	40	EL Appearances	
0	8	0	0	0	0	0	0	3	0	0	0	2	1	2	2	0	5	0	4	10	1	16	5	0	1	6	11	0	EL Sub Appearances	
4	2+1	4	4	0	0	0	0	1	0	4	4	0	4	0	4	0	0	0	0+1	3	0+1	3	3	0	0	0+2	1+1	2	CC Appearances	
0	3	3	3	0	0	0	0	2	0	2	2	1	0+1	0	3	3	2	0	0+1	3	1	2+1	3	0+1	0	0	0	3	FAC Appearances	
1	2+1	3	3	0	0	0	1	0	2	2	1	1	0	0	2	2	1	0	1	3	1	3	0	0	0+1	1+1	2	AWS Appearances	

so Played: (F) Cureton S1(8,14), S3(9,10,12,13) S(16). (M) Dean X1(39), X2(40,41), X(42), S1(43), S(47). (D) Howe X1(31), X2(32,33), S(39,47,56), X(44), S3(45).
(M) Santos S2(27,34,38), S(31,32,36,37,44,46), S1(33). (M) Stephens S3(27).

385

CLUB RECORDS

BIGGEST VICTORIES
League: 7-0 v Swindon Town, Division 3(S), 22.9.1956.
Most Goals Scored in a Cup Tie: 11-0 v Margate, FA Cup,
20.11.1971.

BIGGEST DEFEATS
League: 0-9 v Lincoln City, Division 3, 1.12.1982.
Most Goals conceded in a Cup Tie: 0-7 v Burnley, FA Cup 3rd
Round Replay, 1965-66.
0-7 v Sheffield Wednesday, FA Cup 4th Round, 1931-32.

MOST POINTS
3 points a win: 97, Division 3, 1986-87.
2 points a win: 62, Division 3, 1971-72.

RECORD TRANSFER FEE RECEIVED
£800,000 from Everton for Joe Parkinson, March 1994.

RECORD TRANSFER FEE PAID
£300,000 to Manchester City for Paul Moulden, July 1989.

BEST PERFORMANCES
League: 12th Division 2, 1988-89.
FA Cup: 6th Round, 1956-57.
League Cup: 4th Round, 1961-62, 1963-64.

HONOURS
Division 3 Champions 1986-87.
Associate Members Cup 1983-84.

LEAGUE CAREER
Elected to Div.3(S) 1923, Transferred to Div.3 1957-58, Relegated to
Div.4 1969-70, Promoted to Div.3 1970-71, Relegated to Div.4
1974-75, Promoted to Div.3 1981-82, Promoted to Div.2 1986-87,
Relegated to Div.3 (now Div.2) 1989-90.

INDIVIDUAL CLUB RECORDS

MOST GOALS IN A SEASON
Ted MacDougall - 49, 1970-71 (League 42, FA Cup 7).

MOST GOALS IN A MATCH
Ted MacDougall - 9 v Margate, FA Cup 1st Rnd. (11-0) 20.11.1971
(All time FA Cup record).

OLDEST PLAYER
Harry Kinghorn, 48 years v Brentford, 11.3.1929.

YOUNGEST PLAYER
Jimmy White, 15 years v Brentford, 30.4.1958.

MOST CAPPED PLAYER
Gerry Peyton (Eire) 7.

PREVIOUS MANAGERS

Harry Kinghorn 1920-25, Leslie Knighton 1925-28, Frank Richards
1928-30, Billy Birrell 1930-35, Bob Crompton 1935-36, Charles Bell
1936-39, Harry Kinghorn 1939-47, Harry Lowe 1947-50, Jack
Bruton 1950-56, Freddie Cox 1956-58, Don Welsh 1958-61, Bill
McGarry 1961-63, Reg Flewin 1963-65, Freddie Cox 1965-70, John
Bond 1970-73, Trevor Hartley 1973-75, John Benson 1975-79, Alec
Stock 1979-80, Dave Webb 1980-82, Don Megson 1982, Harry
Redknapp 1983-92, Tony Pullis 1992-94.

ADDITIONAL INFORMATION
Previous League: Southern League.

Previous Names: Boscombe St Johns 1899.
Boscombe FC 1899-1923. Bournemouth & Boscombe AFC 1923-72.

Club colours: Red & black striped shirts, white shorts & white socks.

Change colours: Yellow & blue halves shirts blue shorts & socks.

Reserves League: Avon Insurance League Division 1.

LONGEST LEAGUE RUNS

of undefeated matches:	18 (1982)	of league matches w/out a win:	14 (1973-74)
of undefeated home matches:	33 (1962-63)	of undefeated away matches:	13 (1961)
without home win:	10 (1931-32)	without an away win:	26 (1976-77)
of league wins:	7 (1970)	of home wins:	12 (1968, 1971)
of league defeats:	7 (1955)	of away wins:	5 (1948)

THE MANAGER

MEL MACHIN . . . . appointed September 1994.

PREVIOUS CLUBS
As Manager . . . . Manchester City, Barnsley.
As Asst.Man/Coach . . . . Norwich City.
As a player . . . . Port Vale, Gillingham, Bournemouth, Norwich City.

HONOURS
As a Manager . . . . None.
As a Player . . . . None.

BOURNEMOUTH

PLAYERS NAME / Honours	Ht	Wt	Birthdate	Birthplace / Transfers	Contract Date	Clubs	League	L/Cup	FA Cup	Other	Lge	L/C	FAC	Oth
GOALKEEPERS														
Glass James R	6.1	11.10	01/08/73	Epsom	04/07/91	Crystal Palace								
				Loan	21/12/95	Gillingham								
				Loan	31/01/96	Burnley								
				Free	08/03/96	Bournemouth	13							
Wells David	6.1	13.0	29/12/77	Portsmouth		Bournemouth (T)								
				Loan		Dorchester								
DEFENDERS														
Coll Owen	6.1	11.7	09/04/76	Donegal	01/08/94	Tottenham Hotspur								
					28/03/96	Bournemouth	8							
Cotterill Leo S : S.	5.9	10.0	02.09.74	Cambridge	01/07/93	Ipswich Town (T)	0+2	0+1						
				Free	15/06/96	Bournemouth								
Howe Eddie						Bournemouth (T)	4+1							
Morris Mark iv.4'83.	6.1	13.8	26/09/62	Morden	26/09/80	Wimbledon	167+1	11	11	1+1	9			
				Loan	05/09/85	Aldershot	14		1					
				£35000	21/07/87	Watford	41	5	7		1	1		
				£175000	11/07/89	Sheffield United	53+3	5	5	2	3			
				£100000	31/07/91	Bournemouth	190+2	15	17	9	8	2	1	
Strong Steve	5.7	11.2	15/03/78	Watford		Bournemouth (T)	0+1		0+1					
Young Neil	5.8	10.5	31/08/73	Harlow	17/08/91	Tottenham Hotspur								
				Free	11/10/94	Bournemouth	72	3	5	4				
MIDFIELD														
Beardsmore Russell : u21.5. ESC'91.	5.6	9.0	28/09/68	Wigan	02/10/86	Manchester United	30+26	3+1	4+4	2+5	4			
				Loan	19/12/91	Blackburn Rovers	1+1							
				Free	29/06/93	Bournemouth	102+9	11	7	5	3	1		
Dean Michael						Bournemouth (T)	4+1							
Gordon Dale : B.2, u21.4,Y.S. SPD'92'93. SFAC'92. SLC'93	5.10	11.8	09.01.67	Gt Yarmouth	17.01.84	Norwich City (A)	194+12	21	19	14+2	31	3	6	3
				£1200000	08.11.91	Glasgow Rangers	41+4	1+1	6+1	1	6	1	1	
				£750000	20.07.93	West Ham United	8	1			1			
				Loan	23.03.95	Peterborough Utd	6				1			
					01/07/96	Bournemouth								
Holland Matthew	5.9	11.4	11/04/74	Bury	03/07/92	West Ham United								
				Loan	21/10/94	Bournemouth								
				£150000	18/11/94	Bournemouth	52+7	4	2	2	10			
Ledbury Marcus	5.7	10.02	29/03/76	Bournemouth	01/07/94	Norwich City								
				Free	01/07/95	Bournemouth	2+10	0+1	0+1	1			1	
Rawlinson Mark	5.8	11.11	09/06/75	Bolton	05/07/93	Manchester United								
				Free	01/07/95	Bournemouth	3+16	0+1	1	1				
FORWARDS														
Bailey John						Enfield								
				£10000	05/08/95	Bournemouth	36+8	2+1	3	2+1	4			
Brissett Jason	5.11	11.10	07/09/74	Wanstead		Arsenal								
				Free	14/06/93	Peterborough Utd	27+8	5+1	2+1	3+1		1	1	1
				Free	23/12/94	Bournemouth	67+1	4	3	3	3			2
Cox Ian G a Whyteleafe,Carshalton Athletic	6.0	12.2	25/03/71	Croydon		Crystal Palace								
				£35000	08/03/94	Crystal Palace	2+13		2+1			1		
				Free	28/03/96	Bournemouth	8							
Fletcher Steven	6.0	12.1	26/06/72	Hartlepool	23/08/90	Hartlepool United	19+13	0+2	1+2	2+2	4	1		1
				£30000	28/07/92	Bournemouth	100+13	11	4	3	17	1		
McElhatton Michael	6.1	12.8	16/04/75	Kerry (Eire)	05/07/93	Bournemouth	21+21	3+1	1+2	1			1	
Murray Robert : u21.1.	5.11	11.7	21/10/74	Hammersmith	11/01/93	Bournemouth	68+43	4+2	2+5	1+4	9			2
O'Neill Jon	5.10	10.4	03/01/74	Glasgow		Queens Park BC								
					01/08/91	Queens Park	91				30			
					01/08/94	Celtic	1							
				Free	29/03/96	Bournemouth	2+4							
Robinson Stephen I: B, u21.6,Y.S.	5.8	10.7	10/12/74	Lisburn	27/01/93	Tottenham Hotspur	1+1							
				Free	20/10/94	Bournemouth	66+7	3	4+1	4	13		1	1
Town David	5.8	11.7	09/12/76	Bournemouth	14/07/94	Bournemouth	1+6	0+2		0+1				
Watson Mark			28/12/73	Birmingham		Sutton United								
					01/08/94	West Ham United								
				Loan	04/09/95	Leyton Orient	1				1			
				Loan	27/10/95	Cambridge United	1+3		1	1				
				Loan	02/02/96	Shrewsbury Town	1							
					16/05/96	Bournemouth								

DEAN COURT GROUND

Bournemouth, Dorset BH7 7AF
Tel: 01202 395 381

Capacity ....11,000.

First game ....In the League - 01.09.1923.
First floodlit game ....v Northampton 27.09.1961.

ATTENDANCES
Highest ....28,799 v Manchester United, FA Cup 6th Round, 02.03.1957.
Lowest ....1,218 v Reading, Autoglass Trophy, 05.01.1993.

OTHER GROUNDS ....Castleman Road, Pokedown 1899-1910. Dean Court 1910-

MATCHDAY TICKET PRICES

South Stand (Terrace Standing)	£7.50
Juv/OAP	£4
New Stand (Enclosure Standing)	£7.50
Juv/OAP	£4
Centre Stand (Seating)	£11.50
B Block (Seating)	£10
E Block (Seating)	£10
Juv/OAP	£6.50
F Block (Family Stand - Seating)	£8.50
Juv	£4.50
(Adults must be accompanied by an u16-year-old)	
A Block (Wing Stand - Seating)	£8.50
Juv/OAP	£4.50

Ticket Office Telephone no. 01202 395 381

CLUBCALL
0891 12 11 63
Calls cost 39p per minute cheap rate and 49p per
minute at all other times.
Call costings correct at time of going to press.

HOW TO GET TO THE GROUND

From the North and East
A338 to roundabout junction with A3060. Take second exit, then first
from next roundabout into Littledown Avenue. Turn right into
Thistlebarrow Road for Dean Court.

From the West
A3049 to Bournemouth. In 2 miles after, lights at Wallisdown, turn left
into Talbot Road. Take first exit from roundabout into Queens Park
South Drive, then second exit from next roundabout into Littledown
Avenue. Turn right into Thistle Road for Dean Court.

Car Parking
Parking for 1,500 cars.

Nearest Railway Station
Bournemouth. Tel: 01202 558 216.

MATCHDAY PROGRAMME
(F.D.P. Division Two Programme of the Year 1995/96)

Programme Editor . . . . Mike Cunningham.

Number of pages . . . . 40.

Price . . . . £1.50.

Subscriptions . . . . £43.

Local Newspapers. . . . . Evening Echo.

Local Radio Stations . . . . Two Counties Radio, BBC Radio Solent.

BRENTFORD
(The Bees)
NATIONWIDE LEAGUE DIVISION 2
SPONSORED BY: ERICSSON MOBILE PHONES

Back Row (L-R): J Omigie, G Hurdle, J Bates, B Ashby, R Taylor, C Asaba, C Hutchings, C Campbell, K Burke.
Middle Row: B Booker, M Grainger, D McGhee, P Smith, T Fernandes, K Dearden, D Mundee, P Abraham, I Anderson, R Johnson.
Front Row: J Hooker, D Annon, L Harvey, D Webb, K Lock, N Forster, B Statham, C Ravenscroft.

BRENTFORD
FORMED IN 1889
TURNED PROFESSIONAL IN 1899
LTD COMPANY IN 1901

PRESIDENT: W Wheatley
CHAIRMAN: M M Lange
DIRECTORS
B R Evans, D Tana, J P Herting,
E J Radley-Smith, MS, FRCS, LRCR.

SECRETARY
Polly Kates
MARKETING MANAGER
Peter Gilham

MANAGER: David Webb
ASSISTANT MANAGER: Kevin Lock

YOUTH TEAM MANAGER
Bob Booker
PHYSIOTHERAPIST
Roy Johnson

STATISTICIAN FOR THE DIRECTORY
Frank Coumbe

A fter just missing out on promotion in 1994/95 hopes were high but, after spending a long spell in the relegation zone, Brentford and their supporters were happy to finish in a safe 15th position.

David Webb released experienced players Simon Ratcliffe, Shane Westley, Paul Stephenson and Denny Mundee and this, coupled with injuries, loss of form and suspensions saw some younger reserves brought into the first team, some of whom proved to be not quite good enough.

After a stuttering start the Bees dropped into the bottom four by November, staying there for nearly three months. Three successive wins pulled the club out starting a run of one defeat in eleven games. Only two points in five games saw the alarm bells ringing again but three wins over Easter confirmed safety.

The Bees scored only 43 goals in the League all year compared to 81 the previous campaign.

In the Coca-Cola Cup Walsall were defeated in Round One (5-4) before elimination to Premier Leaguers Bolton (2-4). The FA Cup saw a fine run with Farnborough beaten 4-0, (following a 1-1 draw), Bournemouth (1-0), and First Division Norwich (2-1) before an unlucky reverse at Charlton (2-3). In the AWS Bournemouth (1-0) and Exeter (1-1) were opposed in the group matches before a surprise exit at the hands of Fulham (0-1).

Creditable performances came from goalkeeper Kevin Dearden, Lee Harvey, who played out of position for half the campaign at right-back, captain Jamie Bates, ever present Paul Smith and Player of the Year Robert Taylor. In addition Ijah Anderson and David McGhee emerged as reliable first teamers while Marcus Bent showed promise for the future. The whole squad also showed great character to pull the club out of trouble.

From the performances in the second half of the season there's no reason why the Bees shouldn't mount a promotion challenge in 1996/97.

FRANK COUMBE.

BRENTFORD

League: 15th   FA Cup: 4th Rnd   Coca-Cola Cup: 2nd Rnd   Auto Windscreen Shield: 2nd Rnd

M	DATE	COMP	VEN	OPPONENTS	RESULT	HT	LP	GOAL SCORERS/GOAL TIMES	ATT.
1	A 12	EL	A	York City	D 2-2	1-0	12	Smith 22, Forster 65	(3239)
2	15	CC 1/1	A	Walsall	D 2-2	1-2		Harvey 44, Forster 52	(3549)
3	19	EL	H	Oxford United	W 1-0	1-0	6	Taylor 31	5516
4	22	CC 1/2	H	Walsall	W 3-2	2-1		Taylor 5, Anderson 23, McGhee 68	3149
5	26	EL	A	Burnley	L 0-1	0-1	12		(9586)
6	29	EL	H	Hull City	W 1-0	0-0	11	Taylor 51	4535
7	S 2	EL	H	Swindon Town	L 0-2	0-1	13		7878
8	9	EL	A	Rotherham United	L 0-1	0-1	17		(3061)
9	12	EL	A	Bristol City	D 0-0	0-0	18		(5054)
10	16	EL	H	Walsall	W 1-0	1-0	12	Taylor 7	4717
11	20	CC 2/1	A	Bolton Wanderers	L 0-1	0-0			(5243)
12	23	EL	A	Bristol Rovers	L 0-2	0-1	13		(5131)
13	27	AWS 1/1	A	Bournemouth	W 1-0	1-0		Taylor 17	(1092)
14	30	EL	A	Chesterfield	L 1-2	0-1	18	McGhee 83	4734
15	O 3	CC 2/2	H	Bolton Wanderers	L 2-3	1-0		Forster 36, Grainger 63(pen)	4861
16	7	EL	H	Blackpool	L 1-2	1-0	19	McGhee 44	5313
17	14	EL	A	Stockport County	D 1-1	0-1	19	Smith 83	(6228)
18	17	AWS 1/1	H	Exeter City	D 1-1	1-1		Forster 40	1413
19	21	EL	H	Peterborough United	W 3-0	2-0	16	Bates 13, 45, Grainger 49(pen)	4865
20	28	EL	A	Crewe Alexandra	L 1-3	0-2	18	Forster 90	(3835)
21	N 1	EL	A	Notts County	L 0-4	0-1	20		(4005)
22	4	EL	H	Shrewsbury Town	L 0-2	0-2	21		4104
23	11	FAC 1	H	Farnborough	D 1-1	1-0		Bent 7	4711
24	18	EL	A	Bournemouth	L 0-1	0-0	22		(3894)
25	22	FAC 1R	A	Farnborough	W 4-0	1-0		Smith 30, Taylor 52, 76, Bent 72	(3581)
26	25	EL	A	Bradford City	W 2-1	2-0	21	Taylor 6, 15	4237
27	28	AWS 2	H	Fulham	L 0-1	0-0			3760
28	D 2	FAC 2	A	Bournemouth	W 1-0	1-0		Taylor 12	(4451)
29	9	EL	H	Bristol Rovers	D 0-0	0-0	22		5679
30	16	EL	A	Chesterfield	D 2-2	2-0	22	Smith 26, Ansah 45	(4016)
31	22	EL	A	Wrexham	D 2-2	0-2	21	Taylor 58, Martin 65	(3670)
32	26	EL	H	Brighton & H.A.	L 0-1	0-1	21		5794
33	J 6	FAC 3	A	Norwich City	W 2-1	1-0		Newsome 20(og), Bent 60	(10082)
34	13	EL	A	Oxford United	L 1-2	1-1	12	Ashby 23	(5566)
35	20	EL	H	York City	W 2-0	1-0	22	Bates 16, Taylor 46	3915
36	30	EL	H	Wycombe Wanderers	W 1-0	0-0	19	Taylor 46	4616
37	F 3	EL	H	Burnley	W 1-0	0-0	18	Forster 61	5195
38	7	FAC 4	A	Charlton Athletic	L 2-3	1-2		Ashby 18, Smith 57	(15000)
39	10	EL	A	Carlisle United	L 1-2	0-1	19	Bates 47	(5143)
40	17	EL	H	Bristol City	D 2-2	1-0	19	McGhee 33, Taylor 66	5213
41	21	EL	A	Swindon Town	D 2-2	2-2	19	Abrahams 10, 37	(8814)
42	24	EL	A	Walsall	W 1-0	1-0	19	Abrahams 27	(3506)
43	27	EL	H	Rotherham United	D 1-1	0-0	19	Grainger 65	3446
44	M 2	EL	A	Brighton & H.A.	D 0-0	0-0	19		(5914)
45	5	EL	A	Hull City	W 1-0	0-0	15	Anderson 88	(2284)
46	9	EL	H	Wrexham	W 1-0	1-0	13	Anderson 40	4579
47	12	EL	A	Swansea City	L 1-2	1-0	14	Forster 29	(3538)
48	16	EL	A	Wycombe Wanderers	L 1-2	1-1	17	Forster 27	(4912)
49	19	EL	H	Carlisle United	D 1-1	1-1	15	Grainger 25	3104
50	23	EL	H	Swansea City	D 0-0	0-0	16		4378
51	30	EL	A	Blackpool	L 0-1	0-1	16		(5899)
52	A 2	EL	H	Stockport County	W 1-0	0-0	16	Smith 58	3274
53	6	EL	H	Crewe Alexandra	W 2-1	0-1	14	Taylor 80, 90	4408
54	8	EL	A	Peterborough United	W 1-0	0-0	13	McGhee 85	(4343)
55	13	EL	H	Notts County	D 0-0	0-0	14		4588
56	20	EL	A	Shrewsbury Town	L 1-2	1-2	15	McGhee 44	(2711)
57	26	EL	A	Bradford City	L 1-2	0-1	16	Bent 80	(7730)
58	M 4	EL	H	Bournemouth	W 2-0	0-0	15	Asaba 50, 57	6091

Best Home League Attendance: 7878 v Swindon Town   Smallest: 3104 v Carlisle United   Average: 4790

Goal Scorers:
EL(43):   Taylor(11),Forster(5),McGhee(5),Smith(4),Bates(4),Grainger(3),Abrahams(3),Asaba(2),Anderson(2),Ashby(1),Martin(1),Ansah(1),Bent(1)
CC(7):   Forster(2),McGhee(1),Taylor(1),Harvey(1),Grainger(1),Anderson(1)
FAC(10):   Bent(3),Taylor(3),Smith(2),Ashby(1),Opponent(s)(1)
AWS(2):   Forster(1),Taylor(1)

(F) Abrahams	(D) Anderson	(F) Annon	(M) Ansah	(F) Asaba	(D) Ashby	(D) Bates	(F) Bent	(M) Canham	(M) Davis	(G) Dearden	(G) Fernandes	(F) Forster	(D) Grainger	(D) Greene	(F) Harvey	(F) Hooker	(D) Hurdle	(M) Hutchings	(M) Martin	(F) McGhee	(D) Mundee	(F) Omigie	(F) Ravenscroft	(M) Smith	(D) Statham	(M) Sussex	(F) Taylor	Player	#
S	X			X	X					X	S	X	X		X		X			S				X	X		X	N.Barry	1
S	X			X	X					X	S	X	X		X		X			S				X	X		X	R.Lomas	2
	X			X	X					X	S	X	X		X		X			S	S			X	X		X	A.D'Urso	3
	X		X1	X						X	S	X	X		X		X2			S1	S2			X	X		X	T.Heilbron	4
S	X				X					X	S	X	X		X		X1			X	S1			X	X		X	M.Brandwood	5
S	X			S						X	S	X	X		X					X				X	X		X	I.S.Hemley	6
	X	S2		S1	X					X	S	X1	X		X					X	X2			X	X		X	P.Rejer	7
	X1			S1	X	X				X	S	X	X		X			X		S				X	X		X1	T.Lunt	8
				S1	X	X				X	S	X	X		X			X		S	X	X		X	X		X	A.Wiley	9
				S	X	X			X	X	S	X	X		X		X			S	X			X	X		X	S.Bennett	10
				S	X	X			X	X	S	X	X		X		X			S	X			X	X		X	G.Cain	11
				S1	X	X				X	S	X	X		X1					S2	X2			X	X		X	F.Stretton	12
					X	X				X	S	X	X		X		S			X			S	X	X		X		13
			X1		X	X				X	S	X	X		X				S1	X			S	X	X		X	M.Fletcher	14
	S				X	X			X1	X	S	X	X		S1					X				X	X		X	D.J.Gallagher	15
S1	X			S					X1	X	S	X	X		X					X				X	X		X	K.A.Leach	16
	S				X	X				X	S	X	X		X				S	X	X			X	X		X	P.Richards	17
	S1				X	X				X	S	X	X		X				S2	X	X1			X	X		X2	A.Butler	18
				S1	X	X				X	S	X	X		X				S2	X	X		X1	X2	X			B.Knight	19
	X			S1	X	X				X	S	X	X		X				X1	X	X			X	X		X	A.Leake	20
X	S				X	X				X	S	X	X		X					S	X	X		X	X			J.Rushton	21
	S				X		X		X1	S		X	X		S1	X				X	X			X	X			M.J.Brandwood	22
	S				X		X			S		X	X1		X	S1				X	X			X				B.Knight	23
	S		X				X			S		X			X	S				X	X			X			X	G.Singh	24
	S		X				X			S		X			X	S1				X	X1			X			X	B.Knight	25
			X2		X		X	S1				S			X		X			S2	X		X1	X	X		X	R.Gifford	26
			X		X		X	X1				S			X		S			X	X		S1	X	X		X	C.Wilkes	27
S2					X		X					X		S	X		S1			X	X1			X	X2		X	G.Singh	28
S			X1		X		X	S1				X			S		X			X	X			X			X	G.Barber	29
S			X		X		S					X			S		X			X	X			X		X	X	G.Frankland	30
S			X1		X		S1					X			S		X			X	X			X		X	X	N.Fletcher	31
S			X		X							X			S		X			X	X1		S1	X		X	X	M.E.Pierce	32
S2					X		X	X2				X			S		X1			X	S1			X			X	J.Kirkby	33
S					X		X					X			S		X			X	S1			X1			X	T.West	34
					X	X	X1	X				X			S		X			X	S		S1	X			X	P.Taylor	35
S					X	X	X1	X				X			S		X			X	S1			X			X	G.R.Pooley	36
S					X	X		X				X			S		X			X	X	S		X			X	A.Wiley	37
X					X	X	S					X			S		X			X	X	S		X			X	S.Lodge	38
S					X	X		X				X			S		X			X	X1	S1		X			X	R.Poulain	39
X						X2	X1					X			S		X			X	S1		S2	X			X	F.G.Stretton	40
X	X				X	X	S					X			S		X			X	X		S	X			X	N.Barry	41
X	X				X	X						X			S	X2		X			S2		S1	X1			X	K.Breen	42
X	X				X	X						X			S	X					S1		S	X			X	J.Rushton	43
X	X					X						X	X	X	S	X	X	X			S		S	X			X	M.C.Bailey	44
X	X					X						X	X	X	S	X1	X	X1		X	S1		S	X			X	E.Wolstenholme	45
X1	X					X						X	X	X	S	X	X	X		X	S1		S	X			X	R.B.Gifford	46
X1	X					X						X	X		S	X	X	X			S1		S	X			X	G.Cain	47
	X				X	X			X			X	X		S	X	X1	X			S		S1	X			X	K.A.Leach	48
	X				S1	X		X				X	X	X	S	X1		X			S			X			X	A.D'Urso	49
S1	X				X	X						X	X2	X	S	X1					S2	X		X			X	S.Bennett	50
X	X				X				X			X	X	X	S	X	X	X		S	X		S1	X			X1	M.Fletcher	51
X	X				X				X			X	X	X	S	X	X	X		S	X		S	X			X	I.Hemley	52
X	X				X				X			X	X	X1	S	X	X1	X		S	X		S1	X			X	R.Harris	53
X	X1				X				X			X	S		X	X	X2	X		S2	X		X1	X			X	K.Lynch	54
X					X				X			X	S	S1	X	X	X2			S2	X		X1	X			X	A.R.Leake	55
X1	X				X			S1	X			X	S		X	X	X	S		X				X			X	E.Lomas	56
X			X	X1	X	X						S	X	X		X	X	S1		X			S	X			X	T.West	57
S1			X1	X	X	X						S	X	X		X	X	X		X				X			X	P.Rejer	58
14	25	0	6	5	31	36	8	14	5	41	5	37	33	11	38	4	11	20	14	31	5	3	1	46	17	3	42	EL Appearances	
3	0	1	0	5	2	0	4	0	0	0	0	1	0	0	2	0	3	3	5	5	1	7	0	0	0	0	0	EL Sub Appearances	
0	2	0	0	1	4	4	0	2	4	0	4	4	0	2+1	1	2	0	0	1+1	0	4	4	0	4				CC Appearances	
0	1+2	0	1	1	4	5	4	0	0	3	2	3	5	0	4+1	0+2	0	5	4+1	4	0	0	0	5	1	0	4	FAC Appearances	
0	0+1	0	1	1	3	3	1	0	1	2	1	2	3	0	1	0	0	1+1	2+1	2	0	0	0	3	3	0	3	AWS Appearances	

CLUB RECORDS

BIGGEST VICTORIES
League: 9-0 v Wrexham, Division 3, 15.10.1963.
F.A. Cup: 7-0 v Windsor & Eton (a), 1st Round, 20.11.1982.

BIGGEST DEFEATS
League: 0-7 v Swansea City, Division 3(S), 8.11.1924.
0-7 v Walsall, Division 3, 19.1.1957.
F.A. Cup: 1-7 v Manchester United, 3rd Round, 1927-28.

MOST POINTS
3 points a win: 85, Division 2, 1994-95.
2 points a win: 62, Division 3(S), 1932-33.
62, Division 4, 1962-63.

MOST GOALS SCORED
98, Division 4, 1962-63.

RECORD TRANSFER FEE RECEIVED
£720,000 from Wimbledon for Dean Holdsworth, July 1992.

RECORD TRANSFER FEE PAID
£275,000 to Chelsea for Joe Allon, November 1992.

BEST PERFORMANCES
League: 5th in Division 1, 1935-36.
F.A. Cup: 6th Round, 1938, 1946, 1949, 1989.
League Cup: 4th Round, 1982-83.

HONOURS
Champions Division 3(S), 1932-33.
Champions Division 2, 1934-35.
Champions Division 4, 1962-63.
Champions Division 3, 1991-92.

LEAGUE CAREER
Founder Members of Division 3, 1920.
Division 3(S) 1921-33, Div 2 1932-33, Div 1 1934-35, Div 2 1946-47, Div 3(S) 1953-54, Div 4 1961-62, Div 3 1962-63, Div 4 1965-66, Div 3 1971-72, Div 4 1972,73, Div 3 1977-78, Div 2 (now Div 1) 1991-92, Div 2 1992-

INDIVIDUAL CLUB RECORDS

MOST GOALS IN A SEASON
Jack Holliday: 39 goals in 1932-33. (League 38, FA Cup 1).

MOST GOALS IN A MATCH
5. Jack Holliday v Luton Town, Division 3 (S), (a) 28.1.1933 (5-5).
5. Billy Scott v Barnsley, Division 2, (h) 15.12.1934 (8-1).
5. Peter McKennan v Bury, Division 2, (h) 18.2.1949 (8-2).

OLDEST PLAYER
Dai Hopkins, 39 years 7 months 13 days, 26.5.1947.

YOUNGEST PLAYER
Danis Salman, 15 years 8 months 3days, 15.11.1975.

MOST CAPPED PLAYER
Dai Hopkins (Wales) 12.
Billy Scott & Leslie Smith (England) 1.

PREVIOUS MANAGERS

(Since 1945)
Harry Curtis (Sec./Manager) 1926-49; A.H.'Jackie'Gibbons (Sec./Man.) 1949-52; Jim Bain 1952-53; Tommy Lawton (players/manager) 1953; Bill Dodgin (Senior) 1953-57; Malcolm MacDonald 1957-65; Tommy Cavanagh 1965-66; Billy Gray 1966-67; Jimmy Sirrel 1967-69; Frank Blunstone 1969-73; Mike Everitt 1973-75; John Docherty 1975-76; Bill Dodgin (Junior) 1976-80; Fred Callaghan 1980-84; Frank McLintock 1984-87; Steve Perryman 1987-90; Phil Holder 1990-93;

ADDITIONAL INFORMATION
PREVIOUS NAMES
None.
PREVIOUS LEAGUES
Southern League.
Club colours: Red & white striped shirts, black shorts, black socks with red/white turnover.
Change colours: Black & white striped shirts, white shorts and white socks with red/black turnover.
Reserves League: Springheath Print Capital League.
Youth League: South East Counties.

LONGEST LEAGUE RUNS

of undefeated matches:	16 (1932, 1967)	of league matches w/out a win:	16 (1994)
of undefeated home matches:	24 (1934-35)	of undefeated away matches:	11 (1993)
without home win:	11 (1947)	without an away win:	21 (1965-66)
of league wins:	9 (1932)	of home wins:	21 (1929-30)
of league defeats:	9 (1925,1928)	of away wins:	5 (1956, 1981)

Brentford won all 21 home games in 1929-30, they also played 44 away League games without a draw between 1923-25.

THE MANAGER

DAVID WEBB . . . . appointed in May 1993.

PREVIOUS CLUBS
As Manager . . . . Torquay United, Bournemouth, Southend, Chelsea.
As a player . . . . Leyton Orient, Southampton, Chelsea, Q.P.R., Leicester City, Derby County, ... Bournemouth, Torquay.

HONOURS
As a Manager . . . . None.
As a Player . . . . Chelsea: FA Cup 1970. E.C.W.C. 1971.

BRENTFORD

PLAYERS NAME Honours	Ht	Wt	Birthdate	Birthplace Transfers	Contract Date	Clubs	APPEARANCES				GOALS			
							League	L/Cup	FA Cup	Other	Lge	L/C	FAC	Oth
G O A L K E E P E R S														
Dearden Kevin	5.11	12.8	08/03/70	Luton	05/08/88	Tottenham Hotspur	0+1	1						
				Loan	09/03/89	Cambridge United	15							
				Loan	31/08/89	Hartlepool United	10							
				Loan	23/03/90	Swindon Town	1							
				Loan	24/08/90	Peterborough Utd	7							
				Loan	10/01/91	Hull City	3							
				Loan	16/08/91	Rochdale	2							
				Loan	19/03/92	Birmingham City	12							
				Free	30/09/93	Brentford	119	8	7	11				
Fernandes Tamer	6.3	13.7	07/12/74	Paddington	12/07/93	Brentford	11+3		2	1+2				
E: Y.1.				Loan	12/10/93	Wealdstone								
D E F E N D E R S														
Anderson Ijah			30/12/75	Hackney		Tottenham Hotspur								
						Southend United								
					31/07/95	Brentford	25	2	1+2	0+1	2	1		
Ashby Barry	6.2	13.2	21/11/70	Brent	01/12/88	Watford	101+13	6	4	2+1	3			
FAYC'89.					22/03/94	Brentford	79+2	7	6	8	3		1	
Bates Jamie	6.1	13.0	24/02/68	Croydon	01/06/87	Brentford	295+20	25+3	12+1	35	14	2	1	1
Div.3'92.														
Hurdle Gus	5.9	11.01	14/10/73	Kensington		Fulham								
				Free		Dorchester								
				Free	19/07/94	Brentford	18+5	4	0+1	1				
Myall Stuart	5.10	13.3	12/11/74	Eastbourne	09/07/93	Brighton & H.A. (T)	69+11	4	4	4+1	4			
				Free	06/07/96	Brentford								
Statham Brian	5.8	11.6	21/05/69	Zimbabwe	03/08/87	Tottenham Hotspur	20+4	2	0+1					
E: u21.3,u19.2. Div.3'92.				Loan	28/03/91	Reading	8							
				Loan	20/11/91	Bournemouth	2			1				
				£70000	16/01/92	Brentford	137+10	10	7	13	6		1	
M I D F I E L D														
Davis Paul	5.10	10.13	09/12/61	London	11/07/79	Arsenal	331+20	47+5	22+5	19+1	30	4	3	1
E:B.1,u21.11. LC'87'93.				Free	12/09/95	Brentford	5	2		1				
Div.1'89'91. FAC'93. ECWC'94.														
Hutchings Carl	5.11	11.0	24/09/74	Hammersmith	12/07/93	Brentford	78+13	5+1	8+1	7+3				
Smith Paul W	5.11	13.7	18/09/71	Lenham	16/03/90	Southend United	18+2		0+1		1			
SLP'93. (while on loan with Dover)				Free	06/08/93	Brentford	113	8	9	10	10	1	2	1
F O R W A R D S														
Abrahams Paul	5.8	10.6	31/10/73	Colchester	11/08/92	Colchester United	30+25	2+3	4	3	8		2	2
				£30000	09/03/94	Brentford	21+6			1	6			
				Loan	05/01/96	Colchester United	8			1	2			
Asaba Carl	6.2	13.0	28/01/73	London		Dulwich Hamlet								
					09/08/94	Brentford	5+5	1	1	2	2			1
				Loan	16/02/95	Colchester United	9+3				2			
Bent Marcus						Brentford	8+4		4	1	1		3	
Forster Nicholas	5.9	11.5	08/09/73	Caterham		Shrewsbury Town								
						Gillingham	54+13	3+2	6		24		2	
				£100000	17/06/94	Brentford	83+1	8	5	6+1	29	2		3
Harvey Lee	5.11	11.7	21/12/66	Harlow	05/12/84	Leyton Orient	135+49	13+3	10+4	19+4	23	3	2	3
E: Y.5.				Free	04/08/93	Nottingham Forest	0+2	0+1						
				Free	18/11/93	Brentford	85+6	7+1	8+1	7	2	1		
McGhee David	5.10	11.04	19/06/76	Sussex	15/07/94	Brentford	57+13	5+1	6	3+1	9	1		
McPherson Malcolm	5.10	12.0	09/12/74	Glasgow		Yeovil Town								
						West Ham United								
					06/07/96	Brentford								
Omigie Joe	6.2	13.0	13/06/72	Hammersmith		Donna								
					26/08/94	Brentford	3+7							
				Loan	01/09/95	Woking								
Taylor Robert	6.0	11.6	30/04/71	Norwich	26/03/90	Norwich City								
				Loan	28/03/91	Leyton Orient	0+3							
					31/08/91	Birmingham City								
				Free	21/10/91	Leyton Orient	54+19	1+1	2+1	2+1	20			
				£100000	24/03/94	Brentford	90	8	6	7	36	2	4	1

GRIFFIN PARK
Braemar Road, Brentford, Middx, TW8 0NT
Tel: 0181 847 2511

Capacity...13,800
Covered Standing...6,500
Seating...3,500

First game...v Plymouth Argyle, 1.9.1904.
First floodlit game ....v Chelsea, 5.10.1954.

ATTENDANCES
Highest.......................................39,626 v Preston North End, FA Cup 6th Rnd, 5.3.1938.
Lowest ....1,110 v Swindon Town, AMC, 6.1.1987.

OTHER GROUNDS...None.

MATCHDAY TICKET PRICES

A Block . . . . £9.80 (Juv/OAP £5)

E Block . . . . £13 (Juv/OAP £10.20)

B Block. . . . . £11.50 (Juv/OAP £8.70)

D Block . . . . £14 (Juv/OAP £11.20)

Terraces (Home & away). . . . . £7.80 (Juv/OAP £5)

Away End Seats . . . . £13 (Juv/OAP £10)

Ticket Office Telephone No. . . . . . . 0181 847 2511.

CLUBCALL
0891 12 11 08
Calls cost 39p per minute cheap rate and 49p per minute at all other times.
Call costings correct at time of going to press.

HOW TO GET TO THE GROUND

From the North:
Use M1 or A1 then A406 North Circular Road to Chiswick then follow signs for the South Circular Road. In 0.3 miles turn right A315 (S.P. Brentford). In 0.5 miles turn right into Ealing Road for Brentford FC.

From the East:
Use either A406 North Circular Road then as above or South Circular Road A205. Cross Kew Bridge and turn left A315 (S.P. Brentford). In 0.5 miles turn right into Ealing Road for Brentford FC.

From the South:
Use A240/A3/M3 or A316 to junction with South Circular Road. A205. Cross Kew Bridge and turn left A315 (S.P. Brentford). In 0.5 miles turn right into Ealing Road for Brentford FC.

From the West:
Use M4 until junction 1, leave Motorway and follow signs for South Circular Road. In 0.3 miles turn right A315 (S.P. Brentford). In 0.5 miles turn right into Ealing Road for Brentford FC. Alternative use M25/M4.

Car Parking: Street parking available.
Nearest Railway Station: Brentford or South Ealing (Tube), Piccadilly Line.

MATCHDAY PROGRAMME

Programme Editor . . . . Peter Gilham.

Number of pages . . . . 32.

Price . . . . £1.50.

Subscriptions . . . . £55.

Local Newspapers . . . . . . Brentford & Chiswick Times, Ealing Gazette,
. . . . Middlesex Chronicle, Hounslow Informer, Weekend Recorder.

Local Radio Stations . . . . Capital Gold, London Newstalk.

BRISTOL CITY
(The Robins)
NATIONWIDE LEAGUE DIVISION 2
SPONSORED BY: AUTO WINDSCREENS

Back Row (L-R): Louis Carey, Rob Edwards, Matthew Hewlett, Vegard Hansen, Keith Welch, Mark Shail, Phil Klte, Jason Fowler, Scott Paterson, Matt Bryant, Alan McLeary. **Middle Row:** Dave Bell (Yth Coach), Tony Fawthrop (Chief Scout), Jim Brennan, Dominic Barclay, Paul Agostino, Mark Humphreys, Wayne Brown, Richard Dryden, Gary Owers, Brian Tinnion, Phil Barber, Mike Gibson (Coach), Buster Footman (Physio), Gerry Sweeney (Coach). **Front Row:** Stuart Munro, Dean Higgins, Junior Bent, Scott Partridge, Joe Jordan (Manager), John Gorman (Asst. Manager), David Seal, Martin Kuhl, Rodney McAree, Ian Baird.

BRISTOL CITY
FORMED IN 1894
TURNED PROFESSIONAL IN 1897
LTD COMPANY IN 1897

CHAIRMAN: Scott Davidson
DIRECTORS
John Clapp, Bob Neale
Associate Directors: Gary Williams,
Stephen Lansdown, Keith Dawe, John Lacock
GENERAL MANAGER
Ian Wilson
COMMERCIAL MANAGER
John Cox

MANAGER: Joe Jordan
ASSISTANT MANAGER: Gerry Sweeney

PHYSIOTHERAPIST
Buster Footman

STATISTICIANS FOR THE DIRECTORY
David Woods & David Peacey

It was a season of consolidation, both on and off the field. When a club is relegated it usually bears the burden of being promotion favourite the following season. This was not so for City. Indeed, at one stage, a second successive relegation was a distinct possibility, and it wasn't until the last couple of months of the campaign that relative safety was assured. But, the optimists amongst the Ashton Gate faithful will tell you that the side also flirted briefly with the other end of the table via a play-off spot when 11th place was secured for a month in March.

All in all, a mid-table finish was a fair reflection on a season that, once again, saw more to get excited about off the pitch than on it at times. Things finally came to a head in the close-season with a new share issue floated following yet another shake-up at boardroom level and the promise of a much-improved 'outfit' at both playing and administration levels.

The signs are good. The public have responded positively, with advance season-ticket sales up, manager Joe Jordan already active in the transfer market and a new playing surface set to be ready pre-season. With 30 players used in all competitions last season (only one ever-present: the impressive Martin Kuhl), more consistency will, it is hoped, lead to a more settled and established side. On the plus side, the Aussie strikers David Seal and Paul Agostino shared 20 of the 55 league goals scored by the side.

Failure to mention the one major highlight of the campaign would be tantamount to a criminal offence in the eyes of the die-hard City supporters. It wasn't the visit of Newcastle United in the Coca-Cola Cup, nor the bumper attendance - over 20,000 - for the home game against arch-rivals Rovers. Rather it was the return game played in March. At the eighth attempt - and with Rovers moving home again, possibly the last chance - City finally achieved a league victory at Twerton Park by 4-2.

The club is about to enter its centenary season with the likelihood of much celebration. With the calibre of sides coming into the division from above and below it's going to be a tough season, but the thought of signing off the campaign in style with some silverware to commemorate those 100 years is a realistic one. . .

DAVE PEACEY

BRISTOL CITY

League: 13th   FA Cup: 1st Rnd   Coca-Cola Cup: 2nd Rnd   Auto Windscreen Shield: 2nd Rnd

M	DATE	COMP	VEN	OPPONENTS	RESULT	HT	LP	GOAL SCORERS/GOAL TIMES	ATT.
1	A 12	EL	H	Blackpool	D 1-1	1-1	17	Seal 20	7734
2	15	CC 1/1	A	Colchester United	L 1-2	1-2		Seal 2	(3684)
3	22	CC 1/2	H	Colchester United	W 2-1	1-0		Seal 28, 81	3648
4	26	EL	H	Stockport County	W 1-0	1-0	15	Seal 29	7331
5	29	EL	A	Shrewsbury Town	L 1-4	1-0	16	Agostino 20	(2558)
6	S 2	EL	A	Peterborough United	D 1-1	0-1	16	Seal 63	(4621)
7	9	EL	H	Brighton & H.A.	L 0-1	0-1	22		7585
8	12	EL	H	Brentford	D 0-0	0-0	22		5054
9	16	EL	A	Bradford City	L 0-3	0-1	22		(5165)
10	19	CC 2/1	H	Newcastle United	L 0-5	0-3			15952
11	23	EL	A	Notts County	D 2-2	0-0	23	Agostino 56, Seal 84	(5251)
12	26	AWS 1/2	A	Oxford United	L 0-3	0-3			(2558)
13	30	EL	H	Wycombe Wanderers	D 0-0	0-0	23		5564
14	O 4	CC 2/2	A	Newcastle United	L 1-3	1-0		Agostino 14	(36357)
15	7	EL	A	Swindon Town	L 0-2	0-1	1		(11797)
16	14	EL	H	Hull City	W 4-0	1-0	21	Bent 24, Starbuck 54, Bent 61, Barnard 80	5354
17	17	AWS 1/1	H	Barnet	W 2-0	1-0		Seal 29(pen), Edwards 58	1830
18	21	EL	A	York City	W 1-0	1-0	19	Nugent 24	(3367)
19	28	EL	A	Walsall	L 0-2	0-2	21		6475
20	31	EL	H	Chesterfield	W 2-1	1-1	18	Barnard 14, Morris 53(og)	4408
21	N 4	EL	A	Oxford United	L 0-2	0-0	12		(5665)
22	11	FAC 1	A	Bournemouth	D 0-0	0-0			(5304)
23	18	EL	H	Carlisle United	D 1-1	0-0	20	Nugent 56	5423
24	21	FAC 1R	H	Bournemouth	L 0-1	0-1			5069
25	25	EL	A	Rotherham United	W 3-2	1-1	18	Barnard 25, Owers 64, Seal 65	(2649)
26	28	AWS 2	A	Shrewsbury Town	D 0-0	0-0		(Lost 6-7 on penalties)	(2258)
27	D 5	EL	A	Crewe Alexandra	L 2-4	1-0	19	Nugent 30, Dryden 75	(2977)
28	9	EL	H	Notts County	L 0-2	0-1	20		5617
29	16	EL	A	Wycombe Wanderers	D 1-1	0-1	18	Tinnion 70	(4020)
30	23	EL	A	Burnley	D 0-0	0-0	17		(9327)
31	26	EL	H	Swansea City	W 1-0	0-0	17	Kuhl 90	6845
32	J 6	EL	A	Bournemouth	D 1-1	1-0	16	Maskell 39	(3667)
33	13	EL	H	Crewe Alexandra	W 3-2	2-1	16	Patterson 4, Nugent 25, 67	6790
34	16	EL	H	Bristol Rovers	L 0-2	0-0	16		20007
35	20	EL	A	Blackpool	L 0-3	0-1	16		(4838)
36	23	EL	A	Wrexham	D 0-0	0-0	10		(2637)
37	F 10	EL	H	Bournemouth	W 3-0	2-0	17	Seal 12, Tinnion 20, Agostino 56	6217
38	13	EL	H	Shrewsbury Town	W 2-0	0-0	15	Agostino 69, 89	5217
39	17	EL	A	Brentford	D 2-2	0-1	15	Agostino 48, Barnard 56	(5213)
40	20	EL	H	Peterborough United	L 0-1	0-0	16		5014
41	24	EL	H	Bradford City	W 2-1	1-0	13	Seal 20, Kuhl 79	5400
42	27	EL	A	Brighton & H.A.	W 2-0	1-0	11	Kuhl 37, 49	(4739)
43	M 2	EL	A	Swansea City	L 1-2	0-2	11	Walker 46(og)	(4109)
44	9	EL	H	Burnley	L 0-1	0-1	11		6612
45	16	EL	A	Bristol Rovers	W 4-2	2-1	11	Nugent 9, Hewlett 44, Agostino 59, Seal 86	(8648)
46	19	EL	A	Stockport County	D 0-0	0-0	11		(3713)
47	23	EL	H	Wrexham	W 3-1	1-0	11	Nugent 18, 84, Tinnion 62	6141
48	30	EL	H	Swindon Town	D 0-0	0-0	12		11370
49	A 2	EL	A	Hull City	W 3-2	0-0	11	Hewlett 54, Agostino 66, Seal 81	(2641)
50	6	EL	A	Walsall	L 1-2	1-1	12	Seal 33	(4142)
51	8	EL	H	York City	D 1-1	0-0	12	Kuhl 55(pen)	7512
52	13	EL	A	Chesterfield	D 1-1	1-0	11	Owers 19	(4619)
53	20	EL	H	Oxford United	L 0-2	0-0	13		7674
54	27	EL	H	Rotherham United	W 4-3	1-1	13	Partridge 15, Agostino 46, 48, Kuhl 78	6101
55	M 4	EL	A	Carlisle United	L 1-2	1-2	13	Robinson 22(og)	(5935)

Best Home League Attendance: 20007 v Bristol Rovers   **Smallest: 4408 v Chesterfield**   **Average: 7019**

Goal Scorers:
EL(55):   Agostino(10), Seal(10), Nugent(8), Kuhl(6), Barnard(4), Tinnion(3), Opponent(s)(3), Owers(2), Bent(2), Hewlett(2), Maskell(1), Partridge(1), Starbuck(1), Dryden(1), Patterson(1)
CC(4):   Seal(3), Agostino(1)
FAC(0):
AWS(2):   Seal(1), Edwards(1)

1995-96

	(F) Agostino	(M) Armstrong	(F) Barber	(F) Barclay	(D) Barnard	(F) Bent	(D) Bryant	(F) Carey	(D) Dryden	(G) Dykstra	(M) Edwards	(M) Fowler	(D) Hansen	(M) Hewlett	(G) Kite	(M) Kuhl	(M) Maskell	(D) McLeary	(D) Munro	(F) Nugent	(M) Owers	(F) Partridge	(M) Patterson	(D) Plummer	(F) Seal	(D) Shail	(F) Starbuck	(D) Tinnion	(G) Welch		
	X		X			X			X			S	X			X			X	X				X		S	X	S		X	G.Pooley	1
	X		X			X			X			S2	X		S	X		X	X1			X2			X	S1	X		X	P.Taylor	2
	X3		X1			X	S2		X			X	X2			X		X				S3		S1	X	X		X	G.Barber	3
	X2	X	X1			X	S		X				X			X		X				S2		S1	X	X		X	A.D'Urso	4
	X	X	X2			X	S1		X				X			X		X				S		S2	X	X1		X	U.D.Rennie	5
	X	X				X	X		X			X3			S2	X		X1	X			S3			X	S1		X2	M.Riley	6
	X3	X1				X	X		X			X2				X		X			S1	S3		S2	X	X			G.Singh	7
	X1	X				X2	X		S	X		X		X		X					X	S1		S2	X	X			A.Wiley	8
	S1	X				X	X		X	X		X		X		X		S			X1			S	X		X		T.Heilbron	9
	X					X	X		X	X		X	S1	X	X			X				S	S	X1	X				K.Burge	10
	X				S1	X		X	X	X		X				X		S			X			X1	S2		X		P.Taylor	11
	X2				X	X		X	X	X		X				X		S1			X			S	S2		X		A.Butler	12
						X	X		X	X	X	X	X	S		X		S	X	X1	X		X		S1		X		M.J.Brandwood	13
	X2					X	X		X	X	X	X		X	X	X		S			X	S1	X	S2	X1				J.Kirkby	14
	S1			X		X	X		X	X	X	X		S		S					X	X	X				X1			R.Gifford	15
	S1			X		X	X		X	X	X	X				X2					X	X		X		S	X1	S2		P.Rejer	16
	X2			X		X	X		X	X	X	X				X1					X	X		X	S1	X	S	S2		K.Leach	17
				X		X	X	X	X	X	X	X				X					X	X	X1		S	S1		S		D.Allison	18
	S1			X		X	X	X2	X	X	X	X				X					X	X	X1			S2		S		B.Knight	19
	X1			X		X	X	X	X	X	X	X				X					X	X	X		S1	S		S		D.Orr	20
	X1			X		X	X		X	X		X		S		X		X2			X	X			S2	X		S1		I.Hemley	21
				X		X	X1		X	X		X		S		X					X	X	S1			X			X	G.Barber	22
	S1			X		X	X2		X	X		X				X					X	X	X1	S	S2		X		X	M.Pierce	23
				X	X	X	X		X			X				X					X	X1	S		S	X	X	S1	X	G.Barber	24
				X	X	X	X		X	S1		X				X					X	X	S2		X2	X1		S	X	I.Cruikshanks	25
	S1			X	X	X	X		X	S		X				X					X	X			X	X		X1	X	A.Butler	26
	S			X	X	X	X		X	X		X				X					X	X			S	X		X	X	P.Richards	27
	S1			X2	X	X	X		X	X		X				X			S3		X	X			X1	X3	S2	X	X	R.Gifford	28
	S1			X	X1	X	X					X		X		S	X	S	X		X	X	S			X		X	X	P.Taylor	29
	X2			X		X1	X					X		X		X		X	X		X	X		S1	S	S2		X	X	K.Lynch	30
	X1			X		X	X		S			X		X2		X		X	X		X	X		X	S2	S1		X	X	J.Rushton	31
				X1	S1	X	S		X	S		X		X	X	X	X	X	X		X			X				X	X	I.Hemley	32
	S			X		X	S		X	S		X		X	X	X	X	X	X		X			X	S			X	X	N.Fletcher	33
	S3			S2	S1	X	X		X2			X		X1	X	X3	X	X	X		X	X		X				X	X	G.Singh	34
	S2			S	S1	X	X		X			X		X1	X	X2	X	X	X		X	X		X				X	X	T.West	35
	S1			X1	S	X	X		X	S		X		X	X	X	X	X	X		X	X		X				X	X	A.G.Wiley	36
	X			X	X1	X	X2	S				S2		X		X		X	X		X			S1	X			X	X	K.Leach	37
	X		S	X	X1	X	X						X			X		X	X		X		S	S	X			X	X	B.Knight	38
	X		S	X	X1	X	X						X			X		X	X		X		S1	S	X			X	X	F.G.Stretton	39
	X3			X	X2	X	X					X1		X		X		X	X		X		S3	S1	S2	X		X	X	J.Brandwood	40
	X			X	S1	X	X1			S			X			X		X	X		X		S2	X	X2			X	X	P.Rejer	41
	X			X	X	X	X		S	S				X		X		X	X		X		S1	X	X1			X	X	A.P.D'Urso	42
	X			X	X1	X	X		S	S				X		X		X	X		X		S1	X	X			X	X	G.Pooley	43
	X1			X	X2	X	X		S					S2		X		X	X		X		S1	X	X			X	X	S.G.Bennett	44
	X2			X	X1	X	X		S					S1		X		X	X		X		X	X	S2			X	X	J.Rushton	45
	X			X	X1	X	X		S					S1		X		X	X		X		X	X	S			X	X	J.Kirkby	46
	X3			X	X1	X	S2							S1		X		X2	X		X		X	X	S3			X	X	G.Barber	47
	X			X	X1	X	X		S					S		X		X	X		X		X	X	S1			X	X	I.Hemley	48
	X			X	S	X	S		X					X		X		X	X		X		X	X	S1			X	X	R.Poulain	49
	S1			X	S2	X	X		X	S				X2		X		X	X		X		X		X1			X	X	A.Leake	50
	X		S3	X	X2	X	X1							X		X		X	X		X			S1	S2	X3		X	X	M.Fletcher	51
	X2			X	S1	X	X		S					X		X		X	X		X		X	X	S2			X	X	D.Orr	52
	X2		S2	X	X	X	S							X1		X		X	X		X		X	X	S1			X	X	P.Rejer	53
	X			X	S	X	X					S		X		X		X	X		S		X	X		X		X	X	M.Pierce	54
	X			X		X			X1					S2		X		X	X		X	X	S1	X		S		X2	X	S.Mathieson	55
29	**6**	**3**	**0**	**33**	**33**	**31**	**22**	**17**	**8**	**18**	**6**	**7**	**27**	**3**	**46**	**5**	**30**	**3**	**29**	**34**	**3**	**16**	**1**	**19**	**9**	**5**	**27**	**35**	EL Appearances	
11	0	0	2	1	7	1	1	1	0	1	4	1	0	1	0	0	1	0	5	3	6	2	10	11	3	0	3	0		EL Sub Appearances	
4	0	2	0	0	4	2+1	0	4	0	2	1+1	4	0+1	2	4	0	2	2	0	1	1+2	1	1+2	4	1+1	0	0	2		CC Appearances	
0	0	0	0	0	2	2	1	2	1	0	2	0	0	0	2	0	0	0	2	0+1	0	0	1	0	1	2	0+1	2		FAC Appearances	
2+1	0	0	0	2	3	3	1	2	2	3	0	1	0	0	3	0	0	0	0+1	0	3	0	1	0+1	2+1	1	1+1	1		AWS Appearances	

Also Played: (F) Baird X2(11), X1(12).

397

CLUB RECORDS

BIGGEST VICTORIES
League: 9-0 v Aldershot, Division 3(S), 28.12.1946.
F.A. Cup: 11-0 v Chichester City, Round 1, 5.11.1960.
League Cup: 4-0 v Rotherham United, Round 2, 15.9.1970.
4-0 v Peterborough United, Round 3, 2.10.1979.
5-1 v Cardiff City, Round 1 2nd Leg, 25.8.92.
BIGGEST DEFEATS
League: 0-9 v Coventry City, Division 3(S), 28.4.1934.
F.A. Cup: 0-5 v Preston North End, Round 5 replay, 25.2.1935.
0-5 v Brentford, Round 4, 2nd leg, 31.1.1946.
1-6 v Sunderland, Round 4, 25.1.1964.
League Cup: 0-5 v Everton, Round 2, 13.9.1967.
1-6 v West Ham United, Round 2, 2nd leg, 9.10.1984.
1-6 v Sunderland, Round 2, 2nd leg, 8.10.1990.

MOST POINTS
3 points a win: 91, Division 3, 1989-90.
2 points a win: 70, Division 3(S), 1954-55.
MOST GOALS SCORED
104, Division 3(S), 1926-27.
MOST GOALS CONCEDED
97, Division 2, 1959-60.
MOST FIRST CLASS MATCHES IN A SEASON
64 (League 46, FA Cup 6, Lge Cup 9, AMC 3) 1988-89.
MOST LEAGUE WINS
30, Division 2, 1905-06; Division 3(S), 1954-55.
MOST LEAGUE DRAWS
17, Division 2, 1919-20, 1965-66; Division 4, 1982-83.
MOST LEAGUE DEFEATS
26, Division 2, 1959-60.
BEST PERFORMANCES
League: Champions of Division 2, 1905-06.
Highest Position: Runners-up in Division 1, 1906-07.
F.A. Cup: Runners-up in 1908-09.
League Cup: Semi-Finals in 1970-71, 1988-89.
HONOURS
Champions of Division 2, 1905-06.
Champions of Division 3(S), 1922-23, 1926-27, 1954-55.
Welsh Cup 1933-34. Anglo/Scottish Cup 1977-78.
Freight Rover Trophy 1985-86.

LEAGUE CAREER
Div 2 1901-06, Div 1 06-11, Div 2 11-22, Div 3(S) 22-23, Div 2 23-24, Div 3(S) 24-27, Div 2 27-32, Div 3(S) 32-55, Div 2 55-60, Div 3 60-65, Div 2 65-76, Div 1 76-80, Div 2 80-81, Div 3 81-82, Div 4 82-84, Div 3 84-90, Div 2 (now Div 1) 90-95, Div 2 95-

INDIVIDUAL CLUB RECORDS

MOST GOALS IN A SEASON
Don Clark: 41 goals in 1946-47 (League 36, FAC 5).

MOST GOALS IN A MATCH
6. 'Tot' Walsh v Gillingham, Division 3(S), 15.1.1927 (9-4).

OLDEST PLAYER
Terry Cooper, 40 years 86 days, 6.10.1984.

YOUNGEST PLAYER
Nyrere Kelly, 16 years 8 months, 16.10.1982.

MOST CAPPED PLAYER
Billy Wedlock (England) 26.

PREVIOUS MANAGERS

(Since 1945)
Bob Hewison 1945-49; Bob Wright 1949-50; Pat Beasley 1950-58; J Seed/L Bardsley (caretakers) 1958; Peter Doherty 1958-60; Les Bardsley (caretaker) 1960; Fred Ford 1960-67; Les Bardsley (caretaker) 1967; Alan Dicks 1967-80; T Collins/K Wimshurst (caretaker) 1980; Bob Houghton 1980-82; R Hodgson/G Sharpe (caretaker) 1982; Terry Cooper 1982-88; Joe Jordan 1988-90; Jimmy Lumsden 1990-92; Aizle'd/Osman/Shelton (caretakers) 1992; Denis Smith 1992-93; Russell Osman 1993-94.
ADDITIONAL INFORMATION
PREVIOUS NAMES
Bristol South End 1894-97.
PREVIOUS LEAGUES
Southern League 1897-1901.
Club colours: Red shirts, white shorts, red and white socks.
Change Colours:
Reserves League: The Avon Insurance Football Combination.
Youth League: South East Counties League.

LONGEST LEAGUE RUNS

of undefeated matches:	24 (9.9.1905 -10.2.1906)	of league matches w/out a win:	15 (29.4.1933 - 4.11.1933)
of undefeated home matches:	25 (24.10.1953 - 27.11.1954)	of undefeated away matches:	21 (16.9.1905 - 22.9.1906)
without home win:	10 (17.10.1931 - 5.3.1932)	without an away win:	23 (8.10.1932 - 28.10.1933)
of league wins:	14 (9.9.1905 - 2.12.1905)	of home wins:	12 (24.4.1926 - 29.1.1927)
of league defeats:	7 (5.9.1931- 3.10.1931 & 3.10.1970 - 7.11.71)	of away wins:	6 (16.9.1905 - 25.11.1905)

THE MANAGER

JOE JORDAN . . . . appointed November 1994.

PREVIOUS CLUBS
As Manager . . . . Bristol City, Hearts, Stoke City.
As Asst.Man/Coach . . . . Bristol City.
As a player . . . . Morton, Leeds United, Manchester United, AC Milan, Verona, Southampton, Bristol City.

HONOURS
As a Manager . . . . Division Three runners-up 1989-90.
As a Player . . . . Leeds United: Division 1 Champions 1974.
International Career . . . . 52 full caps and 1 U23 cap for Scotland.

BRISTOL CITY

PLAYERS NAME Honours	Ht	Wt	Birthdate	Birthplace Transfers	Contract Date	Clubs	APPEARANCES				GOALS			
							League	L/Cup	FA Cup	Other	Lge	L/C	FAC	Oth
G O A L K E E P E R S														
Welch Keith	6.2	12.5	03/10/68	Bolton		Bolton Wanderers								
				Free	03/03/87	Rochdale	205	12	10	12				
				£200000	25/07/91	Bristol City	195	12	11	9				
D E F E N D E R S														
Barnard Darren	5.10	12.0	30/11/71	Rintein (Germ)		Wokingham Town								
				£50000	25/07/90	Chelsea	18+11	1+1	1+1		2			
				£75000	06/10/95	Bristol City	33+1		2	2	4			
Bryant Matthew	6.1	12.4	21/09/70	Bristol	01/07/89	Bristol City	201+2	9+1	11	9	7			
				Loan	24/08/90	Walsall	13	4						
Hansen Vergard	6.1	12.12	08/08/69	Drammen		Stromsgodset								
					18/11/94	Bristol City	36+1	4	3	1				
McLeary Alan	5.10	10.9	06/10/64	Lambeth	12/10/81	Millwall	289+18	16+1	24+1	22+1	5		2	2
E: B.2,u21.1,Y.6. AMC'83.				Loan	23/07/92	Sheffield United	3							
Div.2'88.				Loan	16/10/92	Wimbledon	4	2						
				Free	27/05/93	Charlton Athletic	44	2	5	3	2			
				Free	31/07/95	Bristol City	30+1	2						
Plummer Dwayne	6.3	11.6	12/10/76			Bristol City (T)	1+10	1+2		1				
Shail Mark	6.1	13.03	15/10/66	Sweden		Worcester City			2					
E: SP.1.				£5000		Yeovil Town			8					
				£45000	25/03/93	Bristol City	84+6	5+1	10	2	4		1	
Tinnion Mark	5.11	11.5	23/02/68	Stanley	26/02/86	Newcastle United	30+2	5		1+1	2			
				£150000	09/03/89	Bradford City	137+8	12	9	7+1	22	1	4	2
				£180000	23/03/93	Bristol City	111+6	4	8+1	1+1	12		3	
M I D F I E L D														
Brennan Jim	5.9	11.06	08/05/77	Canada		Sora Lazio								
				Free	05/10/94	Bristol City								
Edwards Robert	6.0	11.10	01/07/73	Kendal	10/04/90	Carlisle United	48	4	1	2+1	5			
W: B.2,u21.9,Y.				£135000	27/03/91	Bristol City	104+21	8+1	10+1	8+1	3	1		2
Fowler Jason	6.0	11.12	20/08/74	Bristol	08/07/93	Bristol City	16+9	1+2		1+1				
Hewlett Matthew	6.2	10.11	25/02/76	Bristol	12/08/93	Bristol City	38+2	2+1			2			
E: Y.				Loan	30/12/94	Bath City								
Kuhl Martin	5.11	11.13	10/01/65	Frimley	13/01/83	Birmingham City	103+8	13	8	1+1	5		1	1
					20/03/87	Sheffield United	38	2	1	1	4			
via (19/02/88) Watford 4 Lge App				£125000	30/09/88	Portsmouth	146+11	11	13	3	27	1		
				£650000	26/09/92	Derby County	59	5	6	2	1			1
Loan (09/09/94) Notts County 2 Lge App.				£330000	30/12/94	Bristol City	63	4	4	3	7			
Owers Gary	5.11	11.10	03/10/68	Newcastle	08/10/86	Sunderland	241+8	25+1	10+2	11+1	24	1		1
Div.3'88. FLgeXI.1.				£300000	23/12/94	Bristol City	55+3	1	5	3	4			
Patterson Scott	5.11	11.9	13/05/72	Aberdeen		Cove Rangers								
				£15000	19/03/92	Liverpool								
				Free	04/07/94	Bristol City	18+3	2	1	1	1			
F O R W A R D S														
Agostino Paul						Young Boys of Berne								
				£50000	18/07/95	Bristol City	29+11	4		2+1	10	1		
Barclay Dominic			05/09/76	Bristol	01/08/93	Bristol City	2+2							
Bent Junior	5.5	10.6	01/03/70	Huddersfield	09/12/87	Huddersfield Town	25+11	1	3+1	4	6		1	
				Loan	30/11/89	Burnley	2				3			
				£30000	22/03/90	Bristol City	125+34	9+1	11+3	5+2	17		2	
				Loan	26/03/92	Stoke City	1							
Carey Louis					03/07/95	Bristol City	22+1		2	1				
Nugent Kevin P	6.1	13.03	10/04/69	Edmonton	08/07/87	Leyton Orient	86+8	9+3	9	9+1	19	6	3	1
				£200000	23/03/92	Plymouth Argyle	124+7	11	10	5+3	31	2	3	
				£75000	29/09/95	Bristol City	29+5		2		8			
Partridge Scott	5.9	10.09	13/10/74	Grimsby	10/07/92	Bradford City	0+5	1						
				Free	18/02/94	Bristol City	24+27	3+3	1+3		7			
				Loan	13/10/95	Torquay United	5				2			
				Loan	22/01/96	Plymouth Argyle	6+1				2			
				Loan	08/03/96	Scarborough	5+2							
Seal David	5.11	12.4	26/01/72	Sydney (Aus)		Eendracht Aalst(Bel)								
				£80000	05/10/94	Bristol City	24+15	4	1+1	2+1	10	3		1

ASHTON GATE
Bristol BS3 2EJ
Tel: 01272 632 812

Capacity ....20,832.

First game ....v Bolton W. 3.9.1904.
First floodlit game ....v Wolves 27.1.1953.

ATTENDANCES
Highest ....43,335 v P.N.E. FA Cup 5th Rnd, 16.2.1935.
N.B. Over 50,000 were judged to be in the ground on 30.1.1935 for the FA Cup 4th Rnd replay v Portsmouth, when the gates were rushed and the crowd broke in. Official paid attendance was given as 42,885.
Lowest ....1,515 v Oxford United, Anglo Italian Cup, 7.9.1993.

OTHER GROUNDS ....St John's Lane 1894-1904.

MATCHDAY TICKET PRICES

	MEMBERS	NON-MEM.
Atyeo Stand £9		£10
S.Cit & Students/Juv . . . . £6/£4		£7/£5
Dolmans & Williams Stands . . £11		£12
S.Cit & Students/Juv . . . . £8/£4		£9/£5
Block D in the Dolmans £12		£13
S.Cit & Students/Juv . . . . £9/£4		£10/£5
GWR Family Enclosure £11		£12
S.Cit & Students/Juv . . . . £8/£2		£9/£2
Executive Seating £16		£17
S.Cit & Students/Juv . . . . £11/£6		£12/£7
Database Computers Stand £10		
S.Cit & Students/Juv . . . . £7/£5		
Ticket Office Telephone No. . . . . . 01272 632 812.		

CLUBCALL
0898 12 11 76
Calls cost 39p per minute cheap rate and 49p per minute at all other times.
Call costings correct at time of going to press.

HOW TO GET TO THE GROUND

From the North and West
Use motorway (M5) until junction 16. Leave motorway and follow signs to Bristol (A38). Follow signs to City Centre then follow signs to Taunton (A38). In 1.2 miles cross Cumberland Basin swing bridge, then branch left into Winterstoke Road for Bristol City FC.

From the East
Use motorway (M4), then M32 and follow signs to the City Centre, then follow signs to Taunton A38. In 1.2 miles cross Cumberland Basin swing bridge, then branch left into Winterstoke Road for Bristol City FC.

From the South
Use motorway (M5) until junction 18. Leave motorway and follow signs to Bristol (A4) along Portway then turn right and follow signs to Taunton over Cumberland Basin swing bridge, then branch left into Winterstoke Road for Bristol City FC. To use the Bristol City FC park and ride scheme follow AA signs to 'Bristol City car park', which is in Anchor Road.

Car Parking
There is limited street parking around ground.

Nearest Railway Station
Temple Meads (01272 294 255).

MATCHDAY PROGRAMME

Programme Editor . . . . Paper Plane.

Number of pages . . . . 24.

Price . . . . £1.50.

Subscriptions . . . . £40 (home), £45 (away), £85 all programmes).

Local Newspapers . . . . Bristol Evening Post, Western Daily Press,
. . . . Sunday Independent.

Local Radio Stations . Radio Bristol, GWR/Brunel Radio, Galaxy Radio.

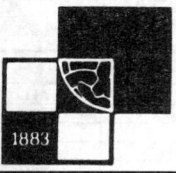

BRISTOL ROVERS
(The Pirates)
NATIONWIDE LEAGUE DIVISION 2
SPONSORED BY: ELITE HAMPERS LTD

1883

1996-97 - Back Row (L-R): Peter Beadle, Marcus Browning, Billy Clark, Andy Collett, Shane Higgs, Paul Miller, Justin Skinner, Andy Tillson.
Middle Row: Lee Martin, Jonathan French, Andy Gurney, Matthew Hayfield, Steve Parmenter, Graeme Power, Dave Pritchard, Lee Archer, Steve Bowey, Tom White. **Front Row:** Stuart Harte, Phil Kite (Physio), Tony Gill (Youth Team Manager/ Centre of Excellence Director), Terry Connor (Reserve Team Manager/ Assistant Centre of Excellence Director), Ian Holloway (Player-Team Manager), Geoff Twentyman (Assistant Manager), Ray Kendall (Kit Manager), John Gingell (Fitness Coach), Roy Dolling (Youth Development Manager), Matthew Lockwood.

BRISTOL ROVERS
FORMED IN 1883
TURNED PROFESSIONAL IN 1897
LTD COMPANY IN 1896

PRESIDENT: Marquis of Worcester
CHAIRMAN: Denis M H Dunford
DIRECTORS
R Craig, G H M Dunford, V B Stokes,
R Andrews, C Jelf, B Bradshaw
SECRETARY
Roger Brinsford
COMMERCIAL MANAGER
Graham Bowen (0117 986 9999)

MANAGER: Ian Holloway
ASSISTANT MANAGER: Geoff Twentyman
RESERVE TEAM MANAGER
Terry Connor
YOUTH TEAM MANAGER
Tony Gill
PHYSIOTHERAPIST
Phil Kite

STATISTICIAN FOR THE DIRECTORY
Mike Jay

Bristol Rovers started the season with the loss of the influential assistant manager Dennis Booth. The £1.6 million transfer of striker Gareth Taylor to Crystal Palace instead of the expected departure of rising star Marcus Stewart unfortunately coincided with the loss through injury of regulars Lee Archer, David Pritchard and Paul Miller. Furthermore Justin Skinner was a broken-leg victim which necessitated three loan signings and also league debuts for three young professionals, Mike Watt, Jon French, Matt Hayfield and Josh Low.

Rovers suffered their most embarrassing FA Cup defeat in the club's history at Hitchin Town. This resulted in manager John Ward's only activity in the transfer market in buying Peter Beadle, who proved to be a success, scoring 12 goals including arguably the best goal of the season in a 2-0 victory at Bristol City.

One of the biggest disappointments was missing out on another Wembley visit when Rovers were defeated by Shrewsbury in the Auto Windscreens Southern Area Final.

Despite the lack of goals - other than from top-scorer Marcus Stewart who managed a remarkable 30 goals (the best from a Rovers player for 32 years) - the team equalled a club record set 40 years ago of scoring in 23 consecutive league matches. However, there were some inconsistent team performances and poor results, particularly at Twerton Park in the first half of the season. Rovers finished the season in tenth position, four points below the amount required to achieve a second successive play-off place. Manager John Ward and his assistant Steve Cross did not have their contracts renewed.

However, supporters' hopes have been raised by the prospect of new player-manager Ian Holloway, a popular Bristol-born player who had two successful previous spells with Rovers before spending five seasons with Queen's Park Rangers. An exciting prospect is the return to Bristol after a ten-year exile in Bath: a 25-year ground-share agreement has been made with Bristol Rugby club to use their 12,000 capacity stadium at the Memorial Ground, which is just one mile from Rovers' former home, Eastville Stadium. It will hopefully result in improved attendances and commercial spin-offs. But it brings sharply into focus the club's lack of progress in securing a new all-seater stadium. This has caused supporters to become very concerned about the club's future. Bristol Rovers' ability to progress, and the likely options available are still very much open to debate.

MIKE JAY

BRISTOL ROVERS

League: 10th		FA Cup: 1st Rnd			Coca-Cola Cup: 2nd Rnd			Auto Windscreen Shield: Southern Final	

M	DATE	COMP	VEN	OPPONENTS	RESULT	HT	LP	GOAL SCORERS/GOAL TIMES	ATT.
1	A 12	EL	A	Carlisle United	W 2-1	1-1	6	Clarke 32, Stewart 62	(8003)
2	15	CC 1/1	A	Gillingham	D 1-1	0-0		Stewart 57	(3827)
3	19	EL	H	Swansea City	D 2-2	0-1	4	Taylor 80, 83	6689
4	23	CC 1/2	H	Gillingham	W 4-2	1-1		Stewart 1, 73, 85, Miller 70	3602
5	26	EL	A	Walsall	D 1-1	0-0	8	Taylor 54	(4851)
6	29	EL	A	Burnley	W 1-0	0-0	3	Taylor 49	5646
7	S 2	EL	H	Wrexham	L 1-2	1-0	7	Stewart 9	6031
8	9	EL	A	York City	W 1-0	0-0	4	Miller 88	(4047)
9	12	EL	A	Rotherham United	L 0-1	0-0	7		(2739)
10	16	EL	H	Swindon Town	L 1-4	1-1	11	Miller 40	7025
11	20	CC 2/1	H	West Ham United	L 0-1	0-1			7103
12	23	EL	A	Brentford	W 2-0	1-0	9	Stewart 42(pen), Paul 67	5131
13	30	EL	A	Oxford United	W 2-1	2-0	11	Browning 16, Stewart 44	(6091)
14	O 4	CC 2/2	A	West Ham United	L 0-3	0-0			(15375)
15	7	EL	A	Bournemouth	L 0-2	0-1	9		5171
16	14	EL	A	Bradford City	W 3-2	1-1	5	Gurney 8, Archer 56, Stewart 61	(5817)
17	17	AWS 1/2	A	Brighton & H.A.	W 2-0	0-0		Davis 46, Archer 47	(1191)
18	21	EL	A	Notts County	L 0-3	0-0	9		6078
19	28	EL	A	Brighton & H.A.	L 0-2	0-1	11		(5658)
20	31	EL	A	Blackpool	L 0-3	0-3	12		(3877)
21	N 4	EL	A	Peterborough United	D 1-1	1-0	13	Gurney 38	4241
22	7	AWS 1/2	H	Cambridge United	W 3-0	0-0		French, Stewart (2)	1805
23	11	FAC 1	A	Hitchin	L 1-2	1-2		Archer 22	(3101)
24	18	EL	A	Wycombe Wanderers	D 1-1	0-1	14	Gurney 69	(4886)
25	25	EL	H	Stockport County	L 1-3	0-0	15	Miller 87	4326
26	28	AWS 2	H	Bournemouth	W 2-1	0-0		Browning, Tilson	1979
27	D 9	EL	A	Brentford	D 0-0	0-0	15		(5679)
28	16	EL	H	Oxford United	W 2-0	0-0	14	Stewart 78, Stewart 90	4051
29	23	EL	H	Crewe Alexandra	L 1-2	0-0	15	Browning 90	4519
30	26	EL	A	Shrewsbury Town	D 1-1	0-0	15	Beadle 58	(4944)
31	J 6	EL	H	Hull City	W 2-1	2-0	14	Stewart 1, Stewart 20	4276
32	9	AWS QF	A	Fulham	W 2-1	1-1		Stewart (2)	(3479)
33	13	EL	A	Swansea City	D 2-2	0-2	15	Gurney 72, Beadle 78	(2956)
34	16	EL	A	Bristol City	W 2-0	0-0	13	Beadle 72, 74	(20007)
35	20	EL	H	Carlisle United	D 1-1	0-1	12	Stewart 70	5196
36	F 3	EL	A	Walsall	W 2-0	0-0	11	Beadle 50, Stewart 88(pen)	4948
37	10	EL	A	Hull City	W 3-1	0-0	7	Stewart 49, Browning 62, Beadle 83	(3311)
38	13	AWS SF	A	Peterborough United	W 1-0	0-0		Stewart	(3761)
39	17	EL	H	Rotherham United	W 1-0	0-0	6	Stewart 46	5416
40	20	EL	A	Wrexham	L 2-3	1-1	7	Beadle 45, Tilson 52	(3235)
41	24	EL	A	Swindon Town	L 1-2	1-1	1	Stewart 12	(11724)
42	27	EL	H	York City	W 1-0	1-0	7	Stewart 4	4013
43	M 2	EL	A	Shrewsbury Town	W 2-1	1-1	7	Gurney 22, Stewart 75(pen)	5004
44	5	AWS SF1	A	Shrewsbury Town	D 1-1	0-0		Matthew 55	(5262)
45	9	EL	A	Crewe Alexandra	W 2-1	0-0		French 47, Stewart 64	(4091)
46	12	AWS SF2	H	Shrewsbury Town	L 0-1	0-0			7050
47	16	EL	H	Bristol City	L 2-4	1-2	7	Gurney 30, Clarke 87	8648
48	23	EL	A	Chesterfield	L 1-2	0-0	10	Stewart 80	(4748)
49	26	EL	H	Chesterfield	W 1-0	0-0	8	Beadle 82	3513
50	30	EL	A	Bournemouth	L 1-2	0-1	9	Miller 46	(4607)
51	A 2	EL	H	Bradford City	W 1-0	0-0	8	Beadle 63	4008
52	6	EL	H	Brighton & H.A.	W 1-0	0-0	8	Beadle 58	5385
53	9	EL	A	Notts County	L 2-4	0-1	9	Stewart 51, Beadle 87	(4661)
54	13	EL	A	Blackpool	D 1-1	1-0	10	Beadle 44	5626
55	20	EL	A	Peterborough United	D 0-0	0-0	10		(4884)
56	23	EL	A	Burnley	W 1-0	0-0	7	Stewart 64	(9368)
57	27	EL	A	Stockport County	L 0-2	0-1	9		(6935)
58	M 4	EL	H	Wycombe Wanderers	W 2-1	1-0	10	Browning 15, Stewart 55	6621

Best Home League Attendance: 8648 v Bristol City — **Smallest: 3513 v Chesterfield** — **Average: 5285**

Goal Scorers:
EL(57): Stewart(21),Beadle(12),Gurney(6),Miller(4),Browning(4),Taylor(4),Clarke(2),Paul(1),French(1),Archer(1),Tilson(1)
CC(5): Stewart(4),Miller(1)
FAC(1): Archer(1)
AWS(11): Stewart(5),Browning(1),Archer(1),Davis(1),Matthew(1),French(1),Tilson(1)

Match	(M) Archer	(D) Armstrong	(F) Beadle	(F) Browning	(D) Channing	(D) Clarke	(G) Collett	(F) Davis	(F) French	(D) Gurney	(D) Hayfield	(G) Higgs	(M) Low	(M) Matthew	(D) McLean	(F) Miller	(D) Morgan	(G) Parkin	(F) Paul	(D) Pritchard	(M) Skinner	(F) Sterling	(F) Stewart	(D) Taylor	(D) Tilson	(M) Tovey	(D) White	(D) Wright	(F) Wyatt
1 G.Cain			X		X		S			X						X		X		X	X	X	X	X	X			S	S
2 B.Knight			X		X		S			X						X		X		X	X	X	X	X	X			S	S
3 A.Wiley			X		S	X				X					S	X		X		X	X	X	X	X	X			S	
4 R.J.Harris			X		S	X	S			X						X		X		X	X	X	X	X	X1			S1	
5 J.Kirkby			X			X	S			X					S	X		X		X	X	X	X	X	X			X	S
6 M.Fletcher			X			X	S			X	S					X		X		X	X	X	X	X	X			X	S
7 A.D'Urso					X	S				X	S1				S	X		X		X	X1	X	X		X			X	X
8 P.Richards	X1		X		S1	X	S			X					S	X		X		X	X		X		X			X	
9 A.R.Leak	S1		X		X		S			X2					S2	X		X		X	X		X	X	X			X	X1
10 E.Wolstenholme	X		X		X		S			X						X		X		X	X		X	S	X			X	S
11 K.Cooper			X		X1	S	S			X						X		X		X	X		X	X	X			S1	
12 F.Stretton			X		X	S1	S									X		X	X	X	X2		X		X			X1	X
13 P.Taylor			X		X	S	S			X	S1					X		X	X1	X	X		X		X			X	
14 R.Gifford			X		X1		S	S1						S		X		X	X	X	X		X		X			X	
15 G.Singh	S1		X		X	S			S									X	X	X1	X	X	X		X			X	
16 A.R.Pearson	X		X		X	S	X	S1											S	X1	X		X		X			X	
17 M.Pierce	X3		X		X			S1		X	S2									X		X	X1	X2	X			X	
18 I.S.Hemley	X		X		X			S1		X	S			S						X1	X	X	X		X			X	
19 P.Rejer	X				X2					X	X3					S1				S3	X	X	X		X			S2	X1
20 M.Riley	X		X1			X				X	X					X		S	X1		X		X		X				S1
21 D.Orr	X					X	S1	X	X	X						X		S			X		X		X			X	S
22	X2					X		X	X1	X						X		S	S2		X		X		X			X1	
23 I.Hemley	X		S1	S	X					X	X1					X		S		X	X		X		X			X	
24 K.Leach		X1	X	X	X			S	S	X	S				X	X	S1	X		X	X		X		X				
25 G.Pooley			X	X	X	S		S	X	X					X1	X		X		S1	X		X		X				
26			X	X	X				S1	X					S	X		X			X		X		X	X1			
27 G.Barber		S1	X	X	X	S				X					S	X		X1			X		X		X	X			
28 C.Wilkes		X	X	X	X	S				X					S	X		X			X		X		X	X			
29 P.D'Urso		X1	X	X	X					X					S	X		X			S1		X		X	X			
30 K.J.Breen			X	X	X	X				X2					S1	X		S			S2		X		X	X1			
31 P.Taylor	S1	X2	X	X	X					X						X		X			S2		X		X	X1			
32 A.Wiley	S	X	X	X	X					X			S			X		X			X1		X		X	S1			
33 R.Gifford			X	X	X	X				X			S	X		X		X				S	X		X			S	
34 G.Singh			X	X	X	X				X			S	X		X		X				S	X		X			S	
35 A.Butler			X	X	X	X					S		S	X		X		X				S	X		X			S	
36 S.G.Bennett			X	X	X	X	X				S		S			X						X	X		X			S	
37 I.Cruickshanks			X	X	X	X	X						S	X		X			S1			X1	X		X			S	
38			X	X	X	X	X						S	X		X			S			X	X		X			S	
39 E.Wolstenholme			X	X	X	X	X		S				S	X		X						X	X		X			S	
40 D.Laws			X	X	X	X	X						S	X		X			S			X	X		X			S	
41 J.Lloyd				X	X	X	X		S				S	X		X						X	X		X			S	
42 I.Hemley		X		X1	X	X	X	X	S1				S			X						X	X		X		X	S	
43 R.J.Harris		X		X	X1	X	X						S			X	X					S1	X		X		X2	S1	
44				X		X	X	X1		X			S	X		X	X		S			X	X		X			S1	
45 K.Leach		X1		X		X	X	X2		X			S			X	X		S1			X	X		X		X	S2	
46 N.Known				X	X	X1	X			X			S			X	X					S	X		X		X	S	
47 J.Rushton				X	X	X	X	S1		X			S			X	X					X	X		X			S	
48 K.J.Breen	S1			X	X	X	X	X		S2	X2		S			X	X					X1	X		X			X	
49 C.Wilkes				X	X	X	X	X		X1	X		S				X					S1	X		X			S	
50 G.Pooley	X	X2		X	X	X	X	X		S1	X1		S			X							X		X			S2	
51 A.Wiley	X1	X		X	X	X	X	X		S1						X						S	X		X			S	
52 R.B.Gifford	X	X1		X	X	X	X	X					S			X						S1	X		X			S	
53 A.D'Urso	X	X		X	X	X	X	X			X1					X						S1	S		X			X	
54 S.Mathieson	S1	X		X	X	X	X	X		X			S				X1						X		X			S	
55 R.Furnandiz	S1	X		X1	X	X	X	X			X1		S			X							X		X		S		
56 G.Cain	S	X		X1	X	X				S1	X2					X							X		X			S2	
57 R.Pearson	S1	X		X	X	X	X			S	X1					X							X		X			S	
58 M.Fletcher	X1	X2		X3	X	X		S2	S1				S3			X							X		X				
EL Appearances	13	13	26	45	35	38	26	1	3	42	3	0	0	8	4	37	5	20	9	12	23	28	44	7	38	8	0	15	3
EL Sub Appearances	6	1	1	0	1	1	0	3	7	1	3	0	1	0	3	1	0	0	4	0	5	2	0	0	0	0	0	2	3
CC Appearances	0	0	0	4	2	2	0	0+1	0	4	0	0	0	0	0	3	0	4	1	4	4	2	4	3	4	0	0	2+1	0+1
FAC Appearances	1	0	0	0	0+1	2	0	1	0	0	1	0	0	0	1	0	0	0	1	0	0	1	1	1	0	0	0	1	0
AWS Appearances	2	0	3	6	5	5	5	0+1	2+1	7	1+1	0	0	2	1	5	2	2	2+1	0	3	6	7	0	7	2+1	0+1	2+1	0

Also Played:

CLUB RECORDS

BIGGEST VICTORIES
League: 7-0 v Swansea City, Division 2, 2.10.1954.
7-0 v Brighton & Hove Albion, Division 3(S), 29.11.1952.
7-0 v Shrewsbury Town, Division 3, 21.3.1964.
F.A. Cup: 6-0 v Merthyr Tydfil, Round 1, 14.11.1987.

BIGGEST DEFEATS
League: 0-12 v Luton Town, Division 3(S), 13.4.1936.
F.A. Cup: 1-8 v Queens Park Rangers, 27.11.1937.

MOST POINTS
3 points a win: 93, Division 3, 1989-90.
2 points a win: 64, Division 3(S), 1952-53.

MOST GOALS SCORED
92, Division 3(S), 1952-53.

RECORD TRANSFER FEE RECEIVED
£1,000,000 from Crystal Palace for Nigel Martyn, November 1989.

RECORD TRANSFER FEE PAID
£370,000 to Queens Park Rangers for Andy Tillson, November 1992.

BEST PERFORMANCES
League: 6th in Division 2, 1955-56, 1958-59.
Highest Position:
F.A. Cup: 6th Round 1950-51, 1957-58.
League Cup: 5th Round, 1970-71, 1971-72.

HONOURS
Division 3 South Cup 1934-35.
Champions of Division 3(S), 1952-53.
Champions of Division 3, 1989-90.

LEAGUE CAREER
Original members of Div 3 1920, Transferred to Div 3 South 1921, Div 2 1952-53, Div 3 1961-62, Div 2 1973-74, Div 3 1980-81, Div 2 (now Div 1) 1989-90, Div 2 1992-93.

INDIVIDUAL CLUB RECORDS

MOST GOALS IN A SEASON
Alfie Biggs: 37 goals in 1963-64 (League 30, FA Cup 1, League Cup 6).

MOST GOALS IN A MATCH
6. Jack Jones v Weymouth, FA Cup, 15-1, 17.11.1900.

OLDEST PLAYER
Jack Evans, 39 years, 9.4.1928.

YOUNGEST PLAYER
Ronnie Dix, 15 years 180 days v Norwich City, 3.3.1928.
(Youngest player to score in the Football League, in his second match).

MOST CAPPED PLAYER
Neil Slatter (Wales) 10, 1983-85.
Geoff Bradford (England) 1, 1955.

PREVIOUS MANAGERS

1899-1920 Alf Homer; 1920-21 Ben Hall; 1921-26 Andrew Wilson; 1926-29 Joe Palmer; 1929-30 David McLean; 1930-36 Albert Prince Cox; 1936-37 Percy Smith; 1938-49 Brough Fletcher; 1950-68 Bert Tann; 1968-69 Fred Ford; 1969-72 Bill Dodgin; 1972-77 Don Megson; 1977-79 Bobby Campbell; 1979-80 Harold Jarman; 1980-81 Terry Cooper; 1981-83 Bobby Gould; 1983-85 David Williams; 1985-87 Bobby Gould, 1987-91 Gerry Francis; 1991 Martin Dobson; 1991-92 Dennis Rofe; 1992-93 Malcolm Allison.

ADDITIONAL INFORMATION
Previous Names: Black Arabs, Eastville Rovers.
Previous Leagues: Southern League.

Club colours: Blue shirts with blue & white quarters & white trim, white shorts, blue socks.
Change colours: Green & white stripes, black shorts, black socks.

Reserves League: Avon Insurance Football Combination.
'A' Team: South East Counties League Div.2.

LONGEST LEAGUE RUNS

of undefeated matches:	32 (1973-74)	of league matches w/out a win:	20 (1980-81)
of undefeated home matches:	34 (1989-90)	of undefeated away matches:	17 (1973-74)
without home win:	10 (1980-81)	without an away win:	23 (1980-81)
of league wins:	12 (1952-53)	of home wins:	10 (1934-35)
of league defeats:	8 (1961-62)	of away wins:	5 (1952-53, 1964)

THE MANAGER

IAN HOLLOWAY . . . . appointed May 1996.

PREVIOUS CLUBS
As Manager . . . . None.
As Asst.Man/Coach . . . . None.
As a player . . . . Bristol Rovers, Wimbledon, Brentford, Torquay (Loan), Bristol Rovers, QPR.

HONOURS
As a Manager . . . . None.
As a Player . . . . **Bristol Rovers:** Division 3 championship medal 1990.

BRISTOL ROVERS

PLAYERS NAME / Honours	Ht	Wt	Birthdate	Birthplace / Transfers	Contract Date	Clubs	APPEARANCES League	L/Cup	FA Cup	Other	GOALS Lge	L/C	FAC	Oth
G O A L K E E P E R S														
Collett Andrew A	5.11	11.3	28/10/73	Stockton	06/03/92	Middlesbrough	2			3				
				Loan	18/10/94	Bristol Rovers								
				£10000	23/03/95	Bristol Rovers	30		1	6				
Higgs Shane	6.2	12.12	13/05/77	Oxford	01/08/94	Bristol Rovers								
D E F E N D E R S														
Channing Justin	5.10	11.3	19/11/68	Reading	27/08/86	Queens Park Rangers	42+13	4+1	2	5	5			
E: Y.2.				£250000	24/10/92	Bristol Rovers	121+9	5	4+1	11+1	9			
Clarke William	6.0	12.3	19/05/67	Christchurch	25/09/84	Bournemouth	4							
					16/10/87	Bristol Rovers	209+12	9+1	8+1	18+2	13		1	
Gurney Andrew	5.7	10.7	25/01/74	Bristol	10/07/92	Bristol Rovers	79+5	5	5	14	7			
Hayfield Matthew			08/08/75	Bristol	13/07/94	Bristol Rovers	3+3		1	1+1				
Pritchard David	5.7	11.4	27/05/72	Wolverhampton		W.B.A.	1+4							
					01/08/92	Telford			2					
				£15000	25/02/94	Bristol Rovers	66	6	4	6				
Tilson Andrew	6.2	12.7	30/06/66	Huntingdon		Kettering Town								
				Free	14/07/88	Grimsby Town	104+1	8	10	5	6			
				£400000	21/12/90	Q.P.R.	27+2	2		1	2			
				Loan	15/09/92	Grimsby Town	4		1					
				£370000	07/11/92	Bristol Rovers	119+1	8	6	13	3	1		1
White Thomas	5.11	12.02	26/01/76	Bristol	13/07/94	Bristol Rovers	4+2			0+1				
M I D F I E L D														
Archer Lee	5.6	9.6	06/11/72	Bristol	18/07/91	Bristol Rovers	54+9	3	2	5	7		2	1
Skinner Justin	6.0	11.6	30/01/69	Hounslow	17/11/86	Fulham	11+24	10+1	5+1	10+1	23	4		1
				£130000	27/08/91	Bristol Rovers	141+8	11	8	14+1	9			1
F O R W A R D S														
Beadle Peter	6.1	11.12	13/05/72	London	05/05/90	Gillingham	42+25	2+4	1+1	1	14	2		
				£300000	04/06/92	Tottenham Hotspur								
				Loan	25/03/93	Bournemouth	9				2			
				Loan	04/03/94	Southend United	8				1			
					12/09/94	Watford	12+11	1			1			
				£30000	17/11/95	Bristol Rovers	26+1			3	12			
Browning Marcus	6.1	13.0	22/04/71	Bristol	01/07/89	Bristol Rovers	128+20	5+3	7	12+3	11		1	3
				Loan	18/09/92	Hereford United	7				5			
French Jon						Bristol City (T)	3+7			2+1	1			1
Miller Paul	6.0	11.0	31/01/68	Woking		Wimbledon								
						Wealdstone								
						Yeovil Town								
					12/08/87	Wimbledon	65+15	3+3	3	1	11			
				Loan	20/10/87	Newport County	6				2			
				Loan	11/01/90	Bristol City	0+3			2				
				£100000	16/08/94	Bristol Rovers	78+2	5	4	11	20	1	4	2
ADDITIONAL CONTRACT PLAYERS														
Bowey Steven						Bristol City (T)								
Low Joshua						Bristol City (T)	0+1							

MEMORIAL GROUND
Horfield, Bristol
Tel: 0117 951 4448

Capacity ....Approx. 7,000 (Hoping for a final capacity of 10,000 when alterations are complete)
Covered Standing ....
Seated ....

First game ....Unknown at time of going to press.
First floodlit game...Unknown at time of going to press.

ATTENDANCES
Highest...Unknown at time of going to press.
Lowest...Unknown at time of going to press.

OTHER GROUNDS ....Eastville. Twerton Park.

MATCHDAY TICKET PRICES

Grandstand £13
Juv/OAP £8.50

Family Stand . . Unknown at time of going to press.
Juv/OAP. . . . . . Unknown at time of going to press.

Family Enclosure . . Unknown at time of going to press.
Juv/OAP. . . . . . Unknown at time of going to press.

Terraces. £8
Juv/OAP £4

Visitors Terracing £8
Juv £8

Telephone no. . . Memorial Ground 0117 951 4448.
(Above number may change)

CLUBCALL 0891 66 44 22

Calls cost 39p per minute cheap rate and 49p per
minute at all other times.
Call costings correct at time of going to press.

HOW TO GET TO THE GROUND

From all directions:
M5,
M4,
M32,
Off at junction 2,
around the roundabout,
turn off into Muller Road,
pass 6 sets of traffic lights (2 pedestrian),
turn left into Filton Avenue at 6th set of lights.

MATCHDAY PROGRAMME

Programme Editor . Pete Francombe (Sports Programme Promotions).

Number of pages . . . . 32.

Price . . . . £1.30.

Subscriptions. . . . . . . £45.50 (inland), £56 (Europe), £90 (Overseas).

Local Newspapers . . . . Western Daily Press, Bristol Evening Post,
. . . . Bath Evening Chronicle, Sunday Independent,
. . . . Kingswood/North Avon Gazette.

Local Radio Stations . . . . Radio Bristol, GWR Radio.

BURNLEY
(The Clarets)
NATIONWIDE LEAGUE DIVISION 2
SPONSORED BY: ENDSLEIGH INSURANCE

Back Row (L-R): Ted McMinn, Adrian Randall, Steve Thompson, Nathan Peel, Mark Winstanley, Tony Philliskirk, Peter Swan, John Pender, Glen Davies, Paul Smith. **Middle Row:** Terry Pashley (Yth Coach), Gary Parkinson, Warren Joyce, Alan Harper, Derek Adams, Wayne Dowell, Marlow Beresford, Wayne Russell, Andy Cooke, Kurt Nogan, Matthew Taylor, John Borland, Brian Miller (Chief Scout). **Front Row:** Harry Wilson (Res. Coach), Adrian Heath, Liam Robinson, Chris Brass, David Eyres, Jamie Hoyland, Jimmy Mullen (Manager), Clive Middlemass (Asst. Manager), Chris Vinnicombe, John Francis, Paul Weller, Gerry Harrison, Andy Jones (Physio).

BURNLEY
FORMED IN 1882
TURNED PROFESSIONAL IN 1883
LTD COMPANY IN 1897

CHAIRMAN: F J Teasdale
VICE-CHAIRMAN
Dr R D Iven MRCS(Eng), LRCOP (Lond), MRCGP
DIRECTORS
R B Blakeborough, C Holt
B M Rothwell, JP
SECRETARY
John W Howarth F.A.A.I. 01282 700000
COMMERCIAL MANAGER
Tom Skelly (01282 700007)

MANAGER: Adrian Heath
ASSISTANT MANAGER: John Ward
RESERVE TEAM MANAGER
Harry Wilson
YOUTH TEAM MANAGER
Terry Pashley/Alan Harper
PHYSIOTHERAPIST
A Jones

STATISTICIAN FOR THE DIRECTORY
Wallace Chadwick

There were few redeeming features to a Turf Moor season which started with hopes of an instant return to the First Division - but Burnley fans are never short on unrealistic optimism - and ended with relief at avoiding the drop to the Third. Several eras ended, most notably the age of terracing and the managerial reign of Jimmy Mullen.

The team that started the season was basically the one that ended 1994/5, except that new-signing Peter Swan replaced record-sale Steve Davis in central defence. Results-wise, it began well enough, but few performances were convincing, even in victory - probably the best early-season show was in an undeserved home defeat at the hands of Leicester in the Coca-Cola Cup - and as the table began to take shape it became clear that Burnley had yet to prove themselves against the best in the division. The beloved Longside Terrace, meanwhile, was demolished after the biggest crowd of the season turned out to say farewell in the game against Hull.

Despite league results remaining good enough to sustain a place in the top six until after Christmas, there were clear warning signs with some abysmal defensive displays and an obvious over-reliance on Kurt Nogan up front. Unrest grew after a 5-0 thrashing at lowly Carlisle in the Auto Windscreens Shield, and Jimmy Mullen left in February after four successive league defeats with no goals scored. Mullen had been the butt of the crowd for some time, and his departure followed an incident which may have been blown up by the press, but which certainly brought no credit to the club or many of its fans.

By the time Adrian Heath returned as manager - following a brief spell as Howard Kendall's assistant at Sheffield United - Burnley had slumped to the bottom half of the table. After a fluke win in his first game in charge (at Bristol City), the next four matches were against the top four sides in the division and brought only one point. The style was changed, with a return to the passing game latterly abandoned by Mullen, followed by the introduction of three at the back, however, results didn't really improve until the last three weeks of the season, by which time relegation was looking a real possibility.

Now that the drop has been avoided, that familiar Burnley optimism has returned: the smart new stand replacing the Longside has opened; a similar structure is being built in the close season to replace the Bee Hole terrace; and the feeling is that Heath - still a hero for his playing abilities - is the man to help the club back to where it belongs. Realistically, his task will not be an easy one: the side needs strengthening in most departments and much will depend in the short term on how much money is made available to the manager and how well he uses it. Improvement isn't much to ask, but this writer will not be among those betting on Burnley for the Second Division title next time round.

WALLACE CHADWICK

BURNLEY

League: 17th   FA Cup: 1st Rnd   Coca-Cola Cup: 2nd Rnd   Auto Windscreen Shield: Quarter Finals

M	DATE	COMP	VEN	OPPONENTS	RESULT	HT	LP	GOAL SCORERS/GOAL TIMES	ATT.
1	A 12	EL	H	Rotherham United	W 2-1	2-1	5	Eyres 25(pen), Philliskirk 39	10156
2	15	CC 1/1	A	Mansfield Town	W 1-0	1-0		Nogan 28	(2544)
3	19	EL	A	Stockport County	D 0-0	0-0	9		(8463)
4	22	CC 1/2	H	Mansfield Town	W 3-1	1-0		Randall 8, Nogan 59, 68	4103
5	26	EL	H	Brentford	W 1-0	1-0	6	Nogan 11	9586
6	29	EL	A	Bristol Rovers	L 0-1	0-0	12		(5646)
7	S 6	EL	H	Walsall	D 1-1	0-0	11	Joyce 90	8778
8	9	EL	A	Carlisle United	L 0-2	0-0	16		(7318)
9	12	EL	A	York City	D 1-1	1-0	15	Cooke 38	(4684)
10	16	EL	H	Hull City	W 2-1	1-0	9	Nogan 41, Allison 89(og)	10613
11	20	CC 2/1	A	Leicester City	L 0-2	0-1			(11142)
12	23	EL	A	Chesterfield	L 2-4	2-2	12	Nogan 17, Eyres 42(pen)	(4933)
13	30	EL	H	Swansea City	W 3-0	1-0	9	Nogan 15, Joyce 54, Eyres 79	8067
14	O 3	CC 2/2	H	Leicester City	L 0-2	0-0			4605
15	7	EL	H	Wycombe Wanderers	D 1-1	1-0	11	Joyce 40	8279
16	14	EL	A	Bournemouth	W 2-0	1-0	7	Vinnicombe 6, Nogan 78	(4954)
17	17	AWS 1/1	A	Rotherham United	D 1-1	1-0		Nogan	(1539)
18	21	EL	H	Brighton & H.A.	W 3-0	3-0	5	Eyres 4, Swan 33, Nogan 36	9018
19	28	EL	A	Bradford City	D 2-2	1-1	6	Harrison 25, Swan 86	(8356)
20	31	EL	A	Peterborough United	W 2-0	2-0	4	McDonald 11, Swan 33	(4737)
21	N 4	EL	H	Notts County	L 3-4	1-2	7	Nogan 4, 85, Cooke 69	10511
22	7	AWS 1/2	H	Chester City	D 1-1	1-0		Nogan	3225
23	10	FAC 1	A	Walsall	L 1-3	1-1		Eyres 35	6525
24	18	EL	A	Shrewsbury Town	L 0-3	0-2	8		(3914)
25	25	EL	H	Wrexham	D 2-2	0-0	8	Nogan 59, Joyce 66	8710
26	29	AWS 2	A	Crewe Alexandra	W 1-0	0-0		Nogan 105	(2596)
27	D 2	EL	A	Carlisle United	W 2-0	1-0	4	Nogan 38, 57	8297
28	9	EL	H	Chesterfield	D 2-2	1-1	6	Nogan 21, 82	8459
29	16	EL	A	Swansea City	W 4-2	1-0	5	Eyres 32, Nogan 54, Cooke 75, 87	(2078)
30	23	EL	H	Bristol City	D 0-0	0-0	5		9327
31	J 6	AWS QF	A	Carlisle United	L 0-5	0-3			(5169)
32	13	EL	H	Stockport County	W 4-3	2-3	5	Vinnicombe 6, Cooke 18, Nogan 69, Francis 78	9113
33	20	EL	A	Rotherham United	L 0-1	0-0	6		(4018)
34	30	EL	H	Oxford United	L 0-2	0-1	6		6815
35	F 3	EL	A	Brentford	L 0-1	0-0	8		(5195)
36	10	EL	H	Crewe Alexandra	L 0-1	0-1	11		9153
37	17	EL	H	York City	D 3-3	0-2	12	Winstanley 50, Francis 60, Nogan 67	8731
38	24	EL	A	Hull City	L 0-3	0-1	15		(4206)
39	M 2	EL	H	Blackpool	L 0-1	0-0	16		10082
40	9	EL	A	Bristol City	W 1-0	0-0	15	Nogan 83	(6612)
41	12	EL	A	Blackpool	L 1-3	1-1	16	Nogan 28	(8941)
42	16	EL	H	Swindon Town	D 0-0	0-0	15		9360
43	19	EL	A	Crewe Alexandra	L 1-3	0-0	17	Winstanley 65	(3393)
44	23	EL	A	Oxford United	L 0-5	0-2	18		(6529)
45	30	EL	A	Wycombe Wanderers	L 1-4	0-2	18	Mahorn 53	(4921)
46	A 2	EL	H	Bournemouth	D 0-0	0-0	19		7912
47	6	EL	H	Bradford City	L 2-3	0-2	20	Robinson 55, Eyres 70(pen)	9714
48	9	EL	A	Brighton & H.A.	L 0-1	0-1	20		(5954)
49	13	EL	H	Peterborough United	W 2-1	0-0	20	Joyce 51, Swan 66	8393
50	17	EL	A	Swindon Town	D 0-0	0-0	20		(10480)
51	20	EL	A	Notts County	D 1-1	1-0	20	Swan 31	(5697)
52	23	EL	H	Bristol Rovers	L 0-1	0-0	20		9368
53	27	EL	A	Wrexham	W 2-0	2-0	19	Robinson 26, Nogan 44	(6664)
54	30	EL	A	Walsall	L 1-3	0-0	19	Nogan 52	(3411)
55	M 4	EL	H	Shrewsbury Town	W 2-1	1-1	17	Weller 15, Winstanley 72	9729

Best Home League Attendance: 10613 v Hull City   Smallest: 6815 v Oxford United   Average: 9050

Goal Scorers:
EL(56): Nogan(20), Eyres(6), Cooke(5), Swan(5), Joyce(5), Winstanley(3), Vinnicombe(2), Robinson(2), Francis(2), Opponent(s)(1), Weller(1), Philliskirk(1), Harrison(1), McDonald(1), Mahorn(1)
CC(4): Nogan(3), Randall(1)
FAC(1): Eyres(1)
AWS(3): Nogan(3)

(G) Beresford	(D) Bishop	(M) Borland	(D) Brass	(D) Cooke	(F) Eyres	(F) Francis	(M) Harper	(M) Harrison	(F) Heath	(F) Helliwell	(M) Hoyland	(M) Joyce	(D) Mahorn	(F) McDonald	(M) McMinn	(F) Nogan	(D) Parkinson	(D) Pender	(F) Philliskirk	(M) Randall	(F) Robinson	(G) Russell	(F) Smith	(D) Swan	(M) Thompson	(D) Vinnicombe	(F) Weller	(D) Winstanley		
X		S2			X	S1						X				X1	X	X	X	X2		S		X		X			K.Lynch	1
X		S			X1	S1	X					X				X	X		X	X		S		X		X			G.Barber	2
X		S				S1	X					X		X1		X	X		X	X		S		X		X		X	N.Barry	3
X	X											X	X			X	X		X	X	S	S	X1	X		X		X	R.Pearson	4
X				S	S1	X						X	X			X	X		X1	X		S		X		X		X	M.Brandwood	5
X			S2		X	S1						X	X1			X	X		X2	X		S		X		X		X	M.Fletcher	6
X		X2	S1		X	X						X	S2			X	X1		X	X		S		X		X		X	R.Dilkes	7
X			S2		X	S1		X1				X	X			X	X2		X	X		S		X		X		X	T.Heilbron	8
X	X		X		X	S1		X				X	X			X1			S			S		X		X		X	U.Rennie	9
X			X	S1								X2		X	X	X			S2			S		X1		X		X	J.Rushton	10
X			S	X	S	X	X	X				X				X	X		X			S		X		X		X	P.Rejer	11
X				X	S2	X	X	X				X		S1		X	X1		X2					X		X		X	G.Frankland	12
X		S	S		X		X					X			X	X	X		X			X		X		X	X1	X	T.West	13
X					X	S2	X	X				X				X	X1		X2			X		X		X		X	M.Riley	14
X			S2		X2	S1						S		X	X1	X	X		X			X		X		X		X	R.Poulain	15
X			S1	X1	X			X				X	X		X	X	X		S			X		X		X		X	M.Pierce	16
X			X1			S1		X				X		X	X	X	X		S	S		X		X		X		X	S.J.Baines	17
X			S	X	S1			X				S2		X	X2	X1	X		X			X		X		X		X	K.Breen	18
X			S3	X1	X	S2		X				X	X2	X3		X	X		S1			X		X		X		X	D.Allison	19
X			S	X	S			X				X	X1		X	X		S1			X		X		X		X	G.Pooley	20
X			S2	X	X	S3		X				X			X3	X1	X	X2	S1			X		X		X		X	R.Pearson	21
X			S2	X2	X	S1		X1				X			X3	X	X		X	X1		X		X		X		X	U.Rennie	22
X	S1		S2	X	S3			X				X2			X3	X	X		X1			X		X		X		X	M.Riley	23
X		S2	S3	X	S1			X				X	X			X	X		X2			X		X3	X1	X		X	S.W.Mathieson	24
X			S	X				X	X			X1	X		S1	X			X			X		X	X	S	X	X	J.Kirkby	25
X			X	S1	X	S		X	X1			X				X			S			X		X	X	X	X	X	R.Furnandiz	26
X			X	S1	X				X1			X	X		S	X	S		X			X		X	X	X		X	J.Rushton	27
X			X	S1	X	X3	S3		X1			X	X			S2	X		X			X		X	X	X2		X	N.Barry	28
X			X	X	X	S		X				X	X1			X			S			X		X	X	X		X	K.A.Leach	29
X			X2	X				X3				X	X			S2	X		X					S1	X1	X		X	K.Lynch	30
X			X2	X	S2			X				X	X			X			S			S		X		X	X1	X	S.Mathieson	31
X			X	X	S1	S2		X				X1				X			S			S		X		X	X2	X	D.Allison	32
X		X1	X	X	X	S1		X				S				X			X			S		X		X		X	A.Poulain	33
X					X	S1		X2				S				X	X1		X			S2	X	X		X		X	A.Butler	34
			S	X	X			X				X				X	X1		X			S1	X	X		X		X	A.Wiley	35
			S2	X	S1			X		X	X	X				X			X			X		X2		X	X2	X	E.Lomas	36
			S2			X		X		X1	X	X				X			S1	X		S		X		X	X2	X	S.Baines	37
			S		S1			X		X1	X	X				X			X	X		X	X	X	X	X	S	X	U.Rennie	38
			S2	X2	S3			X				X				X			X3	X	X	S1	X	X	X	X	X1	X	K.Lynch	39
X					X					X	S1	X				X	X		X	X				S	S1	X	X	X1	S.G.Bennett	40
X					X						S	X				X	X		X	X		S	S1	X	X	X	X	X1	T.Heilbron	41
X		X1			X							X				X	X		X	X		S	S1	X	X	X	X	X	M.Riley	42
X			X	X				S	X			X				X	X		X	X		S	S	X	X	X	X	X	J.Lloyd	43
X		X1			X							X				X	X		X	X		S	S1	X	X	X	X	X	M.Fletcher	44
X	X				X				X	X2		S				X	X		X	X				X	X1	X	S2	X	D.Furnandiz	45
	X				X				X			X				X	X		X	X		S1	X	S	X	X		X	K.Breen	46
	X				X			S	X	S		X				X			S1	X		X	X	X	X	X	X1	X	M.Bailey	47
	X					X1		X				X				X	S		X	X		X	X	X	X	X	S	X	P.Rejer	48
	X				X			X		S1		X				X	X1		X	S		X	X	X	X	X	S	X	B.Burns	49
X	X				X				X	S		X				X	X1		S	X		X		X	X	X	X	X	K.Leach	50
X	X				X			S		S		X				X	X		X	X		X		X	X	X	X	X	R.Gifford	51
X	X				X			S				X				X	S1		X	X		X2		S2	X	X		X1	G.Cain	52
X	X				X			S		S		X				X	S1		X	X		X		X1	X	X		X	S.Bains	53
X					X			S	X			S2				X	X		X	X		X		S1	X	X	X1	X	D.Orr	54
X					X3			S3	X	S1		X2				X	X		X	X		X		S2	X1	X	X	X	R.Poulain	55
36	9	1	7	10	39	4	3	35	5	3	21	42	3	8	7	46	29	1	7	12	11	10	3	31	18	35	24	45	EL Appearances	
0	0	0	2	13	3	1	0	2	1	2	1	5	1	3	0	0	0	1	3	5	0	7	1	0	0	1	0	0	EL Sub Appearances	
4	0	2	0	0	3	0+3	2	2	1	0	1	4	0	0	1	4	4	1	3	2	0	0	0	2	0	4	1	3	CC Appearances	
1	0	0+1	0	0+1	1	0+1	0	1	0	0	1	0	0	0	1	1	1	0	0	1	0	0	0	1	0	1	0	1	FAC Appearances	
4	0	0	2	2+2	2	0+3	0	4	1	0	3	3	0	2	0+1	4	2	0	0	1	0+1	0	0	4	0	4	2	4	AWS Appearances	

Also Played: (M) Adams S(13,14,42), S1(29), S3(30).(F) Duerden S(44). (G) Glass S(35,36). (D) Dowell X(37).

409

CLUB RECORDS

BIGGEST VICTORIES
League: 9-0 v Darwen, Division 1, 9.1.1892.
F.A. Cup: 9-0 v Crystal Palace, 2nd Round, 10.2.1909.
9-0 v New Brighton, 4th Round, 26.1.1957.
9-0 v Penrith, 1st Round (a), 17.11.1984.
League Cup: 6-0 v Grimsby Town, 2nd Round, 10.9.1968.
BIGGEST DEFEATS
League: 0-10 v Aston Villa, Division 1, 29.8.1925.
0-10 v Sheffield United, Division 1, 19.1.1929.
F.A. Cup: 0-11 v Darwen Old Wanderers, 1st Round, 17.10.1885.
League Cup: 0-4 v Peterborough, 5th Round, 17.11.1965.
0-4 v Leeds United, 2nd Round, 6.9.1972.
0-4 v West Ham, 2nd Round, 2.9.1980.
0-4 v Manchester United, 2nd Round, 26.9.1984.
MOST POINTS
3 points a win: 83, Division 4, 1991-92.
2 points a win: 62, Division 2, 1972-73.
MOST GOALS SCORED: 102, Division 1, 1960-61.
MOST GOALS CONCEDED: 108, Division 1, 1925-26.
MOST FIRST CLASS MATCHES IN A SEASON
62 - 1960-61 (League 42, FA Cup 7, League Cup 8, European Cup 4, Charity Shield 1).
MOST LEAGUE WINS: 25, Division 4, 1991-92.
MOST LEAGUE DRAWS: 17, Division 3, 1981-82.
MOST LEAGUE DEFEATS: 23, Division 1, 1975-76.
BEST PERFORMANCES
League: 1972-73: Played 42, Won 24, Drawn 14, Lost 4, Goals for 72, Against 35, Points 62. Champions of Division 2.
Highest Position: Champions of Division 1 - 1920-21, 1959-60.
F.A. Cup: 1913-14: 1st Round South Shields 3-1; 2nd Round Derby County 3-2; 3rd Round Bolton Wanderers 3-0; 4th Round Sunderland 0-0,2-1; Semi-Final Sheffield United 0-0,1-0; Final Liverpool 1-0.
League Cup: Semi-Final in 1960-61, 1968-69.
1982-83: 1st Round Bury 5-3,3-1; 2nd Round Middlesbrough 3-2,1-1; 3rd Round Coventry 2-1; 4th Round Birmingham City 3-2; 5th Round Tottenham 4-1; Semi-Final Liverpool 0-3,1-0.
Europe: European Cup: 1960-61, 2nd Round Reims 2-0,2-3; 3rd Round Hamburg 3-1,1-4.
European Fairs Cup: 1966-67, 1st Round V.F.B.Stuttgart 1-1,2-0;

2nd Round Lausanne-Sports 3-1,5-0; 3rd Round Napoli 3-0,0-0; 4th Round Eintracht Frankfurt 1-1,1-2.
HONOURS: Champions of Division 1, 1920-21, 1959-60.
Champions of Division 2, 1897-98, 1972-73.
Champions of Division 3, 1982-83.Champions of Division 4, 91-92.
FA Cup winners in 1913-14.
Charity Shield winners in 1960-61, shared in 1973-74.
LEAGUE CAREER: Div 1 88-97, Div 2 97-98, Div 1 98-00, Div 2 00-13, Div 1 13-30, Div 2 30-47, Div 1 47-71, Div 2 71-73, Div 1 73-76, Div 2 76-80, Div 3 80-82, Div 2 82-83, Div 3 83-85, Div 4 85-92, Div 3/2 92-94, Div 2/1 94-95, Div.3/2 1995-

INDIVIDUAL CLUB RECORDS

MOST GOALS IN A SEASON
Jimmy Robson: 37 goals in 1960-61 (League 25, FA Cup 5, Lge Cup 4, EC 3).
Willie Irvine: 37 goals in 1965-66 (League 29, FAC 5, Lge Cup 3).
MOST GOALS IN A MATCH
6. Louis Page v Birmingham City (a), Division 1, 10.4.1926.
OLDEST PLAYER
Jerry Dawson, 40 years 282 days, (Christmas Day 1928).
YOUNGEST PLAYER
Tommy Lawton, 16 years 174 days, 28.3.1936.
MOST CAPPED PLAYER
Jimmy McIlroy (Northern Ireland) 51. Bob Kelly (England) 11.

PREVIOUS MANAGERS

Arthur Sutcliffe 1893-96; Harry Bradshaw 1896-99; Ernest Mangnall 1900-03; Spen Whittaker 1903-10; John Haworth 1910-24; Albert Pickles 1925-32; Tom Bromilow 1932-35; Alf Boland 1935-40; Cliff Britton 1945-48; Frank Hill 1948-54; Alan Brown 1954-57; Billy Dougall 1957-58; Harry Potts 1958-70; Jimmy Adamson 1970-76; Joe Brown 1976-77; Harry Potts 1977-79; Brian Miller 1979-83; Frank Casper 1983; John Bond 1983-84; John Benson 1984-85; Martin Buchan 1985; Tommy Cavanagh 1985-86; Brian Miller 1986-89; Frank Casper 1989-91, Jimmy Mullen 1991-96.
ADDITIONAL INFORMATION
Previous Name: Burnley Rovers 1881-82.
Club colours: Claret shirts with light blue sleeves, white shorts & socks. **Change colours:** All yellow.
Reserves League: Pontins Central League Division 2.

LONGEST LEAGUE RUNS

of undefeated matches:	30 (1920-21)	of league matches w/out a win:	24 (1979)
of undefeated home matches:	34 (1911-13)	of undefeated away matches:	15 (1972-73)
without home win:	11 (1979)	without an away win:	31 (1901-03)
of league wins:	10 (1912-13)	of home wins:	17 (1920-21)
of league defeats:	8 (1889-90 & 1895)	of away wins:	7 (1991-92)

THE MANAGER

ADRIAN HEATH . . . . appointed March 1996.

PREVIOUS CLUBS
As Manager . . . . None.
As Asst.Man/Coach . . . . Sheffield United.
As a player . . . . Stoke, Everton, Espanol, Aston Villa, Manchester City, Stoke, Burnley.

HONOURS
As a Manager . . . . None.
As a Player . . . . **Everton:** Division 1 championship 1985'87. FAC'84. CS'84'85'86'87.
. . . . **England:** 8 caps at u21 level. UEFA u21'82.

BURNLEY

PLAYERS NAME Honours	Ht	Wt	Birthdate	Birthplace Transfers	Contract Date	Clubs	League	L/Cup	FA Cup	Other	Lge	L/C	FAC	Oth
G O A L K E E P E R S														
Beresford Marlon	6.1	12.6	02/09/69	Lincoln	23/09/87	Sheffield Wed.								
Loan (25/08/89) Bury 1 Lge App.				Loan	27/09/90	Northampton Town	13			2				
Loan (28/02/91) Crewe Alexandra 3 Lge Apps.				Loan	15/08/91	Northampton Town	15							
					28/08/92	Burnley	166	12	14	11				
Russell Wayne L	6.2	13.7	29/11/67	Cardiff		Ebbw Vale								
					28/10/93	Burnley	16+2		1					
D E F E N D E R S														
Brass Christopher	5.9	11.08	24/07/75	Easington		Burnley	9+5			2				
				Loan	14/10/94	Torquay United	7		2	1				
Dowell Wayne A	5.10	11.2	28/12/73	Durham	27/03/93	Burnley	6	1	2					
				Loan	29/03/96	Carlisle United	2+5							
Hoyland Jamie	6.0	12.8	23/01/66	Sheffield	12/11/83	Manchester City	2	0+1						
E: Y.3.				Free	11/07/86	Bury	169+3	14+1	6	12	35	5		2
				£250000	04/07/90	Sheffield United	72+15	3+3	8+2	2	6	1	1	1
				Loan	04/03/94	Bristol City	6							
Loan (14/10/94) Burnley				£130000	08/11/94	Burnley	51+2	1	5	3	2			
Parkinson Gary	5.10	11.6	10/01/68	Thornaby		Everton								
				Free	17/01/86	Middlesbrough	194+8	20	17	19	5	1	1	
Loan (10/10/92) Southend United 6 Lge Apps.				Free	02/03/93	Bolton Wanderers	1+2			4				
				£80000	27/01/94	Burnley	91+1	8	6	5	3			1
Swan Peter	6.2	14.12	28/09/66	Leeds	06/08/84	Leeds United	43+6	3	3	1+2	11	2		
				£200000	23/03/89	Hull City	76+4	2+3	2	1	24	1		
				£300000	16/08/91	Port Vale	105+6	6	9	12	6		1	1
				£300000	22/07/94	Plymouth Argyle	24+3	2	2		2	1		
				£200000	10/08/95	Burnley	31+1	2	1	4	5			
Vinnicombe Chris	5.9	10.4	20/10/70	Exeter	01/07/89	Exeter City	35+4	5		2	1	1		
E: u21.12.				£150000	03/11/89	Glasgow Rangers	14+9	1	1+1		1			
				£200000	30/06/94	Burnley	64	7	1	4	3			
West Gareth	6.1	11.10	01/08/78	Oldham	01/06/96	Burnley (T)								
Winstanley Mark	6.1	12.7	22/01/68	St Helens	22/07/86	Bolton Wanderers	215+5	19+1	19	26	3			3
				05/08/94		Burnley	89	7	6	4	5			
M I D F I E L D														
Adams Derek	5.8	11.06	25/06/75	Aberdeen		Aberdeen								
					27/10/95	Burnley	0+2							
Borland John	5.8	11.6	28/01/77		01/08/95	Burnley	1	2	0+1					
Harrison Gerald R	5.10	12.12	15/04/72	Lambeth	18/12/89	Watford	6+3			1				
				Free	23/07/91	Bristol City	24+13	2+2	1	4+1	1			
				Loan	24/01/92	Cardiff City	10				1			
				Loan	19/11/93	Hereford United	6	1		1				
Free (24/03/94) Huddersfield Town				Free	05/08/94	Burnley	51+3	3+1	2	4	3			
Joyce Warren	5.9	11.11	20/01/65	Oldham	23/06/82	Bolton Wanderers	180+4	14+1	11	11	17	1	1	2
				£35000	16/10/87	Preston North End	170+7	8	6	19	34	2	1	7
				£160000	19/05/92	Plymouth Argyle	28+2	6	2	2	3	1		
				£140000	07/07/93	Burnley	65+5	7	4	8	9	1	1	1
				Loan	20/01/95	Hull City								
Matthew Damian	5.11	10.10	23/09/70	Islington	13/06/89	Chelsea	13+8	5		1				
E: u21.9. Div.1'94.				Loan	25/09/92	Luton Town	3+2				1			
				£150000	11/02/94	Crystal Palace	17+7	2+1	1		1			
				Loan	12/01/96	Bristol Rovers	8			2				1
				£65000		Burnley								
Thompson Stephen J	5.9	11.0	02/11/64	Oldham	04/11/82	Bolton Wanderers	329+6	27	21	39	49	2	4	2
AMC'89.				£180000	13/08/91	Luton Town	5	2						
				22/10/91		Leicester City	105+3	6	5	11+3	18	2	1	4
				£200000	24/02/95	Burnley	30							
Webster James	5.8	11.3	01/08/78	Burnley	01/06/96	Burnley (T)								
Weller Paul	5.8	10.13	06/03/75	Brighton	01/08/93	Burnley	24+1	1		2	1			
F O R W A R D S														
Cooke Andrew	6.0	12.0	02/01/74	Shrewsbury		Newtown								
					01/05/95	Burnley	10+13		0+1	2+2	5			
Duerden Ian	5.9	12.6	27/03/78	Burnley	01/08/95	Burnley (T)								
Eastwood Philip	5.10	12.2	06/04/78	Blackburn	01/06/96	Burnley (T)								
Eyres David	5.10	11.0	26/02/64	Liverpool		Rhyl								
				£10000	15/08/89	Blackpool	147+11	11+1	11	13+2	38	1	2	4
				£90000	29/07/93	Burnley	122+4	9	10	7	33	3	7	2
Helliwell Ian	6.4	14.8	07/11/62	Rotherham		Matlock Town								
				£10000	23/10/87	York City	158+2	8	5	9+1	40	1		7
				£80000	16/08/91	Scunthorpe United	78+2	8	4	9	22	5	2	2
				£50000	01/08/93	Rotherham United	37+3	3+1	1	1+1	3			
				Loan	12/01/95	Stockport County								
				10/02/95	Stockport County	35+4	4	2		13		1	
				09/02/96	Burnley	3+1							
Nogan Kurt	5.10	11.1	09/09/70	Cardiff	11/07/89	Luton Town	17+16	1+3		1+1	3	1		
W: u21.2.				Free	30/09/92	Peterborough Utd				0+1				
				Free	17/10/92	Brighton & H.A.	71	4	4+1	5	42	2	4	
				£300000	24/02/95	Burnley	57+4	4	1	4	23	3		3
Robinson Spencer L	5.7	11.5	29/12/65	Bradford		Nottingham Forest								
				£10000	05/01/84	Huddersfield Town	17+4				2			
				Loan	18/12/85	Tranmere Rovers	4				3			
				£60000	08/07/86	Bury	248+14	17+3	9	24	89	6	1	4
				£130000	14/07/93	Bristol City	31+10	1	5	1	4	1		
				£250000	26/07/94	Burnley	40+15	4	5	0+1	9	2	1	
Smith Paul	6.0	13.3	22/01/76	Easington	01/08/95	Burnley	3+7							

TURF MOOR

Brunshaw Road, Burnley, Lancs BB10 4BX
Tel: 01282 700000

Capacity 21,100

First game..v Rawtemstall, 17.02.1883.
First floodlit game ....v Blackburn (friendly), .12.1957.

ATTENDANCES
Highest ....54,775 v Huddersfield Town, FA Cup Round 3, 23.2.1924.
Lowest ....1,138 v Darlington, AMC, 13.3.1986.

OTHER GROUNDS ....None.

MATCHDAY TICKET PRICES

Endsleigh Stand (Visitors) . . . . £12.
Concessions . . . . £6.

Bob Lord. . . . . £12.
Concessions . . . . £6.

North Stand . . . . £14/£12.
Concessions . . . . £7/£6.
East Stand . . . . £10/£9.
Concessions . . . . £4.50.

Ticket Office Telephone No. . . . . 01282 700010.

CLUBCALL
0898 12 11 53
Calls cost 39p per minute cheap rate and 49p per minute at all other times.
Call costings correct at time of going to press.

HOW TO GET TO THE GROUND

From the North
Follow signs to Burnley (A56) into Town Centre, at roundabout take first exit into Yorkshire Street, shortly over crossroads into Brunshaw Road for Burnley FC.

From the East:
Follow signs Burnley (A646) then join A671 enter town centre by Todmorden Road and at the end turn right at crossroads into Brunshaw Road for Burnley FC.

From the South:
(or use route from west). Use M62, M66 and A56 signposted Burnley into town centre, then at roundabout take 3rd exit in Yorkshire Street, shortly at crossroads forward into Brunshaw Road for Burnley FC.

From the West and South:
Use M6 to junction 31, then Blackburn bypass and A679 into Burnley town centre and at roundabout take third exit into Yorkshire Street, shortly over crossroads into Brunshaw Road for Burnley FC.

Car Parking
Parks in Church Street and Fulledge Recreation Ground for approx 500 vehicles each (chargeable). Both are five minutes walk from ground.

Nearest Railway Station: Burnley Central.

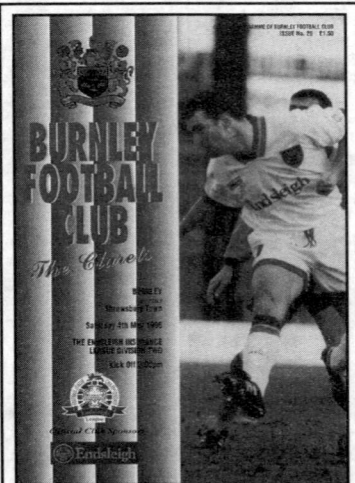

MATCHDAY PROGRAMME

Programme Editor . . . . John Stringer.

Number of pages . . . . 48.

Price . . . .£1.50.

Subscriptions . . . . Apply to club.

Local Newspapers. . . Lancashire Evening Telegraph, Burnley Express.

Local Radio Stations . . . . Radio Lancashire, Red Rose Radio.

BURY
(The Shakers)
NATIONWIDE LEAGUE DIVISION 2
SPONSORED BY: BIRTHDAYS (RON WOOD GREETING CARDS LTD)

Back Row (L-R): Ian Hughes, Mark Sertori, Trevor Matthewson, John Paskin, Ryan Cross, Nick Daws, Chris Lucketti. **Middle Row:** Alan Raw (Physio), Stan Ternent (Asst. Manager), Andy Woodward, Dave Lancaster, Gary Kelly, Michael Jackson, Lee Bracey, Tony Rigby, Dave Johnson, Cliff Roberts (First Team Coach). **Front Row:** Phil Stant, Kevin Hulme, Lenny Johnrose, David Pugh, Mike Walsh (Manager), Jimmy Mulligan, Stuart Bimson, Shaun Reid, Mark Carter.

BURY
FORMED IN 1885
TURNED PROFESSIONAL IN 1885
LTD COMPANY IN 1897

CHAIRMAN: T Robinson
VICE-CHAIRMAN
Canon J R Smith, MA
DIRECTORS
J Smith, C H Eaves FCA, F Mason
SECRETARY
Mr J Heap
COMMERCIAL MANAGER
N Neville (0161 705 2144)

MANAGER: Mike Walsh
ASSISTANT MANAGER: Stan Ternant

PHYSIOTHERAPIST
Alan Raw

STATISTICIAN FOR THE DIRECTORY
Paul Greenlees

Having lost out in last season's play-off final to Chesterfield, Bury were determined to build on there near success and reach Division Two without the cup tie pressure of the end of season mini tournament.

This they did by piping Plymouth Argyle and Darlington to third place with a 3-0 victory over Cardiff City on the last day of the season. A shaky start however could well have seen them fighting at the wrong end of the table, as by mid October they were sitting in 21st place having won just one game.

This unwanted position seemed to kick start Mike Walshs' men into action and an eight game run without defeat put the 'Shakers' back on the right track. Bury secured their automatic promotion spot by putting together a run of 25 games in which they lost only six.

The Cup competitions were short and sweet. The Coca-Cola Cup saw the only progression with victory over Chesterfield (3-1 on aggregate), followed by a fantastic aggregate score of 5-4 against First Division Sheffield United, before losing out to Reading in the 3rd Round (1-2).

In the F.A. Cup Bury were on the wrong end of a 'giant killing' act. Blyth Spartans, of the Unibond Northern Premier League, won the tie 0-2 at Gigg Lane.

Defeat against Scunthorpe (0-4) and a draw against Wigan (0-0) saw the end of their Auto Windscreen Shield hopes.

Bury, having finally claimed a place in the 2nd Division, will be very keen to stay there next season, and with the belief of the manager and his players there is no reason why they shouldn't.

BURY

League: 3rd   FA Cup: 1st Rnd   Coca-Cola Cup: 3rd Rnd   Auto Windscreen Shield: 1st Rnd

M	DATE	COMP	VEN	OPPONENTS	RESULT	HT	LP	GOAL SCORERS/GOAL TIMES	ATT.
1	A 12	EL	A	Northampton Town	L 1-4	1-1	19	Stant 21	(4487)
2	15	CC 1/1	A	Chesterfield	W 1-0	0-0		Stant 64	(2831)
3	19	EL	H	Chester City	D 1-1	1-1	18	Stant 18	3211
4	26	EL	A	Hereford United	W 4-3	1-2	10	Carter 1, 48(pen), Johnrose 59, Rigby 85	(2702)
5	29	EL	H	Preston North End	D 0-0	0-0	12		4682
6	S 2	EL	H	Plymouth Argyle	L 0-5	0-3	14		3040
7	5	CC 1/2	H	Chesterfield	W 2-1	0-1		Carter 69(pen), Daws 83	2565
8	9	EL	A	Wigan Athletic	W 2-1	1-1	12	Carter 26, Stant 28	(3128)
9	12	EL	A	Lincoln City	D 2-2	0-0	13	Wanless 54(og), Johnrose 87	(1851)
10	16	EL	H	Cambridge United	L 1-2	1-0	16	Pugh 16	2762
11	20	CC 2/1	A	Sheffield United	L 1-2	0-1		Stant 72	(4075)
12	23	EL	H	Barnet	D 0-0	0-0	15		2453
13	30	EL	A	Gillingham	L 0-3	0-0	21		(6125)
14	O 3	CC 2/2	H	Sheffield United	W 4-2	2-0		Stant 15, 62, Carter 31, Johnson 85	2888
15	7	EL	H	Leyton Orient	W 2-1	2-1	16	Carter 9, Rigby 45	3025
16	14	EL	A	Fulham	D 0-0	0-0	18		(3803)
17	17	AWS 1/1	A	Scunthorpe United	L 0-4	0-0			(877)
18	21	EL	H	Scarborough	L 0-2	0-1	21		2590
19	28	EL	A	Mansfield Town	W 5-1	1-1	15	Stant 43, 73, 78, 89 (4), Pugh 46	(2356)
20	31	EL	A	Torquay United	W 2-0	1-0	11	Lucketti 34, Stant 68	(1456)
21	N 4	EL	H	Darlington	D 0-0	0-0	11		2964
22	7	CC 3	A	Reading	L 1-2	0-0		Rigby 57	(10329)
23	11	FAC 1	H	Blyth Spartans	L 0-2	0-1			3076
24	14	AWS 1/2	H	Wigan Athletic	D 0-0	0-0			1471
25	18	EL	A	Cardiff City	W 1-0	1-0	9	Johnson 25	(3846)
26	25	EL	H	Exeter City	W 2-0	0-0	8	Johnson 82, Pugh 83	3597
27	D 9	EL	A	Barnet	D 0-0	0-0	9		(1747)
28	16	EL	H	Gillingham	W 1-0	0-0	8	Rigby 67	3035
29	23	EL	H	Colchester United	D 0-0	0-0	9		3559
30	J 1	EL	H	Hartlepool United	L 0-3	0-1	10		2927
31	6	EL	H	Doncaster Rovers	W 4-1	1-1	7	Pugh 34, Johnrose 53, Stant 68, Rigby 89	2606
32	13	EL	A	Chester City	D 1-1	0-1	7	Matthews 66	(3328)
33	20	EL	H	Northampton Town	L 0-1	0-0	8		3074
34	F 10	EL	A	Doncaster Rovers	W 1-0	1-0	10	Matthews 10	(2418)
35	13	EL	A	Rochdale	D 1-1	0-0	9	Carter 79	(3048)
36	17	EL	H	Lincoln City	W 7-1	2-1	7	Matthews 8, Rigby 17, 68, Pugh 50, Carter 53, 70, Daws 73	3096
37	20	EL	A	Plymouth Argyle	L 0-1	0-0	8		(4536)
38	24	EL	A	Cambridge United	W 4-2	1-2	8	Carter 40, 89, Johnson 56, Pugh 78	(2341)
39	27	EL	H	Wigan Athletic	W 2-1	0-0	7	Carter 65(pen), Jackson 78	3800
40	M 2	EL	H	Scunthorpe United	W 3-0	0-0	6	Carter 42(pen), Johnrose 59, Pugh 78	3035
41	9	EL	A	Colchester United	L 0-1	0-0	7		(2832)
42	16	EL	H	Rochdale	D 1-1	1-1	7	Matthews 20	3473
43	19	EL	H	Hereford United	W 2-0	0-0	5	Carter 48, Jackson 84	2280
44	23	EL	A	Hartlepool United	W 2-1	0-1	5	Jackson 47, Pugh 74	(1879)
45	26	EL	A	Preston North End	D 0-0	0-0	5		(12260)
46	30	EL	A	Leyton Orient	W 2-0	0-0	3	Carter 32, 56(pen)	(3421)
47	A 2	EL	H	Fulham	W 3-0	2-0	3	Setori 9, Johnrose 34, West 48	3771
48	6	EL	H	Mansfield Town	L 0-2	0-2	4		3600
49	9	EL	A	Scarborough	W 2-0	2-0	4	Pugh 38, Johnrose 41	(1773)
50	13	EL	H	Torquay United	W 1-0	0-0	3	Carter 71	3247
51	16	EL	A	Scunthorpe United	W 2-1	0-0	3	Jackson 60, Johnson 65	(2132)
52	20	EL	A	Darlington	L 0-4	0-2	3		(4335)
53	27	EL	A	Exeter City	D 1-1	1-0	4	Carter 25(pen)	(3508)
54	M 4	EL	H	Cardiff City	W 3-0	1-0	3	Pugh 25, Johnson 52, Rigby 64	5658

Best Home League Attendance: 5658 v Cardiff City   Smallest: 2280 v Hereford United   Average: 3281

Goal Scorers:
EL(66):   Carter(16),Pugh(10),Stant(9),Rigby(7),Johnrose(6),Johnson(5),Jackson(4),Matthews(4),Lucketti(1),Setori(1),Daws(1),West(1),Opponent(s)(1)
CC(9):   Stant(4),Carter(2),Daws(1),Rigby(1),Johnson(1)
FAC(0):
AWS (0):

	(D) Bimson	(M) Brabin	(G) Bracey	(F) Carter	(D) Cross	(M) Daws	(D) Edwards	(D) Harle	(M) Hughes	(F) Hulme	(D) Jackson	(M) Johnrose	(F) Johnson	(G) Kelly	(F) Lancaster	(D) Lucketti	(F) Matthews	(D) Matthewson	(F) Mulligan	(F) Paskin	(M) Pugh	(D) Reid	(M) Reid	(D) Richardson	(M) Rigby	(D) Setori	(F) Stant	(D) West	(D) Woodward		
	X			X2					S					X		S2	X				S1		X		X	X1	X		X	S.Bennett	1
	X2		X	X		S2			S1		X1	X				S	X				X		X	X2	S1		X			M.Fletcher	2
	X		X	X	X	S2			X				X1			S2	X				X		X	X2	S1		X2			G.Cain	3
	X		X	X	X				X				X			S	X				X		X	X1	S1		X			P.Rejer	4
	X		X	X	X	X1			X				X			S3	X		S2		X		X	S1	X		X2			P.E.West	5
	X		X	X	X	X1			X				X			S	X				X		X	X	S1	X		X		R.Pearson	6
	X		X	X	X				X				X	S		S	X		X		X		X	X	S		X			J.Rushton	7
	X		X	X	X	X2			X			S1				X	X			S2	X		X1			S2	X2			S.Mathieson	8
	X		X	X	X				X			S				X	X		S1		X		X1		X		X			T.Heilbron	9
			X		X				X	S	X1	X				X	X		S2		X		X		X	S1	X	X2		I.G.Cruikshank	10
			X	X	X				X		X1	X3	S1			S2	X				X		X		X	X	X2			J.Brandwood	11
			X	X	X	X			X				S1		S	X				X		X		X	S	X1			M.Riley	12
X1		X	X	X	X				X				S2			X	X				X		X		X	X2	S1			G.Pooley	13
	X		X	X	X	S			X			S1	X			X	X				X		X		X	X	X1			G.Singh	14
X1			X	X					X			S	X			X	X				X		X		X	S	X	S1		U.D.Rennie	15
	X		X1	X					X			S1	X	S2		X	X				X		X1		X	X2	X			B.Knight	16
	X		X1	X					X			S1	X	S3		X	X				X		X		X	S2	X	X3		Not Known	17
	X			X2	S3				X			S1	X	X		X	X				X1		X		X	S2	X	X3		K.M.Lynch	18
	X		X	S					X1			X1	X			X	X				X		X		X		X	S1		R.Poulain	19
	X		X	S1					X1			X2	X			X	X				X		X		X	S	X	S1		G.Barber	20
	X		X	S					X			X2	X			X	X				X1		X		X	S2	X	S1		W.C.Burns	21
	X		S1	X	S2				X			X1	X			X	X				X		X		X2		X			J.Kirkby	22
	X		X	X					X2			S1				X	X				X		X		X1	S2	X	X		R.A.Hart	23
			X	S					X1			X	X			X	X				X		X		X	S	X	S1		G.Cain	24
			S2		S1				X			X	X	X2		X	X				X		X		X1	S	X	X		A.Wyley	25
			S		S				X			X	X	X	X	X	X				X		X		X	S	X	X		N.S.Barry	26
					S			S1	X			X	X	X2	X	X				X		X1		X	S	X	X		J.Rushton	27
					X		S	S	X			X	X	X	X	X				X		X		X	S	X	X		T.West	28
					X		S	S	X			X	X	X	X	S				X		X		X	S	X	X		R.Furnandiz	29
			S1		X			X1	X			X	X	X	X	S				X		S		X	S	X	X		S.W.Mathieson	30
					X			X	X			X	X	X	X	S	X				X		S		X	S	X	X		S.Baines	31
	X				X			X	X			X1	X	X		X	S1				X		S2		X		X2	X		D.Laws	32
	X				X			X1	X	X	X	S1			X	X	S				X		S		X		X	X		I.G.Cruikshanks	33
			S3		X	X		X	X			S1	X		X	X1					X	S2	X2	X3			X		W.Burns	34
			S3		X	X		X	X			S2	X		X	X1			X3	S1	X2		X				X		K.Breen	35
			X2		X3	X		X	X			S2	X		X	X1		S1	X	S3		X		X			X		A.Butler	36
			X		X	X2		X	X			S2	X		X	X		S2	X		X		X1				X		P.Rejer	37
X2			X		X			X	X			S2	X		X	X				X	S1		X1				X		K.Lynch	38
X1			X		X			X	X	S	X		X	X2		X			S2	X	S1		X				X		M.Fletcher	39
			X		X			X	X	X	X	X	X		X	X			S	X	S	X		X			X		M.Brandwood	40
			X		X			S	X	X	X	S2	X		X	X2			S2	X	X2		X1				X		M.C.Bailey	41
			X		X			S	X	X	X	S2	X		X	X2			S	X	X		X				X		E.Lomas	42
	X		X		X			S1	X	X	X	S2	X		X			S	X	X		X1				X		F.Stretton	43
S		X	X		X			X	X	X	X	X1			X					X	X		X1				X		N.Barry	44
S		X	X		X			X	X	X	X	X1			X					X	X			S1	S		X		J.Lloyd	45
	X1		X3		X			X	X	X	X	X2			X					X	X		S1	S2			X		A.Butler	46
S		X	X		X			X	X	X	X	S1			X					X			X1	X2	S2		X		T.West	47
S	X		X		X			X2	X	X	X	X			X	S1				X			X1		S2		X		R.Furnandiz	48
	X		X		X			X	X	X	X3	X			X	X2				X			S2		S3		X		G.Cain	49
	X	X		X2	X			X	X	X	X3				X				S3	X1	X		S1		S2		X		M.Riley	50
	X	X		X2				X	X	X	X1				X		S			X				S1	S		X		U.Rennie	51
	X	X		X2				X3	X	X	X1				X	S1				X				S3	S2		X		R.Poulain	52
	X		X2		X3			X			X	S1			X		X		S2	X	X		S3		X1	X			S.Bennett	53
	X				X			X	X	X1	X		X		X	S				X	X			X	S	S1	X		A.Butler	54
16	5	21	29	13	33	4	0	30	0	31	34	21	25	1	42	11	16	0	0	42	12	21	3	33	3	27	32	1	EL Appearances	
0	0	0	4	0	4	0	1	2	1	0	0	14	0	4	0	5	0	2	11	0	5	1	2	8	7	7	5	0	EL Sub Appearances	
4	0	3	4+1	4	2+1	0	0	2+1	1	1	3	1+2	2	0+1	5	0	4	0	0	5	0	5	0	5	1	2+1	5	0	CC Appearances	
0	0	0	1	1	0	0	0	1	0	0	0	0	0	1	0	1	0	0	1	0	1	0	1	0	0	1	1	0	FAC Appearances	
1	0	0	1	2	0	0	0	2	0	0	1	1+1	2	0+1	2	0	2	0	0	1	0	2	0	2	0+1	2	1+1	0	AWS Appearances	

CLUB RECORDS

BIGGEST VICTORIES
League: 8-0 v Tranmere Rovers, Division 3, 10.1.1970 (Bury have scored eight goals four times in the League).
F.A. Cup: 12-1 v Stockton, 1st Round, 2.2.1897.

BIGGEST DEFEATS
League: 0-8 v Sheffield United, Division 1, 6.4.1896.
0-8 v Swindon Town, Division 3, 8.12.1979.
League Cup: 0-10 v West Ham United, Round 2, 25.10.1983.

MOST POINTS
3 points a win: 84, Division 4, 1984-85.
2 points a win: 68, Division 3, 1960-61.

MOST GOALS SCORED
108, Division 3, 1960-61.

BEST PERFORMANCES
League: 4th in Division 1, 1925-26.
F.A. Cup: Winners in 1900, 1903.
League Cup: Semi-Final 1963.

HONOURS
Champions of Division 2, 1894-95.
Champions of Division 3, 1960-61.
FA Cup winners 1900, 1903.

LEAGUE CAREER
Elected to Div 2 1894, Div 1 1894-95, Div 2 1911-12, Div 1 1923-24, Div 2 1928-29, Div 3 1956-57, Div 2 1960-61, Div 3 1966-67, Div 2 1967-68, Div 3 1968-69, Div 4 1970-71, Div 3 1973-74, Div 4 1979-80, Div 3 1984-85, Div 4/3 1991-92. Div.2 1996-

INDIVIDUAL CLUB RECORDS

MOST GOALS IN A SEASON
Craig Madden: 43 goals in 1981-82 (League 35, FA Cup 4, League Cup 3, Group Cup 1)

MOST GOALS IN A MATCH
5. Ray Pointer v Rotherham United, 6-1, Division 2, 2.10.1965.
5. Eddie Quigley v Millwall (h), 5-2, Division 2, 15.2.1947.

OLDEST PLAYER
Derek Fazackerley, 37 years 182 days, 6.5.1989.

YOUNGEST PLAYER
Brian Williams, 16 years 133 days, 18.3.1972.

MOST CAPPED PLAYER
Bill Gorman (Eire) 11.

PREVIOUS MANAGERS

(Since 1946)
Norman Bullock, John McNeil, Dave Russell, Bob Stokoe, Bert Head, Les Shannon, Jack Marshall, Les Hart, Colin McDonald, Tommy McAnearney, Allan Brown, Bobby Smith, Bob Stokoe, Dave Hatton, Dave Connor, Jim Iley, Martin Dobson, Sam Ellis.

ADDITIONAL INFORMATION
PREVIOUS NAMES
None.

PREVIOUS LEAGUE
Lancashire League.

Club Colours: White shirts, royal blue shorts, royal blue socks.
Change colours: Green & purple striped shirts, purple shorts, purple socks.

Reserves League: Midland Senior League.

LONGEST LEAGUE RUNS

of undefeated matches:	18 (1961)	of league matches w/out a win:	19 (1911)
of undefeated home matches:	25 (1967-68)	of undefeated away matches:	8 (1961)
without home win:	13 (1937, 1978)	without an away win:	42 (1910-1912)
of league wins:	9 (1960)	of home wins:	15 (1894-95)
of league defeats:	6 (1953, 1967)	of away wins:	6 (1960)

THE MANAGER
MIKE WALSH . . . . . appointed November 1990.

PREVIOUS CLUBS
As Manager . . . . None.
As Player/Coach . . . . Blackpool, Bury.
As a player . . . . Bolton W., Everton, Norwich (loan), Burnley (loan), Fort Lauderdale, ... Manchester City, Blackpool, Bury.

HONOURS
As a Manager . . . . 3rd Division play-offs 1990-91.
As a Player . . . . Bolton: Division 2 Championship 1979-80. Blackpool: Promotion to Division 3, 1984-85, ... Bury: Promotion to Division 2, 1995-96.
International . . . . 4 full caps for Eire.

BURY

PLAYERS NAME / Honours	Ht	Wt	Birthdate	Birthplace / Transfers	Contract Date	Clubs	APPEARANCES League	L/Cup	FA Cup	Other	GOALS Lge	L/C	FAC	Oth
G O A L K E E P E R S														
Bracey Lee	6.1	12.8	11/09/68	Barking	06/07/87	West Ham United								
WFAC'91.				Free	27/08/88	Swansea City	99	8	11	10				
				£47500	17/10/91	Halifax Town	73	2	1	2				
				£20000	23/08/93	Bury	86+2	7	2	3				
Kelly Gary	5.11	12.3	03/08/66	Preston	20/06/84	Newcastle United	53	4	3	2				
Ei: B.1, u21.7, FAYC'85.				Loan	07/10/88	Blackpool	5							
				£60000	05/10/89	Bury	223	14	10	23				
D E F E N D E R S														
Bimson Stuart	5.11	11.8	29/09/69	Liverpool		Macclesfield Town								
				£12500	06/02/95	Bury	51	4		4				
Jackson Michael	5.11	11.9	04/12/73	Chester		Crewe Alexandra	5	1	1	2				
E: Y.2,S.				Free	13/08/93	Bury	123+2	6	2	9	10			
Lucketti Chris	6.0	12.1	28/09/71	Littleborough		Rochdale	1							
				Free	23/08/90	Stockport County								
				Free	12/07/91	Halifax Town	73+5	2	2	4	2	1		
				£50000	01/10/93	Bury	150+1	12	8	14	6		1	
Reid Nicky	5.10	12.04	30/10/60	Urmston	04/11/78	Manchester City	211+5	20	17	6	2			
				Free	10/07/87	Blackburn Rovers	160+14	13	6+2	13+1	9			1
				Loan	17/09/92	Bristol City	3+1			1				
				Free	07/11/92	W.B.A.	13+7		2+1	2+1				1
				Free	04/03/94	Wycombe Wand.	6+2		0+1	5				
					15/12/95	Bury	12+5							
West Dean	5.10	11.07	05/12/72	Morley	17/08/91	Lincoln City	86+25	9	6	6+2	19	1	1	1
				Loan	27/08/93	Boston United								
					28/09/95	Bury	32+5		1	1+1	1			
Woodward Andrew	5.10	10.12	23/09/73	Stockport	29/07/92	Crewe Alexandra	9+11	2		0+3				
					13/03/95	Bury	10			3				
M I D F I E L D														
Daws Nicholas	5.11	13.2	15/03/70	Manchester		Altrincham				2+1				
				£10000	13/08/92	Bury	164+17	10+3	9	10+2	6	1		
Hughes Ian	5.10	10.9	02/08/64	Bangor	19/11/91	Bury	141+16	9+1	7+2	16+3	1			
W: u21.11.														
Johnrose Lennie	5.10	11.5	29/11/69	Preston	16/06/88	Blackburn Rovers	20+22	2+1	0+3	2	11	1		
				Loan	21/01/92	Preston North End	1+2				1			
				£50000	28/02/92	Hartlepool United	59+7	5+1	5	5	11	4	1	
					07/12/93	Bury	102+6	7+1	5	7	16		1	
Pugh David	5.10	11.0	19/09/64	Liverpool		Runcorn								
				£35000	21/07/89	Chester City	168+11	13	11+1	9	23			
				£22500	05/07/95	Bury	126	11	6	9	36			2
Reid Shaun	5.8	11.10	13/10/65	Huyton	20/09/83	Rochdale	126+7	10	5	12	4	2	1	
				Loan	12/12/85	Preston North End	3							
				£32500	23/12/88	York City	104+2	7	4	5	7			1
				Free	16/08/92	Rochdale	106	6	7	8+1	10		1	2
				£15000	05/07/95	Bury	21+1	5	1	2				
Rigby Tony	5.7	10.8	10/08/72	Ormskirk		Crewe Alexandra								
via Lancaster City, Burscough				Free	06/01/93	Bury	120+8	5+1	3	10	22	1		
F O R W A R D S														
Carter Mark	5.9	11.6	17/12/60	Liverpool		Bangor City				4				
E: S.P.11.						Runcorn				12				
				£40000	20/02/91	Barnet	62+20	5	4+1	7+2	31	2	6	8
				£6000	10/09/93	Bury	115+13	10+1	5	10+1	66	5		
Jepson Ronald F	6.1	13.2	12/05/63	Stoke		Nantwich Town								
				Free	23/03/89	Port Vale	12+10	1+1	1+1					
				Loan	25/01/90	Peterborough Utd	18				5			
				£80000	12/02/91	Preston North End	36+2	2		3	8			4
				£60000	29/07/92	Exeter City	50+3	6	3	4	21	2	1	1
				£80000	07/12/93	Huddersfield Town	95+12	6+1	4	6	31	2	3	1
				£40000	23/07/96	Bury								
Johnson David	5.6	12.03	15/08/76	Kingston		Manchester United								
				Free	05/07/95	Bury	21+14	1+2	0+1	1+1	5	1		
Lancaster David	6.3	14.0	08/09/61	Preston		Colne Dynamoes								
				Free	15/08/90	Blackpool	7+1	2		0+1	1			
				Loan	26/02/91	Chesterfield	12				4			
				£70000	27/08/91	Chesterfield	66+3	5	2	6	16	3		3
				Free	05/07/93	Rochdale	37+3	4	2	1	14	1		
*Free (20/07/94) Halifax Town				Free	13/03/95	Bury	5+10	0+1		0+1	1			
					19/02/96	Rochdale	13+1				2			
Matthews Robert	6.0	12.5	14/10/70	Slough	26/03/92	Notts County	12+13		1+2	1+1	8			
E: u18.3, S.				£80000	03/03/95	Luton Town	6+5	0+1						
					08/09/95	York City	14+3		1	3	1			
					12/01/96	Bury	11+5				4			
Stant Phil	6.1	12.7	13/10/62	Bolton	19/08/82	Reading	3+1		1		2			
WFAC'93. Div.3'93.				Free	25/11/86	Hereford United	83+6	3	3	11	38	2	2	7
				£175000	18/07/89	Notts County	14+8	2	0+1	3+2	6	1		
				Loan	05/09/90	Blackpool	12				5			
				Loan	05/10/90	Huddersfield Town	5				1			
				Loan	22/11/90	Lincoln City	4							
				£60000	08/02/91	Fulham	19			1	5			
				£50000	01/08/91	Mansfield Town	56+1	4	2	2	32	1		
				£100000	04/12/92	Cardiff City	77+2	2	6+1	10	35	2	4	3
				Loan	12/08/93	Mansfield Town	4	1			1	1		
					26/01/95	Bury	73+15	5	1	7	31	4		

GIGG LANE

Bury, Lancashire, BL9 9HR
Tel: 0161 764 4881

Capacity ....11,614.
Covered Standing ....4,825.
Seating ....6,787.

First game ....Accrington v Church, 18.6.1885.
First floodlit game ....v Wolverhampton Wanderers, 3-1, 6.10.1953.

ATTENDANCES
Highest...35,000 v Bolton Wanderers FA Cup 3rd Round, 9.1.1960.
Lowest ....416 v Tranmere Rovers, AMC, 26.2.1986.

OTHER GROUNDS ....None.

MATCHDAY TICKET PRICES

Main Stand £10
Juv/OAP £5

Family & Cemetery Enclosure £8
Juv/OAP £4
Family Ticket (1+1). £11

South Stand. £9
Juv/OAP £4

Ticket Office telephone no. . . . . 0161 764 4881.

HOW TO GET TO THE GROUND

From the North
Use motorway (M66) until junction 2, then leave motorway and follow signs to Bury A58. In half a mile turn left into Heywood Street and at end forward into Parkhills Road. At end turn left (A56) into Manchester Road, then shortly turn left into Gigg Lane for Bury FC.

From the East, South and West
Use motorway (M62) until junction 17. Leave motorway and follow signs to Bury (A56). In 3.1 miles turn right into Gigg Lane for Bury FC.

Car Parking
Ample side-street parking is available.

Nearest Railway Station
Bury Metro Interchange.

CLUBCALL
0898 12 11 97
Calls cost 39p per minute cheap rate and 49p per minute at all other times.
Call costings correct at time of going to press.

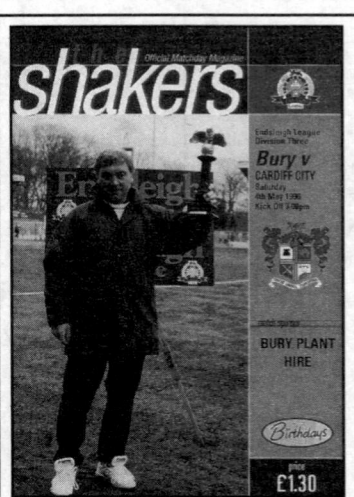

MATCHDAY PROGRAMME

Programme Editor . . . . N Neville.

Number of pages . . . . 32.

Price . . . . £1.20.

Subscriptions . . . . £1.20 per match +50p P&P or SAE.

Local Newspapers . . . . Bury Times, Bolton Evening News,
. . . . Manchester Evening News.

Local Radio Stations . . . . Piccadilly Radio, G.M.R.

CHESTERFIELD
(The Spireites)
NATIONWIDE LEAGUE DIVISION 2
SPONSORED BY: N.DERBYS HEATH AUTH. & G K GROUP

Back Row (L-R): Mark Williams, Kevin Davies, Andy Beasley, Chris Marples, Darren Roberts, Tony Lormor.
Middle Row: Mark Stuart, Jon Howard, Darren Carr, David Moss, Andy Morris, Nicky Laws, Shaun Dyche, Des Hazel, Phil Robinson, Lee Rogers.
Front Row: Mark Jules, Tom Curtis, Chris Perkins, Dave Rushbury (Physio), John Duncan (Manager), Kevin Randall (Assistant Manager), Jon Narbett, Wayne Fairclough, Jamie Hewitt.

CHESTERFIELD
FORMED IN 1866
TURNED PROFESSIONAL IN 1891
LTD COMPANY IN 1871

PRESIDENT
His Grace The Duke of Devonshire MC,DL,JP

CHAIRMAN: J Norton-Lea
VICE-CHAIRMAN: B W Hubbard
DIRECTOR: R F Pepper, Mike Warner
SECRETARY
Mick Horton (01246 209 765)
COMMERCIAL MANAGER
Jim Brown

MANAGER: John Duncan
ASSISTANT MANAGER: Kevin Randall

PHYSIOTHERAPIST
Dave Rushbury

STATISTICIAN FOR THE DIRECTORY
Richard West

Having gained a place in the 2nd Division via the play-of system last season, Chesterfield Football Club and their supporters would have been happy with a good mid-table position. But their final position of 7th excelled everybodies expectations and proved their new status as a 2nd Division club.

A first day defeat by Oxford United (0-1) may well have had the doubts creeping in, but they were soon forgotten when they entertained Carlisle and beat them 3-0. Their form was fairly inconsistent until mid October when only two defeats in ten games saw them reach their highest position in the Division - fourth.

The Spireites hung on to their play-off position for most of the season until a run of three defeats at the end of April saw them sitting in 10th position, with only two games to go. They won both, but the damage had been done and they missed out to eventual play-off winners Bradford City, by one point!

Bury gained sweet revenge for their 1994/95 play-off defeat, by knocking Chesterfield out of the Coca-Cola Cup (1-3 on aggregate). The F.A. Cup saw them defeat Scarborough in the 1st Round (2-0), but then go out to Wrexham (2-3). Auto Windscreen Shield saw get as far as the Northern Semi-Final where they lost out to Carlisle United (0-1).

Chesterfield will be hoping they can maintain their form of last season, but now they are 2nd Division regulars they might find it a little tougher.

CHESTERFIELD

League: 7th   FA Cup: 2nd Rnd   Coca-Cola Cup: 1st Rnd   Auto Windscreen Shield: Semi-Finals

M	DATE	COMP	VEN	OPPONENTS	RESULT	HT	LP	GOAL SCORERS/GOAL TIMES	ATT.
1	A 12	EL	A	Oxford United	L 0-1	0-0	8		(5563)
2	15	CC 1/1	H	Bury	L 0-1	0-0			2831
3	19	EL	H	Carlisle United	W 3-0	2-0	12	Lormor 6, Robinson 38, Morris 87	3634
4	26	EL	A	Swansea City	L 2-3	0-2	16	Davies 82, 89	(3492)
5	29	EL	H	York City	W 2-1	0-1	13	Lormor 75, Morris 77	3419
6	S 2	EL	H	Hull City	D 0-0	0-0	11		4345
7	5	CC 1/2	A	Bury	L 1-2	1-0		Roberts 19	(2565)
8	9	EL	A	Swindon Town	D 1-1	1-1	14	Davies 9	(8687)
9	12	EL	A	Wycombe Wanderers	L 0-1	0-1	16		(3617)
10	16	EL	H	Rotherham United	W 3-0	1-0	10	Lormor 40, Jules 56, Law 69(pen)	5146
11	23	EL	H	Burnley	W 4-2	2-2	7	Hewitt 27, Robinson 42, Lormor 54, Morris 74	4933
12	26	AWS 1/1	A	Stockport County	D 1-1	0-0		Lormor 46	(2152)
13	30	EL	A	Brentford	W 2-1	1-0	7	Curtis 29, Robinson 82	(4734)
14	O 7	EL	H	Crewe Alexandra	L 1-2	0-0	7	Morris 70	4981
15	14	EL	A	Blackpool	D 0-0	0-0	9		(6855)
16	17	AWS 1/2	H	Notts County	W 2-1	0-0		Robinson, Roberts	2150
17	21	EL	H	Shrewsbury Town	W 1-0	1-0	7	Law 21	3920
18	28	EL	A	Stockport County	W 1-0	1-0	4	Law 42(pen)	(6287)
19	31	EL	A	Bristol City	L 1-2	1-1	8	Robinson 6	(4408)
20	N 4	EL	H	Bradford City	W 2-1	1-1	6	Law 44(pen), 75(pen)	5490
21	11	FAC 1	A	Scarborough	W 2-0	0-0		Lormor 52, 75	(2354)
22	18	EL	A	Notts County	L 1-4	1-2	7	Law 26(pen)	(6747)
23	25	EL	H	Bournemouth	W 3-0	2-0	4	Robinson 24, Lormor 38, Robinson 50	4034
24	28	AWS 2	H	Rochdale	W 2-1	0-1		Robinson, Roberts	2344
25	D 2	FAC 2	A	Wrexham	L 2-3	0-2		Davies 56, Davies 90	(4943)
26	9	EL	A	Burnley	D 2-2	1-1	7	Davies 43, Lormor 64	(8459)
27	16	EL	H	Brentford	D 2-2	0-2	7	Bates 50(og), Morris 70	4016
28	22	EL	A	Brighton & H.A.	W 2-0	1-0	4	Robinson 15, Robinson 71	(3629)
29	26	EL	H	Peterborough United	D 1-1	0-1	4	Williams 56	6017
30	J 9	AWS QF	A	Blackpool	W 1-0	0-0		Law (pen)	(2469)
31	13	EL	A	Carlisle United	D 1-1	1-0	6	Narbett 10	(5851)
32	20	EL	H	Oxford United	W 1-0	1-0	5	Lormor 12	4589
33	30	AWS SFN	A	Carlisle United	L 0-1	0-1			(6209)
34	F 3	EL	H	Swansea City	W 3-2	2-2	5	Holland 7, Lormor 33, 70	4050
35	17	EL	H	Wycombe Wanderers	W 3-1	3-0	5	Williams 5, Robinson 18, Lormor 35	4571
36	24	EL	A	Rotherham United	W 1-0	0-0	4	Jules 75	(5712)
37	M 2	EL	A	Peterborough United	W 1-0	1-0	5	Howard 3	(6105)
38	5	EL	A	Wrexham	L 0-3	0-3	5		(2656)
39	9	EL	H	Brighton & H.A.	W 1-0	0-0	5	Williams 47	6233
40	12	EL	A	Hull City	D 0-0	0-0	6		(2832)
41	16	EL	A	Walsall	L 0-3	0-0	6		(4127)
42	19	EL	H	Wrexham	D 1-1	0-0	6	Lormor 62	3760
43	23	EL	H	Bristol Rovers	W 2-1	0-0	6	Howard 50, Lormor 54	4748
44	26	EL	A	Bristol Rovers	L 0-1	0-0	6		(3513)
45	30	EL	A	Crewe Alexandra	L 0-3	0-2	6		(4073)
46	A 2	EL	H	Blackpool	W 1-0	0-0	6	Holland 55	7002
47	6	EL	H	Stockport County	L 1-2	0-1	6	McDougald 61	6090
48	9	EL	A	Shrewsbury Town	D 0-0	0-0	6		(3035)
49	13	EL	H	Bristol City	D 1-1	0-1	6	McDougald 61	4619
50	16	EL	H	Walsall	D 1-1	0-1	6	Lormor 51	4508
51	20	EL	A	Bradford City	L 1-2	1-0	9	McDougald 28	(6803)
52	23	EL	H	Swindon Town	L 1-3	1-2	10	Hewitt 30	5523
53	27	EL	A	Bournemouth	L 0-2	0-1	10		(4483)
54	30	EL	A	York City	W 1-0	0-0	8	Lund 70	(2839)
55	M 4	EL	H	Notts County	W 1-0	0-0	7	Law 69(pen)	6708

Best Home League Attendance: 7002 v Blackpool   **Smallest: 3419 v York City**   **Average: 4884**

Goal Scorers:
EL(56):   Lormor(13),Robinson(9),Law(7),Morris(5),Davies(4),McDougald(3),Williams(3),Holland(2),Jules(2),Howard(2),Hewitt(2),Opponent(s)(1),Lund(1),Narbett(1),Curtis(1)
CC(1):   Roberts(1)
FAC(4):   Lormor(2),Davies(2)
AWS(6):   Robinson(2),Roberts(2),Lormor(1),Law(1)

(G) Beasley	(D) Carr	(M) Curtis	(F) Davies	(D) Dyche	(D) Fairclough	(F) Hatherway	(F) Hazel	(D) Hewitt	(M) Holland	(F) Howard	(F) Jules	(D) Law	(M) Lomas	(F) Lormor	(F) Lund	(D) Madden	(F) McDougald	(G) Mercer	(F) Morris	(M) Moss	(M) Narbett	(D) Perkins	(G) Pierce	(F) Roberts	(M) Robinson	(D) Rogers	(D) Williams		
X		X	X	X			S3			X1	X			X		X3			S2		S1	X2			X		X	G.Barber	1
X		X		X			X1	X		X	S			X2					S2		S1	X			X		X	M.Fletcher	2
X		X	X1	X	S			X		S1				X					X2		X	X		S2	X		X	R.Poulain	3
X		X	X	X				X		S3		X									X3	S1			X2	X1	X	R.Gifford	4
X		X	X	X				X		S1		X		X					X		X	X1		S	X	S	X	F.Stretton	5
X		X	X1	X				X		S2	S1	X		X3					X		X	X		S3	X	X2	X	G.Cain	6
X	X	X	X1	X				X		S		X		X					X		S1	S		X	X		X	J.Rushton	7
X3	X	X	X	X			X2	X		S2	S1	X		X					X			S3		X1	X			M.Pierce	8
		X	X	X			X2	X				X		X					S1		S		X	X1	X	X	X	C.Wilkes	9
		X	X	X			S			S	S	X		X			X	X						S	X	X	X	T.West	10
		X	X1	X				X		S1	X	X		X			X	X		S				S	X	X	X	G.Frankland	11
		X1	X2	X				X		S2	X	X		X			X	X3	S1					S3	X	X	X		12
		X3	X	X				X		S3	X2	X		X1			X	X			S2			S1	X	X	X	M.Fletcher	13
		X	X	X				X		S2		X		X			X	X			S			S1	X1	X2	X	R.Furnandiz	14
		X	X	X				X		S1		X		X1			X	X		S	X			X	S	X		J.Rushton	15
		X	X	X				X		X		X1		S			X	X		S2	S1		X2	X	X	X	X	T.Lunt	16
		X	X	X		S		X		X		X		S1			X	X			S		X1	X	X	X	X	M.Bailey	17
		X	X	X		S1		X		X		X		X1			X	X			S		S	X	X	X	X	I.Cruikshanks	18
		X	X	X		S1		X		X3		X		S2			X2	X		S3			X1	X	X	X	X	D.Orr	19
		X	X	X		S1		X		X		X		X1			X	X		S			S	X	X	X	X	B.Knight	20
X		X	X	X		S1		X		X		X		X			S	S		X1			X	X	X		X	P.Danson	21
X		X	X	X		S		X		X		X		X			S	S		X			X	X	X		X	D.Allison	22
X		X	X	X				X		S		X		X			X			S		X	S	X	X	X	X	S.Mathieson	23
X		X	X	X	S					X2		X		X1			X			S2	X		S1	X		X		24
X		X	X	X	S					S1		X		X1			X			X	X		X2	X		X	E.Lomas	25
X		X	X	X	S		X			X1		X		X			X			X			S	X	X	X	N.Barry	26
		X	X	X				X1				S1	X		X			X2	S				X	X	X	X	G.Frankland	27
		X	X	X			S			S2	X		X1	S1			X			X2	X		X	X	X	X	S.Bennett	28
		X	X3		S3		X1					X		X2	X		X			S1	X		S2	X	X	X	E.Wolstenholme	29
		X					X2				X	X	X	S1	X		X			X	X		X	S2	X1	X	K.Leach	30
		X	S1						X	S	X	X	X	S2	X2		X			X	X	X1		X		X	M.Riley	31
		X	X				S1		X	S	X	X	X	X1			X			X	X	S		X		X	T.Leake	32
		X	X	S3				X	S1	X	X	X		X			X			X1	X		S2	X2		X	P.R.Richards	33
		X	X2	S1		S		X	X	X1	X	X		X			X			X			S2	X	X	X	J.Lloyd	34
		X	X	S2				S1	X1	X	X	X		X			X			X			S	X2		X	W.C.Burns	35
		X	X2	S1		S	X1		X	X	X	X		X			X		S2	X			X	X		X	G.R.Pooley	36
		X	X1	X				X2	X	X	X		X			S2	S1	X		S	X		S	X		X	B.Knight	37
		X	X1	X			S2		S1	X	X2	X		X			S3	X	X		X3		X	R.Pearson	38
		X	X				S	S1	X	X	X		X			S2	X		X2	X1		X	T.West	39
		X	X				X	X	S	X	X		X			S1	X	S	X1			X	A.Barry	40
		X	X	S				X	X	X		X			X	X	X		S			X	S.Mathieson	41
		X	X	S			X	X	X		X			X	X	X		S	S		X	R.Furnandiz	42
		X	X				X	S	X		X1	X		X			S2	S1		X2			X	K.J.Breen	43
			X				X	S	X		X	X		X1			S1	S		X			X	C.Wilkes	44
X		X		X		X3	S1	X	S3	X	X2		X1		X	X					S2	X		X	A.D'Urso	45
		X		X					X	S	X	X			X	X		X	X	X		X1	S	X	G.Frankland	46
		X		X			S	X	X	S	X	X			X	X		X				X	S	X	A.Wiley	47
X		X		X			S	X	S	X	S1	X	X			X		X1			X2	S2		X	K.Leach	48
X		X		X		S	X	X	X	X	X	X			X							S	S	X	D.Orr	49
		X		X		S	X	X	X	S		X			X							S1	S	X	T.Heilbron	50
		X		X			X	X1	S2	X		X			X		X				S1	S	X	I.Cruickshanks	51
		X		X		S	S	X		S		X			X		X		X			X	X	X	D.Allison	52
		X		X			S2	X		X		X			X1	X		X2		S1	X	S	X	J.Lloyd	53
		X		X			X	X		X		X		S	X		X2		S1	X		X	S	X	P.Richards	54
	X	S2	X				X1	S1		X	X	X		X	X		S	X			X		X	T.West	55
11	**1**	**45**	**28**	**39**	**0**	**0**	**15**	**23**	**16**	**14**	**27**	**38**	**0**	**37**	**6**	**1**	**9**	**34**	**14**	**6**	**11**	**18**	**1**	**6**	**38**	**20**	**41**	EL Appearances	
0	0	0	2	2	2	0	5	5	1	14	3	0	0	3	1	0	0	0	2	7	6	4	0	8	1	1	0	EL Sub Appearances	
2	1	2	1	2	0	0	1	2	0	1	0	1	0	2	0	0	0	0+2	0	0+1	0	0+1	1	0	1	1	2	CC Appearances	
2	0	2	2	2	0	0	0+1	0	0	1+1	0	0	2	0	2	0	0	0	1	0	1	1	0	2	2	1	2	FAC Appearances	
1	0	5	4	3	0+1	0	1	1	1	3+2	3	4	0	3+1	1	0	0	4	3	0	2+3	3+1	0	1+4	5	2	5	AWS Appearances	

Also Played:

CLUB RECORDS

BIGGEST VICTORIES
League: 10-0 v Glossop, Division 2, 17.1.1903.
F.A. Cup: 5-0 v Wath Athletic (a), 1st Round, 1925-26.
League Cup: 5-0 v Mansfield (a), 1st Round, 1971-72.
5-0 v Scunthorpe United, 1st Round replay, 1972-73.

BIGGEST DEFEATS
League: 0-10 v Gillingham (a), Division 3, 5.9.1987.
F.A. Cup: 1-8 v West Ham United, 1st Round, 1913-14.
0-7 v Burnley, 3rd Round, 1956-57.

MOST POINTS
3 points a win: 91, Division 4, 1984-85.
2 points a win: 64, Division 4, 1969-70.

MOST GOALS SCORED
102, Division 3(N), 1930-31.

RECORD TRANSFER FEE RECEIVED
£200,000 from Wolves for Alan Birch, August 1981.

RECORD TRANSFER FEE PAID
£150,000 to Carlisle United for Phil Bonnyman, March 1980.

BEST PERFORMANCES
League: 4th Division 2, 1946-47.
F.A. Cup: 5th Round 1932-33, 1937-38, 1949-50.
League Cup: 4th Round 1964-65.

HONOURS
Champions Division 3(N) 1930-31, 1935-36.
Champions Division 4, 1969-70, 1984-85.
Anglo-Scottish Cup winners 1980-81.

LEAGUE CAREER
Elected to Div 2 1899, Failed re-election 1908-09, Re-elected to Div 3(N) 1921-22, Div 2 1930-31, Div 3(N) 1932-33, Div 2 1935-36, Div £(N) 1950-51, Transferred to Div 3 1958, Div 4 1960-61, Div 3 1969-70, Div 4 1982-83, Div 3 1984-85, Div 4 (now Div 3) 1988-89, Div 2 1994-95.

INDIVIDUAL CLUB RECORDS

MOST GOALS IN A SEASON
Jimmy Cookson: 46 goals in 1925-26 (League 44, FA Cup 2).

MOST GOALS IN A MATCH
No player has ever scored more than 4 goals in a match, but this feat has been achieved on 19 occasions.

OLDEST PLAYER
Billy Kidd, 40 years 232 days v Southampton, Division 2, 20.9.1947.

YOUNGEST PLAYER
Dennis Thompson, 16 years 160 days v Notts County, Division 2, 26.12.1950.

MOST CAPPED PLAYER
Walter McMillan (Northern Ireland) 4.

PREVIOUS MANAGERS

1945-49 Bob Brocklebank; 1949-52 Bob Marshall; 1952-58 Ted Davison; 1958-62 Dugald Livingstone; 1962-67 Tony McShane; 1967-73 Jimmy McGuigan; 1973-76 Joe Shaw; 1976-80 Arthur Cox; 1980-83 Frank Barlow; 1983-87 John Duncan; 1987-88 Kevin Randall; 1988-91 Paul Hart; 1991-93 Chris McMenemy.

ADDITIONAL INFORMATION
PREVIOUS NAMES
Chesterfield Municipal until 1915, Chesterfield Town 1919-22.

PREVIOUS LEAGUES
Midland League.

Club colours: Blue shirts, white shorts, blue socks.
Change colours: Green & white striped shirts, navy shorts, navy socks.

Reserves League: Pontins League.

LONGEST LEAGUE RUNS

of undefeated matches:	21 (1994-95)	of league matches w/out a win:	16 (1960-61, 1983)
of undefeated home matches:	27 (1925-26)	of undefeated away matches:	12 (1994-95)
without home win:	9 (1963)	without an away win:	26 (1907-08)
of league wins:	10 (1933)	of home wins:	17 (1929-30)
of league defeats:	9 (1960)	of away wins:	6 (1933)

THE MANAGER

JOHN DUNCAN . . . . appointed February 1993.

PREVIOUS CLUBS
As Manager . . . . Hartlepool United, Chesterfield, Ipswich Town.
As Player Manager . . . . Scunthorpe United.
As a player . . . . Dundee, Tottenham Hotspur, Derby County, Scunthorpe United.

HONOURS
As a Manager . . . . Chesterfield: Division 4 Champions 1985. Promotion to Division 2 via the play-offs 1995.
As a Player. . . . . Scottish Football League.

CHESTERFIELD

PLAYERS NAME / Honours	Ht	Wt	Birthdate	Birthplace / Transfers	Contract Date	Clubs	League	L/Cup	FA Cup	Other	Lge	L/C	FAC	Oth
G O A L K E E P E R S														
Beasley Andy	6.2	12.2	05/02/64	Sedgley	23/02/82	Luton Town								
				Free	06/07/84	Mansfield Town	94	5	3	7				
				Loan	28/07/86	Peterborough Utd	7	3						
				Loan	01/03/88	Scarborough	4							
				Loan	01/11/92	Kettering Town			1					
				Loan	25/03/93	Bristol Rovers	1							
				Free	30/07/93	Doncaster Rovers	37	2	1	2				
				Free	12/08/94	Chesterfield	31+1	3	2	6				
Mercer Billy	6.1	11.0	22/05/69	Liverpool	21/08/87	Liverpool								
					16/02/89	Rotherham United	104	12	12	10				
				£75000	12/10/94	Sheffield United	4							
				Loan	21/03/95	Nottingham Forest								
				£100000	12/12/95	Chesterfield	34			4				
D E F E N D E R S														
Carr Darren	6.2	13.0	04/09/68	Bristol	20/08/86	Bristol Rovers	26+4	2+2	3	2				
					30/10/87	Newport County	9							
				£8000	10/03/88	Sheffield United	12+1	1	3+1	1	1			
				£35000	18/09/90	Crewe Alexandra	96+8	8	12	10	5		2	
				£30000	21/07/93	Chesterfield	64	8	3	7	3			
Dyche Sean	6.0	11.7	28/06/71	Kettering	20/05/89	Nottingham Forest								
				Free	01/02/90	Chesterfield	183+12	7	7	16	8			
Jules Mark	5.10	11.1	05/09/71	Bradford	03/07/90	Bradford City		0+1						
				Free	14/08/91	Scarborough	57+20	6+4	1+1	6	16	2		4
				£40000	21/05/93	Chesterfield	65+21	5+7	1+2	7	3	2		
Law Nicholas E: S.	6.0	13.5	08/09/61	Greenwich	17/07/79	Arsenal								
				Free	04/08/81	Barnsley	113+1	5	6		1			
				Free	28/08/85	Blackpool	64+2	2	2	3	1			
				£40000	12/03/87	Plymouth Argyle	37+1	2	2	0+1	5			
				£70000	17/06/88	Notts County	44+3	4	1	4	4			
				Loan	10/11/89	Scarborough	12		1					
				£35000	01/08/90	Rotherham United	126+2	12	12	7	3	1		
					08/10/93	Chesterfield	104	3	3	10	10			3
Perkins Chris	5.11	10.9	09/01/74	Nottingham	19/11/92	Mansfield Town	3+5			0+1				
				Free	15/07/94	Chesterfield	35+5	2	3	6+3			1	
Rogers Lee	5.11	12.1	28/10/66	Doncaster	27/07/84	Doncaster Rovers				1				
				Free	29/08/86	Chesterfield	294+20	16+1	11+1	27+1	1			
Williams Mark S Div.3'94.	6.0	13.0	28/09/70	Hyde		Newtown								
				Free	27/03/92	Shrewsbury Town	98+6	7+1	6	6	3			1
				£20000	07/08/95	Chesterfield	41	1	2	5	3			
M I D F I E L D														
Curtis Tommy	5.8	11.4	01/03/73	Exeter	01/07/91	Derby County								
				Free	12/08/93	Chesterfield	119+2	10	5	10	6	1		
Hewitt Jamie	5.10	10.8	17/05/68	Chesterfield	22/04/86	Chesterfield	240+9	10	8+1	11+2	14	1		
				Free	01/08/92	Doncaster Rovers	32+1	3+1	1	3		1		
					08/10/93	Chesterfield	89+6	6	2	9	7			
Robinson Phillip Div.4'88. Div.3'89. AMC'88'91.	5.9	10.10	06/01/67	Stafford	08/01/85	Aston Villa	2+1				1			
				£5000	03/07/87	Wolves	63+8	6	3	8+2	8	1		
				£67500	18/08/89	Notts County	65+1	6	1+1	9+1	5	1		
				Loan	18/03/91	Birmingham City	9			2+1				
					01/09/92	Huddersfield Town	74+1	4	8	8	4		1	
					09/12/94	Chesterfield	60+1	1	2	8	17			4
				Loan	30/12/94	Telford								
F O R W A R D S														
Davies Kevin	6.0	12.12	26/03/77	Sheffield	18/04/94	Chesterfield	85+10	5+1	3	9+2	19	1	2	1
Holland Paul	5.11	12.10	08/07/73	Lincoln	04/07/91	Mansfield Town	149	11	7	9	25		3	
					01/06/95	Sheffield United	11+7	2			1	1		
				£200000	05/01/96	Chesterfield	16+1			1	2			
Howard Jonathan	5.10	11.7	07/10/71	Sheffield	10/07/90	Rotherham United	25+11	0+1	4	3+1	5		2	
					09/12/94	Chesterfield	15+25	1	1+1	5+3	3			2
Lormor Anthony	6.0	11.5	29/10/70	Ashington	25/02/88	Newcastle United	6+2				3			
				£25000	29/01/90	Lincoln City	90+10	1+2	4	6	30	2	2	
				Loan	03/03/94	Halifax Town								
				Free	04/07/94	Peterborough Utd	2+3		1	1+1				
				Free	23/12/94	Chesterfield	60+3	2	2	6+1	23		2	3
Lund Gary E: u21.1.	6.0	11.0	13/09/64	Grimsby	22/08/86	Lincoln City	41+3	4	1	3	13	1	1	1
				£40000	17/06/87	Notts County	223+25	15+3	13+3	28+6	63	5	4	8
				Loan	14/08/92	Hull City	11				3			
					27/07/93	Grimsby Town	47+13	6+2	4	2	24	1	5	1
				Loan	23/03/95	Hull City	11				3			
Morris Andrew	6.4	15.7	17/11/67	Sheffield	29/07/85	Rotherham United	0+7	0+1						
					12/01/88	Chesterfield	197+31	15+2	10+1	17+4	51	8	3	3
				Loan	04/03/92	Exeter City	4+3				2			

RECREATION GROUND
Chesterfield S40 4SX
Tel: 01246 209 765

Capacity...11,308
Seating...2,608

First game ....v Lincoln City, 9.9.1899.
First floodlit game...v Lincoln City, 23.10.1967.

Attendances
Highest...30,968 v Newcastle United, Division 2, 7.4.1939.
Lowest...1,053 v Burnley, AMC, 21.1.1986.

Other Grounds...None.

MATCHDAY TICKET PRICES

Centre Stand £10
Juv/OAP £5

Wing Stand £9
Juv/OAP £4.50

Family Stand (1 Adult + 2 children) £11

Terraces. £8
Juv/OAP £4

Ticket Office Telephone no. . . . . . . 01246 209 765.

HOW TO GET TO THE GROUND

From the North
Use motorway (M1) until junction 30, then follow signs to Chesterfield (A619). In town centre follow signs to Old Brampton into Saltergate for Chesterfield FC.

From East and South
Follow signs to Chesterfield (A617) into town centre then follow signs to Old Brampton into Saltergate for Chesterfield FC.

From the West
Follow signs to Chesterfield (A619) then at roundabout take first exit into Foljambe Road at the end turn right into Saltergate for Chesterfield FC.

Car Parking
Street parking near ground allowed. Car parks 0.5 miles from ground in Saltergate.

Nearest Railway Station
Chesterfield (01246 74371)

SPIREITES HOTLINE
0891 55 58 18

Calls cost 39p per minute cheap rate and 49p per minute at all other times.
Call costings correct at time of going to press.

MATCHDAY PROGRAMME

Programme Editor . . . . K Barson.

Number of pages . . . . 36.

Price . . . . £1.30.

Subscriptions . . . . £30 + £5 P&P.

Local Newspapers . . . . Derbyshire Times, Sheffield Star,
. . . . Chesterfield Star.

Local Radio Stations . . . . Radio Hallam, Radio BBC Sheffield.

CREWE ALEXANDRA
(The Railwaymen)
NATIONWIDE LEAGUE DIVISION 2
SPONSORED BY: BOLDON JAMES

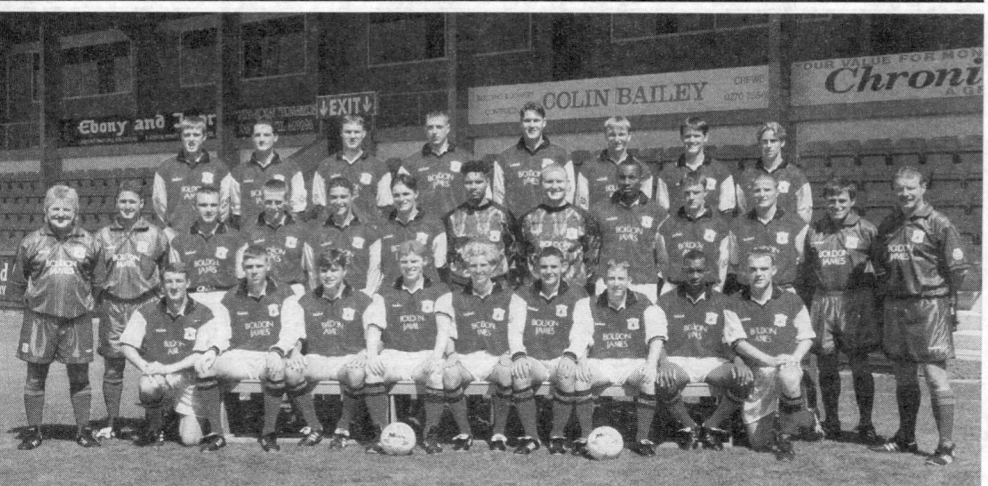

ck Row (L-R): Anthony Hughes, Steve Macauley, Dave Ridings, Danny Collier, Simon Turpin, Francis Tierney, Mark Rivers, Justin Parker.
ddle Row: John Fleet (Kit Manager), Steve Holland (Yth Coach), Rob Edwards, Billy Barr, Lee Unsworth, Steven Pope, Mark Gayle, Mark
nith, Dele Adebola, Ashley Westwood, Shaun Smith, Dario Gradi (Manager), Neil Baker (Asst. Manager).
ont Row: Phil Clarkson, Dale Hawtin, Martyn Booty, Neil Lennon, Robbie Savage, Gareth Whalley, Steve Garvey, Wayne Collins, Danny
urphy.
Photo: Steve Finch LRPS.

CREWE ALEXANDRA
FORMED IN 1877
TURNED PROFESSIONAL IN 1893
LTD COMPANY IN 1892

PRESIDENT: N Rowlinson
CHAIRMAN: J Bowler MPS
VICE-CHAIRMAN
N Hassall FCCA
DIRECTORS
Potts, J McMillan, D Rowlinson, R Clayton,
D Gradi.
SECRETARY
Mrs Gill Palin (01270) 213 014)
MARKETING MANAGER
Alison Bowler

MANAGER: Dario Gradi
ASSISTANT MANAGER: Neil Baker
RESERVE TEAM MANAGER
Neil Baker
YOUTH TEAM MANAGER
Steve Holland
PHYSIOTHERAPIST
Bernadette Oakes
STATISTICIAN FOR THE DIRECTORY
Harold Finch

After seeing their hopes of automatic promotion fade in the later stages of the League programme, Crewe Alexandra once again participated in the play off stages of the promotion battle. Here again, for the second successive season they were unable to progress beyond the Semi-Final stage, this time losing out to Notts County 3-2 on aggregate.

Some consolation can perhaps be gained from the fact that in season 1996-97 they will be appearing in a higher Division for a third successive season following promotion, something the club had not previously managed to do.

Not for the first time, players whose careers have blossomed under manager, Dario Gradi, attracted the attention of other clubs and when Neil Lennon moved to Leicester City, it took a record fee of £750,000 to secure his transfer. Others to move up were Rob Edwards, the leading scorer who went to Huddersfield Town for £150,000 and Martyn Booty to Reading for £70,000.

Another player was to emerge from what has been refered to as "The Crewe Academy", this time it was locally born Mark Rivers who came into the side in October 1995. He quickly made his mark and by the end of the season had become a regular and had also netted 13 League and cup goals. A very promising start in his first ever League season. Newcomer, Ashley Westwood recruited from Manchester United at a fee of £40,000 set by a tribunal, also proved to be an astute signing by the club.

Taking into account cup competitions and the play offs it meant that in all, the club played a total of 60 games. Throughout the whole campaign, just on player, first choice 'keeper Mark Gayle played in them all with Gareth Whalley next with 56. It was perhaps no surprise that Mark was awarded the 'Player of the Year' award from both the senior and junior supporters.

Those cup competitions also gave the players the opportunity of testing themselves against opposition from the Premier League on two occasions. Firstly it was in the Coca-Cola where they played Sheffield Wednesday. Although losing on aggregate 7-4 they acquitted themselves well.

Secondly in the F.A. Cup, after defeated First Division West Bromwich Albion they faced Southampton, at the Dell. They surprised the Saints, holding them to a 1-1 draw. The replay at Gresty Road was an exciting affair, 3-0 down at half-time, Crewe came close to another shock result, coming back to 3-2, the Saints hanging on and hoping for the final whistle.

The clubs disciplinary record was again excellent and the club have secured a hat-trick in winning the Bobby Moore Fair Play Award for a third successive year and making it a double with the Divisional Award from the Endsleigh League. The Manager was also not forgotten, he also won one of the monthly 'Manager of the Month' awards.

HAROLD FINCH.

CREWE ALEXANDRA

M	DATE	COMP	VEN	OPPONENTS	RESULT	HT	LP	GOAL SCORERS/GOAL TIMES	ATT.
1	A 12	EL	A	Wycombe Wanderers	D 1-1	1-0	15	Murphy 13	(5281)
2	23	CC 1/1	H	Darlington	W 4-0	0-0		Unsworth 53, Whalley 61, Collins 70, Adebola 80	2850
3	26	EL	A	York City	W 3-2	1-1	9	Savage 42, Adebola 69, 82	(3880)
4	29	EL	H	Walsall	W 1-0	0-0	8	Edwards 80	4377
5	S 2	EL	A	Stockport County	D 1-1	0-0	8	Tierney 85	(6125)
6	5	CC 1/2	A	Darlington	D 1-1	0-0		Edwards 72	(1084)
7	9	EL	H	Shrewsbury Town	W 3-0	1-0	3	Savage 7, Tierney 54, Westwood 76	3747
8	12	EL	H	Brighton & H.A.	W 3-1	1-0	1	Murphy 42, Savage 47, Macauley 65	3272
9	16	EL	A	Bournemouth	W 4-0	2-0	2	Whalley 32, Morris 34(og), Murphy 57, Savage 67(pen)	(4488)
10	19	CC 2/1	H	Sheffield Wednesday	D 2-2	1-2		Edwards 22, 77	5702
11	23	EL	H	Blackpool	L 1-2	1-0	3	Murphy 32	(7301)
12	26	AWS 1/1	A	Blackpool	L 0-1	0-1			(2560)
13	30	EL	H	Notts County	D 2-2	0-0	4	Westwood 72, Macauley 88	4260
14	O 4	CC 2/2	A	Sheffield Wednesday	L 2-5	2-3		Edwards 9, Lennon 43	(12039)
15	7	EL	A	Chesterfield	W 2-1	0-0	3	Savage 71, Macauley 83	(4981)
16	14	EL	H	Carlisle United	W 2-1	2-1	2	Savage 56(pen), Edwards 59	4512
17	17	AWS 1/1	H	Hartlepool United	W 8-0	0-0		Collins 22, Savage 25, Macauley 27, Whalley 44, Booty 51, Garvey 60, Murphy 69, Rivers 87(pen)	2344
18	21	EL	A	Swindon Town	L 1-2	0-0	3	Garvey 79	(12633)
19	28	EL	H	Brentford	W 3-1	2-0	2	Rivers 15, 38, Westwood 59	3835
20	31	EL	H	Hull City	W 1-0	1-0	2	Edwards 20	3609
21	N 4	EL	A	Rotherham United	D 2-2	1-1	2	Savage 11, Macauley 87	(3328)
22	18	EL	A	Swansea City	W 4-1	2-1	2	Edwards 7, 75, Rivers 38, Murphy 84	3608
23	22	FAC 1	A	Altrincham	W 2-0	0-0		Adebola 63, Unsworth 82	(3062)
24	25	EL	A	Oxford United	L 0-1	0-1	12		(5287)
25	29	AWS 2	A	Burnley	L 0-1	0-0			2596
26	D 2	FAC 2	H	Mansfield Town	W 2-0	1-0		Edwards 39, Rivers 67	3694
27	5	EL	H	Bristol City	W 4-2	0-1	2	Adebola 59, Booty 60, Lennon 85, Edwards 90	2977
28	9	EL	H	Blackpool	L 1-2	1-0	3	Edwards 68	4551
29	16	EL	A	Notts County	W 1-0	1-0	2	Macauley 41	(5869)
30	23	EL	A	Bristol Rovers	W 2-1	0-0	1	Murphy 68, Rivers 72	(4519)
31	26	EL	H	Wrexham	D 0-0	0-0	1		5177
32	J 6	FAC 3	H	West Bromwich Albion	W 4-3	3-1		Adebola 22, Rivers 25, Booty 31, Murphy 58	5750
33	13	EL	A	Bristol City	L 2-3	1-2	2	Booty 18, Westwood 59	(6790)
34	20	EL	H	Wycombe Wanderers	W 2-0	2-0	2	Rivers 37, Lennon 44	4150
35	31	EL	A	Bradford City	L 1-2	0-0	2	Adebola 84	(4095)
36	F 7	FAC 4	A	Southampton	D 1-1	1-0		Whalley 4	(13736)
37	10	EL	A	Burnley	W 1-0	1-0	2	Edwards 22	(9153)
38	13	FAC 4R	H	Southampton	L 2-3	0-3		Edwards 53, Westwood 76	5579
39	17	EL	A	Brighton & H.A.	D 2-2	2-0	2	Edwards 9, 19	(6561)
40	20	EL	H	Stockport County	L 0-1	0-0	3		4241
41	24	EL	H	Bournemouth	W 2-0	0-0	3	Collins 78, Edwards 80	3535
42	27	EL	A	Shrewsbury Town	W 3-2	2-2	3	Murphy 7, Edwards 16, Rivers 89	(3745)
43	M 2	EL	A	Wrexham	W 3-2	2-1	3	Edwards 13, 19, 50	(6112)
44	5	EL	H	York City	D 1-1	0-1	2	Adebola 68	3431
45	9	EL	H	Bristol Rovers	L 1-2	0-0	3	Rivers 51	4091
46	12	EL	A	Walsall	L 2-3	2-1	3	Blissett 8, Whalley 20	(3171)
47	16	EL	A	Peterborough United	L 1-3	0-2	3	Smith 63(pen)	(5004)
48	19	EL	H	Burnley	W 3-1	0-0	3	Garvey 51, Adebola 56, Rivers 88	3393
49	23	EL	H	Bradford City	L 1-2	0-1	3	Adebola 65	3887
50	30	EL	H	Chesterfield	W 3-0	2-0	3	Adebola 5, Murphy 32, 67	4073
51	A 2	EL	A	Carlisle United	L 0-1	0-0	21		(4960)
52	6	EL	A	Brentford	L 1-2	1-0	3	Macauley 3	(4408)
53	8	EL	H	Swindon Town	L 0-2	0-1	4		5162
54	13	EL	A	Hull City	W 2-1	0-0	3	McAllister 61, Murphy 79	(3497)
55	20	EL	A	Rotherham United	L 0-2	0-1	5		3685
56	27	EL	H	Oxford United	L 1-2	0-1	5	Macauley 76	4605
57	30	EL	H	Peterborough United	W 2-1	2-0	5	Rivers 40, Lyttle 42	3206
58	M 4	EL	A	Swansea City	L 1-2	0-1	5	Rivers 58	(2604)
59	12	PO SF1	H	Notts County	D 2-2	2-0		Lyttle 3, Rivers 17	4931
60	15	PO SF2	A	Notts County	L 0-1	0-0			(9640)

Best Home League Attendance: 5177 v Wrexham   Smallest: 2977 v Bristol City   Average: 3973

Goal Scorers:

EL(77): Edwards(15),Murphy(10),Rivers(10),Adebola(8),Macauley(7),Savage(7),Westwood(4),Whalley(2),Booty(2),Garvey(2),Tierney(2),Lennon(2),Opponent(s)(1),Blissett(1), McAllister(1),Collins(1),Lyttle(1),Smith(1)

CC(9): Edwards(4),Unsworth(1),Lennon(1),Whalley(1),Collins(1),Adebola(1)

FAC(11): Edwards(2),Adebola(2),Rivers(2),Unsworth(1),Whalley(1),Westwood(1),Murphy(1),Booty(1)

AWS(8): Collins (1), Savage (1), Macauley (1), Whalley (1), Booty (1), Garvey (1), Murphy (1), Rivers(1)   **PO(2):**   Rivers(1),Lyttle(1)

	(F) Adebola	(M) Barr	(F) Blissett	(D) Booty	(M) Clarkson	(F) Collier	(M) Collins	(F) Edwards	(F) Ellison	(F) Garvey	(G) Gayle	(G) Jones	(D) Lennon	(D) Lightfoot	(M) Lyttle	(D) Macauley	(D) McAllister	(M) Murphy	(M) Pope	(M) Ridings	(D) Rivers	(F) Savage	(D) Smith	(G) Smith	(M) Tierney	(D) Unsworth	(D) Westwood	(M) Whalley	(G) Wilkinson	
S1		X				X	S3		S2	X		X			X		X				X1			X3	X2	X	X			A.Butler 1
S1		X				X			S	X		X			X		X1			X		S		X	X	X	X		S.Baines 2
X2		X				X	S1			X		X			X		S2			X1		S		X	X	X	X		E.Lomas 3
X1						X	S1		S	X		X			X		X			X	S			X	X	X	X		K.Breen 4
S1			X	X1		X	X			X					X		X	S		X		S		X	X	X	X		P.Richards 5
X1			X	S1		X	X			X					X		X					X	S	X	X	X			U.Rennie 6
			X	S2		X1	X			X					X		X			X			S	X2	S1	X	X		G.Cain 7
			X	S2		X1	X2			X					X		X			X			S	X	S1	X	X		K.Lynch 8
			X	S2		X	X2		X						X	X1	X			X			S		S1	X	X		B.Knight 9
			X	S		X	X		X1	X					X		X			X			S		S1	X	X		P.Danson 10
			X	S		X	X			X					X		X			X			S		S1	X	X		R.Pearson 11
X2			X	X1		X		S2	X			X			X		S1			X					X		X		G.Frankland 12
			X			X	X			X		X			X		X			S		X		S	S	X	X		G.Singh 13
			X			X	X			X		X			X		X			S1		X1		S	X	X	X		N.Barry 14
			X			S1	X			X		X			X		X			S		X			X1	X	X		R.Furnandiz 15
			X			X	X1			X	X	X			X		X			S		X			S1	X	X		R.Gifford 16
			X			X	X			X		X			X		X		S	S2		X2			S1	X1	X		17
			X			X	X			X		X		X	X		X			S					S	X	X		G.Barber 18
			X			X	X			X		X		S	X		X			X		X		S	S	X	X		A.Leake 19
			X			X	X			X		X		S	X		X	X1		X2		S2			S1	X	X		D.Allison 20
			X			X	X			X		X		S	X		X			X1	X	S1			S	X	X		F.Stretton 21
S1			X			X	X		S2	X					X		X			X2	X1				X	X	X		P.Taylor 22
S1			X			X2				X		X			X		X			X		X		S2	X	X	X1	S	D.Allison 23
X			X			X	X1		X2	X		X			X		X			S1		X		S	S2	X			U.Rennie 24
S3						X	X		S2	X		X			X		X			X2	X3	X1		S1	X	X		R.Furnandiz 25
X		X			S	X	X1			X		X			X					X					S1	X	X	S	S.Lodge 26
X		X	S			X	X			X		X			X					X	X1	S2			S1	X2	X	S	P.Richards 27
X		X	S			X	X			X		X					X			X			S1		X1	X	X	S	D.Allison 28
X3			X2		S3	X				S1	X		X		X		X			X1			S2			X	X		E.Wolstenholme 29
X1	S		S1			X	X			X2		X			X		X			S2		X				X	X		P.D'Urso 30
X	S					X	X			S1		X			X		X			X1		X				X	X		J.Brandwood 31
X1			X2	S2		X				X		X			X		X			X2		S1			X	X	X	S	G.Cruikshanks 32
X	X		X			X	X1			S1		X			X		X2			X		S		S2		X	X		N.Fletcher 33
X	X				S	X	X2			S1		X			X		X			X1	X	X		S2		X	X		S.Baines 34
X	X					X	X1			S1		X			X		X			X2	S	X		S	S1	X1	X		R.Pearson 35
X	X					X	X2			S2		X			X		X			X	S	X		S1	X1	X	X		P.Alcock 36
X	X				X	X				S2		X			X					X	S	X		X	S1		X1		E.Lomas 37
X	X				X1	X				S1		X			X			S		X	S	X			X	X			P.Alcock 38
X	X					X3				S1		X			X					X2	S2	X		X1	S3	X			I.Hemley 39
X	X					X				S1		X			X					X	X1	S		X1	S	X	X		G.Barber 40
	X					S	X			X		X				S1	X			X1	X	X		X	S	X	X		C.Wilkes 41
	X					X	X2			S2		X				X	X3			S3	X2	X		X	X1	X	X		P.R.Richards 42
	X						X			X3		X				S3	X			S2	X2	X		X	X	X1	X		M.A.Riley 43
S1	X					X	X			X2		X					X			S2	X1	X		X	X		X		B.Knight 44
X	X					S	X			X2		X			S2		X			X	S1	X1		X			X		K.Leach 45
S2	X					S1	X			X		X				X1	X			X	S	X		X2			X		M.Bailey 46
S1	X	X				S				X		X					X	S		X1	X	X		X	X		X		G.Frankland 47
S1	X	X					S2			X		X			X1		X			S3	X3	X		X3	X		X		J.Lloyd 48
X	X	X				S1				X		X	S				X			S2	X2	X		X	X		X		R.Gifford 49
X	X1					S2				X		X	X		S1		X	X2		S	X	X		X	X		X		A.D'Urso 50
	X					S1				X3		X	X1		S2		X			S3	X2	X		X	X		X		J.Kirby 51
X2	X					S1				X		X					X	X		S2	S	X		X1	X		X		R.Harris 52
X1	S	X				X				X		X		S1	X		X	S		X	X	X		X			X		T.Heilbron 53
S2	S1	X1				X				X		X			X		X			X2	X	X		X			X		R.Furnandiz 54
S2		X2				X				X		X			S1	X1	X			X	X	X	S	X			X		S.Mathieson 55
		X1				X		S		X		X			X	X	S1			X	X2	X		X			X		K.Breen 56
						X		S		X		X			X2	X2	X			X	X1	X1		X			X		G.Cain 57
	S2					X			S1	X		X			X	X3	X2	X		X2	X	X		S3	X	X	X1		M.Pierce 58
			S3			S1				X		X			X	X	X	X3		X2	X	X		S2	X	X	X1		D.Allison 59
X	S2					X3				X		X			X	X	X		X2	S1	X	X		S3	X	X			K.Lynch 60
20	15	10	21	1	2	38	29	0	18	46	0	25	5	7	27	13	41	0	1	24	29	24	0	21	15	31	44	0	EL Appearances
9	2	0	0	4	4	5	3	1	11	0	0	0	1	5	2	0	1	0	0	9	2	5	0	1	13	2	0	0	EL Sub Appearances
4	0	0	4	0+1	0	3	3	0	2	4	0	4	0	0	4	0	4	0	0	0+1	0	4	0	0	2	4	4	0	CC Appearances
4+1	2	0	3	0+1	1	4	5	0	0+2	5	0	5	0	0	5	0	3	0	0	5	1	2+2	0	0+1	3+1	5	4	0	FAC Appearances
1+1	0	2	1	0	3	2	0+1	2+1	3	0	3	0	0	3	0	2+1	0	0	1+1	3	1	0	0	1+2	2	3	0		AWS Appearances
1	0+1	1+1	0	0	0	1+1	0	0	2	0	0	2	1	2	2	1	0	1	1+1	2	0	0	0+2	2	2	1	0		PO Appearances

Also Played: (M) Bell S(6). (M) Hawtin S(12,14,44).

CLUB RECORDS

BIGGEST VICTORIES
League: 8-0 v Rotherham United, Division 3(N), 1.10.1932.
F.A. Cup: 7-1 v Gresley Rovers, 1st Round, 12.11.1994.
5-0 v Druids, 1st Round, 1887-88.
5-0 v Billingham Synthonia 1st Round, 1948-49.
6-1 v Wrexham, 1st Round, 14.11.1992.
6-1 v Accrington Stanley, 2nd Round, 5.12.1992.
AMC: 6-0 v Chester City (a), 2nd Round, 29.11.1994.
BIGGEST DEFEATS
League: 1-11 v Lincoln City, Division 3(N), 29.9.1951.
F.A. Cup: 2-13 v Tottenham Hotspur, 4th Round replay, 3.2.1960.

MOST POINTS
3 points a win: 83, Division 2, 1994-95
2 points a win: 59, Division 4, 1962-63.

MOST GOALS SCORED: 95, Division 3(N), 1931-32.

RECORD TRANSFER FEE RECEIVED
£750,000 from Leicester City for Neil Lennon.

RECORD TRANSFER FEE PAID
£80,000 to Barnsley for Darren Foreman, March 1990.
£80,000 to Leicester City for Ashley Ward, December 1992.

BEST PERFORMANCES
League: 10th Division 2, 1892-93.
F.A. Cup: Semi-Final 1888.
League Cup: 3rd Round 1960-61, 1974-75, 1975-76, 1978-79, 1992-93. Welsh Cup: Winners (2).
HONOURS
Welsh Cup Winners 1936, 1937.

LEAGUE CAREER
Original members of Div 2 1892, Failed to gain re-election 1896, re-joined Div 3(N) 1921, Transferred to Div 4 1958, Div 3 1962-63, Div 4 1963-64, Div 3 1967-68, Div 4 1968-69, Div 3 1988-89, Div 4 (now Div 3) 1990-91, Div 2 1993-94.

INDIVIDUAL CLUB RECORDS

MOST GOALS IN A SEASON
Terry Harkin: 35 goals in 1964-65, Division 4.

MOST GOALS IN A MATCH
5. Tony Naylor v Colchester United, 7-1, Division 3, 24.4.1993.

OLDEST PLAYER
Kenny Swain, 39 years 281 days v Maidstone, 5.11.1991.

YOUNGEST PLAYER
Steve Walters, 16 years 119 days v Peterborough United, 6.5.1988.

MOST CAPPED PLAYER
Bill Lewis (Wales) 12.
J.H.Pearson (England) 1.

PREVIOUS MANAGERS

(Since 1946)
George Lillycrop, Frank Hill, Arthur Turner, Harry Catterick, Ralph Ward, Maurice Lindley, Harry Ware, Jimmy McGuigan, Ernie Tagg, Dennis Violete, Jimmy Melia, Ernie Tagg, Harry Gregg, Warwick Rimmer, Tony Waddington, Arfon Griffths, Peter Morris.

ADDITIONAL INFORMATION
PREVIOUS NAMES
None.

PREVIOUS LEAGUES
Central League.

Club colours: Red shirts, white shorts, red socks.
Change colours: White shirts, white or red shorts.

Reserves & 'A' Team League: Lancashire League.

LONGEST LEAGUE RUNS

of undefeated matches:	14 (1990)	of league matches w/out a win:	30 (1956-57)
of undefeated home matches:	28 (1967-68)	of undefeated away matches:	7 (1966-67, 1990, 1993)
without home win:	15 (1979)	without an away win:	56 (1955-57)
of league wins:	7 (1928-29, 1986)	of home wins:	16 (1938)
of league defeats:	10 (1923, 1957-58, 1979)	of away wins:	5 (1986)

THE MANAGER

DARIO GRADI . . . . appointed May 1983.

PREVIOUS CLUBS
As Manager . . . . Wimbledon, Crystal Palace.
As Asst.Man/Coach . . . . Chelsea, Derby County, Wimbledon, Orient (Youth Team).
As a player . . . . Sutton United.

HONOURS
As a Manager . . . . Wimbledon: Promotion to Division 3, 1978-79.
. . . . Crewe: Promotion to Division 3, 1989-90. Promotion to Division 2 (what was Div 3) 1993-94.
As a Player . . . . England Semi-Professional.

CREWE ALEXANDRA

PLAYERS NAME / Honours	Ht	Wt	Birthdate	Birthplace / Transfers	Contract Date	Clubs	League	L/Cup	FA Cup	Other	Lge	L/C	FAC	Oth
GOALKEEPERS														
ayle Mark S R	6.2	12.3	21/10/69	Bromsgrove	01/07/88	Leicester City								
				Free	15/08/89	Blackpool		1						
				Free	01/07/90	Worcester City								
				£15000	08/05/91	Walsall	74+1	8	1	8				
				£35000	21/12/93	Crewe Alexandra	78+1	4	5	9				
DEFENDERS														
ghtfoot Chris	6.1	12.0	01/04/70	Penketh	11/07/88	Chester City	263+14	15+2	16+2	14+2	32	1	1	5
				£87500	13/07/95	Wigan Athletic	11+3	2	2	3	1			
				£50000	22/03/96	Crewe Alexandra	5+1			2				
acauley Steven R	6.1	12.0	04/03/69	Lytham	01/08/86	Fleetwood Town			1					
VC'86.					05/11/87	Manchester City								
				£25000	24/03/92	Crewe Alexandra	121+2	10	8	15	19			3
vers Mark A			26/11/75	Crewe	06/05/94	Crewe Alexandra	24+9	0+1	5	2+2	10		2	2
nith Gareth Shaun	5.10	11.0	09/04/71	Leeds	01/07/89	Halifax Town	6+1			1				
				Free	01/08/90	Emley								
				Free	31/12/91	Crewe Alexandra	142+15	3+1	7+2	15+1	20		2	1
rpin Simon A			11/08/75	Blackburn	10/03/94	Northwich								
					20/08/94	Crewe Alexandra								
				Loan	30/12/94	Chorley								
sworth Lee P			25/02/73	Eccles		Ashton								
					17/02/94	Crewe Alexandra	15+13	2+1	3+1	3+2		1	1	
stwood Ashley	6.0	11.3	31/08/76	Bridgnorth	01/07/94	Manchester United								
				£40000	28/07/95	Crewe Alexandra	31+2	4	5	4	4		1	
MIDFIELD														
rr William J	5.11	10.8	21/01/69	Halifax	06/07/88	Halifax Town	178+18	8+1	11+1	14+3	13	2	2	
				Free	17/06/94	Crewe Alexandra	44+7	2	2	6+1	2			
ll Chris						Crewe Alexandra (T)								
llins Wayne A	6.0	12.0	04/03/69	Manchester		Winsford United								
				£10000	29/07/93	Crewe Alexandra	103+15	5	8+1	14+1	14	1		2
rphy Daniel B	5.9	10.8	18/03/77	Chester	21/03/94	Crewe Alexandra	66+23	5	3	9+2	17		1	2
pe Steven						Crewe Alexandra (T)								
rney Francis	5.10	11.0	10/09/75	Liverpool		Crewe Alexandra (T)								
alley Gareth	5.10	11.6	19/12/73	Manchester	29/07/92	Crewe Alexandra	118+6	9+1	11+1	18	5	1	4	3
FORWARDS														
ebola Bamberdele	6.3	12.6	23/06/75	Liverpool	21/06/93	Crewe Alexandra	45+21	1+2	5+1	6+1	15	1	2	2
				Loan	02/02/94	Northwich								
rvey Stephen H	5.9	10.9	22/11/73	Stalybridge	25/10/91	Crewe Alexandra	51+28	6+4	2+3	7+1	6	2	1	1
tle Colin						Crewe Alexandra (T)	7+5			1	1			1
ralee Jamie	5.11	11.0	02/12/71	Wansworth	03/07/90	Crystal Palace (T)	25+5	4	3		4			
				P.E.	03/09/92	Millwall	56+11	3+1	1	3+1	19	1		
				£450000	13/07/94	Watford	17+8	2+1	2		3			
				Free	06/08/96	Crewe Alexandra								
vage Robert	6.0	10.1	18/10/74	Wrexham	05/07/93	Manchester United								
Y.S. FAYC'92.				Free	22/07/94	Crewe Alexandra	34+3	3	1	5	9			1

GRESTY ROAD

Crewe, Cheshire CW2 6EB
Tel: 01270 213 014

Capacity 6,000

First game...v Basford, 1877.
First floodlit game ....v All Stars XI, 29.10.1958.

ATTENDANCES
Highest ....20,000 v Tottenham, FA Cup 4th Round, 30.1.1960.
Lowest ....994 v Stockport, AMC, 14.1.1986.

OTHER GROUNDS..Earle Street, Edleston Road, Nantwich Road.

MATCHDAY TICKET PRICES

Ringwings Stand	£9.50
Juv/OAP	£5/£7
Family Stand	£9.50
Juv/OAP	£5/£7
South Stand	£9.50
Juv/OAP	£5/£7
Paddock.	£8
Juv/OAP	£5/£6
Gresty Road Visitors Stand	£9.50
Juv/OAP	£7
Ticket Office (Club Shop) 01270 252610	

HOW TO GET TO THE GROUND

From the North
Use motorway (M6) until junction 17 and follow signs to Crewe (A534). At Crewe roundabout follow signs to Chester into Nantwich Road. Then take next turning on left into Gresty Road for Crewe Alexandra FC.

From the East and South
Use A52 then A5020 (sign posted Crewe), then at Crewe roundabout follow signs to Chester into Nantwich Road. Then take next turning on left into Gresty Road for Crewe Alexandra FC.

From the West
Use A534 (sign posted Crewe) and immediately before Crewe Railway Station turn right into Gresty Road for Crewe Alexandra FC.

Car Parking
Barker Street

Nearest Railway Station
Crewe (5mins) 01270 255 245)

CLUB CALL
0891 12 16 47

Calls cost 39p per minute cheap rate and 49p per minute at all other times.
Call costings correct at time of going to press.

MATCHDAY PROGRAMME

Programme Editor . . . . Harold Finch.

Number of pages . . . . 32.

Price . . . . £1.50.

Subscriptions . . . . . Subscription rates on request from the club editor.

Local Newspapers . . . . Crewe Chronicle, Crewe Guardian,
. . . . Evening Sentinel, Hanley.

Local Radio Stations . . . . Radio Stoke (94.6 FM),
. . . . Signal Radio 102.6 & 96.9 FM.

GILLINGHAM
(The Gills)
NATIONWIDE LEAGUE DIVISION 2
SPONSORED BY: INVICTA RADIO FM 103.1 + 102.8

...ck Row (L-R): Dominic Naylor, Joe Dunne, Neil Smith, Richard Carpenter, John Byrne, Jim Stannard, Rusell Eggleton, Steve Brown, ...ott Linsey, Gary Micklewhite, Mark O'Connor. **3rd Row:** Malcolm Machin (Yth De. Officer), Wayne Jones (Physio), Andy Arnott, Darren ...eeman, Dave Martin, Lindsay Parsons (Asst. Manager), Tony Butler, Mark Harris, Richard Green, Simon Ratcliffe, Tony Pullis (Manager), ...vin Bremner. **2nd Row:** Lee Quigley, Sam Tydeman, Paul Watson, Leo Fortune-West, Paul Wilson, Paul Scally (Chairman/Chief ...ecutive), Dennis Bailey, Adrian Foster, Kevin Rattray, Steve Norman, Chris Hall, Craig Roser. **Front Row:** Kevin Clifford, Adam Flanagan, ...e Spiller, Jay Saunders, Darren Smith, Lee Bacon, Tommy Butler, Mark Barnes, Andrew Sambrooke, Roland Edge.

GILLINGHAM
FORMED IN 1893
TURNED PROFESSIONAL IN 1894
LTD COMPANY IN 1893

PRESIDENT: J W Leech
CHAIRMAN/CHIEF EXECUTIVE
Paul Scally

DIRECTORS
A Smith FRICS, P Spokes FCCA
SECRETARY
Gwen Poynter
COMMERCIAL MANAGER
Mike Ling

MANAGER: Tony Pulis
ASSISTANT MANAGER: Lindsay Parsons
YOUTH TEAM MANAGER
Kevin Bremner

PHYSIOTHERAPIST
Javed Mughal

STATISTICIAN FOR THE DIRECTORY
Roger Triggs

What a remarkable story for Gillingham during the 1995/6 season! Having been only two hours from closure during the summer it seems impossible that we will be playing Second Division football this coming season, after businessman Paul Scally turned the club around.

Much of the credit must also go to manager Tony Pulis and his backroom staff. During the summer he made eight new signings, and after four games we had a 100% record and led the table. In fact, Gillingham never dropped below third place - a true record of consistency. Attendances rose by over 100% - often the gates were closed - and this helped the club pay for players of such calibre as Dennis Bailey, Steve Butler and David Puttnam.

The club's success was built around its defensive record: goalkeeper Jim Stannard and his back four conceded only 20 goals, beating Port Vale's record of the 1950s. The only black spot was the club's disciplinary record, where they had over 100 yellow cards and seven red. Tony Pulis has gone on record as saying that we would have won the division by miles had it not been for the suspensions and injuries. At least there was some consolation for him when he was named 'Third Division Manager of the Year'.

Apart from the league, it was only in the FA Cup where the club made any progress, going out to Reading in the third round of an ill-tempered game at Elm Park - but, the club's priority was always the league.

Priestfield Stadium is also getting a new lease of life. The main stand has been gutted with new changing rooms and offices, and plans are advanced for a 2,600-seater stand the whole length of Gordon Road. Exciting times are ahead for Kent's only Football League side!

ROGER TRIGGS

GILLINGHAM

League: 2nd   FA Cup: 3rd Rnd   Coca-Cola Cup: 1st Rnd   Auto Windscreen Shield: 1st Rnd

M	DATE	COMP	VEN	OPPONENTS	RESULT	HT	LP	GOAL SCORERS/GOAL TIMES	ATT.
1	A 12	EL	H	Wigan Athletic	W 2-1	0-1	5	Foster 48, Fortune-West 67	4101
2	15	CC 1/1	H	Bristol Rovers	D 1-1	0-0		Naylor 70	3827
3	19	EL	A	Lincoln City	W 3-0	1-0	2	Fortune-West 44, Bailey 66, Brightwell 81(og)	(2822)
4	23	CC 1/2	A	Bristol Rovers	L 2-4	1-1		Bailey 23, Fortune-West 83	(3602)
5	26	EL	H	Cambridge United	W 3-0	0-0	1	Fortune-West 57, Bailey 67, Rattray 90	5093
6	29	EL	A	Barnet	W 2-0	1-0	1	Rattray 12, Naylor 66	(3077)
7	S 2	EL	H	Colchester United	L 0-1	0-0	1		7684
8	9	EL	A	Scunthorpe United	D 1-1	1-1	1	Bailey 7	(2423)
9	12	EL	A	Hereford United	D 0-0	0-0	1		(1747)
10	16	EL	H	Cardiff City	W 1-0	1-0	2	Fortune-West 35	5317
11	23	EL	A	Chester City	D 1-1	0-0	2	Martin 85	(3886)
12	30	EL	H	Bury	W 3-0	0-0	1	Bailey 51, Fortune-West 79, 82	6125
13	O 7	EL	H	Rochdale	W 1-0	1-0	1	Watson 27	7785
14	14	EL	A	Darlington	L 0-1	0-1	1		(2043)
15	17	AWS 1/2	A	Cardiff City	L 2-3	0-0		Freeman 46, Foster 47	(1034)
16	21	EL	H	Doncaster Rovers	W 4-0	1-0	1	O'Connor 25, Ratcliffe 50, Bailey 63, Harris 77	6307
17	28	EL	A	Hartlepool United	D 1-1	1-0	1	Bailey 40(pen)	(2355)
18	31	EL	A	Exeter City	D 0-0	0-0	1		(3024)
19	N 4	EL	H	Northampton Town	D 0-0	0-0	3		7207
20	7	AWS 1/2	H	Hereford United	D 2-2	0-0		Foster 46, Butler 47	1866
21	13	FAC 1	A	Wycombe Wanderers	D 1-1	0-0		Bailey 79	(5064)
22	18	EL	A	Scarborough	W 2-0	2-0	2	Green 26, Fortune-West 29	(1546)
23	21	FAC 1R	H	Wycombe Wanderers	W 1-0	1-0		Howard 8(og)	8585
24	25	EL	H	Fulham	W 1-0	0-0	2	Fortune-West 85	7704
25	D 2	FAC 2	H	Hitchin	W 3-0	0-0		Fortune-West 53, 84, Ratcliffe 75	7142
26	16	EL	A	Bury	L 0-1	0-0	3		(3035)
27	23	EL	A	Preston North End	D 0-0	0-0	3		(10669)
28	26	EL	H	Plymouth Argyle	W 1-0	0-0	1	Butler 83(pen)	9651
29	J 1	EL	A	Leyton Orient	W 1-0	1-0	1	Fortune-West 22	(7098)
30	6	FAC 3	A	Reading	L 1-3	1-0		Martin 34	(10324)
31	9	EL	H	Chester City	W 3-1	0-0	1	Butler 49, 56, 66	9191
32	13	EL	H	Lincoln City	W 2-0	1-0	1	Fortune-West 14, Ratcliffe 82	8047
33	20	EL	A	Wigan Athletic	L 1-2	1-1	1	Green 2	(2773)
34	30	EL	H	Mansfield Town	W 2-0	2-0	1	Rattray 15, Butler 23	6116
35	F 3	EL	A	Cambridge United	D 0-0	0-0	1		(4114)
36	10	EL	H	Torquay United	W 2-0	2-0	1	Smith 6, Ratcliffe 26	7110
37	13	EL	H	Barnet	W 1-0	1-0	1	Butler 10	6433
38	17	EL	H	Hereford United	D 1-1	0-1	1	Castle 55	6993
39	24	EL	A	Cardiff City	L 0-2	0-0	1		(2994)
40	27	EL	H	Scunthorpe United	D 0-0	0-0	1		5557
41	M 2	EL	A	Plymouth Argyle	L 0-1	0-0	1		(8485)
42	9	EL	H	Preston North End	D 1-1	0-0	1	Harris 72	10602
43	12	EL	A	Torquay United	D 0-0	0-0	1		(1406)
44	16	EL	A	Mansfield Town	W 1-0	1-0	1	Gayle 25	(2698)
45	23	EL	H	Leyton Orient	D 1-1	0-0	1	Gayle 54	8071
46	30	EL	A	Rochdale	L 0-2	0-2	2		(2098)
47	A 2	EL	H	Darlington	D 0-0	0-0	2		6426
48	6	EL	H	Hartlepool United	W 2-0	1-0	2	Butler 39, Bailey 63	6267
49	8	EL	A	Doncaster Rovers	W 1-0	1-0	2	Bailey 10	(1873)
50	13	EL	H	Exeter City	W 1-0	0-0	2	Puttnam 75	7698
51	16	EL	A	Colchester United	D 1-1	0-0	1	Gayle 58	(4952)
52	20	EL	A	Northampton Town	D 1-1	1-0	2	Fortune-West 8	(7427)
53	27	EL	A	Fulham	D 0-0	0-0	2		(10320)
54	M 4	EL	H	Scarborough	W 1-0	1-0	2	Fortune-West 21	10421

Best Home League Attendance: 10602 v Preston North End   Smallest: 4101 v Wigan Athletic   Average: 7213

Goal Scorers:
EL(49): Fortune-West(12),Bailey(8),Butler(5),Rattray(3),Ratcliffe(3),Gayle(3),Green(2),Harris(2),Butler(2),Puttnam(1),Naylor(1),O'Connor(1),Foster(1),Castle(1),
Smith(1),Martin(1),Watson(1),Opponent(s)(1)
CC(3): Bailey(1),Naylor(1),Fortune-West(1)
FAC(6): Fortune-West(2),Bailey(1),Martin(1),Ratcliffe(1),Opponent(s)(1)
AWS(4): Foster(2),Freeman(1),Butler(1)

(F) Ansah	(F) Bailey	(M) Bremner	(F) Brown	(D) Butler	(F) Butler	(M) Carpenter	(M) Castle	(F) Dunne	(F) Fortune-West	(F) Foster	(F) Freeman	(F) Gayle	(D) Green	(M) Harris	(D) Manuel	(D) Martin	(M) Micklewhite	(D) Naylor	(F) O'Connor	(M) Puttnam	(D) Ratcliffe	(M) Rattray	(D) Smith	(G) Stannard	(D) Thomas	(D) Watson	(D) Watson	(F) Wilson	Player	#
		S2		X				X	X	X2			X1	X		X		X3	X		X		X	X	X			S3	P.Taylor	1
	X			X				X1	S1				X	X				X3	X		X		S	X	X			S	B.Knight	2
	X			X1					X2	S2			X	X		X3			X		X		X	S3	X	X		S1	R.Pearson	3
	X			X			S		X	S1			X	X					X		X	X1	X	X	X	X			R.J.Harris	4
	X			X			S		S	S			X	X					X		X	X	X	X	X	X		S	I.Hemley	5
	X1			X			S		X	S1			X	X					X		X	X1	X	X	X	X			G.Barber	6
	X			X		S			X	S1			X	X			S2		X		X	X1	X2	X	X				M.Pearce	7
	X2			X1		S1			X	S2			X	X					X		X	X	X	X	X				S.Baines	8
	X			X			S		X	S1			X	X					X		X	X1	X	X	X		X		J.Lloyd	9
	X								X1	S1			X	X		S	S			X	X	X	X	X	X	X		A.Wiley	10
	X								X	S1			X	X		S2	S	X1			X	X2	X	X	X	X			J.Rushton	11
	X1								X	S1			X	X		S1	S1	X			X	X1	X1	X	X	X			G.Pooley	12
	X								X				X	X		X1					X	X	X	X	X	X			N.D.Durso	13
	X	S2							X				X	X		X3		X	X1	S1	X	S3	X	X		X2			A.Butler	14
				X		X		S1		X2	X		X	X		X	X				X3	X1	S3	X		X				15
	X			S							S		X	X		X	X	X	S		X	X	X	X	X				F.Streeton	16
	X			X					X2					X		X2	S1	X1	X		S2	X		X	X	X			N.Barry	17
	X			X				S	X	S1				X		X	X1	X			X		X	X	X	X2	S2		J.Brandwood	18
	X			S						S1	X1		X	X		X2	S2	X			X		X	X	X	X			M.Pierce	19
		S1		X		X		X		X1	X		X	S		X	X				X		X	S			X			20
	X							S			S2		X	X		X	X1	X	S1		X	X2		X		X	X		D.Gallagher	21
	X			X					X3	S3			X	X		X	X2			S2	X	X1	S1	X1	S3	X	X			T.Heilbron	22
	X			X				S	X				X	X		X	X				X	S1	X	X		X			F.Stretton	23
	X	S2							X	S			X	X		X		X2			S1		X	X			X1		M.Bailey	24
	X	S1							X	S			X	X1		X	X				X		X	X			X		M.Pearce	25
	X			X	X				X				X	X		X2	S2	X			S1	X	X1	X					T.West	26
	X			X	X			S	S1				X	X		X	X	X			X1		X	X					T.Heilbron	27
	X			X	X				S1				X	X		X	X2	X			X1		X	X	S2	X			G.Pooley	28
	X1			X	X				X				X	X		X	S1	X			S		X	X		X			I.Hemley	29
	X			X			S2	S3	X				X	X		X	X1	X2			S1	X3	X	X		X			P.Alcock	30
	X			X1	X2				X				X	X		X	S1	X			S2		X	X		X			I.Hemley	31
	X3			X	X				X2				X	X		X1	S1	X			S2	X	S3	X		X			A.D'Urso	32
	X			X	X1		S2	S		X			X			X					X2	X	X		X	X		S1	A.Pearson	33
	X			X	X1			X3	X2				X	X		S1	X2				S2	X	X		X	X	X	X	A.Wiley	34
S2	X2			X			S1	S2	X				X	X			X3				X1	X	X		X		S3		N.Barry	35
S1	X			X	X1				X				X	X			S1				S	X	X		X	X		S	K.Breen	36
	X3			X	X				X1				X	X			S1				S3	X	X1	X		X	X		G.Barber	37
	X			X	X2	X					S2		X	X		X3	X	S1			S3		X		X	X1			P.Taylor	38
	X			X		S	X				X		X	X		X	X1	X			S1		X		X	X			J.Rushton	39
	X2			X		S	X				S2	X	X	X		X	X1	X			S1		X		X	X			S.Madison	40
	S1			X	X	X		X				X1	X2	X	S	X		X				S2	X	X					G.Singh	41
	X			X1	X	X3			X2		S3		X	X		X		X			S1	S2	X	X					M.Pierce	42
	X			X	X		S1		X2					X		X1	S2	X1			S	X		X		X	X	X	R.Gifford	43
	S2			X			X3		X2			X		X		X	S1	X1			S3	X		X		X	X	X	G.Cain	44
	X1			X		S1	S						X	X		X	S2	X			X2		X		X	X	X		D.Orr	45
	S3			X			X						X	X	X2	X	X1	X			X	S1	X		X				J.Kirkby	46
	S2			X2			X2		X1				X	X	S2	X		X			X	X	X	X					J.Brandwood	47
	S2			X			X2		S3			X3	X1	X	X	X	S1				X	X	X	X					A.Butler	48
S	X			X			X		X		S2	X2	X	S1		X				X		X	X1	X	X				W.Burns	49
	X			X			S1	S	S2			X2	X		X	X				S1	X		X	X	X				G.Pooley	50
S	X			X			S2		X2				X	X	X1	X	X		S1			X	X1	X	X	X			P.Richards	51
	X			X			S1	S3	X1				X	X	X3	X	X2	S2			X	X	X	X	X				D.Allison	52
	X2			S1					X1				X	X		X	X				S2	X	X	X	X			S	R.Gifford	53
	X		X3	S1					X			X1	X	X	X	X1	X				X	X	S1	X	S3				K.Leach	54
0	40	0	0	34	14	7	5	1	36	1	4	9	35	44	6	27	17	30	18	10	41	18	36	46	14	10	3	0	EL Appearances	
2	5	0	1	2	6	5	1	1	4	10	6	0	0	0	4	4	14	1	0	16	0	8	1	0	1	0	5	0	EL Sub Appearances	
0	2	0	2	2	0	0	0	0	2	0+2	0	2	2	0	1	0	2	2	0	2	1	1	2	0	0	0	0	0	CC Appearances	
0	4	0	0	1+1	0	0+1	0	0+1	3	0	0+1	0	4	4	0	4	4	3	2	0+3	3	2	4	4	0	0	0	0	FAC Appearances	
0	0	0+1	0	2	0	2	0	1+1	0	2	2	0	2	0	0	1	2	1	0	1	0	2	0+1	1	0	0	2	0	AWS Appearances	

Also Played: (F) Arnot S1(1), S2(15). (G) Glass S(27,28). (G) Nicholls S(20).

CLUB RECORDS

BIGGEST VICTORIES
League: 10-0 v Chesterfield, Division 3, 5.9.1987 (Div. 3 record).
F.A. Cup: 10-1 v Gorleston (h), 1st Round, 16.11.1957.

BIGGEST DEFEATS
League: 0-8 v Luton Town, Division 3(S), 14.4.1929.
League Cup: 0-6 v Oxford United, 2nd Round, 24.9.1986.

MOST POINTS
3 points a win: 83, Division 3, 1984-85.
2 points a win: 62, Division 4, 1973-74.

RECORD TRANSFER FEE RECEIVED
£300,000 from Tottenham Hotspur for Peter Beadle, June 1992.

RECORD TRANSFER FEE PAID
£102,500 to Tottenham Hotspur for Mark Cooper, October 1987.

MOST GOALS IN A SEASON
Ernie Morgan: 33 goals in 1954-55 (League 31, FA Cup 2).

BEST PERFORMANCES
League: 4th Division 3, 1978-79, 1984-85.
F.A. Cup: 5th Round 1969-70.
League Cup: 4th Round 1963-64.

HONOURS
Champions of Division 4, 1963-64.

LEAGUE CAREER
Original members of Div 3 1920, Transferred to Div 3(S) 1921, Failed to gain re-election 1938, Southern League 1938-44, Kent League 1944-46, Southern League 1946-50, Re-elected to Div 3(S) 1949, Transferred to Div 4 1958, Div 3 1963-64, Div 4 1970-71, Div 3 1973-74, Div 4 (now Div 3) 1988-89, Div 2 1995-96.

INDIVIDUAL CLUB RECORDS

MOST GOALS IN A MATCH
6. Fred Cheesmur v Merthyr Town (h), 6-0, Division 3(S), 26.4.1930.

OLDEST PLAYER
John Simpson, 39 years 137 days.

YOUNGEST PLAYER
Billy Hughes, 15 years 275 days v Southend, 13.4.1976.

MOST CAPPED PLAYER
Tony Cascarino (Eire) 3.

PREVIOUS MANAGERS

(Since 1920)
1920-23 John McMillian, 1923-26 Harry Curtis, 1926-30 Albert Hoskins, 1930-32 Dick Hendrie, 1932-37 Fred Mavern, 1937-38 Alan Ure, 1938-39 Bill Harvey, 1939-58 Archie Clark, 1958-62 Harry Barratt, 1962-66 Freddie Cox, 1966-71 Basil Hayward, 1971-74 Andy Nelson, 1974-75 Len Ashurst, 1975-81 Gerry Summers, 1981-87 Keith Peacock, Paul Taylor 1987-88, 1988-89 Keith Burkinshaw, 1989-92 Damien Richardson, 1992-93 Glenn Roeder, 1993-95 Mike Flanagan, Neil Smillie 1995.

ADDITIONAL INFORMATION
PREVIOUS NAMES
New Brompton 1893-1913.

PREVIOUS LEAGUES
Southern League, Kent League.

Club colours: Blue shirts, white shorts, white socks.
Change colours: Red shirts, red shorts, red socks.

Reserves League: Capital League.
Youth League: South East Counties.

LONGEST LEAGUE RUNS

of undefeated matches:	20 (1973-74)	of league matches w/out a win:	15 (1972)
of undefeated home matches:	48 (1963-65)	of undefeated away matches:	10 (1973-74)
without home win:	9 (1961)	without an away win:	28 (21.3.1992 - 18.9.1993)
of league wins:	7 (1954-55)	of home wins:	10 (1963)
of league defeats:	10 (1988-89)	of away wins:	4 (1953-1981)

Missing seasons in 'away without a win', between 1938-50, was when they were a non-League club.

THE MANAGER

TONY PULIS . . . . appointed July 1995.

PREVIOUS CLUBS
As Manager. . . . . Bournemouth.
As Asst.Man/Coach. . . . . Bournemouth.
As a player . . . . Bristol Rovers, Hong Kong, Bristol Rovers, Newport County, Bournemouth,
. . . . Gillingham, Bournemouth.

HONOURS
As a Manager . . . . Promotion to Division 2, 1995-96.
As a Player. . . . . Newport County: Division 3 Championship 1987.

GILLINGHAM

PLAYERS NAME Honours	Ht	Wt	Birthdate	Birthplace Transfers	Contract Date	Clubs	APPEARANCES League	L/Cup	FA Cup	Other	GOALS Lge	L/C	FAC	Oth
G O A L K E E P E R S														
Stannard James	6.0	13.6	06/10/62	Harold Hill	05/06/80	Fulham	41	3	1					
				Loan	17/09/84	Southend United	6							
				Loan	01/02/85	Charlton Athletic	1							
				£12000	28/03/85	Southend United	103	6	4	5				
				£50000	14/08/87	Fulham	348	22	13	18	1			
				Free	04/08/95	Gillingham	46	2	4	1				
D E F E N D E R S														
Chapman Ian E: S.	5.8	11.6	31/05/70	Brighton	05/06/87	Brighton & H.A. (T)	275+6	18+2	12+2	12+4	13		2	
				Free	19/07/96	Gillingham								
Green Richard E	6.0	12.8	22/11/67	Wolverhampton	19/07/86	Shrewsbury Town	120+5	11	5	5	5	1		1
				Free	25/10/92	Swindon Town								
				Free	06/03/92	Gillingham	161+1	9	13	6	14		1	
Martin David E: Y.4. FAYC'79. FLT'83. FAT'92. (on loan with Colc.)	6.1	12.2	25/04/63	East Ham	10/05/80	Millwall	131+9	10+2	7	4	6	3	1	1
				£35000	14/09/84	Wimbledon	30+5	2	2+1		3			
				Free	23/08/84	Southend United	212+9	25	9+1	10+1	19	4		3
				Free	19/07/93	Bristol City	36+2		5	2	1			
				Loan	13/02/95	Northampton Town	7				1			
				Free	04/08/95	Gillingham	27+4	1	4	1	1		1	
Naylor Dominic FAYC'89.	5.9	13.3	12/08/70	Watford	20/09/88	Watford								
				Loan	06/12/89	Halifax Town	5+1			1+1	1			
					01/08/90	Hong Kong								
				Free	12/08/91	Barnet	50+1	2	5	4			1	
				Free	16/07/93	Plymouth Argyle	84+1	2	8	4+1				
				Free	11/08/95	Gillingham	30+1	2	3	1	1	1		
Ratcliffe Simon E: u19.3, Y.1, S. Div.3'92.	5.11	11.9	08/02/67	Urmston	13/02/85	Manchester United								
				£40000	16/06/87	Norwich City	6+3	2						
				£100000	13/01/89	Brentford	197+17	13+3	9+1	23+2	16			2
				Free	04/08/95	Gillingham	41	2	3		3		1	
Smith Neil J FAYC'90.	5.7	11.10	30/09/71	Lambeth	24/07/90	Tottenham Hotspur								
				£40000	17/10/91	Brentford	162+9	8	16	7+1	9		2	2
Thomas Glen	6.1	11.0	06/10/67	Hackney	09/10/85	Fulham	246+5	21	8	14+1	6			
				Free	04/11/94	Peterborough Utd	6+2		0+1	2				
					23/03/95	Barnet	22+1	2		1				
					15/01/96	Gillingham	14+1							
Watson Paul D	5.8	10.10	04/01/75	Hastings	08/12/92	Gillingham	57+5	4	6	5+3	2			
M I D F I E L D														
Carpenter Richard	6.0	12.0	30/09/72	Sheerness	13/05/91	Gillingham	106+15	2+1	9+1	7	4			1
Harris Mark AGT'94.	6.3	13.11	15/07/63	Reading		Wokingham Town								
				£25000	29/02/88	Crystal Palace	0+2							
				Loan	07/08/89	Burnley	4	2						
				£22500	22/09/89	Swansea City	228	16	18	26	14	1	1	2
O'Connor Mark	5.7	10.2	10/03/63											
Puttnam David P	5.10	11.09	03/02/67	Leicester		Leicester United								
				£8000	09/02/89	Leicester City	4+3	0+1						
				£35000	21/01/90	Lincoln City	160+17	13+1	4	8+1	21	1		
					06/10/95	Gillingham	10+16		0+3	1	1			
Rattray Kevin FAT'94.						Woking								
				£5000	01/08/95	Gillingham	18+8	1	2	2	3			
F O R W A R D S														
Bailey Dennis AMC'91.	5.10	11.6	13/11/65	Lambeth		Barking								
				Free	08/11/86	Fulham								
					01/12/86	Farnborough			1				1	
				£10000	02/12/87	Crystal Palace	0+5				1			
				Loan	27/02/89	Bristol Rovers	17			1+1	9			1
				£80000	03/08/89	Birmingham City	65+10	6	6	3+3	23	2		
				Loan	28/03/91	Bristol Rovers	6				1			
				£175000	02/07/91	Q.P.R.	32+7	5	1+1	1	10	3		
				Loan	29/10/93	Charlton Athletic	0+4			2				1
				Loan	24/03/94	Watford	2+6				4			
				£25000	15/08/95	Gillingham	40+5	2	4		8	1	1	
Butler Steve E: S.P.3. GMVC'89.	6.2	13.00	27/01/62	Birmingham		Wokingham Town								
						Windsor			1					
				Free	19/12/84	Brentford	18+3			2	3			
				Free	01/08/86	Maidstone	76	4	18	10	41	3	7	
				£150000	13/03/91	Watford	40+22	4+3	1	2+1	9			
				Loan	18/12/92	Bournemouth	1							
				£75000	23/12/92	Cambridge United	107+2	4+1	6	3	51		5	
				£100000	15/12/95	Gillingham	14+6				5			
Fortune-West Leo						Stevenage								
				Free	12/07/95	Gillingham	36+4	2	3		12	1	2	
Freeman Darren B A	5.11	13.0	22/08/73	Brighton		Horsham Town								
				Free	31/01/95	Gillingham	4+8		0+1	2				1
O'Connor Mark Div.3'87.	5.7	10.2	10/03/63	Southend	01/06/80	Q.P.R.	2+1							
				Loan	07/10/83	Exeter City	38	2		3	1	1		1
				£20000	13/08/84	Bristol Rovers	79+1	8	7	4	10	1	1	1
				£25000	27/03/86	Bournemouth	115+13	5+3	7	4+1	12			
				£70000	15/12/89	Gillingham	107+9	8	7+1	6+2	8			1
				Free	05/07/93	Bournemouth	56+2	7+1	4	1	3			
				Free	04/08/95	Gillingham	18	2	2		2			

435

PRIESTFIELD STADIUM
Redfern Avenue, Gillingham, Kent ME7 4DD
Tel: 01634 851 854/576 828

Capacity 10,422
Covered Standing 4,823
Seating...1,225

First game ....v Woolwich Arsenal, Friendly, 2.9.1893.
First floodlit game ....v Bury, Lge Cup, 25.9.1963.

ATTENDANCES
Highest ....23,002 v Q.P.R., FA Cup 3rd Rnd, 10.1.1948.
Lowest ....963 v Colchester, AMC, 23.1.1985.

OTHER GROUNDS...None.

MATCHDAY TICKET PRICES

Enclosure £9
OAP. £7
Juv £5

Main Stand £11.50
no concessions

Terraces £7
OAP. £5
Juv £3

Ticket Office Telephone no. . . . . 01634 851 854/576 828.

HOW TO GET TO THE GROUND

Use motorway (M2) until junction 4.
Leave motorway and follow signs to Gillingham.
Straight over two roundabouts, at 3rd roundabout turn left (A2).
In 500 yards straight over roundabout.
Traffic lights in 200 yards Woodlands Road.
Go straight over until next traffic lights.
Stadium on left.
One block street parking.

Nearest Railway Station
Gillingham (10 minutes walk from ground).

CLUBCALL
0891 800 676

Calls cost 39p per minute cheap rate and 49p per
minute at all other times.
Call costings correct at time of going to press.

MATCHDAY PROGRAMME

Programme Editor . . . . Roger Evans.

Number of pages . . . . 32.

Price . . . . £1.20.

Subscriptions . . . . £30 including postage.

Local Newspapers . . . . Kent Today, Medway News and Standard.

Local Radio Stations . . . . BBC Radio Kent, Invicta Radio.

LUTON TOWN
(The Hatters)
NATIONWIDE LEAGUE DIVISION 2
SPONSORED BY: UNIVERSAL SALVAGE AUCTIONS

Back Row (L-R): Ben Chenery, Danny Power, Gary Simpson, Fred Barber, Paul McLaren, Rob Matthews, Gavin Johnson, David Greene, Steve Davis, Kelvin Davis, John Taylor, Trevor Peake, Julian James. **Middle Row:** Chris Green (Director), Cliff Bassett (Director), Clive Goodyear (Physio), Paul Lowe (Yth Dev. Officer), Richard Harvey, Aaron Skelton, David Oldfield, Mitchell Thomas, Des Linton, Marvin Johnson, Bontcho Guentchev, Matthew Woolgar, Wayne Turner (Res coach), John moore (Yth coach), Les Shannon (Scout), Nigel Terry (Director). **Front Row:** Jamie Woodsford, Gary Waddock, Tony Thorpe, Ceri Hughes, Mick McGiven (Asst. Manager), David Kohler (Chairman), Terry Westley (Manager), Scott Oakes, Nathan Jones, Graham Alexander, Dwight Marshall.

LUTON TOWN
FORMED IN 1885
TURNED PROFESSIONAL IN 1890
LTD COMPANY IN 1897

CHAIRMAN: D A Kohler B.Sc(Hons) ARICS

DIRECTORS
C Green, C Bassett, N Terry
SECRETARY
Cherry Newbery
COMMERCIAL MANAGER
Kathy Leather

MANAGER: Lennie Lawrence
FIRST TEAM COACH: Wayne Turner

RESERVE TEAM MANAGER
Trevor Peake
YOUTH TEAM MANAGER
John Moore
PHYSIOTHERAPIST
Clive Goodyear

STATISTICIAN FOR THE DIRECTORY
Vacant

Having gone close in recent seasons, Luton Town finally succumbed to the dreaded drop by finishing bottom of Division 1. With only two wins by October the writing, it would seem, was on the wall, and with only two more wins by December, Luton Town were 24th needing a minor miracle if they were to keep hold of their Division 1 status.

It was then that the Terry Westly was relieved of his managerial post and Lennie Lawrence was brought in.With Lennie's proven track record maybe this appointment was the break the club needed.

A run of eight League games without defeat, that placed them 17th, brought renewed hope to the club and its' supporters. Alas this hope was short lived when only one point was gained from the next seven matches. This left Luton in 23rd and with little hope of escaping the relegation zone. A further eight points was gained from the remaining nine games, which was certainly not enough to keep them up and, with the resurgence going on at local rivals Watford, was not enough to keep them from collecting the 'wooden spoon'.

There was little to cheer in the Cup competitions either. A First Round exit in the Coca-Cola Cup against Bournemouth (2-3 on aggregate) and a Third Round thrashing at Grimsby (1-7) in the F.A. Cup put any ambitions of domestic Cup success to rest.

There was to be little success in Europe too. With three defeats against Perugia (1-4), Genoa (0-4) and Cesena (1-2) all coming in the first three games of the Anglo/Italian Cup, their final match against Ancona saw them record a shock result, when the 'Hatters' convincingly beat the Italian visitors 5-0.

Lennie Lawrence is certainly use to battles and with the chance this season to see Luton through the pre-season preparations, a good start to the 1996/97 season could see them emerge as favourites to reclaim their First Division status. However, they will have to be wary of their arch rivals down at Vicarage Road.

LUTON TOWN

League: 24th   FA Cup: 3rd Rnd   Coca-Cola Cup: 1st Rnd

M	DATE	COMP	VEN	OPPONENTS	RESULT	HT	LP	GOAL SCORERS/GOAL TIMES	ATT.
1	A 13	EL	H	Norwich City	L 1-3	0-0	21	Guentchev 53(pen)	27064
2	15	CC 1/1	H	Bournemouth	D 1-1	0-1		Marshall 70	2728
3	19	EL	A	Southend United	W 1-0	0-0	16	Thorpe 77	(4630)
4	22	CC 1/2	A	Bournemouth	L 1-2	1-1		Johnson 44	(4884)
5	26	EL	H	Leicester City	D 1-1	1-0	18	Hughes 20	7612
6	29	EL	A	Grimsby Town	D 0-0	0-0	12		(4289)
7	S 2	EL	H	Derby County	L 1-2	1-1	20	Marshall 1	6427
8	5	AIC	H	Perugia	L 1-4	1-2		Guentchev 45(pen)	2352
9	9	EL	A	Reading	L 1-3	1-1	19	Marshall 5	(8550)
10	13	EL	A	Millwall	L 0-1	0-0	22		(7354)
11	16	EL	H	Sunderland	L 0-2	0-0	23		6995
12	23	EL	A	Wolverhampton Wand	D 0-0	0-0	24		(23659)
13	30	EL	H	Portsmouth	W 3-1	2-1	22	Marshall 7, Davis 23, Guentchev 59(pen)	7795
14	O 7	EL	A	Tranmere Rovers	L 0-1	0-1	24		(6680)
15	11	AIC	A	Genoa	L 0-4	0-2			(3759)
16	14	EL	H	West Bromwich Albion	L 1-2	1-0	24	Harvey 19	8042
17	22	EL	A	Ipswich Town	W 1-0	1-0	22	Oldfield 24	(9123)
18	29	EL	H	Charlton Athletic	L 0-1	0-1	23		6270
19	N 4	EL	A	Stoke City	L 0-5	0-1	23		(9382)
20	8	AIC	A	Cesena	L 1-2	0-1		Marshall 75	(461)
21	11	EL	A	Oldham Athletic	D 1-1	1-0	23	Douglas 40	6047
22	18	EL	H	Birmingham City	D 0-0	0-0	23		7920
23	21	EL	A	Watford	D 1-1	1-0	23	Davis 25	(10042)
24	25	EL	A	Barnsley	L 0-1	0-0	23		(6437)
25	D 2	EL	H	Tranmere Rovers	W 3-2	1-1	23	Marshall 6, 60, McLaren 71	6025
26	10	EL	H	Wolverhampton Wand	L 2-3	1-3	24	Oakes 31, Marshall 50	6997
27	13	AIC	H	Ancona	W 5-0	2-0		Taylor 22, Oakes 43, Marshall 55, Thorpe 76, Guentchev 85	2091
28	16	EL	A	Portsmouth	L 0-4	0-3	24		(7012)
29	23	EL	H	Huddersfield Town	D 2-2	1-0	24	Marshall 36, Oldfield 79	7076
30	J 6	FAC 3	H	Grimsby Town	L 1-7	1-4		Marshall 39	(5387)
31	13	EL	H	Southend United	W 3-1	1-0	24	Guentchev 45, Oakes 54, 71	6566
32	20	EL	A	Norwich City	W 1-0	1-0	22	Guentchev 33(pen)	(12474)
33	31	EL	A	Sheffield United	W 1-0	1-0	21	Guentchev 39	6995
34	F 3	EL	A	Leicester City	D 1-1	0-0	21	Thorpe 78	(14821)
35	10	EL	H	Grimsby Town	W 3-2	1-1	20	Alexander 7, Guentchev 68, Marshall 74	7158
36	17	EL	A	Millwall	W 1-0	0-0	19	Thorpe 84(pen)	7308
37	21	EL	A	Derby County	D 1-1	0-0	17	Marshall 57	(14825)
38	24	EL	A	Sunderland	L 0-1	0-1	19		(16693)
39	27	EL	H	Reading	L 1-2	1-1	20	Guentchev 5(pen)	6683
40	M 2	EL	H	Crystal Palace	D 0-0	0-0	20		8478
41	9	EL	A	Huddersfield Town	L 0-1	0-0	20		(11950)
42	19	EL	A	Crystal Palace	L 0-2	0-0	23		(13609)
43	23	EL	A	Sheffield United	L 0-1	0-0	23		(14395)
44	30	EL	H	Ipswich Town	L 1-2	0-1	23	Grant 49	9151
45	A 2	EL	A	West Bromwich Albion	W 2-0	1-0	23	Guentchev 22, Grant 84	(15131)
46	5	EL	A	Charlton Athletic	D 1-1	1-0	23	Thorpe 23	(14643)
47	9	EL	H	Stoke City	L 1-2	1-0	23	Grant 45	7689
48	13	EL	A	Birmingham City	L 0-4	0-1	23		(15426)
49	20	EL	H	Watford	D 0-0	0-0	23		9454
50	23	EL	A	Port Vale	L 0-1	0-1	24		(6054)
51	27	EL	A	Barnsley	L 1-3	0-2	24	Thorpe 52	6194
52	30	EL	H	Port Vale	W 3-2	1-1	24	Thorpe 22, 82, Guentchev 78	5443
53	M 5	EL	A	Oldham Athletic	L 0-1	0-0	24		(6623)

Best Home League Attendance: 27064 v Norwich City   Smallest: 5443 v Port Vale   Average: 8060

Goal Scorers:

EL(40): Marshall(9),Guentchev(9),Thorpe(7),Grant(3),Oakes(3),Davis(2),Oldfield(2),McLaren(1),Hughes(1),Douglas(1),Harvey(1),Alexander(1)

CC(2): Marshall(1),Johnson(1)

FAC(1): Marshall(1)

AIC(7): Guentchev(2),Marshall(2),Taylor(1),Thorpe(1),Oakes(1)

(D) Alexander	(G) Davis	(D) Davis	(M) Douglas	(G) Feuer	(F) Grant	(F) Guentchev	(D) Harvey	(M) Hughes	(D) James	(D) Johnson	(D) Johnson	(D) Linton	(F) Marshall	(D) McLaren	(F) Oakes	(M) Oldfield	(D) Patterson	(D) Peake	(F) Riseth	(G) Sommer	(F) Taylor	(D) Thomas	(F) Thorpe	(F) Tomlinson	(D) Vilstrup	(M) Waddock	(F) Wilkinson	(F) Woodsford		
X	X	S				X	X	X			X					X		X		S	S1	X	X1			X			T.West	1
		X				X	X	X		X			X1			X				S	X	X	X	S1			S		G.Singh	2
X2		X				X1	X	X	X		X		X2			X					X	X	S2	S2			S1		G.R.Pooley	3
X		X				X	X3		X		X		X			X1					X	X1	S1			X			D.Orr	4
		X				S2	X	X	X2	X	X		X			X2		S2			X	X1	S1						M.Bailey	5
X	X	X				X	X		X	X	X	X2	X3			X1		S2			S3							S1	W.Burns	6
X3	X	X				X2	X		X	X	X		X			X1		S3			X		S1					S2	J.Brandwood	7
	X	X				X2	X	X	X		X		X			X3							X1			S3		S2	N.Known	8
X	X	X				S1	X		X	X	X	X1	X			X		S								X			K.Leach	9
	X		X			X	X		S1	S	X1	X	X			X		X			S2				X	X			R.Gifford	10
	X		X			S1	X	X	X		X1		X			X		X			S2				X	X2			R.Poulain	11
X	X		X			X	X	X	S		X		X			S2		X			X2				X1	S1			N.Barry	12
X2	X		X			X	X	X	S2		X		X			S		X			X				X1	S1			P.Rejer	13
X	X		X			X1	X		S	S		X	X			S1		X								X		S3	P.Richards	14
S2	X	X				X3			X1		X	X		X	X	X2						S1			X			S3	G.Barber	15
	X	X		X		S	X	S1			X		X	S		X		X1							X		X		G.Barber	16
X	X		X			S3	X2	X		S2		X3		X	X	X									X1	S1			T.West	17
X2	X		X			S2	X	X1			X	S2	X		X	X		X	S1							X2			J.Kirkby	18
X	X		X			X	X	S		X		X	S1	X	S1	X	X	X							X1			J.Lloyd	19
X	X	X	S1			X					X	X	X2	X1	X							S1	X		X		S3			20
X		X	X			X	X	S	X		X2	X1	S1	S2	X	X							X						A.D'Urso	21
X		S1	X			X	X	X		X		X2	X1	X	S	X	X				S2								J.Rushton	22
	X1	S1	X			X	X	X3		X		X1	X	X			S1	X			S3								M.Pierce	23
S1		S1	X			X	X	X		X		X1	X1	X		X	X	X1			S1								A.R.Leake	24
X			X		S	X	X	X		X		X	X	X		X		S			X		X			X			K.Leach	25
S	X	X				S2	X	X2		X		X	X1	X		X					S1		X			X			K.Lynch	26
	X	X				S2	X3			X	X2	X	X1		X						X	S3	S1			X				27
X1		X		X		X2				X		X	X	X1		X					X	S1	S1			X			E.Lomas	28
	X		X			S2	S1			X		X	X2	X	S2	X					X2	X	X1			X			D.Allison	29
S1			X			X2	S		X		X	X	X1	X	X						X	S2				X			P.Richards	30
X		X	X			X	S1		X		X		X2	S2			S				X1	X	X			X			A.Wiley	31
X		X	X			X	X		X		X		X1	S1	S						X	X	S			X			C.Wilkes	32
X		X	X			X	S3	S1		X1		X		X1	S1						X	X	X3			X			D.Orr	33
X		X	X			X	X2				X		S2	S2		X2	X		S1		X1	X	X			X			G.Barber	34
X		X	X			X		X	X		X		S2			S1	X				X1	X	X2			X			B.Knight	35
X2		X	X			X3	S3	X	X		S1					S2	X				X1	X	X			X			J.Rushton	36
X		X	X			S1	X		S		X2					X	X		S2		X	X1	X			X			M.Riley	37
X			X			X	X2	X1	X		X3					X			S3		S2	X	S1			X			A.Butler	38
X		X	X			X			X		X		X		S1	X		X	S2		X2	X	X1	S3		X3			P.Rejer	39
X		X	X			X2	S3	X	X		X		X			X	S2				S1	X	X3			X			J.Kirkby	40
		X	X			X	S		X	S2		X		S1	X1	X					X	X	X			X2			E.Wolstenholme	41
		X	X			X1	S	S1	X	S2		X		X	X	X					X2	X	X			X			P.Taylor	42
X1		X	X			X2	X		X		X		S1	X	X						X	X	S2	S2		X			T.West	43
S1		X	X	X			X		X		X3	X2	X								X	X	S3		X1	X	X		G.Singh	44
X		X	X	X		X	X		S1			S1	X	X1							X	X1				X		X	J.Lloyd	45
X		X	X	X2		X	X1		S1		X		S2	X							X3	S3				X	X	X	B.Burns	46
X	S		X	X		X			X		X		X2	X							S2	X1	S1			X			U.Rennie	47
X		X	X	X		X3	S1		X		X		X3	X							S2	X	S3		X1	X			R.Gifford	48
X		X	X	X		S2	S		S		X		X1	X							X	X2	S1			X			G.Cain	49
X	X	X	X	X		S		S		X		X		X							S	X1	X1			X			R.Furnandiz	50
X3		X	S1	X	X1	X	S3			X				X1		X					S1	X	X			X			J.Brandwood	51
X		X	X2		X3	S2			X						S1		X				S3	X	X			X			N.Barry	52
		S1	X	X1	X					X						X	S	X			X	X	X			X			M.A.Riley	53
35	5	37	3	38	10	25	28	21	23	5	33	6	23	9	26	23	21	15	6	2	18	25	23	1	6	32	3	1	EL Appearances	
2	0	0	5	0	0	10	8	2	4	1	2	4	3	3	3	11	2	3	5	0	10	2	10	6	1	4	0	2	EL Sub Appearances	
1	0	2	0	0	0	2	1	1	1	1	0	2	0	0	2	0	0	0	2	2	1	0+2	0	0	1	0	0	0	CC Appearances	
0+1	0	0	0	1	0	1	0	0	1	0	1	0	1	1	1	1	0	0	0	0	1	0	0+1	0	0	1	0	0	FAC Appearances	
1+1	4	4	0+1	0	0	2+1	3	1	2	0	2	3	2+1	3	3	2	2	0	1	0	1	0+1	1+2	0	2	1+1	0	0+2	AIC Appearances	

Also Played: (D) Chenery S(20,25), X(52), X2(53).(M) Evers S(9,10). X1(52). (D) Greene S(11). (F) Matthews S1(4). (D) Simpson S2(20). (M) Skelton X(8). (M) Upson X(20).

CLUB RECORDS

BIGGEST VICTORIES
League: 12-0 v Bristol Rovers, Division 3 (S), 13.4.1936 (Divisional record).
F.A. Cup: 9-0 v Clapton, 1st Round, 30.11.1927.
League Cup: 7-2 v Mansfield, 2nd Round, 3.10.1989.
BIGGEST DEFEATS
League: 0-9 v Birmingham City, Division 2, 12.11.1898.
F.A. Cup: 0-7 v Crystal Palace, 1st Round, 16.1.1929.
League Cup: 1-5 v Everton, 3rd Round, 1968-69.
MOST POINTS
3 points a win: 88, Division 2, 1981-82.
2 points a win: 66, Division 4, 1967-68.
MOST GOALS SCORED
103, 1936-37.
Payne 55, Stephenson 17, Ball 8, Dawes 8, Roberts 8, Rich 2, Finlayson 2, Fellowes 1, Hancock 1, Hodge 1.
MOST GOALS CONCEDED
95, Division 2, 1898-99.
MOST FIRST CLASS MATCHES IN A SEASON
58 - 1987-88 (League 40, FA Cup 6, League Cup 8, Simod Cup 4).
MOST LEAGUE WINS
27, Division 3(S), 1936-37, Division 4, 1967-68.
MOST LEAGUE DRAWS
21, Division 2/1, 1992-93.
MOST LEAGUE DEFEATS
24, Division 2, 1962-63, Division 3, 1964-65.
RECORD TRANSFER FEE RECEIVED
£2,500,000 from Arsenal for John Hartson, January 1995.
RECORD TRANSFER FEE PAID
£650,000 to Odense for Lars Elstrup, August 1989.
BEST PERFORMANCES
League: 7th in Division 1, 1986-87.
F.A. Cup: Runners-up 1958-59. Lost 1-2 v Nottingham Forest.
League Cup: Winners 1987-88. Won 3-2 v Arsenal.

INDIVIDUAL CLUB RECORDS

MOST GOALS IN A CAREER
Gordon Turner: 265 (1949-64). 243 League, 18 FA Cup, 4 Lge Cup.
MOST GOALS IN A SEASON
Joe Payne: 58 goals in 1936-37 (League 55, FA Cup 3).
MOST GOALS IN A MATCH
10. Joe Payne v Bristol Rovers, 12-0, Division 3(S), 13.4.1936 (League record).
MOST APPEARANCES
Bob Morton: 550 (1948-64). 495 League, 48 FA Cup, 7 Lge Cup.
OLDEST PLAYER
Trevor Peake, 39 years, 17 days, 27.2.96.
YOUNGEST PLAYER
Mike O'Hara, 16 years, 32 days, 1.10.1960.
MOST CAPPED PLAYER
Mal Donaghy (Northern Ireland) 58.

PREVIOUS MANAGERS

George Thomson 1925-27, John McCartney 1927-29, George Kay 1929-31, Harold Wightman 1931-35, Edwin Liddell 1935-38, Neil McBain 1938-39, George Martin 1939-47, Dally Duncan 1947-58, Syd Owen1959-60, Sam Bartram 1960-62) Jack Crompton 1962, Bill Harvey1962-64, George Martin 1964-66) Allan Brown 1966-68, Alec Stock 1968-72, Harry Haslam 1972-78 David Pleat 1978-86, John Moore 1986-87, Ray Harford 1987-90) Jim Ryan 1990-91, David Pleat1991-95, Terry Westley 1995.

ADDITIONAL INFORMATION
PREVIOUS NAMES
None.
PREVIOUS LEAGUES
United League, Southern League.
Club colours: White shirts with blue sleeves, with white & orange trim, blue shorts, blue & white hooped socks.
Change colours: Black & orange striped shirts, black shorts, black socks with orange turnovers.
Reserves League: Neville Ovenden Football Combination.

COMPETITIONS

Div.1	Div.2/1	Div.3/2	Div.3(S)	Div.4	Texaco
1955-60	1897-1900	1920-21	1921-37	1965-68	1974-75
1974-75	1937-55	1963-65			
1982-92	1960-63	1968-70			Wat Cup
	1970-74	1996-			1971
	1975-82				
	1992-96				

HONOURS

Div.2	Div.3(S)	Div.4	Leagues Cup
1981-82	1936-37	1967-68	1987-88

LONGEST LEAGUE RUNS

of undefeated matches:	19 (13.1.68-27.4.68, 7.4.69-11.10.69)	of league matches w/out a win:	16 (1964)
of undefeated home matches:	39 (24.1.1925 - 30.4.1927)	of undefeated away matches:	10 (20.4.1981 - 14.11.1981)
without home win:	10 (26.10.64-25.1.65, 16.9.72-6.1.73)	without an away win:	32 (26.11.1898 - 28.4.1900)
of league wins:	9 (22.1.1977 - 8.3.1977)	of home wins:	15 (1.4.1967 - 26.12.1967)
of league defeats:	8 (11.11.1899 - 6.1.1900)	of away wins:	5 (2.5.1981 - 3.10.1981)

THE MANAGER

LENNIE LAWRENCE . . . . appointed December 1995.
PREVIOUS CLUBS
As Manager. . . . . Plymouth (caretaker), Charlton, Middlesbrough, Bradford.
As Asst.Man/Coach . . . . Plymouth, Lincoln City.
As a player . . . . Croydon, Carshalton Athletic, Sutton United.
HONOURS   As a Manager . . . . Charlton Athletic: Division 2 runners-up 1985-86.
As Asst. Manager . . . . Promotion to Division 3 1980-81.

UTON TOWN

AYERS NAME	Ht	Wt	Birthdate	Birthplace / Transfers	Contract Date	Clubs	League	L/Cup	FA Cup	Other	Lge	L/C	FAC	Oth
O A L K E E P E R S														
vis Kelvin G	6.1	13.2	29/09/76	Bedford	01/07/94	Luton Town	14			4				
				Loan	16/09/94	Torquay United	2	1		1				
uer Anthony	6.5	15.7	20/05/70	Las Vegas, USA										
				£70000	23/03/94	West Ham United								
				Loan	20/02/95	Peterborough Utd	16							
an (11/09/95) Luton Town				£580000	14/12/95	Luton Town	38		1					
E F E N D E R S														
exander Graham	5.10	11.10	10/10/71	Coventry	20/03/90	Scunthorpe United	111+8	9+1	8	11+2	14	2		2
				£100000	08/07/95	Luton Town	35+2	1	0+1	1+1	1			
enery Benjamin R	6.1	11.5	28/01/77	Ipswich	07/03/95	Luton Town	2		1					
vis Stephen M	6.2	12.8	30/10/68	Hexham	06/07/87	Southampton	5+1							
y4'92				Loan	21/11/89	Burnley	7+2							
				Loan	28/03/91	Notts County	6+2							
				£60000	17/08/91	Burnley	119	6	14	13	15	2	1	
				£750000	13/07/95	Luton Town	37	2		4	2			
eene David M	6.2	11.10	26/10/73	Luton	03/09/91	Luton Town	18+1	2	1	0+1				
u21.5				Loan	23/11/95	Colchester United	14				2	1		
				Loan	01/03/96	Brentford	11							
rvey Richard G	5.9	11.10	17/04/69	Letchworth	10/01/87	Luton Town	128+25	8	6+2	8	4	1		
Y3, u19.3				Loan	30/10/92	Blackpool	4+1							
mes Julian C	5.10	11.11	22/03/70	Tring	01/07/88	Luton Town	195+19	9+1	17+1	10+1	12			
u21.2				Loan	12/09/91	Preston North End	6							
hnson Marvin A	5.11	11.6	29/10/68	Wembley	12/11/86	Luton Town	188+13	9+2	9+1	10	4	1		
ton Desmond M	6.1	11.13	05/09/71	Birmingham	09/01/90	Leicester City	6+5	0+1		1				
					22/10/91	Luton Town	62+14	3+1	7	6	1			
Laren Paul	6.0	12.06	17/11/76	Wycombe	31/05/94	Luton Town	9+4		1	3	1			
tterson Darren	6.2	12.07	15/10/69	Belfast	05/07/88	W.B.A.								
8, B, u21, Y				Free	17/04/89	Wigan Athletic	69+28	7+1	5+4	7	6	3	1	
				£225000	01/07/92	Crystal Palace	22	4	6		1			
				£230000	21/08/95	Luton Town	21+2		1	2				
ake Trevor	6.0	12.9	10/02/57	Nuneaton		Nuneaton Borough								
S-P2; FAC'87				£27750	15/06/79	Lincoln City	171	16	7		7	2		
				£100000	06/06/83	Coventry City	277+1	30	17	10	6		1	
				£100000	27/08/91	Luton Town	175+3	7	13	3				
mpson Gary	6.2	14.0	14/02/76	Ashford	05/07/94	Luton Town				0+1				
an (11/08/95) Aylesbury				Loan	28/03/96	Fulham	5+2							
omas Mitchell A	6.0	12.0	02/10/64	Luton	27.08.82	Luton Town (A)	106+1	5	18		1			
B1, u21.3, Y3				£233000	07/07/86	Tottenham Hotspur	136+21	28+1	12		6	1	1	
				£525000	07/08/91	West Ham United	37+1	5	4	2	3			
				Free	12/11/93	Luton Town	75+8	1	5	0+1	1			
I D F I E L D														
ers Sean A					01/06/95	Luton Town	1							
ghes Ceri M	5.9	11.6	26/02/71	Pontypridd	01/07/89	Luton Town	121+18	7	8	4	12		1	
4, B2, Y														
field David	6.0	12.2	30/05/68	Perth (Aus)	16/05/86	Luton Town	21+8	4+2	0+1	2+1	4	2		2
u21.1				£600000	14/03/89	Manchester City	18+8	2+1		0+1	6			1
				£150000	12/01/90	Leicester City	155+19	10+1	6	11+3	25	1	2	2
				Loan	24/02/95	Millwall								
				£150000	21/07/95	Luton Town	23+11	2	1	2	2			
elton Aaron	5.10	11.05	22/11/74	Welwyn G.C.	31/05/94	Luton Town	3+2	0+1		1				
ddock Gary	5.10	11.12	17/03/62	Kingsbury	26/07/79	Q.P.R.	191+12	21+1	14	1	8	2		
21, B, 1, u23.1, u21.1; Div2'83				Free	01/12/87	Charleroi (Belgium)								
				£130000	16/08/89	Millwall	51+7	5+1	5	3	2			1
e (20/12/91) Q.P.R.				Loan	19/03/92	Swindon Town	5+1							
				£100000	07/11/92	Bristol Rovers	70	2	2	2	1			
				Free	09/12/94	Luton Town	72+4	1	5	1+1	1			
O R W A R D S														
ant Kim	5.10	10.12	25/09/72	Ghana	06/03/91	Charlton Athletic	74+49	3+9	8+5	5+2	18	1	5	1
				£250000	28/03/96	Luton Town	10				3			
entchev Bontcho	5.10	11.7	07/07/64	Tcheshevo (Bulg)		Sporting Lisbon								
:				£250000	29/12/92	Ipswich Town	28+17	4	6+2		5		5	
				Free	23/08/95	Luton Town	25+10	2	1	2+1	9			2
rshall Dwight W	5.11	11.8	03/10/65	Jamaica		Grays Athletic								
				£35000	09/08/91	Plymouth Argyle	93+8	8	7+2	7+1	26	1	4	4
				Loan	25/03/93	Middlesbrough	0+3							
				£150000	15/07/94	Luton Town	59+12	3+1	5	2+1	20	2	2	2
lor John	6.1	12.2	24/10/64	Norwich	17/12/82	Colchester United								
3'91				01/08/85	Sudbury Town									
				24/08/88	Cambridge United	139+21	9+2	21	12+2	46	2	10	2
				28/03/92	Bristol Rovers	91+4	4	3	5	44	1		
				£300000	05/07/94	Bradford City								
				£200000	23/03/95	Luton Town	27+10	2		1	3			1
rpe Anthony	5.9	12.0	10/04/74	Leicester	18/08/92	Luton Town	27+20	0+2	1+2	1+2	8		1	1
odsford Jamie	5.9	11.0	09/11/76	Ipswich	07/03/95	Luton Town	2+8		0+2					
DITIONAL CONTRACT PLAYERS														
bey Nathanael					02/05/96	Luton Town (T)								
uglas Stuart					02/05/96	Luton Town (T)								
an Robert S					02/05/96	Luton Town (T)								
dersen Johnny V						Luton Town (T)								
son Matthew J						Luton Town (T)	1							
mott Christopher A					02/05/96	Luton Town (T)								

KENILWORTH ROAD

1 Maple Road, Luton, Beds LU4 8AW
Tel: 01582 411 622

Capacity ....9,970 (All seater)

First game...v Plymouth, 4.9.1905.
First floodlit game ....v Fenerbahce, 7.10.1957.
ATTENDANCES
Highest.......................................30,069 v Blackpool, FA Cup 6th Round replay, 4.3.1959.
Lowest..1,823 v Southend, Anglo Italian Cup, 5.9.1993.

OTHER GROUNDS ....Excelsior Dallow Lane 1885-97, Dunstable Road 1897-05,
....Kenilworth Road 1905-

MATCHDAY TICKET PRICES

	14 days before match	less than 14 days
Main Stand A&E	£14.50	£15.50
Juv/OAP	£7.50	£8
Block F	£11.50	£12.50
Juv/OAP	£5.50	£6
Block G	£7.50	£8
Juv/OAP	£5	£5.50
Main Stand C&G	£11.50	£12.50
Juv/OAP	£5.50	£6
Restricted View B,H&J	£7.50	£8
Juv/OAP	£5	£5.50
Kenilworth Upper tier	£11.50	£12.50
Juv/OAP	£5.50	£6
Kenilworth Lower Tier	£11.50	£12.50
Juv/OAP	£5.50	£6
New Stand	£14.50	£15.50
Juv/OAP	£7.50	£8

Ticket Office Telephone no. 01582 416 976

CLUBCALL 0898 12 11 23

Calls cost 39p per minute cheap rate and 49p per
minute at all other times.
Call costings correct at time of going to press.

HOW TO GET TO THE GROUND

From the North and West
Use motorway (M1) until junction 11 then follow signs to Luton A505 into
Dunstable Road. Forward through one-way system and then turn right into
Kenilworth Road for Luton Town FC.

From the South and East
Use motorway (M1) until junction 10 or A6/A612 into Luton Town centre, then fo
low signs to Dunstable into Dunstable Road A505. Under railway bridge then
turn left into Kenilworth Road for Luton Town FC.

Car Parking
Street parking near ground only available.

Nearest Railway Station
Luton Midland Road (01582 27612).

MATCHDAY PROGRAMME

Programme Editor. . . . . Simon Oxley.

Number of pages . . . . 48.

Price . . . . £1.50.

Subscriptions . . . . Apply to club.

Local Newspapers. . . . . Luton News, The Herald,
. . . . Luton on Sunday.

Local Radio Stations . . . . Chiltern Radio, Three Counties Radio.

MILLWALL
(The Lions)
NATIONWIDE LEAGUE DIVISION 2
SPONSORED BY: SOUTH LONDON PRESS

Back Row (L-R): Mickey Bennett, Kerry Dixon, Tony Witter, Uwe Fuchs, Jason Van Blerk, Chris Malkin, Greg Berry, Anton Rogan, Damian Webber.
Middle Row: Keith Johnstone (Physio), Michael Harle, Keith Stevens, Ricky Newman, Dave Savage, Jimmy Nielsen, Kasey Keller, Dave Wietecha, Alistair Edwards, Bobby Bowry, Maurice Doyle, Richard Cadette, Ian McDonald (Coach).
Front Row: Phil O'Neil, Ben Thatcher, Scott Taylor, Alex Rae, Mick McCarthy (Manager), Ian Evans (First Team Coach), Steve Forbes, Lee McRobert, James Connor, Mark Beard.

MILLWALL
FORMED IN 1885
TURNED PROFESSIONAL IN 1893
LTD COMPANY IN 1894

LIFE PRESIDENT
R I Burr
CHAIRMAN: P Mead
DIRECTORS
B E Mitchell, J D Burnige,
Councillor D Sullivan, Jose Berardo
CHIEF EXECUTIVE/SECRETARY
G I S Hortop (0171 232 1222)
MARKETING MANAGER
Debra Fraser

MANAGER: Jimmy Nicholl
ASSISTANT MANAGER: Martin Harvey
RESERVE /YOUTH TEAM MANAGER
Ian McDonald
PHYSIOTHERAPIST
Keith Johnstone

STATISTICIAN FOR THE DIRECTORY
Richard Lindsay

The season got off to a successful start with a home win over Grimsby Town and an unusual statistic in Millwall's Football League career - three successive away wins. This good form spurred the Lions to the top of the table until a dramatic slump from December onwards saw the club spiral into relegation. The early-season highlight was a 4-2 victory at Goodison Park in the Coca-Cola Cup - 2-0 down to Everton, Millwall staged a dramatic revival with substitute Scot Taylor's two goals helping an extra-time win. Sadly, the fighting spirit and character seemed to desert the players towards the season's end and only a few kept their act together. This coincided with media speculation that the Eire manager's job might be given to Mick McCarthy, which lasted until the end of February - the damage was done by the time Jimmy Nicholl took over in the management hot seat.

Once again midfielder Alex Rae was top scorer, as McCarthy juggled his big-money signings of Malkin and Fuchs, along with the experienced Kerry Dixon - the trio managing 22 goals between them, while Rae scored 16! The lack of goals stood out in the final reckoning, as we finished level with Portsmouth on 52 points, but with 18 goals less. For the first time in the club's Football League history, no more than two goals were scored in any game.

The FA Cup provided no joy either, with Millwall losing on a foggy night at Oxford, after an exciting 3-3 draw at the Den.

The international scene saw Keller add to his impressive total of USA caps, while Van Blerk had a very good game at Hampden Park for Australia and, likewise, young Ben Thatcher had his England under-21 debut after being selected for the squad on numerous occasions previously. Thatcher also won the vote for Player of the Year.

The average home attendance was nearly 2,000 more than in 1994/5, and this will have to be matched next season in order to survive the financial rigours as the club attempt to escape from Division Two. A survey in Matchday magazine showed that Millwall had the second-highest wage bill in the Endsleigh League.

In December we heard the sad news that Lions legend Harry Cripps had passed away aged 54.

MILLWALL FC MUSEUM

MILLWALL

League: 22nd   FA Cup: 3rd Rnd   Coca-Cola Cup: 3rd Rnd

M	DATE	COMP	VEN	OPPONENTS	RESULT	HT	LP	GOAL SCORERS/GOAL TIMES	ATT.
1	A 12	EL	H	Grimsby Town	W 2-1	2-0	8	Rae 9(pen), Malkin 34	8546
2	19	EL	A	Port Vale	W 1-0	0-0	2	Dixon 63	(8202)
3	26	EL	H	Southend United	D 0-0	0-0	3		10536
4	29	EL	A	Reading	W 2-1	0-1	2	Rae 65(pen), Dixon 69	(10143)
5	S 2	EL	A	Portsmouth	W 1-0	1-0	2	Dixon 17	(8023)
6	9	EL	H	Barnsley	L 0-1	0-1	2		9272
7	13	EL	H	Luton Town	W 1-0	0-0	2	Malkin 89	7354
8	16	EL	A	Norwich City	D 0-0	0-0	2		(15952)
9	20	CC 2/1	H	Everton	D 0-0	0-0			12053
10	23	EL	H	Sunderland	L 1-2	0-1	3	Stevens 37	8691
11	O 1	EL	A	Derby County	D 2-2	2-1	3	Rae 6, Black 26	(9590)
12	4	CC 2/2	A	Everton	W 4-2	0-0		Taylor 63,110, Rae 66(pen), Savage 120	(14891)
13	7	EL	A	Watford	W 1-0	0-0	2	Rae 68	(8918)
14	14	EL	H	Tranmere Rovers	D 2-2	0-0	2	Dixon 66(pen), Stevens 85	9293
15	22	EL	A	Crystal Palace	W 2-1	2-1	2	Malkin 3, Fuchs 34	(14338)
16	25	CC 3	H	Sheffield Wednesday	L 0-2	0-1			12822
17	28	EL	H	West Bromwich Albion	W 2-1	1-1	1	Malkin 19, Fuchs 59	9717
18	N 4	EL	A	Birmingham City	D 2-2	0-1	1	Dixon 58, Rae 85	(23016)
19	11	EL	H	Ipswich Town	W 2-1	1-1	1	Malkin 2, Witter 53	11360
20	18	EL	H	Huddersfield Town	D 0-0	0-0	1		9402
21	21	EL	A	Oldham Athletic	D 2-2	0-1	1	Rae 74, Malkin 89	(6161)
22	25	EL	A	Stoke City	L 0-1	0-0	1		(12590)
23	D 2	EL	H	Watford	L 1-2	1-2	1	Malkin 45	8389
24	5	EL	H	Charlton Athletic	L 0-2	0-1	2		11350
25	9	EL	A	Sunderland	L 0-6	0-2	8		(18951)
26	16	EL	H	Derby County	L 0-1	0-1	9		7694
27	26	EL	A	Wolverhampton Wand	D 1-1	0-1	10	Malkin 77	(25593)
28	J 1	EL	H	Leicester City	D 1-1	0-1	10	Malkin 66	9953
29	6	FAC 3	H	Oxford United	D 3-3	0-1		Rae 49, 84, Malkin 65	7564
30	13	EL	H	Port Vale	L 1-2	1-1	11	Rae 33	14220
31	16	FAC 3R	A	Oxford United	L 0-1	0-0			(8122)
32	20	EL	A	Grimsby Town	W 2-1	0-1	6	Rae 61(pen), 65	(4218)
33	27	EL	H	Portsmouth	D 1-1	1-0	6	Van 24	7710
34	F 3	EL	A	Southend United	L 0-2	0-1	9		(7302)
35	10	EL	H	Reading	D 1-1	0-1	8	Newman 59	8875
36	13	EL	A	Sheffield United	L 0-2	0-1	8		(10007)
37	17	EL	A	Luton Town	L 0-1	0-0	9		(7308)
38	24	EL	H	Norwich City	W 2-1	0-0	9	Bowry 58, Fuchs 65	8218
39	27	EL	A	Barnsley	L 1-3	1-0	10	Fuchs 42	(6331)
40	M 2	EL	H	Wolverhampton Wand	L 0-1	0-0	10		9131
41	9	EL	A	Charlton Athletic	L 0-2	0-1	13		(12204)
42	16	EL	H	Sheffield United	W 1-0	0-0	12	Fuchs 54	7795
43	23	EL	A	Leicester City	L 1-2	1-1	15	Rae 37	(12543)
44	30	EL	H	Crystal Palace	L 1-4	0-0	17	Rae 79(pen)	13214
45	A 2	EL	A	Tranmere Rovers	D 2-2	1-0	18	Yuran 22, Malkin 74	(5850)
46	6	EL	A	West Bromwich Albion	L 0-1	0-0	20		(13793)
47	10	EL	H	Birmingham City	W 2-0	1-0	18	Bowry 11, Malkin 53	9271
48	13	EL	A	Huddersfield Town	L 0-3	0-1	18		(11206)
49	20	EL	H	Oldham Athletic	L 0-1	0-0	19		9574
50	27	EL	H	Stoke City	L 2-3	0-2	19	Rae 79(pen), 87	10105
51	M 5	EL	A	Ipswich Town	D 0-0	0-0	22		(17290)

Best Home League Attendance: 14220 v Port Vale   Smallest: 7354 v Luton Town   Average: 9550

Goal Scorers:
EL(43):   Rae(13),Malkin(11),Fuchs(5),Dixon(5),Bowry(2),Stevens(2),Black(1),Newman(1),Yuran(1),Witter(1),Van(1)
CC(4):   Taylor(2),Savage(1),Rae(1)
FAC(3):   Rae(2),Malkin(1)

(F) Black	(M) Bowry	(F) Cadette	(G) Carter	(F) Connor	(F) Dixon	(F) Dolby	(M) Doyle	(M) Forbes	(F) Fuchs	(M) Gordon	(G) Keller	(M) Kulkov	(M) Lavin	(F) Malkin	(M) McRobert	(M) Neill	(M) Newman	(M) Rae	(D) Rogan	(F) Savage	(D) Stevens	(F) Taylor	(D) Thatcher	(D) Van	(D) Webber	(M) Weir	(D) Witter	(M) Yuran		
			S		X		X				X			X			X			S	X		X	X			X		M.Bailey	1
	S1				X3		X		S1		X			X			X		S3	X1	X	S2	X	X2			X		I.Cruikshank	2
	S3				X1		X		S1		X			X	S1		X	X		X	X3		X	X1			X		K.Leach	3
	S1				X		X	X1	S1		X1			X1			X	X3	S3	X1	X		X	X			X		P.Rejer	4
	X				X		X	S1	X1		X			S1			X	X3	S3	X1	X		X	X			X		C.Wilkes	5
	X				X3		S3		X		X			S1	S1		X	X		X3			X	X1			X		J.Rushton	6
	X				X		X	X2	S1	S2	X			S2			X	X		X			X	X1			X		R.Gifford	7
	X				X1		X	S1	S1		X			X	X		X	X		X			X	X1			X		J.Kirkby	8
	X				X1		X	S1	S1		X	X1		X			X	X		X			X	X	S		X		D.Gallagher	9
	X				X1		X3		S1		X			X	X1		X	X		X	S3		X	X1			X		J.Brandwood	10
X1	X				S2				X		X			X2			X	X		S1			X	X	S		X		K.Lynch	11
	X				S3				X3		X			X2			X	X		X	X	S1	X1	X	S2		X		M.Reed	12
	X				S1				X1		X			X			X	X3		S1	X	X1	X	S3			X		E.Wolstenholme	13
S1	X				S2		X		X1		X			X			X	X2		X	X3		X				X		R.Harris	14
S2	X				S1		X		X2		X			X1			X	X		X	X		X				X		D.Orr	15
S1	X				S2		X1	X1	X2		X			X			X	X		X	X3	S3	X				X		P.Durkin	16
X	X				S		X		X		X			X			X	X		X	X		X	X	S1		X1		G.Pooley	17
	X				S1		X1	X2	X1		X			X			X	X		S	X	S2	X				X		J.A.Kirby	18
	X				X1				S1		X			X			X	X		S2	X	X2	X	X	S		X		G.Singh	19
	X		X				X		S1		X			X2			X	X		S2	X	X1	X	X	S		X		J.Brandwood	20
	X				X				X1		X			X			X	X		S1	X		X	X	S1		X1		K.M.Lynch	21
	X				X1				X		X		X	X			S	X		S1	X		X	X			X		P.Taylor	22
	X1				S1				S2		X		X	X			S	X		X2	X	X	X	X			X		M.Bailey	23
							S3	S1	X		X		X	X	S2		X1	X3	X		X	X2	X						M.Pierce	24
						X		X			X		X	X2	S1		S	X1		X	S2	X	X						E.Lomas	25
			S2	S1			X2		X1		X		X	X			S	X		X	X	X	X				X		D.Orr	26
	X				X		S				X		X	X			X	X		X	S	X	X	X			X		R.Gifford	27
	X				X2				S	S2	X		X	X			X	X		S1	X		X	X			X		N.S.Barry	28
	X				X				S	S2	X		X2	X			X	X		S1	X		X	X			X		C.Wilkes	29
	X		X						S3			S1	S	X		X	X			S1	X	X	X1			X	X		U.Rennie	30
	X		X						S			X	S	X	X1	X	X			X	X	X	X			X	X		C.Wilkes	31
	S		X							X	S	X	X		X	X			X	S	X	X			X	X		E.K.Wolstenholme	32
		X	X								X	X	X	S	X		X1	X	S1	X	X			X	X		J.Kirkby	33
		X	X					S2			X	X1	S1		X	X	X	X	X	S	X	X2	R.J.Harris	34
X2			X1					X2		X		X	X		S1	X	S2	X	S2	X	X		I.Hemley	35
S1			X							X1	X	X	X	X1	X1	S3	X	S1	X	X3	X	X	J.Lloyd	36
X				S1						X	X	X	X	X	S	X	X1	X	S	X	X	K.Leach	37
X				S3			X		X2	X		X	S2	S1	X1	X	X	X	X2	K.Leach	38
X				S1				X1		X	S2	X2	X	X	S	X	X	X	W.C.Burns	39
X1				X			X1		X		X	S1	X	X	S	X	S1	X	G.Cain	40
X1				X			X		X		X	S2	X	X	S1	X	X2	X3	X	S3	D.Allison	41
X	S				X		X		X		X		X	X	S1	X1	X	S	X	X	X	R.Gifford	42
S3					X2			X	X3		X	X1	X	X	X1	X	X	S2	X	X	S1	P.Richards	43
			S		X2			S1	X	X	X	X1	X	X	X	X	X	X	S2	X	J.Rushton	44
X					S			X	X	S	X	X	X	X	X	X	S1	X1	X	S.Mathieson	45
X	S	S			S			X	X	X	X	X	X	X	X	X	X	X1	M.Pierce	46
X	S	S			S		X1	X	X	X	X	X	X	X	S1	X	C.Wilkes	47
X	S				S1		X1	X	X	X	S2	X	X	X	X	X2	X	P.Rejer	48
X	S2		X		X1	S3		X	S1	X2	X	X3	X	X	X	G.Pooley	49
X1				X		X1	X	X	X	S1	X	S1	X	X	X	R.Harris	50
X				X		X		X	X	S1	X	S	X1	X	X	X2	S2	K.Lynch	51
2	33	0	4	7	15	6	15	0	21	6	42	5	18	39	1	5	34	37	4	17	39	12	41	42	8	8	30	13	EL Appearances	
2	5	1	0	1	7	4	3	4	11	0	0	1	1	4	6	8	2	0	3	10	0	10	0	8	0	1	0	0	EL Sub Appearances	
0+1	3	0	0	0	1+2	0	2	0+1	2	0	3	0	0	3	1	0	2	2	0	2	0	1	0	0+2	2	3	0+1	0	CC Appearances	
0	2	0	1	0	1	0	0	0	0+1	0	1	0	0	1	0	0	2	1	0	2	2	0	1+1	2	1	1	0	2	FAC Appearances	

so Played: ((M) Bennett X(1), S3(14). (F) Berry X1(28,29). (G) Colgan S(21,22). (M) Keown S1(31). (D) McCarthy X(2). (G) Wietecha S(1).

445

MILLWALL

CLUB RECORDS

BIGGEST VICTORIES
League: 9-1 v Torquay United, Division 3(S), 29.8.1927.
9-1 v Coventry City, Division 3(S) 19.11.1927.
F.A. Cup: 7-0 v Gateshead, 2nd Round, 12.12.1936.
League Cup: 5-1 v Northampton, 3rd Round replay, 16.10.1967.
BIGGEST DEFEATS
League: 1-8 v Plymouth, Division 2, 16.1.1932.
F.A. Cup: 1-9 v Aston Villa, 4th Round, 28.1.1946.
League Cup: 1-7 v Chelsea, 1st Round, 10.10.1960.
MOST POINTS
3 points a win: 90, Division 3, 1984-85.
2 points a win: 65, Division 3(S), 1927-28 & Division 3, 1965-66.
MOST GOALS SCORED
127, Division 3(S) (Record), 1927-28.
MOST GOALS CONCEDED
100, Division 3(S), 1955-56.
MOST FIRST CLASS MATCHES IN A SEASON
61 - 1984-85 (League 46, FA Cup 7, League Cup 4, Freight Rover Trophy 4).
MOST LEAGUE WINS
30, Division 3(S), 1927-28.
MOST LEAGUE DRAWS
18, Division 3(S), 1921-22; Division 3(S), 1922-23.
MOST LEAGUE DEFEATS
26, Division 3(S), 1957-58.
RECORD TRANSFER FEE RECEIVED
£2,300,000 from Crystal Palace for Andy Roberts, July 1995.
RECORD TRANSFER FEE PAID
£800,000 for Paul Goddard from Derby County, December 1989.
BEST PERFORMANCES
League: 10th in Division 1, 1988-89.
F.A.Cup: Semi-finals in 1899-00, 1902-03, 1936-37.
League Cup: 5th Round in 1973-74, 1976-77, 1994-95.

COMPETITIONS

Div.1/P	Div.2/1	Div.3/2	Div.3(S)	Div.4
1988-90	1928-34	1962-64	1920-28	1958-62
	1938-48	1965-66	1934-38	1964-65
	1966-75	1975-76	1948-58	
	1976-79	1979-85		
	1985-88	1996-		FLT
	1990-96			1982-83

INDIVIDUAL CLUB RECORDS

MOST GOALS IN A CAREER
Teddy Sheringham: 111 (1983-91). 93 League, 5 FA Cup, 8 Lge Cup 5 Others.
MOST GOALS IN A SEASON
Richard Parker: 38 goals in 1926-27 (League 37, FA Cup 1).
Peter Burridge: 38 goals in 1960-61 (League 35, FA Cup 2, League Cup 1).
E.Sheringham: 38 goals in 1990-91 (Lge 33, FA Cup 2,Lge Cup 2, FMC 1).
MOST GOALS IN A MATCH
5. Richard Parker v Norwich City, 6-1, Division 3(S), 28.8.1926.
MOST APPEARANCES
Barry Kitchener: 589+7 (1966-82). 518+5 League, 29+2 FA Cup, 42 Lge Cup.
OLDEST PLAYER
Jack Fort, 41 years 8 months.
YOUNGEST PLAYER
David Mehmet, 16 years 5 months.
MOST CAPPED PLAYER
Eamonn Dunphy (Eire) 23.

PREVIOUS MANAGERS

F B Kidd 1894-99, E R Stopher 1899-1900, G A Saunders 1900-11,
H Lipsham 1911-18, R Hunter 1918-33, W McCracken 1933-36,
C Hewitt 1936-40, W Voisey 1940-44, J Cook 1944-48,
C Hewitt 1948-56, R Gray 1956-58, J Seed 1958-59, J Smith 1959-61
R Gray 1961-63, W Gray 1963-66, B Fenton1966-74, G Jago1974-77
G Petchley 1978-80, P Anderson 1980-82, G Graham 1982-86,
I Docherty 1986-90, B Rioch 1990-92, M McCarthy 1992-96.

ADDITIONAL INFORMATION
PREVIOUS NAMES
Millwall Rovers 1885. Millwall Athletic 1889.
PREVIOUS LEAGUES
United, London, Western Leagues. Southern District Combination. Southern League.
Club colours: Blue shirts, white shorts, blue socks.
Change colours: Green & white halved shirts, green shorts.
Reserves League: Avon Insurance Football Combination.

HONOURS

Div.2	Div.3(S)	Div 3(S) KO	Div.4	FLT
1987-88	1927-28	1936-37	1961-62	1982-83
	1937-38			

LONGEST LEAGUE RUNS

of undefeated matches:	19 (27.4.1959 - 7.11.1959)	of league matches w/out a win:	20 (26.12.1989 - 5.5.1990)
of undefeated home matches:	59 (20.4.1964 - 14.1.1967)	of undefeated away matches:	10 (5.3.21-7.9.21, 13.2.88-15.10.88)
without home win:	9 (1.1.1990 - 1.9.1990)	without an away win:	26 (7.11.1979 - 26.12.1980)
of league wins:	10 (10.3.1928 - 26.4.1928)	of home wins:	13 (15.12.1923 - 30.8.1924)
of league defeats:	11 (10.4.1929 - 21.9.1929)	of away wins:	5 (17.3.1928 - 25.4.1928)

THE MANAGER

Jimmy Nicholl . . . . appointed February 1996.

PREVIOUS CLUBS
As Manager . . . . Raith Rovers.
As Asst.Man/Coach . . . . None.
As a player . . . . Manchester United, Toronto, Sunderland, Toronto, West Brom.

HONOURS
As a Managers . . . . Promotion to Scottish Premier Division 1992/93, 1994/95. Scottish Lge Cup 1994/95.
As a Player . . . . Northern Ireland: 73 full caps, 1 u21 & Schools caps.

MILLWALL

PLAYERS NAME / Honours	Ht	Wt	Birthdate	Birthplace / Transfers	Contract Date	Clubs	League	L/Cup	FA Cup	Other	Lge	L/C	FAC	Oth
G O A L K E E P E R S														
Carter Tim	6.2	13.8	05/10/67	Bristol	08/10/85	Bristol Rovers	47	2	2	2				
E: Y3				Loan	14/12/87	Newport County	1							
				£50000	24/12/87	Sunderland	37	9		4				
				Loan	18/03/88	Carlisle United	4							
				Loan	15/09/88	Bristol City	3							
				Loan	21/11/91	Birmingham City	2	1						
				Free	01/08/92	Hartlepool United	18	4	1	2				
				Free	06/01/94	Millwall	8	0+1	1					
Keller Kasey	5.11	11.13	27/11/69	Washington (USA)		Portland University								
USA				Free	20/02/92	Millwall	176	14	8	4				
D E F E N D E R S														
Harle Michael J L	5.10	11.12	31/10/72	Lewisham	01/07/89	Gillingham	1+1				1			
01/08/92 Sittingbourne				£50000	01/08/93	Millwall								
				Loan	08/12/95	Bury								
Rogan Anton	5.11	12.6	25/03/66	Belfast		Distillery								
NI: 17					09/05/86	Celtic	115+12	12+1	18	8	4		1	
				£350000	04/10/91	Sunderland	45+1	1	8	2	1			
					09/08/93	Oxford United	56+2	4	4	2	3			
				Free	11/08/95	Millwall	4+3							
Stevens Keith H	6.0	12.5	21/06/64	Merton	23/06/81	Millwall	442+7	34	28	24	9	1		
Div2'88; FLT'83														
Van Blerk Jason C	6.1	13.0	16/03/68	Sydney		Go Ahead Eagles								
				£300000	08/09/94	Millwall	66+3	5	6		2			
Webber Damian J	6.4	14.0	08/10/68	Rustington		Bognor Regis								
					27/10/94	Millwall	27+11	1+2	2+2		2			
Witter Anthony J	6.2	13.2	12/08/65	London		Grays Athletic								
				£10000	24/10/90	Crystal Palace								
				£125000	19/08/91	Q.P.R.	1							
				Loan	09/01/92	Plymouth Argyle	3				1			
				Loan	11/02/94	Reading	4							
				£100000	14/12/94	Millwall	56+2	4	7		2			
M I D F I E L D														
Bowry Robert	5.8	10.0	19/05/71	Hampstead	08/08/90	Q.P.R.								
Div1'94				Free	04/04/92	Crystal Palace	23+9	7	1		1			
				£220000	05/07/95	Millwall	33+5	3	2		2			
Doyle Maurice	5.8	10.7	17/10/69	Ellesmere Port	11/07/88	Crewe Alexandra	6+2				2			
				£120000	21/04/89	Q.P.R.	6							
				Loan	17/01/91	Crewe Alexandra	6+1							
					17/05/95	Millwall	15+3	2						
Forbes Steven D	6.2	12.6	24/12/75	London		Sittingbourne								
				£45000	11/07/94	Millwall	0+5	0+1						
Lavin Gerard	5.8	10.8	05/02/74	Corby	13/05/92	Watford	121+5	11	6	2+1	3	1		
				£400000	23/11/95	Millwall	18+1		1					
McRobert Lee	5.9	10.12	04/10/72	Bromley		Sittingbourne								
				£35000	17/02/95	Millwall	5+9	1	1		1			
Neill Lucas E	5.9	11.10	01/01/70			Millwall	5+8							
Newman Richard A	5.9	10.7	05/08/70	Guildford	22/01/88	Crystal Palace	43+5	5	5+2	2	3			
Div1'94				Loan	28/02/92	Maidstone	9+1				1			
				£500000	19/07/95	Millwall	34+2	3	2		1			
Nurse David						Manchester C. (T)								
					28/06/96	Millwall								
F O R W A R D S														
Berry Greg J	5.11	12.0	05/03/71	Grays		East Thurrock								
				£2000	03/07/89	Leyton Orient	68+12	6	8+2	5+3	14	3	2	1
				£250000	17/08/92	Wimbledon	6+1		0+1		1			
				£200000	24/03/94	Millwall	10+10	1	1	1	1	2		1
				Loan	24/08/95	Brighton & H.A.	6				2			
				Loan	22/03/96	Leyton Orient	4	3						
Cadette Richard R	5.8	11.7	21/03/65	Hammersmith		Wembley								
B&QC'94				Free	25/08/84	Leyton Orient	19+2	4	1	2	4		1	
				Free	15/08/85	Southend United	90	5+1	4	5	49	1	5	1
				£130000	20/07/87	Sheffield United	26+8	1	2	2	7			
				£80000	22/07/88	Brentford	67+20	10+3	9	14	20	6	1	4
				Loan	22/03/90	Bournemouth	4+4				1			
					09/01/92	Falkirk	74+10	3+1	5+1	4	29	4	1	6
				£135000	13/10/94	Millwall	12+5	2	1		4	1		
Connor James R	6.0	12.9	22/08/74	Twickenham	21/11/92	Millwall	8+1							
Dolby Tony C	5.11	11.4	16/04/74	Greenwich	29/10/91	Millwall	23+22	4		1+1	1			
				Loan	16/02/94	Barnet	13+3				2			
				Loan	16/12/94	Chesham United								
Fuchs Uwe	6.1	12.0	23/07/66	Kaiserslautern		Kaiserslautern								
Div1'95				Loan	27/01/95	Middlesbrough	13+2				9			
				£750000	08/07/95	Millwall	21+11	2+1	0+1		5			
Malkin Chris	6.3	12.0	04/06/67	Hoylake		Stork AFC								
LCD'90				Free	27/07/87	Tranmere Rovers	184+48	20+5	9+4	26+7	59	6	2	8
				£400000	13/07/95	Millwall	39+4	3	2		11		1	
Savage David P T	6.2	12.7	30/07/73	Dublin		Longford Town (Eire)								
Ei: u21.2				£15000	27/05/94	Millwall	48+16	7	3+2		2	1	1	

ADDITIONAL CONTRACT PLAYERS
Aris Steven. Bircham Marc. Canoville Dean. Iga Andrew.
Keown Darren P (0+1 Oth.). Markey Brendon.
Nightingale Lewis. Roche Stephen M.

THE NEW DEN

London SE16 3LN
Tel: 0171 232 1222

Capacity 20,146

First game ....v Sporting Lisbon, 1-2, 4.8.1993.
First floodlit game..As above.

ATTENDANCES
Highest...20,093 v Arsenal, FA Cup 3rd Round, 10.1.1994.
Lowest...4,003 v Charlton Athletic, Anglo Italian Cup, 1.9.1993.

OTHER GROUNDS ....Glengall Road 1885-86. Back of Lord Nelson 1886-90. East Ferry Road 1890-01.
.... North Greenwich 1901-10. The Den 1910-93. The New Den 1993-

MATCHDAY TICKET PRICES

West Stand Upper Tier................... £18
Juv/OAP .... £5/£9

West Stand Lower Tier................... £14
Juv/OAP .... £5/£7

East Stand Upper Tier £16
Juv/OAP .... £5/£8

East Stand Lower Tier £12
Juv/OAP .... £5/£6

South Stand Upper & Lower.............. £10
Juv/OAP £5

Family Enclosure £11
Juv/OAP........................... £3/£4.50

Ticket Office Telephone no........ 0171 231 9999

CLUBCALL 0891 40 03 00

Calls cost 39p per minute cheap rate and 49p per
minute at all other times.
Call costings correct at time of going to press.

HOW TO GET TO THE GROUND

From the North
From motorway M1 and A1 follow signs London A1 then City, then follow signs to
Shoreditch, Whitechapel. Then follow signs to Ring Road, Dover to cross Tower
Bridge. In 1.8 miles at roundabout turn left into Old Kent Road, turn left before
Railway Bridge (Ilderton Road). Take 7th right for new stadium.

From the East
Use A2 sign posted London. At New Cross follow signs, City, Westminster, into
Kendar Street and at end turn left. Turn right at next traffic lights (Ilderton Road)
and then take 7th right for new stadium.

From the South and West
Use A2 sign posted London. At New Cross follow signs, City, Westminster, into
Kendar Street and at end turn left. Turn right at next traffic lights (Ilderton Road)
and then take 7th right for new stadium.

Car Parking
Street parking.

Nearest Railway Station
New Cross Gate BR & tube, New Cross BR & Tube, South Bermondsey BR
(Away) and Surrey Quays tube.

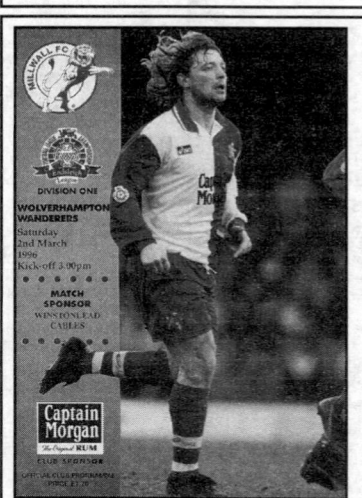

MATCHDAY PROGRAMME

Programme Editor .... Deano Standing.

Number of pages .... 40.

Price .... £1.60.

Subscriptions .... Home League £44, All home games £59,
.... Every game home & away £105

Local Newspapers . South London Press, South East London Mercury,
.... Southwark News.

Local Radio Stations .... Capital Radio.

NOTTS COUNTY
(The Magpies)
NATIONWIDE LEAGUE DIVISION 2
SPONSORED BY: BANK'S BITTER

Back row L-R: Richard Walker, Tony Agana, Steve Slawson, Shaun Murphy, Steve Cherry, Dean Yates, Michael Emenalo, Gary Lund, Colin Hoyle. **Middle:** Dean Thomas, Paul Sherlock, Ron Matthews, Paul Cox, Paul Reece, Gavin Worboys, Michael Johnson, Chris Short, Gary McSwegan. **Front:** Russell Slade (Asst.manager), Tommy Gallagher, Paul Devlin, Derek Pavis (Chairman), Phil Turner, Mick Walker (Manager), Andy Legg, Michael Simpson, Dennis Pettitt (Physio).

NOTTS COUNTY
FORMED IN 1862 (Oldest League Club)
TURNED PROFESSIONAL IN 1885
LTD COMPANY IN 1890

CHAIRMAN: D C Pavis
VICE-CHAIRMAN
J Mounteney
DIRECTORS
W Barrowcliffe, Mrs V Pavis,
D Ward, M Youdell MBE
SECRETARY
Ian Moat

GENERAL MANAGER: Colin Murphy
TEAM MANAGER: Steve Thompson
COACH: Mark Smith

YOUTH TEAM MANAGER
John Gaunt
PHYSIOTHERAPIST
Dennis Pettitt

STATISTICIAN FOR THE DIRECTORY
Ian Moat

The players reported back for pre season training under a new management due of Colin Murphy and Steve Thompson probably unaware of the changes which were to unfold during the course of what turned out to be one of the most eventful season's in the history of the club.

New skipper Gary Stodder had been recruited from W.B.A. and goalkeeper Darren Ward from neighbours Mansfield Town, but this was to be only the start of a massive re-building programme.

The new season kicked off at Wrexham with a spectacular long range goal from Phil Turner securing a well earned first point of the campaign. The much travelled John Burridge sat on the bench for the first time as back-up goalkeeper.

The four League games in August yielded 7 points with 2 wins, 1 draw and 1 defeat. Home and away victories were also achieved against Lincoln City in the Coca-Cola Cup.

The rebuilding of the team continued with the acquisition of Vinny Arkins from Shelbourne, whilst former Notts player Mark Smith re-joined the CLub in a coaching capacity.

The highlight of September was a magnificent 0-0 draw at Elland Road against Leeds United, whilst in the League a further 11 points were gained from six games.

October saw the Magpies valiantly exit the Coca-Cola Cup losing 3-2 to Leeds at Meadow Lane. This was followed by a disappointing defeat at Chesterfield in the Auto Windscreen Shield.

Victories over York, 1-0 (live on Sky) and Telford United 2-0, fixed the Magpies up with a third round tie against Middlesbrough, which the Premiership side won. Defeat against York in the Auto Windscreen Shield also saw the club exit that competition too.

Good League form was maintained in February with a tally of 8 points gained from 2 wins, 2 draws and only one defeat. The effects of the earlier bad weather were now being experienced with no less than nine League games played during March. It proved a productive month, however, with 15 points won from 4 victories, 3 draws and 2 defeats.

April was no less demanding with a further eight games to be played, with 3 wins, 3 draws and 2 defeats accumulating another 12 vital points with the highlights undoubtedly being the four goals scored at home against Bristol Rovers and the injury time equaliser at Oxford.

Defeat against Chesterfield meant that the Magpies missed out on an automatic place in the First Division, but hopes were up for gaining that last place via the play-offs. However, having beaten Crewe in the Semi-Finals they were beaten 0-2 in the final.

NOTTS COUNTY

League: 4th   FA Cup: 3rd Rnd   Coca-Cola Cup: 2nd Rnd   Auto Windscreen Shield: Quarter Finals

M	DATE	COMP	VEN	OPPONENTS	RESULT	HT	LP	GOAL SCORERS/GOAL TIMES	ATT.
1	A 12	EL	A	Wrexham	D 1-1	1-0	13	Turner 26	(4338)
2	15	CC 1/1	H	Lincoln City	W 2-0	2-0		White 28, 42	3494
3	19	EL	H	Wycombe Wanderers	W 2-0	0-0	5	Legg 58, White 80	5552
4	22	CC 1/2	A	Lincoln City	W 2-0	0-0		White 75, 88	(2636)
5	26	EL	A	Peterborough United	W 1-0	1-0	4	White 43	(5618)
6	29	EL	H	Bradford City	L 0-2	0-1	10		6168
7	S 2	EL	A	Brighton & H.A.	L 0-1	0-0	12		(5267)
8	9	EL	H	Bournemouth	W 2-0	0-0	8	White 59, 84(pen)	4875
9	12	EL	H	Stockport County	W 1-0	0-0	5	Devlin 49	4588
10	16	EL	A	Shrewsbury Town	W 1-0	0-0	5	White 74	(2892)
11	19	CC 2/1	A	Leeds United	D 0-0	0-0			(12384)
12	23	EL	H	Bristol City	D 2-2	0-0	4	Legg 48, White 55	5251
13	30	EL	A	Crewe Alexandra	D 2-2	0-0	6	Agana 54, White 80	(4260)
14	O 3	CC 2/2	H	Leeds United	L 2-3	1-1		White 25(pen), 75	12477
15	7	EL	A	Carlisle United	D 0-0	0-0	5		(6058)
16	14	EL	H	Rotherham United	W 2-1	1-1	4	Devlin 13, Gallagher 58	5478
17	17	AWS 1/2	A	Chesterfield	L 1-2	0-0		White	(2150)
18	21	EL	H	Bristol Rovers	W 3-0	1-0	2	Nicol 33, Arkins 57, Legg 73	(6078)
19	28	EL	H	Swindon Town	L 1-3	1-2	3	Legg 15	8725
20	N 1	EL	H	Brentford	W 4-0	1-0	3	Devlin 17, Arkins 58, 88, Murphy 64	4005
21	4	EL	A	Burnley	W 4-3	2-1	3	Arkins 17, Devlin 36(pen), 75, Baraclough 59	(10511)
22	7	AWS 1/2	H	Stockport County	W 1-0	0-0		Devlin	2015
23	12	FAC 1	A	York City	W 1-0	1-0		Legg 25	(4228)
24	18	EL	H	Chesterfield	W 4-1	2-1	3	Gallagher 9, Strodder 40, Nicol 67, Arkins 70	6747
25	25	EL	A	Swansea City	D 0-0	0-0	2		(2327)
26	27	AWS 2	A	Doncaster Rovers	W 3-1	0-0		Murphy, Devlin , Agana	(1714)
27	D 2	FAC 2	A	Telford	W 2-0	1-0		Gallagher 21, Legg 51	(2831)
28	9	EL	H	Bristol City	W 2-0	1-0	2	Strodder 9, White 89	(5617)
29	16	EL	H	Crewe Alexandra	L 0-1	0-1	3		5869
30	23	EL	H	Blackpool	D 1-1	0-0	3	Arkins 48	5522
31	J 6	FAC 3	H	Middlesbrough	L 1-2	0-0		Rogers 52	12671
32	13	EL	A	Wycombe Wanderers	D 1-1	0-0	4	Rogers 86	4980
33	20	EL	A	Wrexham	W 1-0	0-0	4	Arkins 72	5014
34	F 3	EL	H	Peterborough United	W 1-0	0-0	3	Battersby 67	5067
35	9	AWS QF	A	York City	L 0-1	0-0			(2075)
36	10	EL	A	Walsall	D 0-0	0-0	4		(4378)
37	17	EL	A	Stockport County	L 0-2	0-0	4		(6179)
38	24	EL	H	Shrewsbury Town	D 1-1	1-1	5	Rogers 27	4559
39	27	EL	A	Bournemouth	W 2-0	1-0	4	Devlin 29, Hunt 64	(3191)
40	M 2	EL	H	Hull City	W 1-0	0-0	4	Battersby 63	4528
41	6	EL	H	Walsall	W 2-1	1-1	4	Battersby 9, Jones 53	4050
42	9	EL	A	Blackpool	L 0-1	0-1	4		(7187)
43	12	EL	H	York City	D 2-2	2-2	4	Jones 31, Battersby 35	3462
44	16	EL	H	Oxford United	D 1-1	0-1	4	Martindale 65	5140
45	19	EL	A	Bradford City	L 0-1	0-1	5		(3622)
46	23	EL	A	York City	W 3-1	1-1	5	Martindale 7, 63, Jones 71	(3126)
47	26	EL	A	Hull City	D 0-0	0-0	5		(2589)
48	30	EL	H	Carlisle United	W 3-1	2-0	21	Jones 12, Martindale 14, Jones 62	4514
49	A 2	EL	A	Rotherham United	L 0-2	0-0	18		(2750)
50	6	EL	A	Swansea City	L 0-1	0-0	1		(10928)
51	9	EL	H	Bristol Rovers	W 4-2	1-0	4	Strodder 26, Martindale 58, Baraclough 82, Finnan 90	4661
52	13	EL	A	Brentford	D 0-0	0-0	5		(4588)
53	16	EL	A	Oxford United	D 1-1	0-1	3	Murphy 90	(6934)
54	20	EL	H	Burnley	D 1-1	0-1	4	Battersby 64	5697
55	23	EL	H	Brighton & H.A.	W 2-1	1-1	4	Battersby 23, 66	3501
56	27	EL	H	Swansea City	W 4-0	0-0	4	Murphy 47, Agana 63, Martindale 71, Finnan 76	5051
57	M 4	EL	A	Chesterfield	L 0-1	0-0	4		(6708)
58	12	PO SF1	A	Crewe Alexandra	D 2-2	0-2		Finnan 55, Martindale 90	(4931)
59	15	PO SF2	H	Crewe Alexandra	W 1-0	0-0		Martindale 61	9640
60	26	PO F	A	Bradford City	L 0-2	0-1			(39972)

Best Home League Attendance: 8725 v Swindon Town   Smallest: 3462 v York City   Average: 5131

Goal Scorers:
EL(63):   White(8),Arkins(7),Battersby(7),Martindale(6),Devlin(6),Jones(5),Legg(4),Murphy(3),Strodder(3),Finnan(2),Baraclough(2),Gallagher(2),Nicol(2),Rogers(2),
          Agana(2),Turner(1),Hunt(1)
CC(6):   White(6)
FAC(4):   Legg(2),Rogers(1),Gallagher(1)
AWS(5):   Devlin(2),Agana(1),Murphy(1),White(1)   PO(3):   Martindale(2),Finnan(1)

(F) Agana	(D) Atkins	(F) Ashcroft	(F) Baraclough	(F) Battersby	(D) Derry	(F) Devlin	(M) Finnan	(D) Gallagher	(M) Galloway	(F) Hogg	(M) Hunt	(F) Jones	(M) Legg	(M) Martindale	(F) Mills	(D) Murphy	(D) Nicol	(D) Richardson	(M) Rogers	(D) Short	(M) Simpson	(D) Strodder	(M) Turner	(D) Walker	(G) Ward	(F) White	(D) Wilder	(M) Wilks		
X1						X					X		X			X		S				X	X	X	X	X			P.Richards	1
X1						X					X		X			X					S	X	X	X	X	X			M.Bailey	2
X1						X					X		X			X					S	X	X	X	X	X			S.Mathieson	3
											X		X			X	X				X	X	X	X	X	X			T.Leake	4
S1						X1			X		X		X			X	X				S2	X	X	X	X	X			U.Rennie	5
S						X			X		X		X			X	X				S	X	X	X	X	X			E.Wolstenholme	6
X1						X			S		X		X	X	S	X						X	X	X	X	X			G.Barber	7
S1						X	X	S			X1		X		X	X					X	X	X	X	X	X			G.Pooley	8
S2	S					X	X	S1			X2		X			X	X1				X	X	X	X	X	X			G.Cain	9
S2	S1					X	X	S			X2	S	X			X					X	X	X	X	X	X			R.Pearson	10
X	S1					X			X		X	S	X			X		X1			X	X	X	X	X	X			R.Hart	11
S2	X						X	X1			X2	S	X			X		S1			X	X	X	X	X	X			P.Taylor	12
X	X2						X	X			S	S1	X	X1		X		S2			X	X	X	X	X	X			G.Singh	13
X	X1						X	X			X	S	X			X		X				X	X	X	X	X			A.Wilkie	14
X	S1					X	X	X			X	S	X			X					S	X	X	X	X	X1			K.M.Lynch	15
S	X					X	X	S			X		X			X					X	X	X	S	X	X			E.Wolstenholme	16
X	X3					S2	X	X2		S1		S3	X			X			X	X			X1	X	X	X			T.Lunt	17
S		X				X	X1	S			X		X	S1	X	X					X	X			X	X			I.S.Hemley	18
S	X	X				X	X	S			X		X		S	X	X				X	X			X	X			A.Wiley	19
S2	X	X				X	X3	S1			X		X			X	S3	X	X1		X	X			X	X2			J.Rushton	20
S	X	X1				X	X	S			X		X			X	X				X	X			X	S			R.Pearson	21
X	X					X3	X	X2			S2		X1			X					X	X			X	S3			R.Furnandiz	22
S	X	X				X	X	S			X		X			X	X				X	X			X	S			T.Leake	23
X	X	X				X	X	X			X		X			X	X				X	X			X	S			D.Allison	24
X	X	X				X	X	S			X		X			X	X				X	X			X	S			D.Orr	25
X	X	X				X	X	X	X		X		X			X					S	X			X	S			I.G.Cruikshank	26
S	X1	X				X	X	S			X		X			X	X			X	X		X		X	S1			T.West	27
S1	X	X				X	X2	S			X1		X			X	X				X	X	X		X	S2			R.Gifford	28
S	X	X				X	X1	S			X		X			X	X				X	X	X		X	S1			E.Wolstenholme	29
S	X	X				X	S	X			X		X			X1	X				S1	X	X		X	X			M.Bailey	30
S3	X	X				X	X3	X			X2		X			X					S1	X	X1		X	S2			G.Ashby	31
S	S	X	X			X	X	S	X		X		X			X					X	X			X	X			E.Lomas	32
		S1		X		X2	X	S2			X		X			X		X	X		S	X			X	X1	X		G.B.Frankland	33
	X	X	X			X	X	S			X		X			X		X	X1		S1				X	S	X		A.D'Urso	34
S		X				X	X	S	S		X		X	X		X					X	X			X	X			N.Barry	35
X	X	X	X			X	X				X		X			X		X			S				X	X			P.Taylor	36
X	X	X	S			X	X				X		S			S		X			X	X			X		X		U.Rennie	37
S	X1	X	S1	X		X		X			X			S		X					X	X			X		X		I.Hemley	38
X	S	X	X			X	X				X	S	X		S	X					X	X			X		X		S.Bennett	39
X		X	X			X1		S	X	X						X					S1	X			X		X	S	A.Leak	40
X	S1	X	X1		X					S	X	X				X					S	X			X		X		K.Lynch	41
X		X	X	S		S1				S	X	X	X		X						X	X			X		X		G.Cain	42
X		X	X			X1		X	X		S	X	X		S1	X					X	X			X		X		R.J.Harris	43
X	S	X	X1	X		X					S	X	X		S1	X					X	X			X		X		R.Pearson	44
X	X	X	X1			X		X			S1	X	X			X					X	X	S		X		X		W.Burns	45
	S	X	S			X		X		S	X	X	X			X					X	X			X		X		M.Poulain	46
	S	X	S			X		X		X	X		X	X		X					X	X			X		X		P.Richards	47
	S	X	S1	X		X		X		S	X	X				X1					X	X			X		X		J.Lloyd	48
	S	X	X			X		S		X	X		X			X					X	X			X		X		N.Barry	49
S	X1	X	S2	X		S1		X			X		X			X2					X	X			X		X		G.Pooley	50
S1		X1	X			X		S			X2		X			X	X				X	X			X			X	A.D'Urso	51
X	S1	X	S1	S		X		S			X1		X			X	X				X	X			X			X	A.R.Leake	52
X	S1	X1	S2	X		X		S			X2		X			X	X				X	X			X				S.Mathieson	53
X2	S	S2	X	S1		X					X1		X			X	X				X	X			X				R.Gifford	54
	S	X	X	X		X		X	X	X1		S1		X		X		X2			S2				X				J.Rushton	55
X		X	X1	X		X				S		S1		X		X	X			S	X			X				I.Cruikshanks	56
X2	S3	S1	X	X3		X					S2		X1			X		X2			X				X				T.West	57
X		X	X1	X		X		S		X		S		S1		X					X	X			X				D.Allison	58
X		X	X1	X		X		S		X		S		X		X					X	X			X				K.Lynch	59
X		X	X	X		X		S		S		S1		X		X					X	X			X				G.Singh	60
19	**17**	**4**	**34**	**14**	**11**	**26**	**14**	**21**	**7**	**10**	**10**	**16**	**24**	**13**	**12**	**39**	**13**	**15**	**21**	**0**	**18**	**43**	**12**	**11**	**46**	**18**	**9**	**0**	EL Appearances	
8	6	2	0	7	0	0	3	1	2	0	0	2	1	3	2	0	0	0	0	2	5	0	0	0	0	2	0	0	EL Sub Appearances	
3	1+1	0	0	3	0	2	0	1	2	2	0	0	4	0	2	2	1	0	0	2	3	3	4	4	0	0	0	0	CC Appearances	
0+1	3	0	3	0	0	3	0	1	0	0	0	3	0	2	3	1	0	1	1	2+1	2	2	0	3	0+2	0	0	0	FAC Appearances	
3	4	0	0	1	3+1	0	3	3	2	0+2	0	3+1	0	3	3	1	0	1	1+1	3	3	0	1	4	1+1	0	0	0	AWS Appearances	
3	0	0	3	3	0	3	0	0	0	1+1	0	2+1	0	3	3	0	0	3	0	3	3	0	0	3	0	0	0	0	PO Appearances	

Also Played: (G) Burridge S(1,2,4,11). (M) Butler S(4). (F) Hoyle S(14,25,27,45,47), X(41), X1(42). (D) Johnson S1(14). (F) Jemson S(3,8), X(4), S3(5), X1(6), S1(7). (M) Marsden X(1,2,3,7). (F) McSwegan S1(1,2,3,6), S(4,5). (G) Pollitt S(58,59,60). (M) Redmile X(17).

CLUB RECORDS

BIGGEST VICTORIES
League: 10-0 v Port Vale, Division 2, 26.2.1895.
11-1 v Newport County, 15.1.1949.
F.A. Cup: 15-0 v Thornhill (no Rotherham), 1st Round, 24.10.1885.
League Cup: 5-0 v Mansfield, 30.8.1988.
5-0 v Swindon Town, 17.10.1962.
BIGGEST DEFEATS
League: 1-9 v Blackburn Rovers, Division 1, 16.11.1889.
1-9 v Aston Villa, Division 3(S), 29.9.1930.
1-9 v portsmouth, Division 2, 9.4.1927.
0-8 v West Bromwich Albion, Division 1, 25.10.1919.
0-8 v Newcastle United, Division 1, 26.10.1901.
F.A. Cup: 1-8 v Newcastle united, 3rd Round, 8.1.1927.
League Cup: 1-7 v Newcastle United (h), 2nd Round, 5.10.1993.
MOST POINTS: 3 points a win: 87, Division 3, 1989-90.
2 points a win: 69, Division 4, 1970-71.
MOST GOALS SCORED: 107, Division 4, 1959-60.
Newsham 24, Forrest 19, Bircumshaw 17, Roby 11, Joyce 10,
Withers 8, Hateley 8, Horobin 7, Carver 2, Opponents 1.
MOST GOALS CONCEDED: 97, Division 2, 1934-35.
MOST FIRST CLASS MATCHES IN A SEASON
62 - 1993-94 (League 46, FA Cup 3, League Cup 4, Anglo/Italian 9).
MOST LEAGUE WINS: 30, Division 4, 1970-71.
MOST LEAGUE DRAWS: 18, Division 4, 1968-69.
MOST LEAGUE DEFEATS: 28, Division 3, 1963-64.

BEST PERFORMANCES
League: 1970-71: Matches played 46, Won 30, Drawn 9, Lost 7,
Goals for 89, Goals against 36, Points 69. First in Division 4.
Highest Position: 3rd in Division 1, 1890-91, 1900-01.
F.A. Cup: 1893-94: 1st Round Burnley (h) 1-0; 2nd Round Burton
(a) 2-1; 3rd round Nottingham Forest (a) 1-1 (h) 4-1; Semi-final
Blackburn Rovers 1-0; Final Bolton Wanderers 4-1.
League Cup: 5th Round in 1963-64, 1972-73.
Most recent success: 1975-76: 2nd Round Sunderland (h) 2-1;
3rd Round Leeds United (a) 1-0; 4th Round Everton (a) 2-2, (h) 2-0;
5th Round Newcastle United (a) 0-1.
HONOURS: Division 2 Champions 1896-97, 1913-14, 1922-23.
Division 3(S) Champions 1930-31, 1949-50.
Division 4 Champions 1970-71. FA Cup 1893-94.
Anglo-Italian Cup winners in 1994-95. Runners-up 1993-94.
LEAGUE CAREER: Founder member of Football League 1988, Div
2 1892-93, Div 1 1896-97, Div 2 1912-13, Div 1 1913-14, Div 2
1919-20, Div 1 1922-23, Div 2 1925-26, Div 3(S) 1929-30, Div 2
1930-31, Div 3(S) 1934-35, Div 2 1949-50, Div 3 1957-58, Div 2
1958-59, Div 3 1959-60, Div 4 1963-64, Div 3 1970-71, Div 2 1972-
73, Div 1 1980-81, Div 2 1983-84, Div 3 1984-85, Div 2 (now Div 1)
1989-90, Div 2 1994-95.

INDIVIDUAL CLUB RECORDS

MOST GOALS IN A SEASON
Tom Keetley: 41 goals in 1930-31 (League 39, FA Cup 2).

MOST GOALS IN A MATCH
9. Harry Curshaw v Wednesbury Strollers, FA Cup 2nd Round
replay, 10.12.1881.

OLDEST PLAYER: Albert Iremonger, 41 years 320 days.

YOUNGEST PLAYER: Tony Bircumshaw, 16 years 54 days.

MOST CAPPED PLAYER
Kevin Wilson (Northern Ireland) 13.
Harry Curshaw (England) 8.

RECORD TRANSFER FEE RECEIVED
£2,500,000 from Derby County for Craig Short, 9/92.

RECORD TRANSFER FEE PAID
£750,000 for Tony Agana from Sheffield United, 11/91.

PREVIOUS MANAGERS

Albert Fisher 1913-27, Horace Henshall 1927-34, Charles Jones
1934, David Platt 1934, Percy Smith 1935-36; Jim McMullen 1936-
37, Harry Parkes 1938-39, Tony Towe 1939-42, Frank Womack
1942-43, Frank Buckley 1944-46, Arthur Strolley 1946-49, Eric
Houghton 1949-53, George Dryser 1953-57, Tommy Lawton 1957-
58, Frank Hill 1958-61, Tim Coleman 1961-63, Eddie Lowe 1963-65,
Tim Coleman 1965-66, Jack Burkitt 1966-67, Andy Beattie 1967, Bill
Gray 1967-68, Jack Wheeler 1968-69, Jimmy Sirrell 1969-75,
Ronnie Fenton 1975-77, Jimmy Sirrell 1977-82, Howard Wilkinson
1982-83, Larry Lloyd 1983-84, Ritchie Barker 1984-85, Jimmy Sirrell
1985-87, John Barnwell 1987-88, Neil Warnock 1988-92, Mick
Walker 1992-94, Howard Kendal 1995.

ADDITIONAL INFORMATION
PREVIOUS NAMES: None.
PREVIOUS LEAGUES: None.

Club colours: Black and white striped shirts, black shorts, black
socks.

Change colours: Yellow shirts/shorts/socks.

Reserves League: Pontins Central League Division 1.
Youth League: Melville Youth League.

LONGEST LEAGUE RUNS

of undefeated matches:	19 (26.4.1930 - 6.12.1930)	of league matches w/out a win:	18 (26.11.1904 - 8.4.1905)
of undefeated home matches:	25 (17.8.1970 - 14.8.1971)	of undefeated away matches:	10 (24.7.1971 - 30.10.1971)
without home win: 13 (3.12.1904 - 23.9.1905, 24.11.79 - 26.4.80)		without an away win:	24 (23.12.1933 - 30.1.1935)
of league wins:	8 (17.1.1914 - 14.3.1914)	of home wins:	14 (17.9.1959 - 13.2.1960)
of league defeats:	7 (1888-89, 1912, 1933, 1983)	of away wins:	5 (15.9.1896 - 31.10.1896)

GENERAL MANAGER

COLIN MURPHY . . . . appointed July 1995.

PREVIOUS CLUBS
As Manager . . . . . Derby, Lincoln (11 years), Stockport,
. . . . Southend.
As Asst.Man/Coach . . . . Derby, Leicester, Luton.
As a player . . . . Crystal Palace, Cork Hibs, Wimbledon.

HONOURS
As a Manager . . Promotion gained on three occasions.
As a Player . . . . None.

TEAM MANAGER

Steve Thompson . . . . .appointed July 1995.

. . . . .Lincoln, Southend.
. . . . .Doncaster Rovers.
. . . . .Lincoln, Charlton Athletic, Sheffield United.

. . . . .Promotion gained on two occasions.
. . . . .None.

NOTTS COUNTY

PLAYERS NAME Honours	Ht	Wt	Birthdate	Birthplace Transfers	Contract Date	Clubs	League	L/Cup	FA Cup	Other	Lge	L/C	FAC	Oth
							APPEARANCES				**GOALS**			
G O A L K E E P E R S														
Pollitt Michael	6.3	14.1	24/09/72	Farnworth	01/07/90	Manchester United								
				Free	10/07/91	Bury								
				Free	01/12/92	Lincoln City	57	5	2	4				
				Free	11/08/94	Darlington	55	4	3	5				
				£75000	14/11/95	Notts County								
Ward Darren	5.11	12.9	11/05/74	Mansfield	27/07/92	Mansfield Town	81	5	5	6				
				£150000	11/07/95	Notts County	46	4	3	7				
D E F E N D E R S														
Arkins Vincent						Notts County	17+6	1+1	3	4	7			
Derry Shaun						Notts County	11			3				
Forsyth Michael E	5.11	12.2	20/03/66	Liverpool	16/11/83	W.B.A.	28+1	1	2	1				
E: B.1, u21.1, Y.8. Div.2'87.				£25000	28/03/86	Derby County	323+1	36	15+1	29	8	1		
				£200000	23/02/95	Notts County	7							
Gallagher Thomas D	5.10	11.0	25/08/74	Nottingham	25/08/74	Notts County	41+1	1	3	8+2	2		1	
Murphy Shaun P	6.0	12.0	05/11/70	Sydney (Aus)		Perth Italia (Aus)								
					04/09/92	Notts County	84+9	4+2	6	12+1	5			2
Richardson Ian						Dagenham & Red.								
				£60000	23/08/95	Birmingham City	3+4	3+1	2	1+2				
				£200000	22/03/96	Notts County	15			3				
Strodder Gary	6.1	11.4	01/04/65	Cleckheaton	08/04/83	Lincoln City	122+10	7+1	2+1	5+1	6			
				20/03/87	West Ham United	59+6	8	4+2	2	2			
				£190000	22/08/90	W.B.A.	123+17	8+1	7	10	8		1	
				£145000	14/07/95	Notts County	43	3	2	6	3			
Walker Richard N	5.11	10.12	09/11/71	Derby	03/07/90	Notts County	50+1	10		6+1	4			
				Loan	23/03/95	Mansfield Town	4							
Wilder Chris	5.11	10.10	23/09/67	Stockbridge	26/09/85	Southampton								
				Free	20/08/86	Sheffield United	89+4	8+1	7	3	1			
				Loan	02/11/89	Walsall	4		1	2				
Loan (12/10/90) Charlton Athletic 1Lge App.				Loan	28/11/91	Charlton Athletic	2							
				Loan	27/02/92	Leyton Orient	16			1	1			
				£50000	30/07/92	Rotherham United	129+4	11	16+2	6+1	10		1	
				£130000	02/01/96	Notts County	9							
M I D F I E L D														
Galloway Michael A	5.11	11.5	13/10/74	Nottingham	15/06/93	Notts County	13+3	2		3				
Hunt James			17/12/76	Derby	15/07/94	Notts County	10		0+2		1			
Redmile Matthew						Notts County				1				
Rogers Paul A	6.0	12.05	21/03/65	Portsmouth		Sutton United								
E: SP.6. IPL'85'.86.				£35000	29/01/92	Sheffield United	120+5	8+1	4	1	10	1		
					29/12/95	Notts County	21		1	4	2		1	
Simpson Michael	5.9	10.6	28/02/74	Nottingham	01/07/92	Notts County	38+10	4+1	2+1	7+3	3			
Turner Philip	5.8	10.7	12/02/62	Sheffield	05/02/80	Lincoln City	239+2	19	12	5	19	1		
				22/08/86	Grimsby Town	62	6	6	3	9			1
				£42000	19/02/88	Leicester City	18+6	1+1	1		2			
					03/03/89	Notts County	223+14	17+3	15	33+1	16	3		3
Wilks Tim						Notts County(T)								
F O R W A R D S														
Agana Patrick A O	5.11	12.0	02/10/63	Bromley		Weymouth								
E: SP.1.				£35000	13/08/87	Watford	12+3	1+1	2	1	1	2		
				£45000	19/02/88	Sheffield United	105+13	12	14	4+1	42	3	5	1
				£750000	12/11/91	Notts County	96+24	8+1	5+1	17+1	12	2	1	4
				Loan	27/02/92	Leeds United	1+1							
Baraclough Ian	6.1	11.10	04/12/70	Leicester	15/12/88	Leicester City			1	0+1				
E: Fl.ge u18.1.				Loan	22/03/90	Wigan Athletic	8+1				2			
Loan (21/12/90) Grimsby Town 1+3 Lge App.				Free	13/08/91	Grimsby Town	1							
				Free	21/08/92	Lincoln City	68+5	7	4	7	10	1		
				Free	06/06/94	Mansfield Town	47	7	4	4	5			
				£150000	13/10/95	Notts County	34		3	3	2			
Battersby Tony	6.0	12.09	30/08/75	Doncaster	05/07/93	Sheffield United				2+1				1
				Loan	23/03/95	Southend United	6+2				1			
				£200000	08/01/96	Notts County	14+7			4	7			
Hogg Graeme J	6.1	12.4	17/06/64	Aberdeen	01/06/82	Manchester United	82+1	7+1	8	12	1			
AIC'95.				Loan	03/11/87	W.B.A.	7			1				
				£150000	25/08/88	Portsmouth	97+3	2	6	2	2			
				£200000	23/08/91	Hearts	49+8	5	1	4	3		1	
Loan (03/10/94) Notts County				£75000	27/01/95	Notts County	27	2	1	3				
Jones Gary	6.1	12.9	06/04/69	Huddersfield		Rossington Main								
				Free	26/01/89	Doncaster Rovers	10+10	1			2			
£8500 (01/11/89) Grantham				£17500	01/01/90	Kettering Town								
£3000 (01/08/91) Boston United				£25000	03/06/93	Southend United	33+14	1	1	4+1	14			2
Loan (16/08/93) Dagenham & Red.				Loan	17/09/93	Lincoln City	0+4		0+1	2				
				£140000	01/03/96	Notts County	16+2			1+1	5			
Martindale Gary	5.11	11.9	24/06/71	Liverpool		Burscough								
				24/03/94	Bolton Wanderers								
				Free	04/07/95	Peterborough Utd	26+5	4	4	4	15	1		2
				£175000	06/03/96	Notts County	13+3			2+1	6			2

MEADOW LANE

Nottingham NG2 3HJ
Tel: 0115 952 9000

Capacity ....20,300.

First game...v Nottingham Forest, September 1910.
First floodlit game ....v Derby County, 23.3.1953, 1-1, Att: 20,193.

ATTENDANCES
Highest ....47,310 v York City, FACup 6th Round, 10.3.1955.
Lowest...1,616 v Peterborough United, FMC, 12.12.1989.

OTHER GROUNDS ....Park Hallow. Meadows Cricket Ground. Beeston Cricket Ground.
....Castle Cricket Ground. Trent Bridge Cricket Ground.

MATCHDAY TICKET PRICES

Derek Pavis Stand Centre £14

Wings £12

Jimmy Sirrel Stand. £10

Family Stand £10
Juv/OAP £5

Additional Information
Under 10s pay £20 per season for membership and are then admitted free of charge.

Ticket Office Telephone no. 01159 557 210

CLUBCALL
0898 88 86 84

Calls cost 39p per minute cheap rate and 49p per minute at all other times.
Call costings correct at time of going to press.

HOW TO GET TO THE GROUND

From the North
Use motorway (M1) until junction 26, leave motorway and follow signs into Nottingham A610. Follow signs to Melton Mowbray, Trent Bridge A606. On near-side of River Trent turn left into Meadow Lane for Notts County FC.

From the East
Use A52 sign posted Nottingham to Trent Bridge, cross River and then turn right into Meadow Lane for Notts County FC.

From the South
Use motorway (M1) until junction 24, leave motorway and follow signs to NOttingham (South) to Trent Bridge, cross river and then right into Meadow Lane for Notts County FC.

From the West
Use A52 into Nottingham, then follow signs to Melton Mowbray, Trent Bridge A606 on nearside of River Trent turn left into Meadow Lane for Notts County FC.

Car Parking: Limited street parking near ground but ample space in the City of Nottingham Corporation car park only 20 minutes walk.

Nearest Railway Station: Nottingham Midland (all enquiries to Derby Station 01332 32051)

MATCHDAY PROGRAMME

Programme Editor . . . . Terry Bowles.

Number of pages . . . . 40.

Price . . . . £1.30.

Subscriptions . . . . Apply to club.

Local Newspapers. . . . . Nottingham Evening Post.

Local Radio Stations . . . . Radio Nottingham, Radio Trent.

PETERBOROUGH UNITED
(The Posh)
NATIONWIDE LEAGUE DIVISION 2
SPONSORED BY: THOMAS COOK

Back Row (L-R): Kevin Ashley, Simon Clark, Danny Carter, Greg Heald, Lee Power, David Morrison, Neil Le Bihan, Gary Breen, Ryan Semple. **Middle Row:** Keith Oakes (Physio), Sean Farrell, David Gregory, Marcus Ebdon, Billy Manuel, Andy Furnell, Michael Halsall (Asst. Manager). **Front Row:** Lee Williams, Gary Martindale, Mark Tyler, John Still (Manager), Jon Sheffield, Scott McGleish, Tony Spearing.

PETERBOROUGH UNITED
FORMED IN 1934
TURNED PROFESSIONAL IN 1934
LTD COMPANY IN 1934

CHIEF EXECUTIVE: Iain Russell
CHAIRMAN: Roger Terrell
DIRECTORS
B Fry, P Sagar, N Hards, R Terrell,
A Hand, M Vincent.
ASSOCIATE DIRECTORS
M Judson, T Judson, T Elisgood
SECRETARY
Miss Caroline Hand
COMMERCIAL MANAGER
Ben Hallam

DIRECTOR OF FOOTBALL: Barry Fry
ASSISTANT MANAGER: Lil Fuccillo
FIRST TEAM COACH: Mick Halsall
YOUTH TEAM MANAGER
Paul Ashworth
PHYSIOTHERAPIST
Keith Oakes

STATISTICIAN FOR THE DIRECTORY
Mick Robinson

At the end of the 1994/5 season I said the shopping list was: a goalkeeper, if Mark Tyler was not given a chance; a forward to assist Ken Charlery; a midfielder who would score double figures. What happened?

John Still decided that he would not give Mark Tyler a run in goal and bought Jon Sheffield from local rivals Cambridge United for £150,000. Jon played well and was voted Player of the Year. Instead of finding someone to play beside Ken Charlery, he was sold to Birmingham and four attacking players were signed by the club: Carter, Martindale, McGleish and Power. Of the new faces, Carter has scored only once in 45 games, McGleish - who showed in his 6 starts and 12 sub-appearances that he could be a more-than useful player - scored twice and finished the season on loan and scoring at Colchester. Power, who never really looked fit, found the net 7 times in 46 games. This left Gary Martindale, who was signed on a free transfer from Bolton. He scored 18 goals in 43 games and was promptly given away to a Division Two rivals Notts County for £175,000. By the end of the season Charlery was back with the club as player-coach and had scored 7 goals in 20 games.

No midfielder signed, which may have led to John Still's demise. Although a 3-1 victory on the opening day of the season saw Posh top of the table, only on three other occasions did the club find themselves in the top half of the table, offering only five wins in the opening 19 games and no real pattern to the team due to a lack of control in midfield. Jon Still gave in to supporters' pressure and left the club. His last act for the club was to bring Paul Shaw - a midfielder - from Arsenal on loan. Paul added skill and effort to the midfield area and the club for once started to play through the midfield. He scored 5 goals in 12 league games - the club tried to sign him but the price Arsenal were asking was beyond them.

An overview of the season: a poor effort, with relegation only seen off in the last few games. Although the fourth round of the FA Cup and area semi-final of the Auto Windscreens Shield were reached, it was poor fare. The second round of the Coca Cola Cup was achieved after pulling back from a 4-1 defeat in the first round first leg at Swansea.

Predictions for 1996/7: as Barry Fry has bought the club, and as Birmingham had a playing squad bigger than Posh's average attendance, it is anyone's guess what may happen.

M. ROBINSON

PETERBOROUGH UNITED

League: 19th   FA Cup: 4th Rnd   Coca-Cola Cup: 2nd Rnd   Auto Windscreen Shield: Semi-Finals

M	DATE	COMP	VEN	OPPONENTS	RESULT	HT	LP	GOAL SCORERS/GOAL TIMES	ATT.
1	A 12	EL	H	Brighton & H.A.	W 3-1	1-0	3	Clark 39, Farrell 70, Martindale 81	5394
2	15	CC 1/1	A	Swansea City	L 1-4	0-2		Manuel 54	(1862)
3	19	EL	A	Bournemouth	L 0-3	0-1	11		(4175)
4	22	CC 1/2	H	Swansea City	W 3-0	1-0		Manuel 3, 62, Le Bihan 85	1871
5	26	EL	H	Notts County	L 0-1	0-1	17		5618
6	29	EL	A	Blackpool	L 1-2	1-1	20	Heald 28	(3902)
7	S 2	EL	H	Bristol City	D 1-1	1-0	19	Farrell 3	4621
8	9	EL	A	Wycombe Wanderers	D 1-1	0-1	20	Farrell 75	(5637)
9	12	EL	A	Carlisle United	D 1-1	1-0	20	Martindale 41	(6027)
10	16	EL	H	Wrexham	W 1-0	0-0	18	Martindale 55	3817
11	20	CC 2/1	A	Aston Villa	L 0-6	0-3			(19602)
12	23	EL	H	Bradford City	W 3-1	1-1	11	Heald 22, Manuel 52, Martindale 76	4509
13	26	AWS 1/1	A	Plymouth Argyle	W 3-0	1-0		Clark 45, Power 46, McGleish 47	(1818)
14	30	EL	A	Rotherham United	L 1-5	0-2	15	Power 47	(2863)
15	O 3	CC 2/2	H	Aston Villa	D 1-1	1-0		Martindale 39	5745
16	7	EL	A	Walsall	D 1-1	0-0	17	Power 79	(3768)
17	14	EL	H	Swansea City	D 1-1	1-0	16	Carter 34	3834
18	16	AWS 1/1	H	Northampton Town	D 0-0	0-0			3045
19	21	EL	A	Brentford	L 0-3	0-2	17		(4865)
20	28	EL	H	York City	W 6-1	3-0	15	Martindale 19, 44, Morrison 39, 63, Power 54, Shaw 81	4605
21	31	EL	H	Burnley	L 0-2	0-2	17		4737
22	N 4	EL	A	Bristol Rovers	D 1-1	0-1	16	Shaw 55	(4241)
23	11	FAC 1	A	Exeter City	W 1-0	1-0		Le Bihan 10	(3783)
24	18	EL	H	Oxford United	D 1-1	0-1	17	Shaw 65	4720
25	25	EL	A	Hull City	W 3-2	1-1	23	Martindale 12, 48, 81 (3)	(3620)
26	28	AWS 2	A	Swansea City	W 1-0	0-0		Farrell	1952
27	D 2	FAC 2	H	Bognor Regis	W 4-0	3-0		Farrell 25, 44, 45 (3), Ebdon 62	5004
28	9	EL	A	Bradford City	L 1-2	0-1	16	Farrell 56	(4605)
29	16	EL	A	Rotherham United	W 1-0	0-0	15	Spearing 59	3847
30	19	EL	H	Stockport County	L 0-1	0-0	15		3267
31	26	EL	A	Chesterfield	D 1-1	1-0	16	Heald 11	(6017)
32	J 6	FAC 3	H	Wrexham	W 1-0	0-0		Le Bihan 52	5983
33	9	AWS QF	H	Colchester United	W 3-2	0-0		Martindale (2), McGleish 48	2460
34	13	EL	H	Bournemouth	L 4-5	1-2	17	Farrell 15,80, Martindale 54, 64	4596
35	20	EL	A	Brighton & H.A.	W 2-1	1-1	17	Shaw 16, 90	(5572)
36	F 3	EL	A	Notts County	L 0-1	0-0	19		(5067)
37	5	FAC 4	A	Huddersfield Town	L 0-2	0-0			(11629)
38	10	EL	A	Shrewsbury Town	D 2-2	0-0	18	Martindale 57, Basham 70	4985
39	13	AWS SF	H	Bristol Rovers	L 0-1	0-0			3761
40	17	EL	H	Carlisle United	W 6-1	4-0	18	Charlery 8, 43, Ebdon 26, Farrell 37, 54, Martindale 58(pen)	4302
41	20	EL	A	Bristol City	W 1-0	0-0	17	Charlery 55	(5014)
42	24	EL	A	Wrexham	L 0-1	0-0	6		(4011)
43	27	EL	H	Wycombe Wanderers	W 3-0	1-0	15	Martindale 24, 89, Foran 83	3670
44	M 2	EL	H	Chesterfield	L 0-1	0-0	15		6105
45	5	EL	H	Swindon Town	L 0-2	0-1	16		4196
46	9	EL	A	Stockport County	W 1-0	0-0	14	Power 49	(5915)
47	16	EL	H	Crewe Alexandra	W 3-1	2-0	14	Charlery 2, Power 14, Charlery 65	5004
48	19	EL	A	Shrewsbury Town	D 1-1	0-1	12	Ansah 50	(2291)
49	23	EL	A	Swindon Town	L 0-2	0-2	2		(9066)
50	26	EL	H	Blackpool	D 0-0	0-0	13		4425
51	30	EL	H	Walsall	L 2-3	2-2	15	Griffiths 2, Charlery 36	4954
52	A 2	EL	A	Swansea City	D 0-0	0-0	15		(3805)
53	6	EL	A	York City	L 1-3	1-2	16	Ebdon 17(pen)	(3261)
54	8	EL	H	Brentford	L 0-1	0-0	17		4343
55	13	EL	A	Burnley	L 1-2	0-0	19	Heald 68	(8393)
56	20	EL	H	Bristol Rovers	D 0-0	0-0	19		4884
57	27	EL	H	Hull City	W 3-1	1-0	18	Power 25, Farrell 70, Charlery 89	6649
58	30	EL	A	Crewe Alexandra	L 1-2	0-2	18	Grazioli 62	(3206)
59	M 4	EL	A	Oxford United	L 0-4	0-0	19		(7535)

Best Home League Attendance: 6649 v Hull City   **Smallest: 3267 v Stockport County**   **Average: 4655**

Goal Scorers:
EL(59): Martindale(15),Farrell(9),Charlery(7),Power(6),Shaw(5),Heald(4),Ebdon(2),Morrison(2),Griffiths(1),Foran(1),Manuel(1),Spearing(1),Clark(1),Grazioli(1),
Carter(1),Basham(1),Ansah(1)
CC(5): Manuel(3),Martindale(1),Le Bihan (1)
FAC(6): Farrell(3),Le Bihan(2),Ebdon(1)
AWS(7): Martindale(2),McGleish(2),Power(1),Farrell(1),Clark(1)

456

1995-96

	Ashley (D)	Basham (D)	Blount (M)	Breen (D)	Carter (F)	Charley (F)	Clark (D)	Dobson (D)	Ebdon (M)	Farrell (F)	Foran (D)	Gregory (D)	Griffiths (F)	Heald (D)	Hooper (M)	Le Bihan (M)	Manuel (D)	Marindale (F)	McGleish (F)	Morrison (F)	Power (F)	Finch (D)	Robinson (M)	Sedgemore (M)	Shaw (F)	Sheffield (G)	Spearing (D)	Williams.L (M)	Williams.S (M)		
			X	X			X		X	S1				S		S2	X	X		X2	X1					X	X	X		I.S.Hemley	1
			X	X			X		S1					S		S2	X		X2	X1	X					X	X	X		P.Rejer	2
			X	X1			X		S3							S1	X	X2	S2	X	X3					X	X	X		K.Leach	3
				X								S		X		X	X	X1	S1	X2	S1					X		X		N.Barry	4
				X	S1		X		X					X		X1	X	X2	S	X	S2	X				X		X		U.Rennie	5
				X	S2		X		X					X3		X	X	X3	X	X1	X2	X				X		X		J.Lloyd	6
				X	S2		X		X					X		X	X3	X	X1	X2	X					X		X		M.Riley	7
				X	X		S2		X	X1		S		X		X		S1	X2	X1	X					X		X		R.Harris	8
				X	X		X		X	X1		S2		X		S3	X	X3		S1	X					X		X2		R.Pearson	9
				X	X1		X		X			S2		X		X2	X	S3	S1	S1	X					X		X		K.Lynch	10
				X	X1		X		X					X		X2		S1	S2	X					X		X		T.Heilbron	11
			X1	X2			X		X				S1	X		X	X	S	S2	X	X				X		X		S.G.Bennett	12
			X1				X		X					X		X2	X		X	S2	X	X				X		X		P.Rejer	13
S			X	X		X		X					X		X		X	X	X	X				X		X		G.B.Frankland	14
X			X	X		X		X					X		X	X		X	X	X				X		X		G.Ashby	15
X			X	X		X		X					X		X1	X		X	S1	X				X				P.Taylor	16
X			X	X		X		X				S		X		S	X	X	X	S1	X1				X		X		J.Kirkby	17
X			X			X		S				X		X		S	X	X	X	X				X		X		J.Brandwood	18
X			X	S2		X		X1					X		S1	X2	X3	S3					X		X		X		B.Knight	19
X			X	S1		X		X					X		X2			X3	X1	S3			X		X		X		M.Fletcher	20
X			X	S1		X		X					X		X	S2	X2	X					X		X		X1		G.Pooley	21
X			X	X1		X		X					X		X	S1	X		X2	X			X		X		X		D.Orr	22
X			X			X		X	S3		X		X		X1	X3			X2	X					X		S2		A.Wiley	23
X			X			X		X	S1		X		X		X2	X			X1	X			X		X		S2		S.Baines	24
X			X			X		X	S		X		X		S	X	X		X	X			X		X		X		A.Butler	25
X			X			X		X	S1		X		X		S2		X	X1		X2			X		X		X			26
X2			X			X		X	X1		X3		X		X	S3	X	S2		S1	X		X		X		S2		P.Danson	27
X			X			X		X	X		X		X		S			S1	X1		X		X		X		X		P.Richards	28
			X			X		X	X1		X		X	X	S	S	X1		S1				X		X		X		N.S.Barry	29
			X			X		X	X1		X		X	X	S1	S	X		S2				X		X		X2		R.J.Harris	30
S			X			X		X	X		X	X	S1		S	X1							X		X		X		E.Wolstenholme	31
			X	X2		X		X	X		X		X		S1	X1	X	S	X				X		S2		X		T.West	32
			X	X		X		S	X1		X		X		X		S2	X2		S1			X		X		X			33
S			X	X		X		X			X	X1	X		X	S		X		S1			X	X		X		X	S.J.Baines	34
X			X	X		X		S	X2		X		X			X1	S1		S2			X	X	X		X		K.A.Leach	35
X			X	X1		X	X		X		X		X		S			S1	X1	S2			X	X	S	X2		A.D'Urso	36
			X	X1		X	X		X		X		X			S		X	X	S1	S2		X	X	X2		X		J.Rushton	37
X					X	X1	X	X	X	X	X		X		X		S1	X	X	S	S		X	X		X		D.Orr	38
			X	X	X	X	S	X	X	X		X		X		X	X		S	S			X	X		X			39
X			X2	X1	X	S	X	X	X		X		X		S1		X		S2				X	X		X		N.Barry	40
X			X	X	X	X	X	X	X		X		X		S		X		S	X			X	X		X		J.Brandwood	41
X			X	X	X	X	X	X1	X		X		X		X		X		S1	X			X	X		X		I.Cruikshanks	42
X			X	X		X	S	X			X		X		S1	X		X2	X1	X			X	X		X	S2	M.Bailey	43
X			X		X	X	S	X			X		X		S2	X		X1	X				X2	X		X	S1	B.Knight	44
X1			X	X	X	X		X			X		X		S2			X3	X	S1			X2	X		X	S3	A.Butler	45
			X	X	X	X	X		X		X		X				X		X	X			S1	X	S	X	S	D.Laws	46
			X1	X		X		X			X		X			X	X		S	X	X	X		X		X		G.Frankland	47
			X	X	X	X		X			X		X			X	X1	S	X				X		X		S.Bennett	48
S3			X	X	X	X		X			X		X			X	X1		X2				X		X3		T.Heilbron	49
X			X	X	X	X		X			X		X	X	X		X2	S2		X1	S1		X		X		F.Stretton	50
X	S		X	X	X	X		X			X		X				X2	S2		X1	S1		X		X		U.Rennie	51
	X		X	X	X	X		X		S	X	X	X				S	S		X			X		X		C.Wilkes	52
	X		X	X	X	X		X	S1	X	X1	X	X				S	S2		X			X		X	X2	J.Lloyd	53
	X1		X	X	S	X		X	X		X		X		X		X2	S2	S1				X	X		X		K.Lynch	54
			S	X	X	X		X			X		X		X		X	S1	S				X		X	X1	B.Burns	55
X	S		S1	X	X			X			X2		X				S2	X1		X			X		X		R.Furnandiz	56
X	X		X	X	X			X			X		X				X			X			S		X		X	G.Barber	57
			X	X		X		X			X		S2	X	X1	X3			X				S3		X		G.Cain	58
			S1			X	X	X			X		S2	X		X3			X1				X1		X		G.Pooley	59
EL Appearances	13	4	25	30	19	39	4	39	20	17	0	4	40	4	16	13	26	3	21	25	13	5	13	12	46	9	32	0		
EL Sub Appearances	1	1	0	7	0	1	0	0	6	0	3	0	0	0	9	0	5	9	3	13	5	0	4	0	0	0	1	3		
CC Appearances	0	0	4	3	0	3	0	4	0	1	0	3	0	2+1	4	4	0+1	3+1	2+2	2	0	0	4	1	3	0				
FAC Appearances	0	0	4	2	0	4	0	4	3+1	0	1	0	3	2+1	1+1	4	0+1	2	1+2	2+1	1	0	4	1+1	3+1	0				
AWS Appearances	0	0	2	1	0	4	0	2	2+1	0	2	0	5	0	3+1	2	4	3+1	2+1	1	2+1	0	2	5	1	5	0				

Played: (F) Ansah S1(47,48). (M) Codner X1(46), S2(49). (D) Drury S(22), S3(59). (F) Furnell S1(13,23), S(14,15,16,18,21,22,24,25,26), S2(20). (M) Grazioli S(47,48,50,57), S1(49), X(58), X2(59).
Inman X2(58). (M) Meredith S(15), S1(58), X(59). (G) Tyler S(11,13,14,15,16).

PETERBOROUGH UNITED RECORDS AND STATISTICS

CLUB RECORDS

BIGGEST VICTORIES
League: 8-1 v Oldham Athletic, Div 4, 26.11.1969; 7-0 v Barrow, Div 4, 9.10.1971.

MOST GOALS SCORED IN A CUP TIE
9-1 v Rushden, 6.10.45.

BIGGEST DEFEAT
League: 0-7 v Tranmere Rovers, Div 4, 29.10.1985

MOST LEAGUE POINTS
(3pts for win) 82, Div 4, 1981-82
(2pts for win) 66, Div 4,1960-61

MOST LEAGUE GOALS
134, Division 4, 1960-61
Bly 52, Hails 21, Smith 17, Emery 15, McNamee 16, Ripley 5, Dunne 1, Raymor 1,og 6.

RECORD TRANSFER FEE RECEIVED
£350,000 from Watford for Ken Charlery, October 1992.
£350,000 from Birmingham for Ken Charlery, July 1995.

RECORD TRANSFER FEE PAID
£225,000 to POrtsmouth for Carl Griffiths, February 1996.

BEST PERFORMANCES
League: 10th Div 1, 1992/93, FA Cup: 6th rnd. 1964-65
League Cup: Semi Final 1965-66

HONOURS
League Division 4 Champions, 1960-61, 1973-74.

LEAGUE CAREER
Elected to Div 4 1960
Promoted to Div 3 1961
Demoted to Div 4 1968
Promoted to Div 3 1974
Relegated to Div 4 1979
Promoted to Div 3 1990
Promoted to Div 1 1992
Relegated to Div 2 1994

INDIVIDUAL CLUB RECORDS

MOST APPEARANCES
Tommy Robson: League 440+42 + FA Cup 43+2 + League Cup 31+1 +Texaco 3 Total 517+45 (1968-81)

MOST CAPPED PLAYER
A Millington (Wales) 8

RECORD LEAGUE GOALSCORER IN A SEASON
Terry Bly 54 (League 52, FAC 2) 1960-61
4 goals 2 times = 8; 3 goals 5 times = 15; 2 goals 6 times = 12; 1 goal 17times = 17.

RECORD LEAGUE GOALSCORER IN A CAREER
Jim Hall 122 0In All Competitions: JimHall 137 (League 122, FAC 11, Lge Cup 4) 1967-75

OLDEST PLAYER IN A LEAGUE MATCH
Norman Rigby, 38 years 333 days, 21.4.1962.

YOUNGEST PLAYER IN A LEAGUE MATCH
Mark Heeley, 16 years 229 days, 24.4.1976.

PREVIOUS MANAGERS

1934-36 Jock Porter, 1936-37 Fred Taylor, 1937-38 VicPoulter, 1938-48 Sam Haden, 1948-50 Jack Blood, 1950-52 Bob Gurney, 1952-54Jack Fairbrother, 1954-58 George Swindin, 1958-62 Jimmy Hagan, 1962-64 JackFairbrother, 1964-67 Gordon Clark, 1967-69 Norman Rigby, 1969-72 Jim Iley,1972-77 Noel Cantwell, 1977-78 John Barnwell, 1978-79 Billy Hails, 1979-82Peter Morris, 1982-83 Martin Wilkinson, 1983-86 John Wile, 1986-88 NoelCantwell, 1988 89 Mick Jones, 1989-90 Mark Lawrenson, 1990-91 Dave Booth, 1991-93 Chris Turner, 1993-94 Lil Fuccillo, 1994 Chris Turner, 199 John Still.

ADDITIONAL INFORMATION
Previous League: Midland League.
Previous Names: None
Club colours: Blue shirt white sleeve, white shorts, blue & white socks.
Change colours: Red with yellow and green flecks shirt and short red socks.
Reserves League: Capital League.
Youth League: Midland Intermediate.

LONGEST LEAGUE RUNS

of undefeated matches:	17 (17.12.1960 - 15.4.1961)	of league matches w/out a win:	17 (28.9.1978 - 30.12.1978
of undefeated home matches:	32 (21.4.1973 - 9.11.1974)	of undefeated away matches:	8 (28.1.69-19.4.69, 19.3.88-10.9.88
without home win:	9 (1.2.1992 - 14.3.1992)	without an away win:	26 (7.1.1976 - 22.3.1977
of league wins:	9 (1.2.1992 - 14.3.1992)	of home wins:	15 (3.12.1960 - 28.8.1961
of league defeats:	5 (26.12.1988 - 21.1.1989)	of away wins:	5 (22.3.1988 - 7.5.1988

THE MANAGER/DIRECTOR OF FOOTBALL

BARRY FRY. . . . . appointed May 1996.

PREVIOUS CLUBS
As Manager. . . . . Dunstable, Hillingdon, Bedford T, Maidstone, Barnet, Southend Utd, Birmingham City.
As Asst.Man/Coach . . . . None.
As a player . . . . Manchester Utd, Bolton W., Luton, Leyton Orient, Gravesend & Northfleet, Dunstable.

HONOURS
As a Manager. . . . . **Barnet:** GMVC 1990-91. **Birmingham:** Division 2 & AMC 1994-95.
As a Player. . . . . **England:** Schoolboys caps.

PLAYERS NAME / Honours	Ht	Wt	Birthdate	Birthplace / Transfers	Contract Date	Clubs	APPEARANCES League	L/Cup	FA Cup	Other	GOALS Lge	L/C	FAC	Oth
G O A L K E E P E R S														
heffield Jonathan	6.0	12.0	01/02/69	Bedworth	16/02/87	Norwich City	1							
oan (22/09/89) Aldershot 11 Lge, 1 Oth App.				Loan	21/08/90	Aldershot	15			1				
				Free	18/03/91	Cambridge United	56	3	4	6				
				Loan	23/12/93	Colchester United	6							
oan (28/01/94) Swindon Town 2 Lge Apps.				Loan	15/09/94	Hereford United	8	2						
					20/07/95	Peterborough Utd	46	4	4	5				
yler Mark	6.0	12.9	02/04/77	Norwich	07/12/94	Peterborough Utd	4+1			2				
				Loan	25/01/96	Billericay Town								
D E F E N D E R S														
asham Michael	5.10	11.0	27/09/73	Barking	03/07/92	West Ham United								
oan (18/11/93) Colchester United 1 Lge App.				Free	24/03/94	Swansea City	27+2		6	8+2	1			
				Free	18/12/95	Peterborough Utd	13+1				1			
ark Simon	6.1	12.6	12/03/67	London		Stevenage								
				Free	25/05/94	Peterborough Utd	71+1	5	6	4+1	1			1
rury Adam						Peterborough Utd (T)	0+1							
oran Mark	6.4	13.12	30/10/73	Aldershot	03/11/90	Millwall								
oan (01/08/92) Slough 1 FAC App.				£25000	28/08/93	Sheffield United	10+1	1		0+1	1			
oan (26/08/94) Rotherham United 3 Lge Apps.				Loan	13/09/95	Wycombe Wand.	5	2						
					08/02/96	Peterborough Utd	17		1		1			
eald Greg	6.1	12.8	26/09/71	London		Enfield								
				£20000	08/07/94	Peterborough Utd	67+2	4	3	8	4			
earing Tony	5.9	10.12	07/10/64	Romford	11/10/82	Norwich City	67+2	5	4	4				
				Loan	01/11/84	Stoke City	9							
oan (01/02/85) Oxford United 5 Lge Apps.				£100000	12/07/88	Leicester City	71+2	2+1	1	2	1			
				Free	01/07/91	Plymouth Argyle	35	6	1	2+1				
				Free	21/01/93	Peterborough Utd	94+4	5	3+2	6	2			
M I D F I E L D														
odon Marcus	5.9	11.0	17/10/70	Pontypool	16/08/89	Everton								
: u21.2, Y.				Free	15/07/91	Peterborough Utd	124+3	12+1	10+1	11+1	14		1	
razioli Giuliano					19/10/95	Peterborough Utd	2+1				1			
oan (01/11/95) Yeovil Town				Loan	10/02/96	Enfield								
oughton Scott	5.5	11.6	22/10/71		24/08/90	Tottenham Hotspur	0+10	0+2		0+2	2			
Y.7,S. FAYC'90.				Loan	26/03/91	Ipswich Town	7+1				1			
oan (17/12/92) Gillingham 3 Lge Apps.				Loan	26/02/93	Charlton Athletic	6							
				Free	10/08/93	Luton Town	7+9	2+1	0+1	2	1			
				£15000	07/09/94	Walsall	76+2	0+1	10	2	14	1	3	
					05/07/96	Peterborough Utd								
man Niall						Peterborough Utd (T)	1							
e Bihan Neil	5.11	11.1	14/03/76	London		Tottenham Hotspur								
				Free	13/07/94	Peterborough Utd	19+10	2+1	2+1	3+1		1	2	
oan (23/09/94) Bishop Stortford				Loan	10/03/95	Yeovil Town								
eredith Thomas						Peterborough Utd (T)	1+1							
Connor Martin	5.8	10.8	10/12/67			Bromsgrove Rovers								
.P'92.				£25000	26/06/92	Crystal Palace	2			1+1				
				Loan	24/03/94	Walsall	10			2	1			1
				£40000	14/02/94	Walsall	94	6	10	3	21	2	2	1
					05/07/96	Peterborough Utd								
dgemore Ben	5.10	13.11	05/08/75	Wolverhampton	17/05/93	Birmingham City								
				Loan	22/12/94	Northampton Town	1							
				Free	10/01/96	Peterborough Utd	13+4		1					
F O R W A R D S														
arter Darren S	5.11	11.12	29/06/69	Hackney		Billericay Town								
					04/07/88	Leyton Orient	168+20	13+3	10	17+2	22	2	3	1
				£25000	01/08/95	Peterborough Utd	30+7	3	2	3	1			
harley Ken	6.1	13.03	28/11/64	Stepney		Beckton								
a Basildon, Fisher Athletic 1 FAC App.				£35000	01/03/89	Maidstone	41+18	1+3	0+3	5+4	11	1		
				£20000	28/03/91	Peterborough Utd	45+6	10	3	11	19	5	1	7
				£350000	16/10/92	Watford	45+3	3	1	0+1	13			
				£150000	16/12/93	Peterborough Utd	70	2	2+1	2	24		3	1
				£350000	04/07/95	Birmingham City	8+9	3+1		1+1	4	2		
					09/02/96	Peterborough Utd	19			1	7			
arrell Sean	6.1	12.8	28/02/69	Watford	05/03/87	Luton Town	14+11		2+1	1+2	1		1	2
				Loan	01/03/88	Colchester United	4+5				1			
				Loan	13/09/91	Northampton Town	4				1			
				£100000	19/12/91	Fulham	93+1	5+1	2	8	31	3	1	3
				£120000	05/08/94	Peterborough Utd	45+14	3+1	4+1	3+1	17		3	1
iffiths Carl	5.9	10.6	16/07/71	Oswestry	26/09/88	Shrewsbury Town	110+33	7+4	6	7+3	54	3	2	3
: B.1, u21.2, Y. FLge u18.1.				£500000	29/10/93	Manchester City	11+7	0+1			4			
				£200000	17/08/95	Portsmouth	2+13	0+1			2			
				£225000	28/03/96	Peterborough Utd	4				1			
cGleish Scott	5.9	10.08	10/02/74	St Pancras		Edgware Town								
				Free	24/05/94	Charlton Athletic								
				Free	04/07/95	Peterborough Utd	3+9	0+1	0+1	3+1				2
				Loan	23/02/96	Colchester United	10+5			2	6			
orrison David	5.11	12.5	30/11/74	Waltham Forest		Chelmsford								
				£30000	12/05/94	Peterborough Utd	55+11	4+1	2+1	4+1	10	1		
wer Lee	5.10	10.10	30/06/72	Lewisham	06/07/90	Norwich City	28+16	1	0+1	0+2	10			
B.1, u21.12, Y.				Loan	04/12/92	Charlton Athletic	5							
an (13/08/93) Sunderland				Loan	15/10/93	Portsmouth	1+1		1					
				£200000	08/03/94	Bradford City	14+16	0+2	0+2	1+1	3		1	1
an (09/01/95) Millwall				£80000	26/07/95	Peterborough Utd	25+13	2+2	1+2	1	6			1

LONDON ROAD GROUND
Peterborough PE2 8AL
Tel: 01733 53947

Capacity	15,595
Covered Standing	6,000
Seating	9,575

First game	v Gainsborough, 01.09.34.
First floodlit game	v Arsenal, 08.02.60.

ATTENDANCES
Highest	30,096 v Swansea City, FA Cup 5th Round, 20.2.1965.
Lowest	279 v Aldershot, AMC, 17.4.1986.

OTHER GROUNDS: .... None.

MATCHDAY TICKET PRICES

Main Stand	£11
Juv/OAP	£5.50
Wing Stand/Enclosure	£9
Juv/OAP	£4.50
Terraces	£7
Juv/OAP	£3.50

Match & Ticket Inforamtion
Tickets bookable 14 days in advance.

Ticket Office Telephone no 01733 63947

HOW TO GET TO THE GROUND

From the North and West
Use A1 then A47 sign posted Peterborough into town centre. Follow signs to Whittlesey and cross river bridge into London Road for Peterborough United FC.

From East
Use A47 into Peterborough town centre and follow signs to Whittlesey and cross river bridge into London Road for Peterborough United FC.

From the South
Use A1 then A15 sign posted Peterborough into London Road for Peterborough United FC.

Car Parking
Ample parking available at ground.

Nearest Railway Station
Peterborough (01733 68181)

CLUBCALL
0891 12 16 54
Calls cost 39p per minute cheap rate and 49p per minute at all other times.
Call costings correct at time of going to press.

MATCHDAY PROGRAMME

Programme Editor	Russell Plummer.
Number of pages	32.
Price	£1.20.
Subscriptions	Please apply to club.
Local Newspapers	Herald & Post, Evening Telegraph.
Local Radio Stations	Radio Cambridgeshire, Hereward Radio.

PLYMOUTH ARGYLE
(The Pilgrims)
NATIONWIDE LEAGUE DIVISION 2
SPONSORED BY: ROTOLOK

Founded in 1886

ack Row (L-R): Andy Comyn, Keith Hill, Mlck Heathcoat, Kevin Blackwell, Nicky Hammond, Kevin Nugent, Adrian Viveash, Michael Evans.
iddle Row: Mick JOnes (Asst. Manager), Wayne Burnett, Steve McCall, Chris Twiddy, James Dungey, Ronnie Mauge, Mark Patterson, Chris
adbitter, Norman Meadhurst.
ont Row: Mark Saunders, Paul Williams, Micky Ross, Neil Warnock, Dan McCauley (Chairman), Martin Barlow, Adrian Littlejohn, Sam Shilton.

PLYMOUTH ARGYLE
FORMED IN 1886
TURNED PROFESSIONAL IN 1903
LTD COMPANY IN 1903

PRESIDENT: S Rendell
CHAIRMAN: D McCauley
DIRECTORS
P Bloom, G Jasper.
SECRETARY
M Holladay (01752 562 561/2/3)
COMMERCIAL MANAGER
Steve Birley (01752 562561)

MANAGER: Neil Warnock
ASSISTANT MANAGER: Mick Jones
YOUTH TEAM MANAGER
Kevin Blackwell
PHYSIOTHERAPIST
Norman Medhurst

STATISTICIAN FOR THE DIRECTORY
Jonathan Brewer

O n the 25th May a number of Argyle fans realised a dream which they felt may never come to fruition. They saw their team walk out at Wembley, and to top the impossible dream, they saw them win.

The match was of great importance, a play-off final and the chance to regain their second division status at the first time of asking. The final was a tight, evenly contested affair. Argyle won it, and promotion with a training ground move finished beautifully by Ronnie Mauge.

The season preceding the Wembley final was an interesting affair. Neil Warnock's new squad took some time to gel and lost their first six matches before thumping Bury 5-0. From the first victory the team climbed from bottom to fifth in five games. They remained in the play-off positions for the remainder of the season. The team work, from manager, right through the club turned the season around. Argyle missed automatic promotion by one point and were left to rue the twelve points start they gave the teams around them.

The play-off lottery brought up a tie with Colchester and a return to where the season began. The first leg was rearguard action with a 1-0 defeat at Layer Road. This set up an intriguing return at Home Park. Argyle scored early to level the aggregate score, and the roof came off when Chris Leadbitter put Argyle in front with a sweet free kick just before half-time. Then came the emotion swing with Colchester scoring and the thought of a long hard season being wasted on the away goals rule. Yet just as extra time loomed Paul Williams arrived from his left-back role to head home an excellent cross and send the '*Green and White Army*' to Wembley.

The rest is history. However, as Neil Warnock said "the real challenge starts now", but with him at the helm all looks well for the future.

JONATHAN BREWER.

PLYMOUTH ARGYLE

League: 4th **FA Cup: 3rd Rnd** **Coca-Cola Cup: 1st Rnd** **Auto Windscreen Shield: 1st Rnd**

M	DATE	COMP	VEN	OPPONENTS	RESULT	HT	LP	GOAL SCORERS/GOAL TIMES	ATT.
1	A 12	EL	A	Colchester United	L 1-2	0-1	18	Littlejohn 54	(3585)
2	15	CC 1/1	A	**Birmingham City**	L 0-1	0-1			**7964**
3	19	EL	H	Preston North End	L 0-2	0-0	24		6862
4	22	CC 1/2	H	**Birmingham City**	L 1-2	1-0		**Heathcote 45**	**1871**
5	26	EL	A	Chester City	L 1-3	0-1	23	Williams 54	(2660)
6	29	EL	H	Hereford United	L 0-1	0-1	24		5608
7	S 2	EL	A	Bury	W 5-0	3-0	24	Evans 28, 79, Clayton 40, Billy 45, Littlejohn 89	(3040)
8	9	EL	H	Leyton Orient	D 1-1	1-0	23	Evans 19	6292
9	12	EL	H	Doncaster Rovers	W 3-1	2-1	17	Evans 23, Billy 28, Littlejohn 85	4858
10	16	EL	A	Barnet	W 2-1	0-0	13	Evans 67(pen), Littlejohn 88	(2557)
11	23	EL	A	Wigan Athletic	W 1-0	0-0	10	Littlejohn 79	(2631)
12	26	AWS 1/1	H	**Peterborough United**	L 0-3	0-1			**1818**
13	30	EL	H	Lincoln City	W 3-0	3-0	6	Minett 5(og), Evans 6, Littlejohn 20	6643
14	O 7	EL	H	Fulham	W 3-0	2-0	5	Littlejohn 20, Baird 23, Baird 77	6681
15	14	EL	A	Mansfield Town	D 1-1	1-1	5	Heathcote 9	(3164)
16	21	EL	H	Torquay United	W 4-3	2-3	4	Littlejohn 8, 37, 85 (3), Mauge 79	11695
17	28	EL	A	Darlington	L 0-2	0-0	6		(2352)
18	31	EL	A	Scarborough	D 2-2	1-0	7	Littlejohn 15, 47	(1876)
19	N 4	EL	H	Cardiff City	D 0-0	0-0	7		7434
20	7	AWS 1/2	A	**Northampton Town**	L 0-1	0-1			**(2109)**
21	11	FAC 1	A	**Slough**	W 2-0	0-0		og 61, Heathcote 77	**(3013)**
22	18	EL	A	Hartlepool United	D 2-2	2-0	7	Evans 11(pen), Mauge 35	(1830)
23	25	EL	H	Rochdale	W 2-0	0-0	5	Littlejohn 49, Evans 86	6558
24	D 3	FAC 2	A	**Kingstonian**	W 2-1	1-1		**Leadbitter 8, Littlejohn 85**	**(2961)**
25	9	EL	H	Wigan Athletic	W 3-1	1-1	4	Barlow 8, Littlejohn 75, 89	5931
26	16	EL	A	Lincoln City	D 0-0	0-0	5		(2801)
27	23	EL	H	Cambridge United	W 1-0	0-0	4	Mauge 75	7135
28	26	EL	A	Gillingham	L 0-1	0-0	4		(9651)
29	J 1	EL	H	Exeter City	D 2-2	0-2	4	Baird 59, 80	12427
30	6	FAC 3	H	**Coventry City**	L 3	1-0		**Baird 20**	**17721**
31	13	EL	A	Preston North End	L 2-3	1-2	6	Evans 22, Saunders 88	(11126)
32	20	EL	H	Colchester United	D 1-1	0-0	7	Baird 31	5800
33	23	EL	H	Scunthorpe United	L 1-3	0-2	7	Logan 89	4712
34	30	EL	A	Northampton Town	L 0-1	0-1	7		(3911)
35	F 3	EL	H	Chester City	W 4-2	3-0	6	Barlow 12, Mauge 13, Partridge 32, Williams 72	5114
36	10	EL	A	Scunthorpe United	D 1-1	1-1	6	Evans 23	(2789)
37	17	EL	A	Doncaster Rovers	D 0-0	0-0	6		(2338)
38	20	EL	H	Bury	W 1-0	0-0	6	Heathcote 79	4536
39	24	EL	H	Barnet	D 1-1	1-0	6	Partridge 7	6426
40	27	EL	A	Leyton Orient	W 1-0	0-0	4	Logan 63	(3394)
41	M 2	EL	H	Gillingham	W 1-0	0-0	4	Barlow 70	8485
42	9	EL	A	Cambridge United	W 3-2	1-0	3	Billy 9, Logan 69, Baird 81	(2785)
43	16	EL	H	Northampton Town	W 1-0	0-0	3	Evans 82	7001
44	23	EL	A	Exeter City	D 1-1	1-1	4	Clayton 9	(6185)
45	30	EL	A	Fulham	L 0-4	0-1	6		(5667)
46	A 2	EL	H	Mansfield Town	W 1-0	0-0	5	Corazzin 89(pen)	6375
47	6	EL	H	Darlington	L 0-1	0-1	7		8990
48	8	EL	A	Torquay United	W 2-0	1-0	5	Mauge 5, Littlejohn 76	(4269)
49	13	EL	H	Scarborough	W 5-1	1-0	5	Mauge 26, Barlow 46, 77, Littlejohn 71, 89	6949
50	16	EL	A	Hereford United	L 0-3	0-2	5		(4739)
51	20	EL	A	Cardiff City	W 1-0	0-0	4	Evans 60	(3374)
52	27	EL	H	Rochdale	W 1-0	0-0	5	Evans 64	(2355)
53	M 4	EL	H	Hartlepool United	W 3-0	1-0	4	Billy 2, Heathcote 49, Logan 77	11526
54	12	PO SF1	A	**Colchester United**	L 0-1	0-1			**(6511)**
55	15	PO SF2	H	**Colchester United**	W 3-1	2-0		**Evans 3, Leadbitter 41, Williams 85**	**14525**
56	25	PO F	A	**Darlington**	W 1-0	0-0		**Mauge 65**	**(43431)**

Best Home League Attendance: 12427 v Exeter City **Smallest: 4536 v Bury** **Average: 7132**

Goal Scorers:
EL(68): Littlejohn(18),Evans(13),Baird(6),Mauge(6),Barlow(5),Logan(4),Billy(4),Heathcote(3),Williams(2),Partridge(2),Clayton(2),Corazzin(1),Opponent(s)(1),Saunders(1)
CC(1): Heathcote(1)
FAC(5): Baird(1),Opponent(s)(1),Littlejohn(1),Leadbitter(1),Heathcote(1)
AWS(0):
PO(4): Williams(1),Mauge(1),Leadbitter(1),Evans(1)

(F) Baird	(M) Barlow	(F) Billy	(G) Blackwell	(M) Burnett	(G) Cherry	(M) Clayton	(F) Corazzin	(D) Curran	(F) Evans	(G) Hammond	(D) Heathcote	(D) Hill	(M) Hodgson	(M) Leadbitter	(M) Littlejohn	(M) Logan	(F) Magee	(M) Mauge	(D) McCall	(F) Nugent	(F) O'Hagan	(M) Partridge	(D) Patterson	(G) Petterson	(M) Saunders	(F) Twiddy	(D) Williams	(M) Wotton		
		X		X					S1	X	X	X1	S3	X1	X			X		X			X3			S1	X		A.D'Urso	1
		X		X					S	X	X	X	S		X			X		X			X			S	X		J.Lloyd	2
		X		X		X2			S2	X	X	X3	S3	S1				X		X			X1				X		P.Rejer	3
		X		X3		X1			S3	X	X	X			X			X					X2	S2		S1	X	X	C.Wilkes	4
		X		X2		X			S1	X	X			S2				X					X2	S2		X1	X		S.J.Baines	5
		X		X		X			S1	X	X	X		X2				X					X1	S2	S2	X2	X		G.Singh	6
	X	X				X				X	X	X	X	X	X2			X1							S2	S1	X		R.Pearson	7
	X	X				X2				X	X	X	X	X1	X3			X							S2	S1	X		C.Wilkes	8
	X	X	X			X				X	X	X	X		X			X					S		X	S	S	X	K.Leach	9
	X1	X	X1			X				X	X	X	X		X			X					S1		X	S1	X		M.J.Brandwood	10
	X	X	X1			X2				X	X	X	X		X			X					S2		X	S1	S	X	J.Lloyd	11
						X1				X	X	X	X		X			X2		X3					X		X	X	P.Rejer	12
X	X2		X			S1				X	X	X	X		X	S2		X1					X		X	S	S	X	R.B.Gifford	13
X	X		X			S1				X	X	X	X		X			X					X1		X	S	X		A.Wiley	14
X	X1		X			S1				X	X	X	X		X			X					X		X	S	X		K.Lynch	15
X	X1		X			S1				X	X	X	X	X1	X	S1		X					X		X		X		R.Harris	16
X1	S3		X			X3				X	X	X	X		X	X	S2	S1	X2				X		X		X		M.Riley	17
S2	X		X			X				X2		X	X		X	X	X1	S	X				X		X		X	S1	N.Barry	18
X1	S1		X			X				X		X	X		X	X2	X	S2	X				X		X		X	S	S.Mathieson	19
X	X									X	X	X1		S1	X	X	X3	X					X		X	S3	X	X	M.Fletcher	20
S	X1	X				X			X	X	X	X	X	X	X	S1	S	X					X		X		X		J.Rushton	21
S1	X1	X				X			X	X	X	X	X	X	X	S1		X					X		S		X		T.Leake	22
S1	X1	X				X2			X	X	X	X	X		X	S		X					X		S2		X		J.Rushton	23
S1	X2	X				X3			X	X	X	X	X1		S3	S2		X					X		X		X		R.Harris	24
X	X	S				X			X	X	X	X	X		X	S		X					X		S		X		M.Pierce	25
X	S	S				X			X	X	X	X	X		X	X							S		X		X		J.Brandwood	26
X	S	X				X			X	X	X	X	X		X2	X	S1	X1					X		X		X		R.Gifford	27
X	S2	X				X			S	X	X	X	X		X	X2	X	X1					X		X		X		G.Pooley	28
X	S2	X				X2			S1	X	X	X1	X		X2	X	S2	X					X		X		X		K.Leach	29
X1	S	X								X	X	X	X		X	X		X1					X		X	S1	S1	X	G.Willard	30
S1	X	X								X	X	X	X	X1	X	X		X					X		X	S	S	X	N.Barry	31
X	X							S		X	X	X		S2	X1	X2	X	X					X		X	S1	X		D.Orr	32
X	S2	X2						X	X	X		X			X1	S1	X2	X					S2	X	X	X	X		M.Fletcher	33
X	X	S1						X	S	X	X	X				X		X				X	X1	X	X	S	X		A.D'Urso	34
X	X	S1				X1		X	S	X	X	X				X		X			S2	X2	X		X		X		J.Rushton	35
X	X	S				X		X	S	X	X	X				X		X				S	X1	X	X		X		D.Laws	36
X	X	S				X		X	S	X	X	X				X		X				S	X1	X	X		X		J.Lloyd	37
X	X	S1			X				X1	X	X	S				S1		X					X1		X		X		P.Rejer	38
X	X	S			X	X				X	X	S				X		X					S		X		X		M.Fletcher	39
X	X	S			X	X				X	X	X				X		X					S		X		X		G.Pooley	40
X	X	S			X	X				X	X	X				X		X					X		X		X		G.Singh	41
X	X1	X			X	X				X	X	S		S1		X		X					X		X		X		B.Harris	42
X	X	X			X	X				X	X	S				S		X					S		X		X		D.Horr	43
X	X	X			X	X				X	X	S		X		X							X		X		X		S.Mathieson	44
X1	X	X			X	X		S1		X				X		S2		S	X2				X		X		X		K.Leach	45
	X	X1			X	X		S2		X						X2		X					X		X		X		B.Knight	46
	X2	S2			X			X		X		X1		S3		S1		X	X				X				X3		S.Baines	47
	X				X	X			S	X						X		X	X				X	S			X		J.Rushton	48
	X	S2			X	X1		X2		X				X2		X		X	X		S1		X				X		G.Barber	49
	X1	S1			X			S3	X3	X				S1		X		X	X				X				X1		S.Bennett	50
	S	X			X	X1		S	X	X						X		X	X						S		X		I.Hemley	51
	S1	X			X	X1			X	X						X		X	X						S		X		F.Stretton	52
	X	X			X			S1	X1	X2						X3		X	X				S2		S3		X		R.Gifford	53
	X1	X			X			S2	X	X2				S1		X		X	X				X				X		M.Pierce	54
S	S				X				S	X		X				X		X	X				X				X		J.Kirkby	55
S	X	S			X				S	X		X				X		X	X				X				X		B.Burns	56
24	25	22	20	6	16	32	1	6	41	4	44	21	3	29	40	25	0	36	2	4	0	6	42	6	4	1	46	0	EL Appearances	
3	3	10	0	0	0	4	5	2	4	0	0	3	2	4	2	6	4	1	2	2	6	1	1	0	6	1	0	1	EL Sub Appearances	
0	0	2	0	2	0	2	0	0	0+1	2	2	2	0	0	2	0	0	2	0	2	0+1	0	1	0	0+1	1	2	0	CC Appearances	
+1	0	3	3	0	0	0	3	0	3	0	3	3	1+2	0+1	3	0	0	0	0	1	0	1	0	0	0	1+1	1	2	FAC Appearances	
0	1	1	0	0	0	1	0	0	2	1	1	2	0	1+1	0	0	0	0	0	1	0	1	0	1	0	1+1	1	2	AWS Appearances	
0	3	1	0	0	3	0	0+1	3	3	0	3	0+1	0	3	3	3	0	3	0	0	0	3	0	0	0	3	0		PO Appearances	

Also Played: (M) Dawe S2(12). (G) Dungey X(12). (M) Payne S3(12). (M) Richardson S1(12), S2(20). (F) Ross X(12), X2(20). (M) Shilton S3(8).

CLUB RECORDS

BIGGEST VICTORIES
8-1 v Millwall,Division 2, 16.1.1932 8-1 v Hartlepool U. (a),
Division 2, 7.5.1994 7-0 v Doncaster Rovers, Division 2, 5.9.1936
6-0 v Corby, FA Cup Round 3,22.1.1966

BIGGEST DEFEATS
0-9 v Stoke City, Division 2, 17.12.1960
Record Cup Defeat
1-7 v Tottenham Hotspur, FA Cup Rnd 4, 1966-67 0-6 v West Ham
United, League Cup Rnd 2, 26.9.1962

MOST LEAGUE POINTS
(3pts for win) 87, Division 3, 1986-87
(2pts for win)68, Division 3S, 1929-30

MOST LEAGUE GOALS
107, Division 3S, 1925-26 (42 games) 107, Division 3S,1951-52
(46 games)

RECORD TRANSFER FEE RECEIVED
£350,000 from Southend for Gary Poole, July 1993
£350,000 from Crystal Palace for Marc Edworthy, May 1995

RECORD TRANSFER FEE PAID
£300,000 to Port Vale for Peter Swan, July 1994

BEST PERFORMANCES
League: Third in Div 2 1931-32, 1952-53 FA Cup: Semi-Finalists
1983-84
League Cup: Semi-Finalists 1964-65, 1973-74

HONOURS
Champions Division 3S 1929-30, 1951-52 Champions Division 3
1958-59

LEAGUE CAREER
Founder Members of Division 3 1920 Transferred to Division 3S
1921-22
Promoted to Div 2 1929-30 Relegated to Div 3S 1949-50
Promoted to Div 21951-52 Relegated to Div 3S 1955-56
Transferred to Div 3 1958-59 Promoted to Div 2 1958-59
Relegated to Div 31967-68 Promoted to Div 2 1974-75
Relegated to Div 3 1976-77 Promoted to Div 2 1985-86
Relegated to Div 3/21991-92 Relegated to Div 3 1994/95
Promoted to Div 2 1995-96.

INDIVIDUAL CLUB RECORDS

MOST APPEARANCES FOR CLUB
Kevin Hodges (1978-93): League 502+28, FA Cup 39,League Cup
32+3, Other 9+2 Total 582+33

MOST CAPPED PLAYER
Moses Russell (Wales) 20, 1920-28

RECORD GOALSCORER IN A MATCH
Wilf Carter, 5 v Charlton Athletic, 6-4, Div 2,27.12.1960

RECORD LEAGUE GOALSCORER IN A SEASON
Jack Cock, 32, 1926-27 In All Competitions: Jack Cock, 32 (all
league) 1926-27 W Carter 32 (League 26, FA Cup 6) 1957-58
Tommy Tynan, 32 (League 31, FA Cup 1) 1984-85

RECORD LEAGUE GOALSCORER IN A CAREER
Sam Black, 176, 1924-37 In All Competitions: Sam Black, 185
(League 176, FA Cup 9) 1924-37

OLDEST PLAYER IN A LEAGUE MATCH
Peter Shilton, 44 years 21 days v Burnley Div 2, 9.10.1993.

YOUNGEST PLAYER IN A LEAGUE MATCH
Sam Shilton, 16 years 4 months 19 days v Brighton, 10.12.94.

PREVIOUS MANAGERS

1903-05 Frank Brettall 1905-06 Bob Jack 1906-07 Will Fullerton
1910-38 Bob Jack 1938-48 Jack Tresadern 1948-55 Jim Rae
1955-60 Jack Rowley 1960-61 George Taylor/ Neil Dougall
1961-63 Ellis Stuttard 1963 Vic Buckingham 1963-64 Andy
Beattie 1964-65 Malcolm Allison 1965-68 Derek Ufton 1968-
70 Billy Bingham 1970-72 Ellis Stuttard 1972-77 Tony Waiters
1977-78 Mike Kelly 1978 Lennie Lawrence 1978-79 Malcolm
Allison 1979-81 Bobby Saxton 1981-83 Bobby Moncur 1983-
84 John Hore 1984-88 Dave Smith 1988-90 Ken Brown 1990-
92 David Kemp 1992-95 Peter Shilton, 1995 Steve McCall.

ADDITIONAL INFORMATION
Previous Name: Argyle Athletic Club 1886-1903
Club colours: Green & white diagonals with black flashes, black
shorts with green and white trim, green & white hooped socks with
black trim. **Change colours:** Yellow shirts with green & black flashes, green shorts, yellow socks.
Reserves League: Avon Combination

LONGEST LEAGUE RUNS

of undefeated matches:	22 (1929)	of league matches w/out a win:		13 (1962-63)
of undefeated home matches:	47 (1921-23)	of undefeated away matches:		9 (1929)
without home win:	8 (1989-90)	without an away win:		27 (1975-76)
of league wins:	9 (1930,1986)	of home wins:		17 (1922)
of league defeats:	9 (1947)	of away wins:		6 (1929)

THE MANAGER

NEIL WARNOCK . . . . appointed 22nd June 1995.

PREVIOUS CLUBS
As Manager . . . . Gainsborough Trinity, Burton Albion, Scarborough, Notts County, Huddersfield Town.
As Asst.Man/Coach . . . . None.
As a player . . . . Chesterfield, Rotherham United, Hartlepool United, Scunthorpe United, Aldershot, Barnsley,
. . . . York City, Crewe Alexandra.

HONOURS
As a Manager . . . . . . **Scarborough:** Conference League Champions 1987. **Notts County:** Div.2 promotion 1991,
. . . . Div.3 promotion 1990, **Huddersfield:** Promotion to Div.1, 1995. **Plymouth:** Promotion to Div.2, 1995-96.
As a Player . . . . None.

PLYMOUTH ARGYLE

PLAYERS NAME / Honours	Ht	Wt	Birthdate	Birthplace / Transfers	Contract Date	Clubs	APPEARANCES League	L/Cup	FA Cup	Other	GOALS Lge	L/C	FAC	Oth
G O A L K E E P E R S														
Blackwell Kevin	5.11	12.10	21/12/58	Luton		Barnet								
GMVC'87.					01/11/86	Scarborough	44	11	2	2				
				£15000	08/11/89	Notts County								
				Free	15/01/93	Torquay United	18			2				
				Free	05/08/93	Huddersfield Town	3+2	0+1	1	3				
				Free	11/08/95	Plymouth Argyle	20		3					
Cherry Steve	5.11	11.0	05/08/60	Nottingham	22/03/78	Derby County (A)	77	5	8					
E: Y.4.				Loan	26/11/80	Port Vale	4		4					
				£25000	10/08/84	Walsall	71	10	7	6				
				£17000	23/10/86	Plymouth Argyle	73	4	5	1				
				Loan	01/12/88	Chesterfield	10			3				
				£70000	16/02/89	Notts County	266	17	14	31				
				Free	14/07/95	Watford	4							
Loan Plymouth 16 Lge 3 Oth. Apps.				Free	19/05/96	Plymouth Argyle								
Dungey James	5.8	10.1	07/02/78	Plymouth		Plymouth Argyle	3+1		1					
D E F E N D E R S														
Curran Chris	5.11	11.9	17/09/71	Birmingham	13/07/90	Torquay United	145+8	15	8	10	4			1
				£20000	22/12/93	Plymouth Argyle	6+2			3				
Heathcote Micky	6.1	12.7	10/09/65	Kelloe		Spennymoor Utd								
				£15000	19/08/87	Sunderland	6+3			0+1				
				Loan	17/12/87	Halifax Town	7		1		1			
				Loan	04/01/90	York City	3			1				
				£55000	12/07/90	Shrewsbury Town	43+1	6	5	4	6			
				£150000	12/09/91	Cambridge United	123+5	7	5+2	7	13	1	2	2
				£70000	27/07/95	Plymouth Argyle	44	2	3	4	3	1	1	
Patterson Mark	5.10	11.5	13/09/68	Leeds	30/06/86	Carlisle United	19+3	4		1				
				£60000	10/11/87	Derby County	41+10	5+2	4	5+1	3			2
				£85000	23/07/93	Plymouth Argyle	120+2	3	8	9	3			
Williams Paul R C	5.6	10.7	11/09/69	Leicester	01/07/88	Leicester City								
					05/07/89	Stockport County	61+9	3	4	7+5	4			1
				£150000	12/08/93	Coventry City	8+6	3+1	1					
				Loan	19/11/93	W.B.A.	5							
				Loan	17/03/95	Huddersfield Town	9			1				
				£50000	10/08/95	Plymouth Argyle	46	2	3	4	2			1
M I D F I E L D														
Barlow Martin	5.7	10.3	26/06/71	Plymouth	01/07/89	Plymouth Argyle	152+28	6+1	7	12+1	14	2		
Clayton Gary	5.10	11.7	02/02/63	Sheffield		Rotherham United								
E: SP.1.						Burton Albion								
					23/08/86	Doncaster Rovers	34+1	2	3	2	5			
				£10000	02/07/87	Cambridge United	166+13	17+1	9	7	14	3		2
				Loan	25/01/91	Peterborough Utd	4							
				£20000	18/02/94	Huddersfield Town	15+4		0+1	4	1			2
					10/08/95	Plymouth Argyle	32+4	2	2	1	2			
Ilman Neil						Eastwood Town								
					27/03/96	Plymouth Argyle								
				Loan	28/03/96	Cambridge United	1+3							
Leadbitter Chris	5.9	10.6	17/10/67	Middlesbrough	04/09/85	Grimsby Town								
Div.3'91.				Free	21/08/86	Hereford United	32+4	2	2	3	1			
				Free	02/08/88	Cambridge United	144+32	12	16+2	11+2	18	3	3	1
				£25000	16/08/93	Bournemouth	20+7	2+1	3	1				
				Free	27/07/95	Plymouth Argyle	29+4		3	4+1			1	1
Littlejohn Adrian	5.9	10.5	26/09/70	Wolverhampton		W.B.A.								
E: S.				Free	24/05/89	Walsall	26+18	2+1	1+1	4+1	1			
				Free	06/08/91	Sheffield United	44+25	5+1	3+2	1	12		1	1
				£100000	22/07/95	Plymouth Argyle	40+2	2	3	3	18		1	1
Logan Richard A	6.1	13.3	24/05/69	Barnsley		Belper Town								
						Gainsborough T.								
				Free	15/11/93	Huddersfield Town	35+10	3	1	9	1			1
				£20000	26/10/95	Plymouth Argyle	25+6		1+2	4	4			
Mauge Ron	5.10	10.6	10/03/69	Islington	22/07/87	Charlton Athletic								
				Free	21/09/88	Fulham	47+3	4	1	2	2			
				£40000	30/07/90	Bury	92+15	8+2	8	10+2	10	2	2	
				Loan	26/09/91	Manchester City				0+1				
				£40000	22/07/95	Plymouth Argyle	36+1	2	3	4	6			1
Richardson Dominic						Plymouth Argyle (T)				0+2				
Saunders Mark						Tiverton								
				Free	22/08/95	Plymouth Argyle	4+6	0+1	0+1		1			
Wotton Paul				17/08/77	Plymouth		Plymouth Argyle	5+3			2				
F O R W A R D S														
Billy Chris	6.0	10.9	02/01/73	Huddersfield	01/07/91	Huddersfield Town	46+11	5+1	3	9+1	2			
					10/08/95	Plymouth Argyle	22+10	2	3	2	4			
Corazzin Carlo	5.9	12.5	25/12/71	Canada		Vancouver								
				£20000	10/12/93	Cambridge United	104+1	4	5	3	39	2		2
				£150000	28/03/96	Plymouth Argyle	1+5			0+1	1			
Evans Michael	6.0	11.5	11/01/73	Plymouth	30/03/91	Plymouth Argyle	97+33	6+1	7+2	7	27			2
O'Hagan Daniel	6.1	13.8	24/04/76	Truro	29/06/94	Plymouth Argyle	1+8	0+1		1	1			

HOME PARK
Plymouth, Devon PL2 3DQ
Tel: 01752 562 561

Capacity 19,700
Covered Standing 7,000
Seating 6,400

First game .... v Northampton T, Sth Lge, 2-0, 5.9.1903.
First floodlit game .... v Exeter, 26.10.1953.

ATTENDANCES
Highest .... 43,596 v Aston Villa, Division 2, 10.10.1936.
Lowest .... 1,875 v Hull, 11.5.1979.

OTHER GROUNDS .... None.

MATCHDAY TICKET PRICES

Grandstand Centre. £11
OAP. £9
Grandstand Wing £10
Juv/OAP £8
Mayflower £10
OAP. £8
Lynhurst. £9
Juv/OAP £7
Standing
Lynhurst/Devonport £6
Juv/OAP £4.50
Mayflower £6
Juv/OAP £4.50
Barn Park (Visitors) £7
Ticket Office Telephone no. 01752 562 561

HOW TO GET TO THE GROUND

From all directions
Use A38 Plymouth bypass as far as the Tavastock Road (A386).
Then branch left and follow signs to Plymouth (A386).
In 0.7 miles turn right then left (A3041) into Outland Road for Plymouth
Argyle FC.

Car Parking
Free car park adjoining ground, space for 1,000 cars.

Nearest Railway Station
Plymouth (01752 21300)

PILGRIMLINE
0839 44 22 70
Calls cost 39p per minute cheap rate and 49p per
minute at all other times.
Call costings correct at time of going to press.

MATCHDAY PROGRAMME

Programme Editor. . . . . Gordon Sparks.

Number of pages . . . . 48.

Price . . . . £1.50.

Subscriptions. . . . . £46 per year for all home programmes.

Local Newspapers. . . . . Evening Herald, Western Morning News.

Local Radio Stations . . . . Plymouth Sound AM (11.52 Kz).

PRESTON NORTH END
(The Lillywhites)
NATIONWIDE LEAGUE DIVISION 2
SPONSORED BY: BAXI PARTNERSHIP

Back Row (L-R): Gareth Ainsworth, Lee Cartwright, Simon Davey, Allan Smart, Barry Richardson, David Lucas, John Vaughan, Steve Wilkinson, Kevin Magee, Graeme Atkinson. **Middle Row:** Geoff McDougle (Chief Scout), Brian Hickson (Kit Manager), Paul Raynor, Ryan Kidd, Andy Saville, Jamie Squires, John Calligan, Steve Holmes, Kevin Kilbane, Mick Rathbone (Physio), Jim Parker (Yth Physio). **Front Row:** Joe Jakub (Yth Dev. Officer), Chris Borwick, Terry Fleming, Andy Fensome, David Moyes (Player Coach), Gary Peters (Manager), Ian Bryson Capt), Graham Lancashire, Mickey Brown, Raymond Sharp, Chris Sulley (Yth Manager).

PRESTON NORTH END
FORMED IN 1881
TURNED PROFESSIONAL IN 1885
LTD COMPANY IN 1893

PRESIDENT: Tom Finney, OBE,CBE,JP
VICE-PRESIDENT: T C Nicholson, JP,FCIOB
CHAIRMAN: Bryan Gray
VICE-CHAIRMEN
M J Woodhouse, K W Leeming
DIRECTORS
D Shaw (Managing Director)
L King (Company Secretary)
SECRETARY
Mrs Audrey Shaw (01772 902020)

MANAGER: Gary Peters

YOUTH TEAM MANAGER
Chris Sulley
PHYSIOTHERAPIST
Mick Rathbone

STATISTICIAN FOR THE DIRECTORY
Lawrence Bland

A tremendous season, crowned with the Third Division championship. The season started badly with a home defeat in the opening game with Lincoln City, and then the team played 21 league games without defeat, which included 10 away games, nearly breaking the club's record, set up by the old Invincible in 1888-89! The team played some attractive attacking football, scoring 78 goals (only one less than Ipswich Town, top scorers with 79), player of the season Andy Saville leading the way with 29 league goals. The championship was contested most of the season with Gillingham, before three wins in the last three matches sealed both promotion and the title. A huge crowd of 18,700 (with thousands locked out) attended the final game for the presentation of the trophy.

Cup matches took a secondary role to the league. In the Coca - Cola cup we led 2-0 at the eventual 1st Division champions Sunderland, before crashing to three late goals. In the F.A. Cup we lost at Bradford City in a televised game, after winning at Carlisle in Round One. The Auto Windscreens Shield game at Hull attracted only 793! We beat Scarborough to reach Round 2, but lost to old boss John Beck's Lincoln City.

Money raised from the issue of shares, from the flotation of the club on the Alternative Investment Market of the London Stock Exchange, and from the club owners, the Baxi Partnership, combined with the massive attendancefs, produced enough cash for the strengthening of the playing squad and the first stage of the ground re-building programme. The new £4.5 million Tom Finney stand, replacing the old West Stand, containing 7,927 seats (plus five disabled places), was partly opened on December 23rd for the Gillingham game and fully opened on March 16th against Darlington. This is the first part of a complete £10 million re-building of the ground, to provide four seater stands to accommodate 28,000. The Kop/Fulwood End being the next to be developed.

The reserves had their best season for years, finishing 4th in Division 2, clinching promotion, providing there is no reorganisation in the Pontins League. They had an 18 match unbeaten run from November to April. Gary Bennett signed from Tranmere Rovers for £200,000 on March 27th became the club's record signing. Other signings were Dean Barrick (Cambridge United), Kevin Gage(Sheffield United), Tony Grant (Leeds United), Neil McDonald (Bolton Wanderers), Teuvo Moilanen (FF Jaro, Finland), Andy Saville (Birmingham City), Paul Sparrow (Crystal Palace), Russell Wilcox (Doncaster Rovers) and Steve Wilkinson (Mansfield Town). Transfers were - Gareth Ainsworth, Terry Fleming, Steve Holmes, Barry Richardson (all to Lincoln City), Mike Conroy (Fulham), Graham Lancashire (Wigan Athletic), Kevin Magee (Plymouth Argyle), Paul Raynor (Cambridge United) and Mark Sale (Mansfield Town). Loan signings were Paul Birch (Wolves), Charlie Bishop (Barnsley), Alan Johnson (Lincoln City), Jason Kearton (Everton) and Andy Rhodes (St. Johnstone). At the end of the season , Chris Borwick, John Calligan Andy Fensome and John Vaughan were released.

Surprisingly, there was no managerial awards for Gary Paters, although captain Ian Bryson, along with Simon Davey, Andy Saville and Russ Wilcox were in the PFA Divisional side. Coach David Moyes was promoted to assistant manager in February, with Steve Harrison filling the vacant post of coach. Young eplayer of the seasoní Kevin Kilbane was capped by Eire under 21s, with David Lucas gaining England under 18 Youth caps.

There is confidence at the club, that progress to Division one can be achieved in due course. LAWRENCE BLAND.

PRESTON NORTH END

League: Champions | FA Cup: 2nd Rnd | Coca-Cola Cup: 1st Rnd | Auto Windscreen Shield: 2nd Rnd

M	DATE	COMP	VEN	OPPONENTS	RESULT	HT	LP	GOAL SCORERS/GOAL TIMES	ATT.
1	A 12	EL	H	Lincoln City	L 1-2	1-1	17	Saville 35	7813
2	15	CC 1/1	H	**Sunderland**	D 1-1	0-0		Kidd 69	6323
3	19	EL	A	Plymouth Argyle	W 2-0	0-0	12	Squires 64, Bryson 76	(6862)
4	23	CC 1/2	A	**Sunderland**	L 2-3	2-0		**Cartwright 15, Bryson 38**	(7407)
5	26	EL	H	Wigan Athletic	D 1-1	1-1	12	Atkinson 24	6837
6	29	EL	A	Bury	D 0-0	0-0	13		(4682)
7	S 2	EL	H	Cambridge United	D 3-3	1-1	13	Saville 19, Wilkinson 77, Lancashire 79	7034
8	9	EL	A	Hereford United	W 1-0	0-0	10	Saville 52	(3124)
9	12	EL	A	Colchester United	D 2-2	0-1	12	Cartwright 56, Bryson 87	(2869)
10	16	EL	H	Scunthorpe United	D 2-2	1-0	11	Atkinson 27, Bryson 57	7397
11	23	EL	A	Fulham	D 2-2	1-1	11	Bryson 37(pen), Davey 58	(5209)
12	30	EL	H	Chester City	W 2-0	0-0	9	Wilkinson 71, Saville 88	8544
13	O 7	EL	H	Scarborough	W 3-2	1-1	8	Saville 6, Wilkinson 50, Davey 65	7688
14	14	EL	A	Torquay United	W 4-0	2-0	3	Bryson 7, Saville 33, 62, Bryson 87	(4058)
15	17	AWS 1/1	A	**Hull City**	L 0-1	0-0			(793)
16	21	EL	H	Mansfield Town	W 6-0	3-0	2	Wilkinson 14, 39, 76 (3), Saville 34, 69, 85	8981
17	28	EL	A	Doncaster Rovers	D 2-2	1-1	2	Davey 31, 79	(4413)
18	31	EL	A	Northampton Town	W 2-1	1-0	2	Wilcox 33, Saville 88	(4695)
19	N 4	EL	H	Leyton Orient	W 4-0	0-0	1	Saville 50, 78, 87, Davey 60	9823
20	7	AWS 1/2	H	**Scarborough**	W 2-1	1-0		**Atkinson 33, Kidd 61**	5639
21	11	FAC 1	A	**Carlisle United**	W 2-1	0-1		**Cartwright 63, Wilcox 89**	(7046)
22	18	EL	A	Exeter City	D 1-1	0-1	3	Moyes 90	(3550)
23	25	EL	A	Hartlepool United	W 3-0	1-0	3	Moyes 24, Atkinson 61, Saville 87	9449
24	28	AWS 2	A	**Lincoln City**	L 1-2	0-0		**Saville 74**	(1729)
25	D 2	FAC 2	A	**Bradford City**	L 1-2	0-1		**Wilkinson 77**	(7602)
26	9	EL	H	Fulham	D 1-1	0-1	2	Bryson 61	8422
27	16	EL	A	Chester City	D 1-1	1-1	2	Wilkinson 22	(5004)
28	23	EL	H	Gillingham	D 0-0	0-0	1		10669
29	J 1	EL	H	Cardiff City	W 5-0	1-0	3	Davey 18, Brown 46, Saville 51, 61, Atkinson 89	8354
30	6	EL	A	Barnet	L 0-1	0-0	3		(2737)
31	13	EL	H	Plymouth Argyle	W 3-2	2-1	2	Bryson 37, Davey 42, Cartwright 50	11126
32	20	EL	A	Lincoln City	D 0-0	0-0	2		(5185)
33	30	EL	A	Darlington	W 2-1	0-1	2	Cartwright 81, Saville 86(pen)	(2599)
34	F 3	EL	A	Wigan Athletic	W 1-0	0-0	2	Kilbane 83	(5567)
35	10	EL	H	Barnet	L 0-1	0-0	2		9974
36	17	EL	H	Colchester United	W 2-0	2-0	2	Saville 13, 39	9336
37	24	EL	A	Scunthorpe United	W 2-1	0-0	2	Saville 49, Lancashire 70	(3638)
38	27	EL	H	Hereford United	D 2-2	1-1	2	Atkinson 5, Saville 85	9761
39	M 2	EL	H	Rochdale	L 1-2	1-2	2	Saville 14	9697
40	9	EL	A	Gillingham	D 1-1	0-0	2	Davey 49	(10602)
41	12	EL	A	Rochdale	W 3-0	2-0	2	Birch 17, Wilkinson 30, Moyes 61	(4597)
42	16	EL	H	Darlington	D 1-1	1-1	2	Bryson 26	12070
43	23	EL	A	Cardiff City	W 1-0	0-0	2	Saville 70	(3511)
44	26	EL	H	Bury	D 0-0	0-0	1		12260
45	30	EL	A	Scarborough	W 2-1	1-0	1	Davey 5, Bennett 74	(3771)
46	A 2	EL	H	Torquay United	W 1-0	1-0	1	Wilkinson 35	11965
47	6	EL	H	Doncaster Rovers	W 1-0	0-0	1	Birch 62	12773
48	8	EL	A	Mansfield Town	D 0-0	0-0	1		(4626)
49	13	EL	H	Northampton Town	L 0-3	0-1	1		11774
50	16	EL	A	Cambridge United	L 1-2	1-0	2	Saville 20	(2831)
51	20	EL	A	Leyton Orient	W 2-0	1-0	1	Saville 11, 60	(5170)
52	27	EL	A	Hartlepool United	W 2-0	1-0	1	Davey 37, Saville 82	(5076)
53	M 4	EL	H	Exeter City	W 2-0	1-0	1	Saville 7, Wilkinson 70	18700

Best Home League Attendance: 18700 v Exeter City | **Smallest: 6837 v Wigan Athletic** | **Average: 10019**

Goal Scorers:
EL(78): Saville(29),Wilkinson(10),Davey(10),Bryson(9),Atkinson(5),Moyes(3),Cartwright(3),Lancashire(2),Birch(2),Kilbane(1),Wilcox(1),Brown(1),Bennett(1),Squires(1)
CC(3): Kidd(1),Cartwright(1),Bryson(1)
FAC(3): Cartwright(1),Wilcox(1),Wilkinson(1)
AWS(3): Kidd(1),Atkinson(1),Saville(1)

(W) Atkinson	(M) Barrick	(F) Bennett	(M) Birch	(M) Bishop	(F) Brown	(M) Bryson	(M) Cartwright	(F) Davey	(M) Fensome	(F) Fleming	(D) Gage	(D) Holmes	(D) Johnson	(D) Kidd	(D) Kilbane	(F) Lancashire	(F) Magee	(D) McDonald	(M) Molianen	(F) Raynor	(G) Richardson	(F) Saville	(D) Sharp	(D) Sparrow	(D) Squires	(G) Vaughan	(D) Wilcox	(F) Wilkinson		
X						X			X1	X				X			S1	S				X	X		X	S		X	U.Rennie	1
X						X			X1	X				X			S	S1				X	X1		X	X		X	R.Fernandiz	2
X2						X			X1	X				X				X				X	X		X	X	S2	X	P.Rejer	3
X						X	X			X				X			S	X1				X	X		X	X		X	K.M.Lynch	4
X						X	X			X				X			S	X1				X		S	X	X		X	W.Burns	5
X						X	X			X			X	X			S	X				X	S		X	X		X	P.E.West	6
X						X	X		S1	X	X1		X	X			S3	X2		X3	S2	X			X	X		X	A.Wiley	7
X	S1					X	X	X1	X					X	X		S					X	X	X	X	X		X2	P.Taylor	8
X	S1					X	X1	X	X2	S1	X			X	X		S3					X	X		X	X		X	D.Orr	9
X	X					X	X1	X	X2	S1	X			S	X							X			X	X		X	M.Fletcher	10
X	X					X	X	X1	S1	X	X			X								X		S	X	X	X	X	M.Bailey	11
X	X					X	X1	S1	X	X				X					X			X		S	X	X	X	X	I.Cruikshanks	12
X	X					X	X1	X	S1	X	X			S1					X			X			X	X1	X	X	J.Kirkby	13
X2	X					X		X	X	X				S1	S2				X			X			X	X1	X	X	S.Bennett	14
X						X	X	X	X1	S1				X	X				X	X		X2		S2		X		X3	W.Burns	15
X	X					X	X	X1	X					S	S1	S			X			X			X	X1	X	X	T.Heilbron	16
X	X					X	X	X	X					S1	S1				X			X			X	X1	X	X	K.Breen	17
X	X					X	X	X1	X					S	S1				X			X			X	X	X	X	U.Rennie	18
X	X					X	X	X	X					S	S				X			X			X	X	X	X	G.Cain	19
X1	X					X	X3	S1	X	X				S2	S3			X				X			X	X2	X	X	S.Mathieson	20
X	X					X	X	X	X	X				S		S			X			X			X	X	X	X	I.Cruikshanks	21
X	X					X	X	X2	X	X				S1			S2		X			X			X	X1	X	X	F.Stretton	22
X	X				S	X	X2	X	S	X				X		S			X	X		X			X	X		X	P.Rejer	23
X1	X					X	X2	X	S1	X				X		S2			X	X		X	S		X	X		X	I.Hemley	24
X	X					X	X	S1	X	X1				X					X			X			X	X	S	X	A.Wilkie	25
X	X					X	X	X	X	X				S		S		S1	X			X			X	X	X	X	S.Baines	26
X	X					X	X	X	X					S				S1	S	X		X			X	X	X	X1	R.Poulain	27
X	X					X	S	X	X	X				S				S	X			X			X	X	X	X	T.Heilbron	28
X	X					X	S1	X	X	X				X					X			X			X	X	X1	S	T.West	29
X	X					X	S2	X	S1	X2	X1			X					X			X			X	X		X	D.Orr	30
X	X		X	S		X	X	X						S					X			X			X	X		S1	N.Barry	31
X	X		X			X		X1	X	X				S					X			X			S	X	X	S1	S.Mathieson	32
X	X		X			X		X	X	X				S2	X2			X1	X			X			S	X	X	S1	K.Lynch	33
X	X			X		X	X2	X	X					X1	S2				X			X			X	X		S1	D.Allison	34
X1	X					X		X	X				X	X	X		S		X	X		X			S	X		S1	F.Stretton	35
X	X					X	X	X	X1				X	X			S	S	X			X			S	X		X	R.Pearson	36
X	X					X	X	X1	X				X	X			S1		X			X			S1	X		X	J.Kirkby	37
X3	X				S1	X		X	X				X	X	X		S3	X1	X			X			S1	X	X1	X	U.Rennie	38
S3	X				X3	X		X	X				X1	X	X2		X2	X	X			X			S1	X	X	S2	A.Butler	39
X	X		X			X		X	X					S	X				X			X			X	X	X	X	M.Pierce	40
X	X		X			X		X						S	X1				X			X			X	X	X	X	W.C.Burns	41
X	X		X			X		X						S1					X			X			X	X	X1	X	K.Breen	42
X	X		X			X		X	X					S1					X			X		S	X	X		X	A.D'Urso	43
X	X		X			X		X						X					X			X			X	X		X	J.Lloyd	44
X	X	X	X			X		X	X				S		X				X			X			X	X		X	T.Heilbron	45
X	X	X	X			X		X					S1		X				X			X			X1	X		X	I.Cruikshanks	46
X	X	X	X			X		X	X				S		X				X			X			X	X		S	K.Leach	47
X	X	X	X1			X		X					S2		X				X			X			X2	X		S1	J.Lloyd	48
X	X		X			X		X	X				S1		X				X			X			X	X		S1	N.Barry	49
X1	X	S2	X2			X		X					X		S1				X			X			X	X	X	X	G.Pooley	50
	X	S1				X		X	X				X		S	X1			X			X			X	X	X	X	F.Stretton	51
S	X	S				X		X	X				X		S	X			X			X			X	X	X	X	G.Cain	52
S1	X	S2				X		X					X1		S	X2			X			X			X	X	X	X	A.Wiley	53
42	39	5	11	4	6	44	22	37	20	5	4	8	2	23	7	2	4	8	41	2	3	44	1	13	3	40	27	36	EL. Appearances	
2	1	3	0	0	4	0	4	1	0	0	3	0	0	7	4	4	1	3	0	1	0	0	0	0	0	4	0	6	EL Sub Appearances	
2	0	0	0	0	0	2	1	0	1	2	0	0	0	2	0	0	0	0	1+1	0	2	2	0	0	2	2	0	2	CC Appearances	
2	2	0	0	0	0	2	1+1	2	2	0	0	0	0	1	0	0	0	2	0	1	2	0	0	2	0	0	2	2	FAC Appearances	
3	2	0	0	0	1	3	1+2	3	2	0+1	0	0	2+1	1+1	0+1	0	0	2	3	0	1	2	1	0	1+1	2	1	2	AWS Appearances	

Also Played: (F) Ainsworth S1(2,3,4,5), S(10). (D) Grant S(41,43,44,45,46), S1(42). (G) Kearton S(43). (G) Lucas S(37,40,41,42,44,45,46,47,49,50,51), X(52). (D) Moyes S(29,31,35), X(32,33). Rhodes S(18,19,22). (F) Smart S2(9,10), S(12,34), S3(15).

CLUB RECORDS

RECORD LEAGUE VICTORY
10-0 v Stoke City (h), Div 1, 14.9.1889
Most Goals Scored in a Cup Tie
26-0 v Hyde, FA Cup 1st Round, 15.10.1887

RECORD LEAGUE DEFEAT
0-7 v Blackpool (h), Div 1, 1.5.1948   0-7 v Nottingham Forest (a),
Div 2, 9.4.1927
Record Cup Defeat
0-6 v Charlton Athletic, FA Cup Round 5, 1945-46

MOST LEAGUE POINTS
(2pts for win) 61, Div 4, 1970-71
(3pts for win) 90 1986-87

MOST LEAGUE GOALS
100 Div 2, 1927-28   100 Div 1, 1957-58

RECORD TRANSFER FEE RECEIVED
£765,000 Manchester City for Michael Robinson,June 1979

RECORD TRANSFER FEE PAID
£200,000 to Tranmere Rovers for Gary Bennett, March 1996.

BEST PERFORMANCES
League: Champions Div 1 (2)   FA Cup: Winners (2)
League Cup: 4th Round 1963, 1966, 1972, 1981

HONOURS
Champions Div 1 *1888-89 (first winners), 1889-90   Champions
Div 2,1903-04, 1912-13, 1950-51   Champions Div 3 1970-71
Champions Div 3 1995-96. FA Cup Winners *1889,1938
*League and FA Cup Double

LEAGUE CAREER
Original Members of Football League 1888   Relegated to Div
21900-01   Promoted to Div 1 1903-04
Relegated to Div 2 1911-12   Promoted to Div 1 1912-13
Relegated to Div 21913-14   Promoted to Div 1 1914-15
Relegated to Div 2 1924-25   Promoted to Div 1 1933-34
Relegated to Div 21948-49   Promoted to Div 1 1950-51
Relegated to Div 2 1960-61   Relegated to Div 3 1969-70
Promoted to Div 21970-71   Relegated to Div 3 1973-74
Promoted to Div 2 1977-78   Relegated to Div 3 1980-81
Relegated to Div 41984-85   Promoted to Div 3 (now Div 2) 1986-87
Relegated to Div 4/3 1992-93   Promoted to Div 2 1995-96.

INDIVIDUAL CLUB RECORDS

MOST APPEARANCES FOR CLUB
Alan Kelly (1961-75): League 447+Cup games 65 Total512

MOST CAPPED PLAYER: TOM FINNEY, 76 ENGLAND
Record Goalscorer in a Match: Jimmy Ross, 8 v Hyde (h), 26-0, 1s
Round FA Cup,15.10.1887

RECORD LEAGUE GOALSCORER IN A SEASON
Ted Harper 37, Div 2, 1932-33 In All Competitions: Ted Harper 37
(League 37) 1932-33

RECORD LEAGUE GOALSCORER IN A CAREER
Tom Finney 187 In All Competitions: Tom Finney 210 (League 187
+ FA Cup 23) 1946-60

OLDEST PLAYER IN A LEAGUE MATCH
Bob Kelly 40 years 50 days, 5.1.1935 v Everton(h)

YOUNGEST PLAYER IN A LEAGUE MATCH
Steve Doyle, 16 years 166 days, 15.11.1974 v Tranmere Rovers (a)

PREVIOUS MANAGERS

1919 V Hayes   1924 T Lawrence   1925 F Richards   1927 A
Gibson   1931-32 L Hyde   1932-36 No Manager   1936-37 T
Muirhead   1937-49 No Manager   1949-53 W Scott   1953-54 Scot
Symon   1954-56 F Hill   1956-61 C Britton   1961-68 J Milne
1968-70 R Seith   1970-73 A Ball (Snr)   1973 F Lord (Caretaker)
1973-75 R Charlton   1975-77 H Catterick   1977-81 N Stiles   1981
T Docherty   1981-83 G Lee   1983-85 A Kelly   1985 T Booth
1986 B Kidd   1986 J Clark (Caretaker)   J McGrath 1986-90   L
Chapman 1990-92   S Allardyce (Caretaker) 1992   John Beck 1992
94   Gary Peters 1994-
ADDITIONAL INFORMATION
Club colours: White shirts with navy trim, navy shorts, white &
navy hooped socks.
Change colours: Red shirts with navy trim, red shorts, navy & red
hooped socks.
Reserves League: Pontins League Div 2. **Youth:** Lancs Lge 1 & 2.

LONGEST LEAGUE RUNS

of undefeated matches:	23 (1888-89)	of league matches w/out a win:	15 (1923)
of undefeated home matches:	31 (1903-04)	of undefeated away matches:	11 (1888-89)
without home win:	9 (1965-66)	without an away win:	33 (1897-99)
of league wins:	14 (1950-51 - joint League record)	of home wins:	20 (1891-92)
of league defeats:	8 (1983, 1984)	of away wins:	8 (1950-51)

THE MANAGER

GARY PETERS . . . . appointed December 1994.

PREVIOUS CLUBS
As Manager. . . . . None.
As Asst.Man/Coach . . . . Cambridge United, Preston North End.
As a player. . . . . Reading, Fulham, Wimbledon, Aldershot, Reading, Fulham.

HONOURS
As a Manager. . . . . **Preston:** Division 3 Champions 1995-96.
As a Player. . . . . **Reading:** Division 4 championship 1978-79. Division 3 Championship 1985-86.
. . . . **Wimbledon:** Division 4 championship 1982-83.

PRESTON NORTH END

PLAYERS NAME / Honours	Ht	Wt	Birthdate	Birthplace / Transfers	Contract Date	Clubs	League	L/Cup	FA Cup	Other	Lge	L/C	FAC	Oth
G O A L K E E P E R S														
Lucas David A	6.00	11.4	23/11/77	Chapletown	01/07/89	Sheffield United	8+2		1	0+1				
				£40000	24/12/92	Preston North End	48+3		4	4+1				
				Loan	14/10/94	Lincoln City	4			2				
				Loan	12/12/95	Darlington	6							
D E F E N D E R S														
Gage Kevin	5.9	12.8	21/04/64	Chiswick	04/01/82	Wimbledon	135+33	7+2	8+3	0+1	15	1	1	
E: Y.5. Div.4'83.				£100000	17/07/87	Aston Villa	113+2	13	9	8	8	3	1	
				£150000	15/11/91	Sheffield United	107+5	6	10+2	1	7			
				Free	28/03/96	Preston North End	4+3							
Grant Anthony	5.10	11.8	20/08/76	Louth	01/08/94	Leeds United								
				Free	13/11/95	Preston North End	0+1							
Kidd Ryan	5.11	10.0	06/10/71	Radcliffe	12/07/90	Port Vale	1	0+2		0+1				
				Free	15/07/92	Preston North End	103+10	5	5	7+1	4	1		1
Kilbane K D	6.0	13.0	21/10/74	Preston		Cambridge United								
					01/08/93	Preston North End	8+4			1+1	1			
McDonald Neil	5.11	11.4	02/11/65	Wallsend	19/02/83	Newcastle United	163+17	12	10+1	3	24	3	1	
E: u21.5, Y.7, S.				£525000	03/08/88	Everton	76+14	7	17	10+1	4	3		
				£500000	01/10/91	Oldham Athletic	19+5	3	2		1			
				Free	20/07/94	Bolton Wanderers	4			2				
				£40000	06/11/95	Preston North End	8+3		1	2				
Moyes David	6.1	11.5	25/04/63	Blythswood		Celtic	19+5	8+1		2+1				
SPD'92.				Free	28/10/83	Cambridge United	79	3	1	3	1			
				£10000	10/10/85	Bristol City	83	6	5	15	6			
				£30000	30/10/87	Shrewsbury Town	91+5	4	3	5	11		1	
					01/08/90	Dunfermline	105	7	5		13	1		
					01/08/93	Hamilton Acad.	5							
					01/08/95	Preston North End	108	4	9	13	10	1	1	1
Sharp Raymond	5.11	12.6	16/11/69	Stirling	18/08/86	Dunfermline	151				1			
				Loan	01/08/88	Stenhousemuir	5							
					04/10/94	Preston North End	22	2	3	2				
Sparrow Paul	6.1	11.0	24/03/75	London	13/07/93	Crystal Palace	1	0+1						
				£20000	14/03/96	Preston North End	13							
Squires James	6.1	12.0	15/11/75	Preston	26/04/94	Preston North End	18+4			3+1	1			
				Loan	01/08/95	Stafford Rangers								
Wilcox Russell	6.0	11.10	25/03/64	Hemsworth	28/05/80	Doncaster Rovers	1							
E: SP.3. Div.4'87.				Free	01/08/81	Frickley Athletic			7				1	
				£15000	30/06/86	Northampton Town	137+1	6	10	8	9			1
				£120000	06/08/90	Hull City	92+8	5	5	5+1	7		1	
				£60000	30/07/93	Doncaster Rovers	82	5	3	3	6	2		
				£60000	21/09/95	Preston North End	27		1	1	1		1	
M I D F I E L D														
Atkinson Graeme	5.8	10.5	11/11/71	Hull	06/05/90	Hull City	129+20	6+3	4+1	7	23	2	1	
Barrick Dean	5.7	11.7	30/09/69	Hemsworth	07/05/88	Sheffield Wednesday	11				2			
				£50000	14/02/91	Rotherham United	96+3	6	8	5	7			1
				£50000	11/08/93	Cambridge United	88	6	7	6	2	1	1	
Bryson James Ian	5.11	11.11	26/11/62	Kilmarnock		Kilmarnock	194+21	12+7	14+2		40	1	3	
				£40000	24/08/88	Sheffield United	138+17	11+2	18+4	7	36	1	4	3
				£20000	12/08/93	Barnsley	16	2		2	3	1		
				£42500	29/11/93	Preston North End	109+1	3+1	6+1	10	11	1		1
Cartwright Lee	5.8	10.6	19/09/72	Rossendale	30/07/91	Preston North End	160+22	7	12+1	10+4	13	2	1	
McKenna Paul					01/01/96	Preston North End								
Moilanen Tuevo						F.F.Jaro								
				£50000	05/12/95	Preston North End	2							
F O R W A R D S														
Bennett Gary	5.11	11.0	20/09/63	Kirby		Kirby Town								
AMC'85. WFAC'95.				Free	09/10/84	Wigan Athletic	10+10		1	3+1	3			1
				Free	22/08/85	Chester City	109+17	6+4	8+1	10	36	1	5	5
					11/11/88	Southend United	36+6	4	1	2+1	6	4		
				£20000	01/03/90	Chester City	71+9	8	5	4+1	15	2	1	1
				Free	12/08/92	Wrexham	120+1	17	7	9	77	9	3	9
				£300000	13/07/95	Tranmere Rovers	26+3	4			9			
				£200000	27/03/96	Preston North End	5+3				1			
Brown Michael	5.9	10.12	08/02/68	Birmingham	11/02/86	Shrewsbury Town	174+16	17	10	11	9	2	1	
Div.3'94.				£100000	15/08/91	Bolton Wanderers	27+6	0+1	3	2	3			
				£25000	23/12/92	Shrewsbury Town	66+1	8	3	2	11	1		
				£75000	02/12/94	Preston North End	6+4			1	1			
Davey Simon	5.10	11.2	01/10/70	Swansea	03/07/89	Swansea City	37+12	1	1+2	2+3	4		1	
WFAC'91.				Free	05/08/92	Carlisle United	105	10	7	15	18	1	2	2
				£75000	23/02/94	Preston North End	50+1		2	5	13			
Saville Andy	6.0	12.0	12/12/64	Hull	23/09/83	Hull City	74+27	18	3+2	4+2	18	1	1	
				£100000	23/03/89	Walsall	28+10	2		1+1	5			
				£80000	09/03/90	Barnsley	71+11	5+1	2+1	3	21			1
				£60000	13/03/92	Hartlepool United	37	4	4	3	13	1	5	1
				£155000	22/03/93	Birmingham City	51+8	4	1	1	17	1		
				Loan	30/12/94	Burnley	3+1		1		1			
				£100000	28/07/95	Preston North End	44	2	2	2	29			1
Smart Allan	6.2	12.7	08/07/74	Perth		Caledonian								
				£15000	22/11/94	Preston North End	17+4		2	1+1	6		1	
				Loan	21/11/95	Carlisle United	3+1							
Wilkinson Stephen J	5.10	10.9	01/09/68	Lincoln	06/09/86	Leicester City	5+4		1		1			
				Loan	08/09/88	Crewe Alexandra	3+2				2			
				£80000	02/10/89	Mansfield Town	214+18	13+1	10+1	17	83	4	2	1
				£90000	12/06/95	Preston North End	36+6	2	2	2	10		1	

DEEPDALE

Preston PR1 6RU
Tel: 01772 902 020

Capacity..18,700
Seating 9,000
First game...v Eagley (F) 0-1, 5.10.1878.
First floodlit game........................v Bolton W., Lancs Senior Cup 1st Rnd, 3-0, Att: 12,000, 21.10.53.

ATTENDANCES
Highest...42,684 v Arsenal, Div 1, 23.4.1938.
Lowest ....751 v Bury, AMC, 29.1.1986.

OTHER GROUNDS ....None.

MATCHDAY TICKET PRICES

Pavillion Stand £10
Juv/OAP £6

Tom Finney Stand £11
Juv/Oap. £7

Paddocks £8.50
Juv/OAP £5

Kop & Town End £8
Juv/OAP. Juv/OAP £4.50

Ticket Office Telephone no. 01772 902000

HOW TO GET TO THE GROUND

From the North
Use motorway (M6) then M55 until junction 1, leave motorway and follow signs to Preston A6. In 1.9 miles at crossroads turn left A5085 into Blackpool Road. In 0.8 miles turn right A6063 into Deepdale for Preston North End FC.

From the East and South
Use motorway (M6) until junction 31, leave motorway and follow signs Preston A59. In 1 mile at roundabout take 2nd exit into Blackpool Road. In 1.3 miles turn left A6063 into Deepdale for Preston North End FC.

From the West
Use motorway (M55) until junction 1, leave motorway and follow signs Preston A6. In 1.9 miles at crossroads turn left A5085 into Blackpool Road. In 0.8 miles turn right (A6063) into Deepdale for Preston North End FC.

Car Parking
Club park on Deepdale Road (West Stand) side of ground for 500 vehicles. Limited off-street parking Cost (match-days): £1.00.

Nearest Railway Station
Preston (01772 59439)

P.N.E. CLUBCALL
0891 66 02 20

Calls cost 39p per minute cheap rate and 49p per minute at all other times.
Call costings correct at time of going to press.

MATCHDAY PROGRAMME

Programme Editor . . . . Karen Pearson/Sharon Gifford.

Number of pages . . . . 32.

Price . . . . £1.50.

Subscriptions . . . . Home £31. Away £31. Home & Away £62.

Local Newspapers . . . . Lancashire Evening Post.

Local Radio Stations . . . . Red Rose Radio, Radio Lancashire.

ROTHERHAM UNITED
(The Merry Millers)
NATIONWIDE LEAGUE DIVISION 2
SPONSORED BY: PARKGATE RETAIL WORLD (Stadium Development)

ROTHERHAM UNITED
1995-96

ROTHERHAM UNITED
FORMED IN 1884
TURNED PROFESSIONAL IN 1905
LTD COMPANY IN 1920

CHAIRMAN: K F Booth
VICE-CHAIRMAN
R Hull
DIRECTORS
C Luckock, J A Webb
CHEIF EXECUTIVE
P Henson (01709 512434
COMMERCIAL MANAGER
D Nicholls (01709 512 760)

MANAGERS
Archie Gemmill & John McGovern

YOUTH TEAM MANAGER
Bill Russell
PHYSIOTHERAPIST
Ian Bailey

STATISTICIAN FOR THE DIRECTORY
Mike Smith

Rotherham United finished off an otherwise average season with their first ever trip to Wembley Stadium by reaching the final of the Auto Windscreen Shield.   The Yorkshire based club never threatened to challenge for any play-off place and steered clear of any relegation worries with League form that saw them win 14, draw 14 and lose 18, giving them a final position of 16th.

The Second Round of the Coca-Cola Cup was reached via a 6-4 (on aggregate) victory over Scunthorpe, before going out to Bryan Robson's Middlesbrough team 1-3 on aggregate.

The F.A. Cup saw little joy with a First Round exit against Third Division Rochdale (3-5).

It was in the Auto Windscreen Shield though that Rotherham were to make their Wembley Stadium debut, on April 14th against fellow Second Division club Shrewsbury Town.

Initially their journey along the 'Road to Wembley' was hardly convincing though. Victory over Chester City (1-0) was followed by a draw at home to Burnley (1-1). However, this was enough to get them through to the next round where they beat Wigan on penalties, after a 0-0 draw. Lincoln City were next to go, in a well earned 3-1 victory. The Northern Semi-Final paired them off with York City, and by this time the players had belief in their dream of playing at Wembley, seeing off the 'Minster Men' with a 4-1 victory. This brought them a two legged Northern Final against struggerling Carlisle United. Nothing was going to stop the 'Merry Millers' now and four goals, without reply, saw Rotherham through to the final and their first visit to Wembley.

The final itself was affectively over when Nigel Jemson, on loan from Notts County, put Rotherham ahead after 20 minutes. They were not leaving Wembley without the Trophy and it showed. 58 minutes gone and Jemson added to his tally and Rotherham fans were celebrating. Although a late goal from Shrewsbury made the final few minutes tense, the Trophy was going back to South Yorkshire with the 'Merry Millers'.

ROTHERHAM UNITED

League: 16th   FA Cup: 1st Rnd   Coca-Cola Cup: 2nd Rnd   Auto Windscreen Shield: Winners

M	DATE	COMP	VEN	OPPONENTS	RESULT	HT	LP	GOAL SCORERS/GOAL TIMES	ATT.
1	A 12	EL	A	Burnley	L 1-2	1-2	5	Goater 10(pen)	(10156)
2	15	CC 1/1	A	Scunthorpe United	L 1-4	1-1		Hayward 38	(2110)
3	19	EL	H	Hull City	D 1-1	0-0	18	Goater 88(pen)	3754
4	22	CC 1/2	H	Scunthorpe United	W 5-0	1-0		Goater 14, 98, McGlashan 55, Hayward 72, Jeffrey 92	2206
5	26	EL	A	Oxford United	D 1-1	1-0	14	Murphy 29(og)	(4282)
6	29	EL	H	Carlisle United	D 2-2	0-0	19	Goater 63, 82(pen)	3550
7	S 2	EL	A	Bournemouth	L 1-2	1-2	22	Goater 34	(4906)
8	9	EL	H	Brentford	W 1-0	1-0	18	Berry 37	3061
9	12	EL	H	Bristol Rovers	W 1-0	0-0	14	Jeffrey 71	2739
10	16	EL	A	Chesterfield	L 0-3	0-1	17		(5146)
11	20	CC 2/1	A	Middlesbrough	L 1-2	1-2		Goater 44	(13280)
12	23	EL	A	Swindon Town	L 0-1	0-0	19		(8470)
13	26	AWS 1/1	A	Chester City	W 1-0	0-0		Roscoe	(774)
14	30	EL	H	Peterborough United	W 5-1	2-0	13	Goater 41, 49, Berry 44, Jeffrey 80, Roscoe 89	2863
15	O 3	CC 2/2	H	Middlesbrough	L 0-1	0-0			6867
16	7	EL	A	Brighton & H.A.	W 1-0	0-0	13	Jeffrey 75	2950
17	14	EL	A	Notts County	L 1-2	1-1	13	Goater 16	(5478)
18	17	AWS 1/1	H	Burnley	D 1-1	0-1		Hayward	1539
19	21	EL	H	Blackpool	W 2-1	0-0	11	Jeffrey 50, Jeffrey 56	3663
20	28	EL	A	Shrewsbury Town	L 1-3	1-0	13	Garner 14	(2632)
21	31	EL	A	Stockport County	D 1-1	1-0	13	Goater 12	(4070)
22	N 4	EL	H	Crewe Alexandra	D 2-2	1-1	15	Goater 3, Blades 62	3328
23	11	FAC 1	A	Rochdale	L 3-5	0-3		Goater 72(pen), 81, McGlashan 83	(3817)
24	18	EL	A	Wrexham	L 0-7	0-3	15		(3227)
25	25	EL	H	Bristol City	L 2-3	1-1	19	Goater 20, 84	2649
26	28	AWS 2	H	Wigan Athletic	D 0-0	0-0			1008
27	D 2	EL	A	Swansea City	D 0-0	0-0	17		(1788)
28	9	EL	H	Swindon Town	L 0-2	0-0	19		3042
29	16	EL	A	Peterborough United	L 0-1	0-0	20		(3847)
30	26	EL	H	Walsall	L 0-1	0-0	20		3694
31	J 6	EL	H	York City	D 2-2	2-0	20	Goater 20(pen), Richardson 26	2695
32	9	AWS QF	H	Lincoln City	W 3-1	0-0		Berry , Goodwin (2)	1825
33	13	EL	A	Hull City	W 4-1	1-0	18	Berry 29, Goater 50, Goodwin 58, Viljoen 68	(3678)
34	20	EL	A	Burnley	W 1-0	0-0	18	Berry 85	4018
35	23	EL	H	Bradford City	W 2-0	0-0	16	Breckin 63, Roscoe 68	3052
36	F 3	EL	H	Oxford United	W 1-0	0-0	15	Viljoen 73	2842
37	10	EL	A	York City	D 2-2	0-1	16	Richardson 68(pen), Goodwin 76	(3299)
38	13	AWS SF	H	York City	W 4-1	2-1		Goodwin, Garner, Hayward , Roscoe	3913
39	17	EL	A	Bristol Rovers	L 0-1	0-0	17		(5416)
40	20	EL	H	Bournemouth	W 1-0	1-0	15	Hayward 41	2092
41	24	EL	H	Chesterfield	L 0-1	0-0	16		5712
42	27	EL	A	Brentford	D 1-1	0-0	17	Jemson 90	(3446)
43	M 2	EL	A	Walsall	L 1-3	1-1	17	Jemson 27	(3001)
44	5	AWS NF1	H	Carlisle United	W 2-0	0-0		Richardson 46(pen), Goater 47	6848
45	9	EL	H	Swansea City	D 1-1	1-0	19	Jemson 6	2714
46	12	AWS NF2	A	Carlisle United	W 2-0	0-0		Jemson (2)	(6892)
47	16	EL	A	Bradford City	L 0-2	0-0	19		(4047)
48	23	EL	H	Wycombe Wanderers	D 0-0	0-0	19		2775
49	26	EL	A	Carlisle United	L 0-2	0-2	21		(4074)
50	30	EL	A	Brighton & H.A.	D 1-1	1-1	20	Goater 31	(5530)
51	A 2	EL	H	Notts County	W 2-0	0-0	18	Hurst 47, Berry 80	2750
52	6	EL	H	Shrewsbury Town	D 2-2	2-1	18	Goater 3, Goodwin 20	2973
53	8	EL	A	Blackpool	W 2-1	1-1	16	McGlashan 35, Berry 61	6850
54	14	AWS F	H	Shrewsbury Town	W 2-1	1-0		Jemson 20, 58	35235
55	16	EL	A	Wycombe Wanderers	D 1-1	1-0	16	Goater 39	(2836)
56	20	EL	A	Crewe Alexandra	W 2-0	1-0	17	Goodwin 37, Jemson 69(pen)	(3685)
57	23	EL	H	Stockport County	W 2-0	0-0	14	Goater 55(pen), Hayward 80	6920
58	27	EL	A	Bristol City	L 3-4	1-1	15	Jemson 14, Berry 67, McGlashan 88	(6101)
59	M 4	EL	H	Wrexham	L 0-1	0-0	16		4419

Best Home League Attendance: 6920 v Stockport County   **Smallest: 2092 v Bournemouth**   **Average: 3402**

Goal Scorers:

EL(54): Goater(18),Berry(7),Jemson(5),Jeffrey(5),Goodwin(4),McGlashan(2),Richardson(2),Roscoe(2),Viljoen(2),Hayward(2),Garner(1),Breckin(1),Blades(1), Hurst(1),Opponent(s)(1)

CC(7): Goater(3),Hayward(2),Jeffrey(1),McGlashan(1)

FAC(3): Goater(2),McGlashan(1)

AWS(15): Jemson(4),Goodwin(3),Roscoe(2),Hayward(2),Richardson(1),Goater(1),Garner(1),Berry(1)

1995-96

(F) Berry	(D) Blades	(M) Bowyer	(D) Breckin	(G) Clarke	(M) Davies	(F) Davison	(G) Farrelly	(M) Garner	(F) Goater	(D) Goodwin	(F) Hayward	(D) Hurst	(M) James	(F) Jeffrey	(F) Jemson	(M) McGlashan	(D) McIntosh	(D) McLean	(D) Monington	(D) Moore	(G) Muggleton	(G) Pettinger	(D) Pike	(D) Richardson	(M) Roscoe	(D) Smith	(M) Viljoen	(D) Wilder		
	X	X	S	X				X1	X	X	X			X		S1			X			S			X			X	K.Lynch	1
	X	X		X	S	X		X	X	X	X	S				S			X						X			X	J.Rushton	2
	X1	X	S1	X				X	X		X2			X		S2			X3			S3			X			X	A.Butler	3
			X	X				X	X		X	X	S	X		X								X	X			X	M.Bailey	4
	X		X	X				X	X	S1	X1	X		X		X						S		S	X			X	D.Orr	5
	X		X	X				X	X	X	X	X	S	X										S	X			X	S.Mathieson	6
	X		X	X				X	X	X	X1	X	S1	X								S		S	X			X	S.Bennett	7
X1	X		X	X				X	X	S	S	X		X		X								S1	X			X	T.Lunt	8
X1	X		X	X		S		X	X	S		X		X		X								S1	X			X	A.R.Leak	9
S2	X	S1	X	X				X1	X	S		X		X		X								X2	X			X	T.West	10
	X	X	X	X			S	X	X	X	S	S		X		X									X			X	W.Burns	11
X	X	X	X	X				X1	X	X	S	S1		X					S2						X2			X	M.Fletcher	12
X1	X	X	X	X					X	X	S1	S		X					X					X	X	S			E.Wolstenholme	13
X	X	X1	X	X			S		X	X2	S2			X					S1					X	X			X	G.B.Frankland	14
	X	X	X	X			S		X	X	S	S		X					X					X	X			X	P.Danson	15
X	X	X	X	X					X	X1	S			X					S1					X	X	S		X	S.Mathieson	16
	X	X1	X	X					X	X	S2	S1		X					X					X2	X	S		X	E.Wolstenholme	17
S	X		X	X		S		X	X	X	X	X		X											X	S		X	S.J.Baines	18
S	X		X	X				X	X	X	X	X		X		S								S	X			X	W.Burns	19
	X		X	X				X	X	X	X	X		X		S								S	X		S	X	I.S.Helmely	20
	X		X	X				X	X	X	X1	X	S	X		S1									X		S	X	P.Rejer	21
S	X		X					X	X		X	X	S	X		X					X				X		S	X	F.Stretton	22
X	X		X		X			X	X		S1	X1	S	X		X									X		S	X	R.Pearson	23
X	X		X					X	X		S1	X	S	X		X					X				X1	X	S		P.Richards	24
X	X							X	X		S	X		X		X	S		X		X				X	X	S		I.Cruikshanks	25
X	X							X1	X		X	X		X		X	S		X		X			S1		X	S		S.Mathieson	26
X	X							X	X		X	X		X		X	S		X		X			X			S		C.R.Wilkes	27
X			S1					X1			X	X		X		X	S		X		X			X	X2		S2	X	G.Singh	28
X2	X	S1	X	S					X	X	S2	X1		X							X			X	X	X			N.S.Barry	29
X2	X	S1	X	X					X	X	S2	X		X							S			X	X1			X	D.Laws	30
X1	X	X	X	X				S	X	X	S1	X												X	X	X	S		G.Barber	31
X		X1	X	X				X	X	X	S1	X					S							X	X	X	S			32
X		X	X	X			S	X	X	X	S	S1												X	X1	X	X		T.Heilbron	33
X		X	X	X			S	X	X		X	X						X						X	X	S			A.Poulain	34
X			X	X			S	X	X	X	S	X						X						X	X	S	X		D.B.Allison	35
X	S		X	X				X	X	X	S1	X						X						X	X1	S	X		K.Breen	36
X	X	X	S	X				X	X	X	S2	S1						X						X	X1		X2		M.Bailey	37
X	X	X	X	X				X	X2	X1	X	S1												X	X		S2		A.Butler	38
X	X	X	X	X1				X	X	X	S2	S1			X									X	X2		S		E.Wolstenholme	39
X1	X	X	X	X			S	X	X		X	S1			X			X							X		S		A.Leake	40
S1	X	X	X	X					X		X1	X			X			X						X	X1	S	S1		G.R.Pooley	41
X		X	X	X			S				X2	S1			X			X	S2					X	X	X	X1		J.Rushton	42
X	X	X	X	X			S	X	X						X			X	S					X	X		S		E.Cruickshanks	43
X1	X	X	X	X				X	X		S1	X			X				S					X	X2		S2		T.West	44
X	X	X	X	X		S			X		X	X			X				X1						X	S1	S		G.Singh	45
X	X	X	X	X			S		X		X	X			X									X	X	S	S		M.Riley	46
X	X	X	X	X		S			X		X	X			X			X					S		X1		S1		P.Richards	47
X		X	X	X		S			X		S1	X			X					X			S	X	X1	X			G.Cain	48
X	X	X		X					X		X	X			X					X			S	X	X	S	S		R.Pearson	49
X	X	X		X		S			X		X	X			X					X			S1		X1	X	S		P.Taylor	50
X	X1		X	X				X	X	X	S2	X			X2	S				S1				X	X				N.Barry	51
X	X	S	X	X				X	X	X	S1	X			X	S				X					X1				G.Frankland	52
X1	X	X	X	X				X	X	X	X					X2				X					S2	S1	S		K.Breen	53
X	X	S	X	X				X	X	X	S	X			X	S								X	X				D.Allison	54
X		S1	X	X				X	X	X	S	X			X					X				X	X1	S			B.Gifford	55
X1		X	X	X					X	X2	S1	S2			X	X				X					X	X	S		S.Mathieson	56
X			X	X		X1		X2	X		X	X								X			S2	X	X	S1			T.E.West	57
S1		X	X	X		S			X		X	X			X	X				X			S		X1	X			M.Pierce	58
X				X				X	X	X	S1	X			X	X				X			S		X1	X	S		A.D'Urso	59
33	34	23	37	40	0	1	0	31	44	24	22	32	0	22	16	13	0	9	7	10	6	0	0	23	44	11	5	18	EL Appearances	
3	0	4	2	0	0	0	0	0	0	1	14	8	1	0	0	3	0	0	4	1	0	1	2	2	1	3	3	0	EL Sub Appearances	
0	3	3	3	4	0	1	0	3	4	3	2	1	0	3	0	2	0	0	2	0	0	0	0	2	4	0	0	4	CC Appearances	
1	1	0	1	0	1	0	0	1	1	0	0+1	1	0	1	0	1	0	0	0	0	0	0	0	0	1	0	0	1	FAC Appearances	
7	7	5	7	7	0	0	0	6	8	5	4+3	6+1	0	3	3	1	0	0	2	0	1	0	0	6+1	7	2	0+2	1	AWS Appearances	

Also Played: (M) Ayrton S(34,38). (M) Bocken S(4). (M) Boucker S(6). (M) Duffy S(4). (M) Haran S(27). (M) Hudson S(58).

CLUB RECORDS

RECORD LEAGUE VICTORY
8-0 v Oldham Athletic, Div 3N, 26.5.1947
Record Cup Victory and Most Goals Scored in a Cup Tie
6-0 v Spennymoor United,FA Cup Round 2, 1977-78   6-0 v
Wolverhampton Wanderers, FA Cup Round 1,16.11.1985

RECORD LEAGUE DEFEAT
1-11 v Bradford City, Div 3N, 25.8.1928*
* First match of the season. Rotherham United won their second
match at home!
Record Cup Defeat
0-15 v Notts County, FA Cup Round 1, 24.10.1885

MOST LEAGUE POINTS
(2pts for win) 71, Div 3N, 1950-51
(3pts a win) 82, Div4, 1988-89

MOST LEAGUE GOALS
14, Div 3N, 1946-47

RECORD TRANSFER FEE RECEIVED
£325,000 from Sheffield Wednesday for Matt Clarke, July 1996.
RECORD TRANSFER FEE PAID
£110,000 to Wolves for Paul Blades, July 1995.

BEST PERFORMANCES
League: 3rd Div 2, 1954-55
FA Cup: 5th Round 1952-53,1967-68
League Cup: Finalists 1960-61

HONOURS
Division 3N Champions 1950-51
Division 3 Champions 1980-81
Division 4 Champions1988-89
AMC winners 1995-96.

LEAGUE CAREER
Rotherham Town: Elected to Div 2 1893   Not re-elected to Div 2
1896
Rotherham County: Elected to Div 2 1919   Relegated to Div 3N
1923   Promoted to Div 2 1951   Relegated to Div 3 1968
Relegated to Div 4 1973   Promoted to Div 3 1975   Promoted to
Div 2 1981   Relegated to Div 3 1983
Relegated to Div 4 1988   Promoted to Div 3 1989   Relegated to
Div 4 1991   Promoted to Div 3 (now Div 2) 1992

INDIVIDUAL CLUB RECORDS

MOST APPEARANCES FOR CLUB
Danny Williams (1946-60): 459

MOST CAPPED PLAYER
Shaun Goater, Bermuda (6+), Harold Millership, 6 Wales

RECORD GOALSCORER IN A MATCH
No player has scored more than four goals

RECORD LEAGUE GOALSCORER IN A SEASON
Wally Ardron, 38, Div 3N, 1946-47

RECORD LEAGUE GOALSCORER IN A CAREER
Gladstone Guest, 130, 1946-56

OLDEST PLAYER IN A LEAGUE MATCH
Chris Hutchings, 36 years 175 days v Bradford City, Div.2
27.12.1993

YOUNGEST PLAYER IN A LEAGUE MATCH
Kevin Eley, 16 years 72 days v Scunthorpe (h), 3-0, 15.5.1984

PREVIOUS MANAGERS

(Since 1946): Reg Freeman   Andy Smailes   Tom Johnston   Danny
Williams   Jack Mansell   Tommy Docherty   Jimmy McAnearney
Jimmy McGuigan   Ian Porterfield   Emlyn Hughes   George Kerr
Norman Hunter   Dave Cusack   Billy McEwan   Phil Henson

ADDITIONAL INFORMATION
Previous League: Midland League

Previous Names: Thornhill United (1884), Rotherham County
(1905), amalgamated in 1925 with Rotherham Town as Rotherham
United

Club colours: Red and white.

Change colours: Navy /silver.

Reserves League: Pontins Central League Division 2.

Youth League: Northern Intermediate.

LONGEST LEAGUE RUNS

of undefeated matches:	18 (1950-51)	of league matches w/out a win:	14 (1934, 1977-78)
of undefeated home matches:	27 (1939-46-47, 1980-81)	of undefeated away matches:	16 (1950-51)
without home win:	9 (1983)	without an away win:	33 (1894-96-1919 - non-League club)
of league wins:	9 (1982)	of home wins:	22 (1939-46-47)
of league defeats:	8 (1956)	of away wins:	8 (1948)

THE MANAGERS

ARCHIE GEMMILL & JOHN McGOVERN . . . . appointed September 1994.

PREVIOUS CLUBS
As Manager . . . . None for both.
As Asst.Man/Coach . . . . JM - Plymouth.
As a player . . . . AG - Derby, Nottingham Forest. JM - Nottingham Forest.

HONOURS
As a Managers . . . . A.M.C. winners 1995-96.
As a Player . . . . Division 1 championship and European Cup for both, while at Nottingham Forest.
International: (AG-) Full caps for Scotland.

ROTHERHAM UNITED

PLAYERS NAME / Honours	Ht	Wt	Birthdate	Birthplace / Transfers	Contract Date	Clubs	League	L/Cup	FA Cup	Other	Lge	L/C	FAC	Oth
						APPEARANCES					**GOALS**			
G O A L K E E P E R S														
Farrelly Steve				Manchester		Chester City								
						Macclesfield Town								
				£20000	13/07/95	Rotherham United								
D E F E N D E R S														
Blades Paul	6.0	11.0	05/01/65	Peterborough	29/12/82	Derby County	157+9	9+3	12	8+2	1			
E: Y.3. Div.2'87.				£700000	18/07/90	Norwich City	47	8	2	5				
				£325000	14/08/92	Wolves	103+4	4+1	9	6	2		1	
				£110000	18/07/95	Rotherham United	34	3	1	7	1			
Breckin Ian	6.1	12.9	24/02/75	Rotherham	01/11/93	Rotherham United	88+2	4	4	10	2			
Goodwin Shaun	5.7	8.10	14/06/69	Rotherham	01/07/87	Rotherham United	242+16	16+7	16+1	20+2	34	1	3	4
Div.4'89.														
Hurst Paul	5.7	10.4	25/09/74	Sheffield	12/08/93	Rotherham United	43+14	1	3	9+1	1		1	
McIntosh Andrew					27/06/96	Rotherham Utd (T)								
Monington Mark	6.1	13.0	21/10/70	Bilsthorpe	23/03/89	Burnley	65+19	5	4+1	4+2	5		1	
Div.4'92.					28/11/94	Rotherham United	32+4	2		2	2			
Richardson Neil	5.10	13.5	03/03/68	Sunderland		Brandon United								
					18/08/89	Rotherham United	117+10	10+1	4+1	10+2	6			1
Smith Scott	5.8	11.6	06/03/75	Christchurch,NZ	01/10/93	Rotherham United	21+4		2	2+1				
M I D F I E L D														
Bowyer Gary	6.0	12.13	22/06/71	Manchester	01/08/85	Westfields								
WFAC'90.				Free	02/12/89	Hereford United	12+2				2			
				Free	15/09/90	Nottingham Forest								
				Free	02/08/95	Rotherham United	23+4	3		5				
McGlashan John	6.1	13.3	03/06/67	Dundee		Montrose								
				£50000	22/08/90	Millwall	9+7		0+1	1				
				Loan	11/12/92	Fulham	5		1	1	1			
				Loan	15/01/93	Cambridge United	0+1							
				£75000	27/01/93	Peterborough Utd	44+2	4+1	1	2	3	1		
				Free	04/11/94	Rotherham United	40+3	2	1	1	5	1	1	
Garner Darren				Dorchester										
				£30000	01/06/95	Rotherham United	31	3	1	6	1			1
Roscoe Andrew	5.11	12.0	04/06/73	Liverpool		Liverpool								
				Free	17/07/91	Bolton Wanderers	2+1			1+1				
					02/02/95	Rotherham United	75+1	4	1	7	6			2
F O R W A R D S														
Berry Trevor	5.7	10.8	01/08/74	Haslemere		Bournemouth								
					01/08/91	Aston Villa								
				£20000	13/10/95	Rotherham United	33+3		1	7	7			1
Goater Leonardo	5.11	11.4	25/02/70	Bermuda		Manchester United								
Bermuda Int.				Free	25/10/89	Rotherham United	169+40	13+4	12+3	15+5	70	4	7	5
				Loan	12/11/93	Notts County	1							
Hayward Andy	6.0	11.2	21/06/70	Barnsley		Frickley Athletic								
				Free	10/08/94	Rotherham United	55+18	3+1	2+1	6+3	8	3		2
McDougald David	5.11	10.12	12/01/75	Texas	12/07/93	Tottenham Hotspur								
E: S.					12/05/94	Brighton & H.A.	70+7	7	4	6	14	2	3	3
				Loan	10/04/96	Chesterfield	9				3			
				£50000	26/07/96	Rotherham United								
ADDITIONAL CONTRACT PLAYERS														
Hobson Daniel					26/06/96	Rotherham Utd (T)								
Hudson Danny						Rotherham Utd (T)								
Viljoen Nik						Rotherham Utd (T)	5+3		0+2		2			

MILLMOOR GROUND
Rotherham, South Yorkshire S60 1HR
Tel: 01709 612434

Capacity...11,514
Covered Standing...6,951
Seating...4,573

First game...v Tranmere, 31.8.1925.
First floodlit game ....v Bristol Rovers, Lge Cup 2nd Rnd, 23.11.1960.

ATTENDANCES
Highest..25,000 v Sheffield Utd, Div.2, 13.12.1952.
Lowest...1,182 v Scarborough, AMC, 27.11.1990.

OTHER GROUNDS...None.

MATCHDAY TICKET PRICES

Main Stand £10
Juv/OAP £6.50
Millmoor Lane Stand £8
Juv/OAP £5.50
Enclosure Stand £8.50
Juv/OAP £5.50
Tivoli Terrace. £7.50
Juv/OAP £5
Visiting Seats. £10
Juv/OAP £6.50

Ticket Office Telephone no. 01709 512434

CLUBCALL
0891 66 44 42
Calls cost 39p per minute cheap rate and 49p per
minute at all other times.
Call costings correct at time of going to press.

HOW TO GET TO THE GROUND

From the North
Use motorway M1 until junction 34, leave motorway and follow signs to
Rotherham (A6109). Cross railway bridge and then turn right into Millmoor Lane
for Rotherham United FC.

From the East
Use A630 into Rotherham and then follow signs to Sheffield into Masborough
Street, then turn left into Millmoor Lane for Rotherham United FC.

From the South and West
Use motorway M1 until junction 34, leave motorway and follow signs to
Rotherham (A6178). At roundabout take 1st exit into Ring Road and at next
roundabout 1st exit in Masborough Street (A6109). Take 1st turning left into
Millmoor for Rotherham United FC.

Car Parking
There are parks within easy distance of the ground in Kimberworth Road and
Main Street.

Nearest Railway Station
Rotherham Central (Town Centre)

MATCHDAY PROGRAMME

Programme Editor . . . . Dave Nicholls.

Number of pages . . . . 32.

Price . . . . £1.40.

Subscriptions . . . . £35 for full season (includes postage).

Local Newspapers. . . . . Sheffield Morning Telegraph,
. . . . Sheffield Star (including Saturday special), Rotherham Advertiser.

Local Radio Stations . . . . Radio Hallam (194 MWs),
. . . . Radio Sheffield (290 MW).

SHREWSBURY TOWN
(The Town or Blues)
NATIONWIDE LEAGUE DIVISION 2
SPONSORED BY: GREENHOUS LEYLAND DAF & VAUXHALL

Back Row (L-R): Darren Rowbotham, Ian Stevens, Darren Simkin, Martin Jefferies, Ray Woods, Austin Berkley, Nathan King.
Middle Row: Malcolm Musgrove, Dean Spink, Shaun Wray, Mark Hughes, Tony Grenham, Tim Clarke, Paul Edwards, Tommy Lynch, Dave Walton, Steve Anthrobus, Kevin Summerfield. **Front Row:** Chris Withe, Ian Reed, Paul Evans, Mark Taylor, Fred Davies, Kevin Seabury, Richard Scott, Lee Martin, Mark Dempsey.

SHREWSBURY TOWN
FORMED IN 1886
TURNED PROFESSIONAL IN 1905
LTD COMPANY IN 1936

PRESIDENT: F C G Fry
VICE-PRESIDENT: Dr J Millard Bryson
CHAIRMAN: R Wycherley

DIRECTORS
R Bailey,K R Woodhouse,
M J Starkey, W H Richards
SECRETARY
M J Starkey (01743 360 111)
COMMERCIAL MANAGER
M Thomas (01743 356 316)

MANAGER: Fred Davies
COACHES: R Pratley & K Summerfield
PHYSIOTHERAPIST
M Musgrove
STATISTICIAN FOR THE DIRECTORY
Richard & Nicola Stocken

Excitement, frustration, elation and disappointment. A roller coaster season at Shrewsbury had it all. Records were broken, there were flirtations with the play offs and relegation, and a first ever visit to Wembley.

A disastrous start with a just one win in the first 10 league games saw Town in 24th position. The Coca Cola Cup was a memory after an honourable aggregate second round defeat to Derby, but signs of improvement led to a marvellous autumn run, loosing just two league games out of the next 14, including a record equalling seven straight league victories. There were wins at Swindon, Stockport and Brentford and home victory over promoted Oxford. A win on January 2nd at Bournemouth saw Town now in 5th spot.

During this run cup results followed a similar pattern. A new record highest score 11-2 against Marine in the F.A. Cup preceded a replay victory against Scunthorpe in round 2. In the Auto windscreens Shield a 3-1 victory at Leyton Orient led to a penalty victory over Bristol City.That victory at Bournemouth was though the last in the league until York were beaten 2-1 on April 2nd by which time Town had slipped to 17th, 14 league games with no win. To some extent injuries and suspensions had taken their toll on the small squad as did continuing cup success.

In round three of the F.A. Cup Fulham were beaten at the second attempt. With only 10 men for much of the game they came from behind to win 2-1 in the last minute. A dream tie at home to Liverpool followed, or was it? Whether postponements, capacity problems and a ludicrous Police imposed 11 am Sunday Kick off combined to take the sting out of the tie. Town never did themselves justice and lost 0-4.

Progress continued in the AWS with wins over Hereford and Brighton setting up a Regional final against Bristol Rovers. Following a 1-1 draw a fine team performance at Bath including a Paul Edwardís penalty save and Ian Stevens goal was rewarded with a first Wembley appearance.

The run in just provided the points to secure safety but ended in frustration with three final defeats including a 0-6 reverse at Oxford. Eventually 18th place was the final placing after 64 games in League and Cup.

The very pleasant diversion to Wembley saw 16,000 travelling Salopians enjoy a memorable day despite a 1-2 reverse to Rotherham. Yet again Town didn't quite do themselves justice in the big game but Mark Taylor did score a fine goal. The memory of the visit should last in Shropshire until the next time!

Frustration perhaps but on such meagre resources continually forcing manager Davies to shuffle the pack a very memorable season. In the last three seasons Town have now won a championship and a trip to wembley. Quite an achievement. **RICHARD STOCKTON.**

SHREWSBURY TOWN

League: 18th   FA Cup: 4th Rnd   Coca-Cola Cup: 1st Rnd   Auto Windscreen Shield: Runners-up

M	DATE	COMP	VEN	OPPONENTS	RESULT	HT	LP	GOAL SCORERS/GOAL TIMES	ATT.
1	A 12	EL	A	Swansea City	L 1-3	0-2	18	Anthrobus 90	(3498)
2	14	CC 1/1	A	**Doncaster Rovers**	D 1-1	1-0		Seabury 14	(1580)
3	19	EL	H	Walsall	L 0-2	0-0	23		4019
4	22	CC 1/2	H	**Doncaster Rovers**	D 0-0	0-0			1842
5	26	EL	A	Bradford City	L 1-3	1-3	23	Reed 28	(5017)
6	29	EL	A	Bristol City	W 4-1	0-1	18	Reed 47, Spink 55, Dempsey 57, Rowbotham 88	2558
7	S 2	EL	H	Blackpool	L 0-2	0-2	21	3182	
8	9	EL	A	Crewe Alexandra	L 0-3	0-1	23	(3747)	
9	12	EL	A	Wrexham	D 1-1	1-1	23	Taylor 10	(3298)
10	16	EL	H	Notts County	L 0-1	0-0	24		2892
11	19	CC 2/1	H	Derby County	L 1-3	0-2		Lynch 50(pen)	3170
12	23	EL	A	Stockport County	L 1-2	0-0	24	Anthrobus 57	2588
13	26	AWS 1/1	H	**Swansea City**	D 1-1	0-0		Clarke 47	943
14	30	EL	A	Brighton & H.A.	D 2-2	1-1	24	Whiston 43, Rowbotham 76	(5247)
15	O 4	CC 2/2	A	**Derby County**	D 1-1	0-1		Rowbotham 55(pen)	(8825)
16	7	EL	A	Hull City	W 3-2	1-0	23	Rowbotham 44, Spink 73, Rowbotham 80	(3266)
17	14	EL	H	York City	W 2-1	1-0	20	Lynch 24(pen), Spink 80	2827
18	21	EL	A	Chesterfield	L 0-1	0-1	21		(3920)
19	28	EL	H	Rotherham United	W 3-1	0-1	19	Whiston 71, Spink 75, 83	2632
20	31	EL	A	Oxford United	W 2-0	1-0	16	Evans 15, Lynch 78(pen)	2186
21	N 4	EL	A	Brentford	W 2-0	2-0	14	Lynch 24(pen), Scott 27	(4104)
22	7	AWS 1/2	A	**Leyton Orient**	W 3-1	0-0		**Walton 47, Walton 48, Walton 49**	(1437)
23	11	FAC 1	H	**Marine**	W 11-2	4-0		**og 3, Spink 39,48,65, Withe 40, Scott 41,Whiston 47,58 Evans 55, Whiston 58, Stevens 82, Dempsey 86**	2845
24	18	EL	H	Burnley	W 3-0	2-0	11	Evans 8(pen), 35, Scott 59	3914
25	25	EL	A	Swindon Town	W 1-0	0-0	9	Scott 75	(9306)
26	28	AWS 2	H	**Bristol City**	D 0-0	0-0			2258
27	D 2	FAC 2	A	**Scunthorpe United**	D 1-1	0-0		**Scott 50**	(2718)
28	9	EL	A	Stockport County	W 2-0	1-0	9	Rowbotham 20, Dempsey 79	(5530)
29	12	FAC 2R	H	**Scunthorpe United**	W 2-1	2-0		**Scott 35, Rowbotham 41(pen)**	3313
30	16	EL	H	Brighton & H.A.	W 2-1	1-1	8	Rowbotham 42, 59(pen)	3697
31	23	EL	A	Wycombe Wanderers	L 0-2	0-1	9		(4131)
32	26	EL	H	Bristol Rovers	D 1-1	0-0	10	Stevens 81	4944
33	30	EL	H	Carlisle United	D 1-1	0-0	9	Spink 61	2864
34	J 2	EL	A	Bournemouth	W 2-0	1-0	5	Rowbotham 21, Anthrobus 89	(3245)
35	6	FAC 3	A	**Fulham**	D 1-1	0-0		**Evans 60**	(7265)
36	9	AWS QF	H	**Brighton & H.A.**	W 4-2	1-1		**Lynch (4)**	2559
37	13	EL	A	Walsall	L 0-3	0-1	8		5008)
38	16	FAC 3R	H	**Fulham**	W 2-1	0-1		**Anthrobus 49, Dempsey 87**	7983
39	20	EL	H	Swansea City	L 1-2	0-1	9	Stevens 26	6532
40	31	AWS SF	H	**Hereford United**	W 4-1	2-0		**Summerfield 23, 47,48 (3), Brough 40(og)**	4545
41	F 3	EL	H	Bradford City	D 1-1	0-0	9	Berkeley 59	3405
42	10	EL	A	Peterborough United	D 2-2	0-0	18	Anthrobus 46, Currie 65	(4985)
43	13	EL	A	Bristol City	L 0-2	0-0	10		(5217)
44	18	FAC 4	H	**Liverpool**	L 0-4	0-1			7752
45	20	EL	A	Blackpool	L 1-2	0-1	13	Anthrobus 88	(4210)
46	24	EL	A	Notts County	D 1-1	1-1	14	Anthrobus 20	(4559)
47	27	EL	H	Crewe Alexandra	L 2-3	2-2	14	Stevens 18, 42	3745
48	M 2	EL	A	Bristol City	L 1-2	1-1	14	Stevens 7	(5004)
49	5	AWS SF1	H	**Bristol Rovers**	D 1-1	0-0		**Taylor 60**	5262
50	9	EL	H	Wycombe Wanderers	D 1-1	1-1	17	Stevens 21	2866
51	12	AWS SF2	A	**Bristol Rovers**	W 1-0	0-0		**Stevens 87**	(7050)
52	16	EL	A	Carlisle United	D 1-1	0-0	18	Anthrobus 56	(3760)
53	19	EL	H	Peterborough United	D 1-1	1-0	16	Stevens 34	2291
54	23	EL	H	Bournemouth	L 1-2	1-0	17	Stevens 7	2534
55	30	EL	H	Hull City	D 1-1	0-1	17	Anthrobus 79	2347
56	A 2	EL	A	York City	W 2-1	1-1	17	Scott 10, Stevens 67	(2767)
57	6	EL	A	Rotherham United	D 2-2	1-2	17	Anthrobus 25, Stevens 60(pen)	(2973)
58	9	EL	H	Chesterfield	D 0-0	0-0	16		3035
59	14	AWS F	A	**Rotherham United**	L 1-2	0-1		**Taylor 81**	(35235)
60	17	EL	H	Wrexham	D 2-2	2-1	16	Anthrobus 25, Stevens 37	4094
61	20	EL	H	Brentford	W 2-1	2-1	16	Scott 5, 18	2711
62	23	EL	A	Oxford United	L 0-6	0-2	17		(5800)
63	27	EL	H	Swindon Town	L 1-2	1-1	17	Currie 35	4233
64	M 4	EL	A	Burnley	L 1-2	1-1	18	Stevens 42	(9729)

Best Home League Attendance: 6532 v Swansea City   **Smallest: 2186 v Oxford United**   **Average: 3308**

Goal Scorers: EL(58): Stevens(12),Anthrobus(10),Rowbotham(8),Scott(6),Spink(6),Lynch(3),Evans(3),Dempsey(2),Currie(2),Reed(2),Whiston(2),Berkeley(1),Taylor(1)
CC(3): Lynch(1),Rowbotham(1),Seabury(1)   **FAC**(17): Scott(3),Spink(3),Whiston(2),Dempsey(2),Evans(2),Withe(1),Rowbotham(1),Stevens(1),Anthrobus(1),Opponent(s)(1)
AWS(15): Lynch(4),Summerfield(3),Walton(3),Taylor(2),Clarke(1),Stevens(1),Opponent(s)(1)

	Anthrobus (F)	Berkeley (M)	Bowden (D)	Clarke (G)	Cope (M)	Currie (M)	Dempsey (M)	Edwards (G)	Evans (M)	Hughes (D)	Jackson (M)	Kay (D)	King (M)	Lynch (D)	Martin (M)	Megson (F)	Reed (M)	Robinson (M)	Rowbotham (F)	Scott (D)	Seabury (D)	Spink (D)	Stevens (F)	Stewart (D)	Taylor (F)	Walton (D)	Whiston (D)	Withe (D)	Woods (M)	Player	No
	S1		X			X	X	S	X	X									X1	X	S2	X			X	X			X	X2	R.J.Harris	1
	X	S1	X			X	X		X	X								S		X	X	X1			X	X			X		P.Richards	2
	X3	S1	X			X2			X										S3	X	X	X			X	X		X1	X	S2	D.B.Allison	3
	S1	X2	X			X			X								X		X1	X	X	X	S		X	X			X		F.G.Stretton	4
	S2	X2	X			X			S1								X			X	X	X	X1		X	X	X				T.West	5
		X	X			X			X								X		X1	X	X	S	X	S	X	X	X		X	S	U.D.Rennie	6
		X	X			X3			S1								X1		X	X	X	S3	X2		X			X		R.D.Furnandiz	7
		X	X			X			X	X1			X1	S1			X		X	X	S1				X			X		G.Cain	8
	X	X	X			S2			S1				X2				X		X1	X	X				X		X			S.Mathieson	9
	X	X	X			S1			X			S					X		X	X	X	X			X1		X		S	R.Pearson	10
	X	X	X			S1			X	X							X1		S	X	X	X			X			S		J.A.Kirby	11
	X	X	X			X1			X								S			X	X	S			X			S1		A.Wiley	12
	X2		X			X			X								S		S1	X	X	S2			X	X		X1	X	M.Riley	13
		X2	X			S2			X								X2		X	X1	X	X			X	X	X	S1	X	B.Knight	14
		X				S1	X	S				X	X	S2			X2		X	X	X				X	X		X	X1	A.P.D'Urso	15
		X1				S1	X										S		X	X	X2	S2			X	X	X	X	X	K.J.Breen	16
	S2	X1				S1	X										S		X	X	X	X2			X	X	X	X	X	T.Lunt	17
	S2	X	S			S1	X										X2		X	X	X				X1	X	X	X	X	M.Bailey	18
		X				S	X	X									X		X1	X	S2	S1	X			X	X	X2	X	I.S.Hemley	19
	S1	X				S	X	X									X			X	X	X	X1			X	X		X	J.W.Lloyd	20
	S2	X1				S1	X	X									X			X	X	X2				X	X		X	M.J.Brandwood	21
	X	X1				X	X	X									S			X	X	X2				X	X	S1		S.Bennett	22
	S2	X				S1	X	X											X	X1	X2	X			X	X	X	X	X	P.R.Richard	23
	X	X				S	X	X									S		S1	X	X	X1				X	X	X	X	S.W.Mathieson	24
	S1	X1	S			X	X	X									S		X	X	X	X			X	X		X		I.Hemley	25
	X	X	S			X	X	X									S		X	X	X	X			S	X		X		A.Butler	26
	S1	X1				X	X	X									S		X	X	X	X			X	X		X		G.Frankland	27
	X	S				X	X	X									S		X	X	X	X	S		X	X		X		T.West	28
	X	S				X	X	X									X		X	X	X	X	S		X	X	X	X1	X	G.Frankland	29
	X		S			X	X	X									X		X	X	X	S			X	X		X	S	F.G.Stretton	30
	X		S			X	X	X									X		X	X	X	X	S1		X			X1	X	J.Rushton	31
	S3	X3				X											S2		X	X	X2	X	S1		X	X	X	X	X	K.J.Breen	32
	X					X	X							S			X		X	X	X	S	X		X	X	X	X	X	E.Lomas	33
	X	X				S2	X	X											X1	X			S1		X	X	X	X	X2	A.D'Urso	34
	X	X	S			S2	X	X											X1	X		S1			X	X	X	X	X2	G.R.Pooley	35
	S	X				S	X	X												X		X	X		X	X	X	X	X	P.Rejer	36
	S1	X				X	X	X											X	X	S2	X2	X		X	X	X	X	X	R.Harris	37
	X2	X	S			S1	X	X											X1	X		S2			X	X	X	X	X2	G.R.Pooley	38
	X	X	X			S	X	X												X	S1	X			X	X	X1	X	X	K.M.Lynch	39
		X	S	S		S1	X												X	X	X1	X			X	X	X	X	X	J.Kirkby	40
		X	X			S1	X							S2			S		X	X	X	X			X	X	X	X	X1	M.J.Brandwood	41
	S1	X			X2	S2	X							S					X	X	X1	X			X	X	X	X	X	D.Orr	42
	X	X1	X			S	X	X						S					X	X		X			X	X	X	X		B.Knight	43
	X	X				S	X	X	X							S1				X		X			X	X1	X	X	X1	M.Bodenham	44
	S1				X1	X	X												X	X2	X				X	X	X	X	S2	J.L.Lloyd	45
	X	X2	X			S2	X	S1											X	X	X				X	X	X	X	S1	I.Hemley	46
	X	X	X	X			S						S						S	X					X	X	X	X	X	P.R.Richards	47
	X	X3	X				X						S2						S1	X	X1	S3			X	X	X	X	X2	R.J.Harris	48
	X	X1				X	X						X						S1	X		S2	X		X	X	X	X	X2	N.S.Barry	49
	S1	X				X	X	X						X					X	X	S2		X1		X2	X	X	X		A.Leake	50
	X		S				X	X	X					X					S1	X	X	S	X		X1	X	X			D.Orr	51
	S1	X			S	X	X	X						X1					X		S2	X	X2			X		X		I.Cruikshanks	52
					X	X	X	X1						X					X	X	S1	X			X		X		S	S.Bennett	53
	X	X2				X	S							X					X	S2	X	S1	X		X		X1			R.D.Furnandiz	54
	X	X			S3	X3	X	S1			X		X1						S2	X2	X				X	X		X		M.C.Bailey	55
	X	X2				S		X	S1			X							X	X					X1	X	X	X	X	R.Pearson	56
	X		S2			X	X	S1			X		S				X1		X		X				X	X		X	X	G.Frankland	57
			S			X	X	X			X		X			S	S1		X	X	X				X	X		X	X1	K.Leach	58
	S2	X	S			X	X						S1				X1		X		X2	X			X	X	X	X		D.Allison	59
	X	X1			X		X		X				S1				X		X			S			X	X		X	S	G.Cain	60
	X	X1			X		X	X	S1				X				X		X			X			X1	X		X		E.Lomas	61
	X	X1			X		X	S2			X		X				X			X2		X	X3		X	X		X	S3	P.Taylor	62
	X	X			X2		X	X3					S	X1					X	S1	X	X			X	X				J.A.Kirkby	63
					S3	X	X	X3			S2			X2			X1			X	X	X			X	X		X	X	R.Poulain	64
EL Appearances	27	36	5	15	0	11	17	31	25	2	0	7	0	22	0	2	9	2	20	36	26	32	27	4	38	35	28	30	18		
EL Sub Apps	12	2	0	0	1	2	11	0	9	0	1	0	0	3	0	0	2	2	6	0	8	2	5	0	0	0	0	2	5		
CC Appearances	2+1	3	0	3	0	0	2+2	1	2+1	3	0	0	1	2	0+1	0	2	2	2+1	3	4	4	0	0	4	0	0	0	2	1		
FAC Appearances	3+3	5	0	0	0	0	3+3	6	6	3	0	0	1	2	0	0	0	0	0+1	0	4	5	3+1	1+2	0	5	6	5	6	4		
AWS Appearances	5+1	6	0	1	0	0	4+1	7	5	0	0	1	0	3+1	0	0	1	1	1+3	6	4	7+1	6+1	0	6	7	6	7	4+1		

Also Played: (D) Simkin S(31). (M) Summerfield S(21), S2(21,56). (F) Watson X2(41). (M) Wray S1(62,64), S2(63).

CLUB RECORDS

RECORD LEAGUE VICTORY
7-0 v Swindon Town, Div 3S, 6.5.1955
Most Goals Scored in a League Match
7-2 v Luton Town (a), Div 3, 10.3.1965 7-1 v Blackburn Rovers (h), Div 3, 2.10.1971 7-4 v Doncaster Rovers, Div 4,1.2.1975
Most Goals Scored in a Cup Tie
7-1 v Banbury Spencer (h), FA Cup 1st Round,4.11.1961
RECORD LEAGUE DEFEAT
1-8 v Norwich City (h), Div 3S, 13.9.1952 1-8 v Coventry City (a), Div 3, 22.10.1963 0-7 v Bristol Rovers (a), Div 3, 21.3.1964

MOST LEAGUE GOALS
101, Division 4, 1958-59

MOST LEAGUE POINTS
(3pts for win) 79, Div 3, 1993-94
(2pts for win) 62,Division 4, 1974-75

RECORD TRANSFER FEE RECEIVED
£450,000 from Manchester City for Carl Griffiths,29.10.93
RECORD TRANSFER FEE PAID
£100,000 to Aldershot for John Dungworth in November1979.
£100,000 to Southampton for Mark Blake, August 1990

BEST PERFORMANCES
League: 8th Division 2, 1983-84, 1984-85
FA Cup: 6th Round1978-79, 1981-82
League Cup: Semi-Final 1960-61
Welsh Cup: Winners 1891,1938, 1977, 1979, 1984, 1985
HONOURS
Champions Div 3 1978-79, 1993-94
Welsh Cup Winners (6 times)

LEAGUE CAREER
Elected to Div 3N 1950 Reverted to Div 3S 1951 Joined Div4 1958
Promoted to Div 3 1958-59 Relegated to Div 4 1973-74
Promoted to Div 31974-75 Promoted to Div 2 1978-79
Relegated to Div 3 1988-89 Relegated to Div 4 (now Div 3) 1991-92 Promoted to Div 2 1993-94

INDIVIDUAL CLUB RECORDS

MOST APPEARANCES FOR CLUB
Colin Griffin 1975-89: League 402+4 + FA Cup 30 +League Cup 25 + Others 9 Total 466+4 subs

MOST CAPPED PLAYER
Jimmy McLoughlin 5, Northern Ireland & Bernard McNally 5,Northern Ireland For England: None

RECORD GOALSCORER IN A MATCH
Alf Wood 5 v Blackburn Rovers (h), 7-1, Div 3,2.10.1971

RECORD LEAGUE GOALSCORER IN A SEASON
Arthur Rowley 38, Div 3, 1958-59 In All Competitions: Alf Wood 40 (League 35, FA Cup 2, League Cup 3) 1971-72

RECORD LEAGUE GOALSCORER IN A CAREER
Arthur Rowley 152, 1958-65 In All Competitions: Arthur Rowley 167 (League 152, FA Cup 11, League Cup 4) 1958-65

OLDEST PLAYER IN A LEAGUE MATCH
Asa Hartford, 40 years 69 days v Brentford1.1.1991

YOUNGEST PLAYER IN A LEAGUE MATCH
Graham French, 16 years 175 days v Reading (H), 30.09.1961.

PREVIOUS MANAGERS

(Since 1950): 1950-52 Sammy Crooks 1952-54 Walter Rowley 1954-56 Harry Potts 1956-57 John Spuhler 1957-68 Arthur Rowley 1968-72Harry Gregg 1972-74 Maurice Evans 1974-78 Alan Durban 1978 Ritchie Barker 1978-84 Graham Turner 1984-87 Chic Bates 1987 Ken Brown 1987-90 Ian McNeil 1990-91 Asa Hartford 1991-93 John Bond Fred Davies 1993-
ADDITIONAL INFORMATION
Previous League: Shropshire County Lge, Birmingham League Midland League
Club colours: Blue shirts, blue shorts, blue socks.
Change colours: All red with white side stripes and white trim, red socks with white trim.
Reserves League: Pontins League.
'A' Team: Midland Melville Youth Lge.

LONGEST LEAGUE RUNS

of undefeated matches:	16 (30.10.1993 - 26.2.1994)	of league matches w/out a win:	17 (1992)
of undefeated home matches:	31 (1978-79)	of undefeated away matches:	14 (30.10.1993 - 30.4.1994)
without home win:	9 (1992)	without an away win:	20 (1981-82)
of league wins:	7 (1955)	of home wins:	8 (1955, 1975)
of league defeats:	7 (1951-52, 1987)	of away wins:	5 (6.11.1993 - 1.1.1994)

THE MANAGER

FRED DAVIES . . . . appointed May 1993.

PREVIOUS CLUBS
As Manager. . . . . Merthyr Tydfil.
As Asst.Man/Coach . . . . Norwich City, Bournemouth, Blackpool, Swansea, Birmingham, Shrewsbury.
As a player . . . . Wolverhampton, Cardiff, Bournemouth.

HONOURS
As a Manager. . . . . Division 3 Championship 1993-94.
As a Player . . . . None.

SHREWSBURY TOWN

PLAYERS NAME Honours	Ht	Wt	Birthdate	Birthplace Transfers	Contract Date	Clubs	League	L/Cup	FA Cup	Other	Lge	L/C	FAC	Oth
G O A L K E E P E R S														
Edwards Paul	5.11	11.5	22/02/65	Liverpool		Leek Town								
Div.3'94.				Free	24/08/88	Crewe Alexandra	29	4	3	4				
				Free	06/08/92	Shrewsbury Town	146	11	13	14				
D E F E N D E R S														
Lynch Tom	6.0	12.6	10/10/64	Limerick		Limerick								
Div.3'94.				£20000	11/08/88	Sunderland	4			1				
				£20000	16/01/90	Shrewsbury Town	220+14	16	12	17+2	14	1		1
Scott Richard	5.9	10.10	29/09/74	Dudley	17/05/93	Birmingham City	11+1	3+1		3				
					22/03/95	Shrewsbury Town	43+1	3	5	6	7		3	1
Seabury Kevin	5.9	11.6	24/11/73	Shrewsbury	06/07/92	Shrewsbury Town	53+12	4	4	5+1			1	
Simkin Darren	6.0	12.0	24/03/70	Walsall		Blakenhall								
				£10000	03/12/91	Wolves	14+1	1						
				£36000	20/12/94	Shrewsbury Town	10+2							
				Loan	13/10/95	Telford								
Spink Dean	6.1	13.6	22/01/67	Birmingham		Halesowen Town			1					
Div.3'94.				£30000	01/07/89	Aston Villa								
				Loan	20/11/89	Scarborough	3			1	2			
				Loan	01/02/90	Bury	6			1				
				£75000	15/03/90	Shrewsbury Town	205+27	20+2	16+2	17+2	49	1	6	3
Walton David	6.2	13.4	10/04/73	Bedlington		Ashington								
Div.3'94.				Free	15/05/91	Sheffield United								
					05/11/93	Shrewsbury Town	98	5	9	8	8		1	1
Whiston Peter	6.0	11.6	04/01/68	Widnes	17/12/87	Plymouth Argyle	4+6		1	1				
				Free	21/03/90	Torquay United	39+1	5	1	6	1	1		
				£25000	13/09/91	Exeter City	85	7	10	10	7			1
				£30000	01/08/94	Southampton	0+1							
				£50000	20/10/95	Shrewsbury Town	28		5	6	2		2	
M I D F I E L D														
Berkeley Austin	5.9	10.10	28/01/73	Dartford	13/05/91	Gillingham	0+3			0+3				
				Free	16/05/92	Swindon Town	0+1	0+1		3+1				1
				Free	05/09/95	Shrewsbury Town	36+2	3	5	6	1			
Cope James						Shrewsbury Town	0+1							
Currie Darren	5.9	11.07	29/11/74	Hampstead	02/07/93	West Ham United								
				Loan	05/09/94	Shrewsbury Town	10+2				2			
				Loan	03/02/95	Shrewsbury Town	5							
				£70000	07/02/96	Shrewsbury Town	11+2				2			
Dempsey Mark A	5.7	10.9	10/12/72	Dublin	09/08/90	Gillingham	27+21	0+1	5	6	2			
Ei: u21.6.				Free	04/07/94	Leyton Orient	43	2	1+1	5	1			1
				Free	04/07/95	Shrewsbury Town	17+11	2+2	3+3	4+1	2		2	1
Evans Paul S	5.6	10.8	01/09/74	Oswestry	02/07/93	Shrewsbury Town	67+18	7+2	7+1	7	8	1	2	1
Div.3'94.														
Jackson David						Shrewsbury Town	0+1							
Reed Ian	5.8	10.9	04/09/75	Lichfield	04/07/94	Shrewsbury Town	10+5	2	0+1	1	2			
Wray Shaun						Shrewsbury Town	0+3							
F O R W A R D S														
Anthrobus Steve	6.2	12.13	10/11/68	Lewisham	04/08/86	Millwall	19+2	3		1	4			
				Loan	09/02/90	Southend United								
				£150000	16/02/90	Wimbledon	27+1	1	2					
				Loan	21/01/94	Peterborough Utd								
				Loan	26/08/94	Chester City	7							
				£25000	01/08/95	Shrewsbury Town	27+12	2+1	3+3	5+1	10		1	
Rowbotham Darren	5.10	11.5	22/10/66	Cardiff	07/11/84	Plymouth Argyle	22+24	1	0+3	1+1	2		1	
W: Y. Div.4'90.					31/10/87	Exeter City	110+8	11	8	5	46	6	5	1
				£25000	13/09/91	Torquay United	14		3	2	3		1	
				£20000	02/01/92	Birmingham City	31+5	0+1		3+1	6			
				Loan	18/12/92	Mansfield Town	4							
				Loan	25/03/93	Hereford United	8				2			
				Free	06/07/93	Crewe Alexandra	59+2	3	4	6+2	21	1	3	1
				Free	01/06/95	Shrewsbury Town	20+6	2+1	4	1+3	8	1	1	
Stevens Ian	5.9	12.0	21/10/66	Malta	22/11/84	Preston North End	9+2			1	2			
AMC'89.				Free	27/10/86	Stockport County	1+1		0+1	0+1				
					01/12/86	Lancaster City								
				Free	25/03/87	Bolton Wanderers	26+21	1+2	4	3+1	7		2	
				Free	03/07/91	Bury	100+10	3+1	2+2	7+1	38			3
				£20000	01/08/94	Shrewsbury Town	53+17	0+1	2+2	8+2	20		1	11
Taylor R Mark	5.8	11.8	22/02/66	Birmingham	24/07/84	Walsall	100+13	7+1	3+4	10	4			
Div.3'94.				£50000	22/06/89	Sheffield Wed.	8+1	2						
				£70000	13/09/91	Shrewsbury Town	213	15	14	15	14			3

483

GAY MEADOW
Shrewsbury SY2 6AB
Tel: 01743 360 111

Capacity...8,000
Covered Standing..2,000
Seating..3,500

First game ....v Wolves Res. (Birmingham Lge), 10.9.1910.
First floodlit game ....v Q.P.R., Div.3, 21.11.1959.

ATTENDANCES
Highest ....18,917 v Walsall, Div.3, 26.4.1961.
Lowest ....520 v Torquay Utd, 16.1.1991.

OTHER GROUNDS...Old Racecourse. Copthorne.

MATCHDAY TICKET PRICES

Wakeman Stand . . . . (members only) £9
Juv/OAP £5

Centre Stand £10
Juv/OAP £10

Station Stand (away) £10
Family Stand (1+1). £8
Extra child £2, extra adult £10
Terraces. £7
Juv/OAP (members). £4

Ticket Office Telephone no. 01743 360 111

HOW TO GET TO THE GROUND

From the North
Use A49 or A53 and at roundabout take 2nd exit (A5112) into Telford Way. In 0.8 miles at roundabout take 2nd exit. Then at 'T' junction turn right into Abbey Foregate (A458) for Shrewsbury Town FC.

From the East
Use A5 then A458 into Shrewsbury and into Abbey Foregate for Shrewsbury Town FC.

From the South
Use A49 and follow signs Shrewsbury Town centre then at end of Coleham Head turn right in to Abbey Foregate for Shrewsbury Town FC.

From the West
Use A458 then A5 around Shrewsbury Ring Road, Roman Road, then turn left A49 into Hereford Road, and at end of Coleman Head turn right into Abbey Foregate for Shrewsbury Town.

Car Parking
Park adjacent to ground and a public car park five minutes away.

Nearest Railway Station
Shrewsbury (01743 64041)

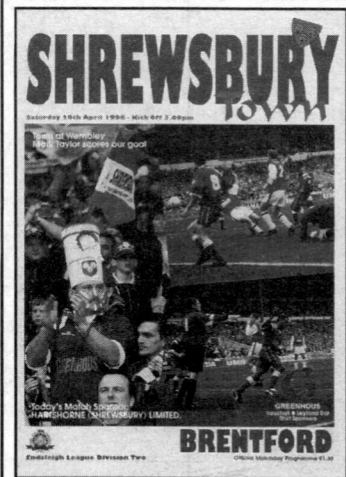

MATCHDAY PROGRAMME

Programme Editor . . . . Pemandos A & M.

Number of pages . . . . 32.

Price . . . . £1.20.

Subscriptions . . . . Aply to club for details.

Local Newspapers . . . . Shropshire Star, Shrewsbury Chronicle.

Local Radio Stations . . . . Radio Shropshire, Beacon Radio.

STOCKPORT COUNTY
(The Hatters)
NATIONWIDE LEAGUE DIVISION 2
SPONSORED BY: FREDERIC ROBINSON LIMITED

ck Row (L-R): Alun Armstrong, Tony Dinning, Richard Landon, Ian Helliwell, Jim Gannon, Matthew Bound, Jeff Eckhardt.
dle Row: Rodger Wylde (Physio), Tom Bennett, Michael Oliver, Neil Edwards, John Sainty (Asst. Manager), Matt Dickins, Chris
aumont, Paul Ware, Dave Philpotts (Yth Manager). **Front Row:** Sean Connelly, Phil Johnson, Gavin Allen, Martyn Chalk, Dave Jones
anager), Michael Flynn (Capt), Lee Marshall, Lee Todd, Marc Lloyd Williams.

STOCKPORT COUNTY
FORMED IN 1883
TURNED PROFESSIONAL IN 1891
LTD COMPANY IN 1908

CHAIRMAN: Brendon Elwood
VICE-CHAIRMAN
Grahame White
DIRECTORS
Mike Baker, Michael H Rains, Brian Taylor,
David Jolley
SECRETARY
Gary Glendenning BA A.C.C.A.
COMMERCIAL MANAGER
John Rutter

MANAGER: David Jones
ASSISTANT MANAGER: John Sainty
RESERVE TEAM MANAGER
Dave Jones/John Sainty
YOUTH TEAM MANAGER
Joe Jakub
PHYSIOTHERAPIST
Rodger Wylde

STATISTICIAN FOR THE DIRECTORY
Ian Watts & Stuart Brennan

A strange season for County, but one that saw good runs in both major cup competitions. Victory over higher division Ipswich was followed by a good performance at Aston Villa in the Coca-Cola Cup. This was eclipsed by the performance in the FA Cup where Everton were pushed very closely at Goodison Park, and to a lesser extent in the replay.

Meanwhile League form stuttered on until after the cup matches. A reasonable start was followed by a very poor spell. Despite an impressive number of away wins - eventually the second best ever - County found themselves struggling in 15th place, mainly due to a home record that saw only four wins by the middle of March. Then the acquisition of one or two players began to pay off and they were quickly back on the verge of play-off places. In the end a final day draw at champions Swindon was not enough and County finished ninth.

Most of the squad remains unaltered for next season, with only two signings made by mid-July. However, the success of the Reserve team in their first outing in the Pontins (Central) League for 60 years has helped two Youth Training Scheme players gain professional contracts - possibly the first time this has ever happened.

The £60,000 signing of Paul Jones should provide the goalkeeper competition the management have been looking for, assuming the out-of-contract Neal Edwards also decides to sign.

The priority for the season would be to have more than one fully-fit forward for the majority of matches. Four players were out of action for substantial periods last season, and better luck with injuries - along with a few more home wins - could produce a more consistent promotion challenge during 1996/7.

IAN WATTS

STOCKPORT COUNTY

League: 9th   FA Cup: 3rd Rnd   Coca-Cola Cup: 3rd Rnd   Auto Windscreen Shield: 1st Rnd

M	DATE	COMP	VEN	OPPONENTS	RESULT	HT	LP	GOAL SCORERS/GOAL TIMES	ATT.
1	A 12	EL	A	Walsall	W 2-0	2-0	4	Helliwell 5, 38	(4884)
2	15	CC 1/1	H	Wrexham	W 1-0	1-0		**Armstrong 2**	3493
3	19	EL	H	Burnley	D 0-0	0-0	8		8463
4	26	EL	A	Bristol City	L 0-1	0-1	13		(7331)
5	29	EL	H	Swansea City	W 2-0	1-0	9	Helliwell 44, Armstrong 78	4433
6	S 2	EL	H	Crewe Alexandra	D 1-1	0-0	9	Armstrong 86	6125
7	5	CC 1/2	A	Wrexham	D 2-2	0-1		**Eckhardt 58, Gannon 70**	(2764)
8	9	EL	A	Blackpool	W 1-0	1-0	5	Armstrong 40	(6602)
9	12	EL	A	Notts County	L 0-1	0-0	8		(4588)
10	16	EL	H	Wycombe Wanderers	D 1-1	1-1	8	Helliwell 17	5588
11	19	CC 2/1	H	Ipswich Town	D 1-1	1-1		**Chalk 5**	4865
12	23	EL	A	Shrewsbury Town	W 2-1	0-0	6	Armstrong 46, 89	(2588)
13	26	AWS 1/1	H	Chesterfield	D 1-1	0-0		**Gannon 47**	2152
14	30	EL	H	Bournemouth	W 3-1	1-0	5	Helliwell 23, 56, Eckhardt 54	5655
15	O 3	CC 2/2	A	Ipswich Town	W 2-1	0-1		**Armstrong 82, Gannon 106**	(8250)
16	7	EL	A	Oxford United	L 1-2	1-2	8	Ware 26	(5646)
17	14	EL	H	Brentford	D 1-1	1-0	8	Landon 25	6228
18	21	EL	A	Hull City	D 1-1	1-0	10	Dewhurst 35(og)	(3496)
19	25	CC 3	A	Aston Villa	L 0-2	0-0			(17679)
20	28	EL	H	Chesterfield	L 0-1	0-1	12		6287
21	31	EL	H	Rotherham United	D 1-1	0-1	11	Gannon 90	4070
22	N 4	EL	A	York City	D 2-2	1-0	10	Helliwell 2, Oliver 46	(3101)
23	7	AWS 1/2	A	Notts County	L 0-1	0-0			(2015)
24	11	FAC 1	H	Lincoln City	W 5-0	3-0		**Eckhardt 21, 33, 56, Barnett 43(og), Armstrong 79**	3952
25	18	EL	H	Swindon Town	D 1-1	0-1	12	Helliwell 85	7196
26	25	EL	A	Bristol Rovers	W 3-1	0-0	10	Thornly 61, Armstrong 71, Eckhardt 82	(4326)
27	D 2	FAC 1	H	Blyth Spartans	W 2-0	2-0		**Eckhardt 3, A.Player 38(og)**	5693
28	9	EL	H	Shrewsbury Town	L 0-2	0-1	12		5530
29	16	EL	A	Bournemouth	L 2-3	1-1	13	Flynn 37, Flynn 46	(3638)
30	19	EL	A	Peterborough United	W 1-0	0-0	10	Bennett 74(pen)	(3267)
31	26	EL	H	Carlisle United	W 2-0	1-0	11	Armstrong 18, Jeffers 78	5941
32	J 1	EL	A	Brighton & H.A.	D 1-1	1-1	11	Eckhardt 19	(5694)
33	7	FAC 3	A	Everton	D 2-2	1-2		**Armstrong 31, Helliwell 61**	(28921)
34	10	EL	H	Bradford City	L 1-2	1-2	11	Jeffers 33	6030
35	13	EL	H	Burnley	L 3-4	3-2	13	Bound 3, Flynn 12, Helliwell 34	(9113)
36	17	FAC 3R	H	Everton	L 2-3	1-0		**Bound 22, Armstrong 88**	11283
37	20	EL	H	Walsall	L 0-1	0-1	15		5870
38	F 6	EL	A	Swansea City	W 3-0	2-0	22	Eckhardt 8, Bound 13, Armstrong 63	(2349)
39	10	EL	A	Bradford City	W 1-0	0-0	10	Landon 73	(5290)
40	13	EL	H	Wrexham	L 2-3	1-1	9	Landon 11, 67	4688
41	17	EL	H	Notts County	W 2-0	0-0	7	Armstrong 85, Williams 88	6179
42	20	EL	A	Crewe Alexandra	W 1-0	0-0	6	Eckhardt 88	(4241)
43	24	EL	A	Wycombe Wanderers	L 1-4	0-3	7	Flynn 49	(4246)
44	27	EL	H	Blackpool	D 1-1	0-0	9	Armstrong 67	7711
45	M 2	EL	A	Carlisle United	W 1-0	0-0	22	Ware 79	(4842)
46	9	EL	H	Peterborough United	L 0-1	0-0	9		5915
47	16	EL	A	Wrexham	W 3-2	1-0	9	Eckhardt 14, Armstrong 72, 80	(4081)
48	19	EL	H	Bristol City	D 0-0	0-0	8		3713
49	23	EL	H	Brighton & H.A.	W 3-1	1-1	7	Bound 35(pen), Ware 58, Mutch 79	5765
50	30	EL	H	Oxford United	W 4-2	2-1	7	Mutch 7, 31, 86, Marsden 81	6096
51	A 2	EL	A	Brentford	L 0-1	0-0	7		(3274)
52	6	EL	A	Chesterfield	W 2-1	1-0	7	Jeffers 17, Bound 83	(6090)
53	8	EL	H	Hull City	D 0-0	0-0	7		5043
54	20	EL	H	York City	W 3-0	2-0	8	Flynn 30, 45, Bound 65(pen)	6286
55	23	EL	A	Rotherham United	L 0-2	0-0	9		(6920)
56	27	EL	H	Bristol Rovers	W 2-0	1-0	7	Armstrong 10, Dinning 64	6935
57	M 4	EL	A	Swindon Town	D 0-0	0-0	9		(14697)

Best Home League Attendance: 8463 v Burnley   Smallest: 3713 v Bristol City   Average: 5902

Goal Scorers:
EL(61): Armstrong(13),Helliwell(9),Flynn(6),Eckhardt(6),Bound(5),Landon(4),Mutch(4),Ware(3),Jeffers(3),Gannon(1),Marsden(1),Oliver(1),Dinning(1),Thornly(1),Bennett(1),Williams(1),Opponent(s)(1)
CC(6): Gannon(2),Armstrong(2),Chalk(1),Eckhardt(1)
FAC(11): Eckhardt(4),Armstrong(3),Opponent(s)(2),Helliwell(1),Bound(1)
AWS(1): Gannon(1)

(F) Allen	(F) Armstrong	(F) Beaumont	(D) Bennett	(D) Bound	(F) Chalk	(D) Connelly	(F) Croft	(G) Dickins	(D) Dinning	(M) Durkan	(D) Eckhardt	(G) Edwards	(M) Flynn	(D) Gannon	(F) Helliwell	(M) Jeffers	(D) Johnson	(G) Jones	(F) Landon	(M) Marsden	(M) Marshall	(F) Mike	(F) Mutch	(M) Oliver	(M) Thornly	(D) Todd	(M) Ware	(F) Williams	Opponent	#
	X	X1	X		X	X		S	S			X	X	X	X											X	X	S1	R.Furnandiz	1
	X	X1	X	X2	X			S	S1			X	X	X	X											X	X	S2	A.Butler	2
	X	X	X	S	X				S		S		X	X	X	X										X	X	X	N.Barry	3
	X	X	X		X						S1	X	X	X	X	X1								S2		X	X	X2	A.D'Urso	4
	X	X	X		S	X1			S1			X	X	X	X	X								S		X		X	R.Poulain	5
	X	X	X		S1	X			S			X	X	X	X	X								S		X		X1	P.Richards	6
	X	X	X		X1	X			S			X	X	X	X	X										X		S1	P.Rejer	7
	X	X	X			X					S1	X	X	X	X	X2				S2						X	X	X1	K.M.Lynch	8
	X	X	X			X			S			X	X	X	X	X				S1						X	X	X1	G.Cain	9
S	X	X	X		X	X			S		S	S	X	X	X	X										X	X		A.Leake	10
S2	X	X2	X		X	X			S		S1	S	X	X	X	X										X	X1		U.Rennie	11
	X	X	X		X	X			S		S	S	X	X	X	X1										X	X	S1	A.Wiley	12
																														13
	X	X	X		S	X			S1			X	X	X1	X	X							S			X	X		T.Lunt	14
	X	X	X1	S2	X				S3			X	X	X3	X	X2								S1		X	X		M.Bailey	15
	X	X	X	S2	X				S			X	X	X	X	X1								S1		X	X		C.Wilkes	16
	X	X	X		X				S			X	X	X	X	X			X1				S1			X	X	S	P.Richards	17
	X	X	X		X	S1			S			X	X	X	X	X			X1				S			X	X		J.Brandwood	18
	X	X	X2		X	X			S3			X	X	X	X				S1				S2			X	X3	X1	D.Gallagher	19
	X	X	X		X				S			X	X	X	X				S2				S1			X	X1	X2	I.Cruikshanks	20
	X	X	X	X1	X	S1			S2			X	X	X	X				X2				X			X	X	S	P.Rejer	21
	X	X2	X		X	S1						X	X	X	X	X1							X			X	X	S2	S.Baines	22
																													R.Furnandiz	23
X2	X	X			X				S3			X	X	X	X3					S2			X1			X	S1		M.Reed	24
	X	X	X		X2				S			X	X	X	X	S2	S1						X	X1	X		X		G.Frankland	25
X1	X	X	X		X				S			X	X	X	X	S1	X						X	X			X	S	G.Pooley	26
	X	X1	X		S1	X						X	X	X	X	X			X1			S	X			X	X		R.Furnandiz	27
	X	X	X		X1		S					X	X	X	X	X2	S2	S1					X	X	X		X		T.West	28
S1	X	X			X							X	X	X	X	S2	X		X				X1	X2	X		X		P.Rejer	29
S1	S2	X	X		X				S			X	X	X1	X	X	X		X				X1		X2	X	X		R.J.Harris	30
	S	X	X		X				S1			X	X1	X	X	X			X				S	X		X	X		S.Baines	31
	X	S1	X		X				S2			X	X	X	X	X2	X		X					X1		X			D.Orr	32
	X	X1	X2	S1	X				S2			X	X	X	X	X	X		X					X		X			G.Poll	33
	X	X	X		X				S1			X	X	X	X	X	X						X	X1	X	S	S	E.Wolstenholme	34
	X	X	X		X							X	X	X	X	X	X1		X				S	S1	X		X		D.Allison	35
	X	X	X	S	X		S					X	X	X	X	X	X		X				S			X	X		G.Poll	36
	X1	X	X		X							X	X	X	X	X3	X		S3	S2				S1		X	X2		P.Richards	37
	X1	X	X	S1	X				S			X	X	X	X		X		X	X						X	S	X	J.Rushton	38
	X	X2	X	S2	X				S1			X	X	X	X		X1		X	X						X		X	A.Butler	39
	X	X	X	S1	X				X1			X	X	X	X				X	X			X			X	S	S	N.Barry	40
	X1	X	X		X	S			S	X	X	X	X	X					X							X		S1	U.Rennie	41
	X	X	X		X	S			S	X	X	X	X	X					X							X		X	G.Barber	42
	X	X	X		X	X			S2	X	X	X		X								S1		S		X	X2	X1	A.D'Urso	43
	X	X	X		X	S			S	X	X	X		X								X1				X	X	X	A.Riley	44
	X	X	X		X				S	X	X	X		X					X			X1		S		X	S1	S	T.Heilbron	45
	X1	X	X		X				S	X	X	X		X					X			S				X	S1	S1	D.Laws	46
	S2	X	X		X				S3	X	X1	X		X					X3			X2				X	S1		D.Allison	47
	S	X	X		X				S	X	X	X		X					X			X				X	X		J.Kirkby	48
	S1	X	X		X				S	X1	X	X		X					X	S		X				X	X		G.Frankland	49
	S1	X	X		X				S	X1	S2	X		X					X			X				X	X2		W.C.Burns	50
	X	X	X		X				S	X1	X	X		X					X			S1	X			X	S		I.Hemley	51
	X	X	X		X				S		X	X		X					X			S	X			X	S		A.Wiley	52
	X	X2	X		X				S2	X1	X	X		X					X			S	X				S1	X	G.Singh	53
X1	X	X	X		X				S1	S	X	X	S2	X2					X			X				X	X		A.Leake	54
	X	X	X		X		S	S2	S1	X	X	X2	S1	X					X			X				X	X1		T.E.West	55
X2	X	X	X		X			S1	S2	X	X	X		X					S			X				X	X1		R.Pearson	56
	X	X2	X3	X	S1				S2	X	X	X1		X					X			X				X	S3		K.Breen	57
0	44	38	24	26	5	42	0	1	1	11	30	45	46	22	18	21	0	0	7	19	0	4	11	7	8	42	22	12	EL Appearances	
0	2	5	0	0	5	1	3	0	9	5	5	0	0	1	4	2	0	0	4	1	0	4	0	2	2	0	5	5	EL Sub Appearances	
0+1	5	5	5	0	4+1	5	0	0	0	2+2	5	5	5	4	0	0	0	0+1	0	0	0	0+2	0	5	4	5	4	1+2	AWS Appearances	
0	4	4	3	2	1+2	4	0	0	0+2	4	4	4	2	2	3	0	0	0	0	0	0+1	0	2	0	4	4	1+1	0	CC Appearances	
0	0	0	0	0	0	0	0	0	0	0	0	0	0	0	0	0	0	0	0	0	0	0	0	0	0	0	0	0	FAC Appearances	

CLUB RECORDS

RECORD VICTORY
13-0 v Halifax Town, Div 3N, 6.1.1934 (Joint League record victory)
Record First Class Cup Victory: 6-2 v West Auckland (a), FA Cup
Round 1, 14.11.1959

RECORD LEAGUE DEFEAT
1-8 v Chesterfield, Div 2, 19.4.1902   0-7 v Burton Utd, Div 2,
10.10.1903   0-7 v Bristol City, Div 2, 20.1.1906   0-7 v Fulham, Div
2,8.3.1913   0-7 v Port Vale, Div 3N, 10.4.1954   0-7 v Aldershot,
Div 4, 22.2.1964   0-7 v Hull City, Div 4, 29.1.1983
Record Cup Defeat: 0-7 v Portsmouth, FA Cup Round 3, 8.1.1949
0-7 v Crystal Palace, League Cup Round 2 2nd leg, 4.9.1979   0-7
v Sheffield Wednesday, League Cup Round 2 2nd leg, 6.10.1986

MOST LEAGUE POINTS
(2pts a win) 64, Div 4, 1966-67
(3pts a win) 85, Div 2, 1993-94

MOST LEAGUE GOALS
115, Div 3N, 1933-34

RECORD TRANSFER FEE RECEIVED
£800,000 from Birmingham City for Kevin Francis, January 1995.

RECORD TRANSFER FEE PAID
£150,000   to Preston North End for Mike Flynn, March 1993.

BEST PERFORMANCES
League: 10th Div 2 1905-06
FA Cup: 5th Round 1935, 1950
League Cup: 4th Round 1972-73
HONOURS: Champions Div 3N 1921-22, 1936-37   Champions Div
4 1966-67 Lancashire League 1899-00   Lancashire Combination
1904-05   Division 3N Cup Winners 1934-35   Autoglass Trophy
Finalists 1992, 1993

LEAGUE CAREER: Elected to Div 2 1900   Failed Re-election
1904   Elected to Div 2 1905 Relegated to Div 3N 1920-21
Promoted to Div 2 1921-22   Relegated to Div 3N 1925-26
Promoted to Div 2 1936-37   Relegated to Div 3N 1937-38
Transferred to Div 3 1958   Relegated to Div 4 1958-59
Promoted to Div 3 1966-67   Relegated to Div 4 1969-70
Promoted to Div 3 (now Div 2) 1990-91

INDIVIDUAL CLUB RECORDS

MOST APPEARANCES FOR CLUB
Andy Thorpe 1978-86 & 1987-92: Lge 484+5 + FAC 14 + Lge Cup
32+1 + Others 18+1. 0Total 548+7

MOST CAPPED PLAYER
Harry Hardy 1, England

RECORD GOALSCORER IN A MATCH
Joe Smith 5 v Southport (h), 6-3, Div 3N,7.1.1928   Joe Smith 5 v
Lincoln City (h), 7-3, Div 3N, 15.9.1928   F Newton 5 v Nelson, 6-1,
Div 3N, 21.9.1929   Alf Lythgoe 5 v Southport, 6-1, Div 3N,
25.8.1934   W McNaughton 5 v Mansfield Town, 6-1, Div 3N,
14.12.1935   Jack Connor 5 v Workington (h), 6-0, Div 3N,
8.11.1952   Jack Connor 5 v Carlisle United (h), 8-1, Div 3N, 7.4.1956

RECORD LEAGUE GOALSCORER IN A SEASON
Alf Lythgoe 46 In All Competitions: Alf Lythgoe 47 (League 46 +
FA Cup 1) 1933-34

RECORD LEAGUE GOALSCORER IN A CAREER
Jack Connor 132   In All Competitions Jack Connor 140 (League
132 + FAC 8) 1951-56

OLDEST PLAYER IN A LEAGUE MATCH
Alec Hard 40 years 47 days, 25.12.1951, Crewe Alexandra (H).

YOUNGEST PLAYER IN A LEAGUE MATCH
Steve Massey 16 years 337 days, 28.02.1975, Darlington (H) (sub).

PREVIOUS MANAGERS

-1895 George Ellis, 1895-1903 Fred Stewart, 1903-04 Sam Ormerod
1904-11 Fred Stewart   1911-14 Harry P Lewis   1914-19 David
Ashworth   1919-24 Albert Williams   1924-26 Fred Scotchbrook
1926-31 Lincoln Hyde   1931-32 No Manager   1932-33 Andrew
Wilson   1933-36 Fred Westgarth   1936-38 Bob Kelly   1938-39 No
Manager   1939-49 Bob Marshall   1949-52 Andy Beattie   1952-56
Dick Duckworth   1956-60 Willie Moir   1960-63 Reg Flewin 1963-65
Trevor Porteous   1965 Bert Trautmann   1965-66 Eddie Quigley
1966-69 Jimmy Meadows   1969-70 Walter Galbraith   1970-71 Matt
Woods 1971-72 Steve Fleet (acting)   1972-74 Brian Doyle   1974-75
Jimmy Meadows 1975-76 Roy Chapman   1976-77 Eddie Quigley
1977-78 Alan Thompson   1978-79 Mike Summerbee   1979-82
Jimmy McGuigan   1982-85 Eric Webster   1985 Colin Murphy   1985-
86 Les Chapman   1986 Jimmy Melia   1986-87 Colin Murphy   1987-
89 Asa Hartford   1989-95 Danny Bergara

ADDITIONAL INFORMATION
Previous Name: Heaton Norris Rovers 1883-88   Heaton Norris
1988-90
Previous League: The Combination 1891-94; Lancashire League
1894-1900; Lancashire Combination 1904-05
Club colours: Blue shirts white trim, white shorts, blue socks.
Change colours: White shirts black trim, black shorts & white
socks.
Reserves League: Pontins League Division Three.
'A'Team: Lancashire League Division 2.

LONGEST LEAGUE RUNS

of undefeated matches:	18 (1933)	of league matches w/out a win:	15 (1989)
of undefeated home matches:	48 (1927-29)	of undefeated away matches:	8 (1921-22, 1929, 1929-30)
without home win:	12 (1986)	without an away win:	37 (1901-03)
of league wins:	8 (1927-28)	of home wins:	13 (1928-29, 1930)
of league defeats:	9 (1908-09)	of away wins:	7 (1951)

THE MANAGER

DAVID JONES . . . . appointed March 1995

PREVIOUS CLUBS
As Manager. . . . . None.
As Asst.Man/Coach . . . . Morecambe, Stockport County.
As a player . . . . Everton, Coventry City, Seiko FC (Hong Kong), Preston North End, Morecambe.

HONOURS
As a Manager . . . . None.
As a Player. . . . . England Under-21. 1 caps, England Youth.

STOCKPORT COUNTY

PLAYERS NAME / Honours	Ht	Wt	Birthdate	Birthplace / Transfers	Contract Date	Clubs	League	L/Cup	FA Cup	Other	Lge	L/C	FAC	Oth
G O A L K E E P E R S														
Edwards Neil	5.10	11.10	05/12/70	Aberdare	10/03/89	Leeds United				1				
W: u21.1,Y.				£5000	03/09/91	Stockport County	163+1	11	11	27				
Jones Paul	6.3	13.2	18/04/67	Chirk		Bridgnorth								
						Kidderminster H.			5					
				£40000	23/07/91	Wolves	33	2	5	4				
				£60000	16/07/96	Stockport County								
D E F E N D E R S														
Bennett Thomas	5.11	11.8	12/12/69	Falkirk	16/12/87	Aston Villa								
				Free	05/07/88	Wolves	103+12	73+1	4+2	3				
				£75000	01/06/95	Stockport County	24	5	3		1			
Bound Matthew	6.2	12.0	09/11/72	Melksham	03/05/91	Southampton	2+3							
				Loan	27/08/93	Hull City	7				1			
				£125000	26/10/94	Stockport County	40		3	2	5		1	1
				Loan	11/09/95	Lincoln City	3+1			1				
Connelly Sean	5.10	11.10	26/06/70	Sheffield		Hallam								
				Free	12/08/92	Stockport County	116+5	9	6+1	8				
Dinning Tony	6.2	12.11	12/04/75	Wallsend	01/10/93	Newcastle United								
				Free	23/06/94	Stockport County	39+11	2+2	0+3	2	2			1
Eckhardt Jeff	6.0	11.7	07/10/65	Sheffield	23/08/84	Sheffield United	73+1	7	2	5	2			
				£50000	20/11/87	Fulham	245+4	13	5+1	15	25			3
				£50000	21/07/94	Stockport County	56+6	6+2	5	1	7	1	4	
Gannon James	6.2	12.6	07/09/68	Southwark		Dundalk								
					27/04/89	Sheffield United								
				Loan	22/02/90	Halifax Town	2							
				£40000	07/03/90	Stockport County	233+7	18	11	31+2	47	3	1	9
					14/01/94	Notts County	2							
Searle Damon	5.11	10.5	26/10/71	Cardiff	20/08/90	Cardiff City (T)	233+2	9	13	29	3	1		
W: B1, u21.7, Y. WFAC'93. Div.3'93.				Free	21/05/96	Stockport County								
Todd Lee	5.5	10.3	07/03/72	Hartlepool		Hartlepool United								
				Free	23/07/90	Stockport County	175+11	15+1	13	24+1	2			2
M I D F I E L D														
Durkan Keiran	5.10	10.05	01/12/73	Chester	16/07/92	Wrexham	43+7	3+1	4+2	15	3		2	1
				£75000	16/02/96	Stockport County	11+5							
Flynn Michael	6.0	11.0	23/02/69	Oldham	07/02/87	Oldham Athletic	37+3	1+1	1	2	1			
E: u19.2.				£100000	22/12/88	Norwich City								
				£125000	04/12/89	Preston North End	134+2	6	6+1	13	7		1	
				£125000	25/03/92	Stockport County	144+1	11	9	12	9			
Jeffers John	5.10	10.10	05/10/68	Liverpool	13/10/86	Liverpool								
				£30000	11/12/88	Port Vale	147+33	8+1	13+2	13+2	10			1
				Loan	06/01/95	Shrewsbury Town	3		2		1			
				Free	16/11/95	Stockport County	21+2		3		3			
Marsden Chris	5.11	10.12	03/01/69	Sheffield	06/01/87	Sheffield United	13+3	1		1	1			
					15/07/88	Huddersfield Town	113+8	15+1	6+2	10	9			
				Loan	02/11/93	Coventry City	5+2							
				£150000	11/01/94	Wolves	8		3					
				£250000	15/11/94	Notts County	10	1		1				1
					16/02/96	Stockport County	19+1				1			
Ware Paul	5.8	11.2	07/11/70	Congelton	15/11/88	Stoke City	92+23	7+1	4+1	12+2	10			4
Div.2'93.														
F O R W A R D S														
Armstrong Alun	6.1	11.13	22/02/75	Gateshead	01/10/93	Newcastle United								
				£50000	23/06/94	Stockport County	84+7	8	4+1	2	27	3	3	
Beaumont Chris	5.11	11.7	05/12/65	Sheffield		Denaby United								
				Free	21/07/88	Rochdale	31+3	0+1	2	2	7	1	1	
				£8000	21/07/89	Stockport County	238+20	14+3	15	32+2	39	3	1	6
Landon Richard	6.3	13.5	22/03/70	Worthing		Bedworth								
				£30000	26/01/94	Plymouth Argyle	21+9	0+1	0+1	2	12			
				£30000	03/08/95	Stockport County	7+4	0+1			4			
Mike Adie	6.0	11.6	16/11/73	Manchester	15/07/92	Manchester City	5+11	1+1	0+1		2			
E: Y,S.				Loan	25/03/93	Bury	5+2				1			
				£60000	18/08/95	Stockport County	4+4		0+1					
Mutch Andy	5.10	11.3	28/12/63	Liverpool		Southport								
E: B.3, u21.1. Div.4'88.					25/02/86	Wolves	277+12	14	11+1	23	99	4	1	4
Div.3'89. AMC'88.				£250000	16/08/93	Swindon Town	34+16	6+1	4	3	6	3	1	2
				Loan	24/08/95	Wigan Athletic	7				1			
					03/04/96	Stockport County	11				4			
ADDITIONAL CONTACT PLAYER														
Villimas Richard					21/05/96	Stockport County (T)								

EDGELEY PARK
Hardcastle Road, Edgeley, Stockport,Cheshire SK3 9DD
Tel: 0161 480 8888

Capacity 12,140

First game...v Gainsborough Trinity 1-1, Div.2, 13.09.02.
First floodlit game ....v Fortuna '54 Geleen (Neth) 0-3, 16.10.56

ATTENDANCES
Highest ....27,833 v Liverpool, FAC 5th Rnd, 11.2.1950.
Lowest...1,000 v Carlisle Utd, AMC, 8.12.1986.

OTHER GROUNDS ....Heaton Norris Rec. Ground 1883-84,
.Heaton Norris W'derers Cricket Ground 1884-85, Chorlton's Farm 1885-87, Wilkes' Field 1887-89,
....Green Lane 1899-1902.

MATCHDAY TICKET PRICES

Main Stand	£10
Juv/OAP	£4
Barlow Stand.	£9
Juv/OAP	£4
Cheadle Stand.	£9
Juv/OAP	£4
Ticket Office Telephone no.	0161 286 8888

HOW TO GET TO THE GROUND

From the North, South and West
Use motorway (M63) until junction 11, sign posted Cheadle (A560). At round-about follow A560 to Stockport and in 0.3 miles turn right at lights, sign posted Stockport County FC). In 1 mile turn right into Caroline Street for Stockport County FC.

From the East
Use A6 into Stockport Town centre and turn left into Greek Street, opposite the Town Hall. At roundabout go straight over and into Mercian Way and in 0.2 miles left into Caroline Street for Stockport County FC.

Car Parking
Ample street parking around the ground.

Nearest Railway Station
Edgeley (short walk to the ground).

CLUBCALL
0891 12 16 38
Calls cost 39p per minute cheap rate and 49p per minute at all other times.
Call costings correct at time of going to press.

MATCHDAY PROGRAMME

Programme Editor . . . . Steve Bellis.

Number of pages . . . . 56.

Price . . . . £1.50.

Subscriptions . . . . £40 inc. postage.

Local Newspapers . . . . Stockport Express Advertiser,
. . . . Stockport Messenger, Edgeley Park Echo.

Local Radio Stations . . . . Radio Piccadilly, G.M.R., Signal Radio.

WALSALL
(The Saddlers)
NATIONWIDE LEAGUE DIVISION 2
SPONSORED BY: BANK'S

Back Row (L-R): Charlie Ntamark, Wayne Evans, Chris Marsh, James Walker, Adrian Thompson, Trevor Wood, Ian Roper, Stuart Ryder, Darren Bradley.
Middle Row: Eric McManus (Youth Team Coach), Stuart Watkiss, Charlie Palmer, Kyle Lightbourne, David Richards, Darren Rogers, Martin Butler, James Rollo, Ray Daniels, Tom Bradley (Physio).
Front Row: Colin Gibson, Scott Houghton, Kevin Wilson, Chris Nicholl (Manager), Martin O'Connor, John Keister, Chris Smith.

WALSALL
FORMED IN 1888
TURNED PROFESSIONAL IN 1888
LTD COMPANY IN 1921

CHAIRMAN: J W Bonser
DIRECTORS
K R Whalley, M N Lloyd, C Welch,
R Tisdale
SECRETARY
Roy Whalley (01922 22791)
COMMERCIAL MANAGER
Roy Whalley
GENERAL MANAGER: Paul Taylor
MANAGER: Chris Nicholl
PLAYER/COACH: Kevin Welson

YOUTH TEAM COACH
Eric McManus
PHYSIOTHERAPIST
Tom Bradley

STATISTICIAN FOR THE DIRECTORY
Mervyn Sargeant

The start of the 1995/6 season was eagerly awaited by many Saddlers fans following the team's promotion the previous year. Hopes were high of another successful season, although the only additions to the squad were free-transfer signings Ray Daniel and Darren Bradley - from Portsmouth and WBA respectively.

Unfortunately, the side struggled in the early part of the season, winning only three of the first 14 games and keeping just one clean sheet in the first sixteen. Although they did not lose an away league game by anything other than a 0-1 scoreline until February, too many points were being thrown away and it was clear that the defence needed strengthening. Adrian Viveash was signed from Swindon Town in October, and he was soon followed by the experienced Derek Mountfield.

Scoring more than once in a game was also a problem, except in cup competitions: five goals were scored in both group games in the Auto Windscreens Shield, and in December an amazing FA Cup replay against Torquay United was won 8-4 after extra time. Early exits were made in both the Coca-Cola Cup and the Auto Windscreens Shield, but Walsall did at least manage to progress to the FA Cup fourth round.

With both new central defenders having settled in a run of just one defeat in eleven league games the promotion play-offs came into sight, but a down-turn in the weather and defeat in the several-times-postponed FA Cup tie at Ipswich seemed to set the Saddlers back on the downwards slope. By early March they had slipped to 19th place and were beginning to get too near to the relegation positions for comfort.

The return to goal-scoring form of Kyle Lightbourne, along with the ability to snatch results when not playing particularly well, averted any further worries and by the end of the season Walsall had climbed to 11th place and were amazingly only four points from a play-off spot. An encouraging end to the season saw them undefeated in the last seven games, and the introduction of exciting prospects Clive Platt and Michael Ricketts from the youth team. With little cash available for major signings it may well be to this avenue that the club looks for new players.

Hopefully the team can maintain the improvement made over the last quarter of 1995/6, and bring on the younger players correctly. Then, having come to terms with the higher division in this season, 1996/7 could well be a season to look forward to.

MERVYN SARGEANT

WALSALL

League: 11th   FA Cup: 4th Rnd   Coca-Cola Cup: 1st Rnd   Auto Windscreen Shield: 2nd Rnd

M	DATE	COMP	VEN	OPPONENTS	RESULT	HT	LP	GOAL SCORERS/GOAL TIMES	ATT.
1	A 12	EL	H	Stockport County	L 0-2	0-2	22		4884
2	15	CC 1/1	H	Brentford	D 2-2	2-1		Wilson 21, O'Connor 28	3549
3	19	EL	A	Shrewsbury Town	W 2-0	0-0	14	Lightbourne 87, Stewart 89(og)	(4019)
4	22	CC 1/2	A	Brentford	L 2-3	1-2		Evans 28, Houghton 89	(3149)
5	26	EL	H	Bristol Rovers	D 1-1	0-0	11	Wright 82(og)	4851
6	29	EL	A	Crewe Alexandra	L 0-1	0-0	15		(4377)
7	S 6	EL	A	Burnley	D 1-1	0-0	17	Lightbourne 77	(8778)
8	9	EL	H	Swansea City	W 4-1	2-0	13	Houghton 6, O'Connor 27, Edwards 67(og), Wilson 74	3788
9	12	EL	H	Oxford United	D 2-2	1-0	12	O'Connor 21, Wilson 66	3905
10	16	EL	A	Brentford	L 0-1	0-1	15		(4717)
11	23	EL	A	York City	L 0-1	0-0	17		(3541)
12	30	EL	H	Carlisle United	W 2-1	2-0	14	O'Connor 10(pen), Wilson 16	4214
13	O 7	EL	H	Peterborough United	D 1-1	0-0	15	Lightbourne 72	3768
14	14	EL	A	Wycombe Wanderers	L 0-1	0-1	18		(4724)
15	17	AWS 1/2	A	Fulham	W 5-2	2-1		Butler 37, 47, Wilson 39, Lightbourne 50, O'Connor 69	(1315)
16	21	EL	H	Wrexham	L 1-2	0-0	20	Wilson 57	4020
17	28	EL	A	Bristol City	W 2-0	2-0	16	Houghton 8, Wilson 33	(6475)
18	31	EL	A	Bradford City	L 0-1	0-0	19		(4310)
19	N 4	EL	H	Bournemouth	D 0-0	0-0	18		3626
20	7	AWS 1/2	H	Wycombe Wanderers	W 5-0	4-0		Lightbourne 12, 19, 21, 30 (4), Viveash 57	2592
21	10	FAC 1	A	Burnley	W 3-1	1-1		Bradley 10, Wilson 49, Houghton 57	(6525)
22	18	EL	A	Brighton & H.A.	W 3-0	2-0	16	Wilson 7, Houghton 29, 66	(4976)
23	25	EL	H	Blackpool	D 1-1	0-0	17	Wilson 51	4459
24	28	AWS 2	H	Brighton & H.A.	L 1-2	1-1		Lightbourne 39	3454
25	D 2	FAC 2	A	Torquay United	D 1-1	0-1		Lightbourne 50	(3552)
26	9	EL	H	York City	W 2-0	2-0	14	Mountfield 31, Marsh 38	3193
27	12	FAC 2R	H	Torquay United	W 8-4	1-1		Marsh 14, 93, Wilson 58, Bradley 71, Lightbourne 96, 119, O'Connor 97, Houghton 104	3230
28	16	EL	A	Carlisle United	D 1-1	0-1	16	Wilson 82	(5308)
29	23	EL	H	Swindon Town	D 0-0	0-0	14		5624
30	26	EL	A	Rotherham United	W 1-0	0-0	14	Wilson 64	(3694)
31	J 6	FAC 3	H	Wigan Athletic	W 1-0	0-0		Pender 76(og)	5672
32	13	EL	A	Shrewsbury Town	W 3-0	1-0	14	Wilson 14, O'Connor 56(pen), Lightbourne 81	5008
33	20	EL	A	Stockport County	W 1-0	1-0	13	Houghton 27	(5870)
34	F 3	EL	A	Bristol Rovers	L 0-2	0-0	14		(4948)
35	10	EL	H	Notts County	D 0-0	0-0	15		4378
36	13	FAC 4	A	Ipswich Town	L 0-1	0-1			(18489)
37	17	EL	A	Oxford United	L 2-3	1-0	16	Butler 24, 80	(4369)
38	24	EL	H	Brentford	L 0-1	0-1	18		3506
39	27	EL	A	Swansea City	L 1-2	0-1	18	Lightbourne 90	(3546)
40	M 2	EL	H	Rotherham United	W 3-1	1-1	18	Lightbourne 23, 89, Wilson 73	3001
41	6	EL	A	Notts County	L 1-2	1-1	19	Lightbourne 17	(4050)
42	9	EL	A	Swindon Town	D 1-1	0-0	1	Houghton 90	(9564)
43	12	EL	H	Crewe Alexandra	W 3-2	1-2	13	Wilson 26, Marsh 63, Lightbourne 90	3171
44	16	EL	H	Chesterfield	W 3-0	0-0	13	Lightbourne 55, O'Connor 72, 81(pen)	4127
45	23	EL	A	Hull City	L 0-1	0-0	14		(3060)
46	30	EL	A	Peterborough United	W 3-2	2-2	13	O'Connor 18, 85, Wilson 45	(4954)
47	A 2	EL	A	Wycombe Wanderers	L 0-1	0-0	14		3252
48	6	EL	H	Bristol City	W 2-1	1-1	13	Nugent 1(og), Bradley 89	4142
49	8	EL	A	Wrexham	L 0-3	0-1	14		(3309)
50	13	EL	A	Bradford City	W 2-1	0-0	13	Lightbourne 46, 57	3679
51	16	EL	A	Chesterfield	D 1-1	1-0	13	Lightbourne 33	(4508)
52	20	EL	A	Bournemouth	D 0-0	0-0	12		4380
53	23	EL	H	Hull City	W 3-0	1-0	11	Butler 25, Lightbourne 47, Platt 85	2752
54	27	EL	A	Blackpool	W 2-1	1-1	11	Butler 15, O'Connor 55	(9148)
55	30	EL	H	Burnley	W 3-1	0-0	11	Wilson 52, Platt 80, Lightbourne 89	3411
56	M 4	EL	H	Brighton & H.A.	W 2-1	1-0	11	Wilson 42, Ricketts 68	4840

Best Home League Attendance: 5624 v Swindon Town   Smallest: 2752 v Hull City   Average: 3982

Goal Scorers:
EL(60): Wilson(15),Lightbourne(15),O'Connor(9),Houghton(6),Butler(4),Opponent(s)(4),Marsh(2),Platt(2),Ricketts(1),Mountfield(1),Bradley(1)
CC(4): Evans(1),Houghton(1),O'Connor(1),Wilson(1)
FAC(13): Lightbourne(3),Wilson(2),Houghton(2),Marsh(2),Bradley(2),Opponent(s)(1),O'Connor(1)
AWS(11): Lightbourne(6),Butler(2),O'Connor(1),Viveash(1),Wilson(1)

(M) Bradley	(F) Butler	(D) Daniel	(D) Evans	(M) Houghton	(M) Keister	(M) Kerr	(F) Lightbourne	(F) Marsh	(D) Mountfield	(M) Ntamark	(M) O'Connor	(D) Palmer	(M) Platt	(F) Richards	(M) Ricketts	(D) Rogers	(F) Rollo	(D) Roper	(D) Ryder	(F) Smith	(D) Viveash	(G) Walker	(D) Watkiss	(F) Wilson	(G) Wood		
X	S	X	X				X	X		X	X					S			X			X	X	X	S	R.Furnandiz	1
X	S	X	X		S		X	X		X	X					S			X			X	X	X		R.Lomas	2
X		X	X	S1			X	X1		X	X	X				S						X	X	X	S	D.B.Allison	3
X		X	X	S1			X1	X		X	X	X						S				X	X	X	S	T.Heilbron	4
X	S	X	X	X	X		X	X			X	X						S				X	X	X		J.Kirkby	5
X		X	X	X	X		X	X		S		X					S					X	X	X	S	K.Breen	6
X	S2	X	X	X1	X		X2	X		S1		X						S3				X	X	X3		R.Dilkes	7
X	S3	X	X	X2			X	X		S2	X	X		S1								X	X1	X3		A.P.D'Urso	8
X	S	X	X	X1			X	X		S1	X	X		S1								X	X	X		E.Wolstenholme	9
X	S1	X	X2	X			X1	X3		S3	X	X		S2							S2	X	X	X		S.Bennett	10
X	S	X	X1				X	X2		S2	X	X		S1								X	X	X		T.West	11
X	X2	X	X	S2			S1	X1		X	X	X		S								X	X1	X		S.G.Stretton	12
X2	X	X	X		S2		S1	X		X	X	X		S								X	X	X		P.Taylor	13
X	X		X				S			X	X1			X1			X					X	X	X		D.Orr	14
	X		X1		X		X	X		S3	X2	S1				X		S2	X3		X			X	X	I.Hemley	15
X	X1		X		S		X	X		S1	X	X				X		S			X			X	X	I.Cruickshanks	16
X3	S3		X2	X			X	X		S2	X	X1				X					X	X	S1	X		B.Knight	17
X	S		X	S			X	X		X	X					X		S			X	X	X	X		T.Lunt	18
X2	X1		X	S2			S1	X		X	X					X		X		S	X	X	X	X		U.Rennie	19
X1	S2		X	X			X2	X		X				S3		X					S1	X	X		X3	A.Butler	20
X3	S1		X1	S2			X2	X		X	X					X		S3			X	X	X	X		M.Riley	21
X2	S1		X1	S2			X2	X		X	X					X		S			X	X		X		A.D'Urso	22
X1	S1		X	S2			X2	X		X	X					X		S			X	X		X		C.Wilkes	23
X	S2		X	S3	S1		X2	X		X	X1					X					X	X		X		E.Wolstenholme	24
X	X1		X	S			S1	X		X	X	X				X					X	X		X	S	D.Gallagher	25
X	S2		X				S1	X	X	X	X1					X					X	X	S	X2		S.W.Mathieson	26
X			X	X2			S2	X	X1	X	X					X					X	X	S1	X	S	D.Gallagher	27
X	S1			X		S		X	X1	X	X	X	S			X						X	X		X	D.Allison	28
X	S	S		X	S		X	X	X	X	X					X					X	X		X	X	S.J.Baines	29
X	S1	S		X1	S		X	X	X	X	X					X					X			X	X	D.Laws	30
X	S1	S		X	S2		X1	X	X	X	X					X					X			X	X	K.Lynch	31
X	S1	S3		X	S2		X1	X2	X	X	X					X3					X			X	X	R.Harris	32
X	X		X	S	S		X1	X	X	X	X	X				X		S1						X	X	P.Richards	33
X		S1		X	S3		S2	X2	X3	X	X	X	X1			X								X	X	S.G.Bennett	34
X		X	S		X		S	X	X1	X	X					X		S1						X	X	P.Taylor	35
X	S3	X	S1	X3			S2	X2	X		X1	X				X								X	X	D.Gallagher	36
X	X	X	X	X	S		X	S		X						X		S			X		S2	X	X	R.Furnandiz	37
X	X2	X1	X	X			S1	X		S						X		X		S2	X			X	X	K.Breen	38
X	X		X	S2			S1	X1	X	X	X	X2	S			X						X		X	X	E.Wolstenholme	39
X1	S2		S	X2	S1		X	X	X	X	X					X						X		X	X	E.Cruickshanks	40
X	S		X	S			X	X	X	X	X	S				X						X		X	X	K.Lynch	41
X	S1		X	S			X	X	X	X	X	S				X1						X		X	X	G.Barber	42
X	S	X	X	S			X	X	X	X	X	S				X						X		X	X	M.Bailey	43
X	S	X	X	S			X	X	X	X	X	S				X						X		X	X	S.Mathieson	44
X	X	X	S	X			X			X	X	X	S								S		X	X		D.Laws	45
X1	X	X	X	S1			X			X	X	X	S								S		X	X	X	U.Rennie	46
X	S2	X	X	S1			X			X2	X1		S			X						X	X	X		F.G.Stretton	47
X	X	X	X	X			X	S1	X	X1						S						X	X	X		A.Leake	48
X	S	X1	X	X			X	S1	X	X						S						X	X	X		P.Richards	49
	S1	X	S	X1	X		X	X	X	X	X					S						X	X	X		C.Wilkes	50
X	X		X				X	X	X	X	X	S				S						X	X	X		T.Heilbron	51
X	S1		S	X2	X		X	X	X	X1			S2			X						X	X	X		P.Taylor	52
X2	X		S3		S2		X3	X	X	X	X		S1			X						X	X		X1	M.Lloyd	53
X	X		S	S			X	X	X	X	X		S			X						X	X		X	R.Poulain	54
X3	X		S3	X2	S1		X	X	X1		S2					X						X	X		X	D.Orr	55
X			S1	X	X		X			X2	X1		S3		S2	X						X	X		X3	I.Cruickshanks	56
45	13	23	20	38	9	0	37	39	28	34	41	15	0	0	0	23	0	3	1	0	31	26	14	46	20	EL Appearances	
0	15	2	3	2	12	1	6	2	0	8	0	0	4	0	1	2	0	2	2	1	0	0	1	0	0	EL Sub Appearances	
2	0	2	2	0+1	0	0	2	2	0	2	2	1	0	0	0	0	0	0	1	0	0	2	2	2	0	CC Appearances	
5	1+3	1	0+1	5	1+2	0+1	3+2	5	3	5	5	0	0	0	0	4	0	1+1	0	0	5	3	1+1	5	2	FAC Appearances	
2	1+2	0	1	2	2+1	0+1	3	3	2	2+1	2	0+1	0	0+1	0	3	0+1	1	0	0+1	3	2	0	3	1	AWS Appearances	

CLUB RECORDS

RECORD LEAGUE VICTORY
10-0 v Darwen,Div 2, 4.3.1899
Most Goals Scored in a First Class Cup Tie: 6-1 v Leytonstone (a),
Round 1,30.11.1946 6-1 v Margate, Round 1, 24.11.1955

RECORD LEAGUE DEFEAT
0-12 v Small Heath, Div 2, 17.12.1892 0-12 v Darwen,Div 2,
26.12.1896
Record Cup Defeat: 0-6 v Wednesday Town, FA Cup Round 2,
1883-84 0-6 v West Bromwich Albion, FA Cup Rnd 1 replay, 1899-
1900 0-6 v Aston Villa, FA Cup Round 1, 1911-12

MOST LEAGUE POINTS
(3pts for win) 83, Div 3, 1994-95.
(2pts for win) 65, Div4, 1959-60

MOST LEAGUE GOALS
102, Division 4, 1959-60

RECORD TRANSFER FEE RECEIVED
£600,000 from West Ham United for David Kelly, August 1988

RECORD TRANSFER FEE PAID
£175,000 to Birmingham City for Alan Buckley, June1979

BEST PERFORMANCES
League: 6th Div 2 1898-99
FA Cup: 5th Round 1939, 1975,1978 and last sixteen 1889
League Cup: Semi-Final 1983-84

HONOURS
Champions Div 4 1959-60

LEAGUE CAREER
Elected to Div 2 1892   Failed to gain re-election 1895
Rejoined Div 2 1896 Failed re-election 1901   Elected as original
members of Div 3N 1921 Transferred to Div 3S 1927
Transferred to Div 3N 1931   Transferred to Div 3S 1936
Joined Div 4 1958 Promoted to Div 3 1959-60
Promoted to Div 2 1960-61   Relegated to Div 3 1962-63
Relegated to Div 41978-79   Promoted to Div 3 1979-80
Promoted to Div 2 1987-88   Relegated to Div 3 1988-89
Relegated to Div 4(now Div 3) 1989-90 Promoted to Div 2 1994-95

INDIVIDUAL CLUB RECORDS

MOST APPEARANCES FOR CLUB
Colin Harrison (1964-82): League 452+15 + FA Cup 36+ League
Cup 19 Total 507+15 subs
Most Capped Player: Mick Kearns 15, Eire For England: None
RECORD GOALSCORER IN A MATCH
Johnny Devlin 5 v Torquay United (h), 7-1, Div3S, 1.9.1949 Gilbert
Alsop 5 v Carlisle Utd (a), 6-1, Div 3N, 2.2.1935 W.Evans 5 v
Mansfield Town, 7-0, Div 3N, 5.10.1935
RECORD LEAGUE GOALSCORER IN A SEASON
Gilbert Alsop 40, Div 3N, 1933-34, 1934-35 In All Competitions:
Gilbert Alsop 44 (League 40 + FA Cup 4) 1934-35
RECORD LEAGUE GOALSCORER IN A CAREER
Tony Richards 184, 1954-63 In All Competitions: Alan Buckley 204
(League 174 + Cups 30) 1973-84
OLDEST PLAYER IN A LEAGUE MATCH
Des Bremner 37 years 240 days v Bristol City, 5.5.1990
YOUNGEST PLAYER IN A LEAGUE MATCH
Geoff Morriss 16 years 218 days v Scunthorpe, 14.9.1965

PREVIOUS MANAGERS

1921-26 J Burchell 1926-27 D Ashworth 1927-28 J Torrance
1928-29 J Kerr 1929-30 S Scholey 1930-32 P O'Rourke 1932-34
W Slade 1934-37 Andy Wilson T Lowes 1937-44 1944-51 Harry
Hibbs 1951-52 G McPhee 1952-53 Brough Fletcher 1953-56
Frank Buckley 1956-57 John Love 1957-64 Bill Moore 1964 Alf
Wood 1964-68 Ray Shaw 1968 Dick Graham 1968-69 Ron Lewin
1969-72 Bob Moore 1972-73 John Smith 1973 Jim McEwan 1973
Ronnie Allen 1973-77 Doug Fraser 1977-78 Dave Mackay 1978
Alan Buckley 1978Alan Ashman 1978 Frank Sibley 1978-81 Alan
Buckley 1981-82 Neil Martin 1982-86 Alan Buckley 1986-88
Tommy Coackley 1988-89 Ray Train 1989-90 John Barnwell 1990
Paul Taylor 1990-94 Kenny Hibbitt 1994-95.

ADDITIONAL INFORMATION
Previous Name: Walsall Swifts (1877) and Walsall Town (1879)
amalgamated and played as Walsall Town Swifts until 1895

Club Colours: Red/black and white trim, black shorts white socks
with red & black hoops.
Change Colours: Jade & white squares, jade shorts, jade socks
with white & yellow hoops.

Reserves League: Pontins League **Youth Team:** Melville Midland Lge

LONGEST LEAGUE RUNS

of undefeated matches:	21 (1979-80)	of league matches w/out a win:		18 (1988-89)
of undefeated home matches:	26 (1960-61)	of undefeated away matches:		13 (1979-80)
without home win:	10 (1988-89, 1989-90)	without an away win:		29 (1953-54)
of league wins:	7 (1933-34)	of home wins:		9 (1973)
of league defeats:	15 (1988-89)	of away wins:	6 (24.4.1993 - 18.9.1993)	

THE MANAGER

CHRIS NICHOLL . . . . appointed September 1994.

PREVIOUS CLUBS
As Manager . . . . Southampton.
As Asst.Man/Coach . . . . Grimsby Town.
As a player . . . . Burnley, Witton Albion, Halifax Town, Luton Town, Aston Villa, Southampton, Grimsby Town.

HONOURS
As a Manager . . . . Division 3 championship 1972. League Cup 1975.
As a Player . . . . None.

WALSALL

PLAYERS NAME Honours	Ht	Wt	Birthdate	Birthplace Transfers	Contract Date	Clubs	League	L/Cup	FA Cup	Other	Lge	L/C	FAC	Oth
							APPEARANCES				**GOALS**			
G O A L K E E P E R S														
Walker James	5.11	11.8	09/07/73	Nottingham	09/07/91	Notts County								
				Free	04/08/93	Walsall	60+1	2	7	3				
Wood Trevor	6.0	12.6	03/11/68	Jersey	07/11/86	Brighton & H.A.								
				Free	08/07/88	Port Vale	42	4	2	2				
				Free	18/07/94	Walsall	59	4	7	3				
D E F E N D E R S														
Daniel Ray	5.10	11.0	10/12/64	Luton	07/09/82	Luton Town	14+8	2	5+1		4			
				Loan	01/09/83	Gillingham	5							
				Free	30/06/86	Hull City	55+3	1	1+1	0+1	3			
				£40000	22/08/89	Cardiff City	56	5	5	1	1			
				£80000	09/11/90	Portsmouth	91+9	7+2	6	6+1	4			1
				Free	03/08/95	Walsall	23+2	2	1					
Evans Wayne D	5.10	12.0	25/08/71	Welshpool		Welshpool								
				Free	13/08/93	Walsall	97+3	7+1	8+1	4		1		
Mountfield Derek	6.1	13.4	02/11/62	Liverpool	04/11/80	Tranmere Rovers	26	2	1		1			
E: B.1,u21.1. Div.1'85'87.				£30000	02/06/82	Everton	100+6	16	17	14+1	19	3	2	1
UEFAu21'84. FAC'84. CS'84'85. ECWC'85.				£450000	06/06/88	Aston Villa	88+2	13	6	11	9	2	1	5
				£150000	07/11/91	Wolves	79+4	4	2	2	4	1		
				Free	03/08/94	Carlisle United	30+1	4+1	4	6	3	1	1	1
				Free	06/11/95	Walsall	28		3	2	1			
Rogers Darren	5.9	11.2	09/04/70	Birmingham	05/07/88	W.B.A.	7+7		0+1	1	1			1
				Free	01/07/92	Birmingham City	15+3	2	0+1	5				
				Loan	05/01/93	Wycombe Wand.	0+1			1				
				Free	19/07/94	Walsall	43+9	4	5+2	5				
Roper Ian	6.4	14.0	20/06/77	Nuneaton	15/05/95	Walsall	3+2		1+1	1				
Ryder Stuart	6.0	12.1	06/11/73	Sutton C'field	16/07/92	Walsall	75+12	4+1	8	4+1				
Viveash Adrian	6.1	11.9	30/09/69	Swindon	14/07/88	Swindon Town	51+3	6+1	0+1	2	3			
				Loan	04/01/93	Reading	5			1				1
				Loan	20/01/95	Reading	6							
				Free	13/11/95	Walsall	31		5	3				1
M I D F I E L D														
Bradley Darren	5.7	11.10	24/11/65	Birmingham	19/12/83	Aston Villa	16+4	3						
E: u19.3, Y.3.					14/04/86	W.B.A.	236+18	13	10	11	9	1	2	1
				Free	01/08/95	Walsall	45	2	5	2	1		2	
Keister John	5.8	11.0	11/11/70	Walsall	18/09/93	Walsall	35+19		5+2	2+2	1			
Sierra Leonne Int.														
Ntamark Charles	5.8	11.12	22/07/64	Paddington		Boreham Wood								
Cameroon Int.				Free	22/08/90	Walsall	220+18	15+1	19	17+1	11	1		1
Platt Clive						Walsall	0+4				2			
Ricketts Michael						Walsall	0+1				1			
F O R W A R D S														
Butler Martin	5.10	11.3	15/09/74	Wordsley	24/05/93	Walsall	23+28	0+1	2+5	2+2	7		2	2
Lightbourne Kyle	6.2	11.0	29/06/68	Bermuda	11/12/92	Scarborough	11+8	1		0+1	3			
Bermuda Int.				Free	17/09/93	Walsall	113+7	6	12+2	6	45	1	8	6
Marsh Chris	6.0	12.10	14/01/70	Sedgley	11/07/88	Walsall	168+30	9+2	16+1	14+1	11		4	
Wilson Kevin	5.7	10.7	18/04/61	Banbury		Banbury United								
NI: 42. Div.2'89. FMC'90.				£20000	21/12/79	Derby County	106+16	8+3	8		30	8	3	
				£100000	05/01/85	Ipswich Town	94+4	8	10	7	34	8	3	4
				£335000	25/06/87	Chelsea	124+28	10+2	7+1	14+5	42	4	1	8
				£225000	27/03/92	Notts County	58+11	3+1	2	5+1	3			
				Loan	13/01/94	Bradford City	5							
				Free	02/08/94	Walsall	88	6	9	5	31	3	5	1

BESCOT STADIUM

Bescot Crescent, Walsall WS1 4SA
Tel: 01922 22791 Fax: 01922 613202

Capacity 9,000
Seating 6,700

First game .... v Aston Villa, Friendly, 18.8.1991.
First floodlit game .... v Cambridge Utd, Lge Cup, 28.8.1991.

ATTENDANCES
Highest .... 10,628, England 'B' v Switzerland, 20.5.1991.
Lowest .... 1,837 v Mansfield Town, AMC Rnd 1, 8.12.1992.

OTHER GROUNDS .... Fellows Park.

MATCHDAY TICKET PRICES

Gilbert Alsop Terrace Advanced £7.50/Matchday £8
Juv/OAP . . . . £5/£6
H.L.Fellows Stand Centre . . . . £11/£12
Juv/OAP Block J,K,Q,R, only . . . . £7/£8
Bank's Family Stand
Family Area (1 adult & 1 child) . . . . £10/£11
Adults . . . . £10/£11
Juv . . . . £2/£2
William Sharp Stand £10
Juv £6
Swifts Club. £20
Reserve Games. £3

OFFICIAL CLUBCALL
0898 55 58 00
Calls cost 39p per minute cheap rate and 49p per
minute at all other times.
Call costings correct at time of going to press.

HOW TO GET TO THE GROUND

From the North
Use A461, sign posted Walsall, then join A4148 Broadway North
around Ring Road. Turn left at traffic lights into Bescot Crescent,
ground on left.

From the East, South and West
Use motorway M6 until junction 9, leave motorway and follow signs
Walsall A461, then turn right A4148 into Broadway West. Turn right at
first set of traffic lights into Bescot Crescent Stadium on left.

Car Parking
Car park for 1,200 vehicles at ground.

Nearest Railway Station
Bescot Stadium Station 70 yards from Ground.

MATCHDAY PROGRAMME

Programme Editor. . . . . Don Stanton.

Number of pages . . . . 32.

Price . . . . £1.50.

Subscriptions . . . . Apply to club shop (01543 480940).

Local Newspapers . . . . Wolverhampton Express & Star,
. . . . Birmingham Evening Mail, Birmingham Post & Mail,
. . . . Walsall Observer.

Local Radio Stations . . . . . . BBC Radio West Midlands, BRMB Radio,
. . . . Beacon Radio.

WATFORD
(The Hornets)
NATIONWIDE LEAGUE DIVISION 2
SPONSORED BY: CTX COMPUTER PRODUCTS

Back Row (L-R): John McDermott (Yth Dev. Officer), David Barnes, Gary Fitzgerald, Robert Page, Colin Simpson, Peter Beadle, Colin Foster, Keith Millen, Robert Calderhead, Richard Johnson, Jamie Moralee, Billy Hails (Physio). **Middle Row:** Len Cheesewright (Chief scout), Ken Brooks (Kit manager), Dominic Ludden, Kevin Phillips, Darren Bazeley, Steve Cherry, Kevin Miller, Paul Wilkerson, David Holdsworth, Craig Ramage, Gerard Lavin, Stuart Murdoch (Reserves Manager), Robert Marshall (Football in Comm. Asst.). **Front Row:** Kenny Sansom (Player/coach), Geoff Pitcher, John White, Gary Porter, Nigel Gibbs (club captain), Glenn Roeder (Manager), Andy Hessenthaler (Capt), Tommy Mooney, David Connolly, Derek Payne, Kenny Jackett (Yth Manager). **Seated:** Paul Robinson, Colin Pluck, Clint Easton, Craig Pearl, Vincent Cave, Mark Rooney, Wayne Andrews, Mark Jones, Chris Johnson, Daniel Grieves, Kevin Belgrave, Andrew Johnson, Darren Ward.

WATFORD
FORMED IN 1891
TURNED PROFESSIONAL IN 1897
LTD COMPANY IN 1909

LIFE PRESIDENT: Elton John CBE
CHAIRMAN: Dr Stuart R Timperley PhD
VICE-CHAIRMAN: Geoff Smith
DIRECTORS
Stuart Lawson Rogers, Jack Petchey,
Charles Lissack, Eddie Plumley
GENERAL MANAGER
Graham Taylor
SECRETARY
John Alexander
HEAD OF SALES & MARKETING
Mark Devlin

MANAGER: Kenny Jackett
ASSISTANT MANAGER: Luther Blissett
DIRECTOR OF YOUTH FOOTBALL
Bobby Downes
YOUTH DEVELOPMENT OFFICER
Jimmy Gilligan
PHYSIOTHERAPIST
Phil Edwards
STATISTICIAN FOR THE DIRECTORY
Audrey Adams

A bitterly disappointing season, which ended with Watford being relegated out of the top two divisions for the first time in 17 years.

In retrospect, one might have feared the worst when Watford's only summer outlay was £2,000 on a new outfit for mascot Harry Hornet, who soon came to resemble the team all too closely: lacking vision up front and wobbly at the back. The two-year failure to sign a big centre-forward to replace Paul Furlong ultimately cost Glenn Roeder his manager's job: the shortage of goals was accompanied by a sudden defensive frailty, and a spate of injuries led to a loss of rhythm and confidence.

Roeder, a patently decent man finally swamped by events, departed in February to be replaced by Graham Taylor, an outstanding success during his first spell at Vicarage Road and still a hero among Watford's supporters. It was a tall order: 18 matches in which to redeem a position seven points away from safety. After a string of draws that were to prove expensive, the team finally came good in April, winning four out of their last six games with a glut of goals and taking the relegation issue to the final Sunday.

Watford departed both Cup competitions to Premiership opposition. The FA Cup clash with Wimbledon featured the unusual sight of identical twins - the Holdsworths, who both started with Watford - in direct opposition.

There were some small consolations. Steve Palmer looked a useful acquisition, while David Connolly and Robert Page of the younger players made significant progress - Connolly all the way to the senior Irish Team. Gary Porter moved to second in Watford's all-time appearance list and Kevin Phillips and Craig Ramage continued to impress - Ramage finishing leading scorer for the second season in a row, despite a poor start. But the Player of the Year was Tommy Mooney, who played with great enthusiasm and to good effect in every left-sided position. One other happy note - not one first-team player was sent off.

On his arrival, Graham Taylor identified various shortcomings in the public image and community role of the club, and at the end of the season he became general manager with the aim of addressing these problems. He nominated Kenny Jackett, Watford-born and a distinguished former player, as the new team manager, with Luther Blissett as his assistant.

A melancholy season closed with the death of Cliff Holton, a strapping centre-forward who once scored 48 goals in a season for Watford as part of a promotion-winning side. The present team would do well to emulate his spirit - and his achievement.

AUDREY ADAMS

WATFORD

League: 23rd   FA Cup: 3rd Rnd   Coca-Cola Cup: 3rd Rnd

M	DATE	COMP	VEN	OPPONENTS	RESULT	HT	LP	GOAL SCORERS/GOAL TIMES	ATT.
1	A 12	EL	H	Sheffield United	W 2-1	2-1	2	Payne 14, Johnson 35	8667
2	19	EL	A	Huddersfield Town	L 0-1	0-0	7		(10556)
3	26	EL	H	Barnsley	L 2-3	1-1	10	Phillips 43, 59(pen)	8409
4	29	EL	A	Charlton Athletic	L 1-2	1-0	13	Mooney 42	(8442)
5	S 2	EL	A	Grimsby Town	D 0-0	0-0	16		(3993)
6	9	EL	H	Stoke City	W 3-0	2-0	24	Ramage 27, 54, Mooney 44	7130
7	12	EL	H	Crystal Palace	D 0-0	0-0	12		8780
8	16	EL	A	Ipswich Town	L 2-4	1-2	17	Phillips 10, Pitcher 81	(11441)
9	19	CC 2/1	H	**Bournemouth**	D 1-1	0-1		**Johnson 62**	5037
10	23	EL	H	Birmingham City	D 1-1	1-1	16	Moralee 7	9422
11	30	EL	A	Tranmere Rovers	W 3-2	1-1		Foster 21, Moralee 59, Mooney 63	(7041)
12	O 3	CC 2/2	A	**Bournemouth**	D 1-1	0-0		**Bazeley 119**	(4365)
13	7	EL	H	Millwall	L 0-1	0-0	22		8918
14	14	EL	A	Sunderland	D 1-1	0-0	20	Moralee 79	(17790)
15	21	EL	H	Wolverhampton Wand	D 1-1	0-1	21	Holdsworth 57	11319
16	24	CC 3	H	**Blackburn Rovers**	L 1-2	1-0		**Phillips 43**	17035
17	28	EL	A	Portsmouth	L 2-4	0-2	22	Phillips 50, Ramage 85	(7025)
18	N 4	EL	H	Southend United	D 2-2	1-1	22	Caskey 21, Phillips 54	7091
19	11	EL	A	Leicester City	L 0-1	0-1	22		(16230)
20	18	EL	A	Port Vale	D 1-1	1-0	22	Ramage 41	(6265)
21	21	EL	H	Luton Town	D 1-1	0-1	22	Phillips 84	10042
22	26	EL	H	Norwich City	L 0-2	0-1	22		7798
23	D 2	EL	A	Millwall	W 2-1	2-1	22	Phillips 24, Phillips 39	(8389)
24	9	EL	A	Birmingham City	L 0-1	0-0	23		(16970)
25	16	EL	H	Tranmere Rovers	W 3-0	1-0	22	Phillips 33(pen), 83, Foster 66	7257
26	23	EL	A	Oldham Athletic	D 0-0	0-0	22		(5878)
27	J 6	FAC 3	H	**Wimbledon**	D 1-1	1-1		**Mooney 36**	11187
28	13	EL	A	Huddersfield Town	L 0-1	0-0	23		7568
29	17	FAC 3R	A	**Wimbledon**	L 0-1	0-0			(5142)
30	20	EL	A	Sheffield United	D 1-1	0-0		Bazeley 80	(12782)
31	F 3	EL	A	Barnsley	L 1-2	0-0	24	Penrice 52	(6139)
32	10	EL	H	Charlton Athletic	L 1-2	1-0	24	Phillips 26	8394
33	17	EL	A	Crystal Palace	L 0-4	0-2	24		(13235)
34	24	EL	H	Ipswich Town	L 2-3	2-0	24	White 21, Palmer 44	11872
35	28	EL	A	Stoke City	L 0-2	0-0	24		(10114)
36	M 2	EL	A	Reading	D 0-0	0-0	24		(8933)
37	5	EL	H	Derby County	D 0-0	0-0	24		8306
38	9	EL	H	Oldham Athletic	W 2-1	1-0	24	Ramage 14, Ramage 49	10961
39	12	EL	A	West Bromwich Albion	D 4-4	2-3	24	Ramage 31, 85, Foster 36, 86	(11836)
40	16	EL	A	Derby County	D 1-1	1-0	24	Foster 22	(15939)
41	23	EL	H	West Bromwich Albion	D 1-1	0-0	24	Ramage 89	10334
42	30	EL	A	Wolverhampton Wand	L 0-3	0-2	24		(25885)
43	A 2	EL	H	Sunderland	D 3-3	1-3	24	Mooney 29, 46, Ramage 75	11195
44	6	EL	A	Portsmouth	L 1-2	1-1	24	Mooney 41(pen)	8226
45	8	EL	A	Southend United	D 1-1	1-0	24	Ramage 40	(5348)
46	13	EL	H	Port Vale	W 5-2	2-1	24	Connolly 2, 31, 80 (pen), White 71, 86	9066
47	16	EL	H	Reading	W 4-2	2-0	24	White 8, 83, Connolly 35, Ramage 87	8113
48	20	EL	A	Luton Town	D 0-0	0-0	24		(9454)
49	23	EL	H	Grimsby Town	W 6-3	4-1	23	Ramage 1, Connolly 13, 19, 70, Ramage 21, Ramage 73	8909
50	27	EL	A	Norwich City	W 2-1	0-0	23	Connolly 2(pen), Porter 67	(14188)
51	M 5	EL	H	Leicester City	L 0-1	0-0	23		20089

Best Home League Attendance: 20089 v Leicester City   Smallest: 7091 v Southend United   Average: 9472

Goal Scorers:
EL(62):   Ramage(15),Phillips(11),Connolly(8),Mooney(6),White(5),Foster(5),Moralee(3),Johnson(1),Holdsworth(1),Bazeley(1),Porter(1),Pitcher(1),Caskey(1),Penrice(1),
            Payne(1),Palmer(1)
CC(3):   Phillips(1),Johnson(1),Bazeley(1)
FAC(1):   Mooney(1)

(D) Barnes	(F) Bazeley	(F) Beadle	(M) Caskey	(G) Cherry	(F) Connolly	(F) Dixon	(D) Foster	(D) Gibbs	(M) Hessenthaler	(D) Holdsworth	(M) Johnson	(M) Lavin	(D) Ludden	(D) Millen	(G) Miller	(F) Mooney	(F) Moralee	(M) Neill	(D) Page	(M) Palmer	(M) Payne	(F) Pennice	(F) Phillips	(G) Pitcher	(M) Porter	(M) Ramage	(F) White	(M) Wilkinson	Opponent ref.	No.
	S	X1		S				X	X	X	X	X		X	X	S1					X		X		X				G.Singh	1
	S2	X1		S				X	X	X	X	X		X	X	S1					X		X2		X				J.Lloyd	2
	X		X	S2					X2	X1	X	X		X	X	S1					X		X		X				M.Pierce	3
	X		X	S1			X	S1			X	X	X1	X	X						X		X		X1				B.Pooley	4
	X		X	X1			X				X	X	S				S1				X		X		X	X	X		J.A.Kirkby	5
	X1			S			X				X	X			X	X1	S1				X		X	S1	X	X		P.Rejer	6
	X			S			X				X	X			X	X	S				X		X	S	X	X		J.Brandwood	7
	X						X				X	X1			X	X	S				X		X	S1	X	X		R.Harris	8
	X	X		S			X				X	S		X	X	X	S1						X1	X	X	X		R.Gifford	9
	X	X1		S	S1		X		S2	X	X	X		X	X	X2							X	X				A.D'Urso	10
	S1			S	S		X				X	X		X	X	X1				X			X	X				A. Butler	11
	S1			S			X				X	X		X	X	X2				X		S2	X1	X				G.Barber	12
	S3						X				X	X		X	X	X3	X1			X		S1	S1	X	X1			E.Wolstenholme	13
	X			S			X				X	S		X	X	X	X			X		X	S	X				K.J.Breen	14
	X			S			X				X	X		X	X	X	X	S		X		X	S	X				T.Lunt	15
	X			S			X				X	X		X	X	X	X	S		X		X	S	X				P.Jones	16
	X1	X	X				X				X	X		X	X	S1	X2			X		X	S2	X				K.Leach	17
	S	X	S				X	X			X	S	X	X	X	X	X		X		X	X		X				P.Rejer	18
		X	S					X	X1	X	S1		X	X	X	X			X		X	X		X1				E.Lomas	19
	S	X						X	X	S2	X		X	X	X	X1			X		S1	X		X2				E.Wolstenholme	20
	S	X						X	X	S	X		X	X	X	S1			X		X1	X		X				M.Pierce	21
	X	X						X	X	S	X		X	X	X		S		X		S	X		S	X			S.Bennett	22
	X					X		X	X	X				X	X		S	X	S1	X	X1					X	M.Bailey	23
	X					X		X	X	X				X	X		S	X	S1	X	X1					X	C.R.Wilkes	24
	X					X		X	X	X			X	X	X		S	X		X	S1					X	A.Wiley	25
	X					X		X	X	X			X	X	X	S2	X2	X		X	S1			X		X	G.Singh	26
	X					X		X	X	X	S1		X	X1	X	X	X			X	X2			X		X	P.Danson	27
	X					X	X		X	S1			X	X1	X	X	S	X2	X	X	S2			X		X	K.Leach	28
	X			S				X	X	X			X	X	X	X	X	S	X	X				X1		X	P.Danson	29
	X1			S	X	X		X	X	X			X	X	X	X	X	X	S1							X	A. D'Urso	30
	X			S	X	X		X				S	X	X	X	X1	X		X		X	S		X			M.Fletcher	31
	X			S		X	X		X		X		X	X	X	X	S	X	X	S				X			J.Brandwood	32
	S1						X	X1	X			S	X	X	X	X	S1	X			X		X1			X	G.Pooley	33
X	S1						S	X	X	X		X	X	X	X			X	X1	X		X		S2	X2		P.Richards	34
X	S1					X	X	X	X	X		X	X	X1				S	X	X1	X			X		X	T.West	35
X	X						X				S1	X	X	X	X	X1	S2	X2	G.Pooley?									E.Wolstenholme	36
X	X						X				X	X1	X	X	X	X		X	X	S1	R.Harris	37
X	X				S1	X		X				X	X	X2	X	X	S	X	S	F.Stretton	38
X	X				S2	X		X				X	X	X2	X	X	S	X1	S1	D.Allison	39
	X				S	X		X		S	X	X	X1	X	X			X	X	S1	C.Wilkes	40
	X				S	X		X		S	X	X1	X2	X	X			X	X	S2	E.Lomas	41
	X				S1	X	X1	X			X	X	X	X	X			X	X	S2	T.Leake	42
	X				S	X		X			X	X	X	X1	X	X			X	X	S	S	R.Gifford	43
	X				X2			X			X	X	X	X	X			X1	X	X	S	R.Poulain	44
X	X				X			X			X	X	X	X	X			X	X3	X1	S	M.Pierce	45
X	X	X1			X			X		S2	X	X	S1	X	X	S		X	X	X	A.D'Urso	46
X2	X	X1				X			S2		X	X	S1	X	X	S		X	X	X	B.Knight	47
	X	X1				X				X	X	S1	X	S2			X2	X	X	G.Cain	48
	X	X				X				X	X	S	X	X			X	X	X	S.Baines	49
X1	X	X1				X		S1		X	X	S	X	X	S		X	X	X	S.Mathieson	50
	X	X1			X1		X	S1	X	X	S1	X	X			X	X	X	S	J.Kirkby	51

10	35	3	6	4	7	8	26	8	30	26	17	16	9	32	42	38	17	1	16	35	9	4	26	2	28	34	9	4	EL Appearances	
0	6	0	0	4	3	0	1	0	1	3	0	3	1	0	4	8	0	3	0	3	3	1	6	1	2	7		0	EL Sub Appearances	
0	2+1	1	0	0	0	3	0	0	2	2	2	0	1+1	2	2	2+1	0	0	2	0	2	1+1	2	3	0	0			CC Appearances	
0	2	0	0	0	0	1	0	0	2	2	0	1	2	1	2	0	2	1	0	2	0	2	0	2	0	0			FAC Appearances	

Also Played: (M) Andrews S(27), S1(37). (M) Hill X(33), (M) Hodge X(25), X1(26). (F) Lowndes S(24,25,26,30), S1(29). ((M) Rooney S(48,49), (F) Simpson S1(44), S(45), (D) Ward X(48). (M) White S(31,37,42,44), (G) Wilkerson S(3)

WATFORD

CLUB RECORDS

BIGGEST VICTORIES
League: 8-0 v Sunderland, Division 1, 25.9.1982
F.A. Cup: 10-1 v Lowestoft, Round 1, 27.11.1927
League Cup: 8-0 v Darlington, Round 2, 6.10.1987
Europe: 3-0 v Kaiserslauten, Round 1, 28.9.1983
BIGGEST DEFEATS
League: 1-8 v Crystal Palace, Division 4, 23.9.1959
1-8 v Aberdare, Division 3S, 2.1.1926
0-7 v Port Vale, Division 3S, 15.9.1947
F.A. Cup: 0-10 v Wolverhampton W., Round 1, 13.12.1912
League Cup: 0-5 v Coventry City, Round 1, 9.12.1980
1-6 v Blackburn Rovers, Round 4, 9.12.1992
Europe: 0-4 v Sparta Prague, UEFA 3, 1983-84
MOST POINTS
3 points a win: 80, Division 2, 1981-82
2 points a win: 71, Division 4, 1977-78
MOST GOALS
92, 1959-60 (Division 4).
Holton 42, Uphill 29, Hartle 6, Benning 5, Gregory 3, Bunce 3, Walter 2, Chung1, og 1.
MOST LEAGUE GOALS CONCEDED
89, Division 3S, 1925-26
MOST FIRST CLASS MATCHES IN A SEASON
60 (46 League, 6 FA Cup, 2 League Cup, 4 Simod Cup, 2 Play-Offs) 1988-89
MOST LEAGUE WINS
30, Division 4, 1977-78
MOST LEAGUE DRAWS
18, Division 3S, 1921-22, Division 1 1995-96.
MOST LEAGUE DEFEATS
28, Division 2, 1971-72
RECORD TRANSFER FEE RECEIVED
£2,300,000 for Paul Furlong from Chelsea, May 1994.
RECORD TRANSFER FEE PAID
£550,000 for Luther Blissett from AC Milan, August 1984.
BEST PERFORMACES
League: 2nd in Division 1, 1982-83.
F.A. Cup: Runners-up 1983-84. Lost 0-2 v Everton.
League Cup: Semi-finals 1978-79, v Nottingham Forest 0-0, 1-3.
Europe (UEFA): 3rd Round 1983-84. Lost 2-3, 0-4 v Sparta Prague.

INDIVIDUAL CLUB RECORDS

MOST GOALS IN CAREER
Luther Blissett: 180 (1975-92 - 3 spells). 148 League, 15 FA Cup, 15 League Cup.
MOST GOALS IN A SEASON
Cliff Holton, 48 (42 League, 6 FA Cup), 1959-60
MOST GOALS IN A MATCH
5, Eddie Mummery v Newport County (8-2), Div 3(S), 5.1.1924
MOST APPEARANCES
Luther Blissett: 443+52 (1975-92 - 3 spells). 369+46 League, 32+2 FA Cup, 41+3 League Cup, 1+1 FMC.
OLDEST PLAYER
Joe Calvert 42 years 25 days
YOUNGEST PLAYER
Keith Mercer 16 years 125 days.
MOST CAPPED PLAYER
John Barnes (England) 31 & Kenny Jackett (Wales) 31

PREVIOUS MANAGERS

John Goodhall 1903-10, Harry Kent 1910-26, Fred Pagnam1926-29
Neil McBain 1929-37, Bill Findlay 1937-47, Jack Bray 1947-48,
Eddie Hapgood 1948-50, Ron Gray 1950-51, Haydn Green1951-52
Len Goulden 1952-55, John Paton 1955-56, Len Goulden 1956,
Neil McBain 1956-59, Ron Burgess 1959-63, Bill McGarry 1963-64
,
Ken Furphy 1964-71, George Kirby 1971-73, Mike Keen 1973-77,
Graham Taylor 1977-87, Dave Bassett 1987-88,
Steve Harrison 1988-90, Colin Lee 1990, Steve Perryman 1990-93,
Glenn Roeder 1993-96.

ADDITIONAL INFORMATION
Previous Names
Watford Rovers until 1891 or amalgamation of West Herts & Watford St. Marys in1898
Previous Leagues
Southern League
Club colours: Red & black striped shirts, white shorts, white socks.
Change colours: Blue/white shirts, white shorts with dark blue trim, white socks, with dark blue tops.
Reserves League: Avon Insurance Football Combination.

COMPETITIONS

Div.1	Div.2/1	Div.3	Div.3(S)	Div.4	UEFA
1982-88	1969-72	1920-21	1921-58	1958-60	1983-84
	1979-82	1960-69		1975-78	
	1988-96	1972-75			
		1978-79			
		1996-			

HONOURS

Division 3	Division 4	Division 3(S) Cup
1968-69	1977-78	1936-37 (shared)

LONGEST LEAGUE RUNS

of undefeated matches:	15 (27.1.34-2.2.35, 11.11.78-10.3.79)	of league matches w/out a win:	19 (27.11.1971 - 8.4.1972)
of undefeated home matches:	27 (15.10.1963 - 19.12.1964)	of undefeated away matches:	12 (17.3.1977 - 16.9.1978)
without home win: 9 (14.12.1971-15.4.1972, 25.8.1990-1.12.1990)		without an away win:	32 (17.4.1971 - 25.11.1972)
of league wins:	7 (17.11.34-29.12.34, 26.12.77-28.1.78)	of home wins:	8 (29.8.31-21.11.31, 3.11.34-2.2.35, 6.9.77-12.11.77)
of league defeats:	9 (26.12.1972 - 27.2.1973)	of away wins:	5 (25.4.1981 - 22.9.1981)

THE MANAGER

Kenny Jackett . . . . appointed 21st May 1996.
PREVIOUS CLUBS
As Manager . . . . None.
As a player . . . . Watford.
HONOURS As a Manager: None As a Player: Promotion to Div.2'79, Div.1'82. **Wales:** 31 full caps, 2 u21 & Youth.

WATFORD

PLAYERS NAME Honours	Ht	Wt	Birthdate	Birthplace Transfers	Contract Date	Clubs	APPEARANCES				GOALS			
							League	L/Cup	FA Cup	Other	Lge	L/C	FAC	Oth
G O A L K E E P E R S														
Chamberlain Alec	6.2	11.11	20/06/64	March		Ramsey Town								
via (27/07/81) Ipswich Town				Free	03/08/82	Colchester United	188	11	10	12				
£80000 (28/07/87) Everton				Loan	01/11/87	Tranmere Rovers	15							
				£150000	27/07/88	Luton Town	138	7	7	7				
				Free	08/07/93	Sunderland	89+1	9	8	1				
Loan (23/03/95) Liverpool				£40000	05/07/96	Watford								
Miller Kevin	6.1	13.0	15/03/69	Falmouth		Newquay								
Div4'90				Free	09/03/89	Exeter City	163	7	12	18				
				£250000	14/05/93	Birmingham City	24	4		2				
				£250000	01/08/94	Watford	86	6	6					
D E F E N D E R S														
Foster Colin	6.4	14.1	16/07/64	Chislehurst	04/02/82	Leyton Orient	173+1	12	19	5	10		5	1
					04/03/87	Nottingham Forest	68+4	8	5	2	5	1		
					22/09/89	West Ham United	88+5	5	9	2+2	5		2	
Loan (10/01/94) Notts County 9 Lge, 2 Oth. Apps.				£100000	23/03/94	Watford	66	6	6		8	1		
Holdsworth David	6.1	12.4	08/11/68	Walthamstow	08/11/86	Watford	249+9	20	14+1	8+2	10	2	1	
E: u21.1, Y.6														
Ludden Dominic	5.8	11.0	30/03/74	Basildon	06/07/92	Leyton Orient	50+8	1	0+1	6	1			1
ESFA u18.4				£100000	01/08/94	Watford	10+3		1+1					
Millen Keith	6.1	12.0	26/09/66	Croydon	07/08/84	Brentford	301+4	26	18	30+1	17	2	1	
Div3'92					22/03/94	Watford	73+1	4	7		1			
M I D F I E L D														
Andrews Wayne						Watford (T)	0+1							
Flash Richard	5.9	11.8	08/04/76	Birmingham	01/08/94	Manchester Utd (A)								
via Wolves				Free	25/07/96	Watford								
Page Robert	6.0	11.8	03/09/74	Llwynypia	19/04/93	Watford	24+4		1+1					
Hessenthaler Andrew	5.7	11.0	17/08/65	Dartford		Dagenham & Red.			5				1	
E: S-P.1. 1LP'91				£65000	12/09/91	Watford	195	13	5	4	12	1	2	
Johnson Richard	5.10	11.4	27/04/74	Newcastle (Aus)	11/05/92	Watford	67+18	6+1	4	0+1	4	1		
Palmer Steve	6.1	12.13	31/03/68	Brighton		Cambridge Uni.								
Div2'92				Free	01/08/89	Ipswich Town	87+24	3	8+3	4+2	2		1	
				£135000	28/09/95	Watford	35	2			1			
Porter Gary	5.6	10.6	06/03/66	Sunderland	06/03/84	Watford	356+38	28+2	25+2	12+1	47	4	3	2
E: u21.12, Y.13. FAYC'82														
Ramage Craig	5.9	11.8	30/03/70	Derby	20/07/88	Derby County	33+9	6+1	3+1	0+3	4	2	1	
E: u21.2				Loan	16/02/89	Wigan Athletic	10			0+1	2			
				£90000	21/02/94	Watford	89+4	7	7		24	2		
Talboys Steve	5.10	11.6	18/09/66	Bristol		Gloucester City				3+2				
				£10000	10/01/92	Wimbledon	19+2	2+1	1+1		1			
				Free	05/07/96	Watford								
F O R W A R D S														
Bazeley Darren	5.10	10.9	05/10/72	Northampton	06/05/91	Watford	101+44	9+4	7+1	3+1	13	2		
Connolly David	5.8	11.4	06/06/77	London	14/11/94	Watford	7+6		1+1		8			
Dixon Kerry	6.0	13.10	24/07/61	Luton	01/07/78	Tottenham Hotspur								
E: 8, u21.1. Div2'84'89.				Free	01/08/79	Dunstable								
ZDC'90				£20000	22/07/80	Reading	110+6	6+1	2+1		51			
				£175000	04/08/83	Chelsea	331+4	40+1	18+2	25	147	24	8	12
				£575000	19/07/92	Southampton	8+1	2	1		2			
				Loan	19/02/93	Luton Town	16+1				3			
				Free	13/08/93	Luton Town	50+8	2	7+2	2	16			1
				£5000	23/03/95	Millwall	24+7	1+2	1		9			
					12/01/96	Watford	8+3							
Lowndes Nathan P	5.11	10.04	02/06/77	Salford	01/08/94	Leeds United								
				£40000	03/10/95	Watford			0+1					
Mooney Thomas	5.11	12.6	11/08/71	Middlesbrough	23/11/89	Aston Villa								
Flg u18.1				Free	01/08/90	Scarborough	96+11	11+2	3	6	29	8		2
				£100000	12/07/93	Southend United	9+5	1+1		2+3	5			
				Loan	17/03/94	Watford	10				2			
					21/07/94	Watford	67+4	7	2+1		9	1	1	
Penrice Gary	5.8	11.1	23/03/64	Bristol		Mangotsfield								
				Free	06/11/84	Bristol Rovers	186+2	11	11	13+2	53	3	7	2
				£500000	14/11/89	Aston Villa	41+2		4		17		1	1
				£1000000	08/03/91	Aston Villa	14+6				1			
				£625000	29/10/91	Q.P.R.	46+17	4+1	2+1	1	17	1	1	
				£300000	15/11/95	Watford	4+3				1			
Phillips Kevin	5.7	11.0	25/07/73	Hitchin		Baldock Town								
				£10000	19/12/94	Watford	41+2	2	2		20	1		
Simpson Colin	6.1	11.05	30/04/76	Oxford	06/07/94	Watford	0+1							
White Devon W	6.3	13.8	02/03/64	Nottingham		Arnold Kingswell								
				Free	14/12/84	Lincoln City	21+8			2+1	4			2
Free (01/10/86) Boston United				Free	21/08/87	Bristol Rovers	190+12	9	10	19	54	2	3	2
				£100000	28/03/92	Cambridge United	157	4	1	1	4	1		1
				£100000	26/01/93	Q.P.R.	15+10	1+1			9			
				£100000	23/12/94	Notts County	16+4		2	3	7		1	
				£100000	16/02/96	Watford	9+7				5			

VICARAGE ROAD STADIUM
Watford WD1 8ER
Tel: 01923 496000

Capacity 22,000

First game...v Millwall, Div 3(S), 0-0, 30.8.1922.
First floodlit game..v Luton Town, Friendly, October 1953.

ATTENDANCES
Highest ....34,099 v Manchester Utd, FAC, 3.2.1969.
Lowest ....1,700 v Southend, ZDS Cup, 2.10.1991.

OTHER GROUNDS ....Cassio Road 1899-1922. Vicarage Road 1922-

MATCHDAY TICKET PRICES

Vicarage Road Stand (north) &
Rookery End (when available)
Adults/Concess....................... £11/£8
Rous Stand (West) £13/N/A
Family Areas (Family Enc., F Block & East Stand)
1st Parent £11
2nd Parent........................... £8
Child aged 13-15..................... £5
12 & Under £1
Wheelchair Areas (Chairbound/Helper) ... £6/£11
Visitors (Rous Stand Lower Tier) .... £11/£8

Ticket Office Telephone no........ 01923 496 010

HORNETS' HOTLINE
0891 10 4 10 4
Calls cost 39p per minute cheap rate and 49p per minute at all other times.
Call costings correct at time of going to press.

HOW TO GET TO THE GROUND

From the North: Exit M1 at junction 5 and take second exit off roundabout, A41, signposted Harrow. Continue short distance to next roundabout and take third exit to Hartspring Lane. Follow this road through a set of traffic lights and continue straight ahead (now Aldenham Road to another roundabout. Go straight over (second exit) still following Aldenham Road, to next traffic lights. When through the lights, move into right-hand lane (marked Watford) and follow one-way system around to Bushey Station, then moving into left-hand lane. Turn left under Bushey Arches, into Eastbury Road. At traffic lights, turn right into Deacons Hill and continue to next traffic lights, turning left into Cardiff Road for visitors' entrance to stadium/coach park.
From the South: Exit M1 at junction 5 and take first exit off roundabout, A41 signposted Harrow (then as North).
From the East: Exit M25 at junction 21A and join the M1 at junction 6. Exit at junction 5 (then as North).
From the West: Exit M25 at junction 19 and take third exit off roundabout, A411 (Hempstead Road), signposted Watford. Continue for approximately two miles and at roundabout go straight across (right-hand lane) to next roundabout, then take third exit into Rickmansworth Road. Take second turning on the left into Cassio Road. Continue through traffic lights, to Merton Road and straight on to Wiggenhall Road. At traffic lights, turn right into Cardiff Road (as North).
Car Parking: No public parking available at ground. There are several multi-story parks in the town centre.
Nearest Railway Station: Watford Junction or Watford High Street (01923 245 001) or Watford Halt. For Bus details phone 0345 788788 - 'Network Watford'.

MATCHDAY PROGRAMME

Programme Editor.................... Ed Coan & Gabriela Lang.

Number of pages .... 32.

Price .... £1.50.

Subscriptions .... Apply to club.

Local Newspapers .... Watford Observer, Watford Review,
.... St Albans Herald and Post, Watford Free Observer,
.... London Evening Standard.

Local Radio Stations .... Chiltern Radio, G.L.R., Capital Radio,
.... BBC Three Counties Radio.

WREXHAM
(The Robins)
NATIONWIDE LEAGUE DIVISION 2
SPONSORED BY: WREXHAM LAGER

Back Row (L-R): Lewis Coady, Karl Connolly, Scott Williams, Barry Jones, Mark Cartwright, Barry Hunter, Andy Marriott, Mark McGregor, Ken Dixon, Paul Jones, Jonathan Cross, Stephen Futcher, Gareth Owen. **Middle Row:** Mel Pejic (Player/Physio), Joey Jones (Coach), Steve Morris, Kieron Durkan, Peter Ward, Wayne Phillips, Mike Cody, Steve Watkin, David Ridler, Craig Skinner, Richard Barnes, Kevin Russell, Mike Buxton (Schoolboy Dev. Officer), Cliff Sear (Yth Dev. Officer). **Front Row:** Steve Weaver (Community Officer), Bryan Hughes, David Brammer, Tony Humes, Kevin Reeves (Asst. Manager), Brian Flynn (Manager), Phil Hardy, Deryn Brace, Richard Rawlins, Dudley Hall (Res. Team Physio).

WREXHAM
FORMED IN 1872
TURNED PROFESSIONAL IN 1912
LTD COMPANY IN 1912

PRESIDENT: G Mytton
CHAIRMAN: W P Griffiths
VICE-CHAIRMAN
B Williams
DIRECTORS
C Griffiths, S F Mackreth, D Rhodes,
C G Paletta
SECRETARY
D Rhodes (01978 262 129)
COMMERCIAL MANAGER
P Stokes (01978 352 536)

MANAGER: Brain Flynn
ASSISTANT MANAGER: Kevin Reeves
COACHES: Brian Prandle & Dudley Hall
**SCHOOLBOY, YOUTH & RESERVE
TEAM MANAGEMENT**
Cliff Sear, Mike Buxton, Joey Jones
PHYSIOTHERAPIST
Mel Pejic

STATISTICIAN FOR THE DIRECTORY
Gareth Davies

Another season of progress up the Second Division table saw the Racecourse team finish up in eight position, an improvement of five places from the previous campaign.

Albeit there is a certain air of disappointment among everyone connected with the club (not least the supporters) that the Play-offs' at least should have been attained as the old 'cliche' 'So near and yet so far' seemed very apt once again, but as manager Brian Flynn rightly pointed out after the final game, "You deserve to be where you finish".

'Consistent inconsistency'! Sums up the team admirably as the chances were presented to them by faltering clubs in the promotion run in, but were sadly spurned by a side who could not 'turn it on' when the chips were down. For example Burnley at home on the penultimate Saturday of the season when three points from a relegation threatened team would have made Wrexham odds on for the final Play-off position.

Strangely, for a side who were among the highest scorers in the whole of the Football League (and Premier Division), this was the area that was lacking in certain matches when after dominating games for long periods the end product was nil due to being unable to capitalise on numerous easy chances in front of goal.

Karl Connolly took over the lamented Gary Bennett's role superbly well (although many fans still prefer to see him perform his talents out on the left) but at times one felt that a stronger physical presence up front would take some pressure away from him and/or perhaps give Flynn an 'option' to change things when the game was not going well, as Wrexham are not a big side but play an excellent, patient passing game, which is very attractive to watch but sadly in the lower division can sometimes encounter problems.

Having said that there are many pluses in the present Wrexham regime under the impressive management team of Brian Flynn, Kevin Reeves, Joey Jones and Cliff Sear, as the squad is improving in quality all the time and must be the strongest since the late 1970s, when the North Wales club was at it's peak.

This was illustrated in the fact that the clubs reserves won the 'Pontins' Third Division at the first time of asking, with the impressive youth side winning honours once again. Thus emphasising the well respected youth policy so ably run at the Racecourse which is the envy of many of the more affluent cheque book waving clubs!

The acquisition of Peter Ward from Stockport County was a major one with 'fine passing of the ball' and 'superb free kicks' a feature of his play and Wayne Phillips surprising many by emerging as a richly deserved 'Player of the Season' with at last 'self belief' added to his game which prompted Wales manager Bobby Gould to include him on the bench for the match against Switzerland in April.

It is to be hoped that the 'Mold Road' side of the Racecourse can accomadate a new stand 'sooner rather than later' as the team and the ground must move together with the times if future success is to be obtained.

GARETH M DAVIES

WREXHAM

League: 8th			**FA Cup: 3rd Rnd**			**Coca-Cola Cup: 1st Rnd**	**Auto Windscreen Shield: 2nd Rnd**		

M	DATE	COMP	VEN	OPPONENTS	RESULT	HT	LP	GOAL SCORERS/GOAL TIMES	ATT.
1	A 10	ECWC P1	H	**Petrolul Ploiesti**	D	0-0	0-0		4308
2	12	EL	H	Notts County	D	1-1	0-1	13	Watkin 67(pen)	4338
3	15	CC 1/1	A	**Stockport County**	L	0-1	0-1		(3493)
4	19	EL	A	Blackpool	L	0-2	0-2	19		(4799)
5	24	ECWC P2	A	**Petrolul Ploiesti**	L	0-1	0-0		(10000)
6	26	EL	H	Brighton & H.A.	D	1-1	0-1	19	Connolly 82	2947
7	29	EL	H	Bournemouth	D	1-1	1-0	21	Russell 35	(4825)
8	S 2	EL	A	Bristol Rovers	W	2-1	0-1	15	Owen 86, Watkin 90	(6031)
9	5	CC 1/2	H	**Stockport County**	D	2-2	1-0		**Russell 30, Watkin 81**	2764
10	9	EL	H	Bradford City	L	1-2	0-0	19	Watkin 60	3268
11	12	EL	H	Shrewsbury Town	D	1-1	1-1	19	Watkin 32	3298
12	16	EL	A	Peterborough United	L	0-1	0-0	20		(3817)
13	23	EL	A	Wycombe Wanderers	D	1-1	1-1	21	Brammer 25	(4649)
14	26	AWS 1/1	A	**Mansfield Town**	D	2-2	1-1		**Hughes 5, Connolly 67**	(1037)
15	30	EL	H	Swindon Town	W	4-3	1-2	16	Connolly 37, 46, 67 (3), Hunter 78	4396
16	O 7	EL	A	York City	L	0-1	0-0	18		(3512)
17	14	EL	H	Oxford United	W	2-1	1-0	14	Humes 6, Phillips 68	3189
18	17	AWS 1/2	H	**York City**	W	1-0	0-0		**Connolly 66**	1411
19	21	EL	A	Walsall	W	2-1	0-0	13	Connolly 88(pen), Hunter 89	(4020)
20	28	EL	H	Swansea City	W	1-0	1-0	10	Connolly 3(pen)	4002
21	31	EL	H	Carlisle United	W	3-2	1-0	9	Russell 14, 81, Brammer 84	2939
22	N 4	EL	A	Hull City	D	1-1	0-0	9	McGregor 89	(3515)
23	11	FAC 1	A	**Hull City**	D	0-0	0-0			(3724)
24	18	EL	H	Rotherham United	W	7-0	3-0	6	Connolly 12,14, Garner 39(og), Ward 64,Skinner 73, Watkin 78,89	3227
25	21	FAC 1R	H	**Hull City**	D	0-0	0-0			4522
26	25	EL	A	Burnley	D	2-2	0-0	7	Skinner 51, Ward 66	(8710)
27	29	AWS 2	H	**Carlisle United**	L	1-2	0-0		**Ward 28**	2225
28	D 2	FAC 2	H	**Chesterfield**	W	3-2	2-0		**Watkin 7, Hunter 31, Connolly 82(pen)**	4943
29	9	EL	H	Wycombe Wanderers	W	1-0	1-0	5	Connolly 30	3468
30	16	EL	A	Swindon Town	D	1-1	0-0	6	Connolly 86	(8418)
31	22	EL	H	Brentford	D	2-2	2-0	7	Russell 14, Connolly 26	3670
32	26	EL	A	Crewe Alexandra	D	0-0	0-0	7		(5177)
33	J 6	FAC 3	A	**Peterborough United**	L	0-1	0-0			(5983)
34	13	EL	H	Blackpool	D	1-1	0-0	9	Watkin 72	5479
35	20	EL	A	Notts County	L	0-1	0-0	10		(5014)
36	23	EL	H	Bristol City	D	0-0	0-0	10		2637
37	F 3	EL	A	Brighton & H.A.	D	2-2	2-1	12	Skinner 22, Phillips 44	(4617)
38	13	EL	A	Stockport County	W	3-2	1-1	8	Ward 43, Connolly 48(og), Humes 89	(4688)
39	20	EL	H	Bristol Rovers	W	3-2	1-1	8	Hunter 25, Channing 55(og), Jones 70	3235
40	24	EL	H	Peterborough United	W	1-0	0-0	6	Brace 76	4011
41	27	EL	A	Bradford City	L	0-2	0-2	8		(3804)
42	M 2	EL	A	Crewe Alexandra	L	2-3	1-2	9	Chalk 35, Humes 80	6112
43	5	EL	H	Chesterfield	W	3-0	3-0	8	Phillips 5, Chalk 22, Connolly 45(pen)	2656
44	9	EL	A	Brentford	L	0-1	0-1	8		(4579)
45	12	EL	H	Bournemouth	W	5-0	3-0	8	Ward 8, Jones 21, 48, Connolly 43, Russell 74	2004
46	16	EL	H	Stockport County	L	2-3	0-1	8	Jones 51, 61	4081
47	19	EL	A	Chesterfield	D	1-1	0-0	7	Ward 90	(3760)
48	23	EL	A	Bristol City	L	1-3	0-1	9	Connolly 66	(6141)
49	30	EL	H	York City	L	2-3	1-2	10	Russell 14, Morris 63	2923
50	A 2	EL	A	Oxford United	D	0-0	0-0	12		(5554)
51	6	EL	A	Swansea City	W	3-1	1-0	10	Owen 29, Ward 74, Jones 87	(4256)
52	8	EL	H	Walsall	W	3-0	1-0	10	Chalk 22, Phillips 66, Connolly 80	3309
53	13	EL	A	Carlisle United	W	2-1	1-0	7	Connolly 40, Jones 86	(7317)
54	17	EL	A	Shrewsbury Town	D	2-2	1-2	7	Chalk 44, Jones 61	(4094)
55	20	EL	H	Hull City	W	5-0	2-0	6	Connolly 12, 53, Russell 31, Phillips 60, Morris 82	3400
56	27	EL	H	Burnley	L	0-2	0-2	8		6664
57	M 4	EL	A	Rotherham United	W	1-0	0-0	8	Morris 59	(4419)

Best Home League Attendance: 6664 v Burnley					**Smallest: 2004 v Bournemouth**			**Average: 3706**	

Goal Scorers:

EL(76): Connolly(18),Jones(8),Russell(7),Watkin(7),Ward(6),Phillips(5),Chalk(4),Opponent(s)(3),Hunter(3),Humes(3),Morris(3),Skinner(3),Brammer(2), Owen(2),Brace(1),McGregor(1)

CC(2): Watkin(1),Russell(1)

FAC(3): Watkin(1),Hunter(1),Connolly(1)

AWS(4): Connolly(2),Hughes(1),Ward(1)

(M) Barnes	(D) Brace	(M) Brammer	(G) Cartwright	(F) Chalk	(M) Coady	(F) Connolly	(M) Cross	(G) Dixon	(F) Durkan	(F) Futcher	(D) Hardy	(F) Hughes	(D) Humes	(D) Hunter	(D) Jones	(L) Jones.L	(G) Marriott	(D) McGregor	(F) Morris	(M) Owen	(M) Phillips	(M) Ridler	(M) Roberts	(F) Russell	(F) Skinner	(D) Thomas	(M) Ward	(F) Watkin		
S	X		S		S	X			X	X	X			X	X		X			X	X		S			S		X	1	
	X					X			S		X	X3		X	X		X				S			X	X		X	X	2	P.Richards
	X					X			S1		X		X	X		X			S2		S3			X	X1		X	X2	3	A.Butler
	X					X			S		X		X	X		X			S2		S1			X	X1		X	X2	4	T.Heilbron
S1			S		S	X	X			X1	X			X	X		X			X	X		S				X		5	
						X			S1		X	X3		X	X		X	S2	X	S3	X			X2	X1		X		6	G.Cane
						X2					X		X		X	X		X	S1	X	X			X	S		X1	S2	7	C.Wilkes
		X				X			X		X		X			X		X	X	X1	X	X	S	X	S			S1	8	A.D'Urso
		X				X			X		X		X		X			X	X	X1	X	X		X	S			S1	9	P.Rejer
		X				X	S2		X1		X		X		X			X	S		X			X2	S1		X		10	E.Lomas
	X1					X	S2		X		X		X		X			X	X		X			X2	S		X		11	S.Mathieson
		X				X	S3		X2		X		X		X			X	X		X1	X		X3	S2		X		12	K.Lynch
	X					X			S		X	X	S	X	X		X			X	X			S1	X			X1	13	B.Knight
	X								S1		X	X	X	X		X		X	X		S		X	X1					14	A.Wiley
	X					X	X		S1		X	X	X	X	X		X		X		S		X	S	X1				15	T.Leake
	X					X	X		S		X	X	X	X	X		X		X		S		X	S	X				16	J.Rushton
	X					X	X2		S		X	X	X1	X		X		X		S1		X	S2	X			X		17	T.West
	X					X	X		S		X	X1	X	X		X		X		S1		X	S	X			X		18	U.Rennie
	X					X	X1				X	X2	X	X	S3		X		X			X	S1	X3		S2			19	I.Cruickshanks
	X					X	X1				X		X	X	X		X		X			S	X	X			X	X	20	S.Baines
	X					X					X		X	X	X	S	X		S			S	X	X			X	S	21	R.Poulain
			S			X					X		X	S	X		X		X	X1			X	X			X	S1	22	T.Lunt
	X			S		X			X		X		X	S1	X		X		X			X1		X2			X	S2	23	K.Breen
	X					X			S		X		X	S2	X2		X		X			X		X1	X		X	S1	24	P.Richards
	X1					X					X		X	S1	X2	S2	X		X			X		S	X		X	X	25	M.J.Brandwood
						X					X		X	S1	X	S	X		X	X	S			X1	X		X	X	26	J.Kirkby
						X		S			X		X	S1	X		X	X1	S1			X		X	X		X	X	27	G.Cain
						X					X		X	S1	X	X	X	X	S	S			X	X		X1	X		28	E.Lomas
						X					X		X	S	X1	X	X	X	S1	S			X	X	X		X	X	29	K.Breen
	S					X					X		X		X	X	X	X	S		S		X	X	X		X	X	30	B.Knight
X						X					X		S	X2	X	X	X	S2	S1			X		X	X		X	X1	31	N.Fletcher
S						X					X		X	S1	X	X	X			S		X1	X	X	X		X	X	32	J.Brandwood
						X			S1		X		X	S	X	X	X	S2	X1		X		X	X2		X			33	T.West
X						X					X		X	S1	X	X	X	X	S	S2		X1		X	X		X	X2	34	J.Rushton
X						X					X		X	S1	X	S3	X	X	X			S2		X3	X	X1	X	X2	35	G.B.Frankland
X						X					X		X	X	X		X	X	X	S2	S1	X2	S	X1	X		X		36	A.G.Wiley
X						X					X		X	S2	X		X	X	S			X		X1	X2		X	S1	37	C.R.Wilkes
X						X			X		X		S		X	X	X	X			S	X		X			X	S1	38	N.Barry
X			X			X					X		S		X	X	X	X	X			S	X	X			X	S	39	D.Laws
X			X		X	X					X		S1		X	X	X	X	X			S	X1	X			X	S	40	I.Cruikshanks
X2			X		X	X3			S1		X	S2	X	X1	X	X	X					X		X			X	S3	41	A.Leake
X			X		X	X					X	X	S	X	X	X	X			S		X1		X2			X	S1	42	M.A.Riley
X			X		X	X					X	S	X	X	X	X	X	X				X		X			X	S	43	R.Pearson
X2			X		X	X					X	S1	X		X	X	X	X	S			X1		X			X	S2	44	R.B.Gifford
X			X		X	X					X	S	X		X	X	X	S		S1		X		X			X	S	45	K.Lynch
X			X		X	X2					X	X1	X		X	X	X	S			S1	X		X				S2	46	D.Allison
			X		X	X					X	S	X	X	X	X	X	X1		S		X		X			X	S1	47	R.Furnandiz
			X		X	X			X2		X		X	S2	X	X	X	X		S	X1	X		X			X	S1	48	G.Barber
			X		X	X1					X		X		X	X	X	X	X	S2	S1	S		X			X	X2	49	E.Wolstenholme
			X2		X	S1					X		X		X	X	X	X	X3	X	X	S3	S2	X			X	X1	50	S.Bennett
			X		X	X					X	S		X	X	X	X	X	X	S	X	X			S		X		51	I.F.Hemley
			X		X	X					X	S		X	X	X	X	X	X	S	X	X			S		X		52	P.Richards
			X		X	X					X	S	S	X	X	X	X	X	X	S	X	X		S			X		53	G.Singh
			X		X	X					X	X	X	X	X	X	X	X	S	X	X			X			S		54	G.Cain
			X		X	X					X	S	S	X	X	X1	X	X	S1	X	X			X			X		55	M.J.Brandwood
			X		X	X					X		X	X	X	X	X	X2	S2	S1	X1			X			X	X1	56	S.Bains
			X		X	X					X		X	X	X	S	X	X	X	S1	X			X	S		X		57	A.D'Urso
0	16	11	0	19	0	45	4	0	6	0	41	11	26	30	39	20	46	27	4	11	43	0	0	37	21	0	33	16		EL Appearances
0	0	0	0	0	0	1	3	0	2	0	1	11	1	1	1	0	0	5	9	8	1	0	0	0	2	0	0	13		EL Sub Appearances
0	1	1	0	0	0	2	0	0	1+1	0	2	1	2	2	2	0	2	0	1+1	1	1+1	0	0	2	1	0	1	1+1		CC Appearances
0	0	2	0	0	0	4	0	0	1+1	0	4	0+3	4	2+1	4	0	4	2+1	1	0	4	0	0	3	3	0	4	2+1		FAC Appearances
0+1	1	0	0	0	0	2	1	0	1	2	2	0	0	2	2	0	2	0	2	2	2	0	0	2	0	0	1	2		ECWC Appearances
0	0	2	0	0	0	2	1+1	0	0	0	3	2	3	0	3	0	3	3	0+1	0+1	3	0	0	2	0	0	1	1		AWS Appearances

Also Played: (M) Rawlins S(5).

CLUB RECORDS

RECORD LEAGUE VICTORY
10-1 v Hartlepool, Div 4, 3.3.1962
Most Goals Scored in a Cup Tie: 11-1 v New Brighton (h), Div 3N Cup, 1933-34
RECORD LEAGUE DEFEAT
0-9 v Brentford, Div 3, 15.10.1963
Record Cup Defeat: 1-9 v Wolverhampton Wanderers, FA Cup Rnd 3, 1930-31
MOST LEAGUE POINTS
(2pts for win) 61, Div 4, 1969-70, Div 3, 1977-78
(3pts for win) 80 Div 3, 1992-93
MOST LEAGUE GOALS
106, Div 3N, 1932-33

RECORD TRANSFER FEE PAID
£210,000 to Liverpool for Joey Jones, Oct 1978
RECORD TRANSFER FEE RECEIVED
£300,000 from Manchester United for Mickey Thomas, Nov 1978
£300,000 from Manchester City for Bobby Shinton, July 1979
£300,000 + further £300,000 on completion of set amount of first team appearances from Liverpool for Lee Jones, March 1992
£300,000 from Tranmere Rovers for Gary Bennett, June 1995.

BEST PERFORMANCES
League: 15th Div 2, 1978-79
FA Cup: 6th Round 1973-74,1977-78
League Cup: 5th Round 1961, 1978   Welsh Cup: Winners (23), Runners-up (22). This is a record number of victories and appearances in the Final
European Cup Winners Cup: Quarter-Final 1975-76
European Competitions entered
European Cup Winners Cup: 1972-73, 1975-76,1978-79, 1979-80, 1984-85, 1986-87, 1990-91
HONOURS
Div 3 Champions 1977-78   Welsh Cup Winners (23)
Welsh Cup Runners-Up (22)

LEAGUE CAREER
Original members of Div 3N 1921   Transferred to Div 3 1958
Relegated to Div 4 1959-60 Promoted to Div 3 1961-62
Relegated to Div 4 1963-64 Promoted to Div 3 1969-70
Promoted to Div 2 1977-78   Relegated to Div 3 1981-82
Relegated to Div 4 1982-83 (now Div 3) Promoted to Div 2 1992-93

INDIVIDUAL CLUB RECORDS

MOST APPEARANCES FOR CLUB
Arfon Griffiths (1959-61 & 1962-79) Total 586+6 subs (not including Cup ties)
MOST CAPPED PLAYER
Joey Jones (Wales) 29   0For England: None
RECORD GOALSCORER IN A MATCH
A Livingstone 7 v Tranmere Rovers, Wartime Football League North, 25.10.1943   T Bamford 6 v New Brighton (h), 11-1, Div3N Cup, 1933-34   T H Lewis 5 v Crewe Alexandra (h) 7-0, Div 3N, 20.9.1930   T Bamford 5 v Carlisle United (h) 8-1, Div 3N, 17.3.1934
RECORD LEAGUE GOALSCORER IN A SEASON
Tommy Bamford, 44, Div 3N, 1933-34
RECORD LEAGUE GOALSCORER IN A CAREER
Tommy Bamford, 175, 1929-35
OLDEST PLAYER IN A LEAGUE MATCH
W. Lot Jones 46 years, 1921-22
YOUNGEST PLAYER IN A LEAGUE MATCH
Ken Roberts 15 years 158 days v Bradford Park Avenue, 1.9.1951
Ken shares this record with Albert Geldard (Bradford P.A.) as the two youngest players to play in the Football League.

PREVIOUS MANAGERS

1924-26 Charles Hewitt   1929-31 Jack Baynes   R Burkinshaw Dec 1931-Jan 1932   1932-36 Ernest Blackburn   Captain Logan 1937-38   1939-42Tommy Morgan   1942-49 Tom W Williams   C Lloyd March-May 1949   1949-50 Leslie J McDowall   1951-54 Peter Jackson   1954-57 Clifford Lloyd   1957-59 John Love   1960-61 Billy Morris   1961-65 Ken Barnes   1965-66 Billy Morris   1966-67Jack Rowley   1967 Cliff Lloyd   1967-8 Alvan Williams   1968-77 John Neal   1977-81 Arfon Griffiths   1981-82 Mel Sutton   1982-85 Bobby Roberts   Dixie McNeil 1985-89   Brian Flynn 1989-

ADDITIONAL INFORMATION
Previous Names: Wrexham Athletic 1881-82.
Wrexham Olympic 1884-88.

Previous Leagues: The Combination, Birmingham League

Club colours: Red shirts, white socks with red trim, red socks.
Change colours: Old gold shirts, black shorts with gold trim, black socks.
Reserves League: Pontins Central League Division 3.

LONGEST LEAGUE RUNS

of undefeated matches:	16 (1966)	of league matches w/out a win:	14 (1923-24, 1950)
of undefeated home matches:	38 (1969-70)	of undefeated away matches:	9 (1992-93)
without home win:	10 (1980-81)	without an away win:	31 (1982-83)
of league wins:	7 (1961, 1978)	of home wins:	13 (19832-33)
of league defeats:	9 (1963)	of away wins:	7 (1961)

THE MANAGER

BRIAN FLYNN . . . . appointed November 1989.

PREVIOUS CLUBS
As Manager. . . . . None.
As Asst.Man/Coach . . . . None.
As a player. . . . . Burnley, Leeds Utd, Cardiff City, Doncaster Rovers, Bury, Limerick, Doncaster Rovers.

HONOURS
As a Manager . . . . Promotion to Division 2, 1992-93.
As a Player. . . . . 66 full caps, 2 U23 and Schools honours for Wales.

WREXHAM

PLAYERS NAME Honours	Ht	Wt	Birthdate	Birthplace Transfers	Contract Date	Clubs	League	L/Cup	FA Cup	Other	Lge	L/C	FAC	Oth
G O A L K E E P E R S														
Cartwright Mark	6.1	12.5	13/01/73	Chester		York City								
				Free	17/08/91	Stockport County								
					05/03/94	Wrexham								
Marriott Andrew	6.1	13.3	11/10/70	Sutton-in-Ashfield	22/10/88	Arsenal								
E: u21.1, Y.2,S. FLge u18.1.				£50000	20/06/89	Nottingham Forest	11	1		1				
Div.4'92. FMC'92.				Loan	06/09/89	W.B.A.	3							
				Loan	29/12/89	Blackburn Rovers	2							
				Loan	21/03/90	Colchester United	10							
				Loan	29/08/91	Burnley	15			2				
				£200000	08/10/93	Wrexham	128	6	10	19				
D E F E N D E R S														
Brace Deryn	5.9	10.8	15/03/75	Haverfordwest	06/07/93	Norwich City								
W: u21.5, Y.				Free	28/04/94	Wrexham	27+4	1	1	5	1			
Carey Brian P	6.3	13.9	31/05/68	Cork		Cork City								
EI: 3, u21.1				£100000	02/09/89	Manchester United								
				Loan	17/01/91	Wrexham	3							
				Loan	24/12/91	Wrexham	13	3	3	1				
				£250000	16/07/93	Leicester City	51+7	3	0+1	4	1			
				£100000	08/07/96	Wrexham								
Hardy Phil	5.10	10.2	09/04/73	Ellesmere Port	24/11/90	Wrexham	217+1	15	17	31				
E: u21.3.														
Humes Tony	5.11	11.0	19/03/66	Blyth	26/05/83	Ipswich Town	107+13	6	4	10	10		1	1
				£40000	27/03/92	Wrexham	125+4	7	10	13	4			
Jones Barry	6.0	12.10	30/06/70	Liverpool		Prescot Cables								
					19/01/89	Liverpool				0+1				
				Free	10/07/92	Wrexham	158+1	12	9	21	4	1		
McGregor Mark	5.10	10.5	16/02/77	Chester		Wrexham	28+5		2+1	3	1			
Thomas Andy						Wrexham (T)				1				
Williams Scott	6.0	11.0	07/08/74	Bangor	02/07/93	Wrexham	20+5	1		2+2				
M I D F I E L D														
Brammer David	5.9	11.0	28/02/75	Bromborough	02/07/93	Wrexham	41+8	4	3	5+2	5			
Coady Lewis	6.1	11.1	20/09/76	Liverpool	01/05/96	Wrexham								
Cross Jonathan	5.10	11.4	02/03/75	Wallasey	15/11/92	Wrexham	79+20	4+2	4+1	9+5	10	1	1	1
Owen Gareth	5.10	11.4	21/10/71	Chester	06/07/90	Wrexham	162+29	6+1	12+2	28+1	20			
W: u21.8.														
Phillips Wayne	5.10	11.0	15/12/70	Bangor	23/08/89	Wrexham	144+17	13+1	10+2	18+5	10		1	1
W: B.1.														
Roberts Neil						Wrexham (T)								
Ward Peter	5.10	11.7	15/10/64	Durham		Chester-Le-Street								
					07/01/87	Huddersfield Town	24+13	1+1	2	1	2			
				Free	20/07/89	Rochdale	83+1	5	7	5	10	1		
					06/06/91	Stockport County	140+2	8	7	26	10	1		6
				Free	01/06/95	Wrexham	33+1	1	4	1	6			1
F O R W A R D S														
Chalk Martyn	5.6	10.0	30/08/69	Louth		Louth United								
				£10000	23/01/90	Derby County	4+3		3	0+1	1		1	
				£40000	30/06/94	Stockport County	24+9	3	1	1+1	6	1		
					01/08/95	Wrexham	19				4			
Connolly Karl	6.1	12.6	09/02/70	Prescot	08/05/91	Wrexham	201+7	14	16	23+1	47	2	4	5
Futcher Steve						Wrexham (T)				2				
Hughes Bryan	5.9	10.0	19/06/76	Liverpool		Wrexham	51+20	2	4+3	14	9		1	3
Morris Steve	5.10	11.01	13/05/76	Liverpool		Liverpool								
				Free	05/09/94	Wrexham	14+11	1+1	1	3+2	5			
Russell Kevin J	5.8	10.10	06/12/66	Brighton		Brighton & H.A.								
E: Y.6. Div.2'93.				£10000	17/07/87	Wrexham	84	4	4	8	43	1		3
				Free	09/10/87	Portsmouth	3+1	0+1	0+1	1+1	1			
				£175000	20/06/89	Leicester City	24+19	0+1	1	5	10			2
				Loan	06/09/90	Peterborough Utd	7				3			
				Loan	17/01/91	Cardiff City	3							
				Loan	07/11/91	Hereford United	3		1		2			
				Loan	02/01/92	Stoke City	5			1				
				£95000	16/07/92	Stoke City	30+10	3	2	4+1	5			1
				£150000	28/06/93	Burnley	26+2	4	4	1	6	1		1
				£125000	03/03/94	Bournemouth	17			1	1			
				£60000	24/02/95	Notts County	9+2							
				£60000	01/06/95	Wrexham	37+3	2	3	2	7	1		
Skinner Craig	5.10	11.0	21/10/70	Heywood	13/06/89	Blackburn Rovers	11+5	0+1	1	3				1
					21/08/92	Plymouth Argyle	42+11	4	5+2	3+1	3		1	
				£50000	01/06/95	Wrexham	21+2	1	3	2	3			
Watkin Stephen	5.10	11.0	16/06/71	Wrexham	24/07/89	Wrexham	143+27	9+2	11+3	17+5	47	4	9	4
W: B.2.														

RACECOURSE GROUND
Mold Road, Wrexham
Tel: 01978 262 129

Capacity...11,500
Covered Standing...6,500
Seating...5,026

First game...v Past & Present Grove Park School, 19.10.1872.
First floodlit game...v Swindon Town (h), Div.3, 30.09.1959.

ATTENDANCES
Highest...34,445 v Manchester United, FA Cup 4th Round, 26.1.1991.
Lowest...627 v Mansfield Town, AMC Preliminary Round, 15.10.1991.

OTHER GROUNDS.............................. Rhosddu Recreation Ground 1880-83. Grosvenor Road 1884.

MATCHDAY TICKET PRICES

Yall Stand (Centre)...................... £10
Yall Stand (Wings)....................... £9
Juv/OAP.............................. £7

Terraces................................ £7
Juv/OAP.............................. £5

Away Supporters
Marston's Stand............. £10/£7 (Juv/OAP)
Marston's Paddock............ £7/£5 (Juv/OAP)

Ticket office Telephone no........ 01978 262 129

CLUBCALL
0898 12 16 42
Calls cost 39p per minute cheap rate and 49p per
minute at all other times.
Call costings correct at time of going to press.

HOW TO GET TO THE GROUND

From the North and West
Use A483 and Wrexham bypass until junction with A541, then branch left and at roundabout follow signs to Wrexham into Mold Road for Wrexham FC.

From the East and South
Follow signs into Wrexham on A543 or A525 then follow signs A541 into Mold Road for Wrexham FC.

Car Parking
Parking at St Marks, Bodhyfryd Square, Eagles Meadow, Old Guild Hall, Hill Street, Holt Street and Town Hall (Hill Street.

Nearest Railway Station
Wrexham General.

MATCHDAY PROGRAMME

Programme Editor.............. D Roberts, G Parry, and P Jones.

Number of pages...................................... 32.

Price.. £1.40.

Subscriptions.......... £49.50 for all 1st team home programmes.
.... £100 for home and away.

Local Newspapers.......... Wrexham Evening Leader, Daily Post,
.... Wrexham Weekly Leader, Shropshire Star.

Local Radio Stations...... Radio City, Marcher Sound, Radio Clwyd,
.... BBC Radio Wales, B.B.C. Radio Cymru.

WYCOMBE WANDERERS
(The Chairboys)
NATIONWIDE LEAGUE DIVISION 2
SPONSORED BY: VERCO OFFICE FURNITURE LTD

Back row (L-R): Jason Soloman, Sean Stevens, Terry Howard, Paul Hyde, Terry Evans, Chuck Moussadik, Matt Crossley, Simon Stapleton, Gary Patterson. **Middle Row:** Dave Jones (Physio), Jim Melvin (Youth Dev. Officer), Miquel Desouza, Tony Hemmings, Keith Ryan, Jason Cousins, Dave Carroll, Steve Thompson, David Kemp (Assistant Manager), Neil Smillie (Youth Team Manager).
Front Row: Steve Brown, Mickey Bell, Paul Hardyman, Alan Smith (Manager), Anthony Clark, Simon Garner, Steve McGavin.

WYCOMBE WANDERERS
FORMED IN 1884
TURNED PROFESSIONAL IN 1974
LTD COMPANY IN 1980

PATRON: J Adams
PRESIDENT: M E Seymour
CHAIRMAN: I L Beeks
DIRECTORS
G Cox, B R Lee, A Parry, G Peart,
G Richards, A Thibault
SECRETARY
John Reardon
COMMERCIAL MANAGER
Mark Austin, BA

MANAGER: Alan Smith
ASSISTANT MANAGER: David Kemp

YOUTH TEAM MANAGER
Neil Smillie
PHYSIOTHERAPIST
Dave Jones

STATISTICIAN FOR THE DIRECTORY
Dave Finch

Following Martin O'Neill was always going to be difficult, and so it proved for new manager Alan Smith in a season of discontent. Finishing 12th in Division Two in only the third season in the Football League is a fine achievement, but unfortunately is not good enough for sections of the Wycombe faithful who have been spoilt with success since the move to Adams park. Their disapproval was reflected in a drop of nearly 1,300 in the average gate.

Admittedly, the league campaign was an inconsistent one with performances going from poor to brilliant then back again in the space of a few days. It started with a rash of dismissals as the players struggled at first to come to terms with new training methods. Then an unbeaten run of 14 games - a Football League record for the club - took them to fourth place in November. However, by January they were down to 12th, where they were to finish - although hopes of a play-off place were raised during a purple patch in March. Three consecutive defeats put paid to this.

The cup competitions saw early exits in both FA Cup and Auto Windscreens Shield, while the second round of the Coca-Cola Cup was reached. After giving Manchester City a difficult time at Adams Park, they were soundly beaten, but not disgraced, at Maine Road.

Despite the general gloom, there were several plusses. Dave Carroll showed superb form and was an all-round better player in his eighth season at the club and a deserving winner of the supporters' Player of the Year. Runner-up Mickey Bell, was converted from a winger to one of the best left-backs in the division. There was also the welcome return from long-term injury of Keith Ryan and the emergence of Gary Patterson in midfield. His wonderful goal in the FA Cup against Gillingham was shown live on television.

The most pleasing aspect, though, has been the form of the youth team who, in their first season as full-time YTS boys, finished fourth in the league. Already two players, Damian Markman and Graham Hall, have been offered professional terms for next season.

Last, but not least, was the commencement of the building of a new £1.8 million, 5,000-seater two-tier stand to replace the Woodland Terrace.

The long-term future certainly looks good.

DAVE FINCH

WYCOMBE WANDERERS

League: 12th   FA Cup: 1st Rnd   Coca-Cola Cup: 2nd Rnd   Auto Windscreen Shield: 1st Rnd

M	DATE	COMP	VEN	OPPONENTS	RESULT	HT	LP	GOAL SCORERS/GOAL TIMES	ATT.
1	A 12	EL	H	Crewe Alexandra	D 1-1	0-1	10	McGavin 72(pen)	5281
2	15	CC 1/1	H	Leyton Orient	W 3-0	2-0		Desouza 11, 20, Crossley 76	3310
3	19	EL	A	Notts County	L 0-2	0-0	16		(5552)
4	22	CC 1/2	A	Leyton Orient	L 0-2	0-1			(2478)
5	26	EL	H	Bournemouth	L 1-2	0-2	22	Desouza 50	4749
6	29	EL	A	Brighton & H.A.	W 2-1	1-1	14	Desouza 29, 71	5360
7	S 2	EL	A	Bradford City	W 4-0	1-0	10	Desouza 36, 75, 85, Castledine 49	(9974)
8	9	EL	H	Peterborough United	D 1-1	1-0	11	Garner 16	5637
9	12	EL	H	Chesterfield	W 1-0	1-0	6	Castledine 37	3617
10	16	EL	A	Stockport County	D 1-1	1-1	7	Castledine 27	(5588)
11	19	CC 2/1	H	Manchester City	D 0-0	0-0			7443
12	23	EL	H	Wrexham	D 1-1	1-1	10	Desouza 8	4649
13	30	EL	A	Bristol City	D 0-0	0-0	10		(5564)
14	O 4	CC 2/2	A	Manchester City	L 0-4	0-2			(11474)
15	7	EL	A	Burnley	D 1-1	0-1	11	Williams 65	8279
16	10	AWS 1	H	Fulham	D 1-1	1-1		Howard 23	2726
17	14	EL	H	Walsall	W 1-0	1-0	10	Carroll 36	4724
18	21	EL	A	Oxford United	W 4-1	3-0	6	Farrell 17, Howard 32, Desouza 36, McGavin 79(pen)	(7731)
19	28	EL	H	Hull City	D 2-2	0-1	7	Evans 65, Bell 76	5021
20	31	EL	H	York City	W 2-1	0-0	5	Desouza 57(pen), Garner 71	4038
21	N 4	EL	A	Swansea City	W 2-1	0-0	4	Garner 62, Carroll 84	(2809)
22	7	AWS 1/2	A	Walsall	L 0-5	0-4			(2592)
23	13	FAC 1	H	Gillingham	D 1-1	0-0		Patterson 56	5064
24	18	EL	H	Bristol Rovers	D 1-1	1-0	4	Farrell 22	4886
25	21	FAC 1R	A	Gillingham	L 0-1	0-1			(8585)
26	26	EL	A	Carlisle United	L 2-4	1-3	5	Carroll 13, 83	(4459)
27	D 9	EL	A	Wrexham	L 0-1	0-1	8		(3468)
28	16	EL	H	Bristol City	D 1-1	1-0	9	Blissett 12	4020
29	23	EL	H	Shrewsbury Town	W 2-0	1-0	8	Blissett 3, Howard 81	4131
30	26	EL	A	Swindon Town	D 0-0	0-0	8		(12976)
31	J 13	EL	H	Notts County	D 1-1	0-0	4	Williams 89	4980
32	20	EL	A	Crewe Alexandra	L 0-2	0-2	11		(4150)
33	23	EL	A	Blackpool	D 1-1	1-1	11	Desouza 76	(3887)
34	30	EL	A	Brentford	L 0-1	0-0	12		(4616)
35	F 3	EL	A	Bournemouth	W 3-2	1-2	7	Williams 15, 87, Patterson 52	(4447)
36	10	EL	H	Blackpool	L 0-1	0-1	9		5285
37	17	EL	A	Chesterfield	L 1-3	0-3	13	Desouza 62	(4571)
38	24	EL	H	Stockport County	W 4-1	3-0	10	Williams 5, 9, 54 (3), Carroll 35	4246
39	27	EL	A	Peterborough United	L 0-3	0-3	12		(3670)
40	M 2	EL	H	Swindon Town	L 1-2	0-2	12	Desouza 58	6457
41	6	EL	H	Brighton & H.A.	L 0-2	0-0	12		3466
42	9	EL	A	Shrewsbury Town	D 1-1	1-1	12	Ryan 11	(2866)
43	16	EL	H	Brentford	W 2-1	1-1	12	Carroll 24, Evans 61	4912
44	23	EL	A	Rotherham United	D 0-0	0-0	12		(2775)
45	26	EL	H	Bradford City	W 5-2	2-1	12	Desouza 23, 64, 74 (3), Ryan 35, Evans 82	3021
46	30	EL	H	Burnley	W 4-1	2-0	11	Ryan 12, 31, Desouza 81, Farrell 90	4921
47	A 2	EL	A	Walsall	W 1-0	0-0	12	Carroll 70(pen)	(3252)
48	6	EL	A	Hull City	L 2-4	0-3		Carroll 50(pen), Desouza 84	(3065)
49	8	EL	H	Oxford United	L 0-3	0-1	11		6727
50	13	EL	A	York City	L 1-2	1-1	12	Skiverton 43	(3113)
51	16	EL	H	Rotherham United	D 1-1	0-1	11	Desouza 81	2836
52	20	EL	H	Swansea City	L 0-1	0-0	11		3672
53	27	EL	H	Carlisle United	W 4-0	1-0	12	Crossley 36, Williams 54, Farrell 62, 75	3964
54	M 4	EL	A	Bristol Rovers	L 1-2	0-1	12	Carroll 73	(6621)

Best Home League Attendance: 6727 v Oxford United   Smallest: 2836 v Rotherham United   Average: 4575

Goal Scorers:
EL(63): Desouza(18),Carroll(9),Williams(8),Farrell(5),Ryan(4),Garner(3),Evans(3),Castledine(3),Blissett(2),Howard(2),McGavin(2),Patterson(1),Bell(1),Crossley(1),Skiverton(1)
CC(3): Desouza(2),Crossley(1)
FAC(1): Patterson(1)
AWS(1): Howard(1)

510

1995-96

(F) Bell	(F) Bissett	(M) Brown	(M) Carroll	(M) Castledine	(F) Clarke	(D) Cousins	(D) Crossley	(F) Desouza	(G) Dykstra	(D) Evans	(F) Farrell	(D) Foran	(F) Garner	(D) Hardyman	(F) Hemmings	(D) Howard	(G) Hyde	(M) Lawrence	(F) McGavin	(M) McGorry	(G) Moussaddik	(M) Patterson	(G) Roberts	(M) Rowbotham	(M) Ryan	(D) Skiverton	(D) Soloman	(F) Williams		
X		X	X1			X	X	X2				X	S1	X	S	S2	X		X									X	A.Butler	1
X		X	X			X	X	X1				X	S1	S	X	S1	S	X				X1							G.Pooley	2
X1		X	X			X	X	X				X			X	S1	S3		X3	X2	S2						X2		S.Mathieson	3
		X	X			X	X	X1	X	X		X	S3	S1	X	X		X3	X2	S2									I.Hemley	4
X3		X	X	X		X		X				X	S1	X1	X3	X	X		X2	S2							X		G.Barber	5
S1		X	X	X	X1		X					X	X2	X		X	X		S2								X		P.Taylor	6
X		X	X	X			X	X				X1	X		X	X	X		S1			S					X		K.Breen	7
X2		X	X	X			X	X				X	X1		S2	X			S1	S3	X	X3					X		R.Harris	8
S		X	X			X1	X				X		S	X		X	X		X	S1		X		X				X	C.Wilkes	9
		X	X			X	X	X			X			X		X	X		S	S		X		X		S	X	A.Leake	10
		X	X				X	X			X			X		X	X		S	S		X		X		S	X	M.Pierce	11
		X	X	X1		X		X			X			X		X	X		S1			S		X		S	X	B.Knight	12
S		X	X				X	X			X			X		X	X		S1	S		X		X			X1	M.J.Brandwood	13
		X1	X				X	X			X			X		X	X		S1		S	X		X		S	X	K.Burge	14
S		X	X				X	X			X			X		X	X		X			S1		X		S	X1	R.Poulain	15
S1		X	X				X	X			X			X1		X	X		X			S				S	X	A.D'Urso	16
X		X	X		S	X		X			X					X	X		X			S1		X		S	X1	D.Orr	17
X		X	X		S2	X		X2		S	X					X	X		X			S1		X			X1	S.Bennett	18
X		X1	X			X		X			X		S2	X	S3	X	X		X3			S1		X			X	J.Lloyd	19
X		X	X		S2	X		X2		X	X			X		X	X		S			S1		X			X1	I.Hemley	20
X		X	X			X		X			X		X2			X	X		S2			S1		X		S	X1	A.G.Wiley	21
X		X	X2			X		X			X		X1			X	X		S2			S1		X		S	X	A.Butler	22
X		X	X			X		X			X					X	X		S			X		X		S	S	D.Gallagher	23
X		X	X			X		X			X		X2			X	X		S2			X1		X		S	S1	K.Leach	24
X		X	X			X		X			X		S1			X	X		S2			X1		X		S	X2	F.Stretton	25
X		X3	X		S2	X		X			X		X2			X			S3			X1		X				T.Lunt	26
X	X		X			X		X		X	X	S1	X		X			X1	X	X2						S	S2	K.Breen	27
X	X		X			X		X		X	X	X1			X			S1	S	X	X							P.Taylor	28
X	X		X					X2		X	X	S1	X		X			X1	X	X	X				S2	S		J.Rushton	29
X	X	X						S		X	X	S			X			X	X	X	X				S			C.Wilkes	30
X		X	X					X1		X	X				X			X2	X	X	X	S1		S2				E.Lomas	31
X		X1	X					X2		X	X				X	S3		X	X	X	X3	S1		S2				S.Baines	32
X		X	X			S		X2		X	X				X			X1	X	X	X	S2		X2				I.Cruikshank	33
X		X	X			X2		X		X	X				X			X1	X	X	X	S1		S2				G.R.Pooley	34
X		X	X			X		S1		X	S	S			X1			X	X	X	X			X			R.Poulaine	35
X		X	X			X		X	S1		X	S			S			X	X	X	X1			X			G.Singh	36
X		X	X1			X		X	S1		X	S2			S			X	X	X	X2			X			W.C.Burns	37
X		X	X			X		X1		X	X				X			S		X	X	S1		S			X	A.D'Urso	38
X		X	X			X		X		X	X				X			X1	X	X				X			X	M.Bailey	39
X		X	X			X		X2		X	X1		S1		X			S	X			X					X	K.Breen	40
X		X	X			X		X		S1	X		S		X			X1	X			S		X			X	M.J.Brandwood	41
X		X				X		S1	X	X		S		X			X		X		S	X		X		X	A.Leake	42
X		X				X		S	X	X	S		X		X			X		X		S	X		X1		K.A.Leach	43
X		X				X		S1	X	X	S		X		X			X		X		S	X		X1		G.Cain	44
X		X				X		X1	X	X	S1		X		X			X		X		S	X			X	I.Hemley	45
X		X				X		X1	X	X	S		S1		X			X		X		S	X			X	D.Furnandiz	46
X1		X	X			X		X	X	X	S		S1		X			X		X			X			X	F.G.Stretton	47
X		X	X			X		X1	X	X	S		S	X2	X			X1		X		X			S2	X	S.Mathieson	48
X		X	X		X	X	X	X	S		S				X			X1		X		X				S1	E.Wolstenholme	49
X		X	X		X		X	X	X	S2	S			S1			X2		X		X	X			X1	J.Kirkby	50
X		X	X				X	X	X	S1	S		X1				X		X		X	X			X	B.Gifford	51
X		X	X				X	X	X	X	S						X		X		X	X1		B.Knight	52
X1		X				X		X	X	X	S1			S			X		X	X	S		X		A.Wiley	53
X		X				X	S1	X	X	X1				S			X		X	X	S		X	M.Fletcher	54

40	4	38	46	7	1	28	12	38	13	26	27	5	8	12	0	36	17	1	22	0	1	31	15	27	18	3	6	23	EL Appearances	
1	0	0	0	0	2	2	0	5	0	2	6	0	5	3	3	3	0	2	9	4	0	6	0	0	5	1	1	6	EL Sub Appearances	
1	0	4	4	0	0	3	3	4	0	0	2	2	0+2	4	0+2	3	4	0	2	2	0	2	0	0	0	0	0	2	CC Appearances	
2	0	2	2	0	0	2	0	2	0	0	2	0	1+1	0	0	2	2	0	2	0	0+1	2	0	2	0	0	0	1	FAC Appearances	
1+1	0	2	2	0	0	2	0	2	0	0	2	0	1	1	0	2	2	0	1+1	0	0	2	0	1	0	0	0	2	AWS Appearances	

Also Played: (M) Hall S(52). (M) Markman S2(41), S1(52). (M) Stapleton S(40,51), X(50). (D) Stevens S(6). (M) Thompson S(7).

CLUB RECORDS

RECORD LEAGUE VICTORY
4-0 v Scarborough (h), Division 3, 2.11.1993
Most Goals Scored in a Cup Tie: 15-1 v Witney Town (h), FA Cup
Prelim Rnd replay,14.9.1955
(First Class) 5-0 v Hitchin Town (a), Second Round, 3.12.1994.
RECORD LEAGUE DEFEAT
2-5 v Colchester United (h) Division 3, 18.9.1993; 0-3 v Mansfield
Town, Division 3, 12.2.1994. 1-4 v Stockport (a) Div.2 24.9.94. 1-4 v
Wrexham (a) Div.2, 1.11.94. 0-3 v Mansfield (a) Div.3, 12.2.94.
0-3 v Birmingham (h) Div.2, 18.3.95.
Record Cup Defeat: 0-8 v Reading (h), FA Cup 1st Qualifying Rnd,
28.10.1899 (First Class) 1-5 v Watford (a), FA Cup 2nd Rnd,
5.12.1959

MOST LEAGUE POINTS
(3pts for win) 78, Division 2 1994-95

MOST LEAGUE GOALS
67, Division 3 1993-94

RECORD TRANSFER FEE RECEIVED
£375,000 from Swindon for Keith Scott, November 1993
RECORD TRANSFER FEE PAID
£140,000 to Birmingham City for Steve McGavin, March 1995.

BEST PERFORMANCES
League: 6th Division 2 1994-95
FA Cup: 3rd Round 1974-75,1985-86, 1993-94
League Cup: 2nd Round 1993-94

HONOURS: Third Division Play-off Winners 1993-94; GM Vauxhall
Conference Champions 1992-93; F.A. Amateur Cup Winners 1930-
31; F.A. Trophy Winners1990-91, 1992-93; Isthmian League
Champions 1955-56, 1956-57, 1970-71, 1971-72, 1973-74, 1974-
75, 1982-83, 1986-87; Spartan League Champions 1919-20,1920-
21; Bob Lord Trophy Winners 1991-92; Anglo-Italian Trophy
Winners1975-76; Conference Shield Winners 1991-92, 1992-93,
1993-94; Hitachi(League) Cup Winners 1984-85; Berks & Bucks
Senior Cup Winners 24 times

LEAGUE CAREER
Promoted to Division 3 1992-93   Promoted to Division 2 1993-94

INDIVIDUAL CLUB RECORDS

MOST APPEARANCES FOR CLUB
Paul Hyde 59 (1993-94)
MOST CAPPED PLAYER
(England Semi-Pro.) Larry Pritchard 26 (1970-74)
RECORD LEAGUE GOALSCORER IN A SEASON
Miquel DeSouza: 20 (1995-96) 18 League 2 League Cup.
RECORD LEAGUE GOALSCORER IN A CAREER
20 - Somon Garner (13 League, 3 FAC, 4 Others) 1993-95.
20 - Miquel DeSouza (18 League 2 League Cup) 1995-96.
MOST GOALS IN A MATCH
3 - Simon Garner v Hitchin Town (a), FAC 2nd Rnd, 3.12.1994.
3 - Miquel DeSouza v Bradford (a) 2.9.95, Bradford (h) 26.3.96.

OLDEST PLAYER IN A LEAGUE MATCH
Cyrille Regis, 37 years 86 days v Leyton Orient (a) Div.2, 6.5.1995.
YOUNGEST PLAYER IN A LEAGUE MATCH
Anthony Clark, 18 years 29 days v Leyton Orient (a) Div.2, 6.5.1995.

PREVIOUS MANAGERS

First coach appointed 1951: (Coaches) 1951-52 James McCormack
1952-61 Sid Cann   1961-62 Graham Adams   1962-64 Don Welsh
1964-68 Barry Darvill   (Managers): 1969-76 Brian Lee   1976-77
Ted Powell   1977-78 John Reardon   1978-80 Andy Williams
1980-84 Mike Keen   1984-86 Paul Bence   1986-87 Alan Gane
1987-88 Peter Suddaby   1988-90 Jim Kelman   1990-95 Martin
O'Neill

ADDITIONAL INFORMATION
Previous League: 1896-1908 Southern Div 2; 1898-99 Bucks &
Contiguous Counties;1901-03 Berks & Bucks Senior; 1908-14 Great
Western Suburban; 1919-21 Spartan;1921-85 Isthmian; 1985-86
Gola; 1986-87 Vauxhall-Opel; 1987-93 GM Vauxhall Conference
Club Colours: Sky & navy striped quarters, sky shorts.
Change Colours: All white.

Reserves League: Springheath Print Capital League
Youth: South East Counties Division Two

LONGEST LEAGUE RUNS

of undefeated matches:	14 (19.8.95 - 26.11.95)	of league matches w/out a win:	8 (21.2.1995 - 25.3.1995)
of undefeated home matches:	11 (1.10.1994 - 4.3.1995)	of undefeated away matches:	9 (14.8.1993 - 27.11.1993)
without home win: 3 (19.4.94-7.5.94, 26.12.95-4.2.95,4.3.95-25.3.95)		without an away win:	9 (11.2.1995 - 19.4.1995)
of league wins:	4 (3.1.1994-25-1.1994, 26.2.1994-19.3.1994)	of home wins:	6 (2.11.1993 - 25.1.1994)
of league defeats:	3 (29.1.1994 - 19.2.1994)	of away wins:	3 (31.8.1993 - 2.10.1993, 26.2.1994 - 19.3.1994)

THE MANAGER

ALAN SMITH . . . . appointed June 1995.

PREVIOUS CLUBS
As Manager . . . . Dulwich Hamlet, Crystal Palace.
As Asst.Man/Coach . . . . Wimbledon (twice), Crystal Palace.
As a player . . . . Brentford.

HONOURS
As a Manager . . . . Crystal Palace: Division 1 Champions 1993-94.
As a Player . . . . None.

WYCOMBE WANDERERS

PLAYERS NAME Honours	Ht	Wt	Birthdate	Birthplace Transfers	Contract Date	Clubs	League	L/Cup	FA Cup	Other	Lge	L/C	FAC	Oth
G O A L K E E P E R S														
Cheesewright John	6.0	11.5	12.01.73	Romford		Tottenham H. (T)								
ree (28/03/91) Southend Utd				Free	28/11/91	Birmingham City	1			1				
ree (07/01/94) Kingsbury Town, via Redbridge, Cobh Ramblers				Free	Free	Braintree Town								
				£10000	13/01/94	Colchester United	40	1	3	2				
				Free	05/06/96	Wycombe Wand.								
Parkin Brian	6.1	12.0	12/10/65	Birkenhead	31/03/83	Oldham Athletic	6	2						
Div.3'90.				Free	30/11/84	Crewe Alexandra	98	7	2	6				
				Free	01/07/88	Crystal Palace	20	3		2				
				Free	11/11/89	Bristol Rovers	241	15	12	23				
				Free		Wycombe Wand.								
D E F E N D E R S														
Cousins Jason	6.0	11.8	04/10/70	Hayes	13/07/89	Brentford	20+1	3		2+2				
MVC'93. FAT'93.				Free	01/07/91	Wycombe Wand.	106+2	9	13	12	3	1		
Crossley Matt	6.2	12.9	18/03/68	Basingstoke		Aldershot								
MVC'93. FAT'91'93.						Newbury Town								
a Overton Town, Basingstoke Town						Wycombe Wand.	86+1	7	14	9	3	1		
Evans Terry	6.4	12.0	12/04/65	Hillingdon Borough		Hillingdon Borough								
Div.3'92.				£5000	22/07/85	Brentford	228+1	15+1	17	23	23	4	2	1
				£40000	26/08/93	Wycombe Wand.	90+4	4	6	4	14	1		1
Hall Graham						Wycombe Wand. (T)								
McCarthy Paul	6.0	13.6	04/08/71	Cork	26/04/89	Brighton & H.A. (T)	180+1	11	13	12	6	1		1
I: u21.10.				£100000	04/07/96	Wycombe Wand.								
Skiverton Terry	5.11	12.4	29/06/75	London	19/05/93	Chelsea								
				Loan	17/02/95	Wycombe Wand.	8+2							
				Free	26/03/96	Wycombe Wand.	3+1			1				
M I D F I E L D														
Brown Stephen	5.10	10.12	06/07/66	Northampton	11/08/83	Northampton Town	14+1			3				
ree (01/08/84) Irthlingborough D.				Free	21/07/89	Northampton Town	145+13	10	12	10+1	19	1	2	1
				£40000	09/02/94	Wycombe Wand.	125+3	7+1	8	3+1	8			
Carroll Dave	6.0	12.0	20/09/66	Paisley		Ruislip Manor								
S. GMVC'93. FAT'91'93.				£6000		Wycombe Wand.	87	8	14	10	15		3	3
Lawrence Matthew	5.10		19/06/74	Northampton		Grays Athletic								
						Wycombe Wand.	1+2							
McGorry Brian	5.10	12.8	16/04/70	Liverpool		Weymouth								
				£30000	13/08/91	Bournemouth	56+5	7	7+3	5	11		2	1
				£60000	10/02/94	Peterborough Utd	44+8	0+2	2	2	6			
				Free	18/08/95	Wycombe Wand.	0+4	1						
Patterson Gary	6.1	12.5	27/10/72	Newcastle	17/07/91	Notts County								
Div.3'94.				Free	02/07/93	Shrewsbury Town	52+5	5	4	3	2			
				£75000	09/12/94	Wycombe Wand.	40+10	2	2	0+1	2		1	
Rowbotham Jason	5.9	11.0	03/01/69	Cardiff	05/07/91	Plymouth Argyle	8+1	0+1						
				Loan	01/10/91	Yeovil Town								
a Penz (Free)				Free	26/03/92	Shrewsbury Town								
					1993/94	Raith Rovers	56				1			
				Free		Wycombe Wand.	27	2	2	1				
Ryan Keith	6.0	11.7	25/06/70	Northampton		Berkhamsted								
MVC'93. FAT'91'93.						Wycombe Wand.	84+5	6	6+3	10+1	9	1	3	
F O R W A R D S														
Bell Michael	5.8	10.4	15/11/71	Newcastle	01/07/90	Northampton Town	133+20	7+1	5	9+2	10		1	1
					21/10/94	Wycombe Wand.	71+1	1	5	2+1	4		2	
Clarke Anthony	5.7		07/04/77	London	01/08/94	Wycombe Wand.	1+2							
				Loan	19/01/96	Hitchin								
Desouza Juan	5.10	11.0	11/02/70	Newham	04/07/89	Charlton Athletic								
				Free	04/07/89	Bristol City								
a (01/08/91) Yeovil Town, (01/08/92) Dorchester					01/08/93	Dagenham & Red.								
				£25000	01/02/94	Birmingham City	5+10	2		1				
				Loan	25/11/94	Bury	2+1							
Ban (25/11/94) Wycombe Wand.1 Lge App 2gls.				£100000	03/02/95	Wycombe Wand.	43+6	4	2	2	22	2		
Farrell David	5.11	11.2	11/11/71	Birmingham		Redditch								
				£45000	06/01/92	Aston Villa	5+1	2						
				Loan	25/01/93	Scunthorpe United	4+1			2	1			
				£100000	14/09/95	Wycombe Wand.	27+6	2	2	2	5			
McGavin Steve	5.10	10.10	24/01/69	North Walsham		Ipswich Town								
MVC'92. FAT'92.						Sudbury Town								
				£10000	28/07/92	Colchester United	55+3	2	6	4	17	2		
				£150000	07/01/94	Birmingham City	6+2				1			
				£175000	20/03/95	Wycombe Wand.	34+9	2+1	0+1	1+1	4			
Markman Damien						Wycombe Wand. (T)								
Williams John	6.2	12.4	11/05/68	Birmingham		Cradley Town								
				£5000	19/08/91	Swansea City	36+3	2	3	1	11			
				£250000	01/07/92	Coventry City	66+14	4	2		11			
				Loan	07/09/94	Notts County	3+2				2			
				Loan	23/12/94	Stoke City	1+3							
				Loan	03/02/95	Swansea City	6+1				2			
				£150000	15/09/95	Wycombe Wand.	23+6	2	1	2	8			

ADAMS PARK
Hillbottom Road, High Wycombe, Buckinghamshire HP12 4HJ
Tel: 01494 472 100

Capacity 10,000
Covered Standing 2,198
Seating 7,802

First game .... 9.8.1990 v Nottingham Forest, friendly.
First floodlit game .... As above.

ATTENDANCES
Highest .... 9,007 v West Ham, FAC 3rd Rnd, 7.1.95.
Lowest .... 2,323 v Barnet, AMC 1st Rnd, 28.9.1993.

OTHER GROUNDS .... Loakes Park, Daws Hill Park, Spring Gardens, The Rye.

MATCHDAY TICKET PRICES

Main Stand £12

VP's £21.50

Away Supporters £12

New Woodlands Stand (Upper) . . . . £8-£12

Lower . . . . £8 (Adults) £5 (Conc.)

AXA Equity & Law Stand Terrace £7

Concessions £4.50

Ticket Office Telephone no 01494 44118

'RINGING THE BLUES'
0891 446 855

Calls cost 39p per minute cheap rate and 49p per
minute at all other times.
Call costings correct at time of going to press.

HOW TO GET TO THE GROUND

From all Directions
Exit M40 at junction 4 and take A4010 John Hall Way, sign posted Aylesbury.
Cross over three mini roundabouts into New Road, continue down hill to two mini
roundabouts at bottom. Turn sharp left at first into Lane End Road and turn right
at next mini roundabout into Hillbottom Road. Continue through industrial Estate
to Adams Park at end.

From Town Centre
Take A40 west, sign posted Aylesbury, after 1.5 miles turn left after second set of
traffic lights into Chapel Lane. Turn right and right again at mini roundabouts into
Lane End Road (then as above).

Car Parking
Club car park (340 spaces) or on adjacent Industrial Estate (some charging).

Nearest Railway Station
High Wycombe (01494 441 561)
London Marylebone to Birmingham Snow Hill Line - 2.9 miles from ground.
Special buses depart station at 1.55pm and 2.25pm Saturdays, 6.35pm and
7.05pm midweek, returning 10 minutes after the match.

MATCHDAY PROGRAMME

Programme Editor . . . . Adrian Wood (01865 63007)

Number of pages . . . . 44.

Price . . . . £1.50.

Subscriptions . . . . Apply to club.

Local Newspapers . . . Bucks Free Press, Wycombe/South Bucks Star.

Local Radio Stations. Chiltern Radio (Dunstable), Radio 210 (Reading)
. . . . Radio Berkshire (Reading), Eleven Seventy Am (High Wycombe).

YORK CITY
(The Minster Men)
NATIONWIDE LEAGUE DIVISION 2
SPONSORED BY: PORTAKABIN LTD

1996-97 - Back Row (L-R): Nigel Pepper, Neil Campbell, Paul Atkin, Tony Barras, Neil Tolson, Steve Tutill, John Sharples, Richard Cresswell, Adrian Randall. **Middle Row:** Jeff Miller (Physiotherapist), Glenn Naylor, Andy McMillan, Martin Reed, Andy Warrington, Wayne Osborn, Alan Pouton, Paul Stephenson, Paul Stancliffe (Assistant Manager). **Front Row:** Darren Williams, Gary Himsworth, Paddy Atkinson, Gary Bull, Alan Little (Manager), Steve Bushell, Scott Jordan, Wayne Hall, Graeme Murty.

YORK CITY
FORMED IN 1922
TURNED PROFESSIONAL IN 1922
LTD COMPANY IN 1922

CHAIRMAN: D M Craig OBE, JP, BSc, FICE
DIRECTORS
B A Houghton, C Webb, E B Swallow,
J E H Quickfall, F.C.A.
SECRETARY
Keith Usher (01904 624 447)
COMMERCIAL MANAGER
Mrs Maureen Leslie (01904 645 941)

MANAGER: Alan Little
ASSISTANT MANAGER: Paul Stancliffe
YOUTH TEAM MANAGER
Derek Bell
PHYSIOTHERAPIST
Jeff Miller

STATISTICIAN FOR THE DIRECTORY
David Batters

1995/96 was a roller coaster season for York City with highs and lows both on and off the field. In the final analysis they just managed to retain their 2nd Division status by winning at Brighton in the last match of their campaign which was extended by five days. This was a result of the original fixture , at the Goldstone Ground on April 27th, being abandoned following crowd disturbances.

City never really recovered from a bad start which saw them collect just two points from their opening eight games and they were the last Endsleigh club to record a victory. Four successive wins followed without conceding a goal but another slump in October, including a 1-6 thrashing at Peterborough, saw them back in the danger zone, where they hovered for the rest of the term.

Notable wins were recorded against Swindon Town and Oxford United and they gained their new customary victory at Blackpool and in the New Year they obtained a number of creditable away draws. On the other side of the coin though poor form at Bootham Crescent continued to be their downfall with a succession of disappointing performances. A home victory over Wycombe Wanderers, however, lifted them to 16th position in the table and apparent safety but four straight defeats without scoring prolonged the agony to the last gasp.

The highlight of the season was undoubtedly the remarkable success over Manchester United in the Coca-Cola Cup. City hit the national headlines with a sensational 3-0 win at Old Trafford in the first leg and they remained the only visiting team to win at United's stronghold in 1995/96. In a tense and thrilling return game at Bootham Crescent they held on to beat the Reds (Cantona et al) on aggregate and then put up a very creditable display at Queens Park Rangers in the next round. They also made good progress in the Auto Windscreen Shield before losing to eventual winners Rotherham United in the area semifinal.

No joy in the F.A. Cup, however, when they lost at home to Notts County and so fell at the first hurdle for the fourth successive season.

The Youth policy continues to flourish at Bootham Crescent, but if a serious promotion challenged is to be mounted in 1996/97 manager, Alan Little, will need to strengthen his senior squad. An experienced leader on the field plus more physical strength up front would appear to be the chief priorities. The close season capture of striker Neil Tolson from Bradford City, for £80,000 will hopefully resolve the latter problem.**DAVID BATTERS**

YORK CITY

League: 20th   FA Cup: 1st Rnd   Coca-Cola Cup: 3rd Rnd   Auto Windscreen Shield: Semi-Finals

M	DATE	COMP	VEN	OPPONENTS	RESULT	HT	LP	GOAL SCORERS/GOAL TIMES	ATT.
1	A 12	EL	H	Brentford	D 2-2	0-1	11	Baker 51, Barnes 80	3239
2	15	CC 1/1	A	Rochdale	L 1-2	0-1		Baker 68	(1390)
3	19	EL	A	Swindon Town	L 0-3	0-2	17		(7746)
4	22	CC 1/2	H	Rochdale	W 5-1	1-0		Baker 2, Barnes 49, 110, Pepper 98, Peverell 117	2130
5	26	EL	H	Crewe Alexandra	L 2-3	1-1	21	Baker 24, Barnes 89	3880
6	29	EL	A	Chesterfield	L 1-2	1-0	23	Pepper 20	(3419)
7	S 3	EL	A	Oxford United	L 0-2	0-2	24		(4304)
8	9	EL	H	Bristol Rovers	L 0-1	0-0	24		4047
9	12	EL	H	Burnley	D 1-1	0-1	24	Barnes 71	4684
10	16	EL	A	Swansea City	W 1-0	1-0	23	Thomas 40(og)	(2422)
11	20	CC 2/1	A	Manchester United	W 3-0	1-0		Barnes 24, 50(pen), Barras 52	(29049)
12	23	EL	H	Walsall	W 1-0	0-0	20	Barnes 49	3541
13	30	EL	A	Hull City	W 3-0	2-0	17	Barnes 3, 62(Pen), Peverell 22	(5273)
14	O 3	CC 2/2	H	Manchester United	L 1-3	1-2		Jordan 39	9386
15	7	EL	H	Wrexham	W 1-0	0-0	14	Barras 84	3512
16	14	EL	A	Shrewsbury Town	L 1-2	0-1	17	Pepper 83	(2827)
17	17	AWS 1/2	A	Wrexham	L 0-1	0-0			(1411)
18	21	EL	H	Bristol City	L 0-1	0-1	18		3367
19	25	CC 3	A	Queens Park Rangers	L 1-3	1-1		Barnes 10	(12972)
20	28	EL	A	Peterborough United	L 1-6	0-3	20	Baker 80	(4605)
21	31	EL	A	Wycombe Wanderers	L 1-2	0-0	21	Barnes 77	(4038)
22	N 4	EL	H	Stockport County	D 2-2	0-1	20	Barnes 51(pen), 71	3101
23	7	AWS 1/2	H	Mansfield Town	W 1-0	0-0		Barras 83	1571
24	12	FAC 1	H	Notts County	L 0-1	0-1			4228
25	18	EL	A	Blackpool	W 3-1	1-1	18	Barnes 3, Matthews 54, Baker 82	(4514)
26	25	EL	A	Brighton & H.A.	W 3-1	0-1	16	Barnes 48, 78, Baker 49	3105
27	28	AWS 2	A	Scunthorpe United	W 3-0	2-0		Barnes 15, 31, Stephenson 77	(1734)
28	D 9	EL	A	Walsall	L 0-2	0-2	18		(3193)
29	16	EL	H	Hull City	L 0-1	0-0	19		3593
30	26	EL	H	Bradford City	L 0-3	0-1	19		5213
31	J 6	EL	A	Rotherham United	D 2-2	0-2	19	Barnes 53, 65	(2695)
32	13	EL	H	Swindon Town	W 2-0	0-0	19	Naylor 59, McMillan 85	3613
33	20	EL	A	Brentford	L 0-2	0-1	20		(3915)
34	F 9	AWS QF	H	Notts County	W 1-0	0-0		Williams 78	2075
35	10	EL	A	Rotherham United	D 2-2	1-0	21	Pepper 32, Naylor 54	3299
36	13	AWS SF	A	Rotherham United	L 1-4	1-2		Peverell 19	(3913)
37	17	EL	A	Burnley	D 3-3	2-0	12	Pepper 12(pen), Naylor 34, Murty 55	(8731)
38	20	EL	H	Oxford United	W 1-0	0-0	21	Barnes 69	2112
39	24	EL	H	Swansea City	D 0-0	0-0	21		2786
40	27	EL	A	Bristol Rovers	L 0-1	0-1	21		(4013)
41	M 2	EL	A	Bradford City	D 2-2	1-2	20	Pepper 11(pen), Cresswell 72	(5208)
42	5	EL	A	Crewe Alexandra	D 1-1	1-0	20	Murty 21	(3431)
43	9	EL	H	Carlisle United	D 1-1	0-1	20	Stephenson 65	3965
44	12	EL	A	Notts County	D 2-2	2-2	21	Pepper 4, Barras 36	(3462)
45	16	EL	A	Bournemouth	D 2-2	0-1	20	Barras 48, Pepper 52	(3505)
46	23	EL	H	Notts County	L 1-3	1-1	21	Bull 2	3126
47	26	EL	H	Bournemouth	W 3-1	1-0	20	Himsworth 30, Naylor 74, 90	2055
48	30	EL	A	Wrexham	W 3-2	2-1	19	Bull 12, 16, 58 (3)	(2923)
49	A 2	EL	H	Shrewsbury Town	L 1-2	1-1	20	Pepper 32	2767
50	6	EL	H	Peterborough United	W 3-1	2-1	19	Naylor 2, Pepper 41, Bull 85	3261
51	8	EL	A	Bristol City	D 1-1	0-0	19	Bull 89	(7512)
52	13	EL	H	Wycombe Wanderers	W 2-1	1-1	16	Bull 36(pen), Naylor 61	3113
53	20	EL	A	Stockport County	L 0-3	0-2	18		(6286)
54	23	EL	A	Carlisle United	L 0-2	0-2	18		(4813)
55	30	EL	H	Chesterfield	L 0-1	0-0	20		2839
56	M 4	EL	H	Blackpool	L 0-2	0-1	21		7147
57	5	EL	A	Brighton & H.A.	W 3-1	0-1	20	Bull 53, Stephenson 56, Jordan 89	(2106)

Best Home League Attendance: 7147 v Blackpool   **Smallest: 2055 v Bournemouth**   **Average: 3537**

Goal Scorers:
EL(58):   Barnes(15),Pepper(9),Bull(8),Naylor(7),Baker(5),Barras(3),Stephenson(2),Murty(2),McMillan(1),Matthews(1),Cresswell(1),Jordan(1),Peverell(1),
         Himsworth(1),Opponent(s)(1)
CC(11):   Barnes(5),Baker(2),Pepper(1),Barras(1),Jordan(1),Peverell(1)
FAC(0):
AWS(6):   Barnes(2),Stephenson(1),Williams(1),Barras(1),Peverell(1)

	(D) Atkinson	(M) Baker	(F) Barnes	(D) Barras	(F) Bull	(M) Bushall	(F) Cresswell	(F) Curtis	(D) Hall	(D) Himsworth	(M) Jordan	(G) Kiely	(F) Matthews	(D) McMillan	(M) Murty	(F) Naylor	(D) Osbourne	(M) Oxley	(M) Pepper	(F) Peverell	(M) Randall	(D) Scaife	(M) Sharples	(F) Stephenson	(D) Tutill	(G) Warrington	(M) Williams		
		X	X	X							X2	X		X	X		X			X1				S	X	X	S1	N.Barry	1
		X	X	X				X			X1	X		X	X			X	X1	X					X	X	S1	S.Mathieson	2
		X	X	X				X			S	X		X	S1				X1	X					X	X	X	M.Bailey	3
	X3	X	X1					X			S2	X		X	X					X				S3	X2	X	X	A.Butler	4
		X	X					X			S	X		X	X		S			X				S3	X	X	X	E.Lomas	5
		X	X					X3		X	S1	X		X	X		S3		X1	S2					X	X	X2	F.Stretton	6
		X2	X					X			S1	X		X	X	S2				X				X		S	X1	R.Poulain	7
	X1	X	X2					X			S	X	S1	X	X					X				X	X		X	P.Richards	8
		X	X					X			S	X	X	X	X	S				X				X	X		X	U.Rennie	9
		X	X					X			S1	X	X1	X	X	S2	S			X				X2	X		X	J.Lloyd	10
	S1	X2	X					X			X	X		X	X					X				X1	X	S	X	J.Rushton	11
	S1	X	X					X			X	X	X1	X	S					X				X1	X		X	T.West	12
	S1	X	X					X			X	X1	X	X	S		S			X				X2	X		X	T.Heilbron	13
	S1	X1	X					X			X	X		X	S2		S			X				X2	X	X	X	J.Winter	14
		X2	X					X			X	X	X	X	S1					X			S2	X1	X	X	J.Rushton	15
	S2	X	X					X			X2	X	X	X	S1								S	X	X	X	T.Lunt	16
		X	X	X	S1			X			X1	X	X	X									S	X	X	X	U.Rennie	17
	S2	X	X	X	S1			X			X1	X	X2	X						X				X	X	X	D.Allison	18
		X	X1	X	X	S	S	X			X	X		X	X					X				X	X	X	M.Bodenham	19
	S3	X		X3				X			X	X	S1	X	X			S2	X1					X	X	X2	M.Fletcher	20
		X	X	X2	S1			X			S2	X1	X	X3					X				X	X	X	I.Hemley	21
		X	X	X	S	S		X			S	X	X	X					X				S	X	X	X	S.Baines	22
	X1	X	X	X2	S1			X			S2	X3	X	X		X			X				S3	X	X	X	R.Pearson	23
		X	X	X	S	S1		X			X	X	X	X		X			X				S	X	X	X1	T.Leake	24
	S	X	X	X				X			X	X	X	X		S			X				S	X	X		R.Pulain	25
	S1	X	X	X				X			X	X1	X	X		S			X				S	X	X		P.Richards	26
	X1	X	X	S3				X			X3	X	X	X	S2				X				S1	X2	X		R.Pearson	27
	X2	X	X	S1				X			X	X	X	X	S2				X1				X	X	X		S.W.Mathieson	28
	X1	X		X				X			S	X	S1	X	X				X				S	X	X		W.Burns	29
	S2	X2		X				X			S	X	X	X					X				S1	X	X		K.Lynch	30
	S1	S2			X			X2			X	X	X	X					X				X	X1	X		G.Barber	31
X1	X			X				S1			S2	X	X	X	X					X				X		X2		I.Cruikshanks	32
X	X			X			S			S3	X	X	X				S2			X1				X1	X2		P.Taylor	33
X	X	X	S			X				S1	X	X	X					S	X1				X		X		N.Barry	34
X	X			S			S			X	X	X	X					X	S1	X			S1	X			M.Bailey	35
X	X		S2	X	X2					S3	X	X	X					X3	X1				X				A.Butler	36
X	X	X	X	S	X1	S				X	X	X	X	X3				X	S3	X2			X				S.Baines	37
X	X	X	X	S2	X1	X				X	X	X	X				X1	X	S3	X2							E.Lomas	38
X	X	X	X	X		S	S			X	X	X	X1	X				X	S1	X							T.Heilbron	39
X	X	X	X	X				X1			X	X	X	X	S			X	S				S1				I.Hemley	40
X		X		X2	S1					X	S2	X	X1	X	X3				X	S3			S1				R.Furnandiz	41
X		X	X	X2	X					X1	X	X	X		X3				X	S3		S	S1				B.Knight	42
S			X	X1	X	X				X1	X	X	X	S1	X			X	S		S		X				U.Rennie	43
X	X		X	X	X2	X1					X	X	X	X3				X	S1	X			X				R.J.Harris	44
X	X	S2	X	X2	X1		S			X	X	X	X	S1	X			X	S2				X				A.D'Orso	45
X	X	S1	S2	X	S	S	X			X	X	X	X	X2			X	X1				X				M.Poulain	46
X	S	X	S	S	X	X				X	X	X	X	X2	S			X	X1		X	X				G.Frankland	47
S	X	X	X	X	S1	S2	X			X	X	X	X2	S				X	X1	X	X	X				E.Wolstenholme	48
S	X	X	X	X	X					X	X	X	X					X	S	X	X						R.Pearson	49
X	X	X		X			X			X	X	X	S	X	S	X	X2			S				J.Lloyd	50
X	X	X	X	S1			X			X	X	X1	X			X	S2		X	X2				M.Fletcher	51
X	X	X	S		X				X	X	X	X			S		X	X				J.Kirkby	52
X2	X	X1		X			X			X	X	X	X			X	S2	S1	X	X3				A.Leake	53
X	X1	X		S2			X			X	X	X	X2			X	S3	X	X3		S			E.Lomas	54
X		X		S1		S			X	X	X	S1	X2			X		X	X1		S		P.Richards	55
X	X1	X		S1			X			X	X	X	X			X		X	X1		S		G.Barber	56
X		X		S1			X			X	X	X	X2	X1		X		S	X		S2	G.Pooley	57
25	20	11	30	32	15	17	9	0	21	7	17	40	14	46	31	20	5	1	39	11	13	0	10	24	25	6	16	EL Appearances	
4	2	7	0	0	0	6	7	1	2	1	8	0	3	0	4	5	1	1	9	3	1	0	3	0	0	2	4+1	EL Sub Appearances	
+3	0	2+2	5	5	0	1	0	0	5	0	4+1	3	0	5	3	0+1	0	1	4	3+1	0	0	0	2	5	2	4+1	CC Appearances	
0	0	1	1	1	0	0	0	0+1	0	0	1	0	1	1	0	0	1	0	0	0	0	1	0	0	0	1	FAC Appearances	
2	2	4	5	3+1	0	3+2	1	0+1	2	0	2+3	3	3	5	3+1	0	1	0	3	2+2	0	0	0	1+1	5	2	3	AWS Appearances	

CLUB RECORDS

RECORD LEAGUE VICTORY
9-1 v Southport,Div 3N, 2.2.1957
Most Goals Scored in a Cup Tie: 7-1 v Horsforth (h), Prelim. Round
FA Cup,1924-25   7-1 v Stockton Malleable (h), FA Cup 3rd
Qualifying Round, 1927-28 7-1 v Stockton (h), FA Cup 1st
Qualifying Round, 1928-29   6-0 v South Shields(a), FA Cup 1st
Round, 1968-69
7-1 v Hartlepool Utd (h), Leyland Daf Cup,1989-90.

RECORD LEAGUE DEFEAT
0-12 v Chester, Div 3N, 1.2.1936
Record Cup Defeat: 0-7 v Liverpool, FA Cup Round 5 replay,
20.2.1985

MOST LEAGUE POINTS
(3pts a win) 101, Div 4, 1983-84
(2pts a win) 62, Div 4,1964-65

MOST LEAGUE GOALS
96, Div 4, 1983-84

RECORD TRANSFER FEE RECEIVED
£450,000 from Port Vale for Jon McCarthy, August 1995.

RECORD TRANSFER FEE PAID
£140,000 for Adrian Randall from Burnley, December 1995.

BEST PERFORMANCES
League: 15th Div 2, 1974-75
FA Cup: Semi-final Replay,1954-55 (as a Third Division club)
League Cup: 5th Round, 1961-2
HONOURS
Champions Div 4, 1983-84

LEAGUE CAREER
Elected to Div 3N 1929   Transferred to Div 4 1958   Promoted to
Div 3 1958-59
Relegated to Div 4 1959-60   Promoted to Div 3 1964-65
Relegated to Div 41965-66   Promoted to Div 3 1970-71
Promoted to Div 2 1973-74   Relegated to Div 3 1975-76
Relegated to Div 41976-77   Promoted to Div 3 1983-84
Relegated to Div 4 (now Div 3) 1987-88   Promoted to Div 2 1992-93

INDIVIDUAL CLUB RECORDS

MOST APPEARANCES FOR CLUB
Barry Jackson (1958-70): League 481 + FA Cup 35 +League Cup
22 Total 538

MOST CAPPED PLAYER
Peter Scott, 7 Northern Ireland   For England: None

RECORD GOALSCORER IN A MATCH
Alf Patrick 5 v Rotherham United, 6-1, Div 3,20.11.1948
RECORD LEAGUE GOALSCORER IN A SEASON
Bill Fenton, 31, Div 3N, 1951-52   Arthur Bottom 1954-55 and 1955
56, Div 3N In All Competitions: Arthur Bottom, 39(League 31, FA
Cup 8) 1954-55
RECORD LEAGUE GOALSCORER IN A CAREER
Norman Wilkinson, 127, 1954-66 In All Competitions: Norman
Wilkinson, 143, (League 127, FA Cup 16) 1954-66

OLDEST PLAYER IN A LEAGUE MATCH
Matt Middleton, 42 years 6 months, May 1950
YOUNGEST PLAYER IN A LEAGUE MATCH
Reg Stockill, 15 years 6 months, Aug 1929

PREVIOUS MANAGERS

1929-30 John Collier   1930-33 G W Sherrington   1933-37John
Collier   1937-50 Tom Mitchell   1950-52 Dick Duckworth   1952-53
Charlie Spencer   1953-54 Jim McCormick   1956-60 Sam Bartram
1960-67 Tom Lockie   1967-68 Joe Shaw   1968-75 Tom Johnston
1975-77 Wilf McGuinness   1977-80Charlie Wright   1980-81 Barry
Lyons   1982-87 Denis Smith   1987-88 Bobby Saxton   1988-91
John Bird   1991-93 John Ward

ADDITIONAL INFORMATION
Previous League: Midland League

Club Colours: Red shirts, navy blue shorts, red stockings
Change Colours: Blue shirts, navy blue shorts, navy blue stocking

Reserves League: Pontins Central League Div 2
`A`Team: Northern Intermediate League

LONGEST LEAGUE RUNS

of undefeated matches:	21(1973-74)	of league matches w/out a win:	17 (May-Oct 1987)
of undefeated home matches:	32 (1970-71)	of undefeated away matches:	10 (1973-74)
without home win:	12 (1981-82)	without an away win:	38 (Sept 1986 - Mar 1988)
of league wins:	7 (1964)	of home wins:	14 (1964-65)
of league defeats:	8 (1966)	of away wins:	5 (1983, 1984)

THE MANAGER

ALAN LITTLE . . . . appointed March 1993.

PREVIOUS CLUBS
As Manager . . . . York City (Caretaker).
As Asst.Man/Coach . . . . Hartlepool United (C), York City (A.M.).
As a player . . . . Aston Villa, Southend United, Barnsley, Doncaster Rovers, Torquay United,
. . . . Halifax Town, Hartlepool United.

HONOURS
As a Manager. . . . . Promotion to Division 2, 1992-93 (via the play-offs).
As a Player . . . . None.

YORK CITY

PLAYERS NAME / Honours	Ht	Wt	Birthdate	Birthplace / Transfers	Contract Date	Clubs	APPEARANCES				GOALS			
							League	L/Cup	FA Cup	Other	Lge	L/C	FAC	Oth
G O A L K E E P E R S														
Kiely Dean	6.1	11.8	10/10/70	Salford	30/10/87	Coventry City								
E: Y.4.					09/03/90	York City	210	9	4	16				
Warrington Andrew	6.3	12.13	10/06/76	Sheffield	11/06/94	York City	6	2	1	2				
D E F E N D E R S														
Atkin Paul	6.0	12.4	03/09/69	Nottingham	06/07/87	Notts County								
E: Y.1,S.					22/03/89	Bury	14+7			2+1	1			
				Free	01/07/91	York City	125+16	4+4	6	10+1	3			
Atkinson Patrick D						York City	20+2			2				
Barras Tony	6.0	12.3	29/03/71	Billingham	06/07/89	Hartlepool United	9+3	2	1	1				
				Free	23/07/90	Stockport County	94+5	2	7	19+1	5			
				Loan	25/02/94	Rotherham United	5				1			
					18/07/94	York City	59+4	7	3	5+1	4	1		1
Hall Wayne	5.8	10.2	25/10/68	Rotherham	19/12/88	Darlington								
				Free	01/01/89	Hatfield Main								
				Free	15/03/89	York City	245+14	15+1	9+1	19	8		1	1
Himsworth Gary	5.7	9.10	19/12/69	Pickering	27/01/88	York City	74+14	5		5+2	8			
				Free	05/12/90	Scarborough	83+9	7+2	1+1	6+1	6	1		
				Free	16/07/93	Darlington	60+6	3+1	3	6	5			4
				£25000	16/02/96	York City	7+1				1			
McMillan Andy	5.10	10.13	22/06/68	South Africa	17/10/87	York City	300+12	16	13	23	4			
Osbourne Wayne						York City	5+1		1	1				
Tutill Steve	5.11	11.0	01/10/69	York	27/01/88	York City	278+6	19	15	21+3	6			1
M I D F I E L D														
Bushall Stephen	5.7	10.5	28/12/72	Manchester	25/02/91	York City	90+13	3	2	9+2	5			1
Jordan Scott	5.10	11.2	19/07/75	Newcastle	21/10/92	York City	50+13	4+1	2	3+4	4	1		
Murty Graeme	5.10	11.2	13/11/74	Middlesbro'	23/03/93	York City	49+7	3		4+1	4			
Pepper Nigel	5.10	10.3	25/04/68	Rotherham	26/04/86	Rotherham United	35+10	1	1+1	3+3	1	1		
				Free	18/07/90	York City	197+9	12+1	9	14+1	28	2	1	
Randall Adrian	5.11	12.04	10/11/68	Amesbury	02/09/86	Bournemouth	3			1+2				
E: Y. Div.4'92.					15/09/88	Aldershot	102+5	3	11	10	12		3	2
				£40000	12/12/91	Burnley	137+20	6	13+3	3	9	1	1	
					28/12/95	York City	13+3							
Sharples John						Ayr								
					28/03/96	York City	10							
Williams Darren			28/04/77	Middlesbro'		York City	16+3	4+1	1	3				1
F O R W A R D S														
Bull Gary	5.9	11.7	12/06/66	Tipton	15/10/86	Southampton								
GMVC'91.					29/03/88	Cambridge United	13+6	0+1		0+2	4			
				£2000	01/03/89	Barnet	83	4	11	8	37	4	3	2
				Free	21/07/93	Nottingham Forest	4+8	2	0+3		1			
				Loan	17/08/95	Brighton & H.A.	10			1	2			2
				Free	29/12/95	Birmingham City	3+3	0+1	0+2	1				1
				Free	04/03/96	York City	15				8			
Cresswell Richard						York City (T)	9+7			1	1			
Stephenson Paul	5.10	10.0	02/01/68			Newcastle United	58+3	3	2	2	1			
E: Y.2.				£300000	10/11/88	Millwall	81+17	3	9	8	6	1	2	1
				Loan	21/11/92	Gillingham	12			2	2			
				£30000	04/03/93	Brentford	70	6	1+1	5	2	1		
					07/08/95	York City	24+3	2		1+1	2			1
Tolsen Neil	6.2	12.4	25/10/73	Walsall	17/12/91	Walsall	3+6		0+1	1+2	1	1		
				£150000	24/03/92	Oldham Athletic	0+3							
					02/12/93	Bradford City	32+31	1+4	3+1	2+2	12	1	1	3
				£80,000	01/07/96	York City								
ADDITIONAL CONTRACT PLAYERS														
Campbell Neil						York City (T)								
Oxley Scott					04/05/96	York City (T)	1+1	1						
Pouton Alan					04/05/96	York City (T)								

BOOTHAM CRESCENT
York YO3 7AQ
Tel: 01904 62447

Capacity 9,534
Covered Standing 5,865
Seating 3,669

First game .... v Stockport County, 1932.
First floodlit game .... v Q.P.R., September 1959.

ATTENDANCES
Highest .... 28,123 v Huddersfield, FAC 6th Rnd, 5.3.1938.
Lowest .... 957 v Carlisle Utd, AMC Prelim Rnd, 22.10.1991.

OTHER GROUNDS .... Fulfordgate 1922-23.

MATCHDAY TICKET PRICES

Main Stand £10
Juv/OAP £6

Popular Stand £8
Juv/OAP £5

Ground £7
Juv/OAP £4
Popular Stand transfer £1

Enclosure. £10
Juv/OAP £6
(Only obtainable from Ticket Office)

Family Stand (max. 3 children) £7.50
Child £4

Ticket Office Telephone no. 01904 624 447

CLUBCALL 0891 66 45 45

Calls cost 39p per minute cheap rate and 49p per
minute at all other times.
Call costings correct at time of going to press.

HOW TO GET TO THE GROUND

From the North
Use A1 then A59, sign posted York. Cross railway bridge and in 1.9 miles turn left into Water End. At end turn right A19, sign posted City Centre. In 0.4 miles turn left into Bootham Crescent for York City FC.

From the East
Use A1079 into York City centre and follow signs for Thirsk (A19) into Bootham. Cross railway bridge and then take 2nd turning on right into Bootham Crescent for York City FC.

From the South
Use A64. Turn left onto by-pass and follow signs for Thirsk (A19). Then turn left sign posted York and then take left into Bootham Crescent for York City FC.

From the West
Use B1224, sign posted York into city centre and follow signs to Thirsk (A19) into Bootham. Cross railway bridge and then take 2nd turning on right into Bootham Crescent for York City FC.

Car Parking
Ample parking in side streets.

Nearest Railway Station: York (01904 642 155)

MATCHDAY PROGRAMME

Programme Editor. . . . . Maureen Leslie.

Number of pages . . . . 32.

Price . . . . £1.50.

Subscriptions . . . . Apply to club.

Local Newspapers . . . . Yorkshire Evening Press.

Local Radio Stations . . . . BBC Radio York & Minster FM.

NATIONWIDE
LEAGUE DIVISION 3

DIVISION THREE 1995-96

FINAL LEAGUE TABLE

		P	W	D	L	F	A	PTS
1	Preston North End (+4)	46	23	17	6	78	38	86
2	Gillingham (+17)	46	22	17	7	49	20	83
3	Bury (+1)	46	22	13	11	66	48	79
4	Plymouth Argyle	46	22	12	12	68	49	78
5	Darlington (+15)	46	20	18	8	60	42	78
6	Hereford United (+10)	46	20	14	12	65	47	74
7	Colchester United (+3)	46	18	18	10	61	51	72
8	Chester City	46	18	16	12	72	53	70
9	Barnet (+2)	46	18	16	12	65	45	70
10	Wigan Athletic (+4)	46	20	10	16	62	56	70
11	Northampton Town (+6)	46	18	13	15	51	44	67
12	Scunthorpe United (-5)	46	15	15	16	67	61	60
13	Doncaster Rovers (-4)	46	16	11	19	49	60	59
14	Exeter City (+8)	46	13	18	15	46	53	57
15	Rochdale (-)	46	14	13	19	57	61	55
16	Cambridge United	46	14	12	20	61	71	54
17	Fulham (-9)	46	12	17	17	57	63	53
18	Lincoln City (-6)	46	13	14	19	57	73	53
19	Mansfield Town (-13)	46	11	20	15	54	64	53
20	Hartlepool United (-2)	46	12	13	21	47	67	49
21	Leyton Orient	46	12	11	23	44	63	47
22	Cardiff City	46	11	12	23	41	64	45
23	Scarborough (-2)	46	8	16	22	39	69	40
24	Torquay United (-11)	46	5	14	27	30	84	29

The figure in brackets denotes the number of places lost or gained on the clubs 1994-95 final position.

NATIONWIDE LEAGUE DIVISION THREE 1996-97

BARNET
(The Bees)
NATIONWIDE LEAGUE DIVISION 3
SPONSORED BY: THE PRINTING COMPANY LTD

Back Row (L-R): Alan Hamlet, Linvoy Primus, Shaun Gale, Mark Cooper, Lee Pearce, Lee Hodges, Alan Pardew, Paul Smith, Kieran Adams. **Middle Row:** Terry Bullivant (First Team Coach), Laird Budge (Kit Manager), Kieran Gallagher, Jamie Campbell, Paul Newell, Glen Thomas, Maik Taylor, Graeme Hall, Terry Harvey (Yth Coach), David Mott (Physio), Terry Gibson (Yth Manager). **Front Row:** Mickey Tomlinson, Terry Robbins, Peter Scott, Ray Clemence (Manager), Paul Wilson, David McDonald, Dougie Freedman (Now Crystal Palace).

BARNET
FORMED IN 1888
TURNED PROFESSIONAL IN 1965

CHAIRMAN: A A Kleanthous

DIRECTORS:
D J Buchler FCA, D B Edwards OBE,
F W Higgins FCA, S Glynne

SECRETARY: A Ashworth

COMMERCIAL MANAGER
Carla Frediani

MANAGER: Ray Clemence

YOUTH TEAM MANAGER
Terry Harvey

PHYSIOTHERAPIST
Gary Gilbert-Anderson

A turbulent first five years in the Football League came to an end with the club on its most stable footing for some time. Despite limited resources the Bees ended the 1995-96 season on a high and can look to the future with justifiable optimism despite a wretched start that bought five losses in the opening eight matches.

Those early miserable weeks, ultimately proved costly, as the play-offs were missed by just two points. The side plummeted to the very foot of the Football League during September, a month that also saw the departure of leading striker, Dougie Freedman who moved to Crystal Palace in a £800,000 deal.

The FA Cup campaign didn't bring any joy either, with a First Round replay loss to Woking for the second consecutive season. Under-fire manager Ray Clemence stuck to his beliefs though and with some astute signings slowly brought the side into the top half of the table. Striker Sean Devine, formerly on Fisher Athletic's books arrived from Cypriot side Omonia Nicosia in OCtober and scored after just seven minutes of his debut. He quickly attained 'cult status' amongst the fans and rewarded them with twenty goals. His partnership with Lee Hodges, who himself hit 18 goals, gave the side a sharp edge to it's attack.

Barnet developed a meanness in defence, particularly at Underhill, and goalkeeper Maik Taylor cemented an impressive first season in league football by lifting the 'Player of the Year' award. In front of him the consistent Linvoy Primus showed the sort of form throughout which will certainly see him playing at a higher level. The manager dealt astutely in the transfer market and apart from Devine, other influential signings included the experienced trio of ALex Dyer, Lee Howarth and Robert Codner, as well as the former Stevenage Borough midfielder Phil Simpson.

With a settled side after Christmas, the play-offs became a real possibility and the team strung together seven wins in eight matches to reach a top seven position for the first time. 22-year-old Lee Hodges achieved the unusual distinction of hitting hat-tricks in consecutive matches, scoring four against Rochdale on Easter Monday and then three against Hartlepool the following Saturday. Late goals proved to be the sides' 'achilles heel' throughout the season an by conceding vital late strikes at Exeter City, Doncaster Rovers and Leyton Orient other results needed to go Barnet's way on the final afternoon. Despite a convincing win over London rivals Fulham, they didn't get the necessary help elsewhere and had to settle for a final ninth place finish.

Much will now depend on whether the nucleus of the side can be kept together for the new campaign. If it can, then there is no reason why the attractive style of play that the manager instills should not bear greater dividends this time round. **DAVID BRACEGIRDLE.**

BARNET

League: 9th   FA Cup: 1st Rnd.   Coca-Cola Cup: 1st Rnd   Auto Windscreens Shield: 1st Rnd.

M	DATE	COMP	VEN	OPPONENTS	RESULT	HT	LP	GOAL SCORERS/GOAL TIMES	ATT.
1	A 12	EL	A	Hereford United	L 1-4	0-3	20	Hodges 54	(2522)
2	15	CC 1/1	H	Charlton Athletic	D 0-0	0-0			1893
3	19	EL	H	Colchester United	D 1-1	0-0	19	Freedman 69	1966
4	22	CC 1/2	A	Charlton Athletic	L 0-2	0-1			(4418)
5	26	EL	A	Scunthorpe United	L 0-2	0-0	21		(1970)
6	29	EL	A	Gillingham	L 0-2	0-1	23		3077
7	S 2	EL	H	Lincoln City	W 3-1	2-1	21	Cooper 20, Freedman 32, 68	1813
8	9	EL	A	Cambridge United	D 1-1	0-0	19	Westley 55(og)	(3054)
9	12	EL	A	Wigan Athletic	L 0-1	0-1	23		(1745)
10	16	EL	H	Plymouth Argyle	L 1-2	0-0	24	Cooper 74	2557
11	23	EL	A	Bury	D 0-0	0-0	23		(2453)
12	30	EL	H	Darlington	D 1-1	0-1	23	Robbins 79	1923
13	O 7	EL	H	Exeter City	W 3-2	2-0	23	Devine 7, Dyer 29, Cooper 86	2146
14	14	EL	A	Cardiff City	D 1-1	1-1	21	Cooper 36	(3342)
15	17	AWS 1/1	A	Bristol City	L 0-2	0-1			(1830)
16	21	EL	H	Rochdale	L 0-4	0-0	22		2039
17	28	EL	A	Northampton Town	W 2-0	0-0	22	Cooper 63, Campbell 89	(5376)
18	31	EL	A	Hartlepool United	D 0-0	0-0	21		(1713)
19	N 4	EL	H	Doncaster Rovers	D 1-1	1-0	22	Devine 2	1913
20	7	AWS 1/2	H	Oxford United	L 2-3	0-0		Cooper 71, Robbins 86	1072
21	11	FAC 1	H	Woking	D 2-2	2-2		Primus 44, Devine 45	3034
22	18	EL	A	Fulham	D 1-1	0-0	21	Dunwell 81	(4369)
23	21	FAC 1R	A	Woking	L 1-2	1-1		Hodges 2	(3535)
24	25	EL	H	Leyton Orient	W 3-0	1-0	17	Dyer 37, Hodges 73, 84	2850
25	D 9	EL	H	Bury	D 0-0	0-0	19		1747
26	16	EL	A	Darlington	D 1-1	0-1	18	Devine 80	(1717)
27	23	EL	A	Chester City	W 2-0	1-0	14	Hodges 31, Devine 62	(3081)
28	26	EL	H	Mansfield Town	D 0-0	0-0	14		2204
29	J 6	EL	H	Preston North End	W 1-0	0-0	13	Wilson 67	2737
30	9	EL	A	Scarborough	D 1-1	1-1	13	Devine 43	(1310)
31	13	EL	A	Colchester United	L 2-3	2-3	15	Primus 22, Cooper 37	(3252)
32	20	EL	A	Hereford United	L 1-3	1-1	16	Hodges 44	1835
33	F 3	EL	H	Scunthorpe United	W 1-0	1-0	15	Hodges 31	1674
34	6	EL	A	Torquay United	D 1-1	0-0	14	Wilson 53	(2262)
35	10	EL	A	Preston North End	W 1-0	0-0	11	Wilson 66	(9974)
36	13	EL	A	Gillingham	L 0-1	0-1	11		(6433)
37	17	EL	H	Wigan Athletic	W 5-0	2-0	10	Hodges 10, Primus 42, Devine 49, 62, Tomlinson 55	2059
38	24	EL	A	Plymouth Argyle	D 1-1	0-0	11	Gale 72	(6426)
39	27	EL	A	Cambridge United	W 2-0	0-0	11	Cooper 63, Wilson 79	1849
40	M 2	EL	A	Mansfield Town	L 1-2	0-0	11	Primus 89	(2146)
41	9	EL	H	Chester City	D 1-1	0-0	12	Tomlinson 56	2195
42	16	EL	H	Torquay United	W 4-0	3-0	11	Devine 20, 77, Simpson 22, Cooper 45	1734
43	19	EL	A	Lincoln City	W 2-1	0-0	10	Devine 53, 57	(1872)
44	23	EL	H	Scarborough	W 1-0	0-0	9	Devine 55	2054
45	30	EL	A	Exeter City	L 0-1	0-0	9		(2726)
46	A 2	EL	H	Cardiff City	W 1-0	0-0	9	Devine 71	2107
47	6	EL	A	Northampton Town	W 2-0	2-0	9	Primus 18, Hodges 35	3135
48	8	EL	A	Rochdale	W 4-0	1-0	8	Hodges 1, 62, 65, 68 (4)	(1442)
49	13	EL	H	Hartlepool United	W 5-1	3-0	7	Hodges 14, 38, 89 (3), Devine 22, 53	2530
50	20	EL	A	Doncaster Rovers	L 0-1	0-0	8		(1579)
51	27	EL	A	Leyton Orient	D 3-3	2-1	10	Devine 17, 19(pen), Hodges 53	(4006)
52	M 4	EL	H	Fulham	W 3-0	1-0	9	Devine 4, 87, Hodges 53	4332

Best Home League Attendance: 4332 v Fulham   Smallest: 1674 v Scunthorpe United   Average: 2281

Goal Scorers:
EL(65): Devine(19),Hodges(17),Cooper(8),Wilson(4),Primus(4),Freedman(3),Dyer(2),Tomlinson(2),Robbins(1),Gale(1),Dunwell(1),Simpson(1),Campbell(1),Opponent(s)(1)
CC (0):
FAC(3): Primus(1),Hodges(1),Devine(1)
AWS(2): Robbins(1),Cooper(1)

(M) Adams	(F) Bradey	(T)Constantiou	(M) Campbell	(M) Charles	(M) Codner	(F) Cooper	(F) Devine	(F) Dunwell	(M) Dyer	(F) Freedman	(D) Gale	(F) Hodges	(D) Howarth	(D) McDonald	(M) Mills	(G) Newell	(M) Pardew	(D) Primus	(F) Robbins	(F) Scott	(M) Simpson	(M) Smith	(D) Stimson	(G) Taylor	(M) Thompson	(D) Thomas	(F) Tomlinson	(D) Wilson		
X1										X	X	X1		X		S	X	X	X1	X		S		X		X	S1		T.Leake	1
			X			S1				X	X	X1		X			X	X	X1	X		S		X		X	S1		D.Orr	2
S			X			S1				X	X1	X2		X			X	X	X	X				X		X	S2		S.G.Bennett	3
			X			S1				X	X	X1		X			X	X1	X					X		X	S1		A.D'Urso	4
			X			X				X	X	X		S			X	X1	X					X		X	S1		R.Pearson	5
			X			X				X	X	X		S			X	X	S	X				X		X	X		G.Barber	6
			S			X	S1			X	X	X1		X			X	X	S	X				X		X	X		B.Knight	7
			X			X	S1			X	X						X	X1	X	S				X		X	X		R.Fernandiz	8
			X			X			X		X	X1		S1	S		X	X	X			S		X		X		X	R.Poulain	9
			S			X			X		X				S	S	X	X	X	X		S		X		X		X	M.J.Brandwood	10
	X		X2	X3					X		X1			S1			X		S3	X	X2		S2	X		X		X2	M.Riley	11
	X		X1	X					X		X			S	S2		X		S1	X				X	X	X		X	C.Wilkes	12
			S3			S1	X3		X1		X			X	S2		X		X2	X				X	X	X		X	G.Pooley	13
			S1			X2	X				X	S2		X	S		X		X1	X				X	X	X		X	F.J.Stretton	14
			S1			X2	X				X	X		X	S2		X		S	X1				X	X	X		X	K.Leach	15
			S1			X	X1				X	X		S	S2		X	X	X2					X	X	X		X	A.Wiley	16
			X			X	X1				X	S2		X	X2		X	X					X		X		S1	X	G.Cain	17
			X			X	X2				X	S2		X	X1		X	X			X	S		X			S1	X	A.Butler	18
			X3			X	X		S3		X	S1		X	X1		X	X			X			X			S1	X	G.P.Barber	19
			S			X	X		X		X1	S1		X	X		X	X	S2	X				X			X	X	D'Urso	20
			X			X	X2		S1		X	S3		X3	X1		X	X		X				X			S2	X	M.Fletcher	21
			X3			X	X2	S2	S3		X	S1		X	X1		X	X		X				X				X	S.Bennett	22
			X			X	X		S		X	X		X	S		X	X		X				X			X1	X	M.Fletcher	23
						X	X		X		X	X		X	S		X	X		X				X			S	X	T.West	24
						X1	X2	S1	X		X	X		X	S2		X	X		X				X		S		X	J.Rushton	25
						X1	X	S1	X		X	X		X	S		X	X		X				X		S		X	D.Laws	26
						X	X1	S1	X		X	X		X	S	S	X	X		X				X				X	E.Lomas	27
						X1	X	S1	X		X	X		X	S2		X	X		X2				X		S		X	I.Hemley	28
						S	X	X1	X		X	X		X	S1		X		X			S		X		X		X	D.Orr	29
						X2	X		X1		X	X		X	S2		X		X					X	S1	X		X	G.Frankland	30
			X			X	X				X	X		X	S1		X	X		X			S	X	S	X1		X	S.G.Bennett	31
			S3			X	X	S1			X	X		X			X3	X	S2	X1				X	X2			X	P.Rejer	32
			X			X		X1	S1		X	X	X		S		X	X		X				X			S	X	E.K.Wolstenholme	33
			X			X1	X	S			X	X	X		S		X	X		X				X				X	C.Wilkes	34
						X	S	S	X		X	X	X	S	S		X	X		X	X			X				X	F.Stretton	35
			S1			X	S3	X			X	X	X	X1			X	X		X2				X			S2	X	G.Barber	36
						S	X2	S1	X		X	X1	X				X	X	S2	X				X			X	X	A.G.Wiley	37
						S1	X		X		X	X1	X				X	X	S1	X				X			X1	X	M.Fletcher	38
			S2			S1	X1		X		X	X	X		S		X	X		X2				X			X	X	B.Knight	39
			X1			S1	X		X		X1	X		X	S1		X	X				S		X			X	X	A.D'Urso	40
			S2			S1	X		X3		X	X1	X	X	S3		X	X						X			X	X2	J.A.Kirkby	41
			S2			X2	X	S2	X		X		X	X	X		X2			S1	X1			X			X		A.R.Leake	42
			S2			X	X1	S	X		X		X	X	X		X	X		X				X			X2		R.Pearson	43
			S3				X	X1	X		X	S1	X	X3	S2		X	X		X				X			X2		G.Singh	44
			S		X		X		X		X	X	X	X	S1		X1	X	S2	X				X			X2		S.Baines	45
			S2		X	S	X		X		X	X	X	X	S1		X	X		X2				X			X1		U.D.Rennie	46
			S1		X	S3	X		X		X	X3	X	X			X	X1		X				X			X2	S2	E.Lomas	47
	S3		S2		X	X3	X		X		X	X1	X	X			X			X2				X				S1	M.Brandwood	48
			S		X	S	X		X		X	X	X	X			X			X				X			X1	S1	A.Wiley	49
			S		X	X1	X		X		X	X	X	X			X			X				X			S1	S	P.Richards	50
					X	S	X		X		X	X	X		S		X	X		X				X			X1	S1	P.Taylor	51
			S		X	S	X		X		X	X	X				X	X		X				X			X	S	M.Bailey	52
1	1	0	14	2	8	26	35	3	30	5	44	34	19	30	5	1	41	42	9	19	24	0	5	45	1	16	17	29	EL Appearances	
0	1	0	10	3	0	7	0	10	5	0	0	6	0	2	14	0	0	6	1	0	1	0	0	1	0	0	8	4	EL Sub Appearances	
0	0	0	2	0	0	0+2	0	0	2	2	2	0	2	0	2	0	2	2	2	2	0	0	2	0	2	0+2	0		CC Appearances	
0	0	0	2	0	0	2	2	2	0	0+1	0	0	2	0	2	1+1	0	2	1	0	2	0	0	2	0	2	1+1	2	FAC Appearances	
0	0	0	0	0+1	0	2	2	0	1	0	2	1+1	0	2	0+1	0	2	1	0	0+1	2	0	0	1	2	0	1	1	AWS Appearances	

CLUB RECORDS

SINCE JOINING THE FOOTBALL LEAGUE
RECORD LEAGUE VICTORY
6-0 v Lincoln City (away), Division 4.9.1992.
Most Goals scored in a Cup tie: 9-0 v Wealdstone, FAC, 1961-62
First Class Cup tie: 6-3 v Brentford, AMC, 17.12.1991.
5-0 v Tiverton Town, FA Cup 1st Round, 16.11.1992.

RECORD LEAGUE DEFEAT
1-5 v York City (h), Division 3, 13.3.1993.

RECORD TRANSFER FEE RECEIVED
£800,000 from Crystal Palace for Dougie Freedman, 1995.

RECORD TRANSFER FEE PAID
£40,000 to Barrow for Kenny Lowe, 1991. £40,000 to Runcorn for
Mark Carter, 1991.

BEST PERFORMANCES
League: 3rd in Division 4/3, 1992-93.
FA Cup: 3rd Round in 1964-65, 1970-71, 1972-73, 1981-82, 1990-
91(As a non-League club) 1991-92, 1993-94 (As a League club).
League Cup: 2nd Round in 1993-94, 1994-95.

HONOURS SINCE JOINING THE FOOTBALL LEAGUE
None.

LEAGUE CAREER
Promoted to Division 4/3 1990-91, Promoted to Division 2 1992-93.

INDIVIDUAL CLUB RECORDS

MOST APPEARANCES
Gary Bull - 106 (1989-93): League 83, FA Cup 11, League Cup 4,
AMC 6, Play-offs 2.

MOST CAPPED PLAYER
No Barnet player has won a full cap.

RECORD GOALSCORER IN A MATCH
4 - Douglas Freedman v Rochdale, 6-2, 13.9.95.
4 - Lee Hodges v Rochdale, 8.4.96.

RECORD LEAGUE GOALSCORER IN A SEASON
Gary Bull 20, 1991-92.
In All Competitions: Mark Carter - 32 (1991-92): League 19, FA Cup
5, League Cup 2, AMC 5, Play-offs 1.

RECORD LEAGUE GOALSCORER IN A CAREER
Gary Bull - 37 (1991-93).
In All Competitions: Mark Carter - 47 (1991-93): League 31, FA Cup
6, League Cup 2, Others 8.

PREVIOUS MANAGERS

(Since 1946): Lester Finch, George Wheeler, Dexter Adams, Tommy
Coleman, Gerry Ward, Gordon Ferry, Brian Kelly, Bill Meadows,
Barry Fry, Roger Thompson, Don McAllister, Barry Fry, Gary
Phillips.

ADDITIONAL INFORMATION
Previous Leagues: Olympian, London Athenian, Southern,
Alliance, Gola, GM Vauxhall Conference.
Previous Name: Barnet Alston F.C.

Club colours: Amber shirts, black shorts, black socks.
Change colours: Green & white stripe, green shorts, green socks.

Reserves League: Springheath Print Capital League.

LONGEST LEAGUE RUNS

of undefeated matches:	12 (1992-93)	of league matches w/out a win:	6 (1993)
of undefeated home matches:	16 (1992-93)	of undefeated away matches:	5 (1992-93)
without home win:	2 (1993)	without an away win:	9 (1991-92)
of league wins:	5 (1993)	of home wins:	8 (1991)
of league defeats:	3 (1992, 1993)	of away wins:	2 (1991, 3 TIMES 1993)

THE MANAGER

Ray Clemence. . . . . appointed in January 1994.

PREVIOUS CLUBS
As a Manager. . . . . None.
As an Asst.Man/Coach. . . . . Tottenham Hotspur, Barnet.
As a player. . . . . Scunthorpe United, Liverpool, Tottenham Hotspur.

HONOURS
As a Manager. . . . . None.
As a Player. . . . . Div.1 championship (x5), FAC (x2), Lge Cup, EC (x3), UEFA (x2), ESC. E: 61, U23-4.

BARNET

PLAYERS NAME Honours	Ht	Wt	Birthdate	Birthplace Transfers	Contract Date	Clubs	League	L/Cup	FA Cup	Other	Lge	L/C	FAC	Oth
G O A L K E E P E R S														
Taylor Maik			08/11/63			Basingstoke Town								
Army Rep. BHLP.						Farnborough								
					13/07/95	Barnet	45	2	2	2				
D E F E N D E R S														
Gale Shaun	6.0	11.6	08/10/69	Reading	12/07/88	Portsmouth	2+1			0+1				
				Free	13/07/94	Barnet	113+2	8	2	5	4			
Howarth Lee	6.1	13.06	03/01/68	Bolton		Chorley								
				Free	16/08/91	Peterborough Utd	56+6	8	3	3+2				1
				£15000	05/08/94	Mansfield Town	39+1	5	3	4	2			
				Loan	26/01/96	Barnet								
				Free	29/02/96	Barnet	19							
McDonald David	5.10	11.0	02/01/71	Dublin	05/08/88	Tottenham Hotspur	2							
Ei: B, u21.2, Y.				Loan	27/09/90	Gillingham	10			2				
				Loan	28/08/92	Bradford City	7							
				Loan	06/03/93	Reading	11							
				Free	13/08/93	Peterborough Utd	28+1	4	2	1				
				Free	24/03/94	Barnet	105+2	8	6	6				
Primus Linvoy	6.0	14.0	14/09/73	Forest Gate	14/08/92	Charlton Athletic	4	0+1		0+1				
				Free	18/07/94	Barnet	123	7+1	6	4	4		1	
Wilson Paul	5.9	10.11	26/09/64	Forest Gate		Billericay Town								
GMVC'91.						Barking								
					01/03/88	Barnet	159+11	6	18+1	8+2	15			
M I D F I E L D														
Adams Kieran	5.10	11.6	20/10/77	St.Ives	01/08/94	Barnet (T)	4+2							
Campbell Jamie	6.1	11.3	21/10/72	Birmingham	01/07/91	Luton Town	10+26	1	1+3	1+2	1			
				Loan	25/11/94	Mansfield Town	3		2		1			
				Loan	10/03/95	Cambridge United	12							
				Free	11/07/95	Barnet	14+10	2	2		1			
Codner Robert	5.11	11.8	23/01/65	Walthamstow		Tottenham Hotspur								
E: SP.1.				Free	17/09/83	Leicester City								
					01/08/84	Dagenham & Red.								
					01/08/86	Barnet			1					
				£125000	08/09/88	Brighton & H.A.	257+9	18+2	11+1	16+1	39	1	4	3
				Free	28/03/96	Barnet	8							
Gallagher Kieran						Barnet (T)								
Mills Danny Raymond	6.0	10.5	13/02/75	Sidcup	01/08/93	Charlton Athletic								
				Free	29/09/95	Barnet	5+14		1	0+1				
Pardew Alan	5.11	11.0	18/07/61	Wimbledon		Yeovil Town								
				£7000	17/03/87	Crystal Palace	111+17	9+3	8	20	8	1	1	2
				Free	21/11/91	Charlton Athletic	98+6	3+1	9+1	6	24		1	1
				Free	31/07/95	Barnet	41	2	2	2				
Simpson Neil						Stevenage								
					27/10/95	Barnet	24				1			
F O R W A R D S														
Brady Matthew	6.0	10.4	27/10/77	London	01/05/95	Barnet (T)	1+3							
Cooper Mark D	6.1	13.0	05/04/67	Watford										
Devine Sean						Famagusta								
				£10000	01/09/95	Barnet	35		2	2	19		1	
Dunwell Richard					10/11/95	Barnet	3+10				1			
Freedman Douglas	5.9	11.2	21/01/74											
Hodges Lee L	5.9	10.9	04/09/73	Epping	29/02/92	Tottenham Hotspur	0+4							
E: Y.4.				Loan	26/02/93	Plymouth Argyle	6+1				2			
				Loan	31/12/93	Wycombe Wand.	2+2		1	1				
				Free	31/05/94	Barnet	100+14	8	3+1	4+1	38		3	
Tomlinson Michael	5.9	10.7	15/09/72	Lambeth	05/07/91	Leyton Orient	7+7	4	1	0+1	1	1		
				Loan	28/01/94	St.Albans								
				Free	21/03/94	Barnet	71+23	3+2	1+4	1+2	5			

Underhill Stadium
Barnet Lane, Herts EN5 2BE
Tel: 0181 441 6932

Capacity. 3,887

First game . . . . v Crystal Palace, 7.9.1907 (London Lge).

ATTENDANCES
Highest . . . . 11,026 v Wycombe W., FA Amateur Cup
. . . . 4th Round, 1951-52.
Lowest. . . . . 248 v Milton Keynes City,Southern League
. . . . First Division North, 1975-76.

MATCHDAY TICKET PRICES

Main Stand. . . . . £12 (Concessions £6)

Family Stand. £10 (£5)

East Terrace. £7 (£3.50)

North & West Terrace. . . . . £5 (Free)

South Stand. £8

Ticket Office Telephone No.. . . . . . . 0181 364 9601

HOW TO GET TO THE GROUND

From North, South, East and West
Use M1 then M25, turn off at junction 23. Follow signs for Barnet (A100). Ground is located at the foot of Barnet Hill, behind the Old Red Lion Public House.

Car Parking
Surrounding roads under police control or HIgh Barnet underground station car park.

Nearest Railway Station
High Barnet (LT Northern Line) New Barnet (British Rail).

CLUBCALL
0891 12 15 44
Calls cost 39p per minute cheap rate and 49p per minute at all other times.
Call costings correct at time of going to press.

MATCHDAY PROGRAMME

Programme Editor . . . . D Bracegirdle.

Number of pages 32

Price £1.50

Subscriptions . . . . Apply to club

Local Newspapers . . . . . . Barnet & Finchley Press, Barnet Advertiser, Barnet Independent, Barnet Borough Times, Hendon & Finchley Times.

Local Radio Stations . . . . LBC, Capital, Chiltern, Three Counties.

BRIGHTON & HOVE ALBION
(The Seagulls)
NATIONWIDE LEAGUE DIVISION 3
SPONSORED BY: AKZO SANDTEX

ck Row (L-R): Peter Smith, Stuart Storer, Paul McCarthy, Mark Ormerod, Nicky Rust, Derek Coughlan, Steve Foster, Simon Fox. **ddle Row:** George Petchey (Youth Dev. Officer), Gerry Ryan (Asst. Manager), Ross Johnson, John Byrne, Kevin McGarrigle, Mark Fox, nn Ryan, Dean Wilkins, Jimmy Case (Coach), Malcolm Stuart (Physio). **Front Row:** Ian Chapman, Stuart Myall, Phillip Andrews, Jeff nton, Liam Brady (Manager), Junior McDougald, James Virgo, Stuart Munday, Stuart Tuck.

**BRIGHTON & HOVE ALBION
FORMED IN 1900
TURNED PROFESSIONAL IN 1901
LTD COMPANY IN 1904**

PRESIDENT: G A Stanley
CHAIRMAN: W A Archer
DIRECTORS
D F Bellotti (Deputy-chairman),
R A Bloom, D Stanley, G A Stanley
SECRETARY:
Derek Allan (01273 778 855)

COMMERCIAL MANAGER
D Bellotti (01273 778 855)

MANAGER: Jimmy Case
CLUB COACH: George Petchey
RESERVE TEAM MANAGER
Jimmy Case
YOUTH DEVELOPMENT OFFICER
John Jackson
PHYSIOTHERAPIST
Malcolm Stuart

STATISTICIAN FOR THE DIRECTORY
James Millen

The season started badly when, during the summer, news was leaked to the local paper that the club had sold the ground to Chartwell Developments and was planning to ground-share with Portsmouth from next season whilst a new site was found and developed. It quickly became apparent that the club's intentions did not satisfy the relevant authorities, particularly the Football League, who had to sanction the proposal. All this angered the fans, who were never consulted and who made their views known vocally at every match throughout the season.

With all this going on, it was always going to be difficult for Liam Brady and his players to concentrate on winning matches - and so it proved. It was seven games before they notched up their first win - this against Notts County, and despite a half-time pitch demonstration which Brady dispersed. Albion's biggest handicap was their failure to consistently pick up points at home, and they only once managed two consecutive wins.

They faired little better in the cup competitions, being dumped out of the Coca-Cola Cup by Fulham (0-5 on aggregate). In the FA Cup Albion managed to beat non-league Canvey Island after a replay, only to face Fulham again. The tie also went to a replay, but Fulham triumphed again, winning through on penalties. And Albion's run in the Auto Windscreens Shield was ended at the quarter-final stage by Shrewsbury.

By this time Brady had resigned and Jimmy Case had taken the helm. Case was latterly given money to strengthen the side, when funds from the sale of the ground were made available. McDonald and Maskell (both Southampton) and Hobson (Hull City) were brought in, while Rowe (Chelsea) and Allan (Southampton) were taken on loan. Despite the players' obvious qualities, it was too late to prevent Albion from being relegated.

The inevitable occurred at the last home match of the season. With the supporters still unsure whether they would have a team to follow next season, let alone where they would be playing, it was no surprise when 15 minutes into the game some 3,000 fans invaded the pitch. Unfortunately, a small element had other ideas besides just a demonstration. The players tunnel was damaged and the goalposts torn down, forcing the game to be abandoned.

By the time the match had been replayed, two things had happened. Firstly, Liam Brady announced that he had a consortium prepared to take over the club and talks were started with the current board; secondly, at the eleventh hour the club agreed with Chartwell to lease back the Goldstone for next season only.

Thanks must go to the Brighton Evening Argus who, through their campaign, kept the fans informed regarding what was actually happening at the club. On the playing front, many fans, I'm sure, will wish to thank Ian Chapman, Steve Foster and Stuart Myall for their services to the club over the past few seasons. All have been released and will be greatly missed.

JAMES MILLEN

BRIGHTON & H.A.

League: 23rd   FA Cup: 2nd Rnd   Coca-Cola Cup: 1st Rnd   Auto Windscreen Shield: Quarter Finals

M	DATE	COMP	VEN	OPPONENTS	RESULT	HT	LP	GOAL SCORERS/GOAL TIMES	ATT
1	A 12	EL	A	Peterborough United	L 1-3	0-1	21	Clark 61(og)	(5394
2	15	CC 1/1	A	Fulham	L 0-3	0-1			(4380)
3	19	EL	H	Bradford City	D 0-0	0-0	22		5471
4	22	CC 1/2	H	Fulham	L 0-2	0-0			3799
5	26	EL	A	Wrexham	D 1-1	1-0	20	Berry 17	(2947)
6	29	EL	A	Wycombe Wanderers	L 1-2	1-1	22	Bull 5	5360
7	S 2	EL	H	Notts County	W 1-0	0-0	17	McDougald 86	5267
8	9	EL	A	Bristol City	W 1-0	1-0	15	Berry 8	(7585)
9	12	EL	A	Crewe Alexandra	L 1-3	0-1	17	Bull 80	(3272)
10	16	EL	H	Blackpool	L 1-2	0-2	19	Chapman 88	6158
11	24	EL	A	Bournemouth	L 1-3	0-2	22	Chapman 89	(4560)
12	26	AWS 1/1	A	Cambridge United	W 4-1	1-0		McCarthy 29, Bull 46(pen), 53, McDougald 57	(1438)
13	30	EL	H	Shrewsbury Town	D 2-2	1-1	22	Foster 4, Thompson-Minton 77	5247
14	O 7	EL	A	Rotherham United	L 0-1	0-0	22		(2950)
15	14	EL	H	Swindon Town	L 1-3	0-3	24	McDougald 53	7808
16	17	AWS 1/2	H	Bristol Rovers	L 0-2	0-0			1191
17	21	EL	A	Burnley	L 0-3	0-3	5		(9018)
18	28	EL	H	Bristol Rovers	W 2-0	0-0	23	Parris 50, Mundee 58(pen)	5658
19	31	EL	H	Swansea City	L 0-2	0-1	23		4230
20	N 4	EL	A	Carlisle United	L 0-1	0-0	24		(5896)
21	12	FAC 1	A	Canvey Island	D 2-2	2-1		McDougald 16, 38	(3500)
22	18	EL	H	Walsall	L 0-3	0-2	24		4976
23	21	FAC 1R	H	Canvey Island	W 4-1	1-0		Byrne 45, 68, McDougald 47, Smith 78	7008
24	25	EL	A	York City	L 1-3	1-0	24	McCarthy 3	(3105)
25	28	AWS 2	A	Walsall	W 2-1	1-1		Storer 14, Mundee 81(pen)	(3454)
26	D 2	FAC 2	H	Fulham	D 0-0	0-0			(8052)
27	9	EL	H	Bournemouth	W 2-0	1-0	23	Myall 27, Thompson-Minton 57	5414
28	14	FAC 2R	H	Fulham	D 0-0	0-0			6209
29	16	EL	A	Shrewsbury Town	L 1-2	1-1	24	Storer 12	(3697)
30	22	EL	H	Chesterfield	L 0-2	0-1	24		3629
31	26	EL	A	Brentford	W 1-0	1-0	23	Wilkins 42	(5794)
32	J 1	EL	A	Stockport County	D 1-1	1-1	23	Chapman 8	5694
33	9	AWS QF	A	Shrewsbury Town	L 2-4	1-1		Scott 26(og), McDougald 79	(2559)
34	13	EL	A	Bradford City	W 3-1	2-0	21	Thompson-Minton 25, Mundee 39, McDougald 50	(5139)
35	20	EL	A	Peterborough United	L 1-2	1-0	24	Mundee 41(pen)	5572
36	23	EL	A	Hull City	D 0-0	0-0	23		(2421)
37	F 3	EL	H	Wrexham	D 2-2	1-2	23	Thompson-Minton 9, Thompson-Minton 63	4617
38	10	EL	A	Oxford United	D 1-1	0-1	13	McDougald 48	(5967)
39	17	EL	H	Crewe Alexandra	D 2-2	0-2	22	Wilkins 47, Smith 82	6561
40	24	EL	A	Blackpool	L 1-2	1-0	22	Storer 18	(4937)
41	27	EL	H	Bristol City	L 0-2	0-1	23		4739
42	M 2	EL	H	Brentford	D 0-0	0-0	23		5914
43	6	EL	A	Wycombe Wanderers	W 2-0	0-0	23	Thompson-Minton 55, McGarrigle 80	(3466)
44	9	EL	A	Chesterfield	L 0-1	0-0	23		(6233)
45	12	EL	H	Oxford United	L 1-2	0-1	23	Maskell 80	3953
46	16	EL	H	Hull City	W 4-0	2-0	23	Maskell 8, 82, Byrne 38, 53,	4910
47	23	EL	A	Stockport County	L 1-3	1-1	23	Parris 44	(5765)
48	30	EL	A	Rotherham United	D 1-1	1-1	23	Wilkins 41	5530
49	A 3	EL	A	Swindon Town	L 2-3	0-1	23	Thompson-Minton 55, Rowe 64	(8610)
50	6	EL	A	Bristol Rovers	L 0-1	0-0	23		(5385)
51	9	EL	H	Burnley	W 1-0	1-0	23	Rowe 19	5954
52	13	EL	A	Swansea City	L 1-2	1-1	23	Ampadu 22(og)	(2373)
53	20	EL	A	Carlisle United	W 1-0	1-0	23	Rowe 7	6131
54	23	EL	A	Notts County	L 1-2	1-1	23	Thompson-Minton 26	(3501)
55	M 4	EL	A	Walsall	L 1-2	0-1	23	Myall 82	(4840)
56	5	EL	H	York City	L 1-3	1-0	23	Maskell 19	2106

Best Home League Attendance: 7808 v Swindon Town   **Smallest: 2106 v York City**   **Average: 5256**

Goal Scorers:
EL(46):   Thompson-Minton(8),McDougald(4),Maskell(4),Rowe(3),Wilkins(3),Chapman(3),Mundee(3),Myall(2),Parris(2),Storer(2),Opponent(s)(2),Berry(2),Bull(2),
                 Byrne(2),Foster(1),Smith(1),McGarrigle(1),McCarthy(1)
CC(0):
FAC(6):   McDougald(3),Byrne(2),Smith(1)
AWS(8):   McDougald(2),Bull(2),Mundee(1),Storer(1),McCarthy(1),Opponent(s)(1)

(D) Allan	(F) Andrews	(F) Berry	(F) Bull	(F) Byrne	(M) Case	(D) Chapman	(D) Foster	(M) Fox	(F) Fox	(D) Hobson	(F) Maskell	(D) McCarthy	(F) McDonald	(F) McDougald	(D) McGarrigle	(D) Munday	(F) Mundee	(D) Myall	(D) Osman	(D) Parris	(M) Rowe	(G) Rust	(D) Smith	(F) Storer	(M) Thompson-Minton	(D) Tuck	(M) Wilkins	(D) Yorke-Johnson	
						X	S1	S2				X		X	X2			X1				X	X	X	X	X	X	X	I.S.Hemley 1
	S3		S1			S2						X		X1	X2	X		X1				X	X3	X	X	X	X	X	R.Harris 2
	S		X	X		X		S1				X		X	X2	X1		S2				X	X	X		X			D.Orr 3
	X			X		X			S1			X			X2			X				X	X1	X		X	X	S	M.Pierce 4
	S	X	X	X	S1	X						X			X			S				X	X	X1		X	X		G.Cane 5
	S2		X	X2		X						X		X	X			S				X	X	X	S1	X	X1		P.Taylor 6
	S2	X2	X	S1		X	X					X		X				X				X	X	X1	S		X		G.Barber 7
	S1	X	X1	S		X	X					X		X				X				X	S	X	X		X		G.Singh 8
	S	X	X	S1		X						X		X1				X				X	S	X	X	X	X		K.Lynch 9
	S2	X2	X			X	X					X		X		X1						X	X1	X	X	X	X		F.Stretton 10
	S1	X1	X			X	X					X		X				S				X	X	S2	X2		X		I.Hemley 11
	S2		X			X2						X		X	X			S1	X			X	S3	X1	X		X3		M.Fletcher 12
		X2				X	X					X		X		S1			X			X	X	S2	X	S	X1		B.Knight 13
		X				X	X					X		X	X2	X1			X			X	X	S1	X	S	S		S.Mathieson 14
	S3					X	X1					X		X	X2				X			X	X	X		X3	S1	S2	G.Pooley 15
	X					X1		S1				X		X	S2				X	X		X	X	X		X2	X	S	M.Pierce 16
	S1					X						X		X	S		X	X	X		X	X	X	X	X1		X	S	K.Breen 17
			S1	S		X						X		X	S		X	X	X		X	X	X	X1		X	X		P.Rejer 18
			S1	S2		X						X		X		X	X3	X	X		X	X	X	X1		X2	X	S3	M.Bailey 19
			X			X						X		X	S		X	X	X	X		X	X	X1	S1		X	S	T.Leeke 20
	S		X			X						X		X		S1	X1	X	X			X	X	X		X	S	X	M.Bailey 21
	S		X			X						X		X		S		X	X	X1		X	X	S		X	X	X	A.D'Urso 22
	S		X			X						X		X		S1	X	X	X1			X	X	S		X	X	X	M.Bailey 23
	S		X			X						X		X	X	X		X	X			X	X	S		X	X	X	P.Richards 24
			X		S							X		X	S	X		X	X			X	X	X		X	S	X	E.Wolstenholme 25
	S1		X1	X		X						X			S			X	X			X	X	X		X	S	X	G.Poll 26
	S		X	X1		X						X		X				X	X			X	X	S1		S1	X	X	R.J.Harris 27
	X		X			X						X		X	S			X1	X2			X	X	S1		S2	X	X	G.Poll 28
	S3		X			X						X		X	S1			X	S			X	X1	X	X		X	S1	F.G.Stretton 29
			X1			X			S2			X		X				X	S1			X	X	X2	X		X		S.Bennett 30
			X			X			S			X		X			S	X	X	S		X	X	X		X	X		M.E.Pierce 31
			X			X			S			X		X				X	S1	X		X	X	X	X1		S	D.Orr 32
			S1			X1			X			X		X			S	X	X			X	X	X		X	S	X	P.Rejer 33
			S			X			X			X		X			S	X	X			X	X	X		X	S	X	P.Taylor 34
			S			X			X1			X		X				X	S	S1		X	X	X		X	X	X	K.A.Leach 35
			S			X			X			X		X				X	S	S		X	X	X		X	X	X	R.Pearson 36
			S1			X			S			X		X		X1		S	X			X	X	X		X1	X	X	C.R.Wilkes 37
			X			X			S			X		X				S1	S			X	X	X	X1		X	X	G.Barber 38
			X1			X			S		X	X	X	X	S			S2				X	X	S1	X		X2	X	I.Hemley 39
			S			X			S	X	X	X	X	S				X	X			X	X		X		X	X	S.Baines 40
			X2			X			S2		X	X	X	S1	S			X1	X			X	X		X		X	X	A.P.D'Urso 41
			X1			X				X	X	X	X	S1	S			X	X2			X	X		X		X	X	M.C.Bailey 42
			S			X				X	X	X	X1	X	S2			X	S1			X	X		X2		X	X	M.J.Brandwood 43
			S			X			S2	X	X1	X		X	S1			X	X			X	X		X2		X	X	T.West 44
			S1			X		S	S	X	X	X	X	X				X	X			X	X		X		X	X	B.Knight 45
			X			X			S	X		X		X	X	S		X	X			X	X		S		X	X	A.G.Wiley 46
			X1			X			S	X		X		X2	X			X	X			X	X		S1	X	S2	X	G.Frankland 47
			S			X			S	X	X			X	S			X	X	X	X	X	X		X	X	X	P.Taylor 48
X						X			X	X					S3	S1	X	X1	X	X	X			S2	X2		X3		A.Leake 49
X						X			X	X						S3	X2	X3	X	X	X			S2	X		S1	X1	R.B.Gifford 50
X			S1			X			X	X							S2	X	X	X	X			X2	X		X1	S	P.Rejer 51
X			S1			X			X	X				S	X			X2	X	X	X			S2	X		X1		G.Cain 52
X			S			X			S	X	X					S1		X	X	X	X				X		X1		S.G.Bennett 53
X			X2			X			S1	X	X						S2	X	X1	X	X				X			S	J.Rushton 54
X			X1			X			S	S	X	X						X	X			X	X	X	S1			X	I.Cruikshanks 55
X			S1			X			S3	X1	X			S2				X2	X		X	X	X	X3	X		X		G.Pooley 56
8	0	6	10	15	0	36	8	0	0	9	15	33	5	33	8	7	30	27	11	38	9	46	28	28	37	7	31	18	EL Appearances
0	8	0	9	2	0	0	2	6	0	0	0	0	3	6	3	1	6	1	0	0	2	0	0	2	2	1	4	2	EL Sub Appearances
0	1+1	0	0	1+1	0	1+1	0	0	0	0	2	0	1	2	1	0	2	0	0	2	2	2	1	2	2				CC Appearances
0	1+1	0	3	0	2	0	0	0	0	0	4	0	3	0	0+2	4	4	2	4	0	4	1+1	4	0	2+1	2			FAC Appearances
0	1+1	0	1	0+1	0	4	0	0	0	0	2	0	4	1+1	1	2	2+1	3	4	0	4	3+1	3	3	1	3	2		AWS Appearances

Also Played: (M) Coughlan S(34), X1(45). (G) Ormerod S(1,16). (M) Virgo S2(4).

CLUB RECORDS

BIGGEST VICTORIES
League: 9-1 v Newport, Division 3(S), 18.4.1951.
9-1 v Southend, Division 3, 27.11.1965.
F.A. Cup: 12-0 v Shoreham, 1.10.1932.
10-1 v Wisbech, FA Cup Round 1, 13.11.1965.

BIGGEST DEFEATS
League: 0-9 v Middlesbrough, Division 2, 23.8.1958.
League Cup: 0-8 v Northampton, 4th Round replay, 1.11.1966.

MOST POINTS
3 points a win: 84, Division 3, 1987-88.
2 points a win: 65, Division 3(S), 1955-56 & Division 3, 1971-72.

MOST GOALS SCORED
112, Division 3, 1955-56.

RECORD TRANSFER FEE RECEIVED
£900,000 from Liverpool for Mark Lawrenson, August 1981.

RECORD TRANSFER FEE PAID
£500,000 to Manchester United for Andy Ritchie, October 1980.

BEST PERFORMANCES
League: 13th Division 1, 1981-82.
F.A. Cup: Runners-up 1982-83. **League Cup:** 5th Round 1978-79.

HONOURS
Charity Shield Winners 1910. Champions Division 3(S) 1957-58.
Champions Division 4, 1964-65.

LEAGUE CAREER
Original members of Division 3 1920, Div 3(S) 1921, Div 2 1957-58,
Div 3 1961-62, Div 4 1962-63, Div 3 1964-65, Div 2 1971-72, Div 3
1972-73, Div 2 1976-77, Div 1 1978-79, Div 2 1982-83, Div 3 1986-
87, Div 2 1987-88, Div 3 (now Div 2) 1991-92, Div 3 1996-97.

INDIVIDUAL CLUB RECORDS

MOST GOALS IN A SEASON
Peter Ward: 36 goals in 1976-77 (League 32, FA Cup 1, League
Cup 3)

MOST GOALS IN A MATCH
6. Arthur Attwood v Shoreham, 12-0, FA Cup, 1.10.1932.

OLDEST PLAYER
Jimmy Case, 41 years 165 days, 31.10.95.

YOUNGEST PLAYER
Simon Fox, 16 years 238 days v Fulham, Div 2, 23.4.1994.

MOST CAPPED PLAYER
Steve Penney (Northern Ireland) 17.

PREVIOUS MANAGERS

(Since 1945) Charles Webb 1919-47; Tommy Cook 1947; Don
Welsh 1947-51; Billy Lane 1951-61; George Curtis 1961-63; Archie
Macauley 1963-68; Freddie Goodwin 1968-70; Pat Saward 1970-73;
Brian Clough 1973-74; Peter Taylor 1974-76; Alan Mullery 1976-81;
Mike Bailey 1981-82; Jimmy Melia 1982-83; Chris Cattlin 1983-86;
Alan Mullery 1986-87; Barry Lloyd 1987-93, Liam Brady 1993-95.

ADDITIONAL INFORMATION
PREVIOUS NAMES
Brighton United 1898-1900.
Brighton & Hove Rangers 1900-1901.
PREVIOUS LEAGUES
Southern League.
Club colours: Blue & white striped shirts, blue shorts, white socks.
Change colours: Red shirts with red & white patterned sleeves,
white shorts, red stockings with white trim.
Reserves League: Avon Insurance Football Combination Div.1.
Youth: South Eastern Counties League Division Two.

LONGEST LEAGUE RUNS

of undefeated matches:	16 (1930-31)	of league matches w/out a win:	15 (1947-48, 1972-73)
of undefeated home matches:	27 (1975-76)	of undefeated away matches:	9 (1938)
without home win:	10 (1972-73)	without an away win:	21 (1982-83)
of league wins:	9 (1926)	of home wins:	14 (1955-56. 1975-76)
of league defeats:	12 (1972-73)	of away wins:	4 (1926, 1936 twice)

THE MANAGER

JIMMY CASE . . . . appointed November 1995.

PREVIOUS CLUBS
As Manager . . . . None.
As Asst.Man/Coach. . . . . Brighton.
As a player . . . . South Liverpool, Liverpool, Brighton, Southampton, Bournemouth, Halifax, Wrexham,
. . . . Darlington, Sittingbourne, Brighton.

HONOURS
As a Manager . . . . None.
As a Player . . . . **Liverpool:** Div.1 championship 1975-76, 1976-77, 1978-79, 1979-80,
. . . . EC 1976-77, 1977-78, 1980-81, UEFA Cup 1975-76.

PLAYERS NAME Honours	Ht	Wt	Birthdate	Birthplace Transfers	Contract Date	Clubs	League	L/Cup	FA Cup	Other	Lge	L/C	FAC	Oth
G O A L K E E P E R S														
Ormerod Mark	6.0	11.05	05/02/76	Bournemouth	21/07/94	Brighton & H.A.								
Just Nicholas	6.0	13.1	25/09/74	Cambridge		Arsenal								
S.				Free	09/07/93	Brighton & H.A.	138	12	6	8				
D E F E N D E R S														
Allan Derek	6.0	10.13	24.12.74	Irvine		Aye United	5							
				£70000	16.03.93	Southampton	0+1							
Apps. with Brighton on Loan 95/96.				Free	14/06/96	Brighton & H.A.	8							
Hobson Gary	6.1	12.10	12/11/71	Hull	17/07/91	Hull City	135+7	13+1	2+2	6				
					27/03/96	Brighton & H.A.	9							
McGarrigle Kevin	5.11	11.05	09/04/77	Newcastle	21/07/94	Brighton & H.A.	25+7	2		1+1	1			
Smith Peter	6.1	12.7	12/07/69	Stone		Alma Swanley								
				Free	08/08/94	Brighton & H.A.	63+5	6+1	5	4+1	2		1	
Tuck Stuart	5.9	10.8	01/10/74	Brighton	09/07/93	Brighton & H.A.	30+12	5	1	4+1				
Mayo Kerry						Brighton & H.A. (T)								
Virgo James				Brighton & H.A.				0+1						
Clarke-Johnson Ross	6.0	12.04	01/02/78	Brighton	22/07/94	Brighton & H.A.	19+3		2	3				
M I D F I E L D														
Cox Mark	5.11	10.11	05/07/57	Basingstoke	21/07/94	Brighton & H.A.	8+15			1	1			
Mundee Denny W	5.10	11.07	10/10/68	Swindon		Q.P.R.								
				Free	21/08/86	Swindon Town								
					01/08/87	Salisbury								
				Loan	07/09/89	Torquay United	9							
				Free	12/08/93	Brentford	59+19	0+3	3	5+3	16			2
					19/10/95	Brighton & H.A.	30+1		4	2	3			1
Parris George M	5.9	13.0	11/09/64	Ilford	09/09/82	West Ham United	211+28	27+3	21	7+1	12	1	4	1
				£150000	12/03/93	Birmingham City	36+3	2	1		1			
				Loan	08/08/94	Brentford	5	2					1	
				Loan	01/12/94	Bristol City	6							
				Loan	09/02/95	Brighton & H.A.	18				2			
					29/09/95	Brighton & H.A.	38		4	4	2			
Peake Jason Y.1.	5.10	11.5	29/09/71	Leicester	09/01/90	Leicester City	4+4			1+1	1			
				Loan	13/02/92	Hartlepool United	5+1				1			
				Free	26/08/92	Halifax Town	32+1		3	1	1		1	
					23/03/94	Rochdale	91+4	3	5	7	6		2	1
					22/07/96	Brighton & H.A.								
Thompson-Minton Jeff	5.6	11.10	28/12/73	Hackney	11/01/92	Tottenham Hotspur	2	0+1			1			
				Free	25/07/94	Brighton & H.A.	74+2	6	5	4	8			
F O R W A R D S														
Andrews Philip	5.11	11.0	14/09/76	Andover	21/07/94	Brighton & H.A.	1+17	1+2	1+2	1+2				
Baird Ian James S. Div.2'90.	6.2	12.12	01/04/64	Rotherham	05/04/82	Southampton (A)	20+2	1+1			5			
				Loan	01/11/80	Cardiff City	12				8			
				£75000	10/03/85	Leeds United	84+1	4	5	7	33		4	
				Loan	01/12/86	Newcastle United	4+1				1			
				£285000	12/08/87	Portsmouth	20	1	1		1			
				£120000	04/03/88	Leeds United	76+1	5	3	6	17	1	2	
				£500000	29/01/90	Middlesbrough	60+3	5+1	3	4	19		1	1
				£400000	31/07/91	Hearts	64	5	7	3	15	2	1	1
				£295000	06/07/93	Bristol City	44+12	3	2	1	11		1	
					29/09/95	Plymouth Argyle	24+3		1+1		6		1	
				£35000	31.07.96	Brighton & H.A.								
Cox Simon	5.10	10.2	28/08/77	Basingstoke		Brighton & H.A.	1+8	0+1		0+1				
Maskell Craig	5.10	11.4	10/04/68	Aldershot	15/04/86	Southampton	2+4				1			
				£20000	31/05/88	Huddersfield Town	86+1	6	8	7	43	4	3	4
				£250000	07/08/90	Reading	60+12	2	5	1	26			
				£225000	09/07/92	Swindon Town	40+7	3+1	2+1	4	21	1		4
				£250000	07/02/94	Southampton	8+9		0+1	1	1			
				Loan	28/12/95	Bristol City	5				1			
				£40000	01/03/96	Brighton & H.A.	15				4			
McDonald Paul	5.7	9.5	20/04/68	Motherwell		Hamilton Acad.								
				£75000	08/06/93	Southampton	0+3		0+1					
				Loan	15/09/95	Burnley	8+1			2	1			
				£25000	16/02/96	Brighton & H.A.	5							
Storer Stuart MC'89.	5.11	11.8	16/01/67	Rugby	23/08/83	Mansfield Town	0+1							
					01/08/84	VS Rugby								
				Free	10/01/85	Birmingham City	5+3	1						
					06/03/87	Everton								
				Loan	23/07/87	Wigan Athletic	9+3	4						
				£25000	24/12/87	Bolton Wanderers	95+28	9+2	7+3	16+5	12		2	1
				£25000	25/03/93	Exeter City	54	4	3	2	6	1	1	
				£15000	02/03/95	Brighton & H.A.	30+9	2	1+1	3	3			1

THE GOLDSTONE GROUND
Newtown Road, Hove, E.Sussex BN3 7DE.
Tel: 01273 778 855 Fax: 01273 321 095

Capacity 18,203
Covered Standing 4,500
Seating 5,110

First game .... v Southampton, 3.9.1898.
First floodlit game .... v Boldklubben Frem, Copenhagen 10.4.61.

ATTENDANCES
Highest .... 36,747 v Fulham, Div 2, 27.12.1958.
Lowest .... 1,150 v Norwich City, Div 3(S), 2.2.1929.

OTHER GROUNDS .... None.

MATCHDAY TICKET PRICES

West Stand £12
Concessions £6

South Stand £10
Concessions £5

Terraces £8
Concessions £4.50

Ticket Office Telephone no. 01273 778 855

ALBION CLUBLINE
0891 44 00 66
Calls cost 39p per minute cheap rate and 49p per minute at all other times.
Call costings correct at time of going to press.

HOW TO GET TO THE GROUND

From the North
Use A23 with Pyecoumbe, then in 2 miles turn right (S.P. Hove). In 1.1 miles bear left into Nevill Road A2023. In 0.9 miles, at cross roads, turn left A27 into Old Shoreham Road for Brighton & Hove Albion.

From the East
From Lewes use A27 to Brighton then follow signs Worthing A27 along Old Shoreham Road for Brighton & Hove Albion.

From West
Use A27 (S.P. Brighton) along Old Shoreham Road for Brighton & Hove Albion.

Car Parking
Available at the Greyhound Stadium (Nevill Road). Limited parking adjacent to ground. Visitors beware - Police tow-away squad on duty on match days.

Nearest Railway Station
Hove (01273 206 755)

MATCHDAY PROGRAMME

Programme Editor . . . . Gareth Roberts (Bishops Printers Ltd).

Number of pages . . . . 32.

Price . . . . £1.30.

Subscriptions . . . . . 23 home programmes £30 (saved) + £9 if posted.
. . . . 23 away programmes £28 (saved) + £9 if posted.

Local Newspapers . . . . Evening Argus.

Local Radio Stations . . . BBC Southern Counties Radio, Southern FM.

CAMBRIDGE UNITED
(The U's)
NATIONWIDE LEAGUE DIVISION 3
SPONSORED BY: PREMIER HOLIDAYS AND TRAVEL

996-97 - Back Row (L-R): Colin Vowden, Marc Joseph, Robbie Turner, David Thompson, Paul wanless, Jody Craddock.
Middle Row: Micah Hyde, Adi Hayes, Tony Richards, Scott Barrett, Danny Granville, Jamie Barnwell-Edinboro, Lenny Pack.
Front Row: David Williamson, Shaun Howes, Paul Raynor, Billy Beall, Matthew Joseph, Keith Oliver.

CAMBRIDGE UNITED
FORMED IN 1919
TURNED PROFESSIONAL IN 1946
LTD COMPANY IN 1948

CHAIRMAN: R H Smart
DIRECTORS
G G Harwood, J S Howard, R F Hunt,
G P Lowe, R T Summerfield.
SECRETARY
Steve Greenall (01223 566 500)
COMMERCIAL MANAGER
Vince Durrant

MANAGER: Tommy Taylor

RESERVE TEAM MANAGER
Paul Clark
YOUTH TEAM MANAGER
David Batch
PHYSIOTHERAPIST
Ken Steggles

STATISTICIAN FOR THE DIRECTORY
Colin Faiers

Cambridge's first year back in Division Three was one of disappointment. Hopes of bouncing back up to the Second Division, from which they jut lost the race for survival in the 1994-95 season, were soon forgotten when their League form suffered.

The season started on the right note however, with a 2-1 win over Scunthorpe United, indeed they only lost once in the League in a run of nine games. Maybe there was hope? However a disastrous October saw them lose four of their five games as the 'U's' slipped from fourth to eleventh.

League form from there on was inconsistent and with another bad sequence of five defeats Cambridge found themselves in 23rd place! The last seven games saw them pick up 14, of the available 21 points which gained them an unsatisfactory, but safe, 16th final position.

The Cup competitions were over as quickly as they had started. First round exits in both the Coca-Cola Cup (·2-3 aggregate to Swindon) and the F.A. Cup again to Swindon (1-4). In the Auto Windscreen Shield they lost to Brighton (1-4) and Bristol Rovers (0-3).

Next season both the fans and club will be expecting to be fighting for the Championship, but a play-off place is probably a more realistic target.

CAMBRIDGE UNITED

League: 16th   FA Cup: 1st Rnd   Coca-Cola Cup: 1st Rnd   Auto Windscreen Shield: 1st Rnd

M	DATE	COMP	VEN	OPPONENTS	RESULT	HT	LP	GOAL SCORERS/GOAL TIMES	ATT.
1	A 12	EL	A	Scunthorpe United	W 2-1	0-1	8	Kyd 79, Butler 85	(2561)
2	15	CC 1/1	H	Swindon Town	W 2-1	1-1		Corazzin 10, 62(pen)	2530
3	19	EL	H	Hereford United	D 2-2	2-1	7	Brough 10(og), Butler 45	2557
4	23	CC 1/2	A	Swindon Town	L 0-2	0-0			(6724)
5	26	EL	A	Gillingham	L 0-3	0-0	13		(5093)
6	29	EL	H	Colchester United	W 3-1	2-0	9	Palmer 15, Joseph 23, Corazzin 60	3476
7	S 2	EL	A	Preston North End	D 3-3	1-1	8	Barrick 38, Corazzin 58, Butler 86	(7034)
8	9	EL	H	Barnet	D 1-1	0-0	9	Butler 84	3054
9	12	EL	H	Exeter City	D 1-1	0-0	11	Butler 85	2365
10	16	EL	A	Bury	W 2-1	0-1	6	Butler 61, Corazzin 86	(2762)
11	23	EL	H	Lincoln City	W 3-1	2-0	4	Perkins 11, Corazzin 24, 84	(2614)
12	26	AWS 1/1	H	Brighton & H.A.	L 1-4	0-1		Adekola 50	1438
13	30	EL	H	Hartlepool United	L 0-1	0-0	7		2895
14	O 7	EL	H	Cardiff City	W 4-2	2-0	4	Corazzin 30, 74, Craddock 74, Adekola 84	2648
15	14	EL	A	Northampton Town	L 0-3	0-2	7		(6301)
16	21	EL	H	Darlington	L 0-1	0-1	8		2730
17	28	EL	A	Rochdale	L 1-3	0-1	11	Butler 57	(2344)
18	30	EL	A	Doncaster Rovers	L 1-2	1-1	11	Watson 27	(1657)
19	N 4	EL	H	Scarborough	W 4-1	2-0	9	Butler 2, Butler 60, Corazzin 9, Middleton 69	2304
20	7	AWS 1/2	A	Bristol Rovers	L 0-3	0-0			(1805)
21	11	FAC 1	A	Swindon Town	L 1-4	0-2		Butler 57	(7383)
22	18	EL	A	Leyton Orient	L 1-3	1-1	11	Raynor 17	(4142)
23	25	EL	H	Torquay United	D 1-1	1-0	11	Butler 38(pen)	2536
24	D 9	EL	H	Lincoln City	W 2-1	1-1	10	Middleton 21, 72	2472
25	16	EL	A	Hartlepool United	W 2-1	1-1	10	Middleton 22, Stock 59	(1612)
26	23	EL	A	Plymouth Argyle	L 0-1	0-0	10		(7135)
27	26	EL	H	Wigan Athletic	W 2-1	0-0	8	Turner 49, Joseph 66	2855
28	J 6	EL	H	Chester City	D 1-1	0-1	8	Turner 49	2643
29	13	EL	A	Hereford United	L 2-5	1-3	9	Middleton 3, Raynor 48	(2548)
30	20	EL	H	Scunthorpe United	L 1-2	0-0	11	Turner 47	2413
31	23	EL	A	Mansfield Town	L 1-2	0-1	11	Raynor 84	(1801)
32	F 3	EL	H	Gillingham	D 0-0	0-0	12		4114
33	13	EL	H	Fulham	D 0-0	0-0	13		2233
34	17	EL	A	Exeter City	L 0-1	0-0	16		(2804)
35	24	EL	H	Bury	L 2-4	2-1	17	Middleton 17, Robinson 34	2341
36	27	EL	A	Barnet	L 0-2	0-0	19		(1849)
37	M 2	EL	A	Wigan Athletic	L 1-3	1-2	22	Craddock 29	(2528)
38	9	EL	H	Plymouth Argyle	L 2-3	0-1	23	Hyde 54, Corazzin 74(pen)	2785
39	16	EL	H	Fulham	W 2-0	1-0	20	Beall 8, Corazzin 47	(3872)
40	19	EL	A	Colchester United	L 1-2	1-1	20	Middleton 30	(2995)
41	23	EL	H	Mansfield Town	L 0-2	0-2	22		2302
42	26	EL	A	Chester City	D 1-1	1-0	21	Beall 10	(1623)
43	30	EL	A	Cardiff City	D 1-1	0-1	21	Richards 81	(2326)
44	A 2	EL	H	Northampton Town	L 0-1	0-0	21		3631
45	6	EL	H	Rochdale	W 2-1	1-1	21	Craddock 6, Barnwell-Edinboro 49	2186
46	8	EL	A	Darlington	D 0-0	0-0	21		(3064)
47	13	EL	H	Doncaster Rovers	D 2-2	0-0	21	Barnwell-Edinboro 62, Middleton 87	2451
48	16	EL	H	Preston North End	W 2-1	0-1	19	Beall 53, 66	2831
49	20	EL	A	Scarborough	L 0-2	0-1	20		(1401)
50	27	EL	A	Torquay United	W 3-0	1-0	18	Wanless 44, Beall 73, Hyde 80	(1853)
51	M 4	EL	H	Leyton Orient	W 2-0	1-0	16	Hyde 28(pen), 87(pen)	3858

Best Home League Attendance: 4114 v Gillingham   Smallest: 2186 v Rochdale   Average: 2768

Goal Scorers:

EL(61): Corazzin(10),Butler(10),Middleton(8),Beall(5),Hyde(4),Craddock(3),Turner(3),Raynor(3),Barnwell-Edinboro(2),Joseph(2),Robinson(1),Barrick(1),Stock(1),Richards(1), Wanless(1),Watson(1),Palmer(1),Adekola(1),Kyd(1),Perkins(1),Opponent(s)(1)

CC(2): Corazzin(2)

FAC(1): Butler(1)

AWS(1): Adekola(1)

(F) Adekola	(F) Barnwell-Edinboro	(G) Barrett	(M) Barrick	(F) Beall	(F) Butler	(F) Corazzin	(D) Craddock	(G) Davies	(M) Granville	(D) Hyde	(D) Jeffrey	(D) Joseph Marc	(D) Joseph Matt	(M) Kyd	(F) Middleton	(M) Pack	(D) Palmer	(D) Rattle	(M) Raynor	(M) Richards	(F) Robinson	(M) Stock	(D) Thompson	(F) Turner	(D) Vowden	(M) Wanless	(F) Watson	(M) Wosahlo		
		X			X	X			X					X		X				X2				X	X				G.Frankland	1
X2		X	X		X	X			S3			X1		X	X3	X	S2							X	X				S.T.Bennett	2
		X		X	X	X			X1			X		X	X	S1	X		X1					X	S				B.Knight	3
X2		X			X1	S			S2					X	S1	X	X					X		X	X				K.Leach	4
		X	S2		X	S3					X			X	S1	X	X2		X1					X	X				I.Hemley	5
		X	X		X	X			S					X	X	X	S1						X1	X	S				A.Butler	6
		X	X		X	X			S1			X1		X	X	S1				X1				X	X				A.Wiley	7
		X			X	X			X1				X2	X	X	S1						S2		X	S				R.Fernandiz	8
S		X			X	X	X							X		X	X		X				X	X	X				N.Barry	9
S2		X			X2	X								X		X	S1		X				X1	X	X				I.G.Cruikshank	10
S		X			X	X								X		X	S2		X			X1		X	S1				S.Mathieson	11
X		X		S1					X		X			X		X			X					X	X				M.Fletcher	12
S2		X			X									X		X	X1		X2			X	S1	X	X				J.Kirkby	13
S2		X			X2	X				X	X			X1		X			X			X		X	S				M.Riley	14
S1		X			X					X	X					X1	S1		X1			X		X	X				J.Lloyd	15
X		X			X				X2	X	X			X		X	S2		X				X1		S				P.Taylor	16
		X			X				S3	X	X			X		X	X2	X3					X1		S1		S2		R.Pearson	17
		X			X				S2	X2	X		X		X	X	X	X					S		X		X1		G.Frankland	18
		X			X				X	X	X			S		X		X	X						X		S		J.Rushton	19
S1							X	X	X	X	X		S	X		X	S2	X	X1					X	X	X2				20
		X					X	X	X	S1	X	X		X	S2	X1		X	X2						S				P.Alcock	21
		X		X	X		X	X	X		X			X2		X		X	X						S		S1		G.Pooley	22
		X		X1	X		X	X	X		X			X		X		X	X						S		S1		A.D'Urso	23
				X	X	X	X		X	X		X	X		X	X	S	X		X1					S				S.Bennett	24
				X	X	X	X		X	S1	S2	X	X		X	X		S	X			S3	X1	X3	X2				P.Richards	25
				X	X	X	X		X	X	X	X		X	X	X	S					S	S2	X1	X	X2			R.Gifford	26
				X	X	X	X		X	X1	X	X	X		X	S1	S2	X2					S3	X3	X				F.Stretton	27
			S		X	X	X		X	X1	X	X			X	X		X					S1	X	X			S2	U.Rennie	28
			X1		X	X	X		X2	X	X				X	X		X	X				S1	X	X				S.Mathieson	29
					X	X	X		X	S1	X2	X	X		X	X		S	X1				S2	X	X				G.Barber	30
					X	X	X		X		S1	X	X		X	X1		X					S	X	X		S		P.Rejer	31
					X	X	X		X1	X	X	S	X		X	X		X						X	X			S	N.Barry	32
					X	X	X		X1	X	X	S	X		X	X		X						X	X		S1		E.Wolstenholme	33
			X1		X	X	X		X		X		X		X	X2		X					S2	X	S		S1		M.Fletcher	34
					X	X	X		X		X	S2	X	X1	X	X		X2					X2			X			K.Lynch	35
					X	X	X		X		X	S2	X1		X	X		X2					X2		X				B.Knight	36
				X	X	X	X		X	X1	S1	X			X	X		S					S2	X2	X				J.Lloyd	37
			X		X	X	X		X	X	X	S1			X	X		X	X1	S2				X	X				B.Harris	38
	X		X		X	X	X		X		X	S1	S		X	X		X2	X1	S2				X	X				R.Poulain	39
	X		X1		X	X	X		X		X	S2			X	X		X	X	S1				X2	X				M.Pierce	40
	X		X1		X	X	X		X		X	S1			X	X	S1	X3	X	X1					X				R.Pearson	41
	X				X	X	X		X		X	S1			X	X		S	X1	X2	S2			X	X				A.Butler	42
	X				X	X	X		X		X				X	X		S	X	X1			X	S	X2	X		S2	S.Bennett	43
	X				X	X	X		X		X	S1			X	X		S		X	S2			X1	X				J.Rushton	44
X	X		X		X				X		X				X			X		X				S1	X	X1			P.Taylor	45
X	X		X		X				X	X					X			X					S1	X1	X2				J.Kirkby	46
X	X		X		X		X1		X	S2					X			X		X			S1	X	X2				S.Baines	47
X	X		X		X				X	X2					X			X		X1			S1	S2	X				G.Pooley	48
X	X		X		X		X		X	X					X			X1							X	X			G.Frankland	49
X	X		X2		X				X	X					X				X1				X2		X	X			P.Rejer	50
X	X1		X		X				X	X		X	X		X				X					S2	S	X			T.Leake	51
1	7	31	2	15	16	31	44	15	31	20	20	10	42	3	38	2	30	7	35	15	4	15	14	10	22	14	1	0	EL Appearances	
4	0	0	1	0	0	0	2	0	4	4	7	2	0	6	2	9	0	2	0	4	13	2	1	0	2	0	3	4	EL Sub Appearances	
0	0	2	1	0	0	2	0	1	0+2	0	1	2	1+1	2	1+1	1	0	0	0	1	0	0	1	2	0	2	0	0	CC Appearances	
0	0	1	0	0+1	0	1	1	1	0	0+1	1	1	0	1	0+1	1	0	1	1	0	0	0	0	0	0	0	0	0	FAC Appearances	
1+1	0	1	0	0+1	0	0	1	1	2	1	1	1	1+1	1	1	1	1	0	2	0	1	0	0	0	0	2	0	0	AWS Appearances	

Also Played: Also Played: (F) Benjamin S1(32,35,36,50,51), S(33). (M) Clark X2(23), X1(31).(M) Fowler S2(1), S1(2,3), X(12). (M) Gutzmore S(12), S2(36), S3(41). (D) Hayes S(12), X49). (F) Howes S2(50). (M) Illman X(46,49,50,51), S2(47), X2(48). (F) Morah X1(22), S2(23), S1(31). (F) Perkins X2(11),S1(14). (M) Pick S2(46), X(43,44), S3(48), S(49). (D) Westley X1(1) X4,5,8). (F) Zumrutel X1(12).

CLUB RECORDS

BIGGEST VICTORIES
League: 6-0 v Darlington, Division 4, 18.9.1971.
6-0 v Hartlepool United, Division 4, 11.2.1989.
7-2 v Cardiff City (a) Division 2, 30.4.1994.
F.A. Cup: 5-1 v Bristol City, 5th Round 2nd replay, 27.2.1990.

BIGGEST DEFEATS
League: 0-6 v Aldershot (a) Division 3, 13.4.1974.
0-6 v Darlington (a), Division 4, 28.9.1974.
0-6 v Chelsea (a), Division 2, 15.1.1983.
League Cup: 0-5 v Colchester United, 1st Round, 1970-71.
0-5 v Derby County, Round 2, 4.10.1989.

MOST POINTS
3 points a win: 86, Division 3, 1990-91.
2 points a win: 65, Division 4, 1976-77.

MOST GOALS SCORED
87, Division 4, 1976-77.

RECORD TRANSFER FEE RECEIVED
£1,000,000 from Manchester United for Dion Dublin, August 1992.

RECORD TRANSFER FEE PAID
£195,000 to Luton Town for Steve Claridge, November 1992.

BEST PERFORMANCES
League: 5th in Division 2, 1991-92.
F.A. Cup: 6th Round 1989-90, 1990-91.
League Cup: 5th Round, 1992-93.

HONOURS
Champions of Division 4, 1976-77.
Champions of Division 3, 1990-91.

LEAGUE CAREER
Elected to Div 4 1970, P. Div 3 1972-73, R. Div 4 1973-74, P. Div 3 1976-77, P. Div 2 1977-78, R. Div 3 1983-84, R. Div 4 1984-85, P. Div 3 1989-90, P. Div 2 (now Div 1) 1990-91, R. Div 2 1992-93, R. Div 3 1994-95.

INDIVIDUAL CLUB RECORDS

MOST GOALS IN A SEASON
David Crown: 27 goals in 1985-86 (League 24, FA Cup 1, Freight Rover Trophy 2).

MOST GOALS IN A MATCH
5. Steve Butler v Exeter City, Division 2, 4.4.1994.

OLDEST PLAYER
John Ryan, 37 years 134 days v Derby County, 1.12.1984.

YOUNGEST PLAYER
Andy Sinton, 16 years 228 days v Wolverhampton W., 2.11.1982.

MOST CAPPED PLAYER
Tom Finney (Northern Ireland) 7.

PREVIOUS MANAGERS

(Since 1951)
Bill Whittaker 1951-55; Gerald Williams 1955; Bert Johnson 1955-59; Bill Craig 1959; Alan Moore (was player coach from 1959-60) 1960-63; Roy Kirk (caretaker) 1963-64; Roy Kirk 1964-66; Matt Wynn (caretaker) 1966-67; Bill Leivers 1967-74; Ray Freeman (caretaker) 1974; Ron Atkinson 1974-78; John Docherty 1978-83; John Ryan 1984-85; John Cozens (caretaker) 1984-85; Ken Shellito 1985-86; Chris Turner 1986-90; John Beck 1990-92; Gary Johnson (caretaker) 1992; Ian Atkins 1992-93; Gary Johnson 1993-95.

ADDITIONAL INFORMATION
PREVIOUS NAMES
Abbey United until 1951.
PREVIOUS LEAGUES
Southern League.
Club Colours: Amber & black quartered shirts, black shorts amber trim, black & amber hooped socks.
Change colours: Blue & green halved shirts, blue shorts, blue & green hooped socks.
Reserves League: Springheath Print Capital League.
Youth League: South East Counties.

LONGEST LEAGUE RUNS

of undefeated matches:	14 (1972)	of league matches w/out a win:	31 (1983-84. A League Record)
of undefeated home matches:	22 (1977-78)	of undefeated away matches:	12 (1990)
without home win:	16 (1983-84. A League Record)	without an away win:	32 (1981-83)
of league wins:	7 (1977)	of home wins:	10 (1977-78)
of league defeats:	7 (1983, 1984, 1984-85, 1985)	of away wins:	4 (20.3.1994 - 30.4.1994)

Cambridge United played 12 successive home league games without conceding a goal in 1982-83.

THE MANAGER

TOMMY TAYLOR . . . . appointed April 1995.

PREVIOUS CLUBS
As Manager . . . . None.
As Asst.Man/Coach . . . . Maidstone.
As a player . . . . West Ham United, Orient.

HONOURS
As a Manager . . . . None.
As a Player . . . . FA Cup 1975.

CAMBRIDGE UNITED

PLAYERS NAME Honours	Ht	Wt	Birthdate	Birthplace Transfers	Contract Date	Clubs	League	L/Cup	FA Cup	Other	Lge	L/C	FAC	Oth
							APPEARANCES				**GOALS**			
G O A L K E E P E R S														
Barrett Scott	6.0	12.11	02/04/63	Ilkeston		Ilkeston Town								
GMVC'92. FAT'92.					27/09/84	Wolves	30	1	1	3				
				£10000	24/07/87	Stoke City	51	2	3	4				
Loan (10/01/90) Colchester Utd13 Lge Apps.				Loan	22/03/90	Stockport County	10			2				
					01/08/91	Colchester United				5				
				Free	14/08/92	Gillingham	47	5	4	2				
				Free	02/08/95	Cambridge United	62	4	2	2				
Davies Martin	6.1	12.4	28/06/74	Swansea	02/07/92	Coventry City								
				Loan	23/11/93	Stafford Rangers								
					02/08/95	Cambridge United	30			2				
D E F E N D E R S														
Craddock Jody	6.0	11.10	25/07/75	Bromsgrove		Christchurch								
				Free	13/08/93	Cambridge United	233+9	6	7	7	6	1		
				Loan	04/10/93	Woking								
Hayes Adi						Cambridge Utd (T)								
Hyde Micah A	5.9	10.5	10/11/74	Newham	19/05/93	Cambridge United	111+30	2	8+2	6+1	18			
Joseph Marc						Cambridge Utd (T)								
Joseph Matthew N A	5.7	10.2	30/09/72	Bethnal Green	17/11/90	Arsenal								
				Free	07/12/92	Gillingham								
					19/11/93	Cambridge United	273	12	12	10	14			
Palmer Lee	6.0	12.4	19/09/70	Croydon	28/07/89	Gillingham	99+11	5+1		7+1	6	4		
				Free	02/08/95	Cambridge United	60	2	2	2	2			
Robinson David			30/10/74	Wrekin		Liverpool								
					01/08/94	Stockport County								
						Cambridge United								
Thompson David	6.3	12.7	20/11/68	Ashington	26/11/86	Millwall	88+9	4	4	6	6		1	
					18/06/92	Bristol City	17	4		5+1				
				Free	01/02/94	Brentford	9+1				1			
Loan (09/09/94) Blackpool					07/11/94	Blackpool								
				Free	23/03/95	Cambridge United	63+2	4						
Vowden Colin	6.0	13.0	13/09/71	Newmarket		Cambridge City								
				£15000	19/05/95	Cambridge United	44+4	4		4				
M I D F I E L D														
Granville Daniel	5.11	12.5	19/01/75	Islington	19/05/93	Cambridge United	145+22	1+4	0+5	9+2	7			
				Loan	12/01/94	Saffron Walden								
Kyd Michael	5.8	12.10	21/05/77	Hackney		Cambridge United	22+33	2+2	0+2	2+2	5			
				Loan	17/11/95	Bishop Stortford								
Pack Lenny	5.10	12.1	27/09/76	Salisbury	01/08/94	Cambridge United	4+18	2+2		2				
Raynor Paul	6.0	12.11	29/04/66	Nottingham	02/04/84	Nottingham Forest	3	1						
WFAC'89'91.				Loan	28/03/85	Bristol Rovers	7+1							
				Free	15/08/85	Huddersfield Town	38+12	3	2+1	1	9			
				Free	27/03/87	Swansea City	170+21	11+1	8+1	15+1	27	3	1	3
				Loan	17/10/88	Wrexham	6							
				Free	10/03/92	Cambridge United	46+3	5	1	2+1	2		1	
				£36000	23/07/93	Preston North End	72+8	4+1	7	10	9		1	2
					11/09/95	Cambridge United	70		2		6			
Richards Tony						Cambridge United								
F O R W A R D S														
Barnwell-Edinboro J	5.10	11.6	26/12/75	Hull	01/08/94	Coventry City								
				Loan	02/02/96	Wigan Athletic	2+8				1			
					28/03/96	Cambridge United	14				4			
Beall Matthew						Cambridge United								
Benjamin Trevor						Cambridge Utd (T)								
Howes Shaun						Cambridge Utd (T)								

ABBEY STADIUM

Newmarket Road, Cambridge CB5 8LN
Tel: 01223 566 500

Capacity 9.667
Covered Standing 6,425
Seating 3,242

First game ....v University Press, Friendly, 31.8.1932.
First floodlit game................................v Great Yarmouth, East Anglian Cup, 21.10.57.

ATTENDANCES
Highest ....14,000 v Chelsea (friendly), 1.5.1970.
Lowest ....857 v Colchester United, AMC 24.11.1987.

OTHER GROUNDS ....None.

MATCHDAY TICKET PRICES

Blocks A & G £10
Juv/OAP/Students £5

Family B Block........................... £7
Juv/OAP/Students £4

Blocks C,D,E £12
Juv/OAP/Student £6

Terraces................................. £7
Juv/OAP/Students £4

Match and Ticket Information
Postal application with payment & SAE one week in advance. (Access & Visa accepted)
Ticket Office Telephone no. 01223 566 500

CLUBCALL
0891 55 58 85
Calls cost 39p per minute cheap rate and 49p per minute at all other times.
Call costings correct at time of going to press.

HOW TO GET TO THE GROUND

From the North
Use A1 and A14 signposted to Cambridge, then follow signs for Newmarket. Leave A14 to join B1047 to Cambridge. Turn right into Newmarket Road for Cambridge United FC.

From the East
Follow signs A14 to Cambridge, use A1303 to Cambridge, then follow signs for Newmarket Road for Cambridge United FC.

From the South
Use A10 or M11, follow signs for A14 to Newmarket. Leave A14 to join B1047 to Cambridge, turn right into Newmarket Road for Cambridge United FC.

From the West
Follow signs A428 to Cambridge, then A14 to Newmarket and as for North.

Car Parking
Limited parking at main entrance. Off-street parking permitted. Also at Coldhams Common for visitors.

Nearest Railway Station
Cambridge (01223 311 999)

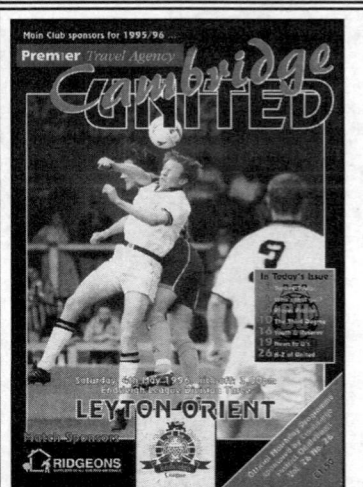

MATCHDAY PROGRAMME

Programme Editor . . . . A Pincher.

Number of pages . . . . 32.

Price . . . . £1.50.

Subscriptions. . . . . £50.00.

Local Newspapers . . . . Cambridge Evening News.

Local Radio Stations . . . . BBC Radio Cambridgeshire, Q103,
. . . . Chiltern Radio.

CARDIFF CITY
(The Bluebirds)
NATIONWIDE LEAGUE DIVISION 3
SPONSORED BY: THE SOUTH WALES ECHO

Back Row (L-R): Chris Davies, Andy Scott, Simon Haworth, Scott Young, Paul Shaw, Derek Brazil. **Middle Row:** Harry Parsons (Kit Manager), Keith Downing, Lee Baddeley, Patrick Mountain, Nathan Wigg, David Williams, Anthony Bird, Steve Williams, Chris Ingram, Bill Coldwell (director of football), Ian Jones, Jimmy Goodfellow (physio). **Front Row:** Ian Rodgerson, Damon Searle, Jason Perry (club captain), Kenny Hibbitt (coach), Paul Harding (captain), Carl Dale, Darren Adams.

CARDIFF CITY
FORMED IN 1899
TURNED PROFESSIONAL IN 1910
LTD COMPANY IN 1910

CHAIRMAN: Samesh Kumar
DIRECTORS
Joan HIll (Cheif Executive)
Rodney East, Will Dixon,

SECRETARY
Jim Finney
MERCHANDISING MANAGER
Kathy Shea

DIRECTOR OF FOOTBALL Kenny Hibbitt
MANAGER: Phil Neal

YOUTH TEAM MANAGER
Gavin Tait

STATISTICIAN FOR THE DIRECTORY
Alan Jenkins

It was another very disappointing season for Cardiff City. After being relegated from Division Two in 1994-5, the Bluebirds plummeted through the third division to finish only two places clear of the relegation zone.

City's form was inconsistent throughout the season: three wins in the first ten league matches were intermixed with three draws and four defeats. Their longest run of consecutive victories was a mere two in February, which sent them up to 16th in the league for a brief spell - from then onwards it was a struggle in the bottom reaches of the table, with City only managing three wins in the last nineteen matches.

There was a positive start to the cup competitions with two victories over first division Portsmouth in the Coca-Cola Cup - unfortunately, this success was short-lived, as Southampton proved to be too much for the Bluebirds, beating them conclusively in both legs of the second round. City's Auto Windscreens Shield campaign also began hopefully, with a high-scoring draw against Hereford and a victory over Gillingham, but was quickly over when Northampton Town won at Ninian Park. And there was another second-round defeat in the FA Cup - this time Swindon dealt the fatal blow.

Striker Carl Dale had an excellent season, scoring a total of 21 goals in the league - more than all the other Cardiff goalscorers put together - and scoring in all three cup competitions.

If the club can put the events of the last two seasons firmly behind them and build upon the potential of such players as Dale, and some of the season's new signings, they should be able to progress up to the top half of the table and begin their campaign to return to the second division.

CARDIFF CITY

League: 22nd   FA Cup: 2nd Rnd   Coca-Cola Cup: 2nd Rnd   Auto Windscreen Shield: 2nd Rnd

M	DATE	COMP	VEN	OPPONENTS	RESULT	HT	LP	GOAL SCORERS/GOAL TIMES	ATT.
1	A 12	EL	A	Rochdale	D 3-3	2-2	13	Bird 31, 41, Dale 59	(2321)
2	16	CC 1/1	A	Portsmouth	W 2-0	1-0		Dale 17, Bird 65	(4203)
3	19	EL	H	Northampton Town	L 0-1	0-1	15		7872
4	22	CC 1/2	H	Portsmouth	W 1-0	0-0		Dale 57	4341
5	26	EL	A	Doncaster Rovers	D 0-0	0-0	19		(2186)
6	29	EL	H	Exeter City	L 0-1	0-1	21		4444
7	S 2	EL	A	Darlington	W 1-0	1-0	16	Dale 13(pen)	(1845)
8	9	EL	H	Torquay United	D 0-0	0-0	17		4231
9	12	EL	H	Scarborough	W 2-1	1-1	14	Todd 1(og), Dale 77	2385
10	16	EL	A	Gillingham	L 0-1	0-1	17		(5317)
11	20	CC 2/1	H	Southampton	L 0-3	0-1			9041
12	23	EL	A	Hartlepool United	L 1-2	1-1	20	Dale 10(pen)	(2172)
13	26	AWS 1/1	A	Hereford United	D 3-3	0-0		Dale (2), Adams	(1411)
14	30	EL	H	Mansfield Town	W 3-0	1-0	15	Ingram 22, Dale 85, 90(pen)	3468
15	O 4	CC 2/2	A	Southampton	L 1-2	1-0		Rodgerson 22	(12709)
16	7	EL	A	Cambridge United	L 2-4	0-2	19	Adams 72, Bird 85	(2648)
17	14	EL	H	Barnet	D 1-1	1-1	20	Dale 16	3342
18	17	AWS 1/2	H	Gillingham	W 3-2	0-0		Dale (2), Adams	1034
19	21	EL	A	Lincoln City	W 1-0	0-0	15	Gardiner 84	(2453)
20	28	EL	H	Colchester United	L 1-2	1-2	19	Adams 30	3207
21	31	EL	H	Scunthorpe United	L 0-1	0-1	20		2024
22	N 4	EL	A	Plymouth Argyle	D 0-0	0-0	21		(7434)
23	11	FAC 1	A	Rushden & Diamonds	W 3-1	2-0		Dale 24, 71, Jarman 28	(4212)
24	18	EL	A	Bury	L 0-1	0-1	22		3846
25	26	EL	A	Hereford United	W 3-1	0-0	19	Dale 46, 81, Adams 52	(3528)
26	28	AWS 2	H	Northampton Town	L 1-2	1-0		Dale 46(pen)	1450
27	D 2	FAC 2	A	Swindon Town	L 0-2	0-0			(8274)
28	9	EL	H	Hartlepool United	W 2-0	0-0	15	Dale 52, 58	2919
29	16	EL	A	Mansfield Town	D 1-1	0-0	14	Searle 86	(1680)
30	19	EL	A	Fulham	L 2-4	2-1	14	Dale 4, Rodgerson 37	(2284)
31	26	EL	H	Chester City	D 0-0	0-0	17		6046
32	J 1	EL	A	Preston North End	L 0-5	0-1	18		(8354)
33	6	EL	H	Leyton Orient	D 0-0	0-0	17		2736
34	13	EL	A	Northampton Town	L 0-1	0-1	20		(4454)
35	20	EL	H	Rochdale	W 1-0	0-0	19	Gardiner 80	2230
36	F 3	EL	H	Doncaster Rovers	W 3-2	1-0	16	Dale 35, 52, 76 (3)	2313
37	10	EL	A	Leyton Orient	L 1-4	1-1	17	Philliskirk 19	(3564)
38	17	EL	A	Scarborough	L 0-1	0-1	21		(1414)
39	20	EL	H	Darlington	L 0-2	0-2	21		2113
40	24	EL	H	Gillingham	W 2-0	0-0	20	Dale 71, Harris 89(og)	2994
41	27	EL	A	Torquay United	D 0-0	0-0	18		(2004)
42	M 2	EL	H	Chester City	L 0-4	0-2	21		(2308)
43	5	EL	H	Wigan Athletic	W 3-0	2-0	16	Gardiner 17, Philliskirk 31, Gardiner 54	1611
44	9	EL	H	Fulham	L 1-4	0-1	18	Dale 68	3019
45	12	EL	A	Exeter City	L 0-2	0-1	18		(2609)
46	16	EL	A	Wigan Athletic	L 1-3	0-0	19	Flack 88	(2897)
47	23	EL	H	Preston North End	L 0-1	0-0	21		3511
48	30	EL	H	Cambridge United	D 1-1	0-0	22	Dale 62(pen)	2326
49	A 2	EL	A	Barnet	L 0-1	0-0	22		(2107)
50	6	EL	A	Colchester United	L 0-1	0-0	22		(3345)
51	8	EL	H	Lincoln City	D 1-1	0-0	22	Dale 50	2657
52	13	EL	A	Scunthorpe United	D 1-1	1-1	22	Dale 45	(2044)
53	20	EL	H	Plymouth Argyle	L 0-1	0-0	22		3374
54	27	EL	H	Hereford United	W 3-2	2-0	22	Dale 29, Philliskirk 45, 58	3751
55	M 4	EL	A	Bury	L 0-3	0-1	22		(5658)

Best Home League Attendance: 7872 v Northampton Town   **Smallest: 1611 v Wigan Athletic**   **Average: 3322**

Goal Scorers:
EL(41):   Dale(21),Philliskirk(4),Gardiner(4),Adams(3),Bird(3),Opponent(s)(2),Flack(1),Rodgerson(1),Searle(1),Ingram(1)
CC(4):   Dale(2),Bird(1),Rodgerson(1)
FAC(3):   Dale(2),Jarman(1)
AWS(7):   Dale(5),Adams(2)

1995-96

(F) Adams	(D) Baddeley	(F) Bird	(D) Brazil	(F) Dale	(M) Dobbs	(M) Downing	(F) Evans	(D) Evans	(M) Flack	(M) Fleming	(F) Gardiner	(M) Harding	(M) Harper	(D) Howarth	(M) Ingram	(M) Jarman	(M) McGorry	(D) Osman	(D) Perry	(F) Philliskirk	(M) Rodgerson	(M) Scully	(D) Searle	(F) Shaw	(M) Wigg	(G) Williams	(G) Williams	(F) Young	Player	#
	X	X	X	X										X			S		X				X		X	X	X	S	S.Baines	1
	X	X	X	X			S1							X		X1			X				X		X	X	S	S	A.D.Urso	2
	X1	X1	X	X										X		S1			X				X	X	X	X		S1	G.Barber	3
	X	X	X	X		S1					X1			X2					X				X		X	X		S2	J.Brandwood	4
	X	X	X	X		S1								X		X2			X				X	X	X1	X			G.Frankland	5
	X	X1	X	X		X								X					X				X		X	S1	X		S	D.Orr	6
	X		X	X	X	X								X		S1			X				X1		X1	X	S	S1	N.Barry	7
	X		X	X	X	X								X					X				X	X1	S1	X	S	S1	M.Fletcher	8
	X	X	X	X	X1									X		X			X				S		X	X	S	S1	P.Rejer	9
S2	X	X	X1	X	X											X2			X				X		X	X		S1	A.Wiley	10
S1	X	X		X	X1						X2			X					X				S2		X	X		X	S.W.Dunn	11
X	X	X1		X			S							X		X	S1		X				X		X	X		X	U.Rennie	12
X2	X			X			S1	S2						X		X1	X		X				X		X	X		X		13
S	X			X				S			X			X		X	X		X				X		X	X	S	X	K.Leach	14
X2	X			X			S2	S1						X		X	X		X1				X		X	X		X	M.Bodenham	15
S1	X			X			X	S2			X			X		X2			X			X1			X	X	S	X	M.Riley	16
S1	X			X			S2	X			X			X		X2	X		X1				X		X	X	S	X	F.J.Stretton	17
S1	X3	X1	X	X							X	X		X2	S2	S3							X		X	X		X		18
X1	X		X								X	X		S1	S2			X				X2		X	X	S	X	R.Poulaine	19
X	X		X								X	X		S2	S1	S		X				X1		X	X		X	J.Rushton	20
X1		S1	X2	X							X			X	X	X		X				S		X	X		X	R.J.Harris	21
X1		S1	X	X						X	X			X	S	X		X				X		X	X		X	S.Mathieson	22
X1		X2	X	X			S1			X	X			X		X		X				X		X	X		X	S.Dunn	23
X		S	X1	X					X	X				S2	X		S1		X				X2	X		X	A.Wyley	24
X	S2	S1		X					X2	X	X			X			X1		X				X		X		X	G.Barber	25
X	X	S1		X					X	X	X		X	S	X			X				S	X		X	X1	P.Jones	26
X1	X	S1		X				X2	X	X			X		X		X			S2	X		X	X	P.Jones	27
S			X				X	X	X	X	S		S	X	X	X		X				X	X	B.Knight	28
S1			X				X	X	X	X	S		X	X1		X				X	X	S.Bane	29
S1			X				X	X	X	X	S		S	X	X1		X				X	X	A.Butler	30
X	S		X				X	X	X	X		S1	S	X		X1	X		X			X	X	G.Singh	31
	S2		X				X	X	X1	X		S1	X2		X	X		X				X		X	T.West	32
	S2		X				X	X2	X1	X	S		X		X	X	X		S1	X		X	X	M.Bailey	33
		X		X			S1	X1		X			X		X	S2	X	X	X2		S	X	X	G.Pooley	34
		S1	X				S	X1	X	X			X		X		X		S	X		X	X	D.Allison	35
	X		X				S1	X	X	X			X		X	S	X	S	X		X	X	M.Pierce	36
		X					S1	X	X1	X			X		X	S2	X2	X		X	X	R.Furnandiz	37
	X		X				S	S	S1	X			X	X		X	X1	X1		X	X	I.G.Cruikshanks	38
	X		X				S	S1	X2	X			X	X		X	X1	S2	X		X	X	R.Harris	39
	X		X				S	X	X	X			X			X	X		X	X	J.Rushton	40
	X		X				S	X	X1	X			X			X	X	X1	X		X	D.Orr	41
		X	X				S	S1	X	X			X			X	X	X1	X		X	G.P.Barber	42
	X		X				S		X	X	X		X			X	S1	X1	S	X		X	P.Taylor	43
	X	X1	X				S	X	X1	X			X			X	X2	X	S1	X		X	J.Brandwood	44
	X		X				S2	X	X	X			X			X	S2	X2	S1	X		X	P.Rejer	45
	X		X				X	X2	S1	X			X			X	S2	X1	X	S	X		X	D.Laws	46
	X		X				X1	S	X			X	X	X		X	S1	S	X		X	A.D'Urso	47
	X		X				X	X1	X1			X	X	S1	X	X	S	X		X	S.Bennett	48
			X				S	S	X1	X		X	X	X	X		X		X	X	U.D.Rennie	49
			X				S	S2	X1	X		X	X	X	X	X2	X		X	X	G.Singh	50
			X				S	S	X	X		X	X	X	X		X	X1	X	X	B.Knight	51
			X				S	S	X	X		X	X	X	X		X	S	X	X	X	T.Heilbron	52
			X				S1		X2	X		X	X	X1	X	X		X	X	X	I.Hemley	53
			X				X	X	X			X	X	X		X	X	X	X	K.Leach	54
S1			X				X	X2	X1			X	X	X	S2	X	X2	X	X	A.Butler	55
8	27	9	19	44	3	3	1	1	5	20	32	36	5	8	4	31	7	14	13	28	28	13	42	6	15	42	4	37	EL Appearances	
6	3	3	1	0	0	1	1	1	5	2	3	0	0	5	4	1	0	1	1	0	6	1	0	0	5	0	0	4	EL Sub Appearances	
1+1	4	3	2	4	1	0+1	0+2	0+1	0	0	4	0	4	1	0	0	4	0	3+1	0	4	0	4	0	3	4	0	2+1	CC Appearances	
2	1	0+1	1	2	0	0	0+1	0	0	2	2	1	0	0	0	2	0	0	0	2	0	2	0	2	1+1	2	0	2	FAC Appearances	
3	1+1	1	3	0	0	0	0+1	0+1	0	1	2	2	1	1	2	1	1+1	1+1	0	1	0	2	0	1	3	0	3	AWS Appearances	

Also Played: (M) Bolesan S2(21). (F) Clarke S(54). (F) Johnson S1(48,49,50,52), X(51). (D) Jones X(6). (M) Misbah S(22). (M) Mountain S(3,4,6,11,12,13,54).(M) Oatway X(19), X2(20), S2(23).(D) Scott S(40,41,42), S2(44). (M) Vick S2(53,55),S(54).

CLUB RECORDS

BIGGEST VICTORIES
League: 7-0 v Burnley, Division 1, 1.9.1928.
9-2 v Thames, Division 3(S), 6.2.1932.
7-0 v Barnsley, Division 2, 7.12.1957.
F.A. Cup: 8-0 v Enfield 1st Round, 1931-32.
(Scored 16 in a Welsh Cup tie, 20.1.1961)
Europe: 8-0 v P.O.Larnaca (Cyprus), ECWC 1st Round, 1970-71.
BIGGEST DEFEATS
League: 2-11 v Sheffield United, Division 1, 1.1.1926.
0-9 v Preston North End, Division 2, 7.5.1966.
F.A. Cup: 1-6 v Aston Villa, 3rd Round, 1928-29.
0-5 v Charlton Athletic, 3rd Round, 1937-38.
MOST POINTS
3 points a win: 86, Division 3, 1982-83.
2 points a win: 66, Division 3(S), 1946-47.
MOST GOALS SCORED: 93, Division 3(S), 1946-47.
RECORD TRANSFER FEE RECEIVED
£215,000 from Portsmouth for Jimmy Gilligan, September 1989.
RECORD TRANSFER FEE PAID
£200,000 to San Jose Earthquakes for Godfrey Ingram, Sept 1982.
BEST PERFORMANCES
League: Runners-up Division 1, 1923-24.
Highest Position: 2nd Division 1, 1923-24.
F.A. Cup: Winners in 1926-27.
League Cup: Semi-Finals in 1965-66.
Welsh Cup: Winners 22 times.
Europe: (ECWC) Semi-Finals in 1967-68
HONOURS
Champions of Division 3(S), 1946-47.
Champions of Division 3, 1992-93.
FA Cup winners in 1926-27.
Charity Shield winners in 1927.
Welsh Cup winners 22 times.
LEAGUE CAREER
Elected to Div 2 1920, Div 1 1920-21, Div 2 1928-29, Div 3(S) 1930-31, Div 2 1946-47, Div 1 1951-52, Div 2 1956-57, Div 3 1959-60, Div 2 1961-62, Div 3 1974-75, Div 2 1975-76, Div 3 1981-82, Div 2 1982-83, Div 3 1984-85, Div 4 1985-86, Div 3 1987-88, Div 4 (now Div 3) 1989-90, Div 2 1992-93, Div 3 1994-95

INDIVIDUAL CLUB RECORDS

MOST GOALS IN A SEASON
John Toshack: 31 goals in 1968-69 (League 22, Cup ties 9).

MOST GOALS IN A MATCH
6. Derek Tapscott v Knighton Town (Welsh FA Cup) 20.01.61.

OLDEST PLAYER
George Latham, 42 v Blackburn Rovers, Division 1, 2.1.1922.

YOUNGEST PLAYER
John Toshack, 16 v Leyton Orient, Division 2, 13.11.1965.

MOST CAPPED PLAYER
Alf Sherwood (Wales) 39.

PREVIOUS MANAGERS

Davy McDougall 1910-11; Fred Stewart 1911-33; Bartley Wilson 1933-34; B Watts Jones 1934-37; Bill Jennings 1937-39; Cyril Spiers 1939-46; Billy McCandless 1946-48; Cyril Spiers 1948-54; Trevor Morris 1954-58; Bill Jones 1958-62; George Swindin 1962-64; Jimmy Schoular 1964-73; Frank O'Farrell 1973-74; Jimmy Andrews 1974-78; Richie Morgan 1978-81; Graham Williams 1981-82; Len Ashurst 1982-84; Jimmy Goodfellow & Jimmy Mullen (caretakers) 1984; Alan Durban 1984-86; Frank Burrows 1986-89; Len Ashurst 1989-91; Eddie May 1991-94; Terry Yorath 1994-95; Eddie May 1995. Kenny Hibbitt 1995-96.

ADDITIONAL INFORMATION
PREVIOUS NAMES
Riverside FC (1899-1908) amalgamated with Riverside Albion (1902). Cardiff City from 1908.

PREVIOUS LEAGUES
Southern League. Cardiff & District F.L. South Wales League.

Club colours: Royal blue shirts with white collar, white shorts, blue stockings.
Change colours: Yellow, black, yellow.
Reserves League: Neville Ovenden Football Combination.

LONGEST LEAGUE RUNS

of undefeated matches:	21 (1946-47)	of league matches w/out a win:	15 (1936-37)
of undefeated home matches:	27 (1939/46/47)	of undefeated away matches:	10 (1946-47)
without home win:	10 (1986-87)	without an away win:	44 (1971-73)
of league wins:	9 (1946)	of home wins:	9 (1922-23, 1951-52)
of league defeats:	7 (1933)	of away wins:	7 (1993)

THE MANAGER

PHIL NEAL . . . . appointed February 1996.

PREVIOUS CLUBS
As Manager . . . . Bolton Wanderers, Coventry City.
As Asst.Man/Coach . . . . None.
As a player . . . . Northampton Town, Liverpool, Bolton wanderers.

HONOURS
As a Manager . . . . **Bolton:** Promotion to Div.3 (1988), AMC'89.
As a Player . . . . **Liverpool:** Div.1'76'77'79'80'82'83'84'86. EUFA Cup'76. EC'77'78'81'84. LC'81'82'83'84.
. . . . **England:** 50 full caps.

CARDIFF CITY

PLAYERS NAME / Honours	Ht	Wt	Birthdate	Birthplace Transfers	Contract Date	Clubs	APPEARANCES League	L/Cup	FA Cup	Other	GOALS Lge	L/C	FAC	Oth
G O A L K E E P E R S														
Williams Stephen	6.3	12.12	16/10/74	Cardigan		Coventry City								
				Free	13/08/93	Cardiff City	28		1	5+1				
D E F E N D E R S														
Baddeley Lee	6.1	12.10	12/07/74	Cardiff	13/08/91	Cardiff City	108+16	4+2	8	23	1			
Howarth Simon	6.1	13.6	03/01/68											
Perry Jason	5.11	10.4	02/04/70	Newport	21/08/87	Cardiff City	243+3	20	13+1	21+1	5			
Scott Andrew M	6.0	12.0	27/06/75	Manchester	04/01/93	Blackburn Rovers								
				Free	09/08/94	Cardiff City	13+1		1	1	1			
M I D F I E L D														
Jack Steve						Cardiff City (T)								
Fleming Hayden						Cardiff City (T)								
Harding Paul	5.10	12.5	06/03/64	Mitcham										
Gorman Lee						Cardiff City (T)								
Asbah Samir						Cardiff City (T)								
Rodgerson Ian	5.8	10.7	09/04/66	Hereford	01/08/55	Cardiff City								
					03/07/85	Hereford United	95+5	7	4	7+1	6			
				£35000	03/08/88	Cardiff City	126+7	11+1	12	8+1	5	1		
				£50000	04/12/90	Birmingham City	87+8	7+1	2	11	13	2		1
				£140000	23/07/93	Sunderland	2+2							
Jack Leigh			08/01/78	Cardiff	01/08/94	Cardiff City (T)	2+2							
Wigg Nathan	5.9	10.5	27/09/74	Pontypool	04/08/93	Cardiff City	41+17	3	1+2	8+3	1			
F O R W A R D S														
Clarke Allan A.						Cardiff City (T)								
Dale Carl	6.0	12.0	24/04/66	Colwyn Bay		Bangor City								
FAC'92'93. Div.3'93.				£12000	19/05/88	Chester City	106+10	7+1	9	6	41		5	2
				£100000	19/08/91	Cardiff City	144+11	9+1	6	17+1	59	4	2	18
Gardner Jimmy						Cardiff City (T)								
Johnson Glenn						Cardiff City (T)								
Williskirk Anthony	6.1	11.2	10/02/65	Sunderland	16/08/83	Sheffield United	62+18	4+1	5	3+2	20	1	1	
S.				Loan	16/10/86	Rotherham United	6				1			
				£25000	13/07/88	Oldham Athletic	3+7	0+2		1	1	1		
					10/02/89	Preston North End	13+1				6			
				£50000	22/06/89	Bolton Wanderers	139+2	18	10	13	52	12	7	5
				£85000	17/10/92	Peterborough United	37+6	2	4	2	15	1	1	1
				£80000	21/01/94	Burnley	33+12	2+2			8			
				Loan	26/10/95	Carlisle United	28				4			
				£60000	01/12/95	Cardiff City	28				4			
Young Scott	6.1	12.0	14/01/76	Pontypridd	04/07/90	Cardiff City	55+14	3+1	2	7+3				1

NINIAN PARK
Sloper Road, Cardiff CF1 8SX
Tel: 01222 398 636

Capacity ....12,695.
Seating ....10,371.

First game ....v Ton Pentre, Southern Lge Div 2, 24.9.1910.
First floodlit game...v Grasshoppers Zurich
....(Friendly) 5.10.1960.

ATTENDANCES
Highest...................61,566 Wales v England, 14.10.1961. 57,893 v Arsenal, Division 1, 22.4.1953.
Lowest ....1,006 v Swansea City, AMC, 28.1.1986. 581 v Taffs Well, Welsh Cup, 25.11.1986.

OTHER GROUNDS: .... None.

MATCHDAY TICKET PRICES

Grandstand C&D £12
Juv/OAP £7

Grandstand elsewhere £10
Juv/OAP £6

Ground £8
Juv/OAP £4

Additional Information
There are sometimes surcharges for important
games of £1 or more per ticket.

Ticket Office Telephone no. 01222 398 636

BLUEBIRDS HOTLINE
0898 12 11 71
Calls cost 39p per minute cheap rate and 49p per
minute at all other times.
Call costings correct at time of going to press.

HOW TO GET TO THE GROUND

From the North
Follow signs to Cardiff (A470) until junction with Cardiff bypass. At roundabout
take 3rd exit A48 (sign posted Port Talbot). In 2 miles at roundabout take 1st ex
(A4161) into Cowbridge Road . In half a mile turn right along Lansdowne Road.
At end at crossroads turn right (A4055) into Leckwith Road. In 0.2 miles turn le
into Sloper Road to Cardiff City FC.

From the East
Use motorway (M4), then A48 into Cardiff bypass. Follow Port Talbot then in 2
miles at roundabout take first exit A4161 into Cowbridge Road. In half a mile tu
right along Lansdowne Road. At end at crossroads turn right (A4055) into
Leckwith Road. In 0.2 miles turn left into Sloper Road for Cardiff City FC.

From the West
Use the M4 and leave at junction 33, taking the A4232 (traffic from the A48 can
also join the A4232 at the Culverhouse Cross junction). Leave the A4232 at the
exit the City Centre, B4267 for Cardiff City FC.

Car Parking
(Shared with the Leckwith athletic stadium) across the road from Ninian Park.

Nearest Railway Station
Cardiff Central (01222 228 000)

MATCHDAY PROGRAMME

Programme Editor . . . . Kathy Shea.

Number of pages . . . . 32.

Price . . . . £1.50.

Subscriptions . . . . Apply to the club.

Local Newspapers . . . . South Wales Echo, Western Mail.

Local Radio Stations. . . . . BBC Radio Wales, Red Dragon Radio,
. . . . BBC Radio Cymru.

CARLISLE UNITED
(The Cumbrians)
NATIONWIDE LEAGUE DIVISION 3
SPONSORED BY: CONWAY VAUXHALL

Back Row (L-R): Marc Clelland, Jeff Thorpe, Lee Peacock, Rory Delap, Paul Conway, David Currie, Tony Gallimore, Will Varty, Gareth McAlindon, Nathan Murray. **Middle Row:** David Wilkes (Yth Coach), Peter Hampton (Physio), Tony Hopper, Richard Prokas, Darren Edmondson, Tony Caig, Tony Elliott, Jamie Robinson, Glynn Snodin, Rod Thomas, Joe Joyce (Coach), Neil Dalton (Asst. Physio). **Front Row:** Warren Aspinall, Steve Hayward, David Reeves (Capt), Mick Wadsworth (Director of Coaching), Michael Knighton (Chairman & Chief Executive), Mervyn Day (Coach), Dean Walling, Derek Mountfield, Paul Murray.

CARLISLE UNITED
FORMED IN 1904
TURNED PROFESSIONAL IN
LTD COMPANY IN 1921
PRESIDENT: J C Monkhouse JP
VICE-PRESIDENTS
J A Doweck, J B Lloyd,
Dr T Gardner, MB ChB MBE, H A Jenkins,
J R Sheffield, R S Liddell FCA, T A Bingley
CHAIRMAN & CHIEF EXECUTIVE
Michael Knighton
DIRECTORS
B Chaytow (Vice-Chairman), A Dowbeck,
R McKnight
SECRETARY
Philip Vine (01228 26237)
COMMERCIAL MANAGER
Donna Wenn (01228 24014)
COACHES: Joe Joyce & Mervyn Day
RESERVE TEAM MANAGER

YOUTH TEAM MANAGER
David Wilkes
PHYSIOTHERAPIST
Peter Hampton
STATISTICIAN FOR THE DIRECTORY
Bill Rodger

The delight of promotion in the 1994-5 season turned to disappointment this year as Carlisle failed to hold on to their place in the second division. Their problems were evident from the opening matches - losing the first three and only managing their first win in September against Burnley at Brunton Park. The undoubted low point of the year was the 1-6 defeat against Peterborough in February, but Carlisle regained their composure in their next match and produced a solid 3-0 victory over Swansea City. The last part of the season was full of contrasts with United winning five and losing five of their last ten matches - the wins were all at home. They kept battling right to the end, but a run of three defeats in mid-April meant that a final-day win over Bristol City was not enough to save them from the drop.

The Cumbrians went out in the first round of both the Coca-Cola and FA Cups, but their run in the Auto Windscreens Shield was a different story, providing the only real success this season. United improved on their two first-round draws, producing a 2-1 win over Wrexham and then going on to a storming 5-0 victory over Burnley - who were a first division side in 1994-5. Chesterfield were then disposed of, to take Carlisle into the Northern Final against Rotherham United - but the run ended here, with defeat in both legs.

David Reeves was top scorer with 13 league goals - he also made his mark in all three cup competitions. David Currie also produced a respectable record, achieving nine league goals, while Aspinall, Bennett and Hayward also contributed to the score sheets.

After a difficult season which showed moments of promise, Carlisle should take a positive attitude this year and use the time to consolidate the team with a view to jumping straight back into Division Two.

CARLISLE UNITED

League: 21st   FA Cup: 1st Rnd   Coca-Cola Cup: 1st Rnd   Auto Windscreen Shield: Northern Final

M	DATE	COMP	VEN	OPPONENTS	RESULT	HT	LP	GOAL SCORERS/GOAL TIMES	ATT.
1	A 12	EL	H	Bristol Rovers	L 1-2	1-1	20	Aspinall 25	8003
2	15	CC 1/1	A	Hull City	W 2-1	0-0		Walling 72, Aspinall 78	(2779)
3	19	EL	A	Chesterfield	L 0-3	0-2	24		(3634)
4	22	CC 1/2	H	Hull City	L 2-4	0-0		Reeves 46, 47	4250
5	26	EL	H	Swindon Town	L 0-1	0-0	24		6325
6	29	EL	A	Rotherham United	D 2-2	0-0	24	Reeves 53, 55	(3550)
7	S 2	EL	A	Swansea City	D 1-1	1-0	23	Peacock 9	(3345)
8	9	EL	H	Burnley	W 2-0	0-0	21	Aspinall 52, Conway 70	7318
9	12	EL	H	Peterborough United	D 1-1	0-1	21	Reeves 49	6027
10	16	EL	A	Oxford United	L 0-4	0-2	6		(5046)
11	23	EL	H	Hull City	W 2-0	2-0	18	Reeves 22, 37	6007
12	30	EL	A	Walsall	L 1-2	0-2	21	Thorpe 53	(4214)
13	O 7	EL	H	Notts County	D 0-0	0-0	21		6058
14	14	EL	A	Crewe Alexandra	L 1-2	1-2	22	Delap 61	(4512)
15	17	AWS 1/2	A	Bradford City	D 1-1	0-0		Thomas 46	(1287)
16	21	EL	H	Bradford City	D 2-2	2-0	22	Reeves 10, Edmondson 31	6274
17	28	EL	H	Bournemouth	L 0-2	0-1	24		4250
18	31	EL	A	Wrexham	L 2-3	0-1	24	Philiskirk 57, Aspinall 85	(2939)
19	N 4	EL	H	Brighton & H.A.	W 1-0	0-0	22	Currie 51	5896
20	7	AWS 1/2	H	Doncaster Rovers	D 1-1	0-1		Currie 46	4421
21	11	FAC 1	H	Preston North End	L 1-2	1-0		Reeves 2	7046
22	18	EL	A	Bristol City	D 1-1	0-0	21	Currie 48	(5423)
23	26	EL	H	Wycombe Wanderers	W 4-2	3-1	21	Aspinall 3, Walling 8, Reeves 22, Gallimore 56(pen)	4459
24	29	AWS 2	A	Wrexham	W 2-1	0-0		Bennett 46, Aspinall 47	(2225)
25	D 2	EL	A	Burnley	L 0-2	0-1	21		(8297)
26	9	EL	H	Hull City	W 5-2	3-2	17	Currie 18, 28, Murray 40, Reeves 48, Bennett 71	(3478)
27	16	EL	H	Walsall	D 1-1	1-0	17	Bennett 2	5308
28	26	EL	A	Stockport County	L 0-2	0-1	18		(5941)
29	30	EL	A	Shrewsbury Town	D 1-1	0-0	18	Currie 85	(2864)
30	J 1	EL	H	Blackpool	L 1-2	0-1	18	Gallimore 62(pen)	7532
31	6	AWS QF	H	Burnley	W 5-0	3-0		Edmondson (2), Reeves (3)	5169
32	13	EL	H	Chesterfield	D 1-1	0-1	20	Law 89(og)	5851
33	20	EL	A	Bristol Rovers	D 1-1	1-0	19	Reeves 14	(5196)
34	30	AWS SFN	H	Chesterfield	W 1-0	0-0		Hayward 3	6209
35	F 3	EL	A	Swindon Town	L 1-2	0-0	20	Delap 83	(8242)
36	10	EL	H	Brentford	W 2-1	1-0	20	Currie 20, Reeves 60	5143
37	17	EL	A	Peterborough United	L 1-6	0-4	20	Reeves 60	(4302)
38	20	EL	H	Swansea City	W 3-0	2-0	19	Peacock 29, Bennett 37, Aspinall 85	4645
39	24	EL	H	Oxford United	L 1-2	0-0	20	Robinson 67	5525
40	M 2	EL	A	Stockport County	L 0-1	0-0	22		4842
41	5	AWS NF1	A	Rotherham United	L 0-2	0-0			(6848)
42	9	EL	A	York City	D 1-1	1-0	22	Currie 8	(3965)
43	12	AWS NF2	H	Rotherham United	L 0-2	0-0			6892
44	16	EL	H	Shrewsbury Town	D 1-1	1-0	22	Currie 1	3760
45	19	EL	A	Brentford	D 1-1	1-1	22	Robinson 31	(3104)
46	23	EL	A	Blackpool	L 1-3	1-1	22	Reeves 2	(8144)
47	26	EL	H	Rotherham United	W 2-0	2-0	21	Bennett 1, Hayward 29	4074
48	30	EL	A	Notts County	L 1-3	0-2	21	Aspinall 48	(4514)
49	A 2	EL	H	Crewe Alexandra	W 1-0	0-0	21	Conway 84	4960
50	6	EL	H	Bournemouth	W 4-0	0-0	21	Currie 49, Hayward 56, Delap 84, Bennett 90	5401
51	8	EL	A	Bradford City	L 1-3	0-1	21	Hayward 78	(6156)
52	13	EL	H	Wrexham	L 1-2	0-1	21	Thomas 78	7317
53	20	EL	A	Brighton & H.A.	L 0-1	0-1	22		(6131)
54	23	EL	H	York City	W 2-0	2-0	21	Walling 29, Reeves 42	4813
55	27	EL	A	Wycombe Wanderers	L 0-4	0-1	21		(3964)
56	M 4	EL	H	Bristol City	W 2-1	2-1	20	Conway 10, Hayward 27(pen)	5935

Best Home League Attendance: 8003 v Bristol Rovers   **Smallest: 3760 v Shrewsbury Town**   **Average: 5716**

Goal Scorers:
EL(57): Reeves(13),Currie(9),Aspinall(6),Bennett(5),Hayward(4),Conway(3),Delap(3),Robinson(2),Peacock(2),Gallimore(2),Walling(2),Edmondson(1),Murray(1),Philiskirk(1), Thomas(1),Thorpe(1),Opponent(s)(1)
CC(4): Reeves(2),Aspinall(1),Walling(1)
FAC(1): Reeves(1)
AWS(10): Reeves(3),Edmondson(2),Hayward(1),Thomas(1),Currie(1),Bennett(1),Aspinall(1)

(F) Allen	(F) Aspinall	(M) Atkinson	(D) Bennett	(G) Caig	(F) Conway	(F) Currie	(M) Delap	(D) Dowell	(D) Edmondson	(G) Elliott	(M) Fuller	(M) Gallimore	(M) Hayward	(M) Hopper	(M) McAlindon	(M) Moore	(D) Mountfield	(D) Murray	(M) Murray	(F) Peacock	(F) Philiskirk	(M) Prokas	(F) Reeves	(M) Robinson	(F) Smart	(F) Thomas	(M) Thorpe	(F) Walling	Opponent	No.
	X1		X		X				X			X	X				S	S2		S1		X2	X		S2	X		X	G.Cain	1
X	X		X		S1	X2			X			X	X					X		X1			X	S2		X		X	W.C.Burns	2
	X2		X		X	X			X	S		X	X						S2	S1			X	X		X1		X	R.Poulain	3
	X1		X		X2	X			X	S		X	X						X	S1			X		S2			X	E.K.Wolstenholme	4
	X		X		S2	X2			X			X	S			X			X	X			X			X1	S1	X	K.Breen	5
	X		X			X1			X	S	X	X	S			X			X				X			X1	S1	X	S.Mathieson	6
	X		X			X			X	S		X	S					X	X	X			X			X1	S1	X	G.Singh	7
	X3		X		S1	X			X			X	S3					X	X	X1			X			X2	S2	X	T.Heilbron	8
	X		X		S2	X1			X			X	S					X	X2	S1			X			X	S2	X	R.Pearson	9
	X		X		S2	X1			X	S	X2	X						X	X				X			X	S1	X	E.Lomas	10
	X		X			X1			X			X	X					X	X	S			X			S1	S	X	J.Kirkby	11
X	X1		X			X2			X			X	X					X3	S2				X			S3	S1	X	S.G.Stretton	12
X	X				S1	X1			X	X		X						X	X2		S		X	S		S2		X	K.M.Lynch	13
	X					S	X		X	X		X						X	X			X	X	S		S1	X1	X	R.Gifford	14
	X					S2	X2		X	X		X		S	X1			X	X			X	S1			X		X	G.Frankland	15
	X					X2			X	X		X		S2	X				X			X	S			X1	S1	X	J.Lloyd	16
	X					X			X	X1		X	S			X		X				X	S				S1	X	P.Taylor	17
	X		X			X			X			X	X		X1			X		S1	X1	X	X				S	X	R.Poulain	18
X2	X		X			X						X	X			S		X	X3	X	X					X3	S1	X	T.Leeke	19
	X		X	S2		X						X1	X			X2		X	S2	X	X					X2	X	X	P.Richards	20
X1			X	S1		X						X	S					X	S2	X	X	X			X2	X	X	I.Cruikshanks	21
X1		X	X			X			X			X	X					X	S	X	X	S			X	X	X	M.Pierce	22
X3		X	X			X2			X			X	X					S3		X	X		X1	S2	S1	X	X	T.Lunt	23
	X		X	S		X1			X			X	X				X		S1	X	X			S	X	X	X	G.Cain	24
	X		X	X		X3			S2			X	X				X			X	X			S1	S3	X1	X	J.Rushton	25
X2		X	X		S2	X1			S1			X	X				X			X	X			X3		S3	X	E.Wolstenholme	26
	X		X	X1		X						X	X	S	S				X		X			X		S1	X	D.Allison	27
X2		X	X	X	X1	S2			X			X	X				S3		X	X3					X	S1	X	S.Baines	28
	X		X	X	X1	X	S1		X			X	X					X	S				S		X1		X	E.Lomas	29
	X		X	S3	X3	S1			X1			X	X2				X	S2		X2	X	S2			S1		X	E.Wolstenholme	30
X2		X	X	S1		S2		X				X	S3				X		X3	X	X1			X			X	S.Mathieson	31
	X		X	X	X2	S2			X			X	X			X1	S	X	X				S1			S1	X	M.Riley	32
	X	X	X	X		X2			X			X	X					X	S	X	X					S1	X	A.Butler	33
	X	X	X	S2	X2	X			X			X						S1	S3	X	X					X3	X	P.R.Richards	34
S2	X1		X			X2	X		X				X					X	S1	X	X	S			X	X	X	T.Leeke	35
S1		X	X		X	X2			X			X	X1	S					S2	X	X					X	X	R.Poulain	36
	X		X	X			X		X			X	X						S1	X	X	S		S	X1	X	N.Barry	37
S1	X2		X1			S2			X	X		X							X	X	X			X3	S3	X	S.Baines	38
S3			X1	S2		X	X		X	X3		X						S1	X	X	X	X		X2			X	G.Frankland	39
X2		X	S		X3	X			X	X		X	S1					X1	S2	X	X			X			X	T.Heilbron	40
	X		X		X1				X	X	X							S	X	X		X		X2			X	T.West	41
S	X				X1		X		X	X	X	X						S1	X	X			S	X1	X	X	U.Rennie	42
S1	X1		S2		X		X		X	X	X							S	X2	X	X			X	S2	X	M.Riley	43
	X		S2	X		X	X		X	S1								S	X	X			X	X1	X	X	I.Cruikshanks	44
	X		S	X1	X	X	X	S										X	X			X	X	X	X	X	A.D'Urso	45
X1	X		S1	X2	S2	X	X		X									X	X			X	S	X	X	X	W.Burns	46
X1	X			X2	S2	X	X		X								S1	X	X			X	X	X	X	X	R.Pearson	47
	X		S	X	S2	S1	X		X									X	X2	X	X1	X	J.Lloyd	48
X1	X	X	X	S	X2	S	X		X				S					X	X	X	X	X	X	J.Kirby	49
	X	X	X2	X1	S3	S2	X		X	S1							X	X	X	X3	X	X	T.West	50
	X	X	X	X1	S2	S1	X		X	S							X	X	X	X2	X	F.Stretton	51
S1	X	X	X1	X		S3	X		X				S2				X	X	X	X3	X3	X2	G.Singh	52
	X	X	X		X	S1	X		X	S2							S3	X	X2	X	X1	X	S.G.Bennett	53
X1	X	X		X2	S2	X	X		X								X	X	X	S1	X	E.Lomas	54
	X	X	S1	X	S3	X	X2		X								X1	X	X3	X	A.Wiley	55
		X	X	X	X1	X			X	S	S1							S	X	X	X	X	S.Mathieson	56

2	36	2	26	32	13	41	5	2	39	14	1	36	36	1	0	12	0	7	16	12	3	17	43	18	3	28	16	43	EL Appearances	
0	5	0	0	0	9	1	14	5	2	0	0	2	4	3	0	0	1	4	10	0+1	0	3	0	2	0+1	8	17	0	EL Sub Appearances	
1	2	0	0	2	1+1	2	0	0	2	0	0	2	2	0	0	0	1	0	2	0+1	0	1	1+1	0	2				CC Appearances	
0	1	0	0	1	0+1	1	0	0	0	0	0	0	1	0	0	0	1	0+1	0	1	0	1	0	1	1	1			FAC Appearances	
0	4+1	1	5	4	0+3	6+1	3+1	0	3	3	0	7	6	1	0	2	0	2	2	2+2	0	5+1	7	2+2	0	4	2+2	7	AWS Appearances	

• Played: (M) Donachie S3(40). (M) Jansen S(54). (D) Joyce X(4) S(41). (M) Varty S2(42), S(47).

CLUB RECORDS

BIGGEST VICTORIES
League: 8-0 v Hartlepool United, Division 3(N), 1.9.1928.
8-0 v Scunthorpe United, Division 3(N), 25.12.1952.
F.A. Cup: 6-1 v Billingham Synthonia, Round 1, 1.17.1956.

BIGGEST DEFEATS
League: 1-11 v Hull City, Division 3(N), 14.1.1939.
F.A. Cup: 0-5 v West Ham United, !st Round replay, 1909-10.
1-6 v Wigan Athletic, 1st Round, 1934-35.
1-6 v Bradford City, 1st Round, 1951-52.
0-5 v Bristol City, 4th Round replay, 28.1.1981.

MOST POINTS
3 points a win: 80, Division 3, 1981-82.
2 points a win: 62, Division 3(N), 1950-51.

RECORD TRANSFER FEE RECEIVED
£275,000 from Vancouver Whitecaps for Peter Beardsley, April 1981.

RECORD TRANSFER FEE PAID
£121,000 to notts County for David Reeves, October 1993.

BEST PERFORMANCES
League: 22nd in Division 1, 1974-75.
F.A. Cup: 6th Round, 1974-75.
League Cup: Semi-Finals in 1969-70.

HONOURS
Champions of Division 3, 1964-65, 1994-95.

LEAGUE CAREER
Elected to Div 3N 1928, Transferred to Div 4 1958, Div 3 1961-62, Div 4 1962-63, Div 3 1963-64, Div 2 1964-65, Div 1 1973-74, Div 2 1974-75, Div 3 1976-77, Div 2 1981-82, Div 3 1985-86, Div 4 (now Div 3) 1986-87, Div 2 1994-95.

INDIVIDUAL CLUB RECORDS

MOST GOALS IN A SEASON
Hugh McIlmoyle: 44 goals in 1963-64 (League 39, League Cup 5).

MOST GOALS IN A MATCH
5. H.Mills v Halifax Town, Division 3(N), 11.9.1937.
5. Jim Whitehouse v Scunthorpe United, 8-0, Division 3(N), 25.12.1952.

OLDEST PLAYER
Bryan 'Pop' Robson, 39 years 321 days v Shrewsbury Town, 28.9.1985.

YOUNGEST PLAYER
Rory Delap, 16 years 306 days v Scarborough, 8.5.1993.

MOST CAPPED PLAYER
Eric Welsh (Northern Ireland) 4.

PREVIOUS MANAGERS

W.Clark; Ivor Broadis; Bill Shankly; Fred Emery; Andy Beattie; Ivor Powell; Alan Ashman; Tim Ward; Bob Stokoe; Ian MacFarlane; Alan Ashman; Dick Young; Bobby Moncur; Martin Harvey; B.S.Robson; Bob Stokoe; Harry Gregg; Aidan McCaffery.

ADDITIONAL INFORMATION
PREVIOUS NAMES
None.

PREVIOUS LEAGUES
North Eastern League.

Club colours: Blue shirts with white pinstripe, white collar with red and blue trim, white shorts and blue stockings.
Change colours: Green, red and white stripes.

Reserves League: Midland Senior League.

'A' Team: Lancashire League Division 2.

LONGEST LEAGUE RUNS

of undefeated matches:	15 (1950-51, 1983-84)	of league matches w/out a win:	14 (1935
of undefeated home matches:	22 (1950-51)	of undefeated away matches:	12 (1950-51
without home win:	8 (1954, 1991-92)	without an away win:	20 (1970-71
of league wins:	6 (1937, 1981-82)	of home wins:	7 (1930-35
of league defeats:	8 (1935)	of away wins:	4 (1964-65

THE MANAGER

MICK WADSWORTH . . . . appointed June 1993.

PREVIOUS CLUBS
As Manager . . . . None.
As Asst.Man/Coach . . . . Carlisle United.
As a player . . . . Scunthorpe United.

HONOURS
As a Manager . . . . None.
As a Player . . . . None.

CARLISLE UNITED

PLAYERS NAME / Honours	Ht	Wt	Birthdate	Birthplace / Transfers	Contract Date	Clubs	League	L/Cup	FA Cup	Other	Lge	L/C	FAC	Oth
G O A L K E E P E R S														
Craig Anthony	6.1	12.0	11/04/74	Whitehaven	10/07/92	Carlisle United	93	6	7	17				
Day Mervyn	6.2	15.1	26/06/55	Chelmsford	01/03/73	West Ham United	194	14	14	10				
E: u23.5, Y. FAC'75. Div.2'90.				£100000	01/07/79	Leyton Orient	170	8	10					
				£15000	12/08/83	Aston Villa	30	3						
				£30000	01/02/85	Leeds United	227	14	11	16				
				Loan	05/03/92	Luton Town	4							
				Loan	01/05/92	Sheffield United	1							
				Free	14/07/93	Carlisle United	16	2	1	2				
D E F E N D E R S														
Edmondson Darren	6.0	12.2	04/11/71	Coniston	17/07/90	Carlisle United	185+8	13	12	20	8	1	2	3
Joyce Joseph	5.9	10.5	18/03/61	Consett		Barnsley	332+2	26+1	24	3	4	1	1	
				Free	20/02/91	Scunthorpe United	91	5		11	2			
				Free	05/08/93	Carlisle United	45+5	5+1	4+1	9				1
				Loan	23/09/93	Darlington	4							
M I D F I E L D														
Delap Rory	6.0	11.11	06/07/76	Coldfield	18/07/94	Carlisle United	9+18			3+2	3			
Hayward Steve	5.10	11.7	08/09/71	Pelsall	17/09/88	Derby County	12+11	0+2	1	2+4	1			
E: Y.13. FLge u18.1.				£100000	13/03/95	Carlisle United	45+2	2		8	6			1
Hopper Tony	5.11	11.07	31/05/76	Carlisle	18/07/94	Carlisle United	6+10			1				
Jansen Matt						Carlisle United (T)								
McAlindon Gareth						Carlisle United (T)	0+3							
Moore David G						Carlisle United (T)	12			2				
Pounewatchy Stephane						Gueugnon (France)								
				Free	06/08/96	Carlisle United								
Prokas Richard	5.8	11.4	22/01/76	Penrith	18/07/94	Carlisle United	54+5	3	4	12+1	1			
Robinson Jamie	6.1	12.3	26/02/72	Liverpool	04/06/90	Liverpool								
				Free	17/07/92	Barnsley	8+1			3				
				Free	28/01/94	Carlisle United	34+2	0+1	1	6+2	3			1
Thorpe Jeffery	5.10	12.8	17/11/72	Cockermouth	02/07/91	Carlisle United	86+58	6+3	4+2	8+12	7			1
Party Will						Carlisle United (T)	0+1							
F O R W A R D S														
Archdeacon Owen	5.7	11.0	04/03/66	Greenock		Gourock United								
S: u21.1, Y.SPD'86					20/08/82	Celtic	38+38	1+4	3+1	1+3	8	1		
				£80000	07/07/89	Barnsley	222+10	15+1	14+1	9+1	23	2	2	4
					10/07/96	Carlisle United								
Aspinall Warren	5.9	11.12	13/09/67	Wigan	31/08/85	Wigan Athletic	39+12	1	2+3	3+5	22		2	4
E: u19.1, Y.2. AMC'85.				£315000	26/08/88	Portsmouth	97+35	8+3	4+5	6+1	21	3	2	2
				£150000	05/05/86	Everton	0+7	0+1		0+2				
				£300000	19/02/87	Aston Villa	40+4	4	1+1		14	2		
				Loan	27/08/93	Bournemouth	4+2				1			
				Loan	14/10/93	Swansea City	5			1				
				£20000	31/12/93	Bournemouth	18		1		5			
				Loan	09/03/95	Carlisle United								
				Free	12/07/95	Carlisle United	36+5	2	1	4+1	6	1		1
Currie David	6.0	11.3	27/11/62	Middlesbrough	05/02/82	Middlesbrough	94+19	6	5+1	2	31	1		
LgeXI.1. Div.2'91.				Free	17/06/86	Darlington	76	6	3	5	33			3
				£150000	26/02/88	Barnsley	80	3	5	1	30	1	4	
				£750000	19/01/90	Nottingham Forest	4+4				1			
				£460000	23/08/90	Oldham Athletic	17+14	2+1	1	0+1	3	2		
				£250000	05/09/91	Barnsley	53+22	2+1	4+1	1+1	12			1
				Loan	15/10/92	Rotherham United	5				2			
				Loan	10/01/94	Huddersfield Town	7		1		1			
				Free	18/07/94	Carlisle United	79+1	5+1	4	13+1	13		1	5
Peacock Lee	6.0	12.8	09/10/76	Paisley	10/03/95	Carlisle United	14+16	0+1	0+1	2+2	2			
S: Y.														
Reeves David	6.0	11.7	19/11/67	Birkenhead	06/08/86	Sheffield Wed.	8+9	1+1	1+1	0+1	2	1		
				Loan	17/12/86	Scunthorpe United	3+1				2			
				Loan	01/10/87	Scunthorpe United	6				4			
				Loan	20/11/87	Burnley	16			2	8			1
				£80000	17/08/89	Bolton Wanderers	111+23	14+1	8+5	9+2	30	1	5	7
				£80000	25/03/93	Notts County	9+4	1+1			2			
					01/10/93	Carlisle United	119	6	9	23	46	4	4	6
Thomas Roderick	5.6	10.6	10/10/70	Brent	03/05/88	Watford	63+21	3+2	0+1	3+1	9			
E: u21.1, Y., S. FAYC'89.				Loan	27/03/92	Gillingham	8			1	1			
				Free	12/07/93	Carlisle United	101+9	7+1	9	20	16	1		8
Walling Dean	6.0	10.8	17/04/69	Leeds		Leeds United								
AV'91.				Free	30/07/87	Rochdale	43+22	3	0+1	1+1	8			
				Free	01/08/90	Guiseley								

BRUNTON PARK
Warwick Road, Carlisle, Cumbria CA1 1LL
Tel: 01228 26237

Capacity..10,925 at present.
By Christmas the capacity will rise to 17,300, and eventually the stadium will accomadate for 28,000 all seated spectators.

First game...Not known.
First floodlit game ....Not known.

ATTENDANCES
Highest ....27,500 v Birmingham City, FA Cup 3rd Round, 5.1.1957
....& Middlesbrough, FA Cup 5th Round, 7.2.1970.
Lowest ....859 v Hartlepool, AMC 1st Round, 15.12.1992.

OTHER GROUNDS: .... None.

MATCHDAY TICKET PRICES

A, B & D £9.50
Juv/OAP £5.50

C Stand £10

Platinum Stand. £10

Terraces £7.50
Juv/OAP £4.50

Foxy's Restaurant
Eat & View (Viewing Gallery) £28
Eat & View (Platinum Stand) £23

Ticket Office Telephone no. 01228 26237

HOW TO GET TO THE GROUND

From the North, East, South
Use Motorway M6 until junction 43. Leave motorway and follow signs to Carlisle (A69) into Warwick Road for Carlisle United FC.

From the West
Follow signs into Carlisle then forward (A69) along Warwick Road for Carlisle United FC.

Car Parking
Car park for 1,500 vehicles next to ground. Entrance in St Aidan's Road. 50p cars, 32.00 coaches. Limited street parking permitted.

Nearest Railway Station
Carlisle Citadel (01228 4471)

CLUBCALL
0891 12 16 32
Calls cost 39p per minute cheap rate and 49p per minute at all other times.
Call costings correct at time of going to press.

MATCHDAY PROGRAMME

Programme Editor. . . . . Jim Thoburn.

Number of pages . . . . 32.

Price . . . . £1.20.

Subscriptions . . . . £28 per season (home), £56 (home & away).

Local Newspapers. . . . . Cumbrian Newspapers.

Local Radio Stations . . . . BBC Radio Cumbria, CFM Radio.

CHESTER CITY
(The Blues)
NATIONWIDE LEAGUE DIVISION 3

Back Row (L-R): Cyrille Regis, Spencer Whelan, Billy Stewart, Ray Newland, John Murphy, Eddie Bishop.
Middle Row: Stuart Walker (Physio), David Rogers, Scott Blenchley, Leroy Chambers, Julian Alsford, Andy Milner, David Flitcroft, Stuart Rimmer, Derek Mann (Yth Coach/Physio).
Front Row: Chris Priest, Iain Jenkins, Gary Shelton (Player/Coach), Roger Preece, Kevin Ratcliffe (Manager), Jason Burnham, Neil Fisher.
Photo: Dale Miles.

CHESTER CITY
FORMED IN 1884
TURNED PROFESSIONAL IN 1902
LTD COMPANY IN 1909

PATRON: Duke of Westminster

CHAIRMAN: M.S Guterman
VICE-CHAIRMAN: I G Morris

SECRETARY
D E Barber J.P. Amitd

GENERAL MANAGER: W Wingrove
MANAGER: Kevin Ratcliffe
PLAYER COACH: Gary Shelton

YOUTH TEAM MANAGER
David Fogg

PHYSIOTHERAPIST
Stuart Walker

STATISTICIAN FOR THE DIRECTORY
John Martin

It was a case of so near yet so far as City just missed out on a play-off spot on the last day of the season.

Earlier in the season it looked as though they were a sure bet for promotion as they not only stayed within the play-off positions but actually led the table for a number of weeks. At the start of the season they lost only one league game in the first nine and soon found themselves amongst the front runners.

Unfortunately, long term injuries to several key players did not help the cause, although the team kept in touch with the leading pack throughout the season.

As far as results were concerned the second half of the season did match the first as only six league games were won between January and May with another ten matches being drawn - if only one of those draws had resulted in a win, City would have made the play-offs.

Apart from the league, City had limited success on the cups front, going out of the FA Cup and Auto Windscreen Shield at the first hurdle. It was the Coca Cola Cup, however, that provided the excitement. Wigan Athletic were comprehensively beaten 7 - 2 on aggregate in the first round - a result which earned City a second round meeting with Tottenham Hotspur. Once again injuries did not help the cause as they lost 7 - 1 on aggregate despite putting up two good performances.

Away from the playing front the club has made great strides and now has a stable base on which to build for the future. The foundations for what is hoped will be a successful Youth Policy are in place as the Club looks to compete with other local clubs to bring in young talent who will hopefully break in to the first team in the future.

On the senior side, most of last season's players have been retained as the club looks to build on the progress made last season.

JOHN MARTIN

CHESTER CITY

League: 8th   FA Cup: 1st Rnd   Coca-Cola Cup: 2nd Rnd   Auto Windscreen Shield: 1st Rnd

M	DATE	COMP	VEN	OPPONENTS	RESULT	HT	LP	GOAL SCORERS/GOAL TIMES	ATT.
1	A 12	EL	H	Hartlepool United	W 2-0	1-0	7	Bishop 30, Priest 79	2286
2	15	CC 1/1	H	**Wigan Athletic**	**W 4-1**	**2-0**		**Whelan 5, Bishop 22, Milner 82, Murphy 86**	**2626**
3	19	EL	A	Bury	D 1-1	1-1	9	Bishop 23	(3211)
4	22	CC 1/2	A	**Wigan Athletic**	**W 3-1**	**2-0**		**Milner 2, 43, Bishop 54**	**(2061)**
5	26	EL	H	Plymouth Argyle	W 3-1	1-0	6	Bishop 45, 64, Regis 85	2660
6	29	EL	A	Wigan Athletic	L 1-2	1-1	8	Rimmer 5	(2555)
7	S 2	EL	H	Hereford United	W 2-1	2-0	4	Regis 5, Noteman 23	3385
8	9	EL	A	Colchester United	W 2-1	0-0	2	Priest 53, Regis 81	(3416)
9	12	EL	A	Scunthorpe United	W 2-0	2-0	1	Richardson 23, Priest 35	(1875)
10	16	EL	H	Lincoln City	W 5-1	3-1	1	Burnham 12, Fisher 32, Milner 40, Priest 79, Murphy 88	3049
11	20	CC 2/1	A	**Tottenham Hotspur**	**L 0-4**	**0-3**			**(17645)**
12	23	EL	H	Gillingham	D 1-1	0-0	1	Flitcroft 54	3886
13	26	AWS 1/1	H	**Rotherham United**	**L 0-1**	**0-0**			**774**
14	30	EL	A	Preston North End	L 0-2	0-1			(8544)
15	O 4	CC 2/2	H	**Tottenham Hotspur**	**L 1-3**	**1-2**		**Chambers 21**	**5372**
16	7	EL	H	Doncaster Rovers	L 0-3	0-0	2		2374
17	14	EL	A	Leyton Orient	W 2-0	1-0	2	Regis 5, Noteman 23	(6037)
18	21	EL	H	Fulham	D 1-1	1-0	3	Bishop 31	2752
19	28	EL	A	Scarborough	D 0-0	0-0	5		(1847)
20	31	EL	A	Rochdale	W 3-1	0-0	3	Regis 22, Noteman 49, Shelton 67	(3018)
21	N 4	EL	H	Torquay United	W 4-1	2-0	2	Regis 8, Milner 38, Whelan 50, Noteman 67(pen)	2535
22	7	AWS 1/2	A	**Burnley**	**D 1-1**	**0-1**		**Richardson 54**	**(3225)**
23	11	FAC 1	A	**Blackpool**	**L 1-2**			**Milner 76**	**(5004)**
24	18	EL	A	Mansfield Town	W 4-3	2-1	1	Rimmer 3, 49, 83 (3), Noteman 40	(2415)
25	25	EL	H	Darlington	W 4-1	1-0	1	Rimmer 37, 73, Priest 55(pen), 84	2652
26	D 16	EL	H	Preston North End	D 1-1	1-1	1	Richardson 34	5004
27	23	EL	H	Barnet	L 0-2	0-1	2		3081
28	26	EL	A	Cardiff City	D 0-0	0-0	2		(6046)
29	30	EL	A	Exeter City	W 2-1	2-0	1	Rimmer 25, Noteman 29	(3324)
30	J 6	EL	A	Cambridge United	D 1-1	1-0	1	Rimmer 20	(2643)
31	9	EL	A	Gillingham	L 1-3	0-0	2	Kenworthy 87	(9191)
32	13	EL	H	Bury	D 1-1	1-0	3	Regis 21	3328
33	20	EL	A	Hartlepool United	L 1-2	1-1	3	Rimmer 25	(1864)
34	F 3	EL	A	Plymouth Argyle	L 2-4	0-3	3	Priest 70, Richardson 84	(5114)
35	17	EL	A	Scunthorpe United	W 3-0	1-0	3	Noteman 15, Fisher 59, Jackson 82	2401
36	20	EL	A	Hereford United	L 0-1	0-0	4		(1827)
37	24	EL	A	Lincoln City	D 0-0	0-0	4		(2533)
38	27	EL	A	Colchester United	D 1-1	0-0	6	Richardson 79	2001
39	M 2	EL	H	Cardiff City	W 4-0	2-0	5	Davidson 25, Priest 41, Rogers 53(pen), Rimmer 82	2308
40	9	EL	A	Barnet	D 1-1	0-0	6	Priest 57	(2195)
41	16	EL	H	Exeter City	D 2-2	1-1	6	Priest 23, Blake 87(og)	2043
42	19	EL	H	Wigan Athletic	D 0-0	0-0	7		2825
43	23	EL	A	Northampton Town	L 0-1	0-1	8		(4810)
44	26	EL	H	Cambridge United	D 1-1	0-1	8	Noteman 60	1623
45	30	EL	A	Doncaster Rovers	W 2-1	0-1	7	Whelan 47, Murphy 90	(1548)
46	A 2	EL	H	Leyton Orient	D 1-1	1-1	7	Rimmer 43	2097
47	6	EL	H	Scarborough	W 5-0	3-0	6	Milner 20, 63, Noteman 21, Priest 38, Rimmer 54	2485
48	8	EL	A	Fulham	L 0-2	0-2	7		(3777)
49	13	EL	H	Rochdale	L 1-2	1-1	9	Ryan 2(pen)	2158
50	20	EL	A	Torquay United	D 1 -1	0-0	10	Priest 52	(2549)
51	23	EL	A	Northampton Town	W 1 -0	0-0	8	Murphy 87	1674
52	27	EL	A	Darlington	L 1-3	0-0	9	Rimmer 69	(4510)
53	M 4	EL	H	Mansfield Town	W 2 -1	0-0	8	Chambers 66, Priest 89	2935

Best Home League Attendance: 5004 v Preston North End   Smallest: 1623 v Cambridge United   Average: 2675

Goal Scorers:

EL(72): Rimmer(13),Priest(13),Noteman(9),Regis(7),Bishop(5),Richardson(4),Milner(4),Murphy(3),Whelan(2),Fisher(2),Ryan(1),Kenworthy(1),Jackson(1),Flitcroft(1),
Rogers(1),Davidson(1),Chambers(1),Burnham(1),Shelton(1),Opponent(s)(1)

CC(8): Milner(3),Bishop(2),Chambers(1),Murphy(1),Whelan(1)

FAC(1): Milner(1)

AWS(1): Richardson(1)

(D) Alsford	(F) Barlow	(M) Bishop	(M) Brenchley	(D) Brien	(D) Brown	(D) Burnham	(F) Chambers	(G) Cutler	(D) Davidson	(M) Fisher	(M) Flitcroft	(D) Jackson	(D) Jenkins	(M) Kenworthy	(F) Milner	(F) Murphy	(F) Noteman	(M) Preece	(M) Priest	(M) Quinn	(F) Regis	(M) Richardson	(F) Rimmer	(M) Rogers	(M) Ryan	(M) Shelton	(G) Stewart	(D) Whelan	Referee	
S		X				X				X	S1	X	X		X	S2		X1	X		X2						X	X	M.Fletcher	1
X	X1	S3				X				X	X				X	S2			X		X2		S1			X3	X	X	K.J.Breen	2
X	X					X				X	X			X1	S				X		X		S1			X	X	X	G.Cain	3
X	X					X				X	X3	X	X2		X	S1			X		X1		S3	S2			X		G.B.Frankland	4
X	X1					X				X	X	X	X		X	S2			X		X2		S1	S			X		S.J.Baines	5
X						X	S2			X	X1	X	X						X		X		X			X2	X	S1	E.Lomas	6
S1						X				X	X2	X	X		S2		X		X		X		X			S	X	X1	F.G.Stretton	7
S3						X				X	S1	X	X1		X3		X		X		X2	X	S2				X	X	B.Knight	8
X						X				X	X	X	X		X2	S1			X		X1	X	X2				X	X	R.Furnandiz	9
S						X				X	X	X	X		X2	S1			X		X1	X	X				X	X	P.R.Richards	10
S1	X					X				X	X	X	X1		X				X				X	S			X		P.E.Alcock	11
X	X2					X				X	X	X	X		X1	S1			X			X	X	S2		S	X		J.Rushton	12
X	X					X				X	X	X	X			X1	S1		X			X	X	S	S		X		E.Wolstenholme	13
X	X					X				X	X	X				S1	X1		X			X	X	X		S	X	X	I.Cruikshanks	14
X	S3	X3				X	X1			X	X				X				X	S1	X2		X	S2		X	X	X	K.J.Breen	15
X	X					X	S			X	X				S2		S1		X		X	X2				X1	X	X	T.E.West	16
X	S2					X				X	X				X1		X		X		X2	S1				X	X	X	A.Wiley	17
X	X					X	S			X	X				X1			S	X		X	X	S1			X	X	X	N.S.Barry	18
X						X	S2			X	X				X		X		X	S1	X2	X				X1	X	X	T.Lunt	19
X	S1					X	S2			X	X				X		X		X		X2	X		S		X1	X	X	G.Cain	20
X						X	S3			X		X2	S2		X		X		X		X3	X1	S1			X	X	X	E.K.Wolstenholme	21
X			S1		X	S3						X			X3		X		X1		X	X2	X				X	X	U.Rennie	22
X					X1					X		X	S1		X		X		X		X	X	S				X	X	J.Kirkby	23
X	S					X	S			X		X			X		X		X		X	X	X			S	X	X	R.Pearson	24
X						X	S1			X		X			X		X		X		X1	X	X			S	X	X	K.J.Breen	25
X						X				X		X		X1	S1	S	X		X		X	X			X1		X	S1	R.Poulain	26
X3			S2		X2	X				X		X		X1	X	S1	X				X	X	S3				X	X	E.Lomas	27
	S					X				X		X		X	X	S	X				X	X					X	X	G.Singh	28
			S1			X				X		X		X	X	S	X		S		X	X1					X	X	C.Wilkes	29
X						X				X		X			X		X1		X		X	X	S1		S		X	X	U.Rennie	30
X						X				X				S1	S2	S	X		X		X2	X	X1				X	X	I.Hemley	31
X						X				X				X1	S1	S	X		X		X	X1	X2				X	X	D.Laws	32
X						X				X				X1	S1	S	X		X		X	X			S		X	X	W.C.Burns	33
					X1		X	X		X		X			S2		X		X		X2	S2	X	S1	X2		X	X	J.Rushton	34
S				S		X			X	X	X			X	X		X		X1		X	S1	X				X	X	K.A.Leach	35
S				S		X			X	X	X			X	X		X		X		X	X	S	X			X	X	C.Wilkes	36
				X		X			X	X	X			X	X	S			X		S	X	X				X	X	M.Bailey	37
			S	X1		X			X	X	X			X	S2	S1	X		X		X	X2	X				X	X	M.J.Brandwood	38
S				S		X			X	X	X			X	S1	X		X			X	X				X	X	G.P.Barber	39
X						X			X	X	X	X1			X		S1		X		X	X	X				X	X	J.A.Kirkby	40
X				S	X	S1			X	X	X			X		X	S1		X		X1	X	X				X	X	F.Stretton	41
				S	X	S			X	X				X		X			X		X1	X	S1	X	X		X	X	G.Frankland	42
			X			X			X2	X				X		S1			X		S	X	X	X1	S	S2	X	X	P.Taylor	43
			X			X			X	X				X		X			X		X	X	S		S	X	X	A.Butler	44
			X			X	S3		X	X		X			X	S1	X1		X		X1	X3	S1			X	X	D.Laws	45
			X			X			X	X		X1			X1	X2	X3		X			X	X2	S3		X	S1	P.Rejer	46
			X			X			X3	X	X1				X2	S2	S1	X2		X		X	X	S2			X	X1	M.Fletcher	47
S			X		X	S			X	X	X			X1	S1					X	X		X		X		P.Richards	48
S			X				S	X	X	X	X	X	X1	S1				X	X		X			R.Harris	49
S			X			X				X	X	X	X		X	S1	X1		X		X	X	S			X	X	A.R.Leake	50
X			X1	X			X		X	X			X		X	S1	X		X	X	S		S	X	X	E.Lomas	51
			X2			X			X	X				X	S2	S1		X		X1	X	S			X	X	E.Wolstenholme	53

Bottom totals

	(D) Alsford	(F) Barlow	(M) Bishop	(M) Brenchley	(D) Brien	(D) Brown	(D) Burnham	(F) Chambers	(G) Cutler	(D) Davidson	(M) Fisher	(M) Flitcroft	(D) Jackson	(D) Jenkins	(M) Kenworthy	(F) Milner	(F) Murphy	(F) Noteman	(M) Preece	(M) Priest	(M) Quinn	(F) Regis	(M) Richardson	(F) Rimmer	(M) Rogers	(M) Ryan	(M) Shelton	(G) Stewart	(D) Whelan
EL Appearances	22	0	7	0	8	1	40	2	1	19	43	7	36	12	5	35	1	27	1	38	0	29	36	30	14	2	10	45	35
EL Sub Appearances	2	0	2	0	0	2	0	6	0	0	1	2	0	1	2	7	17	6	0	1		0	1	0	11	6	2	1	4
CC Appearances	3+1	0+1	4	0+1	0	0	4	1	0	0	4	3	3	2	0	2	1+2	0	3	0+1		3	0	2+2	0+2	0	2	4	3
FAC Appearances	1	0	0	0	1	0	1	0	1	0+1	0	1	1	0	1	0	1	0	1	0		1	0	1	1	0	0	1	1
AWS Appearances	2	0	1	0	0	0+1	2	0+1	0	0	1	1	1	1	0	1	1	1+1	0	2		0	2	2	1	0	0	1	1

Also Played: (M) Brigg S(41). (M) Dobson S(28). (M) Jones S2(22). (G) Newland X(13).

CLUB RECORDS

BIGGEST VICTORIES
League: 12-0 v York City, Division 3(N), 1.2.1936.
F.A. Cup: 6-1 v Darlington, 1st Round, 25.11.1933.
5-0 v Crewe Alexandra, 1st Round, 1964-65.
5-0 v Runcorn (a), 1st Round replay, 28.11.1978.

BIGGEST DEFEATS
League: 0-9 v Barrow, Division 3(N), 10.2.1934.
2-11 v Oldham Athletic, Division 3(N), 19.1.1952.
F.A. Cup: 0-7 v Blackburn Rovers, 2nd Round, 1890-91.
League Cup: 2-9 v Leyton Orient, 3rd Round, 1962-63.

MOST POINTS
3 points a win: 84, Division 4, 1985-86.
2 points a win: 57, Division 4, 1974-75.

MOST GOALS SCORED
119, Division 4, 1964-65.
(in this season 4 players scored 20 goals or more, the only occasion this has ever happened in the Football League. The 119 goals were shared between just 8 players).

RECORD TRANSFER FEE RECEIVED
£300,000 from Liverpool for Ian Rush, May 1980.

RECORD TRANSFER FEE PAID
£120,000 to Barnsley for Stuart Rimmer, August 1991.

BEST PERFORMANCES
League: 5th Division 3, 1977-78.
F.A. Cup: 5th Round replay, 1976-77, 1979-80.
League Cup: Semi-Final 1974-75. Welsh Cup: Winners (3).

HONOURS
Division 3(N) Cup winners 1935-36, 1936-37.
Debenhams Cup winners 1977. Welsh Cup winners (3).

LEAGUE CAREER
Elected to Div 3(N) 1931, Div 4 1957-58, Div 3 1974-75, Div 4 1981-82, Div 3 (now Div 2) 1985-86, Div 3 1992-93.

INDIVIDUAL CLUB RECORDS

MOST GOALS IN A SEASON
Dick Yates: 44 goals in 1946-47 (League 36, Others 8).

MOST GOALS IN A MATCH
5. T.Jennings v Walsall, 5-1, Division 3(N), 30.1.1932.
5. Barry Jepson, York City, 9-2, Division 4, 8.2.1958.

OLDEST PLAYER
Graham Barrow, 39 years 234 days v P.N.E., Division 3, 2.4.1994.

YOUNGEST PLAYER
Aidan Newhouse, 15 years 350 days v Bury, 7.5.1988.

MOST CAPPED PLAYER
Bill Lewis (Wales) 7.

PREVIOUS MANAGERS

1930-36 Charles Hewitt; 1936-38 Alex Raisbeck, 1938-53 Frank Brown; 1953-56 Louis Page; 1956-59 John Harris; 1959-61 Stan Pearson; 1961-63 Bill Lambton; 1963-68 Peter Hauser; 1968-76 Ken Roberts; 1976-82 Alan Oakes; 1982 Cliff Sear*; 1982-83 John Sainty*; 1983-85 John McGrath; 1985-92 Harry McNally; Graham Barrow* 1992-94; Mike Pejic 1994-95; Derek Mann* 1995.
*Includes period as caretaker manager.

ADDITIONAL INFORMATION
PREVIOUS NAMES
Chester until 1983.

PREVIOUS LEAGUES
Cheshire League.

Club colours: Blue & white striped shirts, blue shorts, white socks with blue tops.
Change colours: Yellow shirts, royal blue shorts, yellow socks.

Reserves League: Lancashire League, Pontins League.

LONGEST LEAGUE RUNS

of undefeated matches:	18 (1934-35)	of league matches w/out a win:	26 (1961-62)
of undefeated home matches:	27 (1973-75)	of undefeated away matches:	12 (1939-46)
without home win:	13 (1961-62)	without an away win:	29 (1971-72, 1977-78)
of league wins:	8 (1934, 1936, 1978)	of home wins:	10 (1932, 1963-64)
of league defeats:	9 (7.4.1993 - 21.8.1993)	of away wins:	4 (1934, 1936)

THE MANAGER

KEVIN RATCLIFFE . . . . appointed April 1995

PREVIOUS CLUBS
As Manager . . . . None.
As Asst.Man/Coach . . . . None.
As a player . . . . Everton, Dundee, Cardiff City, Derby County, Chester City.

HONOURS
As a Manager . . . . None.
As a Player . . . . Division 1 championship 1985, 1987. FA Cup 1984. ECWC 1985.
. . . . Charity Shield 1984, 1985, 1986, 1987. Division 3 championship 1993.
International . . . . 56 full caps, 2 U21, Youth and Schoolboy level for Wales.

CHESTER CITY							APPEARANCES				GOALS			
PLAYERS NAME Honours	Ht	Wt	Birthdate	Birthplace Transfers	Contract Date	Clubs	League	L/Cup	FA Cup	Other	Lge	L/C	FAC	Oth
G O A L K E E P E R S														
Sinclair Ronnie	5.9	11.12	19/11/64	Stirling	30.10.82	Nottm. Forest (A)								
S: Y, S. Div2'93.				Loan	01.03.84	Wrexham	11			1				
				£10,000	27.06.86	Leeds United	8	1						
Loan (01/03/87) Halifax 4 Lge App.				Loan	23/12/88	Halifax Town	10			1				
				Free	01/09/89	Bristol City	44	3	5	3				
Loan (05/09/91 Walsall 10 Lge, 1 Oth App.				£25000	21.11.91	Stoke City	77+2	2	4	9				
Loan (26.08.94) Bradford				Free	01/07/96	Chester City								
D E F E N D E R S														
Alsford Julian	6.2	12.11	24/12/72	Poole	30/04/91	Watford	9+4	1		2	1			
				Loan	28/03/94	Slough								
				Free	11/08/94	Chester City	54+5	4+1	3	4	1			
Brown Greg			31/07/78			Chester City (T)								
Davidson Ross	5.10	11.6	13/11/73			Walton & Hersham								
					05/06/93	Sheffield United	2			2				
				Free	26/03/96	Chester City	19				1			
Jackson Peter	6.1	12.6	06/04/61	Bradford	07/04/79	Bradford City	267+11	27	10+1	4	24	1		
Div.3'85.				£250000	23/10/86	Newcastle United	60	3	6	3	3			
				£290000	15/09/88	Bradford City	55+3	7	4	2	5			
				Free	06/09/90	Huddersfield Town	152+3	11	13	18	3		1	1
				Free	23/11/94	Chester City	68	3	2	2	2			
Jenkins Iain	5.10	11.6	24/11/72	Prescot	04/06/91	Everton	3+2	0+1						
				Loan	31/12/92	Bradford City	6			1				
				Free	13/08/93	Chester City	82+5	4+2	6+1	8				
Ratcliffe Kevin	5.11	10.2	04/12/62	Mancot	18/11/78	Everton	356+3	46	57	29+1	2			
W: 59, u21.2, Y,S. Div1'85'87.				Loan	01/08/92	Dundee	4	1						
FAC'84.ECWC'85.CS'84'85'86'87				Free	12/08/93	Cardiff City	25	1		3	1			
				Free	20/01/94	Derby County	6							
				Free	19/07/94	Chester City	23	2	1	2+1				
Whelan Spencer	6.1	11.13	17/09/71	Liverpool		Liverpool								
				Free	03/04/90	Chester City	143+12	9+1	6+1	3+1	3	2		
M I D F I E L D														
Briggs Greg						Chester City (T)								
Dobson Ryan			24/09/78			Chester City (T)								
Fisher Neil	5.10	11.0	07/11/70	St Helens	12/07/89	Bolton Wanderers	7+6	2	1		1			
				Free	01/06/95	Chester City	43+1	4	1	1	2			
Flitcroft David	5.11	12.0	14/01/74	Bolton	02/05/92	Preston North End	4+4	0+1		0+1	2			
				Loan	17/09/93	Lincoln City	2	0+1						
				Free	09/12/93	Chester City	31+18	4	2	3	2			
Jones Jonathan			27/10/78	Wrexham		Chester City (T)								
Preece Roger	5.9	10.4	09/06/69	Much Wenlock		Coventry City								
				Free	15/08/86	Wrexham	89+21	2+1	5	8+1	12			1
				Free	14/08/90	Chester City	165+5	10	8	11	4		1	
Priest Chris	5.10	10.10	18/10/73	Leigh	01/06/92	Everton								
Loan (09/09/94) Chester City				Free	11/01/95	Chester City	60+3	3	1	4	14			
Quinn Philip			05/10/78			Chester City (T)								
Richardson Nick	6.0	12.7	11/04/67	Halifax		Emley								
				Free	15/11/88	Halifax Town	89+12	6+4	2+1	6	17	2	1	1
				£35000	13/08/92	Cardiff City	106+5	7	6	12+2	13			2
Loan (21/10/94) Wrexham 4 Lge Apps. 2gls				Loan	16/12/94	Chester City	6				1			
£22500 (08/08/95) Bury				£40000	07/09/95	Chester City	36+1		1	2	4			1
Rogers Dave	6.0	11.01	25/08/75	Liverpool		Tranmere Rovers								
					01/08/95	Chester City	14+6	0+2		1	1			
Shelton Gary	5.7	10.12	21/03/58	Nottingham	01/03/76	Walsall	12+12	0+1	2+2				1	
E: u21.1.				£80000	18/01/78	Aston Villa	24	2+1			7	1		
				Loan	13/03/80	Notts County	8							
				£50000	25/03/82	Sheffield Wed.	195+3	19	23+1	1	18	3	3	
				£150000	24/07/87	Oxford United	60+5	7+1	5	1	1	2		
					24/08/89	Bristol City	149+1	12	9	9	24			3
Loan (11/02/94) Rochdale 3 Lge Apps.				Free	22/07/94	Chester City	41+3	2	2	2	3			2
F O R W A R D S														
Barlow Brett			06/09/77			Chester City (T)								
Milner Andrew	6.0	11.12	10/02/67	Kendal		Netherfield								
via Manchester City				£20000	18/01/90	Rochdale	103+24	9+4	6+2	4	25	5	1	2
				Free	12/08/94	Chester City	67+11	3+1	2+1	2	12	3	2	
Murphy John	6.1	14.0	18/10/76	Whiston	01/08/94	Chester City	1+17	1+2		1	3	1		
Noteman Kevin	5.10	12.2	15/10/69	Preston	13/06/88	Leeds United	0+1			1				
				£10000	10/11/89	Doncaster Rovers	105+1	4	5+1	11	20	1	2	1
				£25000	27/03/92	Mansfield Town	77+18	7	3	5+1	15	1		
					01/09/95	Chester City	27+6		1	1+1	9			
Regis Cyrille	6.0	13.4	09/02/58	French Guyanna		Molesey								
E: 5, B.3, u21.6. FAC'87.				£5000	01/05/77	W.B.A.	233+4	27+1	25	10	82	16	10	4
				£250000	11/10/84	Coventry City	231+7	24	15+1	4	47	12	3	
				Free	02/07/91	Aston Villa	46+6	3+1	5+2		12			
				Free	03/08/93	Wolves	8+11		1+2	1	2			
				Free	01/08/94	Wycombe Wand.	30+5	2	1		9	1		
				Free	01/08/95	Chester City	29	3	1		7			
Rimmer Stuart	5.8	11.0	12/10/64	Southport	15/10/82	Everton	3							
E: Y3.				£10000	17/01/85	Chester City	110+4	6	4+3	11+1	68	6		3
				£205000	18/03/88	Watford	10	0+1			1	1		
				£200000	10/11/88	Notts County	3+1		2	3	2			
				£150000	02/02/89	Walsall	85+3	6	5	7	31	4	2	7
				£150000	05/03/91	Barnsley	10+5			1	1			
				£150000	15/08/91	Chester City	165+23	11+2	6+2	8+2	56	3		1
Loan (02/09/94) Rochdale 3 Lge Apps.				Loan	05/12/94	Preston North End	0+2							

DEVA STADIUM
Bumpers Lane, Chester, Cheshire
Tel: 01244 371 376

Capacity 6,000
Covered Standing 2,640
Seating..3,094

First game ....v Stockport Co., Lge Cup, 25.8.1992.
First floodlit game ....As above.

ATTENDANCES
Highest ....5,638 v P.N.E., Div 3, 2.4.1994.
Lowest...774 v Rotherham United (AMC) 26.9.1996.

OTHER GROUNDS ....Sealand Road

MATCHDAY TICKET PRICES

Seats................................... £9
Juv/OAP £6

Terraces.............................. £7
Juv/OAP £4.50

Additional Information
£25 membership charge for Supporters Club Lounge.

Ticket Office Telephone no. ...... 01244 371 376.

SPORTSLINES
0891 66 45 54

Calls cost 39p per minute cheap rate and 49p per
minute at all other times.
Call costings correct at time of going to press.

HOW TO GET TO THE GROUND

From the North
Use motorway (M56), A41 or A56 sign posted to Chester, into Town Centre, then follow signs to Queensferry (A548) onto Sealand Road, turn into Bumpers Lane for Chester City FC.

From the East
Use A54 or A51 sign posted Chester, into Town Centre, then follow signs to Queensferry (A548) into Sealand Road as above.

From the South
Use A41 or A483 sign posted Chester Town Centre, then follow signs to Queensferry (A548) into Sealand Road as above.

From the West
Use A55, A494 or A548 sign posted Chester, then follow signs to Queensferry. Follow signs to Birkenhead (A494), then in 1.2 miles branch left to join the A548 Chester into Sealand Road as above.

Car Parking
Parking at the ground.

Nearest Railway Station
British Rail, Chester (01244 340 170)

MATCHDAY PROGRAMME

Programme Editor .... J Stanley.

Number of pages .... 32.

Price .... £1.50.

Subscriptions.............. Available on request (-1244 371 376).

Local Newspapers .... Chester Chronicle, Evening Leader.

Local Radio Stations ...... Radio Merseyside, Marcher Sound Radio.

COLCHESTER UNITED
(The U's)
NATIONWIDE LEAGUE DIVISION 3
SPONSORED BY: SGR FM

Back Row (L-R): Adam Locke, Steve Ball, Tony McCarthy, Carl Emberson, Peter Cawley, Mark Kinsella, Simon Betts.
Middle Row: Steve Foley (Yth Manager), Tony English (Capt), Tony Adcock, Michael Cheetham, Chris Fry, Robbie Reinelt, Nicky Haydon, Paul Gibbs, Brian Owen (Physio).
Front Row: Kelvin Wagner (Kit Manager), Gus Ceaser, Tony Dennis, Steve Mardenborough, Steve Wignall (Manager), Steve Whitton (Asst. Manager), James Siddons, Tony Lock, Jean Dalli, Paul Dyer (Chief Scout).

COLCHESTER UNITED
FORMED IN 1937
TURNED PROFESSIONAL IN 1937
LTD COMPANY IN 1937

CHAIRMAN: Gordon Parker
VICE-CHAIRMAN
Peter Heard
DIRECTORS
Peter Powell, John Worsp,
Steve Gage (Managing Director)
SECRETARY
Marie Partner
MARKETING MANAGER
John Schultz
COMMERCIAL MANAGER
Brian Wheeler
MANAGER: Steve Wignall
ASSISTANT MANAGER: Steve Whitton
RESERVE TEAM MANAGER
Paul Dyer
YOUTH TEAM MANAGER
Steve Foley
PHYSIOTHERAPIST
Brian Owen

STATISTICIAN FOR THE DIRECTORY
Vanessa & Jeff Dunn

Steve Wignall's first full season as Manager at Layer Road, saw the return of old favourite striker, Tony Adcock, who fully justified his return by finishing as top scorer.

The season was the most successful since the U's return to the football league but it also contained one very big low, the exit from the FA Cup in the first round at non-leaguers Gravesend and Northfleet by the score of 2 - 0.

For most of the season the U's were either just in or just out of a play-off place and the season reached a climax at the final home game of the season when a 1 - 0 home win over Doncaster and other helpful results elsewhere meant that Colchester finished seventh and thus in the last play-off place.

The two-legged semi-final against Plymouth Argyle had all the ingredients of a cup tie: although the U's won 1 - 0 at home before a capacity crowd, they regretted the missed chances to increase the margin when in the second leg they lost 3 - 1 - the deciding third goal being scored just four minutes from time.

Both Colchester goals in the play-offs were scored by the outstanding player of the season, Mark Kinsella, whose great work was rewarded by selection for the third division PFA team.

Some inspired loan signings by Steve Wignall kept the supporters' interest throughout the season, notably David Greene during the close season, and Scott McLeish. These, along with other new signings David Barnes (Watford) and old favourite Richard Wilkins (Hereford), make promotion in 1996/7 look a distinct possibility. Fingers are crossed that the club can keep Mark Kinsella for another season.

VANESSA DUNN & JEFF DUNN

COLCHESTER UNITED

League: 7th   FA Cup: 1st Rnd   Coca-Cola Cup: 1st Rnd   Auto Windscreen Shield: 2nd Rnd

M	DATE	COMP	VEN	OPPONENTS	RESULT	HT	LP	GOAL SCORERS/GOAL TIMES	ATT.
1	A 12	EL	H	Plymouth Argyle	W 2-1	1-0	6	Betts 14, Locke 57	3585
2	15	CC 1/1	H	Bristol City	W 2-1	2-1		Adcock 14, Kinsella 16	3684
3	19	EL	A	Barnet	D 1-1	0-0	8	Adcock 81	(1966)
4	22	CC 1/2	A	Bristol City	L 1-2*	0-1		Cheetham 61 (Lost 4-5 on penalties)	(3648)
5	26	EL	H	Lincoln City	W 3-0	2-0	5	Dennis 1, 8, Mardenborough 75	2939
6	29	EL	A	Cambridge United	L 1-3	0-2	7	Adcock 49	(3476)
7	S 2	EL	A	Gillingham	W 1-0	0-0	5	Adcock 75	(7684)
8	9	EL	H	Chester City	L 1-2	0-0	8	Whitton 82	3416
9	12	EL	H	Preston North End	D 2-2	1-0	8	Fry 26, Whitton 48	2869
10	16	EL	A	Darlington	D 2-2	2-0	9	Dennis 11, Cheetham 21	(1685)
11	23	EL	H	Hereford United	W 2-0	1-0	8	Reinelt 21, Reinelt 63	2596
12	26	AWS 1/1	H	Torquay United	W 5-2	2-0		Cawley, Reinelt, Adcock (3)	1121
13	30	EL	A	Scunthorpe United	L 0-1	0-1	10		(2051)
14	O 7	EL	H	Hartlepool United	W 4-1	3-0	9	Locke 9, 54, Adcock 20, Reinelt 25	2618
15	14	EL	A	Rochdale	D 1-1	1-0	8	Reinelt 30	(2193)
16	21	EL	H	Northampton Town	W 1-0	0-0	6	Kinsella 59	3873
17	28	EL	A	Cardiff City	W 2-1	2-1	4	Adcock 13, 15	(3207)
18	31	EL	A	Fulham	D 1-1	1-0	4	Mardenborough 25	(2870)
19	N 4	EL	H	Exeter City	D 1-1	1-0	5	Kinsella 20	3377
20	8	AWS 1/2	H	Swindon Town	L 0-2	0-0			(6222)
21	11	FAC 1	A	Gravesend	L 0-2	0-1			(3218)
22	18	EL	A	Doncaster Rovers	L 2-3	1-2	6	Cheetham 45, Adcock 85	(1603)
23	25	EL	H	Mansfield Town	L 1-2	0-1	7	Adcock 46(pen)	2819
24	D 9	EL	A	Hereford United	D 1-1	0-0	8	Betts 78	(3324)
25	16	EL	H	Scunthorpe United	W 2-1	2-0	7	Ball 19, Kinsella 40	2138
26	23	EL	A	Bury	D 0-0	0-0	8		(3559)
27	26	EL	H	Leyton Orient	D 0-0	0-0	6		4965
28	J 1	EL	A	Torquay United	W 3-2	1-1	5	Kinsella 1, Duguid 77, Betts 90	(2425)
29	9	AWS 2	A	Peterborough United	L 2-3	2-0		Betts 46, Kinsella 47	(2460)
30	13	EL	H	Barnet	W 3-2	3-2	4	Betts 6(pen), Abrahams 10, 18	3252
31	20	EL	A	Plymouth Argyle	D 1-1	0-1	5	Greene 88	(5800)
32	30	EL	A	Wigan Athletic	L -2	0-2	5		(2101)
33	F 3	EL	A	Lincoln City	D 0-0	0-0	7		(2531)
34	6	EL	H	Scarborough	D 1-1	1-0	5	Cawley 5	2299
35	10	EL	H	Wigan Athletic	L 1-2	0-0	7	Adcock 52	3028
36	17	EL	A	Preston North End	L 0-2	0-2	8		(9336)
37	24	EL	H	Darlington	D 1-1	1-0	9	Adcock 38	2653
38	27	EL	A	Chester City	D 1-1	0-0	10	Gibbs 73	(2001)
39	M 2	EL	A	Leyton Orient	W 1-0	1-0	9	Adcock 40	(4049)
40	9	EL	H	Bury	W 1-0	0-0	8	Caeser 75	2832
41	16	EL	A	Scarborough	D 0-0	0-0	8		(1201)
42	19	EL	H	Cambridge United	W 2-1	1-1	8	Adcock 8, McGleish 51	2995
43	23	EL	H	Torquay United	W 3-1	2-0	7	Fry 6, McGleish 46, Betts 73(pen)	2888
44	30	EL	A	Hartlepool United	L 1-2	1-1	8	Gibbs 45	(1364)
45	A 2	EL	H	Rochdale	W 1-0	0-0	8	Reinelt 55	3021
46	6	EL	H	Cardiff City	W 1-0	0-0	8	Kinsella 55	3345
47	8	EL	A	Northampton Town	L 1-2	0-0	9	Reinelt 90	(5021)
48	13	EL	H	Fulham	D 2-2	1-1	8	McGleish 43, 76	3795
49	16	EL	H	Gillingham	D 1-1	0-0	8	McGleish 63	4952
50	20	EL	A	Exeter City	D 2-2	1-2	9	Caeser 6, McGleish 65	(2788)
51	27	EL	A	Mansfield Town	W 2-1	0-0	7	Reinelt 68, Dunne 90	(2073)
52	M 4	EL	H	Doncaster Rovers	W 1-0	1-0	7	Gibbs 45	5038
53	12	PO SF1	H	Plymouth Argyle	W 1-0	1-0		Kinsella 44	6511
54	15	PO SF2	A	Plymouth Argyle	L 1-3	0-2		Kinsella 66	(14525)

Best Home League Attendance: 5038 v Doncaster Rovers   Smallest: 2138 v Scunthorpe United   Average: 3273

Goal Scorers:

EL(61): Adcock(12),Reinelt(7),McGleish(6),Kinsella(5),Betts(5),Locke(3),Gibbs(3),Dennis(3),Mardenborough(2),Fry(2),Whitton(2),Caeser(2),Cheetham(2),Abrahams(2), Cawley(1),Greene(1),Ball(1),Dunne(1),Duguid(1)

CC(3): Kinsella(1),Cheetham(1),Adcock(1)

AWS(7): Adcock(3),Cawley(1),Kinsella(1),Betts(1),Reinelt(1)

PO(2): Kinsella(2)

(*A.E.T.)

1995-96

(M) Abrahams	(F) Adcock	(D) Ball	(D) Betts	(M) Boyce	(D) Caeser	(M) Caldwell	(D) Cawley	(M) Cheetham	(M) Craft	(M) Dennis	(F) Duguid	(F) Dunne	(G) Emberson	(M) English	(M) Fry	(F) Gibbs	(D) Greene	(D) Gregory	(M) Haydon	(M) Kinsella	(M) Lewis	(M) Locke	(F) Mardenborough	(D) McCarthy	(F) McGleish	(G) Petterson	(M) Reinelt	(F) Whitton		
	X		X		X		X	X1		S1			X	X	S					X		X		X			S	X	A.D'Urso	1
	X		X		X		X	X		S			X	X	S					X		X		X			S	X	P.Taylor	2
	X1		X		X		X	X		S			X	X	S					X		X		X			S1	X	S.G.Bennett	3
	X1		X		X		X	X1					X	X	S1					X		X		X				X	G.Barber	4
	X		X		X1		X	X2		X			X		S2					X		X	S1	X			S	X	R.J.Harris	5
	X		X		X1		X	X		X2			X	S1						X		X	S2	X				X	A.Butler	6
	X		X				X	X1		X			X	X	S					X		X	S1	X				X	M.Pearce	7
	X		X			S	X	X1		X			X	X	S2					X		X2		X			S1	X	B.Knight	8
	X		X			S		X		X			X	X	X	S				X		X1		X			S1	X	D.Orr	9
	X		X				X	X		X2			X	X	X	S2				X			S1	X				X1	D.Allison	10
	X	S	X				X	X2					X	X	X	S2				X		X	S1	X			X1		G.Pooley	11
	X	S1	X				X	X					X	X	X	S				X		X1	S	X			X		P.Taylor	12
	X	S3	X				X	X					X		X1	S1				X	X	X3	S2	X			X2		W.Burns	13
	X	S	X				X	X					X	X	X	S				X		X	S	X			X		J.Brandwood	14
	X		X				X	X2		S1			X	X	X	S3				X3		X1	S2	X			X		G.Frankland	15
	X		X		X1		X	X		S1			X	X	X	S				X				X			X		G.R.Pooley	16
	X		X	S2	X		X	X		X			X	X		S1				X1			X2	X					J.Rushton	17
	X		X	S			X	X		X			X	X		X			S	X	S1		X1	X					G.Singh	18
	X		X		S		X	X		X			X	X	X	S				X			X1	X			S1		M.Bailey	19
			X		X1	X		X	S	X				S1	X	X			S	X	X		X	X						20
	X		X		X1		X	X		S			X	X	X	S1				X			X	X					G.R.Pooley	21
	X		X	S1	X		X	X1					X	X	X	S				X	S		X	X					G.Cain	22
	X		X1				X	X		S			X	X	X	S1	X			X			S1	X			X1		K.A.Leach	23
	X	X1	X	S			X	X		S1			X	X	X	S	X			X				X					D.Orr	24
	X	X1	X				X	X		S	S1		X	X	X		X	S		X				X					R.Pulain	25
	X	X1	X				X	X		S1	S		X	X	X		X	S		X				X					I.S.Hemley	26
	X	X1	X				X	X		S1			X	X	X		X	S		X		S		X					R.Furnandiz	27
	X	X2	X				X	X1		S2			X	X	X		X	S		X		S1		X					A.T.D'Urso	28
X	X	S	X				X			X1	S1		X	X	X		X			X				X					G.Barber	29
X1	X	S	X				X			S	S1		X	X	X		X			X		X		X						30
X2			X		S		X	X		S1	S2		X		X		X	X		X		X1		X					S.G.Bennett	31
X	X		X		S		X	S		X	S1		X		X		X	X1		X				X					D.Orr	32
X	X		X		S		X	S1		X2	S2		X		X1		X	X		X				X					T.Heilbron	33
X	X	X1	X		S		X	S					X		S1		X	X		X		X		X					G.Frankland	34
X	X	S	X		S		X	X					X		S		X	X		X		X		X					B.Knight	35
X	X	S1	X		S		X	X2					X				X	X1		X		X		X			S2		J.Kirkby	36
X	X	X2	X3		X			S3		X	S1		X		X	S2	X	X1		X									R.Pearson	37
	X	S	X		X			S		X	X		X		X	X	X			X		X1			S1				D.Orr	38
	X		X		X		X	S1		X	X1		X		X	X				X		S		X	S				M.J.Brandwood	39
	X		X	S	X		X			X	X		X		X1	X2		S1		X				X	S2				S.Baines	40
	X		X		X		X			X	X1				X	X2				X		S		X	S1	X	S2		M.C.Bailey	41
	X		X		X		X			X1	X3				X	X2		S1		X				X	S2	X	S3		T.West	42
	X		X		X		X2				X1				X	X		S2		X		X		X	S1	X	S		M.Pierce	43
	X1		X		X		X			S	S2				X	X2				X		X		X	X	X		S1	G.Pooley	44
			X		X		X				S2	S2			X	X2				X		X		X	X1	X	S1	X2	K.Lynch	45
			X		X		X			X	S	S	X		X	X						X		X	X		S1	X1	R.D.Furnandiz	46
	X		X		X		X			S		S	X		X	X1				X		X		X	X		S1		G.Singh	47
	X		X		X		X1			S3		S1	X		X	S2				X		X3		X	X2		X		S.Bennett	48
	X			S	X			S		X		X	X		X	X		S		X				X	X		X		U.Rennie	49
	X1		X		X		X	S		X		S	X		X	S1				X				X	X		X		P.Richards	50
	X		X		X1		X			X	S2	S1	X		X3	S3				X				X	X		X2		E.Wolstenholme	51
			X	S			X			X	X1	X	X		X1	S1				X		S1		X	X		X		M.Fletcher	52
			X		X1		X			X	S		X		X	X				X		S1		X	X		X2	S2	C.Wilkes	53
			X		X		X			X	S		X		X	X1				X		S1		X	X		X2	S2	M.Pierce	54
	S2		X		X1		X			X			X		X	X3				X		S1		X	X		X2	S3	J.Kirkby	55
8	41	6	45	0	23	0	42	25	0	24	7	2	41	20	35	13	14	7	0	45	1	22	4	44	10	5	12	10	EL Appearances	
0	0	2	0	2	0	0	0	3	0	8	9	3	0	1	3	11	0	3	0	0	1	3	8	0	5	0	10	2	EL Sub Appearances	
0	2	0	2	0	2	0	2	2	0	0	0	0	2	2	0+1	0	0	0	0	2	0	2	0	2	0	0	0	2	CC Appearances	
0	1	0	1	0	1	0	1	1	0	0	0	0	1	1	1	0+1	0	0	0	1	0	0	1	1	0	0	0	0	FAC Appearances	
1	3	1+1	4	0	1	1	3	3	0	1+1	0+1	0	3	3+1	4	1	2	0	0	4	1	2	1	4	0	0	1	0	AWS Appearances	
0	0+1	0	2	0	2	0	2	0	0	2	0	0	2	0	2	2	0	0	0	2	0	0+2	0	2	2	0	2	0+2	PO Appearances	

CLUB RECORDS

BIGGEST VICTORIES
League: 9-1 v Bradford City, Division 4, 30.12.1961.
F.A. Cup: 7-0 v Yeovil Town, 2nd Round, 1958.

BIGGEST DEFEATS
League: 0-8 v Leyton Orient, 15.10.1988.

MOST POINTS
3 points a win:
2 points a win:

RECORD TRANSFER FEE RECEIVED
£120,000 from Wimbledon for P McGee, February 1989.

RECORD TRANSFER FEE PAID
£45,000 to Sporting Lochern for D Tempest, August 1987.

BEST PERFORMANCES
League: 3rd Division 3(S), 1956-57.
Highest Position:
F.A. Cup: 6th Round (shared record for Division 4) 1970-71.
League Cup: 5th Round 1974-75.

HONOURS
GMVC winners 1991-92.
FA Trophy winners 1991-92.

LEAGUE CAREER
Elected to Div.3(S) 1950, Transferred to Div.3 1958, Relegated to Div.4 1960-61, Promoted to Div.3 1961-62, Relegated to Div.4 1964-65, Promoted to Div.3 1965-66, relegated to Div.4 1967-68, Promoted to Div.3 1973-74, Relegated to Div.4 1975-76, Promoted to Div.3 1976-77, relegated to Div.4 1980-81, Relegated to GM Vauxhall Conference 1989-90, Promoted to Div 3 (Old 4) 1991-92.

INDIVIDUAL CLUB RECORDS

MOST GOALS IN A SEASON
Bobby Hunt: 38 goals in 1961-62 (League 37, FA Cup 1).

MOST GOALS IN A MATCH
No one has scored more than four.

OLDEST PLAYER
Benny Fenton, 39 years 6 months.

YOUNGEST PLAYER
Lindsay Smith, 16 years 218 days v Grimsby Town, 24.4.1971.

MOST CAPPED PLAYER
None.

PREVIOUS MANAGERS

(Since joining the Football League)
Ted Fenton; Jimmy Allen, Jack Butler, Benny Fenton, Neil Franklin, Dick Graham, Jim Smith, Bobby Roberts, Allan Hunter, Cyril Lea, Jock Wallace, Mick Mills, Ian Atkins, Roy McDonough, George Burley.

ADDITIONAL INFORMATION
PREVIOUS NAMES
None.

PREVIOUS LEAGUES
Southern League; Alliance Premier (Vauxhall Conference).

Club Colours: Royal blue & white striped shirts, royal blue shorts, white socks.
Change colours: Red & black quarters, black shorts, red socks.

Reserves League: Springheath Print Capital League.

LONGEST LEAGUE RUNS

of undefeated matches:	20 (1956-57)	of league matches w/out a win:	20 (1968
of undefeated home matches:	27 (1956-57)	of undefeated away matches:	9 (1956-57
without home win:	11 (1958)	without an away win:	19 (1950-51, 1959-60
of league wins:	7 (1968-69)	of home wins:	13 (1976-77
of league defeats:	8 (1954)	of away wins:	5 (1981, 1987

THE MANAGER

STEVE WIGNALL . . . . appointed January 1995.

PREVIOUS CLUBS
As Manager . . . . Aldershot.
As Asst.Man/Coach. . . . .
As a player . . . . Doncaster Rovers, Colchester United, Brentford, Aldershot.

HONOURS
As a Manager . . . . None.
As a Player . . . . None.

COLCHESTER UNITED

PLAYERS NAME Honours	Ht	Wt	Birthdate	Birthplace Transfers	Contract Date	Clubs	League	L/Cup	FA Cup	Other	Lge	L/C	FAC	Oth
G O A L K E E P E R S														
Amberson Carl W	6.1	12.5	13/07/73	Epsom	04/05/91	Millwall				1				
				Loan	17/12/92	Colchester United	13							
				Free	06/07/94	Colchester United	60+1	3	2	5				
D E F E N D E R S														
Ball Steven J	6.0	12.1	02/09/69	Colchester	20/09/87	Arsenal								
				Free	29/12/89	Colchester United	3+1			1				1
				Free	18/09/90	Norwich City	0+2	0+2						
				Free	07/08/92	Cambridge United								
				Free	14/09/92	Colchester United	52+12	2	2	15+2	7		3	1
Barnes David	5.10	11.4	16/11/61	Paddington	31/05/79	Coventry (A)	9		4					
E: Y.7. UEFAY'80.				Free	12/04/82	Ipswich Town	16+1							
				£35000	03/10/84	Wolves	86+2	7	6	6	4			
				£25000	22/08/87	Aldershot	68+1	2	2+2	4	1			
				£50000	11/07/89	Sheffield United	82	6	14	4	1			
				£50000	14/01/94	Watford	6		1					
				Free	10/07/96	Colchester United								
Betts Simon R	5.9	11.4	03/03/73	Middlesbrough	02/07/91	Ipswich Town								
				Free	13/08/92	Wrexham								
				Free	03/11/92	Scarborough								
				Free	11/12/92	Colchester United	133+3	3	6+1	12	8			2
Cawley Peter	6.4	14.8	15/09/65	Walton-on-Thames	26/01/87	Wimbledon	1		1					
				Loan	26/02/87	Bristol Rovers	9+1							
				Loan	14/12/88	Fulham	3+2							
				Free	17/07/89	Bristol Rovers	1+2							
				Free	06/07/90	Southend United	6+1	1	1	1	1			
					22/11/90	Exeter City	7							
				Free	08/11/91	Barnet	3		1					
				Free	09/10/92	Colchester United	123+2	2	8	11	7			1
Gregory David	5.11	11.6	23/01/70	Colchester	31/03/87	Ipswich Town	16+16	3+2	1	3+2	2			4
				Loan	09/01/95	Hereford United	2			1				
				Free	04/07/95	Peterborough Utd	0+3	1	1	2				
				Free	08/12/95	Colchester United	7+3							
McCarthy Anthony P	6.0	12.0	09/11/69	Dublin		Shelbourne								
				£100000	25/06/92	Millwall	20+4	3			1			
				Loan	09/12/94	Crewe Alexandra	2							
				Free	17/03/95	Colchester United	54	2	1	6	1			
Partner Andrew N	6.4	13.6	21/10/74	Colchester	24/06/93	Colchester United	1+2			1				
M I D F I E L D														
Caldwell Garett				Princeton, USA										
				Free	26/10/95	Colchester United				1				
Craft Daryl						Colchester Utd (T)								
ry Christopher D	5.9	9.6	23/10/69	Cardiff	03/08/88	Cardiff City	22+33	1+2	0+2	0+2	1			
V: S.				Free	02/08/91	Hereford United	76+14	6+2	8+2	6	10		1	
					24/10/93	Colchester United	71+17	1+1	2+1	6+1	10			
Haydon Nicholas						Colchester Utd (T)								
Kinsella Mark A	5.9	11.2	12/08/72	Dublin		Home Farm								
i: u21.8. GMVC'92. FAT'92.				Free	18/08/89	Colchester United	167+6	8+1	11	12+2	25	2	1	5
Lewis Ben						Colchester Utd (T)								
Lock Anthony C	5.11	11.0	03/09/76	Harlow	18/04/95	Colchester United	0+3				1			
				Loan	15/03/96	Chelmsford								
Locke Adam S	5.10	12.7	20/08/70	Croydon	21/06/88	Crystal Palace								
				Free	06/08/90	Southend United	56+17	5	2+1	6+1	3			
				Loan	08/10/93	Colchester United	4		1					
					23/09/94	Colchester United	42+5	2	4	4+2	4			
Reinelt Robert S	5.10	11.13	11/03/74	Loughton		Aldershot	3+2							
				Free		Wivenhoe Town								
				Free	19/03/93	Gillingham	16+9	1	2+1	2	1	1		
					22/02/95	Colchester United	14+13			3	7			1
F O R W A R D S														
Adcock Tony	5.11	11.9	27/02/63	Bethnal Green	31/03/81	Colchester United	192+18	16+1	12+2	9	98	5	3	6
				£75000	01/06/87	Manchester City	12+3	2+1	2	2	5	1		3
				£85000	25/01/88	Northampton Town	72	6	1	4	30	3		1
				£190000	06/10/89	Bradford City	33+5	1	0+1	2	6			
				£75000	11/01/91	Northampton Town	34+1	1	1	2	10		1	1
				£35000	30/12/91	Peterborough Utd	107+4	8+1	5	3+2	35	3		1
				£20000	04/08/94	Luton Town	0+2		0+1					
				Free	03/08/95	Colchester United	41	2	1	3+1	12	1		4
Duguid Karl						Colchester Utd (T)								
Dunne Joseph J	6.0	11.6	25/05/73	Dublin	09/08/90	Gillingham	108+7	7	5+1	4+2	1			
				Free	27/03/96	Colchester United	2+3				1			
Gibbs Paul	5.10	11.3	26/10/72	Gorleston		Diss Town								
					06/03/95	Colchester United	21+12		0+1	3	3			
Hardenborough Steve	5.8	11.9	11/09/64			Colchester United								
Whitton Stephen P	6.0	12.7	04/12/60	East Ham	15/09/78	Coventry City	64+10	3+2	2		21		2	
Div.2'92.				£175000	11/07/83	West Ham United	35+4	6	1		6	2		
				Loan	31/01/86	Birmingham City	8				2			
				£60000	28/08/86	Birmingham City	94+1	7+1	5	3	28	4		1
				£275000	03/03/89	Sheffield Wednesday	22+10	3	0+1	0+1	4	4		
				£150000	11/01/91	Ipswich Town	80+8	7+1	8+1	4	15	2	2	
				£10000	24/03/94	Colchester United	54+2	4	4	2+2	14		2	

LAYER ROAD GROUND
Colchester, Essex CO2 7JJ
Tel: 01206 574 042

Capacity..7,944
Covered Standing..4,591
Seating...1,950

First game...Not known.
First floodlit game ....Not known.

ATTENDANCES
Highest ....19,073 v Reading, FA Cup Round 1, 27.11.1948.
Lowest...Not known.

OTHER GROUNDS...None.

MATCHDAY TICKET PRICES

Terraces................................... £6
Juniors..................................... £4

Family Enclosure £5
Juniors..................................... £2

Seats................... £6.50, £7.50 or £8
Juniors .... £4.50, £5 or £5.50

Ticket Office Telephone no........ 01206 574 042

CLUBCALL
0891 73 73 00

Calls cost 39p per minute cheap rate and 49p per minute at all other times.
Call costings correct at time of going to press.

HOW TO GET TO THE GROUND

From the North
Follow signs in Colchester on A133/B1508 or A12, then follow signs to Layer B1026 into Layer Road for Colchester United FC.

From the East
Follow signs into Colchester on A604 or A133 then follow signs to Layer B1026 into Layer Road for Colchester United FC.

From the South and West
Follow signs into Colchester on A604 or A12 then follow signs to Layer B1026 into Layer Road for Colchester United FC.

Car Parking
Street parking only.

Nearest Railway Station
Colchester North (01206 564 777)

MATCHDAY PROGRAMME

Programme Editor .... Rob Hadcroft.

Number of pages .... 32.

Price .... £1.50.

Subscriptions .... £75 per season (home & away).

Local Newspapers............ Evening Gazette (Mon-Fri evenings),
.... East Anglian Daily Times (Mon-Fri mornings),
.... Essex County Standard (weekly-Fridays).

Local Radio Stations..................... SGR FM (Colchester),
.... Essex Radio (Southend & Chelmsford) 257 MW.

DARLINGTON
(The Quakers)
NATIONWIDE LEAGUE DIVISION 3
SPONSORED BY: SOCCERDOME

ack Row (L-R): Rui Neves, Andy Crosby, Sean Gregan, Mike Pollitt, Steve Gaughan, Gary Himsworth, Pedro Paulo.
ddle Row: Steohen Morgon (Director), Peter Ellis (Asst. Director), Paul Mattison, Michael Pugh, Robert Blake, Anthony Carrs, Robbie
inter, Simon Shaw, Gavin Worboys, Nigel Carnell (Physio), Gordon Hodgson (Director), Ian Parker (Asst. Director). **Front Row:** Paul
sson, Mattie Appleby, Jim PLatt (Director of Coaching), Bernard Lowery (Chairman), Stephen Weeks (Vice Chairman), David Hodgson
irector of Coaching), Gary Bannister, Phil Brumwell.

DARLINGTON
FORMED IN 1883
TURNED PROFESSIONAL IN 1908
LTD COMPANY IN 1891

PRESIDENT: Alan Noble
CHAIRMAN: B Lowery
VICE-CHAIRMAN
S Weeks
DIRECTORS
Steve Morgan, G Hodgson
COMMERCIAL MANAGER
K Lavery
GENERAL MANAGER
S Morgan

DIRECTOR OF COACHING: Jim Platt
ASSISTANT MANAGER: Danny Begarra

YOUTH TEAM MANAGER
B Askew
PHYSIOTHERAPIST
Mark Riley
STATISTICIAN FOR THE DIRECTORY
Frank Tweddle

Almost a triumphant season! Having finished the League in 5th spot, a play-off place was secured and Darlington were three games away from promotion to the Second Division, five season's after being relegated from, what was then, the Third Division.

A slow start saw Darlington win just one of their opening ten games, however, they only lost three in the same sequence. It was only a matter of time before the 'Quakers' could turn their draws into victories. October was the turning point, five consecutive wins saw them race up the table, moving from 22nd position to 8th.

Darlington maintained this form and lost only three times in the New Year to earn themselves a play-off place.

Hereford United were their opponents in the Semi-Finals in which a final aggregate score of 4-1 saw them comfortably through. Darlington were to meet Neil Warnocks' ambitious Plymouth Argyle in a tight and tense final. The game was decided by the one goal, unfortunately, for Darlington, it was scored at the wrong end, and the Quakers dream of promotion was over.

The Cup competitions brought little cheer. A First Round exit to Crewe (1-5 on aggregate) in the Coca-Cola Cup was followed by an early departure from the Auto Windscreen Shield - Rochdale (2-5), Lincoln City (0-1). In the F.A. Cup a convincing First Round victory over Hartlepool United (4-2) was followed by defeat at the hands of Rochdale (0-1) after a 2-2 draw at The Feethams.

Darlington will again be pushing for League honours next season, and if they convert more of the draws, of which their were 18 last season, into victories then there's no reason why they won't by-pass the play-offs and gain an automatic promotional spot.

565

DARLINGTON

League: 5th | FA Cup: 2nd Rnd | Coca-Cola Cup: 1st Rnd | Auto Windscreen Shield: 1st Rnd

M	DATE	COMP	VEN	OPPONENTS	RESULT	HT	LP	GOAL SCORERS/GOAL TIMES	ATT.
1	A 12	EL	A	Exeter City	W 1-0	1-0	11	Olsson 7	(2934)
2	19	EL	H	Rochdale	L 0-1	0-0	14		2139
3	23	CC 1/1	A	Crewe Alexandra	L 0-4	0-0			(2850)
4	26	EL	A	Leyton Orient	D 1-1	0-0	15	Crosby 85	(4034)
5	29	EL	H	Fulham	D 1-1	0-1	14	Carss 87	1906
6	S 2	EL	H	Cardiff City	L 0-1	0-1	17		1845
7	5	CC 1/2	H	Crewe Alexandra	D 1-1	0-0		Carss 85	1084
8	9	EL	A	Hartlepool United	D 1-1	0-0	16	Carss 84	(2705)
9	12	EL	A	Mansfield Town	D 2-2	2-1	18	Bannister 5, Olsson 29	(2190)
10	16	EL	H	Colchester United	D 2-2	0-2	18	Muir 46, Bannister 80	1685
11	23	EL	H	Scarborough	L 1-2	0-1	21	Himsworth 46	2046
12	30	EL	A	Barnet	D 1-1	1-0	22	Bannister 40	(1923)
13	O 7	EL	A	Lincoln City	W 2-0	1-0	18	Appleby 43, Olsson 70	(2564)
14	14	EL	A	Gillingham	W 1-0	1-0	13	Bannister 20	2043
15	21	EL	A	Cambridge United	W 1-0	1-0	12	Painter 11	(2730)
16	24	AWS 1/1	A	Rochdale	L 2-5	1-2		Olsson 8, Appleby 84	(1055)
17	28	EL	A	Plymouth Argyle	W 2-0	0-0	8	Himsworth 54, Naylor 85	2352
18	31	EL	H	Wigan Athletic	W 2-1	1-0	8	Shaw 16, Appleby 86	2076
19	N 4	EL	A	Bury	D 0-0	0-0	8		(2964)
20	7	AWS 1/2	H	Lincoln City	L 0-1	0-0			984
21	11	FAC 1	A	Hartlepool United	W 4-2	2-1		Brumwell 25, Gaughen 37, Bannister 59, Painter 64	(3834)
22	18	EL	H	Scunthorpe United	D 0-0	0-0	8		2078
23	25	EL	A	Chester City	L 1-4	0-1	9	Barnard 58	(2652)
24	D 2	FAC 2	A	Rochdale	D 2-2	1-0		Shaw 42, Olsson 71	(3732)
25	9	EL	A	Scarborough	W 2-1	0-1	7	Bannister 85, Worboys 87	(1585)
26	12	FAC 2R	H	Rochdale	L 0-1	0-0			4131
27	16	EL	H	Barnet	D 1-1	1-0	9	Guinan 17	1717
28	23	EL	A	Torquay United	W 1-0	1-0	8	Bannister 5	(2405)
29	J 6	EL	A	Northampton Town	L 1-2	0-2	9	Worboys 75	1943
30	13	EL	A	Rochdale	W 2-1	0-1	8	Appleby 75(pen), Olsson 83	(2200)
31	16	EL	H	Doncaster Rovers	L 1-2	0-1	8	Painter 48	1502
32	20	EL	A	Exeter City	W 1-0	0-0	6	Blake 52	1723
33	30	EL	H	Preston North End	L 1-2	1-0	6	Himsworth 22	2599
34	F 3	EL	H	Leyton Orient	W 2-0	0-0	5	Blake 62, McMahon 81	1880
35	10	EL	A	Northampton Town	D 1-1	1-1	5	Painter 39	(4926)
36	17	EL	H	Mansfield Town	D 1-1	0-0	5	Bannister 85	2598
37	20	EL	A	Cardiff City	W 2-0	2-0	5	Barnard 34, Blake 44	(2113)
38	24	EL	A	Colchester United	D 1-1	0-1	5	Blake 71	(2653)
39	27	EL	H	Hartlepool United	W 1-0	0-0	3	Gaughen 83	4333
40	M 2	EL	A	Doncaster Rovers	W 2-1	1-1	3	Bannister 8, Blake 55	(2209)
41	5	EL	A	Fulham	D 2-2	2-0	3	Blake 2, 24	(2534)
42	9	EL	H	Torquay United	L 1-2	0-2	4	Appleby 80	2861
43	16	EL	A	Preston North End	D 1-1	1-1	5	Bannister 41	(12070)
44	23	EL	H	Hereford United	W 1-0	0-0	6	Painter 54	1708
45	30	EL	H	Lincoln City	W 3-2	2-1	4	Gaughen 21, 30, Blake 57	2146
46	A 2	EL	A	Gillingham	D 0-0	0-0	6		(6426)
47	6	EL	A	Plymouth Argyle	W 1-0	1-0	5	Painter 22	(8990)
48	8	EL	H	Cambridge United	D 0-0	0-0	4		3064
49	13	EL	A	Wigan Athletic	D 1-1	1-0	6	Appleby 14	(4473)
50	20	EL	H	Bury	W 4-0	2-0	5	Carmichael 12, Blake 17, Painter 67, 77	4335
51	23	EL	A	Hereford United	W 1-0	1-0	4	Carmichael 43	(5359)
52	27	EL	H	Chester City	W 3-1	0-0	3	Blake 46, Painter 78, Bannister 88	4510
53	M 4	EL	A	Scunthorpe United	D 3-3	0-2	5	Appleby 60(pen), Blake 68, Barnard 87	(4847)
54	12	PO SF1	A	Hereford United	W 2-1	2-1		Gregan 27, Blake 37	(6622)
55	15	PO SF2	H	Hereford United	W 2-1	1-0		Painter 17, Appleby 47(pen)	6584
56	25	PO F	N	Plymouth Argyle	L 0-1	0-0			43431

Best Home League Attendance: 4510 v Chester City | Smallest: 1502 v Doncaster Rovers | Average: 2395

Goal Scorers:
EL(60): Blake(11),Bannister(10),Painter(8),Appleby(6),Olsson(4),Barnard(3),Himsworth(3),Gaughen(3),Carmichael(2),Carss(2),Worboys(2), Muir(1),Naylor(1),McMahon(1),Crosby(1),Shaw(1),Guinan(1)
CC(1): Carss(1)
FAC(6): Bannister(1),Brumwell(1),Gaughen(1),Olsson(1),Painter(1),Shaw(1)
AWS(2): Appleby(1),Olsson(1)   PO(4): Painter(1),Gregan(1),Blake(1),Appleby(1)

1995-96

(D) Appleby	(F) Bannister	(D) Barnard	(F) Blake	(M) Brumwell	(G) Burridge	(F) Carmichael	(M) Carss	(D) Crosby	(M) Gaughen	(D) Gregan	(M) Guinan	(F) Himsworth	(M) Lucas	(M) Mattison	(F) McMahon	(F) Muir	(F) Naylor	(M) Neves	(G) Newell	(M) Olsson	(F) Painter	(M) Paulo	(G) Pollitt	(M) Quetongo	(M) Robinson	(M) Shaw	(M) Twynham	(F) Worboys		
X	X2		X				X3	X	X	X		S1								X	X1		X			X		S2	A.Whiley	1
X1	X		X2	S1			X3	X	X	X		X							S2	X	X		X					S3	J.Kirkby	2
	X		S1				X1	X	X	X		X								X	X		X			X2		S2	S.Baines	3
X	X			S3			S2	X	X	X		X							X1	X3	X2		X			X		S1	M.Fletcher	4
X	X		S3	X			S2	X	X	X		X							S1	X3	X1		X			X2		X	A.Leak	5
X2	X			S2			S	X	X	X		X								X	X		S1	X1		X1		X	N.Barry	6
	X	X	S1	X			X	X	X	X		X							X1	S		S2	X			X2		X	U.Rennie	7
	X	X1		X3			S1	X	X	X		X				X			X2	X			X			S3		S2	J.Lloyd	8
S1	X		S	X1			X2	X	X	X		X				X				X			X			S2		X	I.Hemley	9
X	X		S1	S3			X	X	X3	X		X2				X				X			X			S2		X1	D.Allison	10
X	X	X1	X2	X2			S2	X	S2	X		X								X	X	S1	X						P.Richards	11
X	X	X		S3			X	X	S1			S2			X1				X	X3		X2	X			X			C.Wilkes	12
X	X	X					S	X	X	X		X						S		X	X		X	S	X	X		S	F.Stretton	13
X	X	X		S			X	X	X1	X		X						S		X	X		X			X		S	A.Butler	14
X	X	X		S			X	X	X1	X		X						S1		X	X		X			X		S	P.Taylor	15
X	X1	X		S1			X	X	X3	X		X						S2		X	X		X			X2		S3	S.Baines	16
X	X	X					S	X	S1	X		X						X		X	X1		X			X		S	M.Riley	17
X	X1	X					S1	X	S	X		X						X		X	X1		X			X		S1	R.Furnandiz	18
X	X	X		S			S	X	X	X		X						X		X	X1		X			X		S1	W.C.Burns	19
X	S3	X		X1			X3	X	X	X		X						X		X			X			X		X2	T.Leake	20
X	X			X			X	X	X1	X		X								X	X		X		S1	X		S	W.Burns	21
X	X			S1	X		S	X	X1	X		X								X	X2		X			X		S2	T.West	22
X	X			S2	X		S	X	X1	X		X								X2	X		X		S1	X			K.J.Breen	23
X	X		S1	X	X		X	X	S	X		X								X	X1		X			X			N.Barry	24
X	X	X		X2	X		S3	X	S2			X3								X	X1		X			X		S1	U.D.Rennie	25
X	X		X1	X2	X		S2	X	X			X								X	S1		X			X		X	N.Barry	26
X	X			X			S	X	S2		X1	X	X							X	X		X			X		X2	D.Laws	27
X	X1	X					S2	X	S1	X	X2	X	X							X	X		X			X		S	K.Leach	28
X	X1	X					S2	X	S1	X2	X2	X	X							X	X		X			X		S2	W.Burns	29
X		X	S1	S2				X	X2	X	S	X	X							X	X		X			X		X1	M.Brandwood	30
X		X	S2	X				X	X	X		X	X1	X	S1	X				X2	X		X			X			S.Mathieson	31
X		X	X1	X				S	S	X		X	X	X	S1	X				X	X		X			X			J.Kirby	32
X	X	X	S1	S				X	X			X		S	X	S		X		X1	X		X			X			K.Lynch	33
X	S	X	X	S				X	X	X		X				S1				X	X		X			X1			M.Riley	34
X	S	X	S1	S				X	X	X		X				X1				X	X		X			X			S.Baines	35
X	X	X	X	S				X	X	X		X				S1				X	S	X1	X			X			P.R.Richards	36
X	X	X	X					S	X	X		X								X	X		X			X1			R.Harris	37
X	X	X	X	X1				S1	X	X2						S3				X	X	X3	X			S2		X	D.Orr	38
X	S1	X	X	S				X	X	X				X1	X					X	X		X			S	X	S	G.Cain	39
X	X	X	X	X1				S1	X	X				S	X1					X	X		X			X			P.Rejer	40
X	X	X	X2					X1	S2	X	X			S	X1					X	S1		X			X			M.Fletcher	41
X	X	X	X2	S3				X	X	X		X3		S2						X	X1		X			S1		X	R.Pearson	42
X	X	X		X	S			X	X	X		X		S1						X	X1		X			X			K.Breen	43
X	X	S	X1	S				X	X	X		X		S1						X	X		X			X			A.Leake	44
X	X	X	X1	X				X	S	X		X		S1						X	X		X			X1	S		T.West	45
X	X	X	X1	X				S	X	X		X								X	X		X						J.Brandwood	46
X	S1	X	X	S				X	X	X		X		S2						X	X		X			S	S		S.Baines	47
X	X	X3	X	S2			S1	S3	X	X		X								X	X		X			X2	X1		J.Kirkby	48
X	X	X	S	X			X	X	X	X		X								X	X		X			S1	X1		A.Butler	49
	X	X	X	X1				X	X2	X				S2						X	X		X			S1			R.Poulain	50
X	X2	X	X	X1				X	X	X										X	X		X			S1	S		G.Singh	51
X	X	X	X	S				X	X	X										X	X		X			X	S		E.Lomas	52
X	X	S	X	S				X1	S1	X										X	X		X			X	S		R.Furnandiz	53
X	X	X	X2	S1			X	X1	X	X				S2						X	X		X					S	K.Lynch	54
X	X	X	X	S				X	X	X				S						X	X		X					S	D.Allison	55
X	X	X	X	X			S1	X	X	X1	X			S						X	X		X					S	B.Burns	56
42	39	37	23	16	3	11	13	45	34	38	3	26	6	1	6	4	3	3	21	34	33	4	15	1	0	36	2	6	EL Appearances	
1	2	0	6	12	0	2	14	0	7	0	0	2	0	5	5	0	1	0	0	2	2	0	0	0	0	4	5	8	EL Sub Appearances	
0	2	1	0+2	1	0	0	2	2	2	1	0	2	0	0	0	0	0	2	0	1	0	1+1	2	0	0	2	0	1	CC Appearances	
3	3	0	1+1	3	2	0	1+1	3	2	2	0	3	0	0	0	0	0	3	0	2+1	0	1	0	0+1	3	0	1	FAC Appearances	
2	1+1	2	0	1+1	0	0	1	2	2	2	0	1	0	0	0	0	1+1	0	0	1	1	0	2	0	0	2	0	1+1	AWS Appearances	
3	3	3	2+1	0	2+1	2	3	3	3	0+1	0	0+1	0	0	0	0	0	3	0	3	0	3	0	0	3	0	0	0	PO Appearances	

Also Played: (M) Kirkham S2(20). (M) Johnston S(24). (M) Kirkham S(43). (M) Pepper S(31,46), S1(37).(M) Pugh S1(20), S(26). (G) Stevens X(10).

CLUB RECORDS

BIGGEST VICTORIES
League: 9-2 v Lincoln City, Division 3(N) 7.1.1928.
F.A. Cup: 7-2 v Evenwood, 1st Round, 17.11.1958.
Freight Rover Trophy: 7-0 v Halifax Town, 3.3.1985.

BIGGEST DEFEATS
League: 0-10 v Doncaster Rovers, Division 4, 25.1.1964.

MOST POINTS
3 points a win: 85, Division 4, 1984-85 (87, GMVC, 1989-90).
2 points a win:

RECORD TRANSFER FEE RECEIVED
£200,000 from Leicester City for Jimmy Willis, December 1991.

RECORD TRANSFER FEE PAID
£95,000 to Motherwell for Nick Cusack, January 1992.

BEST PERFORMANCES
League: 15th Division 2, 1925-26.
F.A. Cup: 3rd Round 1910-11, 5th Round 1957-58 (both last 16).
League Cup: 5th Round 1967-68.

HONOURS
Division 3(N) Champions 1924-25.
Division 3(N) Cup 1933-34.
G.M.V.C. Champions 1989-90.
Division 4 Champions 1991.

LEAGUE CAREER
Original member of Div 3(N) 1921, Div 2 1924-25, Div 3(N) 1926-27, Transferred to Div 4 1958, Div 3 1965-66, Div 4 1966-67, Div 3 1984-85, Div 4 1986-87, G.M.V.C. 1988-89, Div 4 1989-90, Div 3 1990-91, Div 4 (now Div 3) 1991-

INDIVIDUAL CLUB RECORDS

MOST GOALS IN A SEASON
David Brown: 39, Division 3(N), 1924-25.

MOST GOALS IN A MATCH
5. Tom Ruddy v South Shields, Division 2, 23.4.1927.
5. Maurice Wellock, Division 3(N), 15.2.1930.

OLDEST PLAYER
Jimmy Case, 39 years 128 days v Wycombe W., Division 3, 23.10.1993.

YOUNGEST PLAYER
Dale Anderson, 16 years 254 days, 4.5.1987.

MOST CAPPED PLAYER
None.

PREVIOUS MANAGERS

(Since 1946)
Bill Forrest, George Irwin, Bob Gurney, Dick Duckworth, Eddie Carr, Lol Morgan, Jimmy Greenhalgh, Ray Yeoman, Len Richley, Frank Brennan, Allan Jones, Ralph Brand, Dick Connor, Bill Horner, Peter Madden, Len Walker, Billy Elliott, Cyril Knowles, Paul Ward (Player/manager), David Booth, Brian Little, Frank Gray, Ray Hankin, Alan Murray, Paul Futcher, Eddie Kyle (Caretaker)

ADDITIONAL INFORMATION
PREVIOUS NAMES
None.

PREVIOUS LEAGUES
Northern League, North Eastern League, G.M.Vauxhall League.

Club colours: Black white hooped shirts,
Change colours: Yellow, blue sleeves.

Reserves League: Pontins League.

LONGEST LEAGUE RUNS

of undefeated matches:	17 (1968)	of league matches w/out a win:	19 (1988-89)
of undefeated home matches:	36 (1923-25)	of undefeated away matches:	14 (1968-69)
without home win:	18 (1988-89)	without an away win:	36 (1952-54)
of league wins:	5 (1922, 1924, 1975, 1985, 1989 (GMVC)	of home wins:	8 (1923-24, 1924, 1935-36)
of league defeats:	8 1985	of away wins:	4 (1948) 5 (1989 GMVC)

THE MANAGER (DIRECTOR OF COACHING)

JIM PLATT . . . . appointed June 1995.

PREVIOUS CLUBS
As Manager . . . . Corlraine.
As Asst.Man/Coach . . . . None.
As a player . . . . Middlesbrough, Liverpool, Sunderland.

HONOURS
As a Manager . . . . None.
As a Player . . . . None.
. . . . **Northern Ireland:** 21 full games, including World Cup 1982 & 1986.

DARLINGTON

PLAYERS NAME Honours	Ht	Wt	Birthdate	Birthplace Transfers	Contract Date	Clubs	League	L/Cup	FA Cup	Other	Lge	L/C	FAC	Oth
G O A L K E E P E R S														
Newell Paul	6.1	12.8	23/02/69	Woolwich	17/06/87	Southend United (T)	15		2	1				
				£5000	06/08/90	Leyton Orient	61	3	3	4				
				Loan	12/08/92	Colchester United	14	2						
				Free	26/07/94	Barnet	15			1				
				Free		Darlington								
Johnston Frank						Darlington (T)								
D E F E N D E R S														
Barnard Mark	6.0	11.10	27/11/75	Sheffield	13/07/94	Rotherham United								
				Free	27/09/95	Darlington	37	1		5	3			
Crosby Andrew K	6.2	13.0	03/03/73	Rotherham		Leeds United								
				Free	04/07/91	Doncaster Rovers	41+10	1+1	2	4+1				1
				Loan	12/10/93	Halifax Town								
				Free	10/12/93	Darlington	105	4	5	7	1			
Faulkner David via USA	6.0	11.12	08/10/75	Sheffield	01/08/92	Sheffield Wed.								
					08/08/96	Darlington								
Gregan Sean M	6.2	12.5	29/03/74	Guisborough	20/12/91	Darlington	113+7	4	6	10+1	4			1
M I D F I E L D														
Atkinson Brian E: u21.6	5.10	11.6	19/01/71	Darlington	21/07/89	Sunderland	119+22	8+2	13	2+3	4		2	
				Loan	19/01/96	Carlisle United	2			1				
					08/08/96	Darlington								
Brumwell Philip	5.7	11.2	08/08/75	Darlington	30/06/94	Sunderland								
				Free	11/08/95	Darlington	16+12	1	3	3+2			1	
Carss Tony	5.11	12.0	31/03/76	Alnwick		Bradford City								
					01/08/94	Blackburn Rovers								
				Free	11/08/95	Darlington	13+14	2	1+1	3	2	1		
Gaughen Steven E	5.11	11.2	14/04/70	Doncaster		Hatfield Main								
				Free	21/01/88	Doncaster Rovers	42+25	2+2	4+1	5+1	3			
				Free	01/07/90	Sunderland								
				£10000	21/01/92	Darlington	159+12	8	6	10+1	15	1		
Johnston Frank						Darlington (T)								
Olsson Paul	5.8	10.11	24/12/65	Hull	07/01/84	Hull City				1				1
				Free	13/03/87	Exeter City	38+5	2	0+1		2			
				Free	17/08/88	Scarborough	34+14	5+1	2	8	5			
				£5000	26/12/89	Hartlepool United	162+19	11+2	10	11+1	13			2
				Free	01/07/90	Darlington	76	3	5	4	8		1	2
Robinson Paul						Darlington (T)								
Shaw Simon R	6.0	12.0	21/09/73	Middlesbrough	14/08/92	Darlington	82+25	4+1	4	4+1	7		1	
Twynham Gary	6.0	12.1	08/02/76	Manchester		Manchester Utd (T)								
						Darlington								
F O R W A R D S														
Blake Robert J	5.11	12.0	04/03/76	Middlesbrough	01/07/94	Darlington	26+12	0+2	1+1	3	11			1
Carmichael Matthew	6.0	12.4	13/05/64	Singapore		Basingstoke Town								
				Free	08/08/89	Lincoln City	113+20	9+1	4+1	7+1	18	1		2
				Free	16/07/93	Scunthorpe United	51+11	1+1	4+3	5	20		2	5
				Loan	23/09/94	Barnet	2+1							
				Free	10/03/95	Preston North End	7+3				3			
					18/08/95	Doncaster Rovers	19+9	0+1	0+1	2+1	4	1		
				Free	29/03/96	Darlington	11+2			2+1	2			
Painter Peter Robert	5.10	11.0	26/01/71	Wigan	01/07/88	Chester City	58+26	2+2	7+1	3	8		3	
				£30000	16/08/91	Maidstone	27+3	2	1+1	0+2	5			
				£25000	27/03/92	Burnley	16+10	2	1		2			
					16/09/93	Darlington	102+7	2	5+1	9	28		2	3

FEETHAMS
Darlington, Co.Durham DL1 5JB
Tel: 01325 465 097

Capacity...7,046
Covered Standing..2,822
Seating...973

First game..1883.
First floodlit game...v Millwall, 19.9.1960.

ATTENDANCES
Highest..21,023 v Bolton, Lge Cup 3rd Rnd, 14.11.1960.
Lowest..657 v Halifax, AMC, 3.3.1985.

OTHER GROUNDS...None.

HOW TO GET TO THE GROUND

From the North
Use motorway (A1M) then A167 sign posted Darlington into town centre, then follow signs to Northallerton into Victoria Road for Darlington FC.

From the East
Use A67 sign posted Darlington into town centre, then follow signs to Northallerton into Victoria Road for Darlington FC.

From the South
Use motorway (A1M) and A66M then A66 sign posted Darlington and at round-about take the fourth exit into Victoria Road for Darlington FC.

From the West
Use A67 sign posted Darlington into town centre and at roundabout take 3rd exit into Victoria Road for Darlington FC.

Car Parking
Adequate space in adjacent side streets.

Nearest railway Station
Darlington (01325 55111)

MATCHDAY TICKET PRICES

Seats................................ £6
Juv/OAP £3

Terraces............................ £6
Juv/OAP £3

Ticket Office Telephone no........ 01325 465 097

CLUBCALL
0898 10 15 55
Calls cost 39p per minute cheap rate and 49p per minute at all other times.
Call costings correct at time of going to press.

MATCHDAY PROGRAMME

Programme Editor .... Ken Lavery.

Number of pages .... 28.

Price .... £1.30.

Subscriptions .... £34 (all home games).

Local Newspapers .... Northern Echo, Evening Gazette.

Local Radio Stations........... BBC Radio Cleveland, T.F.M. Radio.

DONCASTER ROVERS
(The Rovers)
NATIONWIDE LEAGUE DIVISION 3
SPONSORED BY: DONCASTER FREE PRESS

Back Row (R-L): Jason Knight, Kevin Noteman, Mark Proctor, Paul Marquis, Mickey Norbury, Perry Suckling, Graeme Jones, Lee Warren, Darren Moore, Hakan Hayrettin. **Middle Row:** Phil McLoughlin (Physio), Jim Golze (Yth Coach), Ian Clarke, John Schofield, Ian Measham, Mark McCluskie, Warren Hackett, Lee Saunders, Paul Haywood, Duane Darby, Ryan Kirby, Peter Schofield (Chief Scout), George Foster (Coach). **Front Row:** Scott Maxfield, James Meara, Steve Gallen, Ken Richardson, Russ Wilcox, Steve Beaglehole (Asst. Manager), Scott Colcombe, Sean Parrish, Steve Harper, Gary Brabin.

DONCASTER FREE PRESS
FORMED IN 1879
TURNED PROFESSIONAL IN 1885
LTD COMPANY IN 1905 & 1920

DIRECTORS
K Haranl
L Mabbett, J Richardson, R Ashworth
SECRETARY
Mrs K J Oldale (01302 539 441)

MANAGER: Sammy Chung
ASSISTANT MANAGER: Steve Beaglehole
FIRST TEAM COACH
George Foster

RESERVES & YOUTH TEAM MANAGER
Steve Beaglehole

PHYSIOTHERAPIST
Phil McCloughlin

STATISTICIAN FOR THE DIRECTORY
Ernest Wiles

Rovers had an overall disappointing season, not even managing to equal last year's 9th position - 13th wasn't disastrous, but followers of the club had expected greater things from their team.

The season started well with Doncaster remaining unbeaten until 9th September when defeat against Fulham knocked their confidence - losing in the next match meant that they had slipped from second to 10th place in the course of three days. An encouraging 4-1 victory over Leyton Orient in December was unfortunately immediately followed by a defeat of the same margin at Bury. January produced a run of three wins and hopes were high in February when Rovers stayed at third place in the table for most of the month, but March - and losses against Darlington and Exeter City - brought an end to their dream of promotion.

Rovers' cup campaigns were unspectacular: they failed to win any game, going out in the first round of both FA and Coca-Cola Cups, and in the second round of the Auto Windscreens Shield.

Graeme Jones was top scorer with 11 goals in the Endsleigh League, while Cramb and Parrish managed 12 between them.

If Doncaster can reproduce the form of the early part of the season, without tailing off into inconsistency at the end, they should be able to produce a solid promotion challenge in 1996-7.

DONCASTER ROVERS

League: 13th FA Cup: 1st Rnd Coca-Cola Cup: 1st Rnd Auto Windscreen Shield: 2nd Rnd

M	DATE	COMP	VEN	OPPONENTS	RESULT	HT	LP	GOAL SCORERS/GOAL TIMES	ATT.
1	A 12	EL	H	Scarborough	W 1-0	0-0	10	Parrish 74	2523
2	14	CC 1/1	H	Shrewsbury Town	D 1-1	0-1		Wilcox 51	1580
3	19	EL	A	Torquay United	W 2-1	0-0	3	Noteman 49, Jones 70	(2086)
4	22	CC 1/2	A	Shrewsbury Town	D 0-0	0-0			(1842)
5	26	EL	H	Cardiff City	D 0-0	0-0	7		2186
6	29	EL	A	Mansfield Town	D 0-0	0-0	3		(2940)
7	S 2	EL	H	Hartlepool United	W 1-0	0-0	2	Brodie 58	2304
8	9	EL	A	Fulham	L 1-3	1-2	5	Brabin 13	(4920)
9	12	EL	A	Plymouth Argyle	L 1-3	1-2	10	Hill 11(og)	(4858)
10	16	EL	H	Northampton Town	W 1-0	1-0	5	Brabin 45	2353
11	23	EL	H	Rochdale	L 0-3	0-1	3		2217
12	25	AWS 1/1	H	Bradford City	D 1-1	1-1		Clark 15	1014
13	30	EL	A	Leyton Orient	L 1-3	0-2	5	Darby 83	(5524)
14	O 7	EL	A	Chester City	W 3-0	0-0	3	Maxfield 77, Darby 78, Carmichael 88	(2374)
15	14	EL	H	Hereford United	D 0-0	0-0	4		1961
16	21	EL	A	Gillingham	L 0-4	0-1	7		(6307)
17	28	EL	A	Preston North End	D 2-2	1-1	7	Darby 45, Jones 70	4413
18	30	EL	H	Cambridge United	W 2-1	1-1	6	Parrish 7, Darby 67	1657
19	N 4	EL	A	Barnet	D 1-1	1-1	6	Moore 47	(1913)
20	7	AWS 1/2	H	Carlisle United	D 1-1	1-0		Colcombe 36	(4421)
21	11	FAC 1	A	Mansfield Town	L 2-4	0-3		Jones 81(pen), Carmichael 90	(3116)
22	18	EL	H	Colchester United	W 3-2	2-1	5	Colcombe 18, Jones 25, 76	1603
23	25	EL	A	Wigan Athletic	L 0-2	0-2	6		(2879)
24	27	AWS 2	H	Notts County	L 1-3	0-0		Moore 58	1714
25	D 2	EL	H	Exeter City	W 2-0	0-0	4	Brabin 45, Jones 74	1429
26	9	EL	A	Rochdale	L 0-1	0-1	6		(2168)
27	16	EL	H	Leyton Orient	W 4-1	2-1	4	Colcombe 7, Jones 32, 49, 60(pen)	1633
28	J 6	EL	A	Bury	L 1-4	1-1	6	Carmichael 41	(2606)
29	13	EL	H	Torquay United	W 1-0	0-0	5	Carmichael 71	1807
30	16	EL	A	Darlington	W 2-1	1-0	4	Parrish 5, Carmichael 74	(1502)
31	20	EL	A	Scarborough	W 2-0	0-0	4	Cramb 54, 89	(1661)
32	F 3	EL	A	Cardiff City	L 2-3	0-1	4	Jones 49, Colcombe 87	(2313)
33	5	EL	H	Lincoln City	D 1-1	1-0	3	Parrish 33	2083
34	10	EL	H	Bury	L 0-1	0-1	3		2418
35	17	EL	H	Plymouth Argyle	D 0-0	0-0	4		2338
36	20	EL	A	Hartlepool United	W 1-0	0-0	3	Cramb 72(pen)	(1367)
37	24	EL	A	Northampton Town	D 3-3	1-2	3	Schofield 44(pen), Cramb 49, 77	(4738)
38	26	EL	H	Fulham	L 0-2	0-2	3		2331
39	M 2	EL	H	Darlington	L 1-2	1-1	8	Moore 32	2209
40	9	EL	A	Exeter City	L 0-1	0-1	9		(3175)
41	16	EL	H	Scunthorpe United	W 2-0	0-0	8	Marquis 49, Parrish 80	1920
42	23	EL	A	Lincoln City	L 0-4	0-4	10		(3240)
43	25	EL	H	Mansfield Town	D 0-0	0-0	10		1657
44	30	EL	H	Chester City	L 1-2	1-0	10	Williams 44	1548
45	A 2	EL	A	Hereford United	L 0-1	0-1	11		(2060)
46	6	EL	A	Preston North End	L 0-1	0-1	13		(12773)
47	8	EL	H	Gillingham	L 0-1	0-1	13		1873
48	13	EL	A	Cambridge United	D 2-2	0-0	12	Jones 83, Schofield 86	(2451)
49	20	EL	H	Barnet	W 1-0	0-0	12	Clark 90	1579
50	23	EL	A	Scunthorpe United	D 2-2	1-1	12	Cramb 22, 61	(2614)
51	27	EL	H	Wigan Athletic	W 2-1	1-1	12	Schofield 45, 85	2122
52	M 4	EL	A	Colchester United	L 0-1	0-1	13		(5038)

Best Home League Attendance: 4413 v Preston North End   Smallest: 1429 v Exeter City   Average: 2094

Goal Scorers:
EL(51): Jones(11),Cramb(7),Parrish(5),Darby(4),Carmichael(4),Schofield(4),Colcombe(3),Brabin(3),Moore(2),Noteman(2),Brodie(1),Maxfield(1),Williams(1),Marquis(1),Opponent(s)(1),Clark(1)
CC(1): Wilcox(1)
FAC(2): Jones(1),Carmichael(1)
AWS(3): Colcombe(1),Clark(1),Moore(1)

(F) Barker	(M) Brabin	(F) Brodie	(F) Carmichael	(F) Clark	(F) Colcombe	(F) Cramb	(F) Darby	(M) Gore	(D) Hackett	(F) Jones	(D) Kirby	(D) Marquis	(D) Maxfield	(D) Measham	(D) Moore	(D) Murphy	(F) Norbury	(F) Noteman	(M) O'Connor	(M) Parrish	(F) Robertson	(M) Schofield	(M) Smith	(G) Suckling	(F) Warren	(D) Wilcox	(G) Williams	(F) Wright		
			X1				X		X	X	X2			S2	X		S		S	X		X		X		X	S1	X	R.Pearson	1
				S2			X1		X	X					X	X			S1	X2		X		X		X	X	X	P.Richards	2
		S2	S				X		X1	X					X	X				X2		X		X		X	X	X	R.Harris	3
		S1	S3				X1		X	X					X	X				X		X2		X		X	X	X	F.G.Stretton	4
		X	X	X			X				S1		S	X1	X					X		X		X	X	X			G.Frankland	5
X		X	S1	X			X1				X		X1		X				S1	X		X		X	X	X			B.Knight	6
X	X	X	X1	S1							X				X				X			X		X	X	X			A.Leake	7
X	X	X	X1						X	X2		S			X				S1	X		X		X	X	X			S.Bennett	8
X	X	X1							X	X1		S1			X					X		X		X	X	X	X		K.Leach	9
X	X1	S1		X			S		X	X	S1				X					X		X1		X	X	X	X		T.Lunt	10
	X	X	S2	X1		X2	X						S3	X	X3	S1				X		X		X	X				G.Singh	11
	X	X1	X1	X		X			X		X		X	S	S	S1				X		X		X				X	R.Pearson	12
X2		X	X1	X		S2			X	X2	X		S1		X					S2		X		X		X		X	J.Rushton	13
	X	X	S			S2			X	X2	X		S1		X	X1				X		X		X	X				T.E.West	14
S1	X	X				S2			X	X2	X		X		X	S				X1		X		X	X				S.Baines	15
X2	X	X				S1			X	S	X		X	X	X					X		X		X	X1				F.Streeton	16
X	X	X	S			S1			X		X		X1	X	X	S				X		X		X	X				K.Breen	17
X2	X	S1	S2			X			X	X			X	X	X	S				X		X		X	X1				G.Frankland	18
X1	X	S1				X			X3	X			X	X2	S2					X	X			X	S3				G.P.Barber	19
S3	X	S2	X1	X2		S1			X3	X			X	X						X	X			X	X				P.Richards	20
	X2	S1	X	X		S2			X	X			X1	X						X		X		X	X				A.Wilkie	21
	X	X	X2	X		S1			X	X			X1	S2		X				S	X			X	X				G.Cain	22
	X	X	X	X1	S1				X	X			X2			X				S2	X			X			X		M.J.Brandwood	23
	X	X	X						X	S	S		S	X	X	X				X	X			X			X		I.G.Cruikshank	24
	X	X	X2	S2					X	S1	X	X	X	X						X1				X			X		A.Leake	25
	X	X	X	S1					X	X		S	S	X	X					X	X			X1			X		D.Laws	26
	X	S	X	X	X				X	X			S		X	X				X				S		X	X		A.Butler	27
	X	S1	X	S2	X2				X1	X	X	X	S3			X3				X	X			X			X		S.Baines	28
	X	S1	X	X					X	S	X		X	X1						X	X			X			X		E.Wolstenholme	29
	X	X	S1	X2	X				X	S	X1		S2							X	X			X			X		S.Mathieson	30
	X	X	S	X	X				X	S	X1		S1							X	X			X			X		N.Barry	31
	X		X	X1			X	X	X	S1			S				X	X	X	X				X					M.Pierce	32
	X	S1	X	X	X1			X1	X	S	S		X				X	X		X				X2					J.Kirkby	33
	X	S1	X	X				X	X	S2			X				X	X		X				X					W.Burns	34
	X		S					X	X	S			X	X1			X			X		X	X	X					J.Lloyd	35
	X	X	S					X	X	S			X	S1			X		X1	X	X2			X					F.Stretton	36
	X		X	X				X	X				X	S2			X	S2	X	X2	X2			X					M.J.Brandwood	37
	X		X	X				X	X				X3	S1			X	S2	X	X2				X			X		K.Breen	38
	X		S1	X3			X	X2		X1	X		X				X	S3	X		X	X		X			X		P.Rejer	39
	X		S1	X	X1	X	X	X					X				X	X	X					X			X	X	D.Orr	40
	X1		S	S	X	S1		X	X				X	X			X	X	X					X			X	X	P.Taylor	41
	X			X	S1			X	X			X	X				X	X	X	S		X1		X			X	X	U.Rennie	42
	X		S1	S		X		X	S				X				X	X	S1	X		X1	X		X		X	X	T.Heilbron	43
			S	S1		X		X					X				X	X	S		X	X	S	X		X	X	D.Laws	44
	X		S1	X1	X			S2	X				X				X	X	S		X	X	S	X		X	X	M.C.Bailey	45
	X		S3			X		X2	X			X3	S1				X				X			X			X		K.Leach	46
	X		S1			X		X	X	X			X				X				X	X		X			X	X1	W.Burns	47
	X		S	S				X	X	X			X		X	X			X	X		X	X	X			X		S.Baines	48
	X		S1	S	X			X	X	X			X				X		X	X	S	X	X1	X			X		P.Richards	49
	X		S2	X	X2				X	X			X				X			X	S1	X	X1	X			X		M.C.Bailey	50
	X		S2	X	X				X	X			X				X			X	S1	X	X2	X			X	X1	B.Knight	51
	X		X	X				S1	S		X	X1		X						X	X	X2	X	S2	X				C.Wilkes	52
5	31	5	19	14	21	20	9	5	8	32	32	15	12	9	36	16	2	5	8	40	12	41	12	22	41	5	17	13	EL Appearances	
1	0	0	9	9	9	1	9	1	0	0	4	0	6	3	0	6	3	0	2	4	1	1	0	2	0	0	0	0	EL Sub Appearances	
0	0	0	0+1	0+2	0	0	2	0	2	2	0	0	2	0	2	0	0+1	2	0	2	0	2	0	2	0	2	2	0	CC Appearances	
0	1	0	0+1	1	1	0+1	0	0	1	1	0	0	1	1	0	0	1	0	0	1	0	1	0	1	0	1	0	0	FAC Appearances	
0+1	2	0	2+1	3	2	1+1	0	1	2	2	0	1	2	2	0	1	2	2	0+1	2	0	1	2	2	0	3	0	2	AWS Appearances	

Also Played: (D) Ashley X1(45,47), X2(46). (M) Byng S(48). (M) Doling S1(36), S(37). (F) Harper S1(3,11), S2(4). (M) Knight S(7,26), S2(8,17), S1(9), X(18). (M) Meara S(2,5,7,24,25,30), S1(39). (F) Peel X(38), X1(39). (M) Speight X1(48). (M) Utley S(48,51), X(49). (D) Williams S(33), X1(45), X(46), S2(47).

CLUB RECORDS

BIGGEST VICTORIES
League: 10-0 v Darlington, Division 4, 25.1.1964.
F.A. Cup: 7-0 v Blyth Spartans, 1st Round, 1937-38.

BIGGEST DEFEATS
League: 0-12 v Small Heath, Division 2, 11.4.1903.
F.A. Cup: 0-8 v Everton, 4th Round, 1938-39.

MOST POINTS
3 points a win: 85, Division 4, 1983-84.
2 points a win: 72, Division 3(N), 1946-47.

MOST GOALS SCORED
123, Division 3(N), 1946-47.

RECORD TRANSFER FEE RECEIVED
£250,000 from Q.P.R. for Rufus Brevett, February 1991.
£175,000 from Leicester for Jamie Lawrence - Further installments could take the fee to £300,000.

RECORD TRANSFER FEE PAID
£60,000 to Stirling Albion for John Philliben, March 1984.
£60,000 to Hull City for Russ Wilcox, July 1993.

BEST PERFORMANCES
League: 7th in Division 2, 1901-02.
F.A. Cup: 5th Round 1951-52, 1953-54, 1954-55, 1955-56.
League Cup: 5th Round 1975-76.

HONOURS
Division 3(N) champions 1934-35, 1946-47, 1949-50.
Division 4 champions 1965-66, 1968-69.

LEAGUE CAREER
Elected to Div 2 1901, Failed to gain re-election 1903, Re-elected to Div 2 1904, Failed to gain re-election 1905, Re-elected to Div 3(N) 1923, Div 2 1934-35, Div 3(N) 1936-37, Div 2 1946-47, Div 3(N) 1947-48, Div 2 1949-50, Div 3 1957-58, Div 4 1958-59, Div 3 1965-66, Div 4 1966-67, Div 3 1968-69, Div 4 1970-71, Div 3 1980-81, Div 4 1982-83, Div 3 1983-84, Div 4 (now Div 3) 1987-88.

INDIVIDUAL CLUB RECORDS

MOST GOALS IN A SEASON
Clarrie Jodan: 44 goals in 1946-47 (League 42, FA Cup 2).

MOST GOALS IN A MATCH
6. Tom Keetley v Ashington (a), 7-4, Division 3(N), 16.2.1929.

OLDEST PLAYER
Mitchell Downie, 40 years 252 days.

YOUNGEST PLAYER
Alick Jeffrey, 15 years 229 days.

MOST CAPPED PLAYER
Len Graham (Northern Ireland) 14.
Ian Snodin (England U21) 4.

PREVIOUS MANAGERS

(Since 1946)
Bill Marsden, Jackie Bestall, Peter Doherty, Jack Hodgson, Syd Bycroft, Jack Crayston, Jack Bestall, Norman Curtis, Danny Malloy, Oscar Hold, Bill Leivers, Keith Kettleborough, George Raynor, Lawrie McMenemy, Maurice Setters, Stan Anderson, Billy Bremner, Dave Cusack, Dave Mackay, Billy Bremner, Steve Beaglehole, Ian Atkins.

ADDITIONAL INFORMATION
PREVIOUS NAMES
None.

PREVIOUS LEAGUES
Midland League.

Club colours: Red shirts with white sleeves & red/green trim, white shorts, red socks with white/green tops.
Change colours: Dark blue shirts, with white sleeves/red trim, white shorts with red trim, red socks with blue/white tops.

Reserves League: Central League Division 3.

LONGEST LEAGUE RUNS

of undefeated matches:	21 (1968-69)	of league matches w/out a win:	16 (1991-92)
of undefeated home matches:	33 (1931-33)	of undefeated away matches:	17 (1939, 1946)
without home win:	13 (1989)	without an away win:	44 (1902-03, 1904-05, 1923-24)
of league wins:	10 (1947)	of home wins:	11 (1934-35)
of league defeats:	9 (1905)	of away wins:	9 (1939, 1946)

THE MANAGER

SAMMY CHUNG . . . . appointed July 1994.

PREVIOUS CLUBS
As Manager . . . . Wolves, IFK Vastern, Tamworth.
As Asst.Man/Coach . . . . Watford, Ipswich, Wolves, United Arb Em., Stoke, Colchester.
As a player . . . . Reading, Norwich, Watford.

HONOURS
As a Manager. . . . . Wolves: Division 2Champions 1977.
As a Player . . . . None.

DONCASTER ROVERS

PLAYERS NAME Honours	Ht	Wt	Birthdate	Birthplace Transfers	Contract Date	Clubs	League	L/Cup	FA Cup	Other	Lge	L/C	FAC	Oth
G O A L K E E P E R S														
Williams Dean P	6.0	12.8	05/01/72	Lichfield	11/07/90	Birmingham City	4		1					
				Free	01/03/92	Tamworth								
				£2000	08/08/93	Brentford	6+1							
				Free	12/08/94	Doncaster Rovers	50+2	1	1	5				
D E F E N D E R S														
Marquis Paul R	6.1	11.12	29/08/72	Enfield	01/07/91	West Ham United	0+1							
				Free	10/03/94	Doncaster Rovers	26+2			1				
				Loan	12/09/95	Gateshead								
Moore Darren	6.2	12.0	22/04/74	Birmingham	18/11/92	Torquay United	102+1	6	7	8	7		1	2
				£62500	19/07/95	Doncaster Rovers	36	2	1	2	2			1
Murphy James A	6.1	12.7	25/02/73	Manchester	23/08/90	Blackpool	48+7	4	3	2+3	1	1		
				Free	14/09/95	Doncaster Rovers	16+6			2				
M I D F I E L D														
Byng David	6.1	13.0	09/07/77	Coventry		Torquay United (T)	12+12	1+3	1+1	1	3		1	
					06/02/96	Doncaster Rovers								
Doling Stuart	5.6	10.06	26/10/72	Newport I.o.W.	25/06/90	Portsmouth	20+17	4+3	1	4+3	4			1
					13/07/95	Lymington AFC								
					30/10/95	Doncaster Rovers	0+1							
Gore Ian	5.11	12.4	10/01/68	Liverpool	01/05/86	Birmingham City								
					01/08/87	Southport								
					21/01/88	Blackpool	196+4	15+1	11	20+2				
				Free	11/08/95	Torquay United	26	4	1	2	2		1	
				£5000	22/03/96	Doncaster Rovers	5+1							
Hayrettin Hakan GMVC'92'93. FAT'93.	5.9	11.2	04/02/70	Enfield	04/07/88	Leyton Orient (T)	2							
				Free	01/06/89	Barnet								
					01/08/91	KSK (Turkey)								
					06/08/92	Barnet	0+6	0+1	1+2	0+2				
				Loan	15/01/93	Torquay United	3+1							
				Free	25.03.93	Wycombe Wand.	15+4	2+2	2	2	1			
				Free	26/08/94	Cambridge United	15+2			1				
					10/07/95	Doncaster Rovers								
Parrish Sean	5.9	10.0	14/03/72	Wrexham	12/07/90	Shrewsbury Town	1+2	1		3				1
				Free	01/08/91	Telford			4					
				£20000	28/05/94	Doncaster Rovers	40+2	2	1	1	5			
Schofield John D	5.11	11.3	16/05/65	Barnsley		Gainsborough T.								
				Free	10/11/88	Lincoln City	209+10	11	5+2	12+1	10	2		
				Free	18/11/94	Doncaster Rovers	66+3	2	1	2	5			
F O R W A R D S														
Clark Ian David					20/07/95	Doncaster Rovers	14+9	0+2	1	3	1			1
Colcombe Scott	5.5	10.6	15/12/71	West Bromwich	05/07/90	W.B.A.								
				Free	14/08/91	Torquay United	68+11	8+1	4+1	5	1		1	
				Free	10/07/95	Doncaster Rovers	21+9		1	2	3			1
Cramb Colin	6.0	11.09	23/06/74	Lanark	01/08/90	Hamilton Acad.	48				10			
					01/08/93	Southampton	1							
					01/08/94	Falkirk	8				1			
					01/02/95	Hearts	6				1			
					15/12/95	Doncaster Rovers	20+1				7			
Robertson Paul						Runcorn								
					30/10/95	Doncaster Rovers	12+4			2				
Warren Lee A	6.0	11.10	28/02/69	Manchester	27/07/87	Leeds United								
				Free	28/10/87	Rochdale	31		1	2	1			
				£100000	25/08/88	Hull City	141+12	8	5+1	4+1	1		1	
				Loan	20/09/90	Lincoln City	2+1				1			
				Free	21/07/94	Doncaster Rovers	51+6	2	1	3+1	2			
ADDITIONAL CONTRACT PLAYERS														
O'Connor Gary						Doncaster Rov. (T)	8							
Smith Michael						Doncaster Rov. (T)	12+1							
Speight Martyn						Doncaster Rov. (T)	1							
Utley Darren						Doncaster Rov. (T)	1							
Wheeler Adam						Doncaster Rov. (T)								

BELLE VUE GROUND
Doncaster, South Yorkshire DN4 5HT
Tel: 01302 539 441

Capacity...8,608
Covered Standing 2,125
Seating...1,259

First game ....v Gainsborough Trinity, 08/1922.
First floodlit game ....v Hiberbian, 4.3.1952.

ATTENDANCES
Highest ....37,149 v Hull City, Div 3(N), 2.10.1948.
Lowest ....613 v Blackpool, AMC, 17.12.1991.

OTHER GROUNDS..None.

HOW TO GET TO THE GROUND

From the North
Use motorway (A1(N)) then A638 sign posted Doncaster into Town Centre. Then follow signs to Bawtry (A368) and in 1.2 miles at roundabout take 3rd exit into Bawtry Road for Doncaster FC.

From the East
Use motorway (M18) then A630 sign posted Doncaster. In 2.7 miles at round-about take first exit (A18). In 2.5 miles at roundabout take first exit into Bawtry Road (A638) for Doncaster FC.

From the South
Use motorway (M1) then M18, take junction 3, sign posted to Doncaster (A6182) in 2 miles at roundabout take 3rd exit, sign posted Racecourse and Scunthorpe (A18). In 1.25 miles at roundabout take 3rd exit (A638) into Bawtry Road for Doncaster FC.

From the West
Use (A635) in Doncaster Town Centre then follow signs to Bawtry (A638) and in 1.2 miles at roundabout take 3rd exit into Bawtry Road for Doncaster FC.

Car Parking: Very large car and coach park adjacent to ground. Entrance direct from Great North Road.
Nearest Railway Station: Doncaster (01302 340 222)

MATCHDAY TICKET PRICES

Seats.. £8
Juv/OAP/Unemployed £5

Terraces... £7
Juv/OAP/Unemployed £3.50

Ticket Office Telephone no........ 01302 539 441

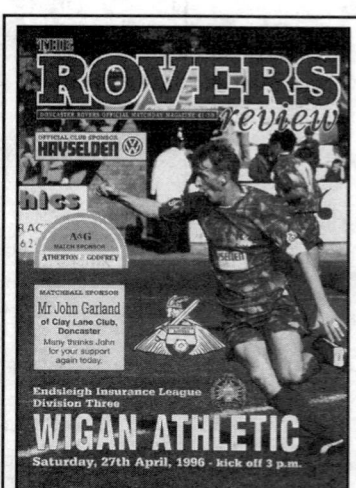

MATCHDAY PROGRAMME

Programme Editor .... K Avis.

Number of pages .... 32.

Price £1.30

Subscriptions .... £30.

Local Newspapers .... Doncaster Star, Yorkshire Post.

Local Radio Stations .... Radio Hallam, Radio Sheffield.

EXETER CITY
(The Grecians)
NATIONWIDE LEAGUE DIVISION 3
SPONSORED BY: ALC WINDOWS

96-97 - Back row L-R: Marcus Dailly, Leon Braithwaite, Sufyan Gwazgwazi, Darren Hughes, Mark Chamberlain.
Middle Row: George Kent (scout), Mike Chapman (Physio), Eamonn Dolan (Community Officer), Jon Richardson, Ashley Bayes, Richard Pears, Mathew Hare, Mike Radford (Youth Development Officer), Noel Blake (Assistant Manager).
Front Row: Nicky Medlin, Danny Bailey, Tim Steele, Peter Fox (Manager), Barry McConnelly, Chris Myers, Gary Rice.

EXETER CITY
FORMED IN 1904
TURNED PROFESSIONAL IN 1908
LTD COMPANY IN 1908

CHAIRMAN: A I Doble
DIRECTORS
M Couch, S Dawe, G Vallance, P Carter,
M Shelbourne
SECRETARY
Margaret Bond (01392 54073)
COMMERCIAL MANAGER
David Bird

MANAGER: Peter Fox
ASSISTANT MANAGER: Noel Blake

YOUTH TEAM MANAGER
Mike Radford (01395 232 784)

STATISTICIAN FOR THE DIRECTORY
Graham Lucas

The survival of Exeter City was one of the season's greatest success stories. With no money, the threat of closure and an inexperienced manager thrown into the job with a squad of youngsters, the Grecians would have settled for 23rd place having finished with the 'wooden spoon' in the previous campaign.

But after a shaky first month, City were never really in the danger zone. Indeed, they were safely camped in mid-table and the experience of Peter Fox and Noel Blake at the heart of the defence managed to inspire the youngsters to produce performances that their supporters wouldn't have dared to believe were possible.

After a home defeat to Darlington in the first match four wins and six draws followed and four games were played within this sequence without conceding a goal!

Ex-manager Terry Cooper's son Mark, who was enjoying his second spell at St James Park, finished the season as club top scorer and sixteen different scorers registered league goals for City as well as four from opponents!

That sort of generosity didn't follow them in the cups however, a Coca-Cola Cup exit at the hands of local rivals Torquay United was particularly disappointing and a home FA Cup defeat by Peterborough United allowed Exeter City to 'concentrate on the league'!

Peter Fox should really have been in the running for managerial awards as he really did produce miracles for his club. Hopefully the worst is over for The grecians but times are tough at St James Park as the club works on a very limited budget, hoping for a new stadium and some sort of financial stability.

Could a 'stop-press' pre-season result of a 2-1 friendly victory over Chelsea be an omen?

TONY WILLIAMS.

EXETER CITY

League: 14th   FA Cup: 1st Rnd   Coca-Cola Cup: 1st Rnd   Auto Windscreen Shield: 1st Rnd

M	DATE	COMP	VEN	OPPONENTS	RESULT	HT	LP	GOAL SCORERS/GOAL TIMES	ATT.
1	A 12	EL	H	Darlington	L 0-1	0-1	24		2934
2	15	CC 1/1	A	Torquay United	D 0-0	0-0			(2473)
3	19	EL	A	Hartlepool United	D 0-0	0-0	21		(2311)
4	23	CC 1/2	H	Torquay United	D 1-1*	1-1		Richardson 22	3763
5	26	EL	H	Scarborough	W 2-0	0-0	14	Came 47, 75	2439
6	29	EL	A	Cardiff City	W 1-0	1-0	11	Pears 4	(4444)
7	S 2	EL	H	Scunthorpe United	W 1-0	1-0	6	Bailey 22	2893
8	9	EL	A	Northampton Town	D 0-0	0-0	6		(5625)
9	12	EL	A	Cambridge United	D 1-1	0-0	5	Turner 90	(2365)
10	16	EL	H	Fulham	W 2-1	1-0	4	Cooper 31, Phillips 88	4440
11	23	EL	H	Leyton Orient	D 2-2	2-1	6	Pears 2, Cooper 20	5507
12	30	EL	A	Rochdale	L 2-4	0-3	8	Phillips 73, Cecere 84	(2052)
13	O 7	EL	A	Barnet	L 2-3	0-2	10	Turner 79, 90	(2146)
14	14	EL	H	Wigan Athletic	L 0-4	0-1	12		3870
15	17	AWS 1/1	A	Brentford	D 1-1	1-1		Bailey 45	(1413)
16	21	EL	A	Hereford United	D 2-2	0-1	13	Blatherwitk 48(og), Buckle 52	(2236)
17	28	EL	H	Lincoln City	D 1-1	1-1	13	Phillips 19	3252
18	31	EL	H	Gillingham	D 0-0	0-0	15		3024
19	N 4	EL	A	Colchester United	D 1-1	0-1	14	Pears 81	(3377)
20	7	AWS 1/2	H	Bournemouth	L 0-2	0-0			1898
21	11	FAC 1	H	Peterborough United	L 0-1	0-1			3783
22	18	EL	H	Preston North End	D 1-1	1-0	14	Saville 26(og)	3550
23	25	EL	H	Bury	L 0-2	0-0	14		(3597)
24	D 2	EL	A	Doncaster Rovers	L 0-2	0-1	14		(1429)
25	9	EL	A	Leyton Orient	W 3-0	2-0	12	Ross 20, Bradbury 36, 86	(3471)
26	16	EL	H	Rochdale	W 2-0	1-0	12	Richardson 14, Gavin 90	3152
27	26	EL	H	Torquay United	D 0-0	0-0	12		6182
28	30	EL	A	Chester City	L 1-2	0-2	12	Ross 80	3324
29	J 1	EL	A	Plymouth Argyle	D 2-2	2-0	12	Came 2, Buckle 45	(12427)
30	6	EL	A	Mansfield Town	D 1-1	1-0	12	Bradbury 16	(1893)
31	20	EL	A	Darlington	L 0-1	0-0	15		(1723)
32	30	EL	H	Hartlepool United	W 1-0	1-0	14	Cooper 37	2468
33	F 3	EL	A	Scarborough	D 0-0	0-0	14		(1307)
34	13	EL	H	Mansfield Town	D 2-2	1-2	15	Bradbury 4, Hackett 69(og)	2507
35	17	EL	H	Cambridge United	W 1-0	0-0	12	Blake 90	2804
36	24	EL	A	Fulham	L 1-2	0-1	12	Braithwaite 75	(4027)
37	27	EL	A	Northampton Town	L 1-2	1-1	12	Gavin 39	2663
38	M 2	EL	A	Torquay United	W 2-0	1-0	12	Bradbury 41, Cooper 76(pen)	(4038)
39	9	EL	H	Doncaster Rovers	W 1-0	1-0	13	Braithwaite 10	3175
40	12	EL	A	Cardiff City	W 2-0	1-0	11	Pears 21, Cooper 54(pen)	2609
41	16	EL	A	Chester City	D 2-2	1-1	12	Came 45, Cooper 90	(2043)
42	23	EL	H	Plymouth Argyle	D 1-1	1-1	12	Logan 19(og)	6185
43	26	EL	A	Scunthorpe United	L 0-4	0-0	12		(1615)
44	30	EL	H	Barnet	W 1-0	0-0	12	Pears 89	2726
45	A 2	EL	A	Wigan Athletic	L 0-1	0-0	13		(2744)
46	6	EL	A	Lincoln City	W 1-0	1-0	12	Sharpe 41	(2723)
47	8	EL	H	Hereford United	L 0-2	0-1	12		3161
48	13	EL	H	Gillingham	L 0-1	0-0	13		(7698)
49	20	EL	H	Colchester United	D 2-2	2-1	13	Braithwaite 11, Chamberlain 25	2788
50	27	EL	H	Bury	D 1-1	0-1	14	Blake 66	3508
51	M 4	EL	A	Preston North End	L 0-2	0-1	14		(18700)

Best Home League Attendance: 6185 v Plymouth Argyle   Smallest: 2439 v Scarborough   Average: 3441

Goal Scorers:
EL(46):   Cooper(6),Bradbury(5),Pears(5),Opponent(s)(4),Came(4),Phillips(3),Turner(3),Braithwaite(3),Blake(2),Ross(2),Gavin(2),Buckle(2),Chamberlain(1),
           Sharpe(1),Richardson(1),Cecere(1),Bailey(1)
CC(1):   Richardson(1)
FAC(0):
AWS(1):   Bailey(1)

(M) Anderson	(M) Bailey	(D) Blake	(M) Bradbury	(M) Braithwaite	(M) Buckle	(D) Came	(F) Cecere	(M) Chamberlain	(M) Cooper	(M) Coughlin	(F) Foster	(G) Fox	(F) Gavin	(M) Hare	(D) Hughes	(M) McConnell	(M) Medlin	(M) Morgan	(M) Myers	(D) Parsley	(F) Pears	(F) Phillips	(D) Rice	(F) Richardson	(F) Ross	(F) Sharpe	(F) Thirlby	(F) Turner	Player	No.
X	X	X				X	X	X				X	S1						S	X		X1		X				X	A.Whiley	1
	X	X				X	X	X				X	X							X	S	X	X				S	S	C.Wilkes	2
	X	X				X		X2	X	S1		X	X1							X	S2	X	X					X	E.Wolstenholme	3
	X2	X				X	X1	X	X		X									X	S3	S1	X3	X		S2		X	G.Singh	4
S	X	X			X1			X	X	X	X	X								X	X	S	X	X				S	B.Knight	5
S2	X	X			X1			X	X	X		X			S1					X2	X		X	X					D.Orr	6
	X	X					X	X	X			X	S		S			X		X	X	X	X	X					R.Gifford	7
	X	X					X	X		X2		X		X						X	X1	S2	X	X				S1	G.Frankland	8
	X	X				S2	X	X				X		X3			S1			X	X2	X	X1	X				S3	N.Barry	9
	X	X				S1	X2	X				X		X			X			X	X1	X	X		S		S2		G.Barber	10
S	X	X					X	X1		S1		X		X						X	X2	X	X	X			S2		M.Pierce	11
X	X	X				X		X2		X		X		X1		S2				X		X	X	X			S1		D.B.	12
	X2							X	X1			X	S1						S2	X	S	X	X1					X	G.Pooley	13
	X				X		X	X				X	S1							X2	S	X	X1					X	G.Singh	14
S	X	X			X		X	X				X	X	X		S	X	S		X		X	X						A.Butler	15
S2	X	X			X		X	S1				X	X	X							X1	X2	X	X					G.Caine	16
	X	X			X		X					X	X	X			S2		S		X2	X	X1	X				S1	R.Harris	17
X	X	X			X		X					X	X	X2		S	S2			X	S1	X		X				X1	J.Brandwood	18
X	X	X			X		X					X			S	S1	S			X1	X	X	S	X					M.Bailey	19
X	X				X		X	S1				X	X	X				S		X1	X	X	S	X				S1	D.Orr	20
S2	X2	X			X		X1					X	X	S3	X					X	X3	X		X				S1	A.Wiley	21
S	X	X			X		X					X	X		X	S1	S			X				X	X			X1	F.Stretton	22
S1	X	X		S2	X		X					X	X	S	X		X1			X				X	X2				N.S.Barry	23
	X2	X		X	X		X		S1	S2		X	X		X					X				X	X1				A.Leake	24
S	X	X		S1	X		X	S		X		X	X		X					X				X	X1				F.Stretton	25
S		X		S	X		X		S1	X		X	X		X					X				X	X1				S.Bennett	26
S	X	X		S2	X		X			S1		X	X2		X					X				X	X1				M.Riley	27
S	S1	X		X	X		X		X	X1		X	X		X					X1					X				C.Wilkes	28
S1	X	X		X	S		X			X		X	X	X1	X					X									K.Leach	29
S1	X	X	X2	S3	X		X1	S2		X		X			X					X		X3							K.Breen	30
X	X	X	S2	X	X			X2				X			X		S1			X			S	X1					J.Kirby	31
S1	X	X	X	S	X		X	X		X		X			X	X1				S2			X						M.Pierce	32
	X	X	X1	X	X		S1					X			X		S2			X			S	X	X2				D.Laws	33
	X1	X	X	X	X			S2	S1			X			X					X			S	X2	X				R.Gifford	34
	X1	X	S1	X	X		X	X				X	X2		X				S				X			S2			M.Fletcher	35
	X	X	X2	S2	X1		X	X3				X			X				S1				X			S3			P.Taylor	36
	X	X	X	X	X		X	X				X			X				S	S			X			S			K.Leach	37
	X	X	X	X1	X		X	X				X			X				S				X						I.Hemley	38
	X	X	X		X		X	X				X			X				S		S		X			S1		X1	D.Orr	39
	X	X	X		X		X	X1				X			X				S2	S1	X2		X			S			P.Rejer	40
	X	X	X		X		X					X	X		X		S1			X	X1		S	X		S			F.Stretton	41
S2	X	X	X		X		X		X1			X	X	X	X		S			X			X			S1			S.Mathieson	42
	X	X	X1		X		X		X1			X	X	X		X3				X		S1	S3			S1			G.Singh	43
	X2	X			X		X		S2			X	X1	X	X	X3		X		X		S1		X		S3			S.Baines	44
	X		S1		X		X		S2			X	X1	X				X		X	S		X	X		X2			T.Heilbron	45
	X	X			X		X				S	X			X		S			X		X	S	X		X			I.Cruikshanks	46
	X1	X			X			X3		X	S1	X	X				S3			S1		X1	X	X		X			R.Gifford	47
	X	X1			X			X2				X			X		S2					X	X1	X	X	X			G.Pooley	48
	X	X			X			X			S1	X	S1								X3	X1	X	X		X1	S3		E.Wolstenholme	49
	X	X			X			X			S2	X		S1		X3				X		X2	X	X		X1	S3		S.Bennett	50
	X	X			X			X			S	X		S			S1			X			X	X1	X	X			A.Wiley	51
5	41	44	14	14	22	38	5	29	26	6	4	46	24	10	24	1	2	2	7	29	19	11	17	43	7	10	0	6	EL Appearances	
7	1	0	0	9	0	0	8	4	1	2	3	0	4	3	1	7	4	3	1	3	3	2	2	0	0	5	2	6	EL Sub Appearances	
0	2	2	0	0	0	2	1	2	2	1	0	2	1	0	0	0	0	0	0	0	0+1	0+1	2	2	0	0	0+1	1	CC Appearances	
0+1	1	1	0	0	1	1	0	0	0	0	0	1	1	0+1	1	0	0	0	0	1	1	1	0	1	0	0	0+1	1	FAC Appearances	
1	2	0	0	0	2	2	0+1	1	0	0	0	2	2	2	0	0	1	0	0	1	0	0	1	2	1	1	0	0	AWS Appearances	

Also Played: (M) Peat S(1).

579

CLUB RECORDS

BIGGEST VICTORIES
League: 8-1 v Coventry, Division 3(S) 4.12.1926.
8-1 v Aldershot, Division 3(S) 4.5.1935.
7-0 v Crystal Palace, Division 3(S) 9.1.1954.
F.A. Cup: 9-1 v Aberdare, 1st Round, 26.11.1927.
Other: 11-6 v Crystal Palace, Division 3(S) Cup, 24.1.1934.

BIGGEST DEFEATS
League: 0-9 v Notts County, Division 3(S), 16.10.1948.
0-9 v Northampton Town, Division 3(S), 12.4.1958.
League Cup: 1-8 v Aston Villa, 2nd Round 7.10.1985.

MOST POINTS
3 points a win: 89, Division 4, 1989-90.
2 points a win: 62, Division 4, 1976-77.

MOST GOALS SCORED: 88, Division 3(S), 1932-33.

RECORD TRANSFER FEE RECEIVED
£300,000 from Glasgow Rangers for Chris Vinicombe, November 1989. (Initial £200,000 + £100,000 for completion of 20 first team appearances paid Oct'91)

RECORD TRANSFER FEE PAID
£10,000 + £5,000 + £125,000 to Bristol Rovers for Richard Dryden, March 1989, May 1989, July 1991.

BEST PERFORMANCES
League: 2nd Division 3(S) 1932-33.
F.A. Cup: 6th Round replay 1930-31.
League Cup: 4th Round.

HONOURS
Champions of Division 4, 1989-90.
Division 3(S) Cup winners 1933-34.

LEAGUE CAREER
Elected to Div 3 1920, Transferred to Div 3(S) 1921, Div 4 1957-58, Div 3 1963-64, Div 4 1965-66, Div 3 1976-77, Div 4 1983-84, Div 3(now Div 2) 1989-90, Div 3 1993-94

INDIVIDUAL CLUB RECORDS

MOST GOALS IN A SEASON
Rod Williams: 37 goals in 1936-37 (League 29, FA Cup 7, Division 3(S) Cup 1).

MOST GOALS IN A MATCH
6. James Bell v Weymouth, 1st Preliminary Rnd., 3.10.1908.
6. Fred Whitlow v Crystal Palace, Division 3(S) Cup, 24.1.1934 (11-6).

YOUNGEST PLAYER
Cliff Bastin, 16 years 31 days v Coventry City, 14.4.1928.

MOST CAPPED PLAYER
Dermot Curtis (Eire) 1.

PREVIOUS MANAGERS

1908-22 Arthur Chadwick, 1923-27 Fred Mavin, 1928-29 David Wilson, 1929-35 Billy McDevitt, 1935-40 Jack English, 1945-52 George Roughton, 1952-53 Norman Kirkman, 1953-57 Norman Dodgin, 1957-58 Bill Thompson, 1958-60 Frank Broome, 1960-62 Glen Wilson, 1962-63 Cyril Spiers, 1963-65 Jack edwards, 1965-66 Ellis Stuttard, 1966-67 Jock Basford, 1967-69 Frank Broome, 1969-76 John Newman, 1977-79 Bobby Saxton, 1979-83 Brian Godfrey, 1983-84 Gerry Francis, 1984-85 Jim iley, 1985-87 Colin Appleton, 1988 John Delve (caretaker), 1988-91 Terry Cooper, 1991-94 Alan Ball.

ADDITIONAL INFORMATION
PREVIOUS NAMES
None.
PREVIOUS LEAGUES
None.

Club colours: Red & white striped shirts, black shorts, red socks.
Change colours: All white.
Reserves League: Avon Combination Division 2.
'A' Team: Devon & Exeter Premier.

LONGEST LEAGUE RUNS

of undefeated matches:	13 (1986)	of league matches w/out a win:	18 (1984)
of undefeated home matches:	23 (1989-90)	of undefeated away matches:	8 (1964)
without home win:	9 (1984)	without an away win:	27 (1986-87)
of league wins:	7 (1977)	of home wins:	13 (1932-33)
of league defeats:	7 (1921, 1923, 1925, 1936, 1984)	of away wins:	6 (1977)

THE MANAGER

PETER FOX . . . . appointed June 1995.

PREVIOUS CLUBS
As Manager . . . . None.
As Asst.Man/Coach . . . . None.
As a player . . . . Sheffield Wednesday, Barnsley, Stoke City.

HONOURS
As a Manager . . . . None.
As a Player . . . . None.

EXETER CITY

PLAYERS NAME / Honours	Ht	Wt	Birthdate	Birthplace / Transfers	Contract Date	Clubs	APPEARANCES League	L/Cup	FA Cup	Other	GOALS Lge	L/C	FAC	Oth
G O A L K E E P E R S														
ox Peter	5.10	12.4	05/07/57	Scunthorpe	01/06/75	Sheffield Wed.	49		3					
MC'92. Div.2'93.				Loan	22/12/77	Barnsley	1	1						
				£15000	04/03/78	Stoke City	409	32	22	14				
				Free	15/07/93	Exeter City	102+1	7	6	4				
D E F E N D E R S														
ake Noel	6.0	13.11	12/01/62	Kingston (Jam)		Sutton Coldfield								
					01/08/79	Aston Villa	4							
				Loan	01/03/82	Shrewsbury Town	6							
				£55000	15/09/82	Birmingham City	76	12	8		5			
				£150000	24/08/84	Portsmouth	144	14	10	5	10	1	2	1
				Free	04/07/88	Leeds United	51	4+1	2	4	4			
				£175000	09/02/90	Stoke City	74+1	6	3+1	4+1	3			
				Loan	27/02/92	Bradford City	6							
				Free	20/07/92	Bradford City	31+1	2	3	3	3		1	
					01/12/93	Dundee United								
					31/08/95	Exeter City	44	2	1		2			
ame Mark R	6.1	13.0	14/09/61	Exeter		Winsford United								
					28/04/84	Bolton Wanderers	188+7	15+4	16+2	27	7	2		2
					04/12/92	Chester City	47	2	3	6	1			1
				Free	14/07/94	Exeter City	70	4	2	3	5			
rsley Neil	5.9	10.12	25/04/66	Liverpool		Witton Albion								
				£20000	08/11/88	Leeds United								
				Loan	13/12/89	Chester City	6			1				
				Free	25/07/90	Huddersfield Town	55+2	6	6	6		1		
				Loan	20/02/91	Doncaster Rovers	2+1							
				£25000	09/09/93	W.B.A.	38+5	3	1	1				
				Free	25/08/95	Exeter City	29+3	2	1	1				
ce Gary			29/09/75	Zambia	07/07/94	Exeter City	22+7	3		2				
M I D F I E L D														
iley Danny	5.9	12.7	21/05/64	Leyton		Bournemouth	1+1							
v.4'90.						Walthamstow Ave.								
				Free	01/03/84	Torquay United	1							
					01/08/85	Wealdstone								
				Free	01/08/89	Exeter City	63+1	8	7	4+1	2		1	1
				£50000	26/12/90	Reading	49+1		3		2			
				Loan	29/07/92	Fulham	2+1							
				Free	07/12/92	Exeter City	111+6	8	6	14	3		1	2
ckle Paul	5.7	10.10	16/12/70	Hatfield	01/07/89	Brentford	42+15	5+1	3+1	6+5	1			
				Free	03/02/94	Torquay United	58+2	8	3	3	10			
				Free	03/11/95	Exeter City	22		1	2	2			
F O R W A R D S														
aithwaite Leon						Exeter City (T)	14+9				3			
ars Richard J	6.0	12.6	16/07/76	Exeter	07/07/94	Exeter City	37+15	1+2	1	2+1	7			
chardson Jonathan	6.0	12.0	29/08/75	Nottingham	07/07/94	Exeter City	85+3	3	3	5	2	1		
ADDITIONAL CONTRACT PLAYERS														
re Matthew						Exeter City (T)	10+3		0+1	2				
Connell Barry						Exeter City (T)	1+7							
dlin Nicky						Exeter City (T)	2+4		1					

St. James Park

Well Street, Exeter, Devon EX4 6PX
Tel: 01392 54073

Capacity 8,960
Covered Standing 3,200
Seating..1,664

First game ....Not Known.
First floodlit game...Not Known.

ATTENDANCES
Highest...................................20,984 v Sunderland, FA Cup 6th Round replay, 4.3.1931.
Lowest ....1,515 v Darlington, Division 4, 30.4.1988.

OTHER GROUNDS..None.

MATCHDAY TICKET PRICES

Seat. £9
Juv/OAP £6

Terraces. £6
Juv/OAP £4

Covered standing £7
Juv/OAP £4

HOW TO GET TO THE GROUND

From the North
Use motorway (M5) until junction 30. Leave motorway and follow signs to City Centre along Sidmouth Road for Heavitree Road, then at roundabout take 4th exit into Western Way and at roundabout take 2nd exit into Old Tiverton Road, then take next turning left into St. James Road for Exeter FC.

From the East
Use A30 sign posted Exeter, into Heavitree Road, then at roundabout take 4th exit into Western Way and at roundabout take 2nd exit into Old Tiverton Road, then take next turning left into St James Road for Exeter FC.

From the South and West
Use A38 and follow signs to the City Centre into Western Way and at roundabo take 3rd exit passing Coach Station, then at next roundabout take 2nd into Old Tiverton Road, and turn left into St James Road for Exeter City FC.

Car Parking
Use City Centre car parks and local street parking.

Nearest Railway Station
Exeter St Davids (01392 33551)

CLUBCALL
0891 44 68 68

Calls cost 39p per minute cheap rate and 49p per minute at all other times.
Call costings correct at time of going to press.

MATCHDAY PROGRAMME

Programme Editor. . . . . Mike Blackstone (01395 274 564).

Number of pages . . . . 48.

Price . . . . £1.

Subscriptions . . . . £39.50 for all home, £39.50 for all away games.

Local Newspapers . . . . Express & Echo, Western Morning News,
. . . . Sunday Independent.

Local Radio Stations . . . . BBC Radio Devon, The New Devonair.

FULHAM
(The Cottagers)
NATIONWIDE LEAGUE DIVISION 3
SPONSORED BY: G.M.B.

996-97 - Back Row (L-R): Terry Angus, Mark Blake, Mark Walton, Danny Cullip, Tony Lange, Simon Stewart, Michael Mison.
Middle Row: Chris Smith (Physio), Darren Freeman, Martin Thomas, Rod McAree, Lea Barkus, Chris Honor, Rory Hamill, Paul Watson, ohn Hamsher, Robbie Herrera, Rob Scott, John Marshall (Youth Team Coach). **Front Row:** Adam Grover, Glenn Cockerill, Nick Cusack, en Walker (Assistant Manager), Micky Adams (Player-Manager), Alan Cork (Reserve Team Coach), Simon Morgan, Mike Conroy, Paul rooker.

FULHAM
FORMED IN 1879
TURNED PROFESSIONAL IN 1898
LTD COMPANY IN 1903

CHAIRMAN: Jimmy Hill
DIRECTORS
W F Muddyman (Vice-Chairman),
D E Shrimpton, C A Swain,
A M Muddyman, T Wilson
SECRETARY
Mrs Janice O'Doherty (0171 736 6561)
CORPORATE AFFAIRS MANAGER
Mrs Annie Bassett

GENERAL MANAGER: Ian Branfoot
PLAYER/MANAGER: Micky Adams
ASSISTANT MANAGER: Len Walker

RESERVE TEAM COACH: Alan Cork
YOUTH MANAGER
John Marshall
PHYSIOTHERAPIST
Chris Smith Grad. Dip. Phys. MCSP.

STATISTICIAN FOR THE DIRECTORY
Dennis Turner

Fulham achieved an unwanted hat-trick in 1995/6, a third year in which they set a new club record for their lowest-ever league position. After relegation to the league basement in 1993/4, the Cottagers finished eighth a year later, and then dropped to 17th last season. It could, however have been so much worse. In February and March, they were languishing in 23rd place, just one off the bottom and uncomfortably close to the GM Vauxhall Conference League.

The turning point came in the darkest hour, when player-coach Micky Adams was given full responsibility for team affairs, Ian Branfoot becoming general manager. The difference was obvious immediately. Skipper Simon Morgan was moved into the back four and Nick Cusack dropped into midfield. Both players benefitted from the switch, and not only did results improve in the closing weeks of the season, but there was a serious attempt to play the type of passing football the Cottage faithful would. In the end, 17th was a position the supporters would have settled for at the turn of the year. They were, moreover, encouraged by the signs that the new manager seemed to put a higher priority on skill than physical strength and that he wanted to play the game on the ground, not in the air.

In fairness to the previous manager, the early months of 1995/6 were not without their highlights, but they were very isolated. In both the major cup competitions, Fulham eliminated teams from a higher division (Brighton twice, and Swansea), and were only denied a money-spinning tie with Liverpool by a late goal in a replay at Shrewsbury. The 7-0 hammering of Swansea was the biggest winning margin in the history of the FA Cup over a side from a higher division. Some of Ian Branfoot's signings look very promising, particularly Rob Scott from Sheffield United and Rod McAree, once of Liverpool and Bristol City. He also gave an opportunity to young Paul Brooker, who excited the crowd with some imaginative wing play.

In the end, it was the league form that was so frustrating. It was not until the end of February that three points were taken from an away game, whilst the home form had slumped alarmingly from the autumn. Of the 23 league games (half the season) played between mid-September and the end of February, only two were won, and Fulham dropped 20 places in the table. A change at the top was necessary and inevitable. In the closing weeks, the potential at the Cottage was revealed. Of the final five home league games, four were won and one drawn, and just one goal conceded.

Fulham seem to have been in transition for the last few years, but a turning point now appears to have been reached. The manager will re-shape the playing squad in the close season, and the early indications of his attitude have been very promising. A public enquiry set up to consider a development application at Craven Cottage will report during the summer. This will have a significant bearing on the club's long-term financial future as they approach their centenary at their famous Thameside ground. The 1996/7 season should be very interesting for all involved with Fulham FC.

DENNIS TURNER

583

FULHAM

League: 17th		FA Cup: 3rd Rnd			Coca-Cola Cup: 2nd Rnd		Auto Windscreen Shield: Quarter Finals		

M	DATE	COMP	VEN	OPPONENTS	RESULT	HT	LP	GOAL SCORERS/GOAL TIMES	ATT.
1	A 12	EL	H	Mansfield Town	W 4-2	1-1	3	Mison 9, 58, Thomas 60, 68	4909
2	15	CC 1/1	H	**Brighton & H.A.**	**W 3-0**	**1-0**		**Mison 3, Conroy 74, Barkus 84**	**4380**
3	19	EL	A	Scarborough	D 2-2	2-1	5	Brazil 4, Thomas 20	(1946)
4	22	CC 1/2	A	**Brighton & H.A.**	**W 2-0**	**0-0**		**Conroy 83, Brazil 89**	**(3799)**
5	26	EL	H	Torquay United	W 4-0	1-0	2	Barkus 44, Adams 55, Hamill 78, Barrow 89(og)	4764
6	29	EL	A	Darlington	D 1-1	1-0	2	Conroy 28	(1906)
7	S 2	EL	A	Leyton Orient	L 0-1	0-0	7		(7248)
8	9	EL	H	Doncaster Rovers	W 3-1	2-1	3	Conroy 8, Blake 26(pen), Cusack 82	4920
9	12	EL	H	Rochdale	D 1-1	1-1	3	Morgan 36	3848
10	16	EL	A	Exeter City	L 1-2	0-1	7	Moore 67	(4440)
11	20	CC 2/1	A	**Wolverhampton Wand**	**L 0-2**	**0-1**			**(20381)**
12	23	EL	H	Preston North End	D 2-2	1-1	9	Thomas 13, Morgan 46	5209
13	30	EL	A	Northampton Town	L 0-2	0-0	12		(5778)
14	O 3	CC 2/2	H	**Wolverhampton Wand**	**L 1-5**	**0-1**		**Cusack 82**	**6625**
15	7	EL	A	Plymouth Argyle	L 0-3	0-2	13		(6681)
16	10	AWS 1	A	**Wycombe Wanderers**	**D 1-1**	**1-1**		**Conroy 4**	**(2726)**
17	14	EL	H	Bury	D 0-0	0-0	16		3803
18	17	AWS 1/2	H	**Walsall**	**L 2-5**	**1-2**		**Morgan (2)**	**1315**
19	21	EL	A	Chester City	D 1-1	0-1	17	Conroy 86	(2752)
20	28	EL	H	Hereford United	D 0-0	0-0	18		3631
21	31	EL	H	Colchester United	D 1-1	0-1	18	Cusack 63	2870
22	N 4	EL	A	Wigan Athletic	D 1-1	1-1	17	Angus 35	(2348)
23	11	FAC 1	H	**Swansea City**	**W 7-0**	**3-0**		**Conroy 3,18,60,(3), Jupp 28,Cusack 68 Brooker 80 Thomas 85**	**4798**
24	18	EL	H	Barnet	D 1-1	0-0	17	Brazil 88	4369
25	25	EL	A	Gillingham	L 0-1	0-0	19		(7704)
26	28	AWS 2	A	**Brentford**	**W 1-0**	**0-0**		**Cusack**	**(3760)**
27	D 2	FAC 2	H	**Brighton & H.A.**	**D 0-0**	**0-0**			**8052**
28	9	EL	A	Preston North End	D 1-1	1-0	20	Bolt 27(pen)	(8422)
29	14	FAC 2R	A	**Brighton & H.A.**	**D 0-0**	**0-0**			**(6209)**
30	16	EL	H	Northampton Town	L 1-3	1-2	20	Angus 39	3421
31	19	EL	H	Cardiff City	W 4-2	1-2	17	Bolt 43(pen), Harding 66(og), Mison 68, Morgan 72	2284
32	26	EL	A	Lincoln City	L 0-4	0-2	20		(3693)
33	J 6	FAC 3	H	**Shrewsbury Town**	**D 1-1**	**0-0**		**Angus 83**	**7265**
34	9	AWS QF	H	**Bristol Rovers**	**L 1-2**	**1-1**		**Jupp**	**3479**
35	13	EL	A	Scarborough	W 1-0	1-0	18	Cusack 42	3557
36	16	FAC 3R	A	**Shrewsbury Town**	**L 1-2**	**1-0**		**Hamill 29**	**(7983)**
37	20	EL	A	Mansfield Town	L 0-1	0-0	21		(2025)
38	30	EL	H	Scunthorpe United	L 1-3	0-1	21	Blake 56	2176
39	F 3	EL	A	Torquay United	L 1-2	1-1	23	Conroy 31	(2594)
40	10	EL	H	Hartlepool United	D 2-2	0-0	23	Barber 18, Blake 54	3700
41	13	EL	A	Cambridge United	D 0-0	0-0	23		(2233)
42	17	EL	A	Rochdale	D 1-1	1-1	23	Conroy 29	(1923)
43	24	EL	H	Exeter City	W 2-1	1-0	22	Scott 6, Scott 70	4027
44	26	EL	A	Doncaster Rovers	W 2-0	2-0	18	Thomas 16, Cusack 31	(2331)
45	M 2	EL	H	Lincoln City	L 1-2	1-2	23	McAree 31	4245
46	5	EL	H	Darlington	D 2-2	0-2	21	Cusack 68, Mison 87	2534
47	9	EL	A	Cardiff City	W 4-1	1-0	15	McAree 32, Scott 53, Conroy 68, 70	(3019)
48	12	EL	A	Hartlepool United	L 0-1	0-1	16		(1198)
49	16	EL	H	Cambridge United	L 0-2	0-1	17		3872
50	23	EL	A	Scunthorpe United	L 1-3	0-1	20	Blake 90(pen)	(1919)
51	26	EL	H	Leyton Orient	W 2-1	0-0	18	Blake 62, Brooker 76	3636
52	30	EL	H	Plymouth Argyle	W 4-0	1-0	17	Scott 5, Morgan 51, Conroy 69, Brooker 84	5667
53	A 2	EL	A	Bury	L 0-3	0-2	17		(3771)
54	6	EL	A	Hereford United	L 0-1	0-1	18		(3276)
55	8	EL	H	Chester City	W 2-0	2-0	16	Morgan 7, Scott 9	3777
56	13	EL	A	Colchester United	D 2-2	1-1	16	Morgan 30, Conroy 47	(3795)
57	20	EL	H	Wigan Athletic	W 1-0	0-0	16	Hamill 78	4657
58	27	EL	H	Gillingham	D 0-0	0-0	16		10320
59	M 4	EL	A	Barnet	L 0-3	0-1	17		(4332)

Best Home League Attendance: 10320 v Gillingham — **Smallest: 2176 v Scunthorpe United** — **Average: 4182**

Goal Scorers:

EL(57): Conroy(9),Morgan(6),Scott(5),Blake(5),Thomas(5),Cusack(5),Mison(4),Hamill(2),McAree(2),Brooker(2),Brazil(2),Bolt(2),Angus(2),Opponent(s)(2), Barber(1),Barkus(1),Adams(1),Moore(1)

CC(6): Conroy(2),Cusack(1),Mison(1),Brazil(1),Barkus(1)

FAC(9): Conroy(3),Jupp(1),Thomas(1),Hamill(1),Cusack(1),Brooker(1),Angus(1)

AWS(5): Morgan(2),Jupp(1),Cusack(1),Conroy(1)

(M) Adams	(D) Angus	(F) Barber	(F) Barkus	(F) Blake	(M) Bolt	(M) Bower	(F) Brazil	(M) Brooker	(F) Conroy	(F) Cusack	(M) Finnigan	(M) Gray	(F) Hamill	(M) Hamsher	(G) Harrison	(D) Herrera	(D) Jupp	(G) Lange	(M) Marshall	(M) McAree	(M) Mison	(D) Moore	(D) Morgan	(F) Scott	(D) Simpson	(M) Taylor	(D) Thomas	(M) Williams	Opponent	No.
X	X		S2	X			X2		X1	S1						X	X	X			X		X			X		X	D.Orr	1
X	X		S2	X			X1		X	S1						X	X	X			X		X				X2		R.Harris	2
X	X		S1	X			X1		X	S1						X	X	X			X		X				X1		W.Rennie	3
X	X		X1	X			S1		X	X						X	X	X			X	S					X		M.Pierce	4
X	X		X1	X			X						S1			S	X	X	X			X	S				X		A.Wiley	5
X	X			X			X		X	S						S	X	X	X			X		X			X		A.Leak	6
X2	X			X			X1		X	S2			S1				X	X	X			X		X			X		K.Leach	7
	X			X	S		X		X	X					S	X	X	X			X	S	X				X		S.Bennett	8
	X			X	S1		X		X	X					S	X	X	X			X	S	X			X1		P.Taylor	9
	X			X	X1		X		X	X						X	X	X			X	S1	X					G.Barber	10
	X			X			X		X	S1			X		S	X	X	X			X1	X				X		R.Lomas	11
	X			X	S		X		X1	X			S1		S	X	X	X			X		X			X		M.Bailey	12
	X			X					X2	X1	S1		S2		S	X	X1				X		X			X	X	E.Wolstenholme	13
	X			X			X		X2	S2	X		X		S	X	X				X1		X			X	X	R.Harris	14
	X		X2	S1			X		X	S2					S	X	X				X	X	X			X1	X	A.Wiley	15
	X		S			X	X	S	X	X	X					X					X		X			X	X	S	A.D'Urso	16
	X	S2		S	X	X	S1	X	X1	X						X					X		X			X	X2		B.Knight	17
	X	X3		S2	X	X		X	S3	X1	X	X				X2					X2		X				X		I.Hemley	18
		S2			X	X2		X	X3	X	S	X	S1				X	X			X		X			X1	X	N.S.Barry	19
		S2			X			X3	X	S3		X	S1			X	X				X1	X	X			X1	X2	A.D'Urso	20
					X	S1	S2	X	X	X		X	X2			X	X			X1	X	X				S	X	G.Singh	21
	X	S			X			X	X	X1		X	S1			X	X				X	X				S	X	M.Riley	22
	X	X1		S2			X2	S1	X	X			S2			X	X				X	X					X	P.Rejer	23
	X		S1			X	X1	X			X	X1				X	X				X	X				S1	S	S.Bennett	24
	X		S1			X1	S2	X	X		X	X2				X	X				X	X				S	X	M.Bailey	25
	X	X1		X3			S1	X		X	X2					S3	X	X			X	X				X		C.Wilkes	26
	X	X1		X			S1	X	X							X	X		X2	X				S	X	S2	G.Poll	27
	X	X2	S	X			S2	X		X1						X	X			X	X				S1	X	S.Baines	28
	X	S1		X			X1	X	X2		X					X	X		S2	X					X		G.Poll	29
	X	X1	S2	X			S1	X2	X							X	X		X2	X				X	S2		M.Pierce	30
X1			S1	X			S	X2	X							X	X		X	X				X	X	S2	A.Butler	31
	X		S2	X3			S3	X	X1		S1					X	X		X2	X				X	X	S2	G.Barber	32
	X		X	X2	X		X1	S1		S2				X3		X	X		S3	X					X		G.R.Pooley	33
	X		X	X	X2		X3	S3		S2				X1	S1	X	X			X					X		A.Wiley	34
	X		X	X2	S1			X		S2				X1		S	X	X	X					X		D.Orr	35
X1			S1	X			S2	X		X				X2		S1	X	X					X	X	S2	G.R.Pooley	36
X1	X	S2	X			X	X2	X	S3	X	S1	X	X3	R.Harris	37
X2	X		X			X		S1		X		X	X	S2	X		X	X2		X1	F.Stretton	38
S	X		X			X		S1		X	X1	X	S2	X	X	X2	G.Singh	39
S	X		X			X		S1		X	X1	X	X	X	S	S.Bennett	40
	X		X			S1	X		X	X	X	X1	X	X2	S	E.Wolstenholme	41
	X		X			X1	X1		S1	X	X	S	X	X	S1	G.Frankland	42
	X1		X			X		S1	X	X	X	S	X	X	X	S2	P.Taylor	43
	X2		X			X			X	X	X2	X1	S1	S	X	X	S	K.Breen	44
	X1		X			X			X	X	X	S1	S	X	X	S	C.Wilkes	45
	X2		X			X		S1	X	X2	S2	X1	X	X	X	M.Fletcher	46
	X		X			S2	X		X	X		X	X2	X	X1	J.Brandwood	47
	X		X			X	X		S2	X	X2	X	S2	X1	S2	X	J.Kirkby	48
S1	X1		X			S1	X		X	X	X1	X	X	X3	S3	R.Poulain	49
X			X	X1		X	X	X		X	X	X	S	X	X	S1	S.Baines	50
X	S		X			X		X	X		X	X	X2	S2	X	X1	S1	B.Knight	51
X2			X			X	X		S1	X	X	X1	S	X	X	S2	K.Leach	52
X1			X			X	X		S3	X	X	X1	X	X3	S1	T.West	53
X2			X			S1	X		S3	X	X3	X		X1	X	X	X	S2	K.J.Breen	54
X			X			X		S	S	X	X		S	X	X	X	D.Orr	55
X	S		X			X	X		S1	X	X	X		X	X1	X	X	U.Rennie	56
X			X	S		X2	X		X	X	X	S1	X1		X	X	S2	A.D'Urso	57
			X			S1	X2	X		X	X	X1	S2	X	X	X	S2	R.Gifford	58
			X3	X		X	X	X		S2	S3	X	X1	X2	X	X	S1	M.Bailey	59

5	30	13	3	35	7	4	17	9	38	38	1	6	6	0	5	42	35	41	14	16	16	17	41	21	5	7	32	2	EL Appearances
0	1	0	6	3	4	0	1	11	2	4	0	1	0	19	3	0	1	1	0	2	1	7	3	0	0	2	5	11	EL Sub Appearances
2	4	0	1+1	4	0	0	3+1	0	4	1+3	1	0	2	0	0	4	3+1	4	0	0	0	4	4	0	0	0	4	0	CC Appearances
0	5	0	2+1	2	4+1	0	2	1+2	4+1	4+1	0	0	2+2	0	0	5	5	5	2	0	1+1	3	3	0	0	0	1	4	0+1	FAC Appearances
0	4	0	2	1	2+1	2	3	0+1	3	2+2	2	1	1+2	0	2	2+2	2	2	1	0+1	2	1	4	0	0	2	3	0	AWS Appearances

Also Played: (M) Bartley S2(26).

585

CLUB RECORDS

BIGGEST VICTORIES
League: 10-1 v Ipswich Town, Division 1, 26.9.1963.
10-2 v Torquay United, Division 3, 10.9.1931.
F.A. Cup: 6-0 v Wimbledon, 1st Round replay, 1930-31.
6-0 v Bury, 3rd Round, 7.1.1939.
8-3 v Luton Town (a), 1st Round, 1907-08.

BIGGEST DEFEATS
League: 0-9 v Wolverhampton Wanderers, Division 1, 16.9.1959.
League Cup: 0-10 v Liverpool, 2nd Round, 23.9.1986.

MOST POINTS
3 points a win: 78, Division 3, 1981-82.
2 points a win: 60, Division 2, 1958-59. Division 3, 1970-71.

MOST GOALS SCORED
111, Division 3(S), 1931-32.

RECORD TRANSFER FEE RECEIVED
£333,333 from Liverpool for Money, May 1980.

RECORD TRANSFER FEE PAID
£150,000 to Orient for Peter Kitchen, February 1979.
£150,000 to Brighton for Teddy Maybank, December 1979.

BEST PERFORMANCES
League: 10th Division 1, 1959-60.
F.A. Cup: Runners-up 1974-75.
League Cup: 5th Round 1967-68, 1970-71.

HONOURS
Champions of Division 3(S) 1931-32.
Champions Division 2, 1948-49.

LEAGUE CAREER
Elected to Div 2 1907, Div 3(S) 1927-28, Div 2 1931-32, Div 1 1948-49, Div 2 1951-52, Div 1 1958-59, Div 2 1967-68, Div 3 1968-69, Div 2 1970-71, Div 3 1979-80, Div 2 1981-82, Div 3 (now Div 2) 1985-86, Div 3 1993-94.

INDIVIDUAL CLUB RECORDS

MOST GOALS IN A SEASON
Frank Newton: 43, Division 3(S), 1931-32.

MOST GOALS IN A MATCH
6. Ronnie Rooke v Bury, 6-0, FA Cup 3rd Round, 7.1.1939.

OLDEST PLAYER
Jimmy Sharpe, 40 years, April 1920 (Played in an emergency and scored his only goal for the club many years after officially retiring!)

YOUNGEST PLAYER
Tony Mahoney, 16 years, 1976.

MOST CAPPED PLAYER
Johnny Haynes (England) 56.

PREVIOUS MANAGERS

1904-09 Harry Bradshaw, 1909-24 Phil Kelso, 1924-26 Andy Ducat, 1926-29 Joe Bradshaw, 1929-31 Ned Liddell, 1931-34 James McIntyre, 1934-35 Jimmy Hogan, 1935 Joe Edelston (acting), 1935-48 Jack Peart, 1948-49 Frank Osborne, 1949-53 Bill Dodgin, 1956-58 Dug Livingstone, 1958-64 Bedford Jezzard, 1964-65 Arthur Stevens (acting), 1965-68 Vic Buckingham, 1968 Bobby Robson, 1968 Johnny Haynes (acting), 1968-72 Bill Dodgin (jnr), 1972-76 Alec Stock, 1976-80 Bobby Campbell, 1980-84 Malcolm MacDonald, 1984-86 Ray Harford, 1986-90 Ray Lewington, 1990-91 Alan Dicks, 1991 Ray Lewington (caretaker), 1991-94 Don Mackay, Ian Branfoot 1994-95.

ADDITIONAL INFORMATION
PREVIOUS NAMES
Fulham St Andrews 1879-98.
PREVIOUS LEAGUES
Southern League.

Club colours: White shirts with black trim, white shorts and white socks with black trim.
Change colours: All red.
Reserves League: Capital League.
Youth League: South East Counties.

LONGEST LEAGUE RUNS

of undefeated matches:	15 (1957, 1970)	of league matches w/out a win:	15 (1950)
of undefeated home matches:	28 (1921-22)	of undefeated away matches:	9 (1958, 1970)
without home win:	9 (8.5.1993 - 6.11.1993)	without an away win:	31 (1964-66)
of league wins:	8 (1963)	of home wins:	12 (1959)
of league defeats:	11 (1961-62)	of away wins:	5 (1966, 1981)

THE MANAGER

MICKY ADAMS . . . . appointed February 1996.

PREVIOUS CLUBS
As Manager . . . . None.
As Asst.Man/Coach . . . . None.
As a player . . . . Gillingham, Coventry, Leeds, Southampton.

HONOURS
As a Manager . . . . None.
As a Player . . . . None.

FULHAM

PLAYERS NAME Honours	Ht	Wt	Birthdate	Birthplace Transfers	Contract Date	Clubs	League	L/Cup	FA Cup	Other	Lge	L/C	FAC	Oth
G O A L K E E P E R S														
Lange Tony	6.0	12.9	10/12/64	West Ham	15/12/82	Charlton Athletic	12			1				
				Loan	22/08/85	Aldershot	7							
				Free	07/07/88	Aldershot	125	5	10	16				
				£150000	13/07/89	Wolves	8	2						
				Loan	23/11/90	Aldershot	2			1				
				Loan	12/09/91	Torquay United	1							
				Free	12/08/92	W.B.A.	45+3	3	1	7				
				Free	27/07/95	Fulham	41	4	5	2				
D E F E N D E R S														
Angus Terence N	6.0	13.9	14/01/66	Coventry		VS Rugby								
				£15000	22/08/90	Northampton Town	115+1	7	5+1	9	6			
				Free	12/07/93	Fulham	79+11	5+1	6	11	4		1	1
Herrera Roberto	5.7	10.6	12/06/70	Torquay	01/03/88	Q.P.R.	4+2	1+2		1+1				
				Loan	17/03/92	Torquay United	11							
				Loan	24/10/92	Torquay United	5							
				Free	29/10/93	Fulham	91+2	7	9	6+1	1			
Morgan Simon C E: u21.2.	5.10	11.7	05/09/68	Birmingham	15/11/84	Leicester City	147+13	14	4+1	3	3	1		
				£100000	12/10/90	Fulham	223+4	15	12	14	33		1	4
Thomas Martin R	5.8	10.8	12/09/73	Lymington	19/06/92	Southampton								
				Free	24/03/94	Leyton Orient	5				2			
				Free	21/07/94	Fulham	53+7	5	4	4	8		1	
M I D F I E L D														
Adams Michael R E: Y.4.	5.6	10.4	08/11/61	Sheffield	01/11/79	Gillingham	85+7	5	6		5			
				£75000	19/07/83	Coventry City	85+5	9	7	2	9	1		
				£110000	23/01/87	Leeds United	72+1	4	6	6	2		1	
				£250000	14/03/89	Southampton	141+3	16	8	6	7			
				Free	24/03/94	Stoke City	10				3			
				Free	14/07/94	Fulham	23+3	3	2	2	8		4	1
Mison Michael	6.3	13.2	08/11/75	London	15/07/94	Fulham	34+17	7	4+1	4+1	5	1		1
F O R W A R D S														
Barkus Lea	5.6	9.13	07/12/74	Reading	13/08/92	Reading	8+7		0+1	1	1			
				£20000	01/07/95	Fulham	3+6	1+1	2+1	2	1	1		
Blake Mark C E: Y.	6.1	12.8	19/12/67	Portsmouth	23/12/85	Southampton	18	2	3	1+2	2			
				Loan	05/09/89	Colchester United	4				1			
				£100000	22/03/90	Shrewsbury Town	142	12	9	12	3			
				Free	16/09/94	Fulham	69+4	6	6	4	8	1	1	
Conroy Michael Div.4'92.	6.0	11.0	31/12/65	Glasgow		Coventry City								
				Free	01/08/84	Clydebank	92+22	4+1	5+2		38			
					01/12/87	St.Mirren	9+1		0+1		1			
				£50000	28/09/88	Reading	65+12	3+2	8+2	2+2	7		1	
				£35000	16/07/91	Burnley	76+1	4	9+1	7+1	30	1	4	4
				£85000	20/08/93	Preston North End	50+7	2+1	7	2+3	22		2	
				£75000	09/08/95	Fulham	38+2	4	4+1	3	9	2	3	1
Cusack Nicholas J	6.0	11.13	24/12/65	Maltby		Alvechurch								
					18/06/87	Leicester City	5+11		0+1	1+1	1			
				£40000	29/07/88	Peterborough Utd	44	4	4	2	10	1	1	
				£100000	02/08/89	Motherwell	68+9	5	3+1	1+1	17	4	2	1
				£95000	24/01/92	Darlington	21				6			
				£95000	16/07/92	Oxford United	48+11	3	4+2	2+1	10	2	1	
				Loan	24/03/94	Wycombe Wand.	2+2				1			
Loan (04/11/94) Fulham				Free	06/01/95	Fulham	64+5	1+3	6+1	4+2	12	1	1	2
Hamill Rory	5.8	12.3	04/05/76	Coleraine		Port Stewart								
				Free	18/11/94	Fulham	24+24	2	2+4	1+3	7		3	
Scott Robert	6.1	11.10	15/08/73	Epsom		Sutton United								
				£20000	01/08/93	Sheffield United	3+5	1+1		2				
				Loan	22/03/95	Scarborough	8				3			
				£30000	10/01/96	Fulham	21				5			
ADDITIONAL CONTRACT PLAYERS														
Brooker Paul						Fulham (T)	9+11		1+2	0+1	2		1	
Hamsher John						Fulham (T)	0+3							
McAree Rodney						Fulham (T)	16+1			0+1	2			
Taylor Mark S						Fulham (T)	7		1	2				

CRAVEN COTTAGE

Stevenage Road, Fulham, London SW6 6HH
Tel: 0171 736 6561

Capacity 14,500

First game..v Minerva, 5-0, Middx Snr Cup, 10.10.1896.
First floodlit game ....v Sheffield Wednesday, 4-1,
....League, September 1962.

ATTENDANCES
Highest...49,335 v Millwall, Div 2, 8.10.1938.
Lowest ....1,108 v Gillingham, Autoglass Trophy, 28.11.1991.

OTHER GROUNDS..None as a professional club.

MATCHDAY TICKET PRICES

Seats......................... £11.50
Juv/OAP......................... £6

Terraces......................... £8
Juv/OAP......................... £4

CLUBCALL
0891 44 00 44

Calls cost 39p per minute cheap rate and 49p per minute at all other times.
Call costings correct at time of going to press.

HOW TO GET TO THE GROUND

From the North
Use motorway (M1) sign posted London then take North Circular Road (A406), sign posted West to Neasden, follow signs to Harlesden (A404), then Hammersmith (A219) and at Broadway follow sign to Fulham and in 1 mile turn right into Harbord Street and at end turn left for Fulham FC.

From the East & South
Use South Circular Road (A205) and take sign to Putney Bridge (A219). Cross bridge and follow sign to Hammersmith and in 0.5 miles turn left into Bishops Park Road and at end turn right for Fulham FC.

From the West
Use motorway (M4) then A4 and in 2 miles branch left, sign posted, other routes into Hammersmith Broadway, follow sign Fulham (A219) and in 1 mile turn right into Harbord Street and at end turn left for Fulham FC.

Car parking
Ample in adjacent streets.

Nearest Railway Station
Putney
Nearest Tube Stations
Putney Bridge or Hammersmith.

MATCHDAY PROGRAMME

Programme Editor .... Ken Myers.

Number of pages .... 32.

Price .... £1.50.

Subscriptions................. All League & Cup matches £45.50.

Local Newspapers.......................... Fulham Chronicle,
..... Hammersmith & Fulham Gazette, Wandsworth Borough News.

Local Radio Stations .... Greater London Radio,
.... Capital & Capital Gold.

HARTLEPOOL UNITED
(The Pool)
NATIONWIDE LEAGUE DIVISION 3
SPONSORED BY: CAMERONS BREWERY COMPANY

1996-97 - Back Row (L-R): Gary Hinchley (Physio.), Joe Allon, Jamie Allinson, Graeme Lee, Glen Davies, Stephen Pears, Steven Howard, Craig Winstanley, Ian McGuckin, Denny Ingram, Brian Honour (Reserve Team Coach), Billy Horner (Youth Team). **Front Row:** Chris Homer, Ian Gallagher, Sean McAuley, Mick Tait (Player-Coach), Keith Houchen (Player-Manager), Chris Beech, David Clegg, Mark Cooper.

HARTLEPOOL UNITED
FORMED IN 1908
TURNED PROFESSIONAL IN 1908
LTD COMPANY IN 1908

PRESIDENT: E Leadbitter
VICE-PRESIDENT: R Boyes, MP
CHAIRMAN: Harold Hornsey
DIRECTORS
A Bamford, D Jukes
CHIEF EXECUTIVE
Stuart Bagnall
COMMERCIAL EXECUTIVE
Frankie Baggs

MANAGER: Keith Houchen
COACH: Mick Tait

YOUTH TEAM MANAGER
Billy Horner
Brian Honour (Assistant Youth Team Coach)

STATISTICIAN FOR THE DIRECTORY
Gordon Small

After three years of decline there were high hopes that 1995/6 would see a change in fortunes for Hartlepool. During the close season there had been major ground improvements, while chairman Harold Hornsey had cleared the club's debts and appointed a new 'gang of four' coaching team.

Unfortunately the optimism was not totally justified, and 1995/6 will have to be seen as a season of consolidation. With a tight budget, Keith Houchen was forced to operate with a small first team squad, and overall there were rather more bad results than good. Hopes were raised at the turn of the year with two successive 3-0 away wins, but throughout the season 'Pool were never out of the bottom half of the table. They maintained a position just clear of the dreaded bottom place, but in April the club's shortcomings were made abundantly clear. The squad had been further pruned down as a cost-cutting exercise, but then injuries and suspensions stretched the club right to its limits - seven of the last eight games were lost, with Keith Houchen being forced to field untried juniors and players not fully fit. The end of the season came as a relief, and really a final position of 20th was about as good as could be expected. Oddly, 1995/6 was a season for the statisticians - in league games over a ten-day period Hartlepool recorded their 1000th win, scored their 4000th goal, but then conceded their 5000th goal.

As in previous years it was the Coca-Cola Cup which provided a welcome diversion. After they had defeated Scarborough in their first ever penalty shoot-out, Hartlepool were paired with Arsenal for the second year running. Inevitably, they were greatly outclassed by the Premiership club, but the financial rewards were ample consolation. The other cup competitions were less memorable: an embarrassing home defeat to neighbours Darlington in the FA Cup came shortly after an even more embarrassing 8-0 drubbing at Crewe in the Auto Windscreens Shield.

Player of the Year was Brian Horne, but really this was a protest vote by the supporters at the way they believed their hero had been treated. Sean McAuley received the ASDA award for performances over the season, while captain Ian McGuckin was another whose consistency was a major strength. Stephen Halliday continued to win praise as a player for the future, but Denny Ingram and Steve Howard must also be considered fine prospects. Joe Allon's return was a little disappointing due to fitness problems, but his nine goals did make him joint top scorer. Fellow striker Keith Houchen worked hard but the worries of management meant he was not the goalscorer he had been in 1994/5. No such problems for 'Duracell Man' Mick Tait, though - he refused to take a back seat and had an exceptional season. Peter Billing and Damian Henderson were both good in spells, while Shane Reddish and Tony Canham were unlucky to have their seasons badly affected by injury. Steven Jones, Chris Lynch and Keith Oliver were others to suffer through a lack of match practice. Hartlepool were unfortunate with their loan signings, but Kenny Lowe was a revelation in midfield before it was decided the club could not afford to sign him. It was pleasing to see the emergence of several promising juniors - Jamie Allinson, Paul Conlon and Graeme Lee all impressed and were offered professional contracts, while a number of first year YTS players also stepped up to gain valuable first-team experience.

During the summer Keith Houchen has been active in the transfer market, but he has also had to battle to retain some of his promising young players. Finances dictate that he will again have to manage with a small squad, but one major problem has been addressed with the re-introduction of a reserve team so that fringe first-teamers can be kept match fit.   **GORDON SMALL**

HARTLEPOOL UNITED

League: 20th   FA Cup: 1st Rnd   Coca-Cola Cup: 2nd Rnd   Auto Windscreen Shield: 1st Rnd

M	DATE		COMP	VEN	OPPONENTS	RESULT		HT	LP	GOAL SCORERS/GOAL TIMES	ATT.
1	A	12	EL	A	Chester City	L	0-2	0-1	23		(2286)
2		15	CC 1/1	A	Scarborough	L	0-1	0-0			(1555)
3		19	EL	H	Exeter City	D	0-0	0-0	20		2311
4		22	CC 1/2	H	Scarborough	W	1-0	1-0		McGuckin 40	2134
5		26	EL	A	Rochdale	L	0-4	0-1	22		(1794)
6		29	EL	H	Northampton Town	W	2-1	1-0	18	Hughes 24(og), McGuckin 90	2390
7	S	2	EL	A	Doncaster Rovers	L	0-1	0-0	23		(2304)
8		9	EL	H	Darlington	D	1-1	0-0	22	Houchen 72	2705
9		12	EL	H	Torquay United	D	2-2	1-0	20	Houchen 37, Lowe 47	1976
10		16	EL	A	Leyton Orient	L	1-4	0-2	22	Houchen 54	(4519)
11		19	CC 2/1	H	Arsenal	L	0-3	0-2			4945
12		23	EL	H	Cardiff City	W	2-1	1-1	19	Lowe 45, Lowe 90	2172
13		30	EL	A	Cambridge United	W	1-0	0-0	16	Howard 69	(2895)
14	O	3	CC 2/2	A	Arsenal	L	0-5	0-2			(27194)
15		7	EL	A	Colchester United	L	1-4	0-3	20	Howard 89	(2618)
16		14	EL	H	Scunthorpe United	W	2-0	0-0	14	Howard 50, Henderson 54	2608
17		17	AWS 1/1	A	Crewe Alexandra	L	0-8	0-0			(2344)
18		21	EL	A	Wigan Athletic	L	0-1	0-0	18		(2104)
19		28	EL	H	Gillingham	D	1-1	0-1	20	Halliday 63	2355
20		31	EL	H	Barnet	D	0-0	0-0	19		1713
21	N	4	EL	A	Lincoln City	D	1-1	0-1	19	Allon 47	(2956)
22		7	AWS 1/2	H	Blackpool	W	3-2	2-2		Allon, Howard (2)	895
23		11	FAC 1	H	Darlington	L	2-4	1-2		Sloan 13, Halliday 76	3834
24		18	EL	H	Plymouth Argyle	D	2-2	0-2	18	Ingram 48, Howard 61	1830
25		25	EL	A	Preston North End	L	0-3	0-1	21		(9449)
26	D	9	EL	A	Cardiff City	L	0-2	0-0	22		(2919)
27		16	EL	H	Cambridge United	L	1-2	1-1	22	Allon 12	1612
28		23	EL	A	Mansfield Town	W	3-0	1-0	22	Houchen 26, 79, Halliday 82	(1979)
29	J	1	EL	A	Bury	W	3-0	1-0	17	Houchen 45, Halliday 62, McGuckin 67	(2927)
30		6	EL	H	Scarborough	D	1-1	0-1	16	Allon 79	2252
31		20	EL	H	Chester City	W	2-1	1-1	18	Halliday 16, Tait 52	1864
32		30	EL	A	Exeter City	L	0-1	0-1	19		(2468)
33	F	3	EL	H	Rochdale	D	1-1	0-0	20	Tait 73	1927
34		10	EL	A	Fulham	D	2-2	0-1	21	Allon 78, 80	(3700)
35		17	EL	A	Torquay United	D	0-0	0-0	20		(2580)
36		20	EL	H	Doncaster Rovers	L	0-1	0-0	20		1367
37		24	EL	H	Leyton Orient	W	4-1	2-0	18	Conlon 2, Allon 45, McGuckin 50, Lynch 83	1915
38		27	EL	A	Darlington	L	0-1	0-0	21		(4333)
39	M	2	EL	A	Scarborough	W	2-1	1-1	15	Conlon 38, 82	(2420)
40		5	EL	H	Hereford United	L	0-1	0-1	17		1473
41		9	EL	H	Mansfield Town	D	1-1	1-0	17	Howard 38	1758
42		12	EL	H	Fulham	W	1-0	1-0	15	Conlon 24	1198
43		19	EL	A	Northampton Town	D	0-0	0-0	15		(3537)
44		23	EL	H	Bury	L	1-2	1-0	16	Ingram 7	1879
45		30	EL	H	Colchester United	W	2-1	1-1	16	Halliday 16, Howard 72	1364
46	A	2	EL	A	Scunthorpe United	L	1-2	1-0	16	Halliday 40	(2100)
47		6	EL	A	Gillingham	L	0-2	0-1	17		(6267)
48		8	EL	H	Wigan Athletic	L	1-2	1-0	19	Canham 8	1877
49		13	EL	A	Barnet	L	1-5	0-3	19	Halliday 48	(2530)
50		20	EL	H	Lincoln City	W	3-0	1-0	19	Henderson 29, Allon 74, 76	3012
51		27	EL	H	Preston North End	L	0-2	0-1	20		5076
52		30	EL	A	Hereford United	L	1-4	0-1	20	Howard 90	(3942)
53	M	4	EL	A	Plymouth Argyle	L	0-3	0-1	20		(11526)

Best Home League Attendance: 5076 v Preston North End   Smallest: 1198 v Fulham   Average: 2114

Goal Scorers:
EL(47): Allon(8),Howard(7),Halliday(7),Houchen(6),Conlon(4),McGuckin(3),Lowe(3),Henderson(2),Ingram(2),Tait(2),Canham(1),Lynch(1),Opponent(s)(1)
CC(1): McGuckin(1)
FAC(2): Halliday(1),Sloan(1)
AWS(3): Howard(2),Allon(1)

(M) Allinson	(F) Allon	(D) Billing	(M) Canham	(F) Conlon	(F) Dixon	(M) Ford	(F) Halliday	(F) Henderson	(M) Homer	(G) Home	(F) Houchen	(M) Howard	(D) Ingram	(G) Jones	(M) Key	(M) Lee	(M) Lowe	(F) Lynch	(D) McAuley	(D) McGuckin	(G) O'Connor	(M) Oliver	(D) Reddish	(G) Roberts	(D) Sloan	(M) Stokoe	(F) Tait	(M) Walton		
		X	X				X	X			X	X	X	X					S	X	X				S		X		M.Fletcher	1
		X	X				X	X2	S		X	X	X1	X				S1	X	X		S2					X		R.Poulain	2
		X	X				X	X		X	X	X	X	S				X1	X	X		S					X		E.Wolstenholme	3
		X	X				X	X		X	X	X2	X1					S1	X	X		S2				S	X		R.Fernandiz	4
		X	X				X	X			X	X1	X2						X	X		X				S1	X		F.Stretton	5
		X	X				X	X	S2		X		X1					X	X2	X		S1	X				X		P.Richards	6
		X	X				X1	X	X1		X	X						X	S1	X	X		S	X			X		A.Leake	7
		X	X			S1	X	X1			X	X						X	S	X	X		S	X			X		J.Lloyd	8
		X	X				X1	X	S		X	X						X2	S1	X	X		S2	X			X		M.Riley	9
		X	X				X1	S1			X	X						X	S	X	X		S	X			X		D.Orr	10
		X	X			S3	X	S2			X	X2						X3	X1	X	X		S1	X			X	S	E.Wolstenholme	11
		X	X2				X	X			X	X1	X	X	S2	S1		X	X	X		X					X		U.Rennie	12
		X					X	X				X1	X2	X				X	S1	X		X					X3		J.Kirkby	13
		X					X	X				X1	X2	X		S2		X	S1	X		X						S.W.Dunn	14
	X1	X	S				X	X	S1			X	X	X				S	X	S	X		X1				X		J.Brandwood	15
	X	X	X				X1	X	S1		S	X	X	X	X				S	X	X						X		S.Mathieson	16
	X	X					X	X	S		X	X	X	X					S	X	X						X			17
	X	X					S	S1	X		X1	X	X						X	S	X						X		C.Wilkes	18
	X	X					S1	X1				X	X	X					X	S	X			X	S		X		N.Barry	19
	X	X					X	X				X1	S1	X					X	X		S	X2	X					A.Butler	20
	X	X					S2	X				X2	S1	X					X	X			X1	X			X		K.Lynch	21
X3	X4	X					X	X		X1		X	X				S1		X	X		X			X1	S2			T.West	22
X2	X						X	X		X		X	X				S		S2	X	X		S1			X			W.Burns	23
		X	X1		X		X	X			X	S2	S1	X			X3		X	X					X2	S3			T.Leake	24
		X	S1		X1		X2	X			X	X	X	X					X	X			S2		S3		X		P.Rejer	25
		X			X1		X	X			X	X	X	X				S		X	X				S1		X		B.Knight	26
	X	X					X	S				X	X1	X				S1	X	X			X		S		X		P.Richards	27
	X	X					X				S2	X1	X2					S	X	X		X	X				X1		P.Taylor	28
	X	X					X				S	X	X1	S	X			X	X	X		X	X		S1				S.W.Mathieson	29
	X	X					X			S	X	X		S		X1		X	X	X		X	X		S1				R.Furnandiz	30
	X	X					X					X	S1	X	S			X	X	X		S	X				X1		W.C.Burns	31
	X	X					X					X	S1	X	S			X1	X	X		S	X				X		M.Pierce	32
X1	X						X1			X	S	X	X	X		S			X	X		S	X		S1		X		T.West	33
	X	X					X1					X	X	X		S			X	X		S	X		S1		X		S.Bennett	34
	X2		X	S2			X			X	X	X	X		S		S1		X	X	X1	X	X				M.Bailey	35
	X		S1	S2			X			X	X	X1	X			S			X	X		X2					X		F.Stretton	36
	X		X2	X			X			X	X	X1	S1	X		S			S2	X						X	X	T.Leake	37
X1			X	X2			X			X	X	X	S1	X		S			S2	X						X	X	G.Cain	38
	X	X	X				X			X	X	X	X		S		S		X	X		S				X	X	D.Allison	39
	X	X		X1			S1			X	X	X	X		S			X	X		S				X	X	R.Poulain	40
	X	X		X1						X	X	X	X		S			X	X		S				X	X	S.Mathieson	41
	S			X			X	X		X	X	X	X		S				X	X					X	X	S	J.Kirkby	42
			S1	X1			X	X		X	X	X	X					X	X						X	X	S	R.Harris	43
			S1	X1			X	X		X	X	X	X	S				X	X						X	X	S	N.Barry	44
S3		S1	X	X2			X	X		X	X	X	X1					X	X3							X	S2	K.Lynch	45
X1		X	X2				X	X		X	X	X					S2		X							X	S1	B.Burns	46
X		X	S				X	X		X1	X	X	X2	S1					X							X	S2	A.Butler	47
X2		X	X1				X	X			X	X		X					X							X	S1	S.Baines	48
	X	X	X	S			X	X			X	X		X				S	X							X	S	A.Wiley	49
	X	X	S2				X	X1				X2	X	X				S1	X	X	X	S					M.Riley	50
	X	S	X	S			X	X			X	X	X					S	X	X						X		G.Cain	51
	X	X	S	S1			X	X				X	X	X				S	X	X						X1		J.Brandwood	52
	X						X	X				X	X2	X				X	X	X							S1	R.Gifford	53
3	**22**	**35**	**25**	**11**	**3**	**2**	**36**	**33**	**1**	**32**	**36**	**32**	**32**	**7**	**1**	**3**	**13**	**13**	**46**	**40**	**1**	**7**	**18**	**4**	**1**	**8**	**38**	**1**	EL Appearances	
1	0	1	4	4	0	1	3	3	4	0	2	7	1	2	0	3	0	5	0	0	0	6	1	0	5	0	1	5	EL Sub Appearances	
0	0	4	3	0	0	0+1	4	3+1	0	2	3	3	3	2	0	0+1	2	1+3	4	4	0	1+3	1	0	0	0	4	0	CC Appearances	
1	0	1	0	0	0	0	1	1	0	1	0	1	1	0	0	0	0	0+1	1	1	0	0+1	0	0	1	0	1	0	FAC Appearances	
1	2	2	1	0	0	2	2	0+1	1	0	2	2	1	0	0	2	1	0	2	1	0	1	2	1	0	1	0	0	AWS Appearances	

Also Played: ((G) De Bont X(16), F) Foster S2(5). (M) Gallagher X(53). (M) Hutt S(52), S2(53). (M) Slater S2(45).

CLUB RECORDS

BIGGEST VICTORIES
League: 10-1 v Barrow, Division 4, 4.4.1959.
F.A. Cup: 6-0 v North Shields, 1st Round, 30.11.1946.
6-1 v Scarborough, 1st Round, 20.11.1971.
6-3 v Marine, 2nd Round replay, 15.12.1975.

BIGGEST DEFEATS
League: 1-10 v Wrexham, Division 4, 3.3.1962.
F.A. Cup: 0-6 v Manchester City, 3rd Round, 3.1.1976.
Other: 1-7 v York City, Leyland Daf Cup 7.11.1989.

MOST POINTS
3 points a win: 82, Division 4, 1990-91.
2 points a win: 60, Division 4, 1967-68.

MOST GOALS SCORED
90, Division 3(N) 1956-57.

RECORD TRANSFER FEE RECEIVED
£250,000 from Plymouth Argyle for Paul Dalton, May 1992.

RECORD TRANSFER FEE PAID
£60,000 to Barnsley for Andy Saville, March 1992.

BEST PERFORMANCES
League: 2nd Division 3(N) 1956-57.
F.A. Cup: 4th Round 1954-55, 1977-78, 1988-89, 1992-93.
League Cup: 4th Round 1974-75.

HONOURS
None.

LEAGUE CAREER
Original members of Div 3(N) 1921, Transferred to Div 4 1958, P. Div 3 1967-68, R. Div 4 1968-69, P. Div 3 (now Div 2) 1990-91.

MOST GOALS IN A SEASON
Joe Allon: 35 goals in 1990-91. (League 28, FA Cup 3, League Cup 2, Leyland Daf 2).

INDIVIDUAL CLUB RECORDS

MOST GOALS IN A MATCH
7. Billy Smith v St Peters Albion (10-1), FA Cup, 17.11.1923.
5. Harry Simmons v Wigan Borough (6-1), Division 3(N), 1.1.1931.
5. Bobby Folland v Oldham Athletic (5-1, Division 3(N), 15.4.1961.

OLDEST PLAYER
Jackie Carr, 39 years 360 days, 21.11.1931.

YOUNGEST PLAYER
John McGovern, 16 years 205 days, 21.5.1966.

MOST CAPPED PLAYER
Amby Fogarty (Eire) 1.

PREVIOUS MANAGERS

1908-12 Fred Priest, 1912-13 Percy Humphreys, 1913-20 Jack Manners, 1920-22 Cecil Potter, 1922-24 David Gordon, 1924-27 Jack Manners, 1927-31 Bill Norman, 1931-35 Jackie Carr, 1935-39 Jimmy Hamilton, 1943-57 Fred Westgarth, 1957-59 Ray Middleton, 1959-62 Bill Robinson, 1962-63 Allenby Chilton, 1963-64 Bob Gurney, 1964-65 Alvan Williams, 1965 Geoff Twentyman, 1965-67 Brian Clough, 1967-70 Angus McLean, 1970-71 John Simpson, 1971-74 Len Ashurst, 1974-76 Ken Hale, 1976-83 Billy Horner, 1983 John Duncan, 1983-86 Mick Docherty, 1983-86 Billy Horner, 1986-88 John Bird, 1988-89 Bobby Moncur, 1989-91 Cyril Knowles, 1991-93 Alan Murray; 1993 Viv Busby, 1993-94 John MacPhail, 1994-95 David McCreery.

ADDITIONAL INFORMATION
PREVIOUS NAMES
Until 1968 Hartlepool United: 1968-77 Hartlepool.
PREVIOUS LEAGUES
North Eastern League.

Club colours: Light blue & white striped shirts, light blue shorts with dark blue trimmings.
Change colours: Red shirts with white trim, red shorts.

Youth League: Northern Intermediate

LONGEST LEAGUE RUNS

of undefeated matches:	17 (1968)	of league matches w/out a win:	18 (1962-63, 1993)
of undefeated home matches:	27 (1967-68)	of undefeated away matches:	8 (1992)
without home win:	8 (1977, 1984, 1986, 1993)	without an away win:	31 (1937-38)
of league wins:	7 (1956, 1968)	of home wins:	12 (1933, 1951)
of league defeats:	8 (1950, 1993)	of away wins:	4 (1921-22, 1979, 1991)

THE MANAGER

KEITH HOUCHEN . . . . appointed April 1995.

PREVIOUS CLUBS
As Manager . . . . None.
As Asst.Man/Coach . . . . None.
As a player . . . . Chesterfield, Hartlepool, Leyton Orient, York City, Scunthorpe Utd, Coventry City, Hibernian, ... Port Vale, Hartlepool United.

HONOURS
As a Manager . . . . None.
As a Player . . . . FA Cup 1987.

PLAYERS NAME Honours	Ht	Wt	Birthdate	Birthplace Transfers	Contract Date	Clubs	League	L/Cup	FA Cup	Other	Lge	L/C	FAC	Oth
GOALKEEPERS														
Horne Brian S	5.11	12.4	05/10/67	Billericay	10/10/85	Millwall (A)	163	14	9	10				
				Loan	28/08/92	Middlesbrough	3+1							
				Loan	02/10/92	Stoke City	1	1						
				Free	24/12/92	Prtsmouth	3			2				
				Free	02/08/94	Hartlepool United	73	5	2	3				
DEFENDERS														
Davies Glen	6.1	12.10	20/02/76	Brighton		Burnley (T)								
				Free	19/06/96	Hartlepool United								
Ingram Stuart Denevan	5.10	11.8	27/06/76	Sunderland	05/07/94	Hartlepool United	80+1	6+1	2	4	2			
McAuley Sean : u21.1.	6.0	11.9	23/06/72	Sheffield	01/07/90	Manchester United								
					22/04/92	St.Johnstone	52+2	3	3					
				Loan	04/11/94	Chesterfield	1		1+1	2	1			
					21/07/95	Hartlepool United	46	4	1	2				
McGuckin Thomas Ian	6.2	12.2	24/04/73	Middlesbrough	20/06/91	Hartlepool United	126+4	12	4	6	9	1		
Reddish Shane	5.10	11.10	05/05/71	Bolsover										
MIDFIELD														
Homer Chris	5.9	11.5	16/04/77		01/08/94	Hartlepool United	1+4			0+1				
Howard Steve						Tow Law Town								
					08/08/95	Hartlepool United	32+7	3	1	2	7			2
FORWARDS														
Allon Joe : Y.1. FAYC'85.	5.11	12.02	12/11/66	Gateshead	16/11/84	Newcastle United	9	1			2			
				Free	06/08/87	Swansea City	27+7	2	2	2	12			1
				Free	29/11/88	Hartlepool United	112	5	6+1	7	51	2	5	2
				£250000	14/08/91	Chelsea	3+11	0+2		1+1	2			1
				Loan	27/07/92	Port Vale	2+4							
				£275000	19/11/92	Brentford	38+7	2	2	7	19		2	7
				Loan	16/09/93	Southend United	2+1							
					24/03/94	Port Vale	13+10	0+1	2		9		1	
				£42500	17/07/95	Lincoln City	3+1	1						
				£50000	13/10/95	Hartlepool United	22			2	8			1
Houchen Keith M AC'87.	6.2	11.4	25/07/60	Middlesbrough		Chesterfield								
				Free	09/02/78	Hartlepool United	160+10	8	4+1		65	1		
				£25000	26/03/82	Leyton Orient	74+2	3	3	0+1	20	1		
				£151000	22/03/84	York City	56+11	6	9+2	4	19	3	3	2
				£40000	28/03/86	Scunthorpe United	9				2			
				£60000	03/07/86	Coventry City	43+11	2+1	5+1	2+1	7		5	
				£100000	29/03/89	Hibernian	51+6	5	6	4	11	1	4	1
				£100000	09/08/91	Port Vale	44+5	2+1	2	1+1	10	1		
				Free	01/08/93	Hartlepool United	102+2	8	2	3	27	1		
Tait Michael P	5.11	12.5	30/09/56	Wallsend	08/10/74	Oxford United	61+3	2+1	2		23	1		
				£65000	03/02/77	Carlisle United	101+5	7	7		20		2	
				£150000	06/09/79	Hull City	29+4		1		3		1	
				£100000	11/06/80	Portsmouth	227+12	33+1	13	2+1	31	1	1	
				£50000	01/09/87	Reading	98+1	9	16	9	10	2		3
				Free	03/08/90	Darlington	79	5	4	3	2			
				Free	31/07/92	Hartlepool United	35	4	2		1			
					01/07/94	Gretna								
				Free	09/09/94	Hartlepool United	58+1	5	1	1	2			
ADDITIONAL CONTRACT PLAYERS														
Nutt Stephen						Hartlepool Utd (T)	0+1							
Lee Graeme						Hartlepool Utd (T)	3+3	0+1		0+1				
Slater Darren						Hartlepool Utd (T)	0+1							
Walton Paul						Hartlepool Utd (T)	1+5							

THE VICTORIA PARK
Hartlepool, Cleveland TS24 8BZ
Tel: 01429 272 584

Capacity 7,229
Seating 3,466
Terrace 3,263

First game .... v Newcastle Utd Res. (F) 6-0, 2.9.1908.
First floodlit game .... v Southend Utd, Div 4, 1-2, 6.1.1967.

ATTENDANCES
Highest .... 17,426 v Manchester Utd, FA Cup 3rd round, 18.1.1957.
Lowest .... 655 v Bradford City, Football League Trophy, 18.8.1982.
.... 790 v Stockport County, Division 4, 5.5.1984.

OTHER GROUNDS .... None.

MATCHDAY TICKET PRICES

Seats £9
Juv/OAP £6

Terraces £7
Juv/OAP £5

Ticket Office Telephone no. 01429 222 077

HOW TO GET TO THE GROUND

From the North
Use A1, A19 then A179, sign posted Hartlepool to Hart. In 2.5 miles at traffic signals forward, then at crossroads turn right into Clarence Road for Hartlepool United FC.

From the South and West
Use A1, A19 and A689 into Hartlepool town centre, then bear right into Clarence Road for Hartlepool United FC.

Car Parking
Side street parking is ample.

Nearest Railway Station
Hartlepool Church Street (01429 274 039).

MATCHDAY PROGRAMME

Programme Editor .... Mike Challards.

Number of pages .... 32.

Price £1.30

Subscriptions .... Please apply to club.

Local Newspapers .... Hartlepool Mail, Northern Echo.

Local Radio Stations .... T.F.M, Radio Cleveland.

HEREFORD UNITED
(United)
NATIONWDIE LEAGUE DIVISION 3
SPONSORED BY: SUN VALLEY

Back Row (L-R): Dean Clarke, Steve White, John Brough, Tony James, Chris McKenzie, Neil Lyne, Kevin Lloyd, Rob Warner.
Front Row: Phil Preedy, Murray Fishlock, Andy Preece, Gary Pick, Graham Turner, Dean Smith, Richard Wilkins, Nicky Cross, Tim Steele.

**HEREFORD UNITED
FORMED IN** 1924
TURNED PROFESSIONAL IN 1924
LTD COMPANY IN 1939

LIFE-VICE-PRESIDENT: A Bush
CHAIRMAN: P S Hill, FRICS
DIRECTORS
D H Vaughan, J Simmons,
R Fry (Managing)
SECRETARY
D H Vaughan (01432 276 666)
PROMOTIONS EXECUTIVE
John Pulling (01432 276666)

DIRECTOR OF FOOTBALL
Graham Turner

STATISTICIAN FOR THE DIRECTORY
Lawrence Appleby

With Hereford's start to the season, you would have hardly thought that it would end with a place in the play-offs and a chance of going to Wembley, with possible further glory in being promoted.

Two wins in their first ten League matches saw them languishing in 17th position. Things were to get worst before they got better when the Winter programme put them in their lowest position of the season - 19th.

This seemed enough to bring United to life as they enjoyed a run of seven games without defeat, this took them to 11th. A slight hic-up away to Bury and Darlington was followed by a sequence of eight games, when only Torquay United (1-1) denied them a 100% winning record - this put them in seventh place.

With four games left they needed to gain one more place to secure a play-off spot, but in the form United were in an automatic promotion could also be achieved. This however, was not to be as they lost to promotion challengers Darlington (0-1) at home and then a surprise defeat at struggling Cardiff City (2-3). However, two victories, against Hartlepool (4-1) and Rochdale (2-0), in the last games of the season was enough to put them into the play-offs.

The play-offs were a bit of anticlimax, with Darlington winning both legs of the semi-final 1-2, thus ending Hereford's hopes.

A run in the Auto Windscreen Shield was enjoyed with Hereford getting to the Southern Semi Final before being knocked out by Chesterfield (1-4), whilst the Third Round was reached in the F.A. Cup, with victories over Stevenage Borough (2-1) and Sutton United (2-0). This set up a dream Cup tie against Tottenham Hotspur at Edgar Street. With Spurs taking an early lead United stood firm and held the Londoners before eventually equalising mid-way through the second-half. Holding on to a very creditable 1-1 draw United were then given a lesson in Premiership Football at White Hart Lane ten days later - losing 1-5.

If Hereford can start the 1996/97 season as they ended the last, then they have a good chance of certainly reaching the play-offs, if not an automatic promotion place.

HEREFORD UNITED

League: 6th   FA Cup: 3rd Rnd   Coca-Cola Cup: 1st Rnd   Auto Windscreen Shield: Semi-Finals

M	DATE	COMP	VEN	OPPONENTS	RESULT	HT	LP	GOAL SCORERS/GOAL TIMES	ATT.
1	A 12	EL	H	Barnet	W 4-1	3-0	2	Smith 32(pen), Brough 41, Mackenzie 43, Pounder 85	2522
2	15	CC 1/1	H	Oxford United	L 0-2	0-1			3021
3	19	EL	A	Cambridge United	D 2-2	1-2	4	Fishlock 2, Lyne 48	(2557)
4	22	CC 1/2	A	Oxford United	L 2-3	0-3		Reece 7, Smith 85	(3571)
5	26	EL	H	Bury	L 3-4	2-1	9	White 41, 46, Preedy 58	2702
6	29	EL	A	Plymouth Argyle	W 1-0	1-0	4	White 32	5608
7	S 2	EL	A	Chester City	L 1-2	0-2	11	Pounder 87	(3385)
8	9	EL	H	Preston North End	L 0-1	0-0	14		3124
9	12	EL	H	Gillingham	D 0-0	0-0	15		1747
10	16	EL	A	Scarborough	D 2-2	1-0	14	Stoker 28, Cross 81	(1449)
11	23	EL	A	Colchester United	L 0-2	0-0	17		(2596)
12	26	AWS 1/1	H	Cardiff City	D 3-3	0-0		Smith, Wilkins (2)	1411
13	30	EL	H	Wigan Athletic	D 2-2	1-1	17	Wilkins 1, White 86	2198
14	O 7	EL	H	Torquay United	W 2-1	1-0	14	White 44, Wilkins 90	2143
15	14	EL	A	Doncaster Rovers	D 0-0	0-0	14		(1961)
16	21	EL	H	Exeter City	D 2-2	0-0	16	White 58, Blatherwitk 84	2236
17	28	EL	A	Fulham	D 0-0	0-0	17		(3631)
18	31	EL	A	Leyton Orient	W 1-0	0-0	14	Cross 46	(3567)
19	N 4	EL	H	Mansfield Town	L 0-1	0-0	15		2193
20	7	AWS 1/2	A	Gillingham	D 2-2	0-0		Smith (pen), Stoker	(1866)
21	11	FAC 1	H	Stevenage	W 2-1	0-1		White 56, Cross 62	3321
22	18	EL	A	Rochdale	D 0-0	0-0	15		(2619)
23	26	EL	H	Cardiff City	L 1-3	0-0	16	White 56	3528
24	29	AWS 2	A	Swindon Town	W 1-0	1-0		White	(6650)
25	D 2	FAC 2	H	Sutton	W 2-0	1-0		White 25, 82	2908
26	9	EL	H	Colchester United	D 1-1	0-0	17	Smith 63	3324
27	16	EL	A	Wigan Athletic	L 1-2	1-0	19	Cross 8	(1962)
28	19	EL	H	Scunthorpe United	W 3-0	1-0	13	Cross 36, White 50, 84	2516
29	26	EL	A	Northampton Town	D 1-1	0-0	15	Smith 60	(5222)
30	J 6	FAC 3	H	Tottenham Hotspur	D 1-1	0-1		Brough 62	8806
31	9	AWS QF	H	Northampton Town	W 1-0	0-0		Cross 60	2905
32	13	EL	A	Cambridge United	W 5-2	3-1	16	White 12, 34, 67, 85 (4), Smith 23(pen)	2548
33	17	FAC 3R	A	Tottenham Hotspur	L 1-5	0-2		Stoker 90	(31534)
34	20	EL	A	Barnet	W 3-1	1-1	13	Stoker 3, Cross 54, White 80	(1835)
35	31	AWS SF	A	Shrewsbury Town	L 1-4	0-2		Cross 46	(4545)
36	F 13	EL	A	Lincoln City	L 1-2	1-0	19	White 38	(1884)
37	17	EL	A	Gillingham	D 1-1	1-0	19	Smith 32	(6993)
38	20	EL	H	Chester City	W 1-0	0-0	17	White 89	1827
39	24	EL	H	Scarborough	D 0-0	0-0	16		2568
40	27	EL	A	Preston North End	D 2-2	1-1	15	Fishlock 20, Smith 66	(9761)
41	M 2	EL	H	Northampton Town	W 1-0	0-0	14	James 89	2822
42	5	EL	A	Hartlepool United	W 1-0	1-0	12	Smith 44	(1473)
43	9	EL	A	Scunthorpe United	W 1-0	0-0	11	Hargreaves 47	(1903)
44	19	EL	A	Bury	L 0-2	0-0	14		(2280)
45	23	EL	A	Darlington	L 0-1	0-0	14		(1708)
46	27	EL	H	Lincoln City	W 1-0	0-0	12	Cross 81	1631
47	30	EL	A	Torquay United	D 1-1	1-1	14	White 29	(2034)
48	A 2	EL	H	Doncaster Rovers	W 1-0	1-0	12	White 15	2060
49	6	EL	H	Fulham	W 1-0	1-0	10	James 36	3276
50	8	EL	A	Exeter City	W 2-0	1-0	10	White 15, 65	(3161)
51	13	EL	H	Leyton Orient	W 3-2	1-0	10	Wilkins 38, 57, 68 (3)	3459
52	16	EL	H	Plymouth Argyle	W 3-0	2-0	9	White 12, 39, 51(pen) (3)	4739
53	20	EL	A	Mansfield Town	W 2-1	1-1	7	White 44(pen), Hargreaves 84	(2358)
54	23	EL	H	Darlington	L 0-1	0-1	7		5359
55	27	EL	A	Cardiff City	L 2-3	0-2	8	White 84, Fishlock 92	(3751)
56	30	EL	H	Hartlepool United	W 4-1	1-0	6	White 6, Smith 58(pen), Cross 77, Stoker 89	3942
57	M 4	EL	H	Rochdale	W 2-0	1-0	6	Cross 45, White 83	5880
58	12	PO SF1	H	Darlington	L 1-2	1-2		Smith 2	6622
59	15	PO SF2	A	Darlington	L 1-2	0-1		White 65	(6584)

Best Home League Attendance: 5880 v Rochdale   Smallest: 1631 v Lincoln City   Average: 2971

Goal Scorers:
EL(65): White(29),Smith(8),Cross(8),Stoker(3),Fishlock(3),Wilkins(3),James(2),Pounder(2),Hargreaves(2),Preedy(1),Brough(1),Blatherwitk(1),Lyne(1),Mackenzie(1)
CC(2): Smith(1),Reece(1)
FAC(6): White(3),Brough(1),Cross(1),Stoker(1)
AWS(8): Wilkins(2),Cross(2),Smith(2),White(1),Stoker(1)
PO(2): Smith(1),White(1)

(M) Medford	(D) Blatherwick	(M) Brough	(F) Clarke	(F) Cross	(G) De Bont (L)	(M) Downing	(D) Evans	(D) Fishlock	(F) Hall	(F) Hargreaves	(D) James	(D) Lloyd	(F) Lyne	(G) Mackenzie	(M) Pick	(M) Pitman	(M) Pounder	(D) Preedy	(M) Reece	(M) Smith	(D) Smith	(M) Steele	(M) Stoker	(D) Watkiss	(F) White	(M) Wilkins			
S	X		S					X				X	X	X	S		X		X		X		X		X	X		T.Leake	1
S	X		S					X				X	X	X	S		X		X		X		X		X	X		R.Gifford	2
S		X1	S2					X				X	X2	X	S1		X		X		X		X		X	X		B.Knight	3
			S2				X1					X	X2	X	X		X	S1	X		X		X		X	X		A.Wiley	4
S			S2					X				X1	X	X	X2		X	S1	X		X		X		X	X		P.Rejer	5
		X	X					X	S				X	X	S1		X	X	X		X				X1	X		G.Singh	6
S		X	X					X	S			X1	X	X	S1		X	X	X		X				X	X		F.G.Stretton	7
S		X1						X	S2			X	X	X	X		X	S1	X2		X		X			X		P.Taylor	8
S	X	X1	X					X	S			X	X	X	X		X		S1		X				X	X		J.Lloyd	9
	X		X		X	X	X					S	X	X	X		X	S1					X1			X		G.B.Frankland	10
S	X		X	X2	X	X						X	X	X	S2		X	S1					X1			X		G.Pooley	11
S	X	X1	X	X	X							X	X	X			X	S					X	S1		X			12
S	X	X	S	X	X							X	X	X			X	S1					X1		X	X		R.Poulain	13
S	X		X	X	X							X		X	X1		S1						X		X	X		A.Butler	14
S	X		X	X	X							X	X	S			X						X		X	X		S.Baines	15
	X		X	X	X							X	X	X			X	S1					X1		X	X		G.Caine	16
	X		X1	X	X							X	S1	X			X						S		X	X		A.D'Urso	17
	X	S	X	X	X							X		X	X		X						S		X	X		M.Peirce	18
	X	S	X	X1	X	X						X		X	X2		X	S1					S2		X	X		D.B.Allison	19
	X		X1	X	X	X						X		X	X2		X	S1					S2		X	X			20
		S	X	X		X						S	X	X	X		X	X				S	X		X	X		G.Ashby	21
		S	X	X		X						S	X	X	X		X	X				S	X		X	X		M.Riley	22
			X	X		X						S	X	X	X		X	X				S	X		X	X		G.Barber	23
	X		X	X		X	X	S				X	X	X			S1					S	X		X1	X			24
	X		X1	X		X	X					X	X	X			S1					S	X		X	X		P.Rejer	25
	X		X	X		X	X	S				X	X	X			S1					S	X		X1	X		R.Pulain	26
	X		X	X		X	X					X	X	X			S1					S	X	S1	X	X		I.Cruikshanks	27
	X		X	X		X	X	X				X	X	X			X1					S	X	S1	X	X		A.Wiley	28
	X		X	X		X	X	X				X	X	X			X					S	X	S	X	X		P.Richards	29
	X		X	X		X	X	X				X	X	X			X					S	X	S	X	X		M.A.Riley	30
	X1		X	X		X	X	X				X	X	X			X					S	X	S1	X	X		P.Richards	31
	X		X1	X1		X	X	X				X	X	X			X					S	X	S1	X	X		S.Mathieson	32
	X		X1	X		X	X	X				X	X	X			X2					S	S2	S1	X	X		S.Dunn	33
	X	S	X			X						X	X	X	X		X					S	X	X	X			P.Rejer	34
	X	S	X			X	X	X				X	X	X1			X					S	S1		X	X			35
	X	S	X			X						X	X	X		X1	X					X	S1	X1	X			B.Burns	36
	X		S2			X	X					S	X2	X	X		X1					X	S1	X	X	X		P.Taylor	37
	X					X						S	X	X	S	X1	X					X		X	X	X	X	C.Wilkes	38
	X					X	X	X	S1			S	S1	X			X					X		S	X	X	X	E.Wolstenholme	39
	X					X	X	X	X			S	S	X			X					X	S	X	X	X	X	U.Rennie	40
			S2			X	X	X	X2		X	S	S1	X			X1					X		X	X	X	X	M.Fletcher	41
						X	X	X	S		X	X	X	X			S					X		X	X	X	X	R.Poulain	42
						X	X	X	X			X	X	X			S					X		S	X	X	X	G.Frankland	43
			X1			X	X3	X	X		X	S2	X	X2	S2		S3					X			X	S1	X	F.Stretton	44
			X2	X	X			X1			X	X	X2	S1	S2		X	S2				X			X	X	X	A.Leake	45
	S		S1	X	X	S			X1		X	X	X	X			X					X			X	X	X	J.Rushton	46
	X		X	X	X			X				S	X	X			X					S	S1	X1	X	X	X	B.Knight	47
	X		X	X		X		S				X	X	X			X					S	S	X	X	X	X	M.C.Bailey	48
	X		X					S1	X			X		X	X1		X					S	S	X	X	X	X	K.J.Breen	49
	X		X			X			X		X	S		X			X	S				S	S	X	X	X	X	R.Gifford	50
			X	X		X			X			X	X	X	S		X					S	S1	X	X	X1	X	J.Lloyd	51
	X		X	X		X			X1		X	X	X	S1			X					S	S1	X	X	X1	X	S.Bennett	52
	X		X	X		X		S	X		X	X	X2	S2			X					X	S1	X	X	X	X	K.Lynch	53
	X		X	X	X		X	S1	X		X	X2	S2	S2			S					X1	X	X2	X	X	X	G.Singh	54
	X		X	X	X1			X	X		X	X	X	S1	S		X					S2	X	X2	X	X	X	K.Leach	55
			X1					X	X		X	X	S1	X			X	S				X		X	X	X	X	J.Brandwood	56
		X	X	S				X	X		X	X	S1	X			X					X		X	X	X	X	S.Baines	57
	S		X	S				X	X1		X	S1	X	X			X					X		X	X2	X	X	K.Lynch	58
	S2		X	S				X				X	X	X			X1	S1				X		X	X2	X	X	D.Allison	59
0	10	22	6	32	8	29	24	26	0	15	17	25	22	38	10	12	31	5	6	0	39	0	30	19	39	42		EL Appearances	
0	0	0	5	0	0	0	1	1	2	0	2	0	8	0	4	1	3	9	0	0	1	6	3	0	1	0		EL Sub Appearances	
0	1	1	0	0+1	0	0	0	2	0	0	0	2	2	2	1	0	2	0+1	2	0	2	0	2	0	2	2		CC Appearances	
0	0	3	0	4	0	3	4	3	0	0	0	1	3	4	1	0	3+1	1	0	0	4	0+1	2+1	0	4	4		FAC Appearances	
0	2	3	0	5	0	4	5	2	0	0	0	3	4	5	2	0	4+1	0+1	0	0	5	0+2	3+1	0	4+1	4		AWS Appearances	
0	0	0+1	0	2	0	0	0	2	0	0	0	1	1+1	2	0	2	0+1	0	0	0	2	0	2	2	2	2		PO Appearances	

HEREFORD UNITED

RECORDS AND STATISTICS

CLUB RECORDS

BIGGEST VICTORIES
League: 6-0 v Burnley (a), Division 4, 24.1.1987.
F.A. Cup: 6-1 v Queens Park Rangers, 2nd Round, 7.12.1957.

BIGGEST DEFEATS
League: 0-6 v Rotherham United (a), Division 4, 29.4.1989.
F.A. Cup: 2-7 v Arsenal, 3rd Round replay, 21.1.1985.
League Cup: 0-5 v Newport County 1st round, 11.8.1981.
0-5 v Nottingham Forest 2nd Round, 7.10.1987.
0-5 v Torquay United, 1st round 2nd leg, 25.8.1992.

MOST POINTS
3 points a win: 77, Division 1, 1984-85.
2 points a win: 63, Division 3, 1974-75.

MOST GOALS SCORED
86, Division 3, 1975-76.

RECORD TRANSFER FEE RECEIVED
£250,000 from Q.P.R. for Darren Peacock, March 1991, plus another £240,000 after moving to Newcastle United from QPR, March 1994.

RECORD TRANSFER FEE PAID
£75,000 to Walsall for Dean Smith, July 1994.

BEST PERFORMANCES
League: 22nd Division 2, 1976-77.
F.A. Cup: 4th Round 1971-72, 1976-77, 1981-82, 1989-90, 1991-92.
League Cup: 3rd Round, 1974-75.
Welsh Cup: Finalists (4 times), Winners 1989-90.

HONOURS
Division 3, 1975-76.
Welsh FA Cup 1989-90.

LEAGUE CAREER
Elected to Div 4 1972, Div 3 1972-73, Div 2 1975-76, Div 3 1976-77, Div (now Div 3) 1977-78.

INDIVIDUAL CLUB RECORDS

MOST GOALS IN A SEASON
'Dixie' McNeil: 37 goals in 1975-76 (League 35, FA Cup 2).

MOST GOALS IN A MATCH
4.'Dixie' McNeil v Chester, Division 3, 10.3.1976.

OLDEST PLAYER
John Jackson, 40 years 6 days.

YOUNGEST PLAYER
Stuart Phillips, 16 years 112 days.

MOST CAPPED PLAYER
Brian Evans (Wales) 1.

PREVIOUS MANAGERS

(Since joining the Football League)
1971-74 Colin Addison, 1974-78 John Sillett, 1978 Tony Ford, 1978-79 Mike Bailey, 1979-82 Frank Lord, 1982-83 Tommy Hughes, 1983-87 John Newman, 1987-90 Ian Bowyer, 1990-91 Colin Addison, 1991-92 John Sillett, 1992-94 Greg Downs, John Layton 1994-95.

ADDITIONAL INFORMATION
PREVIOUS NAMES
None.

PREVIOUS LEAGUES
Southern League, Birmingham Lge, Birmingham Combination.

Club colours: White shirts with black trim, black shorts with white trim, black socks with white hooped tops.
Change colours: red/white/black/diamond pattern, white shorts, white socks.

Reserves League
Avon Insurance Football Combination. (Youth Team)

LONGEST LEAGUE RUNS

of undefeated matches:	14 (1972-73, 1984)	of league matches w/out a win:	13 (1977-78, 1978)
of undefeated home matches:	21 (1972-73)	of undefeated away matches:	6 (1972-73, 1984)
without home win:	11 (1981-82)	without an away win:	28 (1977-78)
of league wins:	5 (twice 1984)	of home wins:	12 (1973)
of league defeats:	8 (1986-87)	of away wins:	3 (1975-76, 1976-77, 1984-85, 1987-88)

THE MANAGER

GRAHAM TURNER . . . . appointed Summer 1995.

PREVIOUS CLUBS
As Manager . . . . Shrewsbury Town, Aston Villa, Wolverhampton Wanderers.
As Asst.Man/Coach . . . . None.
As a player . . . . Wrexham, Chester City, Shrewsbury Town.

HONOURS
As a Manager . . . . Shrewsbury Town: Division 3 Championship 1979.
. . . . Wolves: Division 4 Championship 1987-88. Sherpa Van Trophy 1987-88. Division 3 Champions 1988-89.
As a Player . . . . None.

HEREFORD UNITED

PLAYERS NAME Honours	Ht	Wt	Birthdate	Birthplace Transfers	Contract Date	Clubs	APPEARANCES				GOALS			
							League	L/Cup	FA Cup	Other	Lge	L/C	FAC	Oth
G O A L K E E P E R S														
Mackenzie Christopher	6.0	12.6	14/05/72	Northampton		Corby								
				Free	20/07/94	Hereford United	59+1	2	4	7	1			
				Loan	07/10/94	Rushden & Dia.								
D E F E N D E R S														
Fishlock Murray	5.7	11.0	23/09/73	Marlborough		Trowbridge								
				Free	30/09/94	Hereford United	38+3	3	3	6	3			
James Anthony C	6.3	13.8	27/06/67	Sheffield		Gainsborough T.								
				£20000	22/08/88	Lincoln City	24+5	2		0+1				
				£150000	23/08/89	Leicester City	79+28	6	2	3+1	11			
				Free	25/07/94	Hereford United	35	4	1	5	4			1
Preedy Phillip	5.10	10.8	20/11/75	Hereford	13/07/94	Hereford United	29+14	4+1	3	1+1	2			1
Smith Dean	6.1	12.0	19/03/71	West Brom	01/07/89	Walsall	137+5	10	4	10	2			
				£75000	17/06/94	Hereford United	74+4	6	6	10+1	11	1		4
Warner Robert M	5.9	11.07	20/04/77	Stratford	18/01/95	Hereford United	15+1							
M I D F I E L D														
Brough John	6.0	12.6	08/01/73	Ilkeston	09/07/91	Notts County								
				Free	06/07/92	Shrewsbury Town	7+9	1+1	1	1	1			
					01/08/93	Telford								
				Free	04/11/94	Hereford United	38+2	1	3	3+3	2		1	
Downing Keith	5.8	11.0	23/07/65	Oldbury		Mile Oak Rovers								
				Free	16/05/84	Notts County	23				1			
				Free	06/08/87	Wolves	169+22	9+3	7	15+3	8		2	1
				Free	22/07/93	Birmingham City	1	1						
				Free	09/08/94	Stoke City	16	2	1	3+2				
				Free	01/09/95	Hereford United	29		3	4				
Pitman Jamie	5.9	10.09	06/01/76	Trowbridge	08/07/94	Swindon Town	2+1							
				Free	16/02/96	Hereford United	12+1			2				
Stoker Gareth	5.9	10.10	22/02/73	Bishop Auckland		Leeds United								
				Free	13/09/91	Hull City	24+6	3	2+1	0+2	2			
					16/03/95	Hereford United	40+3	2	2+1	5+1	3		1	1
Wilkins Richard J Div.3'91.	6.0	11.6	28/05/65	Lambeth		Haverhill Rovers								
				Free	20/11/86	Colchester United	150+2	6	7+2	9+3	24		4	3
				£65000	25/07/90	Cambridge United	79+2	6	8+1	9	7			
				Free	20/07/94	Hereford United	76+1	6	6	8	5			2
F O R W A R D S														
White Stephen J Div.2'82.	5.10	11.4	02/01/59	Chipping Sodbury		Mangotsfield								
				Free	11/07/77	Bristol Rovers	46+4	2	3		20	1	3	
				£200000	24/12/79	Luton Town	63+9	3+1	2+1		25	1		
				£150000	30/07/82	Charlton Athletic	29	2			12			
				Loan	28/01/83	Lincoln City	2+1							
				Loan	24/02/83	Luton Town	4							
				£45000	26/08/83	Bristol Rovers	89+12	8	7+1	5+2	24	2	2	1
				Free	08/07/86	Swindon Town	200+44	21+8	9+2	22+6	83	11	2	15
				Free	26/08/94	Hereford United	70+6	5	6	9+2	43	2	4	3

EDGAR STREET
Hereford HR4 9JU
Tel: 01432 276 666

Capacity 8,843
Covered Standing 6,082
Seating 2,761

First game .... v Atherstone (2-3), 30.8.24.
First floodlit game .... v Merthyr (3-1), 14.3.53

ATTENDANCES
Highest .... 18,114 v Sheffield Wednesday, FA Cup 3rd Round, 4.1.1958.
Lowest .... 662 v Shrewsbury, AMC 1st Round, 22.12.1992.

OTHER GROUNDS .... None.

MATCHDAY TICKET PRICES

Merton Stand (A/B) . . . . £8/£9
*Juv/OAP . . . . £5/£6

Len Weston Stand . . . . £8/£9
*Juv/OAP . . . . £5/£6

Ground . . . . £6/£7
*Juv/OAP . . . . £3/£4

*Concessionary prices are only available to holders
of 'Bulls Membership' otherwise full prices apply.

Ticket Office Telephone no. . . . . . . 01432 276 666.

CLUBCALL
0898 55 58 08
Calls cost 39p per minute cheap rate and 49p per
minute at all other times.
Call costings correct at time of going to press.

HOW TO GET TO THE GROUND

From the North
Use A49 (sign posted Hereford) into Edgar Street for Hereford United FC.

From the East
Use A465 or A438 (sign posted Hereford) into town centre, then follow signs
Leominster A49 into Edgar Street for Hereford United FC.

From the South
Use A49 or A465 (sign posted Hereford) into town centre, then follow signs
Leominster A49 into Edgar Street for Hereford United FC.

From the West
Use A438 (sign posted Hereford) into town centre, then follow signs Leominster
A49 into Edgar Street for Hereford United FC.

Car Parking
Available near ground for 1,000 cars (approx)

Nearest Railway Station
Hereford (01432 266 534)

MATCHDAY PROGRAMME

Programme Editor . . . . Gary Watts.

Number of pages . . . . 48.

Price . . . . £1.50.

Subscriptions . . . . £36 (All home & away programmes)

Local Newspapers . . . . Hereford Times, Evening News.

Local Radio Stations . . . . . Radio Wyvern, BBC Hereford & Worcester.

HULL CITY
(The Tigers)
NATIONWIDE LEAGUE DIVISION 3
SPONSORED BY: I B C LTD

1996-97 - Back Row (L-R): Paul Wharton, Scott Maxfield, Simon Trevitt, Andy Mason, Steve Wilson, Roy Carroll, Jamie Marks, Duane Darby, Michael Quigley, Kenny Gilbert. **Middle Row:** Rod Arnold (Youth Coach), Antonio Doncel, Mark Greaves, Ian Wilkinson, Andy Brown, Neil Allison, Gavin Gordon, Ian Wright, Paul Fewings, Jeff Radcliffe (Physio), Billy Legg (U16 Manager). **Front Row:** Gregor Rioch, Adam Lowthorpe, Warren Joyce, Terry Dolan (Manager), Martin Fish (Chairman), Jeff Lee (Assistant Manager), Tony Brien, Neil Mann, Richard Peacock.

HULL CITY
FORMED IN 1904
TURNED PROFESSIONAL IN 1904
LTD COMPANY IN 1904

PRESIDENT: T C Waite, FIMI, MIRTE
CHAIRMAN: M W Fish
SECRETARY
M W Fish
COMMERCIAL MANAGER
Simon Cawkill

MANAGER: Terry Dolan
ASSISTANT MANAGER: Jeff Lee
RESERVE TEAM MANAGER

YOUTH TEAM MANAGER
Rod Arnold
PHYSIOTHERAPIST
Jeff Radcliffe MCSP, SRP

STATISTICIAN FOR THE DIRECTORY
Vacant

After finishing a promising eighth last season, Hull had a depressing year which culminated in relegation to the third division. Indeed, the drop looked a distinct possibility from late September when the Tigers had notched up only one win in their ten opening matches. Five consecutive defeats took them to an ominous 23rd in the table by mid October - a position which they were not to improve upon for the remainder of the campaign. There were two runs of three and one of four defeats, and the final five consecutive losses thoroughly confirmed City's fate and brought a very negative end to the year. Throughout the season, only Blackpool, York City, Burnley, Walsall and Wycombe went down against City in the league - a very poor record.

The cup competitions held little in the way of consolation. City lost in a penalty shoot-out against Wrexham in the first round of the FA Cup, and were put out of the Coca-Cola Cup in the second round by Premiership Coventry City. The second round was also the limit for Hull in the Auto Windscreens Shield where, after two good wins - away at Scarborough and at home to Preston North End - Blackpool dealt the fatal blow with a 2-1 victory at Boothferry Park.

Richard Peacock was top scorer with only seven league goals, closely followed by Gregory Abbott with six, while Fewings and Windass both managed to get on the score sheet in both the FA Cup and Auto Windscreens Shield.

It may be difficult for Hull to recover from such a dismal season, particularly with the financial worries that a falling attendance brings, but memories of the 1994-5 season should provide inspiration for the campaign to return to Division Two.

HULL CITY

League: 24th   FA Cup: 1st Rnd   Coca-Cola Cup: 2nd Rnd   Auto Windscreen Shield: 2nd Rnd

M	DATE	COMP	VEN	OPPONENTS	RESULT	HT	LP	GOAL SCORERS/GOAL TIMES	ATT.
1	A 12	EL	H	Swindon Town	L 0-1	0-0	1		6525
2	15	CC 1/1	H	Carlisle United	L 1-2	0-0		Windass 73	2779
3	19	EL	A	Rotherham United	D 1-1	0-0	3	Windass 85	(3754)
4	22	CC 1/2	A	Carlisle United	W 4-2	0-0		Allison, Fewings, Windass (2)	(4250)
5	26	EL	H	Blackpool	W 2-1	1-1	3	Brown 30, Mason 52	4755
6	29	EL	A	Brentford	L 0-1	0-0	5		(4535)
7	S 2	EL	A	Chesterfield	D 0-0	0-0	6		(4345)
8	9	EL	H	Oxford United	D 0-0	0-0	9		4608
9	12	EL	H	Swansea City	D 0-0	0-0	11		3519
10	16	EL	A	Burnley	L 1-2	0-1	14	Fewings 90	(10613)
11	20	CC 2/1	A	Coventry City	L 0-2	0-2			(8915)
12	23	EL	A	Carlisle United	L 0-2	0-2	16		(6007)
13	26	AWS 1/1	A	Scarborough	W 2-0	0-0		Lawford 46, Mann 47	(893)
14	30	EL	A	York City	L 0-3	0-2	20		5273
15	O 4	CC 2/2	H	Coventry City	L 0-1	0-1			6929
16	7	EL	H	Shrewsbury Town	L 2-3	0-1	20	Abbott 46, Windass 78(pen)	3266
17	14	EL	A	Bristol City	L 0-4	0-1	23		(5354)
18	17	AWS 1/1	H	Preston North End	W 1-0	0-0		Fewings 46	793
19	21	EL	H	Stockport County	D 1-1	0-1	23	Abbott 79	3496
20	28	EL	A	Wycombe Wanderers	D 2-2	1-1	22	Windass 41, Lee 57	(5021)
21	31	EL	A	Crewe Alexandra	L 0-1	0-1	22		(3609)
22	N 4	EL	H	Wrexham	D 1-1	0-0	23	Abbott 84	3515
23	11	FAC 1	H	Wrexham	D 0-0	0-0			3724
24	18	EL	A	Bradford City	D 1-1	1-0	23	Windass 37	(5830)
25	21	FAC 1R	A	Wrexham	D 0-0*	0-0		(Lost on penalties.)	(4522)
26	25	EL	A	Peterborough United	L 2-3	1-1	23	Davison 31, Peacock 58	3620
27	28	AWS 2	H	Blackpool	L 1-2	0-0		Windass 46	1422
28	D 9	EL	H	Carlisle United	L 2-5	2-3	24	Peacock 14, 16	3478
29	16	EL	A	York City	W 1-0	0-0	23	Fewings 84	(3593)
30	23	EL	A	Bournemouth	L 0-2	0-1	23		(3491)
31	J 6	EL	A	Bristol Rovers	L 1-2	0-2	24	Davison 63 (pen)	(4276)
32	13	EL	H	Rotherham United	L 1-4	0-1	24	Abbott 78	3678
33	20	EL	A	Swindon Town	L 0-3	0-0	24		(8118)
34	23	EL	H	Brighton & H.A.	D 0-0	0-0	24		2421
35	F 3	EL	A	Blackpool	D 1-1	0-1	24	Allison 62	(4713)
36	10	EL	H	Bristol Rovers	L 1-3	0-0	24	Davison 54	3311
37	17	EL	A	Swansea City	D 0-0	0-0	24		(1909)
38	24	EL	H	Burnley	W 3-0	1-0	24	Peacock 4, 83, Davison 69	4206
39	27	EL	A	Oxford United	L 0-2	0-1	24		(4650)
40	M 2	EL	A	Notts County	L 0-1	0-0	24		(4528)
41	5	EL	H	Brentford	L 0-1	0-0	24		2284
42	9	EL	H	Bournemouth	D 1-1	1-1	24	Graham 33	2853
43	12	EL	H	Chesterfield	D 0-0	0-0	24		2832
44	16	EL	A	Brighton & H.A.	L 0-4	0-2	24		(4910)
45	23	EL	H	Walsall	W 1-0	0-0	24	Abbott 79	3060
46	26	EL	H	Notts County	D 0-0	0-0	24		2589
47	30	EL	A	Shrewsbury Town	D 1-1	1-0	24	Peacock 13	(2347)
48	A 2	EL	H	Bristol City	L 2-3	0-0	24	Gordon 71, Mann 82	2641
49	6	EL	H	Wycombe Wanderers	W 4-2	3-0	24	Wilkinson 6, Peacock 16, Quigley 35, Abbott 53	3065
50	8	EL	A	Stockport County	D 0-0	0-0	24		(5043)
51	13	EL	H	Crewe Alexandra	L 1-2	0-0	24	Gordon 83	3497
52	20	EL	A	Wrexham	L 0-5	0-2	24		(3400)
53	23	EL	A	Walsall	L 0-3	0-1	24		(2752)
54	27	EL	A	Peterborough United	L 1-3	0-1	24	Allison 87	(6649)
55	M 4	EL	H	Bradford City	L 2-3	2-2	24	Gordon 10, Darby 17	8965

Best Home League Attendance: 8965 v Bradford City   **Smallest: 2284 v Brentford**   **Average: 3802**

Goal Scorers:

EL(36): Peacock(7),Abbott(6),Windass(4),Davison(4),Gordon(3),Fewings(2),Allison(2),Wilkinson(1),Mann(1),Lee(1),Mason(1),Darby(1),Brown(1),Quigley(1),Graham(1)

CC(5): Windass(3),Fewings(1),Allison(1)

FAC(0):

AWS(4): Mann(1),Windass(1),Lawford(1),Fewings(1)

(M) Abbott	(D) Allison	(F) Brown	(G) Carroll	(D) Dakin	(F) Darby	(F) Davison	(D) Dewhurst	(G) Fettis	(F) Fewings	(M) Gilbert	(F) Gordon	(D) Graham	(D) Hobson	(M) Humphries	(D) Lawford	(M) Lee	(F) Lowthorpe	(M) Mann	(D) Marks	(F) Mason	(M) Peacock	(M) Quigley	(D) Trevitt	(M) Wharton	(D) Wilkinson	(M) Williams	(G) Wilson	(M) Windass	Opponent	#
	X2	X1					X	S					X	X		X	X			S1	X	X					X	X2	E.Lomas	1
	X1						X		S1				X	X	S3	X3	X	X			S2	X2	X2				X	X	W.C.Burns	2
	X	X					X		S2				X	X	S1	X				S	X2	X1					X	X	A.Butler	3
	X						X	S	X				X	X		X	X	S		X	S1	X					X	X1	E.K.Wolstenholme	4
	X	X1					X	S	X				X	X	S1	X	S	X	X	X							X		I.G.Cruikshanks	5
	X	X2					X		S3		X1		X	X	S2	X		X		X	S1						X		I.S.Hemley	6
	X	X1											X	X	X2	X	S	X		X	S1	S2				X	X	X	G.Cain	7
	X	X1					X	S					X	X		X		X2	X2	X	S1	X				X	X	X	M.Riley	8
	X1						X	S					X	X	S	X	S1	X		X	X					X	X	X	G.B.Frankland	9
	X						X		S2				X		X	S1	X1	S	X		X	X2				X	X	X	J.Rushton	10
X							X	S3	X3		S1		S2	X2		X		X		X1						X	X	X	R.Poulain	11
X	S						X		X		X	X1	X	X2	X	S1			S2				X	X	X	J.Kirkby	12
X	X		S				X					S2	X		X	X	X1	S1				X	X	X2		13
X3	X1						X	S3	X				X		S2	X	X2			S1					X	X	X	T.Heilbron	14
X		X2						X3		S2	X	X	X	X	S3	S1		X1	X	X	S.J.Lodge	15
X	S2	X					X	X	S3	X	X2	X	X	X1	X3	S1	X	X	K.J.Breen	16
X	X2						S2	X1	X	X	X	S1	S3	X	X3	X	X	X	P.Rejer	17
X	X	X1	S				S1	X	X	X	X	X	X	S	X	X	W.Burns	18
X	X		S				X	X	X	X1	X	S1	X	S2	X	X2	J.Brandwood	19
X	X	S					X	X	S	X	S	X	X	X	X	X	J.Lloyd	20
X	X		S				X	X	S1	X	X1	X	X	X	S	X	D.Allison	21
X	X	X3	S1		X1	X	S3	X	X	S2	X2	X	X	T.Lunt	22
X	S2			X		X2	X	X	X	X	S	X	X	X	X1	K.Breen	23
X		S		X		S2	X	X	X	X	S1	X2	X	X	X1	M.Fletcher	24
X	X	S1		X		X	X1	X	S2	X	X2	X	X	M.J.Brandwood	25
X2	X	X	X			X	X	X	S	S2	S1	X	X1	X	A.Butler	26
X	X	X1	X		X	X	X2	S	S2	S1	X	X	X	T.Leake	27
X	X3	S3	X		X	X2	X	S1	X	X	X1	X	E.Wolstenholme	28
X1	X		S		S	X1	S	X	X	S1	S2	X	X	X	W.Burns	29
X		S1	X	X1	S	X	X2	X	S2	X	X	X	A.Wiley	30
X	S1	S	X	X	X	X	X	S	X	X	X1	X	P.Taylor	31
X	X	S1	X	S3	S2	X3	X1	X	X2	X	X	X	T.Heilbron	32
X	X	X	X	X1	X	X	X2	S2	S1	X	S	G.Cain	33
X	X	X	X1	X	X	X	S1	X2	X	S2	S	X	R.Pearson	34
X	X	X	X	S	X	S	X	X	X	X	S	E.Lomas	35
X1	X	X	X	S1	X	X2	X	S2	X	X	S	I.Cruikshanks	36
X	X	X1	X	S1	X	S	S	X	X	X	X	K.J.Breen	37
X	X	S	X	S2	X	S1	X1	X2	X	X	U.Rennie	38
X1	X	S1	S2	X	X	S3	X3	X2	X	X2	X	R.Gifford	39
X1	X	X	S	X	S2	X	X	X2	X	X	S1	X	A.Leak	40
X2	X	X	S2	S	X	X	X1	X	S1	X	E.Wolstenholme	41
X2	X	X	S2	X	X	S1	X3	X1	X	S3	X	X	P.R.Richards	42
X	X	X	S	X	X	X	X1	X	S	X	X	X	A.Barry	43
X	X	X1	X	S1	X	X	X	X	X	S	A.G.Wiley	44
X	X	X	X1	S1	X	X	S	X	X	X	X	S	X	D.Laws	45
X	X	X	X2	S2	X	X	S	X	X	S1	X	X1	X	X	P.Richards	46
X1	X	X	X3	S2	X	X	X	X2	X	X	X	M.C.Bailey	47
X	X	X	S1	X	X2	S2	X	X	X	X1	X	X	S	R.Poulain	48
X2	X	X	X	S	X	X	X	X1	S2	X	X	S.Mathieson	49
X	X	X	X	S	X	X	X	X1	X	S	X	X	G.Singh	50
X	X	X	X	S2	X2	X	X	X	S	X1	X1	S1	X	R.Furnandiz	51
X	X	X	X	S2	X1	X	X	X2	X	X3	X	X	M.J.Brandwood	52
X	X	X	X	X	X	X	X	X	S	M.Lloyd	53
X	X	X	X1	X	X	X	S1	X	S	G.Barber	54
X	X	X	S2	X	X1	X	X2	X	X	X	S	S1	U.Rennie	55

31	34	21	23	2	8	11	16	4	16	6	3	24	28	9	21	25	15	32	4	10	39	9	25	7	7	33	19	16	EL Appearances	
0	1	1	0	4	0	0	0	2	9	7	10	0	1	3	10	3	4	4	1	10	6	4	0	2	1	1	0	0	EL Sub Appearances	
2	1	2	0	0	0	3	0+1	3+1			0	0	2	3+1	2	2+1	2	3		4	0	1+3	2+1	1	0	0	0	2	4	4	CC Appearances	
1	1	1+1	0	0+1	0	1	1	1	0+1		0+1	0	1+1	0	0+1	2	2	2		0	2	0	1+1	1+1	0	1	2	1	FAC Appearances	
2	3	2	0	1	0	1	1	1	1	0+1	0	0+1	2	1	3	2	1	2+1		1+1	1+1	1	0	1	0	0	2	3	AWS Appearances	

Also Played: (M) Capuano S(53,54). (D) Fiddler S2(28). (M) Hennessy S(53). (D) Maxfield S1(52), X(53,54,55). (M) Pridmore X1(23). (M) Watson X(18,19,20,21).

CLUB RECORDS

BIGGEST VICTORIES
League: 10-0 v Halifax Town, Division 3(N), 26.12.1930.
11-1 v Carlisle United, Division 3(N), 14.1.1939.
F.A. Cup: 8-2 v Stalybridge Celtic, 1st Round, 26.11.1932.

BIGGEST DEFEATS
League: 0-8 v Wolverhampton Wndrs, Division 2, 4.11.1911.
F.A. Cup: 0-5 v Fulham, 3rd Round, 9.1.1960.
League Cup: 0-5 v Lincoln City, 1st round, 9.8.1980.
0-5 v Manchester United, 2nd Round 1st leg, 23.9.1987.

MOST POINTS
3 points a win: 90, Division 4, 1982-83.
2 points a win: 69, Division 3, 1965-66.

RECORD TRANSFER FEE RECEIVED
£750,000 from Middlesbrough for Andy Payton, November 1991.
(Installments could take fee to £1,000,000)

RECORD TRANSFER FEE PAID
£200,000 to Leeds United for Peter Swan, March 1989.

BEST PERFORMANCES
League: 3rd Division 2, 1909-10.
F.A. Cup: Semi-Finalists 1929-30.
League Cup: 4th Round 1973-74, 1975-76, 1977-78.

HONOURS
Champions of Division 3(N) 1932-33, 1948-49.
Champions of Division 3 1965-66.

LEAGUE CAREER
Elected to Div 2 1905, Div 3(N) 1930-31, Div 2 1933-34, Div 3(N) 1936-37, Div 2 1948-49, Div 3(N) 1956-57, Transferred to Div 3 1958-59, Div 2 1959-60, Div 3 1960-61, Div 2 1966-67, Div 3 1978-79, Div 4 1981-82, Div 3 1983-84, Div 2 1985-86, Div 3 (now Div 2) 1990-91.

INDIVIDUAL CLUB RECORDS

MOST GOALS IN A SEASON
Bill McNaughton: 42 goals in 1932-33 (League 39, FA Cup 3).

MOST GOALS IN A MATCH
5. Ken McDonald v Bristol City, 5-1, Division 2, 17.11.1928.
5. Slim Raleigh v Halifax Town, 10-0, Division 3(N), 26.12.1930.

OLDEST PLAYER
Eddie Burbanks, 40 years 15 days, 16.4.1953.

YOUNGEST PLAYER
Matthew Edeson, 16 years 63 days v Fulham, 10.10.1992.

MOST CAPPED PLAYER
Terry Neill (Northern Ireland) 15.

PREVIOUS MANAGERS

1905-13 Ambrose Langley, 1913-14 Harry Chapman, 1914-16 Fred G Stringer, 1916-21 David M Menzies, 1921-23 P Lewis, 1923-31 Bill McCracken, 1931-34 Hayden Green, 1934-36 Jack Hill, 1936 David Menzies, 1936-46 Ernie Blackburn, 1946-48 Major Buckley, 1948-51 Raich Carter, 1952-55 Bob Jackson, 1955-61 Bob Brocklebank, 1961-70 Cliff Britton, 1970-74 Terry Neill, 1974-77 John Kaye, 1977-78 Bobby Collins, 1978-79 Ken Houghton, 1980-82 Mike Smith, 1982-84 Colin Appleton, 1984-88 Brian Horton, 1988-90 Eddie Gray, 1990 Colin Appleton, 1990-91 Stan Ternant.

ADDITIONAL INFORMATION
PREVIOUS NAMES
None.

PREVIOUS LEAGUES
None.

Club colours: Amber shirts, black shorts, amber socks.
Change colours: Maroon shirts, maroon shorts, maroon socks.

Reserves League: Pontins Central League Division 2.

LONGEST LEAGUE RUNS

of undefeated matches:	15 (1964-65, 1983)	of league matches w/out a win:	27 (1990)
of undefeated home matches:	25 (1932-33, 1965-66)	of undefeated away matches:	13 (1948-49)
without home win:	15 (1990)	without an away win:	35 (1979-81)
of league wins:	10 (1948, 1966)	of home wins:	19 (1965-66)
of league defeats:	8 (1934)	of away wins:	5 (Several occasions)

THE MANAGER

TERRY DOLAN. . . . . appointed April 1991.

PREVIOUS CLUBS
As Manager. . . . . Bradford City, Rochdale.
As Asst.Man/Coach . . . . Bradford City.
As a player. . . . . Bradford P.A., Huddersfield Town, Bradford City, Rochdale.

HONOURS
As a Manager . . . . Bradford City: Promotion to Division 2, 1988.
As a Player . . . . None.

HULL CITY

PLAYERS NAME Honours	Ht	Wt	Birthdate	Birthplace Transfers	Contract Date	Clubs	League	L/Cup	FA Cup	Other	Lge	L/C	FAC	Oth
G O A L K E E P E R S														
Carroll Roy						Hull City	23							
Wilson Stephen L	5.10	10.7	24/04/74	Hull	13/07/92	Hull City	79	7	5	7				
D E F E N D E R S														
Allison Neil J	6.2	11.10	20/10/73	Hull	13/07/92	Hull City	85+10	7	3	6+1	3	1		
Dewhurst Robert M	6.3	12.0	10/09/71	Keighley	15/10/90	Blackburn Rovers	13	2		1				
				Loan	20/12/91	Darlington	11		1	1				
				Loan	02/10/92	Huddersfield Town	7							
				Free	05/11/93	Hull City	84	5	5	4	10			
Doncel Antonio						Deportivo La Coruna								
					07/08/96	Hull City								
Marks Jamie	5.9	10.13	18/03/77	Belfast	01/08/94	Leeds United								
				Free	13/02/96	Hull City	4+1							
Maxfield Scott	5.8	10.7	13/07/76	Doncaster	08/07/94	Doncaster Rovers	32+6		0+1	1	1			
					27/03/96	Hull City	3+1							
Trevitt Simon	5.11	11.10	20/12/67	Dewsbury	16/06/86	Huddersfield Town	216+13	23	13	19+1	3	1		
				Free	21/12/95	Hull City	25			1				
Wilkinson Ian	6.2	13.0	19/09/77			Hull City	7+1				1			
M I D F I E L D														
Gilbert Kenny					12/01/96	Hull City	6+7							
Mann Neil	5.10	12.0	19/11/72	Nottingham		Notts County								
				Free	06/09/90	Grimsby Town								
					01/08/91	Spalding United								
					01/08/92	Grantham								
				Free	30/07/93	Hull City	63+9	5+2	3	4+2	3			1
Peacock Richard J	5.11	11.0	29/10/72	Sheffield	14/10/93	Hull City	71+22	4+1	3	3+1	13	1		
Pridmore Lee						Hull City			1					
Quigley Michael	5.7	9.13	02/10/70	Manchester	01/07/89	Manchester United	3+9				1			
					05/07/95	Hull City	9+4	1			1			
Wharton Paul	5.4	9.9	26/06/77	Newcastle	01/08/94	Leeds United								
				Free	13/02/96	Hull City	7+2							
F O R W A R D S														
Brown Andrew S	6.3	13.0	11/10/76	Edburgh	01/08/94	Leeds United (T)								
					13/05/96	Hull City								
Darby Duane	5.11	11.2	17/10/73	Birmingham	03/07/92	Torquay United	60+48	4+3	1+4	5+3	26	1		2
					27/03/96	Hull City	8				1			
Fewings Paul	5.11	11.7	18/02/78	Hull		Hull City	16+11	3+1	2	0+1	2	1		1
Lowthorpe Adam	5.7	10.06	07/08/75	Hull	02/07/93	Hull City	36+5	4	2	1				
Mason Andrew	5.11	11.11	22/11/74	Bolton	21/05/93	Bolton Wanderers								
					01/06/95	Hull City	10+10	1+3		1+1	1			
ADDITIONAL CONTRACT PLAYERS														
Greaves Mark					07/06/96	Hull City								

BOOTHFERRY PARK
Boothferry Road, Hull, North Humberside HU4 6EU
Tel: 01482 51119

Capacity..12,996
Covered Standing...4,851
Seating..5,495

First game..31st August 1946.
First floodlit game..19th January 1953.

ATTENDANCES
Highest.................................55,019 v Manchester United, FA Cup 6th Round, 26.2.1949.
Lowest..890 v Doncaster Rovers. AMC, 27.9.1994.

OTHER GROUNDS...The Boulevard, Dairycoates, Anlaby Road.

MATCHDAY TICKET PRICES

Best Stand £10
Juv/OAP £5

Family Stand £8
Juv/OAP £4

South Stand. £8
Juv/OAP £4

Ground £7
Juv/OAP £3

Ticket office Telephone no. 01482 351119

CLUBCALL
0898 88 86 88

Calls cost 39p per minute cheap rate and 49p per
minute at all other times.
Call costings correct at time of going to press.

HOW TO GET TO THE GROUND

From the North
Use A1 or A19 then A1079, sign posted Hull, into town centre. Then follow signs
to Leeds (A63) into Anlaby Road. At roundabout take first exit into Boothferry
Road for Hull City AFC.

From the West
Use motorway (M62) then A63, sign posted Hull, into Boothferry Road for Hull
City AFC.

From the South
Use motorway (M1), M18 then M62 and A63, sign posted Hull, into Boothferry
Road for Hull City AFC.

Car Parking
Limited parking in front of ground.

Nearest Railway Station
Hull Paragon (01482 260 33) or Boothferry Halt by the ground.

MATCHDAY PROGRAMME

Programme Editor . . . . Rob Smith.

Number of pages . . . . 32.

Price . . . . £1.50.

Subscriptions . . . . £45.

Local Newspapers . . . . Hull Daily Mail.

Local Radio Stations . BBC Radio Humberside (95.5FM, MW1485KHZ)
. . . . Viking Radio (96.6 FM)

LEYTON ORIENT
(The O's)
NATIONWIDE LEAGUE DIVISION 3
SPONSORED BY: H.E.A.T.

Back Row (L-R): Danny Chapman, Ian Hendon, Lee Shearer, Peter Caldwell, Colin West, Mark Warren, Kevin Austin.
Middle Row: Tommy Cunningham (Director of Coaching), Roger Stanislaus, Barry Lakin, Glen Wilkie, Darren Purse, Paul Hague, Alex Inglethorpe, Joe Baker, Andy Taylor (Physio).
Front Row: Tony Flynn (Kit Manager/Asst. Physio), Lee Williams, Tony Kelly, Glenn Cockerill, Pat Holland (Manager), Barry Hearn (Chairman), Gary Bellamy, Shaun Brooks, Andy Gray, Steve Shorey (Youth Dev. Officer).

LEYTON ORIENT
FORMED IN 1881
TURNED PROFESSIONAL IN 1903
LTD COMPANY IN 1906

CHAIRMAN: Barry Hearn
VICE-CHAIRMAN
D L Weinrabe
CHIEF EXECUTIVE: Bernard Goodall
DIRECTORS
S J Dawson, D R Dodd, R P Cousens,
J Goldsmith (Friba), H Linney, V Marsh,
T.Wood

SECRETARY
David Burton (0181 539 2223)
COMMERCIAL MANAGER
F Woolf

MANAGER: Pat Holland
RESERVE TEAM COACH
Tommy Cunningham
DIRECTOR OF COACHING: Paul Brush
PHYSIOTHERAPIST
Andy Taylor

STATISTICIAN FOR THE DIRECTORY
Don Hales

Disappointing is probably the word that best describes Leyton Orients season. With a new backbone to the club, under the direction of Sporting Promoter Barry Hearn, the club started the 1995-96 season on a high, both on and off the field.

The sparkle however, was to fade as initial promise, culminating in 3rd position, faltered and the 'O's' started to slip down the table.

There was little to cheer about in Cup competitions either as Leyton Orient went out in the First Round of each. In the Coca-Cola Cup they lost out to Wycombe Wanderers (2-3), whilst in the F.A. Cup struggling Torquay United beat them 0-1 down at Plainmoor. A draw against Swansea City (0-0), followed by a defeat at home to Shrewsbury Town (1-3) saw their Auto Windscreen Shield run end.

The New Year only brought five victories which in turn saw the club sink to 21st position, the position they were to finish the season in.

The 1996/97 season could be their year though. With matters off the pitch now in order time can be spent on getting it right on the pitch, and when they do the 'O's' will be pushing for the play-offs.

LEYTON ORIENT

League: 21st   FA Cup: 1st Rnd   Coca-Cola Cup: 1st Rnd   Auto Windscreen Shield: 1st Rnd

M	DATE	COMP	VEN	OPPONENTS	RESULT	HT	LP	GOAL SCORERS/GOAL TIMES	ATT.
1	A 12	EL	H	Torquay United	W 1-0	0-0	9	Brooks 70	8221
2	15	CC 1/1	A	**Wycombe Wanderers**	L 0-3	0-2			(3310)
3	19	EL	A	Mansfield Town	D 0-0	0-0	10		(2565)
4	22	CC 1/2	H	**Wycombe Wanderers**	W 2-0	1-0		**Austin 23, West 52(pen)**	2478
5	26	EL	H	Darlington	D 1-1	0-0	8	Inglethorpe 49	4034
6	30	EL	A	Scarborough	L 1-2	1-1	14	Cockerill 32	(1797)
7	S 2	EL	H	Fulham	W 1-0	0-0	10	Inglethorpe 77	7248
8	9	EL	A	Plymouth Argyle	D 1-1	0-1	11	Watson 81	(6292)
9	12	EL	A	Northampton Town	W 2-1	0-1	4	Hendon 48, Inglethorpe 90	(5072)
10	16	EL	H	Hartlepool United	W 4-1	2-0	3	Inglethorpe 7, Bellamy 9, West 68, 84	4519
11	23	EL	A	Exeter City	D 2-2	1-2	5	Inglethorpe 33, 66	(5507)
12	30	EL	H	Doncaster Rovers	W 3-1	2-0	3	West 13, Kelly 15, Chapman 48	5524
13	O 7	EL	A	Bury	L 1-2	1-2	6	West 26	(3025)
14	14	EL	H	Chester City	L 0-2	0-2	9		6037
15	17	AWS 1/1	A	**Swansea City**	D 0-0	0-0			(796)
16	21	EL	A	Scunthorpe United	L 0-2	0-1	10		(2315)
17	28	EL	H	Wigan Athletic	D 1-1	1-1	10	Brooks 12	4562
18	31	EL	H	Hereford United	L 0-1	0-0	12		3567
19	N 4	EL	A	Preston North End	L 0-4	0-0	13		(9823)
20	7	AWS 1/2	H	**Shrewsbury Town**	L 1-3	0-0		**Hendon 46**	1437
21	11	FAC 1	A	**Torquay United**	L 0-1	0-0			(2434)
22	18	EL	A	Cambridge United	W 3-1	1-1	10	West 2, Inglethorpe 47, West 51	4142
23	25	EL	A	Barnet	L 0-3	0-1	12		(2850)
24	D 9	EL	H	Exeter City	L 0-3	0-2	14		3471
25	16	EL	A	Doncaster Rovers	L 1-4	1-2	16	Chapman 13	(1633)
26	22	EL	H	Rochdale	W 2-0	1-0	13	West 3, 53	5399
27	26	EL	A	Colchester United	D 0-0	0-0	13		(4965)
28	J 1	EL	H	Gillingham	L 0-1	0-1	13		7098
29	6	EL	A	Cardiff City	D 0-0	0-0	15		(2736)
30	13	EL	H	Mansfield Town	W 1-0	0-0	13	Kelly 70	3461
31	16	EL	H	Lincoln City	L 0-1	0-0	13		(1841)
32	20	EL	A	Torquay United	L 1-2	1-0	14	Hendon 10	(2212)
33	F 3	EL	A	Darlington	L 0-2	0-0	19		(1880)
34	10	EL	H	Cardiff City	W 4-1	1-1	15	West 26, 49, 56(pen) (3), Inglethorpe 89	3564
35	17	EL	H	Northampton Town	W 2-0	1-0	13	West 23, Arnott 77	4444
36	24	EL	A	Hartlepool United	L 1-4	0-2	14	Kelly 90	(1915)
37	27	EL	H	Plymouth Argyle	L 0-1	0-1	16		3394
38	M 2	EL	H	Colchester United	L 0-1	0-1	18		4049
39	9	EL	A	Rochdale	L 0-1	0-1	21		(1934)
40	16	EL	H	Lincoln City	W 2-0	0-0	16	Austin 64, Inglethorpe 89	3129
41	19	EL	H	Scarborough	W 1-0	0-0	16	Warren 90	2121
42	23	EL	A	Gillingham	D 1-1	0-0	15	Arnott 87	(8071)
43	26	EL	A	Fulham	L 1-2	0-0	15	Shearer 86	(3636)
44	30	EL	H	Bury	L 0-2	0-1	19		3421
45	A 2	EL	A	Chester City	D 1-1	1-1	20	West 29	(2097)
46	6	EL	A	Wigan Athletic	L 0-1	0-0	20		(3081)
47	8	EL	H	Scunthorpe United	D 0-0	0-0	20		2814
48	13	EL	A	Hereford United	L 2-3	0-1	20	West 53, 90	(3459)
49	20	EL	H	Preston North End	L 0-2	0-1	21		5170
50	27	EL	H	Barnet	D 3-3	1-2	21	Hanson 43, Arnott 61, West 87	4006
51	M 4	EL	A	Cambridge United	L 0-2	0-1	21		(3858)

Best Home League Attendance: 8221 v Torquay United   **Smallest: 2121 v Scarborough**   **Average: 4495**

Goal Scorers:
EL(44):   West(16),Inglethorpe(9),Arnott(3),Kelly(3),Chapman(2),Brooks(2),Hendon(2),Shearer(1),Bellamy(1),Cockerill(1),Austin(1),Warren(1),Watson(1),Hanson(1)
CC(2):   Austin(1),West(1)
FAC(0):
AWS(1):   Hendon(1)

608

1995-96

(F) Arnott	(D) Austin	(M) Ayorinde	(M) Baker	(D) Bellamy	(F) Berry	(M) Brooks	(G) Caldwell	(M) Chapman	(M) Cockerill	(M) Currie	(M) Everitt	(D) Fearon	(D) Gray	(D) Hague	(M) Hanson	(D) Hendon	(F) Inglethorpe	(F) Kelly.R (L)	(F) Kelly.T	(F) Lakin	(D) McCarthy	(D) Purse	(D) Shearer	(D) Stanislaus	(F) Warren	(M) Watson	(F) West	(M) Williams		
	X1		S1	X		X	X	X	X			S	X			X	X						S	X	X				F.G.Stretton	1
	X		S1	X		X	X	X	X			S				X	X						X	X1	X				G.Pooley	2
	X					X	X	X	X			S				X	X		X		X		S		X		X		R.Furnandiz	3
	X		S2			X2	X	X	X							X	X		X		X		S1		X1		X	S	I.Hemley	4
	X		S1	X		X	X	X	X			S				X	X1		X		X		S				X		M.Fletcher	5
	X		S1	X		X	X	X1	X			S					X		X		X		X				X		D.Allison	6
	S		S	X		X	X	X	X			S				X	X		X		X			X			X		K.Leach	7
	S1			X		X	X	X	X							X1	X2		X		X			X		S2	X		C.Wilkes	8
	S2		S1	X		X	X	X	X2							X	X		X1		X			X			X		A.N.Butler	9
	S			X		X	X	X	X			S				X	X		X		X			X		S	X		D.Orr	10
	S1			X		X2	X	X	X							X	X		X1		X			X		S	X		M.Pierce	11
	S2			X		X2	X	X	X							X	X		X1		X			X	S1	S	X		J.Rushton	12
	X1			X			X	X				S			S2	X	X		X2		X	S1		X	X		X		U.D.Rennie	13
	S2		S1	X2			X	X								X	X		X	X	X	S		X	X		X1		A.Wiley	14
	S		S1	X			X	X							X	X	X		X	X	X1	S		X	X					15
	X		S1	X			X	X							X	X	X1		X		X	S		X	X				E.Lomas	16
	S2			X1		X	X	X2	X						S	X	X		X		X			X	S1		X		G.Barber	17
	S			S		X	X	X	X						X	X	X		X		X	S		X	X				M.Peirce	18
	X		X1	S		X	X	X	X						X2	X			X		X	X		S1	S2				G.Cain	19
	X		S2	X		X2		X	X			X			X1	X			X		X	S1		S				X		20
	X		S1	X		X1	S	X	X			X				X			X					X			X	X	D.Orr	21
	X			X		X1			X	X		X			S	X	X2		X		S1			X			X	S2	G.Pooley	22
	X			X		X1			X	X		X			S	X	X			X2	S2			X			X	S1	T.West	23
	X					S1			X	X		X	S2			X	X			X1	S	X		X			X	X2	F.Stretton	24
	X1			X		S1		X	X	X		X				X	X				X	S		X			X		A.Butler	25
				X		S		X	X	X		X			S	X	X		X		X		S	X			X		P.Rejer	26
	X1			X		X2			X			X	S1		S2		X		X		X	X	S	X			X		A.T.D'Urso	27
				X		X			X	X		X	S		S1		X1		X		X	X	S	X			X		I.Hemley	28
	S1		S	X		X			X	X		X	X1		X				X		X	X		X					M.Bailey	29
	X			X3		S1		X	X	X2		X	S2		X1	X			X		X	S3					X		B.Knight	30
	X		S1	X		X		X	X1	S2		X	X2			X			X		X	S					X		M.Fletcher	31
	X		S2	X		X		X		X1		X	S1			X	X		X2		X	X	S						A.Wiley	32
X	S1		S2	X		X	X		X							X	X		X2		X	X1					X		M.Riley	33
X	X		S	X		X			X1			X				X	X		X		X	S1					X	S	R.Furnandiz	34
X	X		S	X				X	X			X				X	X		X		X	S					X	S	B.Harris	35
X	X			X		S1		X	X			X				X	X1		X		X						X	S	T.Leake	36
X	X		S2	X		S1		X2	X			X				X	X1		X		X						X	S	G.Pooley	37
X	X			X		X		X	X			X				X			X1		X		S		S1		X	S	S.Baines	38
X	X			X		X1	X	X	X2		S								X		S1	X	S2		X		X		J.Rushton	39
X	X		S1	X		S2	X	X							X		X		X1		X	X2	S		X				S.Bennett	40
X	X		S	X		S1	X	X							S2	X	X2		X1		X				X		X		T.Leake	41
X3	X				S1	X	X	X2	X							X			S2	S3	X		X		X1		X		D.Orr	42
X	X				S1	X1	X	X	X							X			S2	S	X		X		X2		X		B.Knight	43
X	X		S1		X2	X1	X	X	X							X		S2			X		X		S		X		A.Butler	44
X	X		S1			X	X	X	X							X		X		S	X		S		X1		X		P.Rejer	45
X	X		S2		S1	X2	X	X	X									X		X1	X		S		X		X		U.Rennie	46
X	X1		X		X	X	X	X								X		X			X		S		S1		X		A.Wiley	47
X	X		S1		X	X	X	X				S								X1	X	S	X		X		X		J.Lloyd	48
X	X1		S1		X	X	X	X2	X							X		X		S2	X				S		X		F.Stretton	49
X	X		X			X		X	X2			X			X3	X				S2	X1		S3		S1		X		P.Taylor	50
X	S1	X	X			X2		X	X			X			S	X		X1					S2		X		X		T.Leake	51
19	32	1	4	32	4	34	28	38	38	9	0	18	3	0	7	38	30	5	32	5	40	9	5	20	15	0	39	1	EL Appearances	
0	9	0	16	0	3	7	0	0	0	1	0	0	4	0	4	0	0	1	2	3	3	3	3	1	6	1	0	2	EL Sub Appearances	
0	2	0	0+2	1	0	2	2	2	2	0	0	0	0	0	0	2	2	0	1	0	1	0	1	1	2	0	1	0	CC Appearances	
0	1	0	0+1	1	0	1	0	1	1	0	0	1	0	0	0	1	0	0	1	0	0	0	0	1	0	0	1	1	FAC Appearances	
0	1	0	0+2	2	0	1	1	2	1	0	0	1	0	0	2	2	1	0	2	1	2	0+1	0	1	1	0	0	1	AWS Appearances	

lso Played: (M) Jones S(47).

CLUB RECORDS

BIGGEST VICTORIES
League: 9-2 v Aldershot, Division 3(S), 10.2.1934.
8-0 v Crystal Palace, Division 3, 12.11.1955.
8-0 v Rochdale, Division 4, 20.10.1987.
8-0 v Colchester United, Division 4, 15.10.1988.
League Cup: 9-2 v Chester, 3rd Round, 15.10.1962.

BIGGEST DEFEATS
League: 1-7 v Torquay United (A) Division 3(S), 16.4.1949.
1-7 v Stoke City (a), Division 2, 7.9.1956, also 0-6 on seven occasions.
F.A. Cup: 0-8 v Aston Villa, 4th Round, 30.1.1929.

MOST POINTS
3 points a win: 75, Division 4, 1988-89.
2 points a win: 66, Division 3, 1955-56.

MOST GOALS SCORED
106, Division 3(S), 1955-56.

RECORD TRANSFER FEE RECEIVED
£600,000 from Notts County for John Chiedozie, August 1981.

RECORD TRANSFER FEE PAID
£175,000 to Wigan Athletic for Paul Beesley, October 1989.

BEST PERFORMANCES
League: 22nd Division 1, 1962-63.
F.A. Cup: Semi-final 1977-78.
League Cup: 5th Round 1963.

HONOURS
Champions of Division 3(S), 1955-56.
Champions of Division 3, 1969-70.

LEAGUE CAREER
Elected to Div 2 1905, Div 3(S) 1928-29, Div 2 1955-56, Div 1961-62, Div 2 1962-63, Div 3 1965-66, Div 2 1969-70, Div 3 1981-82, Div 4 1984-85, Div 3 (now Div 2) 1988-89.

INDIVIDUAL CLUB RECORDS

MOST GOALS IN A SEASON
Tom Johnston: 36 goals in 1957-58 (League 35, FA Cup 1).

MOST GOALS IN A MATCH
5. R Heckman v Lovells Athletic (h), 7-1, 1st Round, 19.8.1955.

OLDEST PLAYER
John Rutherford, 42 years v Portsmouth (h) Division 2, 2.4.1927.

YOUNGEST PLAYER
Chris Bart-Williams, 16 years 232 days v Tranmere Rovers (h), Division 3, 2.2.1991.

MOST CAPPED PLAYER
John Chiedozie (Nigeria) 8.
J Townrow & O Williams (England) 2.

PREVIOUS MANAGERS

S Ormerod 1905-07; W Holmes 1907-22; P Proudfoot 1923-28; A Grimsdell 1929-30; P Proudfoot 1930-31; J Seed 1931-33; D Pratt 1933-35; P Proudfoot 1935-39; W Wright 1939-40; W Hall 1945; W Wright 1945-46; C Hewitt 1946-48; N McBain 1948-49; A Stock 1949-56; L Gore (caretaker) 1956; A Stock 1956-57; L Gore (caretaker)1957-58; A Stock 1958-59; J Carey 1961-63; L Gore (caretaker) 1963; B Fenton 1963-64; L Gore (caretaker) 1964-65; D Sexton 1965; L Gore (caretaker) 1965-66; R Graham 1966-68; J Bloomfield 1968-71; G Petchey 1971; J Bloomfield 1971-81; P Went 1981; K Knighton 1981-83; Frank Clark 1983-91; Peter Eustace 1991-94; John Sitton & Chris Turner 1994

ADDITIONAL INFORMATION
Previous Names: 1881-86 Glyn Cricket & Football Club, 1886-88 Eagle FC, 1888-98 Orient FC, 1898-1946 Clapton Orient, 1946-67 Leyton Orient, 1967-87 Orient, 1987 Leyton Orient.
Previous Leagues: None.

Club colours: Red with white shirts, white shorts, red socks.
Change colours: Yellow with blue shirts, blue shorts, yellow socks.
Reserves League: Capital League. **Youth League:** S.E. Counties.

LONGEST LEAGUE RUNS

of undefeated matches:	14 (1954-55)	of league matches w/out a win:	23 (1962-63)
of undefeated home matches:	25 (1913-14)	of undefeated away matches:	9 (1954-55)
without home win:	14 (1962-63)	without an away win:	34 (1938-47)
of league wins:	10 (1956)	of home wins:	12 (1954)
of league defeats:	8 (1927-28)	of away wins:	6 (1956)

THE MANAGER

PAT HOLLAND . . . . appointed April 1995.

PREVIOUS CLUBS
As Manager . . . . None.
As Asst.Man/Coach . . . . Leyton Orient.
As a player . . . . West Ham, Bournemouth (Loan).

HONOURS
As a Manager . . . . None.
As a Player . . . . FA Cup winner 1975. ECEC runners-up 1976.

LEYTON ORIENT

PLAYERS NAME / Honours	Ht	Wt	Birthdate	Birthplace / Transfers	Contract Date	Clubs	League	L/Cup	FA Cup	Other	Lge	L/C	FAC	Oth
G O A L K E E P E R S														
Caldwell Peter	6.1	12.3	05/06/72	Dorchester	09/03/90	Q.P.R.								
				Free	03/07/95	Leyton Orient	28	2		1				
D E F E N D E R S														
Austin Kevin	5.9	10.12	12/02/73	London		Saffron Walden								
				£1000	19/08/93	Leyton Orient	101+9	4	6	7	3	1		
Hendon Ian M	6.0	12.0	05/12/71	Ilford	20/12/89	Tottenham Hotspur	0+4	1		0+2				
E: u21.7, Y.19. FAYC'90. CS'91				Loan	16/01/92	Portsmouth	1+3							
				Loan	26/03/92	Leyton Orient	5+1							
				Loan	17/03/93	Barnsley	6							
				£50000	09/08/93	Leyton Orient	102+1	6	5	11	4		1	
				Loan	23/03/95	Birmingham City	4							
McCarthy Alan	5.11	12.10	11/01/72	Wandsworth	08/12/89	Q.P.R.	8+3		0+1	1				
E: Y.1.				Loan	26/11/93	Watford	8+1							
				Loan	11/02/94	Plymouth Argyle	1+1							
					14/08/95	Leyton Orient	40+3	1		2				
Purse Darren J	6.0	12.4	14/02/77	London	22/02/94	Leyton Orient	85+8	4	2	14+1	6			4
Shearer Lee			23/10/77	Southend	01/08/94	Leyton Orient	7+3	1+1			1			
M I D F I E L D														
Baker Joseph P J			19/04/77	London		Charlton Athletic								
				Free	01/06/95	Leyton Orient	4+16	0+2	0+1	0+2				
Chapman Danny	5.11	13.6	21/11/74	Deptford	18/03/93	Millwall	4+8	0+1						
				Free	03/07/95	Leyton Orient	38	2	1	2	2			
Hanson David						Leyton Orient	7+4			2	1			
				Loan	16/02/96	Welling								
F O R W A R D S														
Arnott Andy	6.1	12.0	18/10/73	Chatham	13/05/91	Gillingham	40+23	2+3	10+2	3+2	12		1	
				Free	25/01/96	Leyton Orient	19				3			
Inglethorpe Alex M	5.11	11.0	14/11/71	Epsom	01/07/90	Watford	2+10	1+2		1+1	2			1
					18/05/95	Leyton Orient	30	2		1	9			
Kelly Tony	5.9	10.12	14/02/66	Meridan		Bristol City	2+4				1			
						Dulwich Hamlet								
						Cheshunt								
						Enfield								
						St.Albans								
				£20000	29/01/90	Stoke City	33+25	5+4		3+3	5	3		
				Loan	30/01/92	Hull City	6				1			
				Loan	30/10/92	Cardiff City	5				1			
				£10000	17/09/93	Bury	53+4	0+1	1+1	8	10			3
				Free	07/07/95	Leyton Orient	32+2	1	1	2	3			
Warren Mark W	5.9	10.5	12/11/74	Clapton	06/07/92	Leyton Orient	15+6	2		1	1			
E: Y.2.														
West Colin	6.1	13.2	13/11/62	Wallsend	09/07/80	Sunderland	88+14	13+4	3+1		21	5	2	
				£115000	28/03/85	Watford	45	2+1	8		20		3	
				£180000	23/05/86	Glasgow Rangers	4+6	2	0+1	0+2	2	1		
				£150000	07/09/87	Sheffield Wed.	40+5	6	6	3	8	3	1	1
					24/02/89	W.B.A.	64+9	2	4	2	22		1	1
				Loan	01/11/91	Port Vale	5				1			
				Free	05/08/92	Swansea City	29+4	0+1	5	3+2	12		2	1
				Free	26/07/93	Leyton Orient	108+4	3	5	5	39	1	1	4
ADDITIONAL CONTRACT PLAYERS														
Ayorinde Samuel					24/04/96	Leyton Orient	1							
Jones David						Leyton Orient (T)								
Jones Tony					07/07/95	Leyton Orient (T)								
Williams Michael						Leyton Orient (T)	1+2		1	1				
Weaver Luke D					26/06/96	Leyton Orient								

BRISBANE ROAD

Leyton, London E10 5NE
Tel: 0181 539 2223

Capacity 18,869
Seating 7,171

First game .... v Cardiff City, 28.8.1937.
First floodlit game .... v Brighton & Hove Albion, 10.9.1959.

ATTENDANCES
Highest .... 34,345 v West Ham United, FA Cup 4th Round, 25.1.1964.
Lowest .... 749 v Brentford, AMC, 15.12.1986.

OTHER GROUNDS .... None.

MATCHDAY TICKET PRICES

Main Centre £11
Juv/OAP £6

Main North (members) £9
Juv/OAP £4.50

Main South £9
Juv/OAP £4.50

Terraces £7
Juv/OAP £3.50

Ticket Office Telephone no. 0181 539 2223

CLUBCALL
0891 12 11 50
Calls cost 39p per minute cheap rate and 49p per
minute at all other times.
Call costings correct at time of going to press.

HOW TO GET TO THE GROUND

From the North and West
Use A406 North Circular Road (sign posted Chelmsford) to Edmonton, then in
2.6 miles at roundabout take 3rd exit A112 (sign posted Leyton). Pass Leyton
Midland Road Station and in half-a-mile turn right into Windsor Road, then turn
left into Brisbane Road for Leyton Stadium.

From the East
Use A12 (sign posted London then City) to Leytonstone and follow signs
Hackney into Grove Road. At Leyton cross main road and forward into Ruckholt
Road, then turn right then left into Leyton High Road and in 0.2 miles turn left
into Buckingham Road then right into Brisbane Road for Leyton Orient FC.

Car Parking
Street parking around the ground.

Nearest Railway Station
Leyton Central.

Nearest Tube Station
Leyton (Central Line).

MATCHDAY PROGRAMME

Programme Editor . . . . Tim Reder.

Number of pages . . . . 42.

Price . . . . £1.50.

Subscriptions . . . . Rates obtainable from the shop manager.

Local Newspapers . . . . Waltham Forest Guardian, Ilford Recorder,
. . . . Hackney Gazette, East London Advertiser, Stratford Express.

Local Radio Stations . . . . Radio Goodmayes,
. . . . Whipps Cross Hospital Radio.

LINCOLN CITY
(The Red Imps)
NATIONWIDE LEAGUE DIVISION 3
SPONSORED BY: LINCOLNSHIRE ECHO

1996-97 - Back Row (L-R): Colin Alcide, Jason Minett, Andy Leaning (left club), Jonathan Whitney, Barry Richardson, Paul Wanless (left club), Ian Johnson (left club). **Middle Row:** Roger Cleary (Physio), Neil Davies, Steve Williams (left club), Phil Daley (left club), Grant Brown, Shane Westley, Matt Carbon (left club), David Johnson (left club), John Robertson. **Front Row:** Terry Fleming, Gareth Ainsworth, Jason Barnett, John Beck (Manager), John Still (Asst. Manager), Ben Dixon (left club), Steve Brown, Tony Daws (left club), Paul Mudd (left club).

LINCOLN CITY
FORMED IN 1884
TURNED PROFESSIONAL IN 1885
LTD COMPANY IN 1895

PRESIDENT: H Dove
CHAIRMAN: K J Reames
VICE-CHAIRMAN
G R Davey
DIRECTORS
H C Sills, J Hicks, N Woolsey, P Jackson
SECRETARY
G R Davey
COMMERCIAL MANAGER
G R Davey

MANAGER: John Beck
ASSISTANT MANAGER: John Still

YOUTH DEVELOPMENT OFFICER
Ian Whyte

PHYSIOTHERAPIST
Roger Cleary

STATISTICIAN FOR THE DIRECTORY
Ian Nannestad

1995/6 was an eventful and at times traumatic season for the Imps and their supporters, with the spectre of relegation to the Vauxhall Conference uppermost in the minds of all at the club for much of the campaign.

The season began promisingly with a victory at eventual champions Preston, but this proved something of an illusion with the uninspiring performances which followed leading to the dismissal of manager Sam Ellis at the beginning of September. Ellis was replaced by Steve Wicks who was given the new title of 'Head Coach'. With his excellent communication skills and a change of tactics to open attacking football, Wicks quickly made himself popular with the fans. Unfortunately, although sometimes exciting to watch, the new style brought few goals, and with the defence leaking badly at the other end the team gained just one point from eight league games. Forty-two days after his appointment, with the side four points adrift at the bottom of the table, Wicks was relieved of his duties.

The new manager was John Beck who immediately began to reshape the side, bringing in Barry Richardson and Steve Holmes, from his former club Preston, for his first match. The Imps were soon off the bottom and a run of 10 points from four matches earned Beck the divisional Manager of the Month award for November. Slowly but surely the side was rebuilt with a series of low-budget signings and as results improved the prospect of relegation receded. Beck's team generally played a version of the long-ball game, a style known to be difficult to counter and made more attractive to the Imps' fans with an added emphasis on wing play. City developed into a hard-working side, strong in defence and difficult to break down - although there were exceptions, notably a 7-1 defeat at Bury. The attacking sparkle came from former Preston North End man Gareth Ainsworth who finished top scorer with 12 goals, and the skillful Dutch recruit Gijsbert Bos whose spectacular goal in the 2-1 home victory over Mansfield will long be remembered.

Beck's success in turning the situation around was achieved despite the sale of young stars Darren Huckerby to Newcastle (£400,000) and Matt Carbon to Derby County (£385,000) - necessary to stabilise a growing financial deficit. In the end City were satisfied with 18th position, 24 points ahead of bottom club Torquay. However, in the nine seasons since their return to league football the Imps have only once finished higher than tenth, and it is not since 1992/3 that they have appeared regularly in the top half of the table - a fact that the ever-patient supporters will be looking for Beck and his men to rectify in the 1996/7 campaign.

IAN NANNESTAD

LINCOLN CITY

League: 18th   FA Cup: 1st Rnd   Coca-Cola Cup: 1st Rnd   Auto Windscreen Shield: Quarter Finals

M	DATE	COMP	VEN	OPPONENTS	RESULT	HT	LP	GOAL SCORERS/GOAL TIMES	ATT.
1	A 12	EL	A	Preston North End	W 2-1	1-1	4	Puttnam 36, West 51	(7813)
2	15	CC 1/1	A	Notts County	L 0-2	0-2			(3494)
3	19	EL	H	Gillingham	L 0-3	0-1	13		2822
4	22	CC 1/2	H	Notts County	L 0-2	0-0			2636
5	26	EL	A	Colchester United	L 0-3	0-2	17		(2939)
6	28	EL	H	Scunthorpe United	D 2-2	0-0	14	Daws 88, Onwere 89(pen)	2674
7	S 2	EL	A	Barnet	L 1-3	1-2	20	Huckerby 4	(1813)
8	9	EL	H	Rochdale	L 1-2	0-1	24	Onwere 73	2408
9	12	EL	H	Bury	D 2-2	0-0	21	Onwere 68(pen), Daws 75	1851
10	16	EL	A	Chester City	L 1-5	1-3	23	Daws 25	(3049)
11	23	EL	H	Cambridge United	L 1-3	0-2	24	Johnson 68	2614
12	26	AWS 1/1	H	Rochdale	W 4-3	1-1		Johnson (2), Huckerby (2)	1238
13	30	EL	A	Plymouth Argyle	L 0-3	0-3	24		(6643)
14	O 7	EL	H	Darlington	L 0-2	0-1	24		2564
15	14	EL	A	Scarborough	D 0-0	0-0	24		(1848)
16	21	EL	H	Cardiff City	L 0-1	0-0	24		2453
17	28	EL	A	Exeter City	D 1-1	1-1	24	Barnett 33	(3252)
18	N 1	EL	A	Mansfield Town	W 2-1	1-0	24	Onwere 38(pen), Holmes 78	(2398)
19	4	EL	H	Hartlepool United	D 1-1	1-0	23	Huckerby 29	2956
20	7	AWS 1/2	A	Darlington	W 1-0	0-0		Brown 46	(984)
21	11	FAC 1	A	Stockport County	L 0-5	0-3			(3952)
22	18	EL	A	Torquay United	W 2-0	1-0	23	Ainsworth 28, 47	(2553)
23	25	EL	H	Northampton Town	W 1-0	0-0	22	Brown 89	3287
24	28	AWS 2	H	Preston North End	W 2-1	0-0		Onwere, Brown	1729
25	D 9	EL	H	Cambridge United	L 1-2	1-1	23	Westley 37	(2472)
26	16	EL	H	Plymouth Argyle	D 0-0	0-0	23		2801
27	23	EL	A	Wigan Athletic	D 1-1	0-0	23	Brown 71	(2334)
28	26	EL	H	Fulham	W 4-0	2-0	22	Brown 33, Ainsworth 37, 81, Whitney 87	3693
29	J 9	AWS QF	A	Rotherham United	L 1-3	0-0		Ainsworth	(1825)
30	13	EL	A	Gillingham	L 0-2	0-1	23		8047
31	16	EL	H	Leyton Orient	W 1-0	1-0	22	Carbon 32	1841
32	20	EL	H	Preston North End	D 0-0	0-0	22		5185
33	F 3	EL	H	Colchester United	D 0-0	0-0	22		2531
34	5	EL	A	Doncaster Rovers	D 1-1	0-1	21	Minett 88(pen)	(2083)
35	13	EL	H	Hereford United	W 2-1	0-1	22	Minett 48(pen), Whitney 55	1884
36	17	EL	A	Bury	L 1-7	1-2	22	Carbon 11	(3096)
37	24	EL	H	Chester City	D 0-0	0-0	23		2533
38	27	EL	A	Rochdale	D 3-3	1-2	23	Carbon 19, Ainsworth 46, Stuart 74(og)	(1253)
39	M 2	EL	A	Fulham	W 2-1	2-1	20	Ainsworth 6, 12	(4245)
40	5	EL	A	Scunthorpe United	W 3-2	1-0	15	Ainsworth 16, 76, Daley 86	(2411)
41	9	EL	H	Wigan Athletic	L 2-4	1-1	16	Alcide 10, Ainsworth 70	3282
42	16	EL	A	Leyton Orient	L 0-2	0-0	18		(3129)
43	19	EL	H	Barnet	L 1-2	0-0	18	Bos 49	1872
44	23	EL	H	Doncaster Rovers	W 4-0	4-0	17	Alcide 8, 20, Minett 10, 29	3240
45	27	EL	A	Hereford United	L 0-1	0-0	20		(1631)
46	30	EL	A	Darlington	L 2-3	1-2	20	Bos 24, Ainsworth 56	(2146)
47	A 2	EL	H	Scarborough	W 3-1	2-1	18	Bos 13, 16, Ainsworth 89	2010
48	6	EL	H	Exeter City	L 0-1	0-1	19		2723
49	8	EL	A	Cardiff City	D 1-1	0-0	18	Alcide 76	(2657)
50	13	EL	H	Mansfield Town	W 2-1	0-0	18	Eustace 67(og), Bos 82	2992
51	20	EL	A	Hartlepool United	L 0-3	0-1	18		(3012)
52	27	EL	A	Northampton Town	D 1-1	0-0	19	Minett 72(pen)	(5166)
53	M 4	EL	H	Torquay United	W 5-0	1-0	18	Alcide 2, 57, Barnett 55(pen), Storey 75, Holmes 86	5814

Best Home League Attendance: 5814 v Torquay United   **Smallest: 1841 v Leyton Orient**   **Average: 2870**

Goal Scorers:

EL(57): Ainsworth(12), Alcide(6), Minett(5), Bos(5), Onwere(4), Carbon(3), Brown(3), Daws(3), Whitney(2), Barnett(2), Opponent(s)(2), Holmes(2), Huckerby(2), Puttnam(1), Daley(1), West(1), Storey(1), Johnson(1), Westley(1)

CC(0):
FAC(0):
AWS(8): Johnson(2), Huckerby(2), Onwere(1), Brown(1), Brown(1), Ainsworth(1)

(F) Ainsworth	(F) Alcide	(F) Barnett	(F) Bos	(D) Brightwell	(D) Brown	(F) Brown	(D) Carbon	(F) Daley	(F) Daws	(M) Dixon.B	(D) Fleming	(D) Holmes	(M) Huckerby	(F) Hulme	(D) Johnson	(F) Johnson	(G) Key	(G) Leaning	(M) Minett	(M) Mudd	(M) Onwere	(F) Putnam	(G) Richardson	(D) Robertson	(M) Wanless	(M) West	(D) Westley	(D) Whitney		
				X						X				X			X		X	S1	X	X1				X			U.Rennie	1
				X						X				X				X	X	S1	X	X1				X			M.Bailey	2
				X			X1		S2	X				X				X	X	S	X					X			R.Pearson	3
				X			X1		S1	X				X		S		X	X	S	X					X			T.Leake	4
				X			X		S	X				X		S1	X		X	X1	X	S				X			R.J.Harris	5
				X			X		S1	X				X		X	X		X	S	X	X1				X			S.Bennett	6
				X	X1		X			X				X		X	X		X	S1	X				S1	X			B.Knight	7
							X	X	X	X				X		X		X	X	S	X				X	X	X		I.Hemley	8
							X	X	X	X				X		X		X	X		X	X1			X	X	S1		T.Heilbron	9
							X	X1	X	X				X		X		X	X		X2				X			P.R.Richards	10
							X	X	X	X				X		S2	X	S3	X			S1			X	X			S.Mathieson	11
							X1	S1		X				X		X		X	X		X					X			T.West	12
							X	S	S1	X				X	X1	X	X	X	X		X				X			R.B.Gifford	13
					X				S1	X2				X	X	X1	X	X	X		X				X			F.Stretton	14
				X			X	S	X					X	X			X	X		X				X	X		R.Furnaulds	15
				X	S1		X	X	S	X			X	X	X1	X			X		X	X		S	X			R.Poulaine	16
		X		X	S2		X	X	X2				X	X	X	S			X		X1	X			X			R.Harris	17
X	X1			X			X	S	S1	X			X		X				X2		X	X			X	S2		T.West	18
X	X			X			X	S					X		X	X1			S1		X	X			X	X	X	K.Lynch	19
X	X			X	X		X	X					X			X			X	S	X			S	S	X	X	T.Leake	20
X	X			X			X		S1				X		X1	X			X		X	X			X	X	X	M.Reed	21
X	X			X	X		X	X					X			S	X		X	S	X	X		S	X	X	X	P.Rager	22
X	X			X	X	X	X	X					X			S			X		X	X		X1	X	X	X	R.Furnandiz	23
X	X			X	X		X	X							S1			X	X		X	X			X	X	X	I.Hemley	24
X	S1			X	X1	X1				X				X				S1	X		X	X			X	X	X1	S.Bennett	25
X		X		X	X	X2		S				X	X				S1	S2	X		X				X	X	X	J.Brandwood	26
X	X1	X		X	X	X2				X	X		X	X	S	S1		S2	X		X	X			X		X	G.Frankland	27
X	X1	X2		X	X		S1			X	X		X		S2	S			X		X	X			X		X	G.Barber	28
X	X	X1			X	X	S			X	X	X	X		X	S	X	X	X		X				X		X		29
X	X	S1		X	X	S		X1				X	X		X	S			X		X	X			X	X	X	A.D'Urso	30
X	X1	S2		X	X2	X		S	X			X	X		X	S1			X		X	X			X	X	X	M.Fletcher	31
X1	X	X		X	X	X		X	X				X		S	S			X		X	X			X	X	X	S.Mathieson	32
X	X	X		X	X	X		X	X	S	S		X						X	X		X			X	X	X	G.Frankland	33
X	X	X		X	X1	X	X	S					X		S1				X	S	X				X	X	X	J.Kirkby	34
X1	S1	X		X	X	X	X	X					X		S	S			X		X	X			X	X	X	B.Burns	35
X1	S	X		X	X	X	X	X					X		S1	S			X		X	X			X	X	X	A.Butler	36
X	X	X		X	X1		X	X1					X		X				X		X	S	S		X	X	X	M.Bailey	37
X	S1	X2		X			X	X1					X			S2			X		X				X	X	X	K.Lynch	38
X	S2	X2		X			X	X	S1				X			X1			X		X				X	X	X	C.Wilkes	39
X	X	X		X	S1		X	X		S2			X			X2			X		X1				X	X	X	P.Richards	40
X	X	X		X			X	X		S1			X			X			X		X1				X	X	X	P.Rejer	41
	X2	X1		X	X		X	X					X	S1	S2	X			X		X				X	X	X	S.Bennett	42
X	X	X	S1	X	S		X	S					X		X1	X			X		X				X	X	X	R.Pearson	43
X3	X		X	X	X2		X						X	X	S1	S2			X		X				X	X	X1	U.Rennie	44
X	X	S1	X1	X	X2		X						X	S2	S				X		X				X	X	X	J.Rushton	45
X	X1	X	X	X	X1		X	S	S				X		S1				X		X				X	X	X	T.West	46
X	X	S1	X	X1			X	S					S1		S				X		X				X	X	X	E.Lomas	47
X	X	X	X	X			X	S					S		X				X		X				X	S	X	I.Cruikshanks	48
X	S1	S1	X	X			X1	X1					X		X				X		X1				X	X	X	B.Knight	49
X	X2	S1	X					X					S		X				X		X1				X		X	I.Hemley	50
X	X	X	X1	X	S		X	S	S				X		X				X		S1				X		X	M.Riley	51
X	X	X	X1	X	S		X2	S					S1	X	X				X		X	X	S2				X	A.D'Urso	52
X	X	X	X		X		X	S					X	X	X				X1	S		X	X				X	G.Frankland	53
31	22	26	10	5	34	22	26	6	8	10	17	23	16	4	16	15	5	7	39	2	33	4	33	21	7	7	8	25	EL Appearances	
0	5	5	1	0	0	4	0	6	2	2	5	0	0	1	5	9	0	0	3	2	2	1	0	1	1	1	0	1	EL Sub Appearances	
0	0	0	0	2	0	0	1	0	0+1	2	0	0	2	0	0	0	2	2	0+1	2	1	0	0	1	0	0	0	0	CC Appearances	
1	0	1	0	0	1	0	1	0	0+1	0	0	0	0	1	1	0	0	0	4	1	1	0	1	0	0	0	1	1	FAC Appearances	
3	1	3	0	0	2	3	2+1	0+1	0	1	0	2	1	1+1	0	2	1	0	4	1	1	2	0	0	1	2	0	1	3	AWS Appearances	

lso Played: (F) Allon X2(1,3,11), X(2), S1(10).(M) Appleton (L) X(10,11,12,13,14). (D) Bound X(9,10,12), X1(11), S2(14), S(15). (M) Davis X(8,11,12,13). (M) Dixon.A S(9,12,13). (M) Dyer X(4,5).
(M) Gibson S(24). (D) Greenall X(1,2,3,4,5,6). (M) Megson X(1,2,3,4). (D) Platnauer S2(1). (M) Storey S2(50), S1(53). (F) Williams S(1,6,8,9,12,14,15) S2(2,10), S1(3,7).

CLUB RECORDS

BIGGEST VICTORIES
League: 11-1 v Crewe Alexandra, Division 3(N), 29.9.1951.
F.A. Cup: 13-0 v Peterborough (a), 1st Qualifying Round, 12.10.1895.
8-1 v Bromley, 2nd Round, 10.12.1938.
BIGGEST DEFEATS
League: 3-11 v Manchester City, Division 2, 23.3.1895.
0-8 v Notts County, Division 2, 23.1.1897.
0-8 v Preston North End, Division 2, 28.12.1901.
1-9 v Wigan Borough, Division 3(N), 3.3.1923.
0-8 v Stoke City, Division 2, 23.2.1957.
F.A. Cup: 0-5 v Grimsby Town, 4th Qualifying Round, 10.12.1892.
0-5 v Stoke City, 1st Round, 11.01.1907.
League Cup: 0-5 v Leicester City, 3rd Round, 05.10.1966.
Others: 2-7 v Doncaster Rovers, Division 3(N) Cup Round 1, 28.10.1937.

MOST POINTS: 3 points a win: 77, Division 3, 1981-82.
2 points a win: 74, Division 4, 1975-76.
MOST GOALS SCORED: 121, Division 3(N), 1951-52.
RECORD TRANSFER FEE RECEIVED
£400,000 + appearance payment from Newcastle Utd for Darren Huckerby, November 1995.
RECORD TRANSFER FEE PAID
£63,000 to Leicester City for Grant Brown, January 1990.
BEST PERFORMANCES
League: 5th Division 2, 1901-02.
F.A. Cup: Equivalent 5th Round 1886-87, 18889-90, 1901-02.
League Cup: 4th Round 1967-68.
HONOURS
Champions of Division 3(N), 1931-32, 1947-48, 1951-52.
Champions of Division 4, 1975-76. Champions of GMVC 1987-88.
LEAGUE CAREER: Original members of Div 2 1892, Not re-elected to Div 2 1908, re-elected Div 2 1909, Not re-elected 1911, Re-elected Div 2 1912, Not re-elected 1920, Re-elected Div 3(N) 1921, Div 2 1931-32, Div 3(N) 1933-34, Div 2 1947-48, Div 3(N) 1948-49, Div 2 1951-52, Div 3 1960-61, Div 4 1961-62, Div 3 1975-76, Div 4 1978-79, Div 3 1980-81, Div 4 1985-86, GMVC 1986-87, Div (now Div 3) 1987-88.

INDIVIDUAL CLUB RECORDS

MOST GOALS IN A SEASON
Allan Hall: 42 goals in 1931-32, Division 3(N).

MOST GOALS IN A MATCH
6. Andy Graver v Crewe Alexandra (h) 11-1, Division 3(N), 29.9.1951.
6. Frank Keetley v Halifax Town (h) 9-1, Division 3(N), 16.1.1932.

OLDEST PLAYER
John Burridge, 42 years 57 days v Rochdale, Division 3, 29.1.1994.

YOUNGEST PLAYER
Shane Nicholson, 16 years 112 days, League Cup v Charlton, 23.9.1986.

MOST CAPPED PLAYER
David Pugh (Wales) 3.
George Moulson (Eire) 3.

PREVIOUS MANAGERS

(since 1947)
Bill Anderson 1947-64; Con Moulson (coach) 1965; Roy Chapman (player/coach) 1965-66; Ron Gray 1966-70; Bert Loxley 1970-71; David Herd 1971-72; Graham Taylor 1972-77; George Kerr 1977; Willie Bell 1977-78; Colin Murphy 1978-85; John Pickering 1985; George Kerr 1985-87; Peter Daniel (caretaker) 1987; Colin Murphy 1987-90; Alan Clarke 1990; Steve Thompson 1990-93; Keith Alexander 1993-94, Sam Ellis 1994-95.

ADDITIONAL INFORMATION
PREVIOUS NAMES
None.
PREVIOUS LEAGUES
None.
Club colours: red and white striped shirts, black shorts with red trim, red socks with black & white trim.
Change colours: Blue shirts yellow trim, blue shorts, blue socks.
Reserves League: Pontins League.
Youth League: (Juniors) Midland Purity Youth League.

LONGEST LEAGUE RUNS

of undefeated matches:	18 (1980)	of league matches w/out a win:	19 (1978)
of undefeated home matches:	35 (1975-76)	of undefeated away matches:	12 (1980)
without home win:	11 (1978-79)	without an away win:	35 (1896-98)
of league wins:	10 (1930)	of home wins:	14 (1982)
of league defeats:	12 (1896-97)	of away wins:	5 (1968, 1975, 1989, 1992)

THE MANAGER

JOHN BECK . . . . appointed October 20th 1995.

PREVIOUS CLUBS
As Manager . . . . Cambridge United, Preston North End.
As Asst.Man/Coach . . . . None.
As a player . . . . QPR, Coventry, Fulham, Bournemouth, Cambridge Utd.

HONOURS
As a Manager . . . . Promotion to Div.3 1990. Div.3 champions 1991, Div.3 Manager of the Year 1991..
As a Player . . . . **Bournemouth:** F.M.C. 1984.

LINCOLN CITY

PLAYERS NAME Honours	Ht	Wt	Birthdate	Birthplace Transfers	Contract Date	Clubs	APPEARANCES				GOALS			
							League	L/Cup	FA Cup	Other	Lge	L/C	FAC	Oth
G O A L K E E P E R S														
Richardson Barry	6.1	12.1	05/08/69	Wallsend	20/05/88	Sunderland								
					21/03/89	Scunthorpe United								
				Free	03/08/89	Scarborough	30	1		1				
				Free	16/06/91	Stockport County								
				Free	10/09/91	Northampton Town	96	4	5	8				
				£20000	25/07/94	Preston North End	20	2	3	2				
				£20000	20/10/95	Lincoln City	33		1					
D E F E N D E R S														
Brown Grant A	6.0	11.12	19/11/69	Sunderland	01/07/88	Leicester City	14	2						
				£63000	20/08/88	Lincoln City	254	13	10	15	11	1		2
Fleming Terry	5.9	10.09	05/01/73	Marston Green	02/07/91	Coventry City	8+5	0+1						
				Free	03/08/93	Northampton Town	26+5	2	0+1	0+1	1			
				Free	18/07/94	Preston North End	20+7	2	0+1	3+1	2			
					07/12/95	Lincoln City	17+5							
Holmes Steve	6.2	13.0	13/01/71	Middlesbrough	17/07/89	Lincoln City								
					01/01/90	Gainsborough T.								
					01/01/92	Guisborough T.								
				£10000	14/03/94	Preston North End	13		3	3	1			
				Loan	31/03/94	Bromsgrove Rovers								
				Loan	10/03/95	Hartlepool United	5			2				
				£30000	15/03/96	Lincoln City	23			2	2			
Robertson John	6.2	12.8	08/01/74	Liverpool	06/07/92	Wigan Athletic	94+4	10	6+1	8+1	3			
					05/12/95	Lincoln City	21+1			1				
Westley Shane L M	6.2	13.08	16/06/65	Canterbury	08/06/83	Charlton Athletic	8		1					
				£15000	01/03/85	Southend United	142+2	10+1	5	7	10	1		1
				£150000	19/06/89	Wolves	48+2	5		2	1	1		
				£100000	30/10/92	Brentford	61+3	5	5	6	1	2		
				Loan	03/02/95	Southend United	4+1							
					01/08/95	Lincoln City	8		1	1	1			
Whitney Jonathan D	5.10	12.3	23/12/70	Nantwich		Wigan Athletic								
						Skelmersdale Utd								
				Free		Winsford United			1					
				£10000	21/10/93	Huddersfield Town	14			4				
				Loan	17/03/95	Wigan Athletic	12							
					01/08/95	Lincoln City	25+1		1	3	2			
M I D F I E L D														
Davis Darren						Fleetwood Town								
				Free	01/06/95	Lincoln City	3		1					
Gibson Lee						Lincoln City (T)								
Minett Jason	5.9	10.4	12/08/71	Peterborough	04/07/89	Norwich City	0+3							
				Loan	19/03/93	Exeter City	11+1			1				1
				Free	21/07/93	Exeter City	42+4	4	6	6	3			1
				Free	10/07/95	Lincoln City	39+3	2	1	4	5			
Wanless Paul	6.1	13.4	14/12/73	Banbury	03/12/91	Oxford United	9+13	0+3		1+1		1		
				Free	07/07/95	Lincoln City	7+1			2				
				Loan	25/01/96	Woking								
				Loan	11/04/96	Cambridge United	14			1				
F O R W A R D S														
Ainsworth Gareth	5.9	11.9	10/05/73	Blackburn		Blackburn Rovers								
				Free	31/10/91	Northwich								
					21/01/92	Preston North End	2+3				1			
				Free	17/08/92	Cambridge United	1+3	0+1			1			
				Free	23/12/92	Preston North End	76+6	3+2	3+1	8+1	12		1	
				£50000	31/10/95	Lincoln City	31		1	3	12			1
Alcide Colin						Emley								
				£15000	05/12/95	Lincoln City	22+5			1	6			
Barnett Jason V	5.9	10.10	21/04/76	Shrewsbury	04/07/94	Wolves								
				£5000	26/10/95	Lincoln City	26+5		1	3	2			
Bos Gijsbert						Ysseelmeervogels								
				£10000	19/03/96	Lincoln City	10+1				5			
Brown Steve	6.0	11.6	06/12/73	Southend	10/07/92	Southend United	10		0+1	1	2			
				Free	05/07/93	Scunthorpe United								
				Free	27/08/93	Colchester United	56+6	2	5	5	17		1	1
					22/03/95	Gillingham	8+1				1			
				£20000	06/10/95	Lincoln City	22+4		1	3	3			1
Williams Steven R	6.1	11.7	03/11/75			Lincoln City								

SINCIL BANK

Lincoln LN5 8LD
Tel: 01522 522 224

Capacity 10,918

ATTENDANCES
Highest ....23,196 v Derby County, League Cup 4th Round, 15.11.1967.
Lowest ....1,003 v Scunthorpe, AMC, 25.11.1986.

OTHER GROUNDS ....None.

MATCHDAY TICKET PRICES

St Andrews Stand Ticket Sales Tel: 01522 522224
Adult £8
Juv/OAP £6
Family 1+1 . . . . £10
1+2 - £13 . . . . 1+3 - £16
Stacey West Stand (Covered seating or standing)
Adult £6
Juv/OAP £4.50
Family 1+1 . . . . £8
1+2 - £11.50 . . . . 1+3 - £15
Linpave Stand (inc. visitors) £8
Juv/OAP £6
South Park Stand
Adult £8
OAP. £6
E.G.T. Family Stand: Family 1+1 . . . . £8
1+2 - £11.50 . . . . 1+3 - £15

HOW TO GET TO THE GROUND

From the North, East and West
Use A15, A57, A46 or A158 into Lincoln City centre then follow Newark (A46) in High Street, left into Scorer Street and right into Cross Street for Lincoln City FC.

From South
Use A1 then A46 (sign posted Lincoln) then following signs city centre into High Street and turn right into Scorer Street and right again into Cross Street for Lincoln City FC.

Car Parking
Club Car Park £2, plus street parking available.

Nearest Railway Station
Lincoln Central (01522 539502).

IMPSLINE 0891 66 46 66

Calls cost 39p per minute cheap rate and 49p per minute at all other times.
Call costings correct at time of going to press.

MATCHDAY PROGRAMME

Programme Editor . . . . David Teague.

Number of pages . . . . 32.

Price . . . . £1.50.

Subscriptions . . . . £45.

Local Newspapers . . . . Lincolnshire Echo, Lincoln Standard.

Local Radio Stations . . . . BBC Radio Lincolnshire, Lincs FM.

MANSFIELD TOWN
(The Stags)
NATIONWIDE LEAGUE DIVISION 3
SPONSORED BY: ABACUS - MANSFIELD BREWERY

Back Row (L-R): Iffy Onoura, Matt Carmichael, Jason Trinder, Lee Howarth, Ian Bowling, Mark Gale, Mark Peters.
Middle Row: Paul Handford, John Dodlan, Chris Timmons, Scott Eustace, Ian Baraclough, Steve Slawson, Stewart Hadley, Kevin Lampkin.
Front Row: Keith Alexander (Asst. Manager), Bob Shaw (Chief Scout), Aidy Boothroyd, Steve Parkin, Andy King (Manager), Paul Sherlock, Simon Ireland, Barry Statham (Physio).

MANSFIELD TOWN
FORMED IN 1910
TURNED PROFESSIONAL IN 1910
LTD COMPANY IN 1921

CHAIRMAN: Keith Haslam
DIRECTOR
M Haslam
SECRETARY
Christine Reynolds (01623 23567)
COMMERCIAL MANAGER
Mick Saxby

MANAGER: Andy King
RESERVE/YOUTH TEAM MANAGER
Steve Parkin

PHYSIOTHERAPIST
Barry Statham

STATISTICIAN FOR THE DIRECTORY
Vacant

Mansfield's sixth-place finish to the 1994-5 season was succeeded by a disappointing 19th position this year, dashing the earlier hopes of a promotion challenge. The campaign began badly with the Stags only managing one win in the first ten matches - although their eleventh game produced a satisfying 6-2 victory over Wigan Athletic in which Stewart Hadley achieved a hat-trick. Hadley repeated his feat against Chester City just over a month later, but his three goals were not enough to claim the vital three points.

A low of 22nd in the table in mid January made the prospect of possible relegation all too real, but the Stags won the next match - at home to Fulham - and gained enough victories in the remainder of the season to ensure they stayed well out of the drop zone.

Mansfield went out in the first round of the Coca-Cola Cup, losing to Burnley in both legs, and similarly disappeared out of the Auto Windscreens Shield, drawing with Wrexham and losing to York City. The FA Cup campaign began more promisingly with a 4-2 win over Doncaster Rovers at Field Mill Ground, but hopes were soon to be dashed by a 2-0 defeat at the hands of Crewe Alexandra.

The number of goalscorers in the league (19) reflects the inconsistency of the line-up throughout the year. A more settled side in the forthcoming season may be able to produce a better promotion prospect.

MANSFIELD TOWN

League: 19th   FA Cup: 2nd Rnd   Coca-Cola Cup: 1st Rnd   Auto Windscreen Shield: 1st Rnd

M	DATE	COMP	VEN	OPPONENTS	RESULT	HT	LP	GOAL SCORERS/GOAL TIMES	ATT.
1	A 12	EL	A	Fulham	L 2-4	1-1	14	Carmichael 30, Sherlock 71	(4909)
2	15	CC 1/1	H	Burnley	L 0-1	0-1			2544
3	19	EL	H	Leyton Orient	D 0-0	0-0	17		2565
4	22	CC 1/2	A	Burnley	L 1-3	0-1		Sale 61	(4103)
5	26	EL	A	Northampton Town	D 3-3	2-1	18	Sale 16, 32, Baraclough 56	(4797)
6	29	EL	H	Doncaster Rovers	D 0-0	0-0	18		2940
7	S 2	EL	A	Torquay United	D 1-1	1-1	19	Sale 8	(2041)
8	9	EL	H	Scarborough	W 2-0	0-0	15	Baraclough 72, Ireland 89	2419
9	12	EL	H	Darlington	D 2-2	1-2	16	Slawson 10, Sale 50	2190
10	16	EL	A	Rochdale	D 1-1	0-0	15	Slawson 69	(2173)
11	23	EL	H	Scunthorpe United	D 1-1	0-0	14	Ireland 89	2478
12	26	AWS 1/1	H	Wrexham	D 2-2	0-0		Doolan 46, Hadley 47	1037
13	30	EL	A	Cardiff City	L 0-3	0-1	18		(3468)
14	O 7	EL	A	Wigan Athletic	W 6-2	2-1	12	Hadley 2, 74,77 (3),Peters 23, Harper 48, Doolan 52	(2084)
15	14	EL	H	Plymouth Argyle	D -1	1-1	15	Ireland 30	3164
16	21	EL	H	Preston North End	L 0-6	0-3	19		(8981)
17	28	EL	H	Bury	L 1-5	1-1	21	Doolan 36	2356
18	N 1	EL	H	Lincoln City	L 1-2	0-1	22	Sale 61	2398
19	4	EL	A	Hereford United	W 1 -0	0-0	20	Harper 70	(2193)
20	7	AWS 1/2	A	York City	L 0-1	0-0			(1571)
21	11	FAC 1	H	Doncaster Rovers	W 4-2	3-0		Harper 33, Sherlock 44, Parkin 45, Doolan 80	3116
22	18	EL	H	Chester City	L 3-4	1-2	20	Hadley 38, 60, 64 (3)	2415
23	25	EL	A	Colchester United	W 3-1	1-0	15	Hadley 41, Boothroyd 50(pen), Ireland 70	(2819)
24	D 2	FAC 2	A	Crewe Alexandra	L 0-2	0-1			(3694)
25	9	EL	A	Scunthorpe United	D 1-1	0-0	16	Barber 61	(2522)
26	16	EL	H	Cardiff City	D 1-1	0-0	17	Parkin 64	1680
27	23	EL	H	Hartlepool United	L 0-3	0-1	21		1979
28	26	EL	A	Barnet	D 0-0	0-0	18		(2204)
29	J 6	EL	H	Exeter City	D 1-1	0-1	19	Harper 61	1893
30	13	EL	A	Leyton Orient	L 0-1	0-0	22		(3461)
31	20	EL	H	Fulham	W 1-0	0-0	20	Slawson 64	2025
32	23	EL	H	Cambridge United	W 2-1	1-0	16	Sale 38, Sherlock 58	1801
33	30	EL	A	Gillingham	L 0-2	0-2	17		(6116)
34	F 3	EL	H	Northampton Town	D 0-0	0-0	18		2981
35	13	EL	A	Exeter City	D 2-2	2-1	17	Hackett 36, Onuora 41	(2507)
36	17	EL	A	Darlington	D 1-1	0-0	18	Ireland 66	(2598)
37	27	EL	A	Scarborough	D 1-1	1-1	22	Slawson 37	(1304)
38	M 2	EL	H	Barnet	W 2-1	0-0	17	Hackett 52, Peters 75	2146
39	9	EL	A	Hartlepool United	D 1-1	0-1	18	Slawson 52	(1758)
40	16	EL	H	Gillingham	L 0-1	0-1	21		2698
41	23	EL	A	Cambridge United	W 2-0	2-0	18	Timons 21, Sale 36	(2302)
42	25	EL	A	Doncaster Rovers	D 0-0	0-0	17		(1657)
43	30	EL	A	Wigan Athletic	W 1-0	0-0	18	Hackett 90	2369
44	A 2	EL	A	Plymouth Argyle	L 0-1	0-0	18		(6375)
45	6	EL	A	Bury	W 2-0	2-0	16	Harper 32, Wood 36	(3600)
46	8	EL	H	Preston North End	D 0-0	0-0	16		4626
47	13	EL	A	Lincoln City	L 1-2	0-0	18	Ireland 84	(2992)
48	16	EL	H	Rochdale	D 2-2	1-0	16	Boothroyd 13, Williams 75	1814
49	20	EL	H	Hereford United	L 1-2	1-1	17	Harper 31	2358
50	23	EL	H	Torquay United	W 2-0	1-0	16	Williams 12, 77	1674
51	27	EL	H	Colchester United	L 1-2	0-0	17	Eustace 49	2073
52	M 4	EL	A	Chester City	L 1-2	0-0	19	Williams 82	(2935)

Best Home League Attendance: 4626 v Preston North End   **Smallest: 1674 v Torquay United**   **Average: 2393**

Goal Scorers:
EL(54):   Hadley(7),Sale(7),Ireland(6),Harper(5),Slawson(5),Williams (4),Hackett(3),Baraclough(2),Peters(2),Sherlock(2),Boothroyd(2),Doolan(2),Parkin(1),
           Carmichael(1),Eustace(1),Barber(1),Onuora(1),Timons(1),Wood(1)
CC(1):   Sale(1)
FAC(4):   Doolan(1),Harper(1),Parkin(1),Sherlock(1)
AWS(2):   Hadley(1),Doolan(1)

(F) Baraclough	(F) Barber (L)	(D) Boothroyd	(G) Bowling	(D) Doolan	(M) Clarke	(F) Eustace	(D) Hackett	(F) Hadley	(F) Harper	(D) Howarth	(M) Ireland	(M) Kerr (L)	(D) Kilcline	(M) Lampkin	(M) Onuora	(D) Parkin	(F) Peel (L)	(M) Peters	(M) Robinson	(F) Sale	(M) Sedgemore	(M) Sherlock	(F) Slawson	(D) Timons	(M) Todd	(G) Trinder	(M) Williams	(M) Wood		
X		X	X	X						X	X					S1				X		X	X						D.Orr	1
X		X	X	X				X		X	X		S3			X				S2		X		X2	X1		S		G.Barber	2
X		X	X	X		S		X		X	X					X						X	X		S				R.Furnandiz	3
X		X	X	X				X		X	X2					X				X	S	X		X1					R.Pearson	4
X		X	X	X				X		X	X					X			S1	X	X	S		X1			S		P.Taylor	5
X		X	X	X				X		X	X			X1		X				X	X	S2		S1					B.Knight	6
X		S	X	X				S1	X2	X	X					X				X	X	X	S2	X1					S.Mathieson	7
X		S2	X	X				X	X3	X	X					X2				X	X	S1	X1	S3					T.Leake	8
X		X	X	X				S1	X1	X	X								S	X	X	S1		X			S		I.Hemley	9
X		X	X	X				S			X1	X	X			X				X	X	S1		X					W.C.Burns	10
X		X	X	X				S1	X1	X	X	X2				X				X	X			X			S		K.Breen	11
X		X	S	X	X	X		X	X	X		S	S			X				X		X			X				A.Wiley	12
X		X	X	X		S		X	X	X			S1							X	X	X1		X					K.Leach	13
X		X	X	X1			X3	X		X		X2				X				X	S3	S1	S2						N.Barry	14
		X	X	X				X	X	X		X		X		X				X			X	S	S		S		K.Lynch	15
		X	X	X		S2	X	X	X2	X		X1				X				X				S1			S		T.Heilbron	16
		X	X	X			S		X		X					S1	X	X1		X			X	S					R.Poulain	17
		X	X	X3			X		X2		X					S3	X	X1		X		S1		X	S2				T.West	18
X	X	X	X			X		X		X	X	X				S	X			S		X					S		D.B.Allison	19
X	X	X	X			X			S	X	X		X			X		X		X		X					S		R.Pearson	20
		X	X	X		X		X	X1	X						S1				X		S	X				S		A.Wilkie	21
S		X		X			X	X2	X1		X					S2				X		S1	X			X			R.Pearson	22
X	X			X			X		X		X					X				X	X	X		X					K.A.Leach	23
		X	X				S		X	X	X	X				X				X		X							S.Lodge	24
	X		X	X			S		X	X	X	X		X		X				X		X	S				S		M.Riley	25
	S		X	X	X		S		X		X	X			X		X			X		X							S.Bane	26
	S		X	X			S1	X	X1		X				X		X			X			X1	S1					P.Taylor	27
	S		X	X			X	X	X		X		X		X				S	X	X			S					I.Hemley	28
	X	X	X			X	X	X	X		X1					X			X2		X			S1	S				K.Breen	29
	X	X	X			X	X	X	X		X					X			X2		X1	S1		S			S2		B.Knight	30
	X	X	X			X	X	X1	X2	S						X					X	S2	X				S		R.Harris	31
	X	X	X			X	X	X		S						X		S		X		X1	X						P.Rejer	32
	X	X	X			X	X	X			X					X		S1		X		X1	X	S			S		A.Wiley	33
	X	X	X			X	X	S2			X1			X		X	X			X		S1	S	X2					S.Mathieson	34
	X	X	X	S		X	X	X					X		X					X		X	S	X			S		R.Gifford	35
	X	X	X			X	X	X			X		X1		S					X		X	S1	X					P.R.Richards	36
	X	X		S		X	X		X		S2				X			X2		X	X		X	X	X1		S1		R.Poulain	37
	X	S		X		X	X		X		X				X			S	X	X		X	X				S		A.D'Urso	38
	X	X		X		X	X		X		X			S1		X		S2	X1	X2		X					S		S.Mathieson	39
	X	X	X			X	X		X		X		X		X					X			X				X		G.Cain	40
	X		X			X	X		X		X					X				X		X1	X	S1			S		R.Pearson	41
	X	X	X			X	S1	X			X		X2			X				X		X1	X	S			S2		T.Heilbron	42
	X	X	X	S		X	X	X			X					X						X1	X	X		S1	X	X	I.Cruikshanks	43
	X	X	X	S		X	X	X			X					S1						X1	X	X		S	X	X	B.Knight	44
	X	X	X		X		X		X		X		X	S1		S						X	X1	X	X		X	X	R.Furnandiz	45
	X	X	X		X		X		X		X2			S1		S2						X	X1	X	X		X	X	J.Lloyd	46
	X	X	X		X		X		X		X		X	S		X1						X1	X	X2		S		X	I.Hemley	47
	X	X	X	S		X	X		X		X		S2									X1	X	X2		S1	X	X	N.Barry	48
	X	X	X	S2		X	X	X2			X1		S									X	S1	X			X	X2	K.Lynch	49
	X	X	X	S2		X	X	X1			X					X			X1			S	X				X		S.Bennett	50
	X	X	X			X	X	X1			X		S1	X								S	X			X	X		M.Fletcher	51
	X	X1	X			X		S			X2		X	X	X			S1					X			S2	X		E.Wolstenholme	52
11	4	42	44	42	1	25	32	27	29	17	38	4	18	2	7	25	2	4	21	24	4	14	20	16	10	1	5	9	EL Appearances	
0	0	1	0	0	2	2	0	5	0	0	1	1	1	4	7	1	0	5	0	3	4	4	8	1	2	0	5	1	EL Sub Appearances	
2	0	2	2	2	0	0	0	2	0	2	2	0	0	0+1	0	2	0	0+1	1	2	0	1	2	0	0	0	0	0	CC Appearances	
0	0	2	2	1	0	1	2	2	2	1	2	0	0	0	0	2	0	0	0	2	1	0	2	1	0	0	0	0	FAC Appearances	
1	1	2	1	2	0	2	0	1	2	1	1	1	0	0	0	1	0	1	1	0	1	0	0	1	0	0	0	0	AWS Appearances	

Also Played: (F) Alexander S1(2), S2(29). (D) Brien (L) X(36,37,38,39). (F) Carmichael X2 (1). (D) Clifford X(40), S(46). (M) Clance S(51). (M) Thompson S(26). (F) Varadi X1(1), S(2). (M) Weaver S(13), X(41).

CLUB RECORDS

BIGGEST VICTORIES
League: 9-2 v Rotherham United, Division 3(N), 27.12.1932.
8-1 v Q.P.R., Division 3, 15.3.1965.
7-0 v Scunthorpe United, Division 4, 21.4.1975.
F.A. Cup: 8-0 v Scarborough (a), 1st Round, 22.11.1952.
9-2 v Hounslow, 1st Round replay, 5.11.62.

BIGGEST DEFEATS
League: 1-8 v Walsall, Division 3(N), 19.1.1933.
F.A. Cup: 0-5 v Sheffield Wednesday (a), 3rd Round 10.1.1946.
0-5 v Bristol Rovers (a), 3rd Round, 4.1.1958.
League Cup: 0-5 v Chesterfield (h), 1st Round replay 23.8.1971.
0-5 v Notts County (a) 1st Round, 30.8.1988.
2-7 v Luton Town (a), 2nd Round, 3.10.1989.

MOST POINTS
3 points a win: 81, Division 4, 1985-86.
2 points a win: 68, Division 4, 1974-75.

MOST GOALS SCORED
108, Division 4, 1962-63.

RECORD TRANSFERS FEE RECEIVED
£638,500 from Swindon Town for Colin Calderwood (£27,000 7/85 + £611,500 8/93 when Calderwood moved on to Tottenham).

RECORD TRANSFER FEE PAID
£80,000 to Leicester City for Steve Wilkinson, Oct 1989 & to Notts County for Wayne Fairclough, March 1990.

BEST PERFORMANCES
League: 21st Division 2, 1977-78.
F.A. Cup: 6th Round, 1968-69.
League Cup: 5th round 1975-76.

HONOURS
Division 4 champions 1974-75.
Division 3 champions 1976-77.
Freight Rover Trophy winners 1986-87.

LEAGUE CAREER: Elected to Div 3(S) 1931, Transferred to Div 3(N) 1932, Transferred to Div 3(S) 1937, Transferred to Div 3(N) 1947, Transferred to Div 3 1958, Div 4 1959-60, Div 3 1962-63, Div 4 1971-72, Div 3 1974-75, Div 2 1976-77, Div 3 1977-78, Div 4 1979-80, Div 3 1985-86, Div 4 1990-91, Div 3 (now Div 2) 1991-92, Div 3 1992-93.

INDIVIDUAL CLUB RECORDS

MOST GOALS IN A SEASON
Ted Harston: 58 goals in 1936-37 (League 55, FA Cup 3).

MOST GOALS IN A MATCH
7. Ted Harston v Hartlepool United, Division 3(N), 8-2, 23.1.1937.

OLDEST PLAYER
David Owen 'Dai' Jones, 38 years 207 days v Wrexham (a), Division 3(N), 4.5.1949.

YOUNGEST PLAYER
Cyril Poole, 15 years 351 days v New Brighton (h), Division 3(N), 27.2.1937.

MOST CAPPED PLAYER
John McClelland (Northern Ireland) 6.

PREVIOUS MANAGERS

J Baynes 1922-25; E Davison (player/manager) 1926-27; J Hickling 1928-33; H Martin 1933-35; C Bell 1935; H Wightman 1936; H Parkes 1936-38; J Poole 1938-44; C Barke 1944-45; R Goodall 1945-49; F Steele 1949-51; G Jobey 1952-53; S Mercer 1953-56; C Mitten 1956-58; S Weaver 1958-60; R Carter 1960-63; T Cummings 1963-67; T Eggleston 1967-70; J Basford 1970-71; D Williams 1971-74; D Smith 1974-76; P Morris 1976-78; B Bingham 1978-79; M Jones 1979-81; S Boam 1981-83; I Greaves 1983-89; George Foster 1989-93.

ADDITIONAL INFORMATION
PREVIOUS NAMES
None.
PREVIOUS LEAGUES
Midland League.
Club colours: Amber with royal blue stripe down sides, royal blue collar
Change colours: White shirts with thin blue stripes, short as shirt, white socks.
Reserves League: Pontins League Division 2.
'A' Team: Midland Purity Youth League.

LONGEST LEAGUE RUNS

of undefeated matches:	20 (1976)	of league matches w/out a win:	12 (1959, 1974, 1979-80)
of undefeated home matches:	38 (1976-77)	of undefeated away matches:	8 (1976, 1991)
without home win:	11 (1959)	without an away win:	37 (1931-33)
of league wins:	7 (1962, 1991)	of home wins:	10 (1949)
of league defeats:	7 (1947)	of away wins:	7 (1976, 1991)

THE MANAGER

ANDY KING . . . . appointed November 1993.

PREVIOUS CLUBS
As Manager . . . . None.
As Asst.Man/Coach . . . . Luton Town.
As a player . . . . Luton, Everton, QPR, WBA, Everton, Wolves, Cambuut (Netherlands), Luton, Aldershot.

HONOURS
As a Manager . . . . None.
As a Player . . . . 2 caps for England U21.

MANSFIELD TOWN

PLAYERS NAME Honours	Ht	Wt	Birthdate	Birthplace Transfers	Contract Date	Clubs	League	L/Cup	FA Cup	Other	Lge	L/C	FAC	Oth
							APPEARANCES				GOALS			
G O A L K E E P E R S														
Bowling Ian	6.3	13.11	27/07/65	Sheffield		Gainsborough T.								
				Free	23/10/88	Lincoln City	59	3	2	4				
				Loan	17/08/89	Hartlepool United	1							
				Loan	25/03/93	Bradford City	7							
				£27500	28/07/93	Bradford City	29	2	2+1	1				
				Free	11/08/95	Mansfield Town	44	2	2	1				
D E F E N D E R S														
Clifford Mark			11/09/77			Mansfield Town (T)								
Doolan John	6.1	12.10	07/05/74	Liverpool	01/06/92	Everton								
				Free	02/09/94	Mansfield Town	63+3	4	3	3+1	3		1	1
Hackett Warren J	6.0	12.5	16/12/71	Plaistow		Tottenham Hotspur								
FAYC'90.				Free	03/07/90	Leyton Orient	74+2	4	8	7	3		1	
				Free	26/07/94	Doncaster Rovers	47	4	1	4				
				£50000	20/10/95	Mansfield Town	32		2		3			
Kilcline Brian	6.2	12.0	07/05/62	Nottingham	01/04/80	Notts County	156+2	16	10		9	1	2	
E: u21.2. FAC'87. Div.1'93.				£60000	11/06/84	Coventry City	173	16+1	15	8	28	4	3	
				£400000	01/08/91	Oldham Athletic	8	2						
				£250000	19/02/92	Newcastle United	20+12	3+2	1+2	5				
				£90000	20/01/94	Swindon Town	16+1	3		4				
					01/12/95	Mansfield Town	18+1							
Parkin Stephen J	5.6	10.7	07/11/65	Mansfield	12/11/83	Stoke City	104+9	9	9	6	5			
E: u21.5, Y.6, S.				£190000	16/06/89	W.B.A.	44+4	3		2+1	2			
				Free	16/07/92	Mansfield Town	84+3	6	5+1	6+1	3		1	
Peters Mark	6.0	11.3	06/07/72	St.Asaph	05/07/90	Manchester City								
W: B.1, u21.3.				Free	02/09/92	Norwich City								
				Free	10/08/93	Peterborough Utd	17+2	2		2				
				Free	30/09/94	Mansfield Town	46+1	3	4	5	6			
M I D F I E L D														
Ireland Simon P	5.10	10.7	23/11/71	Barnstaple	01/07/90	Huddersfield Town	10+9	1	0+1	1+1		1		
E: u18.4.				Loan	11/03/92	Wrexham	2+3							
				£200000	03/11/92	Blackburn Rovers	0+1							
				Loan	18/03/94	Mansfield Town	8+1				1			
				£60000	12/08/94	Mansfield Town	76+3	7	6	4	11	1	1	
Onuora Ifem	6.0	11.10	28/07/67	Glasgow	28/07/89	Huddersfield Town	115+50	10+6	12+3	13+3	30	4	3	3
				Free	20/07/94	Mansfield Town	17+11		0+1	1	8			
Wood Simon	5.9	11.8	24/09/76	Hull	01/08/93	Coventry City								
					15/03/96	Mansfield Town	9+1				1			
F O R W A R D S														
Eustace Scott	6.0	13.6	13/06/75	Leicester	09/07/93	Leicester City	0+1							
				Free	01/06/95	Mansfield Town	25+2		1	2	1			
Hadley Stewart	6.0	11.7	30/12/72	Dudley	06/07/92	Derby County								
					09/02/94	Mansfield Town	69+16	5+2	5	4	26		1	2
Harper Steve	5.10	11.12	03/02/69	Newcastle-u-L.	29/06/87	Port Vale	16+12	1+2		1+1	2			
Div.4'92.					23/03/89	Preston North End	57+20	1+1	1+2	6+1	10			1
				Free	23/07/91	Burnley	64+5	1+2	10	8	8		3	
				Free	07/08/93	Doncaster Rovers	56+10	2+1	3	4	11	1		
				£20000	08/09/95	Mansfield Town	29		2	2	5		1	
Sale Mark	6.5	13.8	27/02/72	Burton-on-Trent	10/07/90	Stoke City	0+2							
				Free	31/07/91	Cambridge United								
					26/03/92	Birmingham City	11+10	2		3+1		1		2
				£10000	05/03/93	Torquay United	30+14	1	2	3+1	8		1	
				£20000	26/07/94	Preston North End	10+3	1+1	0+1	4	6			
				Free	31/07/95	Mansfield Town	24+3	2	1	1	7	1		

FIELD MILL GROUND
Quarry Lane, Mansfield, Nottingham NG18 5DA
Tel: 01623 23567

Capacity 7,033
Covered Standing 1,638
Seating 3,329

First game ....v Swindon Town, August 1931.
First floodlit game...v Cardiff City, (friendly), 5.10.1961.
An experimental match under artificial lights took place at Field Mill on 22.2.1930.
ATTENDANCES
Highest..24,467 v Nott'm Forest, FAC Rnd 3, 10.1.1963.
Lowest ....1,086 v Darlington, AMC, 22.2.1984.

OTHER GROUNDS: ....None.

MATCHDAY TICKET PRICES

Seats................................... £10
Juv/OAP £5

Family Stand £10
Juv £5

Terraces............................... £8
Juv/OAP £3

Ticket Office Telephone no........ 01623 23567.

CLUBCALL
0891 12 13 11
Calls cost 39p per minute cheap rate and 49p per minute at all other times.
Call costings correct at time of going to press.

HOW TO GET TO THE GROUND

From the North
Use motorway M1 until junction 29. Leave motorway and follow signs to Mansfield A617. In 6.3 miles turn right into Rosemary Street B6030. In 1 mile turn right into Quarry Lane for Mansfield Town FC.

From the East
Use A617 to Rainworth. In 3 miles, at crossroads, turn left (B6030) into Windsor Road. At end turn right into Nottingham Road. Shortly turn left into Portland Street, then turn left into Quarry Lane for Mansfield Town FC.

From the South and West
Use motorway M1 until junction 28 then follow signs to Mansfield (A38). In 6.4 miles at crossroads turn right into Belvedere Street (B6030). In 0.4 miles turn right into Quarry Lane for Mansfield Town FC.

Car Parking
Space for 500 cars at the ground.

Nearest Railway Station
Mansfield Alfreton Parkway.

MATCHDAY PROGRAMME

Programme Editor............................. Mick Saxby.

Number of pages .... 32.

Price .... £1.20.

Subscriptions .... £32 per person.

Local Newspapers . . . Chronicle Advertiser, Nottingham Evening Post.

Local Radio Stations .... Radio Trent, Radio Nottingham.

NORTHAMPTON TOWN
(The Cobblers)
NATIONWIDE LEAGUE DIVISION 3
SPONSORED BY: LOTTO

1996-97 - Back Row (L-R): Michael Whittaker, Ali Gibb, Sean Parrish, Chris Lee, Garry Thompson, Lee Maddison, Claudio Devito, Jason White, Michael Warner. **Middle Row:** Dennis Casey (Physio), Dean Peer, Mark Cooper, Andy Woodman, Ian Sampson, Billy Turley, Chris Burns, David Rennie, Paul Curtis (Youth Team Coach). **Front Row:** Ian Clarkson, Roy Hunter, Neil Grayson, Ian Atkins (Manager), Ray Warburton, Lee Colkin, Danny O'Shea. Photo: Pete Norton.

NORTHAMPTON TOWN
FORMED IN 1897
TURNED PROFESSIONAL IN 1901
LTD COMPANY IN 1922

CHAIRMAN: B J Ward
DIRECTORS
B Hancock, B Stonhill, D Kerr, B Collins,
B Lomax, M Church.
SECRETARY
Rebecca Kerr
COMMERCIAL MANAGER
Bob Gorrill

MANAGER: Ian Atkins
PLAYER COACH: Garry Thompson
ASSISTANT MANAGER: Danny O'Shea

YOUTH TEAM MANAGER
Paul Curtis
PHYSIOTHERAPIST
Dennis Casey

STATISTICIAN FOR THE DIRECTORY
Frank Grande

Having taken the club off the bottom of the League, last season, new manager Ian Atkins set about building the side into promotion seeking unit.

He paid ˜35,000 to Scarborough for striker, Jason White and then bought goalkeeper William Turley from Evesham on a pay as you play basis, Roy Hunter(West Brom), Christian Lee (Doncaster) and Jason Beckford (Millwall) all arrived on a free transfer.

The start could not have been better, a 4-1 win over Bury, the team that had beat us 5-0, twice the previous season, and as a bonus, Neil Grayson hit a hattrick, the first by a Cobbler's player since October 1988.

Those early days saw the club riding high, but injuries and suspensions took their toll and by Christmas they were on familiar grounds near the bottom of the division, however, the manager continued his search for the right players and brought in Lee Maddison a left-back from Bristol Rovers and Ali Gibb aright sided midfield player from Norwich for a combined fee of ˜55,000 and slowly but surely they club climbed up the league, and in the final few weeks of the season there was a chance of reaching the play offs, but this disappeared when the club picked up only five points from its last four games.

Ironically the last few games of the season were against the top clubs, and Northampton won the reputation of 'party poopers', when they beat Preston at Deepdale, for the first time ever, stopping them from claiming the championship on that day, held Gillingham to a draw, meaning they still needed a point to clinch automatic promotion, and then beat Wigan in the last game of the season,knocking them out of the 'play off zone', it also meant the club had beaten all the Lancashire clubs on their own grounds.

The cup competitions brought their own customary results the Coca-Cola saw the club fail to clear the first hurdle, West Brom, the F.A. Cup bought groans from the fans when they saw yet again non-League opposition in the first round,with Hayes, but they were defeated, only for Northampton to be drawn away to Oxford in the next round, where they made their exit. The AWS, saw the club reach the area Quarter-final for the third time, but went out to bogey side,Hereford.

One coincidence had a sad conclusion when Lee Maddison turned on his ankle and broke a bone in his leg, in February putting him out for the rest of the season, Mark Taylor was signed from Fulham to replace him and after one game he did the same thing.

Eleventh in the League was what most supporters expected this season, and all agree with manager Ian Atkins words 'our opponents respect us now'. **FRANK GRANDE.**

NORTHAMPTON TOWN

League: 11th   **FA Cup: 2nd Rnd**   **Coca-Cola Cup: 1st Rnd**   **Auto Windscreen Shield: Quarter Finals**

M	DATE	COMP	VEN	OPPONENTS	RESULT	HT	LP	GOAL SCORERS/GOAL TIMES	ATT.
1	A 12	EL	H	Bury	W 4-1	1-1	1	Grayson 14, 47, 48 (3), Burns 50(pen)	4487
2	15	CC 1/1	A	West Bromwich Albion	D 1-1	0-1		Colkin 72	(6489)
3	19	EL	A	Cardiff City	W 1-0	1-0	1	Peer 42	(7872)
4	22	CC 1/2	H	West Bromwich Albion	L 2-4	0-1		Burns 76(pen), Peer 86	7083
5	26	EL	H	Mansfield Town	D 3-3	1-2	4	White 9, Burns 64, 73(pen)	4797
6	29	EL	A	Hartlepool United	L 1-2	0-1	5	Thompson 47	(2390)
7	S 2	EL	A	Rochdale	W 2-1	1-0	3	Burns 25, White 72	(2139)
8	9	EL	H	Exeter City	D 0-0	0-0	4		5625
9	12	EL	H	Leyton Orient	L 1-2	1-0	7	Williams 57	5072
10	16	EL	A	Doncaster Rovers	L 0-1	0-1	12		(2353)
11	23	EL	A	Torquay United	L 0-3	0-1	13		(2314)
12	30	EL	H	Fulham	W 2-0	0-0	11	Grayson 49, White 85	5778
13	O 7	EL	A	Scunthorpe United	D 0-0	0-0	11		(2455)
14	14	EL	H	Cambridge United	W 3-0	2-0	10	Grayson 41, Burns 45, Colkin 81	6301
15	16	AWS 1/1	A	Peterborough United	D 0-0	0-0			(3045)
16	21	EL	A	Colchester United	L 0-1	0-0	11		(3873)
17	28	EL	H	Barnet	L 0-2	0-0	12		5376
18	31	EL	H	Preston North End	L 1-2	0-1	16	Gibb 66	4695
19	N 4	EL	A	Gillingham	D 0-0	0-0	16		(7207)
20	7	AWS 1/2	H	Plymouth Argyle	W 1-0	1-0		Burns 19(pen)	2109
21	11	FAC 1	H	Hayes	W 1-0	0-0		Warburton 67	5389
22	18	EL	H	Wigan Athletic	D 0-0	0-0	16		4102
23	25	EL	A	Lincoln City	L 0-1	0-0	18		(3287)
24	28	AWS 2	A	Cardiff City	W 2-1	0-1		Hunter 17, Grayson 47	(1450)
25	D 2	FAC 2	A	Oxford United	L 0-2	0-1			(6348)
26	9	EL	H	Torquay United	D 1-1	1-0	18	White 7	3656
27	16	EL	A	Fulham	W 3-1	2-1	13	Thompson 14, White 20, 86	(3421)
28	23	EL	A	Scarborough	L 1-2	0-0	16	White 51	(1404)
29	26	EL	H	Hereford United	D 1-1	0-0	16	White 52	5222
30	J 6	EL	A	Darlington	W 2-1	2-0	14	White 31, 33	(1943)
31	9	AWS QF	A	Hereford United	L 0-1	0-0			(2905)
32	13	EL	H	Cardiff City	W 1-0	1-0	12	Armstrong 20	4454
33	20	EL	A	Bury	W 1-0	0-0	10	White 51	(3074)
34	30	EL	H	Plymouth Argyle	W 1-0	1-0	9	Sampson 16	3911
35	F 3	EL	A	Mansfield Town	D 0-0	0-0	9		(2981)
36	10	EL	H	Darlington	D 1-1	1-1	9	White 32	4926
37	17	EL	A	Leyton Orient	L 0-2	0-1	11		(4444)
38	20	EL	H	Rochdale	W 2-1	0-0	10	Warburton 83, Worboys 86	3090
39	24	EL	H	Doncaster Rovers	D 3-3	2-1	10	Sampson 10, Doherty 23, White 90(pen)	4738
40	27	EL	A	Exeter City	W 2-1	1-1	9	Warburton 38, Grayson 90	(2663)
41	M 2	EL	A	Hereford United	L 0-1	0-0	10		(2822)
42	9	EL	H	Scarborough	W 2-0	1-0	10	White 33, Sampson 62	4621
43	16	EL	A	Plymouth Argyle	L 0-1	0-0	10		(7001)
44	19	EL	H	Hartlepool United	D 0-0	0-0	11		3537
45	23	EL	H	Chester City	W 1-0	1-0	11	Burns 26	4810
46	30	EL	H	Scunthorpe United	L 1-2	0-0	11	Grayson 63	4290
47	A 2	EL	A	Cambridge United	W 1-0	0-0	10	White 53	(3631)
48	6	EL	A	Barnet	L 0-2	0-2	11		(3135)
49	8	EL	H	Colchester United	W 2-1	0-0	11	Grayson 65, Gibb 82	5021
50	13	EL	A	Preston North End	W 3-0	1-0	11	Grayson 14, 71, 78 (3)	(11774)
51	20	EL	H	Gillingham	D 1-1	0-1	11	Burns 66	7427
52	23	EL	A	Chester City	L 0-1	0-0	11		(1674)
53	27	EL	H	Lincoln City	D 1-1	0-0	11	Warburton 56	5166
54	M 4	EL	A	Wigan Athletic	W 2-1	1-1	11	Sampson 27, White 86	(5089)

Best Home League Attendance: 7427 v Gillingham   **Smallest: 3090 v Rochdale**   **Average: 4830**

Goal Scorers:
EL(51): White(16),Grayson(11),Burns(7),Sampson(4),Warburton(3),Gibb(2),Thompson(2),Doherty(1),Colkin(1),Armstrong(1),Peer(1),Williams(1),Worboys(1)
CC(3): Burns(1),Colkin(1),Peer(1)
FAC(1): Warburton(1)
AWS(3): Burns(1),Grayson(1),Hunter(1)

1995-96

(F) Aldridge	(M) Armstrong	(F) Beckford	(M) Burns	(F) Cahill	(D) Colkin	(M) Doherty	(M) Gibb	(M) Grayson	(D) Hughes	(M) Hunter	(M) Lee	(D) Maddison	(D) Mountfield	(D) Norton	(D) O'Shea	(M) Peer	(D) Sampson	(M) Scott	(M) Smith	(M) Taylor	(F) Taylor	(F) Thompson	(G) Turley	(D) Warburton	(F) White	(F) Williams	(G) Woodman	(F) Worboys	Name	
			X		X			X2	X2	S2				X	X	X	X					S1		X		X	X	X	S.Bennett	1
			X	S	X			X1		S				X	X	X	X		X			S1		X		X	X	X	J.Kirkby	2
			X		X			X1		S2				X	X	X	X		X					X		X	S1	X2	X	G.Barber	3
			X		X			X1		S				X	X	X	X1					S2		X		X	S1	X2	X	T.West	4
		S	X		X				S2					X	X	X	X1	X2				X		X		X	X	X		P.Taylor	5
			X		X			X1	X1	S1				X	X	X	X					S1		X		X	X	X	P.Richards	6
		S	X		X			X	S1					X	X	X	X					S2		X	X2	X1	X		N.Fletcher	7
			X		X		S2	X	S					X	X1	X	X					S1		X	X2		X		G.Frankland	8
	S1		X		X2			X	X					X	S	X	X					S2		X	X	X1	X		A.N.Butler	9
			X		S1			X	X					X	X	X1	X					S2		X	X	S	X		T.Lunt	10
			X		X1		X2	X	X					X	X	S2	X					S1		X	X	S	X		C.Wilkes	11
			X		S1		X2	X				S3	X	X	S2	X	X					X1		X	X3		X		E.Wolstenholme	12
			X		S		X1	X				S	X	X		X						X		X	X	X	S1	X	A.R.Leake	13
			X		S1		X2	X					X	X	X	X	S3					X1		X	X3	S2	X		J.Lloyd	14
	S1		X	S	X		X			X	X	X1		X		X	X							X	X	X			J.Brandwood	15
			X		X2		X	X				X	X	X3		X	X1							X1	X	S3	S2	X	G.R.Pooley	16
			X		S2		X	X				X	X	X3		X	S1			X2		S2		X1	X	S3	X		G.Cain	17
			X		X2		X2	X	S1			X		X	X	X	X			S2				X	S2	X1	X		U.Rennie	18
			X		X1		X3	X	S2			X2		X	X	X	X							X	S1	X	X		M.Pierce	19
S2			X	S	X		X	X	X2			X		X	S1	X	X1							X	X		X		M.Fletcher	20
	S		X		S1			X	X1	X		X		X	X	X	X							X	X	X	X		P.Jones	21
	S		X		X1			X	S	X	X	X1		X	X	X	X							X	X	X	X		N.Barry	22
S					S1			X	X	S		X	X	X	X			X						X	X1	X	X		R.Furnandiz	23
S1	S2		S					X	X	X		X	X	X	X	X		X						X	X1	X	X		K.Leache	24
	S3		X	S2	X2			X	X	X	S1	X	X3	X	X									X	X1	X	X		M.Reed	25
			X	X1	S1			X	S	X	S	X	X	X	X		X2					S2		X	X	X	X		M.Bailey	26
					X				S1	S2	X	X	X	X	X		X1					X2	X	X	X	X	X		M.Pierce	27
	S		S1		X			S2		X	X	X	X	X	X	X1					X2		X	X	X	X		R.Pearson	28
			X2		S1			X	X1	X	X	X	X	X			X					X1		X	X	X	S2	X	P.Richards	29
	X		X1				X1	X	X	X	X	X		X	X	X					S1		X	X	S1	X		W.Burns	30
	X		X1	S			X	X	X	X	X	X2		X	X	X					S1		X	X	S2	X		P.Richards	31
	X		S1	S3		X3	X	X	X	X	S2		X	X	X						X1		X	X	X2	X		G.Pooley	32
			X	S			X	X	S	X	X	X	X1	X			X					X		X	X	S1	X	S2	I.G.Cruikshanks	33
X			X1				X	X	X	X		X	X1	X			X					X2	X	X	X	X		S2	A.D'Urso	34
X1			S1				X	X	S	X	X	X	S2	X								X	X	X		X2		S.Mathieson	35
	X						X	X	X	X	S3	X2	X	X								X	X	S3	X	X1		S.Baines	36
	X			S1	S1	X3	X	X	X1	X	X										X	X	S3	X	X1	X	B.Harris	37
	X			S2	X3	X	X	X1	X	X	X	X			S1						X2	X	X	X	S3		R.Gifford	38
	X3			X	S3	S1	X	X2	X	X	X										X1	X	X	X	S2		M.J.Brandwood	39
				X1	S	S1	X	X	X	X	X	X		X			X					X2	X	X	X	S2		K.Leach	40
				X1	S	S1	X	X	X	X	X	X									X2	X	X	X	S2		M.Fletcher	41
				S	S	X	X	X	X	X	X										X	X	X	X	X		A.Wiley	42
			X1		S1	S1	X1	X	X	X	X	X									X1	X	X	X	S1		D.Horr	43
			X2		S2	S2	X2	X	X	X		X									S1	X	X	X	X1		R.Harris	44
			X		S1	S1	X	X	X	X	X	S									X1	X	X	X	S1		P.Taylor	45
			X		S1	X	X1	X	X3	X	X	S3									X2	X	X	X	S2		C.Wilkes	46
			X		S	S	X	X	X	X	X										S1	X	X	X	X1		J.Rushton	47
			X		S3	S1	X	X	X	X1	X	X									X2	X	X3	X	S2		E.Lomas	48
			X		S1	S1	X	X	S3		X	X	X1								X3	X	X1	X	X		S.Bennett	49
			X	S	S	X	X	X	X	X										S	X	X	X	X		N.Barry	50
			X	S	S1	X	X	X	X1	X	X1	X								S1	X	X	X	X		D.Allison	51
			X	S3	S2	X	X3	X	X	X1	X									S1	X	X2	X	X		A.R.Leake	52
			X	X1	S1	X1	X		S1	X	S	X									X	X	X	X		A.D'Urso	53
			X	S	S2		X2	X	X1	X	X	X	X								X	S1	X	X		R.Pearson	54
0	4	0	40	2	14	3	12	37	7	26	1	21	4	42	37	37	30	5	2	1	1	21	2	44	40	25	44	4	EL Appearances	
0	0	1	3	1	10	6	11	5	1	7	4	0	0	2	1	5	3	0	0	0	1	13	0	0	5	10	0	9	EL Sub Appearances	
0	0	0	2	0	0	2	0	0	0	2	0	2	0	2	2	2	2	0	0	0	0	2	0	2	2	2	2	0	CC Appearances	
0	0	0+1	2	0+1	1+1	0	0	1	0	2	1+1	0	2	2	2	0	0	0	0	0	0	2	0	0+2	1+2	0+1	0+2	0	FAC Appearances	
0+2	1	0+2	3	0	2	0	2	2	1	4	2	2	0	3	2+1	4	2	1	0	0	0	0+1	0	4	3	2+1	4	0	AWS Appearances	

Also Played: (M) Atkinson S(15). (M) Warner S(29).

CLUB RECORDS

BIGGEST VICTORIES
League: 10-0 v Walsall, Division 3(S), 5.11.1927.
F.A. Cup: 10-0 v Sutton, 7.12.1907.
League Cup: 8-0 v Brighton, 1.11.1966.

BIGGEST DEFEATS
League: 0-10 v Bournemouth, Division 3(S), 2.9.1939.
F.A. Cup: 2-8 v Manchester United (h), 5th Round, 7.2.1970.
League Cup: 0-5 v Fulham, 13.10.1965.
0-5 v Ipswich, 30.8.1977.

MOST POINTS
3 points a win: 99, Division 4, 1986-87.
2 points a win: 68, Division 4, 1975-76.

MOST GOALS SCORED
109, Division 3(S), 1952-53, Division 3, 1962-63.

RECORD TRANSFER FEE RECEIVED
£265,000 from Watford for Richard Hill, March 1987.

RECORD TRANSFER FEE PAID
£85,000 to Manchester City for Tony Adcock, January 1988.

BEST PERFORMANCES
League: 21st Division 1, 1965-66.
F.A. Cup: 5th Round 1911-12, 1933-34, 1949-50, 1969-70.
League Cup: 5th Round 1964-65, 1966-67.

HONOURS
Champions Division 3, 1962-63.
Champions Division 4, 1986-87.

LEAGUE CAREER
Original members of Division 3 1920, Transferred to Div 3(S) 1921, Div 4 1957-58, Div 3 1960-61, Div 2 1962-63, Div 1 1964-65, Div 2 1965-66, Div 3 1966-67, Div 4 1968-69, Div 3 1975-76, Div 4 1976-77, Div 3 1986-87, Div 4 (now Div 3) 1989-90.

INDIVIDUAL CLUB RECORDS

MOST GOALS IN A SEASON
Cliff Holton: 39 goals in 1961-62 (League 36, FA Cup 3).

MOST GOALS IN A MATCH
5. R Hoten v Crystal Palace (h) 8-1, Division 3(S), 27.10.1928.
5. A Dawes v Lloyds Bank (h) 8-1, FA Cup 1st Round, 26.11.1932.

OLDEST PLAYER
E Lloyd-Davies, 42 years, 1919.

YOUNGEST PLAYER
Adrian Mann, 16 years 297 days v Bury, 5.5.1984.

MOST CAPPED PLAYER
E Lloyd-Davies (Wales) 12.
1903-12 Herbert Chapman, 1912-13 Walter Bull, 1913-19 Fred

PREVIOUS MANAGERS

Lessons, 1920-25 Bob Hewison, 1925-31 Jack Tresadern, 1931-36 Jack English Snr., 1936-37 Sid Puddlefoot, 1937-War Warney Cresswell, War-1949 Tom Smith, 1949-55 Bob Dennison, 1955-59 Dave Smith, 1959-63 Dave Bowen, 1963 Jack Jennings (caretaker), 1963-67 Dave Bowen, 1967-68 Tony Marchi, 1968-69 Ron Flowers, 1969-72 Dave Bowen, 1972-73 Bill Baxter, 1973-76 Bill Dodgin, 1976-77 Pat Crerand, 1977 Committee*, 1977-78 John Petts, 1978-79 Mike Keen, 1979-80 Clive Walker, 1980-81 Bill Dodgin, 1981-84 Clive Walker, 1984-85 Tony Barton, 1985-90 Graham Carr, 1990-92 Theo Foley, 1992-93 Phil Chard, 1993- 94 John Barnwell.
*Committee: 1 director, 1 coach, 2 senior players.

ADDITIONAL INFORMATION
PREVIOUS NAMES
None.
PREVIOUS LEAGUES
Northants League and Midland League.
Club colours: Claret shirts, with white shoulders, white shorts, claret socks.
Change colours: White shirts with claret shoulders, claret shorts, white socks
Youth Team League: Midland Melville Youth League.

LONGEST LEAGUE RUNS

of undefeated matches:	21 (1986-87)	of league matches w/out a win:	18 (1969)
of undefeated home matches:	29 (1932-33, 1975-76)	of undefeated away matches:	12 (1986-87)
without home win:	11 (1989-90)	without an away win:	33 (1921-23)
of league wins:	8 (1960)	of home wins:	12 (1927)
of league defeats:	8 (1935)	of away wins:	5 (1978)

THE MANAGER

IAN ATKINS . . . . appointed January 1995.

PREVIOUS CLUBS
As Manager . . . . Colchester United (player-manager), Cambridge United (player-manager), Doncaster Rovers.
As Asst.Man/Coach . . . . Birmingham City.
As a player . . . . Shrewsbury Town, Sunderland, Everton, Ipswich Town, Birmingham.

HONOURS
As a Manager . . . . **Birmingham:** Promotion.
As a Player . . . . **Everton:** Div.1 champions, ECWC winner. **Shrewsbury:** Promotion from Div.4, Div.3 champions.

NORTHAMPTON TOWN

PLAYERS NAME / Honours	Ht	Wt	Birthdate	Birthplace / Transfers	Contract Date	Clubs	APPEARANCES League	L/Cup	FA Cup	Other	GOALS Lge	L/C	FAC	Oth
G O A L K E E P E R S														
Turley Billy			15/07/73			Evesham								
				Free	01/06/95	Northampton Town	2							
Woodman Andrew	6.1	12.4	11/08/71	Camberwell	01/07/89	Crystal Palace								
				Free	04/07/94	Exeter City	6	1	1	2				
				Free	10/03/95	Northampton Town	54	2	2	4				
D E F E N D E R S														
Colkin Lee	5.11	11.1	15/07/74	Nuneaton	31/08/92	Northampton Town	73+20	5	2+1	3	3	1		
Maddison Lee	5.11	11.0	05/10/72	Bristol	18/07/91	Bristol Rovers	68+5	4	2	6+1				
				Loan	15/01/93	Bath City								
				Loan	22/09/95	Northampton Town								
				Free	26/10/95	Northampton Town	21		2	2				
O'Shea Daniel E Div.3'91.	6.0	12.8	26/03/63	Kennington	23/12/80	Arsenal	6	3						
				Loan	23/02/84	Charlton Athletic	9							
				Free	24/08/84	Exeter City	45	2	2	2	2			
				£5000	09/08/85	Southend United	116+2	8	5+1	6	12			
				Free	18/08/89	Cambridge United	186+17	18+1	15+3	12+2	1			
				Free	23/03/95	Northampton Town	44+1	2	2	2+1	1			
Sampson Ian	6.2	12.8	14/11/68	Wakefield		Goole Town								
					13/11/90	Sunderland	13+4	1	0+2	0+1	1			
				Loan	08/12/93	Northampton Town	8							
				Free	05/08/94	Northampton Town	72+3	4	1	5	6			
Warburton Raymond	6.0	11.5	07/10/67	Rotherham	05/10/85	Rotherham United	3+1		2	2				
				Free	08/08/89	York City	86+4	8	6	7	9	1	1	
				£35000	04/02/94	Northampton Town	100	4	3	7	7		1	1
M I D F I E L D														
Burns Christopher	6.0	12.0	09/11/67	Manchester		Cheltenham Town								
				£25000	15/03/91	Portsmouth	78+12	7+2	7	9+1	9	2		
				Loan	17/12/93	Swansea City	4				1			
				Loan	11/03/94	Bournemouth	13+1				1			
				Free	25/11/94	Swansea City	3+2		0+1					
				Free	13/01/95	Northampton Town	56+4	2	2	3	9	1		1
Gibb Alistair	5.9	10.08	17/02/76	Salisbury	01/07/94	Norwich City								
				Loan	22/09/95	Northampton Town								
				£15000	05/02/96	Northampton Town	12+11			2	2			
Grayson Neil	5.10	12.4	01/01/64	York		Rowntree Mac.								
				Free	22/03/90	Doncaster Rovers	21+8		1+1	2+1	6			1
				Free	26/04/91	York City	0+1							
					16/08/91	Chesterfield	9+6	2	1	1				
					01/08/92	Gateshead								
					01/08/93	Boston United								
					19/06/94	Northampton Town	71+9	4	2	5	19			3
Hunter Roy	5.9	10.12	29/10/73	Middlesbrough	04/03/92	W.B.A.	3+6			4+1	1			
				Free	01/06/95	Northampton Town	26+7		2	4				1
Lee Christian						Doncaster Rovers								
					13/07/95	Northampton Town	1+4		1+1	2				
Peer Dean AMC'91.	6.2	11.5	08/08/69	Stourbridge	09/07/87	Birmingham City	106+14	14+1	2+1	11+1	8	3		
				Loan	18/12/92	Mansfield Town	10			1				
				Free	16/11/93	Walsall	41+4	2	4+2	3	8			
				Free	01/06/95	Northampton Town	37+5	2	2	4	1	1		
Warner Michael						Tamworth								
					01/06/95	Northampton Town								
				Loan	16/02/96	Telford								
F O R W A R D S														
Cahill Oliver F	5.10	11.2	29/09/75	Clonmel		Clonmel								
					02/09/94	Northampton Town	7+4		0+1	1+2	1			
Thompson Garry L E: u21.6. FMC'91.	6.1	13.13	07/10/59	Birmingham	29/06/77	Coventry City	127+7	12+1	11		38	7	4	
				£225000	17/02/83	W.B.A.	91	9	5		39	5	1	
				£450000	12/08/85	Sheffield Wed.	35+1	2+1	5		7	1	1	
				£450000	05/06/86	Aston Villa	56+4	6	4	3	17	2		
				£325000	24/12/88	Watford	24+10	0+1	7+1		8			
				£200000	24/03/90	Crystal Palace	17+3	0+1		0+1	3			
				£125000	19/08/91	Q.P.R.	10+9	3+2		1	1	3		
				Free	15/07/93	Cardiff City	39+4	2	5+2	6+3	5		1	3
				Free	10/02/95	Northampton Town	36+13	0+2		0+1	6			
White Jason	6.2	12.0	19/10/71	Meriden	04/07/91	Derby County								
				Free	06/09/91	Scunthorpe United	44+24	1+1	3+3	4+4	16		1	1
				Loan	20/08/93	Darlington	4				1			
				Free	10/12/93	Scarborough	60+3	2+1	5	1	20		1	
					01/06/95	Northampton Town	40+5	0+1	2	3	16			

SIXFIELDS

Upton Way, Northampton NN5 4EG
Tel: 01604 75 77 73

Capacity...7,653.

First game ....v Barnet, Division 3, 15.10.1994.
First floodlit game ....v Barnet, AMC, 1.11.1994.

ATTENDANCES
Highest..7,461 v Barnet, Division 3, 15.10.1994.
Lowest..2,109 v Plymouth Argyle, AMC, 07.11.95.

OTHER GROUNDS ....County Ground 1897-94.

MATCHDAY TICKET PRICES

West Stand Upper Centre £11
Upper Wing. £10.50
Concessions £7.50
Family Tandem. £14
Family Tricycle. £17.50
Family Two+Two £25
Lower Centre £10
Lower Wing £9
Concessions £6.50
East Stand
Adult £9.50
Family Tandem. £11
Family Tricycle £13
Family Two+Two £21
Concessions £4
North Stand £8.50
Concessions £5.50
Away Section £8.50
Concessions £5.50
Ticket Office Telephone no. 01604 75 77 73

CLUBCALL 0839 66 44 77

Calls cost 39p per minute cheap rate and 49p per
minute at all other times.
Call costings correct at time of going to press.

HOW TO GET TO THE GROUND

From the North and West
M1 to junction 16. Take A45 (signposted Northampton/Duston). After approx.
3.25 miles there is a roundabout; take the fourth exit onto Upton Way for the
ground.

From the South
M1 to junction 15a, then A43 (signposted Northampton) to A45 Northampton
Ring Road. Bear left (signposted Daventry) at second roundabout, then take first
exit into Upton Way and the ground is immediately on the left.

From the East
Either A43 or A428 to A45. Once on the A45, follow signs for Daventry until you
pass the Rugby Ground (Franklin Gardens). At the second roundabout after this,
take the first exit into Upton Way for the ground.

Car Parking
There is on-site parking at Sixfields with six overflow car parks to take the strain
on busy days.

Nearest Railway Station
Castle Station (01908 370 883 - Milton Keynes Enqs.)

MATCHDAY PROGRAMME

Programme Editor . . . .

Number of pages . . . . 48.

Price . . . . £1.60.

Subscriptions . . . . Apply to club.

Local Newspapers . . . . Chronicle and Echo, Evening Telegraph,
. . . . Northants Post.

Local Radio Stations . . . . Northants Radio, Radio Northampton.

ROCHDALE
(The Dale)
NATIONWIDE LEAGUE DIVISION 3
SPONSORED BY: CARCRAFT

Back Row (L-R): Steve Whitehall, Mark Stewart, Paul Butler, Paul Williams, Ian Thompstone, Peter Valentine, David Bayliss.
Middle Row: Jimmy Robson, Graham Shaw, Darren Ryan, Ian Gray, Chris Clarke, Dean Martin, John Deary, Mick Docherty.
Front Row: Derek Hall, Jason Peeke, Dave Thompson, Kevin Formby, Alex Russell, Jamie Taylor, Andy Thackery.

ROCHDALE
FORMED IN 1907
TURNED PROFESSIONAL IN 1907
LTD COMPANY IN 1910

PRESIDENT: Mrs L Stoney
CHAIRMAN: D F Kilpatrick
DIRECTORS
K Clegg (Managing Director)
J Marsh, G Morris, C Dunphy,
M Mace, G R Brierley,
SECRETARY
Miss Karen Smyth
COMMERCIAL MANAGER
Stephen Walmsley (01706 47521)

MANAGER: Graham Barrow
FIRST TEAM COACH
Joe Hinnighan
YOUTH TEAM MANAGER
Jimmy Robson
PHYSIOTHERAPIST
Joe Hinnighan

STATISTICIAN FOR THE DIRECTORY
Stephen Birch

The last time Rochdale played outside of the League's basement Ted HEath was Prime Minister, the miners were on strike and a good proportion of the current regular attendance, as well as some of the current team, were not born. But 1995-96 saw the Dale playing the type of football that seemed sure to end the 21 year stay in the basement.

The first 17 games produced 29 points and 32 goals including a first ever win in London, a wait of 87 years, 4-0 at Barnet. Form was maintained in the FA Cup as Second Division Rotherham were sent packing in devastating style. A highly entertaining draw with Darlington in Round Two was followed by a tense replay with both teams knowing that victory meant a dream trip to Anfield. Another disciplined performance saw Dale through with a late goal - the sixth away victory of the season - and much, perhaps too much, rejoicing.

Not only did Rochdale fail to win at Liverpool - being demolished 7-0 - the team failed to win any of the 15 League games played in the three months to follow - a dismal stretch that coincided with a season ending injury to goalkeeper Gray and some poor performances by his replacements.

By the start of March Rochdale had fallen twelve places in the league table to 15th, goals had dried up (six in twelve games) and attendances fell below 2,000. The end of the slump, if anything, was even less expected than its onset, with a 2-1 victory at table-topping Preston. Goalkeeper Pilkington, signed on loan from Manchester United, finally provided confidence at the back and the Dale saw out the season playing 'win one - lose one' football including an impressive home win over Gillingham and two draws with high-flying neighbours, Bury.

The other two cup competitions saw early exits. York scored four in extra-time after two close games in the Coca-Cola Cup, before going on to greater things at Old Trafford, while Chesterfield came from behind in the Auto Windscreen competition.

Whitehall and Peake played in all 55 games. Whitehall, who broke the twenty league goal barrier with the help of penalty kicks, together with Stuart provided almost two thirds of the team's goals. The seven League wins on opponents grounds were the best for 25 years. The continuation of the downward slide of recent seasons doesn't bode well for the future, especially since the six figure windfall from the Liverpool tie was used to pay off accumulated debts.

With the real prospect of further development of Spotland ground the fans can only hope that corresponding improvements on the field will not be far behind. **STEPHEN BIRCH.**

ROCHDALE

League: 15th FA Cup: 3rd Rnd Coca-Cola Cup: 1st Rnd Auto Windscreen Shield: 2nd Rnd

M	DATE	COMP	VEN	OPPONENTS	RESULT	HT	LP	GOAL SCORERS/GOAL TIMES	ATT.
1	A 12	EL	H	Cardiff City	D 3-3	2-2	12	Whitehall 13, Whitehall 26(pen), Thompson 81	2321
2	15	CC 1/1	H	York City	W 2-1	2-0		Shaw 13, Thompstone 72	1390
3	19	EL	A	Darlington	W 1-0	0-0	6	Whitehall 79(pen)	(2139)
4	22	CC 1/2	A	York City	L 1-5	0-1		Tutill 70(og)	(2130)
5	26	EL	H	Hartlepool United	W 4-0	1-0	3	Taylor 24, Taylor 54, Thompson 55, Taylor 79	1794
6	29	EL	A	Torquay United	L 0-1	0-0	6		(2139)
7	S 2	EL	H	Northampton Town	L 1-2	0-1	12	Butler 80	2139
8	9	EL	A	Lincoln City	W 2-1	1-0	7	Whitehall 21(pen), Stuart 83	2408
9	12	EL	A	Fulham	D 1-1	1-1	6	Deary 38	(3848)
10	16	EL	H	Mansfield Town	D 1-1	0-0	8	Stuart 77	2173
11	23	EL	A	Doncaster Rovers	W 3-0	1-0	7	Whitehall 23(pen), Schofield 72(og), Stuart 87	(2217)
12	26	AWS 1/1	A	Lincoln City	L 3-4	1-1		Whitehall 44, Peake 83, Deary 84	(1238)
13	30	EL	H	Exeter City	W 4-2	3-0	6	Stuart 6, Deary 21, Whitehall 32, Peake 70	2052
14	O 7	EL	A	Gillingham	L 0-1	0-1	7		(7785)
15	14	EL	H	Colchester United	D 1-1	0-1	6	Stuart 67	2193
16	21	EL	A	Barnet	W 4-0	0-0	5	Peake 49, Stuart 70, Stuart 74, Whitehall 85	(2039)
17	24	AWS 1/1	H	Darlington	W 5-2	2-1		Whitehall 7, Gregan 33(og), Moulden 55, 73, 74 (3)	1055
18	28	EL	H	Cambridge United	W 3-1	1-0	3	Moulden 4, Whitehall 47, 69	2344
19	31	EL	H	Chester City	L 1-3	0-1	5	Peake 64	3018
20	N 4	EL	A	Scunthorpe United	W 3-1	2-0	4	Stuart 2, Whitehall 39, 89	(3003)
21	11	FAC 1	H	Rotherham United	W 5-3	3-0		Moulden 9, 74, Whitehall 14(pen), Peake 19, 49	3817
22	18	EL	H	Hereford United	D 0-0	0-0	4		2619
23	25	EL	A	Plymouth Argyle	L 0-2	0-0	4		(6558)
24	28	AWS 2	A	Chester City	L 1-2	1-0		Whitehall 9	(2344)
25	D 2	FAC 2	H	Darlington	D 2-2	0-1		Deary 66, 85	3732
26	9	EL	H	Doncaster Rovers	W 1-0	1-0	5	Whitehall 33(pen)	2168
27	12	FAC 2R	A	Darlington	W 1-0	0-0		Martin 80	(4131)
28	16	EL	A	Exeter City	L 0-2	0-1	6		(3152)
29	22	EL	A	Leyton Orient	L 0-2	0-1	6		(5399)
30	J 2	EL	A	Wigan Athletic	L 0-2	0-0	9		(2624)
31	6	FAC 3	A	Liverpool	L 0-7	0-3			(28126)
32	13	EL	H	Darlington	L 1-2	1-0	10	Whitehall 23	2200
33	20	EL	A	Cardiff City	L 0-1	0-0	12		(2230)
34	23	EL	A	Scarborough	D 1-1	0-0	12	Peake 69	(1401)
35	F 3	EL	A	Hartlepool United	D 1-1	0-0	13	Whitehall 69	(1927)
36	10	EL	H	Scarborough	L 0-2	0-0	14		1662
37	13	EL	H	Bury	D 1-1	0-0	14	Butler 63	3048
38	17	EL	H	Fulham	D 1-1	1-1	15	Stuart 13	1923
39	20	EL	A	Northampton Town	L 1-2	0-0	15	Thompstone 80	(3090)
40	27	EL	H	Lincoln City	D 3-3	2-1	13	Whitehall 36(pen), Stuart 45, 57	1253
41	M 2	EL	A	Preston North End	W 2-1	2-1	13	Whitehall 2, Stuart 38	(9697)
42	9	EL	H	Leyton Orient	W 1-0	1-0	14	Lancaster 14	1934
43	12	EL	H	Preston North End	L 0-3	0-2	14		4597
44	16	EL	A	Bury	D 1-1	1-1	14	Butler 2	(3473)
45	19	EL	H	Torquay United	W 3-0	1-0	13	Deary 32, Whitehall 72(pen), Thompson 80	1206
46	23	EL	H	Wigan Athletic	L 0-2	0-1	13		2870
47	30	EL	H	Gillingham	W 2-0	2-0	13	Stuart 11, Thompson 37	2098
48	A 2	EL	A	Colchester United	L 0-1	0-0	14		(3021)
49	6	EL	A	Cambridge United	L 1-2	1-1	15	Lancaster 45	(2186)
50	8	EL	H	Barnet	L 0-4	0-1	15		1442
51	13	EL	H	Chester City	W 2-1	1-1	15	Whitehall 39, 84	(2158)
52	16	EL	A	Mansfield Town	D 2-2	0-1	15	Hall 76, Whitehall 82	(1814)
53	20	EL	H	Scunthorpe United	D 1-1	1-0	15	Deary 3	1654
54	27	EL	H	Plymouth Argyle	L 0-1	0-0	15		2355
55	M 4	EL	A	Hereford United	L 0-2	0-1	15		(5880)

Best Home League Attendance: 4597 v Preston North End **Smallest: 1206 v Torquay United** Average: 2220

Goal Scorers:

EL(57): Whitehall(20),Stuart(13),Deary(4),Thompson(4),Peake(4),Butler(3),Taylor(3),Lancaster(2),Moulden(1),Thompstone(1),Hall(1),Opponent(s)(1)

CC(3): Shaw(1),Thompstone(1),Opponent(s)(1)

FAC(8): Peake(2),Deary(2),Moulden(2),Whitehall(1),Martin(1)

AWS(9): Moulden(3),Whitehall(3),Deary(1),Peake(1),Opponent(s)(1)

(D) Bayliss	(D) Butler	(G) Clarke	(M) Deary	(M) Formby	(G) Gray	(M) Hall	(M) Hardy	(G) Key	(F) Lancaster	(M) Lyons	(M) Martin	(M) Mitchell	(F) Moulden	(M) Peake	(G) Pilkington	(M) Price	(F) Proctor	(M) Russell	(M) Ryan	(F) Shaw	(F) Stuart	(F) Taylor	(M) Thackeray	(F) Thompson	(M) Thompstone	(D) Valentine	(F) Whitehall	(F) Williams	Player	
	X	S		X	X						X1			X				X	S1	X2				X	X	X	X	S2	S.Baines	1
X	X		X	X		S								X				X	S	X				X	X	X	X	S	S.Mathieson	2
X	X		X	X		S1								X				X	S2	X3				X2	X1	X	X	S3	J.Kirkby	3
X1	X2		X	X							S2			X				X	S1					X		X	X	X	A.Butler	4
X	X		X	X	X						X		S1	X				X	S				X2	X			X1	S2	F.Stretton	5
X3	X		X	X	X		S1				X1			X				X	S3				X1	X	S1		X		R.Gifford	6
X1	X		X	S	X		X				X		S2	X				X			S1	X2		X			X	S2	N.Fletcher	7
X	X		X	X	X						X			X				X2			S1	X		X1			X	X1	I.Hemley	8
X	X		X		X		X				X		S1	X				S		X			X				X	X1	P.Taylor	9
X	X		X		X	X2					X		X1	X				S2		X2	S1		X	X	X1	S2	X3		W.C.Burns	10
X	X		X		X	X2					X			X				S1		X			X	X1	S2		X3		G.Singh	11
X	X		X	X	X	S					X1			X						S	S		X	X	X		X	S1	T.West	12
X	X		X	X	X						S1			X						X	X2		X1	X	S		X	S2	D.B.	13
X	X		X	X	X						X1		S1	X3			S3			S1	X		X	X			X1		N.D.Durso	14
X2	X		X	X	X						S			X						X1	X	S2	X	X	X	S	X	X	G.Frankland	15
	X		X	X	X						X			X						S1	X		X	X1	S3	X	X3		A.Wiley	16
	X		X	X	X						S2		X	X						S1	X		X	X	X	X	X	X	S.Baines	17
	X		X	X	X						S		X	X						S	X		X	X	X	S1	X	X	R.Pearson	18
	X		X2	X	X						S		X1	X						S2	X		X	X	X	S1	X	X	G.Cain	19
	X		X	X	S						X		S	X						S1	X		X1	X	X	X	X	X	R.D.Furnandiz	20
	X		X	X							X		X	X						S1	X1		X3	X3	X3	X2	X	X	R.Pearson	21
S2			X	X	X						X			X			X	X			S2		X2	X	X1	X1	X	X	M.Riley	22
S	X		X	X	X	S1					X		S2	X1				X					X	X	X	S	X		J.Rushton	23
X	X		X	X	X	X					X		X1	X					S1	X	S		X	X	X	X	X			24
S	X		X	X	X	S					X		X1					S1	S1				X	X	X	X	X		N.Barry	25
	X		X	X	X						S1	X1	S	X				X	X2				X	X	X	X	X	S2	D.Laws	26
	X		X	X	X						X			X				S1	X	X	S		X	X1	X	X	X		N.Barry	27
X		X	X								X	X1		X				X	X2	S1		S2		X		X	X2	S2	S.Bennett	28
S	X	X	X								X	S1	X1	X				X	X1				X	X		X	X	S1	P.Rejer	29
S3	X	X	X								X	X2		X				X1			S1		X	X3	S3	X	X	S2	U.Rennie	30
	X	X	X								X		X1	X1						S1	S1		X	X3	S3	X	X	X	K.Leach	31
	X	X	X				X				X		X1	X2						S2	S2	X	X2	S1	X	X	X		M.Brandwood	32
X1	X		X						S1		X		S3	X				X			S2	X3	X2	X	X	X	X		D.Allison	33
X			X					X			X			X	X	S		X		X	X	S	X	X			X	X	S.Baines	34
S1	X		X								X2			X	X	X2		X		X	S2			X	S2	X1	X1	X	T.West	35
S	X		X								S2	X1		X2	X	X2		X		X				X	S		X		S.Mathieson	36
X	X		X								X	S	X	X		X	X	X		X	S			X	S		S	X	K.Breen	37
X2	X1		X								X2	S2	X	X				X		X		S2		X		S1	X	X	G.Frankland	38
	X		X						X		X	X	X	X				X		X1	S	S		X1		S1	X	X	R.Gifford	39
X1	X		X						X		X1	X	X	X				X			X	S1		X		S1	X	S	K.Lynch	40
S	X		X					X	X		X			X				S		X			X	X	S	X	X	X	A.Butler	41
	X		X					X	X		X1			X				S2		X			X	X	X2	S1	X1	S3	J.Rushton	42
	X		X					X	X		X			X				S3		X			X	X	X3	X1	X		W.C.Burns	43
	X		X				S1				X	X		X				S		X		X	X	X		X1	X		E.Lomas	44
	X		X				X	X	S		X			X						X	S1	X	X	X			S		T.Heilbron	45
X	X		X				S	X	X		S1			X				X1		X	S	S	X	X			X		F.Wolstenholme	46
S1	X		X				S2	X	X		X			X						X	S	S	X	X		X1	X		J.Kirkby	47
	X		X			X		X3			X			X		S1		S1			X	X1	X	X			X1		R.D.Furnandiz	48
	X		X			X		X			X			X		S1		X2		X2	X1	X		X			X		P.Taylor	49
	X		X			X		X	X2		X			S3		S1				X	S2	X		X			X		M.Brandwood	50
	X		X			X		X	S	S	S			X						X	S	X		X			X		P.Richards	51
X	X		X			X		X	S2	S	X1			X						X	S1	X		X			X		N.Barry	52
X	X		X2			X		X	X	S2				X						X	S	X1		X			X		R.Pearson	53
X1	X		X			X		X	X	S				X						X	S	X1		X1	X2		X		F.Stretton	54
	X		X			X			S2	X	S1			X						X	X1	X2		X			X		S.Baines	55
25	38	5	36	18	20	9	5	14	13	1	33	3	6	45	6	3	1	20	4	9	32	8	27	42	11	22	46	1	EL Appearances	
3	0	0	0	0	0	5	2	0	1	2	4	1	10	1	0	0	2	5	3	8	2	8	2	0	0	14	1	11	EL Sub Appearances	
2	2	0	1	2	2	0	0	0	0	0	2	1	1	0	0	0	0	2	0+1	1	0	0	0	2	1	2	2	1	CC Appearances	
1+1	3	1	3	4	3	0	0	0	0	0	4	0	3	4	0	0	0	0+1	1+2	0+3	1	0	2	4	2+2	4	4	0	FAC Appearances	
2	3	0	3	3	3	0	0	0	0	0	2+1	0	2	2	0	0	0	0	0+1	1+1	2	0	2	3	1+1	1	3	0+1	AWS Appearances	

Also Played: (D) Barlow S2(49), X1(50). (D) Powell S3(48), S2(49).

CLUB RECORDS

RECORD LEAGUE VICTORY
8-1 v Chesterfield, Div 3N, 18.12.1926   7-0 v Walsall,Div 3N, 24.12.1921   7-0 v York City (a), Div 3N, 14.1.1939   7-0 v Hartlepool,Div 3N, 2.11.1957

RECORD LEAGUE DEFEAT
1-9 v Tranmere Rovers, Div 3N, 25.12.1931   0-8 v Wrexham(a), Div 3, 28.9.1929   0-8 v Leyton Orient (a), Div 4, 20.10.1987
Record Cup Defeat
0-6 v Wigan Athletic, Freight Rover Trophy, 28.1.1986

MOST LEAGUE POINTS
(2pts a win) 62 Div 3N, 1923-24
(3pts a win) 67 Div 4,1991-92

MOST LEAGUE GOALS
105, Div 3N, 1926-27

RECORD TRANSFER FEE RECEIVED
£200,000 plus 25% of any future fee from Bristol City for Keith Welch, July 1991

RECORD TRANSFER FEE PAID
£80,000 to Scunthorpe Utd for Andy Flounders, July 1991

BEST PERFORMANCES
League: 9th Div 3, 1969-70   FA Cup: 5th Round, 1989-90
League Cup: Runners-Up 1962 (4th Div Record)

HONOURS
None

LEAGUE CAREER
Elected to Div 3N 1921   Transferred to Div 3 1958
Relegated to Div 4 1958-59   Promoted to Div 3 1968-69
Relegated to Div 4 (now Div 3) 1973-74

INDIVIDUAL CLUB RECORDS

MOST APPEARANCES FOR CLUB
Graham Smith (1966-74): League 316+1, FA Cup 15,League Cup 13 Total 344+1 sub

MOST CAPPED PLAYER
No Rochdale player has won an international cap

RECORD GOALSCORER IN A MATCH
Tommy Tippett 6 v Hartlepool (a), 8-2, Div 3N,21.4.1930

RECORD LEAGUE GOALSCORER IN A SEASON
Albert Whitehurst 44 (1926-27) In All Competitions: Albert Whitehurst, 46 (League 44 + FA Cup 2)

RECORD LEAGUE GOALSCORER IN A CAREER
Reg Jenkins 119 In All Competitions: Reg Jenkins 130 (League 119 + FA Cup 5 + League Cup 6) 1964-73

MOST GOALS SCORED IN A FIRST CLASS MATCH
Record League Victory (above)   8-2 v Crook Town (h), 1st Round FA Cup, 26.11.1927   8-2 v Hartlepool United (a), Div3N, 22.4.1930

OLDEST PLAYER IN A LEAGUE MATCH
Jack Warner (player/manager) 41 years 195 days v Chesterfield, Div 3N, 4.4.1953

YOUNGEST PLAYER IN A LEAGUE MATCH
Zac Hughes, 16 years 105 days v Exeter City, Div 4, 19.9.1987

PREVIOUS MANAGERS

1920-21 William Bradshaw   1921-22 No appointment made   1922-23 Thomas C Wilson   1923-30 Jack Peart   1930 Harry Martin (caretaker)   1930-31 William Smith Cameron   1931-32 Vacant   1932-34 Herbert Hopkinson   1934-35 William H Smith   1935-37 Ernest Nixon (caretaker)   1937-38 Sam Jennings   1938-52 Ted Goodier   1952 Jack Warner   1953-58 Harry Catterick   1958-60 Jack Marshall   1960-67 Tony Collins   1967-68 Bob Stokoe   1968-70 Len Richley   1970-73 Dick Connor   1973-76 Walter Joyce   1976-77 Brian Green   1977-78 Mike Ferguson   1978-79 Peter Madden (caretaker)   1979 Doug Collins   1979-83 Peter Madden   1983-84 Jimmy Greenhoff   1984-86 Vic Halom   1986-88Eddie Gray   1988-89 Danny Bergara   1989-91 Terry Dolan   1991-94 Dave Sutton 1994- Mick Docherty (caretaker).

ADDITIONAL INFORMATION
Club colours: Blue shirts, white shorts, blue socks.

Change colours: Green shirt, black shorts, green socks.

Reserves League: Pontins League.

LONGEST LEAGUE RUNS

of undefeated matches:	20 (1923-24)	of league matches w/out a win:	28 (1931-32)
of undefeated home matches:	34 (1923-25)	of undefeated away matches:	9 (1923-24)
without home win:	16 (1931-32)	without an away win:	37 (1977-78)
of league wins:	8 (1969)	of home wins:	16 (1926-27)
of league defeats:	17 (1931-32)	of away wins:	4 (1923-24, 1926, 1946, 1947, 1969)

THE MANAGER

GRAHAM BARROW . . . . appointed May 1996.

PREVIOUS CLUBS
As Manager . . . . Chester City, Wigan Athletic
As Asst.Man/Coach . . . . Chester City.
As a player . . . . Altrincham, Wigan Athletic, Chester City.

HONOURS
As a Manager. . . . . Northern Sports Writers Manager of the Year 1993/94.
As a Player . . . . Promoted with both Wigan and Chester. Autoglass Trophy winner.

ROCHDALE

PLAYERS NAME Honours	Ht	Wt	Birthdate	Birthplace Transfers	Contract Date	Clubs	APPEARANCES				GOALS			
							League	L/Cup	FA Cup	Other	Lge	L/C	FAC	Oth
G O A L K E E P E R S														
Gray Ian J	6.2	12.0	25/02/75	Manchester	16/07/93	Oldham Athletic								
				Loan	18/11/94	Rochdale	12			3				
				£20000	17/07/95	Rochdale	20	2	3	3				
D E F E N D E R S														
Bayliss David	5.8	11.0	08/06/76	Liverpool		Rochdale	26+3	2	1+1	2				
Butler Paul	6.3	13.0	02/11/72	Manchester	05/07/91	Rochdale	151+7	8+1	6+2	12+1	10			
M I D F I E L D														
Deary John	5.10	11.11	18/10/62	Ormskirk	13/03/80	Blackpool	285+18	20	16+2	14	43	5	4	1
Div.4'92.				£30000	18/07/89	Burnley	209+6	13+3	20+1	21	23	1	2	1
					30/01/95	Rochdale	53	1	3	6	5		2	1
Formby Kevin	5.11	12.0	22/07/71	Ormskirk		Burscough								
RN rep.				Free	24/03/94	Rochdale	47+4	4	5	10				
Lyons Paul						Rochdale	1+2							
Martin Dean	5.10	10.2	09/09/67	Halifax	10/09/85	Halifax Town	149+4	7	10	12	7			3
				Free	08/07/91	Scunthorpe United	100+6	8	7	13+1	7	1		1
					13/01/95	Rochdale	45+7	0+1	4	2+1			1	
Russell Alex	5.8	11.7	17/03/73	Crosby		Liverpool								
				Free	01/03/93	Stockport County								
					01/08/93	Burscough								
				£4000	11/07/94	Rochdale	22+10	2	0+1	1+2	1			
Thackeray Andy	5.9	11.0	13/02/68	Huddersfield	15/02/86	Manchester City								
FAYC.				Free	01/08/86	Huddersfield Town	2		0+1					
				£5000	27/03/87	Newport County	53+1	3+1	1	2+1	4			1
				£5000	20/07/88	Wrexham	139+13	10	6	13+2	14	1		
				£15000	15/07/92	Rochdale	144+4	8	7	10+2	13			2
F O R W A R D S														
Stuart Mark R	5.10	10.11	15/12/66	Chiswick	03/07/84	Charlton Athletic	89+18	7+3	1	9+1	28	2	1	
				£150000	04/11/88	Plymouth Argyle	55+2	4	3	2	11			1
				Loan	22/03/90	Ipswich Town	5				2			
				£80000	03/08/90	Bradford City	22+7	6	0+1	1+1	5	1		
				Free	30/10/92	Huddersfield Town	9+6		2	4	3			1
				Free	05/07/93	Rochdale	99+8	5+1	4	5+3	28	1	1	1
				Loan	07/08/95	Chesterfield								
Taylor Jamie	5.6	9.12	11/01/77	Bury	12/01/94	Rochdale	10+25	0+1		0+2	4			1
Thompson Dave S	5.9	11.6	27/05/62	Manchester	26/09/81	Rochdale	147+8	7	7+1	6	13			
					22/08/86	Notts County	52+3	3+1	3	2	8			
				£35000	20/10/87	Wigan Athletic	107+1	5	3+1	6	16	2		1
				£77500	01/08/90	Preston North End	39+7	1+1		3+1	4			
				Free	14/08/92	Chester City	70+10	4	5	4	9			
				£6000	08/08/94	Rochdale	80+2	4	4	10	10			
Whitehall Steve	5.10	11.0	08/12/68	Bromborough		Southport								
					23/07/91	Rochdale	185+18	9+3	11+2	14	65	3	3	10

SPOTLAND
Willbutts Lane, Rochdale OL11 5DS
Tel: 01706 44648

Capacity 6,448
Covered Standing 3,837
Seating 2,611

First game .... v Oldham Ath., Friendly, 3.9.1907.
First floodlit game .... v St. Mirren, 16.2.1954.

ATTENDANCES
Highest .... 24,231 v Notts County, FAC 2nd Rnd, 10.12.1949
Lowest .... 588 v Cambridge Utd, Div 3, 5.2.1974
(played on a Tuesday afternoon during power cuts)

OTHER GROUNDS .... None.

MATCHDAY TICKET PRICES

Ground £7
Juv/OAP £4
Main Stand £9
Juv/OAP £5
Family Stand £9
Children under 16 . . . . £1 (max. 2)

All matches will be categorised A, B or C. The above prices apply to '**Category A**' (low) and the club reserves the right to increase prices for higher category matches and those where extra security is required.

Ticket Office Telephone no. 01706 44648

CLUBCALL
0891 55 58 58
Calls cost 39p per minute cheap rate and 49p per minute at all other times.
Call costings correct at time of going to press.

HOW TO GET TO THE GROUND

From all directions
Use motorway M62 until junction 20 then follow signs to Rochdale.
On to A627 (M), at first roundabout keep left and at second go straight ahead signed Blackburn.
At traffic lights after 1 mile go straight ahead into Sandy Lane.
Ground on right after half-a-mile.

Car Parking
Street parking only.

Nearest Railway Station
Rochdale.

MATCHDAY PROGRAMME

Programme Editor . . . . Stephen Walmsley.

Number of pages . . . . 32.

Price . . . . £1.50.

Subscriptions . . . . £31 for home matches.

Local Newspapers . . . Rochdale Observer, Manchester Evening News.

Local Radio Stations . . . . Radio Manchester, Radio Piccadilly.

SCARBOROUGH
(The Boro)
NATIONWIDE LEAGUE DIVISION 3
SPONSORED BY: YORKSHIRE COAST RADIO

Back Row (L-R): Don Page, Lee Thew, Craig Boardman, Kevin Martin, Gavin Kelly, Stuart Hicks, Ian Ironside, Jason Rockett, Lee Harper, Neil Trebble. **Front Row:** Oliver Heald, Steve Charles, David D'Auria, Andy Ritchie, Ian Kerr, Phil Chambers, Ray McHale, John Murray, Darren Knowles, Mark Wells, Richard Lucas, Alex Willgrass.

SCARBOROUGH
FORMED IN 1879
TURNED PROFESSIONAL IN 1926
LTD COMPANY IN 1933

PRESIDENT & CHIEF EXECUTIVE
J R Birley
CHAIRMAN: J Russell
DIRECTORS
Mrs G Russell
SECRETARY
Mrs G Russell

MANAGER: Miek Wadsworth
ASSISTANT MANAGER: Ray McHale

RESERVE TEAM MANAGER
&
YOUTH TEAM MANAGER
Ray McHale

PHYSIOTHERAPIST
J Murray

The 1995/96 season proved to be Scarborough's toughest since joining the League from the Vauxhall Conference back in 1987.This may well have been exaggerated by the lack of threat of relegation, this due to Stevenage Borough's ground not being upto scratch in time for the deadline set by the League. This meant that unless Macclesfield could mount a late challenge Stevenage would win the Vauxhall Conference but not be promoted to the Third Division.

It has to be said though that Scarborough were in trouble before Stevenage's exceptence to the Division was denied. Having won only five games leading up to the New Year, they started 1996 in 20th position. The run-in to the end of the season was to prove no better. With a run, starting in mid-March, of eight defeats, interrupted by a 2-0 victory over Cambridge United, cementing the Boro to 23rd place. But as mentioned before it must be very difficult for the management to motivate their players when there is no threat of relegation.

There was no joy in the Coca-Cola Cup. Though a first leg victory against Hartlepool (1-0) was encouraging, the second leg was lost (0-1) and Hartlepool went through on penalties. The FA. Cup saw a First Round exit against Chesterfield, whilst a defeat against Hull (0-2) and preston (1-2) knocked them out of the Auto Windscreen Shield.

Scarborough will again find it hard next season, but hopefully with the possibility of relegation from the Third Division, the club might find the threat of going down enough of an incentive to better their fortunes.

SCARBOROUGH

League: 23rd   FA Cup: 1st Rnd   Coca-Cola Cup: 1st Rnd   Auto Windscreen Shield: 1st Rnd

M	DATE	COMP	VEN	OPPONENTS	RESULT	HT	LP	GOAL SCORERS/GOAL TIMES	ATT.
1	A 12	EL	A	Doncaster Rovers	L 0-1	0-0	22		(2523)
2	15	CC 1/1	H	Hartlepool United	W 1-0	0-0		D'Auria 55	1555
3	19	EL	H	Fulham	D 2-2	1-2	16	Ritchie 31, Heald 75	1946
4	22	CC 1/2	A	Hartlepool United	L 0-1	0-1			(2134)
5	26	EL	A	Exeter City	L 0-2	0-0	20		(2439)
6	30	EL	H	Leyton Orient	W 2-1	1-1	17	Page 4, 75	1797
7	S 2	EL	H	Wigan Athletic	D 0-0	0-0	15		1949
8	9	EL	A	Mansfield Town	L 0-2	0-0	20		(2419)
9	12	EL	A	Cardiff City	L 1-2	1-1	24	Charles 43	(2385)
10	16	EL	H	Hereford United	D 2-2	0-1	21	Rockett 62, Gardner 75	1449
11	23	EL	H	Darlington	W 2-1	1-0	18	Page 26, Rockett 59	(2046)
12	26	AWS 1/1	H	Hull City	L 0-2	0-0			893
13	30	EL	H	Torquay United	W 2-1	1-0	14	Charles 7, D'Auria 67	1395
14	O 7	EL	A	Preston North End	L 2-3	1-1	17	Page 3, Ritchie 47	(7688)
15	14	EL	H	Lincoln City	D 0-0	0-0	19		1848
16	21	EL	A	Bury	W 2-0	1-0	14	Page 36, Todd 86	(2590)
17	28	EL	H	Chester City	D 0-0	0-0	16		1847
18	31	EL	H	Plymouth Argyle	D 2-2	0-1	17	Charles 67, Trebble 89	1876
19	N 4	EL	A	Cambridge United	L 1-4	0-2	18	Ritchie 67	(2304)
20	7	AWS 1/2	A	Preston North End	L 1-2	0-1		Kelly 56	(5639)
21	11	FAC 1	H	Chesterfield	L 0-2	0-0			2354
22	18	EL	H	Gillingham	L 0-2	0-2	19		1546
23	25	EL	A	Scunthorpe United	D 3-3	0-2	20	Trebble 58, Wells 73, Rockett 79	(2231)
24	D 9	EL	H	Darlington	L 1-2	1-0	21	Charles 9	1585
25	16	EL	A	Torquay United	D 0-0	0-0	21		(1680)
26	23	EL	H	Northampton Town	W 2-1	0-0	20	Trebble 50, Ritchie 64	1404
27	J 6	EL	A	Hartlepool United	D 1-1	1-0	20	Magee 18	(2252)
28	9	EL	H	Barnet	D 1-1	1-1	19	Ritchie 24	1310
29	13	EL	A	Fulham	L 0-1	0-1	21		(3557)
30	20	EL	H	Doncaster Rovers	L 0-2	0-0	23		1661
31	23	EL	H	Rochdale	D 1-1	0-0	22	Trebble 68	1401
32	F 3	EL	H	Exeter City	D 0-0	0-0	21		1307
33	6	EL	A	Colchester United	D 1-1	0-1	21	Trebble 66	(2299)
34	10	EL	A	Rochdale	W 2-0	0-0	20	Toman 53, Midgley 55	(1662)
35	17	EL	H	Cardiff City	W 1-0	1-0	17	Toman 17	1414
36	20	EL	A	Wigan Athletic	L 0-2	0-2	18		(2208)
37	24	EL	A	Hereford United	D 0-0	0-0	19		(2568)
38	27	EL	H	Mansfield Town	D 1-1	1-1	17	Ritchie 11(pen)	1304
39	M 2	EL	H	Hartlepool United	L 1-2	1-1	19	Hicks 42	2420
40	9	EL	A	Northampton Town	L 0-2	0-1	22		(4621)
41	16	EL	H	Colchester United	D 0-0	0-0	23		1201
42	19	EL	A	Leyton Orient	L 0-1	0-0	23		(2121)
43	23	EL	A	Barnet	L 0-1	0-0	23		(2054)
44	30	EL	H	Preston North End	L 1-2	0-1	23	Ritchie 79	3771
45	A 2	EL	A	Lincoln City	L 1-3	1-2	23	Robertson 6(og)	(2010)
46	6	EL	A	Chester City	L 0-5	0-3	23		(2485)
47	9	EL	H	Bury	L 0-2	0-2	23		1773
48	13	EL	A	Plymouth Argyle	L 1-5	0-1	23	Ritchie 90(pen)	(6949)
49	20	EL	H	Cambridge United	W 2-0	1-0	23	Rockett 21, Charles 89	1401
50	27	EL	H	Scunthorpe United	L 1-4	1-3	23	Knowles 40	1738
51	M 4	EL	A	Gillingham	L 0-1	0-1	23		(10421)

Best Home League Attendance: 3771 v Preston North End   Smallest: 1201 v Colchester United   Average: 1710

Goal Scorers:
EL(39):   Ritchie(8), Trebble(5), Charles(5), Page(5), Rockett(4), Toman(2), Todd(1), Wells(1), Midgley(1), Knowles(1), Hicks(1), Heald(1), Gardner(1), D'Auria(1), Magee(1), Opponent(s)(1)
CC(1):   D'Auria(1)
FAC(0):
AWS(1):   Kelly(1)

1995-96

(D) Boardman	(F) Charles	(F) Curtis	(M) D'Auria	(D) Fairclough	(M) Gardner	(F) Heald	(D) Hicks	(G) Ironside	(G) Kelly	(F) Kinnaird	(M) Knowles	(M) Lucas	(F) Magee	(D) Meyer	(F) Midgley	(M) Myers	(F) Page	(F) Partridge	(F) Ritchie	(M) Rockett	(F) Sansam	((F) Sunderland	(M) Thew	(M) Todd	(M) Toman	(F) Trebble	(M) Wells	(M) Willgrass		
S	X		X			S	X	X			X	X					X		X	X			X	X					R.Pearson	1
S	X	X2	X				X		X		X	X					X		X1	X			X	X				S1	R.Poulain	2
S	X		X			S1	X		X		X	X					X		X	X			X	X1				S	W.Rennie	3
	X		X			S1	X		X		X	X					X		X1	X			X	X				S	R.Fernandiz	4
S3	X		X			S2	X3		X		X	X					S1		X	X			X	X2		X1			B.Knight	5
S	X		X		S1	S2	X		X		X	X					X		X2	X			X1	X1					D.Allison	6
S	X		X		X	S	X		X		X	X					X		X	X			S1	X1					A.Butler	7
	X1		X		X	S1	X		X		X	X					X		X	X				X		X		S	T.Leake	8
	X	X1	X		X	S1	X		X		X	X					X		X	X				X				S	P.Rejer	9
	X		X		X	S	X	X			X	X					X		X1	X			S2	X2		S1			G.B.Frankland	10
X	X		X		X	S		X			X	X					X			X			X			X		S	P.Richards	11
																														12
S	X		X			S2	X		X		X	X					X1		X2	X			X1	X		S1			K.J.Breen	13
S1	X		X			S1	X		X		X	X					X1		X1	X			X1	X		S1			J.Kirkby	14
S	X		X			S	X		X		X	X					X		X	X			X1	X		S1			R.Furnaulds	15
S	X		X				X	X		X	X	X					X		X	X			S	X		S			K.M.Lynch	16
S	X		X			S2	X		X		X	X					X2		X1	X			X			S1			T.Lunt	17
S	X		X			S	X		X		X	X					X1		S1	X			X			X			N.Barry	18
S2	X		X				X	X		X	X						S1		X2	X			S	X		X			J.Rushton	19
																													S.Mathieson	20
X	X		X			S2	X	X		X1	X	X					X		X2					X	S	S1			P.Danson	21
S	X		X			X	X	X		X	X						X		X	X			S	X		X		S	T.Heilbron	22
S	X1		X				X	X		X	X						X2		X	X			S2	X		X		S1	R.Poulain	23
	X						X	X		X	X	X	X		X		S1		X1	X			X			X		S	U.D.Rennie	24
	X						X	X		X	X	X	X		X		X		X	X			S	X		X		S	M.Fletcher	25
	X						X	X		X	X	X	X				S		X	X			S	X		X		S	R.Pearson	26
X	X						X		X	X	X	X					S		X	X			S	X		X			R.Furnandiz	27
X	X						X		X	X	X	X					S		X	X			X1			X1		S1	G.Frankland	28
X	X						S2	X		X	X	X	X1		X		S1		X	X			X3			X1			D.Orr	29
X3	X						S1	X		X	X	X		X2			S2		X	X			X1			X		S3	N.Barry	30
	X	X1					X	X		X	X	X		X		S1	X	X3					S1	X		X1			S.Baines	31
	X	X1					X	X		X	X	X	X		X	S1	X		S				S	X					D.Laws	32
	X	S					X	X		X	X	X		X		X1	X	S1	X				X	X					B.Knight	33
	X						X	X		X	X	X	X	S	X	X	S	X					X	X					S.Mathieson	34
	X1	S					X	X		X	X	X	X		X	S1	X	S	X				X	X					I.G.Cruikshanks	35
	X	S1					X	X		X	X	X		X1	X1	X	S1	X					X	X					K.Breen	36
	X	S					X	X		X	X	X	X	X		X	S	X	X				X	X					E.Wolstenholme	37
	X	S2					X	X		X	X	X	X1		X	X	S1	X2	X				X	X					R.Poulain	38
	X	S					X	X		X	X	X	X	X		X	S	X	X				X	X					D.Allison	39
	X1						X	X		X	X	X		X		X	X	X	X				X1	S1		S1			A.Wiley	40
	X	S					X	X		X	X	X	X1		S	X	X	X					X	X	X	S1			T.West	41
	X						X	X		X	X	X		X		S2	X			S1			X2	X	X1	X		S1	T.Leake	42
X2	X						X	X		X	X	X		X		X				X			X1	S2	X	S1			G.Singh	43
X2	X		X				X	X		X	X	X		X		S1	X	X1					X1	X					T.Heilbron	44
	X		X				X	X		X	X	S1		S2	X1	X		X	X	X	X	S				X2			E.Lomas	45
	X		X				X	X		X	X	S1		X	S1	X		X1	X1				X1			X1			M.Fletcher	46
	X		X				X	X		X	X	X		S1		X	X1	X2	X2				S2			S2			G.Cain	47
	X		X				X	X		X	X	X		S2		X	X2	X1	S1							X	S		G.Barber	48
	X		X				X	X		X	X	X		X		X	X	S	S							X			G.Frankland	49
	X		X				X	X		X	X	X		X		X		S	S				S1			X	X1		E.Wolstenholme	50
X1	X						X	X		X	X	X		X			X		X			X2	S1			X	S2		K.Leach	51
6	41	3	18	7	5	1	39	40	6	3	46	44	26	3	14	5	26	5	33	39	5	3	9	23	12	25	10	2	EL Appearances	
3	0	2	0	0	1	7	2	0	0	0	0	0	2	0	2	1	10	2	4	0	1	1	4	0	4	7	3	5	EL Sub Appearances	
0	2	0	2	0	0	0+1	2	0	2	0	2	2	0	0	0	0	2	0	2	2	0	0	2	2	0	0	0	0+1	CC Appearances	
1	1	0	1	0	0	0+1	1	1	0	1	1	1	0	0	0	0	1	0	1	0	0	0	0	1	0	0+1	0	0	FAC Appearances	
																													AWS Appearances	

Also Played: (M) Anthony X(37,40), S(38,39). (M) Carr S(51). (M) Cook X(43,50), S(49). (D) Foreman S2(43), X(45), S3(46). (M) O'Riordan S(24), X2(43). (M) O'Riordan S2(8), X1(19).

CLUB RECORDS

RECORD LEAGUE VICTORY & MOST GOALS SCORED
4-0 v BoltonWanderers, Division 4, 29.8.1987 4-0 v Newport County (a), Division 4,12.4.19880 4-0 v Doncaster R., Division 3, 23.4.94 5-2 v Torquay Utd,Division 4, 29.9.1988
Most Goals Scored in a First Class Cup Tie
6-0 v Rhyl Athletic, FA Cup Round1, 29.11.1930

RECORD LEAGUE DEFEAT
1-5 v Barnet, Division 4, 8.2.1992
Record Cup Defeat
0-8 v Mansfield Town (h), FA Cup Rnd 1, 22.11.1952

MOST LEAGUE GOALS
67, Division 4, 1988-89

MOST LEAGUE POINTS
(3pts for win) 77, Division 4, 1988-89

RECORD TRANSFER FEE RECEIVED
£350,000 (￣100,000 7/89 + ￣250,000 9/92) from Notts County for Craig Short

RECORD TRANSFER FEE PAID
£100,000 to Leicester City for Martin Russell,February 1989

BEST PERFORMANCES
League: 5th Division 4, 1988-89 FA Cup: Third Round (1931,1938, 1976, 1978) League Cup: Fourth Round, 1992-93

HONOURS
FA Trophy Winners 1973, 1976, 1977 (Record) GM Vauxhall ConfereneceChampions 1987 Midland League Champions 1930 Scarborough & District LeagueChampions 1946 North Easter League Champions 1963 Vauxhall Floodlit League Winners 1973, 1975 Northern Premier League Cup Winners 1977 Bob Lord TrophyWinners 1984 North Eastern Counties League Cup Winners 1963 East Riding CupWinners (8 times) 1888, 1889, 1891, 1892, 1893, 1897, 1901, 1902 North RidingSenior Cup Winners 1909, 1929, 1939, 1948, 1956, 1959, 1961, 1962, 1969, 1973,1974, 1977, 1978, 1981, 1982, 1985, 1988 Festival of Football Winners 1990

INDIVIDUAL CLUB RECORDS

MOST APPEARANCES FOR CLUB
Steve Richards (1987-91): (League 164 + FA Cup 5 +League Cup 15 + Others 12) 0Total 196

MOST CAPPED PLAYER
Kyle Lightbourne, Bermuda

RECORD GOALSCORER IN A MATCH
Darren Foreman 3 v Northampton, Div 3, 10.10.1992(4-2) & Darren Foreman 3 v York City, Div 3, 19.12.1992 (4-2)

RECORD LEAGUE GOALSCORER IN A SEASON
(Football League only) Darren Foreman 27,Div 4/3, 1992-93
In All Competitions: Darren Foreman, 31 (League 27, Lge Cup 2, Autoglass 2)1992-93

RECORD LEAGUE GOALSCORER IN A CAREER
(Football League only) Darren Foreman,34, 1991-93
In All Competitions: Darren Foreman 40 (League 34, League Cup 4, Others 2)1991-93

OLDEST PLAYER TO PLAY IN A LEAGUE MATCH
John Burridge, 41 years 338 days v Doncaster Rovers, Division 3, 6.11.1993

YOUNGEST PLAYER IN A LEAGUE MATCH
Lee Harper, v Scunthorpe Utd, Division 3,2.10.1993

PREVIOUS MANAGERS

(Since the war): G Hall H Taylor F Taylor A Bell RHalton C Robson G Higgins A Smailes E Brown A Frank S Myers GShaw C Appleton K Houghton C Appleton J McAnearney J Cottam H Dunn N Warnock R McHale P Chambers B Ayre

ADDITIONAL INFORMATION
Previous Leagues: Northern (1898-1910) Yorkshire Combination (1910-14) Northern (1914-26) Yorkshire (1926-27) Midland (1927-40) Scarborough &District (1945-46) Midland (1946-60) Northern Counties (1960-62) NorthEastern (1962-63) Midland (1963-68) Northern Premier (1968-79) Alliance Premier (1979-87) Football League (1987-)
Club colours: Red & white, white shorts, red socks.
Change colours: All blue.

Reserves League: Pontins Division 3, Northern Intermediate.

LONGEST LEAGUE RUNS

of undefeated matches:	9 (1988, 1990, 1990-91)	of league matches w/out a win:	6 (1989)
of undefeated home matches:	13 (1992)	of undefeated away matches:	6 (1.5.1993 - 2.10.1993)
without home win:	13 (23.3.1993 - 16.10.1993)	without an away win:	11 (1990,1992)
of league wins: 3 (x2 1987-88, 1988-89, x2 1989-90, x2 1992-93,94)		of home wins:	6 (1987)
of league defeats:	6 (1989)	of away wins:	3 (1992)

THE MANAGER

MICK WADSWORTH . . . . appointed July 1996.

PREVIOUS CLUBS
As Manager . . . . Carlisle United.
As Asst.Man/Coach . . . . Barnsley, Norwich City.
As a player . . . . Scunthorpe United.

HONOURS
As a Manager . . . . **Carlisle**: Division 3 Champions 1994/95.
As a Player . . . . None.

SCARBOROUGH

PLAYERS NAME / Honours	Ht	Wt	Birthdate	Birthplace Transfers	Contract Date	Clubs	APPEARANCES				GOALS			
							League	L/Cup	FA Cup	Other	Lge	L/C	FAC	Oth
G O A L K E E P E R S														
Ironside Ian	6.1	11.9	08/03/64	Sheffield	17/09/82	Barnsley								
				Free	01/08/83	North Ferriby								
				Free	08/03/88	Scarborough	88	2	2	10				
				£80000	15/08/91	Middlesbrough	12+1	2						
				Loan	05/03/92	Scarborough	7							
					23/09/93	Stockport County	17+2		1	1				
				Free	23/03/95	Scarborough	49		1					
Martin Kevin	6.0	12.8	26/06/76	Bromsgrove	01/08/94	Scarborough	3		2	1				
				Loan	24/11/95	Guiseley								
D E F E N D E R S														
Bennett Gary E	6.1	12.1	04/12/61	Manchester		Ashton United								
				Free	08/09/79	Manchester City								
				Free	16/09/81	Cardiff City	85+2	6	3		11	1		
				£65,000	26/07/84	Sunderland	362+7	34+1	17+1	21	23	1		1
				Free		Carlisle United	26			5	5			1
				Free	10/07/96	Scarborough								
Hicks Stuart	6.1	12.6	30/05/67	Peterborough	10/08/84	Peterborough Utd								
					01/08/85	Wisbech								
				Free	24/03/88	Colchester United	57+7	2	5	5			1	
				Free	19/08/90	Scunthorpe United	67	4	4	8	1		1	
				Free	10/08/92	Doncaster Rovers	36	2	1	2				
					27/08/93	Huddersfield Town	20+2	3	3	1	1			
					24/03/94	Preston North End	3+1			1				1
					22/02/95	Scarborough	45+2	2	1		1			
M I D F I E L D														
Knowles Darren	5.6	10.1	08/10/70	Sheffield	01/07/89	Sheffield United								
				£3000	14/09/89	Stockport County	51+12	2+4		14+1				
				Free	04/08/93	Scarborough	127	8	8	4	2			
Lucas Richard	5.10	11.4	22/09/70	Chapletown	01/07/89	Sheffield United	8+2		1	0+1				
				£40000	24/12/92	Preston North End	47+3		4	4+1				
					05/07/95	Scarborough	44	2	1					
Rockett Jason	5.11	11.5	26/09/69	London	25/03/92	Rotherham United								
				Free	04/08/93	Scarborough	99+1	6	5	3	4			
Willgrass Alex			08/04/76	Scarborough	01/08/94	Scarborough	2+5	0+1						
F O R W A R D S														
Daws Anthony \ E: Y.1.	5.8	11.10	10/09/66	Sheffield	18/09/84	Notts County	6+2				1			
				Free	21/08/86	Sheffield United	7+4		1	0+1	3			
				Free	02/07/87	Scunthorpe United	166+17	15+1	9	23+1	63	4	2	3
				£50000	25/03/93	Grimsby Town	14+2	2		1+1	1			1
				£50000	15/02/94	Lincoln City	42+8	0+1	1	1	13			
				Loan	15/03/96	Halifax Town								
				Free	06/07/96	Scarborough								
Ritchie Andy \ E: u21.1, Y.4, S. Div.2'91.	5.10	11.10	28/11/60	Manchester	05/12/77	Manchester United	26+7	3+2	3+1		13			
				£500000	17/10/80	Brighton & H.A.	82+7	3+1	9		23	1	2	
				£150000	25/03/83	Leeds United	127+9	11	9	2+1	40	3	1	
				£50000	14/08/87	Oldham Athletic	187+30	18+2	8+2	3	83	18	4	
				Free	03/08/95	Scarborough	33+4	2	1		8			
Sansom Christian	6.0	11.7	26/12/75	Hull	23/12/75	Scunthorpe United	10+11		2+1	1+4	1			
					01/03/96	Scarborough								
Sunderland Jon	5.11	11.9	02/11/75	Newcastle	18/07/94	Blackpool	0+2			0+1				
				Loan	12/10/95	Northwich Victoria								
				Free	28/03/96	Scarborough	3+1							

THE McCAIN STADIUM
Seamer Road, Scarborough YO12 4HF
Tel: 01723 375 094

Capacity 5,900
Covered Standing 1,000
Seating..3,500.
Terracing...1,400.

First game..Not known.
First floodlit game ....Not known.

ATTENDANCES
Highest ....11,162 v Luton Town, FAC 3rd Rnd, 1938.
Lowest ....412 v Scunthorpe Utd, AMC, 27.9.1993.

OTHER GROUNDS...None.

HOW TO GET TO THE GROUND
The ground is situated on the main Scarborough-York Road (A64).
Half-a-mile on left past B&Q going into Town.

Car Parking
In streets around the ground.

Nearest Railway Station
Scarborough Central (2 miles)

MATCHDAY TICKET PRICES
Main Stand £9.50

Terraces. £7
OAP £3.50
Juv. £1.50

Ticket Office Telephone no. . . . . . . 01723 375 094.

MATCHDAY PROGRAMME

Programme Editor. . . . . Eric Pickup.

Number of pages . . . . 36.

Price . . . . £1.30.

Subscriptions . . . . £30.

Local Newspapers . . . . Scarborough Evening News, The Mercury.

Local Radio Stations. . . . . Radio York, Y.C.R. Radio.

SCUNTHORPE UNITED
(The Iron)
NATIONWIDE LEAGUE DIVISION 3
SPONSORED BY: PLEASURE ISLAND

996-97 - Back Row (L-R): Paul Wilson, Kirk Jackson, Mark Samways, Lee Turnbull, Mario Ziccardi, Russell Bradley, Chris Hope.
iddle Row: Paul Wilson (Youth Development Officer), Mark Sertori, Andy McFarlane, Alan Knill, David Moss, Michael Walsh, Nigel Adkins (Physiotherapist).
Front Row: Jamie Paterson, David D'Auria, Phillip Clarkson, Mick Buxton (Manager), Don Rowing (Chief Executive), John Eyre, Steven Housham, Andrew Murfin.

SCUNTHORPE UNITED
FORMED IN 1904
TURNED PROFESSIONAL IN 1912
LTD COMPANY IN 1912

CHAIRMAN: K Wagstaff
VICE-CHAIRMAN
R Garton
DIRECTORS
B Borrill, C Plumtree, B Collen, S Wharton,
J Godfrey
CHIEF EXECUTIVE/SECRETARY
A D Rowing (01724 848 077)

MANAGER: Mick Buxton
YOUTH TEAM MANAGER
Paul Wilson

STATISTICIAN FOR THE DIRECTORY
Michael Norton

With 15 wins, 15 draws and 16 defeats, Scunthorpe United finished the 1995-96 season in 12th position, nether chasing for a play-off place or fighting off relegation.

Having missed the 1994-95 play-off finals by three points, finishing in seventh, expectations of going one better were high. These hopes were soon laid to rest when only one victory could be obtained from their first nine matches. Three straight wins in October however, lifted the club to 9th position from 20th, and showed just what the side could achieve. This was followed by more inconsistency leading up to January when the side proved, yet again, that they had what it takes by going undefeated in the opening month of 1997. Four straight victories, with 14 goals scored and only 4 against, if only they could maintain that form.

Alas they didn't and it wasn't until March 23rd that they recorded their next victory, followed by another...and another...in fact they put together a run of five victories, including a 4-0 thrashing of Exeter City. The Club only lost one in their last twelve which was pleasing to the supporters, if only a little to late. But it did see them rise from 20th position to their final resting place of 12th.

There was no success in any of the Cup competitions either. A Coca-Cola First Round 1st Leg tie at home to Rotherham United was won 4-1 and should have been enough to see them through to the next round. It wasn't - Rotherham won the 2nd Leg 0-5! A 1-1 draw against Wigan and a 0-4 defeat at home to Bury saw them exit the Auto Windscreen Shield. In the F.A. Cup non-League Northwich were defeat (2-1), which in turn brought Shrewsbury to Glanford Park in the Second Round. A 1-1 draw was followed by a 1-2 defeat in the replay.

If Scunthorpe can maintain the form they showed in flashes in the 1995-96 season, they should be able to put in a good promotion challenge.

SCUNTHORPE UNITED

League: 12th   FA Cup: 2nd Rnd   Coca-Cola Cup: 1st Rnd   Auto Windscreen Shield: 2nd Rnd

M	DATE	COMP	VEN	OPPONENTS	RESULT	HT	LP	GOAL SCORERS/GOAL TIMES	ATT.
1	A 12	EL	H	Cambridge United	L 1-2	1-0	16	Eyre 36	2561
2	15	CC 1/1	H	Rotherham United	W 4-1	1-1		Eyre 20, 84, McFarlane 56, Ford 67	2110
3	19	EL	A	Wigan Athletic	L 1-2	1-1	22	Turnbull 44	(3153)
4	22	CC 1/2	A	Rotherham United	L 0-5	0-1			(2206)
5	26	EL	H	Barnet	W 2-0	1-0	16	Thomas 49(og), McFarlane 90	1970
6	28	EL	A	Lincoln City	D 2-2	0-0	10	Graham 74, Eyre 90	(2674)
7	S 2	EL	A	Exeter City	L 0-1	0-1	18		(2893)
8	9	EL	H	Gillingham	D 1-1	1-1	18	Hope 6	2423
9	12	EL	H	Chester City	L 0-2	0-2	22		1875
10	16	EL	A	Preston North End	D 2-2	0-1	20	Bullimore 58(pen), Sansam 84	(7397)
11	23	EL	A	Mansfield Town	D 1-1	0-0	22	McFarlane 90	(2478)
12	26	AWS 1/1	A	Wigan Athletic	D 1-1	0-0		Housham 46	(1064)
13	30	EL	H	Colchester United	W 1-0	1-0	20	Eyre 15	2051
14	O 7	EL	H	Northampton Town	D 0-0	0-0	21		2455
15	14	EL	A	Hartlepool United	L 0-2	0-0	22		(2608)
16	17	AWS 1/1	H	Bury	L 0-4	0-0		McFarlane (2), Eyre, Bracey (og)	877
17	21	EL	H	Leyton Orient	W 2-0	1-0	20	Paterson 13, Hope 81	2315
18	28	EL	A	Torquay United	W 8-1	4-1	14	McFarlane 12, 34, 45 67 (4), Eyre 30, 87, Knill 52, Ford 53	(2137)
19	31	EL	A	Cardiff City	W 1-0	1-0	9	McFarlane 15	(2024)
20	N 4	EL	H	Rochdale	L 1-3	0-2	12	Ford 84	3003
21	11	FAC 1	A	Northwich	W 3-1	0-0		Ford 55, McFarlane 66, 88	(2685)
22	18	EL	A	Darlington	D 0-0	0-0	13		(2078)
23	25	EL	H	Scarborough	D 3-3	2-0	13	Ford 27, Clarkson 37, Bullimore 53(pen)	2231
24	28	AWS 2	H	York City	L 0-3	0-0			1734
25	D 2	FAC 2	H	Shrewsbury Town	D 1-1	0-0		Eyre 67	2718
26	9	EL	H	Mansfield Town	D 1-1	0-0	13	McFarlane 57	2522
27	12	FAC 2R	A	Shrewsbury Town	L 1-2	0-2		Paterson 76	(3313)
28	16	EL	A	Colchester United	L 1-2	0-2	15	Young 63	(2138)
29	19	EL	A	Hereford United	L 0-3	0-1	16		(2516)
30	J 13	EL	H	Wigan Athletic	W 3-1	1-0	17	Jones 29, D'Auria 58, McFarlane 67	2288
31	20	EL	A	Cambridge United	W 2-1	0-0	17	McFarlane 52, Wilson 90(pen)	(2413)
32	23	EL	A	Plymouth Argyle	W 3-1	2-0	13	Hope 20, Turnbull 33, McFarlane 81	(4712)
33	30	EL	A	Fulham	W 3-1	1-0	11	D'Auria 22, Jones 69, Paterson 72	(2176)
34	F 3	EL	A	Barnet	L 0-1	0-1	11		(1674)
35	10	EL	H	Plymouth Argyle	D 1-1	1-1	12	McFarlane 4	2789
36	17	EL	A	Chester City	L 0-3	0-1	14		(2401)
37	24	EL	H	Preston North End	L 1-2	0-0	14	Jones 51	3638
38	27	EL	A	Gillingham	D 0-0	0-0	14		(5557)
39	M 2	EL	A	Bury	L 0-3	0-1	16		(3035)
40	5	EL	H	Lincoln City	L 2-3	0-1	17	Eyre 51, Clarkson 64	2411
41	9	EL	H	Hereford United	L 0-1	0-0	20		1903
42	16	EL	A	Doncaster Rovers	L 0-2	0-0	22		(1920)
43	23	EL	H	Fulham	W 3-1	0-0	19	Knill 32, Ford 51, D'Auria 69	1919
44	26	EL	H	Exeter City	W 4-0	0-0	16	Eyre 50, 89, Ford 55, McFarlane 69	1615
45	30	EL	A	Northampton Town	W 2-1	0-0	15	Clarkson 48, McFarlane 50	(4290)
46	A 2	EL	H	Hartlepool United	W 2-1	1-1	15	Ford 10, Bradley 81	2100
47	6	EL	H	Torquay United	W 1-0	1-0	14	Ford 34	2247
48	8	EL	A	Leyton Orient	D 0-0	0-0	14		(2814)
49	13	EL	H	Cardiff City	D 1-1	1-1	14	Knill 11	2044
50	16	EL	H	Bury	L 1-2	0-0	14	Nicholson 84	2132
51	20	EL	A	Rochdale	D 1-1	0-1	14	Clarkson 64	(1654)
52	23	EL	H	Doncaster Rovers	D 2-2	1-1	13	Turnbull 25, Clarkson 82	2614
53	27	EL	A	Scarborough	W 4-1	3-1	13	McFarlane 5, Clarkson 29, D'Auria 34, 57(pen)	(1738)
54	M 4	EL	H	Darlington	D 3-3	2-0	12	Eyre 4, 34, McFarlane 86	4847

Best Home League Attendance: 4847 v Darlington   Smallest: 1615 v Exeter City   Average: 2432

Goal Scorers:

EL(67): McFarlane(16), Eyre(10), Ford(7), Clarkson(6), D'Auria(5), Turnbull(3), Jones(3), Knill(3), Hope(3), Paterson(2), Bullimore(2), Bradley(1), Opponent(s)(1), Young(1), Wilson(1), Graham(1), Sansam(1), Nicholson(1)

CC(4): Eyre(2), Ford(1), McFarlane(1)

FAC(5): McFarlane(2), Paterson(1), Ford(1), Eyre(1)

AWS(5): McFarlane(2), Housham(1), Eyre(1), Opponent(s)(1)

(D) Bradley	(M) Bullimore	(G) Butler	(M) Clarkson	(M) D'Auria	(M) Eyre	(M) Field	(M) Ford	(G) Germaine	(M) Graham	(D) Hope	(M) Housham	(M) Jones	(D) Knill	(M) McFarlane	(F) Murfin	(F) Nicholson	(D) O'Halleron	(F) Paterson	(G) Samways	(M) Sansam	(M) Thornber	(M) Turnbull	(F) Varadi	(D) Walsh	(D) Wilson	(M) Wilson	(F) Young	(M) Ziccardi		
X	S				X		X			S			X	X		X			X		X	X		X	X				G.Frankland	1
X	S1				X		X						X1	X		X3			X		X2	X		X	X		S2		J.Rushton	2
X	S1				X		X				X			X		X3			X1		X1	X		X	X		S2	S	K.Lynch	3
X			X1		X2						X			X		X			X		X	X		X	X		S1	S	M.Bailey	4
X	X				X				S	X	X		X	X		X			X	S	X				X		S		R.Pearson	5
X1	X				X				S1	X	X		X	X		X			X	S	X				X		S		S.Bennett	6
	X				X				X	X	X		X	X1	X				X	S	S	S		X			S1		R.Gifford	7
X	X				X		S1		S	X	X		X	X		X1			X		X				X		S1		S.Baines	8
X1	X				X		S1		S2	X	X3		X	X		X			X		X2				X		S3		R.Furnandiz	9
S3	X		X1		X					X	X		X	X		X			S1		X3			X	X		X2		M.Fletcher	10
S3	X		X		X					X	X		X	X		X			S1		X1			X3	X		X1		K.Breen	11
X					X	S				X	X		X	X		X			S1		X	X			X		X1	S	D.Allison	12
X			X3		X					X	X		X	X		X3	S3	S2			X1	X	S1		X		X2		W.Burns	13
X			X2		X					X	X		X	X		X		S2	S1		X2	X	S2		X		X1		A.R.Leake	14
X	S1				X					X	X		X	X		X		S2	X		S2	X2			X1		X2		S.Mathieson	15
X2	X				X					X	X		X	X		X		S2	X3	S1	X						S3			16
S	X				X					X	X		X	X		X		S2	X2		X				X		S1		E.Lomas	17
	X1				X					X	X		X	X3		X		S3	X		X			S1	X		S2		M.Pierce	18
X		X			X					X	X		X	X1		X		S2	X2		X			S1	X		S		R.J.Harris	19
X1	S1	X			X					X	X		X	X		X		S	X		X			X	X		S		R.D.Furnandiz	20
X	X				X		X1			X	X		X	X		X		S1	X		X			X	X			S	S.Lodge	21
X	X	X			X					X	X		X	X		X		S	X		X	S1		X1	X		S		T.West	22
X	X2	X			X					X	S1		X1	X		S2			X		X			X	X		S		R.Poulain	23
X	X2				X					X	X1			X		S1			X		X	X		X	X		S2	S	R.Pearson	24
X				X	X					X	X			X		X			X		X	X		X	X		S	S	G.Frankland	25
X	S		X		X					X	X			X2		X1			X		X	S1		X	X		S2		M.Riley	26
X	X				X1					X	X			X		S1			X		X			X	X	X		S	G.Frankland	27
X			X		X					X	X			X		S1			X		X			X	X1	X	X	S	I.S.Hemley	28
X			X		X					X	X			X		S1			X		X	S2		X2	X		X1	S	A.Wiley	29
X			X	X	X					X			X	X	S	X2			S1		X1	X		S2	X		X		G.Singh	30
X			X	X2	X					X			X	X	S	S1			X1		X1			S2	X		X		G.Barber	31
X			X	X	X					X	S1	X1	S	X	X	X			X		X			X	X				M.Fletcher	32
X			X	X	X					X	S2	X2	X	X		X			X		X	X1		X	X		S		F.Stretton	33
			X	X	S1					X	S2	X	X	X		X1			X		X	S	X2	X	X				E.K.Wolstenholme	34
X		X	X	X1	S1					S		X	X	X		X			X		S			X	X				D.Laws	35
X		X	X	X						S	S	X	X	X		X			S1		S			X	X1				K.A.Leach	36
		X	X	S2	X					X	S1	X3	X	X2		S3			X	X				X1					J.Kirkby	37
X		S	X	X	X					X	X	X	X	X		X			S		S	S							S.Madison	38
X			X	X	X					X	X	X	X	X		X			S		S	S							M.Brandwood	39
X			X1	X	X					S	X1		X	X		X			X		S1			X	X				P.Richards	40
X			X	X	X1	X				S3	X2	X3	X	X		X			X1		S2			X	X				G.Frankland	41
X			S1	X	X					X			X	X		X1		S			S1			X1	X				P.Taylor	42
X			X	X	X					X	S1		X	X		S		S			X			X1					S.Baines	43
X			S1	X	X					X	S		X	X		S		S			X1				X				G.Singh	44
X			X	X	X					X	S		X	X		S		S			X				X				C.Wilkes	45
X			X	X	X					X	S		X	X		S		S			X				X				B.Burns	46
			X	X	X					X	X		X2	X		X1		S2	X	S1	S				X				A.P.D'Urso	47
			X	X	X					X	X1		X	X		X		S1	X		X				X		X	S	A.Wiley	48
			X	X	X1	X2				X			X	X		X		S2	X	S1	S				X				T.Heilbron	49
X			S1	X		X1				X			X	X		X		S1			X1				X				U.Rennie	50
X			X	X						X	X		S2	X		X		S1	X2	S2	X				X	X2			R.Pearson	51
X1			X	X	X		S			X	X2		X2	X		X		S1	S2	X	X			X					M.C.Bailey	52
X			X	X2	S1		S			X	X		X	X		X1		X			X				X		S		E.Wolstenholme	53
X			X	X	X					X	X		X1	X		X		S1			X	S			X		S		R.Furnandiz	54
36	11	2	21	27	36	0	35	11	1	38	21	11	38	41	1	13	6	23	33	2	14	16	0	22	40	0	7	0	EL Appearances	
2	3	0	3	0	3	0	3	0	2	2	6	0	0	5	0	22	1	2	0	3	2	6	2	2	0	0	7	0	EL Sub Appearances	
2	0+1	0	0	0	2	0	2	0	1	0	0	1	0	2	0	0	2	0	2	0	2	2	2	2	0	0	0+2	0	CC Appearances	
3	2	0	0	0	3	0	3	0	0	2	1	0	1	2	0	1+2	0	3	3	0	1	2	0	2	3	0	1	0	FAC Appearances	
3	2	0	0	0	2	0	3	0	0	3	2	0	2	3	0	0+3	0	2	3	1+1	2	1	0	1	2	0	1+2	0	AWS Appearances	

CLUB RECORDS

RECORD LEAGUE VICTORY
8-1 v LutonTown, Div 3, 24.4.1965
Most Goals Scored in a Cup Tie
9-0 v Boston United, FA Cup 1st Round,21.11.1953

RECORD LEAGUE DEFEAT
0-8 v Carlisle United, Div 3N, 25.12.1952
Record Cup Defeat
0-7 v Coventry City, FA Cup Round 1, 29.11.1934

MOST LEAGUE POINTS
(3pts a win) 83, Div 4, 1982-83
(2pts a win) 66, Div 3N,1957-58

MOST LEAGUE GOALS
88, Div 3N, 1957-58

RECORD TRANSFER FEE RECEIVED
£400,000 from Aston Villa for Neil Cox, February1991

RECORD TRANSFER FEE PAID
£80,000 to York City for Ian Helliwell, August 1991

BEST PERFORMANCES
League: 4th Div 2, 1961-62 FA Cup: 5th Round 1957-58,1969-70
League Cup: Never beyond 3rd Round

HONOURS
Div 3N Champions 1957-58

LEAGUE CAREER
Elected to Div 3N 1950   Promoted to Div 2 1957-58
Relegated to Div 3 1963-64
Relegated to Div 4 1967-68   Promoted to Div 3 1971-72
Relegated to Div 41972-73   Promoted to Div 3 1982-83
Relegated to Div 4 (now Div 3) 1983-84

INDIVIDUAL CLUB RECORDS

MOST APPEARANCES FOR CLUB
Jack Brownsword (1950-65): League 597 + Cup 54 Total 651

MOST CAPPED PLAYER
No Scunthorpe player has won an international cap

RECORD GOALSCORER IN A MATCH:
Barrie Thomas 5 v Luton Town (h), 8-1, Div 3,24.4.1965

RECORD LEAGUE GOALSCORER IN A SEASON
Barrie Thomas 31, Div 2, 1961-62   In AllCompetitions: Barrie Thomas, 31 (all league)

RECORD LEAGUE GOALSCORER IN A CAREER
Steve Cammack 110   In All Competitions: Steve Cammack 120
(League 110, FA Cup 6, League Cup 2, AMC 2) 1979-81 & 1981-86

OLDEST PLAYER IN A LEAGUE MATCH
Jack Brownsword, 41 years, 1965

YOUNGEST PLAYER IN A LEAGUE MATCH
Mike Farrell, 16 years 240 days, 8.11.1975

PREVIOUS MANAGERS

Leslie Jones 1950-51   Bill Corkhill 1951-56   Ron Stuart1956-58
Tony Macshane 1958-59   Bill Lambton (3 days) 1959   Frank Soo
1959-60 Dick Duckworth 1960-64   Freddie Goodwin 1964-67
Ron Ashman 1967-73 Ron Bradley 1973-74   Dickie Rooks 1974-76   Ron Ashman 1976-81   John Duncan1981-83   Allan Clarke
1983-84 Frank Barlow 1984-87 Mick Buxton 1987-91 Bill Green
1991-93   Richard Money 1993-95   Dave Moore 1994-96.

ADDITIONAL INFORMATION
Previous League: Midland League
Previous Name: Merged with Lindsey United in 1910 to become
Scunthorpe and Lindsey United. Dropped the name Lindsey in 1958
Club colours: Sky blue shirts claret stripes, sky blue shorts & socks.
Change colours: Yellow & navy quarters.
Reserves League: Pontins Central League Div 3.

LONGEST LEAGUE RUNS

of undefeated matches:	15 (1957-58, 1971-72)	of league matches w/out a win:	14 (1973-74-1974-75)
of undefeated home matches:	21 (1950-51)	of undefeated away matches:	9 (1981-82-1982-83)
without home win:	7 (1963-64, 1972-73, 1989)	without an away win:	30 (1977-78)
of league wins:	6 (1954, 1965)	of home wins:	7 (1984-85, 1987)
of league defeats:	7 (1972-73)	of away wins:	5 (1965-66)

THE MANAGER

MICK BUXTON . . . . appointed March 1996.

PREVIOUS CLUBS
As Manager . . . . Huddersfield, Scunthorpe Utd, Sunderland.
As Asst.Man/Coach . . . . Halifax (player), Southend Utd, Scunthorpe Utd, Wimbledon..
As a player . . . . Burnley, Halifax.

HONOURS
As a Manager . . . . Division 4 champions 1980. Promotion to Division 2 1983.
As a Player . . . . **Burnley:** 1st Division Championship 1960.

SCUNTHORPE UNITED

PLAYERS NAME / Honours	Ht	Wt	Birthdate	Birthplace Transfers	Contract Date	Clubs	APPEARANCES League	L/Cup	FA Cup	Other	GOALS Lge	L/C	FAC	Oth
G O A L K E E P E R S														
Samways Mark	6.0	11.12	11/11/68	Doncaster	20/08/87	Doncaster Rovers	121	3	4	10				
					26/03/92	Scunthorpe United	155	8	13	16				
D E F E N D E R S														
Bradley Russell	6.2	12.5	28/03/66	Birmingham		Dudley Town								
WFAC'90.					20/05/88	Nottingham Forest								
				Loan	13/11/88	Hereford United	12		1	3	1			
				£15000	26/07/89	Hereford United	75+2	7		5+1	3			
				£45000	06/09/91	Halifax Town	54+2	2	3	4	3			
				Free	30/06/93	Scunthorpe United	94+3	4	10	9	4			
Hope Chris	6.1	12.7	14/11/72	Sheffield		Darlington								
				Free	23/08/90	Nottingham Forest								
				£50000	05/07/93	Scunthorpe United	97+8	3	8	8	3		1	
Knill Alan	6.2	11.7	08/10/64	Slough	14/10/82	Southampton								
W: 1, Y. WFAC'89.				Free	13/07/84	Halifax Town	118	6	6	6	6			
				£15000	14/08/87	Swansea City	89	4	5	7	3			
				£95000	18/08/89	Bury	141+3	7	8	14+1	9		1	1
				Loan	24/09/93	Cardiff City	4							
					05/11/93	Scunthorpe United	102	3	9	6	8			
Walsh Michael	6.0	12.4	05/08/77	Rotherham	01/08/94	Scunthorpe United	25+2	2	2	1				
Wilson Paul	5.10	11.8	02/08/68	Bradford	12/06/86	Huddersfield Town	15	1						
				£30000	23/07/87	Norwich City								
				£30000	12/02/88	Northampton Town	132+9	10	7	6+3	6	1		
				£30000	19/12/91	Halifax Town	45	2	1	2	7			
					01/02/93	Burnley	31		0+1					
				Loan	06/10/94	York City	5							
					09/10/94	York City	16+1		2	1				
					09/08/95	Scunthorpe United	40	2	3	2	1			
M I D F I E L D														
Clarkson Philip I	5.10	10.8	13/11/68	Garstang		Fleetwood Town				1				
				£22500	15/10/91	Crewe Alexandra	76+22	6+2	3+2	7+5	27	1	2	1
					13/03/96	Scunthorpe United	21+3				6			
D'Auria David	5.8	11.0	26/03/70	Swansea	02/08/88	Swansea City	27+18	2+2	1	4	6			
					22/08/92	Scarborough	49+3	3+2	4+1	1	8	1		
				Free	06/12/95	Scunthorpe United	27				5			
Eyre John R	6.1	11.3	09/10/74	Hull	16/07/93	Oldham Athletic	4+6	0+2			1			
				Loan	15/12/94	Scunthorpe United	9				8			
				£40000	04/07/95	Scunthorpe United	36+3	2	3	2	10	2	1	1
Housham Steve	5.10	11.7	24/02/76	Gainsborough	23/12/93	Scunthorpe United	25+6		1	2+1				1
McFarlane Andy	6.3	12.6	30/11/68	Wolverhampton		Cradley Heath								
GT'94.				£20000	20/11/90	Portsmouth	0+2							
				£20000	06/08/92	Swansea City	33+22	3	0+6	7+5	8	1	3	2
				£15000	04/08/95	Scunthorpe United	41+5	2	2	3	16	1	2	2
Turnbull Lee	6.0	11.9	27/09/67	Stockton	07/09/85	Middlesbrough	8+8	0+1		1+1	4			1
					24/08/87	Aston Villa								
				£17500	03/11/87	Doncaster Rovers	108+15	3+1	5+1	9+1	21	2		2
				£35000	14/02/91	Chesterfield	80+7	2+3	3	5	26	1	1	
					08/10/93	Doncaster Rovers	10+1		2	1	1			
				£20000	21/01/94	Wycombe Wan000d.	8+3	0+1	1	1	1	1		
				Loan	06/03/95	Scunthorpe United	10				3			
				£12000	01/06/95	Scunthorpe United	16+6	2	2	1	3			
Riccardi Marino						Scunthorpe United								
F O R W A R D S														
Paterson Jamie	5.4	10.00	26/04/73	Dumfries		Halifax Town								
					01/08/94	Falkirk	4							
					13/10/95	Scunthorpe United	23+2		3	2	2		1	

GLANFORD PARK
Doncaster Road, Scunthorpe DN15 8TD
Tel: 01724 848 077

Capacity..9,200
Covered Standing...2,773
Seating..6,427

First game...v Hereford Utd, League, 27.8.1988.
First floodlit game..Huddersfield, Lge Cup, 30.8.1988.

ATTENDANCES
Highest..8,775 v Rotherham, Div 4, 1.5.1989.
Lowest...859 v Chesterfield, AMC, 18.12.1990.

OTHER GROUNDS...Old Show Ground.

MATCHDAY TICKET PRICES

British Steel Stand (home terrace)........£6.50
Juv/OAP..£3.30
Clugston Stand (all seated)..................£8
Juv/OAP..£4
Evening Telegraph Stand (all seated)......£9
Juv/OAP..£5.50
South Stand (Away supporters)...........£8.50
Juv/OAP..£5
Executive
Members..£11
OAP..£8
Non-Members....................................£13.50
OAP..£9
Family tickets (1+1) available if reserved in advance.
With membership card.
Ticket Office Telephone no.......01724 848 077.

HOW TO GET TO THE GROUND

From all Directions
Use motorway (M18) to junction 5, exit on to M180, at junction 3 exit on to M181, at roundabout take third exit.
The ground can clearly be seen on the right as you approach the roundabout.

Car Parking
Club park adjacent to ground for 800 vehicles.
£1 per car.

Nearest Railway Station
Scunthorpe.

CLUBCALL 0891 12 16 52

Calls cost 39p per minute cheap rate and 49p per minute at all other times.
Call costings correct at time of going to press.

MATCHDAY PROGRAMME

Programme Editor...................John Curtis & Andy Skeels.

Number of pages..32.

Price..£1.50.

Subscriptions.....................Home & away combined £70.

Local Newspapers................Scunthorpe Evening Telegraph.

Local Radio Stations............Radio Humberside, Viking Radio.

SWANSEA CITY
(The Swans)
NATIONWIDE LEAGUE DIVISION 3
SPONSORED BY: The South Wales Evening Post

Back Row (L-R): Denis Spiteri, Darren Perrett, Lee Jones, Roger Freestone, Ben Miles, David Barnhouse, Jamie Rickard.
Middle Row: Mark Clode, David Thomas, Michael Basham, Christian Edwards, Stephen Torpey, Carl Heggs, Keith Walker, Jason Price, Shaun Chapple.
Front Row: David Beresford, Jonathan Coates, John Hodge, Colin Pascoe, John Cornforth, David Penney, Andy Cook, Kwame Ampadu, Stephen Jenkins

SWANSEA CITY
FORMED IN 1900
TURNED PROFESSIONAL IN 1912
LTD COMPANY IN 1912

PRESIDENT: Ivor Pursey MBE
CHAIRMAN: D J Sharpe
VICE-CHAIRMAN
D G Hammond FCA MBIM
DIRECTORS
M Griffiths
OFFICE MANAGER
Miss Vicky Townsend (01792 474114)
PLAYER/MANAGER: Jan Molby
ASSISTANT MANAGER: Billy Ayre

YOUTH TEAM MANAGER
Alan Curtis
PHYSIOTHERAPIST
Mike Davenport

STATISTICIAN FOR THE DIRECTORY
Colin Jones

After the first three matches of the 1995/6 season, the Swans held the third place in the developing league table. On 22 February when the club welcomed their new player-manager they were 22nd. Between those two dates pathos, farce and incredulity had been the order of the day: Frank Burrows resigned in October; Bobby Smith had been given the chance to replace the popular Scot but within weeks had left; Jimmy Rimmer had stood in; and a millionaire mystery man, Michael Thompson, had emerged as the new 'owner-elect' of the club.

The new man told the media that he was going to bring in a manager of quality. In addition he spoke of plans which would take the Swans to the Premier League by the year 2000. Swans fans were delighted with the idea, but that delight turned sour when the chairman-elect (the legal hand-over date had not been reached) appointed a manager without football league experience. At the time, Chairman Doug Sharpe was out of the country, but on hearing the news returned immediately. Within days the new manager had left and Sharpe moved quickly to bring Jan Molby to the Vetch as player-manager. Meanwhile, when the due date arrived for completion of the take-over, Thompson was not able to meet the requirements.

By then the Swans were 23rd in the league table, and in the five matches before Molby arrived they had failed to score. With just fourteen games to play, Molby knew that he had a tough job on his hands. The question was, could he perform a miracle? At first it seemed that he could: of the first four games three were won and one drawn but, following a defeat by Blackpool, other losses were to follow. In the end, despite fine wins over Wycombe and Crewe, the Swans failed to gain enough points to avoid relegation.

Inevitably, this caused some dismay at the Vetch, but Molby let it be known that he was going to strengthen his squad ready for the campaign ahead. Whilst at the time of writing we do not know what will evolve, we can be certain that Jan Molby will have worked hard to stamp his brand upon the Vetch Field squad. Fitness and skill will be the order of the day and, whenever possible, fluent and attractive football will be played by the men in white.

Notwithstanding the fact that the 1995/6 season was disappointing, the new manager had seen enough to feel that there was talent at the Vetch. The presence of Jan himself had given the team a new dimension. Youngsters like Christian Edwards had emerged to show their potential, Steve Torpey had scored 15 league goals, and late signings Linton Brown, Colin McDonald, Steve Jones and Shaun Garnett had done enough to suggest that they would contribute in the season ahead. Coupled with the talents of players like Keith Walker, Roger Freestone, David Penney and the promised newcomers, every Swans fan will be hoping that their team will play winning, attractive football and retrieve their position in Division Two at the first time of asking. However, no one at the Vetch underestimates the extent of that task - 23 other sides will have the same objective in mind.

COLIN JONES

SWANSEA CITY

League: 22nd   FA Cup: 1st Rnd   Coca-Cola Cup: 1st Rnd   Auto Windscreen Shield: 2nd Rnd

M	DATE	COMP	VEN	OPPONENTS	RESULT	HT	LP	GOAL SCORERS/GOAL TIMES	ATT.
1	A 12	EL	H	Shrewsbury Town	W 3-1	2-0	18	Heggs 35, Cornforth 43, Freestone 82(pen)	3498
2	15	CC 1/1	H	Peterborough United	W 4-1	2-0		Ampadu 18, Hodge 23, 56, Torpey 77	1862
3	19	EL	A	Bristol Rovers	D 2-2	1-0	2	Torpey 17, Basham 86	(6689)
4	22	CC 1/2	A	Peterborough United	L 0-3	0-1			(1871)
5	26	EL	H	Chesterfield	W 3-2	2-0	2	Freestone 36(pen), Torpey 39, Edwards 64	3492
6	29	EL	A	Stockport County	L 0-2	0-1	4		(4433)
7	S 2	EL	H	Carlisle United	D 1-1	0-1	5	Heggs 65	3345
8	9	EL	A	Walsall	L 1-4	0-2	12	Palmer 76(og)	(3788)
9	12	EL	A	Hull City	D 0-0	0-0	13		(3519)
10	16	EL	H	York City	L 0-1	0-1	16		2422
11	23	EL	H	Oxford United	D 1-1	0-1	14	Heggs 65	2505
12	26	AWS 1/1	A	Shrewsbury Town	D 1-1	0-0		Torpey 46	(943)
13	30	EL	A	Burnley	L 0-3	0-1	9		8067
14	O 7	EL	H	Bradford City	W 2-0	1-0	16	Torpey 12, 61	2207
15	14	EL	A	Peterborough United	D 1-1	0-1	15	Ampadu 71	(3834)
16	17	AWS 1/1	H	Leyton Orient	D 0-0	0-0			796
17	21	EL	H	Bournemouth	D 1-1	0-1	15	Heggs 62	1988
18	28	EL	A	Wrexham	L 0-1	0-1	17		(4002)
19	31	EL	A	Brighton & H.A.	W 2-0	1-0	15	Torpey 13, Lampard 57	(4230)
20	N 4	EL	H	Wycombe Wanderers	L 1-2	0-0	17	Torpey 58	2809
21	11	FAC 1	A	Fulham	L 0-7	0-3			(4798)
22	18	EL	A	Crewe Alexandra	L 1-4	1-2	19	Pascoe 12	(3608)
23	25	EL	H	Notts County	D 0-0	0-0	20		2327
24	28	AWS 2	A	Peterborough United	L 0-1	0-0			(1952)
25	D 2	EL	H	Rotherham United	D 0-0	0-0	20		1788
26	9	EL	A	Oxford United	L 1-5	0-0	21	Torpey 69	(4674)
27	16	EL	H	Burnley	L 2-4	0-1	21	Hurst 61, Torpey 63	2078
28	26	EL	A	Bristol City	L 0-1	0-0	22		(6845)
29	J 10	EL	A	Swindon Town	L 0-3	0-1	22		(6555)
30	13	EL	H	Bristol Rovers	D 2-2	2-0	22	Torpey 24, Edwards 30	2956
31	20	EL	A	Shrewsbury Town	W 2-1	1-1	21	Heggs 11, Cornforth 76	(6532)
32	F 3	EL	A	Chesterfield	L 2-3	2-2	22	Torpey 31, 43	(4050)
33	6	EL	H	Stockport County	L 0-3	0-2	22		2349
34	10	EL	H	Swindon Town	L 0-1	0-1	23		4452
35	13	EL	A	Blackpool	L 0-4	0-2	23		(4092)
36	17	EL	H	Hull City	D 0-0	0-0	23		1909
37	20	EL	A	Carlisle United	L 0-3	0-2	19		(4645)
38	24	EL	A	York City	D 0-0	0-0	23		(2786)
39	27	EL	H	Walsall	W 2-1	1-0	22	Torpey 36, Hodge 59	3546
40	M 2	EL	H	Bristol City	W 2-1	2-0	21	Chappell 9, Molby 28	4109
41	9	EL	A	Rotherham United	D 1-1	0-1	18	Torpey 55	(2714)
42	12	EL	H	Brentford	W 2-1	0-1	20	Chappell 73, Molby 90(pen)	3538
43	16	EL	H	Blackpool	L 0-2	0-0	22		4478
44	23	EL	A	Brentford	D 0-0	0-0	20		(4378)
45	30	EL	A	Bradford City	L 1-5	0-0	22	Chapman 88	(4183)
46	A 2	EL	H	Peterborough United	D 0-0	0-0	22		3805
47	6	EL	H	Wrexham	L 1-3	0-1	22	Torpey 58	4256
48	9	EL	A	Bournemouth	L 1-3	1-1	22	Chapman 2	(4049)
49	13	EL	H	Brighton & H.A.	W 2-1	1-1	22	Ampadu 6, Chapman 74	2373
50	20	EL	A	Wycombe Wanderers	W 1-0	0-0	21	Chapman 55	(3672)
51	27	EL	A	Notts County	L 0-4	0-0	22		(5051)
52	M 4	EL	H	Crewe Alexandra	W 2-1	1-0	22	Torpey 35, Thomas 86	2604

Best Home League Attendance: 4478 v Blackpool   Smallest: 1788 v Rotherham United   Average: 2992

Goal Scorers:
EL(43): Torpey(15), Heggs(5), Chapman(4), Freestone(2), Cornforth(2), Edwards(2), Ampadu(2), Chappell(2), Molby(2), Lampard(1), Hurst(1), Basham(1), Thomas(1), Pascoe(1), Hodge(1), Opponent(s)(1)
CC(4): Hodge(2), Ampadu(1), Torpey(1)
FAC(0):
AWS(1): Torpey(1)

1995-96

(F) Ampadu	(M) Barnhouse	(M) Barwell-Edritoro	(D) Basham	(M) Beresford	(F) Brown	(F) Chapman	(M) Chappell	(M) Clode	(F) Coates	(D) Cook	(M) Comforth	(M) Dennison	(D) Edwards	(G) Freestone	(D) Garnett	(F) Heggs	(F) Hodge	(D) Jenkins	(D) Jones.S	(M) Lampard	(M) McDonald	(M) Molby	(F) Pascoe	(M) Penney	(F) Perrett	(F) Thomas	(F) Torpey	(M) Walker		
S1	X		X2					X2		X		X	X	X	X	X	X	X						X1			X	X	R.J.Harris	1
X	X						S2	X1		X		X	X	X	X	X	X	X							S1	S	X	X2	P.Rejer	2
X	X	S1	X1					S2		X		X	X	X	X	X	X2	X									X	X	A.Wiley	3
X	X1						X	S1	S2	X		X	X	X	X	X	X2	X							S	X	X	N.Barry	4
X	S		X					S	X	X		X	X	X	X	X	X	X						S			X	X	R.Gifford	5
X	S2	X1	S1				X2			X		X	X	X	X	X	X	X									X		R.Poulain	6
X	S	X	X1					S1	X	X2		X	X	X	X	X	X	X						S2		X			G.Singh	7
X	X	X	X				S	S1	X	X		X	X	X	X	X1	X	X						S2				X2	A.P.D'Urso	8
X1	X						X	S	X	X		X	X	X	X	X	X	X					X	S1			X		G.B.Frankland	9
X	X						S1	S2	X1	X		X	X	X	X	X	X	X		X2			X	X			X		J.Lloyd	10
X	X	S					X	X1		X		X	X	X	X	X	X	X						S1		X	X	X	G.Cain	11
X	X	S1					X1	X		X		X	X	X	X	X	X	X						S		X	X	X	T.West	12
X	X	S1					X	X1		X		X	X	X	X	X	X	X						S1		X	X	X	T.West	13
X		S1							X	X2	X3	X	X	X	X	X	X	X	X1					S2	S3		X	X	G.P.Barber	14
X	S3							X		X1		X	X	X	X	X	X	X	X3				S1		S2	X2	X	X	J.Kirkby	15
X		S1						X		X		X	X2	X3	X		X	X		X			S2		S3		X	X1		16
X	S1		X					S2	X2	X	X1		X3	X		X	X	X		X			S3				X		M.Fletcher	17
X	X1		X				S2		S1	X		X	X	S	X	X	X	X		X2							X		S.Baines	18
X	X		X				S1		X2			X	X	X	X	X	X	X		X1					S2	S	X		M.Bailey	19
X	X		X					X2	S2	X		X	X	X	X	X3	S1			X			X1			S3	X		A.G.Wiley	20
	X	X1				X		X	X	X		X	X	X	X	X	X			X			X		S1	S	X		P.Rejer	21
	X1						S		X	X	X		X	X	X	X	X1		X	X			X	X			X	X	P.Taylor	22
							S		S2	X1	X		X	X	X	X	X2	S1		X	X		X	X			X	X	D.Orr	23
X							S		X1	X		X2	X	X	X		S1		X	S2			X	X			X	X		24
X							S		S	X		X	X	X	X		X1		X	S1			X	X	X1		X	X	C.R.Wilkes	25
X							S1		X	X		X	X	X			S2		X				X	X		S	X	X1	J.Brandwood	26
X	X	X					S		X1	X		X	X	X			S1		X				X2	S2			X	X	K.A.Leach	27
X	S	X					S2	X		X		X	X	X	X				X				S1	X2			X	X	J.Rushton	28
X	X	S2						X1		X		X	X	X		X2	S3		X				S1	X3			X	X	M.Pierce	29
X		S					S	X1		X		X	X	X		X	X		S1				X	X			X	X	R.Gifford	30
X		S2					S3	X2		X	X3		S1	X	X	X	X	X1					X				X	X	K.M.Lynch	31
X							S	X	S1	X	X		X	X	X1	X	X						X				X	X	J.Lloyd	32
X							S1	X2	S2	X	X1		X	X	X	X	X	S					X				X	X	J.Rushton	33
X1	S						X	S1		X		X	X	X	X	X	X	X					X			S	X	X	P.Rejer	34
	X1						X	X	S	X		X	X	X	X	X	X	X					X			S1	X	X	U.Rennie	35
X							X	X	S	X		X	X	X	X	X	X	X					X		S	X	X	X	K.J.Breen	36
X							X1	X	S1	X		X	X	X	X2	X	X	X		S			X			S2	X	X	S.Baines	37
S1							X	X	X	X	X		X	X	X	X	X	S				X	X		X1		X	X	T.Heilbron	38
X							X	X	S	X	X		X	X	X	X	X1	S				X	X		S1		X		E.Wolstenholme	39
X2							X	X	S2	X	X		X1	X		X	X3						X		S3	X	S1	X	G.Pooley	40
X							X	X	S	X	X		X	X	X	X	X			S			X		S	S	X	X	G.Singh	41
X							X	X	X	X		X	X	X	X	S1	X1						X		S	X	X	X	G.Cain	42
X							X	X	X	X		X	X	X	X	S1	X						X		S	X	X	S	A.Butler	43
S2			X				X	X1		X2		X	X	X	S				S1	X			X		X		X	X	S.Bennett	44
X			X	X	X	X	X			X		X	X	X	S2	X1	S		S1	X			X				X	X	E.Lomas	45
X			X1	X2	X	X			S1			X	X3	X				S3	X			X			S2		X	X	C.Wilkes	46
X2				X	X1	X		S2				X	X	X				S1	X			X			S	X	X	X	I.F.Hemley	47
X			X	X	S1	X1				X	X		X	X			S2		X	X2			X		S	X	X	X	B.Harris	48
X			X	S2	X			S3		X	X1		X	X			X	X		X2			X		S	X	X	X	G.Cain	49
X			X	S	X	X				X			X	X		S	X			X			S	X			X	X	B.Knight	50
X				X2	S	S1		X			X	X1		X			X			S2	X		X				X	X	I.Cruikshanks	51
X	X		S1				S3		X3			X		X			X			X2			X		S2	X1	X	X	M.Pierce	52
40	12	2	9	5	3	7	15	25	7	30	17	9	35	45	9	28	34	15	16	8	3	12	9	28	2	3	41	32	EL Appearances	
3	3	2	2	1	1	0	7	5	11	3	0	0	2	0	0	4	7	0	1	1	5	0	4	1	2	13	1	1	EL Sub Appearances	
2	2	0	0	0	0	0	1	0+2	0	1	0	2	0	2	2	2	2	0	0	0	0	0	0	0	0	2	2	2	CC Appearances	
0	1	0	1	0	0	0	0	1	0	1	1	0	1	1	0	1	1	0	0	0	0	0	0	1	0	0+1	0	1	FAC Appearances	
3	2	0	0+2	0	0	0	0	1	2	2	0	2	3	3	0	2	2+1	1	1	1+1	0	0	1+1	1	0+1	0	3	3	AWS Appearances	

Iso Played: (M) Hurst X(27), X1(28). (G) Jones.L X(52). (F) Mardenborough X(26). (D) Miles S(1,3,6,9,10,11,12,13). (D) O'Leary X2(45). (M) Price S(21,35).

CLUB RECORDS

RECORD LEAGUE VICTORY
8-0 v Hartlepool United, Div 4, 1.4.1978
Most Goals Scored in a Cup Tie: 12-0 v Sliema Wanderers (Malta),
1st rnd 1st leg, European Cup Winners Cup, 15.9.1982
RECORD LEAGUE DEFEAT
1-8 v Fulham, Div 2, 22.1.1938 1-8 v Newcastle United,Div 2,
2.9.1939 0-7 v Tottenham Hotspur, Div 2, 3.12.1932 0-7 v Bristol
Rovers, Div 2, 2.10.1954 0-7 v Workington, Div 3, 4.10.1960
Record Cup Defeat
0-8 v Liverpool, FA Cup Round 3 replay, 9.1.1990 0-8 v Monaco,
ECWC 1st rnd 2nd leg, 1.10.1991
European Competitions entered: European Cup Winners Cup
1961-62, 1966-67, 1981-82, 1982-83, 1983-84, 1989-90, 1991-92
MOST LEAGUE POINTS
(3pts a win) 73, Division 2 1992-93
(2pts a win) 62, Div3S, 1948-49
MOST LEAGUE GOALS
92, Div 4, 1976-77
RECORD TRANSFER FEE RECEIVED
£375,000 from Crystal Palace for Chris Coleman, June 1991 (Fee
paid in installments. Final payment made when Coleman played his
50th game for Palace). £375,000 from Nott'm Forest for Des Lyttle,
July 1993
RECORD TRANSFER FEE PAID
£340,000 to Liverpool for Colin Irwin, Aug 1981
BEST PERFORMANCES
League: 6th Div 1 1981-82
FA Cup: Semi-finals 1926, 1964
League Cup: 4th Round 1964-65, 1976-77
European Cup Winners Cup: 2nd round
Welsh Cup Winners (10)
HONOURS
Champions Div 3S 1924-25, 1948-49 Welsh Cup Winners (10
times) Autoglass Trophy 1993-94
LEAGUE CAREER
Original Members of Div 3 1920 Promoted to Div 2 1924-25
Relegated to Div 3S 1946-47 Promoted to Div 2 1948-49
Relegated to Div 31964-65 Relegated to Div 4 1966-67
Promoted to Div 3 1969-70 Relegated to Div 4 1972-73
Promoted to Div 31977-78 Promoted to Div 2 1978-79
Promoted to Div 1 1980-81 Relegated to Div 2 1982-83
Relegated to Div 31983-84 Relegated to Div 4 1985-86
Promoted to Div 3 (now Div 2) 1987-88 Relegated to Div 3 1995-96

INDIVIDUAL CLUB RECORDS

MOST APPEARANCES FOR CLUB
'Wilfy' Milne (1920-37): League 585 + FA Cup 44 +Welsh Cup 28
Total 657

MOST CAPPED PLAYER
Ivor Allchurch, 42 Wales For England: None

RECORD GOALSCORER IN A MATCH
Jack Fowler 5 v Charlton Athletic, 6-1 Div 3S,27.9.1924
RECORD LEAGUE GOALSCORER IN A SEASON
Cyril Pearce 35, 1931-32 In All Competitions: Cyril Pearce 39 (Lge
35 + Welsh Cup 4)
RECORD LEAGUE GOALSCORER IN A CAREER
Ivor Allchurch 166 (1949-58 & 1965-68) In All Competitions: Ivor
Allchurch, 189 (League 166 + FA Cup 9 + League Cup 4+ Welsh
Cup 10)

OLDEST PLAYER IN A LEAGUE MATCH
Tommy Hutchison 43 years 171 days v Southend,12.3.91
YOUNGEST PLAYER IN A LEAGUE MATCH
Nigel Dalling, 15 years 10 months

PREVIOUS MANAGERS

1912-14 Walter Whittaker 1914-15 William Bartlett 1919-26 Joe
Bradshaw 1927-31 James Thompson 1934-39 Neil Harris 1939-
47 Haydn Green 1947-55 Billy McCandless 1955-58 Ron
Burgess 1958-65 Trevor Morris 1965-66 Glyn Davies 1967-69
Billy Lucas 1969-72 Roy Bentley 1972-75 Harry Gregg 1975-78
Harry Griffiths 1978-84 John Toshack 1984 Colin Appleton
1985-86 John Bond 1986-89 Terry Yorath 1989-90 Ian Evans
1990-91 Terry Yorath 1991-95 Frank Burrows.
In addition B Watts-Jones, Joe Sykes, Walter Robins, Doug
Livermore, Wyndham Evans, Les Chappel, Tommy Hutchison,
Bobby Smith and Jimmy Rimmer all acted in a 'caretaker' capacity
for short periods.

ADDITIONAL INFORMATION
Previous Name: Swansea Town (until Feb 1970)
Previous League: Southern League.
Club Colours: All white.
Change Colours: Orange & white shirts, blue shorts.
Reserves League: Neville Ovenden Football Combination.

LONGEST LEAGUE RUNS

of undefeated matches:	19 (1970-71)	of league matches w/out a win:		15 (1989)
of undefeated home matches:	28 (1925-27)	of undefeated away matches:		12 (1970-71)
without home win:	9 (1938)	without an away win:		46 (1982-84)
of league wins:	8 (1961)	of home wins:		17 (1948-49)
of league defeats:	9 (1990-91)	of away wins:	4 (1955-56, 1987-88, 1993)	

THE MANAGER (PLAYER)

JAN MOLBY . . . . appointed 22nd February 1996.

PREVIOUS CLUBS
As Manager . . . . None.
As a player . . . . Kolding, Ajax, Liverpool, Norwich (Loan).

HONOURS
As a Manager . . . . None.
As a Player . . . . **Liverpool:** Div 1 championship 1985-86, 1987-88, 1989-90. FA Cup winners 1986, 1992.
. . . . **Denmark:** 34 full caps and u21 & Youth caps.

SWANSEA CITY

PLAYERS NAME / Honours	Ht	Wt	Birthdate	Birthplace / Transfers	Contract Date	Clubs	APPEARANCES League	L/Cup	FA Cup	Other	GOALS Lge	L/C	FAC	Oth
G O A L K E E P E R S														
Freestone Roger	6.2	14.6	19/08/68	Newport	02/04/86	Newport County	13			1				
W: u21.1. Div.2'89. AMC'94.				£95000	10/03/87	Chelsea	42	2	3	6				
				Loan	29/09/89	Swansea City	14			1				
				Loan	09/03/90	Hereford United	8							
				£50000	05/09/91	Swansea City	223+1	14	16	27	3			
Jones Lee	6.3	14.4	09/08/70	Pontypridd		AFC Porth								
				£7500	24/03/94	Swansea City	3			1				
D E F E N D E R S														
Cook Andy	5.9	10.12	10/08/69	Romsey	06/07/87	Southampton	11+5	4	1	1	1			
				£50000	13/09/91	Exeter City	70	2	7	6	1		1	1
				£125000	23/07/93	Swansea City	54+8	2	3	9+1				2
Edwards Christian	6.3	11.7	23/11/75	Caerphilly	20/07/94	Swansea City	44+2	2	1	4+1	2			
Barnett Shaun	6.2	11.0	22/11/69	Wallasey	15/06/88	Tranmere Rovers	93+1	12	3	15+2	5	1		
AMC'90.				Loan	01/10/92	Chester City	9							
				Loan	11/12/92	Preston North End	10		1	2				
				Loan	26/02/93	Wigan Athletic	13			1				
Jones Steve R						Swansea City	16+1			1				
M I D F I E L D														
Chappell Shaun	5.10	12.3	14/02/73	Swansea	15/07/91	Swansea City	59+26	3+1	8+2	8+2	9	1		1
W: u21.6.														
Clode Mark	5.7	10.6	24/02/73	Plymouth	30/03/91	Plymouth Argyle								
AMC'94.				Free	23/07/93	Swansea City	84+7	6+2	3	8	2			
McDonald Colin	5.7	10.8	10/04/74	Edinburgh	01/08/91	Hibernian								
					01/08/93	Falkirk	47			10				
					01/03/96	Swansea City	3+5							
Molby Jan	6.1	14.07	04/07/63	Kolding, Jutland		Ajax								
Danish Int. Div.1'86'90.				£575000	24/08/84	Liverpool	195+23	25+3	24+4	16+2	44	9	4	4
AC'86'92. CS'86.				Loan	18/09/95	Barnsley	4							
				Loan	29/12/95	Norwich City	3	2					1	
					22/02/96	Swansea City	12			2				
Penney David	5.8	10.7	17/08/64	Wakefield		Pontefract								
WFAC'91.				£1500	26/09/85	Derby County	6+13	2+3	1	1+3		1	1	1
				£175000	23/06/89	Oxford United	76+34	10+1	2+2	3+1	15		1	
				Loan	28/03/91	Swansea City	12			3				
				£20000	24/03/94	Swansea City	68+7	3+1	5	9	7	2	1	
Price Jason						Aberavon								
				Free	01/06/95	Swansea City								
Walker Keith	6.0	11.9	17/04/66	Edinburgh		Stirling Albion	82+9	5	5		16	3	2	
						St.Mirren	41+2	3	1	3	6			
				£80000	23/11/89	Swansea City	191+8	8	20	21	5		1	
F O R W A R D S														
Ampadu Kwame	5.10	10.10	20/12/70	Bradford	19/11/88	Arsenal	0+2							
I: u21.4, u17.2, Y.1. AMC'94.				Loan	31/10/90	Plymouth Argyle	6			1	1			
				£50000	24/06/91	W.B.A.	27+22	6+1	1	5	4			1
				£15000	16/02/94	Swansea City	87+13	5+1	3	12	8	1	1	1
Brown Linton	5.9	11.0	12/04/68	Driffield		Guiseley								
				Loan	18/12/92	Halifax Town	3							
				Free	08/01/93	Hull City	111+9	6	4+1	4	11			
					01/03/96	Swansea City	3+1							
Coates Jonathan	5.8	10.4	27/06/75	Swansea	08/07/93	Swansea City	7+20	1+1	1	2	1			
Heggs Carl	6.0	11.10	11/10/70	Leicester		Leicester United								
					22/08/91	W.B.A.	13+27	2	0+1	6+3	3			1
				Loan	27/01/95	Bristol Rovers	2+3				1			
				£60000	01/06/95	Swansea City	28+4	2	1	2	5			
Hodge John	5.6	10.0	01/04/69	Skelmersdale		Falmouth Town								
AMC'94.				Free	12/09/91	Exeter City	57+8	3	2	8+2	10	1		1
				£20000	14/07/93	Swansea City	87+25	6+2	6	13+4	10	3		
Thomas David	5.10	11.7	26/09/75	Caerphilly	25/07/94	Swansea City	5+15			0+3	1			1
Torpey Stephen	6.3	13.3	08/12/70	Islington	14/02/89	Millwall	3+4	0+1						
AMC'94.				£70000	21/11/90	Bradford City	86+10	6	2	8	22		6	
				£80000	03/08/93	Swansea City	114+9	8+1	8	13+2	35	2	4	5

VETCH FIELD
Swansea SA1 3SU
Tel: 01792 474 114

Capacity 16,550
Covered Standing 13,003
Seating 3,547

ATTENDANCES
Highest ....32,796 v Arsenal, FA Cup 4th Round, 17.2.1968.
Lowest ....1,311 v Brentford, Division 4, 26.4.1976.

OTHER GROUNDS..None.

MATCHDAY TICKET PRICES

Centre Stand £10

East Stand . . . . Adult £9
. . . . 1+1 - £14, 1+2 - £16

Jewson Stand . . . . Adult £10
. . . . 1+1 £12.50, 1+2 - £14.50

Wing Stand £8.50
OAP £3.50

Terraces £6.50
Juv/OAP £3.50

Ticket Office Telephone no. 01792 462 584

HOW TO GET TO THE GROUND
ive minutes walk from city bus station or take South Wales Transport Co Ltd from High Street General Station to Lowere Oxford Street. Car parking near ground at Quadrant.

Car Parking
Car park 200 yards from ground in the Kingsway. Covered supervised parking within 75 yards.
There is also ample street parking.

Nearest Railway Station
Swansea HIgh Street (01792 467 777)

CLUBCALL
0891 12 16 39
Calls cost 39p per minute cheap rate and 49p per minute at all other times.
Call costings correct at time of going to press.

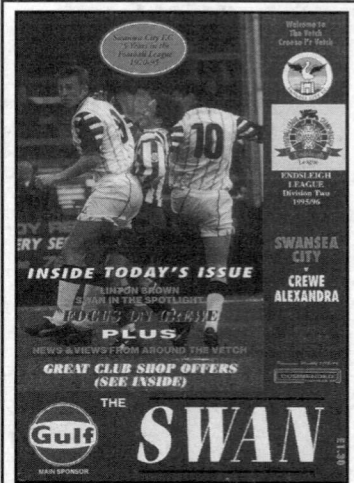

MATCHDAY PROGRAMME

Programme Editor . . . . Major Reg Pike, I.S.M, T.D.

Number of pages . . . . 32.

Price . . . . £1.50.

Subscriptions . . . . Please contact club (01792 462 584)

Local Newspapers . . . . Evening Post, Western Mail.

Local Radio Stations . . . . Swansea Sound, BBC Radio Wales.

TORQUAY UNITED
(The Gulls)
NATIONWIDE LEAGUE DIVISION 3
SPONSORED BY: MOD DEC WINDOWS

Back Row (L-R): Michael Preston, Simon Travis, Neil Aggett, Scot Kaasikmae, Lee Barrow, Ellis Laight, Richard Hancox, Scott Stamps, Michael Shannon, Damien Davey (Physio), Lee Setter. **Middle Row:** Paul Compton (Yth Dev. Officer), Neil Povey, Matthew Wright, Neil Male, Matthew Gregg, Ashley Bayes, Paul Beswick, David Byng, Darren Horn, Robert King, John James (Scout). **Front Row:** Paul Buckle, Mark Hall, Chris Curran, Don O'Riordan (Manager), Mike Bateson (Chairman), Kevin Hodges (Coach), Gregory Goodridge, Tom Kelly, Ian Hathaway

TORQUAY UNITED
FORMED IN 1898
TURNED PROFESSIONAL IN 1921
LTD COMPANY IN 1921

CHAIRMAN: M Bateson
DIRECTORS
Mrs S Bateson, D Turner, M Beer, M Benney,
I Hayman, H Kindeleit, T Lilley, B Palk,
W Rogers
SECRETARY
Mike Bateson (01803 328 666)
COMMERCIAL REP.
Cedric Munslow
ADMINISTRATION
Ann Sandford
TEAM COACH: Kevin Hodges

YOUTH TEAM COACH
Steve McCall
PHYSIOTHERAPIST
Damien Davey

STATISTICIAN FOR THE DIRECTORY
John Lovis

Torquay United broke many club records during the 1995-96 league season. Unfortunately these were all unwanted records; including fewest ever wins(5), fewest goals scored (30), most defeats (27) and most goalless games (25).

The club entered the campaign totally ill-prepared and the signs of struggle were there for all to see (except perhaps the management). Players who had been sold were replaced by untried youngsters and players who quite frankly were just not up to the rigours of a physically demanding Third Division.

Don O'Riordan paid the price after the 1-8 defeat at home by Scunthorpe (yet another record!). Eddie May took over the reins and whilst he brought in more experienced players there was no dramatic improvement. He also had to contend with an horrendous injury list but it would be too easy to blame bad luck on the kind of season which tries the patience of even the most devoted follower.

Remarkably the supporters stayed most loyal to the club and they alone deserve the life line of league survival thrown to them by Stevenage's failure to bring their ground up to standard by the 31st December 1995 deadline.

Eddie May has now left the club together with assistant manager Paul Compton and there needs to be major surgery done to ensure that we do not endure the same miseries next season.

One of May's signings, midfielder Charlie Oatway, was a major success and he won the "Player of the Year Award". If some of the players had performed with Oatway's skill and enthusiasm the club might have escaped the "wooden spoon"position.

JOHN LOVIS.

TORQUAY UNITED

League: 24th   FA Cup: 2nd Rnd   Coca-Cola Cup: 2nd Rnd   Auto Windscreen Shield: 1st Rnd

M	DATE	COMP	VEN	OPPONENTS	RESULT	HT	LP	GOAL SCORERS/GOAL TIMES	ATT.
1	A 12	EL	A	Leyton Orient	L 0-1	0-0	21		(8221)
2	15	CC 1/1	H	**Exeter City**	D 0-0	0-0			2473
3	19	EL	H	Doncaster Rovers	L 1-2	0-0	23	Buckle 57(pen)	2086
4	23	CC 1/2	A	**Exeter City**	D 1-1	1-1		**Hawthorne 23**	(3763)
5	26	EL	A	Fulham	L 0-4	0-1	24		(4764)
6	29	EL	H	Rochdale	W 1-0	0-0	20	Stamps 52	2139
7	S 2	EL	H	Mansfield Town	D 1-1	1-1	22	Buckle 3(pen)	2041
8	9	EL	A	Cardiff City	D 0-0	0-0	21		(4231)
9	12	EL	A	Hartlepool United	D 2-2	0-1	19	Gore 50, Buckle 90(pen)	(1976)
10	16	EL	H	Wigan Athletic	D 1-1	0-1	19	Curran 89	2188
11	19	EL	H	Doncaster Rovers	L 1-2	0-1	19	Buckle 57(pen)	2086
12	20	CC 2/1	A	**Norwich City**	L 1-6	0-3		**Hathaway 56**	(7542)
13	23	EL	H	Northampton Town	W 3-0	1-0	16	Ndah 5, Mateau 55, Buckle 90(pen)	2314
14	26	AWS 1/1	H	**Colchester United**	L 2-5	0-2		**Hathaway 68(pen), Stamps 79**	(1121)
15	30	EL	A	Scarborough	L 1-2	0-1	19	Hicks 71(og)	(1395)
16	O 4	CC 2/2	H	**Norwich City**	L 2-3	0-0		**Barrow 61, 73**	1790
17	7	EL	A	Hereford United	L 1-2	0-1	22	Hathaway 84	(2143)
18	14	EL	H	Preston North End	L 0-4	0-2	23		4058
19	17	AWS 1/2	H	**Swindon Town**	D 1-1	1-1		**Curran 36**	1135
20	21	EL	A	Plymouth Argyle	L 3-4	3-2	23	Ndah 16, 23, Partridge 40	(11695)
21	28	EL	H	Scunthorpe United	L 1-8	1-4	23	Partridge 32	2137
22	31	EL	H	Bury	L 0-2	0-1	23		1456
23	N 4	EL	A	Chester City	L 1-4	0-2	24	Laight 57	(2535)
24	11	FAC 1	H	**Leyton Orient**	W 1-0	0-0		**Byng 64**	2434
25	18	EL	H	Lincoln City	L 0-2	0-1	24		2553
26	25	EL	A	Cambridge United	D 1-1	0-1	24	Gore 85	(2536)
27	D 2	FAC 2	H	**Walsall**	D 1-1	1-0		**Hathaway 2**	3552
28	9	EL	A	Northampton Town	D 1-1	0-1	24	Newhouse 66	(3656)
29	12	FAC 2R	A	**Walsall**	L 4-8	1-1		**Hancox 36, Barrow 53, Gore 65, Mateau 101**	(3230)
30	16	EL	H	Scarborough	D 0-0	0-0	24		1680
31	23	EL	H	Darlington	L 0-1	0-1	24		2405
32	26	EL	A	Exeter City	D 0-0	0-0	24		(6182)
33	J 1	EL	H	Colchester United	L 2-3	1-1	24	Jack 35, Newhouse 50	2425
34	13	EL	A	Doncaster Rovers	L 0-1	0-0	24		(1807)
35	20	EL	H	Leyton Orient	W 2-1	0-1	24	Baker 52, Watson 90	2212
36	F 3	EL	H	Fulham	W 2-1	1-1	24	Baker 2, Garner 82	2594
37	6	EL	H	Barnet	D 1-1	0-0	24	Baker 71(pen)	2262
38	10	EL	A	Gillingham	L 0-2	0-2	24		(7110)
39	17	EL	H	Hartlepool United	D 0-0	0-0	24		2580
40	24	EL	A	Wigan Athletic	L 0-3	0-1	24		(2697)
41	27	EL	H	Cardiff City	D 0-0	0-0	24		2004
42	M 2	EL	H	Exeter City	L 0-2	0-1	24		4038
43	9	EL	A	Darlington	W 2-1	2-0	24	Watson 12, Jack 14	(2861)
44	12	EL	H	Gillingham	D 0-0	0-0	24		1406
45	16	EL	A	Barnet	L 0-4	0-3	24		(1734)
46	19	EL	A	Rochdale	L 0-3	0-1	24		(1206)
47	23	EL	A	Colchester United	L 1-3	0-1	24	Laight 86	(2888)
48	30	EL	H	Hereford United	D 1-1	1-1	24	Hancox 39	2034
49	A 2	EL	A	Preston North End	L 0-1	0-1	24		(11965)
50	6	EL	A	Scunthorpe United	L 0-1	0-1	24		(2247)
51	8	EL	H	Plymouth Argyle	L 0-2	0-1	24		4269
52	13	EL	A	Bury	L 0-1	0-0	24		(3247)
53	20	EL	H	Chester City	D 1-1	0-0	24	Baker 71	2549
54	23	EL	A	Mansfield Town	L 0-2	0-1	24		(1674)
55	27	EL	H	Cambridge United	L 0-3	0-1	24		1853
56	M 4	EL	A	Lincoln City	L 0-5	0-1	24		(5814)

Best Home League Attendance: 4269 v Plymouth Argyle   **Smallest: 1406 v Gillingham**   Average: 2390

Goal Scorers:
EL(31):   Buckle(5),Baker(4),Ndah(3),Jack(2),Partridge(2),Newhouse(2),Laight(2),Watson(2),Gore(2),Mateau(1),Hancox(1),Garner(1),Curran(1),Stamps(1), Hathaway(1),Opponent(s)(1)
CC(4):   Barrow(2),Hathaway(1),Hawthorne(1)
FAC(6):   Mateau(1),Hathaway(1),Hancox(1),Gore(1),Byng(1),Barrow(1)
AWS(3):   Hathaway(1),Curran(1),Stamps(1)

(F) Baker	(D) Barrow	(G) Bayes	(M) Buckle	(F) Byng	(M) Coughlin	(D) Curran	(F) Garner	(M) Gore	(F) Hall	(M) Hancox	(F) Hathaway	(M) Hawthorne	(M) Jack	(D) Kelly	(F) Laight	(F) Mateau	(F) Ndah	(G) Newland	(M) O'Riordan	(M) Oatway	(F) Partridge	(M) Preston	(D) Ramsey	(F) Stamps	(M) Travis	(D) Watson	(F) Williams	(M) Winter		
	X	X	X2	X		X		X		S1	X	X	X		X1									X	S2				F.G.Stretton	1
	X	X	X2	X1		X		X		X	X	X	X	X	X										X1	S1			C.Wilkes	2
	X	X	X3	S2		X		X		X	X	X		X	X2										X1	S1			R.Harris	3
	X	X	X	S3		X		X	X1		X3	X	X	X2			S1		S2					X					G.Singh	4
	X	X	X	S3		X		X	X	X2	S1	X1		X			X3		S2					X					A.Wiley	5
	X	X	X	S3		X		X3		X	S1		X				X		X1					X2	S2			X	R.Gifford	6
	X	X	X	S2		X		X		X2	S		X				X		X1					X				X	S.Mathieson	7
S1	X	X	S2			X		X1					X	X			X3							X				X	M.Fletcher	8
S2	X1	X	S1			X		X					X	X2			X							X				X	M.Riley	9
S3	X		X1			X		X	S1		X			X			X		S2					X				X3	P.Rejer	10
	X	X	X2	S2		X		X	S1	X	X		X	X2			X							X		X1	S1		R.Harris	11
	X	X	X	S2		X		X	S3	S1	X		X				X		X1		X				X			S	R.D.Furnandiz	12
	X	X	X2			X		X		S3	S1	X	X1	X			X		X2	X					X			X	C.Wilkes	13
	X	X			X1		X	S3	X2	X	X				S2	X3			X					S1				X	P.Taylor	14
	X	X			S2		X	S1		X	X	X				X	X		X1									X2	K.J.Breen	15
	X	X	S1			X	X1		X	X	X		X	S3	S1	X1								X				X	J.Rushton	16
	X	X1		S1		X	X	S1	X	X1	X	X	X	S1										X	X1			X	A.Butler	17
	X	X		X	S		X	S	X	X	X	X	X	S1					X									X	S.Bennett	18
	X		X	X	X		X		X	X	X	X	X	S1	X1		X											X	C.Wilkes	19
	X		X	X	X		X		X	X	X	S2	S	X1	X2		X											X	R.Harris	20
	X	X3	X		X		S1		X	X1	X	S2		X	X2	X				S3								X	M.Pierce	21
	X	X2	X		X			S2	S3	X	X3	X2	X		X1	X								X	X1			X	G.Barber	22
	X	X	X		X	S2	S1		X	X3	X2		X		X1	X												X	E.K.Wolstenholme	23
	X		X		X	S3		X		X	X1		X	X	X	X								X				X	D.Orr	24
	X	X2			X		X	S2	X1	S1	X		X		X	X							X		X			X	P.Rager	25
S	X	S1	S2		X	X	X2		X	X	X		X											X		X		X	A.D'Urso	26
	X	X	X	X		X1		X1	X1	X	X	S1	S1													X		X	D.Gallagher	27
	X	S1	S2		X	X1	S	X	X2		X	X		S1								X				X		X	M.Bailey	28
	X	X	X		X	X1	X	X	X1		S1															X		X	D.Gallagher	29
S	X	X	X	S	X	X		X	S1														X	X1		X		X	M.Fletcher	30
S3	X	X2	X	X	X	X1	S1	S2	X															X3		X	X	M.Riley	31
S1	X	X	S	X	X	X	X	X															X	S	X	X1	M.Riley	32
S	X	X	X	S1	X	X		X	S1					X1					X	S1	X	X	X	G.Barber	33
	X	X	X1	X	X	X1		X		X		X		X		X2	S1	X	X	E.Wolstenholme	34
X	S2	X	X	X	X1	X		X	X		X2	S1	X	X	A.Wiley	35
X	X	X	X1	S1	S2	X2	S	X	S	X	X	X	X	X	X	X	G.Singh	36

so Played: (D) Barnes S1(7). (F) Bedeau S3(8), S1(29,34) S2(43). (M) Canham X(23,25), X1(26). (F) Cooke X1(18), S(19). (M) Croft S2(2,11), S3(3). (G) Gregg X(10), S(12).
4) Haddaoui S2(48,50), S(51). (M) Hodges S1(20), S2(24), X(56). (M) Kaasiknae X(14). (D) Monk X(2347,55,56), S(27), S1(41). (F) Moors S3(23), S3(24), S(25). (F) Newhouse X(28,30,32,33).
4) Povey X2(8,10), X(9). (M) Thomas S1(40,53,56), X1(47), S2(54), S3(55).

EL Appearances	20	36	29	12	4	22	18	10	26	22	16	23	18	12	27	9	5	16	17	6	24	5	4	18	21	4	29	9	36
EL Sub Appearances	0	6	0	10	3	2	1	0	7	10	4	5	2	5	12	5	1	2	0	0	4	0	3	0	0	0	0	0	0
CC Appearances	0	4	4	4	1+2	0	3	0	4	3	2+1	4	3	0	4	0+2	0+1	2+1	0	1+1	0	0	0	3	1	0	0	0	1
FAC Appearances	0	3	3	0	1+1	3	3	0	1	2+1	1	3	2	3	1	1+1	0	1	0	1	0	0	0	0	0	0	1	2	0	1
AWS Appearances	0	2	2	0	1	1	2	0	2	0+1	1	2	1	1	2	1	0+2	2	0	0	2	0	0	0	0+1	0	0	0	1

CLUB RECORDS

RECORD LEAGUE VICTORY
9-0 v Swindon Town, Div 3S, 8.3.1952
Record Cup Victory and Most Goals Scored in a Cup Tie: 7-1 v
Northampton Town(h), FA Cup 1st Round, 14.11.1959 (all goals
scored by Torquay-born players:Graham Bond (3), Ernie Pym (3),
and Tommy Northcott)
6-0 v Canterbury City, FA Cup Round 1, 1964-65

RECORD LEAGUE DEFEAT
2-10 v Fulham, Div 3S, 7.9.1931   2-10 v Luton Town, Div3S,
2.9.1933   1-9 v Millwall, Div 3S, 29.8.1927
Record Cup Defeat: 0-7 v Southend United, Leyland Daf Sth Q-
Final, 26.02.1991

MOST LEAGUE POINTS
(3pts a win) 77, Div 4, 1987-88
(2pts a win) 60, Div 4,1959-60

MOST LEAGUE GOALS
89, Div 3(S), 1956-57

RECORD TRANSFER FEE RECEIVED
£185,000 from Manchester United for Lee Sharpe, June 1988

RECORD TRANSFER FEE PAID
£60,000 to Dundee for Wes Saunders, July 1990

BEST PERFORMANCES
League: 2nd Div 3S 1956-57
FA Cup: 4th Round 1948-49,1954-55, 1970-71, 1982-83, 1989-90
League Cup: Never past 3rd Round

HONOURS
Sherpa Van Trophy Finalists 1989

LEAGUE CAREER
Elected to Div 3S 1927   Original Members of Division 4 1958
Promoted to Div 3 1960   Relegated to Div 4 1962
Promoted to Div 3 1966   Relegated to Div 4 1972
Promoted to Div 3 1991   Relegated to Div 4/3 1992

INDIVIDUAL CLUB RECORDS

MOST APPEARANCES FOR CLUB
Dennis Lewis (1947-59): League 443 + FA Cup 30 Total473

MOST CAPPED PLAYER
Gregory Goodridge, Barbados International

RECORD GOALSCORER IN A MATCH
Robin Stubbs 5 v Newport County, 8-3, Div 4,19.10.1963

RECORD LEAGUE GOALSCORER IN A SEASON
Sammy Collins, 40, Div 3S, 1955-56   In All Competitions: Sammy
Collins 42 (League 40 + FA Cup 2)

RECORD LEAGUE GOALSCORER IN A CAREER
Sammy Collins 204, 1948-58   In All Competitions: 219 (League
204 + FA Cup 15)

OLDEST PLAYER IN A LEAGUE MATCH
David Webb, 38 years 8 months v Crewe Alexandra, Div 4,
5.1.1985
YOUNGEST PLAYER IN A LEAGUE MATCH
David Byng, 16 years 36 days v Walsall, Div3, 14.8.1993

PREVIOUS MANAGERS

(Since 1946): John Butler   John McNeil   Bob John   Alex Massie
Eric Webber   Frank O'Farrell   Allan Brown   Jack Edwards
Malcolm Musgrove   Frank O'Farrell   Mike Green   Frank O'Farrell
Bruce Rioch   David Webb   John Sims   Stuart Morgan   Cyril
Knowles   David Smith   John Impey   Ivan Golac   Paul Compton,
Don O'Riordan, Eddie May.

ADDITIONAL INFORMATION
Previous League: Southern League
Previous Name: Torquay Town (1910), Amalgamated with
Babbacombe in 1920

Club Colours: Yellow & navy blue stripes, navy shorts with white
trim, yellow socks with navy blue top
Change Colours: Blue & white stripes, white shorts

LONGEST LEAGUE RUNS

of undefeated matches:	15 (1960, 1990)	of league matches w/out a win:	17 (1938)
of undefeated home matches:	31 (1956-57)	of undefeated away matches:	7 (1976, 1990)
without home win:	11 (1961)	without an away win:	28 (1991-1992)
of league wins:	6 (1953, 1990)	of home wins:	13 (1966-67)
of league defeats:	8 (1948, 1971)	of away wins:	5 (1959)

TEAM COACH

KEVIN HODGES . . . . appointed May 1996.

PREVIOUS CLUBS
As Manager . . . . None.
As Reserve team manager . . . . Torquay.
As a player . . . . Plymouth Argyle, Torquay United.

HONOURS
As a Manager . . . . None.
As a Player . . . . None.

PLAYERS NAME Honours	Ht	Wt	Birthdate	Birthplace Transfers	Contract Date	Clubs	League	L/Cup	FA Cup	Other	Lge	L/C	FAC	Oth
G O A L K E E P E R S														
Gregg Matthew						Torquay United (T)	1							
Newland Raymond J	6.3	13.10	19/07/71	Liverpool	12/09/91	St. Helens								
				Free	03/07/92	Plymouth Argyle	25+1	1	2					
				Free	18/07/94	Chester City	9+1			2				
				Free	12/01/96	Torquay United	17							
D E F E N D E R S														
Barrow Lee	5.11	12.5	01/05/73	Belper	09/07/91	Notts County								
				Free	03/08/92	Scarborough	11	2		1				
				Free	18/02/93	Torquay United	110+7	9	9	5	5	2	1	
Gittens Jon	5.11	12.6	22/01/64	Birmingham		Paget Rangers								
				£10000	16/10/85	Southampton	18	4	1					
				£40000	22/07/87	Swindon Town	124+2	15+1	9	13+1	6			1
				£400000	28/03/91	Southampton	16+3	4		1				
				Loan	19/02/92	Middlesbrough	9+3							
				£200000	27/07/92	Middlesbrough	13	0+1	1					
				Free	09/08/93	Portsmouth	81+2	10	3	3	2			
				Free	02/08/96	Torquay United								
Monk Garry						Torquay United (T)	4+1							
Watson Alex E: Y.4. CS'89.	6.0	11.9	05/04/68	Liverpool	18/05/85	Liverpool	3+1	1+1	1+1	1				
				Loan	30/08/90	Derby County	5							
				£150000	18/01/91	Bournemouth	145+6	14	12	5	5	1	1	
				Loan	11/09/95	Gillingham	10			1				
				£50000	23/11/95	Torquay United	29		2		2			
M I D F I E L D														
Hancox Richard	5.10	13.0	04/10/68	Wolverhampton		Stourport Swifts								
				Free	18/03/93	Torquay United	51+21	6+1	2+3	3	10	3	2	
Oatway Anthony						Torquay United (T)	24							
Preston Michael						Torquay United (T)	4+4							
Thomas Wayne						Torquay United (T)	1+5							
Winter Steven				Taunton Town										
					25/08/95	Torquay United	36	1	1	1				
F O R W A R D S														
Baker David P						Torquay United	20				4			
Hathaway Ian	5.8	10.6	22/08/68	Wordsley		Bedworth								
				£8000	08/02/89	Mansfield Town	21+23	1+1	1	3+1	2			1
					22/03/91	Rotherham United	5+8			0+1	1			
				Free	30/07/93	Torquay United	94+12	9	9	4+3	13	1	2	1
				Loan	09/04/96	Chesterfield								
Jack Rodney A						Torquay United (T)	12+2		3	1	2			
Ndah Jamie						Kingstonian								
				£20000	22/08/95	Torquay United	16	2+1	1		3			
Stamps Scott	5.11	11.0	20/03/75	Birmingham	06/07/93	Torquay United	51+6	5	1	1+1	2			1

PLAINMOOR GROUND
Torquay, Devon TQ1 3PG
Tel: 01803 328 666

Capacity 6,490
Covered Standing 4,131
Seating...2,359

First game..(As Torquay Town) v St Austell, 2-0, 03.09.1910.
First floodlit game..v Birmingham City (F) 2-3, 22.11.1954.

ATTENDANCES
Highest...21,908 v Huddersfield, FAC 4th Rnd, 29.1.1955.
Lowest..601 v Swansea, AMC, 2.12.1986.
....967 v Chester, Division 4, 2.5.1984.

OTHER GROUNDS..None.

MATCHDAY TICKET PRICES
SEATS & TERRACES

League games............................... £8

Juv/OAP £4

Ticket Office Telephone no........ 01803 328 666

CLUBCALL
0891 66 45 65
Calls cost 39p per minute cheap rate and 49p per
minute at all other times.
Call costings correct at time of going to press.

HOW TO GET TO THE GROUND

From the North
Use A38 then A380 to Kingskerswell. In 1 mile at roundabout take 1st exit. In 1 mile turn left (A3022) sign posted Babbacombe. In 0.8 miles turn left then right into Westhill Road and Warbro Road for Torquay United FC.

From the West
Use A380 into Torquay town centre then follow signs to Teignmouth (A379) into Lymington Road, then turn right into Upton Hill, keep forward into Bronshill Road. Take 2nd turning on left into Derwent Road and at end turn right then turn right again into Marnham Road for Torquay United FC.

Car Parking
Street parking. Coaches park at Lymington Road Coach Station.

Nearest Railway Station
Torquay (01752 221 300)

MATCHDAY PROGRAMME

Programme Editor... Ann Sandford.

Number of pages .... 32.

Price .... £1.50.

Subscriptions .... Home only £38, Away only £38, Home & away £68.

Local Newspapers......... Herald Express, Western Morning News.

Local Radio Stations .... BBC Radio Devon, Geminin Radio.

WIGAN ATHLETIC
(The Latics)
NATIONWIDE LEAGUE DIVISION 3
SPONSORED BY: JJB SPORTS

ack Row (L-R): Ian Benjamin, John Butler, Neil Ogden, Chris Lightfoot, Simon Farnworth, David Felgate, Martin Haley, David Miller, Mark eonard, John Robertson. **Middle Row:** Joe Hinnigan (Coach), Paul Tait, Roberto Martinez, Ian Kilford, Tony Kelly, Paul West, John Doolan, ndy Lyons, Michael Millett, David Crompton (Yth Dev. Officer), Alex Cribley (Coach/Physio). **Front Row:** Tony Black, Jesus Seba, Neill immer, Graham Barrow (Manager), Andy Farrell, Isidro Diaz, Matthew Carragher.
Photo: Derek Davies.

**WIGAN ATHLETIC
FORMED IN** 1932
TURNED PROFESSIONAL IN 1932
LTD COMPANY IN 1932

PRESIDENT: T Hitchen
CHAIRMAN: Dave Whelan
DIRECTORS
B Ashcroft, S Jackson, C Ronnie,
D Sharpe, J Winstanley, P Williams
CHIEF EXECUTIVE/SECRETARY
Mrs Brenda Spencer
ASSISTANT SECRETARY
Gordon Allan

MANAGER: John Deehan
ASSISTANT MANAGER: John Benson
YOUTH DEVELOPMENT OFFICER
David Crompton MSc, BSc (Econ), BA
YOUTH TEAM COACH: Alex Cribley
PHYSIOTHERAPIST
Simon Farnworth
FOOTBALL CO-ORDINATOR: Frank Lord

STATISTICIAN FOR THE DIRECTORY
Geoffrey Lea

Anyone who only watched Wigan Athletic at Springfield Park in 1995/96 would have wondered how the club failed to gain a play-off place.

Regular away supporters however, saw the other side, as the contrast between the team's home and away form was a constant mystery. Ironically it was the inability to win their last home game of the season that cost a play-off place ending the season in tenth place.

The summer of 1995 saw the club astound the football world with the capture of three Spaniards, Isidro Diaz, Roberto Martinez and Jesus Seba. The three Amigo's were joined by Chris Lightfoot, with Chairman and owner Dave Whelan pledging his commitment to provide funds as the record transfer fee was broken paying manager Graham Barrow's old club, Chester City, ¨87,500 for his services.

An indifferent start to the campaign saw victories recorded at home over Scunthorpe United and Barnet with defects in both legs of the first round of the Coca-Cola Cup against Chester City.

September witnessed the tragic death of Michael Millett which was too overshadow the club's year. Rated as one the brightest prospects to develop through the youth system, the former England youth international died in a car crash the day before his 18th birthday.

A month later following a luminating 2-6 home defeat by Mansfield Town, manager Barrow paid the ultimate price for the performance, his dismissal after just thirteen months in charge. Former Norwich City manager John Deehan was appointed in charge promising a play-off target and a more passing style of football.

Potential giant-killing embarrassment were crushed with wins over non-League sides Runcorn and Barrow, but any possibility of a money spinning tie against Premier League opponents came to an end following defeat in the 3rd Round at Walsall. Progress in the Auto Windscreens Trophy was to end against eventual winners Rotherham United in a penalty shoot out in the 2nd Round.

The turn of the year saw an impressive run of performance at Springfield Park resulting in a run of eight matches without defeat. However, on their travels indifferent displays were recorded with just three wins up to the end of March.

A new record transfer deal of ¨100,000 saw former England youth international Kevin Sharpe arrive at the club, white striker Graham Lancashire was signed following a successful loan period. Sadly a serious knee injury at Lincoln was to end his season in his first game following his transfer, while Tony Black's season ended after suffering a broken ankle a fortnight later.

After allowing previous record signing Chris Lightfoot to move onto Crewe Alexandra, the record transfer fee was broken for the three time, when striker David Lowe returned after an eight year absence on transfer deadline day for ¨125,000.

Immediately repaying part of the large fee paid, Lowe scored three goals in as many games to push Latics into an automatic promotion place following the Easter fixtures. Sadly just one point in the last four games was to ensure the season was to end in disappointment.

The close season has seen release of six players as Deehan's rebuilding exercise continued. Financial backing will again be produced to achieve the Chairman's ultimate dream of top flight football in a new stadium at Robin Park.

GEOFFREY LEA.

WIGAN ATHLETIC

League: 10th FA Cup: 3rd Rnd Coca-Cola Cup: 1st Rnd Auto Windscreen Shield: 2nd Rnd

M	DATE	COMP	VEN	OPPONENTS	RESULT	HT	LP	GOAL SCORERS/GOAL TIMES	ATT.
1	A 12	EL	A	Gillingham	L 1-2	1-0	15	Martinez 22	(4101)
2	15	CC 1/1	A	Chester City	L 1-4	0-2		Martinez 67	(2626)
3	19	EL	H	Scunthorpe United	W 2-1	1-1	11	Seba 25, Lightfoot 80	3153
4	22	CC 1/2	H	Chester City	L 1-3	0-2		Lyons 66(pen)	2061
5	26	EL	A	Preston North End	D 1-1	1-1	11	Mutch 18	(6837)
6	29	EL	H	Chester City	W 2-1	1-1	10	Diaz 27, Lyons 58	2555
7	S 2	EL	A	Scarborough	D 0-0	0-0	9		(1949)
8	9	EL	H	Bury	L 1-2	1-1	11	Kilford 42	3128
9	12	EL	H	Barnet	W 1-0	1-0	9	Kilford 6	1745
10	16	EL	A	Torquay United	D 1-1	1-0	10	Diaz 28	(2188)
11	23	EL	A	Plymouth Argyle	L 0-1	0-0	12		2631
12	26	AWS 1/1	H	Scunthorpe United	D 1-1	0-0		Benjamin 53	1064
13	30	EL	A	Hereford United	D 2-2	1-1	13	Diaz 44, Greenall 86	(2198)
14	O 7	EL	H	Mansfield Town	L 2-6	1-2	15	Diaz 33, 67	2084
15	14	EL	H	Exeter City	W 4-0	1-0	11	Diaz 39, Seba 48, 84, Leonard 55	(3870)
16	21	EL	H	Hartlepool United	W 1-0	0-0	9	Diaz 90	2104
17	28	EL	A	Leyton Orient	D 1-1	1-1	9	Martinez 20	(4562)
18	31	EL	A	Darlington	L 1-2	0-1	10	Butler 85	(2076)
19	N 4	EL	H	Fulham	D 1-1	1-1	10	Robertson 43	2348
20	11	FAC 1	A	Runcorn	D 1-1	1-0		Martinez 38	(2844)
21	14	AWS 1/2	A	Bury	D 0-0	0-0			(1471)
22	18	EL	A	Northampton Town	D 0-0	0-0	12		(4102)
23	21	FAC 1R	H	Runcorn	W 4-2	2-2		Leonard 41, Diaz 42, Martinez 69, og 74	3224
24	25	EL	H	Doncaster Rovers	W 2-0	2-0	10	Leonard 13, Biggins 18	2879
25	28	AWS 2	A	Rotherham United	D 0-0*	0-0		(Lost 1-4 on Penalties)	(1008)
26	D 2	FAC 2	A	Barrow	W 4-0	0-0		Diaz 57, Black 61, 71, Martinez 70	(3630)
27	9	EL	A	Plymouth Argyle	L 1-3	1-1	11	Farrell 13	(5931)
28	16	EL	H	Hereford United	W 2-1	0-1	11	Sharp 55, Martinez 62	1962
29	23	EL	H	Lincoln City	D 1-1	0-0	11	Martinez 52	2334
30	26	EL	A	Cambridge United	L 1-2	0-0	11	Kilford 73	(2855)
31	J 2	EL	A	Rochdale	W 2-0	1-0	10	Diaz 63, Martinez 68	2624
32	6	FAC 3	A	Walsall	L 0-1	0-0			(5672)
33	13	EL	A	Scunthorpe United	L 1-3	0-1	11	Sharp 71	(2288)
34	20	EL	H	Gillingham	W 2-1	1-1	9	Lancashire 6, Diaz 66	2773
35	30	EL	H	Colchester United	W 2-0	2-0	8	Johnson 14, 37	2101
36	F 3	EL	H	Preston North End	L 0-1	0-0	8		5567
37	10	EL	A	Colchester United	W 2-1	0-0	8	Lancashire 64, 86	(3028)
38	17	EL	A	Barnet	L 0-5	0-2	9		(2059)
39	20	EL	H	Scarborough	W 2-0	2-0	7	Martinez 7, 26	2208
40	24	EL	H	Torquay United	W 3-0	1-0	7	Diaz 43, Black 65, Pender 69	2697
41	27	EL	A	Bury	L 1-2	0-0	8	Black 69	(3800)
42	M 2	EL	H	Cambridge United	W 3-1	2-1	7	Martinez 10(pen), Sharp 28, Barnwell 70	2528
43	5	EL	A	Cardiff City	L 0-3	0-2	7		(1611)
44	9	EL	A	Lincoln City	W 4-2	1-1	6	Greenall 8, Johnson 60, Sharp 63(pen), Leonard 71	(3282)
45	16	EL	H	Cardiff City	W 3-1	0-0	4	Sharp 49, 67, Leonard 51	2897
46	19	EL	A	Chester City	D 0-0	0-0	4		(2825)
47	23	EL	A	Rochdale	W 2-0	1-0	3	Peake 25(og), Biggins 65	(2870)
48	30	EL	A	Mansfield Town	L 0-1	0-0	5		(2369)
49	A 2	EL	H	Exeter City	W 1-0	0-0	4	Leonard 81	2744
50	6	EL	H	Leyton Orient	W 1-0	0-0	3	Lowe 56	3081
51	8	EL	A	Hartlepool United	W 2-1	0-1	3	Lowe 60, Leonard 69	(1877)
52	13	EL	H	Darlington	D 1-1	0-1	4	Lowe 82	4473
53	20	EL	A	Fulham	L 0-1	0-0	6		(4657)
54	27	EL	A	Doncaster Rovers	L 1-2	1-1	6	Martinez 14	(2122)
55	M 4	EL	H	Northampton Town	L 1-2	1-1	10	Leonard 11	5089

Best Home League Attendance: 5567 v Preston North End   **Smallest: 1745 v Barnet**   **Average: 2856**

Goal Scorers:
EL(62): Diaz(10),Martinez(9),Leonard(7),Sharp(6),Lancashire(3),Lowe(3),Kilford(3),Johnson(3),Seba(3),Black(2),Greenall(2),Biggins(2),Farrell(1), Lightfoot(1),Lyons(1),Barnwell(1),Mutch(1),Pender(1),Robertson(1),Butler(1),Opponent(s)(1)
CC(2): Lyons(1),Martinez(1)
FAC(9): Martinez(3),Diaz(2),Black(2),Opponent(s)(1),Leonard(1)
AWS(1): Benjamin(1)

(*A.E.T.)

(F) Barnwell	(F) Benjamin	(F) Biggins	(F) Black	(D) Butler	(D) Carragher	(F) Diaz	(D) Doolan	(G) Farnworth	(M) Farrell	(G) Felgate	(D) Greenall	(D) Johnson	(M) Kelly	(M) Kilford	(F) Lancashire	(F) Leonard	(D) Lightfoot	(F) Lowe	(F) Lyons	(M) Martinez	(F) Miller	(M) Mutch	(F) Ogden	(D) Pender	(M) Rimmer	(D) Robertson	(F) Seba	(M) Sharp		
			X		S2	S1	X1	S	X	X						X	X			X2	X	X					X	X	P.Taylor	1
			X1		S1	X	X2		X	X						X	X			S2	X	X					X	X	K.J.Breen	2
		S1			X	X		S	X	X						X	X			X	X			X			X	X1	K.Lynch	3
			S		X	X			X	X						X	X			X	X	X1	S1				X	X2	G.B.Frankland	4
				X	X	X1		X	X								X			X			X	S		X	X	S1	W.Burns	5
		S1		X	X	X1		X	X								X			X			X	X		S	X	S	E.Lomas	6
				X	X1	X	S	X	X								X			X2			X	X		X	S1	S2	A.Butler	7
				S2	X	X		X	S2		X	X		X2						X1			X	X		X2	X	S1	S.Mathieson	8
				S	X	X		X	X		X	X		X		X				S1	X		X	X	S	X1	X	S	R.Poulain	9
				S1	X	X		X	X		X	X		X						S1	X	S	X	X	S	X1	X	S	P.Rejer	10
S3					X	X		X	X		X	X		X2			X			S1			X3	X	X	X1		S2	J.Lloyd	11
X			S		X	X	S	X	X		X	X	X	X		X				X				X	X			S	D.Allison	12
X					S1	X	X	X	X		X	X	X							X			X1	X	X			S	R.Poulain	13
S2		S1		X		X		X	S		X	X				X				X1			X2	X	X				N.Barry	14
				X		X		X			X					X	X1			X			X2	S2	S1	X	X		G.Singh	15
			S2		X			X	S		X			X		X	X1			S1			X	X		X	X2		C.Wilkes	16
			S	X		X		X	S		X			X		X				S			X	X		X	X1		G.Barber	17
		S1		X		X		X	S		X			X2		X				S2			X	X		X	X1		R.Furnandiz	18
		S1				X		X			X			X		X	S2			X	X2		X	X1		X	S		M.Riley	19
				X1	X	X		X	S		X			X		X				S1			X	X		X			S.Baines	20
		S1		X	X	X1		X	X		X			X		X				X			X	X		X			G.Cain	21
	X	X1	X	X	X3			X	X					X2		X	S1	S2	S3	X			X	X			X		N.Barry	22
		S		X	X	X1		X			X2			S		X	X			X	X	S		X		X1	S2		S.Baines	23
	X	S1		X	X1	X		X	X		X			X		X	X	X	S	X			X						M.J.Brandwood	24
		S		X	X	X		X	X2		X			X	X1	X	X	S2		X			X			X			S.Mathieson	25
				X	X	X		X	X		S1			X		X				X			X1			X	S		T.Heilbron	26
	X	S2	X2	X	X1			X	X		X			S1		X				X			X	S				X	M.Pierce	27
	X1	S1	X	S		X		X	X		X	X		X		X				X			X	X				X	I.Cruikshanks	28
		X1			X	S1		X	S		X	X		X2		X				X			X	S2				X	G.Frankland	29
				X	S1			X	X1		X2	X		S2		X				X	X	X	X	S		X		X	F.Stretton	30
				X	X	X		X	S		X	X				X				X	X	X	X	X			X	X	U.Rennie	31
				X	X			X	X2	S	X			X		X				X	X			S2	X	X1	S1	X	K.Lynch	32
				X	X	X		X	S1		X	X		X	X	X2				X1	X3	S3		X		X	S2	X	G.Singh	33
		S	S	X	X	X		X	X		X	X		X	X	X				S1	X1			X	X			X	A.Pearson	34
	S1		S	X	X	X		X	S		X	X		X1		X				X				X	X			X	T.Heilbron	35
S1	X		S	X		X		X	X		X	X		X		X				X				X	X			X1	D.Allison	36
S1	X1		S	X		X		X	X		X	X	X			X				X				X	X			X	J.Kirkby	37
S1	X1			X2	S2			X	X		X	X				X			S3	X3				X	X			X	A.G.Wiley	38
S1		X1				X		X	X		X	X	S			X				S	X			X	X			X	K.Breen	39
S2	X1	S1	X		X			X	X2		X	X		S3		X				X3				X	X			X	R.Furnandiz	40
S1		X	X			S2		X			X	X				X	X1			X	S			X	X			X2	M.Fletcher	41
S2		X2	X3		X			X			X	X		S3		X	S1			X				X1	X		X	X	J.Lloyd	42
X1		S1		X		X		X			X	X				X	X			X2	X			X	S2		S	X	P.Taylor	43
				X	X2	X		X	S2		X	X			X1	S1	X			X				X				X	P.Rejer	44
		S2	X2	X		X		X	X1		X	X		S2		X				X				X	X		S1	X	D.Laws	45
S1		X	S	X				X	X		X	X	X			X1				X				X	X				G.Frankland	46
X1		X	S1	X	S1			X	X		X	X		X						X1				X	X				F.Wolstenholme	47
	X	S1	X	S2				X	X1		X	X		X		X				X2				X	X		S3		I.Cruikshanks	48
	X		X	S	X1			X	X		X	X		X2		X			S2	X	X			X	X		S1		T.Heilbron	49
X2				X	S2			X			X	X		S1		X	X			X			S	X	X		X	X1	U.Rennie	50
				X	X			X	S2		X	X		X1		X	X			X2				X	X			S1	S.Baines	51
				X1	X	X2		X	S		X	X				X				X			S2	X	X			S1	A.Butler	52
				S	X			X	X1		X	X		S1		X1				X	X		X	X	X			S1	A.D'Urso	53
	X			X	X		S	X	X	S	X	X		X						S	X			X	X			X	B.Knight	54
				X1	S1	X		X	S		X	X		X		X				X				X	X		S2	X2	R.Pearson	55
2	1	15	8	32	22	31	2	43	21	3	37	27	2	18	5	32	11	7	14	42	4	7	10	40	27	14	8	20	EL Appearances	
8	2	3	13	0	6	1	0	2	0	0	0	0	0	0	0	7	0	3	0	8	0	3	0	0	0	0	12	0	EL Sub Appearances	
0	0	0	0	1	1+1	2	1	0	2	2	0	0	0	0	0	2	0	2	0	1+1	2	2	0	0+1	0	0	2	0	CC Appearances	
0	0	0	2	3	4	4	0	4	2+1	0	3	0	0	1+1	0	4	2	0	3+1	4	0	0	0	4	1	0	0+2	1	FAC Appearances	
0	0	0	0+1	3	2	3	0	3	2+1	0	2+1	0	1	2	0	2	3	0	3	2	0+1	0	1	3	0	0	1	0	AWS Appearances	

Also Played: (G) Butler X(19). (D) Millett S(3), S2(4).

CLUB RECORDS

RECORD LEAGUE VICTORY
7-2 v Scunthorpe Utd, (a), Div 4, 12.3.1982   5-0 v Peterborough Utd, (h), Div 4, 19.1.1982   5-0 v Swansea City, (h), Div 3, 18.1.1986   6-1 v Swansea City (a),Div 3,6.4.1991
Most Goals Scored in a Cup Tie: 6-0 v Carlisle United, FA Cup Rnd 1, 24.11.1934 6-0 v Rochdale, Freight Rover Trophy (Northern Section), 28.1.1986

RECORD LEAGUE DEFEAT
0-5 v Bristol Rovers, Div 3, 26.2.1983   1-6 v Bristol Rovers, Div 3, 3.3.1990
Record Cup Defeat: 0-5 v Chelsea (h), FA Cup Round 3 replay, 26.1.1985

MOST LEAGUE POINTS
(3pts a win) 91, Div 4, 1981-82
(2pts a win) 55, Div 4,1978-79, 1979-80

MOST LEAGUE GOALS
83, Div 3, 1985-86

RECORD TRANSFER FEE RECEIVED
£350,000 from Coventry City for Peter Atherton, August 1991

RECORD TRANSFER FEE PAID
£150,000 for Graeme Jones from Doncaster Rovers, July 1996.

BEST PERFORMANCES
League: 4th Div 3 1985-86 & 1986-87
FA Cup: 6th Round1986-87
League Cup: 4th Round 1981-82

HONOURS
Freight Rover Trophy 1985

LEAGUE CAREER
Elected to Div 4 1978   Promoted to Div 3 (now Div 2) 1982
Relegated to Div 3 1992-93

INDIVIDUAL CLUB RECORDS

MOST APPEARANCES FOR CLUB
Kevin Langley (1982-86 & 1990-1994): League 307+10 +FA Cup 27+1 + League Cup 21 + Other Competitions 27 Total 382+11 sub
MOST CAPPED PLAYER
None
RECORD GOALSCORER IN A MATCH
Paul Jewell 4 v Aldershot, Div 3, 1.3.1988
RECORD LEAGUE GOALSCORER IN A SEASON
Warren Aspinal 21, Div 3, 1985-86   In All Competitions: Warren Aspinal 27 (League 21 + Cup Competitions 6)
RECORD LEAGUE GOALSCORER IN A CAREER
Peter Houghton 62, 1978-83   In All Competitions: Peter Houghton 68 (League 62 + FA Cup 3 + League Cup 3)

OLDEST PLAYER IN A LEAGUE MATCH
Joe Jakub, 38 years, 76 days v Exeter City, Division 3, 21.2.95.
YOUNGEST PLAYER IN A LEAGUE MATCH
Steve Nugent, 16 years 132 days v Leyton Orient, Division 3, 16.9.1989

PREVIOUS MANAGERS

Charlie Spencer 1932-37   Jimmy Milne 1946-47   Bob Pryde 1949-52 Ted Goodier 1952-54   Walter Crook 1954-55   Ron Suart 1955-56 Billy Cooke 1956   Sam Barkas 1957   Trevor Hitchen 1957-58 Malcom Barrass 1958-59   Jimmy Shirley 1959   Pat Murphy 1959-60 Allenby Chilton 1960   Johnny Ball 1961-63   Allan Brown 1963-66   Alf Craig 1966-67   Harry Leyland 1967-68   Alan Saunders 1968   Ian McNeill 1968-70   Gordon Milne 1970-72   Les Rigby 1972-74   Brian Tiler 1974-76   Ian McNeill 1976-81   Larry Lloyd 1981-83   Harry McNally 1983-85   Bryan Hamilton 1985-86   Ray Mathias 1986-89 Bryan Hamilton 1989-91   Dave Philpotts 1991-93, Kenny Swain 1993-94 Graham Barrow 1994-95.

ADDITIONAL INFORMATION
Previous Name: None.
Previous League: Northern Premier.

Club Colours: White shirts with broad blue & narrow green striped sleeves, blue shorts with white & green trim, blue & white socks.
Change Colours: Yellow shirts with blue pin stripes, yellow shorts, yellow socks.
Reserves League: Pontins League Division Three.

LONGEST LEAGUE RUNS

of undefeated matches:	21 (1981-82)	of league matches w/out a win:	14 (1989)
of undefeated home matches:	25 (1985-86)	of undefeated away matches:	11 (1986)
without home win:	6 (1988, 1989)	without an away win:	15 (1988)
of league wins:	6 (1986, 1993)	of home wins:	8 (1978-79)
of league defeats:	7 (1993)	of away wins:	4 (1987, 1988)

THE MANAGER

JOHN DEEHAN . . . . appointed 1st November 1995.
PREVIOUS CLUBS
As Manager . . . . Norwich City.
As Asst.Man/Coach. . . . . Norwich City.
As a player. . . . . Aston Villa, West Brom, Norwich, Ipswich, Manchester City, Barnsley.
HONOURS
As a Manager . . . . None.
As a Player . . . . **Norwich City:** League Cup 1984-85. Div.2 championship 1985-86.
. . . . **England:** 7 caps at u21 level & youth caps.

WIGAN ATHLETIC

PLAYERS NAME / Honours	Ht	Wt	Birthdate	Birthplace / Transfers	Contract Date	Clubs	League	L/Cup	FA Cup	Other	Lge	L/C	FAC	Oth
G O A L K E E P E R S														
Butler Lee	6.2	13.0	30/05/66	Sheffield	16/06/86	Lincoln City	30	1	1					
Loan (18/03/91) Hull City 4 Lge Apps.				£100000	21/08/87	Aston Villa	8			2				
Loan (05/02/96) Scunthorpe 2 Lge Apps.				£165000	22/07/91	Barnsley	118+2	5	9	4				
				Free	01/06/96	Wigan Athletic								
Farnworth Simon	5.11	11.0	28/10/63	Chorley	05/09/81	Bolton Wanderers	113	11	6	8				
E: S.				Loan	11/09/86	Stockport County	10	2						
Loan (09/01/87) Tranmere Rovers 7 Lge Apps.				Free	12/03/87	Bury	105	11	3	5				
				Free	01/07/90	Preston North End	81	6	3	7				
				Free	27/07/93	Wigan Athletic	167	10	10	13				
D E F E N D E R S														
Bishop Charlie	6.0	12.11	16/02/68	Nottingham			Stoke City								
via Free 17/04/86 Watford				Free	17/04/86	Watford								
				Free	10/08/87	Bury	104+10	5	4	12+1	6		1	
				£50000	24/07/91	Barnsley	136+7	14+1	9	5	1			
Loan (12/01/96) Preston North End 4 Lge Apps				Loan	28/03/96	Burnley	9							
					28/06/96	Wigan Athletic								
Butler John	5.11	11.7	07/02/62	Liverpool			Prescot Cables								
AMC'92. Div.2'93.				£100	15/01/82	Wigan Athletic	238+7	17+1	20+1	18	15		2	
				£100000	23/12/88	Stoke City	258+4	19	11	26+1	7			2
				Free	17/06/95	Wigan Athletic	32	1	3	3	1			
Carragher Matthew	5.9	10.7	14/01/76	Liverpool	25/11/93	Wigan Athletic	90+11	4+1	10	7+1		1	2	
Greenall Colin	5.10	11.06	30/12/63	Billinge	17/01/81	Blackpool	179+4	12	9	2	9	2		
E: Y.5.				£285000	15/02/88	Oxford United	67	4	1	2	2			
				£40000	10/09/88	Gillingham	62	3	6	9	5	1	1	2
Loan (04/01/90) Bury 3 Lge, 1 Oth App.				£125000	16/07/90	Bury	66+2	3	2	8	5			1
				£50000	27/03/92	Preston North End	29				1			
				Free	13/08/93	Chester City	42	2	4	4	1			1
				Free	27/07/94	Lincoln City	43	6	3	2	3	1		
					19/09/95	Wigan Athletic	37		3	2+1	2			
Johnson Gavin	5.11	11.7	10/10/70	Eye	01/03/89	Ipswich Town	100+15	8+1	12	3+1	11	2		1
					04/07/95	Luton Town	5+1	1						
					16/02/96	Wigan Athletic	27				3			
Moore Andy	5.9		02/05/78	Liverpool			Wigan Athletic								
Pender John	6.0	13.12	19/11/63	Luton	08/11/81	Wolves	115+2	5	7		3		1	
Ei: u21.1, Y. Div.4'92.				£35000	23/07/85	Charlton Athletic	41	1	1	2				1
				£50000	30/10/87	Bristol City	83	11	8	12	3			
				£70000	18/10/90	Burnley	171	11	19	21	9	1	1	1
				£30000	22/08/95	Wigan Athletic	40+1		4	3	1			
Salt Daniel	5.10		17/11/77	Warrington			Wigan Athletic								
M I D F I E L D														
Fearns Terry	5.11		24/10/77	Liverpool			Wigan Athletic								
Kilford Ian	5.10	10.5	06/10/73	Bristol	03/04/91	Nottingham Forest	0+1							
					23/12/93	Wigan Athletic	60+8	4	3+2	5	11		1	1
Love Michael J	5.11	12.4	27/11/73	Stockport			Hinckley Athletic								
					15/01/96	Wigan Athletic								
Martinez Roberto	5.11	11.12	13/07/73	Balaguer			CF Balaguer (Spain)								
				Free	25/07/95	Wigan Athletic	42	2	4	2	9	1	3	
Sharp Kevin	5.9	10.7	19/09/74	Canada			Auxerre (France)								
E: Y.S. UEFA Yth'93. FAYC'93.				£60000	20/10/92	Leeds United	11+6		0+1					
				£100000	30/11/95	Wigan Athletic	20		1		6			
F O R W A R D S														
Biggins Wayne	5.11	11.0	20/11/61	Sheffield	22/11/79	Lincoln City	8				1			
Div.2'88. AMC'92.					01/08/80	Kings Lynn								
01/08/82 Matlock Town				£7500	04/02/84	Burnley	78	6	3	7	29	1	1	5
				£40000	17/10/85	Norwich City	66+13	6	4	6+2	16	2		3
				£150000	15/07/88	Manchester City	29+3	4	2		9	1		
				£250000	10/08/89	Stoke City	120+2	10	6	10	46	2		5
				£200000	02/10/92	Barnsley	44+3		3+1		16			
					25/11/93	Celtic	4+5		0+1					
				£125000	24/03/94	Stoke City	18+9	1+1		3+1	6			2
				Free	06/07/95	Oxford United	8+2	3+1		0+1	1	1		
					18/12/95	Wigan Athletic	15+3				2			
Black Tony	5.8	11.0	15/07/69	Barrow			Bamber Bridge								
					22/03/95	Wigan Athletic	17+13		2	0+1	2		2	
Diaz Isidro	5.7	9.4	15/05/72	Valencia			CF Balaguer (Spain)								
				Free	25/07/95	Wigan Athletic	31+6	2	4	3	10		2	
Jones Graeme A	6.0	12.12	13/03/70	Gateshead			Bridlington								
NPL Div.1'93. FA Vase'93.				£10000	02/08/93	Doncaster Rovers	81+11	4+1	2+1	5	27	1	2	1
				£150000	05/07/96	Wigan Athletic								
Lancashire Graham	5.10	11.12	19/10/72	Blackpool	01/07/91	Burnley	11+19		2+2	2+4	8		1	
Div.4'92.				Loan	20/11/92	Halifax Town	2		1+1					
				Loan	21/01/94	Chester City	10+1				7			
				£55000	23/12/94	Preston North End	11+12		1+1		3			
					08/03/96	Wigan Athletic	5				3			
Lowe David A	5.10	11.4	30/08/65	Liverpool	01/06/83	Wigan Athletic	179+9	8	16+1	18	40		4	9
E: u21.2, Y.7. AMC'85.				£80000	26/06/87	Ipswich Town	121+13	10	3	10+2	37	2		6
Div.2'92.				Loan	19/03/92	Port Vale	8+1				2			
				£250000	13/07/92	Leicester City	68+26	4+3	2+2	3	22	1		
				Loan	18/02/94	Port Vale	18+1				5			
				£125000	28/03/96	Wigan Athletic	7				3			
Seba Jesus	5.6	9.13	11/04/74	Zaragoza			Real Zaragoza								
Spanish u21 Int.				Free	25/07/95	Wigan Athletic	8+12	2	0+2	1	3			
Tyrell Kevin	5.10		05/10/77	Warrington			Wigan Athletic								

SPRINGFIELD PARK
Wigan, Lancashire WN6 7BA
Tel: 01942 244 433

Capacity...7,097
Covered Standing...2,967
Seating...1,109

First game (As Wigan Ath.) ....5,106 v Port Vale Reserves. Cheshire Lge.
First ever game..Wigan County v Burton Swifts, 1.9.1897.
ATTENDANCES
Highest ....527,526 v Hereford Utd, FA Cup 2nd Rnd.,2.12.1953.
....(*Record for two non-League clubs outside of Wembley*)
Lowest ....983 v Bury, AMC, 19.10.1993.

OTHER GROUND...None.

MATCHDAY TICKET PRICES

Phoenix Stand £9

Juv/OAP £6

Cable North West Family Stand £9

U16 . . . . £4

Ground

Adult £7

U16/OAP £4

Junior Latics £3

Ticket Office Telephone no. 01942 244433

CLUBCALL 0891 12 16 55
Calls cost 39p per minute cheap rate and 49p per
minute at all other times.
Call costings correct at time of going to press.

HOW TO GET TO THE GROUND

From the North: Exit M6 at junction 27 and turn left at end of slip road. Turn right at T-junction, signposted Shevington. After 1 mile turn left into Old Lane (signed B5375 Standish Lower Ground). The road winds through countryside for approx. 2 miles. Go straight on at cross roads (you can see floodlights ahead). After 0.75 miles, turn left at traffic lights into Springfield Road, take second left (First Avenue) into ground.
From the South & West: Exit M6 at junction 25. At end of slip road (approx. 1 mile) turn left, signposted Wigan A49. Follow signs for Wigan A49 for 1.8 miles to complex junction (Homestyle warehouse is ahead of you). Turn left at traffic lights into Robin Park Road. Go straight on for 1 mile to crossroads, then turn right. After 0.75 miles, turn left at traffic lights into Springfield Road. Take second left (First Avenue) into ground.
From the East: Exit M61 at junction 6 (signposted Chorley, Horwich A6027) and take first exit at roundabout. NB: do not exit at junction 5 which is signposted Wigan. At next round-about, take first left (signposted Westhoughton A6, Wigan B5238) into Chorley Road. After 0.3 miles turn right (signposted Wigan B5238). After 1.8 miles turn left at Aspull War Memorial (signposted Wigan B5238). After 2.2 miles just after *Earl of Balcarres pub* turn right at traffic lights (Central Park, Wigan RLFC, is now facing you). Turn left at lights and get in right hand lane. Go straight through three sets of lights until Morrisons is on left hand side, BBC North on right hand side, and the college ahead and to the right (building has a large wheel on wall). Turn right as lights into Parsons Walk, thus passing the college on your left. Follow this road for 0.7 miles tosecond setof traffic lights. Turn right into Springfield Road, then second left (First Avenue) into ground.
Car Parking: Parking in nearby side streets.
Nearest Railway Station: Wigan Wallgate or Wigan Northwestern (01942 242 231)

MATCHDAY PROGRAMME

Programme Editor . . . . Derek Davies.

Number of pages . . . . 32.

Price . . . . £1.50.

Subscriptions . . . . £45 inc. P&P.

Local Newspapers . . . . Wigan Observer, Wigan Evening Post,
. . . . Wigan Reporter.

Local Radio Stations . . . . Piccadilly Gold, BBC GMR,
. . . . Red Rose Gold, Fortune Radio, City FM.

1946-47

1. Northern Ireland   A   W 7-2   Goalscorers: Carter, Finney, Langton, Lawton, Mannion (3).

Swift	Scott	Hardwick	W Wright	Franklin	Cockburn	Finney	Carter	Lawton	Mannion	Langton

2. Republic of Ireland   A   W 1-0   Goalscorers: Finney.

Swift	Scott	Hardwick	W Wright	Franklin	Cockburn	Finney	Carter	Lawton	Mannion	Langton

3. Wales   H   W 3-0   Goalscorers: Lawton, Mannion (2).

Swift	Scott	Hardwick	W Wright	Franklin	Cockburn	Finney	Carter	Lawton	Mannion	Langton

4. Holland   H   W 8-2   Goalscorers: Carter (2), Finney, Lawton (4), Mannion.

Swift	Scott	Hardwick	W Wright	Franklin	Johnston	Finney	Carter	Lawton	Mannion	Langton

5. Scotland   H   D 1-1   Goalscorers: Carter.

Swift	Scott	Hardwick	W Wright	Franklin	Johnston	S Matthews	Carter	Lawton	Mannion	Mullen

6. France   H   W 3-0   Goalscorers: Carter, Finney, Mannion.

Swift	Scott	Hardwick	W Wright	Franklin	Lowe	Finney	Carter	Lawton	Mannion	Langton

7. Switzerland   A   L 0-1

Swift	Scott	Hardwick	W Wright	Franklin	Lowe	S Matthews	Carter	Lawton	Mannion	Langton

8. Portugal   A   W 10-0   Goalscorers: Finney, Lawton (4), S Matthews, Mortensen (4).

Swift	Scott	Hardwick	W Wright	Franklin	Lowe	S Matthews	Mortensen	Lawton	Mannion	Finney

1947-48

9. Belgium   A   W 5-2   Goalscorers: Mortensen, Lawton (2).

Swift	Scott	Hardwick	Ward	Franklin	W Wright	S Matthews	Mortensen	Lawton	Mannion	Finney

10. Wales   A   W 3-0   Goalscorers: Finney (2), Lawton, Mortensen.

Swift	Scott	Hardwick	P Taylor	Franklin	W Wright	S Matthews	Mortensen	Lawton	Mannion	Finney

11. Switzerland   H   W 6-0   Goalscorers: Haines (2), Hancocks (2), Milburn, J Rowley

Ditchburn	Ramsey	Aston	W Wright	Franklin	Cockburn	S Matthews	J Rowley	Milburn	Haines	Hancocks

12. Scotland   H   L 1-3   Goalscorer: Milburn

Swift	Aston	J Howe	W Wright	Franklin	Cockburn	S Matthews	Mortenson	Milburn	Pearson	Finney

13. Sweden   A   L 1-3   Goalscorer: Finney

Ditchburn	Shimwell	Aston	W Wright	Franklin	Cockburn	Finney	Mortenson	Bentley	J Rowley	Langton

14. Norway   A   W 4-1   Goalscorers: Finney, Morris, Mullen, Opponents

Swift	Ellerington	Aston	W Wright	Franklin	Dickinson	Finney	MOrris	Mortenson	Mannion	Mullen

15. France   A   W 3-1   Goalscorers: Morris (2)

Williams	Ellerington	Aston	W Wright	Franklin	Dickinson	Finney	Morris	J Rowley	Mannion	Mullen

1949-50

16. Eire   H   L 0-2

Williams	Mozley	Aston	W Wright	Franklin	Dickinson	P Harris	Morris	Pye	Mannion	Finney

17. Wales   A   W 4-1   Goalscorers: Milburn (3), Mortenson

Williams	Mozley	Aston	W Wright	Franklin	Dickinson	Finney	Mortenson	Milburn	Shackleton	Hancocks

18. Northern Ireland   A   W 9-2   Goalscorers: J Froggatt, Mortensen, Pearson (2), J Rowley (4)

Streten	Mozley	Aston	Watson	Franklin	W Wright	Finney	Mortenson	J Rowley	Pearson	J Froggatt

19. Italy   H   W 2-0   Goalscorers: J Rowley, W Wright

Williams	Ramsey	Aston	Watson	Franklin	W Wright	Finney	Mortenson	J Rowley	Pearson	J Froggatt

20. Scotland   A   W 1-0   Goalscorers: Bentley

Williams	Ramsey	Aston	W Wright	Franklin	Dickinson	Finney	Mannion	Mortenson	Bentley	Langton

21. Portugal   A   W 5-3   Goalscorers: Finney (4), Mortenson

Williams	Ramsey	Aston	W Wright	W H Jones	Dickinson	Milburn	Mortenson	Bentley	Mannion	Finney

22. Belgium   A   W 4-1   Goalscorers: Bentley, Mannion, Mortenson, Mullen

Williams	Ramsey	Aston	W Wright	W H Jones	Dickinson	Milburn[1]	Mortenson	Bentley	Mannion	Finney	Mullen[1]

23. Chile   N   W 2-0   Goalscorers: Mannion, Mortenson

Williams	Ramsey	Aston	W Wright	L Hughes	Dickinson	Finney	Mannion	Bentley	Mortenson	Mullen

24.	USA	N	L	0-1							
Williams	Ramsey	Aston	W Wright	L Hughes	Dickinson	Finney	Mannion	Bentley	Mortensen	Mullen	

25.	Spain	N	L	0-1							
Williams	Ramsey	Eckersley	W Wright	L Hughes	Dickinson	S Matthews	Mortensen	Milburn	E Baily	Finney	

1950-51

26. Northern Ireland   A   W 4-1   Goalscorers: E Baily (2), J Lee, W Wright

Williams	Ramsey	Aston	W Wright	Chilton	Dickinson	S Matthews	Mannion	J Lee	E Baily	Langton

27. Wales   H   W 4-2   Goalscorers: E Baily (2), Mannion, Milburn

Williams	Ramsey	L Smith	Watson	L Compton	Dickinson	Finney	Mannion	Milburn	E Baily	Medley

28. Yugoslavia   H   D 2-2   Goalscorers: Lofthouse (2)

Williams	Ramsey	Eckersley	Watson	L Compton	Dickinson	Hancocks	Mannion	Lofthouse	E Baily	Medley

29. Scotland   H   L 2-3   Goalscorers: Finney, Hassall

Williams	Ramsey	Eckersley	Johnston	J Froggatt	W Wright	S Matthews	Mannon	Mortensen	Hassall	Finney

30. Argentina   H   W 2-1   Goalscorers: Milburn, Mortensen

Williams	Ramsey	Eckersley	W Wright	J Taylor	Cockburn	Finney	Mortensen	Milburn	Hassall	Metcalfe

31. Portugal   H   W 5-2   Goalscorers: Finney, Hassall, Milburn (2), Nicholson

Williams	Ramsey	Eckersley	Nicholson	J Taylor	Cockburn	Finney	Pearson	Milburn	Hassall	Metcalfe

1951-52

32. France   H   D 2-2   Goalscorers: Medley, Opponents

Williams	Ramsey	Willis	W Wright	Chilton	Cockburn	Finney	Mannion	Milburn	Hassall	Medley

33. Wales   A   D 1-1   Goalscorers: E Baily

Williams	Ramsey	L Smith	W Wright	Barrass	Dickinson	Finney	T Thompson	Lofthouse	E Baily	Medley

34. Northern Ireland   H   W 2-0   Goalscorers: Lofthouse (2)

Merrick	Ramsey	L Smith	W Wright	Barrass	Dickinson	Finney	Sewell	Lofthouse	Phillips	Medley

35. Austria   H   D 2-2   Goalscorers: Lofthouse, Ramsey

Merrick	Ramsey	Eckersley	W Wright	J Froggatt	Dickinson	Milton	Broadis	Lofthouse	E Baily	Medley

36. Scotland   A   W 2-1   Goalscorers: Pearson (2)

Merrick	Ramsey	Garrett	W Wright	J Froggatt	Dickinson	Finney	Broadis	Lofthouse	Pearson	J Rowley

37. Italy   A   D 1-1   Goalscorers: Broadis

Merrick	Ramsey	Garrett	W Wright	J Froggatt	Dickinson	Finney	Broadis	Lofthouse	Pearson	Elliott

38. Austria   A   W 3-2   Goalscorers: Lofthouse (2), Sewell

Merrick	Ramsey	Eckersley	W Wright	J Froggatt	Dickinson	Finney	Sewell	Lofthouse	E Baily	Elliott

39. Switzerland   A   W 3-0   Goalscorers: Lofthouse (2), Sewell

Merrick	Ramsey	Eckersley	W Wright	J Froggatt	Dickinson	R Allen	Sewell	Lofthouse	E Baily	Finney

1952-53

40. Northern Ireland   A   D 2-2   Goalscorers: Elliott, Lofthouse

Merrick	Ramsey	Eckersley	W Wright	J Froggatt	Dickinson	Finney	Sewell	Lofthouse	E Baily	Elliott

41. Wales   H   W 5-2   Goalscorers: Bentley, J Finney, Froggatt, Lofthouse (2)

Merrick	Ramsey	L Smith	W Wright	J Froggatt	Dickinson	Finney	R Froggatt	Lofthouse	Bentley	Elliott

42. Belgium   H   W 5-0   Goalscorers: Elliott (2), Lofthouse (2), R Froggatt

Merrick	Ramsey	L Smith	W Wright	J Froggatt	Dickinson	Finney	Bentley	Lofthouse	R Froggatt	Elliott

43. Scotland   H   D 2-2   Goalscorers: Broadis (2)

Merrick	Ramsey	L Smith	W Wright	Barrass	Dickinson	Finney	Broadis	Lofthouse	R Froggatt	J Froggatt

44. Argentina   A   D 0-0

Merrick	Ramsey	Eckersley	W Wright	Johnston	Dickinson	Finney	Broadis	Lofthouse	T Taylor	Berry

45. Chile   A   W 2-1   Goalscorers: Lofthouse, T Taylor

Merrick	Ramsey	Eckersley		Johnston	Dickinson	Finney	Broadis	Lofthouse	T Taylor	Berry

46. Uruguay   A   L 1-2   Goalscorer: T Taylor

Merrick	Ramsey	Eckersley		Johnston	Dickinson	Finney	Broadis	Lofthouse	T Taylor	Berry

47. USA   A   W 6-3   Goalscorers: Broadis, Finney (2), R Froggatt, Lofthouse (2)

Ditchburn	Ramsey	Eckersley	W Wright	Johnston	Dickinson	Finney	Broadis	Lofthouse	R Froggatt	J Froggatt

1953-54

48. Wales   A   W 4-1   Goalscorers: Lofthouse (2), Wilshaw (2)

Merrick	Garrett	Eckersley	W Wright	Johnston	Dickinson	Finney	Quixall	Lofthouse	Wilshaw	Mullen

49. FIFA H D 4-4 Goalscorers: Mortensen, Mullen (2), Ramsey
Merrick Ramsey Eckersley W Wright Ufton Dickinson S Matthews Mortensen Lofthouse Quixall Mullen

50. Ireland H W 3-1 Goalscorers: Hassall (2), Lofthouse
Merrick Rickaby Eckersley W Wright Johnston Dickinson S Matthews Quixall Lofthouse Hassall Mullen

51. Hungary H L 3-6 Goalscorers: Mortensen, Ramsey, Sewell
Merrick Ramsey Eckersley W Wright Johnston Dickinson S Matthews E Taylor Mortensen Sewell Robb

52. Scotland A W 4-2 Goalscorers: R Allen, Broadis, Mullen, Nicholls
Merrick Staniforth R Byrne W Wright H Clarke Dickinson Finney Broadis R Allen Nicholls Mullen

53. Yugoslavia A L 0-1
Merrick Staniforth R Byrne W Wright Owen Dickinson Finney Broadis R Allen Nicholls Mullen

54. Hungary A L 1-7 Goalscorer: Broadis
Merrick Staniforth R Byrne W Wright Owen Dickinson P Harris Sewell Jezzard Broadis Finney

55. Belgium N D 4-4 Goalscorers: Broadis (2), Lofthouse (2)
Merrick Staniforth R Byrne W Wright Owen Dickinson S Matthews Broadis Lofthouse T Taylor Finney

56. Switzerland N W 2-0 Goalscorers: Mullen, Wilshaw
Merrick Staniforth R Byrne McGarry W Wright Dickinson Finney Broadis T Taylor Wilshaw Mullen

57. Uruguay N L 2-4 Goalscorers: Finney, Lofthouse
Merrick Staniforth R Byrne McGarry W Wright Dickinson S Matthews Broadis Lofthouse Wilshaw Finney

---

1954-55

58. Northern Ireland A W 2-0 Goalscorers: Haynes, Revie
Wood Foulkes R Byrne Wheeler W Wright Barlow S Matthews Revie Lofthouse Haynes Pilkington

59. Wales H W 3-2 Goalscorers: Bentley (3)
Wood Staniforth R Byrne Phillips W Wright Slater S Matthews Bentley R Allen Shackleton Blunstone

60. West Germany H W 3-1 Goalscorers: R Allen, Bentley, Shackleton
Williams Staniforth R Byrne Phillips W Wright Slater S Matthews Bentley R Allen Shackleton Finney

61. Scotland H W 7-2 Goalscorers: Lofthouse (2), Revie, Wilshaw (4)
Williams Meadows R Byrne Armstrong W Wright Edwards S Matthews Revie Lofthouse Wilshaw Blunstone

62. France A L 0-1
Williams P Sillett R Byrne Flowers W Wright Edwards S Matthews Revie Lofthouse Wilshaw Blunstone

63. Spain A D 1-1 Goalscorer: Bentley
Williams P Sillett R Byrne Dickinson W Wright Edwards S Matthews Bentley Lofthouse Quixall Wilshaw

64. Portugal A L 1-3 Goalscorer: Bentley
Williams P Sillett R Byrne Dickinson W Wright Edwards S Matthews Bentley Lofthouse[1] Wilshaw Blunstone Quixall[1]

1955-56

65. Denmark A W 5-1 Goalscorers: Bradford, Lofthouse (2), Revie (2)
Baynham Hall R Byrne McGarry W Wright Dickinson Milburn Revie Lofthouse Bradford Finney

66. Wales A L 1-2 Goalscorer: Opponents
Williams Hall R Byrne McGarry W Wright Dickinson S Matthews Revie Lofthouse Wilshaw Finney

67. Northern Ireland H W 3-0 Goalscorers: Finney, Wilshaw (2)
Baynham Hall R Byrne Clayton W Wright Dickinson Finney Haynes Jezzard Wilshaw Perry

68. Spain H W 4-1 Goalscorers: Atyeo, Finney, Perry (2)
Baynham Hall R Byrne Clayton W Wright Dickinson Finney Atyeo Lofthouse Haynes Perry

69. Scotland A D 1-1 Goalscorer: Haynes
R Matthews Hall R Byrne Dickinson W Wright Edwards Finney T Taylor Lofthouse Haynes Perry

70. Brazil H W 4-2 Goalscorers: Grainger (2), T Taylor (2)
R Matthews Hall R Byrne Clayton W Wright Edwards S Matthews Atyeo T Taylor Haynes Grainger

71. Sweden A D 0-0
R Matthews Hall R Byrne Clayton W Wright Edwards Berry Atyeo T Taylor Haynes Grainger

72. Finland A W 5-1 Goalscorers: Astall, Haynes, Lofthouse (2), Wilshaw
Wood Hall R Byrne Clayton W Wright Edwards Astall Haynes T Taylor[1] Wilsahw Grainger Lofthouse[1]

73. West Germany A W 3-1 Goalscorers: Edwards, Grainger, Haynes
R Matthews Hall R Byrne Clayton W Wright Edwards Astall Haynes T Taylor Wilshaw Grainger

---

1956-57

74. Northern Ireland A D 1-1 Goalscorer: S Matthews
R Matthews Hall R Byrne Clayton W Wright Edwards S Matthews Revie T Taylor Wilshaw Grainger

75. **Wales**   H   W   3-1   **Goalscorers: Brooks, Finney, Haynes**
Ditchburn Hall   R Byrne   Clayton   W Wright   Dickinson   S Matthews   Brooks   Finney   Haynes   Grainger

76. **Yugoslavia**   H   W   3-0   **Goalscorers: Brooks, T Taylor (2)**
Ditchburn Hall   R Byrne   Clayton   W Wright   Dickinson   S Matthews   Brooks   Finney   Haynes[1]   Blunstone   T Taylor[1]

77. **Denmark**   H   W   5-2   **Goalscorers: Edwards (2), T Taylor (3)**
Ditchburn Hall   R Byrne   Clayton   W Wright   Dickinson   S Matthews   Brooks   T Taylor   Edwards   Finney

78. **Scotland**   H   W   2-1   **Goalscorers: Edwards, Kevan**
Hodgkinson Hall   R Byrne   Clayton   W Wright   Edwards   S Matthews   T Thompson   Finney   Kevan   Grainger

79. **Eire**   H   W   5-1   **Goalscorers: Atyeo (2), T Taylor (3)**
Hodgkinson Hall   R Byrne   Clayton   W Wright   Edwards   S Matthews   Atyeo   T Taylor   Haynes   Finney

80. **Denmark**   A   W   4-1   **Goalscorers: Atyeo, Haynes, T Taylor (2)**
Hodgkinson Hall   R Byrne   Clayton   W Wright   Edwards   S Matthews   Atyeo   T Taylor   Haynes   Finney

81. **Eire**   A   D   1-1   **Goalscorer: Atyeo**
Hodgkinson Hall   R Byrne   Clayton   W Wright   Edwards   Finney   Atyeo   T Taylor   Haynes   Pegg

---

1957-58

82. **Wales**   A   W   4-0   **Goalscorers: Finney, Haynes (2), Opponents**
Hopkinson D Howe   R Byrne   Clayton   W Wright   Edwards   Douglas   Kevan   T Taylor   Haynes   Finney

83. **Northern Ireland**   H   L   2-3   **Goalscorers: A'Court, Edwards**
Hopkinson D Howe   R Byrne   Clayton   W Wright   Edwards   Douglas   Kevan   T Taylor   Haynes   A Court

84. **France**   H   W   4-0   **Goalscorers: R Robinson (@), T Taylor (2)**
Hopkinson D Howe   R Byrne   Clayton   W Wright   Edwards   Douglas   R Robson   T Taylor   Haynes   Finney

85. **Scotland**   A   W   4-0   **Goalscorers: R Charlton, Douglas, Kevan (2)**
Hopkinson D Howe   Langley   Clayton   W Wright   Slater   Douglas   R Charlton   Kevan   Haynes   Finney

86. **Portugal**   H   W   2-1   **Goalscorers: R Charlton (2)**
Hopkinson D Howe   Langley   Clayton   W Wright   Slater   Douglas   R Charlton   Kevan   Haynes   Finney

87. **Yugoslavia**   A   L   0-5
Hopkinson D Howe   Langley   Clayton   W Wright   Slater   Douglas   R Charlton   Kevan   Haynes   Finney

88. **USSR**   A   D   1-1   **Goalscorer: Kevan**
McDonald D Howe   T Banks   Clamp   W Wright   Slater   Douglas   R Robson   Kevan   Haynes   Finney

89. **USSR**   N   D   2-2   **Goalscorers: Finney, Kevan**
McDonald D Howe   T Banks   Clamp   W Wright   Slater   Douglas   R Robson   Kevan   Haynes   Finney

90. **Brazil**   N   D   0-0
McDonald D Howe   T Banks   Clamp   W Wright   Slater   Douglas   R Robson   Kevan   Haynes   A'Court

92. **Austria**   N   D   2-2   **Goalscorers: Haynes, Kevan**
McDonald D Howe   T Banks   Clamp   W Wright   Slater   Douglas   R Robson   Kevan   Haynes   A'Court

92. **USSR**   N   L   0-1
McDonald D Howe   T Banks   Clayton   W Wright   Slater   Brabrook   Broadbent   Kevan   Haynes   A'Court

---

1958-59

93. **Northern Ireland**   A   D   3-3   **Goalscorers: R Charlton (2), Finney**
McDonald D Howe   T Banks   Clayton   W Wright   McGuinness   Brabrook   Broadbent   R Charlton   Haynes   Finney

94. **USSR**   H   W   5-0   **Goalscorers: R Charlton, Haynes (3), Lofthouse**
McDonald D Howe   G Shaw   Clayton   W Wright   Slater   Douglas   R Charlton   Lofthouse   Haynes   Finney

95. **Wales**   H   D   2-2   **Goalscorers: Broadbent (2)**
McDonald D Howe   G Shaw   Clayton   W Wright   Flowers   Clapton   Broadbent   Lofthouse   Haynes   A'Court

96. **Scotland**   H   W   1-0   **Goalscorer: R Charlton**
Hopkinson D Howe   G Shaw   Clayton   W Wright   Flowers   Douglas   Broadbent   R Charlton   Haynes   Holden

97. **Italy**   H   D   2-2   **Goalscorers: Bradley, R Charlton**
Hopkinson D Howe   G Shaw   Clayton   W Wright   Flowers   Bradley   Broadbent   R Charlton   Haynes   Holden

98. **Brazil**   A   L   0-2
Hopkinson D Howe   Armfield   Clayton   W Wright   Flowers   Deeley   Broadbent   R Charlton   Haynes   Holden

99. **Peru**   A   L   1-4   **Goalscorer: Greaves**
Hopkinson D Howe   Armfield   Clayton   W Wright   Flowers   Deeley   Greaves   R Charlton   Haynes   Holden

100. **Mexico**   A   L   1-2   **Goalscorer: Kevan**
Hopkinson D Howe   Armfield   Clayton   W Wright   McGuinness[1]   Holden[2]   Greaves   Kevan   Haynes   R Charlton   Flowers[1],
Bradley[2]

102. **USA**   A   W   8-1   **Goalscorers: Bradley, R Charlton (3), Flowers (2), Haynes, Kavan**
Hopkinson D Howe   Armfield   Clayton   W Wright   Flowers   Bradley   Greaves   Kevan   Haynes   R Charlton

1959-60

103. Wales   A   D   1-1   **Goalscorer: Greaves**

Hopkinson   D Howe   A Allen   Clayton   T Smith   Flowers   Connelly   Greaves   Clough   R Charlton   Holliday

104. Sweden   H   L   2-3   **Goalscorers: R Charlton, Connelly**

Hopkinson   D Howe   A Allen   Clayton   T Smith   Flowers   Connelly   Greaves   Clough   R Charlton   Holliday

105. Northern Ireland   H   W   2-1   **Goalscorers: Baker , Parry**

R Springett   D Howe   A Allen   Clayton   Brown   Flowers   Connelly   Haynes   Baker   Parry   Holliday

106. Scotland   A   D   1-1   **Goalscorer: R Charlton**

R Springett   Armfield   Wilson   Clayton   Slater   Flowers   Connelly   Broadbent   Baker   Parry   R Charlton

107. Yugoslavia   H   D   3-3   **Goalscorers: Douglas, Greaves (2), Haynes**

R Springett   Armfield   Wilson   Clayton   Swan   Flowers   Douglas   Haynes   Baker   Greaves   R Charlton

108. Spain   A   L   0-3

R Springett   Armfield   Wilson   R Robson   Swan   Flowers   Brabrook   Haynes   Baker   Greaves   R Charlton

109. Hungary   A   L   0-2

R Springett   Armfield   Wilson   R Robson   Swan   Flowers   Douglas   Haynes   Baker   Viollet   R Charlton

1960-61

110. Northern Ireland   A   W   5-2   **Goalscorers: R Charlton, Douglas, Greaves (2), R Smith**

R Springett   Armfield   McNeil   R Robson   Swan   Flowers   Douglas   Greaves   R Smith   Haynes   R Charlton

111. Luxembourg   A   W   9-0   **Goalscorers: R Charlton (3), Greaves (3), Haynes, R Smith**

R Springett   Armfield   McNeil   R Robson   Swan   Flowers   Douglas   Greaves   R Smith   Haynes   R Charlton

112. Spain   H   W   4-2   **Goalscorers: Douglas, Greaves, R Smith (2)**

R Springett   Armfield   McNeil   R Robson   Swan   Flowers   Douglas   Greaves   R Smith   Haynes   R Charlton

113. Wales   H   W   5-1   **Goalscorers: R Charlton, Greaves (2), Haynes, R Smith**

Hodgkinson   Armfield   McNeil   R Robson   Swan   Flowers   Douglas   Greaves   R Smith   Haynes   R Charlton

114. Scotland   H   W   9-3   **Goalscorers: Douglas, Greaves (3), Haynes (2), R Robson, R Smith (2)**

R Springett   Armfield   McNeil   R Robson   Swan   Flowers   Douglas   Greaves   R Smith   Haynes   R Charlton

115. Mexico   H   W   8-0   **Goalscorers: R Charlton (3), Douglas (2), Flowers, Hitchens, R Robson**

R Springett   Armfield   McNeil   R Robson   Swan   Flowers   Douglas   Kevan   Hitchens   Haynes   R Charlton

116. Portugal   A   D   1-1   **Goalscorer: Flowers**

R Springett   Armfield   McNeil   R Robson   Swan   Flowers   Douglas   Greaves   R Smith   Haynes   R Charlton

117. Italy   A   W   3-2   **Goalscorers: Greaves, Hitchens(2)**

R Springett   Armfield   McNeil   R Robson   Swan   Flowers   Douglas   Greaves   Hitchens   Haynes   R Charlton

118. Austria   A   L   1-3   **Goalscorer: Greaves**

R Springett   Armfield   Angus   Miller   Swan   Flowers   Douglas   Greaves   Hitchens   Haynes   R Charlton

1961-62

119. Luxembourg   H   W   4-1   **Goalscorers: R Charlton (2), Pointer, Viollet**

R Springett   Armfield   McNeil   R Robson   Swan   Flowers   Douglas   Fantham   Pointer   Viollet   R Charlton

120. Wales   A   D   1-1   **Goalscorer: Douglas**

R Springett   Armfield   Wilson   R Robson   Swan   Flowers   Connelly   Douglas   Pointer   Haynes   R Charlton

121. Portugal   H   W   2-0   **Goalscorers: Connelly, Pointer**

R Springett   Armfield   Wilson   R Robson   Swan   Flowers   Connelly   Douglas   Pointer   Haynes   R Charlton

122. Northern Ireland   H   D   1-1   **Goalscorer: R Charlton**

R Springett   Armfield   Wilson   R Robson   Swan   Flowers   Douglas   J Byrne   Crawford   Haynes   R Charlton

123. Austria   H   W   3-1   **Goalscorers: Crawford, Flowers, Hunt**

R Springett   Armfield   Wilson   Anderson   Swan   Flowers   Connelly   Hunt   Crawford   Haynes   R Charlton

124. Scotland   A   L   0-2

R Springett   Armfield   Wilson   Anderson   Swan   Flowers   Douglas   Greaves   R Smith   Haynes   R Charlton

125. Switzerland   H   W   3-1   **Connelly, Flowers, Hitchens**

R Springett   Armfield   Wilson   R Robson   Swan   Flowers   Connelly   Douglas   Hitchens   Haynes   R Charlton

126. Peru   A   W   4-0   **Goalscorers: Greaves (3), Flowers**

R Springett   Armfield   Wilson   Moore   Norman   Flowers   Douglas   Greaves   Hitchens   Haynes   R Charlton

127. Hungary   N   L   1-2   **Goalscorer: Flowers**

R Springett   Armfield   Wilson   Moore   Norman   Flowers   Douglas   Greaves   Hitchens   Haynes   R Charlton

128. Argentina   N   W   3-1   **Goalscorers: R Charlton, Flowers, Greaves**

R Springett   Armfield   Wilson   Moore   Norman   Flowers   Douglas   Greaves   Peacock   Haynes   R Charlton

129. Bulgaria   N   D   0-0

R Springett, Armfield, Wilson, Moore, Norman, Flowers, Douglas, Greaves, Peacock, Haynes, R Charlton

130. Brazil — N, L 1-3. Goalscorer: Hitchens
R Springett, Armfield, Wilson, Moore, Norman, Flowers, Douglas, Greaves, Hitchens, Haynes, R Charlton

1962-63

131. France — H, D 1-1. Goalscorer: Flowers
R Springett, Armfield, Wilson, Moore, Norman, Flowers, Hellawell, Crowe, Charnley, Greaves, A Hinton

132. Northern Ireland — A, W 3-1. Goalscorers: Greaves, O'Grady (2)
R Springett, Armfield, Wilson, Moore, Labone, Flowers, Hellawell, F Hill, Peacock, Greaves, O'Grady

133. Wales — H, W 4-0. Goalscorers: Connelly, Greaves, Peacock (2)
R Springett, Armfield, G Shaw, Moore, Labone, Flowers, Connelly, F Hill, Peacock, Greaves, Tambling

134. France — A, L 2-5. Goalscorers: R Smith, Tambling
R Springett, Henry, Moore, Labone, Flowers, Connelly, Tambling, R Smith, Greaves, R Charlton

135. Scotland — H, L 1-2. Goalscorer: Douglas
G Banks, Armfield, G Byrne, Moore, Flowers, Douglas, Greaves, R Smith, Melia, R Charlton

136. Brazil — H, D 1-1. Goalscorer: Douglas
G Banks, Armfield, Wilson, Milne, Norman, Moore, Douglas, Greaves, R Smith, Eastham, R Charlton

137. Czechoslovakia — A, W 4-2. Goalscorers: R Charlton, Greaves (2), R Smith
G Banks, Shellito, Wilson, Milne, Norman, Moore, Paine, Greaves, R Smith, Eastham, R Charlton

138. East Germany — A, W 2-1. Goalscorers: R Charlton, Hunt
G Banks, Armfield, Wilson, Milne, Norman, Moore, Paine, Hunt, R Smith, Eastham, R Charlton

139. Switzerland — A, W 8-1. Goalscorers: J Byrne (2), R Charlton (3), Douglas, Kay, Melia
R Springett, Armfield, Wilson, Kay, Moore, Flowers, Douglas, Greaves, J Byrne, Melia, R Charlton

1963-64

140. Wales — A, W 4-0. Goalscorers: R Charlton, Greaves, R Smith (2)
G Banks, Armfield, Wilson, Milne, Norman, Moore, Paine, Greaves, R Smith, Eastham, R Charlton

141. Rest of World — H, W 2-1. Goalscorers: Greaves, Paine
G Banks, Armfield, Wilson, Milne, Norman, Moore, Paine, Greaves, R Smith, Eastham, R Charlton

142. Northern Ireland — H, W 8-3. Goalscorers: Greaves (4), Paine (3), R Smith
G Banks, R Thomson, Wilson, Milne, Norman, Moore, Paine, Greaves, R Smith, Eastham, R Charlton

143. Scotland — A, L 0-1.
G Banks, Armfield, Wilson, Milne, Norman, Moore, Paine, Hunt, J Byrne, Eastham, R Charlton

144. Uruguay — H, W 2-1. Goalscorers: J Byrne (2)
G Banks, Cohen, Wilson, Milne, Norman, Moore, Paine, Greaves, J Byrne (2), Eastham, R Charlton

145. Portugal — A, W 4-3. Goalscorers: J Byrne (3), R Charlton
G Banks, Cohen, Wilson, Milne, Norman, Moore, P Thompson, Greaves, J Byrne, Eastham, R Charlton

146. Eire — A, W 3-1. Goalscorers: J Byrne, Eastham, Greaves
Waiters, Cohen, Wilson, Milne, Flowers, Moore, P Thompson, Greaves, J Byrne, Eastham, R Charlton

147. USA — A, W 10-0. Goalscorers: R Charlton, Hunt (4), Paine (2), Pickering (3)
G Banks, Cohen, R Thomson, M Bailey, Norman, Flowers, Paine, Hunt, Pickering, Eastham[1], P Thompson, R Charlton [1]

148. Brazil — A, L 1-5. Goalscorer: Greaves
Waiters, Cohen, Wilson, Milne, Norman, Moore, P Thompson, Greaves, J Byrne, Eastham, R Charlton

149. Portugal — N, D 1-1. Goalscorer: Hunt
G Banks, R Thomson, Wilson, Flowers, Norman, Moore, Paine, Greaves, J Byrne, Hunt, P Thompson

150. Argentina — N, L 0-1.
G Banks, R Thomson, Wilson, Milne, Norman, Moore, P Thompson, Greaves, J Byrne, Eastham, R Charlton

1964-65

152. Northern Ireland — A, W 4-3. Goalscorers: Greaves (3), Pickering
G Banks, R Thomson, Milne, Norman, Moore, Greaves, Pickering, R Charlton, P Thompson

153. Belgium — H, D 2-2. Goalscorers: Pickering, Opponents
Waiters, Cohen, R Thomson, Milne, Norman, Moore, P Thompson, Greaves, Pickering, Venables, A Hinton

154. Wales — H, W 2-1. Goalscorers: Wignall (2)
Waiters, Cohen, R Thomson, M Bailey, Flowers, Young, P Thompson, Hunt, Wignall, J Byrne, A Hinton

155. Holland — A, D 1-1. Goalscorer: Greaves
Waiters, Cohen, R Thomson, Mullery, Norman, Flowers, P Thompson, Greaves, Wignall, Venables, R Charlton

156. Scotland — H, D 2-2. Goalscorers: R Charlton, Greaves

G Banks | Cohen | Wilson | Stiles | J Charlton | Moore | P Thompson | Greaves | Bridges | J Byrne | R Charlton

157. Hungary   H   W   1-0   **Goalscorer: Greaves**

G Banks | Cohen | Wilson | Stiles | J Charlton | Moore | Paine | Greaves | Bridges | Eastham | Connelly

158. Yugoslavia   A   D   1-1   **Goalscorer: Bridges**

G Banks | Cohen | Wilson | Stiles | J Charlton | Moore | Paine | Greaves | Bridges | Ball | Connelly

159. West Germany   A   W   1-0   **Goalscorer: Paine**

G Banks | Cohen | Wilson | Flowers | J Charlton | Moore | Paine | Ball | M Jones | Eastham | Temple

160. Sweden   A   W   2-1   **Goalscorers: Ball, Connelly**

G Banks | Cohen | Wilson | Stiles | J Charlton | Moore | Paine | Ball | M Jones | Eastham | Connelly

---

1965-66

161. Wales   A   D   0-0

R Springett | Cohen | Wilson | Stiles | J Charlton | Moore | Paine | Greaves | Peacock | R Charlton | Connelly

162. Austria   H   L   2-3   **Goalscorers: R Charlton, Connelly**

R Springett | Cohen | Wilson | Stiles | J Charlton | Moore | Paine | Greaves | Bridges | R Charlton | Connelly

163. Northern Ireland   H   W   2-1   **Goalscorers: Baker, Peacock**

G Banks | Cohen | Wilson | Stiles | J Charlton | Moore | P Thompson | Baker | Peacock | R Charlton | Connelly

164. Spain   A   W   2-0   **Goalscorers: Baker, Hunt**

G Banks | Cohen | Wilson | Stiles | J Charlton | Moore | Ball | Hunt | Baker[1] | Eastham | R Charlton | Hunter[1]

165. Poland   H   D   1-1   **Goalscorer: Moore**

G Banks | Cohen | Wilson | Stiles | J Charlton | Moore | Ball | Hunt | Baker | Eastham | G Harris

166. West Germany   H   W   1-0   **Goalscorer: Stiles**

G Banks | Cohen | K Newton[1] | Moore | J Charlton | Hunter | Ball | Hunt | Stiles | G Hurst | R Charlton | Wilson[1]

167. Scotland   A   W   4-3   **Goalscorers: R Charlton, Hunt (2), G Hurst**

G Banks | Cohen | K Newton | Stiles | J Charlton | Moore | Ball | Hunt | R Charlton | G Hurst | Connelly

168. Yugoslavia   H   W   2-0   **Goalscorers: R Charlton, Greaves**

G Banks | Armfield | Wilson | Peters | J Charlton | Hunter | Paine | Greaves | R Charlton | G Hurst | Tambling

169. Finland   A   W   3-0   **Goalscorers: J Charlton, Hunt, Peters**

G Banks | Armfield | Wilson | Peters | J Charlton | Hunter | Callaghan | Hunt | R Charlton | G Hurst | Ball

170. Norway   A   W   6-1   **Goalscorers: Connelly, Greaves (4), Moore**

R Springett | Cohen | G Byrne | Stiles | Flowers | Moore | Paine | Greaves | R Charlton | Hunt | Connelly

171. Denmark   A   W   2-0   **Goalscorers: J Charlton, Eastham**

Bonetti | Cohen | Wilson | Stiles | J Charlton | Moore | Ball | Greaves | G Hurst | Eastham | Connelly

172. Poland   A   W   1-0   **Goalscorer: Hunt**

G Banks | Cohen | Wilson | Stiles | J Charlton | Moore | Ball | Greaves | R Charlton | Hunt | Peters

173. Uruguay   H   D   0-0

G Banks | Cohen | Wilson | Stiles | J Charlton | Moore | Ball | Greaves | R Charlton | Hunt | Connelly

174. Mexico   H   W   2-0   **Goalscorers: R Charlton, Hunt**

G Banks | Cohen | Wilson | Stiles | J Charlton | Moore | Paine | Greaves | R Charlton | Hunt | Peters

175. France   H   W   2-0   **Goalscorers: Hunt (2)**

G Banks | Cohen | Wilson | Stiles | J Charlton | Moore | Callaghan | Greaves | R Charlton | Hunt | Peters

176. Argentina   H   1-0   **Goalscorer: G Hurst**

G Banks | Cohen | Wilson | Stiles | J Charlton | Moore | Ball | G Hurst | R Charlton | Hunt | Peters

177. Portugal   H   2-1   **Goalscorers: R Charlton (2)**

G Banks | Cohen | Wilson | Stiles | J Charlton | Moore | Ball | G Hurst | R Charlton | Hunt | Peters

178. West Germany   H   4-2   **Goalscorers: G Hurst (3), Peters**

G Banks | Cohen | Wilson | Stiles | J Charlton | Moore | Ball | G Hurst | R Charlton | Hunt | Peters

---

1966-67

179. Northern Ireland   A   W   2-0   **Goalscorers: Hunt, Peters**

G Banks | Cohen | Wilson | Stiles | J Charlton | Moore | Ball | G Hurst | R Charlton | Hunt | Peters

180. Czechoslovakia   H   D   0-0

G Banks | Cohen | Wilson | Stiles | J Charlton | Moore | Ball | G Hurst | R Charlton | Hunt | Peters

181. Wales   H   W   5-1   **Goalscorers: J Charlton, R Charlton, G Hurst (2), Opponents**

G Banks | Cohen | Wilson | Stiles | J Charlton | Moore | Ball | G Hurst | R Charlton | Hunt | Peters

182. Scotland   H   L   2-3   **Goalscorers: J Charlton, G Hurst**

G Banks | Cohen | Wilson | Stiles | J Charlton | Moore | Ball | Greaves | R Charlton | G Hurst | Peters

183. Spain   H   W   2-0   **Goalscorers: Greaves, Hunt**

Bonetti | Cohen | K Newton | Stiles | Labone | Moore | Ball | Greaves | G Hurst | Hunt | Hollins

184. Austria A W 1-0 Goalscorer: Ball
Bonetti | K Newton | Wilson | Mullery | Labone | Moore | Ball | Greaves | G Hurst | Hunt | Hunter

1967-68

185. Wales A W 3-0 Goalscorers: Ball, R Charlton, Peters
G Banks | Cohen | K Newton | Mullery | J Charlton | Moore | Ball | Hunt | R Charlton | G Hurst | Peters

186. Northern Ireland H W 2-0 Goalscorers: R Charlton, G Hurst
G Banks | Cohen | Wilson | Mullery | Sadler | Moore | P Thompson | Hunt | R Charlton | G Hurst | Peters

187. USSR H D 2-2 Goalscorers: Ball, Hunt
G Banks | C Knowles | Wilson | Mullery | Sadler | Moore | Ball | Hunt | R Charlton | G Hurst | Peters

188. Scotland A D 1-1 Goalscorer: Peters
G Banks | K Newton | Wilson | Mullery | Labone | Moore | Ball | G Hurst | Summerbee | R Charlton | Peters

189. Spain H W 1-0 Goalscorer: R Charlton
G Banks | C Knowles | Wilson | Mullery | J Charlton | Moore | Ball | Hunt | Summerbee | R Charlton | Peters

190. Spain A W 2-1 Goalscorers: Hunter, Peters
Bonetti | K Newton | Wilson | Mullery | Labone | Moore | Peters | R Charlton | Hunt | Hunter

191. Sweden H W 3-1 Goalscorers: R Charlton, Hunt, Peters
Stepney | K Newton | C Knowles | Mullery | Labone | Moore | Bell | Peters | R Charlton[1] | Hunt | Hunter | G Hurst[1]

192. West Germany A L 0-1
G Banks | K Newton | C Knowles | Hunter | Labone | Moore | Ball | Bell | Summerbee | G Hurst | P Thompson

193. Yugoslavia N L 0-1
G Banks | K Newton | Wilson | Mullery | Labone | Moore | Ball | Peters | R Charlton | Hunt | Hunter

194. USSR N W 2-0 Goalscorers: R Charlton, G Hurst
G Banks | T wright | Wilson | Stiles | Labone | Moore | Hunter | Hunt | R Charlton | G Hurst | Peters

1968-69

195. Romania A D 0-0
G Banks | T Wright[1] | K Newton | Mullery | Labone | Moore | Ball | Hunt | R Charlton | G Hurst | Peters | McNab[1]

196. Bulgaria H D 1-1 Goalscorer: G Hurst
West | K Newton[1] | McNab | Mullery | Labone | Moore | Bell | R Charlton | G Hurst | Peters | Reaney

197. Romania H D 1-1 Goalscorer: J Charlton
G Banks | T Wright | McNab | Sties | J Charlton | Hunter | Radford | Hunt | R Charlton | G Hurst | Ball

198. France H W 5-0 Goalscorers: O'Grady, G Hurst (3), F Lee
G Banks | K Newton | Cooper | Mullery | J Charlton | Moore | F Lee | Bell | G Hurst | Peters | O'Grady

199. Northern Ireland A W 3-1 Goalscorers: G Hurst, F Lee, Peters
G Banks | K Newton | McNab | Mullery | Labone | Moore | F Lee | R Charlton | G Hurst | Peters

200. Wales H W 2-1 Goalscorers: R Charlton, F Lee
West | K Newton | Cooper | Moore | J Charlton | Hunter | F Lee | Bell | Astle | R Charlton | Ball

201. Scotland H W 4-1 Goalscorers: G Hurst (2), Peters (2)
G Banks | K Newton | Cooper | Mullery | Labone | Moore | Ball | R Charlton | G Hurst | Peters

202. Mexico A D 0-0
West | K Newton[1] | Cooper | Mullery | Labone | Moore | F Lee | Ball | R Charlton | G Hurst | Peters | T Wright[1]

203. Uruguay A W 2-1 Goalscorers: G Hurst, F Lee
G Banks | T Wright | K Newton | Mullery | Labone | Moore | F Lee | Bell | G Hurst | Ball | Peters

204. Brazil A L 1-2 Goalscorer: Bell
G Banks | T Wright | K Newton | Mullery | Labone | Moore | Ball | Bell | R Charlton | G Hurst | Peters

1969-70

205. Holland A W 1-0 Goalscorer: Bell
Bonetti | T Wright | E Hughes | Mullery | J Charlton | Moore | F Lee[1] | Bell | R Charlton | G Hurst | Peters | P Thompson[1]

206. Portugal H W 1-0 Goalscorer: J Charlton
Bonetti | Reaney | E Hughes | Mullery | J Charlton | Moore | F Lee | Bell[1] | Astle | R Charlton | Ball | Peters[1]

207. Holland H D 0-0
G Banks | K Newton | Cooper | Peters | J Charlton | Hunter | F Lee[1] | Bell | M Jones[2] | R Charlton | Storey-Moore | Mullery[1], G Hurst[2]

208. Belgium A W 3-1 Goalscorers: Ball (2), G Hurst
G Banks | T Wright | Cooper | Moore | Labone | E Hughes | F Lee | Ball | Osgood | G Hurst | Peters

209. Wales A D 1-1 Goalscorer: F Lee

G Banks | T Wright | E Hughes | Mullery | Labone | Moore | F Lee | Ball | R Charlton | G Hurst | Peters

210. Northern Ireland   H   W 3-1   Goalscorers: R Charlton, G Hurst, Peters

G Banks | K Newton[1] | E Hughes | Mullery | Moore | Stiles | Coates | Kidd | R Charlton | G Hurst | Peters | Bell[1]

211. Scotland   A   D 0-0

G Banks | K Newton | E Hughes | Stiles | Labone | Moore | P Thompson[1] | Ball | Astle | G Hurst | Peters | Mullery[1]

212. Colombia   A   W 4-0   Goalscorers: Ball, R Charlton, Peters (2)

G Banks | K Newton | Cooper | Mullery | Labone | Moore | F Lee | Ball | R Charlton | G Hurst | Peters

213. Ecuador   A   W 2-0   Goalscorers: Kidd, F Lee

G Banks | K Newton | Cooper | Mullery | Labone | Moore | F Lee[1] | Ball | R Charlton[2] | G Hurst | Peters | Kidd[1], Sadler[2]

214. Romania   N   W 1-0   Goalscorer: G Hurst

G Banks | K Newton[1] | Cooper | Mullery | Labone | Moore | F Lee[1] | Ball | R Charlton | G Hurst | Peters | T Wright[1], Osgood[2]

215. Brazil   N   L 0-1

G Banks | T Wright | Cooper | Mullery | Labone | Moore | F Lee[1] | Ball | R Charlton[2] | G Hurst | Peters | Astle[1], Bell[2]

216. Czechoslovakia   N   W 1-0   Goalscorer: A Clarke

G Banks | K Newton | Cooper | Mullery | J Charlton | Moore | Bell | R Charlton[1] | Astle | A Clarke[2] | Peters | Ball[1], Osgood[2]

217. West Germany   N   L 2-3   Goalscorers: Mullery, Peters

Bonetti | K Newton | Cooper | Mullery | Labone | Moore | F Lee | Ball | R Charlton[2] | G Hurst | Peters[2] | Bell[1], Hunter[2]

1970-71

218. East Germany   H   W 3-1   Goalscorers: A Clarke, F Lee, Peters

Shilton | E Hughes | Cooper | Mullery | Sadler | Moore | F Lee | Ball | G Hurst | A Clarke | Peters

219. Malta   A   W 1-0   Goalscorer: Peters

G Banks | Reaney | E Hughes | Mullery | McFarland | Hunter | Ball | Chivers | Royle | Harvey | Peters

220. Greece   H   W 3-0   Goalscorers: Chivers, G Hurst, F Lee

G Banks | Storey | E Hughes | Mullery | McFarland | Moore | F Lee | Ball[1] | Chivers | G Hurst | Peters | Coates[1]

221. Malta   H   W 5-0   Goalscorers: Chivers (2), A Clarke, F Lee, Lawler

G Banks | Lawler | Cooper | Moore | McFarland | E Hughes | F Lee | Coates | Chivers | A Clarke | Peters[1] | Ball[1]

222. Northern Ireland   A   W 1-0   Goalscorer: A Clarke

G Banks | Madeley | Cooper | Storey | McFarland | Moore | F Lee | Ball | Chivers | A Clarke | Peters

223. Wales   H   D 0-0

Shilton | Lawler | Cooper | T Smith | Lloyd | E Hughes | F Lee | Coates[1] | G Hurst | Coaters | Peters | A Clarke[1]

224. Scotland   H   W 3-1   Goalscorers: Chivers (2), Peters

G Banks | Lawler | Cooper | Storey | McFarland | Moore | F Lee[1] | Ball | Chivers | G Hurst | Peters | A Clarke[1]

1971-72

225. Switzerland   A   W 3-2   Goalscorers: Chivers, G Hurst, Opponents

G Banks | Lawler | Cooper | Mullery | McFarland | Moore | F Lee | Madeley | Chivers | G Hurst[1] | Peters | Radford[1]

226. Switzerland   H   D 1-1   Goalscorer: Summerbee

Shilton | Madeley | Cooper | Storey | Lloyd | Moore | Summerbee[1] | Ball | G Hurst | F Lee[2] | E Hughes | Chivers[1], Marsh[2]

227. Greece   A   W 2-0   Goalscorers: Chivers, G Hurst

G Banks | Madeley | E Hughes | Bell | McFarland | Moore | F Lee | Ball | Chivers | G Hurst | Peters

228. West Germany   H   L 1-3   Goalscorer: F Lee

G Banks | Madeley | E Hughes | Bell | Moore | Hunter | F Lee | Ball | Chivers | G Hurst[1] | Peters | Marsh[1]

229. West Germany   A   D 0-0

G Banks | Madeley | E Hughes | Storey | McFarland | Moore | Ball | Bell | Chivers | Marsh[1] | Hunter[2] | Summerbee[1], Peters[2]

230. Wales   A   W 3-0   Goalscorers: Bell, E Hughes, Marsh

G Banks | Madeley | E Hughes | Storey | McFarland | Moore | Summerbee | Bell | MacDonald | Marsh | Hunter

231. Northern Ireland   H   L 0-1

Shilton | Todd | E Hughes | Storey | Lloyd | Hunter | Summerbee | Bell | MacDonald[1] | Marsh | Currie[2] | Chivers[1], Peters[2]

232. Scotland   A   W 1-0   Goalscorer: Ball

G Banks | Madeley | E Hughes | Storey | McFarland | Moore | Ball | Bell | Chivers | Marsh[1] | Hunter | MacDonald[1]

1972-73

233. Yugoslavia   H   D 1-1   Goalscorer: Royle

Shilton | M Mills | Lampard | Storey | Blockley | Moore | Ball | Channon | Royle | Bell | Marsh

234. Wales   A   W 1-0   Goalscorer: Bell

Clemence | Storey | E Hughes | Hunter | McFarland | Moore | Keegan | Chivers | Marsh | Bell | Ball

235. Wales   H   D 1-1   Goalscorer: Hunter

Clemence Storey E Hughes Hunter McFarland Moore Keegan Bell Chivers Marsh Ball

236. Scotland A W 5-0 Goalscorers: Chivers[1], A Clarke (2), Shannon, Opponents

Shilton Storey E Hughes Bell Madeley Moore Ball Channon Chivers A Clarke Peters

237. Northern Ireland A W 2-1 Goalscorers: Chivers(2)

Shilton Storey Nish Bell McFarland Moore Bell Channon Chivers Richards Peters

238. Wales H W 3-0 Goalscorers: Channon, Chivers, Peters

Shilton Storey E Hughes Bell McFarland Moore Ball Channon Chivers A Clarke Peters

239. Scotland H W 1-0 Goalscorer: Peters

Shilton Storey E Hughes Bell McFarland Moore Ball Channon Chivers A Clarke Peters

240. Czechoslovakia A D 1-1 Goalscorer: A Clarke

Shilton Madeley Storey Bell McFarland Moore Ball Channon Chivers A Clarke Peters

241. Poland A L 0-2

Shilton Madeley E Hughes Storey McFarland Moore Ball Bell Chivers A Clarke Peters

242. USSR A W 2-1 Goalscorers: Chivers, Opponents

Shilton Madeley E Hughes Storey McFarland Moore Currie Channon[3] Chivers A Clarke[1] Peters[2] M'cDonald[1], Hunter[2], Sumerbe[3]

243. Italy A L 0-2

Shilton Madeley E Hughes Storey McFarland Moore Currie Channon Chivers A Clarke Peters

1973-74

243. Austria H W 7-0 Goalscorers: Bell, Channon (2), Chivers, A Clarke (2), Currie

Shilton Madeley E Hughes Bell McFarland Hunter Currie Channon Chivers A Clarke Peters

244. Poland H D 1-1 Goalscorer: A Clarke

Shilton Madeley E Hughes Bell McFarland Hunter Currie Channon Chivers[1] A Clarke Peters Hector[1]

245. Italy H L 0-1

Shilton Madeley E Hughes Bell McFarland Moore Currie Channon Osgood A Clarke[1] Peters Hector[1]

246. Portugal A D 0-0

Parkes Nish Pejic Dobson Watson Todd Bowles Channon MacDonald[1] Brooking Peters Ball[1]

247. Wales A W 2-0 Goalscorers: Bowles, Keegan

Shilton Nish Pejic E Hughes McFarland Todd Keegan Bell Channon Weller Bowles

248. Northern Ireland H W 1-0 Goalscorer: Weller

Shilton Nish Pejic E Hughes McFarland[1] Todd Keegan Weller Channon Bell Bowles[2] Hunter[1], Worthington[2]

249. Scotland A 0-2

Shilton Nish Pejic E Hughes Hunter[1] Todd Channon Bell Worthington[2] Weller Peters Watson[1], MacDonald[2]

250. Argentina H D 2-2 Goalscorers: Channon, Worthington

Shilton E Hughes Lindsay Todd Watson Bell Keegan Channon Worthington Weller Brooking

251. East Germany A D 1-1 Goalscorer: Channon

Clemence E Hughes Lindsay Todd Watson Dobson Keegan Channon Worthington Bell Brooking

252. Bulgaria A W 1-0 Goalscorer: Worthington

Clemence E Hughes Todd Watson Lindsay Dobson Brooking Bell Keegan Channon Worthington

253. Yugoslavia A D 2-2 Goalscorers: Channon, Keegan

Clemence E Hughes Lindsay Todd Watson Dobson Keegan Channon Worthington[1] Bell Brooking MacDonald[1]

1974-75

254. Czechoslovakia H W 3-0 Goalscorers: Bell (2), Channon

Clemence Madeley E Hughes Dobson[1] Watson Hunter Bell G Francis Worthington[2] Channon Keegan Brooking[1], Thomas[2]

255. Portugal H D 0-0

Clemence Madeley Watson E Hughes Cooper[1] Brooking G Francis Bell Thomas Channon A Clarke[2] Todd[1], Worthington[2]

256. West Germany H W 2-0 Goalscorers: Bell, MacDonald

Clemence Whitworth Gillard Bell Watson Todd Ball MacDonald Channon Hudson Keegan

257. Cyprus H W 5-0 Goalscorers: MacDonald (5)

Shilton Madeley Watson Todd Beattie Bell Ball Hudson Channon[1] MacDonald Keegan Thomas[1]

258. Cyprus A W 1-0 Goalscorer: Keegan

Clemence Whitworth Beattie[1] Watson Todd Bell Thomas Ball Channon MacDonald Keegan[2] E Hughes[1], Tueart[2]

259. Northern Ireland A D 0-0

Clemence Whitworth E Hughes Bell Watson Todd Ball Viljoen MacDonald[1] Keegan Tueart Channon[1]

260. Wales H D 2-2 Goalscorers: Johnson (2)

Clemence Whitworth Gillard G Francis Watson Todd Ball Channon[1] Johnson Viljoen Thomas Little[1]

261. Scotland H W 5-1 Goalscorers: Beattie, Bell, G Francis (2), Johnson

Clemence Whitworth Beattie Bell Watson Todd Ball Channon Johnson G Francis Keegan[1] Thomas[1]

262. Switzerland A W 2-1 Goalscorers: Channon, Keegan
Clemence Whitworth Todd Watson Beattie Bell Currie G francis Channon Johnson[1] Keegan MacDonald[1]

263. Czechoslovakia A L 1-2 Goalscorer: Channon
Clemence Madeley Gillard G Francis McFarland[1] Todd Keegan Channon[2] MacDonald A Clarke Bell Watson[1], Thomas[2]

264. Portugal A D 1-1 Goalscorer: Channon
Clemence Whitworth Beattie G Francis Watson Todd Keegan Channon MacDonald[2] Brooking Madeley[1] A Clarke[1], Thomas[2]

265. Wales A W 2-1 Goalscorers: Kennedy, P Taylor
Clemence Cherry[1] M Mills Neal P Thompson Doyle Keegan Channon[2] Boyer Brooking Kennedy Clement[1], P Taylor[2]

266. Wales A W 1-0 Goalscorers: P Taylor
Clemence Clement M Mills Towers B Greenoff P Thompson, Keegan G francis Pearson Kennedy P Taylor

267. Northern Ireland H W 4-0 Goalscorers: Channon (2), G Francis, Pearson
Clemence Todd M Mills P Thompson B Greenoff R Kennedy Keegan[2] G Francis Pearson Channon P Taylor[1] Towers[1], Royle[2]

268. Scotland A L 1-2 Goalscorer: Channon
Clemence Todd M Mills P Thompson McFarland[2] R Kennedy Keegan G Francis Pearson[1] Channon P Taylor Cherry[1], Doylet[2]

269. Brazil N L 0-1
Clemence Todd Doyle P Thompson Doyle G Francis Cherry Brooking Keegan Pearson Channon

270. Italy N W 3-2 Goalscorers: Channon (2), P Thompson
Rimmer[1] Clement Neal[2] P Thompson Doyle Towers Wilkins Brooking Royle Channon Hill Corrigant[1], M Mills[2]

271. Finland A W 4-1 Goalscorers: Channon, Keegan (2), S Pearson
Clemence Todd M Mills P Thompson Madeley Cherry Keegan Channon S Pearson Brooking G Francis

1976-77

272. Eire H D 1-1 Goalscorer: Pearson
Clemence Todd Madeley Cherry McFarland Greenhoff Keegan Wilkins Pearson Brooking George[1] Hill[1]

272. Finland H W 2-1 Goalscorers: Royle, Tueart
Clemence Todd Beattie P Thompson Greenoff Wilkins Keegan Channon Royle Brooking[1] Tueart[2] M Mills[1], Hill[2]

273. Italy A L 0-2
Clemence Clement[1] M Mills B Greenoff McFarland E hughes Keegan Channon Bowles Cherry Brooking Beattie[1]

274. Holland H L 0-2
Clemence Clement Beattie Doyle Watson Madeley[2] Keegan Greenoff[1] T francis Bowles Brooking Todd[1], S Pearson[2]

275. Luxembourg H W 5-0 Goalscorers: Channon (2), T Francis, Keegan, Kennedy
Clemence Gidman Cherry Kennedy Watson E Hughes Keegan Channon Royle[1] T francis Hill Mariner[1]

276. Northern Ireland A W 2-1 Goalscorers: Channon
Shilton Cherry M Mills Greenhoff Watson Todd Wilkins[1] Channon Mariner Brooking Tueart Talbot[1]

277. Wales H L 0-1
Shilton Neal M Mills Greenhoff Watson E Hughes Keegan Channon Pearson Brooking[1] R Kennedy Tueart[1]

278. Scotland H L 1-2 Goalscorer: Channon
Clemence Neal M Mills Greenhoff[1] Watson E Hughes T Francis Channon Pearson Talbot R Kennedy[2] Cherry[1], Tueart[2]

279. Brazil A D 0-0
Clemence Neal Cherry B Greenhoff Watson E Hughes Keegan T Francis Pearson[1] Wilkins[2] Talbot Channon[1], R Kennedy[2]

280. Argentina A D 1-1 Goalscorer: Pearson
Clemence Neal Cherry B Greenhoff[1] Watson E Hughes Keegan Channon Pearson Wilkins Talbot R Kennedy[1]

281. Uruguay A D 0-0
Clemence Neal Cherry B Greenhoff Watson E Hughes Keegan Channon Pearson Wilkins Talbot

1977-78

282. Switzerland H D 0-0
Clemence Neal Cherry McDermott Watson E Hughes Keegan Channon[1] T Francis R Kennedy Callaghan[2] Hill[1], Wilkins[2]

283. Luxembourg A W 2-0 Goalscorers: R Kennedy, Mariner
Clemence Cherry Watson[2] E Hughes R Kennedy Callaghan McDermott[1] Wilkins T Francis Mariner G Hill Whymark[1], Beattie[2]

284. Italy H W 2-0 Goalscorers: Brooking, Keegan
Clemence Neal Cherry Wilkins Watson E Hughes Keegan[2] Coppell R Latchford[1] Brooking P Barnes Pearson[1], T Francis[2]

285. West Germany A L 1-2 Goalscorer: S Pearson
Clemence Neal M Mills Wilkins Watson E Hughes Keegan[1] Coppell S Pearson Brooking P Barnes T Francis[1]

286. Brazil H D 1-1 Goalscorer: Keegan
Corrigan M Mills Cherry B Greenhoff Watson Currie Keegan Coppell R Latchford T Francis P Barnes

287. Wales A W 3-1 Goalscorers: P Barnes, Currie, R Latchford
Shilton M Mills Cherry[1] B Greenhoff Watson Wilkins Coppell T Francis R Latchford[2] Brooking P Barnes Currie[1], Mariner[2]

288. Northern Ireland   H   W   1-0   **Goalscorer: Neal**
Clemence | Neal | M Mills | Wilkins | Watson | E Hughes | Currie | Coppell | Pearson | Woodcock | B Greenhoff

289. Scotland   A   W   1-0   **Goalscorer: Coppell**
Clemence | Neal | M Mills | Currie | Watson | E Hughes[1] | Wilkins | Coppell | Mariner[2] | T Francis | P Barnes | B Greenhoff[1], Brooking[2]

290. Hungary   H   W   4-1   **Goalscorers: P Barnes, Currie, T Francis, Neal**
Shilton | Neal | M Mills | Wilkins | Watson[1] | E Hughes | Keegan | Coppell[2] | T Francis | Brooking | P Barnes | B Greenhoff[1], Currie[2]

1978-79

291. Denmark   A   W   4-3   **Goalscorers: Keegan (2), Latchford, Neal**
Clemence | Neal | M Mills | Wilkins | Watson | E Hughes | Keegan | Coppell | Latchford | Brooking | P Barnes

292. Eire   A   D   1-1   **Goalscorer: Latchford**
Clemence | Neal | M Mills | Wilkins | Watson[1] | E Hughes | Keegan | Coppell | Latchford | Brooking | P Barnes[2] | P Thompson[1], Woodcock

293. Czechoslovakia   H   W   1-0   **Goalscorer: Coppell**
Shilton | Anderson | Cherry | P Thompson | Watson | Wilkins | Keegan | Coppell | Woodcock[1] | Currie | P Barnes | Latchford[1]

294. Northern Ireland   H   W   4-0   **Goalscorers: Keegan, Latchford (2), Watson**
Clemence | Neal | M Mills | Currie | Watson | E Hughes | Keegan | Coppell | Latchford | Brooking | P Barnes

295. Northern Ireland   A   W   2-0   **Goalscorers: Coppell, Watson**
Clemence | Neal | M Mills | P Thompson | Watson | Wilkins | Coppell | Wilkins | Latchford | Currie | P Barnes

296. Wales   H   D   0-0
Corrigan | Cherry | Sansom | [2] | Watson | E Hughes | Keegan[1] | Wilkins | Latchford | McDermott | Cunningham | Coppell[1], Brooking[2]

297. Scotland   H   W   3-1   **Goalscorers: P Barnes, Coppell, Keegan**
Clemence | Neal | M Mills | P Thompson | Watson | Wilkins | Keegan | Coppell | Latchford | Brooking | P Barnes

298. Bulgaria   A   W   3-0   **Goalscorers: P Barnes, Keegan, Watson**
Clemence | Neal | M Mills | P Thompson | Watson | Wilkins | Keegan | Coppell | Latchford[1] | Brooking | P Barnes[2] | T Francis[1], Woodcock[2]

299. Sweden   A   D   0-0
Shilton | Anderson | Cherry | McDermott[1] | Watson | E Hughes | Keegan | T Francis[2] | Latchford | Woodcock | Cunningham | Wilkins[1], Brooking[2]

300. Austria   A   L   3-4   **Goalscorers: Coppell, Keegan, Wilkins**
Shilton[1] | Neal | M Mills | P Thompson | Watson | Wilkins | Keegan | Coppell | Latchford[2] | Brooking | P Barnes[3] | Clemence[1], T Francis[2], Cunningham[3]

1979-80

301. Denmark   H   W   1-0   **Goalscorer: Keegan**
Clemence | Neal | M Mills | P Thompson | Watson | Wilkins | Coppell | McDermott | Keegan | Brooking | P Barnes

302. Northern Ireland   A   W   5-1   **Goalscorers: T Francis (2), Woodcock (2), Opponents**
Shilton | Neal | M Mills | P Thompson | Watson | Wilkins | Coppell | T Francis | Brooking[1] | Woodcock | McDermott[1]

303. Bulgaria   H   W   2-0   **Goalscorers: Hoddle Watson**
Clemence | Anderson | Sansom | P Thompson | Watson | Wilkins | Reeves | Hoddle | T Francis | Kennedy | Woodcock

304. Eire   H   W   2-0   **Goalscorer: Keegan (2)**
Clemence | Cherry | Sansom | P Thompson | Watson | Robson | Keegan | McDermott | Johnson | Woodcock[1] | Cunningham | Coppell[1]

305. Spain   A   W   2-0   **Goalscorers: T Francis, Woodcock**
Shilton | Neal[1] | M Mills | P Thompson | Watson | Wilkins | Keegan | Coppell | T Francis[2] | R Kennedy | Woodcock | E Hughes[1], Cunningham[2]

306. Argentina   H   W   3-1   **Goalscorers: Johnson (2), Keegan**
Clemence | Neal[1] | Sansom | P Thompson | Watson | Wilkins | Keegan | Coppell | Johnson[2] | Woodcock | R Kennedy[3] | Cherry[1], Birtles[1], Brooking[3]

307. Wales   A   L   1-4   **Goalscorer: Mariner**
Clemence | Neal[1] | Cherry | P Thompson | Lloyd[2] | R Kennedy | Coppell | Hoddle | Mariner | Brooking | Barnes | Sansom[1], Wilkins[2]

308. Northern Ireland   H   D   1-1   **Goalscorer: Johnson**
Corrigan | Cherry | Sansom | E Hughes | Watson | Wilkins | Reeves[1] | Wilkins | Johnson | Brooking | Devonshire | Mariner[1]

309. Scotland   A   W   2-0   **Goalscorers: Brooking, Coppell**
Clemence | Cherry | Sansom | P Thompson | Watson | Wilkins | Coppell | McDermott | Johnson | Mariner[1] | Brooking | E Hughes[1]

310. Australia   A   W   2-1   **Goalscorers: Hoddle, Mariner**
Corrigan | Cherry | Lampard | Talbot | Osman | Butcher | Robson[1] | Hoddle | Mariner | | Armstrong[3] | B Greenhoff[1], Ward[2], Devonshire[3]

311. Belgium   N   D   1-1   **Goalscorers: Wilkins**
Clemence | Neal | Sansom | P Thompson | Watson | Wilkins | Keegan | Coppell[1] | Johnson[2] | Woodcock | Brooking | McDermott[1], R Kennedy[2]

312. Italy   A   L   0-1
Shilton | Neal | Sansom | P Thompson | Watson | Wilkins | Keegan | Coppell | Birtles[1] | R Kennedy | Woodcock | Mariner[1]

313. Spain   N   W   2-1   **Goalscorers: Brooking, Woodcock**
Clemence | Anderson | M Mills[1] | P Thompson | Watson | Wilkins | McDermott | Hoddle[2] | Keegan | Woodcock | Brooking | Cherry[1], Mariners[2]

314. Norway H W 4-0 Goalscorers: Mariner, McDermott (2), Woodcock
Shilton Anderson Sansom P Thompson Watson Robson Gates McDermott Mariner Woodcock Rix

315. Romania A L 1-2 Goalscorer: Woodcock
Clemence Neal Sansom P Thompson Watson Robson Rix McDermott Birtles[2] Woodcock Gates[1] Cunningham[1], Coppell[2]

316. Switzerland H W 2-1 Goalscorers: Mariner, Opponents
Shilton Neal Sansom Robson Watson M Mills Coppell McDermott Mariner Brooking[1] Woodcock Rix[1]

317. Spain H L 1-2 Goalscorer: Hoddle
Clemence Neal Sansom Robson Butcher Osman Keegan T Francis[1] Mariner Brooking[2] Hoddle P Barnes[1], Wilkins[2]

318. Romania H D 0-0
Shilton Anderson Sansom Robson Watson Osman Wilkins Brooking Coppell T Francis Woodcock[1] McDermott[1]

319. Brazil H L 0-1
Clemence Neal Sansom Robson Martin Wilkins Coppell McDermott Withe Rix P Barnes

320. Wales H D 0-0
Corrigan Anderson Sansom Robson Watson Wilkins Coppell Hoddle Withe[1] Rix P Barnes Woodcock[1]

321. Scotland H L 0-1
Corrigan Anderson Sansom Wilkins Watson[1] Robson Coppell Hoddle Withe Rix Woodcock[2] Martin[1], T Francis[2]

322. Switzerland A L 1-2 Goalscorer: McDermott
Clemence M Mills Sansom Wilkins Watson[2] Osman Keegan Robson Keegan Mariner T Francis[1] McDermott[1], P Barnes[2]

323. Hungary A W 3-1 Goalscorers: Brooking (2), Keegan
Clemence Neal M Mills P Thompson Watson Robson Keegan McDermott Mariner Brooking[1] T Francis Wilkins[1]

324. Norway A L 1-2 Goalscorer: Robson
Clemence Neal M Mills P Thompson Osman Robson Keegan T Francis Mariner[1] Hoddle[2] McDermott Withe[1], P Barnet[2]

325. Hungary H W 1-0 Goalscorer: Mariner
Shilton Neal M Mills P Thompson Martin Robson Keegan Coppell[1] Mariner Brooking McDermott Morley[1]

326. Northern Ireland H W 4-0 Goalscorers: Hoddle, Keegan, Robson, Wilkins
Clemence Anderson Sansom Wilkins Watson Foster Keegan Robson T Francis[1] Hoddle Morley[2] Regis[1], Woodcock[2]

327. Wales A W 1-0 Goalscorer: T Francis
Corrigan Neal Sansom P Thompson Butcher Robson Wilkins T Francis[1] Withe Hoddle[2] Morley McDermott[1], Regis[2]

328. Holland H W 2-0 Goalscorers: Mariner, Woodcock
Shilton Neal Sansom P Thompson Foster Robson Wilkins Devonshire[1] Mariner[2] McDermott Woodcock Rix[1], Barnes[2]

329. Scotland A W 1-0 Goalscorer: Mariner
Shilton M Mills Sansom P Thompson Butcher Robson Keegan[1] Coppell Mariner[2] Brooking Wilkins McDermott[1], T Francis[2]

330. Iceland A D 1-1 Goalscorer: Goddard
Corrigan Anderson Neal Watson Osman McDermott Hoddle Devonshire[1] Withe Regis[1] Morley Perryman[1], Goddard[2]

331. Finland A W 4-1 Goalscorers: Mariner (2), Robson (2)
Clemence M Mills Sansom P Thompson Martin Robson[1] Keegan Coppell[2] Mariner Brooking[3] Wilkins Rix[1], T Francis[2], Woodcock[3]

332. France N W 3-1 Goalscorers: Mariner, Robson (2)
Shilton M Mills Sansom[1] P Thompson Butcher Robson Coppell T Francis Mariner Rix Wilkins Neal[1]

333. Czechoslovakia N W 2-0 Goalscorers: T Francis, Opponents
Shilton M Mills Sansom P Thompson Butcher Robson[1] Coppell T Francis Mariner Rix Wilkins Hoddle[1]

334. Kuwait N W 1-0 Goalscorer: T Francis
Shilton Neal M Mills P Thompson Foster Hoddle Coppell T Francis Mariner Rix Wilkins

335. West Germany N D 0-0
Shilton M Mills Sansom P Thompson Butcher Robson Coppell T Francis[1] Mariner Rix Wilkins Woodcock[1]

336. Spain A D 0-0
Shilton M Mills Sansom P Thompson Butcher Robson Rix[1] T Francis Mariner Woodcock[2] Wilkins Brooking[1], Keegan[2]

347. Denmark A D 2-2 Goalscorers: T Francis (2)
Shilton Neal Sansom Wilkins Osman Butcher Morley[1] Robson Mariner T Francis Rix Hill[1]

348. West Germany H L 1-2 Goalscorer: Woodcock
Shilton Mabbutt Sansom P Thompson Butcher Wilkins R Hill Regis Mariner[1] Armstrong[2] Devonshire[3] Woodcock[1], Blissett[2], Rix[3]

349. Greece A W 3-0 Goalscorers: S Lee, Woodcock (2)
Shilton Neal Sansom P Thompson Martin Robson S Lee Mabbutt Mariner Woodcock Morley

350. Luxembourg   H   W   9-0   Goalscorers: Blissett (3), Chamberlain, Coppell, Hoddle, Neal, Woodcock, Opponents

Clemence — Neal — Sansom — Robson — Martin — Butcher — Coppell[1] — S Lee — Woodcock — Blissett — Mabbutt[2] — Chamberlain[1], Hoddle[2]

351. Wales   H   W   2-1   Goalscorers: Butcher, Neal

Shilton — Neal — Statham — S Lee — Martin — Butcher — Mabbutt — Blissett — Mariner — Cowans — Devonshire

352. Greece   H   D   0-0

Shilton — Neal — Sansom — S Lee — Martin — Butcher — Coppell — Mabbutt — T Francis — Woodcock[1] — Devonshire[2] — Blissett[1], Rix[2]

353. Hungary   H   W   2-0   Goalscorers: T Francis, Withe

Shilton — Neal — Sansom — S Lee — Martin — Butcher — Mabbutt — T Francis — Withe — Blissett — Cowans

354. Northern Ireland   A   D   0-0

Shilton — Neal — Sansom — Hoddle — Roberts — Butcher — Mabbutt — T Francis — Withe — Blissett[1] — Cowans — J Barnes[1]

355. Scotland   H   W   2-0   Goalscorers: Cowans, Robson

Shilton — Neal — Sansom — Roberts — Butcher — Robson[1] — T Francis — Withe[2] — Hoddle — Cowans — Mabbutt[1], Blissett[2]

356. Australia   A   D   0-0

Shilton — Thomas — Statham[1] — Williams — OSman — Butcher — Barham — Gregory — Blissett[2] — T Francis — Cowans — J Barnes[1], Walsh[2]

357. Australia   A   W   1-0   Goalscorer: Walsh

Shilton — Neal — Statham[1] — Barham — Osman — Butcher — Gregory — T Francis — Walsh — Cowans — J Barnes — Williams[1]

358. Australia   A   D   1-1   Goalscorer: T Francis

Shilton[1] — Neal[2] — Pickering — S Lee — Osman — Butcher — Gregory — T Francis — Walsh[3] — Cowans — J Barnes — Spink[1], Thomas[2], Blissett[3]

1983-84

359. Denmark   H   L   0-1

Shilton — Neal — Sansom — S Lee[1] — Osman — BUtcher — Wilkins — Gregory — Mariner — T Francis — J Barnes[2] — Blissett[1], Chamberlain[2]

360. Hungary   A   W   3-0   Goalscorers: Hoddle, S Lee, Mariner

Shilton — Gregory — Sansom — S Lee — Martin — Butcher — Robson — Hoddle — Mariner — Blissett[1] — Mabbutt — Withe[1]

361. Luxembourg   A   W   4-0   Goalscorers: Butcher, Mariner, Robson (2)

Clemence — Duxbury — Sansom — S Lee — Martin — Butcher — Robson — Hoddle — Mariner — Woodcock[1] — Williams — J Barnes[1]

362. France   A   L   0-2

Shilton — Duxbury — Sansom — S Lee[1] — Roberts — Butcher — Robson — Stein[2] — Walsh — Hoddle — Williams — J Barnes[1], Woodcock[2]

363. Northern Ireland   H   W   1-0   Goalscorer: Woodcock

Shilton — Anderson — A Kennedy — S Lee — Roberts — Butcher — Robson — Wilkins — Woodcock — T Francis — Rix

364. Wales   A   L   0-1

Shilton — Duxbury — A Kennedy — S Lee — Martin[1] — Wright — Wilkins — Gregory — Walsh — Woodcock — Armstrong[2] — Fenwick[1], Blissett[2]

365. Scotland   A   D   1-1   Goalscorer: Woodcock

Shilton — Duxbury — Sansom — Wilkins — Roberts — Fenwick — Chamberlain[1] — Robson — Woodcock[2] — Blissett — J Barnes — Hunt[1], Lineker[2]

366. USSR   H   L   0-2

Shilton — Duxbury — Sansom — Wilkins — Roberts — Fenwick — Chamberlain — Robson — T Francis[1] — Blissett — J Barnes[2] — Hateley[1], Hunt[2]

367. Brazil   A   W   2-0   Goalscorers: J Barnes, Hateley

Shilton — Duxbury — Sansom — Wilkins — Watson — Fenwick — Robson — Chamberlain — Hateley — Woodcock[1] — J Barnes — Allen[1]

368. Uruguay   A   L   0-2

Shilton — Duxbury — Sansom — Wilkins — Watson — Fenwick — Robson — Chamberlain — Hateley — Allen[1] — J Barnes — Woodcock[1]

369. Chile   A   D   0-0

Shilton — Duxbury — Sansom — Wilkins — Watson — Fenwick — Robson — Chamberlain[1] — Hateley — Allen — J Barnes — S Lee[1]

1984-85

370. East Germany   H   W   1-0   Goalscorer: Robson

Shilton — Duxbury — Sansom — Williams — Wright — Butcher — Robson — Wilkins — Mariner[1] — Woodcock[2] — J Barnes — Hateley[1], T Francis[2]

371. Finland   H   W   5-0   Goalscorers: Hateley (2), Robson, Sansom, Woodcock

Shilton — Duxbury[1] — Sansom — Williams — Wright — Butcher — Robson[2] — Wilkins — Hateley — Woodcock — J Barnes — G Stevens[1], Chamberlain[2]

372. Turkey   A   W   8-0   Goalscorers: Anderson, J Barnes (2), Robson (3), Woodcock (2)

Shilton — Anderson — Sansom — Williams[1] — Wright — Butcher — Robson — Wilkins — Withe — Woodcock[2] — J Barnes — G Stevens[1], Francis[2]

373. Northern Ireland   A   W   1-0   Goalscorer: Hateley

Shilton — Anderson — Sansom — Steven — Martin — Butcher — Robson — Wilkins — Hateley — Woodcock[1] — J Barnes — T Francis[1]

374. Eire   H   W   2-1   Goalscorers: Lineker, Steven

Bailey — Anderson — Sansom — Steven — Wright — Butcher — Robson — Wilkins — Hateley[1] — Lineker — Waddle[2] — Hoddle[1], Davenport[2]

375. Romania   A   D   0-0

Shilton — Anderson — Sansom — Steven — Wright — Butcher — Robson — Wilkins — Mariner[1] — T Francis — J Barnes[2] — Lineker[1], Waddle[2]

376. Finland   A   D   1-1   Goalscorer: Hateley

Shilton — Anderson — Sansom — Steven[1] — Fenwick — Butcher — Robson — Wilkins — Hateley — T Francis — J Barnes — Waddle[1]

377. Scotland A L 0-1

Shilton	Anderson	Sansom	Hoddle[1]	Fenwick	Butcher	Robson	Wilkins	Hateley	T Francis	J Barnes[2]	Lineker[1], Waddle[2]

378. Italy N L 1-2 — Goalscorer: Hateley

Shilton	Stevens	Sansom	Steven[1]	Wright	Butcher	Robson	Wilkins	Hateley	T Francis[2]	Waddle[3]	Hoddle[1], Lineker[2], J Barnes[3]

379. Mexico A L 0-1

Bailey	Anderson	Sansom	Hoddle[1]	Fenwick	Watson	Robson	Wilkins[2]	Hateley	T francis	J Barnes[3]	K Dixon[1], Reid[2] Waddle[3]

380. W. Germany N W 3-0 — Goalscorers: K Dixon (2), Robson

Shilton	Stevens	Sansom	Hoddle	Wright	Butcher	Robson[1]	Reid	K Dixon	Lineker[2]	Waddle	Bracewell[1], J Barnes[2]

381. USA A W 5-0 — Goalscorers: K Dixon (2), Lineker (2), Steven

Woods	Anderson	Sansom[1]	Hoddle[2]	Fenwick	Butcher	Robson[3]	Bracewell	K Dixon	Lineker	Waddle"	Watson[1], Steven[2], Reid[3]
											J Barnes"

1985-86

382. Romania H D 1-1 — Goalscorer: Hoddle

Shilton	Stevens	Sansom	Reid	Wright	Fenwick	Robson	Hoddle	Hateley	Lineker[1]	Waddle[2]	Woodcock[1], J Barnes[2]

383. Turkey H W 5-0 — Goalscorers: Lineker (3), Robson, Waddle

Shilton	Stevens	Sansom	Hoddle	Wright	Fenwick	Robson[1]	Wilkins	Hateley[2]	Lineker	Waddle	Steven[1], Woodcock[2]

384. N.Ireland H D 0-0

Shilton	GStevens	Sansom	Hoddle	Wright	Fenwick	Bracewell	Wilkins	K Dixon	Lineker	Waddle	

385. Egypt A W 4-0 — Goalscorers: Cowans, Steven, Wallace, Opponents

Shilton	Stevens	Sansom	Cowans	Wright	Fenwick	Steven	Wilkins	Hateley	Lineker	Wallace	

386. Israel A W 2-1 — Goalscorer: Robson (2)

Shilton[1]	Stevens	Sansom	Hoddle	Martin	Butcher	Robson	Wilkins	Dixon[2]	Beardsley[3]	Waddle	Woods[1], Woodcock[2], J Barnes[3]

387. USSR A W 1-0 — Goalscorer: Waddle

Shilton	Anderson	Sansom	Hoddle	Wright	Butcher	Cowans[1]	Wilkins	Beardsley	Lineker	Waddle[2]	Hodge[1], Steven[2]

388. Scotland H W 2-1 — Goalscorers: Butcher, Hoddle

Shilton	Stevens	Sansom	Hoddle	Watson	Butcher	Wilkins[1]	T Francis	Hateley	Hodge[2]	Waddle	Reid[1], G Stevens[2]

389. Mexico N W 3-0 — Goalscorers: Beardsley, Hateley (2)

Shilton	Anderson	Sansom	Hoddle	Fenwick	Butcher	Robson[1]	Wilkins[2]	Hateley[3]	Beardsley	Waddle"	G Stevens[1], Steven[2]
											K Dixon[3], J Barnes"

390. Canada A W 1-0 — Goalscorer: Hateley

Shilton[1]	Stevens	Sansom	Hoddle	Martin	Butcher	Hodge	Wilkins[2]	Hateley	Lineker[3]	Waddle"	Woods[1], Reid[2], Beardsley[3]
											J Barnes"

391. Portugal N L 0-1

Shilton	Stevens	Sansom	Hoddle	Fenwick	Butcher	Robson[1]	Wilkins	Hateley	Lineker	Waddle[2]	Hodge[1], Beardsley[2]

392. Morocco N D 0-0

Shilton	Stevens	Sansom	Hoddle	Fenwick	Butcher	Robson[1]	Wilkins	Hateley[2]	Lineker	Waddle	Hodge[1], G Stevens[2]

393. Poland N W 3-0 — Goalscorer: Lineker (3)

Shilton	Stevens	Sansom	Hoddle	Fenwick	Butcher	Hodge	Reid	Beardsley[1]	Lineker[2]	Steven	Waddle[1], K Dixon[2]

394. Paraguay N W 3-0 — Goalscorers: Beardsley, Lineker (2)

Shilton	Stevens	Sansom	Hoddle	Martin	Butcher	Hodge	Reid[1]	Beardsley[2]	Lineker	Steven	G Stevens[1], Hateley[2]

395. Argentina N L 1-2 — Goalscorer: Lineker

Shilton	Stevens	Sansom	Hoddle	Fenwick	Butcher	Hodge	Reid[1]	Beardsley	Lineker	Steven[2]	Waddle[1], J Barnes[2]

1986-87

396. Sweden A L 0-1

Shilton	Anderson	Sansom	Hoddle	Martin	Butcher	Steven[1]	Wilkins	K Dixon	Hodge	J Barnes[2]	Cottee[1], Waddle[2]

397. N. Ireland H W 3-0 — Goalscorers: Lineker (2), Waddle

Shilton	Anderson	Sansom	Hoddle	Watson	Butcher	Robson	Hodge	Beardsley[1]	Lineker	Waddle	Cottee[1]

398. Yugoslavia H W 2-0 — Goalscorers: Anderson, Mabbutt

Woods	Anderson	Sansom	Hoddle	Wright	Butcher	Mabbutt	Hodge[1]	Beardsley	Lineker	Waddle[2]	Wilkins[1], Steven[2]

399. Spain A W 4-2 — Goalscorer: Lineker (4)

Shilton[1]	Anderson	Sansom	Hoddle	Adams	Butcher	Robson	Hodge	Beardsley	Lineker	Waddle[2]	Woods[1], Steven[2]

400. N. Ireland A W 2-0 — Goalscorers: Robson, Waddle

Shilton[1]	Anderson	Sansom	Mabbutt	Wright	Butcher	Robson	Hodge	Beardsley	Lineker	Waddle	Woods[1]

401. Turkey A D 0-0

Woods	Anderson	Sansom	Hoddle	Adams	Mabbutt	Robson	Hodge[1]	Allen[2]	Lineker	Waddle	J Barnes[1], Hateley[2]

402. Brazil H D 1-1 — Goalscorer: Lineker

Shilton	Stevens	Pearce	Reid	Adams	Butcher	Robson	J Barnes	Beardsley	Lineker[1]	Waddle	Hateley[1]

403. Scotland A — D — 0-0

Woods · Stevens · Pearce · Hoddle · Wright · Butcher · Robson · Hodge · Beardsley · Hateley · Waddle

---

1987-88

404. W. Germany A — L — 1-3 — **Goalscorer: Lineker**

Shilton · Anderson · Sansom[1] · Hoddle[2] · Adams · Mabbutt · Reid · J Barnes · Beardsley · Lineker · Waddle[3] · Pearce[1], Webb[2], Hateley[3]

405. Turkey H — W — 8-0 — **Goalscorers: J Barnes (2), Beardsley, Lineker (3), Robson, Webb**

Shilton · Stevens · Sansom · Stevens[1] · Adams · Butcher · Robson · Webb · Beardsley[2] · Lineker · J Barnes · Hoddle[1], Regis[2]

406. Yugoslavia A — W — 4-1 — **Goalscorers: Adams, J Barnes, Beardsley, Robson**

Shilton · Stevens · Sansom · Steven · Adams · Butcher · Robson[1] · Webb[2] · Beardsley · Lineker · J Barnes · Reid[1], Hoddle[2]

407. Israel A — D — 0-0

Woods · Stevens · Pearce · Webb · Watson · Wright[1] · Allen[2] · McMahon · Beardsley · J Barnes · Waddle · Fenwick[1], Harford[2]

408. Holland H — D — 2-2 — **Goalscorers: Adams, Lineker**

Shilton · Stevens · Sansom · Steven · Adams · Watson[1] · Robson · Webb[2] · Beardsley[3] · Lineker · J Barnes · Wright[1], Hoddle[2] Hateley[3]

409. Hungary A — D — 0-0

Woods · Anderson · Pearce[1] · Steven · Adams · Pallister · Robson · McMahon · Beardsley[2] · Lineker[3] · Waddle" · Stevens[1], Hateley[2], Cottee[3] Hoddle"

410. Scotland H — W — 1-0 — **Goalscorer: Beardsley**

Shilton · Stevens · Sansom · Webb · Watson · Adams · Robson · Steven[1] · Beardsley · Lineker · J Barnes · Waddle[1]

411. Colombia H — D — 1-1 — **Goalscorer: Lineker**

Shilton · Anderson · Sansom · McMahon · Wright · Adams · Robson · Waddle[1] · Beardsley[2] · Lineker · J Barnes · Hoddle[1], Hateley[2]

412. Switzerland A — W — 1-0 — **Goalscorer: Lineker**

Shilton[1] · Stevens · Sansom · Webb · Wright · Adams[2] · Robson[3] · Steven" · Beardsley · Lineker · J Barnes · Woods[1], Watson[2], Reid[3], Waddle"

413. Eire N — L — 0-1

Shilton · Stevens · Sansom · Webb[1] · Wright · Adams · Robson · Waddle · Beardsley[2] · Lineker · J Barnes · Hoddle[1], Hateley[2]

414. Holland N — L — 1-3 — **Goalscorer: Robson**

Shilton · Stevens · Sansom · Hoddle · Wright · Adams · Robson · Steven[1] · Beardsley[2] · Lineker · J Barnes · Waddle[1], Hateley[2]

415. USSR N — L — 1-3 — **Goalscorer: Adams**

Woods · Stevens · Sansom · Hoddle · Watson · Adams · Robson · Steven · McMahon[1] · Lineker[2] · J Barnes · Webb[1], Hateley[2]

1988-89

416. Denmark H — W — 1-0 — **Goalscorer: Webb**

Shilton[1] · Stevens · Pearce · Rocastle · Adams[2] · Butcher · Robson · Webb · Harford[3] · Beardsley" · Hodge · Woods[1], Walker[2], Cottee[3] Gascoigne"

417. Sweden H — D — 0-0

Shilton · Stevens · Pearce · Webb · Adams[1] · Butcher · Robson · Beardsley · Waddle · Lineker · J Barnes[2] · Walker[1], Cottee[2]

418. Saudi Arabia A — D — 1-1 — **Goalscorer: Adams**

Seaman · Sterland · Pearce · M.Thomas[1] · Adams · Pallister · Robson · Rocastle · Beardsley[2] · Lineker · Waddle[3] · Gascoigne[1], A Smith[2] Marwood[3]

419. Greece A — W — 2-1 — **Goalscorers: J Barnes, Robson**

Shilton · Stevens · Pearce · Webb · Walker · Butcher · Robson · Rocastle · A Smith[1] · Lineker · J Barnes · Beardsley[1]

420. Albania A — W — 2-0 — **Goalscorers: J Barnes, Robson**

Shilton · Stevens · Pearce · Webb · Walker · Butcher · Robson · Rocastle · Waddle[1] · Lineker · J Barnes · Beardsley[1], A Smith[2]

421. Albania H — W — 5-0 — **Goalscorers: Beardsley (2), Gascoigne, Lineker, Waddle**

Shilton · Stevens[1] · Pearce · Webb · Walker · Butcher · Robson · Rocastle[2] · Beardsley · Lineker[3] · Waddle · Parker[1], Gascoigne[2]

422. Chile H — D — 0-0

Shilton · Parker · Pearce · Webb · Walker · Butcher · Robson · Gascoigne · Clough · Fashanu[1] · Waddle · Cottee[1]

423. Scotland A — W — 2-0 — **Goalscorers: Bull, Waddle**

Shilton · Stevens · Pearce · Webb · Walker · Butcher · Robson · Steven · Fashanu[1] · Cottee[2] · Waddle · Bull[1], Gascoigne[2]

424. Poland H — W — 3-0 — **Goalscorers: J Barnes, Lineker, Webb**

Shilton · Stevens · Pearce · Webb · Walker · Butcher · Robson · Waddle[1] · Beardsley[2] · Lineker · J Barnes · Rocastle[1], A Smith[2]

425. Denmark A — D — 1-1 — **Goalscorer: Lineker**

Shilton[1] · Parker · Pearce · Webb[2] · Walker · Butcher · Robson · Rocastle · Beardsley[3] · Lineker · J Barnes" · Seaman[1], McMahon[2]

Bull[3], Waddle"

1989-90

426. Sweden A — D — 0-0

Shilton · Stevens · Pearce · Webb[1] · Walker · Butcher · Beardsley · McMahon · Waddle · Lineker · J Barnes[2] · Gascoigne[1], Rocastle[2]

427. Poland A D 0-0

| Shilton | Stevens | Pearce | McMahon | Walker | Butcher | Robson | Rocastle | Beardsley | Lineker | Waddle | |

428. Italy H D 0-0

| Shilton[1] | Stevens | Pearce[2] | McMahon[3] | Walker | Butcher | Robson" | Waddle | Beardsley" | Lineker | J Barnes | Beasant[1], Winterburn[2] Hodge[3], Phelan", Platt" |

429. Yugoslavia H W 2-1 Goalscorer: Robson (2)

| Shilton[1] | Parker | Pearce | Thomas | Walker | Butcher | Robson | Rocastle | Bull | Lineker | Waddle | Beasant[1], Dorigo[2], Platt[3] McMahon", Hodge" |

430. Brazil H 1-0 Goalscorer: Lineker

| Shilton[1] | Stevens | Pearce | McMahon | Walker | Butcher | Platt | Waddle | Beardsley[2] | Lineker | J Barnes | Woods[1], Gascoigne[2] |

431. Czechoslovakia H W 4-2 Goalscorers: Bull (2), Gascoigne, Pearce

| Shilton[1] | Dixon | Pearce[2] | Steven | Walker[3] | Butcher | Robson" | Gascoigne | Bull | Lineker | Hodge | Seaman[1], Dorigo[2], Wright[3], McMahon[3] |

432. Denmark H W 1-0 Goalscorer: Lineker

| Shilton[1] | Stevens | Pearce[2] | McMahon[3] | Walker | Butcher | Hodge | Gascoigne | Waddle" | Lineker" | J Barnes | Woods[1], Dorigo[2], Platt[3] Rocastle", Bull" |

433. Uruguay H L 1-2 Goalscorer: Lineker

| Shilton | Parker | Pearce | Hodge[1] | Walker | Butcher | Robson | Gascoigne | Waddle | Lineker[2] | J Barnes | Beardsley[1], Bull[2] |

434. Tunisia A D 1-1 Goalscorer: Bull

| Shilton | Stevens | Pearce | Hodge[1] | Walker | Butcher[2] | Robson | Waddle[3] | Gascoigne | Lineker" | J Barnes | Beardsley[1], Wright[2], Platt[3], Bull" |

435. Eire N D 1-1 Goalscorer: Lineker

| Shilton | Stevens | Pearce | Gascoigne | Walker | Butcher | Waddle | Robson | Beardsley | Lineker[1] | J Barnes[2] | McMahon[1], Bull[2] |

436. Holland N D 0-0

| Shilton | Parker | Pearce | Wright | Walker | Butcher | Robson[1] | Waddle[2] | Gascoigne | Lineker | J Barnes | Platt[1], Bull[2] |

437. Egypt N W 1-0 Goalscorer: Wright

| Shilton | Parker | Pearce | Gascoigne | Walker | Wright | McMahon | Waddle[1] | Bull[2] | Lineker | J Barnes | Platt[1], Beardsley[2] |

438. Belgium N W 1-0 Goalscorer: Platt

| Shilton | Parker | Pearce | Wright | Walker | Butcher | McMahon[1] | Waddle | Gascoigne | Lineker | J Barnes[2] | Platt[1], Bull[2] |

439. Cameroon N W 3-2 Goalscorers: Lineker (2), Platt

| Shilton | Parker | Pearce | Wright | Walker | Butcher[1] | Platt | Waddle | Gascoigne | Lineker | J Barnes | Steven[1], Beardsley[2] |

440. W. Germany N D 1-1 Goalscorer: Lineker   *West Germany won 4-3 on penalties.*

| Shilton | Parker | Pearce | Wright | Walker | Butcher[1] | Platt | Waddle | Gascoigne | Lineker | Beardsley | Steven[1] |

441. Italy A L 1-2 Goalscorer: Platt

| Shilton | Stevens | Dorigo | Parker | Walker | Wright[1] | Platt | Steven | McMahon[2] | Lineker | Beardsley | Waddle[1], Webb[2] |

1990-91

442. Hungary H W 1-0 Goalscorer: Lineker

| Woods | Dixon | Pearce[1] | Parker | Walker | Wright | Platt | Gascoigne | Bull[2] | Lineker | J Barnes | Dorigo[1], Waddle[2] |

443. Poland H W 2-0 Goalscorers: Beardsley, Lineker

| Woods | Dixon | Pearce | Parker | Walker | Wright | Platt | Gascoigne | Bull[1] | Lineker[2] | J Barnes | Beardsley[1], Waddle[2] |

444. Eire A D 1-1 Goalscorer: Platt

| Woods | Dixon | Pearce | Adams | Walker | Wright | Platt | Cowans | Beardsley | Lineker | McMahon | |

445. Cameroon H W 2-0 Goalscorer: Lineker (2)

| Seaman | Dixon | Pearce | Steven | Walker | Wright | Robson[1] | Gascoigne[2] | I Wright | Lineker | J Barnes | Pallister[1], Hodge[2] |

446. Eire H D 1-1 Goalscorer: Dixon

| Seaman | Dixon | Pearce | Adams[1] | Walker | Wright | Robson | Platt | Beardsley | Lineker[2] | J Barnes | Sharpe[1], I Wright[2] |

447. Turkey A W 1-0 Goalscorer: Wise

| Seaman | Dixon | Pearce | Wise | Walker | Pallister | Platt | G Thomas[1] | A Smith | Lineker | J Barnes | Hodge[1] |

448. USSR H W 3-1 Goalscorers: Platt, A Smith

| Woods | Stevens | Dorigo | Wise[1] | Parker | Wright | Platt | G Thomas | A Smith | I Wright | J Barnes | Batty[1], Beardsley[2] |

449. Argentina H D 2-2 Goalscorers: Lineker, Platt

| Seaman | Dixon | Pearce | Batty | Walker | Wright | Platt | G Thomas | A Smith | Lineker | J Barnes[1] | Clough[1] |

450. Australia A W 1-0 Goalscorer: Opponents

| Woods | Parker | Pearce | Batty | Walker | Wright | Platt | G Thomas | Clough | Lineker[1] | Hirst[2] | Wise[1], Salako[2] |

451. New Zealand A W 1-0 Goalscorer: Lineker

| Woods | Parker | Pearce | Batty[1] | Walker | Barrett | Platt | G Thomas | Wise | Lineker | Walters[2] | Deane[1], Salako[2] |

452. New Zealand A W 2-0 Goalscorers: Hirst, Pearce

| Woods | Charles | Pearce | Wise | Walker | Wright | Platt | G Thomas | Deane[1] | I Wright | Salako | Hirst |

453. **Malaysia** A W 4-2 Goalscorers: Lineker (4)

Woods — Charles — Pearce — Batty — Walker — Wright — Platt — GThomas — Clough — Lineker — Salako

1991-92

454. **Germany** H L 0-1

Woods — Dixon — Dorigo — Batty — Pallister — Parker — Platt — Steven[1] — A Smith — Lineker — Salako[2] | Stewart[1], Merson[2]

455. **Turkey** H W 1-0 Goalscorer: A Smith

Woods — Dixon — Pearce — Batty[1] — Walker — Mabbutt — Robson — Platt — A Smith — Lineker — Waddle

456. **Poland** A D 1-1 Goalscorer: Lineker

Woods — Dixon — Pearce — Gray[1] — Walker — Mabbutt — PLatt — G Thomas — Rocastle — Lineker — Sinton[2] | A Smith[1], Daley[2]

457. **France** H W 2-0 Goalscorers: Lineker, Shearer

Woods — R Jones — Pearce — Keown — Walker — Wright — Webb — G Thomas — Clough — Shearer — Hirst[1] | Lineker[1]

458. **Czechoslovakia** A D 2-2 Goalscorers: Keown, Merson

Seaman — Keown — Pearce — Rocastle[1] — Walker — Mabbutt[2] — Platt — Merson — Clough[3] — Hateley — J Barnes" | Dixon[1], Lineker[2], Stewart[3], Dorigo"

459. **CIS** A D 2-2 Goalscorers: Lineker, Steven

Woods[1] — Stevens — Sinton[2] — Palmer — Walker — Keown — Platt — Steven[3] — Shearer" — Lineker — Daley | Martyn[1], Curle[2], Stewart[3], Clough"

460. **Hungary** A W 1-0 Goalscorer: Webb

Martyn[1] — Stevens — Dorigo — Curle[2] — Walker — Keown — Webb[3] — Palmer — Merson" — Lineker" — Daley | Seaman[1], Sinton[2], Batty[3], A Smith", I Wright"

461. **Brazil** H D 1-1 Goalscorer: Platt

Woods — Stevens — Dorigo[1] — Palmer — Walker — Keown — Daley[2] — Steven[3] — Platt — Lineker — Sinton" | Pearce[1], Merson[2], Webb[3], Rocastle"

462. **Finland** A W 2-1 Goalscorer: Platt (2)

Woods — Stevens[1] — Pearce — Keown — Walker — Wright — Platt — Steven[2] — Webb — Lineker — J Barnes[3] | Palmer[1], Daley[2], Merson[3]

463. **Denmark** N D 0-0

Woods — Curle[1] — Pearce — Palmer — Walker — Keown — Platt — Steven — A Smith — Lineker — Merson[2] | Daley[1], Webb[2]

464. **France** N D 0-0

Woods — Batty — Pearce — Palmer — Walker — Keown — Platt — Steven — Shearer — Lineker

465. **Sweden** N L 1-2 Goalscorer: Platt

Woods — Batty — Pearce — Keown — Walker — Palmer — Platt — Webb — Sinton[1] — Lineker — Daley | Merson[1], A Smith[2]

1992-93

466. **Spain** A L 0-1

Woods — Dixon — Pearce — Ince — Walker — Wright — White[3] — Platt — Clough — Shearer — Sinton" | Bardsley[1], Palmer[2], Merson[3], Dean"

467. **Norway** H D 1-1 Goalscorer: Platt

Woods — Dixon[1] — Pearce — Batty — Walker — Adams — Platt — Gascoigne — Shearer — I Wright[2] — Ince | Palmer[1], Merson[2]

468. **Turkey** H W 4-0 Goalscorers: Gascoigne (2), Pearce, Shearer

Woods — Dixon — Pearce — Palmer — Walker — Adams — Platt — Gascoigne — Shearer — I Wright — Ince

469. **San Marino** H W 6-0 Goalscorers: Ferdinand, Palmer, Platt (4)

Woods — Dixon — Dorigo — Palmer — Walker — Adams — Platt — Gascoigne — Ferdinand — J Barnes — Batty

470. **Turkey** A W 2-0 Goalscorers: Gascoigne, Platt

Woods — Dixon[1] — Sinton — Palmer — Walker — Adams — Platt — Gascoigne — J Barnes — I Wright[2] — Ince | Clough[1], Sharpe[2]

471. **Holland** H D 2-2 Goalscorers: J Barnes, Platt

Woods — Dixon — Keown — Palmer — Walker — Adams — Platt — Gascoigne[1] — Ferdinand — J Barnes — Ince | Merson[1]

472. **Poland** A D 1-1 Goalscorer: I Wright

Woods — Bardsley — Dorigo — Palmer[1] — Walker — Adams — Platt — Gascoigne[2] — Sheringham — J Barnes — Ince | I Wright[1], Clough[2]

473. **Norway** A L 0-2

Woods — Dixon — Pallister — Palmer — Walker[1] — Adams — Platt — Gascoigne — Ferdinand — Sheringham[2] — Sharpe | Clough[1], I Wright[2]

474. **U.S.A.** A L 0-2

Woods — Dixon — Dorigo — Palmer[1] — Pallister — Batty — Ince — Clough — Sharpe — Ferdinand[2] — J Barnes | Walker[1], I Wright[2]

475. **Brazil** D 1-1 Goalscorer: Platt

Flowers — Barrett — Dorigo — Walker — Pallister — Batty[1] — Ince[2] — Clough[3] — I Wright — Sinton — Sharpe | Platt[1], Palmer[2], Merson[3]

476. **Germany** N L 1-2 Goalscorer: Platt

Martyn — Barrett — Sinton — Walker — Pallister[1] — Ince — Platt — Clough[2] — Sharpe[3] — J Barnes — Merson | Keown[1], I Wright[2], Winterburn[3]

1993-94

477. Poland H W 3-0 Goalscorers: Ferdinand, Gascoigne, Pearce
Seaman Jones Pearce Ince Pallister Adams Platt Gascoigne Ferdinand Wright Sharpe

478. Holland A L 0-2
Seaman Parker Dorigo INce Pallister Adams Platt Palmer[1] Shearer Merson[2] Sharpe Sinton[1], I Wright[2]

479. San Marino A W 7-1 Goalscorers: Ferdinand, Ince (2), I Wright (4)
Seaman Dixon Pearce INce Pallister Walker Platt Ripley Ferdinand I Wright Sinton

480. Denmark H W 1-0 Goalscorer: Platt
Seaman Parker Le Saux Ince[1] Adams Pallister Platt Gascoigne[2] Shearer Beardsley Anderton Batty[1], Le Tissier[2]

481. Greece H 5-0 W Goalscorers: Anderton, Beardsley, Platt (2), Shearer
Flowers Jones[1] Le Saux Richardson Bould Adams Platt Merson Shearer Beardsley[2] Anderton[3] Pearce[1], I Wright[2], Le Tissier[3]

482. Norway H D 0-0
Seaman Jones Le Saux Ince[1] Bould Adams Platt Wise Shearer Beardsley Anderton[2] Le Tissier[1], I Wright[2]

1994-95

483. U.S.A. H W 2-0 Goalscorer: Shearer (2)
Seaman Jones Le Saux Venison Adams Pallister Platt J Barnes Shearer[1] Sheringham[2] Anderton Ferdinand[1], I Wright[2]

484. Romania H D 1-1 Goalscorer: Lee
Seaman Jones[1] Le Saux Ince Adams Pallister Lee[2] I Wright[3] Shearer J Barnes Le Tissier Pearce[1], Wise[2], Sheringham[3],

485. Nigeria H W 1-0 Goalscorer: Platt
Flowers Jones Le Saux Lee[1] Howey Ruddock PLatt Beardsley[2] Shearer[3] J Barnes Wise McManaman[1], Le Tissier[2], Sheringham[3]

486. Eire A 0-1 *Game abandoned after 27 minutes.*
Seaman Barton Le Saux Ince Adams Pallister Platt Beardsley Shearer Le Tissier Anderton

487. Uruguay H D 0-0
Flowers Jones Le Saux[1] Venison Adams Pallister Platt Beardsley[2] Sheringham[3] J Barnes Anderton McManaman[1], Barmby[2], Cole[3]

488. Japan H W 2-1 Goalscorers: Anderton, Platt
Flowers Neville Pearce Batty[1] Scales Unsworth Platt Beardsley[2] Shearer Collymore[3] Anderton McManaman[1], Gascoigne[2], Sheringham[3]

489. Sweden H D 3-3 Goalscorers: Anderton, Platt, Sheringham
Flowers Barton Le Saux J Barnes[1] Cooper Pallister[2] Platt Beardsley[3] Shearer Sheringham Anderton Gascoigne[1], Scales[2], Barmby[3]

490. Brazil H L 1-3 Goalscorer: Le Saux
Flowers Neville Pearce Batty[1] Cooper Scales[2] Platt Le Saux Shearer Sheringham[3] Anderton Gascoigne[1], Barton[2], Collymore[3]

1995-96

491. Colombia H D 0-0
Seaman G Neville Le Saux Redknapp[3] Adams Howey Barmby Gascoigne[1] Shearer[2] McManaman Wise J Barnes[1], Sheringhamt[2], Lee[3]

492. Norway H D 0-0
Seaman G Neville Pearce Redknapp[3] Adams Pallister Barmby[1] Lee Shearer McManaman Wise[2] Sheringham[1], Stone[2]

493. Switzerland H W 3-1 Goalscorers: Quentin (og), Sheringham, Stone.
Seaman G Neville Pearce Redknapp[1] Adams Pallister Lee Gascoigne Shearer Sheringham McManaman Stone[1]

494. Portugal H D 1-1 Goalscorer: Stone.
Seaman G Neville Pearce Wise[2] Adams Howey Barmby[1] Gascoigne Shearer Ferdinand[3] Stone McManaman[1], Southgate[2], Beardsley[3]

495. Bulgaria H W 1-0 Goalscorer:
Seaman G Neville Pearce Ince Southgate Howey McManaman Gascoigne[1] Ferdinand[2] Sheringham[3] Stone Lee[1], Fowler[2], Platt[3]

496. Croatia H D 0-0
Seaman G Neville Pearce Ince Wright McManaman Platt Gascoigne Fowler Sheringham Stone

497. Hungray H W 3-0 Goalscorers: Anderton (2), Platt
Seaman[4] G Neville Pearce Ince[5] Wright[3] Lee Platt[2] Wilcox Ferdinand[1] Sheringham Anderton Shearer[1], Wise[2], Southgate[3], Walker[4], Campbell[5]

498. **China** **A** **W** **3-0** **Goalscorers: Barnby (2), Gascoigne**

Flowers[1] G Neville P Neville Redknapp Adams Southgate Barmby[2] Gascoigne Shearer[3] McManaman[4] Anderton Walker[1], Beardsley[2], Fowler[3], Stone[4],

499. **Switzerland H** **D** **1-1** **Goalscorer: Shearer**

Seaman G Neville Pearce Ince Adams Southgate McManaman[1] Gascoigne Shearer Sheringham[2] Anderton Stone[1], Barmby[2]

500. **Scotland** **H** **W** **2-0** **Goalscorers: Shearer (Pen), Gascoigne**

Seaman G Neville Pearce[1] Ince[3] Adams Southgate McManaman Gascoigne Shearer Sheringham Anderton Redknapp[1,2], Campbell[2], Stone[3]

501. **Holland** **H** **W** **4-1** **Goalscorers: Shearer (2, [1 pen]), Sheringham (2)**

Seaman G Neville Pearce Ince[3] Adams Southgate McManaman Gascoigne Shearer[2] Sheringham[1] Anderton Barmby[1], Fowler[2], Platt[3]

502. **Spain** **H** **D** **0-0** *(England won 4-3 on penalties)*

Seaman G Neville Pearce McManaman[1] Adams Southgate Platt Gascoigne Shearer Sheringham[2] Anderton[3] Barmby[1], Stone[2], Fowler[3]

503. **Germany** **H** **D** **1-1** **Goalscorers: Shearer** *(Germany won 6-5 on penalties)*

Seaman McManaman Pearce Ince Adams Southgate Platt Gascoigne Shearer Sheringham Anderton

CLUB INDEX

Printed and bound by Unwin Brothers Ltd.,
The Gresham Press, Old Woking, Surrey GU22 9LH
A Member of the Martins Printing Group